THE VONNEGUT ENCYCLOPEDIA

An Authorized Compendium

Marc Leeds

Foreword by Kurt Vonnegut

GP

GREENWOOD PRESS
Westport, Connecticut • London

Library of Congress Cataloging-in-Publication Data

Leeds, Marc.
The Vonnegut encyclopedia : an authorized compendium / Marc Leeds.
p. cm.
Includes index.
ISBN 0-313-29230-2 (alk. paper)
1. Vonnegut, Kurt—Encyclopedias. I. Title.
PS3572.05Z755 1995
813'.54—dc20 94-16122

British Library Cataloguing in Publication Data is available.

Library of Congress Catalog Card Number: 94-16122
ISBN: 0-313-29230-2

First published in 1995

Greenwood Press, 88 Post Road West, Westport, CT 06881
An imprint of Greenwood Publishing Group, Inc.

Printed in the United States of America

The paper used in this book complies with the Permanent Paper Standard issued by the National Information Standards Organization (Z39.48-1984).

10 9 8 7 6 5 4 3 2 1

Copyright Acknowledgments

The author and publisher are grateful for permission to reprint excerpts from the following copyrighted materials:

Kurt Vonnegut, *Hocus Pocus* (New York: G. P. Putnam's Sons, 1990). Copyright © 1990 by Kurt Vonnegut.

Kurt Vonnegut, *Fates Worse Than Death: An Autobiographical Collage of the 1980s* (New York: G. P. Putnam's Sons, 1991). Copyright © 1991 by Kurt Vonnegut.

In addition, excerpts from the following copyrighted titles by Kurt Vonnegut have been reprinted by permission of Dell Publishing: *Bluebeard; Galápagos; Deadeye Dick; Palm Sunday: An Autobiographical Collage; Jailbird; Slapstick or Lonesome No More!; Wampeters, Foma & Granfalloons; Breakfast of Champions; Happy Birthday, Wanda June; Welcome to the Monkey House; Slaughterhouse-Five or The Children's Crusade: A Duty-Dance with Death; God Bless You, Mr. Rosewater or Pearls Before Swine; Cat's Cradle; Mother Night; The Sirens of Titan;* and *Player Piano.*

John Masefield, "C.L.M.," in *Poems* by John Masefield (New York: Macmillan, 1967). Reprinted by permission of The Society of Authors as the literary representative of the Estate of John Masefield.

Contents

Foreword by Kurt Vonnegut	ix
Preface	xi
Acknowledgments	xiii
A Note About the Text	xv
The Encyclopedia	1
Index	659

Foreword

A working-class Englishman named Ned Ludd, early in the nineteenth century, smashed up some machinery that was making his skills redundant, thus giving our already rich language a word for a person wary of newfangled contraptions, such as myself, which is "Luddite." A common irony, a virtually unavoidable irony in these times, is for a Luddite to be a beneficiary of a technological advance. I myself now find my life's work as a writer, which I made with ink on bleached and flattened wood pulp, transmogrified into something as insubstantial, ephemeral, and yet immortal as the ghost of Hamlet's father on a parapet at Elsinor. Electrons. Ah me. What is one to think?

My most recent opus in the Gutenberg medium, *Fates Worse Than Death*, isn't at this writing all that recent anymore (1991). I set to work on another one, to be called *Timequake*, but I have been unable to complete it to my own satisfaction, so perhaps it will never be. Civilization will survive in any case. I hoped it to be a tragicomedy (what a language!) about the externalization in the form of compact, reasonably priced, and readily available electronic devices of all that is amusing or economically valuable about the nervous systems of human beings. Memory, given the circumstances that inspire this little essay, is the human capability that first comes to mind. Thanks to my good friend and Professor Marc Leeds, Ph.D., who fed my words to a computer, some machine will remember the two of us long after human beings have stopped giving a damn whether we lived or not.

Ha!

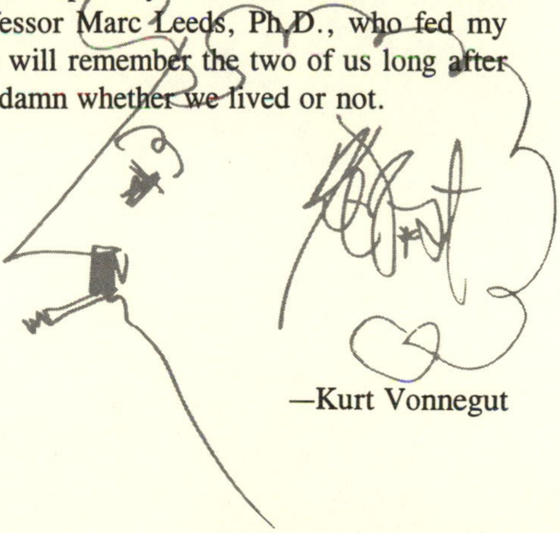

—Kurt Vonnegut

Preface

I am an unabashed Kurt Vonnegut fan. In the academic marketplace this may not get me very far, but I spent the last five years working on this book, mostly for myself. The idea for this collection came while working on my dissertation at the University of Buffalo. At the time, I was trying to juggle my way across twelve of Vonnegut's books. I never could make all my reading notes work the way I needed, nor could I get to them if I were out of the house. I needed portability and accuracy. And then it hit me. I looked up from the desk and saw on the bookshelf my invaluable copy of Michael and Molly Hardwick's *Dickens Encyclopedia*. I thought, "If I ever finish this dissertation. . . ."

The day I received the bound copy of my dissertation in the mail, I wrote to Mr. Vonnegut asking his permission to put together the collection. I felt that since I planned a fair amount of concordance work, I needed the author's permission for such extensive quotation. I received his reply in less than one week. Gracious and reassuring, he wished me well on the work. Moreover, he offered any assistance I needed. Since then, we have met and often written. For his initial encouragement and continuing friendship, a simple "thank you" is barely enough. I hope Kurt accepts this book as a gift and that he writes another dozen books so I can make a truly significant revision of this text.

But why make such a compendium now? There is merit to the notion that such a work should have the benefit of the author's entire collection, and since Vonnegut is well and actively publishing, this work may seem premature. For most authors, I would agree. However, Vonnegut's fictional world and his readers are unique. For his part, Vonnegut's characters, themes, phrasing, and imagery are forever reappearing. The readership has always been there, and you probably know from your own experience that conversations about his work are as much about the various reappearances of familiar friends and notions as they are about anything else.

My purpose was to organize and identify a good portion of Vonnegut's most frequently reappearing images and all his characters. I wanted to present the information in such a way that anyone could quickly find the passages in their books. Fortunately, most of Vonnegut's reprints are based on first editions, so I decided to cite the page and line numbers for every reference made.

There are two types of references: encyclopedia entries and concordance entries. They are meshed to form one running collection. The concordance entries are based on the input of many scholars who answered my queries. Most of their suggestions made it into the book. As for the encyclopedia entries, I tried to include every named character no matter how small the part. I also tried to include the many locations, institutions, and so on that any Vonnegutian needs to know about. I'm sure I missed something somewhere. Any omissions or errors are mine, and I would be glad to hear from readers suggesting additions or corrections.

When it came to writing about individual novels, I tried to work around strict plot summary. More often, I chose to look at major themes of the novels. With the amount of information provided in the encyclopedia, I felt it would be redundant to restructure the texts. Short story descriptions are generally made through character references rather than titles.

Acknowledgments

There are a number of people who directly or indirectly remained constant sources of inspiration while I wrote this text. I hate not being able to enumerate the ways in which they assisted my efforts, but I hope my long toils have not badly strained my relationship with Peter Reed, Joyce Lawrence, Jeff Gold, Norma Nutter, or Robert Forrey. For technical assistance above and beyond the call of duty, I need to thank Reed Sturdivant, Bruce Ottens, Gary Stottlemyer, Wendel and Carol Hester, Marcia Tackett, Mike Pinson, and Joyce Lawrence, again.

Loree Rackstraw and Asa Pieratt have remained fixed in my mind throughout this endeavor, providing a constant source of inspiration. Jerry Holt and Jim Flavin, my chairs in the English department at Shawnee State University, were most accommodating and resourceful.

A special note of thanks is due to Leslie Fiedler. Though I kept him in the dark about my progress with this project, I always felt the presence of my old advisor waiting for me to finish. Whenever I think of Professor Fiedler, I want to be more productive than the day before.

I would be remiss if I failed to thank my lawyer Donald Farber. He has persevered without the promise for much remuneration.

A special word of thanks goes to Bob Hagelstein, president of Greenwood Press, and the rest of his staff. Cynthia Harris calmed me down and let me prepare for the production phase of the project. Katie Chase did a wonderful job copy-editing the manuscript. Production editor Jude Grant deserves a medal for getting me through all the finer points, keeping track of all the details, maintaining her good humor and mine while I commuted across five states and moved just before the deadline.

Of the many scholars who answered my queries I want to particularly thank John Boni, Lawrence Broer, Ken Davis, William Godshalk, David Hayman, David Ketterer, Jerome Klinkowitz, Donald Lawler, Charles Lonie,

Robert Merrill, Asa Pieratt, Loree Rackstraw, Peter Reed, Mary Doyle Springer, William Veeder, and Lee F. Werth. Professor Broer sent along a brief index developed by his students and they deserve to be noted as well: Jessy Bennet, Eileen Butler, Sarah Cannon, Tom Cordy, Judy Delapenha, Chris Duffy, Marshall Flax, Shari Goldman, Diana Guzy, Patricia Lebeda, E. Snow Martin, Peter Mayer, Keith Morelli, Marianne Love, Joe Puccio, Hoe Richichi, David Rutman, Margie Stopak, and Darlene Wedler.

A special note of thanks goes to Angela Campbell and Cynthia Sequin, Presidential Scholars at Shawnee State University. I also want to thank President Clive Veri and Provost A.L. Addington of Shawnee State University for their support.

My older brother Don played a special role in the text's development. In 1968 he shunned his peers and took his little brother on a trip to Greenwich Village. There, in the basement of a bookstore, I was struck by the cover of *Mother Night* and Vonnegut's note about the firebombing of Dresden. This was news to me, and ever since I have been enthralled with his work. Years later, my brother mentioned to Bob Hagelstein that his brother wrote this book and is looking for a publisher. Here we are. I like my big brother a lot.

Above all, I want to thank my wife, Saralyn Gold, and our daughters, Marisa and Whitney, for their constant support, patience, and good humor about this manic obsession. And they have this promise: I shall not take the computer on our next vacation. You may even hide it.

A Note About the Text

I tried to maintain a consistent use of type styles as governed by the following rules:

ITALICS are used for:

1. My original commentary including original material inserted within Vonnegut quotations.
2. Book titles
3. Vonnegut's original italics are retained.

EXCEPTION to this rule is made for book titles to appear in plain face when used within my original italicized commentary.

BOLD FACE is used at the beginning of an entry and with each of its appearances within the noted citations.

EXCEPTION is made when I use the referenced term within my original commentary. When an entry is a book title, the reference is both italicized and bold faced.

QUOTATION MARKS are used for short quotes from Vonnegut within my commentary and around short story titles or short essays. Quotation marks are not used when flowing from original italicized commentary into Vonnegut's words. In this case my material is italicized and Vonnegut's is in plain face.

EXCEPTIONS were made when citing a short story/essay title within a parenthesized reference, i.e.: (*PS* 50:L17 *Obscenity*). In this example the reference comes from the book *Palm Sunday* page 50, line 17 in the essay called "Obscenity."

PAGE AND LINE NUMBERS are usually found within parenthetical references as illustrated above. In cases where a reference is frequently made within the same quoted material, I have included the lines for the entire reference. For instance, 50:L17-26 means numerous references are included within lines 17 through 26.

PLACEMENT OF PARENTHETICAL CITATIONS varies. A typical entry without commentary is preceded by the parenthetical material. In cases where original commentary flows into Vonnegut's material, the parenthetical citation comes at the end of the sentence before the end of line punctuation, in accordance with the Modern Language Association guidelines.

ASTERISKS are used for footnotes (very few, indeed) and whenever Vonnegut uses them, principally in *Galápagos* to note characters no longer living.

BOOK TITLES within parenthetical references are abbreviated as follows (the list is chronological):

Player Piano	*PP*	1952
The Sirens of Titan	*ST*	1959
Mother Night	*MN*	1962
Cat's Cradle	*CC*	1963
God Bless You, Mr. Rosewater	*GBR*	1965
Welcome to the Monkey House	*MH*	1968
Slaughterhouse-Five	*SL5*	1969
Happy Birthday, Wanda June	*WJ*	1970
Breakfast of Champions	*BC*	1973
Wampeters, Foma & Granfalloons	*WFG*	1974
Slapstick	*Slap*	1976
Jailbird	*JB*	1979
Palm Sunday	*PS*	1981
Deadeye Dick	*DD*	1982
Galápagos	*Gal*	1985
Bluebeard	*Blue*	1987
Hocus Pocus	*HP*	1990
Fates Worse Than Death	*FWD*	1991

Between Time and Timbuktu (*TIM*) presents an exceptional case. Vonnegut did not write the script. He did, however, provide an introductory note to the text, and that is the only material referenced in this text.

SOURCE MATERIALS for citations are based on the first edition Delta reprints and original first editions. First edition formatting is most commonly used in Vonnegut's reprints.

A

Aamons, Celia. *Though Celia's maiden name is not provided in* Cat's Cradle, *she married Nestor Aamons when he came to San Lorenzo to design and build the House of Hope and Mercy in the Jungle for Julian Castle. Nestor and Celia are the parents of Mona.*

Aamons, Nestor. (*CC* 102:L12) **Nestor Aamons** *(a native Finn)* was captured by the Russians, then liberated by the Germans during the Second World War. He was not returned home by his liberators, but was forced to serve in a *Wehrmacht* engineer unit that was sent to fight the Yugoslav partisans. He was captured by Chetniks, royalist Serbian partisans, and then by Communist partisans who attacked the Chetniks. He was liberated by Italian parachutists who surprised the Communists, and he was shipped to Italy.

The Italians put him to work designing fortifications for Sicily. He stole a fishing boat in Sicily, and reached neutral Portugal. *In Portugal, Nestor Aamons met Julian Castle, who convinced him to go to San Lorenzo where he designed Castle's hospital, the House of Hope and Mercy in the Jungle, "married a native woman named Celia, fathered a perfect daughter* [Mona], *and died."*

A-bomb, **American bomb**, **atomic bomb**, **atom-bombed**, **atom-bombing**, **atombombed**, **atomic weapons**, **hydrogen bomb**, **the bomb** (when clearly meaning a nuclear device), **neutron bomb**. *Vonnegut's frequent references to nuclear devices run throughout each one of his books. In* Player Piano *the supercomputer EPICAC is in charge of the technocracy's nuclear arms.* (*PP* 101:L32) EPICAC could consider the merits of high-explosive bombs as opposed to **atomic weapons** for tactical support, and keep in mind at the same time the availability of explosives as opposed to fissionable materials, the spacing of enemy foxholes, the labor situation in the respective processing industries, the probable mortality of planes in the face of enemy antiaircraft technology, and on and on, if it seemed at all important, to the number of cigarettes and Cocoanut Mound Bars and Silver Stars required to support a high-morale air force.

Cat's Cradle*'s narrator John/Jonah originally intends to write* an account of what important Americans had done on the day when the first **atomic bomb** was dropped on Hiroshima, Japan (*CC* 13:L17). *In* Slaughterhouse-Five *Vonnegut makes frequent comparisons between the firebombing of Dresden and the destruction of Hiroshima and Nagasaki, noting that more people were killed in Dresden than in the other two cities. His point has to do with the economy of destructive forces.* (*SL5* 162:L20) (British Air Marshal Sir Robert Saundby quoted in David Irving's *The Destruction of Dresden*) *The advocates of nuclear disarmament seem to believe that, if they could achieve their aim, war would become tolerable and decent. They would do well to read this book and ponder the fate of Dresden, where 135,000 people died as the result of an air attack with conventional weapons. On the night of March 9th, 1945, an air attack on Tokyo by American heavy bombers, using incendiary and high explosive bombs, caused the death of 83,793 people. The* ***atom bomb*** *dropped on Hiroshima killed 71,379 people.*

Similarly, Vonnegut speaks in his own voice about the bombing as a technological achievement in Palm Sunday . . . and when I feel most lost in this world, I comfort myself by visiting a hardware store. I meditate there. I do not buy anything. A hammer is still my Jesus, and my Virgin Mary is still a cross-cut saw.

But I learned how vile that religion of mine could be when the **atomic bomb** was dropped on Hiroshima... There was nothing in the bombs or the airplanes, after all, which could not, essentially, be bought at a small hardware store (*PS* 69:L13 *When I Lost My Innocence*). *Vonnegut creates the contrast in his mind between the bombings of Dresden and Hiroshima. Dresden's conventionally engineered destruction was not beyond imagination because of its reliance on everyday materials. Hiroshima's immolation reflected a leap in materials acquisition and application.*

Colonel Looseleaf Harper in Happy Birthday, Wanda June *is said to be the pilot who dropped the bomb on Nagasaki.* Deadeye Dick *has at its core the neutron bombing of Midland City and the suggestion that the government authorized its destruction as a test of the weapon.* (*DD* 234:L26, 31) My own guess is that the American Government had to find out for certain whether the **neutron bomb** was as harmless as it was supposed to be. So it set one off in a small city which nobody cared about, where people weren't doing all that much with their lives anyhow, where businesses were going under or moving away. The Government couldn't test a **bomb** on a foreign city, after all, without running the risk of starting World War Three.

Galápagos *chronicles humanity's evolutionary return to the sea as a partial consequence of the genetically altered Hisako Hiroguchi (her mother survived the Hiroshima bombing). Warden Hiroshi Matsumoto (whose first name and first two letters of his last name spell "Hiroshima") of* Hocus Pocus is also a survivor of the Hiroshima bombing. *See also: MN* 68:L10; 115:L23; *CC* 13:L17; 17:L9; 17:L13,15,21,23; 18:L4,14-15; 19:L2,10-13,22,24,28; 20:L12; 22:L35; 23:L25,33; 24:L1,9,34,36; 25:L2; 27:L18; 31:L26; 32:L7; 37:L32; 41:L23; 57:L30-31; 63:L22; 66:L13; 93:L4; 111:L32; 190:L22; *SL5* 159:L25; 160:L4-5,7,11,14,16,29; *MH—Report on the Barnhouse Effect* 157:L12; 158:L1; 159:L31; 161:L31; 163:L10; *WJ* 2:L27; 4:L3; 55:L7; 161:L11; 162:L12; *BC* 156:L14; 269:L12; *WFG—Address to the American Physical Society* 98:L7,13; *WFG—Address to P.E.N. Conference in Stockholm, 1973* 226:L29; *WFG—Playboy Interview* 266:L25; *Slap* 96:L25; *JB* xi:L4; xxi:L1; 60:L21-22,30-31; *PS—When I Lost My Innocence* 66:L9-10; *PS—Jekyll And Hyde Updated* 285:L5; *DD* xii:L30; xiii:L14,17-18; 33:L2,5,7,9-10,14; 58:L14; 92:L5-6; 100:L16-17; 104:L14; 114:L7; 115:L9; 150:L5-6; 209:L24; 214:L30-31; 225:L1-2; 226:L16; 229:L18; 232:L21-22; 235:L2; *Gal* 39:L6; 40:L22; 58:L9; 94:L23; 145:L27-28; 156:L19,22; *Blue* 35:L1; 218:L28; *HP* 57:L12; 118:L16; 128:L34-35; 218:L24-26; 223:L15; 227:L8-9,L26; 243:L19; 267:L11; 281:L30; 294:L18; 296:L19,23-24; 299:L9; *FWD* 97:L4; 100:L12-13; 139:L4,8.

"Adam" (1954). *Reprinted in* Welcome to the Monkey House, *this is the short story about the birth of Peter Karl Knechtmann, the only child of Heinz and Avchen Knechtmann, both survivors of the Nazi death camps. As Heinz looks into the small face of his son, he senses the child's natural resemblance to all the family members he lost in the Holocaust.* (*MH* 279:L21-24 *Adam*) "Little Peter, little Kroll," he said softly, "little Friederich—and there's Helga in you, too. Little spark of Knechtmann, you little treasure house. Everything is saved in you." *The story of the Knechtmanns' personal and cultural triumph is set against Mr. Souza's wait for a son. His wife delivers their seventh daughter.*

Adams, James Carmalt (also **James Carmalt Adams, Jr.**). *Vonnegut's brother-in-law married to his sister Alice. The two died within two days of each other. He was killed in a commuter train accident and she died of cancer. This episode is recounted in the prologue to* Slapstick *and in* Palm Sunday.

James Carmalt Adams, Jr. is one of their sons adopted by Vonnegut and his first wife Jane. He became a goat farmer and Vonnegut recounts the realization his adopted son made about the fading memory of his parents, "tapping his forehead with his fingertips, 'It isn't the museum it should be'" (*Slap* 15:L12-13).

Adams, Steve. *One of Vonnegut's nephews adopted by him after the deaths of his sister and brother-in-law. Steve Adams and Mark Vonnegut (Kurt's son) were the same age and became "artificial twins" as did Kurt Adams and Edith Vonnegut.*

Steve Adams is also the name of the captain of the basketball team in Deadeye Dick *who stole away Sally Freeman from Felix Waltz just before the senior prom. This prompted Felix to ask Celia Hildreth to escort him.*

Adams, Tiger. *The pilot for Fred T. Barry, he had once dated Celia Hildreth in high school, though she later married Dwayne Hoover. One evening, while* "coming in for a night landing at Will Fairchild Memorial Airport . . . he had to pull up at the last second because there was somebody out on the runway" (*DD* 155:L15). *The person was Celia whom Tiger described as looking like the Wicked Witch of the West in* The Wizard of Oz.

Adult Correctional Institution at Shepherdstown. *Located on the opposite side of Route 103 from the Quality Motor Court, the correctional facility is famous for its dentistry program and its Sexual Offenders' Wing. In* Breakfast of Champions, *the latter is the source of great fear for transvestite Harry LeSabre, the Pontiac salesman who is terrorized by the taunts of his employer Dwayne Hoover, though Hoover didn't know Harry's secret. Shepherdstown was also the place of incarceration for Wayne Hoobler. The institution was destroyed during the neutron bombing of Midland City in* Deadeye Dick.

afterlife (see also **blue tunnel**). *Vonnegut has always made a point of emphasizing his family's deeply felt atheism. (FWD* 238:L11) I am a fourth generation German American religious skeptic ("Freethinker"). Like my essentially puritanical forebears, I believe that God has so far been unknowable and hence unservable, hence the highest service one can perform is to his or her community, whose needs are quite evident. I believe that virtuous behavior is trivialized by carrot-and-stick schemes, such as promises of highly improbable rewards or punishments in an improbable afterlife. *Eugene Debs Hartke, the narrator of* Hocus Pocus, *echoes Vonnegut's own upbringing and sentiments.* (*HP* 16:L19) I am in fact pretty much an Atheist like my mother's father, although I kept that to myself. Why argue somebody else out of the expectation of some sort of an **Afterlife**? (*HP* 175:L36) I have looked up who the Freethinkers were. They were members of a short-lived sect, mostly of German descent, who believed, as did my Grandfather Wills, that nothing but sleep awaited good and evil persons alike in the **Afterlife**.

Nevertheless, the idea of an afterlife is at the core of both Slapstick *and* Galápagos. *In* Slapstick *Wilbur Swain has the existence of an afterlife confirmed for him when he uses "The Hooligan" to speak with Eliza, his dearly departed twin. Swain's knowledge of the afterlife doesn't make its prospect too appealing. (Slap* 231:L17) The talkers *(on the other end of The Hooligan)* identified themselves as persons in the **afterlife**. They were backed by a demoralized chorus of persons who complained to each other of tedium and social slights and minor ailments, and so on. *Prompted by all the background cackling and complaining, Swain renames the afterlife "The Turkey Farm."*

Galápagos*' narrative comes from the afterlife.* (*Gal* 219:L21) I *(Leon Trout)* was painlessly decapitated one day by a falling sheet of steel while working inside the hull of the Bahía de Darwin, at which time I refused to set foot in the blue tunnel leading into the Afterlife. *Trout goes on to say that from time to time his father, famed science fiction author Kilgore Trout, would come to the mouth of the blue tunnel to prompt him inside. Leon continuously refuses, and instead writes the ensuing text with nothing more substantial than his finger scribbling in thin air. See also: WFG—In a Manner That Must Shame God Himself* 205:L18; *Slap* 11:L1; 45:L3; 60:L9; 205:L27; 237:L14; *Gal* 5:L2; 65:L16; 73:L11; 98:L26-27; 118:L23; 147:L4; 159:L12; 163:L5; 166:L6; 199:L24; 229:L3; 251:L18; 257:L2; *FWD* 159:L22.

Agnes and Agnes (Barbara and Martha). *These are two barflies Ed Finnerty picks up at the bar in Homestead.* (*PP* 89:L1, 5) "Paul—I'd like you to meet my cousin Agnes from Detroit," said Finnerty. He rested his hand on the knee of a fat and determinedly cheerful redhead sitting next to him. "And this," he said, pointing across the table at a tall, homely brunette, "is *your* cousin Agnes." *They order double scotches which are actually nothing more than water. They are found out when Paul casually picks up one of their shot glasses. They are awed and resentful of Ed and Paul when they find out they are engineers from across the river,* Barbara still kept her distance from Paul and looked at him distastefully. "What are you doing over here—having a good laugh at the dumb bunnies?"

Agnew, Spiro. *Vice-President Spiro Agnew is one of about forty people at a White House meeting shortly after the May 4, 1970, shooting of four students at Kent State University.* (*JB* 31:L21) Vice-President **Spiro T. Agnew** was there. He would eventually plead *nolo contendere* to charges of accepting bribes and evading income taxes.

Aïda. (*GBR* 39:L2) That evening, he *(Eliot Rosewater)* and Sylvia went to the Metropolitan Opera for the opening of a new staging of ***Aïda***. . . .

Everything was fine until the last scene of the opera, during which the hero and heroine were placed in an airtight chamber to suffocate. As the doomed pair filled their lungs, Eliot called out to them, "You will last a lot longer, if you don't try to sing." Eliot stood, leaned far out of his box, told the singers, "Maybe you don't know anything about oxygen, but I do. Believe me, you must not sing."

(*GBR* 41:L1) Norman Mushari learned that, on the night of ***Aïda***, Eliot disappeared again, jumped out of his homeward-bound cab at Forty-second Street and Fifth Avenue.

Aiken, Conrad. *Like Vonnegut, this Pulitzer Prize winner was also the child of a suicide. In fact, Aiken's father committed a murder suicide involving the*

author's mother. Aiken was the literary editor of Emily Dickinson's Selected Poems. (*PS* 251:L26, 29, 32 *Children*) And **Conrad Aiken**, the poet, the one time I met him, told me that a child will compete with its father in an area where the father is weak, in an area where the father mistakenly believes himself to be quite accomplished. **Aiken** himself did this, by his own account. His father was a Renaissance man, a surgeon, an athlete, something of a musician, something of a poet, and on and on. **Aiken** said that he himself became a poet because he realized that his father's poetry really wasn't very good.
(*Blue* 260:L13, 16-17, 19) He *(Terry Kitchen)* said that the poet **Conrad Aiken** had lectured at Yale when Kitchen was in law school there, and had said that sons of gifted men went into fields occupied by their fathers, but where their fathers were weak. **Aiken's** own father had been a great physician and politician and ladies' man, but had also fancied himself a poet. "His poetry was no damn good, so **Aiken** became a poet," said Kitchen. "I could never do such a thing to my old man."

Ainus. (*HP* 212:L5) TO understand how the lower ranks of guards at Athena in those days felt about White people, and never mind Black people, you have to realize that most of them were recruited from Japan's northernmost island, Hokkaido. On Hokkaido the primitive natives, the **Ainus**, thought to be very ugly because they were so pallid and hairy, were White people. Genetically speaking, they are just as white as Nancy Reagan. Their ancestors long ago had made the error, when humiliated by superior Asiatic civilizations, of shambling north instead of west to Europe, and eventually, of course, to the Western Hemisphere.
(*HP* 219:L18) I misread him *(Hiroshi Matsumoto)* completely, not knowing then that the Japanese considered themselves to be as genetically discrete from other Orientals as from me or Donner or Nancy Reagan or the pallid, hairy **Ainus**, say.

air-raid, **air raid**, **air-raid shelter**, **air-raid siren** (also **raid** and **raids** as they refer to Dresden or to war-time bombing). *Vonnegut took shelter during the firebombing of Dresden in an underground slaughterhouse meatlocker. Not so surprisingly, a number of his characters are forced to take refuge in similar structures.* Player Piano*'s Paul Proteus is taken prisoner by the Ghost Shirt Society in an old Ilium air-raid shelter. Eliot Rosewater purchases an air-raid siren from Berlin for the Rosewater County volunteer fire department. Billy Pilgrim and Howard Campbell take refuge in the slaughterhouse meatlocker of* Slaughterhouse-Five. *Within that seminal text, Professor Rumfoord is hard at work on condensing the* Official History of the Army Air Force in World War Two *into one volume. (SL5* 165:L6) The thing was, though, there was almost nothing in the twenty-seven volumes about the Dresden raid, even though it had been such a howling success. *This represents a fictional follow-up of Vonnegut's own search for official information about the Dresden raid which* *was still classified as top secret years after the event.*

Vonnegut recalls that despite whatever he was writing at the time, he was always struggling with writing a book about Dresden (SL5 9:L5). *His vision of the world became fixed during this underground episode, and aside from the explicit move to an air-raid shelter by Paul Proteus, Billy Pilgrim, and Howard Campbell, other leading characters who specifically take refuge or have a transforming underground experience include: Malachi Constant in the caves of Mercury (ST); John/Jonah in Papa Monzano's oubliette on San Lorenzo during the ice-nine freezing of the Earth (CC); Wilbur Swain stores his various scientific and social treatises in the underground mausoleum of his grandfather (Slap); Walter Starbuck's White House office is in its third subbasement, and he is jailed for the second time in the basement cell of a New York City police precinct before tending to the the mortally wounded Mary Kathleen O'Looney in the abandoned tunnels of Grand Central Station (JB); Rudy Waltz is jailed in the basement cell of Midland City's police department after unintentionally killing Eloise Metzger (DD); Leon Trout is decapitated while constructing the hull of the* Bahía de Darwin *and refuses to enter the blue tunnel into the afterlife (Gal); Rabo Karabekian's one-time masterpiece "Windsor Blue Number Seventeen" degrades due to the fatally flawed Sateen Dura-luxe, but after retrieving the sixty-four foot tryptich, he paints his photo-realistic masterpiece "Now It's the Women's Turn," the scene depicting the image Vonnegut saw when released from the German POW camp (Blue); Eugene Debs Hartke earned his silver star by going down the mouth of a Viet Cong tunnel and killing three supposed combatants, only to find out they were a mother, her child, and the child's grandmother (HP). See also: PP* 252:L35-36; 253:L4; *MN* 182:L10; *GBR* 92:L23; *SL5* 9:L5; 9:L10; 10:L4; 141:L19; 152:L28; 165:L14; *MH—Unready To Wear* 237:L24; 238:L19; *WJ* 72:L15; *PS—Self-Interview* 89:L25; 94:L23-24; *PS—A Nazi Sympathizer Defended At Some Cost* 296:L27; *PS—A Nazi City Mourned At Some Profit* 302:L5; *DD* 42:L18; *FWD* 100:L21.

A.J. Topf und Sohn. *Warden Hiroshi Matsumoto purchased crematoria ovens from this German firm located in Essen, and which had built the crematorium at Auschwitz during World War II. The warden needed to buy the ovens when the Mafia, using the AIDS epidemic as the reason, doubled its price for disposing of convicts' bodies. When the prisoners broke out they destroyed the facility.* (*HP* 229:L15-22) The postwar **Topf** models all had state-of-the-art smoke scrubbers on their smokestacks, so people in Scipio, unlike the people living near Auschwitz, never knew that they had a busy corpse carbonizer in the neighborhood.

We could have been gassing and incinerating convicts over there around the clock, and who would know?

Who would care?

Ajax. *In the* Iliad, *Ajax is the son of Telamon and second in bravery to Achilles of the Greeks who besieged Troy. Kilgore Trout wonders about the juxtaposition of such a literary reference used as the logo written across a tractor trailer.* (*BC* 90:31-33, 92:L1-2) Trout wondered what a child who was just learning to read would make of a message like that *(the Pyramid logo written across a tractor trailer)*.

Akbahr, Abdullah. *When Hartke meets him in the warden's waiting room, Abdullah is reading* The Protocols of the Elders of Zion. *He is part of the Black Brothers of Islam, the ruling gang at the Athena prison, and is instrumental in assisting Hartke with his prison literacy program whose principal text is* The Protocols of the Elders of Zion. *Abdullah Akbahr, a Marine veteran of the Vietnam War, was imprisoned for committing three murders as part of a drug war.* (*HP* 234:L24) His name was **Abdullah Akbahr**. With my *(Eugene Debs Hartke)* encouragement, he would write several interesting short stories. One, I remember, was supposedly the autobiography of a talking deer in the National Forest who has a terrible time finding anything to eat in winter and gets tangled in barbed wire during the summer months, trying to get at the delicious food on farms. He is shot by a hunter. As he dies he wonders why he was born in the first place. The final sentence of the story was the last thing the deer said on Earth. The hunter was close enough to hear it and was amazed. This was it: "What the blankety-blank was that supposed to be all about?" (*HP* 235:L2-5) He himself would be shot dead with buckshot and slugs after the prison break, while carrying a flag of truce, by Whitey VanArsdale, the mechanic, and Lyle Hooper, the Fire Chief.

Al. *One of the Ghost Shirt Society members who participates in the destruction of some of the physical facilities in Ilium.* (*PP* 283:L21-22) "And, by God, here'sh ol' **Al** to go with us. Where you been, y'ol' horsethief?"

"Blew up the goddam sewage 'sposal plant," said **Al** proudly.

Albanian Flu. *Along with the Green Death, these two plagues took many lives after the Chinese experiments destabilized gravity in* Slapstick.

Alberti, Leon Battista (1402-1472). *The Florentine Renaissance writer, architect, and humanist.* (*Blue* 213:L5-6) She was only four blocks away—in a palazzo designed for Innocenzo "the Invisible" de Medici by **Leon Battista Alberti** in the middle of the fifteenth century.

Algonquin Hotel. (*Blue* 111:L27-28) I *(Rabo Karabekian)* spent an uneventful late evening watching pornographic TV programs in my room at the **Algonquin Hotel**. I watched and didn't watch at the very same time.

Algonquins. (*PP* 3:L8) He *(Paul Proteus)* was showing the cat an old battlefield at peace. Here *(the Ilium Works)*, in the basin of the river bend, the

Mohawks had overpowered the **Algonquins**, the Dutch the Mohawks, the British the Dutch, the Americans the British.

Algren, Nelson (1909-1981). *The Chicago novelist noted for his realistic portrayals of urban poverty.* (*Blue* 46:L7) While I was at it, I asked them if they recognized the names of Jackson Pollock, Mark Rothko, or Terry Kitchen, or Truman Capote, or **Nelson Algren**, or Irwin Shaw, or James Jones, all of whom had figured not only in the history of arts and letters but in the history of the Hamptons. They did not. So much for achieving immortality via the arts and letters. *Rabo asked Celeste and her friends by the swimming pool if they knew who any of these people were as a sort of cultural quiz to satisfy his own misgivings about teenagers.*

Nelson Algren and Vonnegut met in 1965 while both were teaching at the Iowa Writer's Workshop. (*FWD* 35:L12) I am able to follow the three rules for a good life set down by the late writer **Nelson Algren**, a fellow depressive, and another subject of the study of writers made at the University of Iowa. The three rules are, of course: Never eat at a place called Mom's, never play cards with a man named Doc, and most important, never go to bed with anybody who has more troubles than you do. *Vonnegut refers to Algren a number of times in* Fates Worse Than Death, *including the introduction he wrote for the 1987 reprint of Algren's* Never Come Morning.

Alice in Wonderland. (*PP* 251:L20) "Wait until he sits in on some meetings," said Finnerty. "They're like something out of ***Alice in Wonderland***, Paul." *Finnerty refers to meetings of the Ghost Shirt Society.*

In The Sirens of Titan, *Vonnegut refers to the undersized side entrance door (four-and-a-half feet high) to the Rumfoord estate as an "Alice-in-Wonderland door."* *ST* 10:L19-20; 13:L2; 15:L18; 94:L6; 234:L17-18; 239:L7-8.

The author of the classic tale is cited by Wanda June as another resident of heaven who avidly plays shuffleboard (WJ 136:L2). *See also:* BC 252:L33-253:L1; *WFG—A Political Disease* 233:L2-3; *Blue* 138:L15.

"**All the King's Horses**" (1953). *Reprinted in* Welcome to the Monkey House, *this cold war short story chronicles the capture of Colonel Bryan Kelly, his wife, children and military escort after their plane crashes in an unnamed country in the orient. Pi Ying, the sadistic outpost commander forces Kelly into a chess match using his family and captured soldiers as the chess pieces. Captured pieces are to be summarily executed. Ying is killed by his mistress, and Major Barzov, Ying's Soviet advisor, releases the captives.*

All-Night Sam. *In the short story "Next Door," All-Night Sam is the radio disc jockey listened to by Lemuel Harger and his mistress in the apartment adjacent to Paul Leonard's. Young Paul calls All-Night Sam to dedicate a record from Mr. Harger to his wife Rose. Sam obliges by playing Eartha Kitt's*

"Somebody Bad Stole De Wedding Bell!" This drives a wedge between Harger and his mistress and brings back Rose.

Allen, Lester (see also **Ginsberg**). *The former newspaperman Vonnegut knows from Cape Cod who was one of the many writing books about the murderer Tony Costa and recounted in "There's a Maniac Loose Out There" in* Wampeters, Foma & Granfalloons.

Amphibious Pioneers Society (also **Amphibians**) *An organization of the first five thousand followers of the teachings of Dr. Ellis Konigswasser in the 1953 short story "Unready to Wear." The amphibians have learned how to isolate their psyches and leave the physical confines of their bodies.*

Anderson Trailer. *Among the first investments of Noel Constant, the father of Malachi,* ***Anderson Trailer*** *helped him complete financial transactions which demanded he invest according to stock acronyms which spell out the text of the Bible.* (*ST* 74:L16) His very first investment was International Nitrate. After that came Trowbridge Helicopter, Electra Bakeries, Eternity Granite, Indiana Novelty, Norwich Iron, National Gelatin, Granada Oil, Del-Mar Creations, Richmond Electroplating, **Anderson Trailer**, and Eagle Duplicating.

Anschluss. (*JB* 228:L24) In accordance with my wife's will *(Ruth, Walter Starbuck's wife)*, incidentally, Juan and his brother, Geraldo, were receiving reparations from West Germany for the confiscation of my wife's father's bookstore in Vienna by the Nazis after the ***Anschluss***, Germany's annexation of Austria in Nineteen-hundred and Thirty-eight. *Juan and Geraldo are the grandsons of Walter and Ruth Starbuck.*

anthropoids. (*CC* 56:L1) "Hello, fellow **anthropoids** and lily pads and paddlewheels," he *(Lyman Enders Knowles)* said to Miss Faust and me. "Yes, yes!"

(*Blue* 202:L2-3) The clitoris, so goes the speculation in the paper *(The New York Times)*, is the last vestige of the inseminating organ of a conquered, enslaved, trivialized and finally emasculated race of weaker, but not necessarily dumber, **anthro-poids**!

Cancel my subscription!

anthropological, anthropologist, anthropology. *Vonnegut studied for a master's degree in anthropology at the University of Chicago and supported himself during that time by working as a police reporter for the Chicago City News Bureau. Through his thesis he sought to graph simple tales of good and evil, but it was rejected. After publishing* Cat's Cradle, *however, the university awarded him the degree. There are two anthropology instructors in his books: Robert Pefko returns from Korea and becomes an anthropology instructor at West Point (BC); Arthur von Strelitz is Walter Starbuck's Harvard* *anthropology professor, and he permits his young student to use his apartment for a lovers' tryst with Mary Kathleen O'Looney.*

More importantly, the Vonnegut Freethinker legacy dovetails with his understanding of anthropology and is everywhere apparent. (*WFG* 283:L7 *Playboy Interview*) All my books are my effort to answer that question and to make myself like life better than I do. I'm trying to throw out all the trashy merchandise adults put in my head when I was a little kid. I want to put a culture up there. People will believe anything, which means *I* will believe anything. I learned that in **anthropology**. I want to start believing in things that have shapeliness and harmony.
(*PS* 101:L5 *Self-Interview*) INTERVIEWER: Did the study of **anthropology** later color your writings?
VONNEGUT: It confirmed my atheism, which was the faith of my fathers anyway. Religions were exhibited and studied as the Rube Goldberg inventions I'd always thought they were. We weren't allowed to find one culture superior to any other. We caught hell if we mentioned races much. It was highly idealistic.

Vonnegut frequently mentions his mentor at the University of Chicago who strongly influenced the core of his novels, especially as they concern folk societies and extended families. (*PS* 116:L24 *Self-Interview*) VONNEGUT: And when I went to the University of Chicago, and I heard the head of the Department of anthropology, Robert Redfield, lecture on the folk society, which was essentially a stable, isolated extended family, he did not have to tell me how nice that could be. (*FWD* 122:L1) When I studied anthropology long ago at the University of Chicago, my most famous professor was Dr. Robert Redfield... He said that he could describe to every fair-minded person's satisfaction one (and only one) stage every society had passed through or would pass through. He called this inevitable stage and his essay on it "The Folk Society." (*FWD* 31:L21) "I hold a master's degree in **anthropology** from the University of Chicago. Students of that branch of poetry are taught to seek explanations for human comfort or discomfort—wars, wounds, spectacular diseases, and natural disasters aside—in culture, society, and history. And I have just named the villains in my books, which are never individuals. The villains again: culture, society, and history—none of them strikingly housebroken by lithium, Thorazine, Prozac, or Tofranil. *See also: PP* 23:L18; 78:L1-3; *SL5* 7:L9,20; *BC* 153:L11; *WFG—There's A Maniac Loose Out There* 69:L23; *WFG—Address to the National Institute of Arts and Letters, 1971* 174:L5; 176:L1,5,22,26; 177:L1-2; 180:L26; *WFG—Playboy Interview* 287:L6; *Slap* 129:L28; *JB* 163:L21; *PS—Triage* 74:L12,15-16,18; 76:L30; *PS—Self-Interview* 95:L13; 101:L27,29; 103:L7; 105:L7; *PS—Religion* 211:L22; *PS—Children* 240:L30; 241:L1-9,19; *PS—The Sexual Revolution* 312:L13; *Gal* 154:L10; *FWD* 34:L33; 65:L11; 77:L24; 90:L5; 126:L11,16,19; 129:L7; 146:L32; 191:L20.

anthropomorphic. (*PP* 112:L5) "Garth's a fine man," said Paul. Garth was, too: four-square, desperate to please, and he seemed to have an **anthropomorphic** image of the corporate personality. Garth stood in relation to that image as a lover, and Paul wondered if this prevalent type of relationship had ever been given the consideration it deserved by sexologists. On second thought, he supposed that it had—the general phenomenon of a lover's devotion to the unseen—in studies of nuns' symbolic marriages to Christ. At any rate, Paul had seen Garth at various stages of his love affair, unable to eat for anxiety, on a manic crest, moved to maudlin near-crying at recollections of the affair's tender beginnings. In short, Garth suffered all the emotional hazards of a perennial game of she-loves-me, she-loves-me-not. To carry out directions from above—an irritating business for Paul—was, for Garth, a favor to please a lady. "I'd like to see him get the job."
(*Gal* 106:L14) Mary used to shut up then. There would be no more **anthropomorphic** jokes.

anti-gerasone. *In the short story "Tomorrow and Tomorrow and Tomorrow," anti-gerasone is the anti-aging potion which allows people to seemingly live forever. Because it prevents death by natural causes, it is the cause of a severe housing shortage.*

apocalyptic. (*ST* 216:9) The church, which squatted among the headstones like a wet mother dodo, had been at various times Presbyterian, Congregationalist, Unitarian, and Universal **Apocalyptic**. It was now the Church of God the Utterly Indifferent.
(*MN* vi:4) More bombs were dropped to keep firemen in their holes, and all the little fires grew, joined one another, became one **apocalyptic** flame.
(*Gal* 126:4) And this **apocalyptic** warning so suited the wiring of the Captain's brain, even before his father came down with Huntington's chorea, that he would ever after believe that that was indeed the most likely way in which humanity would be exterminated: by meteorites. *Captain Adolf Von Kleist had learned of the destructive power of meteors while a student at the United States Naval Academy.*

Arapahos. *Vonnegut uses the Arapahos as a metaphor for the inferior state of the white man in America when compared with the new elite, the dominant culture of the Japanese. Even the prison guards from Hokkaido, the white Ainus—considered the lowest strata among Japanese culture—look down upon the whites.* (*HP* 212:L12-19) Those White people on Hokkaido had sure missed a lot. They were way behind practically everybody. And when the man who wanted to teach shop and I presented ourselves at the gate to the road that led through the National Forest to the prison, the 2 guards on duty there were fresh from Hokkaido. For all the respect our being Whites inspired in them, we might as well have been a couple of drunk and disorderly **Arapahos**.

Archangel Gabriel (also **Gabriel horns**). *Acting as a messenger of God, one of the seven archangels, Gabriel is the angel of the Annunciation and the herald of good news and comfort.* (*ST* 86:L1-2) The Wilburhampton Hotel was a frumpish, three-story Tudor structure across the street from the Magnum Opus Building, standing in relation to that building like an unmade bed at the feet of the **Archangel Gabriel**. Pine slats were tacked to the stucco exterior of the hotel, simulating half-timbered construction. The backbone of the roof had been broken intentionally, simulating great age. The eaves were plump and low, tucked under, simulated thatch. The windows were tiny, with diamond-shaped panes. *The Wilburhampton Hotel is where Noel Constant dreamed up his "divinely inspired" investment strategy. By contrast, Winston Niles Rumfoord's estate has horns which blare for the coming of the Space Wanderer, considered a messiah by the Church of God the Utterly Indifferent. Rumfoord, acting like a God, speaks to the crowd through his estate's horns.* (*ST* 240:L20) "*Bring the Space Wanderer here!*" blatted Rumfoord's voice from the **Gabriel horns** on the walls. (*ST* 242:L23) "Welcome, Space Wanderer," blatted Rumfoord's oleomargarine tenor from the **Gabriel horns** on the wall. "How meet it is that you should come to us on the bright red pumper of a volunteer fire department. I can think of no more stirring symbol of man's humanity to man than a fire engine. . . ." (*ST* 248:L29-30) His voice *(Rumfoord's)* came not from the tree but from the **Gabriel horns** on the walls.

Eliot Rosewater, another messiah figure, tailors himself in seemingly celestial attire. (*GBR* 32:L33) But he *(Eliot)* was off again in a month, carousing with firemen in Clover Lick, West Virginia, one night, and in New Egypt, New Jersey, the next. And on that trip he traded clothes with another man, swapped a four-hundred-dollar suit for a 1939 double-breasted blue chalkstripe, with shoulders like Gibraltar, lapels like the wings of the **Archangel Gabriel**, and with the creases in the trousers permanently sewed in.

Archimedes screw. *An ancient apparatus for raising water consisting of either a spiral tube around an inclined axis, or an inclined tube containing a tight-fitting, broad-threaded screw. Senator Rosewater makes mention of this old device to continue lecturing Eliot about the metaphorical Money River.* (*GBR* 105:L1) "The Money River, where the wealth of the nation flows. We were born on the banks of it—and so were most of the mediocre people we grew up with, went to private schools with, sailed and played tennis with. We can slurp from that mighty river to our hearts' content. And we even take slurping lessons, so we can slurp more efficiently. . . . From lawyers! From tax consultants! From customers' men! We're born close enough to the river to drown ourselves and the next ten generations in wealth, simply using dippers and buckets. But we still hire the experts to teach us the use of aqueducts, dams, reservoirs, siphons, bucket brigades, and the **Archimedes' screw**. And our teachers in turn become rich, and their children become buyers of lessons in slurping."

Aristotle. (*ST* 68:L28, 30-32) *(Ransom K.)* Fern read two books a day. It has been said that **Aristotle** was the last man to be familiar with the whole of his own culture. Ransom K. Fern had made an impressive attempt to equal **Aristotle**'s achievement. He had been somewhat less successful than **Aristotle** in perceiving patterns in what he knew.
(*MN* 38:L24) I *(Howard Campbell)* have at hand a clipping from the New York *Herald Tribune* of March third, about two weeks ago, in which a critic says of Kraft as a painter: Here at last is a capable and grateful heir to the fantastic inventiveness and experimentation in painting during the past hundred years. **Aristotle** is said to have been the last man to understand the whole of his culture. George Kraft is surely the first man to understand the whole of modern art—to understand it in his sinews and bones.
(*GBR* 103:L4) "You want me to start buying paintings for museums again? Would you be prouder of me, if I'd contributed two and a half million dollars to buy Rembrandt's *Aristotle Contemplating a Bust of Homer?*"

"Don't reduce the argument to an absurdity." *This is a piece of conversation between Eliot and his father concerning the manner in which Eliot expresses his philanthropy.*
(*FWD* 114:L4) They said, as most of them do today, that the country was falling apart because the young people were no longer required to read Plato and **Aristotle** and Marcus Aurelius and St. Augustine and Montaigne and the like, whose collective wisdom was the foundation of any decent and just and productive society.

Arnold, General Benedict. (*Blue* 193:L5-6) He *(Paul Slazinger)*, incidentally, was from a very old American family. The first Slazinger on this continent was a Hessian grenadier serving as a mercenary with General John Burgoyne, the British general who was defeated by forces commanded in part by the rebel **General Benedict Arnold**, who would later desert to the British, at the second Battle of Freeman's Farm, north of Albany, two hundred years ago. Slazinger's ancestor was taken prisoner during the battle, and never went home, which was in Wiesbaden, Germany, where he had been the son of—guess what?

A cobbler.

In defense of his teaching and the scurrilous stories attributed to him at the meeting of the Board of Trustees, Eugene Debs Hartke invokes the image of the notorious traitor. (*HP* 131:L24-32) "Mr. Moellenkamp, sir—" I said, "you know darn well, and so does everybody else here, that you can follow the most patriotic, deeply religious American who ever lived with a tape recorder for a year, and then prove that he's a worse traitor than **Benedict Arnold**, and a worshipper of the Devil. Who doesn't say things in a moment of passion or absentmindedness that he doesn't wish he could take back? So I ask again, am I the only one this was done to, and if so, why?"

Arthur, Chester Alan (*Slap* 114:L4) I *(Wilbur Swain)* was then not only a stupid Bobby Brown, but a conceited one. Though only a first-year medical student with the genitalia of an infant field mouse, I was the master of a great house on Beacon Hill. I was driven to and from school in a Jaguar—and I had already taken to dressing as I would dress when President of the United States, like a medical mountebank during the era of **Chester Alan Arthur**, say.

Ashland, Captain Bryant. *Cited as the "second man in space" by Mikhail Ivankov, father of Soviet Major Stepan Ivankov, in the short story "The Manned Missiles." Both military astronauts meet their deaths in space. Ashland was sent into orbit to observe and photograph the Soviet capsule. The two spaceships got too close and crashed, stranding both astronauts in space for eternity.*

Ashland, Charlene. *The twin sister of Colonel Bryant Ashland who dies in space in the short story "The Manned Missiles." She works for the telephone company in Jacksonville, Florida. Charlene asks that when her father writes to Mr. Ivankov he tell him the story which shows Bud's humanity and that conveys the humor all families enjoy repeating when they gather.* (*MH* 263:L9-16 *The Manned Missiles*) When Bud and **Charlene** were about eight, why I came home one night with a fish bowl and two goldfish. There was one goldfish for each twin, only it was impossible to tell one fish from the other one. They were exactly alike. So one morning Bud got up early, and there was one goldfish floating on top of the water dead. So Bud went and woke up **Charlene**, and he said, "Hey, **Charlene**—your goldfish just died." That's the story **Charlene** asked me to tell you, Mr. Ivankov.

Ashland, Charles. *The father of Captain Bryant Ashland, one of title characters in the short story "The Manned Missiles." Described as a "petroleum merchant in Titusville, Florida," he and Mikhail Ivankov, the father of Soviet Major Stepan Ivankov, exchange letters of regret and commiseration about their sons' fates, expressing hope that their sons' eternal orbits will bind mankind together and halt the arms/space race.* (*MH* 261:L26-31 *The Manned Missiles*) "May Major Stepan Ivankov and Captain Bryant Ashland serve to reproach us, whenever we look at the sky, for making a world in which there is no trust. May the two men be the beginning of trust between peoples. May they mark the end of the time when science sent our good, brave young men hurtling to meet in death."

Asimov, Isaac. (*WFG* 85:L18) Good science-fiction writers of the present are not necessarily as eager as Arthur C. Clarke to found kindergartens on Jupiter, to leave the poor Maine ape and his clam rake far behind. **Isaac Asimov**, who is a great man, perceives three stages so far in the development of American science fiction, says we are in stage three now:

1. Adventure dominant.

2. Technology dominant.

3. Sociology dominant.

I can hope that this is a prophetic outline of Earthling history, too. I interpret "sociology" broadly—as a respectful, objective concern for the cradle natures of Earthlings on Earth.

"Asleep at the Switch" (see **Albert Einstein**, **Dr. Robert Fender**, and **Kilgore Trout**).

Astor, Madelaine. *A member of the Tarkington College Board of Trustees and former graduate of the school. She turned out to be as dim-witted as Kimberley Wilder (another Tarkington student and daughter of Jason Wilder who acted as a spy to gather evidence against Eugene Debs Hartke).* (*HP* 127:L19, 21) But that was the only time they *(the board members)* defended me, although 1 of them had been my student, **Madelaine Astor**, née Peabody, and 5 of them were parents of those I had taught. **Madelaine** dictated a letter to me afterward, explaining that Jason Wilder had promised to denounce the college in his column and on his TV show if the Trustees did not fire me.

Atlas, Charles. *Vonnegut and Bokonon were both alumni of the Charles Atlas physical fitness program operating on the principle of "dynamic tension"* (*WFG* 254:L5 *Playboy Interview*). *In* Cat's Cradle *Bokonon takes Charles Atlas' idea of pitting opposing muscle groups in tension against each other to describe the social theory he and Corporal McCabe employ to coax the people of San Lorenzo into positive activities.*

(*CC* 90:L3) It was the belief of **Charles Atlas** that muscles could be built without bar bells or spring exercisers, could be built by simply pitting one set of muscles against another.

It was the belief of Bokonon that good societies could be built only by pitting good against evil, and by keeping the tension between the two high at all times.

Augustus, Caesar. *Referred to by Senator Lister Ames Rosewater in his famous and often used speech on the Golden Age of Rome. Caesar Augustus is appreciated by the senator as a "great humanitarian" for his ruthless measures intended to regain control over the moral decline of Rome. Through Senator Rosewater, Vonnegut creates an analogy between ancient Rome and modern America that predates the hard line Republican Party rhetoric of the late 1970s and early 1980s.* (*GBR* 34:L8-9, 35:L14, 27) I should like to speak of the Emperor Octavian, of **Caesar Augustus**, as he came to be known. This great humanitarian, and he was a humanitarian in the profoundest sense of the word, took command of the Roman Empire in a degenerate period strikingly like our own. Harlotry, divorce, alcoholism, liberalism, homosexuality, pornography, abortion, venality, murder, labor racketeering, juvenile delinquency, cowardice, atheism, extortion, slander, and theft were the height of fashion. Rome was a paradise for gangsters, perverts, and the lazy working man, just as America is now. As in America now, forces of law and order were openly attacked by mobs, children were disobedient, had no respect for their parents or their country, and no decent woman was safe on any street, even at high noon! And cunning, sharp-trading, bribing foreigners were in the ascendency everywhere. And ground under the heels of the big city money-changers were the honest farmers, the backbone of the Roman Army and the Roman soul.

What could be done? Well, there were soft-headed liberals then as there are bubble-headed liberals now, and they said what liberals always say after they have led a great nation to such a lawless, self-indulgent, polyglot condition: "Things have never been better! Look at all the freedom! Look at all the equality! Look how sexual hypocrisy has been driven from the scene! Oh boy! People used to get all knotted up inside when they thought about rape or fornication. Now they can do both with glee!"

And what did the terrible, black-spirited, non-fun-loving conservatives of those happy days have to say? Well, there weren't many of them left. They were dying off in ridiculed old age. And their children had been turned against them by the liberals, by the purveyors of synthetic sunshine and moonshine, by the something-for-nothing political strip-teasers, by the people who loved everybody, including the barbarians, by people who loved the barbarians so much they wanted to open all the gates, have all the soldiers lay their weapons down, and let the barbarians come in!

That was the Rome that **Caesar Augustus** came home to, after defeating those two sex maniacs, Antony and Cleopatra, in the great sea battle of Actium. And I don't think I have to re-create the things he thought when he surveyed the Rome he was said to rule. Let us take a moment of silence, and let each think what he will of the stews of today...

And what methods did **Caesar Augustus** use to put this disorderly house in order? He did what we are so often told we must never, ever do, what we are told will never, ever work: he wrote morals into law, and he enforced those unenforceable laws with a police force that was cruel and unsmiling. He made it illegal for a Roman to behave like a pig. Do you hear me? It became illegal! And Romans caught acting like pigs were strung up by their thumbs, thrown down wells, fed to lions, and given other experiences that might impress them with the desirability of being more decent and reliable than they were. Did it work? You bet your boots it did! Pigs miraculously disappeared! And what do we call the period that followed this now-unthinkable oppression? Nothing more nor less, friends and neighbors, than "The Golden Age of Rome."

Aurelius, Marcus. (*MN* 83:L22) *(Werner)* Noth's house, said Westlake, had been demolished by Russian artillery, but Noth had continued to live in one undamaged room in the back. Westlake took an inventory of the room, found it to contain a bed, a table, and a candlestick. On the table were framed photographs of Helga, Resi, and Noth's wife.

There was a book. It was a German translation of *The Meditations of Marcus Aurelius*.

Auschwitz. (*MN* 5:L6) Andor *(Gutman)* is a sleepy, not very bright Estonian Jew. He spent two years in the extermination camp at **Auschwitz**.
(*MN* 5:L11) Sonderkommando means special detail. At **Auschwitz** it meant a very special detail indeed—one composed of prisoners whose duties were to shepherd condemned persons into gas chambers, and then to lug their bodies out. When the job was done, the members of the Sonderkommando were themselves killed.
(*MN* 6:L15) He went away for a little while, after having confessed that. And he thought about **Auschwitz**, the thing he liked least to think about. *Gutman could never understand why he joined the Sonderkommando and he wonders out loud about this to Campbell while on guard in the Old Jerusalem basement jail.*
(*MN* 12:L4) Mengel *(Bernard Mengel, another of Campbell's jailers)* was speaking of Rudolf Franz Hoess, the commandant of the extermination camp at **Auschwitz**. In his tender care, literally millions of Jews were gassed.
(*MN* 13:L1) I, too, knew Rudolf Hoess, Commandant of **Auschwitz**. I *(Howard Campbell)* met him at a New Year's Eve party in Warsaw during the war—the start of 1944.
(*MN* 25:L14-16) *Dr. Epstein complains about anyone's reminiscence of Nazi horrors.* "They should fade," said young Dr. Epstein. "They belong to a period of insanity that should be forgotten as quickly as possible."

"**Auschwitz**," said his mother.

"Forget **Auschwitz**," said Dr. Epstein.

"Do you know what **Auschwitz** was?" his mother asked me.

"Yes," I said.
(*MN* 125:L26) "Do you feel that you're guilty of murdering six million Jews?" I *(Campbell)* said.

"Absolutely not," said the architect of **Auschwitz**, the introducer of conveyor belts into crematoria, the greatest customer in the world for the gas called Cyklon-B.

Campbell's explanation for Hoess' war crimes, and all such nightmarish crimes, was schizophrenia which he likened to a "cuckoo clock in Hell." (*MN* 169:L27-28) That was how Rudolf Hoess, Commandant of **Auschwitz**, could alternate over the loudspeakers of **Auschwitz** great music and calls for corpse-carriers—
(*MN* 192:L2-3, 24-26) When I reached the landing outside the door of young Dr. Abraham Epstein, a man who had spent his childhood in **Auschwitz**, the stench stopped me. . . .

"I'd like to surrender to an *Auschwitzer*," I said. This made him mad. "Then find one who thinks about **Auschwitz** all the time!" he said. "There are plenty who think about nothing else. I never think about it!"
(*MN* 194:L14) "This is not the first time you've seen eyes like that," she said to her son in German, "not the first man you've seen who could not move unless someone told him where to move, who longed for someone to tell him what to do next, who would do anything anyone told him to do next. You saw thousands of them at **Auschwitz**."
(*MN* 196:L21) What she crooned was this, a command she had heard over the loudspeakers of **Auschwitz**—had heard many times a day for years.

"*Leichentrager zu Wache*," she crooned. *(Mrs. Epstein, the doctor's mother.)*

In Cat's Cradle *Julian Castle tells John/Jonah*, "After death, the body turns black—coals to Newcastle in the case of San Lorenzo. When the plague was having everything its own way, the House of Hope and Mercy in the Jungle looked like **Auschwitz** or Buchenwald. We had stacks of dead so deep and wide that a bulldozer actually stalled trying to shove them toward a common grave" (*CC* 134:L14).
(*CC* 153:L26) "He *(Dr. Schlichter von Koenigswald)* was in the S.S. for fourteen years. He was a camp physician at **Auschwitz** for six of those years."
(*CC* 193:L22) Dr. von Koenigswald, the humanitarian with the terrible deficit of **Auschwitz** in his kindliness account, was the second to die of ice-nine.
(*WFG* 142:L4 *Biafra: A People Betrayed*) I admire Miriam, though I am not grateful for the trip she gave me. It was like a free trip to **Auschwitz** when the ovens were still going full blast. I now feel lousy all the time.
(*PS* 234:L19 *Obscenity*) He was right. It was impossible for her to think coherently about assholes or **Auschwitz** or anything else that might be upsetting to a little girl. *After returning from World War II, Vonnegut had a discussion with his father about one of their relations who had married a German officer before the war and had come to identify with the plight of the Germans over her native America.*
(*PS* 242:L27 *Children*) "There is this psychiatrist, you see. He is a colonel in the German SS in Poland during World War Two. His name is Vonnegut. That is a good German name. Colonel Vonnegut is supposed to look after the mental health of SS people in his area, which includes the uniformed staff at **Auschwitz**."
(*PS* 243:L10 *Children*) "Lieutenant Dampfwalze, who could be played by Peter O'Toole, feels that he can't cut the mustard anymore on the railroad platform at **Auschwitz**, where boxcars of people are unloaded day after day. He is sick and tired of it, but he has the wisdom to seek professional help. Dr. Vonnegut is an eclectic worker in the field of mental health, incidentally, a pragmatic man. He is a little bit Jungian, a little bit Freudian, a little bit Rankian—and so on. He has an open and inquiring mind."

Eugene Debs Hartke muses about the state of mankind: (*HP* 225:L12) And the worst flaw is that we're just plain dumb. Admit it!

You think **Auschwitz** was intelligent?

(*HP* 226:L19) My body, as I understand it, is attempting to contain the TB germs inside me in little shells it builds around them. The shells are calcium, the most common element in the walls of many prisons, including Athena. This place is ringed by barbed wire. So was **Auschwitz**.

(*HP* 229:L14, 17) There wasn't a Japanese manufacturer of crematoria, so Warden Matsumoto bought one from A.J. Topf und Sohn in Essen, Germany. This was the same outfit that had made the ovens for **Auschwitz** in its heyday.

The postwar Topf models all had state-of-the-art smoke scrubbers on their smokestacks, so people in Scipio, unlike the people living near **Auschwitz**, never knew that they had a busy corpse carbonizer in the neighborhood. *The crematoria was bought to incinerate the bodies of convicts who died from AIDS.*

(*HP* 280:L21, 26) I remember a lecture Damon Stern gave about his visit with several Tarkington students to **Auschwitz**, the infamous Nazi extermination camp in Poland during the Finale Rack. Stern used to make extra money taking trips to Europe with students whose parents or guardians didn't want to see them over Christmas or during the summertime. He caught a lot of heck for taking some to **Auschwitz**. He did it impulsively and without asking permission from anyone. It wasn't on the schedule, and some of the students were very upset afterward.

(*HP* 281:L3) The buildings *(of Auschwitz)* had been put up years before World War I, he said, as a comfortable outpost for soldiers of the Austro-Hungarian Empire. Among the many titles of that Emperor, he said, was Duke of **Auschwitz**.

Referring to elements in his unpublished manuscript entitled SS Psychiatrist, *Vonnegut recalls:* "This was about an MD who had been psychoanalyzed, and he was stationed at **Auschwitz**. His job was to treat the depression of those members of the staff who did not like what they were doing there. Talk therapy was all he or anybody had to offer back then. This was before the days of—Never mind" (*FWD* 32:L1).

(*FWD* 44:L19) "And could any moralist have called for a more appropriate reaction by painters to World War II, to the death camps and Hiroshima and all the rest of it, than pictures without persons or artifacts, without even allusions to the blessings of Nature? A full moon, after all, had come to be known as a 'bomber's moon.' Even an orange could suggest a diseased planet, a disgraced humanity, if someone remembered, as many did, that the Commandant of **Auschwitz** and his wife and children, under the greasy smoke from the ovens, had had good food every day."

(*FWD* 84:L6) "The United States of America had human slavery for almost one hundred years before that custom was recognized as a social disease and people began to fight it. Imagine that. Wasn't that a match for **Auschwitz**? What a beacon of liberty we were to the rest of the world when it was perfectly acceptable here to own other human beings and treat them as we treated cattle.

Who told you we were a beacon of liberty from the very beginning? Why would they lie like that?"
(*FWD* 99:L9) "When I was liberated in May, I was in the Russian zone. I spent some time with concentration camp survivors and heard their stories before returning to the American lines. I have since visited **Auschwitz** and Birkenau and have seen the collections there of human hair and children's shoes and toys and so on. I know about the Holocaust. Elie Wiesel and I are friends."
(*FWD* 118:L31) "Hitler dreamed of killing Jews, Gypsies, Slavs, homosexuals, Communists, Jehovah's Witnesses, mental defectives, believers in democracy, and so on, in industrial quantities. It would have remained only a dream if it hadn't been for chemists as well educated as my brother, who supplied Hitler's executioners with the cyanide gas known as Cyklon-B. It would have remained only a dream if architects and engineers as capable as my father and grandfather hadn't designed extermination camps—the fences, the towers, the barracks, the railroad sidings, and the gas chambers and crematoria—for maximum ease of operation and efficiency. I recently visited two of those camps in Poland, **Auschwitz** and Birkenau. They are technologically perfect. There is only one grade I could give their designers, and that grade is A-plus. They surely solved all the problems set for them."
(*FWD* 172:L24) "As I say, color the people in old photographs of **Auschwitz** all shades of brown and black and you will be looking at what he sees every day." *Vonnegut wrote this for a piece about Mozambique).*

Auschwitzer. (*MN* 192:L24) "I'd like to surrender to an ***Auschwitzer***," I said. *Howard Campbell is speaking to Dr. Abraham Epstein who, along with his mother, survived Auschwitz.*

Auschwitzian. (*PS* 257:L14 *Jonathan Swift Misperceived*) In *Gulliver's Travels*, Swift sets such high standards for unsentimentality about human beings that most of us can meet those standards only in wartime, and only briefly even then. He shrinks us, urinates on us, expands us and peers into all our nauseating apertures, encourages us to demonstrate our stupidity and mendaciousness, makes us hideously old. On paper he subjects us to every humiliating test that imaginative fiction can invent. And what is learned about us in the course of these **Auschwitzian** experiments? Only this, according to Swift's hero, Captain Gulliver: that we are disgusting in the extreme.

Averageman, John. *In the morality play performed at the engineers' annual retreat to The Meadows in* Player Piano, *John Averageman is the pawn caught in the cross-examination by the Radical and the Young Engineer. The Radical attempts to show that John's purchasing power, standard of living, and employment status have all been compromised by the engineers. The Young Engineer counters by showing John that he has more creature comforts and health protection than Caesar, Napoleon, Henry VIII, or Charlemagne.*

Avondale. *Vonnegut has created two Avondale communities, one outside of Rosewater, Indiana, and the other outside of Midland City, Ohio. In the novel* God Bless You, Mr. Rosewater, *Avondale is where* the few highly paid agronomists, engineers, brewers, accountants and administrators who did all that needed doing lived in a defensive circle of expensive ranch homes in another cornfield near New Ambrosia, a community named, for no reason whatsoever, "**Avondale**." All had gas-lit patios framed and terraced with railroad ties from the old Nickel Plate right-of-way (*GBR* 52:L6). *When Eliot and Sylvia went to live in Indiana, all the Avondale residents—employees of the Rosewater Corporation—tried to court the Rosewaters but their efforts were rebuffed. They became enraged, grew snobbish, and behaved disrespectfully toward their neighbors.*

In Deadeye Dick, *Avondale is an inexpensive community of tract homes developed by Marco and Gino Maritimo. After Otto Waltz passed away in 1960, Rudy and his mother were given a terrific deal by the Maritimo brothers on one of the model homes. Rudy frequently calls Avondale a "jumble of little shitboxes." Their house had an ornate concrete mantelpiece built with radioactive cement from the Manhattan Project in Oak Ridge, Tennessee. Mrs. Waltz eventually died from exposure to radiation emitted by the concrete. Vonnegut adds that Avondale had once been John Fortune's dairy farm and later became a testing ground for tanks produced by Fred T. Barry.*

B

B-1. (*FWD* 135:L30) "A word about appeasement, something World War II, supposedly taught us not to practice: I say to you that the world has been ruined by appeasement. . . . Appeasement of the compulsive war-preparers. I can scarcely name a nation that has not lost most of its freedom and wealth in attempts to appease its own addicts to preparations for war.

"And there is no appeasing an addict for very long: 'I swear, man, just lay enough bread on me for twenty multiple-reentry vehicles and a fleet of **B-1** bombers, and I'll never bother you again.'"

B-17. (*HP* 32:L13) When I *(Eugene Debs Hartke)* was 2 years old, we moved to Midland City, Ohio, where a washing-machine company named Robo-Magic Corporation was beginning to make bomb-release mechanisms and swivel mounts for machine guns on **B-17** bombers. The plastics industry was then in its infancy, and Father was sent to Robo-Magic to determine what synthetic materials from Du Pont could be used in the weapons systems in place of metal, in order to make them lighter.

B-36. (*WJ* 169:L6) HAROLD . . . . Looseleaf delivered a lecture on maintenance procedures for the hydraulic system of a **B-36**.

B-52. (*HP* 208:L26) "A **B-52** . . . . Gore and guts everywhere." *Eugene Debs Hartke uses the image of the B-52 bomber to describe the kind of destruction wrought by those on high in the administration of Tarkington College*. (*HP* 226:10) If the Trustees were bad, the convicts were worse. I would be the last person to say otherwise. They were devastators of their own communities with gunfights and robberies and rapes, and the merchandising of brain-busting chemicals and on and on.

But at least they saw what they were doing, whereas people like the Trustees had a lot in common with **B-52** bombardiers way up in the stratosphere. They seldom saw the devastation they caused as they moved the huge portion of this country's wealth they controlled from here to there.

Babel (also **Tower of Babel**). *The discovery of the chrono-synclastic infundibula halted the launching of* The Whale, *built by Malachi Constant's Galactic Spacecraft corporation. Since the appearance of the chrono-synclastic infundibulum indicated that all that ever will be, already was—the question it poses for man is* "What makes you think you're going anywhere?" (*ST* 30:3-31:L) *This offers the opportunity to look at the space program in larger, biblical terms, and, as the narrator goes on to describe, draw a parallel between the efforts necessary for space exploration and the Tower of Babel.* (*ST* 31:L20, 28, 32:L7) It was a situation made to order for American fundamentalist preachers. They were quicker than philosophers or historians or anybody to talk sense about the truncated Age of Space. Two hours after the firing of *The Whale* was called off indefinitely, the Reverend Bobby Denton shouted at his Love Crusade in Wheeling, West Virginia:

"'And the Lord came down to see the city and the tower, which the children of men builded. And the Lord said, "Behold, the people is one, and they have all one language; and this they begin to do; and now *nothing will be restrained from them, which they have imagined to do*. Go to, let us go down, and there confound their language, that they may not understand one another's speech." So the Lord scattered them abroad from thence upon the face of all the earth; and they left off to build the city. Therefore is the name of it called **Babel**; because the Lord did there confound the language of all the earth: and from thence did the Lord scatter them abroad upon the face of the earth.'"

Bobby Denton spitted his audience on a bright and loving gaze, and proceeded to roast it whole over the coals of its own iniquity. "Are these not Bible times?" he said. "Have we not builded of steel and pride an abomination far taller than the **Tower of Babel** of old? And did we not mean, like those builders of old, to get right into Heaven with it? And haven't we heard it said many times that the language of scientists is international? They all use the same Latin and Greek words for things, and they all talk the language of numbers. . . .

"'So why should we cry out in surprise and pain now when God says to us what He said to the people who builded the **Tower of Babel**: 'No! Get away from there! You aren't going to Heaven or anywhere else with that thing! Scatter, you hear? Quit talking the language of science to each other! Nothing will be restrained from you which you have imagined to do, if you all keep on talking the language of science to each other, and I don't want that! I, your Lord God on High want things restrained from you, so you will quit thinking about crazy towers and rockets to Heaven, and start thinking about how to be better neighbors and husbands and wives and daughters and sons! Don't look to rockets for salvation—look to your homes and churches!'"

Babylon, Babylonian. (*CC* 150:L8) My hair stood on end, as though Angela were rolling on the floor, foaming at the mouth, and babbling fluent **Babylonian**. *This is John/Jonah's reaction to hearing Angela Hoenikker play the clarinet.*
(*GBR* 21:L33) And Noah begat Samuel, who married Geraldine Ames Rockefeller. Samuel became even more interested in politics than his father had been, served the Republican Party tirelessly as a king-maker, caused that party to nominate men who would whirl like dervishes, bawl fluent **Babylonian**, and order the militia to fire into crowds whenever a poor man seemed on the point of suggesting that he and a Rosewater were equal in the eyes of the law.
(*MH* 65:L31 *The Foster Portfolio*) And then Herbert Foster, looking drab and hunted, picked his way through the crowd. His expression was one of disapproval, of a holy man in **Babylon**. He was oddly stiff-necked and held his arms at his sides as he pointedly kept from brushing against anyone or from meeting any of the gazes that fell upon him. There was no question that being in the place was absolute, humiliating hell for him.
(*WFG* 83:L2 *Excelsior! We're Going to the Moon! Excelsior!*) I used to talk to G.E. scientists sometimes about exciting stuff I had read in *Scientific American*. I was reading it regularly in those days. I thought it was part of my job—to keep up. If the article I was discussing wasn't related to my listener's field, he would doze. I might as well have been speaking **Babylonian**.
(*JB* xxxv:L11) The chief cast his spell. His shouted words bounced off the buildings, warred with their own echoes, and sounded like **Babylonian** by the time they reached Alexander's ears. *This is Walter Starbuck's description of that moment just before the Cuyahoga Massacre when the Cleveland Chief of Police read the Riot Act to the striking workers.*
(*HP* 179:L17) Darius, King of Persia, he told me, crucified 3,000 people he thought were enemies in **Babylon**. *After viewing the mutilated body of Tex Johnson, Eugene Debs Hartke has an informative discussion about crucifixion with the State Police forensic medicine specialist.*

Bach, Johann Sebastian. *Vonnegut uses Bach to score a scene in* Slaughterhouse-Five *which, in retrospect for Billy Pilgrim, gains new significance because of its Tralfamadorian fourth-dimensionality.* (*SL5* 27:L10-11) One time on maneuvers Billy was playing "A Mighty Fortress Is Our God," with music by **Johann Sebastian Bach** and words by Martin Luther. It was Sunday morning. Billy and his chaplain had gathered a congregation of about fifty soldiers on a Carolina hillside. An umpire appeared. There were umpires everywhere, men who said who was winning or losing the theoretical battle, who was alive and who was dead.

The umpire had comical news. The congregation had been theoretically spotted from the air by a theoretical enemy. They were all theoretically dead now. The theoretical corpses laughed and ate a hearty noontime meal.

Remembering this incident years later, Billy was struck by what a Tralfamadorian adventure with death that had been, to be dead and to eat at the same time.

bacteria, bacterium. (*SL5* 73:L15) The Americans' clothes were meanwhile passing through poison gas. Body lice and **bacteria** and fleas were dying by the billions. So it goes.
(*MH* 158:L1 *Report on the Barnhouse Effect*) As a weapon, then, dynamopsychism has an impressive advantage over **bacteria** and atomic bombs, beyond the fact that it costs nothing to use: it enables the professor to single out critical individuals and objects instead of slaughtering whole populations in the process of maintaining international equilibrium.
(*Gal* 186:L6) If people can swim as fast and far as fur seals now, what is to prevent their swimming all the way back to the mainland, whence their ancestors came? Answer: nothing.

Plenty have tried it or will try it during periods of fish shortages or overpopulation. But the **bacterium** which eats human eggs is always there to greet them.
(*Blue* 14:L16) And I told Mrs. Berman this about my mother: "She died when I was twelve—of a tetanus infection she evidently picked up while working in a cannery in California. The cannery was built on the site of an old livery stable, and tetanus **bacteria** often colonize the intestines of horses without hurting them, and then become durable spores, armored little seeds, when excreted. One of them lurking in the dirt around and under the cannery was somehow exhumed and sent traveling. After a long, long sleep it awakened in Paradise, something we would all like to do. Paradise was a cut in my mother's hand."
(*Blue* 256:L22) So I could not bring myself to put them *(Karabekian's art collection)* in the barn, which was then a musty place, having been home for so long for nothing but potatoes and the earth and **bacteria** and fungi which so loved to cling to them.
(*HP* 173:L33) He *(mortician Norman Updike)* went on to tell me with bow-wow cheerfulness back in 1987 that people were generally mistaken about how quickly things rot, turn into good old dirt or fertilizer or dust or whatever. He said scientists had discovered well-preserved meat and vegetables deep in city dumps, thrown away presumably years and years ago. Like Hermann and Sophia Shultz, these theoretically biodegradable works of Nature had failed to rot for want of moisture, which was life itself to worms and fungi and **bacteria**.

Baer (see also **Kroner**). *Baer is chief engineer of the Eastern Division of the National Industrial, Commercial, Communications, Foodstuffs, and Resources ruling technocracy*. (*PP* 14:L31) It was Kroner and **Baer** who would decide who was to get the most important job in their division, a job left vacant two weeks ago by death—the managership of the Pittsburgh Works.

Kroner always appears to reserve his comments, making him hard to read, yet Baer is no political slouch, though his outward appearance borders on buffoonery. (*PP* 36:L33) The other, **Baer**, slight and nervous, noisily and unconvincingly extroverted, laughed, nudged, and clapped shoulders, and maintained a continuous commentary on whatever was being said: "Fine, fine, right, sure, sure, wonderful, yes, yes, exactly, fine, good."
(*PP* 38:L10, 16, 18-19) **Baer** was a social cretin, apparently unaware that he was anything but suave and brilliant in company. Someone had once mentioned his running commentary on conversations to him, and he hadn't known what they were talking about. Technically, there wasn't a better engineer in the East, including Finnerty. There was little in the Division that hadn't been master-minded by **Baer**, who here seemed to Kroner what a fox terrier seems to a St. Bernard. Paul *(Proteus)* had thought often of the peculiar combination of Kroner and **Baer**, and wondered if, when they were gone, higher management could possibly duplicate it. **Baer** embodied the knowledge and technique of industry; Kroner personified the faith, the near-holiness, the spirit of the complicated venture. Kroner, in fact, had a poor record as an engineer and had surprised Paul from time to time with his ignorance or misunderstanding of technical matters; but he had the priceless quality of believing in the system, and of making others believe in it, too, and do as they were told.
(*PP* 71:L36) The civic managers were the career administrators who ran the city. They lived on the same side of the river as the managers and engineers of the Ilium Works, but the contact between the two groups was little more than perfunctory and, traditionally, suspicious. The schism, like so many things, dated back to the war, when the economy had, for efficiency's sake, become monolithic. The question had arisen: who was to run it, the bureaucrats, the heads of business and industry, or the military? Business and bureaucracy had stuck together long enough to overwhelm the military and had since then worked side by side, abusively and suspiciously, but, like Kroner and **Baer**, each unable to do a whole job without the other.
(*PP* 168:L11) Paul reflected that **Baer** was possibly the most just, reasonable, and candid person he'd ever known—remarkably machinelike in that the only problems he interested himself in were those brought to him, and in that he went to work on all problems with equal energy and interest, insensitive to quality and scale.

"Bagladies" (see **Pamela Ford Hall**).

Bagnialto (see also ***The Barring-gaffner of Bagnialto***). (*BC* 128:25, 30) Kilgore Trout was suddenly woozy with deja vu. The truck driver was reminding him of the premise of a book he hadn't thought about for years. The driver's toilet paper in Libertyville, Georgia, had been *The Barring-gaffner of Bagnialto*, or *This Year's Masterpiece*, by Kilgore Trout.

The name of the planet where Trout's book took place was **Bagnialto**, and a "Barring-gaffner" there was a government official who spun a wheel of chance once a year. Citizens submitted works of art to the government, and these were given numbers, and then they were assigned cash values according to the Barring-gaffner's spins of the wheel.

Bahía de Darwin. *Spanish for "Darwin Bay," it is the cruise ship built for trips to the Galápagos Islands. Captained by Adolf von Kleist, it was scheduled for "The Nature Cruise of the Century" on Friday, November 28, 1986. It winds up as the last refuge for the remaining biped humans.*

During the construction of the ship in Malmö, Sweden, Leo Trout, the son of Kilgore Trout, was decapitated by a sheet of falling steel. His ghost is the narrator of Galápagos.

Baku. *In* Player Piano, *these are mud and straw figures once made by the now extinct Surrasi, considered an infidel tribe by the Shah of Bratpuhr. Baku are viewed as false gods, and the Shah equates America's faith in EPICAC with the Surrasi's faith in Baku.*

Baltra. *One of the first sights of conflict leading to the end of mankind as we know it, also one of the islands in the Galápagos chain.* (*Gal* 180:3) It was at about that time that Peru declared war on Ecuador. Two of Peru's fighter bombers were then over Ecuadorian territories, one with its rocket tuned to the radar signals coming from Guayaquil International Airport, and the other with its rocket tuned to radar signals coming from the naval base on the Galápagos Island of **Baltra**, lair of a sail training ship, six Coast Guard ships, two oceangoing tugs, a patrol submarine, a dry dock, and, high and dry in the dry dock, a destroyer. The destroyer was the largest ship in the Ecuadorian Navy, save for one—the *Bahía de Darwin*.
(*Gal* 233:1) If they had ever reached **Baltra**, which they never did, they would have found it devastated and depopulated by yet another airmailed package of dagonite.

The Bannister. *The Midland City movie theater is first mentioned in* Breakfast of Champions, *though there is no direct connection with George Hickman Bannister's family. In* Deadeye Dick, *Rudy Waltz recalls the building was originally Midland City's Opera House, but became a movie theater in 1927. When the downtown area became a haven for the homeless and local business moved out, the building was taken over by The Empire Furniture Company—controlled by gangsters.*

Bannister, George Hickman (also **Bannister Memorial Fieldhouse**). *The Midland City high school football player killed in the 1924 Thanksgiving Day game. Buried in Calvary Cemetery, his grave was marked by a sixty-two-foot obelisk bought by contributions from the community. A city ordinance made* *it illegal for any structure to be built taller than Bannister's commemorative obelisk. Only the need to construct a radio tower for a local station changed the law. The new fieldhouse, which was under construction at the time of his death, was named in his honor. Bannister's family moved from Midland City before the obelisk was erected. Though most of the references to Bannister are made in* Breakfast of Champions, *in* Deadeye Dick *Rudy Waltz visits the grave after the neutron bombing of Midland City, just before Hippolyte Paul de Mille's resurrection of the nearby interred aviator Will Fairchild.*

Bannister, Lucy. *The sister of George Hickman Bannister. She and her parents left Midland City before the commemorative sixty-two-foot obelisk was erected by the Midland citizenry in honor of her brother, in* Breakfast of Champions.

baptism, baptismal, Baptist, baptized, baptizing. *When Malachi/Unk creates an explosive diversion to seek out Bea and Chrono, Boaz is left by himself.* (*ST* 137:L13) As they stood, Boaz stood, too. "God damn, buddy," he said, "I guess we done had a **baptism** of fire."

(*MN* 19:L3) I, Howard W. Campbell, Jr., was born in Schenectady, New York, on February 16, 1912. My father, who was raised in Tennessee, the son of a **Baptist** minister, was an engineer in the Service Engineering Department of the General Electric Company.

(*GBR* 18:L19) It was common gossip in the office that the very first president of the Foundation, Eliot Rosewater, the Senator's son, was a lunatic. This characterization was a somewhat playful one, but as Mushari knew, playfulness was impossible to explain in a court of law. Eliot was spoken of by Mushari's co-workers variously as "The Nut," "The Saint," "The Holy Roller," "**John the Baptist**," and so on.

The following is a telephone conversation between an anonymous caller and Eliot Rosewater after the former called the Rosewater hotline. (*GBR* 90:L23-33, 91:L1-8) "But what *are* you anyway—some kind of religion?"

"**Two-Seed-in-the-Spirit Predestinarian Baptist**."

"What?"

"That's what I generally say when people insist I must have a religion. There happens to be such a sect, and I'm sure it's a good one. Foot-washing is practiced, and the ministers draw no pay. I wash my feet, and I draw no pay."

"I don't get it," said the caller.

"Just a way of trying to put you at ease, to let you know you don't have to be deadly serious with me. You don't happen to be a **Two-Seed-in-the-Spirit Predestinarian Baptist**, do you?"

"Jesus, no."

"There are two hundred people who are, and sooner or later I'm going to say to one of them what I've just said to you." Eliot took a drink. "I live in dread of that moment—and it's sure to come."

In a conversation between Eliot Rosewater and his wife Sylvia, Norman Mushari listens in on an extension phone and hears the following. (*GBR* 109:L13-14, 24) "Congratulate Mary Moody on her twins."

"I will, I'll be **baptizing** them tomorrow."

"**Baptizing**?" This was something new. . . .

Mushari did not register disappointment. The **baptism** would hold up very well in court as evidence that Eliot thought of himself as a Messiah.

In a conversation between Eliot Rosewater and his wife Sylvia, Norman Mushari listens in on an extension phone and hears the following. (*GBR* 109:L13-14, 24) Congratulate Mary Moody on her twins."

"I will, I'll be **baptizing** them tomorrow."

"**Baptizing**?" This was something new. . . .

Mushari did not register disappointment. The **baptism** would hold up very well in court as evidence that Eliot thought of himself as a Messiah.

(*GBR* 120:L82) And George begat Abraham, who became a Congregationalist minister. Abraham went as a missionary to the Congo, where he met and married Lavinia Waters, the daughter of another missionary, an Illinois **Baptist**.

(*SL5* 15:L26) *Now, in 1760, Dresden underwent siege by the Prussians. On the fifteenth of July began the cannonade. The Picture-Gallery took fire. Many of the paintings had been transported to the Konigstein, but some were seriously injured by splinters of bombshells,—notably Francia's "**Baptism** of Christ."*

In a Kilgore Trout novel about Delmore Skag, Skag was a bachelor in a neighborhood where everyone had large families. Skag was also a scientist and invented a way to reproduce himself by shaving cells from his right hand and mixing it in chicken soup exposed to cosmic rays. (*BC* 21:L24) Pretty soon, Delmore was having several babies a day, and inviting his neighbors to share his pride and happiness. He had mass **baptisms** of as many as a hundred babies at a time. He became famous as a family man.

(*Slap* opening inscription) *"Call me but love and I'll be new **baptiz'd** . . ."*
—ROMEO

(*JB* 37:L19, 22, 24, 27) I myself was nothing. My father had been secretly **baptized** a Roman Catholic in Poland, a religion that was suppressed at the time. He grew up to be an agnostic. My mother was **baptized** a Greek Orthodox in Lithuania, but became a Roman Catholic in Cleveland. Father would never go to church with her. I myself was **baptized** a Roman Catholic, but aspired to my father's indifference, and quit going to church when I was twelve. When I applied for admission to Harvard, old Mr. McCone, a **Baptist**, told me to classify myself as a Congregationalist, which I did.

(*FWD* 156:L35) My second wife is another Episcopalian, and like my first one thinks that I have no religion and am a spiritual cripple on that account. When Jill's and my daughter Lily was **baptized** by the Bishop of New York in the biggest Gothic church in the world (in a neighborhood so poor that the Bishop couldn't get cable service for his TV), I did not attend. (There is a sound reason for hating me right there, but I think the main reason is cigarettes.)

Barber, Kensington. *The Provost of Tarkington College suspected by Eugene Debs Hartke of killing Letitia Smiley, the winner of the 1922 Women's Barefoot Race and crowned Lilac Queen for her effort. Hartke's imprisonment allows him to research the events surrounding the Lilac Queen's disappearance and concludes that Barber had probably impregnated Letitia and killed her the night of her victory. Barber is quoted in newspaper articles from the period that* "Letitia had been deeply troubled by a stormy romance with a much older man down in Scipio" (*HP* 182:L16-18). *He sent his family on their scheduled European vacation without him that summer so he could assist with the investigation. Barber experienced a nervous breakdown toward the end of the summer and was committed to the State Hospital for the Insane in Batavia.*

Barca-Lounger, Barcalounger. *Though most memorable as the seat of last repose for those entering the Ethical Suicide Parlors in the short story "Welcome to the Monkey House," (MH* 28:L2 *Welcome to the Monkey House) the Barcalounger is referred to in other tales, as well. In* Slaughterhouse-Five *the Tralfamadorians anesthetize Billy Pilgrim and strap him to a yellow barcalounger they stole from Sears & Roebuck and later use to furnish his dome on their planet* (*SL5* 66:L26).

Kilgore Trout's 2BR02B, *a thematic cross between* Player Piano *and "Welcome to the Monkey House" also has Ethical Suicide Parlors outfitted with pretty hostesses and Barca-Loungers.* (*GBR* 30:L8) All serious diseases had been conquered. So death was voluntary, and the government, to encourage volunteers for death, set up a purple-roofed Ethical Suicide Parlor at every major intersection, right next to an orange-roofed Howard Johnson's. There were pretty hostesses in the parlor, and **Barca-Loungers**, and Muzak, and a choice of fourteen painless ways to die.

In a sense, Rudy Waltz's mother met her death as she sat in her Barcalounger in front of the fireplace which had been built with radioactive cement from the Manhattan Project. (*DD* 219:L18) So we did not panic *(while men from the Nuclear Regulatory Commission dressed in space suits took all sorts of readings of the house and neighborhood)*. Good citizens don't. We waited calmly for Fred T. Barry. I was at the picture window, peering out at the street between slats of the Venetian blinds. Mother was reclining in the **Barcalounger** my brother Felix had given her three Christmases ago. She was vibrating almost imperceptibly, and a reassuring drone came from underneath her. She had the massage motor turned on low.

Barker, General Honus. *General Barker is one of the ranking officers and chaperones for Professor Barnhouse during Operation Brainstorm, a test of the professor's dynamopsychic abilities intended to destroy a number of practice targets scattered throughout the Western Hemisphere. General Barker later* *warns Congress that it is impossible to defend against the Barnhouse Effect. This all occurs in "Report on the Barnhouse Effect" reprinted in* Welcome to the Monkey House.

Barkley, Ben. *Dr. Remenzel's black chauffeur is also a good friend to Remenzel's son, Eli, in the short story "The Lie" reprinted in* Welcome to the Monkey House. *Barkley drives both to the Whitehill School for Boys, a private prep school in North Marston, Mass.*

Barlow, Frank X. *One of the pseudonyms attributed to Dr. Bob Fender, a veterinarian who writes science fiction while incarcerated at Finletter Air Force Base with Walter Starbuck in* Jailbird. *Another of his pseudonyms is Kilgore Trout.*

Barnhouse, Professor Arthur (see also **dynamopsychism**). *In Vonnegut's short story "Report on the Barnhouse Effect," thirty-nine-year-old Professor Arthur Barnhouse accidentally discovers that one's mental powers of concentration (what Barnhouse terms "dynamopsychism") can be developed into the most powerful weapon on earth. The press preferred to use the term "Barnhouse Effect." Barnhouse first realized he possessed such powers while playing his initial game of craps with other enlisted men in his barracks. He rolled "sevens" ten times in a row. Without his participation or endorsement, The First Church of Barnhouse is established in Los Angeles.* (*MH* 157:L17-18) There is an understandable tendency to look upon **Professor Barnhouse** as a supernatural visitation. **The First Church of Barnhouse** in Los Angeles has a congregation numbering in the thousands. He is godlike in neither appearance nor intellect. The man who disarms the world is single, shorter than the average American male, stout, and averse to exercise. His I.Q. is 143, which is good but certainly not sensational. He is quite mortal, about to celebrate his fortieth birthday, and in good health. If he is alone now, the isolation won't bother him too much. He was quiet and shy when I knew him, and seemed to find more companionship in books and music than in his associations at the college.

Barnhouse uses this ability to demand universal disarmament. Those nations who fail to agree face destruction of their arms. Consequently, most governments—including the United States—seek to get rid of him. At one time he offered his services to the Secretary of State, but he eventually changed his mind when he felt universal disarmament would serve a better purpose. (*MH* 167:L32) *"Gentlemen,"* I read aloud, *"As the first superweapon with a conscience, I am removing myself from your national defense stockpile. Setting a new precedent in the behavior of ordnance, I have humane reasons for going off.* ***A. Barnhouse.****" See also: MH—Report on the Barnhouse Effect* 156:L18; 157:L1; 157:L32; 158:L16; 158:L26-27.

Barnstable, Barnstable First Church of God the Utterly Indifferent, West Barnstable, West Barnstable Volunteer Fire Department. *Vonnegut wrote many of his early novels while living on Cape Cod in West Barnstable, Massachusetts. The location is used a number of times throughout his work. In* The Sirens of Titan *Reverend C. Horner Redwine leads the Barnstable First Church of God the Utterly Indifferent, also known as The Church of the Weary Space Wanderer. Winston Niles Rumfoord had prophesied* "a lone straggler from the Army of Mars would arrive at Redwine's church some day" (*ST* 218:L8-10). *It is where Malachi Constant/Unk/the Weary Space Wanderer arrives before being sent off to Titan as a symbolic religious sacrifice (accompanied by Beatrice and Chrono).* (*ST* 216:L25-28) The church . . . had been at various times Presbyterian, Congregationalist, Unitarian, and Universal Apocalyptic. *The town's volunteer fire department is comprised mostly of Redwine's followers.*

The short story "Welcome to the Monkey House" takes place in Barnstable County, and Frank Wirtanen, captain of the Kennedy yacht Marlin *in "Brief Encounters on the Inland Waterway" (reprinted in* Wampeters, Foma & Granfalloons*), is a resident of West Barnstable. Also in* Wampeters, *Vonnegut notes that serial killer Anthony Costa is jailed in the Barnstable County House of Correction in his essay "There's a Maniac Loose Out There."*

barracks humor (see **humor**).

barring-gaffner, *The Barring-gaffner of Bagnialto*, or *This Year's Masterpiece* *The Kilgore Trout novel used as toilet paper in Libertyville, Georgia, and later discussed by the truck driver when he offers a ride to the hitchhiking author.* (*BC* 128:L29-33, 129:L1-21) The name of the planet where Trout's book took place was *Bagnialto*, and a "**Barring-gaffner**" there was a government official who spun a wheel of chance once a year. Citizens submitted works of art to the government, and these were given numbers, and then they were assigned cash values according to the **Barring-gaffner**'s spins of the wheel.

The viewpoint of the character of the tale was not the **Barring-gaffner**, but a humble cobbler named Gooz. Gooz lived alone, and he painted a picture of his cat. It was the only picture he had ever painted. He took it to the **Barring-gaffner**, who numbered it and put it in a warehouse crammed with works of art.

The painting by Gooz had an unprecedented gush of luck on the wheel. It became worth eighteen thousand *lambos*, the equivalent of one billion dollars on Earth. The **Barring-gaffner** awarded Gooz a check for that amount, most of which was taken back at once by the tax collector. The picture was given a place of honor in the National Gallery, and people lined up for miles for a chance to see a painting worth a billion dollars.

There was also a huge bonfire of all the paintings and statues and books and so on which the wheel had said were worthless. And then it was discovered that the wheel was rigged, and the **Barring-gaffner** committed suicide.

Barry, Fred T. *Appearing in* Breakfast of Champions *and* Deadeye Dick, *Fred T. Barry is Chairman of the Midland City Arts Festival, the wealthiest man in Midland City, exactly the same age as Kilgore Trout, founder and Chairman of the Board of Barrytron, Ltd.—his successor company to Robo-Magic, and sole benefactor of the Mildred Barry Memorial Center for the Arts.*
(*BC* 33:L4, 6) **Fred T. Barry**, incidentally, was exactly the same age as Trout. They had the same birthday. But they certainly didn't look anything alike. **Fred T. Barry** didn't even look like a white man anymore, even though he was of pure English stock. As he grew older and older and happier and happier, and all his hair fell out everywhere, he came to look like an ecstatic old Chinaman.
(*BC* 243:L9) People who had horrible jobs during the week used to call Monday "Blue Monday" sometimes, though, because they hated to return to work after a day of rest. When **Fred T. Barry** made up the Robo-Magic motto as a young man *("Goodbye Blue Monday")*, he pretended that Monday was called "Blue Monday" because doing the laundry disgusted and exhausted women.
(*BC* 246:L10) **Fred T. Barry** wrote these ads himself, and he predicted at the time that Robo-Magic appliances of various sorts would eventually do what he called "all the Nigger work of the world," which was lifting and cleaning and cooking and washing and ironing and tending children and dealing with filth.
(*DD* 151:L8) I keep wanting to say that **Fred T. Barry** was the grandest neuter I ever saw. He certainly had no sex life. He didn't even have friends. It was all right with him if life ended at any time, obviously, since this was a suicidal flight we were on *(into Midland City after the great snow storm)*.

Barry, Mildred (also **The Mildred Barry Memorial Center for the Arts**). *The mother of Fred T. Barry and the namesake of Midland City's Mildred Barry Memorial Center for the Arts,* a translucent sphere on stilts, and it was illuminated from the inside. . . .(*BC* 64:4) *It sat above Sugar Creek and served as the home for the Midland City Symphony Orchestra.*

Barry, Roland. *Roland Barry has a 100% disability pension for the nervous breakdown he suffered ten minutes after being sworn into the Army, when he was told to take a shower with a hundred other men. He visits Eliot Rosewater daily, but Eliot doesn't remember him from one meeting to the next. Barry is indebted to Eliot because he was the only one not to think what happened to him was funny. Just before Eliot leaves Rosewater, Roland Barry gives him this poem:* (*GBR* 194:L10-27) "Lakes, carillons, / Pools and bells, / Fifes and freshets, / Harps and wells; / Flutes and rivers, / Streams, bassoons, / Geysers, trumpets, / Chimes, lagoons. / Hear the music, / Drink the water, / As we poor lambs / All go to slaughter. / I love you Eliot. / Good-bye. I cry. / Tears and violins. / Hearts and flowers, / Flowers and tears. / Rosewater, good-bye."

Barrytron. *First appearing in* Breakfast of Champions, *Barrytron Limited (an electronics firm in Midland City involved in secret weapons work) was originally called The Midland City Ordnance Company and later The Robo-Magic Corporation. Barrytron, Ltd. was founded in its present form by Fred T. Barry, the Chairman of the Board. Though Barrytron is a publicly held company in* Breakfast of Champions *(Dwayne Hoover holds stock in it and Kilgore Trout receives a single stock certificate as part of his honorarium), in* Deadeye Dick *it is wholly owned by Fred T. Barry. In* Hocus Pocus, *Eugene Debs Hartke's father worked for Barrytron through World War II. It was later bought by Du Pont.*

(*BC* 224:L14, 29) The company was manufacturing a new anti-personnel bomb for the Air Force. The bomb scattered plastic pellets instead of steel pellets, because the plastic pellets were cheaper. They were also impossible to locate in the bodies of wounded enemies by means of x-ray machines.

Barrytron had no idea it was dumping this waste into Sugar Creek. They had hired the Maritimo Brothers Construction Company, which was gangster-controlled, to build a system which would get rid of the waste. . . .

Barrytron would be absolutely sick when it learned what a polluter it had become. Throughout its history, it had attempted to be a perfect model of corporate good citizenship, no matter what it cost.

(*HP* 32:L20) By the time the war was over, the company had gotten out of the washing-machine business entirely, had changed its name to **Barrytron, Limited**, and was making weapons, airplanes, and motor vehicle parts composed of plastics it had developed on its own. My father had become the company's Vice-President in Charge of Research and Development.

Barus, Karl. *One of Kurt Vonnegut's great-grandparents. Noted by John Rauch in* Palm Sunday *as* "'Professor' **Karl Barus**, 'the first real professional teacher of voice, violin, and piano in the city,' according to Uncle John, and his wife, Alice Mollman. . . . He was well educated and a definite intellectual. He never engaged in trade or business but made a good income by his teaching and lived well. **Professor Barus** originally settled in Cincinnati in the early fifties, where he was appointed Musical Director of the Cincinnati Sangverein.

"In 1858 **Dr. Barus** was invited to come to Indianapolis to conduct the mixed chorus of German singing societies from Indianapolis, Louisville, Cincinnati, and Columbus, Ohio, at a great Musical Festival. In 1882 he was invited by Das Deutsche Haus to come to Indianapolis to be musical director of the Maennerchor, in which position he remained until 1896" (*PS* 34:L10, 18, 21, *Roots*).

(*PS* 35:L8 *Roots*) AND **Professor Karl Barus** the musician, and his wife Alice begat another Alice Barus, who, according to Uncle John, "is said to have been the most beautiful and accomplished young lady in Indianapolis. She played the piano and sang; also composed music, some of which was published."

She was my mother's mother.

Barzov, Major. *The Soviet army military observer assisting Pi Ying, a Far Eastern Communist guerilla chief in the short story "All The King's Horses" reprinted in* Welcome to the Monkey House. *Barzov stands by while Pi Ying prepares to have a chess match with Colonel Kelly involving the sixteen captured Americans as Kelly's chess pieces. When Kelly's "pieces" are taken, they are condemned to death.* (*MH* 83:L33-34 *All The King's Horses*) To Pi Ying's right, indistinct in the shadows, stood **Major Barzov**, the taciturn Russian military observer. He acknowledged Kelly's stare with a slow nod. Kelly continued to stare fixedly. The arrogant, bristle-haired major became restless, folding and unfolding his arms, repeatedly rocking back and forth in his black boots. "I wish I could help you," he said at last. *During the course of the game Pi Ying is killed, and Barzov takes over for him.* (*MH* 95:L14 *All The King's Horses*) **Major Barzov** wasn't above the kind of entertainment Pi Ying had found so diverting. But Kelly sensed the difference between the major's demeanor and that of the guerrilla chief. The major was resuming the game, not because he liked it, but because he wanted to prove that he was one hell of a bright fellow, and that the Americans were dirt. Apparently, he didn't realize that Pi Ying had already lost the game. Either that, or Kelly had miscalculated.

In an ominous geo-political metaphor, the Soviet major expresses the kind of Cold-War notion which continued to nag the west until very recently. (*MH* 98:L11-14) "There will be others like Pi Ying eager to play you with live men, and I hope I will again be privileged to be an observer." He smiled brightly. "When and where would you like it to be?"

basement (see also **air-raid shelter**, **cellar**, and **subbasement**). *In a curious plot repetition, Vonnegut places a number of major characters and incidents in basements and other underground dwellings.** *In a number of passages throughout his work Vonnegut recalls taking refuge in the underground meatlocker in Dresden during its firebombing. He usually includes his participation in "corpse mining" after the attack (digging bodies and valuables out of charred basements). Among the many textual citations, there are some passages in the fiction of particular note. In* Player Piano *Paul Proteus is kidnapped by The Ghost Shirt Society and secreted in an abandoned Ilium air-*

---

*See the author's doctoral dissertation "What Goes Around Comes Around: The Naïve, Schizophrenic, Resurrected Cycle in the Novels of Kurt Vonnegut" (1987).

raid shelter. He is later captured by the ruling technocracy and held for trial in the basement cell of the Ilium Police Headquarters.

Mother Night*'s Howard Campbell writes his memoirs from the basement cell of an Old Jerusalem jail. Earlier in the text the Soviet plot to kidnap Campbell from the basement of Dr. Jones' building is foiled by his Blue Fairy Godmother, Colonel Frank Wirtanen.*

Cat's Cradle*'s Franklin Hoenikker lived in the basement of Jack's Hobby Shop where he built a scale model of an island society (foreshadowing his impact on San Lorenzo). He also had a long term love affair with Jack's wife down in his basement apartment.*

In God Bless You, Mr. Rosewater, *Fred Rosewater goes down to his basement and finds the Merrihue Rosewater account of the family's history which prompts him to plot his own suicide. Back in Rosewater County, the Dresden fire alarm ("the loudest fire alarm in the Western Hemisphere") prompts Bella of Bella's Beauty Nook to suffer a mild heart attack in her basement shop.*

In Slaughterhouse-Five, *Vonnegut recalls his early days as a news reporter and having to report on the gruesome death of a veteran who was squashed to death by an elevator headed to the basement when he got his wedding ring stuck in the door. Within the text's story, Billy Pilgrim writes from his basement rumpus room about his time-tripping experiences in a letter addressed to the* Ilium News Leader. *Science fiction writer Kilgore Trout is said to live in a basement apartment two miles from Pilgrim's house in Ilium, New York. In* Breakfast of Champions *Trout lives in a basement apartment in Cohoes, New York.*

Jailbird*'s Walter Starbuck is jailed in the basement cell of a New York City police station. Having once ignorantly implicated Leland Clewes of un-American activities (just prior to the McCarthy hearings in the 1950s), Starbuck later visits Leland and Sarah Clewes in their Tudor City basement apartment. Mary Kathleen O'Looney dies in a subbasement of Grand Central Station after having been struck by a taxi.*

Deadeye Dick*'s Rudy Waltz is placed in the basement holding cage of the Midland City Police Department. It is there that patrolman Anthony Squires nicknames him "Deadeye Dick" for killing Eloise Metzger. Other officers brought curious gawkers to view the young sniper until they cleared the room for a visit by the grieved George Metzger. Later, after the tremendous snow storm which nearly wiped out Midland City, Rudy locates his mother in a hastily arranged ward in the hospital's basement—near the morgue which once held Eloise Metzger.*

Bluebeard*'s Rabo Karabekian often took his meals in the basement while an apprentice to Dan Gregory. Later, Rabo stored sixty-three gallons of the unstable Sateen Dura-Luxe in his Long Island basement. In his later years, Rabo was asked to reclaim the remains of "Blue Windsor Number Seventeen," his sixty-four-foot Abstract Expressionist triptych which fell victim to the faulty paint. The painting was stored in the third subbasement of the GEFFCo*

Building. After cleaning the canvasses, Rabo painted his masterpiece "Now It's The Women's Turn."

Hocus Pocus' *Eugene Debs Hartke's father informs him in their basement that he will enter his son in the school science fair and proceeds to take full control of its development. The duplicity of the father and the unwitting, uncaring obedience of the son result in an odd series of events leading to Eugene's admission to West Point, the start of his long and distinguished military career.* *PP* 8:L4-5; 10:L28; 28:L1; 247:L33; 248:L9; 264:L11; *MN* 117:L1; 118:L12; 121:L1; 132:L3; 136:L10; 161:L4; 165:L4; *CC* 40:L30; 68:L10,16-17; 84:L8,11-12; *GBR* 67:L34; 162:L30; 174:L22; *SL5* 8:L12; 23:L33; 114:L8; 142:L22; *MH—The Foster Portfolio* 64:L37; 65:L5-6; *MH—More Stately Mansions* 128:L37; *WJ* 55:L14; *BC* 20:L1; 30:L5; 52:L24; 77:L7; 100:L9; 154:L24-25; 198:L23; 244:L2; 281:L1-2,8; *JB* 183:L17,25; 200:L19; 221:L5,8; 228:L11; 231:L22; *PS—from Roots—"Account of the Ancestry of Kurt Vonnegut, Jr., by an Ancient Friend of His Family"—formal essay by the late John G. Rauch of Indianapolis* 54:L29; *PS—Self-Interview* 90:L17, 19; *PS—PLAYMATES* 145:L6; *DD* 11:L8; 73:L9; 76:L11,14,27; 77:L18; 81:L5; 82:L2,9,19; 83:L25; 84:L4; 88:L15; 164:L14,16-17; 173:L5; 189:L3; 213:L24; *Blue* 38:L14-15,23; 59:L30; 89:L4; 96:L8; 109:L16,26; 114:L9; 128:L9; 171:L4; 177:L6; 210:L21; 244:L30; 272:L18; *HP* 34:L15-16; 36:L27; 39:L6; 42:L18,20-21; 117:L33; 268:L15; *FWD* 19:L13.

Bassett, Earnest S. *Doctor Bassett was the manager of the Pittsburgh Works who passed away, setting in motion the jockeying for his replacement. Kroner uses The Meadows and the old oak tree as a setting for a brief eulogy.* (*PP* 172:L29) "Ernie was manager of the Philadelphia Works for five years, of the Pittsburgh Works for seven. He was my friend; he was *our* friend: a great American, a great engineer, a great manager, a great pioneer at the head of the procession of civilization, opening new, undreamed-of doors to better things, for better living, for more people, at less cost. . . . He gave himself unstintingly engineeringwise, managershipwise, personalitywise, Americanwise, and—" Kroner paused to look impressively from face to face. Again he talked to the clouds—"heartwise."

Batavia. *In* Hocus Pocus, *the small city in Western New York where Eugene Debs Hartke's wife and mother-in-law are confined in a "lunatic asylum" after his imprisonment. It is also the home for Clarence Daffodil-11 Johnson, the Chief of Police of Batavia, New York, a relative of Wilbur Swain's by government decree* (Slapstick).

Batten, Barton, Durstine & Osborn. *In* Deadeye Dick, *Felix Waltz's soon-to-be employers, a large advertising agency which actually does exist in New York City.*

Battle of Boca Raton. *In* Sirens of Titan*, the battle in which Sergeant Brackman of Unk and Boaz's Martian assault team was badly wounded. He was the only Martian survivor—twenty-three others were killed.*

Battle of the Bulge. *The final great assault of the German Army in December 1944, during which Vonnegut and his friend Bernard V. O'Hare were taken prisoner. They were eventually sent to work in Dresden and there they witnessed the famous firebombing. Billy Pilgrim endures this central episode in* Slaughterhouse-Five *and the events leading up to Vonnegut's actual capture are recounted in various places in* Fates Worse Than Death.

Bauerbeck, Nelson. *Bauerbeck is the old art teacher who rejects taking on Rabo Karabekian as a student at the Art Students League in New York, on the basis of his technically correct, but passionless, portfolio.* (*Blue* 190:L2-7) "On the basis of the very first picture in your portfolio," he said. "It told me, 'Here is a man without passion.' And I asked myself what I now ask you: 'Why should I teach him the language of painting, since there seems to be absolutely nothing which he is desperate to talk about?'"

Bavaria. *In* God Bless You, Mr. Rosewater, *Eliot Rosewater's first nervous breakdown occurred after bayoneyting three volunteer fireman in a smoke-filled clarinet factory in Bavaria. He was led to believe the building was filled with S.S. troops.*

Bay State Progressive. *As a Harvard student, Walter Starbuck was cochairman of this radical weekly newspaper. While working there he first met Mary Kathleen O'Looney who volunteered her services and was put to work as the circulation manager,* "handing out the paper at factory gates and along breadlines and so on" (*JB* 138:L9-10). *When Alexander Hamilton McCone found out about Starbuck's participation with the paper, he cut him off from support. Starbuck was able to graduate because McCone had already paid up the year's tuition.*

Beagle, Her Majesty's Ship (also ***The Voyage of the Beagle***). *The vessel upon which Charles Darwin sailed as the unpaid naturalist during its voyage to the Galápagos Islands. Based on that excursion Darwin wrote* The Voyage of the Beagle*, the text which first set down his theory of evolution. The ship, Darwin, and his text are all frequently cited in* Galápagos.

Beame, Timothy. *The one-time Assistant Secretary of Agriculture under Franklin Delano Roosevelt and Harvard alum who berates Walter Starbuck for his failure to protect the powers above him during the Watergate scandals. Beame is a former Rhodes Scholar and still actively running the law firm of Beame, Mearns, Weld and Weld.* (*JB* 75:L11-17, 19-21) "You ninny, you Harvard abortion, you incomparably third-rate little horse's ass," he said, and he arose from his chair. "You and Clewes have destroyed the good reputation of the most unselfish and intelligent generation of public servants this country has ever known! My God—who can care about you now, or about Clewes? Too bad he's in jail! Too bad we can't find another job for you! . . . The most important thing they teach at Harvard," he said, "is that a man can obey every law and still be the worst criminal of his time."

Bearse, Alfy. (*BC* 104:L30-34) When he *(Kilgore Trout)* lived on Cape Cod, for instance, the only person he could greet warmly and by name was **Alfy Bearse**, who was a one-armed albino. "Hot enough for you, **Alfy**?" he would say. "Where you been keeping yourself, **Alfy**?" he'd say. "You're a sight for sore eyes, **Alfy**," he'd say.

Beelzebub. *The Devil, also known as Lord of the Flies. The great series of bowls outside the Rumfoord mansion are described in such comparative terms, and the largest of the Lutz Carillon bells at Tarkington College is named for him. Franklin Hoenikker is also compared to him for the power he possesses over his trapped bugs.* (*CC* 72:L3) And then, one day, one Sunday, I found out where the fugitive from justice, the model-maker, the Great God Jehovah and **Beelzebub** of bugs in Mason jars was—where Franklin Hoenikker could be found. *See also: ST* 19:L15; *HP* 63:L20; 66:L7; *FWD* 192:L2.

Beethoven (also **Beethoven's Ninth Symphony**). *In* God Bless You, Mr. Rosewater *the clingy and classless Caroline Rosewater plays an endless rack of Beethoven records at a much higher speed than is required.*

Breakfast of Champions' *Rabo wears a Beethoven sweatshirt to the bar in the Holiday Inn prior to the Midland City Arts Festival.*

Beethoven is frequently referred to in Galápagos *not simply as the measure of creative genius, but as the hallmark of "oversized brains." At the passing of a number of characters it is remarked, "Oh, well—he wasn't going to write Beethoven's Ninth Symphony anyway." First uttered by Hjalmar Arvid Boström at the funeral of Per Olaf Rosenquist and later at the funeral for the decapitated Leon Trout, Trout goes on to mark the passing of dogs and people with the same pronouncement. Near the end of Trout's one thousand millennia walking the earth, when humanity has evolved into nothing more cunning than sea lions, he looks forward to entering the "blue tunnel" to the afterlife.* (*Gal* 259:L22-23) Nothing ever happens around here anymore that I haven't seen or heard so many times before. Nobody, surely, is going to write **Beethoven's Ninth Symphony**—or tell a lie, or start a Third World War.
(*FWD* 73:L15) (Speaking of composers: My sister Alice asked our father when she was about ten years old if he and Mother used to dance to **Beethoven**.)

begat, beget, begetting. *In Vonnegut's own playful way, he describes the birth of various fictional characters, machines, explosives, and his own ancestors in*

biblical terms. *(GBR* 21:L28) And Noah **begat** Samuel, who married Geraldine Ames Rockefeller.
(*GBR* 22:L15) And Samuel **begat** Lister Ames Rosewater, who married Eunice Eliot Morgan.
(*GBR* 23:L3) That he *(Senator Lister Ames Rosewater)* is or ever was an Indiana person is a tenuous political fiction. And Lister **begat** Eliot.
(*GBR* 23:L17) And Eliot became a drunkard, a Utopian dreamer, a tinhorn saint, an aimless fool.

Begat he not a soul.

(*GBR* 120:L5) And George **begat** Abraham, who became a Congregationalist minister.
(*GBR* 120:L9) In the jungle, Abraham **begat** Merrihue.
(*GBR* 120:L28) But, before he did that *(Merrihue Rosewater, the Parson's son who shot out his brains)*, he wrote a family history and he **begat** poor Fred, the insurance man.
(*Slap* 241:L30) The boy **begat** Melody at the age of fourteen.
(*PS* 35:L9) AND Professor Karl Barus the musician, and his wife Alice **begat** another Alice Barus, who, according to Uncle John, "is said to have been the most beautiful and accomplished young lady in Indianapolis. She played the piano and sang; also composed music, some of which was published."

She was my mother's mother.

(*PS* 35:L15) Yes, and Peter Lieber, the limping war veteran, and his wife Sophia **begat** Albert Lieber, who became an Indianapolis brewer and *bon vivant*.

He was my mother's father.

(*PS* 35:L20) Henry Schnull, the merchant and banker, and his wife Matilda **begat** Nanette Schnull, who, according to Uncle John, "was a very beautiful woman in her prime, and had a lovely speaking and singing voice. She often sang in public. She laughed readily, enjoyed people, and was greatly admired by a host of friends."

She was my father's mother.

(*PS* 35:L28) And Clemens Vonnegut, the Free Thinker and founder of the Vonnegut Hardware Company, and his wife Katarina **begat** Bernard Vonnegut, who, Uncle John says, "was from earliest youth artistic."
(*Gal* 58:L1, 3-4) *Zenji Hiroguchi **begat** Gokubi one million and five years ago, and then, one million years ago, this young genius **begat** Mandarax. Yes, and at the time of his **begetting** of Mandarax, his wife was about to give birth to his first human child.
(*Gal* 59:L1) *The only human being *Zengi Hiroguchi would ever* **beget** was a darling but furry daughter *(Akiko)* he would never see.
(*Gal* 212:L21) Glacco **begat** dagonite, so to speak, and both were descendants of Greek fire and gunpowder and dynamite and cordite and TNT.

beginning, middle . . . and end. (*PP* 160:L3-4) "Descent into the Maelstrom," he thought wearily, and closed his eyes, and gave himself over to

the one sequence of events that had never failed to provide **a beginning, a middle, and a satisfactory end**. *The descent Proteus thinks of is his sexual relationship with Anita.*
(*MN* 141:L11-12) "I admire form," I *(Howard W. Campbell)* said. "I admire things with **a beginning, a middle, an end**—and, whenever possible, a moral, too."
(*SL5* 76:L19-20) "There are no telegrams on Tralfamadore. But you're right: each clump of symbols is a brief, urgent message—describing a situation, a scene. We Tralfamadorians read them all at once, not one after the other. There isn't any particular relationship between all the messages, except that the author has chosen them carefully, so that, when seen all at once, they produce an image of life that is beautiful and surprising and deep. There is **no beginning, no middle, no end**, no suspense, no moral, no causes, no effects. What we love in our books are the depths of many marvelous moments seen all at one time." *The Tralfamadorians explain to Billy the nature of their narrative texts.*
(*BC* 209:L26-27) I had no respect whatsoever for the creative works of either the painter or the novelist. I thought Karabekian with his meaningless pictures had entered into a conspiracy with millionaires to make poor people feel stupid. I thought Beatrice Keedsler had joined hands with other old-fashioned storytellers to make people believe that life had leading characters, minor characters, significant details, insignificant details, that it had lessons to be learned, tests to be passed, and **a beginning, a middle, and an end**. *Vonnegut makes these remarks after he enters the text and watches his characters discuss art in the bar of the Midland City Holiday Inn.*

Begum, Arjumand Banu. (*DD* 174:L33) It *(the Taj Mahal)* was a memorial to something Fred T. Barry never had, and which I have never had, which is a wife. Her name was **Arjumand Banu Begum**. She died in childbirth. Her husband, who ordered the Taj Mahal to be built at any cost, was the Mogul emperor Shah Jahan.

belfry (see also **cupola** and **tower**). *Aside from references to characters having "bats in their belfries," such structures have plot significance in* Jailbird *and* Hocus Pocus. *It was from the belfry of the Cuyahoga Bridge and Iron Company that Daniel McCone was joined by his sons Alexander and John to watch on Christmas morning as their hired thugs and the civil authorities put down a peaceful union demonstration, resulting in the Cuyahoga Massacre, in* Jailbird.

In Hocus Pocus *the belfry high atop the library on the Tarkington campus offers college president Tex Johnson the opportunity to snipe at the marauding convicts who had escaped the prison across the lake in Scipio. Johnson is eventually captured by the convicts and crucified for the many deaths he caused. See also: JB* xxv:L21, 25; xxxiv:L30-31; xxxv:L1-2; *HP* 27:L14; 64:L22; 65:L12; 77:L18; 155:L13,16,19; 203:L31; 262:L16.

belief. *The sincere as well as arbitrary nature of various belief systems is a hallmark of Vonnegut's work. In* Player Piano, *Paul Proteus' name is forged to a letter from the Ghost Shirt Society reaffirming their belief in the need for a society with purposeful human activity at its core.* (*PP* 262:L15) "You perhaps disagree with the antique and vain notion of Man's being a creation of God.

"But I find it a far more defensible **belief** than the one implicit in intemperate faith in lawless technological progress—namely, that man is on earth to create more durable and efficient images of himself, and, hence, to eliminate any justification at all for his own continued existence.

"Faithfully yours,

"Doctor Paul Proteus"

The central philosophy of Bokononist teaching is encapsulated in this short analogy: (*CC* 90:L3,6) It was the **belief** of Charles Atlas that muscles could be built without bar bells or spring exercisers, could be built by simply pitting one set of muscles against another.

It was the **belief** of Bokonon that good societies could be built only by pitting good against evil, and by keeping the tension between the two high at all times.

Vonnegut went to observe the 1972 Republican National convention and made this observation. (*WFG* 187:L16 *In a Manner That Must Shame God Himself*) That may not really be the message in the *(William F.)* Buckley smile. But I guarantee you that it was the monolithic **belief** that underlay the Republican National Convention in Miami Beach, Florida, in 1972. *Vonnegut phrases that belief as follows, "Yes, oh yes, my dear man—I understand what you have said so clumsily. But you know in your heart what every Winner knows: that one must behave heartlessly toward Losers, if one hopes to survive."*

Vonnegut takes such a simple view of his own belief system that he is bewildered anyone would find him threatening. (*PS* 122:L17 *The People One Knows*) THE **beliefs** I have to defend are so soft and complicated, actually, and, when vivisected, turn into bowls of undifferentiated mush. I am a pacifist, I am an anarchist, I am a planetary citizen, and so on.

(*PS* 195:L9, 12 *Religion*) How proud I became of our **belief** *(his family's legendary belief in freethinking atheism)*, how pigheadedly proud, even, is the most evident thing in my writing, I think. Haven't I already attributed the breakup of my first marriage in part to my wife's failure to share my family **belief** with me?

(*PS* 196:L28, 30, 32 *Religion*) "I have said that one guess is as good as another, but that is only roughly so. Some guesses are crueler than others—which is to say, harder on human beings, and on other animals as well. The **belief** that God wants heretics burned to death is a case in point. Some guesses are more suicidal than others. The **belief** that a true lover of God is immune to the bites of copperheads and rattlesnakes is a case in point. Some guesses are greedier and more egocentric than others. **Belief** in the divine right of kings and presidents is a case in point."

(*FWD* 194:L6) It is my serious **belief** that those of us who become humorists (suicidal or not) feel free (as most people do not) to speak of life itself as a dirty joke, even though life is all there is or ever can be.

We do, doodily do, doodily do, doodily do
What we must, muddily must, muddily must, muddily must:
Muddily do, muddily must, muddily do, muddily must,
Until we bust, bodily bust, bodily bust, bodily bust.

This refrain first appears thirty-two years earlier in Sirens of Titan, *but Vonnegut doesn't make mention of that when repeating it here. See also: PP* 99:L33; 107:L18; 249:L37; *ST* 238:L27; *CC* 90:L3; 90:L6; 159:L10; *SL5* 24:L13; 160:L20; *BC* 25:L30; 40:L10; 197:L10; *JB* 4:L7, 9; 13:L24; *PS—Preface* xviii:L1; *PS—The People One Knows* 135:L8; *PS—Religion* 195:L8; *DD* 83:L31; 232:L8; *Gal* 158:L7; 180:L29; *Blue* 42:L20; 152:L1; 155:L15; *HP* 148:L21; *FWD* 77:L24; 114:L16; 121:L21; 177:L15.

Bella (also **Bella's Beauty Nook**). *Bella was the child of a Nickel Plate Railroad brakeman, weighed 314 pounds, and founded Bella's Beauty Nook in the cellar of the Rosewater County Courthouse, one of the rare successful enterprises in town. She suffers a mild heart attack when Eliot sets off "the loudest fire alarm in the Western Hemisphere" atop the volunteer fire department at high noon.*

Bergeron, Bruce. *A graduate of Tarkington's Class of 1985 and the son of Ed Bergeron, a Trustee of Tarkington College, the homosexual Bruce became a chorus boy for the Ice Capades. He often went over to Eugene Debs Hartke's home to dance with his crazy mother-in-law. Bruce was found dead, strangled and stabbed to death in a motel outside Dubuque, Iowa.*

When Bruce had Hartke as his music appreciation teacher at Tarkington, he set to music his experience as a child when he was caught in an elevator at Bloomingdale's with his Haitian nanny. Since they were stuck for such a long time and he was just a small child, he imagined he was at the center of an important national happening. When the elevator was freed and no one from Bloomingdale's or the media was there to greet the captives' release, he felt sullen and disappointed, and the nanny made him promise never to tell where they had been since she wasn't supposed to have been there. Hartke told him his musical description perfectly described his own return from Vietnam.

Bergeron, Ed. *A member of Tarkington College's Board of Trustees, though he resigned after his friend Eugene Debs Hartke was fired and before the prison breakout which overran the college, and father of Bruce Bergeron—the homosexual ice skater strangled and bludgeoned to death in Dubuque, Iowa.*

Hartke considered Ed his "doomsday pal" since they often spoke about the economic and environmental plight of the earth. Bergeron often debated Jason Wilder, the conservative talk show host who was eventually killed by the prisoners who took over the college. (*HP* 138:L8-14) His wealth was as old as the Moellenkamps', and was based on ancestral oil fields and coal mines and railroads which he had sold to foreigners in order to devote himself full-time to nature study and conservation. He was President of the Wildlife Rescue Federation, and his photographs of wildlife on the Galápagos Islands had been published in *National Geographic*.
(*HP* 140:L17) **Bergeron**'s epitaph for the planet, I remember, which he said should be carved in big letters in a wall of the Grand Canyon for the flying-saucer people to find, was this:

WE COULD HAVE SAVED IT,
BUT WE WERE TOO DOGGONE CHEAP.

Only he didn't say "doggone."
(*HP* 140:L29-33) One thing he used to say to me *(Hartke)*, and to a class of mine he spoke to one time, was that man was the weather now. Man was the tornadoes, man was the hailstones, man was the floods. So he might have said that Scipio was Pompeii, and the escapees were a lava flow.

The two misfortunes which forced Ed Bergeron's resignation were financial and personal. (*HP* 141:L1-15) A company he inherited made all sorts of products out of asbestos, whose dust proved to be as carcinogenic as any substance yet identified, with the exception of epoxy cement and some of the radioactive stuff accidentally turned loose in the air and aquifers around nuclear weapons factories and power plants. He felt terrible about this, he told me, although he had never laid eyes on any of the factories that made the stuff. He sold them for practically nothing, since the company in Singapore that bought them got all the lawsuits along with the machinery and buildings, and an inventory of finished materials which was huge and unsalable in this country. The people in Singapore did what **Ed** couldn't bring himself to do, which was to sell all those floor tiles and roofing and so on to emerging nations in Africa. *Shortly after this episode his son Bruce, a chorus boy in the Ice Capades, was strangled and stabbed to death in a motel outside Dubuque.*

Bergeron, George and Hazel. *The parents of the outlaw Harrison Bergeron who watch his execution on television but barely know it due to the incessant government manipulation of their minds.* (*MH* 7:L14-21 *Harrison Bergeron*) **Hazel** had a perfectly average intelligence, which meant she couldn't think about anything except in short bursts. And **George**, while his intelligence was way above normal, had a little mental handicap radio in his ear. He was required by law to wear it at all times. It was tuned to a government transmitter. Every twenty seconds or so, the transmitter would send out some sharp noise to keep people like George from taking unfair advantage of their brains.

Bergeron, Harrison. *The title character of the short story reprinted in* Welcome to the Monkey House, *Harrison had been jailed by the Handicapper General's office for "suspicion of plotting to overthrow the government." The story takes place in 2081, when all people were made equal due to the imposition of constitutionally mandated handicaps on all who were above average intellectually or physically. Though only fourteen and described as an under-handicapped genius and athlete, Harrison escapes from jail and breaks into a television studio where a ridiculous ballet of lead-weighted ballerinas is airing. He encourages one of the dancers to be his dance partner without the government-issued weights, bullies the orchestra to remove its handicaps to play its best, and declares* "Even as I stand here—" he bellowed, "crippled, hobbled, sickened—I am a greater ruler than any man who ever lived! Now watch me become what I *can* become!"

Harrison tore the straps of his handicap harness like wet tissue paper, tore straps guaranteed to support five thousand pounds.

Harrison's scrap-iron handicaps crashed to the floor.

Harrison thrust his thumbs under the bar of the padlock that secured his head harness. The bar snapped like celery. **Harrison** smashed his headphones and spectacles against the wall.

He flung away his rubber-ball nose, revealed a man that would have awed Thor, the god of thunder (*MH* 11:L29-38, 12:L1-2). *Handicapper General Diana Moon Glampers then breaks into the studio and kills Harrison and his partner. All this was viewed by his father watching television, but the head-splitting radio waves transmitted to his handicap receiver wipe out any recognition of exactly what happened.*

Berman, Abe. *In* Bluebeard, *the brain surgeon husband of Circe Berman who died six months before she met Rabo Karabekian. Circe is the author of romance novels, and she tells Rabo that what gives her books a ring of authenticity for her readers is that she always wrote to her husband's tastes.*

Berman, Circe. *Rabo Karabekian dedicates his memoirs,* Bluebeard, *to Circe Berman. She is the forty-three-year-old fabulously successful romance novelist (using the pen name Polly Madison) who becomes Karabekian's housemate in the Hamptons on Long Island. Her husband died six months before she met Rabo. He was Abe Berman, a brain surgeon who died of a cerebral hemorrhage. Circe is the daughter of a suicide—her father hanged himself after his clothing factory went bankrupt. It is because of her prodding that Rabo decides to write his memoirs and to pick up painting again. Rabo credits her with his resurrection.* (*Blue* 299:L6) "Twice now I've been a Lazarus," I said. "I died with Terry Kitchen, and Edith brought me back to life again. I died with dear Edith, and **Circe Berman** brought me back to life again."

Berringer, Fred and Dave. *A subordinate of Paul Proteus' at the Ilium Works, Fred Berringer challenges his boss' checker championship with his* *father's invention, the robot "Checker Charley." Dave Berringer is considered one of the top "computer-machine" men in the country. Fred's ignorance about his father's invention leads to its undoing. Ed Finnerty noticed some of Checker Charley's connections were loose, and they eventually cause the robot to fail allowing Paul to retain his championship.* (*PP* 40:L3) **Fred Berringer**, a short, heavy, slit-eyed blond, seemed to be their leader. He was a wealthy, extroverted, dull boy from a good family of engineers and managers in Minneapolis. He had squeaked through college, and was just barely acceptable to the personnel machines. Ordinarily, nobody would have hired him. But Kroner, who knew his bloodlines, had taken him on anyway and sent him to Ilium to be trained. The break had done anything but teach him humility. He took it as evidence that his money and name could beat the system any time and, paraphrased, he'd said as much. The hell of it was that his attitude won grudging admiration from his fellow engineers, who had got their jobs the hard way. Paul supposed, gloomily, that beaters of systems had always been admired by the conventional. At any rate, Kroner still believed in the boy, so Paul had no choice but to keep him on, and to pair a smarter man with him to backstop his mental apparatus.

Fred Berringer is also present in court when Paul is tried for treason.

Bert (see also **Bert Quinn**; **Bert Wright**). *The Nova Scotian captain of the yacht* Charity Anne Browning. (*WFG* 14:L1-4, 31) He was sixty years old, had bright blue eyes and the complexion of a used footlocker. He was master of the *Charity Anne Browning*, a sixty-eight-foot yawl. . . . **Bert** kept the ship immaculate inside by the simple expedient of not letting anybody use anything. He kept us off the couch. I made the mistake of using an ashtray, and he took it away immediately, washed it, and put it carefully into a cupboard.

When the Charity Anne Browning *is tied up at dock overnight, Bert and his crew are seen using the toilets in the marina rather than dirty their own.*

Beryllium. *The unnamed member of the Beryllium clan is killed while attempting to deliver a letter to Wilbur Swain. The letter from Wilma Pachysandra-17 von Peterswald, wife of the inventor of The Hooligan (a device to speak with the dead), tells Wilbur about her many conversations with his dead sister Eliza who expresses a great desire to communicate with him. The Beryllium is killed by Byron Hatfield on the new border between Tennessee and West Virginia. Hatfield mistook the Beryllium for Newton McCoy, an hereditary enemy. The Beryllium agreed to deliver the letter while on his way to join his clan in Maryland. Hatfield abides by his dying wish to deliver the letter to Wilbur.*

Beskudnikov. *Beskudnikov, engraver of the plates for Imperial bonds and paper currency in Russia, he and his wife took in the five-year-old Dan Gregory. Gregory became his apprentice and was forced to prove his technical competence by copying the engraving plates Beskudnikov made. The master* *engraver torments his apprentice by destroying copies Gregory worked on for months and years because he said they were deficient. Eventually, Gregory fools his master by offering him the genuine article rather than his copy.*

Gregory later torments the young Rabo Karabekian by having him create a photo-realistic painting of Gregory's attic.

Betelgeuse (also **Betelguese**). *A bright red star 527 light years from Earth in the constellation Orion.* (*ST* 13:L24) Winston Niles Rumfoord had run his private space ship right into the heart of an uncharted chrono-synclastic infundibulum two days out of Mars. Only his dog had been along. Now Winston Niles Rumfoord and his dog Kazak existed as wave phenomena—apparently pulsing in a distorted spiral with its origin in the Sun and its terminal in **Betelgeuse**. . . .
(*ST* 266:L24-25) Winston Niles Rumfoord and his dog Kazak were wave phenomena—pulsing in distorted spirals, with their origins in the Sun and their terminals in **Betelgeuse**. Whenever a heavenly body intercepted their spirals, Rumfoord and his dog materialized on that body.
(HP 260:L20) Imagine the same sort of thing happening on a huge rocket ship bound for **Betelgeuse**. *This is Hartke's idle wondering about the human waste disposal problem posed by the prison break at Scipio. The state's response was to annex Tarkington College in part for its toilet facilities. See also:* ST 21:L13; 36:L13, 20; 179:L11.

Bethlehem (also **Star of Bethlehem**). *Kilgore Trout's explanation that God is not necessarily a benign overseer is illustrated by his analogy to the Star of Bethlehem—the example itself goes against Christian theology.* (*BC* 85:1) "I realized . . . that God wasn't any conservationist, so for anybody else to be one was sacrilegious and a waste of time. You ever see one of His volcanoes or tornadoes or tidal waves? Anybody ever tell you about the Ice Ages he arranges for every half-million years? How about Dutch Elm disease? There's a nice conservation measure for you. That's God, not man. Just about the time we got our rivers cleaned up, he'd probably have the whole galaxy go up like a celluloid collar. That's what the **Star of Bethlehem** was, you know."

In Vonnegut's "Address to the National Institute of Arts and Letters," reprinted in Wampeters, *he takes this same example and repeats it to reinforce his biochemical-anthropological theory of cosmic existence.* (*WFG* 179:2) It *(the sun)* will wish to collapse even more, but the atomic nuclei will prevent this. An irresistible force will meet an immovable object, so to speak. There will be a tremendous explosion. Our sun will become a supernova, a flash such as the **Star of Bethlehem** is thought to have been. Earth Day cannot prevent this.

Bethune. Mother Night*'s Howard W. Campbell, Jr.'s residence in the United States after the war is 27 Bethune Street, New York City.*

BIBEC. *In* Jailbird, *a rising new international conglomerate based in Monaco but suspected of being Soviet in origin. It purchases American Telephone and Telegraph Company, which had just hired away Arpad Leen, the president and chairman of the board of The RAMJAC Corporation. The United States had begun liquidating RAMJAC to cover the nation's short-term economic problems.*

Bierce, Ambrose. (*Gal* 65:L18-23) If Mandarax were still around, it would have had mostly unpleasant things to say about matrimony, such as:

> *Marriage: a community consisting of a master a*
> *mistress, and two slaves, making in all, two.*
> **Ambrose Bierce** (1842-?)

The Big Board. *Billy Pilgrim finds this Kilgore Trout novel in a Times Square bookstore. After skimming its opening, Billy realized he read it before.* (*SL5* 174:L1-29) It was about an Earthling man and woman who were kidnapped by extra-terrestrials. They were put on display in a zoo on a planet called Zircon-212.

These fictitious people in the zoo had a **big board** supposedly showing stock market quotations and commodity prices along one wall of their habitat, and a news ticker, and a telephone that was supposedly connected to a brokerage on Earth. The creatures on Zircon-212 told their captives that they had invested a million dollars for them back on Earth, and that it was up to the captives to manage it so that they would be fabulously wealthy when they were returned to Earth.

The telephone and the **big board** and the ticker were all fakes, of course. They were simply stimulants to make the Earthlings perform vividly for the crowds at the zoo—to make them jump up and down and cheer, or gloat, or sulk, or tear their hair, to be scared shitless or to feel as contented as babies in their mothers' arms.

The Earthlings did very well on paper. That was part of the rigging, of course. And religion got mixed up in it, too. The news ticker reminded them that the President of the United States had declared National Prayer Week, and that everybody should pray. The Earthlings had had a bad week on the market before that. They had lost a small fortune in olive oil futures. So they gave praying a whirl.

It worked. Olive oil went up.

big eye. (*ST* 276:L13, 15-16, 23, 26, 31) The Earthlings behaved at all times as though there were a **big eye** in the sky—as though that **big eye** were ravenous for entertainment.

The **big eye** was a glutton for great theater. The **big eye** was indifferent as to whether the Earthling shows were comedy, tragedy, farce, satire, athletics, or vaudeville. Its demand, which Earthlings apparently found as irresistible as gravity, was that the shows be great...

The **big eye** was the only audience that Earthlings really cared about. The fanciest performances that Salo had seen had been put on by Earthlings who were terribly alone. The imagined **big eye** was their only audience.

Salo, with his diamond-hard statues, had tried to preserve some of the mental states of those Earthlings who had put on the most interesting shows for the imagined **big eye**.

"The Big Space Fuck" (1972). *Reprinted in the "Obscenity" chapter of* Palm Sunday, *this science fiction short story is set against the July 4, 1989, launch of the space ship* Arthur C. Clarke *filled with eight hundred pounds of freeze-dried sperm and heading for the Andromeda Galaxy. It was an attempt to ensure the survival of man, which was living in an increasingly polluted—if not toxic—environment. Society had also lost all decorum. Profanity was so common that even the president called the operation "The Big Space Fuck." Sperm donors needed a 115 I.Q. in order to qualify.*

The main part of the story concerns Elk Harbor, Ohio, residents Dwayne and Grace Hoobler who were being sued by their daughter Wanda June for being lousy parents and ruining her prospects as an adult. At the close of the story Dwayne, Grace, and the Sheriff were all eaten by an overgrown Lamprey, which had to leave its Great Lakes environs due to the pollution.

Bigley, Homer and **Clara**. *The barber shop proprietor in* Player Piano *who gets to cut the hair of the Shah of Bratpuhr. Homer and Clara are childless.* (*PP* 175:L21) While Halyard brooded, **Homer Bigley**, with the reflexes born of a life of barbering, selected his scissors, clicked them in air about the sacred head, and, as though his right hand were serviced by the same nerve as his diaphragm and voicebox, he began to cut hair and talk-talked to the uncomprehending Shah after the fashion of an extroverted embalmer chatting with a corpse.

Bijou Theater. *In* Bluebeard *Rabo Karabekian's father died in the* ***Bijou Theater*** *in San Ignacio, California, in 1938.*

Bikini Atoll. *The South Pacific site of atomic bomb testing conducted in the late 1940s and early 1950s. In* Galápagos, *Roy Hepburn, suffering from inoperable brain cancer, imagines that he had been a victim of the United States atomic bomb tests at Bikini Atoll, preventing his having children with his wife Mary. He also believes he helped tie up all sorts of exotic animals in preparation for the bomb tests.* (*Gal* 40:L20) To hear him tell it, he had tethered peacocks and snow leopards and gorillas and crocodiles and albatrosses to the stakes. In his big brain, **Bikini** became the exact reverse of Noah's ark. Two of every sort of animal had been brought there in order to be atom-bombed.

Bill (Kilgore Trout's parakeet). *Bill is Kilgore Trout's faithful companion with whom Trout discusses his trepidation about the fate of the planet. Trout's theory that the atmosphere would soon become unbreathable prompted some macabre musings (comparable to Vonnegut's view of writers as canaries in a coal mine—these sensitive souls serve as early warning devices to those who pay attention).* (*BC* 18:L24-28) Trout supposed that when the atmosphere became poisonous, **Bill** would keel over a few minutes before Trout did. He would kid **Bill** about that. "How's the old respiration, **Bill**?" he'd say, or, "Seems like you've got a touch of the old emphysema, **Bill**," or, "We never discussed what kind of a funeral you want, **Bill**. You never even told me what your religion is." And so on.

Trout recognizes the power he possesses over Bill's life and when he understands that the fungi eating his tuxedo mindlessly know what they want, he plays with Bill by offering the parakeet his freedom. When Bill resists flying out of his open cage and out the open window, Trout sees this as true wisdom. (*BC* 35:L28-32) Trout closed the door of the cage and latched it. "That's the most intelligent use of three wishes I ever heard of," he told the bird. "You made sure you'd still have something worth wishing for—to get out of the cage."

Trout sees the lure of the Midland City Arts Festival as a wish he should avoid to save his fantasy—much as he understood Bill's reticence to leave his cage. (*BC* 36:L25) Trout shook his head. "I'm not going, **Bill**. I don't want out of my cage. I'm too smart for that. Even if I did want out, though, I wouldn't go to Midland City to make a laughing stock of myself—and my only fan."

Trout confides in Bill his uneasiness about the nature of the universe, that he just may be the fictional whim of someone else. (*BC* 241:L1) Trout was aware of me *(Vonnegut)*, too, what little he could see of me. I made him even more uneasy than Dwayne did. The thing was: Trout was the only character I ever created who had enough imagination to suspect that he might be the creation of another human being. He had spoken of this possibility several times to his parakeet. He had said, for instance, "Honest to God, **Bill**, the way things are going, all I can think of is that I'm a character in a book by somebody who wants to write about somebody who suffers all the time."

Billy the Poet. *In "Welcome to the Monkey House," the notorious "nothinghead" who attempts to seduce Ethical Suicide Parlor hostesses by preventing them from taking their ethical birth control pills, allowing normal sexual urges to return. Billy agrees with the world's rulers that over-reproduction endangers world stability. He points out, however, that reproduction and sexuality should not be confused. After weaning the hostesses from their ethical birth control pills, Billy shares a "traditional wedding night" with them—complete with silk pajamas. He leaves them with birth control pills that prevent reproduction but don't interfere with one's sexuality.*

biochemical-anthropological, **anthropology and biology**, **biochemistry**, **biochemists**. (*WFG* 174:L5-6, 12 *Address to the National Institute of Arts and Letters, 1971*) I can be as serious as anyone here, with a few obvious exceptions. And I will prove it. I will speak of happiness it's true—but I will speak of **anthropology and biochemistry** and unhappiness as well.

I wish in particular to call your attention to the work of Dr. M. Sydney Margoles, a Los Angeles endocrinologist, who is able to distinguish between male homosexuals and heterosexuals by means of urinalysis. He doesn't ever have to meet them. What other sweet mysteries of life are chemicals? All of them, I believe. **Biochemistry** is everything. The speculations of artists about the human condition are trash.

(*WFG* 180:L32 *Address to the National Institute of Arts and Letters, 1971*) As I have said before, I can explain *everything* in terms of this **biochemical-anthropological** theory of mine.

(*PS* 63:L22-23 *When I Lost My Innocence*) "I eventually wound up on academic probation. I was accelerating my course at the time—because of the war. My instructor in organic chemistry was my lab partner in **biochemistry**. He was fit to be tied."

(*PS* 156:L14 *Playmates*) No offense intended, but it would never occur to me to look for the best minds in any generation in an undergraduate English department anywhere. I would certainly try the physics department or the music department first—and after that **biochemistry**.

(*FWD* 33:L23) "He *(Mark Vonnegut)* isn't as enthusiastic about megavitamins as he used to be, before he himself became a doctor. He still sees a whole lot more hope in **biochemistry** than in talk.

(*FWD* 93:L3) The Class of 1940 of Shortridge High School had its Fiftieth Reunion recently, and those in charge sent out a list of members who had vanished entirely as far as Indianapolis was concerned. I was able to report back that one of them was anything but a ghost to fellow **biochemists** in Boston, where he was an expert on the aging process.

In an appendix to Fates Worse Than Death, *Vonnegut includes the updated afterword his son Mark wrote for his critically acclaimed account of his own breakdown.* (*FWD* 205:L3) The events described in *The Eden Express* took place nearly twenty years ago. Some things have changed. The notion that mental illness has a large **biochemical** component is no longer very radical. Things have come full circle, to the point where it's unusual to hear anyone say that mental illness is all mental. The view that going crazy is caused by bad events in childhood and that talk and understanding offer the best hope for a cure seems very out of date. This is a change for the better, although it has by no means brought an end to the shame, blame, and guilt which continue to compound the suffering of the mentally ill and their families.

biodegradable (*HP* 173:L32) Like Hermann and Sophia Shultz, these theoretically **biodegradable** works of Nature *(meat and vegetables found deep* *in landfills)* had failed to rot for want of moisture, which was life itself to worms and fungi and bacteria.

Birch (John Birch Society). *Billy Pilgrim's father-in-law belonged to this right-wing political group. Billy's Cadillac El Dorado Coupe de Ville is decorated with bumper stickers given to him by his father-in-law.* (*SL5* 49:L25) "Support Your Police Department," said another. There was a third. "Impeach Earl Warren," it said. The stickers about the police and Earl Warren were gifts from Billy's father-in-law, a member of the **John Birch Society**.

bird, birdhouses, birdlike (see also **Titanic Bluebird**). *Birds and bird imagery appear throughout Vonnegut's work. Perhaps the most memorable occurrences appear in* Slaughterhouse-Five, *in which birds offer a rather stultifying commentary on man's inhumanity to man.* (*SL5* 17:L8-9) Everything is supposed to be very quiet after a massacre, and it always is, except for the **birds**.

And what do the **birds** say? All there is to say about a massacre, things like "*Poo-tee-weet?*"

Upon emerging from the oubliette after the ice-nine freezing of the planet, John/Jonah writes, I was recalled from this dream by the cry of a darting **bird** above me. It seemed to be asking me what had happened. "Poo-tee-phweet?" it asked.

We all looked up at the **bird**, and then at one another (*CC* 211:L7, 10).

Hiroshi Matsumoto, the Japanese prison warden and Hiroshima bombing victim, expresses his frustration over man's inability to act without malice when he declares "I wish I had been born a **bird** instead. . . . I wish we had all been born **birds** instead" (*HP* 301:L3-4).

Vonnegut's views about the social utility of authors is phrased within his "canary in a coal mine vision." (*WFG* 238:L18-19 *Playboy Interview*) Writers are specialized cells doing whatever we do, and we're expressions of the entire society. . . . And when a society is in great danger, we're likely to sound the alarms. I have the canary-**bird**-in-the-coal-mine theory of the arts. You know, coal miners used to take **birds** down into the mines with them to detect gas before men got sick. The artists certainly did that in the case of Vietnam. They chirped and keeled over. But it made no difference whatsoever. Nobody important cared. But I continue to think that artists—all artists—should be treasured as alarm systems.

Birds become emblematic of a freedom separating one from the horrors of mankind as well as the embodiment of that which is most glorious in the human spirit. When Walter Starbuck first meets Ruth, a victim of the Nazi concentration camps and his future bride, he notes that, Her plan was to roam alone and out-of-doors forever, from nowhere to nowhere in a demented sort of religious ecstasy. "No one ever touches me," she said, "and I never touch anyone. I am like a **bird** in flight. It is so beautiful. There is only God—and me" (*JB* 21:L17).

(*JB* 70:L22) It may be that Ruth protected herself from dread of the gathering storm, or, more accurately, from dread of the gathering silence, by reverting during the daytime, when I was at work, to the Ophelia-like elation she had felt after her liberation—when she had thought of herself as a **bird** all alone with God.

(*FWD* 82:L11) I am even more offended, though, by his *(George Bush's)* failure to take notice of the most beautiful and noble and brilliant and poetical and sacred accomplishment by Americans to date. I am speaking about the exploration of the Solar System by the camera-bearing space probe *Voyager 2*. This gallant **bird** (so like Noah's dove) showed us all the outer planets and their moons! We no longer had to guess whether there was life on them or not, or whether our descendants might survive on them! (Forget it.) As *Voyager 2* departed the Solar System forever ("My work is done"), sending us dimmer and dimmer pictures of what we were and where we were, did our President invite us to love it and thank it and wish it well? No. He spoke passionately instead of the necessity of an Amendment to the Constitution (Article XXVII?) outlawing irreverent treatment of a piece of cloth, the American flag. Such an Amendment would be on a nutty par with the Roman Emperor Caligula's having his horse declared a Consul.

Birds are also seen as loyal and admirable. Boaz terms his relationship with Unk as the happiness of two birds, "`And there they go, happy as two **birds**!'" He chuckled and cooed about the happy, **birdlike** pair (*ST* 121:L13-14). *The Titanic Bluebirds (comparable in size to eagles) accept the teenaged Chrono into their community as one of their own. While Malachi buries his beloved Beatrice,* the sky was filled with **Titanic Bluebirds**. There must have been ten thousand, at least, of the great and noble **birds**.

Not one **bird** cried out (*ST* 312:L6-7).

Chrono finds sanctuary with the Titanic Bluebirds in part because the only other beings on Titan were his parents. Earlier, in Player Piano, *Edgar Rice Burroughs Hagstrohm seeks to be free from his perfectly average surroundings and a bird sanctuary offers him a way out of his predicament.* (*PP* 228:L10) "Hagstrohm cut up his M-17 home in Chicago with a blowtorch, went naked to the home of Mrs. Marion Frascati, the widow of an old friend, and demanded that she come to the woods with him. Mrs. Frascati refused, and he disappeared into the **bird** sanctuary bordering the housing development. There he eluded police, and is believed to have made his escape dropping from a tree onto a passing freight—"

Another bird sanctuary appears in the short story "The Lie" (reprinted in Welcome to the Monkey House*), donated to the exclusive private school Whitehill by the generous Remenzel family. In the short story "The Big Space Fuck" (reprinted in* Palm Sunday*), one romantic and hopeful soul who aligns himself with birds sees his efforts worthy of a very special recognition. Amateur birdhouse-maker Dwayne Hoobler (his specialty was houses made from Clorox bottles) hopes his apparent humanitarianism would qualify him along with the world's genius population to contribute sperm for the spaceship*

Arthur C. Clark, *headed for interstellar intercourse. Birds become the savior of mankind in* Galápagos *as narrator Leon Trout recalls,* These **birds** *(blue-footed boobies)* would later become crucial to the survival of the little human colony on Santa Rosalia. If those **birds** hadn't been so stupid, so incapable of learning that human beings were dangerous, the first settlers would almost certainly have starved to death (104:L13, 15).

If the multitude of bird imagery is to be fully appreciated, one must consider Vonnegut's recent account of the mixed messages his foreign readers encounter. (*FWD* 180:L30, 35) The trouble I caused translators by naming a book ***Jailbird*** is worth an essay by itself. It turns out that countries older than my own have no word for persons who find themselves locked up again and again, since the penitentiary system, an invention of American Quakers, is so new. The closest European languages could come was with their words "gallows **bird**." This failed to describe the habitual criminal I had written about, since a person cannot be hanged again and again. *See also: PP* 110:L19; 138:L37; *ST* 17:L7; 47:L23; 188:L27; 192:L23; 240:L32; 241:L6; 281:L8, 13; 286:L1; 288:L17-18; 312:L17; *MN* 138:L11; *CC* 28:L5; 123:L8; 150:L16, 19; 173:L34; 212:L1; 219:L4; 223:L24; *GBR* 147:L20; 203:L5; 204:L9,16-17,31; *SL5* 80:L22; 86:L16; 99:L24; 186:L23-24; *MH—Where I Live* 4:L12 ; *MH—Welcome to the Monkey House* 31:L34; 40:L16; *MH—The Lie* 221:L25; 222:L19; 223:L24; *MH—The Kid Nobody Could Handle* 254:L29, 31; *WJ* 168:L31; *BC* 35:L30; 48:L31; 52:L3; 84:L31; 156:L7; 162:L3; 250:L4; 251:L2,24,29, 31; 252:L3,5,13; 287:L17; *WFG—Brief Encounters on the Inland Waterway* 17:L17; 19:L27; *WFG—Fortitude* 46:L28; 48:L19; *WFG—Excelsior! We're Going to the Moon! Excelsior!* 81:L22; *WFG—The Mysterious Madame Blavatsky* 126:L11; *WFG—Biafra: A People Betrayed* 156:L28; *WFG—Address to P.E.N. Conference in Stockholm, 1973* 227:L9; *Slap* 58:L5,10; 82:L22; 105:L2, 7; 106:L2, 8,22; 158:L5; 162:L11; 201:L17; 242:L5; *JB* 36:L29; 73:L6; 84:L23, 25; 123:L24; 146:L32; 147:L11; 155:L30, 32; 156:L3; 157:L3; *PS—The First Amendment* 11:L9; *PS—Obscenity,* containing the short story *"The Big Space Fuck"* 227:L20, 22; 228:L31; 233:L2; *PS—Jekyll And Hyde Updated* 285:L20; 288:L1; *DD* 14:L21, 23-26; 111:L23, 28; 149:L27; 157:L18-19, 21; 201:L4; *Gal* 33:L18, 20, 24, 29, 31; 34:L4; 40:L5; 91:L7; 104:L23; 106:L14, 16,20, 24-25; 107:L11; 109:L11-12,18, 21, 27; 110:L2,11,29; 111:L2; 131:L14; 132:L3,15; 133:L9,15,18; 134:L6,8,21; 213:L16,21; 222:L24; 223:2; 224:L14,27; 250:L26; 262:L9; *Blue* 7:L3; 272:L29; *HP* 59:L2; 189:L22; *FWD* 142:L3; 144:L33; 171:L21; 196:L23.

birth (see also **ethical birth control**). *Vonnegut's birth imagery provides a constant source of speculation about matters social, psychological, and literary. Perhaps his most memorable and imaginative application occurs in the science fiction short story "Welcome to the Monkey House," in which J. Edgar Nation, a Grand Rapids pharmacist, invents the ethical birth control pill* *as a partial response to overpopulation. The pills made people numb from the waist down and was a legal requirement of all sexually mature individuals. In order to control population growth, ethical birth control pills were paired with institutionalized Ethical Suicide Parlors.* (*MH* 28:L3 *Welcome to the Monkey House*) One pronging was the encouragement of ethical suicide, which consisted of going to the nearest Suicide Parlor and asking a Hostess to kill you painlessly while you lay on a Barcalounger. The other pronging was compulsory ethical **birth** control.

In Breakfast of Champions, *the book in which Vonnegut squares off with images of his father and his own psyche, Dwayne Hoover's mother dies during his birth. In* Deadeye Dick, *the book which makes a criminal act of Rudy Waltz's errant shot from the family home's cupola window (an act Vonnegut himself committed as a youngster but without such grave consequences), birth is termed a peephole interrupting an eternity. While at the Midland City Police Department after the shooting of Eloise Metzger, Rudy* was taken to a much smaller cellblock on the top floor, the third floor, which was reserved for women and for children under the age of sixteen. There was only one other prisoner up there, a black woman from out of town, who had been taken off a Greyhound bus after beating up the white driver. She was from the Deep South, and she was the one who introduced me to the idea of **birth's** being an opening peephole, and of death's being when that peephole closes again (*DD* 73:L17).

A more conventional but no less meaningful image occurs when the aspiring artist Rabo Karabekian travels cross country by train to become an apprentice to world-famous illustrator Dan Gregory. (*Blue* 67:L31) Yes, and when the Twentieth Century Limited from Chicago plunged into a tunnel under New York City, with its lining of pipes and wires, I was out of the womb and into the **birth** canal.

Vonnegut's concern for and exploration of an individual's psychological development is at the core of Mother Night. *The following material highlights his interest in the inextricable nature of good and evil, the inextricable nature of our futures bound to our past, and the need to start life with positive models.* (*MN* x:L22) The title of the book is Campbell's. It is taken from a speech by Mephistopheles in Goethe's *Faust*. As translated by Carlyle F. MacIntyre (New Directions, 1941), the speech is this:

> I am a part of the part that at first was all, part of the darkness that gave **birth** to light, that supercilious light which now disputes with Mother Night her ancient rank and space, and yet can not succeed; no matter how it struggles, it sticks to matter and can't get free.

(*MN* 1:2) I *(Howard Campbell)* am an American by **birth**, a Nazi by reputation, and a nationless person by inclination.

(*MN* 200:L6) My own feeling is that a child should start experimenting with real people and real communities from the moment of **birth**, if possible. If, for some reason, these materials are not available, then playthings must be used.

Vonnegut frequently writes about writing and art as giving birth to the imagination. (*WFG* xxvi:L31 *Preface*) If a person with a demonstrably ordinary mind, like mine, will devote himself to giving **birth** to a work of the imagination, that work will in turn tempt and tease the ordinary mind into cleverness.
(*PS* 134:L26 *The People One Knows*) To accept a new myth about ourselves is to simplify our memories—and to place our stamp of approval on what might become an epitaph for our era in the shorthand of history. This, in my opinion, is why critics often condemn our most significant books and poems and plays when they first appear, while praising feebler creations. The **birth** of a new myth fills them with primitive dread, for myths are so effective.
(*Blue* 84:L12, 19) Let me *(Rabo Karabekian)* put it yet another way: life, by definition, is never still. Where is it going? From **birth** to death, with no stops on the way. Even a picture of a bowl of pears on a checkered tablecloth is liquid, if laid on canvas by the brush of a master. Yes, and by some miracle I was surely never able to achieve as a painter, nor was Dan Gregory, but which was achieved by the best of the Abstract Expressionists, in the paintings which have greatness **birth** and death are always there. *See also: PP* 37:L34; 160:L32; *CC* 29:L5; 157:L1; *GBR* 22:L29; 26:L20; 64:L26; 120:L10; *SL5* 20:L7; 99:L14; 102:L15; 147:L14; 159:L16; *MH—Welcome to the Monkey House* 28:L16-17; 31:L3; 32:L15,26; 35:L2; *WJ* 66:L12; *BC* 46:L4; 162:L11; 218:L32; *WFG—Good Missiles, Good Manners, Good Night* 104:L18; *WFG—Address to Graduating Class at Bennington College, 1971* 160:L6; *Slap* 3:L31; 5:L14; 28:L10-11; 50:L11; 68:L2; *JB* 24:L19; 65:L1; *PS—Roots* 55:L29; *PS—The People One Knows* 120:L5; *PS—Religion* 210:L20; 211:L13; *PS—A Nazi Sympathizer Defended At Some Cost* 298:L31; *PS—The Sexual Revolution* 316:L17; *PS—In The Capital Of The World* 323:L10; *DD* 21:L23; 104:L4; *Gal* 58:L5; 61:L9; 63:L6,17; 72:L11; 95:L22; 99:L29; 124:L7; 146:L20; 147:L20; 183:L1; 207:L1; 229:L4; 230:L24; *Blue* 16:L23; 84:L20; 201:L2; 224:L31; 293:L5; *HP* 16:L29; 32:L5; 98:L3; 240:L34; 241:L2; 286:L28,31-32; 292:L26,30; 301:L26; *FWD* 26:L16; 44:L33; 63:L3; 85:L5; 88:L20; 92:L3; 96:L16; 101:L18; 107:L35; 120:L6; 125:L30; 187:L4; 199:L30.

Black Brothers of Islam. *The leading prison gang at the Athena prison in* Hocus Pocus. *Headed by Abdullah Akhbahr, the gang's literacy program is based on the anti-Semitic* Protocols of the Elders of Zion, *hundreds of copies of which are supplied by their Libyan supporters.*

Black Cat Café. *Considered a whorehouse by the Tarkington College crowd, the Black Cat Café is a well-respected, tightly protected community business. Owned and operated by Lyle Hooper,* "he would never admit that the availability of prostitutes in his parking lot accounted in large measure for the business he did in liquor and snacks, and for the condom machine in the men's room" (*HP* 202:L10-13). *Eugene Debs Hartke tries to pass on to Tarkington* *freshmen the importance and position of the bar in local circles,* "I had told them, too, that they were never to go into the **Black Cat Café**, which the townspeople considered their private club. It was one place they could go and not be reminded of how dependent they were on the rich kids on the hill, but I didn't say that. Neither did I say that free-lance prostitutes were sometimes found there, and in the past had been the cause of outbreaks of venereal disease on campus" (*HP* 113:L7).

Black Garterbelt (see also ***Plague on Wheels***). *The pornographic magazine which published Kilgore Trout short stories as filler for their photographs. Before traveling to the Midland City Arts Festival in* Breakfast of Champions, *Trout rummages through the old book and magazine bin of a Times Square book store and purchases the April 1962 edition containing his short story "Plague on Wheels." He wasn't aware it had been published.*

In Hocus Pocus, *Jack Patton had given a copy of the porn magazine to Eugene Debs Hartke as a gift while the two served in Vietnam. Hartke stored it, unopened, in his footlocker. Sixteen years after fleeing Vietnam on the last helicopter to leave the American Embassy in Saigon, Hartke and his army footlocker were reunited by United Parcel Service. When he opened it, he finally had a chance to read the short story "The Protocols of the Elders of Tralfamadore." Though no mention of the author is made, its science fiction motif and references to Tralfamadore are similar to other Kilgore Trout stories. See also: BC* 56:L10; 58:L6; *HP* 135:L15-16; 153:L30; 154:L22,32; 155:L3; 187:L8,32; 188:L13; 194:L6; 234:L14; 235:L25; 253:L20.

black humor (see **humor**).

Blackbeard. *Philip Castle's book* San Lorenzo: The Land, the History, the People *reveals that Bokonon's grandfather discovered* one quarter of a million dollars in buried pirate treasure, presumably a treasure of **Blackbeard**, of Edward Teach.

Blackbeard's treasure was reinvested by Bokonon's family in asphalt, copra, cacao, livestock, and poultry (*CC* 90:L35-36, 91:L1-4).

Blake, William (1757-1827). *Howard Campbell recalls the epigraph to his* Memoirs of a Monogamous Casanova *is from Blake.* (*MN* 97:L10) It is a poem by **William Blake** called "The Question Answered": What is it men in women do require? / The lineaments of Gratified Desire. / What is it women do in men require? / The lineaments of Gratified Desire.

On the stairway of the volunteer fire department in Rosewater, Eliot and his father exchange Blake's poetry on the walls. (*GBR* 64:L20, 65:L3) Eliot had painted out the messages *(from the dentist who previously occupied the space)*. He had written a new one, a poem by **William Blake**. This was it, as broken up so as to fit twelve risers: The Angel / that presided / o'er my / birth said, / "little creature, / form'd of / Joy & Mirth, / Go love / Without the / help of / any Thing / on Earth."

At the foot of the stairs, written in pencil on the wall, by the Senator himself, was the Senator's rebuttal, another poem by **Blake**: Love seeketh only Self to please, / To bind another to Its delight, / Joys in another's loss of ease, / And builds a Hell in Heaven's despite.

(*SL5* 90:L12) One thing Trout said that Rosewater liked very much was that there really *were* vampires and werewolves and goblins and angels and so on, but that they were in the fourth dimension. So was **William Blake**, Rosewater's favorite poet, according to Trout. So were heaven and hell.

(*PS* 95:L15 *Self-Interview*) VONNEGUT: My education was as a chemist at Cornell and then an anthropologist at the University of Chicago. Christ—I was thirty-five before I went crazy about **Blake**, forty before I read *Madame Bovary*, forty-five before I'd even heard of Céline. Through dumb luck, I read *Look Homeward, Angel* exactly when I was supposed to.

Blank, Katarina. *She was a café waitress when she married Clemens Vonnegut in 1852. Together they had Bernard Vonnegut, Kurt's grandfather.* (*PS* 25:L24-29 *Roots*) She was one of seven children of a German immigrant family of peasants who came from Urloffen in Baden and settled on a farm in Wayne Township, Marion County, just west of Indianapolis. They were struggling to get their farm to be productive after felling the forest trees and draining the land.

Blankenship, Dr. Martin Peale. *In* Hocus Pocus, *the Rhodes Scholar and University of Chicago economist was scheduled to be the graduation speaker at Tarkington College. His niece in the graduating class was Hortense Mellon. Blankenship is also close friends with talk show host and conservative newspaper columnist Jason Wilder.*

BLINC System. *The Blast Interval Normalization Computer, which was derived from the Robo-Magic washing machine and became the essential component in the bomb sight release mechanism produced during World War II.* (*BC* 247:3-4) The Robo-Magic dream was interrupted by World War Two... All that survived of the Robo-Magic itself was its brain, which had told the rest of the machine when to let the water in, when to let the water out, when to slosh, when to rinse, when to spin dry, and so on.

That brain became the nerve center of the so-called "**BLINC System**" during the Second World War. It was installed on heavy bombers, and it did the actual dropping of bombs after a bombardier pressed his bright red "bombs away" button. The button activated the **BLINC System**, which then released the bombs in such a way as to achieve a desired pattern of explosions on the planet below. "**BLINC**" was an abbreviation of "**Blast Interval Normalization Computer**."

blivit. *This is Vonnegut's tongue-in-cheek introductory description of the collection composing* Palm Sunday. *He likens the broad range of material covered in that text to his brother's adolescent radio experiments which could be detected across all the radio frequencies in Indianapolis.* (*PS* xvi:L25, 29, 32, xvii:L1) THIS is certainly that kind of masterpiece, and a new name should be created for such an all-frequencies assault on the sensibilities. I propose the name ***blivit***. This is a word which during my adolescence was defined by peers as "two pounds of shit in a one-pound bag."

I would not mind if books simpler than this one, but combining fiction and fact, were also called **blivits**. This would encourage *The New York Times Book Review* to establish a third category for best sellers, one long needed, in my opinion. If there were a separate list for **blivits**, then authors of **blivits** could stop stepping in the faces of mere novelists and historians and so on.

. . .

THIS book is not only a **blivit** but a collage. It began with my wish to collect in one volume most of the reviews and speeches and essays I had written since the publication of a similar collection, *Wampeters, Foma & Granfalloons*, in 1974. But as I arranged those fragments in this order and then that one, I saw that they formed a sort of autobiography, especially if I felt free to include some pieces not written by me. To give life to such a golem, however, I would have to write much new connective tissue. This I have done.

Blue Fairy Godmother (see also **Frank Wirtanen**). *Howard W. Campbell calls Harold J. Sparrow, alias Colonel Frank Wirtanen, his Blue Fairy Godmother because no one believes he was an American agent recruited and maintained by Colonel Wirtanen. The U.S. government neither confirms nor denies Wirtanen's existence.*

In Slaughterhouse-Five *there is another Blue Fairy Godmother. The red-headed British POW who beats up Paul Lazzaro had also played the part of Cinderella's Blue Fairy Godmother in a production by the British prisoners. His silver-painted airman's boots are taken by Billy Pilgrim when he, Lazzaro, and Edgar Derby are quartered in the barracks with the stage set.*

blue tubing, blue tunnel (also **tunnel** and **tube** when used to mean the **blue tunnel of the Afterlife**; see also **Afterlife** and **funnel**). *Throughout* Galápagos *narrator Leon Trout informs the reader about what awaits each new person as they pass away.* (*Gal* 219:L21) I (*Leon Trout*) was painlessly decapitated one day by a falling sheet of steel while working inside the hull of the *Bahía de Darwin*, at which time I refused to set foot in the **blue tunnel** leading into the Afterlife.

(*Gal* 65:L16) When the first Santa Rosalia marriage was performed by Kamikaze and Akiko in the year 2027, all of the original colonists had long since vanished into the sinuous **blue tunnel** which leads into the Afterlife.

(*Gal* 251:L30 252:L3) The question the **blue tunnel** implies by appearing is one only I can answer: Have I at last exhausted my curiosity as to what life is all about? If so, I need only step inside what I liken to a vacuum cleaner. If there is indeed suction within the **blue tunnel**, which is filled with a light much like that cast off by the electric stoves and ovens of the *Bahía de Darwin*, it does not seem to trouble my late father, the science fiction writer Kilgore Trout, who can stand right in the nozzle and chat with me. *See also: Gal* 73:L2; 98:L26; 118:L22; 135:L6; 147:L3; 159:L12; 163:L5; 165:L29; 166:L3,6,16; 168:L4; 199:L23-24; 229:L2-3; 251:L17; 255:L14-15; 257:L2,26; 258:L13; 259:L12-13,17.

Bluebeard, *Bluebeard* (see **Rabo Karabekian** for a discussion of the novel). *The namesake for whom Rabo Karabekian titles his memoirs and with whom he draws the following analogy.* (*Blue* 46:L12-33, 47:L1-6) So: **Bluebeard** is a fictitious character in a very old children's tale, possibly based loosely on a murderous nobleman of long ago. In the story, he has married many times. He marries for the umpteenth time, and brings his latest child bride back to his castle. He tells her that she can go into any room but one, whose door he shows her.

Bluebeard is either a poor psychologist or a great one, since all his new wife can think about is what might be behind the door. So she takes a look when she thinks he isn't home, but he really *is* home.

He catches her just at the point she is gazing aghast at the bodies of all his former wives in there, all of whom he has murdered, save for the first one, for looking behind the door. The first one got murdered for something else.

So—of all the people who know about my locked potato barn, the one who finds the mystery most intolerable is surely Circe Berman. She is after me all the time to tell her where the six keys are, and I tell her again that they are buried in a golden casket at the foot of Mount Ararat.

I said to her the last time she asked, which was about five minutes ago: "Look: think about something else, anything else. I am **Bluebeard**, and my studio is my *forbidden chamber* as far as *you're* concerned."

(*FWD* 41:L10) I would eventually write a book about a painter, ***Bluebeard***. I got the idea for it after *Esquire* asked me for a piece about the Abstract Expressionist Jackson Pollock. The magazine was putting together a fiftieth-anniversary issue to consist of essays on fifty native-born Americans who had made the biggest difference in the country's destiny since 1932. I wanted Eleanor Roosevelt but Bill Moyers already had her.

(*FWD* 45:L26) The Franklin Library asked me to provide a special preface to its expensive edition of ***Bluebeard*** (illustrated by my daughter Edith Squibb). So I blathered on some more about painting, which my father and I both did badly.

(*FWD* 107:L17) Our guards had disappeared, and the Russian Army had not yet arrived, and we found ourselves in the valley I describe at the end of my novel ***Bluebeard*** (called *Bluebird* in the meticulously edited *New York Times*).

The scene is recreated by Rabo Karabekian in his 8' x 64' triptych "Now It's the Women's Turn."
(*FWD* 171:L16) (In my novel ***Bluebeard*** I describe a valley full of refugees at the end of WW II. It wasn't imaginary. It was real. O'Hare and I were there.)
(*FWD* 217:L19) In my novel ***Bluebeard*** I described the valley we have just left behind. It is being stripped of everything edible, as though by a locust plague, by liberated prisoners of war like ourselves, by convicts, lunatics, concentration camp victims, and slave laborers, and by armed German soldiers.

Bluebird Farm. *In* Breakfast of Champions, *the location of Sacred Miracle Cave, once owned by the maternal ancestors of ambulance driver Eddie Key and later owned by Dwayne Hoover in partnership with the twins Lyle and Kyle Hoover.*

Boaz. *The twenty-three-year-old Private, First Class, who is one of the eight hundred real commanders of the Army of Mars in* The Sirens of Titan. *Boaz was fourteen when recruited for the Army of Mars. He and Unk (Malachi Constant) are paired together as part of the buddy system. In Boaz's right front trouser pocket was a control box capable of transmitting all sorts of signals to the antennas placed in the skulls of the Martian forces. As one of the real commanders, Boaz did not have his mind erased. He was in charge of one-tenth of the force assigned to attack the United States. He and Unk avoid the massacre which awaited the others in his command who fell in the Battle of Boca Raton. Rumfoord had fixed the automatic pilot of their ship to take them to the caves of Mercury where Boaz fell in love with the gentle Harmoniums. He decides to stay with the Harmoniums rather than leave with Unk because he feels he can do good deeds for them whereas he doesn't know how to behave well with people nor do others know how to treat him well.*

Bob (see **Wild Bob**).

Bob & Ray. *Comedians Bob Goulding and Ray Elliott are among Vonnegut's all-time favorite comedians. The nature of his affinity for them and the similarity of their work with his is revealed in this passage reprinted in* Palm Sunday. (*PS* 140:L7-18, 142:L17-32 *The People One Knows*) AND here is what I said about my friends **Bob Elliott** and **Ray Goulding**, perhaps the most significant and ridiculous American comedy team alive today, as an introduction to their book *Write If You Get Work: The Best of Bob & Ray* (Random House, 1975):

> It is the truth: Comedians and jazz musicians have been more comforting and enlightening to me than preachers or politicians or philosophers or poets or painters or novelists of my time. Historians in the future, in my opinion, will congratulate us on very little other than our clowning and our jazz. . . .

It occurs to me, too, as I look through this marvelous book, that **Bob** and **Ray's** jokes are singularly burglar-proof. They aren't like most other comedians' jokes these days, aren't rooted in show business and the world of celebrities and news of the day. They feature Americans who are almost always fourth-rate or below, engaged in enterprises which, if not contemptible, are at least insane.

And while other comedians show us persons tormented by bad luck and enemies and so on, **Bob** and **Ray's** characters threaten to wreck themselves and their surroundings with their own stupidity. There is a refreshing and beautiful innocence in **Bob's** and **Ray's** humor.

Man is not evil, they seem to say. He is simply too hilariously stupid to survive.

And this I believe.

Cheers.

Bockman, Dr. Fred and **Marion**. *The physicist from Wyandotte College and his wife in the short story "The Euphio Question," reprinted in* Welcome to the Monkey House, *who develops a radio telescope which transmits a pleasantly incapacitating hiss from empty areas of space. Bockman is asked to be a guest on Lew Harrison's radio talk show when he first airs the sounds from space. The sociology professor who got the two men together develops the term "Bockman's Euphoria" to describe the cosmic hiss. He develops the euphoriaphone ("euphio") at the urging of Harrison who sees the opportunity to cash in on one's conscious incapacitation.*

Bodovskov, Stepan. *The Russian corporal was an interpreter among the first troops to enter Berlin in* Mother Night. *He found Howard Campbell's theater trunk full of unpublished poems, plays, and one novel. Bodovskov started publishing the poems and gained fame with the theater production of "The Goblet," a particular favorite of Stalin's. The novel was* Memoirs of a Monogamous Casanova, *Campbell's homage to the love he shared with his wife Helga, and this became a widely distibuted and often-translated underground classic. Despite a magnificent career as a professional plagiarist, Bodovskov is eventually executed for writing an original satire of the Red Army. George Kraft/Iona Potapov turned him in once his friendship with Howard Campbell convinced him Bodovskov was a fraud. Bodovskov's home was searched and the offending original material brought about his execution.*

Bohn, Arthur. (*PS* 41:L22-23 *Roots*) "Returning to Indianapolis in 1883, he engaged in the practice of architecture, first in his own office and later with **Arthur Bohn** in what became the well-known firm of **Vonnegut & Bohn**, whose successors are in practice today. This firm designed and supervised construction of many fine residences and public buildings in Indianapolis, including the first Chamber of Commerce, the Athenaeum, the John Herron Art Museum, the L.S. Ayres store, the Fletcher Trust Building, and many others. (*PS* 46:2 *Roots*) "At the age of nineteen he was well prepared in a solid foundation of secondary education, and was admitted to the Massachusetts Institute of Technology, where he studied architecture and took his degree of Bachelor of Science in 1908—the year in which his father died. He then went with his widowed mother and his sister, Irma, to Berlin, and continued his architectural studies with the best masters. He returned to Indianapolis in 1910, and joined his father's surviving partner, **Arthur Bohn**, in the well-established firm of **Vonnegut & Bohn**. He was thus launched upon what promised to be a comfortable and successful career. His family had a prominent position in the community. They had plenty of money.

Boko-maru, boko-maruing (see also **Bokononism**). (*CC* 132:L13) . . . the Bokononist ritual of *boko-maru*, or the mingling of awarenesses.

We Bokononists believe that it is impossible to be sole-to-sole with another person without loving the person, provided the feet of both persons are clean and nicely tended.

The basis for the foot ceremony is this "Calypso": We will touch our feet, yes, / Yes, for all we're worth, / And we will love each other, yes, / Yes, like we love our Mother Earth.

Dr. Julian Castle is convinced he couldn't operate his House of Hope and Mercy in the jungle without aspirin and boko-maru.

Bokonon. *The black founder and prophet of Bokononism whose real name is Lionel Boyd Johnson, the youngest of six children born and educated in the Episcopalian schools of Tobago. His family's wealth was based on one of Blackbeard's treasures found by his grandfather. In 1911 Johnson set sail alone for London in the sloop* Lady's Slipper, *in search of higher education. By his own admission he was a carouser and womanizer in his youth, prompting his own analogy between his later role as a religious leader with the admissions of Saint Augustine.* (*CC* 91:L11-18) When I was young, / I was so gay and mean, / And I drank and chased the girls / Just like young St. Augustine. / Saint Augustine, / He got to be a saint. / So, if I get to be one, also, / Please, Mama, don't you faint.

In 1922 Johnson and Corporal Earl McCabe set sail in the Lady's Slipper *for Tobago, but were shipwrecked and washed ashore on San Lorenzo. When they saw how impoverished the people were despite the wealth of Castle Sugar and the Catholic Church, they sought political power to reform the country. Castle Sugar withdrew since their dreams of cultivating the hard clay had failed. McCabe overhauled the economy and civil laws, and Bokonon designed a new religion.* (*CC* 109:L3-10) I wanted all things / To seem to make some sense, / So we all could be happy, yes, / Instead of tense. / And I made up lies / So that they all fit nice, / And I made this sad world / A par-a-dise.

The lies, "foma," Bokonon made up were included in his ongoing tract The Books of Bokonon. *Bokonon and McCabe based their plan of development for San Lorenzo on the theory of "Dynamic Tension," which Bokonon learned from ads for Charles Atlas' fitness and muscle building system. Bokonon was, in fact, an alumnus of the Charles Atlas program.* (*CC* 90:L3-8) It was the belief of Charles Atlas that muscles could be built without bar bells or spring exercisers, could be built by simply pitting one set of muscles against another.

It was the belief of **Bokonon** that good societies could be built only by pitting good against evil, and by keeping the tension between the two high at all times.

Bokononism, Bokononist. *The outlawed religion conceived by Lionel Boyd Johnson and Earl McCabe and practiced exclusively on the island of San Lorenzo. Practitioners of the religion run the risk of death on the hook. The truth is that everyone on San Lorenzo is a Bokononist. The religion was developed by Johnson (Bokonon) and McCabe as part of their theory of dynamic tension.* (*CC* 14:L1-6) **Bokononists** believe that humanity is organized into teams, teams that do God's Will without ever discovering what they are doing. Such a team is called a *karass* by Bokonon, and the instrument, the *kan-kan*, that brought me into my own particular karass was the book I never finished, the book to be called *The Day the World Ended*.
(*CC* 16:L7-12) The first sentence in *The Books of Bokonon* is this:

"All of the true things I am about to tell you are shameless lies."

My **Bokononist** warning is this:

Anyone unable to understand how a useful religion can be founded on lies will not understand this book either.
(*CC* 50:L35-37, 51:L1-12) Which brings me to the **Bokononist** concept of a *wampeter*.

A *wampeter* is the pivot of a *karass*. No *karass* is without a *wampeter*, Bokonon tells us, just as no wheel is without a hub.

Anything can be a *wampeter*: a tree, a rock, an animal, an idea, a book, a melody, the Holy Grail. Whatever it is, the members of its *karass* revolve about it in the majestic chaos of a spiral nebula. The orbits of the members of a *karass* about their common *wampeter* are spiritual orbits, naturally. It is souls and not bodies that revolve. As Bokonon invites us to sing:

> Around and around and around we spin,
> With feet of lead and wings of tin. . . .

And *wampeters* come and *wampeters* go, Bokonon tells us.

At any given time a *karass* actually has two *wampeters*—one waxing in importance, one waning.
(*CC* 53:L28) As a **Bokononist**, of course, I would have agreed gaily to go anywhere anyone suggested. As Bokonon says: "Peculiar travel suggestions are dancing lessons from God."

(*CC* 61:L23) *Busy, busy, busy,* is what we **Bokononists** whisper whenever we think of how complicated and unpredictable the machinery of life really is.
(*CC* 64:L1-5) It was in the tombstone salesroom that I had my first *vin-dit*, a **Bokononist** word meaning a sudden, very personal shove in the direction of **Bokononism**, in the direction of believing that God Almighty knew all about me, after all, that God Almighty had some pretty elaborate plans for me.

The following excerpt is a reference to Bokononism as part of the grand theory of dynamic tensions: (*CC* 90:L9-16) And, in Castle's book, I read my first **Bokononist** poem, or "Calypso." It went like this: "Papa" Monzano, he's so very bad, / But without bad "Papa" I would be so sad; / Because without "Papa's" badness, / Tell me, if you would, / How could wicked old Bokonon / Ever, ever look good?
(*CC* 132:L12-16) What I had seen, of course, was the **Bokononist** ritual of *boko-maru*, or the mingling of awarenesses.

We **Bokononists** believe that it is impossible to be sole-to-sole with another person without loving the person, provided the feet of both persons are clean and nicely tended.
(*CC* 156:L33-36, 157:L1-10) I learned some things, but they were scarcely helpful. I learned of the **Bokononist** cosmogony, for instance, wherein *Borasisi*, the sun, held *Pabu*, the moon, in his arms, and hoped that *Pabu* would bear him a fiery child.

But poor *Pabu* gave birth to children that were cold, that did not burn; and *Borasisi* threw them away in disgust. These were the planets, who circled their terrible father at a safe distance.

Then poor *Pabu* herself was cast away, and she went to live with her favorite child, which was Earth. Earth was *Pabu*'s favorite because it had people on it; and the people looked up at her and loved her and sympathized.

And what opinion did Bokonon hold of his own cosmogony? "*Foma!* Lies!" he wrote. "A pack of *foma!*"
(*CC* 163:L3-7) "Do you know anybody who *might* want the job?" Frank was giving a classic illustration of what Bokonon calls *duffle*. *Duffle*, in the **Bokononist** sense, is the destiny of thousands upon thousands of persons when placed in the hands of a *stuppa*. A *stuppa* is a fogbound child.
(*CC* 165:L9-15) All things conspired to form one cosmic *vin-dit*, one mighty shove into **Bokononism**, into the belief that God was running my life and that He had work for me to do.

And, inwardly, I *sarooned*, which is to say that I acquiesced to the seeming demands of my *vin-dit*.

Inwardly, I agreed to become the next President of San Lorenzo.
(*CC* 173:L12-17) "What *is* sacred to **Bokononists**?" I asked after a while.

"Not even God, as near as I can tell."

"Nothing?"

"Just one thing."

I made some guesses. "The ocean? The sun?"

"Man," said Frank. "That's all. Just man."

(*CC* 179:L33-34) "I *(Dr. von Koenigswald)* agree with one **Bokononist** idea. I agree that all religions, including **Bokononism**, are nothing but lies."
(*CC* 193:L30-34) "Pain, ice, Mona-everything. And then 'Papa' said, 'Now I will destroy the whole world.'"

"What did he mean by that?"

"It's what **Bokononists** always say when they are about to commit suicide."
(*CC* 228:L35-36, 229:L1-6) When I hadn't been writing, I'd been poring over *The Books of Bokonon*, but the reference to midgets had escaped me. I was grateful to Newt for calling it to my attention, for the quotation captured in a couplet the cruel paradox of **Bokononist** thought, the heartbreaking necessity of lying about reality, and the heartbreaking impossibility of lying about it.

Midget, midget, midget, how he struts and winks,
For he knows a man's as big as what he hopes and thinks!

Bolivar. *San Lorenzo's capital, and only, city. Despite the flattering advertising of Bolivar as a modern city, Bolivar is a third world mess complete with a useless state-of-the-art hotel amidst the squalor of tin can and wooden crate abodes.* (*CC* 113:L4) **Bolivar** had had many names: Caz-ma-cas-ma, Santa Maria, Saint Louis, Saint George, and Port Glory among them. It was given its present name by Johnson and McCabe in 1922, was named in honor of Simón Bolívar, the great Latin-American idealist and hero.

When Johnson and McCabe came upon the city, it was built of twigs, tin, crates, and mud-rested on the catacombs of a trillion happy scavengers, catacombs in a sour mash of slop, feculence, and slime.

That was pretty much the way I *(John/Jonah)* found it, too, except for the new architectural false face along the water front.

bomb, bomb proof, bomb shelter, bombed, bombed-out, bombing, bombproof, bombshells, timebomb. (These **bomb** references are for non-nuclear devices only. See **A-bomb** for all other references to nuclear bombs.) *Vonnegut's introduction to* Mother Night *includes his most direct account of what it was like in the slaughterhouse meatlocker during the firebombing of Dresden.* (*MN* vi:L19, 23, 30) But high explosives were dropped on Dresden by American and British planes on the night of February 13, 1945, just about twenty-one years ago, as I now write. There were no particular targets for the **bombs**. The hope was that they would create a lot of kindling and drive firemen underground.

And then hundreds of thousands of tiny incendiaries were scattered over the kindling, like seeds on freshly turned loam. More **bombs** were dropped to keep firemen in their holes, and all the little fires grew, joined one another, became one apocalyptic flame. Hey presto: fire storm. It was the largest massacre in European history, by the way. And so what?

We didn't get to see the fire storm. We were in a cool meat-locker under a slaughterhouse with our six guards and ranks and ranks of dressed cadavers of cattle, pigs, horses, and sheep. We heard the **bombs** walking around up there. Now and then there would be a gentle shower of calcimine. If we had gone above to take a look, we would have been turned into artifacts characteristic of fire storms: seeming pieces of charred firewood two or three feet long—ridiculously small human beings, or jumbo fried grasshoppers, if you will.

The reality of this episode is offset by Billy Pilgrim's Tralfamadorian vision of the war in reverse while watching a war movie on late night television. (*SL5* 64:L7) The formation flew backwards over a German city that was in flames. The bombers opened their **bomb** bay doors, exerted a miraculous magnetism which shrunk the fires, gathered them into cylindrical steel containers, and lifted the containers into the bellies of the planes. The containers were stored neatly in racks. The Germans below had miraculous devices of their own, which were long steel tubes. They used them to suck more fragments from the crewmen and planes. But there were still a few wounded Americans, though, and some of the bombers were in bad repair. Over France, though, German fighters came up again, made everything and everybody as good as new.

Vonnegut creates the contrast between Dresden's conventionally engineered destruction (which relied on ordinary materials) and Hiroshima's immolation (which reflected a leap in materials acquisition and application). (*PS* 69:L13 *When I Lost My Innocence*) But I learned how vile that religion of mine could be when the atomic bomb was dropped on Hiroshima.... Only six months before, as a captured American foot soldier, I had been in Dresden when it was burned to the ground by a purposely set firestorm. I was still innocent after that. Why? Because the technology which created that firestorm was so familiar to me... There was nothing in the **bombs** or the airplanes, after all, which could not, essentially, be bought at a small hardware store.

Vonnegut has the decorated Vietnam veteran Eugene Debs Hartke comment on the insanity of such vengeful warfare. (*HP* 54:L9-10) When I married Margaret, their mother seemed perfectly OK still, except for a mania for dancing, which was a little scary sometimes, but harmless. Dancing until she dropped wasn't nearly as loony as wanting to **bomb** North Vietnam back to the Stone Age, or **bombing** anyplace back to the Stone Age. *And in this exchange between Hartke and Hiroshima bombing victim Hiroshi Matsumoto, Hartke fills the silence between them with more commentary.* (*HP* 298:L30-32) "I was in Hiroshima when it was **bombed**," he said.

I am sure there was an implied equation there: The **bombing** of Hiroshima was as unforgivable and as typically human as the Rape of Nanking. *Hartke also calls special attention to the unique difference between the effectiveness of the infantry as opposed to the firepower of an air attack.* (*HP* 52:L32-33, 35) What a footsoldier can do to a body with his pipsqueak technology is nothing, of course, when compared with the ordinary, unavoidable, perfectly routine effects of aerial **bombing** and artillery. One time I saw the severed head of a bearded old man resting on the guts of an eviscerated water buffalo, covered with flies in a **bomb** crater by a paddy in Cambodia. The plane whose **bomb** made the crater was so high when it dropped it that it couldn't even be seen from the ground. But what its **bomb** did, I would have to say, sure beat the ace of spades for a calling card.

Vonnegut recalls an incident which occurred while speaking at the National Air and Space Museum on the topic "The Legacy of Strategic Bombing." (*FWD* 156:L26) During the question-and-answer period following my speech. . . . I was asked what being **bombed** strategically had done to my personality. I replied that the war had been a great adventure for me, which I wouldn't have missed for anything, and that the principal shapers of my personality were probably neighborhood dogs when I was growing up. *Within* Fates Worse Than Death *Vonnegut goes on to relate the sentiments of his long-time friend and fellow Dresden survivor Bernard V. O'Hare.* (*FWD* 108:L23) I said to him, "What did you learn?" The future DA O'Hare replied, "I will never again believe my Government." This had to do with our Government's tall tales of delicate surgery performed by bombers equipped with Sperry and Norden bombsights. These instruments were so precise, we had been told, that a bombardier could drop his billets-doux down the chimney of a factory if ordered to. There were solemn charades performed for newsreels in which military policemen with drawn .45 automatics escorted bombardiers carrying bombsights to their planes. That was how desperate the Germans and the Japanese were (so went the message) to learn and make use of the secret of our **bombings**' diabolical accuracy themselves.

The notion of a bomb is not completely negative for Vonnegut, as this book review indicates. (*MH* 106:L15-16 *New Dictionary*) And now I have this enormous and beautiful new **bomb** from Random House. I don't mean "**bomb**" in a pejorative sense, or in any dictionary sense, for that matter. I mean that the book is heavy and pregnant, and makes you think. *See also: PP* 66:L15; 101:L32; 162:L39; 172:L4; 193:L33; 259:L12; 286:L36; *ST* 51:L16; *MN* 87:L2; 88:L7; 131:L6; 144:L11-12; 181:L12; 182:L15,22; 183:L5,26; *CC* 70:L30; 187:L4; 209:L10; 213:L1; *GBR* 130:L29; 192:L19; 200:L21; *SL5* 12:L19; 15:L25,31; 52:L2,5,7; 98:L31; 115:L30; 127:L9; 128:L14; 129:L8; 135:L20; 136:L31; 152:L22; 159:L2; 162:L3; 164:L33; 167:L4; 183:L19; *MH—Welcome to the Monkey House* 30:L9; *MH—All The King's Horses* 85:L32; *MH—The Manned Missiles* 264:L30; *BC* 8:L10; 43:L6; 103:L2; 224:L10; 246:L21-23; *WFG—Brief Encounters on the Inland Waterway* 11:L19; *WFG—Yes, We Have No Nirvanas* 41:L12; *WFG—Excelsior! We're Going to the Moon! Excelsior!* 78:L2; 88:L9,10; *WFG—Torture and Blubber* 170:L1; *WFG—In a Manner That Must Shame God Himself* 186:L25; 188:L21; *WFG—Thinking Unthinkable, Speaking Unspeakable* 208:L6,12; *WFG—Address to P.E.N. Conference in Stockholm, 1973* 226:L30; *WFG—Playboy Interview* 262:L1,22; 262:L32; 264:L13,16; *JB* 25:L29; 99:L5; *PS—When I Lost My Innocence* 64:L29; 69:L28; *PS—Self-Interview* 89:L16; 91:L13,27,32; 92:L1; 93:L29,30; *PS—Jonathan Swift Misperceived* 258:L9; *PS—Jekyll and Hyde Updated* 281:L20,23,26; 282:L10,22,24; *DD*

152:L28; 167:L16; 191:L11; *Gal* 146:L20-21; 179:L4-6; *Blue* 240:L5; *HP* 40:L31; 62:L21; 129:L31; 227:L21; 242:L22; 244:L36; 245:L3; 253:L34; 254:L31; 255:L9,32-33; 257:L9-10; 286:L11; *FWD* 88:L31; 98:L22; 99:L1,4,17; 102:L1; 104:L18-29; 105:L31; 109:L1,5; 151:L17; 154:L10; 217:L11; 222:L20.

bombardier. (*BC* 246:L21) That brain became the nerve center of the so-called "BLINC System" during the Second World War. It was installed on heavy bombers, and it did the actual dropping of bombs after a **bombardier** pressed his bright red "bombs away" button.
(*PS* 64:L28 *When I Lost My Innocence*) "When I was a freshman here, I didn't know or care where the life of Ginger Rogers ended and the life of General Douglas MacArthur began. The senior senator from California was Mickey Mouse, who would serve with great distinction as a **bombardier** in the Pacific during the Second World War. Commander Mouse dropped a bomb right down the smokestack of a Japanese battleship. The captain of the battleship was Charlie Chan. Boy, was he mad.
(*PS* 91:L22 *Self-Interview*) VONNEGUT: There was all this hokum about the Norden bombsight. You'd see a newsreel showing a **bombardier** with an MP on either side of him holding a drawn 45. That sort of nonsense, and hell, all they were doing was just flying over cities, hundreds of airplanes, and dropping everything.
(*Blue* 284:L14, 28) "He *(a figure within Rabo Karabekian's "Now It's the Women's Turn")* is a Canadian **bombardier** who was shot down over an oil field in Hungary. He doesn't know who I am. He can't even see my face. All he can see is a thick fog which isn't there, and he's asking me if we are home yet. . . .

"That is a concentration-camp guard who threw away his SS uniform and stole the suit from a scarecrow," I said. I pointed out a group of concentration camp victims far away from the masquerading guard. Several of them were on the ground and dying, like the Canadian **bombardier**. . . .
(*Blue* 293:L12) "The **bombardier** clinging to my leg: that's his face, as I remember it. These two Estonians in German uniforms are Laurel and Hardy. This French collaborator here is Charlie Chaplin. These two Polish slave laborers on the other side of the tower from me are Jackson Pollock and Terry Kitchen." *Rabo responds to Circe's question about his 64' painting, "How many of these are portraits of actual people?"*
(*HP* 226:L31) But at least they *(the convicts)* saw what they were doing, whereas people like the Trustees had a lot in common with B-52 **bombardiers** way up in the stratosphere. They seldom saw the devastation they caused as they moved the huge portion of this country's wealth they controlled from here to there.

bombardment. (*SL5* 162:L11) *That the bombing of Dresden was a great tragedy none can deny. . . . Those who approved it were neither wicked nor*

cruel, though it may well be that they were too remote from the harsh realities of war to understand fully the appalling destructive power of air ***bombardment*** *in the spring of 1945* (as quoted from *The Destruction of Dresden*).
(*WFG* 146:L31 *Biafra: A People Betrayed*) General Ojukwu described a typical Nigerian attack for us: "They pound a position with artillery for twenty-four hours, then they send forward one armored car. If anybody shoots at it, it retreats, and another twenty-four hours of **bombardment** begins. When the infantry move forward, they drive a screen of refugees before them."

bombenfest. (*SL5* 16:L9) *The devastation of Dresden was boundless. When Goethe as a young student visited the city, he still found sad ruins: "Von der Kuppel der Frauenkirche sah ich diese leidigen Trummer zwischen die schone stadtische Ordnung hineingesat; da ruhmte mir der Kuster die Kunst des Baumeisters, welcher Kirche und Kuppel auf einen so unerwunschten Fall schon eingerichtet und* ***bombenfest*** *erbaut hatte. Der gute Sakristan deutete mir alsdann auf Ruinene nach allen Seiten und sagte bedenklich lakonisch: Das hat der Feind gethan!"* (as quoted from Mary Endell's *Dresden, History, Stage, and Gallery*)

bomber, **fighter bomber**, **fighter-bomber** (see also **fighter plane**). (*ST* 170:L31) . . . the only Martians left free and standing on the face of the Earth were the Parachute Ski Marines. . . . They were told by loudspeaker that their situation was hopeless, that **bombers** were overhead.
(*SL5* 63:L29; 64:L1, 4, 7, 15, 20) He *(Billy Pilgrim)* came slightly unstuck in time, saw the late movie backwards, then forwards again. It was a movie about American **bombers** in the Second World War and the gallant men who flew them. . . .

Over France, a few German fighter planes flew at them backwards, sucked bullets and shell fragments from some of the planes and crewmen. They did the same for wrecked American **bombers** on the ground, and those planes flew up backwards to join the formation.

The formation flew backwards over a German city that was in flames. The **bombers** opened their bomb bay doors, exerted a miraculous magnetism which shrunk the fires, gathered them into cylindrical steel containers, and lifted the containers into the bellies of the planes... But there were still a few wounded Americans, though, and some of the **bombers** were in bad repair. Over France, though, German fighters came up again, made everything and everybody as good as new.

When the **bombers** got back to their base, the steel cylinders were taken from the racks and shipped back to the United States of America, where factories were operating night and day, dismantling the cylinders, separating the dangerous contents into minerals.
(*SL5* 136:L8) The city was blacked out because **bombers** might come, so Billy didn't get to see Dresden do one of the most cheerful things a city is capable of doing when the sun goes down, which is to wink its lights on one by one.

(*SL5* 158:L8) When she *(Valencia)* arrived at the hospital, people rushed to the windows to see what all the noise was. The Cadillac, with both mufflers gone, sounded like a heavy **bomber** coming in on a wing and a prayer.

(*SL5* 161:L29) *I deeply regret that British and U.S.* ***bombers*** *killed 135,000 people in the attack on Dresden, but I remember who started the last war and I regret even more the loss of more than 5,000,000 Allied lives in the necessary effort to completely defeat and utterly destroy nazism.* (This italicized excerpt is from the foreword to *The Destruction of Dresden*.)

(*SL5* 162:L18) *The advocates of nuclear disarmament seem to believe that, if they could achieve their aim, war would become tolerable and decent... On the night of March 9th, 1945, an air attack on Tokyo by American heavy* ***bombers,*** *using incendiary and high explosive bombs, caused the death of 83,793 people. The atom bomb dropped on Hiroshima killed 71,379 people.* (This excerpt is from Air Marshal Saundby as quoted in *The Destruction of Dresden*.)

(*MH* 71:L16 *Miss Temptation*) "He's out west, ma—with the Strategic Air Command," said Fuller. The little dining room became as lonely as a **bomber** in the thin, cold stratosphere.

(*MH* 164:L17, 23 *Report On The Barnhouse Effect*) "One hundred and twenty of them! At the same time, ten V-2s are being readied for firing in New Mexico, and fifty radio-controlled jet **bombers** are being equipped for a mock attack on the Aleutians. Just think of it!" Happily he reviewed his orders. "At exactly 1100 hours next Wednesday, I will give you the order to *concentrate*; and you, professor, will think as hard as you can about sinking the target ships, destroying the V-2s before they hit the ground, and knocking down the **bombers** before they reach the Aleutians! Think you can handle it?"

(*MH* 166:L1, 5 *Report On The Barnhouse Effect*) *The television screens showed, from left to right, the stretch of desert which was the rocket target, the guinea-pig fleet, and a section of the* Aleutian sky through which the radio-controlled **bomber** formation would roar.

Ninety minutes before H-hour the radios announced that the rockets were ready, that the observation ships had backed away to what was thought to be a safe distance, and that the **bombers** were on their way.

(*MH* 166:L18, 35 *Report On The Barnhouse Effect*) "**Bombers** sighted!" cried the Aleutian observers.

. . . The Aleutian sky was streaked with the smoke trails of **bombers** screaming down in flames.

(*BC* 246:L20) That brain became the nerve center of the so-called "BLINC System" during the Second World War. It was installed on heavy **bombers**, and it did the actual dropping of bombs after a bombardier pressed his bright red "bombs away" button.

(*WFG* 105:L3 *Good, Missiles, Good Manners, Good Night*) My newest book was about utterly pitiful things that happened to unarmed human beings on the ground when our **bombers** went about their technical duties in the sky.

(*WFG* 142:L28 *Biafra: A People Betrayed*) The Russians were helpful in a lot of ways: They gave the Nigerians Ilyushin **bombers** and MIGs and heavy artillery.
(*PS* 89:L1 *Self-Interview*) British mosquito **bombers** attacked us at night a few times.
(*PS* 91:L12 *Self-Interview*) VONNEGUT: It was a fancy thing to see, a startling thing. It was a moment of truth, too, because American civilians and ground troops didn't know American **bombers** were engaged in saturation bombing.
(*PS* 129:L17 *The People One Knows*) The company that made a movie out of Joseph Heller's first novel, *Catch-22*, had to assemble what became the 11th or 12th largest **bomber** force on the planet at the time.
(*Gal* 122:L9) "If Mrs. Onassis were to go there now," said Donoso, "people would receive her as though she were a rescuer, a worker of miracles. She would be expected to summon ships laden with food to Guayaquil—and to have United States **bombers** drop cereal and milk and fresh fruit for the children by parachute!"
(*Gal* 145:L19) One thing which made the Air Force such a high morale unit was that its equipment, bought on credit and delivered before the bankruptcy, was so up to date. It had eight new French **fighter-bombers** and each of these planes, moreover, was equipped with an American air-to-ground missile with a Japanese brain which could home in on radar signals, or on heat from an engine, depending on instructions from the pilot.
(*Gal* 180:L15) Two of Peru's **fighter bombers** were then over Ecuadorian territories, one with its rocket tuned to the radar signals coming from Guayaquil International Airport, and the other with its rocket tuned to radar signals coming from the naval base on the Galápagos Island of Baltra, lair of a sail training ship, six Coast Guard ships, two oceangoing tugs, a patrol submarine, a dry dock, and, high and dry in the dry dock, a destroyer.
(*Gal* 187:L3) There was this Peruvian pilot a million years ago, a young lieutenant colonel who had his **fighter-bomber** skipping from wisp to wisp of finely divided matter at the very edge of the planet's atmosphere. His name was Guillermo Reyes. . . .
(*Gal* 196:L17-18) If he had let them run long enough to get really hot, that temperature anomaly might have attracted the electronic attention of a Peruvian **fighter-bomber** in the stratosphere.
(*HP* 32:L13-14) When I was 2 years old, we moved to Midland City, Ohio, where a washing-machine company named Robo-Magic Corporation was beginning to make bomb-release mechanisms and swivel mounts for machine guns on B-17 **bombers**.
(*HP* 62:L20) He *(Ernest Hubble Hiscock)* was a Tarkington graduate who at the age of 21 was a nose-gunner on a Navy **bomber** whose pilot crashed his plane with a full load of bombs onto the flight deck of a Japanese aircraft carrier in the Battle of Midway during World War II.

The Bombing of Germany. *In* God Bless You, Mr. Rosewater *Hans Rumpf's text is kept in secret by Eliot Rosewater while living in Indiana. Eliot so often read the description of the Dresden fire-storms that after reading Kilgore Trout's* Pan-galactic Three Day Pass *on his journey to meet Sylvia, he went catatonic and silently recalled the passage. When he gazed out the window of the bus, he envisioned Indianapolis consumed by a fire-storm.*

bomb-release. (*HP* 32:L12) When I was 2 years old *(Eugene Debs Hartke)*, we moved to Midland City, Ohio, where a washing-machine company named Robo-Magic Corporation was beginning to make **bomb-release** mechanisms and swivel mounts for machine guns on B-17 bombers.

bombsight. (*PS* 91:L21 *Self-Interview*) VONNEGUT: There was all this hokum about the Norden **bombsight**. You'd see a newsreel showing a bombardier with an MP on either side of him holding a drawn 45. That sort of nonsense, and hell, all they were doing was just flying over cities, hundreds of airplanes, and dropping everything.
(*FWD* 108:L16) The future DA O'Hare replied, "I will never again believe my Government." This had to do with our Government's tall tales of delicate surgery performed by bombers equipped with Sperry and Norden **bombsights**. These instruments were so precise, we had been told, that a bombardier could drop his billets-doux down the chimney of a factory if ordered to. There were solemn charades performed for newsreels in which military policemen with drawn .45 automatics escorted bombardiers carrying **bombsights** to their planes. That was how desperate the Germans and the Japanese were (so went the message) to learn and make use of the secret of our bombings' diabolical accuracy themselves. *Bernard V. O'Hare was Vonnegut's long-time friend and also a survivor of Dresden's firebombing.*

Bonesana, Cesare, Marchese di Beccaria. (*Gal* 175:1-4) And, as long as there was anybody on Santa Rosalia curious as to why his or her ancestors had come there—and that sort of curiosity would finally peter out only after about three thousand years—that was the story: They were driven off the mainland by a shower of meteorites.

Quoth Mandarax:
Happy is the nation without a history.
Cesare Bonesana, Marchese di Beccaria (1738-1794)

booby trap, **booby-trap**, **booby-trapped**, **boobytrapped**. *Vonnegut frequently alludes to the seemingly impossible task of completely innocent activity, as though the world were rigged for failure. As Rudy Waltz terms it,* I wasn't to touch anything on this planet, man, woman, child, artifact, animal, vegetable, or mineral—since it was very likely to be connected to a push-pull detonator and an explosive charge (*DD* 112:23-27). *Aside from references to physical,* *intentionally designed booby traps, Vonnegut frequently refers to the booby traps he sees inherent in human relationships.*

(*PP* 50:L32) Paul took two more of Berringer's pieces and made his own piece a king. "This must be the trickiest **booby trap** in history," he laughed. He was enjoying himself immensely. *Fred Berringer challenged Paul Proteus' checker championship with his faulty Checker Charley robot.*

(*PP* 215:L1) The lights on the **booby-trap** mirror flashed on.

(*PP* 259:L15) His hands *(Bud Calhoun's)* were working in air, fashioning a **booby trap** for a coke machine. "See? Take a li'l ol' coke bottle, only fill her full of nitro. Then we run a li'l ol'—"

(*BC* 153:L16, 20-21) After that, Francine followed Robert to Midland City, where Robert oversaw the manufacture of a new sort of **booby trap**. A **booby trap** was an easily hidden explosive device, which blew up when it was accidentally twiddled in some way. One of the virtues of the new type of **booby trap** was that it could not be smelled by dogs. Various armies at that time were training dogs to sniff out **booby traps**.

(*WFG* 154:L4 *Biafra: A People Betrayed*) Whenever I did something clumsy or unlucky, a Biafran was sure to say that: "Sorry, sah!" He would be genuinely sorry. He was on my side, and against a **booby-trapped** universe.

(*DD* 133:L33) People talk a lot about all the homosexuals there are to see in Greenwich Village, but it was all the neuters that caught my eye that day. These were my people—as used as I was to wanting love from nowhere, as certain as I was that almost anything desirable was likely to be **booby-trapped**.

(*Blue* 107:L2) It sounded good. But guess what? She was assembling a **booby trap**. *Rabo Karabekian refers to Circe Berman's suggestion that he visit New York City again to get his creative juices flowing once more.*

(*HP* 16:L33) The biggest **booby trap** Fate set for me, though, was a pretty and personable young woman named Margaret Patton, who allowed me to woo and marry her soon after my graduation from West Point, and then had 2 children by me without telling me that there was a powerful strain of insanity on her mother's side of the family.

(*HP* 17:L12) I *(Eugene Debs Hartke)* realize that my speaking of my first and only wife as something as inhuman as a **booby trap** risks my seeming to be yet another infernal device.

(*HP* 55:L3) But they *(Hartke's children)* haven't reproduced, and with their knowing what they do about their **booby-trapped** genes, I doubt that they ever will.

(*HP* 61:L2-3) I turned to Jack Patton, who was there with his **booby-trapped** sister and mother and his normal father, and I asked him, "What do you think of us now, Lieutenant Patton?"

(*FWD* 164:L29) "And stay clear of the Ten Commandments, as do the television evangelists. Those things are **booby-trapped**, because right in the middle of them is one commandment which would, if taken seriously, cripple modern religion as show business. It is this commandment: 'Thou shalt not kill.'"

book-banning. (*PS* 8:L19 *The First Amendment*) Here is how I propose to end **book-banning** in this country once and for all: Every candidate for school committee should be hooked up to a lie-detector and asked this question: "Have you read a book from start to finish since high school? Or did you even read a book from start to finish in high school?"

If the truthful answer is "no," then the candidate should be told politely that he cannot get on the school committee and blow off his big bazoo about how books make children crazy.

Whenever ideas are squashed in this country, literate lovers of the American experiment write careful and intricate explanations of why all ideas must be allowed to live. It is time for them to realize that they are attempting to explain America at its bravest and most optimistic to orangutans. From now on, I intend to limit my discourse with dim-witted Savonarolas to this advice: "Have somebody read the First Amendment to the United States Constitution out loud to you, you God damned fool!"

Boone, Michael. *Born Miklós Gömbös, this is the Hungarian paternal grandfather of Kentuckian Mary Hepburn in* Galápagos. *She was a distant relative of Daniel Boone's, but on her mother's side. Miklós changed his name when he came to America.*

Borasisi. (see also **Bokononism**). (*CC* 156:L35, 157:L2) I learned *(from The Books of Bokonon)* of the Bokononist cosmogony, for instance, wherein ***Borasisi***, the sun, held *Pabu*, the moon, in his arms, and hoped that *Pabu* would bear him a fiery child.

But poor *Pabu* gave birth to children that were cold, that did not burn; and ***Borasisi*** threw them away in disgust. These were the planets, who circled their terrible father at a safe distance.

Borders, Lance and **Leora** (see also **Pulsifer**). *Walter Starbuck's secretary at RAMJAC and her husband attend his going away party prior to returning to prison.* (*JB* 233:L30-31) My devoted secretary, **Leora Borders**, and her husband, **Lance**, were there. **Lance** was just getting over a radical mastectomy. He told me that one mastectomy in two hundred was performed on a man. Live and learn!

Boris. *The chess computer given to Walter Starbuck by Clyde Carter and Leland Clewes before he returns to prison at the close of* Jailbird. *Starbuck notes that had "Boris" existed when he was raised in the Alexander Hamilton McCone household, it is doubtful he would have been befriended by his parents' employer.* (*JB* 237:L4) I agreed to be his chess-playing machine. If **Boris** had existed in those days, I probably would have gone to Western Reserve, and then become a tax assessor or an office manager in a lumberyard, or an insurance salesman, or some such thing. Instead, I am the most disreputable Harvard graduate since Putzi Hänfstaengl, who was Hitler's favorite pianist.

Borisoglebsk. *In* Mother Night, *the Soviet town in which George Kraft's (also known as Iona Potapov) wife Tanya has resided for twenty-five years without him.*

Bormann, Martin. *The Nazi war criminal tried and convicted in absentia was the commanding officer of the father of Arthur von Strelitz, the Harvard associate professor of anthropology in* Jailbird.

born again, born-again. (*BC* 218:L31) And now comes the spiritual climax of this book, for it is at this point that I, the author, am suddenly transformed by what I have done so far. This is why I had gone to Midland City: to be **born again**. And Chaos announced that it was about to give birth to a new me by putting these words in the mouth of Rabo Karabekian: *"What kind of man would turn his daughter into an outboard motor?"*
(*Blue* 67:L17) So I *(Rabo Karabekian)* went to New York City to be **born again**.
(*PS* 235:L2 *Children*) MY first wife and both my daughters are **born-again** Christians now—working white magic through rituals and prayers. That's all right.

Borzoi Dance Company. *In* Cat's Cradle, *the company for which Zinka the Ukrainian midget danced. She was wooed by Newt Hoenikker, claimed political asylum in the United States, and a week later appeared at the Russian Embassy wanting to return home. Zinka was a Soviet agent trying to get hold of ice-nine.*

Boström, Hjalmar Arvid. *In* Galápagos, *the Swedish ship welder credited by Leon Trout with perpetuating the saying,* "Oh, well—he wasn't going to write Beethoven's Ninth Symphony anyway." This wry comment on how little most of us were likely to accomplish in life, no matter how long we lived (*Gal* 244:L6-9), *was passed down from his World War I* German grandfather in charge of burying the dead on the Western Front. . . . It was common for soldiers new to that sort of work to wax philosophical over this corpse or that one, into whose face he was about to shovel dirt, speculating about what he might have done if he hadn't died so young. There were many cynical things a veteran might say to such a thoughtful recruit, and one of those was: "Don't worry about it. He wasn't going to write Beethoven's Ninth Symphony anyway" (*Gal* 244:L25, 245:L1-8). *These were also the words uttered by Boström at the funeral of Leon Trout, his co-worker in the Swedish shipyard.*

Boyden, Hay. *In "The Hyannis Port Story," Boyden is a building mover who chastises Robert Taft Rumfoord for downing the Kennedys. Boyden had also* *purchased a bathtub enclosure from the story's narrator, and to save $7.50 he installed it himself. Unfortunately, he did a poor job and his dining room ceiling collapsed. The resulting conversation with the narrator led to a meeting with Commodore Rumfoord, Robert's father.*

Boyer, Richard O. *Along with co-author Herbert M. Morais, Boyer wrote* Labor's Untold Story, *the text which Vonnegut uses in* Jailbird *to quote Judge Thayer's comments as presiding judge at the trial of Sacco and Vanzetti.*

Boyle, Raymond. *The name Raymond Boyle appears in the short story "The Hyannis Port Story" and later in* God Bless You, Mr. Rosewater. *In the short story, Boyle is a Secret Service Agent attached to the Kennedy household in Hyannis Port and is known as the resident Rumfoord Specialist, "or the Ambassador to Rumfoordiana." It is Boyle's duty to call "Commodore" William Rumfoord and inform him that his son was caught trying to use the Kennedy yacht* Marlin *for a love tryst with President Kennedy's fourth cousin Sheila, from Ireland. The Rumfoords are Goldwater Republicans.*

In God Bless You, Mr. Rosewater, *Sergeant Raymond Boyle is the central figure of Kilgore Trout's novel* Pan-Galactic Three-Day Pass. *Boyle is the lone Earthling on an expedition of voyagers from 200 galaxies. Boyle served as an English teacher since the other races used telepathy to communicate. The commanding officer, a Tralfamadorian, and the chaplain from Glinko-X-3, have the sad duty of telling Boyle that the Milky Way died. This apocalyptic tale is read by Eliot Rosewater while on a bus to Indianapolis and is connected in his mind with the Hans Rumpf book* The Bombing of Germany. *The next thing Eliot sees/imagines is Indianapolis engulfed in a fire-storm.*

Brackman, Sergeant Henry. *In* Sirens of Titan, *Unk's (Malachi Constant's) platoon leader in the Martian Army. His real name is Private Francis J. Thompson and he was abducted from Fort Bragg while walking his post around the motor pool. He was the sole Martian survivor of the Battle of Boca Raton. Later, he has the concession booth next to Bee and Chrono outside the Rumfoord estate. He sells $17 replicas of the famous bowl fountain inside the estate's walls.*

Brainard (see **Bullard**).

Braxton, Carter. *Historically, Carter Braxton was one of the representatives from Virginia who signed the Declaration of Independence. In* Galápagos, *Leon Trout explains that he was related to Braxton on his mother's side of the family.*

Breakfast of Champions (1973). *The narrative structures of Vonnegut's first six novels are modeled after autobiographical experiences giving rise to his* *own unique awareness of the forces at work within and around us (the interaction of one's biochemical composition in conjunction with the external environment).* Breakfast of Champions *marks a break with previous narratives by concentrating on a single character's odyssey. Vonnegut squares off with himself, alternately examining that secret part of himself which fears insanity and his more public character as a writer with seemingly rational explanations for our collective state of being.* "This is a tale of a meeting of two lonesome, skinny, fairly old white men on a planet which was dying fast. . . . One of them was a science-fiction writer named Kilgore Trout. . . . The man he met was an automobile dealer, a *Pontiac* dealer name Dwayne Hoover. Dwayne Hoover was on the brink of going insane (*BC* 7:L1-10). *Rounding out their planned meeting in Midland City, Ohio, is Vonnegut, who* "had come to the Arts Festival incognito. I was there to watch a confrontation between two human beings I had created: Dwayne Hoover and Kilgore Trout" (*BC* 192:L14-16). *Hoover and Trout harbor very specific motives for attending the festival. Together, they represent some of Vonnegut's various views of himself. To be sure, Vonnegut is the protagonist.*

Hoover wanted to avoid going crazy the way his wife Celia did (having committed suicide by eating Drano), in much the same way Vonnegut feared schizophrenia and the legacy of his own mother's suicide. (*BC* 195:L10-18) Dwayne was hoping that some of the distinguished visitors to the Arts Festival, who were all staying at the Inn, would come into the cocktail lounge. He wanted to talk to them, if he could, to discover whether they had truths about life which he had never heard before. Here is what he hoped new truths might do for him: enable him to laugh at his troubles, to go on living, and to keep out of the North Wing of the Midland County General Hospital, which was for lunatics.

Prior to presenting Hoover and the nature of his own purpose in the text, Vonnegut muses on his own vexation. (*BC* 193:L28-33, 194:L1-6) There in the cocktail lounge, peering out through my leaks *(mirrored sunglasses)* at a world of my own invention, I mouthed this word: *schizophrenia*.

The sound and appearance of the word had fascinated me for many years. It sounded and looked to me like a human being sneezing in a blizzard of soapflakes.

I did not and do not know for certain that I have that disease. This much I knew and know: I was making myself hideously uncomfortable by not narrowing my attention to details of life which were immediately important, and by refusing to believe what my neighbors believed.

Vonnegut refuses to believe in the isolation of experience. As he had already explained in Slaughterhouse-Five, "All moments, past, present and future, always have existed, always will exist. . . . It is just an illusion we have here on Earth that one moment follows another one, like beads on a string, and that once a moment is gone it is gone forever" (*SL5* 23:L16-24). *Though Vonnegut doesn't offer Hoover this particular explanation of the structured moment, he still maintains that as for himself,* "I had come to the conclusion that there was nothing sacred about myself or about any human being, that we were all machines, doomed to collide and collide and collide. For want of anything better to do, we became fans of collision" (*BC* 219:L30-33, 220:L1).

As an exponent of Vonnegut's sense of fatalism, it falls to Kilgore Trout to inform Hoover of this mechanistic philosophy. (*BC* 103:L3-12) . . . his head no longer sheltered ideas of how things could be and should be on the planet, as opposed to how they really were. There was only one way for the Earth to be, he thought: the way it was.

Everything was necessary. He saw an old white woman fishing through a garbage can. That was necessary. He saw a bathtub toy, a little rubber duck, lying on its side on the grating over a storm sewer. It *had* to be there.

And so on.

The limitations of such a world view may preclude hope, but it does allow Trout to admit that all artists don't necessarily find truth (or even satisfying explanations). He accepts the invitation to the festival because he wishes to point out to the organizers that perhaps there is failure in art. (*BC* 37:L29-33) "I'm going out there to show them what nobody has ever seen at an arts festival before: a representative of all the thousands of artists who devoted their entire lives to a search for truth and beauty—and didn't find doodley-squat!"

Though Trout may think his mechanistic philosophy is bleak, his literature is appreciated in some quarters for the tribulations suffered to produce his vision. Milo Maritimo, the gay clerk at the Holiday Inn who has read much of Trout's work, greets Trout with the same longing that compels Dwayne Hoover to seek out the arts. (*BC* 233:L22-27) Oh, Mr. Trout, teach us to sing and dance and laugh and cry. We've tried to survive so long on money and sex and envy and real estate and football and basketball and automobiles and television and alcohol—on sawdust and broken glass!

Trout, spiritual guru of Eliot Rosewater, Billy Pilgrim, and Milo Maritimo, rejects such adoration as falsely believing in the same empty symbols he wishes to strip bare. Just as Vonnegut frequently rejected his status as a cult figure for the flower children of the 1960s, Trout protests that his truths may do no more than prolong Midland City's desolation and desperation. Even so, Maritimo sees in Trout "a man who is terribly wounded—because he had dared to pass through the fires of truth to the other side, which we have never see. And then he has come back again—to tell us about the other side" (*BC* 234:L5-9). *Everything Vonnegut writes comes from the far side of the fires of Dresden.*

There in the lounge of the Holiday Inn, Vonnegut sets up yet another collision. Only this time, instead of fabled enemies or ancient institutions, the crash dummies are Vonnegut's psychic surrogates: Dwayne Hoover and Kilgore Trout. In response to Dwayne's desire for truth, which he desperately hoped would prevent him from going insane, Vonnegut supplies him with Trout's novel, Now It Can Be Told. *It is the same unsatisfying, mechanistic philosophy Trout/Vonnegut laments,* Dear Sir, poor sir, brave sir. . . . You are an experiment of the Creator of the Universe. You are the only creature in the entire Universe who has free will. You are the only one who has to figure out what to do next—and *why*. Everybody else is a robot, a machine.

You are pooped and demoralized. . . . Why wouldn't you be? Of course it is exhausting, having to reason all the time in a universe which wasn't meant to be reasonable. . . .

You are surrounded by loving machines, hating machines, greedy machines, brave machines, cowardly machines, truthful machines, funny machines, solemn machines. . . . Their only purpose is to stir you up in every conceivable way, so the Creator of the Universe can watch your reactions (*BC* 253:17-28, 254:L1-7).

As sincerely as Milo Maritimo expected Trout to show him truth, Dwayne Hoover interprets Trout's novel as defining his personal existence. Outraged over the depressing knowledge that there existed no spiritual bond among men, that all the sufferings and sacrifices throughout history were for enlightenment of a supposedly benignant Creator, Hoover assaults a number of people before he is finally subdued.

Beyond the obvious confrontation Vonnegut presents between Hoover and Trout is his own purpose for entering the text. He, too, rejects a mechanistic view which puts man in the center of a rat's maze to be observed and judged by a supposedly paternalistic and loving God. "And now the spiritual climax of this book, for it is at this point that I, the author, am suddenly transformed by what I have done so far. This is why I had gone to Midland City: to be born again" (*BC* 218:L28-31). *He owes his rebirth to another surrogate artist, Abstract Expressionist painter Rabo Karabekian.*

Karabekian's philosophy of art disregards any considerations of the eternal collisions of man, of the mechanistic view described by Trout which made man subject to the awareness of a Creator. Instead, man's awareness of his own circumstances is all that can be appreciated. His $50,000 painting of Saint Anthony, nothing more than a single vertical band of luminescent color, raises the ire of the locals, but his explanation modifies Vonnegut's uneasiness. (*BC* 221:L7-20) I now give you my word of honor . . . that the picture your city owns shows everything about life which truly matters, with nothing left out. It is a picture of the awareness of every animal. It is the immaterial core of every animal—the 'I am' to which all messages are sent. . . . Our awareness is all that is alive an maybe sacred in any of us. Everything else about us is dead machinery. *Karabekian's (Vonnegut's) message is clear: whatever the state of one's existence, accepting those circumstances is easier if unencumbered by wishes for divine intervention.*

For Trout, the collision of his life occurs when his creator, Vonnegut, exposes himself. (*BC* 293:L9-23) "Mr. Trout—*Kilgore*—I hold in my hand a symbol of wholeness and harmony and nourishment. It is Oriental in its simplicity, but we are *Americans*, Kilgore, and not Chinamen. We Americans require symbols which have not been poisoned by great sins our nation has committed, such as slavery and genocide and criminal neglect, or by tinhorn commercial greed and cunning."

"Look up, Mr. Trout," I said, and I waited patiently. "Kilgore—?"

The old man looked up, and he had my father's wasted face when my father was a widower—when my father was an old old man.

He saw that I held an apple in my hand.

The apple Vonnegut extends to Trout is a symbol of knowledge which satisfies our demands for intellectual freedom (especially when confronted with Trout's mechanistic theory, or the chrono-synclastic infundibulum of The Sirens of Titan*), yet it simultaneously implies the liability and consequence of discovery, of knowledge (particularly as it is pursued in* Cat's Cradle*). Trout understands this symbol and the consequent legacy of intellectual freedom, and he shrinks from the offering by wishing for youthful renewal, "Make me young, make me young, make me young!" as if there were refuge in a pre-lapsarian state* (*BC* 295:L2-3). Youth only awaits becoming old; it is all part of a larger continuum.

After Trout's plea, the novel ends with "ETC." *because Vonnegut acknowledges the inability to escape into youth, as well as the irrelevance of thinking of youth as somehow protected from the mythical archetypes man creates for himself. Indeed, it is during childhood that myths are presented and perpetuated. ETC is an expression of the inevitable. For Vonnegut, writing about the inevitable requires associating the forces around and within us in terms which have prior significance: the events of life which symbolize our most identifiable concerns. Vonnegut forever returns to his youth and beyond for those moments which enable an orderly discussion of the present.*

Breed, Dr. Asa. *In* Cat's Cradle, *the Vice-president in charge of the Research Laboratory of the General Forge and Foundry Company—Felix Hoenikker's boss. John/Jonah, the narrator of the text, makes an appointment with Dr. Breed to help research his proposed text,* The Day The World Ended. (*CC* 33:L5-8, 10-15) **Breed** was a pink old man, very prosperous, beautifully dressed. His manner was civilized, optimistic, capable, serene. I, by contrast, felt bristly, diseased, cynical. I had spent the night with Sandra. . . . I thought the worst of everyone, and I knew some pretty sordid things about **Dr. Asa Breed**, things Sandra had told me. Sandra told me everyone in Ilium was sure that **Dr. Breed** had been in love with Felix Hoenikker's wife. She told me that most people thought **Breed** was the father of all three Hoenikker children.

During the interview, Breed explains to John/Jonah the nature of "pure research." (*CC* 42:L26-36, 43:L1-9) "It isn't looking for a better cigarette filter or a softer face tissue or a longer-lasting house paint, God help us. Everybody talks about research and practically nobody in this country's doing it. We're one of the few companies that actually hires men to do pure research. When most other companies brag about their research, they're talking about industrial hack technicians who wear white coats, work out of cookbooks, and dream up an improved windshield wiper for next year's Oldsmobile."

"But here. . . ?"

"Here, and shockingly few other places in this country, men are paid to increase knowledge, to work toward no end but that."

"That's very generous of General Forge and Foundry Company."

"Nothing generous about it. New knowledge is the most valuable commodity on earth. The more truth we have to work with, the richer we become."

Had I been a Bokononist then, that statement would have made me howl.

Breed is responsible for telling John/Jonah about the "theoretical" ice-nine, illustrating its effects with reference to cannonballs on courthouse lawns. (*CC* 45:L29-36, 46:L1-33) That old man with spotted hands invited me to think of the several ways in which cannonballs might be stacked on a courthouse lawn, of the several ways in which oranges might be packed into a crate.

"So it is with atoms in crystals, too; and two different crystals of the same substance can have quite different physical properties."

He told me about a factory that had been growing big crystals of ethylene diamine tartrate. The crystals were useful in certain manufacturing operations, he said. But one day the factory discovered that the crystals it was growing no longer had the properties desired. The atoms had begun to stack and lock—to freeze—in a different fashion. The liquid that was crystallizing hadn't changed, but the crystals it was forming were, as far as industrial applications went, pure junk.

How this had come about was a mystery. The theoretical villain, however, was what **Dr. Breed** called "a seed." He meant by that a tiny grain of the undesired crystal pattern. The seed, which had come from God-only-knows-where, taught the atoms the novel way in which to stack and lock, to crystallize, to freeze.

"Now think about cannonballs on a courthouse lawn or about oranges in a crate again," he suggested. And he helped me to see that the pattern of the bottom layer of cannonballs or of oranges determined how each subsequent layer would stack and lock. "The bottom layer is the seed of how every cannonball or every orange that comes after is going to behave, even to an infinite number of cannonballs or oranges."

"Now suppose," chortled **Dr. Breed**, enjoying himself, "that there were many possible ways in which water could crystallize, could freeze. Suppose that the sort of ice we skate upon and put into highballs—what we might call *ice-one*—is only one of several types of ice. Suppose water always froze as *ice-one* on Earth because it had never had a seed to teach it how to form *ice-two, ice-three, ice-four*... ? And suppose," he rapped on his desk with his old hand again, "that there were one form, which we will call *ice-nine*—a crystal as hard as this desk—with a melting point of, let us say, one-hundred degrees Fahrenheit, or, better still, a melting point of one-hundred-and-thirty degrees."

"All right, I'm still with you," I said.

Breed, Marvin and Avram. (*CC* 60:L14-15) "When you put it in a cemetery, it is." Marvin Breed was a sleek and vulgar, a smart and sentimental man. *Marvin is the brother of Asa Breed, Felix Hoenikker's supervisor in* Cat's Cradle. *Marvin is the tombstone salesman in Ilium who runs the Avram Breed and Sons establishment, the great-great grandfather of the scientist and salesman. While John/Jonah interviews Marvin, he learns that Emily Hoenikker had been his girlfriend until Asa wooed her away, and then she hooked up with Felix—much to Marvin's bewilderment.*

John/Jonah also has his first Bokononist experience while with Marvin. The narrator is taken with a stone angel decorated with mistletoe and Christmas lamps. Old Avram Breed had carved the image for John/Jonah's ancestor. (*CC* 64:L1-9) It was in the tombstone salesroom that I had my first *vin-dit*, a Bokononist word meaning a sudden, very personal shove in the direction of Bokononism, in the direction of believing that God Almighty knew all about me, after all, that God Almighty had some pretty elaborate plans for me.

The *vin-dit* had to do with the stone angel under the mistletoe. (*CC* 66:L27-36, 67:L1-5, 14-16) "It was never *paid* for. The story goes: this German immigrant was on his way West with his wife, and she died of smallpox here in Ilium. So he ordered this angel to be put up over her, and he showed my great-grandfather he had the cash to pay for it. But then he was robbed. Somebody took practically every cent he had. All he had left in this world was some land he'd bought in Indiana, land he'd never seen. So he moved on—said he'd be back later to pay for the angel."

"But he never came back?" I asked.

"Nope." Marvin Breed nudged some of the boughs aside with his toe so that we could see the raised letters on the pedestal. There was a last name written there. "There's a screwy name for you," he said. "If that immigrant had any descendants, I expect they Americanized the name. They're probably Jones or Black or Thompson now."

"There you're wrong," I murmured. . . .

"You know some people by that name?"

"Yes."

The name was my last name, too.

Breedlove, Don. *The ironically named* "gas-conversion unit installer" *who* "rapes Patty Keene outside the Bannister Memorial Fieldhouse at the County Fairgrounds after the Regional High School Basketball Playoffs. She never reported it to the police. She never reported it to anybody, since her father was dying at the time" (*BC* 139:L8).

Vonnegut provides the dimensions of Breedlove's penis: "five and seven-eighths inches long and one and seven-eighths inches in diameter" (BC 145:L8-9).

Breedlove makes Gloria Browning pregnant and she endures a botched abortion followed by a hysterectomy. Later, while repairing a defective gas oven in the Holiday Inn, he is victimized by Dwayne Hoover, who first grasps his hand in a handshake and then slams him in the ear, making him deaf on one side.

Breedlove wasn't well liked by too many people since one of the neighborhood children dumped maple sugar in his Pontiac Ventura.

Breslaw. *The University of Pennsylvania buys Breslaw, the University of Wisconsin football star, for $43,000 in one of the many Ivy League attempts to knock down the PE-003 rating of Cornell's coach, Doctor Roseberry, in* Player Piano.

Brewer, Ansel (also **Irving Buchanon** and **Eddie McCarty**). *Howard W. Campbell is attacked in front of his brownstone in Greenwich Village when the* New York Daily News *picks up the story about his whereabouts from* The White Christian Minuteman. *Brewer, Buchanon and McCarty are used as the reason for violent retribution by an unnamed New Yorker on Campbell.* (*MN* 110:10-111:12) And then a bald, bristly fat man carrying a shopping bag came in. He shouldered Resi and me away from the mailboxes with a hoarse, unapologetic bully's apology. . . . The man hit me right through the newspaper before I could comment. . . .

"That one was for Private **Irving Buchanon**," he said.

"Is that who you are?" I said.

"Buchanon is dead," he said. "He was the best friend I ever had. Five miles in from Omaha Beach, the Germans cut his nuts off and hung him from a telephone pole."

He kicked me in the ribs, holding Resi off with one hand. "That's for **Ansel Brewer**," he said, "run over by a Tiger tank at Aachen."

He kicked me again. "That's for **Eddie McCarty**, cut in two by a burp gun in the Ardennes," he said. "Eddie was gonna be a doctor."

briquet. *In* Mother Night, *Campbell's prison guard Andor Gutman uses this term to describe those Jews who seemingly went to the gas chambers without making any attempts to fight back and save themselves. He avoided becoming a "briquet" by getting false papers, then joining the Hungarian S.S. and killing off as many Nazis as he could without being revealed.*

Brokenshire, Dr. David. *In* Deadeye Dick, *the British doctor who had been imprisoned by the Japanese and who came upon John Fortune in his last days in Nepal. Before dying of double pneumonia, Fortune gave Brokenshire a letter which wasn't forwarded to the* Midland City Bugle-Observer *until long after his* *death. Brokenshire wrote a book about Fortune and included a map of Katmandu and the location of Fortune's grave. Brokenshire traveled through Nepal, Tibet, Burma, and China where the Japanese imprisoned him under suspicion of being a spy. When Rudy Waltz writes a play about John Fortune, one of the characters is Dr. David Brokenshire.*

Bromley, Milford S. (General of the Armies). *In* Player Piano, *one of the dignitaries accompanying the Shah of Bratpuhr. He is constantly distressed by the Shah's characterization of Americans, civilians and military personnel alike, as "Takaru"—slaves. Bromley tries to explain Americans work hard because they have patriotism.*

Brown, Betty and Bobby. *Eliza and Wilbur Swain's stupendous intellect is effective only when they literally put their heads together. Whenever they were separated, they each felt as dim-witted as the other. When this happened, they thought of themselves in the third person, as "Betty and Bobby Brown." Before dying in the Martian avalanche, Eliza asked that her tombstone read "HERE LIES BETTY BROWN." Among the many theoretical papers they wrote together, one was a manual on childrearing, which they signed as Betty and Bobby Brown. The original title was* The Cry of the Nocturnal Goatsucker, *but that was conceived in one of their fits of creativity. Later, when Wilbur was a practicing pediatrician in Vermont, it was renamed* So You Went and Had a Baby, *with the pen name Dr. Eli W. Rockmell, M.D.*

Brown, Dr. Ed. (*GBR* 54:L2) Sylvia was placed in a private mental hospital in Indianapolis, was taken there by Eliot and Charley Warmergran, the Fire Chief. They took her in the Chief's car, which was a red Henry J with a siren on top. They turned her over to a **Dr. Ed Brown**, a young psychiatrist who later made his reputation describing her illness. In the paper, he called Eliot and Sylvia "*Mr. and Mrs. Z,*" and he called the town of Rosewater "*Hometown, U.S.A.*" He coined a new word for Sylvia's disease, "*Samaritrophia,*" which he said meant, "hysterical indifference to the troubles of those less fortunate than oneself."

(*GBR* 55:L9-18) I *(Dr. Brown)* made it the goal of my treatments, then, to keep her conscience imprisoned, but to lift the lid of the oubliette ever so slightly, so that the howls of the prisoner might be very faintly heard. Through trial and error with chemotherapy and electric shock, this I achieved. I was not proud, for I had calmed a deep woman by making her shallow. I had blocked the underground rivers that connected her to the Atlantic, Pacific, and Indian Oceans, and made her content with being a splash pool three feet across, four inches deep, chlorinated, and painted blue.

Dr. Brown also treats Eliot in the insane asylum and is present for the final scene along with Eliot, Kilgore Trout, Senator Rosewater, and Thurmond McAllister.

Brown, Payton. *In* Breakfast of Champions, *the fifteen-year-old black man who died in the electric chair at Shepherdstown. Dwayne Hoover tried to save him though his efforts are not enumerated. He mentions Payton Brown while bragging to parolee Wayne Hoobler about the advancements he sought for black people as County Executive for the Boy Scouts of America.*

Brown Bomber (see **Karl Heinz**).

Browning, Gloria. *In* Breakfast of Champions, *the twenty-five year old cashier at Dwayne Hoover's Exit Eleven Pontiac Village who fills in at Francine Pefko's desk while she and Dwayne go for an afternoon rendezvous at a local motel. Gloria had been raped by Don Breedlove and was forced to undergo a hysterectomy after enduring a botched abortion at the Green County Ramada Inn.*

Buchanon, Irving (see **Brewer**).

Buchenwald. *The German concentration camp is referred to in* Cat's Cradle, Slaughterhouse-Five, *and* "The Euphio Question" *in* Welcome to the Monkey House *when referring to piles of dead bodies.*

Buffalo Works. *In* Player Piano, *one of the main industrial centers of the ruling technocracy. The manager of the plant is Fred Garth. The Buffalo Works is one of many sites which suffer sabotage.*

bugger, buggered, buggery. (*PP* 262:L35) "Well, it just don't seem like nobody feels he's worth a crap to nobody no more, and it's a hell of a screwy thing, people gettin' **buggered** by things they made theirselves."
(*GBR* 36:L30) And so on. The Senator said that the carrot and the stick had been built into the Free Enterprise System, as conceived by the Founding Fathers, but that do-gooders, who thought people shouldn't ever have to struggle for anything, had **buggered** the logic of the system beyond all recognition.
(*MH* XIV:L25 *Preface*) I have already put the question to a college professor, who, climbing down into his Mercedes-Benz 300SL *gran turismo*, assured me that public relations men and slick writers were equally vile, in that they both **buggered** truth for money.
(*MH* 274:L17 *EPICAC*) I had hoped to sleep late the next morning, but an urgent telephone call roused me before eight. It was Dr. von Kleigstadt, EPICAC's designer, who gave me the terrible news. He was on the verge of tears. "Ruined! *Ausgespielt*! Shot! *Kaput*! **Buggered**!" he said in a choked voice. He hung up.

(*SL5* 173:L1) In the window there were hundreds of books about fucking and **buggery** and murder, and a street guide to New York City, and a model of the Statue of Liberty with a thermometer on it. Also in the window, speckled with soot and fly shit, were four paperback novels by Billy's friend, Kilgore Trout.
(*WJ* 22:L13) SHUTTLE: She's my date tonight. What do you want her to do—bring the poor old jaguars back to life with a bicycle pump? **Bugger** off! Ask Paul what he thinks.
(*BC* 170:L11) So the Earthlings infiltrated the ad agency which had the shazzbutter account, and they **buggered** the statistics in the ads. They made the average for everything so high that everybody on the planet felt inferior to the majority in every respect.
(*BC* 179:L6,7) Listen: Bunny Hoover went to Prairie Military Academy for eight years of uninterrupted sports, **buggery** and fascism. **Buggery** consisted of sticking one's penis in somebody else's asshole or mouth, or having it done to one by somebody else. Fascism was a fairly popular political philosophy which made sacred whatever nation and race the philosopher happened to belong to. It called for an autocratic, centralized government, headed up by a dictator. The dictator had to be obeyed, no matter what he told somebody to do.
(*BC* 249:L7) Let's see: I have already explained Dwayne's uncharacteristic ability to read so fast. Kilgore Trout probably couldn't have made his trip from New York City in the time I allotted, but it's too late to **bugger** around with that. Let it stand, let it stand!
(*BC* 253:L8) Trout made no reply. He had hoped to get through what little remained of his life without ever having to touch another human being again. Dwayne's chin on his shoulder was as shattering as **buggery** to Trout.
(*WFG* 57:L11 *Fortitude*) FRANKENSTEIN (to LITTLE): You keep her right there. I'm gonna check things over. Maybe there's been a little huggery **buggery**. (To GLORIA) How would you like to be in court for attempted murder, eh?
(*Slap* 233:L16) "**Bugger** . . . defecate . . . semen . . . balls," said the boy. *The boy is David Daffodil-11 von Peterswald, a victim of Tourette's Disease.*
(*DD* 136:L31) There was a young man from Dundee, / Who **buggered** an ape in a tree. / The results were most horrid, / All ass and no forehead, / Three balls and a purple goatee.

Bugle-Observer (also ***Midland City Bugle-Observer***). *The main newspaper in Midland City mentioned in both* Breakfast of Champions *and* Deadeye Dick. *In* Deadeye Dick *the paper's city editor is George Metzger, husband of Eloise Metzger, the victim of Rudy's mindless shooting from his home's cupola.*

Building 58 Suite. *Paul Proteus' perception of the rhythm of the machinery in Thomas Edison's old laboratory at the Ilium Works. The music intoxicates him, separates him from all his anxieties. Paul enchants himself with thinking the machinery is representative of a time when technological innovation was* *brought about by man's direct involvement and signaled a triumph of spirit and intellect, representative of an era less tainted by the technology's direct impact on society.* (*PP* 10:L23) At the door, in the old part of the building once more, Paul paused for a moment to listen to the music of Building 58. He had had it in the back of his mind for years to get a composer to do something with it—***the Building 58 Suite***. It was wild and Latin music, hectic rhythms, fading in and out of phase, kaleidoscopic sound. He tried to separate and identify the themes. There! The lathe groups, the tenors: "*Furrazz-ow-ow-ow-ow-ow-ak! ting! Furr-azz-ow-ow. . .*" The welders, the baritones: "*Vaaaaaaa-zuzip! Vaaaaaaa-zuzip!*" And, with the basement as a resonating chamber, the punch presses, the basses: "*Aw-grumph! tonka-tonka. Aw-grump! tonka-tonka. . .*" It was exciting music, and Paul, flushed, his vague anxieties gone, gave himself over to it.

When Paul is drugged by members of the Ghost Shirt Society before his interrogation, he dreamily retreats to the rhythms of the Building 58 Suite, *projecting himself at the center of an erotic ballet with Anita his wife, who eventually lays amidst a nest of electrical wires with Kroner and Shepherd. Paul awakens from his drug-induced haze by Ed Finnerty, his Ghost Shirt interrogator.*

Bullard, Dr. Brainard Keyes. *The President of Wyandotte College who in the short story "Tomorrow and Tomorrow and Tomorrow" says* "that most of the world's ills can be traced to the fact that Man's knowledge of himself has not kept pace with his knowledge of the physical world" (*MH* 289:L37, 290:L1-3).

Bullard, Harold K. *One of the two old men in the short story "Tom Edison's Shaggy Dog." He and his Labrador retriever go searching for new acquaintances in a Tampa, Florida, park each day. He longs to tell everyone about the five fortunes he made and lost throughout his life,* "Two in real estate, one in scrap iron, and one in oil and one in trucking" (*MH* 100:L8-9 *Tom Edison's Shaggy Dog*). *But Bullard became the butt of his unnamed companion's ire who told him about his days with Thomas Edison when he was trying to figure out a proper element to use for a light bulb filament. As the man explains, Edison's dog Sparky told him to use carbonized cotton thread. When the eavesdropping dogs heard Sparky reveal the true intelligence of dogs, threatening the subservient relationship they had cultivated with humans, they tore Sparky to shreds. Bullard apparently swallows the entire story.*

Bunker, Archie. *The racist patriarch of the sitcom "All in the Family." Using Archie as the American Everyman, Vonnegut reveals the source of the subtitle for* Slapstick. (*WFG* 273:L32-33) PLAYBOY: If you had been the Democratic nominee *(in the 1972 election)*, how would you have campaigned against Nixon?
VONNEGUT: I would have set the poor against the rich. I would have made the poor admit that they're poor. **Archie Bunker** has no sense of being poor,

but he obviously is a frightened, poor man. I would convince **Archie Bunker** that he was poor and getting poorer, that the ruling class was robbing him and lying to him. I was invited to submit ideas to the McGovern campaign. Nothing was done with my suggestions. I wanted Sarge Shriver to say, "You are not happy, are you? Nobody in this country is happy but the rich people. Something is wrong. I'll tell you what's wrong. We're lonesome!"

Mary Kathleen O'Looney, the eccentric and secretive philanthropic owner of The RAMJAC Corporation, appreciates America's passion for the views of Archie and other media stars, but she understands their actions and philosophies to be in opposition of the public good and acts accordingly. (*JB* 158:L25) "It's all such crap," she said. "I find this magazine called *People* in garbage cans," she said, "but it isn't about people. It's about crap. . . . Jackie Onassis and Frank Sinatra and the Cookie Monster and **Archie Bunker** make their moves," she said, "and then I study what they have done, and then I decide what Mary Kathleen O'Looney had better do.

Buntline, Amanita. *Amanita is the mother of Lila, the wife of Stewart Buntline, and the "Lesbian friend" of Caroline Rosewater. She passes down her old clothes and accessories to Caroline and buys her all sorts of nonsensical gifts simply because she can, including a seventeen-dollar toilet paper cover from Mexico.*

Buntline, Castor. *The great-grandfather of Stewart Buntline and founder of the company which produced the Buntline Union Beacon Broom, Castor Buntline did not serve in the military during the Civil War. His corporate intentions to employ disabled veterans were egocentric and mercenary. The disabled General George Rosewater went to work for Buntline and became the namesake of the "General George Rosewater" whiskbroom.* (*GBR* 119:L16-24) **Buntline** perceived correctly that blind veterans would make very agreeable employees, that **Buntline** himself would gain a place in history as a humanitarian, and that no Northern patriot, for several years after the war, anyway, would use anything but a *Buntline Union Beacon Broom*. Thus was the great **Buntline** fortune begun. And, with broom profits, **Castor Buntline** and his spastic son Elihu went carpetbagging, became tobacco kings.

Castor Buntline also founded an orphanage in Pawtucket in 1878, and he wrote the oath of service for the "fortunate" few. (*GBR* 154:L12-22) When it was founded, the **Buntlines** required three things: That all orphans be raised as Christians, regardless of race, color, or creed, that they take an oath once a week, before Sunday supper, and that, each year, an intelligent, clean female orphan enter domestic service in a **Buntline** home. . . in order to learn about the better things in life, and perhaps to be inspired to climb a few rungs of the ladder of culture and social grace. *The oath of service is as follows:* (*GBR* 154:L30-32, 155:L1-11) I do solemnly swear that I will respect the sacred private property of others, and that I will be content with whatever station in life God Almighty may assign me to. I will be grateful to those who employ me, and will never complain about wages and hours, but will ask myself instead, "What more can I do for my employer, my republic, and my God?" I understand that I have not been placed on Earth to be happy. I am here to be tested. If I am to pass the test, I must be always unselfish, always sober, always truthful, always chaste in mind, body, and deed, and always respectful to those to whom God has, in His Wisdom, placed above me. If I pass the test, I will go to joy everlasting in Heaven when I die. If I fail, I shall roast in hell while the Devil laughs and Jesus weeps.

Buntline, Elihu. *In* God Bless You, Mr. Rosewater, *Elihu is the spastic son of Castor Buntline, founder of the Buntline Union Beacon Broom company. He and his father invested their earnings and made a fortune in tobacco. He is also Stewart Buntline's grandfather.*

Buntline, Lila. *In* God Bless You, Mr. Rosewater, *Stewart and Amanita Buntline's daughter is the celebrated thirteen-year-old sailor at the Pisquontuit Yacht Club as well as the pornography and fireworks peddlar to the wealthy youth in Newport, Rhode Island. She bought the latest erotic novels from the local news store and sold them at huge profits to her friends. She was so good at this that a local civic club commended the store for apparently not stocking smut, when in reality, Lila had scooped up the stock.*

Buntline, Stewart. *Just shy of forty, the husband of Amanita and father of Lila is a depressed rich man whose sole interest, however slight, is in studying the Civil War. Stewart is, in some ways, afflicted with the same anxieties as Eliot Rosewater. He was orphaned at sixteen and came into a fourteen-million-dollar tobacco fortune (currently earning over $800,000 per year) under the conservatorship of Reed McAllister, senior partner in the law firm McAllister, Robjent, Reed and McGee—the same firm representing the Senator and Eliot Rosewater. Twenty years earlier he went to Old McAllister feeling ashamed of all his unearned wealth, asking how he could put his money to use for the poor. McAllister chastised him for his naivete, apologized for the lack of real-world education he received at Harvard, and explained that it was Stewart's duty and sole source of personal fulfillment to cherish the fortune. Old McAllister tells him,* (*GBR* 140:L20-27, 4-11) I have to offer what is perhaps an insult. Here it is, like it or not: Your fortune is the most important single determinant of what you think of yourself and of what others think of you. Because of the money, you are extraordinary. Without it, for example, you would not now be taking the priceless time of a senior partner in McAllister, Robjent, Reed and McGee. . . .

"Cling to your miracle, Mr. Buntline. Money is dehydrated Utopia. This is a dog's life for almost everybody, as your professors have taken such pains to point out. But, because of your miracle, life for you and yours can be a paradise! Let me see you smile! Let me see that you already understand what they do not teach at Harvard until the junior year: That to be born rich and to stay rich is something less than a felony."

Bunty. *The name of the yacht belonging to Stewart and Amanita Buntline in* God Bless You, Mr. Rosewater.

Burch, Captain Arnold. *The nominal company commander of Boaz and Unk (Malachi Constant) while serving in the Martian Army, Burch is actually under Boaz's control. It is during his appearance in their barracks that Vonnegut first explains the remote control box Boaz has in his pants.* (*ST* 115:L22-32, 116:L1-3, 6-11) Only one man was slow about coming to attention. That man was Boaz. And when he did come to attention, there was something insolent and loose and leering about the way he did it.

Captain Burch, finding Boaz's attitude profoundly offensive, was about to speak to Boaz about it. But the Captain no sooner got his mouth open than pain hit him between the eyes.

The captain closed his mouth without having made a sound.

Under the baleful gaze of Boaz, he came smartly to attention, did an about-face, heard a snare drum in his head, and marched out of the barrack in step with the drum... He *(Boaz)* had a small control box in his right front trouser pocket that could make his squadmates do just about anything. The box was the size of a one-pint hip flask. Like a hip flask, the box was curved to fit a body curve. Boaz chose to carry it on the hard, curved face of his thigh.

Burger, Knox. *Vonnegut's first literary editor who eventually becomes the literary agent for Mark Vonnegut. Burger received Vonnegut's first short story, "Report on the Barnhouse Effect," at* Collier's. *Vonnegut dedicated his short story collection to Burger.* (*MH* dedication) FOR / **KNOX BURGER** / TEN DAYS OLDER THAN I AM. / HE HAS BEEN A VERY GOOD / FATHER TO ME.

(*PS* 112:L2-3, 10 *Self-Interview*) When I was working for General Electric, I wrote a story, "Report on the Barnhouse Effect," the first story I ever wrote. I mailed it off to *Collier's*. **Knox Burger** was fiction editor there. Knox told me what was wrong with it and how to fix it. I did what he said, and he bought the story for seven hundred and fifty dollars, six weeks' pay at G.E. I wrote another, and he paid me nine hundred and fifty dollars, and suggested that it was perhaps time for me to quit G.E. Which I did. I moved to Provincetown. Eventually, my price for a short story got up to twenty-nine hundred dollars a crack. Think of that. And **Knox** got me a couple of agents who were as shrewd about storytelling as he was—Kenneth Littauer, who had been his predecessor at Collier's and Max Wilkinson, who had been a story editor for MGM. And let it be put on the record here that **Knox Burger**, who is about my age, discovered and encouraged more good young writers than any other editor of his time. I don't think that's ever been written down anywhere. It's a fact known only to writers, and one that could easily vanish, if it isn't somewhere written down.

Burgoyne, General John. *In* Bluebeard, *the commanding officer of Paul Slazinger's first ancestor in America, a Hessian soldier from Wiesbaden, Germany, serving as a mercenary with the British.*

Butler, Nicholas Murray. *The president of Columbia University whom Rudy Waltz met as a child in* Deadeye Dick. *Since there was next to nothing of interest to see or do in Midland City, visiting celebrities were taken to the in-home art studio of Rudy's father.*

C

calcimine. (*PP* 6:L34) It soothed him *(Paul Proteus)* to look up at the wooden rafters *(of Building 58)*, uneven with ancient adze marks beneath flaking **calcimine**, and at the dull walls of brick soft enough for men—God knows how long ago—to carve their initials in: "KTM," "DG," "GP," "BDH," "HB," "NNS."
(*MN* 6:L31) We heard the bombs walking around up there. Now and then there would be a gentle shower of **calcimine**.
(*MN* 183:L6) A bomb crashed down close by, shook loose from the ceiling a snowfall of **calcimine**, brought the woman to her feet shrieking, and her husband with her.
(*SL5* 152:L25) The meat locker was a very safe shelter. All that happened down there was an occasional shower of **calcimine**.

Caldwell Foundation. *In* Slapstick, *the foundation sponsored the 1959 playwriting contest won by Rudy Waltz's "Katmandu." The play was brought to the Theatre de Lys in Greenwich village and closed in one night (the same theater which produced Vonnegut's* "Happy Birthday, Wanda June"*). The actors and sponsors were so infuriated by the inability of Rudy to explain the play that the foundation never sponsored another playwriting contest.*

Calhoun, Doctor Bud. *Though the manager of the petroleum terminal in Ilium, Calhoun is a subordinate of Paul Proteus'. The sweet talking Georgian spends his spare time on the couch in the reception area of Proteus' office flirting with Dr. Katharine Finch, Paul's secretary. Bud is a single-minded inventor and this passage captures Paul's appreciation of Calhoun's talents and place within an historical scheme.* (*PP* 4:L20-27) Paul sometimes wondered if he wouldn't have been more content in another period of history, but the rightness of **Bud**'s being alive now was beyond question. **Bud**'s mentality was one that had been remarked upon as being peculiarly American since the nation had been born—the restless, erratic insight and imagination of a gadgeteer. This was the climax, or close to it, of generations of **Bud Calhouns**, with almost all of American industry integrated into one stupendous Rube Goldberg machine.

Calhoun is so accomplished at inventing new labor-saving devices that he invents himself and seventy-two other people out of their jobs. Faced with unemployment, Bud joins the Ghost Shirt Society and is valued for the technical expertise he provides to the fledgling revolutionaries. Paul doesn't understand Bud's involvement with the group, since **Bud** wasn't at all interested in political action and was without capacity for resentment. As **Bud** had said of himself, "All Ah want is time an' equipmen' to faht around with, and Ah'm happy as a pig in mud"(*PP* 254:L5-6). *The truth of this statement is later borne out when Bud and one of the road workers from the "Reeks and Wrecks" repair the nearly destroyed Orange-O machine, a symbol of man's growing inability to feed itself.* (*PP* 293:L1-5) The man (Bud) had been desperately unhappy then. Now he was proud and smiling because his hands were busy doing what they liked to do best, Paul supposed—replacing men like himself with machines. He hooked up the lamp behind the Orange-O sign. "There we are."

Calvary Cemetery (see also **Golgotha**). *Among the many references to Calvary Cemetery, named to commemorate the place of Christ's crucifixion, one is particularly interesting. At the close of* Deadeye Dick, *Haitian hotel chef Hippolyte Paul De Mille visits Midland City's Calvary Cemetery and resurrects the ghost of Will Fairchild, the barnstorming aviator killed when he forgot to wear his parachute. Both of Rudy's parents were buried there, as well.* (*DD* 172:L9) Father was buried in **Calvary Cemetery**, not all that far from Eloise Metzger. We buried him in a painter's smock, and with his left thumb hooked through a palette. Why not?
(*DD* 226:L20) Felix and I had run into the same sort of ignorance when it was time to bury Mother next to Father in **Calvary Cemetery**. People refused to believe that she herself wasn't radioactive. They were sure that she would make all the other bodies glow in the dark, and that she would seep into the water supply and so on.
(*DD* 235:L10) At the end of our third day in Midland City, Felix became tearful and risked the displeasure of Captain Julian Pefko by asking him if we could please, on the way to the main gate, have our purple school bus make a slight detour past **Calvary Cemetery**, so we could visit our parents grave.
(*DD* 236:L1) **Calvary Cemetery** has never been any comfort to me, so I almost stayed in the purple school bus.

Calvary Cemetery is also where Felix Waltz and Bucky Morissey went for some unatuhorized target shooting. (*DD* 60:L21-22) I wasn't about to say so, but I had some doubts at that point about the gun safety habits of Felix, and of his friend Bucky Morissey, too—the son of the chief of police. For the past couple of years, anyway, Felix and Bucky, without Father's knowledge, had been helping themselves to various weapons in the gun room, and had picked off crows perched on headstones in **Calvary Cemetery**, and had cut off telephone service to several farms by shooting insulators along the Shepherdstown Turnpike, and had blasted God-only-knows how many mailboxes all over the county, and had actually loosed a couple of rounds at a herd of sheep out near Sacred Miracle Cave.

In Breakfast of Champions, *Vonnegut writes about one particular Midland City luminary.* (*BC* 139:L21) The Bannister Memorial Fieldhouse was named in honor of George Hickman Bannister, a seventeen-year-old boy who was killed while playing high school football in 1924. George Hickman Bannister had the largest tombstone in **Calvary Cemetery**, a sixty-two-foot obelisk with a marble football on top.
(*BC* 141:L24) **Calvary Cemetery**, where George Hickman Bannister was at rest, was named in honor of a hill in Jerusalem, thousands of miles away. Many people believed that the son of the Creator of the Universe had been killed on that hill thousands of years ago.

Calvin, Ned. *One of the many ill and stricken residents of Rosewater County whose name is invoked by Diana Moon Glampers as proof of Eliot's curative powers in the hope he will remain in town.* (*GBR* 74:L6) **Ned Calvin** had that twitch in his eye since he was a little boy, and you made it stop.

Calypso. *The name of the Bokononist poems which make up most of the writings of* The Books of Bokonon, *in* Cat's Cradle.

Campbell, Archibald. *He possesses an ignominious place in Rosewater family history as recounted in* A History of the Rosewaters of Rhode Island, *by Merrihue Rosewater.* (*GBR* 163:L21) The Old World home of the Rosewaters was and is in the Scilly Islands, off Cornwall. The founder of the family there, whose name was John, arrived on St. Mary Island in 1645, with the party accompanying the fifteen-year-old Prince Charles, later to become Charles the Second, who was fleeing the puritan Revolution. The name Rosewater was then a pseudonym. Until John chose it for himself, there were no Rosewaters in England. His real name was John Graham. He was the youngest of the five sons of James Graham, Fifth Earl and First Marquis of Montrose. There was need for a pseudonym, for James Graham was a leader of the Royalist cause, and the Royalist cause was lost. James, among other romantic exploits, once disguised himself, went to the Scotch Highlands, organized a small, fierce army, and led it to six bloody victories over the far greater forces of the Lowland Presbyterian Army of **Archibald Campbell**, the Eighth Earl of Argyll. James was also a poet. So every Rosewater is in fact a Graham, and has the blood of Scotch nobility in him. James was hanged in 1650.

Campbell, Howard W., Jr. *The main character of* Mother Night *also appears in* Slaughterhouse-Five. Mother Night *is Campbell's confessional text* *which reveals a severe lack of any sincere commitment outside his "nation of two," his passionate love relationship with his wife Helga Noth. His rededication of the text is to himself,* a man who served evil too openly and good too secretly, the crime of his times (*MN* xii:L10-11).

Born an only child in Schenectady, New York, on February 16, 1912, the grandson of a Tennessee Baptist minister and the son of an engineer working for General Electric's Service Engineering Department, Campbell's family moved to Berlin, Germany, when his father was transferred by GE. Only eleven years old at the time of the move, Campbell was sent to the German public schools and became bilingual. He became a playwright—writing in German—and married German actress Helga Noth, the elder daughter of Werner Noth, Berlin's Chief of Police. In 1939 Campbell's parents left Germany when war in Europe broke out.

Prior to America's entry into World War II he was approached by Harold J. Sparrow (alias Frank Wirtanen, alias Blue Fairy Godmother) to become a secret agent for the United States. His silent agreement to pass along information was facilitated by becoming a writer and broadcaster of Nazi propaganda to the English-speaking world. I was the leading expert on American problems in the Ministry of Popular Enlightenment and Propaganda (*MN* 21:L11-14). *Campbell's method of transmitting information to the "enemy" included a series of coughs and verbal cues in his radio broadcasts. However, he never knew what information was disclosed, including the information about his own wife's death in the Crimea. Seven women who fed him information were eventually found out and executed.*

Neither a Nazi nor an American patriot, Campbell was captured by Lieutenant Bernard B. O'Hare near Hersfeld on April 12, 1945. Only President Roosevelt and Campbell's Blue Fairy Godmother knew his true identity and contribution to the war effort. (*SL5* 139:L9-11) Campbell was the inventor and commander of the unit *(The Free American Corps)*, which was supposed to fight only on the Russian front. *Since his venomous radio broadcasts made him such a widely known and hated individual, the most that could be done for him was a quiet release into the civilian sector.*

He settled in Greenwich Village and was befriended by George Kraft, a sleeper Russian agent whose real name is Iona Potapov. Kraft/Potapov arranges for Campbell's kidnapping to the Soviet Union by notifying the American Legion—and former Lieutenant O'Hare—of his whereabouts, arranging for Resi Noth's impersonation of her older sister, and encouraging Campbell to leave the country since he found his wife and would never be accepted by America. The plot is foiled when the Blue Fairy Godmother learns of Kraft's involvement.

The duplicity of the people and events in his life leads Campbell to surrender to the Israeli authorities. Unsure of his crimes against humanity, Campbell is quite convinced about his "crimes against himself." He leaves the text intimating he will commit suicide, an event confirmed by his appearance in Slaughterhouse-Five.

canary, canary-in-the-coal-mine, canary-bird-in-the-coal-mine. *Vonnegut's theory about writers acting as society's proverbial canary-in-the-coal-mine is clarified in two essays.* (*WFG* 92:L25, 28 *Address to the American Physical Society*) Many of you are physics teachers. I have been a teacher, too. I have taught creative writing. I often wondered what I thought I was doing, teaching creative writing, since the demand for creative writers is very small in this vale of tears. I was perplexed as to what the usefulness of any of the arts might be, with the possible exception of interior decoration. The most positive notion I could come up with was what I call the **canary-in-the-coal-mine** theory of the arts. This theory argues that artists are useful to society because they are so sensitive. They are supersensitive. They keel over like **canaries** in coal mines filled with poison gas, long before more robust types realize that any danger is there.
(*WFG* 238:L18 *Playboy Interview*) PLAYBOY: What *is* in control?
VONNEGUT: Mankind's wish to improve itself.
PLAYBOY: In a Darwinian sense?
VONNEGUT: I'm not very grateful for Darwin, although suspect he was right. His ideas make people crueler. . . . But forget Darwin. Writers are specialized cells doing whatever we do, and we're expressions of the entire society—just a the sensory cells on the surface of your body are in the service of your body as a whole. And when a society is in great danger, we're likely to sound the alarms. I have the **canary-bird-in-the-coal-mine** theory of the arts. You know, coal miners used to take birds down into the mines with them to detect gas before men got sick. The artists certainly did that in the case of Vietnam. The chirped and keeled over. But it made no difference whatsoever. Nobody important cared. But I continue to think that artists—all artists—should be treasured as alarm systems. *See also:* *ST* 177:L9; *WFG* 76:L4.

Canby, Sarah Horne. *The author of the fourth most popular book in the days of the chrono-synclastic infundibula. The text is a children's book entitled* Unk and Boaz in the Caves of Mercury. (*ST* 197:L9-13) The publisher's bland analysis of **Mrs. Canby**'s book's success appears on the dust jacket: "What child wouldn't like to be shipwrecked on a space ship with a cargo of hamburgers, hot dogs, catsup, sporting goods, and soda pop?"

Capone, Al. (*BC* 229:L19) As it happened, the only other person in the lobby at the time was the beautiful young desk clerk, Milo Maritimo. . . . He was the homosexual grandson of Guillermo "Little Willie" Maritimo, a bodyguard of the notorious Chicago gangster, **Al Capone**.
(*JB* 178:L24) **Al Capone**, the famous Chicago gangster, thought Sacco and Vanzetti should have been executed. He, too, believed that they were enemies of the American way of thinking about America. He was offended by how ungrateful to America these fellow Italian immigrants were.

Carlsbad Caverns (also **cavern**). *The home of EPICAC, the computer which controls the industrial output of society in* Player Piano. *(In "EPICAC" the short story, the computer is housed in on the fourth floor of the physics building of Wyandotte College.)* (*PP* 8:L20) Shepherd, who was sick today, would then set the controls for a new batch of refrigerator backs—however many backs EPICAC, a computing machine in **Carlsbad Caverns**, felt the economy could absorb.
(*PP* 100:L2, 6) THE SHAH OF BRATPUHR, looking as tiny and elegant as a snuffbox in one end of the vast **cavern**, handed the *Sumklish* bottle back to Khashdrahr Miasma. He sneezed, having left the heat of summer above a moment before, and the sound chattered along the walls to die whispering in bat roosts deep in **Carlsbad Caverns**.
(*PP* 102:L8) Through the war, and through the postwar years to the present, EPICAC's nervous system had been extended outward through **Carlsbad Caverns**—intelligence bought by the foot and pound and kilowatt.
(*PP* 105:L6) The Shah dropped to his knees on the platform and raised his hands over his head. The small, brown man suddenly seemed to fill the entire **cavern** with his mysterious, radiant dignity, alone there on the platform, communing with a presence no one else could sense.
(*PP* 106:L19) President Lynn squinted at the **cavern** roof thoughtfully.
(*PP* 139:L4) The request *(the Shah of Bratpuhr had asked to visit "the home of a typical* Takaru, *". . . . an "average man.")* had been made as they were passing through Chicago from **Carlsbad Caverns**, and Halyard had stopped off at the local personnel office for the name of a representative American in the neighborhood.
(*PP* 175:L13-14) The letter, from the personnel officer of the State Department, had pursued him from New York to Utica to Niagara Falls to Camp Drum to Indianapolis to St. Louis to Fort Riley to Houston to Hollywood to the Grand Canyon to **Carlsbad Caverns** to Hanford to Chicago to Miami Beach.

In Slaughterhouse-Five, *Billy Pilgrim time-trips to his family's excursion to the famous caverns, a terrifying experience during which he feared the ceiling would fall in.* (*SL5* 77:L17, 19) And Billy took a very short trip through time, made a peewee jump of only ten days, so he was still twelve, still touring the West with his family. Now they were down in **Carlsbad Caverns**, and Billy was praying to God to get him out of there before the ceiling fell in.

A ranger was explaining that the **Caverns** had been discovered by a cowboy who saw a huge cloud of bats come out of a hole in the ground.

Carlsbad Caverns is also a suspected hideout for Professor Barnhouse in the short story bearing his name. (*MH* 168:L10 *Report on the Barnhouse Effect*) During last week alone, three publications carried articles proving variously that he was hiding in an Inca ruin in the Andes, in the sewers of Paris, and in the unexplored lower chambers of **Carlsbad Caverns**.

In Jailbird, *Mary Kathleen O'Looney's hideaway is in the great subbasements of Grand Central Station. Walter Starbuck recalls that* Mary

Kathleen opened the iron door on an iron staircase going down, down, down. There was a secret world as vast as **Carlsbad Caverns** below. It was used for nothing anymore. It might have been a sanctuary for dinosaurs. It had in fact been a repair shop for another family of extinct monsters—locomotives driven by steam (*JB* 145:L12).
(*JB* 212:L13) His voice came to me as though from the place where I was going next, the great **cavern** under Grand Central Station. "No problem," he said.
(*JB* 213:L3) The next thing I knew, I, all alone, having made certain that no one was following me, was descending the iron staircase into the **cavern**.
(*Gal* 13:L10) Darwin continued: "The entire surface. . . . seems to have been permeated, like a sieve, by the subterranean vapours: here and there the lava, whilst soft, had been blown into great bubbles; and in other parts, the tops of **caverns** similarly formed have fallen in, leaving circular parts with steep sides."

The Carlyle Hotel. *A RAMJAC hotel in* Jailbird.

Caroline. *In the short story "The Hyannis Port Story," a "Caroline" is a waffle with a scoop of ice cream served at the First Family Waffle Shop.*

Caroline Islands. *In the short story "Report on the Barnhouse Effect," 120 target ships are towed to the islands as part of Operation Brainstorm, a test of Professor Barnhouse's dynamopsychic abilities.*

Carpathia. *The title of the novel by Felicia Tarkington, youngest daughter of Aaron Tarkington,* about a headstrong, high-born young woman in the Mohiga Valley who fell in love with a half-Indian lock-tender on that same canal (*HP* 21:L19-21), *the Onondaga Canal.*

Carroll, Madeleine. *The movie actress with whom Rabo Karabekian compares his first impressions of Marilee Kemp.* (*Blue* 148:L3) One thing, surely, which prevented my being effusive, was my sense of my own homeliness and powerlessness and virginity. I was unworthy of her, since she was as beautiful as **Madeleine Carroll**, the most beautiful of all movie stars. *When Rabo later establishes himself as a working artist he has an opportunity to use his photo-realistic painting skills to portray the actress stepping from a Cord automobile in front of the ocean liner* Normandie.

Carson, Johnny. *In* Galápagos, *the Tonight Show host interviews Captain von Kleist and finds out that according to the captain, the Ecuadorian navy has four submarines which never surface and maintain constant radio silence.*

Carter, Clyde and Claudia. *Clyde is the guard who befriends Walter Starbuck at the Finletter federal prison.* (*JB* 6:L17-29) The guard's name was

Clyde Carter. He was one of the few friends I had made in prison. Our chief bond was that we had taken the same correspondence course in bartending from a diploma mill in Chicago, The Illinois Institute of Instruction, a division of The RAMJAC Corporation. On the same day and in the same mail each of us had received his Doctor of Mixology degree. **Clyde** had then surpassed me by taking the school's course in air conditioning, as well. **Clyde** was a third cousin to the President of the United States, Jimmy Carter. He was about five years younger than the President, but was otherwise his perfect spit and image. He had the same nice manners, the same bright smile. *His friendship with Starbuck was rewarded by Mary Kathleen O'Looney with a vice-presidency of the Chrysler Air Temp Division of RAMJAC. He and Leland Clewes chip in for the chess-playing computer Boris as a going away gift for Starbuck, due to return to prison. Aside from briefly mentioning Claudia's presence, there is no description of her.*

Carver, George Washington/George Washington Carver High School. *The second high school built in Midland City after World War II intended to serve mostly the black population. As a character in his own text, Vonnegut makes a mental note to explain to Kilgore Trout the significance of the high school jackets he will see in the emergency room of the hospital after Dwayne Hoover went on a rampage.* (*BC* 250:L9-10) And when another Nigger high school was built after the Second World War, it was named after **George Washington Carver**, a black man who was born into slavery, but who became a famous chemist anyway. He discovered many remarkable new uses for peanuts.

But the black people wouldn't call that school by its proper name, either. On the day it opened, there were already young black people wearing jackets *with the inscription "Peanut University" on their backs.*

Casa Mona. *The one hotel on San Lorenzo owned by Philip Castle and named in honor of Mona Aamons Monzano. H. Lowe Crosby derisively called it "The Pissant Hilton" before demanding quarters in the American embassy. John/Jonah recalls:* My room was a pleasant one. It faced, as did all the rooms, the Boulevard of the Hundred Martyrs to Democracy, Monzano Airport, and Bolivar harbor beyond. The **Casa Mona** was built like a bookcase, with solid sides and back and with a front of blue-green glass. The squalor and misery of the city, being to the sides and back of the **Casa Mona**, were impossible to see.

My room was air-conditioned. It was almost chilly. And, coming from the blamming heat into that chilliness, I sneezed.

There were fresh Bowers on my bedside table, but my bed had not yet been made. There wasn't even a pillow on the bed. There was simply a bare, brand-new Beautyrest mattress. And there weren't any coat hangers in the closet; and there wasn't any toilet paper in the bathroom (*CC* 131:1-14).

When John/Jonah meets Bokonon at the end of the novel, the prophet is wearing a blue and white bedspread imprinted with the words "Casa Mona."

Casey, Dwight. *The Tarkington College English teacher who hated his department chair so much that when Eugene Debs Hartke is fired from his physics position, he asks the board for a transfer to fill the slot. That allowed Muriel Peck to take Casey's position and she subsequently died during the prison break. Casey's own fortunes were quite different.* (*HP* 248:L21-24, 249:L1-4) **Dwight Casey** is still alive, I think. His wife came into a great deal of money soon after he replaced me. He quit at the end of the academic year and moved to the south of France.

His wife's family was big in the Mafia. She could have taught but didn't. She had a Master's Degree in Political Science from Rutgers. All he had was a BS in Hotel Management from Cornell.

Castle, Dr. Julian. *John/Jonah's original focus for the magazine article that took him to San Lorenzo was sixty-year-old Dr. Julian Castle,* an American sugar millionaire who had, at the age of forty, followed the example of Dr. Albert Schweitzer by founding a free hospital in a jungle, by devoting his life to miserable folk of another race.

Castle's hospital was called the House of Hope and Mercy in the Jungle. Its jungle was on San Lorenzo, among the wild coffee trees on the northern slope of Mount McCabe. . . .

In his selfish days he had been as familiar to tabloid readers as Tommy Manville, Adolf Hitler, Benito Mussolini, and Barbara Hutton. His fame had rested on lechery, alcoholism, reckless driving, and draft evasion. He had had a dazzling talent for spending millions without increasing mankind's stores of anything but chagrin (*CC* 76:L4-11, 15-20).

As a draft dodger residing in Portugal during World War II, he met Finnish architect Nestor Aamons and invited him on his journey to San Lorenzo to design the House of Hope and Mercy in the Jungle.

Upon first meeting him years later, John/Jonah notes that, **Castle** wore a baggy white linen suit and a string tie. He had a scraggly mustache. He was bald. He was scrawny. He was a saint, I think (*CC* 138:L3-5). *He runs the hospital by relying on aspirin and boko-maru, and he provides this analysis of just how and why Bokononism works,* when it became evident that no governmental or economic reform was going to make the people much less miserable, the religion became the one real instrument of hope. Truth was the enemy of the people, because the truth was so terrible, so Bokonon made it his business to provide the people with better and better lies (*CC* 143:L2-7). *His one offspring is Philip Castle.*

Castle, Dr. Morris N. *The physician on Mars who serves as the Director of Mental Health, responsible for wiping out the memory of new recruits. He is proud to make the pronouncement that* "We can make the center of a man's memory virtually as sterile as a scalpel fresh from the autoclave. But grains of new experience begin to accumulate on it at once. These grains in turn form themselves into patterns not necessarily favorable to military thinking.

Unfortunately, this problem of recontamination seems insoluble" (*ST* 106:L1-7).

Castle, Philip. *The son of Julian Castle, the great-grandson of the founder of Castle Sugar, and the manager and owner of Casa Mona, San Lorenzo's one hotel, as well as Castle Transportation, Inc.*, a hearselike 1939 Chrysler limousine with jump seats (*CC* 124:L8-9). *Philip authored the text* San Lorenzo: The Land, the History, the People. *The text chronicled the role Castle Sugar had on the island as well as the impact brought about by Bokonon's appearance.*

Castle Sugar, Incorporated. *The multinational corporation owned by millionaire Julian Castle, who also built the House of Hope and Mercy in the Jungle. The San Lorenzo branch was opened in 1916 by Julian's grandfather who sought to capitalize on the sugar demands brought about by World War I. When Bokonon and McCabe arrived on the island in 1922, anything worth owning on San Lorenzo was owned either by the Catholic Church or Castle Sugar. As Bokonon says in his calypsos,* "Oh, a very sorry people, yes, / Did I find here. / Oh, they had no music, / And they had no beer. / And, oh, everywhere / Where they tried to perch/ Belonged to Castle Sugar, Incorporated, / Or the Catholic church" (*CC* 106:L7-14).

The brutal imperialism wielded by Castle Sugar at its zenith is further elaborated by Philip Castle in San Lorenzo: The Land, the History, the People, "The form of government was anarchy, save in limited situations wherein **Castle Sugar** wanted to own something or to get something done. In such situations the form of government was feudalism. The nobility was composed of **Castle Sugar**'s plantation bosses, who were heavily armed white men from the outside world. The knighthood was composed of big natives who, for small gifts and silly privileges, would kill or wound or torture on command. The spiritual needs of the people caught in this demoniacal squirrel cage were taken care of by a handful of butterball priests." (*CC* 106:L25-34).

catacombs. (*CC* 113:L10-11) When Johnson and McCabe came upon the city, it was built of twigs, tin, crates, and mud—rested on the **catacombs** of a trillion happy scavengers, **catacombs** in a sour mash of slop, feculence, and slime.

(*SL5* 186:L7) Somewhere in there the poor old high school teacher, Edgar Derby, was caught with a teapot he had taken from the **catacombs**. He was arrested for plundering. He was tried and shot.

(*JB* 122:L5) Little did I dream that I would soon be scuttling through the **catacombs** beneath the station, and that I would learn the secret purpose of The RAMJAC Corporation down there.

(*JB* 146:L16) And then out of the **catacombs** we climbed. *(Mary Kathleen O'Looney and Walter Starbuck exiting Grand Central Station.)*

(*FWD* 162:L14) "I will say that you *(Unitarian Universalists)*, in terms of numbers, power, and influence, and your spiritual differences with the general population, are analogous to the earliest Christians in the **catacombs** under Imperial Rome. I hasten to add that your hardships are not the same, nor are you in any danger. Nobody in the power structure thinks children of the Age of Reason amount to a hill of beans. That is the extent of your discomfort. That sure beats being crucified upside down or being fed to the carnivorous menagerie at the Circus Maximus.
(*FWD* 163:L26) "When I say that the Unitarian Universalists, the people who know pure baloney when they hear it, are something like the early Christians in the **catacombs**, am I suggesting that contempt for baloney will someday be as widespread as Christianity is today? Well the example of Christianity is not encouraging, actually, since it was nothing but a poor people's religion, a servant's religion, a slave's religion, a woman's religion, a child's religion, and would have remained such if it hadn't stopped taking the Sermon on the Mount seriously and joined forces with the vain and rich and violent. I can't imagine that you would want to do that, to give up everything you believe in order to play a bigger part in world history."

Cathcart, Sally. *The dim-witted Judy Garland look-alike cheerleader and girlfriend of Jerry Rivers, president of the student body, in the play "The Chemistry Professor." She doubles as the streetwalker in the "Dr. Jekyll" play-within-the-play.*

Cathedral of Whispers (see **Sacred Miracle Cave**).

Cat's Cradle (1963) (see also **John/Jonah**). *Vonnegut's first three novels are principally concerned with the psychological hardships endured by pivotal characters whose fates are largely determined by the compelling tug of historical and cosmic forces. In the name of the ruling governmental technocracy, Kroner and Baer* (Player Piano) *dissociate Paul Proteus from his father's legacy. He, in turn, is forced to stage his own turnabout in an attempt to establish a moral foundation for civilizing communal activities among men—one more significant than simply facilitating technological and economic "progress." The compounding of governmental and industrial power is seen as inevitable evolution as man develops a community based on manufacturing efficiency and national security. The historical precedents in* Player Piano *(especially the Ghost Shirt Society) provide an understanding of the eternal conflicts which Vonnegut works out on a more global scale. The conflict is predetermined; the future is captive to the past's inertia.*

In The Sirens of Titan, *Vonnegut validates the captivity of the future to an historical past by creating the chrono-synclastic infundibulum. While Winston Niles Rumfoord is split in time and simultaneously inhabits two points in space, Malachi Constant, subject to the designs of Tralfamadore, is forced to assume three different identities. The destiny of man is at the mercy of powers unseen, poorly understood, and forever in motion.*

Vonnegut continues his emphasis on the individual's response to the competing and compelling historical forces in Mother Night. "Tell them the things a man does to stay alive" *expresses in simple terms Arpad Kovacs' intuitive grasp of how to survive the eternal chain of conflict which brings out the ambiguous dichotomies of nearly every character in the novel. The "things" necessary for survival turn out to be deeds perpetrated after a retreat from conditions which induce a form of schizophrenia.*

The endings of all three novels dwell on individuals' final responses to their environment. Proteus weighs the historical record and decides to paint his identity with the broad mythologizing (obfuscating) brush of the revolutionary; Constant is delivered to his eternal rest under the hypnotically induced benign delusion that he is under the protective care of the murdered Stony Stevenson; Howard Campbell's despondency for crimes committed against himself (that is, for his failure to do what no one else had been capable of doing—acting without pretension or deception) brings him to the brink of suicide.

Vonnegut shifts the emphasis in Cat's Cradle *from pivotal characters whose impact on each tale is profoundly impotent in its repercussions, to the writer as naive observer, waiting for a grossly ironic illumination to describe the nature of human endeavor. John/Jonah's attempt to write* The Day the World Ended *is a naive, unselfconscious search for dissociative symptoms among those scientists who shaped the great physical (therefore political) forces which brought World War II to a close. John was looking for the ironical backyard barbecue on the day Hiroshima was roasted. His literary search for the compelling irony of man's deeds and home life is a search for the more obviously "schizophrenic." Though relinquishing his original research into the men behind "the bomb," John discovers the roots of human conflict on the island of San Lorenzo, where artificial factions among men are created by necessarily dissociative types attempting to promote a new communal order. The discomforting truths and lies of Bokononism reveal the schizophrenia of all creative—and destructive—elements in society.*

Whereas Mother Night *chronicles the crippling effects of schizophrenia as the sole method of survival,* Cat's Cradle *bares the civilizing influence as nothing more than a grander manifestation of the same dissociative symptoms. This leaves John/Jonah in a cataleptic trance analogous to that of Howard Campbell but with one major difference. Declining any consideration of suicide, John's trance is manifested in the narrative by use of "∴" before each chapter. This symbol is the mathematical expression meaning "therefore." Since ∴ is the first word of the text (along with every chapter), the effect creates a spherical closure of the narrative placing the end of the world (after ice-nine) at the beginning. The recapitulation of the tale as the logical outcome of the events contained therein establishes a time-looped scenario with the finite boundaries similar to Billy Pilgrim's journey. The narrative-in-the-round is another manifestation of Vonnegut's structured moment theory.*

John's destiny is to be a chronicler of the events which unfold (have already unfolded) in the text. As he says shortly before the opening . . . . . . somebody or something has compelled me to be certain places at certain time, without fail. Conveyances and motives, both conventional and bizarre, have been provided. And, according to plan, at each appointed second, at each appointed place this Jonah was there (*CC* 13:L6-10).

John's preface to the story results from his meeting with Bokonon at the close of the novel. As the fate of the Earth becomes enveloped in ice-nine, staggered by his knowledge of the people behind this latest apocalypse, John cries out at his inability to place himself within the current of events. (*CC* 230:L15-20) "Here it is, the end of the world; and here I am, almost the very last man; and there it is, the highest mountain in sight. I know now what my *karass* has been up to, Newt. It's been working night and day for maybe half a million years to get me up that mountain." I wagged my head and nearly wept. "But what, for the love of God, is supposed to be in my hands?"

His question is quickly answered by Bokonon, who tells him that "If I were a younger man, I would write a history of human stupidity." (*CC* 231:L15-16) *It is at this point Vonnegut has John make the crossover from witness to reporter-with-a-cause. (It could be argued that Vonnegut's Dresden experience turned him into a writer with a cause: discounting any faith in man-made establishments of peace, avoiding any belief in a beneficent supernatural being paternalistically caring for man's eternity both on Earth and in heaven.)*

Wishing to reorganize the communal (primarily economic) relationships among men, Bokonon and McCabe help establish Vonnegut's premise that the foundations of power are schizophrenically conceived. Exposing this symbiosis is John's task. Before Cat's Cradle, *Vonnegut saw schizophrenia as a learned survival skill among those who became tossed by the great entropizing forces (nationalism/ethnocentrism) in our century. Part of* Cat's Cradle*'s importance is that Vonnegut characterizes the formation of power (both religious and political) as an act requiring dissociation.*

Though John journeys to San Lorenzo to write a travel piece, what he finds is a society structurally assembled on the principle of "dynamic tensions": bodybuilding entrepreneur Charles Atlas' theory that muscles could be built by pitting one set of muscles against another without the use of bar bells or spring exercisers. It was the belief of Bokonon that good societies could be built only by pitting good against evil, and by keeping the tension between the two high at all times (*CC* 90:L6-8).

The culmination of John's revelations is that schizophrenia is the engine of activity (both creative and destructive): that the nature of power is schizophrenic, and that schizophrenia is the revealed state of powerful forces. Bokonon's appearance in the final chapter draws to a close The Books of Bokonon *with this:* If I were a younger man, I would write a history of human stupidity; and I would climb to the top of Mount McCabe and lie down on my back with my history for a pillow; and I would take from the ground some of the blue-white poison that makes statues of men; and I would make a statue of myself, lying on my back, grinning horribly, and thumbing my nose at You Know Who (*CC* 231:L15-21).

Striking such a theatrical pose for posterity may seem comical, but it is the measure of a refined vision gained at great personal expense. As Bokonon had written earlier, "Maturity. . . . is a bitter disappointment for which no remedy exists, unless laughter can be said to remedy anything" (*CC* 162:L23-26). *The history he advises John (and any other Bokononists) to write is one which would deny the cosmic paternalism of religion and, by implication, and benevolent paternalistic constructions designed by man. This is precisely the history John had been writing all along.*

Together with Bokonon's closing directive, John's revelation brings about a poised state of insight and impotence which is expressed by the cataleptic "∴". Stuck in his moment of time, his lot in life has been and forever will be to delineate the ambiguous explanations concerning the nature of power and the whimsy of science that forms—and takes—life. The narrative is the revelation of the naive journalist confronted by the awful truths—and lies—about the establishment of power and the motivations of communal man. As it turns out, man is seen as reactive, unable to create goodness without a corresponding evil.

Vonnegut recalls the essence of the novel's plot and the genesis for its idea in Wampeters, Foma & Granfalloons *and* Palm Sunday. (*WFG* 96:L9-33, 97:L1-22 *Address to the American Physical Society*) It is about an old-fashioned scientist who isn't interested in people. In the midst of a terrible family argument, he asks a question about turtles. Nobody has been talking about turtles. But the old man suddenly wants to know: When turtles put in their heads, do their spines buckle or contract?

This absentminded old man, who doesn't give a damn for people, discovers a form of ice which is stable at room temperature. He dies, and some idiots get possession of the substance, which I call Ice-9. The idiots eventually drop some of the stuff into the sea, and the waters of the earth freeze—and that is the end of life on earth as we know it.

I got this lovely idea while I was working as a public relations man at General Electric. I used to write publicity releases about the research laboratory there, where my brother worked. While there, I heard a story about a visit H. G. Wells had made to the laboratory in the early Thirties.

General Electric was alarmed by the news of his coming, because they did not know how to entertain him. The company told Irving Langmuir, who was a most important man in Schenectady, the only Nobel Prize winner in private industry, that he was going to have to entertain Wells. Langmuir didn't want to do it, but he dutifully tried to imagine diversions that would delight Mr. Wells. He made up a science-fiction story he hoped Mr. Wells would want to write. It was about a form of ice which was stable at room temperature. Mr. Wells was not stimulated by the story. He later died, and so did Langmuir. After Langmuir died, I thought to myself, well, I think maybe I'll write a story. While I was writing that story about Ice-9, I happened to go to a cocktail party where I was introduced to a crystallographer. I told him about this ice which was stable at room temperature. He put his cocktail glass on the mantelpiece. He sat down in an easy chair in the corner. He did not speak to anyone or change expression for half an hour. Then he got up, came back over to the mantelpiece, and picked up his cocktail glass, and he said to me, "Nope." Ice-9 was impossible.

Be that as it may, other scientific developments have been almost that horrible. The idea of Ice-9 had a certain moral validity at any rate, even though scientifically it had to be pure bunk.

(*PS* 101:L16, 26; 102:L2 *Self-Interview*) INTERVIEWER: Did the study of anthropology later color your writings?

VONNEGUT: It confirmed my atheism, which was the faith of my fathers anyway. Religions were exhibited and studied as the Rube Goldberg inventions I'd always thought they were. We weren't allowed to find one culture superior to any other. We caught hell if we mentioned races much. It was highly idealistic.

INTERVIEWER: Almost a religion?

VONNEGUT: Exactly. And the only one for me. So far.

INTERVIEWER: What was your dissertation?

VONNEGUT: ***Cat's Cradle***.

INTERVIEWER: But you wrote that years after you left Chicago, didn't you?

VONNEGUT: I left Chicago without writing a dissertation—and without a degree. All my ideas for dissertations had been rejected, and I was broke, so I took a job as a P.R. man for General Electric in Schenectady. Twenty years later, I got a letter from a new dean at Chicago, who had been looking through my dossier. Under the rules of the university, he said, a published work of high quality could be substituted for a dissertation, so I was entitled to an M.A. He had shown ***Cat's Cradle*** to the Anthropology Department, and they had said it was halfway decent anthropology, so they were mailing me my degree. I'm Class of 1972 or so. . . .

INTERVIEWER: Some of the characters in ***Cat's Cradle*** were based on people you knew at G.E., isn't that so?

VONNEGUT: Dr. Felix Hoenikker, the absent-minded scientist, was a caricature of Dr. Irving Langmuir, the star of the G.E. Research Laboratory. I knew him some. My brother worked with him. Langmuir was wonderfully absent-minded. He wondered out loud one time whether, when turtles pulled in their heads, their spines buckled or contracted. I put that in the book. One time he left a tip under his plate after his wife served him breakfast at home. I put that in. His most important contribution, though, was the idea for what I called "Ice-9," a form of frozen water that was stable at room temperature. He didn't tell it directly to me. It was a legend around the Laboratory about the time H.G. Wells came to Schenectady. That was long before my time. I

was just a little boy when it happened—listening to the radio, building model airplanes.
INTERVIEWER: Yes?
VONNEGUT: Anyway—Wells came to Schenectady, and Langmuir was told to be his host. Langmuir thought he might entertain Wells with an idea for a science-fiction story—about a form of ice that was stable at room temperature. Wells was uninterested, or at least never used the idea. And then Wells died, and then, finally, Langmuir died. I thought to myself: "Finders, keepers—the idea is mine." Langmuir, incidentally, was the first scientist in private industry to win a Nobel Prize.

The title is also the central image of this apocalyptic novel. Early in the text Dr. Felix Hoenikker takes the string from a manuscript, makes the traditional cat's cradle string formation, and tries to convince Newt that he should see the cradle where the little cat sleeps. Later, in the cave beneath the waterfall on San Lorenzo, Newt explains to John/Jonah that his mostly black abstract painting is a cat's cradle. (*CC* 137:L15-33) "Hello," I said. "I like your painting."

"You see what it is?"

"I suppose it means something different to everyone who sees it."

"It's a **cat's cradle**."

"Aha," I said. "Very good. The scratches are string. Right?"

"One of the oldest games there is, **cat's cradle**. Even the Eskimos know it."

"You don't say."

"For maybe a hundred thousand years or more, grownups have been waving tangles of string in their children's faces."

"Um."

Newt remained curled in the chair. He held out his painty hands as though a **cat's cradle** were strung between them. "No wonder kids grow up crazy. A **cat's cradle** is nothing but a bunch of X's between somebody's hands, and little kids look and look and look at all those X's.

"And?"

"No damn cat, and no damn cradle."

cave, cave dweller. *Along with basements, subbasements, and underground meatlockers, caves have a prominent role to play in many of Vonnegut's tales. Sirens of Titan has two distinctive references. The first is the description of Malachi Constant's physical appearance, which is repeated by Vonnegut when describing Malachi's new incarnation as Unk.* (*ST* 17:L15) The freshening sea breeze ruffled Constant's blue-black hair. He was a well-made man—a light heavyweight, dark-skinned, with poet's lips, with soft brown eyes in the shaded **caves** of a Cro-Magnon brow-ridge. He was thirty-one.
(*ST* 98:L25) Unk was a well-made man—a light heavyweight, dark-skinned, with poet's lips, with soft brown eyes in the shaded **caves** of a Cro-Magnon brow ridge. Incipient baldness had isolated a dramatic scalplock. *The second*

reference is a major plot element. Winston Niles Rumfoord arranged to strand Unk and Boaz in the caves of Mercury for three years as part of the grand Tralfamadorian scheme to deliver a crucial replacement part for Salo's spaceship. While Unk struggles to discover a way out of the caves, Boaz becomes entranced by the ever-present Harmoniums. (*ST* 184:chapter preface) The harmonium is a **cave-dweller**. A more gracious creature would be hard to imagine. *—A Child's Cyclopedia of Wonders and Things to Do.*

(*ST* 185:L3, 8, 11, 13, 15, 21) There are creatures *(Harmoniums)* in the deep **caves** of Mercury. . . . The creatures cling to the singing walls of their **caves**. . . . The **caves** of Mercury are cozily warm in their depths. . . . The walls of the **caves** in their depths are phosphorescent. They give off a jonquil-yellow light. . . . The creatures in the **caves** are translucent. When they cling to the walls, light from the phosphorescent walls comes right through them. The yellow light from the walls, however, is turned, when passed through the bodies of the creatures, to a vivid aquamarine. . . . The creatures in the **caves** look very much like small and spineless kites. They are diamond-shaped, a foot high and eight inches wide when fully mature. *Rumfoord arranged the colorful and translucent Harmoniums to spell out various messages to the trapped pair. He finally reveals the secret to their escape, which has them turn the ship upside down to take advantage of the unique one-way sensors in the ship's navigational system.* (*ST* 211:L15,19) Thanks to a power winch and the feeble tug of gravity in the **caves** of Mercury, Unk had the ship turned over by the time Boaz got back. All that remained to be done for the trip out was to press the *on* button. The upside-down ship would then blunder against the **cave** floor, give up, retreat from the floor under the impression that the floor was a ceiling.

In Cat's Cradle, *Franklin Hoenikker has a house beneath a waterfall and it is here that he offers narrator John/Jonah the presidency of San Lorenzo.* (*CC* 159:L32) So we went down steps cut into a cliff and into a natural **cave** that was beneath and behind the waterfall.

(*CC* 164:L12) And here, by God, was Secret Agent X-9, a Major General, offering to make me king. . . . in a **cave** that was curtained by a tropical waterfall. *After ice-nine is released on the world, the cave takes on a new appearance.*

(*CC* 222:L2) They took me to what was left of Franklin Hoenikker's house at the head of the waterfall. What remained was the **cave** under the waterfall, which had become a sort of igloo under a translucent, blue-white dome of *ice-nine*.

In the short story "Next Door," Vonnegut draws on the image of a cave to describe the fearfulness of the young hero. (*MH* 118:L19, 24 *Next Door*) Paul ran back into his apartment, jumped into bed, and pulled the covers up over his head. In the hot, dark **cave** of the bed, he cried because he and All-Night Sam had helped to kill a man. . . . Numb, Paul crept out of the hot, dark **cave**, and answered the door. Just as he did, the door across the hall opened, and there stood Mr. Harger, haggard but whole.

Sacred Miracle Cave occupies a good deal of Dwayne Hoover's attention in Breakfast of Champions. (*BC* 113:L25, 30) The **cave** was Sacred Miracle **cave**, a tourist trap just south of Shepherdstown, which Dwayne owned in partnership with Lyle and Kyle *(Dwayne's younger twin stepbrothers)*. . . . who lived in identical yellow ranch houses on either side of the gift shop which sheltered the entrance to the **cave**.
(*BC* 116:L12, 19) The underground stream which passed through the bowels of Sacred Miracle **Cave** was polluted by some sort of industrial waste which formed bubbles as tough as ping-pong balls. . . . The bubbles would soon engulf *Moby Dick* and invade the *Cathedral of Whispers*, which was the main attraction at the **cave**.

Vonnegut returns to cave imagery as part of another physical description with much the same harshness he employed in Sirens of Titan. (*Slap* 87:L17) I still remember what an ear, nose and throat specialist said when he looked up into Eliza's enormous sinus cavities with a flashlight. "My God, nurse— he said, "call up the National Geographic Society. We have just discovered a new entrance to Mammoth **Cave**!"

Sacred Miracle Cave makes its return in Deadeye Dick. *Felix Waltz and Bucky Morissey* had been helping themselves to various weapons in the gun room, . . . and had actually loosed a couple of rounds at a herd of sheep out near Sacred Miracle **Cave** (*DD* 60:L27). *Since the cave is outside the immediate blast area of ground zero (Midland City), Rudy and Felix Waltz and Hippolyte Paul de Mille stay at the Quality Motor Court nearby Sacred Miracle Cave.*

In Bluebeard, *Rabo Karabekian combines two of Vonnegut's favorite themes, anthropology and the arts.* (*Blue* 76:L8) I think that *(one's natural talents for story-telling, singing, dancing, etc.)* could go back to the time when people had to live in small groups of relatives.... And evolution or God or whatever arranged things genetically, to keep the little families going, to cheer them up, so that they could all have somebody to tell stories around the campfire at night, and somebody else to paint pictures on the walls of the **caves**, and somebody else who wasn't afraid of anything and so on.
(*Blue* 265:L8) If I'd lived ten thousand years ago, I might have wowed the **cave dwellers** of Lascaux, France—whose standards for draughtsmanship must have been on about the same level as those of San Ignacio.

Eugene Debs Hartke and his father are shamed into defeat at the hands of Mary Alice French, whose crystallography exhibit stole the Cleveland Science Fair. (*HP* 47:L4) As it happened, she too had an exhibit about crystallography. She, however, had either grown her own or gathered specimens herself from creek beds and **caves** and coal mines within 100 kilometers of her home. *See also: ST* 187:L71; 190:L23; 193:L19,24; 194:L11,21; 196:L23; 197:L7,31; 198:L12; 200:L26; 205:L12,19; 206:L29-30; 207:L1; 208:L4,23,37; 209:L2; 211:L13; 214:L11; 252:L20; 258:L25; 288:L29; 296:L14; *CC* 160:L1,4,6; 162:L203; 165:L1; 166:L30; 225:L32; 227:L28; *BC* 113:L22,33; 116:L3,26; 117:L29; 118:L1,6,11; 150:graphic;

172:graphic; 176:L14-15; 186:graphic; 187:L1; 198:L9; 227:L33; 270:L10; *DD* 230:L32; 233:L24; *Blue* 78:L5.

Caz-ma-cas-ma. *One of the many names for the city of Bolivar on the island of San Lorenzo, in* Cat's Cradle.

Cedar Tavern. *An popular bar with artists in New York City, and the place where Rabo Karabekian hung out with Jackson Pollock and Terry Kitchen. Collectively, they were known as the "Three Musketeers"* (*Blue* 150:L33).

Céline, Louis-Ferdinand. *Vonnegut makes frequent reference to Louis-Ferdinand Céline (the pseudonym for Louis-Ferdinand Destouches). One of the two books Vonnegut took to read on the trip to Dresden in preparation for writing* Slaughterhouse-Five *was Erika Ostrovsky's* Céline and His Vision. (*SL5* 18:L23) **Céline** was a brave French soldier in the First World War—until his skull was cracked. After that he couldn't sleep, and there were noises in his head. He became a doctor, and he treated poor people in the daytime, and he wrote grotesque novels all night. No art is possible without a dance with death, he wrote.

The truth is death, he wrote. *I've fought nicely against it as long as I could . . . danced with it, festooned it, waltzed it around decorated it with streamers, titillated it. . .*

(*WFG* 218L:L12-27 *Address at Rededication of Wheaton College Library, 1973*) About good and evil again—and your library. The books and the films and the records and the tapes and the pictures you have in there have come from the best part of human beings who have often, in real life, been contemptible in many ways. The best example I know of goodness from vileness is the body of humane writing produced by **Louis-Ferdinand Céline**, a French physician and novelist, who was a convicted war criminal after World War Two. **Louis-Ferdinand Céline** was his pen name. His real name was Louis-Ferdinand Destouches. He was the son of poor people. He spent most of his adult life as a badly paid physician who treated the poor. I read his early novels without knowing anything about his vicious anti-Semitism. He kept it out of his early books. The internal evidence of those books persuaded me, and many others, too, that I was in the presence of a great man.

(*PS* 106:L *Self-Interview*) VONNEGUT: I have other things *(than love)* I want to talk about. Ralph Ellison did the same thing in *Invisible Man*. If the hero in that magnificent book had found somebody worth loving, somebody who was crazy about him, that would have been the end of the story. **Céline** did the same thing in *Journey to the End of the Night:* He excluded the possibility of true and final love—so that the story could go on and on and on.

(*PS* 292:L9-20 *A Nazi Sympathizer Defended at Some Cost*) He considered himself at least the equal of any living writer. I am told that he once said of the Nobel prize: "Every Vaseline-ass in Europe has one. Where's mine?"

And yet, compulsively, with no financial gain in prospect, and understanding that many people will believe that I share many of his authentically vile opinions, I continue to say that there were good things about this man. And my name is most snugly tied to his in the Penguin paperback editions of his last three books, *Castle to Castle*, *North*, and *Rigadoon*. My name is on each cover: "With a new introduction," it says, "by Kurt Vonnegut, Jr."
(*PS* 295:L31, 296:L1-19 *A Nazi Sympathizer Defended at Some Cost*) I know when he began to influence me. I was well into my forties before I read him. A friend was startled that I didn't know anything about **Céline**, and he initiated me with *Journey to the End of the Night*, which flabbergasted me. I assigned it for a course in the novel which I was giving at the University of Iowa. When it was time for me to lecture for two hours about it, I found I had nothing to say.

The book penetrated my bones, anyway, if not my mind. And I only now understand what I took from **Céline** and put into the novel I was writing at the time, which was called *Slaughterhouse-Five*. In that book, I felt the need to say this every time a character
died: 'So it goes.' This exasperated many critics, and it seemed fancy and tiresome to me, too. But it somehow had to be said.

It was a clumsy way of saying what **Céline** managed to imply so much more naturally in everything he wrote, in effect: "Death and suffering can't matter nearly as much as I think they do. Since they are so common, my taking them so seriously must mean that I am insane. I must try to be saner."
(*PS* 298:L17-25, 299:L8-14 *A Nazi Sympathizer Defended at Some Cost*) There is at least one significant document by **Céline** that is out of print in English. And it would be punctilious of me to say that it was written not by **Céline** but by Dr. Destouches. It is the doctoral thesis of Destouches, "The Life and Work of Ignaz Philipp Semmelweis," for which he received a bronze medal in 1924. It was written at a time when theses in medicine could still be beautifully literary, since ignorance about diseases and the human body still required that medicine be an art.

And young Destouches, in a spirit of hero-worship, told of the futile and scientifically sound battle fought by a Hungarian physician named Semmelweis (1818-1865) to prevent the spread of childbed fever in Viennese hospital maternity wards. The victims were poor people, since persons with decent sorts of dwellings much preferred to give birth at home. . . .

The jealousy and ignorance of Semmelweis's colleagues, however, caused him to be fired, and the mortality rate went up again.

The lesson Destouches learned from this true story, in my opinion, if he hadn't already learned it from an impoverished childhood and a stretch in the army, is that vanity rather than wisdom determines how the world is run.
(*FWD* 69:L2, 16) (Trivia: Aldous Huxley died on the same day as John F. Kennedy. **Louis-Ferdinand Céline** died two days after Ernest Hemingway.)

. . . It *(a requiem mass for the dead)* begins and ends unobjectionably enough, "Requiem aeternam dona eis, Domine; et lux perpetua luceat eis," which means in English, "Rest eternal grant them, O Lord, and let light perpetual shine upon them." (A credulous and literal-minded person might conclude from this that Huxley and Kennedy and **Céline** and Hemingway and my sister and my first wife Jane and all the rest of the dead are now trying to get some sleep with the lights on.)

(*FWD* 182:L14) (The French writer **Louis-Ferdinand Céline** wrote about a doctor friend who was obsessed with expiring with dignity and who died in convulsions under a grand piano.)

(*FWD* 195:L21, 24) **Louis-Ferdinand Céline**, the French fascist (and physician) about whom I wrote in *Palm Sunday*, may have tried to achieve a little immortality with deliberate, absolutely outrageous immorality. I was talking to Saul Steinberg about **Céline** once, and I cried out in astonishment that a writer so funny and wise and gifted would intersperse what could have been masterpieces with loathsome attacks on Jews in general and, if you can believe it, jeers at the memory of Anne Frank in particular. "Why, why, why did he have to besmirch the sublimely innocent ghost of Anne Frank?" I said.

Steinberg pointed his right index finger at my breastbone. He said, "He wanted *you* to remember him."

cell, **cellblock** (see also **jail** and **organism**). *Vonnegut places a number of characters in jail cells and frequently discusses the writer's place in society as part of a biological metaphor.*

(*PP* 165:L10) Was it chance or ignorance or some subtle plot that had put him *(Paul Proteus)* in the same **cell** with Garth, the other candidate for Pittsburgh?

(*PP* 252:L35) HISTORY, PERSONIFIED AT this point in the life of Doctor Paul Proteus by Ed Finnerty and the Reverend James J. Lasher, let Paul out of his **cell** in an old Ilium air-raid shelter only in order for him to eliminate the wastes accrued in the process of his continued existence as an animal.

(*PP* 265:L16) The irregular tapping came from the other side of the sheetmetal wall that separated Paul's and Harold's barred **cell** from the totally enclosed tank for desperados next door.

(*ST* 186:L3) There is no need for a circulatory system in the creatures *(Harmoniums)*. They are so thin that life-giving vibrations can make all their **cells** tingle without intermediaries.

(*MN* 2:L22) *(Howard W. Campbell, Jr. observes:)* And sometimes, when I look out through my **cell** window at the gay and brassy youth of the infant Republic of Israel, I feel that I and my war crimes are as ancient as Solomon's old gray stones.

(*MN* 124:L30) About that reunion: I was locked up in Tel Aviv for twenty-four hours. On my way to my **cell** there, the guards stopped me outside Eichmann's **cell** to hear what we had to say to each other, if anything.

(*MN* 197:L1) So here I am in Israel, of my own free will, though my **cell** is locked and my guards have guns.

(*SL5* 134:L1) In my prison **cell** I sit, / With my britches full of shit, / And my balls are bouncing gently on the floor. / And I see the bloody snag / When she bit me in the bag. / Oh, I'll never fuck a Polack any more.
(*SL5* 138:L24) A moment went by, and then every **cell** in Billy's body shook him with ravenous gratitude and applause. *This occurs when Billy Pilgrim sneaks a spoonful of the malt-enriched vitamin syrup while a prisoner of war.*
(*MH* 159:L19 *Report on the Barnhouse Effect*) He might have dismissed the phenomenon with a low whistle. But. . . . There was one single factor in common: on both occasions, the same thought train had flashed through his mind just before he threw the dice. It was that thought train which aligned the professor's brain **cells** into what has since become the most powerful weapon on earth.
(*MH* 297:L21 *Tomorrow and Tomorrow and Tomorrow*) Em and Lou were in adjacent four-by-eight **cells**, and were stretched out peacefully on their cots.
(*BC* 21:L18, 20) And Skag was a scientist, and he found a way to reproduce himself in chicken soup. He would shave living **cells** from the palm of his right hand, mix them with the soup, and expose the soup to cosmic rays. The **cells** turned into babies which looked exactly like Delmore Skag. *Delmore Skag appears in an unnamed Rabo Karabekian novel which, as with so many of Trout's novels, were published with pornographic photographs.*
(*BC* 98:L2) He *(Wayne Hoobler)* had a photograph of Dwayne in his wallet. He used to have photographs of Dwayne on the walls of his **cell** at Shepherdstown.
(*BC* 146:L13) Dwayne forgot all about Patty Keene, but she certainly hadn't forgotten him. She would get up enough nerve that night to call him on the telephone, but Dwayne wouldn't be home to answer. He would be in a padded **cell** in the County Hospital by then.
(*BC* 173:L23, 26) And the experimental creature wasn't killed after the banquet. He was transferred to a virgin planet instead. Living **cells** were sliced from the palms of his hands, while he was unconscious. . . . And then the **cells** were stirred into a soupy sea on the virgin planet. *The experimental creature is the main character of Trout's* Now It Can Be Told .
(*WFG* 228:L3-5, 7, 20-21 *Address to P.E.N. Conference in Stockholm, 1973*) All artists are specialized **cells** in a single, huge organism, mankind. Those **cells** have to behave as they do, just as the **cells** in our hearts or our fingertips have to behave as they do.

We here are some of those specialized **cells**. Our purpose is to make mankind aware of itself, in all its complexity, and to dream its dreams. We have no choice in the matter. . . .

Where do these external signals come from? *(The question is prompted by Vonnegut's observation that "The best of our stuff draws information and energy and wholeness from outside ourselves.")* I think they come from all the other specialized **cells** in the organism. Those other **cells** contribute to us energy and little bits of information, in order that we may increase the organism's awareness of itself—and dream its dreams.

(*WFG* 237:L11-12 *Playboy Interview*) VONNEGUT: Writers are specialized **cells** in the social organism. They are evolutionary **cells**. Mankind is trying to become something else; it's experimenting with new ideas all the time. And writers are a means of introducing new ideas into the society, and also a means of responding symbolically to life. I don't think we're in control of what we do.

(*WFG* 238:L13, 15 *Playboy Interview*) Writers are specialized **cells** doing whatever we do, and we're expressions of the entire society—just as the sensory **cells** on the surface of your body are in the service of your body as a whole.

(*WFG* 245:L27 *Playboy Interview*) Clumps of cancer **cells** are probably forming in us all the time and petering out—because the clumps are below a certain size.

(*WFG* 255:L32 *Playboy Interview*) One of my favorite cartoons—I think it was by Shel Silverstein—shows a couple of guys chained to an eighteen-foot **cell** wall, hung by their wrists, and their ankles are chained, too. Above them is a tiny barred window *that a mouse couldn't crawl through. And one of the guys says to the other, "Now here's my plan. . . ."*

(*WFG* 283:L19 *Playboy Interview*) PLAYBOY: So your books have been therapy for yourself.

VONNEGUT: Sure. That's well known. Writers get a nice break in one way, at least: They can treat their mental illnesses every day. If I'm lucky, the books have amounted to more than that. I'd like to be a useful citizen, a specialized **cell** in the body politic.

(*JB* 183:L13-14) The police station was so busy that there wasn't even an ordinary **cell** for me *(Walter Starbuck)*. I was given a chair in the corridor outside the **cells**. It was there that the rioters insulted me from behind bars, imagining that I would enjoy nothing so much as making love to them.

(*JB* 183:L17) I was eventually taken to a padded **cell** in the basement. It was designed to hold a maniac until an ambulance could come for her or him.

(*JB* 188:L15) Yes, and there in my padded **cell** I told myself a joke I had read in *The Harvard Lampoon* when a freshman. It had amazed me back then because it seemed so dirty. . . . This was it:

SHE: How dare you kiss me like that?

HE: I was just trying to find out who ate all the macaroons.

(*JB* 189:L21, 26) So all the **cells** were checked. I wasn't in any of them, of course. The people who had brought me in and the man who had locked me up had all gone off-duty. None of them could be reached at home.

But then the detective who was trying to placate my lawyer remembered the **cell** downstairs and decided to have a look inside it, just in case.

(*PS* 227:L31 *Obscenity—"The Big Space Fuck"*) The powder certainly didn't look like much, and Dwayne Hoobler said so—but there were several hundred million sperm **cells** in there, in suspended animation.

(*PS* 241:L15 *Children*) My own son Mark found it *("that bed of Procrustes")* so uncomfortable that he tried to beat his brains out on it, and had to be put in a padded **cell**.
(*PS* 258:L25 *Jonathon Swift Misperceived*) Mr. Turner tells us, for example: "The scale of Lilliput is one inch to a foot of the ordinary world. Mogg mentions [F. Mogg, Scientific American, Vol. CLXXIX, 1948] some biological difficulties: a Lilliputian would have room for far fewer cortical **cells** (so far less intelligence) than a chimpanzee; his head would be too small to carry useful eyes; and he would need eight times as many calories per ounce of body-weight as a full-scale man needs—twenty-four meals a day instead of three."
(*DD* 73:L9-10) But he was led off to **cells** in the basement of police headquarters, and I was taken to a much smaller **cellblock** on the top floor, the third floor, which was reserved for women and for children under the age of sixteen. *Rudy Waltz recounts the events following his arrest and his father's in the accidental killing of Eloise Metzger.*
(*DD* 197:L19, 33) There in the back of the church, I daydreamed a theory of what life was all about. I told myself that Mother and Felix and the Reverend Harrell and Dwayne Hoover and so on were **cells** in what was supposed to be one great big animal. There was no reason to take us seriously as individuals. Celia in her casket there, all shot through with Drano and amphetamine, might have been a dead **cell** sloughed off by a pancreas the size of the Milky Way.
(*DD* 198:L1, 18) How comical that I, a single **cell**, should take my life so seriously!

. . . To whoever might be watching our insignificant lives under an electron microscope: We **cells** have names, and, if we know little else, we know our names.
(*Gal* 26:L22) But now her own big brain *(Mary Hepburn's)* was urging her to take the polyethylene garment bag from around a red evening dress in her closet there in Guayaquil, and to wrap it around her head, thus depriving her **cells** of oxygen.
(*Gal* 59:L30) Gokubi and Mandarax both had pressure-sensitive buttons on their backs. . . . On the face of each was an identical screen on which images could be caused to appear, and which also functioned as a solar **cell**, charging tiny batteries which, again, were exactly the same in Gokubi and Mandarax.
(*HP* 69:L23, 70:L1-2) At the Athena state prison, as I would discover when I went to work over there, there were 6 men to each **cell** and each **cell** had been built for 2. Each 50 **cells** had a recreation room with one Ping-Pong table and one TV.
(*HP* 236:L3) That summer I would start a literacy program in the prison, using people like Abdullah Akbahr as proselytizers for reading and writing, going from **cell** to **cell** and offering lessons.
(*FWD* 32:L18) "I think I was invited here mostly because of what happened to my dear son Mark Vonnegut, now Dr. Vonnegut. He had a very fancy crack-up, padded-**cell** stuff, straitjacket stuff, hallucinations, wrestling matches

with nurses, and all that. He recovered and wrote a book about it called *The Eden Express*, which is about to be reissued in paperback by Dell, with a new Afterword by him. You should have hired him instead of me. He would have been a heck of a lot cheaper, and he knows what he is talking about. *See also: PP* 266:L21; 266:L25; 290:L30; *MN* 177:L12; *BC* 189:L12; 216:L18,20; *Slap* 18:L3; *JB* 113:L26; 192:L5-6; *DD* 74:L24; *FWD* 33:L2.

cellar. *Vonnegut often recalls his corpse-mining experience in the cellars of Dresden after its firebombing.* (*MN* vii:L5) The malt syrup factory was gone. Everything was gone but the **cellars** where 135,000 Hansels and Gretels had been baked like gingerbread men.

(*SL5* 5:L29) The rabid little American I call Paul Lazzaro in this book had about a quart of diamonds and emeralds and rubies and so on. He had taken these from dead people in the **cellars** of Dresden. So it goes.

(*FWD* 102:L3, 6) "After the raid, the corpses, most of them in ordinary **cellars**, were so numerous and represented such a health hazard that they were cremated on huge funeral pyres, or by flamethrowers whose nozzles were thrust into the **cellars**, without being counted or identified. Many friends and relatives of refugees newly arrived in Dresden can say of them nowadays only that they somehow disappeared near the end of World War II. The town was full of Polish slave laborers. Their friends and relatives must be saying of them nowadays simply that they were taken off to Germany somewhere and never came home again.

(*FWD* 102:L22, 32) "Among the unidentified, not-even-counted dead in the **cellars** of Dresden there were, without doubt, war criminals or loathsomely proud relatives of war criminals, SS and Gestapo, and so on. Whatever they got was too good for them. Maybe most of the Germans killed in Dresden, excepting the infants and children, of course, got what was coming to them. I asked another great German writer, Heinrich Böll, what he thought the dangerous flaw in the character of so many Germans was, and he said, 'Obedience.'

"But I have to say that I felt no pride or satisfaction while carrying corpses from **cellars** to great funeral pyres while friends and relatives of the missing watched."

Rabo Karabekian's masterpiece, "Now It's the Women's Turn," is Vonnegut's vision of what he saw the day he was released from Dresden. The painting contains a cut-away view of a cellar used for shelter which he explains to Circe Berman. (*Blue* 285:L29-30, 32) We went to the extreme right end for a look. . . . There was a farmhouse down at the bottom of both ends: each one buttoned up tight like a little fort, its high gates closed, and all the animals in the courtyard. And I had made a schematic cut through the earth below them, so as to show their **cellars**, too, just as a museum display might give away the secrets of animals' burrows underground.

"The healthy women are in the **cellar** with the beets and potatoes and turnips," I said. "They are putting off being raped as long as possible, but they have heard the history of other wars in the area, so they know that rape will surely come."

Other significant uses of cellars include the one in the home of Mother Night*'s Dr. Lionel J.D. Jones, who uses it for meetings of the Iron Guard of the White Sons of the American Constitution, headed by August Krapptauer. When Howard Campbell takes refuge there as part of the kidnap conspiracy launched by Soviet agent George Kraft/Iona Potapov, Campbell's Blue Fairy Godmother spearheads his release and reveals the true identities of Kraft and Resi Noth. Rather than face incarceration or deportation as a (reluctant) Soviet agent, Resi commits suicide by taking cyanide.*

God Bless You, Mr. Rosewater*'s Fred Rosewater goes down to the cellar of his Pisquontuit, Rhode Island, home where he contemplates suicide until he finds the manuscript of his ancestor Merrihue Rosewater (a suicide victim) entitled* A History of the Rosewaters of Rhode Island. *The text traces the family back to nobility in Great Britain, and though Fred is momentarily buoyed by the revelation, he again thinks about hanging himself when he turns the first few pages and realizes his family chronicle has been eaten by worms.*

In Breakfast of Champions, *Vonnegut recalls having his mother (another suicide) tour him around Indianapolis, an attempt to instill pride in the family history.* (*BC* 288:L6, 12) I thought instead of my paternal grandfather, who had been the first licensed architect in Indiana. He had designed some dream houses for Hoosier millionaires. They were mortuaries and guitar schools and **cellar** holes and parking lots now. I thought of my mother, who drove me around Indianapolis one time during the Great Depression, to impress me with how rich and powerful my maternal grandfather had been. She showed me where his brewery had been, where some of his dream houses had been. Every one of the monuments was a **cellar** hole.

And then there is the lighter side of such an image as it comes to Billy Pilgrim. (*SL5* 116:L20) Billy sniffed. His hot bed smelled like a mushroom **cellar**. He had had a wet dream about Montana Wildhack. *See also: PP* 24:L22; 131:L31; 231:18; *MN* 66:L7; 114:L9,11,14,29; 120:L1; 159:L3; 167:L21; 171:L2; *GBR* 51:L2; 121:L11; 160:L28; 162:L19; 165:L15,21; 167:L16; *SL5* 129:L11; *BC* 145:L33; 146:L16; *JB* 98:L4; *DD* 4:L2.

chaos, chaotic. (*PP* 103:L24) Halyard yawned, and was annoyed to think that Lynn, who had just read "order out of **chaos**," as "order out of koze" made three times as much money as he did.

(*ST* 39:L11) "Things fly this way and that, my boy," he *(Rumfoord)* said, "with or without messages. It's **chaos**, and no mistake, for the Universe is just being born. It's the great becoming that makes the light and the heat and the motion, and bangs you from hither to yon.

(*CC* 45:L3) Anything can be a *wampeter*: a tree, a rock, an animal, an idea, a book, a melody, the Holy Grail. Whatever it is, the members of its *karass* revolve about it in the majestic **chaos** of a spiral nebula. The orbits of the

members of a *karass* about their common *wampeter* are spiritual orbits, naturally. It is souls and not bodies that revolve.
(*BC* 181:L7) Listen: Bunny's mother and my mother were different sorts of human beings, but they were both beautiful in exotic ways, and they both boiled over with **chaotic** talk about love and peace and wars and evil and desperation, of better days coming by and by, of worse days coming by and by. And both our mothers committed suicide. Bunny's mother ate Drano. My mother ate sleeping pills, which wasn't nearly as horrible.
(*BC* 210:L16, 20-21, 24) Once I understood what was making America such a dangerous, unhappy nation of people who had nothing to do with real life, I resolved to shun storytelling. . . . Let others bring order to **chaos**. I would bring **chaos** to order, instead, which I think I have done.

If all writers would do that, then perhaps citizens not in the literary trades will understand that there is no order in the world around us, that we must adapt ourselves to the requirements of **chaos** instead.

It is hard to adapt to **chaos**, but it can be done. I am living proof of that: It can be done.

Adapting to **chaos** there in the cocktail lounge, I now had Bonnie MacMahon, who was exactly as important as anybody else in the Universe, bring more yeast excrement to Beatrice Keedsler and Karabekian.
(*BC* 218:L31) This is why I had gone to Midland City: to be born again. And **Chaos** announced that it was about to give birth to a new me by putting these words in the mouth of Rabo Karabekian: "What kind of man would turn his daughter into an outboard motor?"
(*WFG* 200:L18 *In a Manner That Must Shame God Himself*) I'll say this: Their religions *(those of the American Indians)* couldn't possibly be more **chaotic** than the Christianity reinvented every day by Dr. D. Elton Trueblood, Professor at Large.
(*PS* 199:L19 *Religion*) Our country is now jammed with human beings who say out loud that life is **chaos** to them, and that it doesn't seem to matter what anybody does next. This is worse than being seasick.
(*PS* 321:L16 *In The Capital Of The World*) If any of us came up with good answers, I now have no idea what they might have been. His answer was this: "The artist says, 'I can do very little about the **chaos** around me, but at least I can reduce to perfect order this square of canvas, this piece of paper, this chunk of stone.'" *The answer is provided by Vonnegut's mentor from the University of Chicago.*
(*Gal* 125:L8) I *(Leon Trout)* did not know that humanity was about to be diminished to a tiny point, by luck, and then, again by luck, to be permitted to expand again. I believed that the **chaos** involving billions of big-brained people thrashing around every which way, and reproducing and reproducing, would go on and on.
(*Gal* 200:L27) The most *Siegfried hoped to find was a peaceful stopping place in **chaos**.

(*Blue* 241:L26, 29) I have dug one of hers *(Marilee Kemp's letters)* from the archives here. It is dated three years after our reunion, June 7, 1953, and says that we have failed to paint pictures of nothing after all, that she easily identifies **chaos** in every canvas.

I answered that letter with a cable, of which I have a copy. "NOT EVEN **CHAOS** IS SUPPOSED TO BE THERE," it reads. "WE'LL COME OVER AND PAINT IT OUT. ARE OUR FACES RED. SAINT PATRICK." (*HP* 276:L13) Every so often, in the midst of **chaos**, you come across an amazing, inexplicable instance of civic responsibility. Maybe the last shred of faith people have is in their firemen. *See also: GBR* 94:L5; *MH—The Lie* 219:L21; *BC* 116:L2.

Chaplin, Charlie. *Vonnegut very much enjoys the work of Charlie Chaplin and in a number of instances he manages to work in Chaplinesque images. In his preface to the script of* Timbuktu *(a text he did not author) Vonnegut cites the influence Chaplin and others have had on him.* (*TIM* xvii:L6-16) I would like to say something about American comedians: they are often as brilliant and magical as our best jazz musicians, and they have probably done more to shape my thinking than any writer. When people ask me who my culture heroes are, I express pious gratitude for Mark Twain and James Joyce and so on. But the truth is that I am a barbarian, whose deepest cultural debts are to Laurel and Hardy, Stoopnagel and Bud, Buster Keaton, Fred Allen, Jack Benny, **Charlie Chaplin**, Easy Aces, Henry Morgan, and on and on.

Howard Campbell evokes the following image while walking with Helga/Resi on the streets of New York after the war. (*MN* 99:L1-2) I was not wearing war-surplus clothing. I was wearing the clothes I had put on after seeing Berlin, after shucking off the uniform of the Free American Corps. I was wearing the cloth fur-collared impresario's cloak and blue serge suit—I had been captured in. I was also carrying, for whimsy, a cane. I did marvelous things with the cane: rococo manuals of arms, **Charlie Chaplin** twirls, polo strokes at orts in the gutter.

After capturing George Kraft/Iona Potapov, an FBI officer engages Kraft in some playful, derisive banter about his long spy career coming to an end, that perhaps they could make a movie of his life. The FBI officer suggests that only Charlie Chaplin could play Kraft in the movie. (*MN* 172:L16-19) "Who else could play a spy who was steadily drunk from 1941 until 1948? Who else could play a Russian spy who built an apparatus composed almost entirely of American agents?"

As Eliot Rosewater lapses into a trance preceding his departure from the town, he becomes a Chaplinesque caricature. (*GBR* 185:L1-11) Something there was in Eliot, though, that watched the clock. Ten minutes before his bus was due at the Saw City Kandy Kitchen, he thawed, arose, pursed his lips, picked some lint from his suit, went out his office door. He had no surface memory of the fight with his father. His step was jaunty, that of a **Chaplinesque** *boulevardier*.

He bent to pat the heads of dogs who welcomed him to street level. His new clothes hampered him, bound him in the crotch and armpits, crackled as though lined with newspaper, reminded him of how nicely turned out he was.
(*WFG* 112:L15 *Why They Read Hesse*) A magic theater fantasy in which Harry Haller takes part proves, incidentally, that Hesse might have been one of the most screamingly funny men of his time. It may be that he was so anguished as he wrote *Steppenwolf* that his soul could get relief only by erupting into **Charlie Chaplin** comedy. The fantasy is about two men who climb a tree by a road. They have a rifle. They declare war on all automobiles and shoot them as they come by.
(*PS* 115:L17-22 *Playboy Interview*) INTERVIEWER: You seem to prefer Laurel and Hardy over **Chaplin**. Is that so?
VONNEGUT: I'm crazy about **Chaplin**, but there's too much distance between him and his audience. He is too obviously a genius. In his own way, he's as brilliant as Picasso, and this is intimidating to me.

Rabo Karabekian identifies some of the people he included in his final masterpiece "Now It's the Women's Turn." (*Blue* 293:L15) "How many of these are portraits of actual people?" she said.

"The bombardier clinging to my leg: that's his face, as I remember it. These two Estonians in German uniforms are Laurel and Hardy. This French collaborator here is **Charlie Chaplin**. These two Polish slave laborers on the other side of the tower from me are Jackson Pollock and Terry Kitchen."

Charity Anne Browning. *Belonging to "a Nova Scotian named Bert," the* Charity Ann Browning *is a sixty-eight-foot yawl encountered by the skipper of the* Marlin, *Frank Wirtanen of West Barnstable, Cape Cod. He and the narrator are taking the* Marlin, *which belongs to President Kennedy, down the Inland Waterway from Hyannis Port to West Palm Beach. The* Charity Ann Browning *is used as a point of maritime comparison, one of the chief narrative devices in the story.* (*WFG* 14:L19 *Brief Encounters on the Inland Waterway*) The ***Charity Anne Browning*** looked from the outside like a very businesslike sailing vessel, possibly engaged in the copra trade. Below decks she was like the bridal suit in the newest motor lodge in Reno—thick carpets, three tiled baths, a fifteen-foot couch covered with panther skin and steam heat. In the owner's cabin there was a king-size bed with the covers turned back. The sheets and pillow cases were dotted with forget-me-nots.

Charlestown Prison. *The place of imprisonment and execution of Sacco and Vanzetti as recounted in* Jailbird.

Charley. *In the short play "Fortitude" reprinted in* Wampeters, Foma & Granfalloons, *Charley is the technician in the control room of the hospital ministering to the live heads of Sylvia and her medical miracle worker Dr. Frankenstein. Charley makes sure to adjust their mood altering drugs and when they are finally united as a pair of talking heads, he plays the Jeanette*

MacDonald-Nelson Eddy duet, "Ah, Sweet Mystery of Life" as Frankenstein had requested.

Charlotte. *In the short story "Next Door" reprinted in* Welcome to the Monkey House, *Charlotte is the woman with whom Lemuel K. Harger is having an affair and whose loudness plays on the conscience of the young Paul next door. When Paul calls All-Night Sam to dedicate a record for Mrs. Harger in Lemuel's name, Charlotte hears the radio dedication and storms out of the apartment but not before firing three shots at Lemuel and bribing Paul with a large wad of money. Though she didn't hit Harger, Paul thought he contributed to his death.* (*MH* 118:L4-5) She was a big, blonde woman, all soft and awry, like an unmade bed.

Chasens, Henry Stewart (see **Newt** and **Catharine**). *In the short story "Long Walk to Forever," Chasens is the unseen fiancé of Catharine (no last name).*

Checker Charley. *The invention of Dave Berringer, one of the top "computer-machine" men in the country, and used by Fred Berringer to challenge Paul Proteus' checker championship. Fred's ignorance about his father's invention leads to its undoing. Ed Finnerty noticed a couple of Checker Charley's connections were loose, and they eventually caused the robot to fail allowing Paul to retain his championship.*

chemical, chemically *Vonnegut's first protracted treatment of his concern with the volatile chemistry of humans occurs during a conversation between Howard Campbell and a New York City policeman assigned to protect his vandalized apartment. Campbell is mostly a straight man while listening to the officer.* (*MN* 178:L28) "Getting down in the dumps," he said. "Isn't that what they're finding out—that a lot of that's **chemicals**?"
(*MN* 179:L1, 3, 5,13, 17, 19, 21) "They can give a man certain **chemicals**, and he goes crazy," he said. "That's one Of the things they're working with. Maybe it's all **chemicals**. . . . Maybe it's different **chemicals** that different countries eat that makes people act in different ways at different times. . . . It *has* to be **chemicals**, doesn't it?" he said. . . . "I think about **chemicals** all the time. . . . Sometimes I think I should go back to school and find out all the things they've found out so far about **chemicals**. . . . Maybe, when they find out more about **chemicals**," he said, "there won't have to be policemen or wars or crazy houses or divorces or drunks or juvenile delinquents or women gone bad or anything any more."
(*MN* 180:L1-2, 7) "Certain **chemicals** get loose, and the woman can't help but act that way. Sometimes a certain **chemical** will get loose after a woman's had a baby, and she'll kill the baby. That happened four doors down from here just last week. . . . Most unnatural thing a woman can do is kill her own baby, but she did it," he said. "Certain **chemicals** in the blood made her do it, even though she knew better, didn't want to do it at all."

"Um," I said.

"You wonder what's wrong with the world—" he said, "well, there's an important clue right there."

Vonnegut continues this discourse when thinking of his mother, extends it further to explain the suicidal impulses of Dwayne Hoover, and rambles on about the prevalence of recreational drug use. (*BC* 4:L2, 11, 19) I tend to think of human beings as huge, rubbery, test tubes, too, with **chemical** reactions seething inside. . . . My own mother wrecked her brains with **chemicals**, which were supposed to make her sleep. . . . So it is a big temptation to me, when I create a character for a novel, to say that he is what he is because of faulty wiring, or because of microscopic amounts of **chemicals** which he ate or failed to eat on that particular day.

(*BC* 14:L1-2, 6) Dwayne's incipient insanity was mainly a matter of **chemicals**, of course. Dwayne Hoover's body was manufacturing certain **chemicals** which unbalanced his mind. But Dwayne, like all novice lunatics, needed some bad ideas, too, so that his craziness could have shape and direction. . . . Bad **chemicals** and bad ideas were the Yin and Yang of madness. Yin and Yang were Chinese symbols of harmony.

(*BC* 70:L3, 5, 8) Trout wandered out onto the sidewalk of Forty-second Street. It was a dangerous place to be. The whole city was dangerous—because of **chemicals** and the uneven distribution of wealth and so on. A lot of people were like Dwayne: they created **chemicals** in their own bodies which were bad for their heads. But there were thousands upon thousands of other people in the city who bought bad **chemicals** and ate them or sniffed them—or injected them into their veins.

(*BC* 71:L1, 14, 21) Sometimes they even stuffed bad **chemicals** up their assholes. . . . People took such awful chances with **chemicals** and their bodies because they wanted the quality of their lives to improve. They lived in ugly places where there were only ugly things to do. . . . So they did their best to make their insides beautiful instead. . . . The results had been catastrophic so far—suicide, theft, murder, and insanity and so on. But new **chemicals** were coming onto the market all the time.

(*BC* 133:L11, 14, 17) Dwayne certainly wasn't alone, as far as having bad **chemicals** inside of him was concerned. He had plenty of company throughout all history. In his own lifetime, for instance, the people in a country called Germany were so full of bad **chemicals** for a while that they actually built factories whose only purpose was to kill people by the millions.

Vonnegut continues to discuss his appreciation of the human chemical question outside his fiction, touching on his often touted extended families theory. (*WFG* 174:L15 *Address to the National Institute of Arts and Letters, 1971*) Happiness is **chemical**. Before I knew that, I used to investigate happiness by means of questions and answers.

(*WFG* 178:L26, 28-29 *Address to the National Institute of Arts and Letters, 1971*) And I say to you that we are full of **chemicals** which require us to belong to folk societies, or failing that, to feel lousy all the time. We are

chemically engineered to live in folk societies, just as fish are **chemically** engineered to live in clean water—and there aren't any folk societies for us anymore.

(*WFG* 179:L6 *Address to the National Institute of Arts and Letters, 1971*) Here is what women really want: They want lives in folk societies, wherein everyone is a friendly relative, and no act or object is without holiness. **Chemicals** make them want that. **Chemicals** make us all want that.

(*WFG* 179:L8, 10-11 *Address to the National Institute of Arts and Letters, 1971*) **Chemicals** make us furious when we are treated as things rather than persons. When anything happens to us which would not happen to us in a folk society, our **chemicals** make us feel like fish out of water. Our **chemicals** demand that we get back into water again. If we become increasingly wild and preposterous in modern times—well, so do fish on river banks, for a little while.

(*WFG* 180:L2 *Address to the National Institute of Arts and Letters, 1971*) The American Academy of Arts and Letters and the National Institute of Arts and Letters don't really give a damn for arts and letters, in my opinion. They, too, are **chemically**-induced efforts to form a superstitious, affectionate clan or village or tribe. To them I say this, "Lots of luck, boys and girls."

Moving beyond our internal chemistries, Vonnegut responds to the military-industrial complex's experiments. (*PS* 71:L15 *When I Lost My Innocence*) "We have discovered a brand-new method for committing suicide—family style, Reverend Jim Jones style, and by the millions. What is the method? To say nothing and do nothing about what some of our businessmen and military men are doing with the most unstable substances and the most persistent poisons to be found anywhere in the universe.

"The people who play with such **chemicals** are so *dumb*!"

Eugene Debs Hartke (whose father was a chemical engineer) refers to the explanations he had to make for military assaults made by officers intoxicated with alcohol and marijuana. (*HP* 36:L35) Several of the most gruesome accidents I had to explain to the press during my last year over there were caused by people who had rendered themselves imbecilic or maniacal by ingesting too much of what, if taken in moderation, could be a helpful **chemical**.

Vonnegut frequently discusses mental illness as chemically induced, including his mother's suicide and his son Mark's breakdown. (*PS* 242:L6 *Children*) Schizophrenia is an internal **chemical** catastrophe. It is a case of monstrously bad genetic luck, bad luck of a sort encountered in absolutely every sort of society—including the Australian aborigines and the middle class of Vienna, Austria, before the Second World War.

(*PS* 309:L29 *The Sexual Revolution*) He *(Vonnegut's son Mark)* never blamed me or his mother, as I have said before. His generous wish not to blame us was so stubborn that he became almost a crank on the subject of **chemical** and genetic causes of mental illness.

(*FWD* 28:L23) "I made the strong suggestion in *Palm Sunday* that my mother's untreated, unacknowledged insanity was caused by bad **chemicals** she swallowed rather than created within herself, principally alcohol and unlimited quantities of prescribed barbituates. (She did not live long enough to have a doctor pep her up with some sort of amphetamine.) I am willing to believe that her ailment was hereditary, but I have no American ancestors (fully accounted for in *Palm Sunday*) who were clinically crazy. In any case, what the heck? I didn't get to choose my ancestors, and I look upon my brain and the rest of my body as a house I inhabit which was built long before I was born."

(*FWD* 33:L25, 27, 31) "Long before Mark went crazy, I thought mental illness was caused by **chemicals**, and said so in my stories. I've never in a story had an event or another person drive a character crazy. I thought madness had a **chemical** basis even when I was a boy, because a close friend of our family, a wise and kind and wryly sad man named Dr. Walter Bruetsch, who was head of the State's huge and scary hospital for the insane, used to say that his patients' problems were **chemical**, that little could be done for them until that chemistry was better understood."

(*FWD* 34:L1-2) "So when my mother went crazy, long before my son went crazy, long before I had a son, and finally killed herself, I blamed **chemicals**, and I still do, although she had a terrible childhood. I can even name two of the **chemicals**: phenobarbital and booze. Those came from the outside, of course, the phenobarbs from our family doctor, who was trying to do something about her sleeplessness. When she died, I was a soldier, and my division was about to go overseas."

(*FWD* 133:L12, 14, 25) "The AA *(Alcoholics Anonymous)* scheme, which, again, can work only if the addicts regularly admit that this or that **chemical** is poisonous to them, is now proving its effectiveness with compulsive gamblers, who are not dependent on **chemicals** from a distillery or a pharmaceutical laboratory. This is no paradox. Gamblers, in effect, manufacture their own dangerous substances. God help them, they produce chemicals that elate them whenever they place a bet on simply anything. . . .

"Whether the meeting I was standing before was of Gamblers Anonymous or Alcoholics Anonymous, I would be encouraged to testify as to how the **chemicals** I had generated within myself or swallowed had alienated my friends and relatives, cost me jobs and houses, and deprived me of my last shred of self-respect."

(*FWD* 134:L1) "I now wish to direct your attention to another form of addiction, which has not been previously identified. It is more like gambling than drinking, since the people afflicted are ravenous for situations that will cause their bodies to release **chemicals** into their bloodstreams. I am persuaded that there are among us people who are tragically hooked on preparations for war."

(*FWD* 184:L22, 25) "Jokes work this way: The jokester frightens the listener just a little bit, by mentioning something challenging, such as sex or physical danger, or suggesting that the listener is having his or her intelligence tested.

Step two: The jokester makes clear that no intelligent response is required of the listener. This leaves the listener stuck with useless fight or flee **chemicals** in his or her bloodstream, which must be gotten rid of somehow, unless the listener wants to slug the jokester or do jumping jacks.

"What the listener most likely will do is expel those **chemicals** through the lungs with quick expansions and contractions of the chest cavity, accompanied by grotesque facial expressions and barking sounds." *See also: ST* 265:L8; *MN* 176:chapter title; *CC* 44:L13; 194:L3; 213:L5; *GBR* 179:L9,16; *MH—Welcome To The Monkey House* 37:L25; *MH—Deer In The Works* 211:L26; *MH—Unready To Wear* 237:L1; *WJ* 147:L23; *BC* 39:L7; 46:L10; 49:L18,22; 64:L10; 85:L31; 86:L2; 95:L13; 99:L21; 133:L6,17; 142:L25-26; 159:L8; 164:L33; 216:L1,3; 254:L23; 272:L27; *WFG—Fortitude* 51:L24; *WFG—Address to the American Psychological Society* 92:L11; 100:L31; *WFG—Address to the National Institute of Arts and Letters, 1971* 174:L12; *WFG—Playboy Interview* 248:L6; *Slap* 65:L25-26,28; 162:L12; 223:L30; *JB* 55:L10; 235:L16; *PS—Self-Interview* 99:L21; *PS—Jekyll and Hyde Updated* 267:L19; 269:L21; 282:L22; *DD* 184:L32; *Blue* 19:L4; 152:L12; 242:L4-5; *HP* 14:L28,33; 32:L7; 39:L18; 43:L26,29,34; 63:L36; 188:L30; 189:L4; 205:L20; 226:L20; 241:L24; 241:L28; *FWD* 220:4.

chemist (see also **chemical**). (*ST* 33:L15) "God told us what *we* had to do on this wonderful space ship. He wrote the rules so anybody could understand them. You don't have to be a physicist or a great **chemist** or an Albert Einstein to understand them.
(*MN* 50:L4) Working with a **chemist** named Dr. Lomar Horthy, Jones developed Viverine, an embalming fluid, and Gingiva-Tru, a wonderfully lifelike, gum-simulating substance for false teeth.
(*CC* 30:L19) He then told me who Horvath was. "The famous surface **chemist**," he said, "the one who's doing such wonderful things with films."
(*BC* 228:L3-4) The man who told me how to diagram a segment of a molecule of plastic was Professor Walter H. Stockmayer of Dartmouth College. He is a distinguished physical **chemist**, and an amusing and useful friend of mine.
(*BC* 251:L11) And when another Nigger high school was built after the Second World War, it was named after George Washington Carver, a black man who was born into slavery, but who became a famous **chemist** anyway. He discovered many remarkable new uses for peanuts.
(*WFG* 93:L7, 31 *Address to the American Physical Society*) I was a chemistry major in college. H. L. Mencken started out as a **chemist**. H. G. Wells did, too. My father said he would help to pay for my college education only if I studied something serious. . . . So I went to Cornell University, and I studied chemistry and German. . . .

Back in my days as a chemistry student I used to be quite a technocrat. I used to believe that scientists would corner God and photograph Him in Technicolor by 1951. I used to mock my fraternity brothers at Cornell who were wasting their energies on insubstantial subjects such as sociology and

government and history. And literature. I told them that all power in the future would rest properly in the hands of **chemists** and physicists and engineers.
(*PS* 61:L10 *When I Lost My Innocence*) He *(Vonnegut's father)* and my older brother, who had become a **chemist**, urged me to study chemistry instead.
(*PS* 63:L12 *When I Lost My Innocence*) "It was not Cornell's fault that I did not like this place much. . . . It was my father's fault. He said I should become a **chemist** like my brother, and not waste my time and his money on subjects he considered so much junk jewelry—literature, history, philosophy."
(*PS* 66:L8 *When I Lost My Innocence*) "Well—I am more sentimental about this occasion than I have so far indicated. We **chemists** can be as sentimental as anybody. Our emotional lives, probably because of the A-bomb and the H-bomb, and the way we spell 'Ethel,' have been much maligned."
(*PS* 95:L13 *Self-Interview*) VONNEGUT: My education was as a **chemist** at Cornell and then an anthropologist at the University of Chicago.
(*PS* 159:L17 *Playmates*) "Until that moment of truth, I had agreed with the Nobel-prize **chemist**, the late Irving Langmuir, who once said within my hearing, 'Any person who can't explain his work to a fourteen-year-old is a charlatan.'"
(*Blue* 145:L9) The cook who had begrudgingly fed me my first supper in New York City, and who kept asking, "What next, what next?" died two weeks after I got there. That finally became what was going to happen next: she would drop dead in Turtle Bay **Chemists**, a drugstore two blocks away.
(*HP* 97:L34) When we passed a Catholic church, I recalled, he said, "You think your dad's a good **chemist**? They're turning soda crackers into meat in there. Can your dad do that?"
(*FWD* 93:L14) (I didn't go to the reunion. I was afraid of it because, like everybody else, I had had some really lousy times in high school. I probably would have gone anyway and had a swell time and lots of laughs. But then I was lucky enough to come down with the disease of the moment in the Hamptons, which was Lyme disease. I get sick only when it's useful, knock on wood. Viral pneumonia got me out of trying to be a **chemist** in 1942. I went briefly apeshit in the 1980s in an effort to get out of life entirely, and wound up playing Eightball in a locked ward for thirty days instead.)
(*FWD* 118:L23) "Hitler dreamed of killing Jews, Gypsies, Slavs, homosexuals, Communists, Jehovah's Witnesses, mental defectives, believers in democracy, and so on, in industrial quantities. It would have remained only a dream if it hadn't been for **chemists** as well educated as my brother, who supplied Hitler's executioners with the cyanide gas known as Cyklon-B. It would have remained only a dream if architects and engineers as capable as my father and grandfather hadn't designed extermination camps—the fences, the towers, the barracks, the railroad sidings, and the gas chambers and crematoria—for maximum ease of operation and efficiency. I recently visited two of those camps in Poland, Auschwitz and Birkenau. They are technologically perfect. There is only one grade I could give their designers, and that grade is A-plus. They surely solved all the problems set for them.

chemistry (see also **chemical** and **chemist**). (*WFG* 2:L4 *Science Fiction*) English majors are encouraged, I know, to hate **chemistry** and physics, and to be proud because they are not dull and creepy and humorless and war-oriented like the engineers across the quad. . . . So it is natural for them to despise science fiction.

(*WFG* 93:L5-6,24 *Address to the American Physical Society*) I've had the same formal education you people have had, more or less. I was a **chemistry** major in college. H. L. Mencken started out as a chemist. H. G. Wells did, too. My father said he would help to pay for my college education only if I studied something serious. This was in the late Thirties. *Reader's Digest* magazine was in those days celebrating the wonderful things Germans were doing with chemicals. **Chemistry** was obviously the coming thing. So was German. So I went to Cornell University, and I studied **chemistry** and German. . . .

Back in my days as a **chemistry** student I used to be quite a technocrat. I used to believe that scientists would corner God and photograph Him in Technicolor by 1951.

(*WFG* 252:L11 *Playboy Interview*) I wasn't taking a whole lot of it *(Vonnegut was taking Ritalin for his depression)*, but it puzzled me so much that I could be depressed and just by taking this damn little thing about the size of a pinhead, I would feel much better. I used to think that I was responding to Attica or to the mining of the harbor of Haiphong. But I wasn't. I was obviously responding to internal **chemistry**.

(*WFG* 253:L1 *Playboy Interview*) VONNEGUT: In this book I've just finished, *Breakfast of Champions*, the motives of all the characters are explained in terms of body **chemistry**. You know, we don't give a shit about the characters' childhoods or about what happened yesterday—we just want to know what the state of their bloodstreams is. They're up when their bloodstreams are up and they're down when their bloodstreams are down.

(*PS* 105:L6 *Self-Interview*) VONNEGUT: I'm on the New York State Council for the Arts now, and every so often some other member talks about sending notices to college English departments about some literary opportunity, and I say, "Send them to the **chemistry** departments, send them to the zoology departments, send them to the anthropology departments and the astronomy departments and physics departments, and all the medical and law schools. That's where the writers are most likely to be."

(*HP* 154:L1) I *(Eugene Debs Hartke)* would have been dead if it weren't for that great gift to civilization from the **Chemistry** Department of Harvard, which was napalm, or sticky jellied gasoline.

(*FWD* 54:2) My father, as I have said elsewhere ad nauseam, said I could go to college only if I studied **chemistry**. How flattered I would have been if he had said instead that I, too, should become an architect.

(*FWD* 163:L113) "Like the early Christians, you are part of a society dominated by superstitions, by pure baloney. During Roman Imperial times, though, pure baloney was all that was available about the size of the planet, about its place in the cosmos, about the natures of its other inhabitants, about the probable origins of life, about the causes and cures of diseases, about **chemistry**, about physics, about biology, and on and on. Everybody, including the early Christians, had no choice but to be full of baloney. That is not the case today. And my goodness, do we ever have a lot of information now, and proven techniques for creating almost anything in abundance and for moderating all sorts of catastrophes.

(*FWD* 194:L3) I am now prepared to say that suicidal persons can be divided into two sorts. Styron's sort blames the wiring and **chemistry** of his brain, which could easily fit into a salad bowl. My sort blames the Universe. (Why mess around?) I don't offer this insight as yet another joke ("Why is cream more expensive than milk?"). It is my serious belief that those of us who become humorists (suicidal or not) feel free (as most people do not) to speak of life itself as a dirty joke, even though life is all there is or ever can be.

We do, doodily do, doodily do, doodily do
What we must, muddily must, muddily must, muddily must:
Muddily do, muddily must, muddily do, muddily must,
Until we bust, bodily bust, bodily bust, bodily bust.

(*FWD* 214:L7) If I am apathetic about most academic critics of literature, the ennui is surely mutual. Whereas I find almost nothing of use to a working fiction writer in academic criticism, I have seldom met an academic critic at all interested in asking a writer why and how he does what he does. To me this is like a chemistry professor's being proud of snubbing the element oxygen.

See also: *PP* 236:L4; *MN* 178:L25; *CC* 36:L21; *MH—Unready To Wear* 236:L13; *MH—The Kid Nobody Could Handle* 250:L31; *WFG—Preface* xxvii:L10; *WFG—Science Fiction* 5:L20; *WFG—Address to the American Physical Society* 100:L23-24; *JB* dedication; xi:L8; 3:L23; 28:L18; 55:L10; *PS—Roots* 53:L31; 54:L8; *PS—When I Lost My Innocence* 61:L11; 62:L10; 63:L22; *PS—Triage* 73:L1; 74:L23; 76:L29; *PS—Self-Interview* 99:L20; 100:L21; *PS—Children* 251:L25; *PS—Jekyll And Hyde Updated* 260:L11; 264:L12; 264:L30; 272:L9; 287:L11; 288:L19; *DD* 29:L25; *HP* 25:L9; 39:L2; *HP* 191:L27; *FWD* 33:L32; 88:L30; 117:L5.

"The Chemistry Professor." *Reprinted in* Palm Sunday, *this short play is Vonnegut's updated version of Robert Louis Stevenson's "Dr. Jekyll and Mr. Hyde." In this version Dr. Jekyll is a chemistry professor at Sweetbread College who concocts a potion to increase the growth of chickens as a way to raise funds for the bankrupt institution. He drinks the potion, turns into a human-sized homicidal chicken, and is shot dead by Fred Leghorn. This plot line occurs while the students are rehearsing a production of Stevenson's original story to raise funds for the college.*

Vonnegut records that in 1978 he was asked by Broadway producer Lee Guber (both were then serving on the New York State Council of the Arts) to write a musical updated version of the classic. It was never produced.

Chessman, Caryl. *When prison guard Clyde Carter becomes exasperated with Walter Starbuck's "It's all right," easy going attitude about the fact his son didn't come to visit or meet him for his release, Carter likens Walter's attitude with that of Caryl Chessman.* (*JB* 49:L2) **Caryl Chessman** was a convicted kidnapper and rapist, but not a murderer, who spent twelve years on death row in California. He made all his own appeals for stays of execution, and he learned four languages and wrote two best-selling books before he was put into an airtight tank with windows in it, and made to breathe cyanide gas.

And his last words were indeed, as Clyde said, "It's all right."

Chetniks. *During World War II Nestor Aamons, a Finnish architect and father of the much-sought-after Mona,* was captured by the Russians, then liberated by the Germans during the Second World War. He was not returned home by his liberators, but was forced to serve in a *Wehrmacht* engineer unit that was sent to fight the Yugoslav partisans. He was captured by **Chetniks**, royalist Serbian partisans, and then by Communist partisans who attacked the **Chetniks**. He was liberated by Italian parachutists who surprised the Communists, and he was shipped to Italy (*CC* 102:L16, 18).

Chevy Chase, MD. *After Walter Starbuck returned from Europe with his new wife Ruth, they moved into this Washington, D.C. suburb. Ruth eventually had a small draperies business which she ran from home. Walter had to sell the house to finance his defense for his part in the Watergate scandal.*

chimney, **chimneylike**. (*ST* 23:L28) It was ten feet long, six feet wide, and had a ceiling, like the rest of the rooms in the mansion, twenty feet high. The room was like a **chimney**. *This "architectural accident" was the room Winston Niles Rumfoord "really wanted with all my heart when I was a boy—this little room."*

(*ST* 35:L2) "Well—" murmured Malachi Constant, there in the **chimneylike** room under the staircase in Newport, "it looks like the messenger is finally going to be used."

(*ST* 46:L29) The little door had been a dreamy touch. . . . the dry fountain another and the huge painting of the all white pony. . . . touch-me-not little girl with the all white pony. . . . and the **chimneylike** room under the spiral staircase and the photograph of the three sirens on Titan and Rumfoord's prophecies. . . . and the discomfiture of Beatrice Rumfoord at the top of the stairs. . . .

(*ST* 190:L26) It had delivered its cargo to the floor of a cave one hundred and sixteen miles below the surface of Mercury. It had threaded its way down through a tortuous system of **chimneys** until it could go no deeper. *This is in reference to the space ship carrying Unk/Malachi and Boaz.*

(*ST* 211:L21) It would go up the system of **chimneys** under the impression that it was going down. And it would inevitably find the way out, under the impression that it was seeking the deepest possible hole. *Since the space ship* *could only travel "downwards," Unk had turned the ship upside down so its navigational system would read "up" as "down," thereby allowing him to escape the caves of Mercury.*

(*SL5* 80:L9-10) There was this difference, though: the sheds had tin **chimneys**, and out of the **chimneys** whirled constellations of sparks. *The shed doors were about to swing open to a rousing welcome of "Hail, Hail, the Gang's All Here" from the British POWs to the new American arrivals, Billy Pilgrim included.*

(*MH* 138:L9 *The Hyannis Port Story*) "They *(tourists)* don't even get to look at a Kennedy **chimney** up above the trees. All the glamour they'll get out of this administration is an overpriced waffle named *Caroline*."

(*MH* 160:L3 *Report on the Barnhouse Effect*) By the time of his discharge in 1945, he could knock bricks loose from **chimneys** three miles away. *This describes Barnhouse's early abilities exercising dynamopsychism.*

(*JB* xxiv:L9) By the end of November the **chimneys** of the factory were belching smoke again.

(*JB* 184:L11) When *(Kenneth)* Whistler came home, there was smoke coming out of his **chimney**. There was a hot meal waiting for him inside. *The mine worker and union organizer is surprized by Mary Kathleen O'Looney's arrival at his home in Kentucky.*

(*PS* 20:L1 *Roots*) When I published my first short story, which was "Report on the Barnhouse Effect," in *Collier's*, its hero was a man who could control dice by thinking hard about them, and who could eventually loosen bricks in **chimneys** a mile away, and so on—and Uncle John said, "Now you will hear from every nut in the country. They can all do that."

(*Blue* 89:L11-12) I remembered the long table and the corner cupboard full of pewter and the rustic fireplace with a blunderbuss resting on pegs driven into its **chimney** breast, from a painting he had done of Thanksgiving at Plymouth Colony. *Rabo Karabekian reminisces about a room in Dan Gregory's home.*

(*Blue* 95:L29) I stopped at the head of the stairs, and perceived an impossibility: six free-standing **chimneys** and fireplaces, with a coal fire glowing in the hearth of every one. *Dan Gregory had purchased three connected townhouses and had removed the walls separating them.*

(*Blue* 101:L2) *Dan Gregory is speaking to Rabo of his rearing by Beskudnikov's wife:* "I was just one more job to do, like shoveling ashes from the stoves or cleaning the lamp **chimneys** or beating the rugs."

(*FWD* 14:L15) Here are the last words he *(Heinrich Böll)* would ever say to me in this life (and he was on two canes and still smoking like a **chimney**, and about to board a taxicab to the airport in a cold London drizzle): "Oh, Koort, it is so hard, so hard." He was one of the last shreds of native German sorrow and shame about his country's part in World War II and its prelude. He told me off camera that he was despised by his neighbors for remembering when it was time to forget.

(*FWD* 108:L18) During the question-and-answer period following my great speech I found an opportunity to quote O'Hare. When a Liberty Ship (the

Lucretia C. Mott, named for a women's rights advocate) had wallowed us back to the United States through severe storms in the North Atlantic, and it was time for me and my buddy to say good-bye for a while (a condition now quite permanent), I said to him, "What did you learn?" The future DA O'Hare replied, "I will never again believe my Government." This had to do with our Government's tall tales of delicate surgery performed by bombers equipped with Sperry and Norden bombsights. These instruments were so precise, we had been told, that a bombardier could drop his billets-doux down the **chimney** of a factory if ordered to. There were solemn charades performed for newsreels in which military policemen with drawn .45 automatics escorted bombardiers carrying bombsights to their planes. That was how desperate the Germans and the Japanese were (so went the message) to learn and make use of the secret of our bombings' diabolical accuracy themselves.

Christ, **Jesus Christ**, (see also **The Church of Jesus Christ the Kidnapped**).
(*PP* 112:L11) "Garth's a fine man," said Paul. Garth was, too: four-square, desperate to please, and he seemed to have an anthropomorphic image of the corporate personality. Garth stood in relation to that image as a lover, and Paul wondered if this prevalent type of relationship had ever been given the consideration it deserved by sexologists. On second thought, he supposed that it had—the general phenomenon of a lover's devotion to the unseen—in studies of nuns' symbolic marriages to **Christ**.
(*ST* 50:L10,18) In the year Ten Million, according to Koradubian, there would be a tremendous house-cleaning. All records relating to the period between the death of **Christ** and the year One Million A.D. would be hauled to dumps and burned. . . .

The million-year period to which the burned junk related would be summed up in history books in one sentence, according to Koradubian: *Following the death of* ***Jesus Christ****, there was a period of readjustment that lasted for approximately one million years.*
(*MN* 51:L11-12) And he *(Dr. Lionel J.D. Jones)* wrote and published at his own expense a book that combined not only dentistry and theology, but the fine arts as well. The name of the book was ***Christ** Was Not a Jew*. He proved his point by reproducing in the book fifty famous paintings of **Jesus**. According to Jones, not one painting showed Jewish jaws or teeth.
(*CC* 19:L23) "It so happens I know where the string he *(Felix Hoenikker, inventor of ice-nine)* was playing with came from. . . . The novel was about the end of the world in the year 2000, and the name of the book was *2000 A.D.* It told about how mad scientists made a terrific bomb that wiped out the whole world. There was a big sex orgy when everybody knew that the world was going to end, and then **Jesus Christ** Himself appeared ten seconds before the bomb went off.
(*GBR* 134:L10) There was a photograph of Trout. He was an old man with a full black beard. He looked like a frightened, aging **Jesus**, whose sentence to crucifixion had been commuted to imprisonment for life.

(*GBR* 212:L6) "Think of the sacrilege of a **Jesus** figure redeeming stamps." *Kilgore Trout worked at a stamp redemption center in Cohoes, New York.*
(*SL5* Preface) *The cattle are lowing, / The Baby awakes. / But the little Lord* ***Jesus*** */ No crying He makes.*
(*SL5* 26:L29) He *(Billy Pilgrim)* was a valet to a preacher, expected no promotions or medals, bore no arms, and had a meek faith in a loving **Jesus** which most soldiers found putrid.
(*SL5* 94:L14-15, 27; 95:L3) The flaw in the **Christ** stories, said the visitor from outer space, was that **Christ**, who didn't look like much, was actually the Son of the Most Powerful Being in the Universe. Readers understood that, so, when they came to the crucifixion, they naturally thought, and Rosewater read out loud again:

Oh, boy—they sure picked the wrong guy to lynch that *time!*

And that though had a brother: *"There are* right people *to lynch."* Who? People not well connected. So it goes.

The visitor from outer space made a gift to Earth of a new Gospel. In it, **Jesus** really *was* a nobody, and a pain in the neck to a lot of people with better connections than he had. He still got to say all the lovely and puzzling things he said in the other Gospels.

So the people amused themselves one day by nailing him to a cross and planting the cross in the ground. There couldn't possibly be any repercussions, the lynchers thought. The reader would have to think that, too, since the new Gospel hammered home again and again what a nobody **Jesus** was.

And then, just before the nobody died, the heavens opened up, and there was thunder and lightning. The voice of God came crashing down. He told the people that he was adopting the bum as his son, giving him the full powers and priveleges of The Son of the Creator of the Universe throughout all eternity. God said this: *From this moment on, He will punish horribly anybody who torments a bum who has no connections!*
(*SL5* 170:L22, 26) Billy cried very little, though he often saw things worth crying about, and in that respect, at least, he resembled the **Christ** of the carol: *The cattle are lowing, / The Baby awakes. / But the little Lord* ***Jesus*** */ No crying He makes.*
(*SL5* 174:L33 175:L1, 7, 30, 32; 176:L4, 7, 13-14, 22) Another Kilgore Trout book there in the window was about a man who built a time machine so he could go back and see **Jesus**. It worked, and he saw **Jesus** when **Jesus** was only twelve years old. **Jesus** was learning the carpentry trade from his father.

Two Roman soldiers came into the shop with a mechanical drawing on papyrus of a device they wanted built by sunrise the next morning. It was a cross to be used in the execution of a rabble-rouser.

Jesus and his father built it. They were glad to have the work. And the rabble-rouser was executed on it. . . .

So Billy moved a little farther back, but not as far as the part for adults only. He moved because of absentminded politeness, taking a Trout book with him—the one about **Jesus** and the time machine.

The time-traveler in the book went back to *Bible* times to find out one thing in particular: Whether or not **Jesus** had really died on the cross, or whether he had been taken down while still alive, whether he had really gone on living. The hero had a stethoscope along.

Billy skipped to the end of the book, where the hero mingled with the people who were taking **Jesus** down from the cross. The time-traveler was the first one up the ladder, dressed in clothes of the period, and he leaned close to **Jesus** so people couldn't see him use the stethoscope, and he listened. . . .

The time-traveler, whose name was Lance Corwin, also got to measure the length of **Jesus**, but not to weigh him. **Jesus** was five feet and three and a half inches long. . . .

"**Jesus Christ**, where did you find this thing?" and so on, and he had to tell the other clerks about the pervert who wanted to buy the window dressing. *The clerk in a pornographic book store is shocked that Billy Pilgrim wants to buy a Kilgore Trout novel rather than one of the standard pornographic offerings.*

(*SL5* 182:L13) On Tralfamadore, says Billy Pilgrim, there isn't much interest in **Jesus Christ**.

(*WJ* 136:L10, 13) WANDA JUNE Walt Disney, who gave us Snow White and the Seven Dwarfs, plays shuffleboard. **Jesus Christ** plays shuffleboard.
VON KONIGSWALD It was almost worth the trip—to find out that **Jesus Christ** in Heaven was just another guy, playing shuffleboard. I like his sense of humor, though—you know? He's got a blue-and-gold warm-up jacket he wears. You know what it says on the back? "Pontius Pilate Athletic Club." Most people don't get it. Most people think there really is a Pontius Pilate Athletic Club.

(*BC* 73:L28;) The prostitutes worked for a pimp now. He was splendid and cruel. He was a god to them. He took their free will away from them, which was perfectly all right. They didn't want it anyway. It was as though they had surrendered themselves to **Jesus**, for instance, so they could live unselfishly and trustingly—except that they had surrendered to a pimp instead.

(*WFG* 246:L13 *Playboy Interview*) PLAYBOY: You speak of gentle people, but somehow all this talk of **Jesus** freaks and extended families bring Charles Manson to mind.
VONNEGUT: Yes, it does. His, of course, was an extended family. He recruited all these dim-witted girls, homeless girls, usually—girls who felt homeless, at any rate—and the family meant so much to them that they would do anything for it. They were simple and they were awfully young.

(*Slap* 25:L27) They finally came up with an answer. Melody does most of the talking for them, and this is what she said in all seriousness: "You, and **Jesus Christ**, and Santa Claus." *This is in response to Wilbur Swain's question as to who were the three most important human beings in history.*

(*JB* 171:L28) When I was a young man, I expected the story of Sacco and Vanzetti to be retold as often and as movingly, to be as irresistible, as the story of **Jesus Christ** some day. Weren't modern people, if they were to marvel creatively at their own lifetimes, I thought, entitled to a Passion like Sacco and Vanzetti's, which ended in an electric chair?

(*PS* 325:L27-8, 326:L1-27 *In the Capital of the World*) "Now, as to the verses about Palm Sunday Eve: I choose them because **Jesus** says something in the eighth verse which many people I have known have taken as proof that **Jesus** himself occasionally got sick and tired of people who needed mercy all the time. I read from the Revised Standard Bible rather than the King James, because it is easier understand. Also, I will argue afterward that **Jesus** was only joking, and it is impossible to joke in King James English. The funniest joke in the world, if told in King James English, is doomed to sound like Charlton Heston.

"I read:

"'Six days before the Passover, **Jesus** came to Bethany, where Lazarus was, whom **Jesus** had raised from the dead. There they made him a supper; Martha served, but Lazarus was one of those at table with him.

"'Mary took a pound of costly ointment of pure nard and anointed the feet of **Jesus** and wiped his feet with her hair; and the house was filled with the fragrance of the ointment.

"'But Judas Iscariot, one of his disciples (he who was to betray him), said, "Why was this ointment not sold for three hundred denarii and given to the poor?" This he said, not that he cared for the poor but because he was a thief, and as he had the money box he used to take what was put into it. **Jesus** said, "Let her alone, let her keep it for the day of my burial. The poor you always have with you, but you do not always have me.'"

"Thus ends the reading, and although I have promised a joke, there is not much of a chuckle in there anywhere. The reading, in fact, ends with at least two quite depressing implications: That **Jesus** could be a touch self-pitying, and that he was, with his mission to earth about to end, at least momentarily sick and tired of hearing about the poor."

(*PS* 329:L1-20 *In the Capital of the World*) Mary begins to massage and perfume the feet of **Jesus Christ** with an ointment made from the spikenard plant. **Jesus** has the bones of a man and is clothed in the flesh of a man-so it must feel awfully nice, what Mary is doing to his feet. Would it be heretical of us to suppose that **Jesus** closes his eyes? . . .

"To which **Jesus** replies in Aramaic: 'Judas, don't worry about it. There will still be plenty of poor people left long after I'm gone.' . . .

"If **Jesus** did in fact say that, it is a divine black joke, well suited to the occasion. It says everything about hypocrisy and nothing about the poor. It is a Christian joke, which allows **Jesus** to remain civil to Judas, but to chide him about his hypocrisy all the same.

"'Judas, don't worry about it. There will still be plenty of poor people left long after I'm gone.'"

(*Blue* 127:L27) "I brought you back to life," she said *(Circe Berman)*. "You're my Lazarus. All **Jesus** did for Lazarus was bring him back to life. I not only brought you back to life—I got you writing your autobiography."

(*Blue* 200:L29) Slazinger, high as a kite, says that every successful revolution, including Abstract Expressionism, the one I took part in, had that cast of characters at the top Pollock being the genius in our case, Lenin being the one in Russia's, **Christ** being the one in Christianity's.

(*HP* 14:L14,18) From the time I *(Eugene Debs Hartke)* was 21 until I was 35 I was a professional soldier, a Commissioned Officer in the United States Army. During those 14 years I would have killed **Jesus Christ** Himself or Herself or Itself or Whatever, if ordered to do so by a superior officer. . . .

During that war *(Vietnam)*, which was about nothing but the ammunition business, there was a microscopic possibility, I suppose, that I called in a white-phosphorus barrage or a napalm air strike on a returning **Jesus Christ**.

(*HP* 96:L31) "I heard you said **Jesus Christ** was un-American," she said, her tape recorder running all the time. *Hartke explains that his socialist Grandfther Wills had quoted Marx to him, "From each according to his abilities, to each according to his needs," and continued on by saying "What could be more un-American Gene, than sounding like the Sermon on the Mount?"*

(*HP* 226:L10) Think again about the crucifixions of **Jesus** and the 2 thieves, and the 6,000 slaves who followed the gladiator Spartacus. *Hartke says this as an analogy to all societies which believe their punitive measures are designed to protect the welfare of the state and preserve property.*

(*FWD* 11:inscription) O God who hast hitherto supported me, enable me to proceed in this labor & in the whole task of my present state that when I shall render up at the last day an account of the talent committed to me I may receive pardon for the sake of **Jesus Christ**. Amen.

—SAMUEL JOHNSON
diary entry for April 3, 1753,
when he was working on his
*Dictionary of the English Language**
*April 3, therefore, might be called "Writer's Day."

(*FWD* 80:L3) The first story of mine which got into trouble with the sincerely Christian far right was about time-travelers who went back to Bible times and discovered that **Jesus Christ** was five feet, two inches tall. I think I liked **Jesus** more than the story's naysayers did, since I was asserting that I didn't care how tall or short He was.

(*FWD* 163:L22) "How tragic it is, then, that the major impulses in this and several other societies nowadays should be in the direction of the pure baloney and cruel entertainments of thousands of years ago, which almost inevitably lead to the antithesis of beauty and the good life and Christianity as taught by **Jesus Christ**, which is war."

(*FWD* 189:L15) I mentioned Abbie Hoffman in that piece about books as mantras for meditation. I realize that most people nowadays don't know who he was or what he did. He was a clowning genius, having come into the world that way, like Lenny Bruce and Jack Benny and Ed Wynn and Stan Laurel and

W. C. Fields and the Marx Brothers and Red Skelton and Fred Allen and Woody Allen and so on. He was a member of my children's generation. He is high on my list of saints, of exceptionally courageous, unarmed, unsponsored, unpaid souls who have tried to slow down even a little bit state crimes against those **Jesus Christ** said should inherit the Earth someday. (*FWD* 238:L16) I am a fourth generation German American religious skeptic ("Freethinker"). Like my essentially puritanical forebears, I believe that God has so far been unknowable and hence unservable, hence the highest service one can perform is to his or her community, whose needs are quite evident. I believe that virtuous behavior is trivialized by carrot-and-stick schemes, such as promises of highly improbable rewards or punishments in an improbable afterlife. (The punishment for counterfeiting in Henry VIII's reign, incidentally, was being boiled alive in public.) The Bible is a useful starting point for discussions with crowds of American strangers, since so many of us know at least a little something about it. It has the added virtue of having for contributors at least two geniuses Moses and **Christ**. *See also: PP* 50:L24; 77:L3; 194:L7,9-10; 206:L17; 219:L39; 222:L19; 232:L35; 241:L15; 283:L9; *ST* 99:L2; *MN* 3:L13-14; 29:L23; 41:L6; 102:L12; 124:L18; *CC* 63:L13; 70:L26; 80:L8; 88:L32; 111:L12,28 139:L3,6; 140:L4,6; 154:L15-16,18; *GBR* 91:L4; 108:L1; 155:L11; 170:L27; *SL5* 15:L26; 33:L13,15; 41:L21; 95:L18; 120:L20; 169:L10; *WJ* 2:L23; 44:L10; 56:L8,25; 57:L9; 118:L22; 128:L18; 159:L17; 160:L9,16; 162:L5-6; *BC* 62:L6; 109:L33; 120:L29; 212:L7; *WFG—Yes, We Have No Nirvanas* 39:L4,11,13,16,18,30; 41:L30,31; *WFG—Why They Read Hesse* 108:L3; *WFG—Playboy Interview* 245:L14; *Slap* 47:L9; 126:L12; 134:L29; 184:L14; 185:L8,21,24; 186:L12; 188:L17; 220:L10,14; 237:L30; 239:L25; *JB* xix:L18; 31:L25; 34:L9; 35:L7,15; 38:L10,18,26; 41:L7,31; 42:L1; 194:L19; 196:L26; *PS—When I Lost My Innocence* 69:L10; *PS—Self-Interview* 117:L13; *PS—The People One Knows* 143:L21; *PS—Mark Twain* 167:L28,31; *PS—Religion* 211:L20; 216:L30; 217:L13-31; *PS—Jekyll and Hyde Updated* 266:L32; 267:L11; 268:L31; *PS—In the Capital of the World* 326:L31; 327:L16,28; 328:L6,14,24; *DD* 66:L33; 86:L34; 153:L33; 154:L5-6,16; 213:L13-14; 229:L29; *Gal* 207:L4; *Blue* 10:L31; 16:L23; 99:L32; 214:L2; 268:L26; 270:L1,4; 287:L21,24; 296:L19; *HP* 13:L14; 98:L3; 156:L26; 180:L17; *FWD* 59:L30; 69:L10; 70:L5; 77:L18; 87:L20; 88:L20; 120:L6; 137:L9; 141:L10; 156:L3; 223-226 translation of Latin Mass.

christen. (*MN* 130:L20) *The following is a conversation held by Resi Noth and Howard Campbell about the new identities they will assume once they leave the United States*. Have you decided on a name yet?" she said.

"Name?" I said.

"Your new name—the name of the new writer whose beautiful works come mysteriously out of Mexico," she said. "I will be Mrs.—"

"*Senora—*" I said.

"Senora who?" she said. "Senor and Senora who?"

"**Christen** us," I said.
(*CC* 90:L33) He *(Bokonon)* was **christened** Lionel Boyd Johnson.
(*MH* xiv:L3 *Preface*) She was **christened** "Alice," but she used to deny that she was really an Alice. I agreed. Everybody agreed. Sometime in a dream maybe I will find out what her real name was. *Vonnegut refers to his sister Alice.*
(*MH* 262:L31 *The Manned Missiles*) You are lucky you have a son left, Mr. Ivankov. Hazel and I don't. Bryant was the only son Hazel and I had. We didn't call him Bryant after he was **christened**. We called him Bud.
(*Slap* 27:L7, 11) I was born right here in New York City. I was not then a *Daffodil*. I was **christened** Wilbur *Rockefeller* Swain. . . .

We were **christened** in a hospital rather than in a church, and we were not surrounded by relatives and our parents' friends. The thing was: Eliza and I were so ugly that our parents were ashamed.

Christian (also **Young Men's Christian Association**, **Christian Scientists**; see also **The White Christian Minuteman**). (*MN* 45:L17) I opened the newspaper first, found it to be ***The White Christian Minuteman***, a scabrous, illiterate, anti-Semitic, anti-Negro, anti-Catholic hate sheet published by the Reverend Doctor Lionel J.D. Jones, D.D.S.
(*CC* 13:L19;) The book was to be an account of what important Americans had done on the day when the first atomic bomb was dropped on Hiroshima, Japan.

It was to be a **Christian** book. I was a **Christian** then. I am a Bokononist now.
(*GBR* 139:L28) "Every year at least one young man whose affairs we manage comes into our office, wants to give his money away. He has completed his first year at some great university. It has been an eventful year! He has learned of unbelievable suffering around the world. He has learned of the great crimes that are at the roots of so many family fortunes. He has had his **Christian** nose rubbed, often for the very first time, in the Sermon on the Mount." *The speaker is McAllister, Stewart Buntline's attorney.*
(*SL5* 94:L4) It *(Kilgore Trout's* Gospel From Outer Space*)* was about a visitor from outer space, shaped very much like a Tralfamadorian, by the way. The visitor from outer space made a serious study of Christianity, to learn, if he could, why **Christians** found it so easy to be cruel.
(*WFG* 39:L16 *Yes, We Have No Nirvanas*) He suggested that Jesus might have been onto something like Transcendental Meditation, but that it was garbled and lost by his followers. A few moments later he said that Jesus and the early **Christian** saints had mistakenly allowed their minds to wander. "You must have control," he said. The wandering minds of Jesus and the saints had led to what Maharishi called "an absurdity," an emphasis on faith.
(*JB* 16:L12) My late wife Ruth, the grandmother of these children, was born in Vienna. Her family owned a rare-book store there before the Nazis took it away from them. . . . She herself was hidden by a **Christian** family, but was

discovered and arrested, along with the head of that family, in Nineteen-hundred and Forty-two.

(*JB* 38:L17) This is it: "Depart from me, you cursed, into the eternal fire prepared for the devil and his Angels" *(Quoted by Emil Larkin, Matthew 25:41)*

These words appalled me then, and they appall me now. They are surely the inspiration for the notorious cruelty of **Christians**.

(*PS* 167:L15 *Mark Twain*) "I now quote a previous owner of this house: 'When I find a well-drawn character in fiction or biography, I generally take a warm personal interest in him, for the reason that I have known him before—met him on the river.'

"I submit to you that this is a profoundly **Christian** statement, an echo of the Beatitudes. It is constructed, as many jokes are, incidentally, with a disarmingly pedestrian beginning and an unexpectedly provoking conclusion."

(*PS* 216:L26; 217:L7, 9 *Religion*) "I have spoken of the long tradition of religious skepticism in my family. One of my two daughters has recently turned her back on all that. Living alone and far from home, she has memorized an arbitrary **Christian** creed, Trinitarianism, by chance. She now has her human dignity regularly confirmed by the friendly nods of a congregation. I am glad that she is not so lonely anymore. This is more than all right with me.

"She believes that Jesus was the Son of God, or perhaps God Himself—or however that goes. I have had even more trouble with the Trinity than I had with college algebra. I refer those who are curious about it to what is known about the Council of Nicea, which took place in anno Domini 325. It was there that the Trinity was hammered into its present shape. Unfortunately, the minutes have been lost. It is known that the emperor Constantine was there, and probably spoke a good deal. He gave us the first **Christian** army. He may have given us the Holy Ghost as well.

No matter. I do not argue with my **Christian** daughter about religion at all. Why should I?

(*PS* 235:L2 *Children*) MY first wife and both my daughters are born-again **Christians** now—working white magic through rituals and prayers. That's all right. I would be a fool to say that the Free Thinker ideas of Clemens Vonnegut remain as enchanting and encouraging as ever—not after the mortal poisoning of the planet, not after two world wars, with more to come.

(*PS* 256:L19, 21 *Jonathan Swift Misperceived*) His motives were invariably serious, however, and I now suggest that *Gulliver's Travels* can be read as a series of highly responsible sermons, delivered during a crisis in **Christian** attitudes, one that is far from over yet. The crisis is this, in my opinion: It simply will not do for adult **Christians** to think of themselves as God's little lambs anymore.

(*HP* 128:L12-14) So I happened to sit in on a class where he talked about Hitler's being a devout Roman Catholic. He said something I hadn't realized before, something I have since discovered most **Christians** don't want to hear: that the Nazi swastika was intended to be a version of a **Christian** cross, a cross made out of axes. Stern said that **Christians** had gone to a lot of trouble denying that the swastika was just another cross, saying it was a primitive symbol from the primordial ooze of the pagan past.

(*FWD* 59:L30) "It seems to me now that Algren's pessimism about so much of earthly life was **Christian**. Like Christ, as we know Him from the Bible, he was enchanted by the hopeless, could not take his eyes off them, and could see little good news for them in the future, given what they had become and what Caesar was like and so on, unless beyond death there awaited something more humane."

(*FWD* 76:L6, 31) When I was new at such discussions I insouciantly asked a fundamentalist **Christian** opponent ("Oh, come on now, Reverend") if he knew of anyone who had been ruined by a book. (Mark Twain claimed to have been ruined by salacious parts of the Bible.)

. . . The books he and his supporters wanted out of the schools, one of mine among them, were not pornographic, although he would have liked our audience to think so. (There is the word "motherfucker" one time in my *Slaughterhouse-Five*, as in "Get out of the road, you dumb motherfucker." Ever since that word was published, way back in 1969, children have been attempting to have intercourse with their mothers. When it will stop no one knows.) The fault of *Slaughterhouse-Five*, James Dickey's *Deliverance*, J. D. *Salinger's Catcher in the Rye*, several books by Judy Blume, and so on, as far as the Reverend was concerned, was that neither their authors nor their characters exemplified his notion of ideal **Christian** behavior and attitudes.

(*FWD* 80:L2) (The first story of mine which got into trouble with the sincerely **Christian** far right was about time-travelers who went back to Bible times and discovered that Jesus Christ was five feet, two inches tall. I think I liked Jesus more than the story's naysayers did, since I was asserting that I didn't care how tall or short He was.

(*FWD* 158:L22, 24) "I was an Infantry Private during World War II and fought against the Germans in Europe. My religion as well as my blood type was stamped into my dogtags. The Army decided my religion was P, for 'Protestant.' There is no room on dogtags for footnotes and a bibliography. In retrospect, I think they should have put S on my dogtags, for 'Saracen,' since we were fighting **Christians** who were on some sort of utterly insane Crusade. They had crosses on their flags and uniforms and all over their killing machines, just like the soldiers of the first **Christian** Emperor Constantine. And they lost, of course, which has to be acknowledged as quite a setback for Christianity."

(*FWD* 160:L32) The **Christian** quick trip from love to hate and murder is our principal entertainment. We might call it 'Christianity Fails Again,' and how satisfying so many of us have been trained to find it when it fails and fails.

(*FWD* 161:L31) And should any **Christian** be sorry that we killed Qaddafi's baby daughter? Well Jerry Falwell should speak to this issue, since he knows all the verses in the Bible which make murder acceptable. My own theory is that the little girl, by allowing herself to be adopted by a dark-skinned Muslim absolutely absolutely nobody watching American television could love, in effect committed suicide. *See also: PP* 16:L15; 204:L3; *MN* 46:L21,29; 48:L4; 50:L12; 51:L6,15; 52:L19; 53:L7; 114:L13; 133:L28; *CC* 61:L26; 83:L8; 115:L3; 116:L14; 120:L33; 175:L15; 176:L3,23; 177 paragraph title; 179:L5,10; 187:L10; *GBR* 19:L21; 154:L14; *MH—Welcome To The Monkey House* 33:L15; *MH—Miss Temptation* 76:L7; *MH—More Stately Mansions* 129:L26; *BC* 217:L30; 218:L2; 248:L23; 253:L15; *WFG—Yes, We Have No Nirvanas* 39:L9; *WFG—Biafra: A People Betrayed* 139:L15; *WFG—Address to the National Institute of Arts and Letters, 1971* 180:L8; *Slap* 41:L9; 125:L17; 197:L2; *JB* 69:L7; 150:L4; *PS—Roots* 31:L10; *PS—Religion* 199:L6; 215:L31-32; *PS—Jekyll And Hyde Updated* 290:L13; *PS—The Sexual Revolution* 307:L21; *PS—In The Capital Of The World* 329:L18; *DD* 154:L9,17; 169:L20; *Blue* 217:L11; 217:L27; 240:L7; *HP* 98:L17; 127:L30; 128:L25-26; 129:L24; 219:L2; *FWD* 77:L17; 158:L33; 161:L9,11; 169:L8.

Christianity. (*SL5* 14:L14) *History in her solemn page informs us that the crusaders were but ignorant and savage men, that their motives were those of bigotry unmitigated, and that their pathway was one of blood and tears. Romance, on the other hand, dilates upon their piety and heroism, and portrays, in her most glowing and impassioned hues, their virtue and magnanimity, the imperishable honor they acquired for themselves, and the great services they rendered to* **Christianity**. *(Vonnegut quotes Charles Mackay's* Extraordinary Popular Delusions and the Madness of Crowds.*)*
(*SL5* 44:L10) He *(Roland Weary)* dilated upon the piety and heroism of "The Three Musketeers," portrayed, in the most glowing and impassioned hues, their virtue and magnanimity, the imperishable honor they acquired for themselves, and the great services they rendered to **Christianity**.
(*SL5* 94:L4) . . . *The Gospel from Outer Space*, by Kilgore Trout. It was about a visitor from outer space, shaped very much like a Tralfamadorian, by the way. The visitor from outer space made a serious study of **Christianity**, to learn, if he could, why Christians found it so easy to be cruel. He concluded that at least part of the trouble was slipshod storytelling in the New Testament. He supposed that the intent of the Gospels was to teach people, among other things, to be merciful, even to the lowest of the low.
(*WFG* 239:L30 *Playboy Interview*) VONNEGUT: But as far as improving the human condition goes, our minds are certainly up to that. That's what they were designed to do. And we do have the freedom to make up comforting lies. But we don't do enough of it. One of my favorite ministers was a guy named Bob Nicholson. . . . Every time one of his parishioners died, he went all to pieces. He was outraged by death. So it was up to his congregation and the relatives of the deceased to patch him up, get him pumped up on **Christianity** sufficiently to get through the funeral service. I liked that very much: Nothing he was going to say in the standard Episcopalian funeral oration was going to satisfy him. He needed better lies.

(*WFG* 245:L16, 19-20, 31-32; 246:L1, 5, 9-10 *Playboy Interview*) PLAYBOY: This longing for community may explain, at least in part, the Jesus-freak movement among young people. But why do you think they're attracted to fundamentalist **Christianity**?
VONNEGUT: Well, the choice of a core for an artificial extended family is fairly arbitrary. I've already mentioned the arts and jism and blood and spaghetti. **Christianity** is equally commonplace and harmless, and therefore good. Do you know what nucleation is? I don't, but I'll pretend I do. It has to do with how big something has to be in order to grow rather than die out. The standard example is starting a fire in a coal furnace. If the fire you start is below a certain size, it will go out. If it's larger than that, it will spread until all the fuel is on fire. Clumps of cancer cells are probably forming in us all the time and petering out—because the clumps are below a certain size. In America, it's easy to form a large clump of people who know something about **Christianity**, since there has always been so much talk about **Christianity** around. It wouldn't be easy to get a large clump of Zoroastrians, for instance. But there are very big clumps of **Christianity**. There are very big clumps of race hatred. It's easy to make either one of them grow, especially in a society as lonesome as this one is. All kinds of clumps.
PLAYBOY: So you don't admire **Christianity** any more or less than, say, a communal bowl of spaghetti every evening? Or anything else that might hold an extended family together?
VONNEGUT: I admire **Christianity** more than anything—**Christianity** as symbolized by gentle people sharing a common bowl.
(*WFG* 247:L10 *Playboy Interview*) PLAYBOY: Do you have any suggestions on how to put together healthier extended families than *(Charles)* Manson's?
VONNEGUT: Sure. Put **Christianity** or spaghetti instead of murder at their core. I recommend this for countries, too.
(*PS* 199:L17 *Religion*) "What makes me think we need a new religion? That's easy. An effective religion allows people to imagine from moment to moment what is going on and how they should behave. **Christianity** used to be like that. Our country is now jammed with human beings who say out loud that life is chaos to them, and that it doesn't seem to matter what anybody does next. This is worse than being seasick."
(*Blue* 16:L25) Armenians, incidentally, were the first people to make **Christianity** their national religion.
(*Blue* 200:L29) Slazinger, high as a kite, says that every successful revolution, including Abstract Expressionism, the one I took part in, had that cast of characters at the top—Pollock being the genius in our case, Lenin being the one in Russia's, Christ being the one in **Christianity's**.
(*FWD* 77:L8) So the Reverend was not a hypocrite. He was perfectly willing to say in so many words that there was nothing sacred about the First Amendment, and that many images and ideas other than pornography should be taken out of circulation by the police, and that the official religion of the whole country should be his sort of **Christianity**. He was sincere in believing

that my *Slaughterhouse-Five* might somehow cause a person to wind up in a furnace for all eternity (see the mass promulgated by Pope St. Pius V), which would be even worse (if you consider its duration) than being raped, murdered, and then mutilated by a man maddened by dirty pictures.

(*FWD* 132:L4-5) Further on in the preface I went after American Eastern Seaboard prep schools again. (I am bughouse on that subject.) I said that those schools were clones of British prep schools, and that their idea of character was the so-called "muscular **Christianity**" exhibited by aristocratic imperialists in the time of Queen Victoria. (Those old-timers sure knew how to deal with monkeys without tails.) And then along comes *Masterpiece Theatre* on so-called "Public Television," dramatizing stories about the beauty and charm and wittiness not only of British imperialism but of the British class system as well. The British class system is as subversive of what the United States once hoped to be and might have been and should have been as *Das Kapital* or *Mein Kampf*. (Why is it, do you suppose, that the lower social orders don't watch more Public TV?)

(*FWD* 158:L26) "I was an Infantry Private during World War II and fought against the Germans in Europe. My religion as well as my blood type was stamped into my dogtags. The Army decided my religion was P, for 'Protestant.' There is no room on dogtags for footnotes and a bibliography. In retrospect, I think they should have put S on my dogtags, for 'Saracen,' since we were fighting Christians who were on some sort of utterly insane Crusade. They had crosses on their flags and uniforms and all over their killing machines, just like the soldiers of the first Christian Emperor Constantine. And they lost, of course, which has to be acknowledged as quite a setback for **Christianity**.

(*FWD* 160:L5) "So there you have my scheme for making **Christianity**, which has killed so many people so horribly, a little less homicidal: substituting the word 'respect' for the word 'love.' And as I said, I have been in actual battle with people who had crosses all over themselves. They were sure no fun.

(*FWD* 160:L34; 161:L7) "I have little hope that my simple reform will attract any appreciable support during my lifetime, anyway, or in the lifetimes of my children. The Christian quick trip from love to hate and murder is our principal entertainment. We might call it '**Christianity** Fails Again,' and how satisfying so many of us have been trained to find it when it fails and fails.

"In America it takes the form of the cowboy story. A goodhearted, innocent young man rides into town, with friendly intentions toward one and all. Never mind that he happens to be wearing a loaded Colt .44 on either hip. The last thing he wants is trouble. But before he knows it, this loving man is face to face with another man, who is so unlovable that he has absolutely no choice but to shoot him. **Christianity** Fails Again."

(*FWD* 161:L17, 19) "Very early British versions are tales of the quests of the Christian knights of King Arthur's Camelot. Like Hermann Göring, they have crosses all over them. They ride out into the countryside to help the weak, an admirably Christian activity. They are certainly not looking for trouble.

Never mind that they are iron Christmas trees decorated with the latest in weaponry. And before they know it, they are face to face with other knights so unlovable that they have absolutely no choice but to chop them up as though they were sides of beef in a butcher shop. **Christianity** Fails Again. What fun! And I point out to you that there was an implied promise that our own government would entertain us with failures of **Christianity** when John F. Kennedy allowed his brief Presidency to be called Camelot.
(*FWD* 162:L29-30, 32) "You are like them, as I have already said, in that you live in a time when killing is a leading entertainment form. According to the American Academy of Pediatrics, the average American child watches 18,000 TV murders before it graduates from high school. That kid has seen **Christianity** fail with pistols and rifles and shotguns and machine guns. It has seen **Christianity** fail with guillotines and gallows and electric chairs and gas chambers. That youngster has seen **Christianity** fail with fighter planes and bombers and tanks and battleships and submarines-with hatchets and clubs and chain saws and butcher knives.
(*FWD* 163:L22) "How tragic it is, then, that the major impulses in this and several other societies nowadays should be in the direction of the pure baloney and cruel entertainments of thousands of years ago, which almost inevitably lead to the antithesis of beauty and the good life and **Christianity** as taught by Jesus Christ, which is war.
(*FWD* 175:L11) (The photograph at the head of this chapter shows me in action in Mozambique, demonstrating muscular **Christianity** in an outfit that might have been designed by Ralph Lauren. The aborigines didn't know whether to shit or go blind until I showed up. And then I fixed everything.)
(*FWD* 238:L25) As for the preaching of formal Christianity, I am all for it.
See also: CC 176:L5; 176:L19-20; *BC* 217:L30; 218:L2,13; *JB* 148:L28; *PS—Religion* 201:L8; 208:L6; 216:L1; *PS—The Sexual Revolution* 315:L31; *HP* 98:L12; *FWD* 152:L27; 160:L5; 161:L28; 163:L27-28.

Chrono. *The son of Beatrice Rumfoord and Malachi Constant, Chrono is born on Mars and lives his first eight years there. Chrono was named for one of the twenty-one months in the Martian calendar. He picked up a piece of scrap metal at one of the manufacturing plants on Mars, and this became the long-awaited spare part for the Tralfamadorian messenger, Salo.*

Chrono is the best German batball player at school and is feared by the other children. He and his mother are diverted from the main part of the Martian invasion and crash-land in the Amazon Rain Forest. They are the only two survivors of the crash and become initiated into the Gumbo tribe. (*ST* 234:L6-12) During the initiation, mother and son had been staked at the ends of tethers in the middle of the village, with **Chrono** representing the Sun and Bee representing the Moon, as the Sun and the Moon were understood by the Gumbo people.

As a result of their experiences, Bee and **Chrono** were closer than most mothers and sons.

Chrono lives out his life the sole human being on Titan. He joined the Titanic bluebirds. (*ST* 304:L10-16) At the age of seventeen, young **Chrono** had run away from his palatial home to join the Titanic bluebirds, the most admirable creatures on Titan. **Chrono** now lived among their nests by the Kazak pools. He wore their feathers and sat on their eggs and shared their food and spoke their language.

chrono-synclastic infundibula. *Vonnegut's cosmogonic theory that all things are as they once were, will be as they have always been, that all is balanced as they always will be. He wrote about this perception in his opening comments about* Happy Birthday, Wanda June*:* "This intolerable balancing of characters and arguments reflected my true feelings: I felt and I still feel that everybody is right, no matter what he says. I had, in fact, written a book about everybody's being right all the time, *The Sirens of Titan*. And I gave a name in that book to a mathematical point where all opinions, no matter how contradictory, harmonized. I called it a ***chrono-synclastic infundibulum***.

"I live in one" (*WJ* ix:L12).

The primary use of the chrono-synclastic infundibulum occurs in The Sirens of Titan, *in which it is explained in the following manner.* (*ST* 14:L5-32, 15:L1-16) *CHRONO-SYNCLASTIC INFUNDIBULA*—Just imagine that your Daddy is the smartest man who ever lived on Earth, and he knows everything there is to find out, and he is exactly right about everything, and he can prove he is right about everything. Now imagine another little child on some nice world a million light years away, and that little child's Daddy is the smartest man who ever lived on that nice world so far away.

And he is just as smart and just as right as your Daddy is.

Both Daddies are smart, and both Daddies are right.

Only if they ever met each other they would get into a terrible argument, because they wouldn't agree on anything. Now, you can say that your Daddy is right and the other little child's Daddy is wrong, but the Universe is an awfully big place. There is room enough for an awful lot of people to be right about things and still not agree.

The reason both Daddies can be right and still get into terrible fights is because there are so many different ways of being right. There are places in the Universe, though, where each Daddy could finally catch on to what the other Daddy was talking about. These places are where all the different kinds of truths fit together as nicely as the parts in your Daddy's solar watch. We call these places **chrono-synclastic infundibula**.

The Solar System seems to be full of **chrono-synclastic infundibula**. There is one great big one we are sure of that likes to stay between Earth and Mars. We know about that one because an Earth man and his Earth dog ran right into it.

You might think it would be nice to go to a **chrono-synclastic infundibulum** and see all the different ways to be absolutely right, but it is a very dangerous thing to do. The poor man and his poor dog are scattered far and wide, not just through space, but through time, too.

Chrono (kroh-no) means time. **Synclastic** (sin-class-tick) means curved toward the same side in all directions, like the skin of an orange. **Infundibulum** (infun-dib-u-lum) is what the ancient Romans like Julius Caesar and Nero called a funnel. If you don't know what a funnel is, get Mommy to show you one.

Because of the revelation of eternal and recurring circumstances, The discovery of the **chrono-synclastic infundibula** said to mankind in effect: "What makes you think you're going anywhere?" (*ST* 30:L32, 31:L1-2) *Winston Niles Rumfoord and his dog Kazak travel through time and space by riding the wave of the chrono-synclastic infundibulum.*

In the short story "The Big Space Fuck," reprinted in Palm Sunday, *the plan is to aim the sperm-loaded spaceship* Arthur C. Clarke *directly into one of the eighty-seven known chrono-synclastic infundibulae insuring that* "the ship and its load would be multiplied a trillion times, and would appear everywhere throughout space and time.

"If there's any fecundity anywhere in the Universe," the scientist promised, "our seed will find it and bloom" (*PS* 230:L12-16 *Obscenity*).

Chrysler Building. *The home of RAMJAC's American Harp Company (top floor) in* Jailbird. *In* Galápagos, *Bobby King, mastermind of The Nature Cruise of the Century,* "moved into new offices within the hollow crown of the **Chrysler Building**, formerly the showroom of a harp company which found itself bankrupt" (*Galápagos* 90:L5).

In Bluebeard, *Rabo Karabekian considers it* the most beautiful skyscraper in the world (*Blue* 187:L28-29).
(*FWD* 15:L18) Q: What is your favorite building?
A: The Chrysler Building in Manhattan.

Chung, Lowell. (*HP* 70:L33-34) The most successful athlete ever to come from Tarkington, arguably, was a horseman from my own time, **Lowell Chung**. He won a Bronze Medal as a member of the United States Equestrian Team in Seoul, South Korea, back in 1988. *Chung graduated with an Associate of Arts degree in 1984.*

Chung, Mrs. *Lowell's mother, a member of Tarkington's Board of Trustees, and whom Eugene Debs Hartke describes as owning half of Honolulu without being able to read, write or do math. She spoke only Chinese and used John W. Fedders, Jr., another Tarkington Trustee, as her interpreter for college meetings. She died of tetanus, having never been inoculated against it in her home in China.*

Church of God the Utterly Indifferent. *Founded and presided over by Winston Niles Rumfoord in the days following the failed Martian invasion, the* *church has over three billion followers worldwide. Predicated on Rumfoord's knowledge of the chrono-synclastic infundibulum and on the Tralfamadorians' manipulation of earth history through the Universal Will to Become,* "To us of the **Church of God the Utterly Indifferent**, there is nothing more cruel, more dangerous, more blasphemous that a man can do than to believe that—that luck, good or bad, is the hand of God!" (*ST* 252:L6-10) Members of the church were made to wear bags of buckshot and other handicapping devices to enforce equality, a device Vonnegut previously used in the short story "Harrison Bergeron."

Church of Jesus Christ the Kidnapped. (*Slap* 184:L15-17) ". . . a tiny cult in Chicago, but destined to become the most popular American religion of all time." *In a leaflet about the new sect Wilbur Swain sees and reads the following:* At the very top of the leaflet was a primitive picture of Jesus, standing and with His Body facing forward, but with His Face in profile—like a one-eyed jack in a deck of playing cards.

He was gagged. He was handcuffed. One ankle was shackled and chained to a ring fixed to the floor. There was a single perfect tear dangling from the lower lid of His Eye.

QUESTION: What is your name?

ANSWER: I am the Right Reverend William Uranium-8 Wainwright, Founder of the **Church of Jesus Christ the Kidnapped** at 3972 Ellis Avenue, Chicago, Illinois.

QUESTION: When will God send us His Son again?

ANSWER: He already has. Jesus is here among us.

QUESTION: Why haven't we seen or heard anything about Him?

ANSWER: He has been kidnapped by the Forces of Evil.

QUESTION: What must we do?

ANSWER: We must drop whatever we are doing, and spend every waking hour in trying to find Him. If we do not, God will exercise His Option.

QUESTION: What is God's Option?

ANSWER: He can destroy Mankind so easily, any time he chooses to (*Slap* 185:L17-30, 186:L1-4). *Upon Wilbur's return to the Empire State Building, he sees a painting of Jesus Christ the Kidnapped in the lobby.*

Churchill, Winston. *The British wartime prime minister is held out by Eugene Debs Hartke as proof that even those in supremely responsible positions sometimes behaved in seemingly irresponsible ways. He does this as a way of defending his own high school behavior, which included smoking marijuana when he should have been paying attention to more important matters.* (*HP* 40:L31) I make no apologies for having been zapped during my darkest days in high school. **Winston Churchill** was bombed out of his skull on brandy and Cuban cigars during the darkest days of World War II.

Hartke later invokes Churchill as being one of the many people who everyday walk around with one drug habit or another. (*HP* 107:L3) When you dare to think about how huge the illegal drug business is in this country, you have to suspect that practically everybody has a steady buzz on, just as I did during my last 2 years in high school, and just as General Grant did during the Civil War, and just as **Winston Churchill** did during World War II.

Cincinnati Bengals. *In* Bluebeard *Rabo Karabekian owns one-quarter share of the Cincinnati Bengals, an inheritance from his wife Edith.*

Cinderella. *"Cinderella" is an important image as well as concept for Vonnegut. Upon arrival at the POW camp, Billy Pilgrim and the other newly captured Americans are treated to a roughhouse performance of the play by the British POWs. When midnight strikes in the play and Cinderella exclaims,* "Goodness me, the clock has struck— / Alackday, and fuck my luck," *Billy falls into hysterics and is led from the barracks to a hospital where he is shot up with morphine* (*SL5* 85:L9-10). *Edgar Derby went to care for Billy in the hospital and Paul Lazzaro joined them when he was knocked unconscious by the Blue Fairy Godmother of the play. They were the only three Americans not included in dividing the camp's provisions among the allied prisoners. Consequently, they were forced to sleep on the stage, and it is there Billy finds Cinderella's slippers and appropriates them for himself.* (*SL5* 125:L23-25, 32-33, 126:L1-5) **Cinderella**'s slippers, which were airman's boots painted silver, were capsized side by side under a golden throne. . . . Billy, curled in his azure nest, found himself staring at **Cinderella**'s silver boots under a throne. . . . And then he remembered that his shoes were ruined, that he *needed* boots. He hated to get out of his nest, but he forced himself to do it. He crawled to the boots on all fours, sat, tried them on.

The boots fit perfectly. Billy Pilgrim was **Cinderella**, and **Cinderella** was Billy Pilgrim.

In Breakfast of Champions, *Vonnegut again creates a Cinderella of sorts when Patty Keene senses that Dwayne Hoover could be her Blue Fairy Godmother because he could solve all her money worries. She lives under the burden of paying for her father's medical bills who is dying of cancer* (*BC* 137:L8).

Celia Hildreth is sarcastically characterized as another incarnation of Cinderella when she is asked to the prom by Felix Waltz, only to be later victimized by the antics of Otto Waltz. (*DD* 40:L29) But miracles do happen. A new **Cinderella** is born every minute. One of the richest, cutest boys in town, and the president of the senior class, no less, invited her to the senior prom.

Overriding the relative importance of these references within his fiction is Vonnegut's appreciation of Cinderella's narrative structure. In his "Self-Interview" reprinted in Palm Sunday, *Vonnegut defends simple plots like* Cinderella*'s by saying,* "I guarantee you that no modern story scheme, even plotlessness, will give a reader genuine satisfaction, unless one of those old fashioned plots is smuggled in somewhere. I don't praise plots as accurate representations of life, but as ways to keep readers reading. . . . When you exclude plot, when you exclude anyone's wanting anything, you exclude the reader, which is a mean-spirited thing to do" (*PS* 110:L14-18, 31-32, 111:L1-3). *This is a later reflection of Vonnegut's rejected master's thesis in anthropology at the University of Chicago. In "The Sexual Revolution," also reprinted in* Palm Sunday, *Vonnegut recounts his graphical appreciation of the tale with other similar tales.* (*PS* 315:L1-32, 316:L1-4) But then I had another look at a graph I had drawn of Western civilization's most enthusiastically received story, which is "***Cinderella***." At this very moment, a thousand writers must be telling that story again in one form or another. This very book is a **Cinderella** story of a kind.

I confessed that I was daunted by the graph of "**Cinderella**," and was tempted to leave it out of my thesis, since it seemed to prove that I was full of shit. It seemed too complicated and arbitrary to be a representative artifact—lacked the simple grace of a pot or a spearhead. . . .

The steps, you see, are all the presents the fairy godmother gave to **Cinderella**, the ball gown, the slippers, the carriage, and so on. The sudden drop is the stroke of midnight at the ball. **Cinderella** is in rags again. All the presents have been repossessed. But then the prince finds her and marries her, and she is infinitely happy ever after. She gets all the stuff back, and *then* some. A lot of people think the story is trash, and, on graph paper, it certainly looks like trash.

But then I said to myself, Wait a minute—those steps at the beginning look like the creation myth of virtually every society on earth. And then I saw that the stroke of midnight looked exactly like the unique creation myth in the Old Testament. And then I saw that the rise to bliss at the end was identical with the expectation of redemption as expressed in primitive Christianity.

The tales were identical.

I was thrilled to discover that years ago, and I am just as thrilled today. The apathy of the University of Chicago is repulsive to me.

They can take a flying fuck at the mooooooooooooooon.

civic, civic managers, civics, junior civics. (*PP* 71:L25) The **civic managers** were the career administrators who ran the city. They lived on the same side of the river as the managers and engineers of the Ilium Works, but the contact between the two groups was little more than perfunctory and, traditionally, suspicious. The schism, like so many things, dated back to the war, when the economy had, for efficiency's sake, become monolithic.

(*WFG* 272:L29 273:L6 *Playboy Interview*) PLAYBOY: Do you consider yourself a radical in any sense?

VONNEGUT: No, because everything I believe I was taught in **junior civics** during the Great Depression at School 43 in Indianapolis, with full approval of the school board. School 43 wasn't a radical school. America was an idealistic, pacifistic nation at that time. I was taught in the sixth grade to be proud that we had a standing Army of just over a hundred thousand men and that the generals had nothing to say about what was done in Washington. I was taught to be proud of that and to pity Europe for having more than a million men under arms and spending all their money on airplanes and tanks. I simply never unlearned **junior civics**. I still believe in it. I got a very good grade.

(*PS* 42:L5 *Roots*) "Aside from his attachment to his profession, Bernard *(Vonnegut's paternal grandfather)* took little participation in the social or **civic** life of the community."

(*PS* 97:L32 *Self-Interview*) INTERVIEWER: You just laughed about something.

VONNEGUT: It was something dumb I remembered about high school. It doesn't have anything to do with writing.

INTERVIEWER: You care to share it with us anyway?

VONNEGUT: Oh—I just remembered something that happened in a high school course on **civics**, on how our government worked. The teacher asked each of us to stand up in turn and tell what we did after school . . . a guy name J.T. Alburger . . . kept nudging me, urging me, daring me to tell the truth about what I did after school. He offered me five dollars to tell the truth. He wanted me to stand up and say, "I make model airplanes and jerk off."

(*PS* 279:L26, 29 *Jekyll And Hyde Updated*) Dr. Jekyll played by JERRY comes out of his house, the image of **civic** decency, and is recognized and adored by all. He is trying to get into his secret lab without being observed. While biding his time, he performs acts of **civic** virtue which are noted and admired by one and all.

(*HP* 276:L14) Every so often, in the midst of chaos, you come across an amazing, inexplicable instance of **civic** responsibility. Maybe the last shred of faith people have is in their firemen. *See also:* *PP* 71:L23,37; *MN* 177:L31; *MH—Where I Live* 5:L33; *PS—Roots* 27:L29.

Claessen. *Dan Gregory's Belgium canvas supplier. Marilee Kemp was sending Rabo Karabekian supplies from Dan Gregory's own stockpile while he was still in San Ignacio.* (*Blue* 60:L10-11) "No other artist west of the Rockies had such priceless art supplies!"

Claggett, Noble. *The student of Mary Hepburn's who wrote a poem for extra credit about the courtship dance of the blue-footed boobies after viewing a film of their mating rituals. Though later killed in Vietnam, his poem was memorized by Mary and later taught to Mandarax. This is what he had to say about the blue-footed boobies: Of course I love you, / So let's have a kid / Who will say exactly / What its parents did; / "Of course I love you, / So let's have a kid / Who will say exactly / What its parents did; / 'Of course I love you, / So let's have a kid/ Who will say exactly / What its parents did—'" / Et cetera.* **Noble Claggett** (1947-1966) (*Gal* 109:L3)

clan. (*WFG* 178:L3 *Address to the National Institute of Arts and Letters, 1971*) The American Academy of Arts and Letters and the National Institute of Arts and Letters don't really give a damn for arts and letters, in my opinion. They, too, are chemically-induced efforts to form a superstitious, affectionate **clan** or village or tribe. To them I say this, "Lots of luck, boys and girls."
(*PS* 47:L27, 30 *Roots*) The marriage *(of Edith and Kurt Sr. occurred on November 22, 1913)* was approved by both families; but the Schnull-Vonnegut **clan** was slightly condescending. In the pecking order in the social hierarchy of the community, and particularly in the German group it was generally understood that the Schnull-Vonnegut **clan** ranked ahead of the Lieber-Barus **clan**.
(*PS* 51:L9, 15 *Roots*) The couple *(Vonnegut's parents, Edith and Kurt Sr.)* were married by the Reverend Frank S. C. Wicks, a Unitarian clergyman, in an evening ceremony in the First Unitarian Church attended by members of the two families—Lieber and Vonnegut—and a bevy of lovely bridesmaids and handsome ushers. But these families in three generations were then numerous and both **clans** had many friends. The Liebers and the Vonneguts with the Hollwegs, Mayers, Severeins, Schnulls, Rauchs, Frenzels, Pantzers, Haueisens, Kipps, Kuhns, Metzgers, and Kothes were the leading German families of the city. . . . And they loved to celebrate weddings, particularly between congenial **clans** of a common heritage and cultural background. The nuptials qualified to be celebrated in accordance with the best German traditions: food, drink, dancing, music, and song.
(*PS* 52:L6 *Roots*) "In addition to the numerous relatives of the Lieber-Vonnegut **clans** Albert had a host of friends, a rigid selection of whom had to be invited. About six hundred of them came."
(*PS* 207:L30 *Religion*) "We thought we could do without tribes and **clans**. Well, we can't."
(*FWD* 77:L26, 33) (I had studied anthropology, after all, and so knew in my bones that human beings can't like life very much if they don't belong to a **clan** associated with a specific piece of real estate.)

The Attorney General's Commission on Pornography, a traveling show about dirty books and pictures put on the road during the administration of Ronald Reagan, was something else again. At least a couple of the panel members would later be revealed as having been in the muck of financial or sexual atrocities. There was a **clan** feeling, to be sure, but the family property in this case was the White House, and an amiable, sleepy, absentminded old movie actor was its totem pole.

Clarke, Arthur C. *Influenced by Olaf Stapledon, Arthur Charles Clarke, author of many seminal science fiction works such as* 2001: A Space Odyssey, Childhood's End, The City and the Stars, The Exploration of Space, *and* Voices from the Sky, *is noted for blending hard science and evolutionary mysticism. Clarke was trained in physics and mathematics and wrote about both space flight and underwater research. He was twice chairman of the*

British Interplanetary Society. Vonnegut refers to him in a number of instances and names a space ship in his honor in the short story "The Big Space Fuck."
(*WFG* 80:L9, 16 *Excelsior! We're Going to the Moon! Excelsior!*) We have spent something like $33 billion on space so far. We should have spent it on cleaning up our filthy colonies here on earth. There is no urgency whatsoever about getting somewhere in space, much as **Arthur C. Clarke** wants to discover the source of the terrific radio signals coming from Jupiter. It isn't as though we aren't already going somewhere in space. Every passing hour brings the whole solar system 43,000 miles closer to Globular Cluster M13 in Hercules. . . .

Brilliant space enthusiasts like **Arthur C. Clarke** are treasures, of course, to the thousands of persons in the enormously profitable spaceship trade. He speaks more enchantingly than they do. His art and their commercial interests coincide. "The discovery that Jupiter is quite warm and has precisely the type of atmosphere in which life is believed to have arisen on Earth may be the prelude to the most significant biological findings of this century he wrote recently in *Playboy*.
(*WFG* 84:L5 *Excelsior! We're Going to the Moon! Excelsior!*) "The Earth is our cradle, which we are about to leave," says **Arthur C. Clarke**. "And the Solar System will be our kindergarten." Most of us will never leave this cradle, of course, unless death turns out to be a form of astronautics.
(*WFG* 85:L16 *Excelsior! We're Going to the Moon! Excelsior!*) Good science-fiction writers of the present are not necessarily as eager as **Arthur C. Clarke** to found kindergartens on Jupiter, to leave the poor Maine ape and his clam rake far behind.
(*PS* 174:L23 *Funnier on Paper Than Most People*) "Perhaps you have read the novel *Childhood's End* by **Arthur C. Clarke**, one of the few masterpieces in the field of science fiction. All of the others were written by me. In **Clark's** novel, mankind suddenly undergoes a spectacular evolutionary change. The children become very different from the parents, less physical, more spiritual—and one day they form up into a sort of column of light which spirals out into the universe, its mission unknown. The book ends there."
(*PS* 227:L10 *Obscenity - The Big Space Fuck*) This was a period of great permissiveness in matters of language, so even the President was saying shit and fuck and so on, without anybody's feeling threatened or taking offense. It was perfectly OK. He called the Space Fuck a Space Fuck and so did everybody else. It was a rocket ship with eight hundred pounds of freeze-dried jizzum in its nose. It was going to be fired at the Andromeda Galaxy, two-million light years away. The ship was named the ***Arthur C. Clarke***, in honor of a famous space pioneer.
(*PS* 228:L26 *Obscenity - The Big Space Fuck*) "The way I understand it," the sheriff replied, "I'd have to sit there for more than two million years. My old lady might wonder what's become of me." He was a lot smarter than Dwayne. He had jizzum on the ***Arthur C. Clarke***, and Dwayne didn't. You had to have an I.Q. of over 115 to have your jizzum accepted.

(*PS* 230:L11 *Obscenity - The Big Space Fuck*) There were at least eighty-seven chrono-synclastic infundibulae, time warps, between Earth and the Andromeda Galaxy. If the ***Arthur C. Clarke*** passed through any one of them, the ship and its load would be multiplied a trillion times, and would appear everywhere throughout space and time.
(*PS* 233:L13-14 *Obscenity - The Big Space Fuck*) While all the human beings were in their houses, watching the Big Space Fuck, lampreys were squirming out of the ooze and onto land. Some of them were nearly as long and thick as the ***Arthur C. Clarke***.
(*HP* 301:L23) Subtract the title of the science fiction movie based on a novel by **Arthur C. Clarke** *(2001: A Space Odyssey)* which I saw twice in Vietnam. Do not panic. This will give you a negative number, but Arabs in olden times taught us how to deal with such. *This is part of the math riddle Hartke weaves throughout the text to reveal the number of people he knowingly killed in war, which is equal to the number of women with whom he has made love.*

Clarke, Arthur K. *This Arthur Clarke is more like the late Malcolm Forbes, publisher of* Fortune *magazine, than the science fiction novelist.* (*HP* 166:L4-5) It was a motorcade of highly successful Americans, most on motorcycles, but some in limousines, led by **Arthur Clarke**, the fun-loving billionaire. He himself was on a motorcycle, and on the saddle behind him, holding on for dear life, her skirt hiked up to her crotch, was Gloria White, the 60-year-old lifelong movie star!
(*HP* 166:L19) This wasn't Arthur C. Clarke, the science fiction writer who wrote all the books about humanity's destiny in other parts of the Universe. This was **Arthur K. Clarke**, the billionaire speculator and publisher of magazines and books about high finance.
(*HP* 167:L36) **Arthur K. Clarke** was coming to Tarkington to get an honorary Grand Contributor to the Arts and Sciences Degree.
(*HP* 168:L14) Everybody knew **Arthur Clarke** was going to get a meaningless certificate. But only Tex Johnson and the campus cops and the Provost had advance warning of the spectacular entrance he planned to make. It was a regular military operation. The motorcycles, and there were about 30 of them, and the balloon had been trucked into the parking lot behind the Black Cat Café at dawn.
(*HP* 168:L35, 169:L4) Clarke's big arrival wasn't a half-bad dress rehearsal for Judgment Day. St. John the Divine in the Bible could only imagine such an absolutely knockout show with noise and smoke and gold and lions and eagles and thrones and celebrities and marvels up in the sky and so on. But **Arthur K. Clarke** had created a real one with modern technology and tons of cash!
(*HP* 169:L12) **Arthur Clarke**, astride his bike, was looking in my direction. That was because great pals of his on the Board of Trustees were waving to him from the building right behind me. I found myself deeply offended by his proof that big money could buy big happiness.

(*HP* 198:L23) I parked the bike in plain view in front of the Black Cat Café, noting several champagne corks on the sidewalk and in the gutter. . . . This was where **Arthur K. Clarke** had formed up his motorcycle gang for its unopposed assault on Tarkington.
(*HP* 208:L1) **Arthur K. Clarke** had provided everything but water and toilets. So Muriel *(Peck)* had dared to ask some of them who they were and what they did.
(*HP* 208:L35) So **Arthur K. Clarke**, along with all his other activities, was a whimsical people-collector. He invited people he didn't really know, but who had caought his eye for 1 reason or another, to his parties, and they came, they came.

Claycomb, Judge and Moon. *The Indianapolis judge who had been entertained by Powers Hapgood the morning before Vonnegut met him at lunch with his Uncle Alex and his father as recounted in the preface to* Jailbird. *Moon Claycomb was a high school classmate of Vonnegut's. After listening all morning to labor union war stories from Powers Hapgood, Judge Claycomb, enthralled with Hapgood's tales, asked* "why would such a man from such a distinguished family and with such a fine education choose to live as you do?"

"Why?" said Hapgood, according to Hapgood. "Because of the Sermon on the Mount, sir."

And **Moon Claycomb**'s father said this: "Court is adjourned until two P.M." (*JB* xix:L8-14) *This allows Vonnegut to explain the significance of the Sermon on the Mount and how it relates to the events at the Cuyahoga Massacre.*

Cleveland Science Fair. *In* Hocus Pocus, *the place of humiliation for Eugene Debs Hartke and his father when the judges quickly determined Eugene's crystal display was the work of his father. However, it was there that Eugene met Sam Wakefield, who recruited him for West Point and who later hired him to teach at Tarkington College.*

Clewes, Dr. Alan. (*HP* 25:L13) The Episcopalian priest, **Dr. Alan Clewes**, a graduate of Harvard, would teach Latin, Greek, Hebrew, and the Bible *(at The Mohiga Valley Free Institute, eventually to become Tarkington College).*
(*HP* 26:L15) One week before the first class was held, which was in Latin, taught by the Episcopalian priest **Alan Clewes**, Andre Lutz the Belgian arrived at the mansion with 3 wagons carrying a very heavy cargo, a carillon consisting of 32 bells.

Clewes, Leland and Sarah (see also **Sarah Wyatt**). *Walter Starbuck met Leland Clewes when the two rowed crew for Harvard and Yale at the Henley Regatta—Starbuck a coxswain and Clewes a bowman. They met years later when they had adjoining cubicles at the Department of Agriculture. They became tennis buddies. Their friendship halted when Clewes married Sarah*

Wyatt. He and Sarah had a daughter (unnamed in the text) three years older than Starbuck's son.

During the heyday of McCarthyism, Starbuck was questioned by then Congressman Richard Nixon for the names of known members of the Communist Party who worked for the U.S. government. (*JB* 45:L12-16) I named a number of men who were known to have been communists during the Great Depression, but who had proved themselves to be outstanding patriots during World War Two. On that roll of honor I included the name of **Leland Clewes**.

Clewes at first denied having been a communist, insisted on testifying before Congress. (*JB* 46:L4) Two horrible years later **Leland Clewes** was convicted on six counts of perjury. He became one of the first prisoners to serve his sentence in the then new Federal Minimum Security Adult Correctional Facility on the edge of Finletter Air Force Base—thirty-five miles from Atlanta, Georgia.

Clewes and his wife came to appreciate the positive effects brought out by the prison experience. As they later explained to Starbuck, "Sarah and I have often talked about what we would like to say most to you. . . . "And it's this:" he said, "'Thank you very much, Walter. My going to prison was the best thing that ever happened to Sarah and me.' I'm not joking. Word of honor: It's true."

I was amazed. "How can that be?" I said.

"Because life is supposed to be a test," he said. "If my life had kept going the way it was going, I would have arrived in heaven never having faced any problem that wasn't as easy as pie to solve. Saint Peter would have had to say to me, 'You never lived, my boy. Who can say what you are?'"

"I see," I said.

"Sarah and I not only have love," he said, "but we have love that has stood up to the hardest tests" (*JB* 135:L26-27, 29-32, 136:L1-8).

For the wrong committed by Starbuck against Clewes and for the magnanimous manner by which he rebounded, Mary Kathleen O'Looney makes him a vice-president in the Diamond Match Division of The RAMJAC Corporation. Before Starbuck is sent back to jail, Leland and Sarah host a going-away party in his honor. (*JB* 231:L21-30) They have not moved out of their basement apartment in Tudor City, nor has Sarah given up private nursing, although **Leland** is now pulling down about one hundred thousand dollars a year at RAMJAC. Much of their money goes to the Foster Parents Program, a scheme that allows them to support individual children in unfortunate circumstances in many parts of the world. They are supporting fifty children, I think they said. They have letters and photographs from several of them, which they passed around. *He and Clyde Carter buy Walter "Boris," a chess-playing computer, as a going-away gift. Leland and Sarah live in the basement apartment of the same Tudor City building as Starbuck's son.*

Clinton Street. *In* Galápagos *Clinton Street is revealed as the main street in Ilium, New York, and in* Hocus Pocus *Clinton Street is the name of the main street in Scipio and Athena, New York. The name is a common one in New York because of the high esteem held out for Governor DeWitt Clinton.*

Clough and Higgins. *The accounting firm servicing Noel Constant's Magnum Opus Corporation, in* The Sirens of Titan.

Clowes, Henry. (*DD* xiii:L11) This is fiction, not history, so it should not be used as a reference book. I say, for example, that the United States Ambassador to Austria-Hungary at the outbreak of the First World War was **Henry Clowes**, of Ohio. The actual ambassador at that time was Frederic Courtland Penfield of Connecticut.

In 1914 Otto Waltz was trying to gain an art education in Europe and was so taken with the seeming romanticism of German militarism that he asked friends if they could secure him a post in the Hungarian Life Guard, whose officers' uniforms included a panther skin. . . .

He was summoned by the American Ambassador to the Austro-Hungarian Empire, **Henry Clowes**, who was a Cleveland man and an acquaintance of Father's parents. Father was then twenty-two years old. **Clowes** told Father that he would lose his American citizenship if he joined a foreign army, and that he had made inquiries about Father, and had learned that Father was not the painter he pretended to be, and that Father had been spending money like a drunken sailor, and that he had written to Father's parents, telling them that their son had lost all touch with reality, and that it was time Father was summoned home and given some honest work to do. (*DD* 7:L13-18, 8:L1-7) *Clowes informed Otto Waltz his parents were aware of his waywardness and threatened to cut him off if he failed to return to Midand City. Waltz returned home.*

Club Cybernetics. *In* Player Piano, *Dr. Ewing J. Halyard is in the Club Cybernetics when he witnessed what he thought to be unbecoming behavior on the part of Cornell football coach Doctor Roseberry and other members of the team. Halyard sends his letter to Cornell president Doctor Albert Herpers. Halyard eventually pays for this tattling when he returns to Cornell to make up a missing physical education course.*

Coates, Arnold. *After Rabo Karabekian received a telegram signed by Dan Gregory (though in actuality it was surreptitiously sent by Marilee Kemp) to come to New York as his apprentice, Rabo reveals his good luck to Arnold Coates.* (*Blue* 65:L1-12) The first person I told about this magnificent opportunity was the old newspaper editor for whom I had been drawing cartoons. His name was **Arnold Coates**, and he said this to me:

"You really are an artist, and you have to get out of here or you'll shrivel up like a raisin. Don't worry about your father. He's a perfectly contented, self-sufficient zombie, if you'll pardon my saying so.

"New York is just going to be a stopover for you," he went on. "Europe is where the real painters are, and always will be."

He was wrong about that.

cocoon. (*ST* 298:L6, 8) The spiral telescoped slightly, making a curtsey. And then it began to revolve around Rumfoord, spinning a continuous **cocoon** of green light. . . .

"All I can say," said Rumfoord from the **cocoon**, "is that I have tried my best to do good for my native Earth while serving the irresistible wishes of Tralfamadore. *This sounds very much like Howard Campbell's serving good too secretly and evil too openly. The spiral is the chrono-synclastic infundibulum about to take Rumfoord out of the Solar System.*

(*ST* 298:L20, 27-28, 32, 299:L5) The green **cocoon** left the ground, hovered over the dome. "Remember me as a gentleman of Newport, Earth, and the Solar System," said Rumfoord. He sounded serene again, at peace with himself, and at least equal to any creature that he might encounter anywhere.

"In a punctual way of speaking," came Rumfoord's glottal tenor from the **cocoon**, "good-by."

The **cocoon** and Rumfoord disappeared with a *pft*. . . .

Old Salo came bounding into the courtyard just as Rumfoord and his **cocoon** disappeared. . . .

He looked up at the place where the **cocoon** had hovered.

(*MN* 40:L27) And the thick, bristly, olive-drab **cocoon** I *(Howard Campbell)* had built for myself was frayed a little, was weakened enough to let some pale light in.

(*Gal* 222:L16-17, 28) When young Mary stuck her head out of her **cocoon**, out of her sleeping bag, she saw rotting logs and an undammed stream. . . .

The bird call was coming from a thicket of briars and sumac fifty paces away. She was glad for this alarm clock, for it had been her intention when she went to sleep to awake this early, and to think of her sleeping bag as a **cocoon**, and to emerge from it sinuously and voluptuously, as she was now doing, a vivacious adult.

Coggin's Pond. *The retirement home of Colonel Harold J. Sparrow—alias Frank Wirtanen, and referred to by Howard W. Campbell as his Blue Fairy Godmother in* Mother Night. *It is from this location, "six miles west of Hinkleyville, Maine," that he offers his oath to the Israeli authorities that Campbell's public wartime persona was part of his covert work for the United States.*

Cohen, Abe. (*BC* 235:L15) **Abe Cohen**, the jeweler, said to Karabekian, "If artists would explain more, people would like art more. You realize that?"

(*BC* 255:L24) Only one person noticed her sufficiently to comment out loud. He was **Abe Cohen**, the jeweler. He said this about Mary Alice *(Mary Alice Miller, the Women's Breast Stroke Champion of the World and Queen of the Midland City Arts Festival)*, despising her sexlessness and innocence and empty mind: "Pure tuna fish!"

Cohen, Isadore Raspberry-19. (*Slap* 22:L14) I *(Wilbur Swain)* inhabit the first floor of the Empire State Building with my sixteen-year-old granddaughter, who is Melody Oriole-2 von Peterswald, and with her lover, **Isadore Raspberry-19 Cohen**. The three of us have the building all to ourselves.

Cohen, Israel (also **Cohen Rink**). (*HP* 70:L16) In my time, students didn't skate on the lake anymore, but on an indoor rink given in 1971 by the **Israel Cohen** Family. But they still had sailboat races and canoe races on the lake. (*HP* 78:L30) That morning, with the phones dead and the electricity cut off, with unburied bodies everywhere, and with all the food in Scipio already consumed as though by a locust plague, he *(Alton Darwin)* had gone up to **Cohen Rink** and put on ice skates for the first time in his life. After a few tottering steps, he had found himself gliding around and around, and around and around.

Cohn, Roy. *Senator Joe McCarthy's legal assistant and chief counsel of the Senate Permanent Investigating Committee was idolized by Norman Mushari as a child.* (*GBR* 33:L24) Little Norman Mushari was only twelve in those troubled days, was assembling plastic model airplanes, masturbating, and papering his room with pictures of Senator Joe McCarthy and **Roy Cohn**.
(*JB* xx:L1-8) There is another minor character, whom I call "**Roy M. Cohn**." He is modeled after the famous anticommunist and lawyer and businessman named, straightforwardly enough, one would have to say, **Roy M. Cohn**. I include him with his kind permission, given yesterday (January 2, 1979) over the telephone. I promised to do him no harm and to present him as an appallingly effective attorney for either the prosecution or the defense of anyone. *When Walter Starbuck is arrested for possession of the stolen clarinet parts, The RAMJAC Corporation hires Cohn to defend him.*

Cohoes. (*BC* 20:L2) In 1972, Trout lived in a basement apartment in **Cohoes**, New York. He made his living as an installer of aluminum combination storm windows and screens.

In Galápagos, *Leon Trout remembers growing up in Cohoes.* (*Gal* 149:L30) When I was a child in **Cohoes**, my mother took me to see the circus in Albany one time, although we could not afford it and Father did not approve of circuses.

(*Gal* 157:L10) When I was a little boy in **Cohoes**, and could detect nothing in the life of our little family about which I could be proud, my mother told me that I had the blood of French noblemen flowing in my veins.
(*Gal* 256:L11) Oh, yes, and there was one other thing I could be proud of, and this really counted for something in **Cohoes**: My father had been a United States Marine.
(*Gal* 256:L21) I was then flunking every course but art at school. Nobody flunked art at **Cohoes** High School. That was simply impossible. And I ran away to find my mother, which I never did.

coil. (*PP* 60:L33) Paul returned to the garage, **coiled** the siphon hose in the glove compartment, and drove off.
(*WFG* 76:L11 *There's a Maniac Loose Out There*) In his (*Antone "Tony" C. Costa's*) closet in the rooming house where he helped Patricia Walsh and Mary Ann Wysocki with their luggage, police found a **coil** of stained rope.
(*MH* 271:L26 *Epicac*) "Is this poetry?" he asked. He began clicking away. . . . EPICAC had found himself. The spool of paper ribbon was unwinding at an alarming rate, feeding out **coils** onto the floor. I asked him to stop, but EPICAC went right on creating.
(*MH* 274:L21 *Epicac*) The ceiling over EPICAC was blackened with smoke, and my ankles were tangled in **coils** of paper ribbon that covered the floor.
(*MH* 275:L8 *Epicac*) Oblivious to all else around me, I reeled up the tangled yards of paper ribbon from the floor, draped them in **coils** about my arms and neck, and departed for home.
(*BC* 159:L7) Dwayne mimicked her cruelly in a falsetto voice: "'I don't even know what you think I asked you for,'" he said. He looked about as pleasant and relaxed as a **coiled** rattlesnake now. It was his bad chemicals, of course, which were compelling him to look like that.
(*Slap* 100:L2) Mother did not say anything at first. But she had clearly become subhuman in the finest sense. She was a **coiled** female panther, suddenly willing to tear the throats out of any number of childrearing experts—in defense of her young.
(*Gal* 260:L23) There were still ten meters of stern line, of white nylon umbilical cord, **coiled** by a cleat on the main deck. The Captain tied knots in this, and then he and Mary climbed down it to the shoal, and waded ashore to gather eggs and kill lower animals who had no fear of them.
(*HP* 152:L3) "'To die, to sleep; to sleep: perchance to dream: ay, there's the rub; for in that sleep of death what dreams may come when we have shuffled off this mortal **coil**, must give us pause.'" *Eugene Debs Hartke recites Shakespeare's lines as he prepares to defiantly leave the meeting of Tarkington's Board of Trustees, which was convened to dismiss him.*

college humor (see **humor**).

Collier's. *Vonnegut's first short story, "Report on the Barnhouse Effect," was published in* Collier's *magazine. The fiction editor was Knox Burger, and he introduced Vonnegut to literary agent Kenneth Littauer and Max Wilkinson.*
(*FWD* 26:2) "I sold my first story to ***Collier's***. Received my check ($750 minus a 10% agent's commission) yesterday noon. It now appears that two more of my works have a good chance of being sold in the near future." *This is part of a letter Vonnegut wrote to his father concerning his first paycheck as a writing.*

Colson, Charles W. *The Watergate co-conspirator who eventually served time and later dedicated his life to Jesus Christ, Colson is referred to by Walter Starbuck as a fellow jailbird. Colson is also attributed with nicknaming Starbuck "The Geek"* (*JB* 41:L20-21).

The Columbia Conserve Company. *As described in* Jailbird, *the company was established in 1903 and sold off in 1953, though it struggled for survival after 1931—the victim of economics during the Great Depression. It was a cannery specializing in tomato soup, chili, and catsup. Created by Norman, William, and Hutchins Hapgood, the company was an "experiment in industrial democracy" in that it had a seven-member council of workers advising on wages and working conditions. The company developed a retirement plan, sick pay, and stock-bonus plans. This information is catalogued in Vonnegut's prologue to the text and he takes pains to state that the three brothers who attempted this noble experiment were all Harvard men, as were Starbuck, McCone, and so many of the Watergate criminals.*

column. (*PP* 4:L35) Gingerly, Paul pressed a button on the steering **column**. A motor purred, gears grumbled softly, and the two front seats lay down side by side like sleepy lovers.
(*ST* 40:L28) "Yes," said Constant from below, "that Mr. Constant is still here." He was in plain view, leaning against a **column** in the arch that opened onto the foyer. But he was so low in the composition, so lost in architectural details as to be almost invisible.
(*ST* 235:L19-32) The rube made a show of being a judicious shopper. He compared the toy with the real article it was supposed to represent. The real article was a Martian space ship on top of a **column** ninety-eight feet tall. The **column** and space ship were inside the walls of the Rumfoord estate—in the corner of the estate where the tennis courts had once been.

Rumfoord had yet to explain the purpose of the space ship, whose supporting **column** had been built with the pennies of school children from all over the world. The ship was kept in constant readiness. What was reputedly the longest free-standing ladder in history leaned against the **column**, led giddily to the door of the ship.
(*ST* 250:L4) The Space Wanderer's gaze climbed the ladder to the tiny door of the space ship on top of the **column**.

(*ST* 283:L28) Rumfoord stood bolt upright, his eyes popping, a fiery **column**.
(*MN* 144:L5) "There is every chance," I said, "that I would have become a sort of Nazi Edgar Guest, writing a daily **column** of optimistic doggerel for daily papers around the world. And, as senility set in—the sunset of life, as they say—I might even come to believe what my couplets said: that everything was probably all for the best."
(*MN* 181:L3) While the **column** of air enclosed by the stairs had carried in the past a melancholy freight of coal dust and cooking smells and the sweat of plumbing, that air was cold and sharp now. . . . All warm gases had been whisked up the stairwell and out my windows, as though up a whistling flue.
(*CC* 219:L17) I wasn't half so curious about the living, probably because I sensed accurately that I would first have to contemplate a lot of dead. I saw no **columns** of smoke from possible camp fires; but they would have been hard to see against an horizon of worms.
(*GBR* 50:L18) The town of Rosewater was in the dead center of the county. In the dead center of town was a Parthenon built of honest red brick, **columns** and all. Its roof was green copper.
(*GBR* 200:L29, 31) As the many fires broke through the roofs of the burning buildings, a **column** of heated air rose more than two and a half miles high and one and a half miles in diameter. . . . This **column** was turbulent, and it was fed from its base by in-rushing cooler ground-surface air. One and one and a half miles from the fires this draught increased the wind velocity from eleven to thirty-three miles per hour. *Vonnegut notes he is quoting from Hans Rumpf's* The Bombing of Germany.
(*GBR* 201:L13, 15) Eliot, rising from his seat in the bus, beheld the firestorm of Indianapolis. He was awed by the majesty of the **column** of fire, which was at least eight miles in diameter and fifty miles high. The boundaries of the **column** seemed absolutely sharp and unwavering, as though made of glass. Within the boundaries, *helixes* of dull red embers turned in stately harmony about an inner core of white. The white seemed holy.
(*SL5* 35:L9, 23) The woman and the pony were posed before velvet draperies which were fringed with deedlee-balls. They were flanked by Doric **columns**. In front of one **column** was a potted palm. . . . Le Fevre argued that the picture was fine art, and that his intention was to make Greek mythology come alive. He said the **columns** and the potted palm proved that. *Vonnegut's description of what is supposed to be the first pornographic photograph—a daguerrotype.*
(*MH* 35:L18 *Welcome to the Monkey House*) The view was blocked by the backside of a mocked-up thermometer twenty feet high, which faced the street. It was calibrated in billions of people on Earth, from zero to twenty. The make-believe **column** of liquid was a strip of translucent red plastic. It showed how many people there were on Earth. Very close to the bottom was a black arrow that showed what the scientists thought the population ought to be.
(*BC* 1:L15) She was rich *(Phoebe Hurty—to whom* Breakfast of Champions *is dedicated)*, but she had gone to work every weekday of her adult life, so she

went on doing that. She wrote a sane and funny advice-to-the-lovelorn **column** for the Indianapolis *Times*.
(*WFG* 72:L27 *There's a Maniac Loose Out There*) Here is what she (*Evelyn Lawson*) wrote in her **column** after the district attorney held a sensational press conference about the bodies.
(*WFG* 144:L12 *Biafra: A People Betrayed*) The worst sufferers there were the children of refugees, driven from their homes, then driven off the roads and into the bush by MIGs and armored **columns**.
(*WFG* 188:L16 *In a Manner That Must Shame God Himself*) Art Buchwald said he came to the convention in order to see his pals, mostly other news people. He told our table about a **column** he had just written. The comical premise was that the Republican party had attracted so many campaign contributions that it found itself with two billion dollars it couldn't spend. It decided to buy something nice for the American people. Here was the gift: a free week's bombing of Vietnam.
(*WFG* 218:L1 *Address at Rededication of Wheaton College Library, 1973*) William F. Buckley said in a recent **column** that I would be overjoyed by Nixon's political defeat, since I had made a career of despising America. That proves he hasn't read me much.
(*Slap* 180:L15) The news **columns** told of triumphs by various relatives, and warned against others who were child molesters or swindlers and so on. *The news columns were in government-sponsored family newspapers recounting the expolits of the various extended families established by the government.*
(*JB* 29:L4-5) We named our son Walter F. Starbuck, Jr. Little did we dream that the name would become as onerous as Judas Iscariot, Jr., to the boy. He would seek legal remedy when he turned twenty-one, would have his name changed to Walter F. Stankiewicz, the name that appears over his **columns** in *The New York Times*.
(*JB* 32:L25) The President himself *(Richard Nixon)* at last noticed the **column** of smoke rising from my place *(Walter Starbuck's)*, and he stopped all business to stare at me. He had to ask Emil Larkin who I was.
(*JB* 155:L20) So there Mary Kathleen and I were—among all those harps. They are very strange-looking instruments, now that I think about them, and not very far from poor Ruth's idea of civilization even in peacetime—impossible marriages between Greek **columns** and Leonardo da Vinci's flying machines.
(*JB* 226:L18) If you can believe the gossip **columns**, there is to be a talent search for an actress to play the Irish immigrant girl.
(*PS* 118:L10 *The People One Knows*) He *(William F. Buckley)* can do a **column** in 20 minutes, he tells us, and turn out 150 a year. . . .
(*PS* 174:L28 *Funnier on Paper Than Most People*) "Perhaps you have read the novel *Childhood's End* by Arthur C. Clarke, one of the few masterpieces in the field of science fiction. All of the others were written by me. In Clark's novel, mankind suddenly undergoes a spectacular evolutionary change. The children become very different from the parents, less physical, more spiritual—and one

day they form up into a sort of **column** of light which spirals out into the universe, its mission unknown. The book ends there."

(*DD* 173:L23, 28) According to a gossip **column** Mother and I *(Rudy Waltz)* read, he and his fourth wife had divided the penthouse in half with a line of chairs. Neither one was supposed to go in the other one's territory.

Felix was also due to be fired any day, according to the same **column**, because the ratings of NBC prime time television shows were falling so far behind those of the other networks.

(*Gal* 117:L32) There were forty-two of them, counting mates or companions who were nonentities, but they had organized themselves into a few dinner parties, duly reported in gossip **columns** that day, in order to pass pleasantly the hours remaining until limousines came to cushion and muffle them away to Kennedy International Airport—

(*Blue* 67:L10) Nowadays, of course, just about our only solvent industry is the merchandising of death, bankrolled by our grandchildren, so that the message of our principal art forms, movies and television and political speeches and newspaper **columns**, for the sake of the economy, simply has to be this: War is hell, all right, but the only way a boy can become a man is in a shoot-out of some kind, preferably, but by no means necessarily, on a battlefield.

(*Blue* 213:1) She was only four blocks away *(Marilee, Countess Portomaggiore—the coal miner's daughter who was responsible for bringing Rabo Karabekian to Dan Evan's attention)*—in a palazzo designed for Innocenzo "the Invisible" de Medici by Leon Battista Alberti in the middle of the fifteenth century. It was a cruciform structure whose four wings abutted on a domed rotunda twelve meters in diameter and in whose walls were half embedded eighteen Corinthian **columns** four and a half meters high. Above the capitals of the **columns** was a clerestory, a wall pierced with thirty-six windows. Above this was the dome—on whose underside was an epiphany, God almighty and Jesus and the Virgin Mary and angels looking down through clouds, painted by Paolo Uccello.

(*Blue* 216:L25) The second puzzle was this: why were the vast rectangles between the encircling **columns** at ground level blank?

(*Blue* 240:L1) She said that our unexpected reunion was a stroke of luck for her, since she thought I might have brought the solution to an interior decorating problem which had been nagging at her for many years, namely: what sort of pictures, if any, should she put on the inane blanks between the **columns** of her rotunda? "I want to leave some sort of mark on this place while I have it," she said, "and the rotunda seems the place to do it."

(*HP* 99:L13) I thought she had noted her father's conviction, often expressed in his **columns** and on his TV show, and no doubt at home, that a few teachers who secretly hated their country were making young people lose faith in its future and leadership.

(*HP* 109:L27) I knew who he *(Jason Wilder)* was, of course, and something of how his mind worked, having read his newspaper **column** and watched his television show from time to time.

(*HP* 111:L1) I read your **columns** and watch your TV show regularly.
(*HP* 127:L23) Madelaine dictated a letter to me afterward, explaining that Jason Wilder had promised to denounce the college in his **column** and on his TV show if the Trustees did not fire me.
(*HP* 240:L13) As I say, every **column** adds up to 3,888.

Combat Respiratory Rations (also called **CRR's** or **goofballs**). *Enriched oxygen pills needed by recruits of the Martian army. It was necessary to take the pills every six hours.* (*ST* 148:L15-16) The bloodstream takes on this oxygen through the wall of the small intestine rather than through the lungs. *Beatrice Rumfoord taught the proper use of the goofballs in conjunction with the Schliemann Breathing method.*

comedians. *Vonnegut's great appreciation for comedy's comforts, structure, and cultural significance is encapsulated in the following excerpts:* (*PS* 114:L24) And I want to say, too, that humorists are very commonly the youngest children in their families. When I was the littlest kid at our supper table, there was only one way I could get anybody's attention, and that was to be funny. I had to specialize. I used to listen to radio **comedians** very intently, so I could learn how to make jokes. And that's what my books are, now that I'm a grownup—mosaics of jokes.
(*PS* 140:L13) It is the truth: **Comedians** and jazz musicians have been more comforting and enlightening to me than preachers or politicians or philosophers or poets or painters or novelists of my time. Historians in the future, in my opinion, will congratulate us on very little other than our clowning and our jazz.
(*TIM* xvii:L7) I would like to say something about American **comedians**: they are often as brilliant and magical as our best jazz musicians, and they have probably done more to shape my thinking than any writer. When people ask me who my culture heroes are, I express pious gratitude for Mark Twain and James Joyce and so on. But the truth is that I am a barbarian, whose deepest cultural debts are to Laurel and Hardy, Stoopnagel and Bud, Buster Keaton, Fred Allen, Jack Benny, Charlie Chaplin, Easy Aces, Henry Morgan, and on and on.

They made me hilarious during the Great Depression, and all the lesser depressions after that. When Bob Elliot and Ray Goulding agreed to work on this TV show, I nearly swooned.
(*FWD* 87:L28) (Except that the minister and I would become good friends, and he would invite me to say a few words during a Christmas Eve service along with the **comedian** Joey Adams, and he and the congregation would eventually come to a parting of the ways, and one of his offenses, supposedly, was having lent the pulpit to a known atheist, who was me and not Joey Adams.)
(*FWD* 183:L33) "My generalization is happily or unhappily confirmed in a book called *Punchlines* (Paragon House, 1990) by William Keough of the English Department of Fitchburg State College in Massachusetts. The subtitle

is *The Violence of American Humor*. Mr. Keough, by means of essays on Mark Twain, Ring Lardner, Ambrose Bierce, myself, **comedians** in the movies (both silents and talkies), and radio and TV and nightclub comics right up to the present, persuades me that the most memorable are responses to the economic and physical violence of this society."
(*FWD* 201:L19) (The second funniest clean joke in the world was told to me personally by the great **comedian** Rodney Dangerfield. We were in a movie together. He said he had a great uncle who was admired for his cleanliness. He was the talk of the neighborhood. This old man took six, seven, eight, sometimes as many as twelve baths or showers every day. After he died, his whole funeral cortege went through a car wash on the way to the cemetery.)

common decency. (*BC* 28:L14-15) "And then Earthlings discovered tools. Suddenly agreeing with friends could be a form of suicide or worse. But agreements went on, not for the sake of **common** sense or **decency** or self-preservation, but for friendliness."
(*Slap* 2:L18) I have had some experiences with love, or think I have, anyway, although the ones I have liked best could easily be described as "**common decency**." I treated somebody well for a little while, or maybe even for a tremendously long time, and that person treated me well in turn. Love need not have had anything to do with it.
(*Slap* 3:L20-23) I wish that people who are conventionally supposed to love each other would say to each other, when they fight, "Please—a little less love, and a little more **common decency**."

. . . My longest experience with **common decency**, surely, has been with my older brother, my only brother, Bernard, who is an atmospheric scientist in the State University of New York at Albany.
(*Slap* 5:L23) It is lucky, too, for human beings need all the relatives they can get—as possible donors or receivers not necessarily of love, but of **common decency**.
(*PS* 171:L22) Only a genius *(Mark Twain)* could have misrepresented our speech and our wittiness and our common sense and our **common decency** so handsomely to ourselves and the outside world.

cone, cone-shaped, conical. (*PP* 182:L28) An old man, with a white beard reaching to his waist, wearing a long white robe and golden sandals and a blue **conical** hat speckled with golden stars, sits atop an extraordinarily tall stepladder. *The old man is the Sky Manager in the play produced at the annual summer games in the Meadows.*
(*ST* 16:L29) The fountain itself was. . . . a **cone** described by many stone bowls of decreasing diameters. The bowls were collars on a cylindrical shaft forty feet high.
(*ST* 188:L24) He imagined a remarkable fountain, a **cone** described by descending bowls of increasing diameters. It wouldn't do.

(*MH* 4:L12-13 *Where I Live*) To get bass, one follows the birds, looks for **cone-shaped** formations of them, casts his lure to the place where the **cone** points. Bass will be feeding there.
(*BC* 11:L2) There were pictures and statues of this supposed imaginary beacon for children to see. It was sort of an ice-cream **cone** on fire.
(*JB* 55:L19-20, 22) "When they are very young," Dr. Fender writes in the persona of Frank X. Barlow, "barnacles can drift or creep whence-so-ever they hanker, anywhere in the seven seas and the brackish estuaries thereof. Their upper bodies are encased in **cone-shaped** armor. Their little tootsies dangle from the **cones** like clappers from dinnerbells.

"But there comes a time for every barnacle, at childhood's end, when the rim of its **cone** secretes a glue that will stick forever to whatever it happens to touch next. So it is no casual thing on Earth to say to a pubescent barnacle or to a homeless soul from Vicuna, 'Sit thee doon, sit thee doon.'" *Here, Vonnegut echoes "The Rhyme of the Ancient Mariner."*
(*JB* 236:L2, 10, 15, 22) Israel Edel gave me a rubber ice-cream **cone** with a squeaker in it—a plaything for my little dog, who is a female Lhasa apso, a golden dustmop without a handle. . . . *Vonnegut's next book,* Palm Sunday, *has a cover photograph of him with his Lhasa apso.*

I have never bred her, but now, according to the veterinarian, Dr. Howard Padwee, she is experiencing a false pregnancy and believes the rubber ice-cream **cone** to be a puppy. . . .

I observe how profoundly serious Nature has made her about a rubber ice-cream **cone**—brown rubber **cone**, pink rubber ice cream. I have to wonder what equally ridiculous commitments to bits of trash I myself have made. . . . The human condition in an exploding universe would not have been altered one iota if, rather than live as I have, I had done nothing but carry a rubber ice-cream **cone** from closet to closet for sixty years.
(*DD* 8:L18) I do not believe he would have stayed in Midland City, if it weren't for what remained of his childhood home, which was its fanciful carriage house. It was hexagonal. It was stone. It had a **conical** slate roof.
(*DD* 10:L33) A hexagonal loft encircled and overhung the great chamber. This was partitioned off into bedrooms and bathrooms and a small library.

Above that was an attic under the **conical** slate roof. Father had no immediate use for the attic, so it was left in its primitive condition.
(*DD* 16:L12) They *(the Maritimo brothers)* could either await death, or they could invent something to do. They invented. They saw a **conical** slate roof on the other side of the river, and they walked toward that. In order to keep putting one foot in front of the other, they pretended that it was of utmost importance that they reach that structure and no other.
(*DD* 153:L11, 13) It was the **conical** slate roof of my childhood home, only a few blocks away. The peak of the **cone**, where the cupola used to be, was capped with very light gray tar roofing, with bits of sand stuck to it. In the light of a full moon, it was glittering white—like snow.

(*DD* 158:L4) We had circled over the city, so we approached the **conical** roof from the north. Wind had piled snow halfway up the big north window.
(*Gal* 5:L5) A million years later, they (*the Galápagos Islands*) do possess white beaches and blue lagoons. But when this story begins, they were still ugly humps and domes and **cones** and spires of lava, brittle and abrasive, whose cracks and pits and bowls and valleys brimmed over not with rich topsoil or sweet water, but with the finest, driest volcanic ash.

Conestoga. *As chronicled in* Hocus Pocus, *the name of the covered wagons pioneers took on their westward journeys, named for the location of their original construction, the Conestoga Valley of Pennsylvania. Eugene Debs Hartke points out two sidelights to the myth of the Conestoga: the cigars transported by the pioneers picked up the name "stogies" as representative of the Conestoga wagon, and that* By 1830, the sturdiest and most popular of these wagons were in fact made by the Mohiga Wagon Company right here in Scipio, New York (*HP* 20:L13-15). *The founder of the company was the dyslexic inventor and manufacturer Aaron Tarkington.*

Conners, Harrison C. *Once a laboratory assistant to Felix Hoenikker in* Cat's Cradle, *Conners went to Indianapolis where he founded and became President of Fabri-Tek, a company dealing in weapons technology. After his old mentor passed away he returned to Hoenikker's home, spoke with Angela about old times, and two weeks later they were married. Conners proves to be a lousy husband, a drunk, and womanizer.*

conspiracy. (*PP* 270:L8, 13) "Doctor Proteus," said the prosecutor nastily. The television cameras closed in on his sneer and panned to the beads of sweat on Paul's forehead. "You have pleaded guilty to **conspiracy** to advocate the commission of sabotage, isn't that so? . . .

"This **conspiracy**, of which you are the head, has as its method, and I quote from your famous letter, 'We are prepared to use force to end the lawlessness, if other means fail.' Those are your words, Doctor?"
(*MN* 37:L29) It was dumb luck that brought us together. No **conspiracy** was involved at first. It was I who knocked on his door, invaded his privacy. If I hadn't carved that chess set, we never would have met. *Campbell speaks about his meeting George Kraft, also known as Colonel Iona Potapov, a Soviet agent.*
(*MN* 47:L4) Howard W. Campbell, Jr., a great writer and one of the most fearless patriots in American history, now lives in poverty and loneliness in the attic of 27 Bethune Street. Such is the fate of thinking men brave enough to tell the truth about the **conspiracy** of international Jewish bankers and international Jewish Communists who will not rest until the bloodstream of every American is hopelessly polluted with Negro and/or Oriental blood. *This is from an item printed in* The White Christian Minuteman.

(*BC* 209:L20-21) I had no respect whatsoever for the creative works of either the painter or the novelist. I thought Karabekian with his meaningless pictures had entered into a **conspiracy** with millionaires to make poor people feel stupid. I thought Beatrice Keedsler had joined hands with other old-fashioned storytellers to make people believe that life had leading characters, minor characters, significant details, insignificant details, that it had lessons to be learned, tests to be passed, and a beginning, a middle, and an end.
(*WFG* 22:L27 *Hello, Star Vega*) Let me hasten to say: They are quite certain that we are not being visited now. *(Carl)* Sagan served this year on a committee that reviewed the handling by the Air Force of UFO reports, and he is able to state:

The saucer myths represent a neat compromise between the need to believe in a traditional paternal God and the contemporary pressures to accept the pronouncements of science. . . . Repeated sightings of UFOs and the persistence of the United States Air Force and members of the responsible scientific community in explaining the sightings away have suggested to some that a **conspiracy** exists to conceal from the public the true nature of the UFOs. But precisely because people desire so intensely that unidentified flying objects be of a benign, intelligent, and extraterrestrial origin, honesty requires that. . . . we accept only the most rigorous logic and the most convincing evidence.
(*WFG* 134:L10 *The Mysterious Madame Blavatsky*) Colonel Olcott was for a while so respected for his soundness of mind that he was made a member of an elite committee of three, whose purpose was to discover the extent of the **conspiracy** that led to the death of Abraham Lincoln.
(*WFG* 270:L3 *Playboy Interview*) PLAYBOY: You said it was sexual. *The interviewer is referring to Vonnegut's sense of the space program.*
VONNEGUT: It's a tremendous space fuck, and there's some kind of **conspiracy** to suppress that fact. That's why all the stories about launches are so low-key. The never give a hint of what a visceral experience it is to watch a launch. How would the taxpayers feel if they found out they were buying orgasms for a few thousand freaks within a mile of the launch pad? And it's an extremely satisfactory orgasm. I mean, you are shaking and you do take leave of your senses. And there's something about the sound that comes shuddering across the water. I understand that there are certain frequencies with which you can make a person involuntarily shit with sound. So it does get you in the guts.
(*HP* 202:L29) The Townies protected the image he *(Lyle Hooper)* had of himself, in spite of State Police raids and visits from the County Health Department, as a family man who ran a place of refreshment whose success depended entirely on the quality of the drinks and snacks he served. This kindly **conspiracy** protected Lyle's son Charlton, as well. Charlton grew to be 2 meters tall, and was a New York State High School All-Star basketball center in his senior year at Scipio High School, and all he ever had to say about his father was that he ran a restaurant.

conspiratorial. (*PP* 71:L6) "I love *you*, Anita. Goodbye." He looked up at Finnerty. "O.K., let's go." He felt somehow **conspiratorial**, and got a small lift from the feeling. Being with Finnerty had often had that effect. Finnerty had an air of mysteriousness about him, an implication that he knew of worlds unsuspected by anyone else—a man of unexplained absences and shadowy friends. Actually, Finnerty let Paul in on very little that was surprising, and only gave him the illusion of sharing in mysteries—if, indeed, there were any. The illusion was enough. It filled a need in Paul's life, and he went gladly for a drink with the odd man.
(*PP* 124:L20) "Paul, about this Finnerty and Lasher business—" His *(Dr. Kroner's)* playfully **conspiratorial** tone implied that the proposed prosecution of these two was sort of a practical joke. "Just wanted to tell you that I called Washington about it, to let them in on what we're going to do, and they say we should hold off for a while. They say the whole thing ought to be well planned at the top level. It's apparently bigger stuff than I thought." His voice dropped to a whisper. "It's beginning to look like a problem nationwise, not just Iliumwise."

conspirators. (*PP* 40:L36) The others laughed like **conspirators**. Apparently something special had been cooked up, and one or two of the older engineers seemed to be sharing in the high expectations. *Berringer and his engineer friends taunt Proteus about a proposed championship match with Checker Charlie.*
(*PP* 253:L8) It wasn't a brilliant-looking aggregation of **conspirators**, on the whole, but a righteous and determined one.
(*ST* 318:L28) The **conspirators** presumably fled. *The "sleeper" in the house nearby Malachi's bus stop on the outskirts of Indianapolis presumes he chased away some dangerous prowlers when he hears Salo's ship lift off.*
(*FWD* 20:L14) He told us about the time he emptied a New York subway car in three stops by boarding it with a large number of friends who pretended to be strangers to one another. This was in the wee hours following New Year's Eve. Each **conspirator** was carrying a copy of the *Daily News* with the bold headline: HOOVER OUT, ROOSEVELT IN. Troy had saved the papers from Roosevelt's landslide victory about a year before. (That would have been back at the very start of 1934, I guess, when I was eleven years old, the fourth year of the Great Depression.)

conspire. (*PP* 224:L23) She'd *(Anita Proteus)* have to leave New York State, of course, since the only grounds for divorce there were adultery, and incitement to **conspire** to advocate sabotage. A case could be made for either, he supposed, but not with dignity.
(*PP* 270:L3) Paul had pleaded guilty to **conspiring** to advocate the commission of sabotage, but was now being tried for treason, three weeks after his arrest.
(*ST* 69:L22) His situation, working for Noel Constant and then Malachi, **conspired** nicely to make almost anything he might say bitterly funny—for he

was superior to Constant *pere* and *fils* in every respect but one, and the respect excepted was the only one that really mattered. The Constants—ignorant, vulgar, and brash—had copious quantities of dumb luck.
(*ST* 142:L14) The fielders and Miss Fenstermaker dodged the ball as though it were a red-hot cannonball. When the ball came to a stop of its own accord, the fielders went after it with a sort of ritual clumsiness. Clearly, the point of their efforts was not to hit Chrono with the ball, was not to put him out. The fielders were all **conspiring** to increase the glory of Chrono by making a show of helpless opposition.
(*ST* 279:L29) Rumfoord held his hands high, and his fingers were spread. Streaks of pink, violet, and pale green Saint Elmo's fire streamed from his fingertips. Short streaks of pale gold fizzed in his hair, **conspiring** to give him a tinsel halo.

The following is a list of indictments against Dr. Lionel J.D. Jones, D.D.S., D.D. and twenty-seven others: **Conspiring** to destroy the morale and faith and confidence of the members of the military and naval forces of the United States and the people of the United States in their public officials and republican form of government; **conspiring** to seize upon and use and misuse the right of freedom of speech and of the press to spread their disloyal doctrines, intending and believing that any nation allowing its people the right of freedom of speech is powerless to defend itself against enemies masquerading as patriotic; and seeking to obstruct, impede, break down and destroy the proper functioning of its republican form of government under the guise of honest criticism; **conspiring** to render the Government of the United States bereft of the faith and confidence of the members of the military and naval forces and of the people, and thereby render that government powerless to defend the nation or the people against armed attack from without or treachery from within (*MN* 52:L1, 4, 10).
(*CC* 165:L9) All things **conspired** to form one cosmic *vin-dit*, one mighty shove into Bokononism, into the belief that God was running my life and that He had work for me to do.
(*SL5* 64:L33) The American fliers turned in their uniforms, became high school kids. And Hitler turned into a baby, Billy Pilgrim supposed. That wasn't in the movie. Billy was extrapolating. Everybody turned into a baby, and all humanity, without exception, **conspired** biologically to produce two perfect people named Adam and Eve, he supposed. *Billy had become "slightly unstuck in time" and watched a war movie on television—backwards.*

Constant, Benjamin. (*ST* 72:L2) The family could trace its line back through an illegitimacy to **Benjamin Constant**, who was a tribune under Napoleon from 1799 to 1801, and a lover of Anne Louise Germaine Necker, Baronne de Stael-Holstein, wife of the then Swedish ambassador to France.

Constant, Malachi. *The son of Noel Constant and Florence Whitehill, Malachi is chairman of Magnum Opus, Inc., when he is invited to the*

Rumfoord estate for one of Winston Niles Rumfoord's chrono-synclastic infundibulated materializations. He had been thrown out of the University of Virginia in his freshman year, but was still the richest American—and a notorious rakehell (*MN* 11:L25-26).

Malachi's name actually means "constant messenger" and he believes he is destined for some great use, but when he is told he will visit Mars and Titan, mate with Beatrice Rumfoord and sire a son, Malachi goes on a nearly two-month alcohol binge and loses all the wealth he and his father had compiled.

He is subject to all of Rumfoord's predictions and at various times is known as Malachi, Unk, or the Space Wanderer. He and Boaz are trapped in a cave on a moon, and when he finally extricates himself and returns to Earth, he is hailed as the long-prophesied Space Wanderer—only to become the object of scorn and ritual religious sacrifice to Rumfoord and his Church of God the Utterly Indifferent. All this was predetermined by the plotting Tralfamadorians who sought to get a spare part to their intergalactic messenger, Salo. Malachi's son, Chrono, is the unknowing guardian of the part, which is nothing more than a piece of sheet metal he carried as his good luck charm.

Malachi dies at a bus stop on the outskirts of Indianapolis, under a blanket of snow and in the midst of a posthypnotic illusion suggested by Salo. In a complete transformation from his former hedonism, he wanted to end his life in Indianapolis because it "is the first place in the United States of America where a white man was hanged for the murder of an Indian. The kind of people who'll hang a white man for murdering an Indian—" said **Constant**, "that's the kind of people for me" (*ST* 314:L32, 315:L1-5).

Constant, Noel. *The founder of Magnum Opus and father of Malachi Constant. A native of New Bedford, Massachusetts, he was a traveling salesman of copper-bottomed cookware. At the age of thirty-nine, while in room 223 of the Wilburhampton Hotel, he devised his unique method of investment. In the dresser of the hotel room was a Gideon Bible and a fourteen-year-old page with stock-market quotations.* (*ST* 73:L1-10, 17-32, 74:L1-11) Magnum Opus was built with a pen, a check book, some check-sized Government envelopes, a Gideon Bible, and a bank balance of eight thousand, two hundred and twelve dollars. The bank balance was **Noel Constant**'s share in the estate of his anarchist father. The estate had consisted principally of Government bonds.

And **Noel Constant** had an investment program. It was simplicity itself. The Bible would be his investment counselor. . . . he increased his fortune to a million and a quarter.

Noel Constant did it without genius and without spies. His system was so idiotically simple that some people can't understand it, no matter how often it is explained. The people who can't understand it are people who have to believe, for their own peace of mind, that tremendous wealth can be produced only by tremendous cleverness.

This was **Noel Constant**'s system:

He took the Gideon Bible that was in his room, and he started with the first sentence in Genesis.

The first sentence in Genesis, as some people may know, is: "In the beginning God created the heaven and the earth." **Noel Constant** wrote the sentence in capital letters, put periods between the letters, divided the letters into pairs, rendering the sentence as follows: "I.N., T.H., E.B., E.G., I.N., N.I., N.G., G.O., D.C., R.E., A.T., E.D., T.H., E.H., E.A., V.E., N.A., N.D., T.N., E.E., A.R., T.H."

And then he looked for corporations with those initials, and bought shares in them. His rule at the beginning was that he would own shares in only one corporation at a time, would invest his whole nest-egg in it, and would sell the instant the value of his shares had doubled.

Noel Constant has an infrequent but regular affair with Florence Whitehill, who gives birth to their son Malachi. At his one and only meeting with his son he advises him in terms more blunt than Polonius' advice to his son that "My father gave me only two pieces of advice," he said, "and only one of them has stood the test of time. They were: 'Don't touch your principal,' and 'Keep the liquor bottle out of the bedroom'" (*ST* 82:L13-16).

Constant, Sylvanus. *The father of Noel Constant and grandfather of Malachi was* a loom fixer in the New Bedford Mills of the Nattaweena Division of the Grand Republic Woolen Company. He was an anarchist, though he never got into any trouble about it, except with his wife (*ST* 71:L29-32).

Cooley, Franklin. *In* Bluebeard, *this father of six sits astride a riding lawn mover and causes Rabo Karabekian to wonder if he has any idea about the cultural revolution Rabo was carrying on in his potato barn as he transformed the fatally flawed "Blue Windsor Number Seventeen" into "Now It's The Women's Turn." Regardless, by the time Rabo is prepared to show Circe Berman the painting, they can only reach the barn by following the path cut out by Cooley.*

Cooper, Oveta and **Mary Selwyn Kirk**. *In* Slapstick, *these are the practical nurses long attending the malformed but brilliant twins Wilbur and Eliza Swain at the family's Vermont estate. Once the twins agreed to show the world they were indeed intelligent, they first revealed their true characters to Oveta Cooper, assuring her all the staff would remain employed for all the kindness they showed over the years.*

Corbett, General William K. *The camp commander who plays host to the visiting Shah of Bratpuhr* (*PP* 56:L2-3).

Cordiner, Dr. Cordelia Swain. *The world-renowned psychologist who is hired to test the intelligence of Wilbur and Eliza Swain and recommends they* *should be permanently separated. She has three doctoral degrees and heads a private testing firm which bills three billion dollars a year. In remembering the impact Dr. Cordiner had on him, Wilbur cites Dostoyevsky and extrapolates further.* (*Slap* 90:L3-8) "One sacred memory from childhood is perhaps the best education." I can think of another quickie education: Meeting a human being who is tremendously respected by the adult world, and realizing that that person is actually malicious.

(*Slap* 91:L6-10, 15-18) **Dr. Cordelia Swain Cordiner** was invariably impressive and gracious when in the presence of grownups. She was elaborately dressed the whole time she was in the mansion—in high-heeled shoes and fancy dresses and jewelry. . . .

When she got Eliza and me alone, though, she seethed with paranoia.

"None of your tricks, no more of your snotty little kid millionaire tricks with me," she would say.

Dr. Cordiner insisted on testing the twins separately to prevent Wilbur and Eliza from using their mental telepathy. They tested poorly and insisted they take the test again—together. Their mother insisted Dr. Cordiner retest them. They answered every question correctly but the physical frenzy brought on by their telepathy drove away their parents and caused the doctor to faint.

cork, corkscrew-shaped, corkscrews. (*ST* 234:L24) The man who had the booth next to Bee's was Harry Brackman. . . . He had a **cork** leg and a stainless steel right hand.

(*MH* 3:L6 *Where I Live*) The course was built on the lawn of what had once been an American Legion Post—and, right in the middle of the cunning little bridges and granulated **cork** fairways was a Sherman tank, set there in simpler and less enterprising days as a memorial to the veterans of World War Two.

(*MH* 112:L12 *Next Door*) "If I could hear Harger pulling a **cork**, he can certainly hear you," said his father.

(*BC* 3:L7-8, 23) Those people *(syphilitics)* were infested with carnivorous little **corkscrews** which could be seen only with a microscope. The victims' vertebrae were welded together after the **corkscrews** got through with the meat between. . . .

Here was his problem: his brains, where the instructions to his legs originated, were being eaten alive by **corkscrews**. The wires which had to carry the instructions weren't insulated anymore, or were eaten clear through. Switches along the way were welded open or shut.

(*BC* 79:L31) Around the toilet seat was a band of paper. . . . This loop of paper *(marked "SANITARY")* guaranteed Dwayne that he need have no fear that **corkscrew-shaped** little animals would crawl up his asshole and eat up his wiring. That was one less worry for Dwayne.

(*WFG* 213:L25, 27 *Address at Rededication of Wheaton College Library, 1973*) Here I am, due to become fifty years old two days from now. I have imagined during most of that half century that I was responding to life around me as a just and sensitive man, blowing my **cork** with good reason from time to time.

Only recently, with the help of a physician, have I realized that I have blown my **cork** every twenty days, no matter what is really going on.
(*WFG* 252:L18 *Playboy Interview*) PLAYBOY: Do you experience manic periods as well depressive ones?
VONNEGUT: Until recently, about every twenty days, I blew my **cork**. I thought for a long time that I had perfectly good reasons for these periodic blowups; thought people around me had it coming to them. But only recently have I realized that this has been happening regularly since I've been six years old.
(*Blue* 160:L12) Marilee Kemp wasn't the only one who was trapped like Nora in *A Doll's House* before Nora blew her **cork**. I (*Rabo Karabekian*) was another one.

Cormody. *A screw machine operator occupying booth seven in the short story "Deer in the Works."*

Cornell University (also ***Cornell Daily Sun***). *Vonnegut often speaks of the two years he spent at Cornell before going into the army shortly after the attack on Pearl Harbor. The "Roots" chapter in* Palm Sunday *contains John Rauch's history of the Vonnegut family complete with his father's instructions to study the sciences, especially chemistry. By his own admission, Vonnegut was not a good student. While at Cornell he wrote a humor column for the* Cornell Daily Sun *and was a member of the Delta Upsilon fraternity. Throughout his fiction Vonnegut has sprinkled Cornellians. In* Player Piano *the pompous realtor Dr. Pond holds a Doctor of Realty degree from Cornell's Graduate School. All of Dr. Ewing J. Halyard's Cornell degrees are temporarily rescinded because a degree audit revealed he did not complete his undergraduate physical education requirement. Cornell football coach Dr. Harold Roseberry was the subject of a nasty letter Halyard wrote five years earlier, and Roseberry is given the opportunity to exact revenge by Cornell President Dr. Albert Herpers who passes along the note before Halyard's make-up exam.*

Cat's Cradle*'s narrator John/Jonah is a Cornell alum as well as a member of Delta Upsilon. Through the course of the novel he learns that H. Lowe Crosby is his fraternity brother and Cornell graduate, and Newt Hoenikker was a DU pledge when he flunked out of Cornell.* God Bless You, Mr. Rosewater*'s Norman Mushari is a graduate of Cornell's Law School.* Slapstick*'s Professor Elihu Swain is crediited with starting Cornell's Department of Civil Engineering at the age of twenty-two.* Galápagos*' Siegfried von Kleist is another graduate of the Cornell Hotel School as is* Hocus Pocus*' Dwight Casey, a Tarkington College English teacher. Tarkington was one of Cornell's athletic rivals.*

Corpus Christi. (*HP* 131:L7) His father *(Tex Johnson's)*, whose name certainly wasn't Johnson, was a Lithuanian second mate on a Russian freighter

who jumped ship when it put in for emergency repairs at **Corpus Christi**. Zuzu told me that Tex's father was not only an illegal immigrant but the nephew of the former Communist boss of Lithuania.
(*HP* 134:L33) I wonder if his father would have jumped ship in **Corpus Christi** if he had known what an unhappy end his only son would come to under American Free Enterprise.

Cortes, Hernando. (*CC* 107:L6-12) **Hernando Cortes** was the first man to have his sterile conquest of San Lorenzo recorded on paper. **Cortes** and his men came ashore for fresh water in 1519, named the island, claimed it for Emperor Charles the Fifth, and never returned. Subsequent expeditions came for gold and diamonds and rubies and spices, found none, burned a few natives for entertainment and heresy, and sailed on.

Cortez, Major Ricardo. *The Peruvian jet pilot in* Galápagos *who mistakenly destroys the Colombian freighter* San Mateo, *thinking it was the* Bahía de Darwin.

Corwin, Lance. *When Billy Pilgrim visits a pornographic bookstore in New York's Times Square, he comes upon a Kilgore Trout novel* about a man who built a time machine so he could go back and see Jesus. . . . The time-traveler in the book went back to *Bible* times to find out one thing in particular: Whether or not Jesus had really died on the cross, or whether he had been taken down while still alive, whether he had really gone on living. The hero had a stethoscope along.

Billy skipped to the end of the book, where the hero mingled with the people who were taking Jesus down from the cross. The time-traveler was the first one up the ladder, dressed in clothes of the period, and he leaned close to Jesus so people couldn't see him use the stethoscope, and he listened.

There wasn't a sound inside the emaciated chest cavity. The Son of God was dead as a doornail.

So it goes.

The time-traveler, whose name was **Lance Corwin**, also got to measure the length of Jesus, but not to weigh him. Jesus was five feet and three and a half inches long (*SL5* 174:L31-33, 175:L31-33, 176:L1-14).

Costa, Antone C. *The subject of Vonnegut's essay "There's a Maniac Loose Out There." Costa had killed four women on Cape Cod and was known by Vonnegut's daughter Edith.* (*WFG* 66:L29-33) My nineteen-year-old daughter Edith knows **Tony Costa**. She met him during a crazy summer she spent on her own in Provincetown, knew him well enough to receive and decline an invitation he evidently extended many girls: "Come and see my marijuana patch."

Cotuit Harbor. *In* God Bless You, Mr. Rosewater, *Eunice Morgan Rosewater drowns in the harbor when her son, Eliot, accidentally knocks her overboard with the boom of their sailboat.*

Coulomb, Marc. *When Rabo Karabekian was no longer Dan Gregory's apprentice, he earned money drawing caricatures of people in Central Park.* (*Blue* 186:L13-17) When he struck up a conversation with me in Central Park, **Marc Coulomb** was only twenty-five, and had been sent from Paris to find an advertising agency to make his family's services better known in the U.S.A. *Coulomb is a Bulgarian-Armenian whose original name, Marktich Kouyoumdjian, is later "Frenchified." Coulomb Frères et Cie is the family business.* (*Blue* 186:L25-31) Purely on the basis of race prejudice, I think, one Armenian taking care of another, he bought me a suit, a shirt, a necktie, and a new pair of shoes, and took me to the advertising agency he liked best, which was Leidveld and Moore. He told them they could have the **Coulomb** account if they would hire me as an artist. Which they did.

When Germany invaded France, Coulomb Frères et Cie went out of business and the advertising agency released Karabekian. Karabekian then joined the U.S. Army, specializing in camouflage techniques.

While in the process of writing his memoirs, Rabo reads Coulomb's obituary in The New York Times. (*Blue* 187:L2-6) He was a hero of the French Resistance, they say, and was, at the time of his death, chairman of the board of **Coulomb Frères et Cie**, the most extensive travel organization in the world.

Count Dracula. *In what Wilbur describes as his mother's temporary fit of insanity on the eve of the twins' fifteenth birthday, she declares* "How can I love **Count Dracula** and his blushing bride?"—meaning Eliza and me (*Slap* 67:L10-11).

Rabo Karabekian describes his trip with Floyd Pomerantz from Manhattan to East Hampton in Pomerantz' stretch Cadillac limousine as "coffin*like"—which he says is better than "womblike." Rabo went to New York at the prodding of Circe Berman who insisted he go to prove he* was still a healthy man, in no way in need of assistance, in no way an invalid. So Floyd Pomerantz's chauffeur delivered me to the first flagstone of my doorpath. I clambered out of our fancy casket like **Count Dracula**, blinded by the setting sun. I groped my way to my front door and entered (*Blue* 114:L3). *It was only after his return did he find out about the early demise of his "Blue Windsor Number Seventeen" and replaced it with his singular masterpiece "Now It's the Women's Turn."*

counter-clockwise, counterclockwise. (*ST* 40:L7) She was behaving like an invalid—tottering, blinking hard, making her voice like wind in the treetops. She wore a long white dressing gown whose soft folds formed a **counter-clockwise** spiral in harmony with the white staircase. The train of the

gown cascaded down the top riser, making Beatrice continuous with the architecture of the mansion.
(*ST* 141:L1-2) The child's hair was jet black, bristly—and the black bristles grew in a violently **counter-clockwise** swirl. *This is the beginning of a longer description of Chrono, the son of Malachi and Beatrice.*
(*CC* 154:L14) He pointed them out, **counterclockwise**. "House of Hope and Mercy in the Jungle, 'Papa's palace, and Fort Jesus." *Frank Hoenikker points out some of the significant establishments on San Lorenzo.*

Cowper, William. (*DD* 100:L21) When we heard about that fatal flash back home, in fact, I had quoted the words of **William Cowper**, which a sympathetic English teacher had given me to keep from killing myself when I was young: God moves in a mysterious way / His wonders to perform; / He plants his footsteps in the sea, / And rides upon the storm.

Crimea. *In* Mother Night, *Helga Noth died in the Crimea when the Russians recaptured it from the Nazis. Howard Campbell was unaware of her death though he had transmitted the news in code to his American contacts. When Resi Noth poses as her sister, she claims to have been captured in the Crimea and raped by Russian soldiers before being sent to the Ukraine.*

Crispus Attucks High School. *Vonnegut makes a mental note to explain to Kilgore Trout the significance of the high school jackets he will see in the hospital after he is victimized by Dwayne Hoover during his rampage.* (*BC* 249:L31-32, 250:L2, 5-6) Let's see, let's see. Oh, yes—I have to explain a jacket Trout will see at the hospital. *The jacket has the inscription "INNOCENT BYSTANDER H.S."*

Here is the explanation: There used to be only one Nigger high school in Midland City, and it was an all Nigger high school still. It was named after **Crispus Attucks**, a black man who was shot by British troops in Boston in 1770. There was an oil painting of this event in the main corridor of the school. Several white people were stopping bullets, too. **Crispus Attucks** himself had a hole in his forehead which looked like the front door of a birdhouse.

But the black people didn't call the school ***Crispus Attucks High School*** anymore. They called it *Innocent Bystander High*.

Undoubtedly, Vonnegut appropriated the name of the school from the predominantly African-American Indianapolis high school of his youth.

Crocker, Harry. *The plumber in the short story "Go Back to Your Precious Wife and Son," who chides the narrator for not personally measuring movie starlet Gloria Hilton for her customized shower door.*

Crocker, Pete. *In the short story "Welcome to the Monkey House," Crocker is sheriff of Barnstable County participating in the manhunt for the "notorious nothinghead named Bill the Poet."*

Crocker, Virginia. (*MN* 20:L10) My *(Howard Campbell's)* mother was the former **Virginia Crocker**, the daughter of a portrait photographer from Indianapolis. She was a housewife and an amateur cellist. She played cello with the Schenectady Symphony Orchestra, and she once had dreams of my playing the cello, too.

Crone, Joe (see also **Billy Pilgrim**). *In* Fates Worse Than Death, *Vonnegut reveals that Joe Crone was his model for* Slaughterhouse-Five*'s Billy Pilgrim.*

Crosby, H. Lowe and Hazel. *The Chicago bicycle manufacturer and his wife who travel to San Lorenzo in hopes of opening a new manufacturing plant. He is a Cornell graduate and she is from Indiana, both sources of great pride and granfalloonery. The Crosbys took refuge from the errant attack on the presidential palace and the ensuing outbreak of ice-nine in a palace oubliette along with Frank and Newt Hoenikker. Hazel instantly became fond of John/Jonah, insisting he call her "Mom." They are among the few survivors at the close of* Cat's Cradle.

Crown Hill Cemetery. *The Indianapolis cemetery where the Vonnegut family plot holds the remains of his parents, his sister Alice, as well as the remains of John Dillinger, James Whitcomb Riley, and his first mother-in-law.* (*JB* 10:L4, *PS* 57:L23; 220:L14)

crucifix. (*SL5* 33:L10) Billy, after all, had contemplated torture and hideous wounds at the beginning and the end of nearly every day of his childhood. Billy had an extremely gruesome **crucifix** hanging on the wall of his little bedroom in Ilium. A military surgeon would have admired the clinical fidelity of the artist's rendition of all Christ's wounds—the spear wound, the thorn wounds, the holes that were made by the iron spikes. Billy's Christ died horribly. He was pitiful.

(*SL5* 33:L19, 25, 30) Billy wasn't a Catholic, even though he grew up with a ghastly **crucifix** on the wall. His father had no religion. His mother was a substitute organist for several churches around town. She took Billy with her whenever she played, taught him to play a little, too. She said she was going to join a church as soon as she decided which one was right.

She never *did* decide. She did develop a terrific hankering for a **crucifix**, though. And she bought one from a Santa Fe gift shop during a trip the little family made out West during the Great Depression. Like so many Americans, she was trying to construct a life that made sense from things she found in gift shops.

And the **crucifix** went up on the wall of Billy Pilgrim.

(*WFG* 39:L31-32 *Yes, We Have No Nirvanas*) I went outside the hotel after that, liking Jesus better than I had ever liked Him before. I wanted to see a **crucifix**, so I could say to it, "You know why You're up there? It's Your own fault. You should have practiced Transcendental Meditation, which is easy as pie. You would also have been a better carpenter."

(*HP* 180:L22) But I would tell him now, if he hadn't been killed while trying to save the horses, that the most important message of a **crucifix**, to me anyway, was how unspeakably cruel supposedly sane human beings can be when under orders from a superior authority.

crucifixion, crucify, crurifragium (also **"Crucifixion in Rome"**). (*GBR* 134:L10) There was a photograph of Trout. He was an old man with a full black beard. He looked like a frightened, aging Jesus, whose sentence to **crucifixion** had been commuted to imprisonment for life.

(*SL5* 94:L18) The flaw in the Christ stories, said the visitor from outer space, was that Christ, who didn't look like much, was actually the Son of the Most Powerful Being in the Universe. Readers understood that, so, when they came to the **crucifixion**, they naturally thought, and Rosewater read out loud again:

Oh, boy—they sure picked the wrong guy to lynch this time!

(*WJ* 173:L26) WOODLY Oh—look at the poor, **crucified** violin, would you?
HAROLD It died for your sins.
WOODLY This little corpse is intended as a lesson?

(*JB* 72:L16) I told my poor wife during those first months of unemployment that, yes, that was certainly an option we held, in case all else failed: that I could at any time raise my arms like a man **crucified**, so to speak, and fall backward into General Motors or General Electric or some such thing.

(*PS* 218:L9 *Religion*) "Now a rich Roman tourist, a man, a successful speculator in Mesopotamian millet futures, comes upon the scene. I make him rich, because everybody hates rich people so much. He is blase about **crucifixions**, since he has seen so many strangers **crucified** all over the Roman Empire. Crosses then were as common as lampposts are today."

(*PS* 312:L25 *The Sexual Revolution*) Anyone can graph a simple story if he or she will **crucify** it, so to speak, on the intersecting axes.

(*DD* xii:L12) There really was a John Rettig, and his painting in the Cincinnati Art Museum, **"Crucifixion in Rome,"** is as I have described it.

(*DD* 154:L7) Joseph brought the goblet to the **crucifixion**, and some of Christ's blood fell into it. Joseph was arrested for his Christian sympathies. He was thrown into prison without food or water, but he survived for several years. He had the goblet with him, and every day it filled up with food and drink.

(*DD* 168:L5-6, 9, 26-27) One of the ten greatest paintings in the world, as far as he *(Rudy's father)* was concerned, was **"Crucifixion in Rome,"** by John Rettig, which he had bought for a song in Holland, during his student days. It now hangs in the Cincinnati Art Museum.

"**Crucifixion in Rome**," in fact, was one of the few successes in the art marketplace, or in any sort of marketplace, which Father experienced in his threescore years and eight. . . .

But the only painting anybody wanted was "**Crucifixion in Rome**." The Cincinnati Art Museum bought it for not much money, and the museum wanted it not because its greatness was so evident, I'm sure, but because it had been painted by a native of Cincinnati. It was a tiny thing, about the size of a shirt cardboard—about the size of Father's work in progress, the nude in his Vienna studio.

(*DD* 169:L11, 16) "**Crucifixion in Rome**" is signed "John Rettig," and it is dated 1888. So it was painted four years before Father was born. Father must have bought it in 1913 or so. Felix thinks there is a possibility that Hitler was with Father on that skylarking trip to Holland. Maybe so.

"**Crucifixion in Rome**" is indeed set in Rome, which I have never seen. I know enough, though, to recognize that it is chock-a-block with architectural anachronisms.

(*Blue* 269:L31) I had better explain to young readers that the *Shroud of Turin* is a linen sheet in which a dead person has been wrapped, which bears the imprint of an adult male who has been **crucified**, which the best scientists of today agree may indeed be two thousand years old. It is widely believed to have swaddled none other than Jesus Christ, and is the chief treasure of the Cathedral of San Giovanni Battista in Turin, Italy.

(*Blue* 287:L21) Mrs. Berman told me a legend about Gypsies I had never heard before: "They stole the nails from the Roman soldiers who were about to **crucify** Jesus," she said.

(*HP* 40:L16) I remained philosophical, thanks to marijuana and alcohol, while the community decided whether to **crucify** me as a fraud or to crown me as a genius. *Hartke speaks of the authorities at the Cleveland Science Fair.*

(*HP* 65:L17-18, 22) Even though he *(Tex Johnson, the President of Tarkington College)* was dead when the convicts got to him, they were so outraged that they **crucified** him in the loft of the stable where the students used to keep their horses, at the foot of Musket Mountain.

So a President of Tarkington, my mentor Sam Wakefield, blew his brains out with a Colt .45. And his successor, although he couldn't feel anything, was **crucified**.

(*HP* 102:L11) I think I felt what could be called love for Zuzu Johnson, whose husband was **crucified**.

(*HP* 133:L14) In the folder was a report by a private detective hired by Wilder to investigate my sex life. . . . He didn't miss a thing Zuzu and I did during the second semester. There was only 1 misunderstood incident: when I went up into the loft of the stable, where the Lutz Carillon had been stored before there was a tower and where Tex Johnson was **crucified** 2 years ago. *The misunderstood incident involved Hartke and the architect aunt of a student who visited the tower with him to look at the beam work. The detective mistakenly assumed they made love in the tower.*

(*HP* 134:L31) He *(Tex Johnson)* was a cuckold in the present, and **crucifixion** awaited him in the future.
(*HP* 165:L27) The joke was that Tex Johnson, the College President, having seen one too many motorcycle movies, believed that the campus might actually be assaulted by Hell's Angels someday. This fantasy was so real to him that he had bought an Israeli sniper's rifle, complete with a telescopic sight, and ammunition for it from a drugstore in Portland, Oregon. . . . That was the same weapon which would eventually get him **crucified**.
(*HP* 179:L5, 9, 16, 18-20, 30-31) He was especially fascinated by Tex Johnson's body. He had seen almost everything in his line of work, he told me, but never a man who had been **crucified**, with spikes through the palms and feet and all.

He told me one thing I'd never realized: that the Jews, not just the Romans, also **crucified** their idea of criminals from time to time. Live and learn!

Darius, King of Persia, he told me, **crucified** 3,000 people he thought were enemies in Babylon. After the Romans put down the slave revolt led by Spartacus, he said, they **crucified** 6,000 of the rebels on either side of the Appian Way! . . .

As I said at the beginning of this book, if I had been a professional soldier back then, I probably would have **crucified** people without thinking much about it, if ordered to do so.
(*HP* 180:L2, 4, 7, 9) I might have taught recruits who had never had anything to do with **crucifixions**, who maybe had never even seen one before, a new word from the vocabulary of military science of that time. The word was ***crurifragium***. . . .

It is a Latin word for "breaking the legs of a **crucified** person with an iron rod in order to shorten his time of suffering." But that still didn't make **crucifixion** a country club.
(*HP* 193:L19, 21) In the story, the Elders of Tralfamadore were indifferent, to say the least, to all the suffering going on. When 6,000 rebellious slaves were **crucified** on either side of the Appian Way back in good old 71 B.C., the elders would have been delighted if a **crucified** person had spit into the face of a centurion, giving him pneumonia or TB.
(*HP* 198:L18) I straddled the banana-shaped saddle, which turned out to be surprisingly considerate of my sensitive crotch and hindquarters. Sailing down a hill on that bicycle in the sunshine wasn't anything like being **crucified**.
(*HP* 204:L3) When I visited Lyle up there, he knew the story of those holes, knew the sniper had been **crucified** in the stable loft.
(*HP* 226:L9) Think again about the **crucifixions** of Jesus and the 2 thieves, and the 6,000 slaves who followed the gladiator Spartacus.
(*HP* 276:L21) I also supervised the exhumation of the bodies next to the stable. They had been buried for only a few days, but then the Government, personified by a Coroner and the Medical Examiner from the State Police who knew so much about **crucifixions**, ordered us to dig them up again.

(*HP* 299:L29) That must have been for him like walking down the Appian Way back in 71 B.C., when 6,000 nobodies had just been **crucified** there. Some little kid or maybe a lot of little kids may have walked down that road back then. What could a little kid say on such an occasion? "Daddy, I think I have to go to the bathroom"?
(*FWD* 137:L9) (Even Jesus Christ, if He hadn't been **crucified**, would have started repeating Himself.)
(*FWD* 140:L26-27, 29, 32) "But suppose we foolishly got rid of our nuclear weapons, our Kool-Aid, and an enemy came over here and **crucified** us. **Crucifixion** was the most painful thing the ancient Romans ever found to do to anyone. They knew as much about pain as we do about genocide. They sometimes **crucified** hundreds of people at one time. That is what they did to all the survivors of the army of Spartacus, which was composed mostly of escaped slaves. They **crucified** them all. There were several miles of crosses.
(*FWD* 141:L3) "We know of one person who was **crucified** in olden times, who was supposedly as capable as we or the Russians are of ending life everywhere. But He chose to endure agony instead. All He said was, 'Forgive them, Father—they know not what they do.'"
(*FWD* 141:L14, 17, 20) "I don't believe that we *are* about to be **crucified**. No potential enemy we now face has anywhere near enough carpenters. Not even people at the Pentagon at budget time have mentioned **crucifixion**. I am sorry to have to put that idea into their heads. I will have only myself to blame if, a year from now, the Joint Chiefs of Staff testify under oath that we are on the brink of being **crucified**.
(*FWD* 143:L30-31) "So I haven't had much luck, have I, in identifying fates worse than death? **Crucifixion** is the only clear winner so far, and we aren't about to be **crucified**. We aren't about to be enslaved, either to be treated the way white Americans used to treat black Americans. And no potential enemy that I have heard of wants to come over here to treat all of us the way we still treat American Indians.
(*FWD* 162:L19) "I will say that you, in terms of numbers, power, and influence, and your spiritual differences with the general population, are analogous to the earliest Christians in the catacombs under Imperial Rome. I hasten to add that your hardships are not the same, nor are you in any danger. Nobody in the power structure thinks children of the Age of Reason amount to a hill of beans. That is the extent of your discomfort. That sure beats being **crucified** upside down or being fed to the carnivorous menagerie at the Circus Maximus."

cruciform. (*Blue* 213:L7) She was only four blocks away—in a palazzo designed for Innocenzo "the Invisible" de Medici by Leon Battista Alberti in the middle of the fifteenth century. It was a **cruciform** structure whose four wings abutted on a domed rotunda twelve meters in diameter and in whose walls were half embedded eighteen Corinthian columns four and a half meters high. Above the capitals of the columns was a clerestory, a wall pierced with thirty-six windows.

Cruz, Hernando. *The first mate on the* Bahía de Darwin, *Cruz was an experienced seaman having made fifty cruises to the Galápagos Islands. He was part of the skeleton crew which brought the* Bahía de Darwin *from Sweden and supervised its outfitting in Guayaquil. His wife was expecting their twelfth child when he decided to walk away from his ship and return to his family. According to the story's narrator, Leon Trout, Cruz's decision was a momentous one for humanity.* (*Gal* 139:L28-32, 140:L1-5) That left Adolf von Kleist completely in charge, although he did not know shit from Shinola about navigation, the Galápagos Islands, or the operation and maintenance of a ship that size.

The combination of the Captain's incompetence and the decision of **Hernando Cruz** to go to the aid of his own flesh and blood, although the stuff of low comedy at the time, has turned out to be of incalculable value to present-day humankind. So much for comedy. So much for supposedly serious stuff. *Leon Trout characterized the relationship between Captain von Kleist and Hernando Cruz as a common symbiotic pairing of politesse and practicality. Trout surmises that had Cruz stayed aboard ship it would never have been run aground by von Kleist which, as it turns out, was the saving grace of humanity.*

The Cry of the Nocturnal Goatsucker. *Written pseudonomously under the names Betty and Bobby Brown, this childrearing text was the result of one of the telepathic binges of Eliza and Wilbur Swain in* Slapstick. *When Wilbur later became a pediatrician he had it published under the pseudonym Dr. Eli W. Rockmell, M.D., an amalgamation of his and his sister's name. The publisher retitled the text* So You Went and Had a Baby.

cuckold, cuckolding. (*ST* 261:L12) He *(Winston Niles Rumfoord)* was so well supplied with great material that he could actually let his voice trail off as he announced that the one-eyed, gold-toothed woman was his wife, and that he had been **cuckolded** by Malachi Constant.
(*GBR* 53:L18) Avondale's clammy respect for the monarchy turned to incredulous contempt, and then to savagery. Yahooism, drinking, **cuckolding**, and self-esteem all took sharp upturns.
(*Blue* 170:L23) *Rabo writes of his affair with Marilee Kemp that* The man we were about to **cuckold** *(Dan Gregory)* or whatever was fifty-three, with only seven more years to go, a mere stripling in retrospect.
(*HP* 134:L31) He *(Tex Johnson)* was a **cuckold** in the present, and crucifixion awaited him in the future.

cuckoo clock in Hell. (*MN* 168:L31-32, 169:L1-32, 170:L1-4) I have never seen a more sublime demonstration of the totalitarian mind, a mind which might be likened unto a system of gears whose teeth have been filed off at random. Such a snaggle-toothed thought machine, driven by a standard or even by a substandard libido, whirls with the jerky, noisy, gaudy pointlessness of a **cuckoo clock in Hell**. . . .

Jones wasn't completely crazy. The dismaying thing about the classic totalitarian mind is that any given gear, though mutilated, will have at its circumference unbroken sequences of teeth that are immaculately maintained, that are exquisitely machined.

Hence the **cuckoo clock in Hell**—keeping perfect time for eight minutes and twenty-three seconds, jumping ahead fourteen minutes, keeping perfect time for six seconds, jumping ahead two seconds, keeping perfect time for two hours and one second, then jumping ahead a year.

The missing teeth, of course, are simple, obvious truths, truths available and comprehensible even to ten-year-olds, in most cases.

The willful filing off of gear teeth, the willful doing without certain obvious pieces of information—

That was how a household as contradictory as one composed of Jones, Father Keeley, Vice-Bundesfuehrer Krapptauer, and the Black Fuehrer could exist in relative harmony—

That was how my father-in-law could contain in one mind an indifference toward slave women and love for a blue vase—

That was how Rudolf Hoess, Commandant of Auschwitz, could alternate over the loudspeakers of Auschwitz great music and calls for corpse-carriers—

That was how Nazi Germany could sense no important differences between civilization and hydrophobia—

That is the closest I can come to explaining the legions, the nations of lunatics I've seen in my time. And for me to attempt such a mechanical explanation is perhaps a reflection of the father whose son I was. *Am*. When I pause to think about it, which is rarely, I am, after all, the son of an engineer.

Culver Military Academy. *Wilbur Swain travels to Indiana for a summit meeting of sorts with the King of Michigan, Stewart Oriole-2 Mott, and the setting is drawn from Vonnegut's childhood.* (*Slap* 46:L21) My interview with the King took place, incidentally, in his palace on Lake Maxinkuckee, in northern Indiana, where **Culver Military Academy** had once stood. I was still nominally the President of the United States of America, but I had lost control of everything. There wasn't any Congress any more, or any system of Federal Courts, or any Treasury or Army or any of that.
(*FWD* 52:L9-10, 13) "She asked me on our honeymoon what influence **Culver Military Academy**, which I haven't even mentioned, had on my thinking when I was a child. It was at the head of the lake, after all, and was the principal employer of the town, which is also called **Culver**. It was like a little West Point and Annapolis combined, with a Cavalry troop and a big fleet of sailboats and noisy parades and so on. They fired a cannon every night at sunset.

cupola (see also **belfry** and **tower**). (*GBR* 69:L10-11) When a fire call came in, Eliot would push a red button mounted on the wall under his commission as a Notary Public. The button activated a doomsday bullhorn under the **cupola** on top of the firehouse. Eliot had paid for the horn, and the **cupola**, too.

(*SL5* 50:L11) A siren went off, scared the hell out of him. He was expecting World War Three at any time. The siren was simply announcing high noon. It was housed in a **cupola** atop a firehouse across the street from Billy's office. *The siren shriek from the firehouse cupola prompted another jump in time for Billy Pilgrim.*

(*DD* 17:L4, 6) After they had eaten, he took them up into the attic above the loft, the future gun room. There were two old cots up there. Light and air came from windows in a **cupola** at the peak of the roof. A ladder, its bottom bolted to the center of the attic floor, led up into the **cupola**. Father told the brothers that they could make the attic their home, until they found something better.

(*DD* 24:L29) Father and Mother also bought the enormous weather vane from the gatehouse of the von Furstenberg estate, and put it atop their **cupola** back home, making the studio taller than anything in the county, except for the dome of the county courthouse, a few silos, the Fortunes' dairy barn, and the Midland County National Bank.

(*DD* 61:L22) I liked it so much, and it liked me so much, since I had fired it so well that morning, that I took it with me when I climbed the ladder up into the **cupola**. I wanted to sit up there for a while, and look out over the roofs of the town, supposing that my brother might be going to his death, and hearing and feeling the tanks in the street below. Ah, sweet mystery of life.

(*DD* 63:L14) Father came upstairs to find out if I was all right. I was better than that. I was at one with the universe. I heard him coming, but I was unconcerned—even though I was still at an open window in the **cupola** with the Springfield in my arms.

(*DD* 64:L2) I took my own sweet time about descending from the **cupola**. Firing the Springfield over the city was now part of my treasure-house of memories.

(*DD* 66:L30) Father knew exactly where it had come from. He had heard the bang. He had seen me at the top of the ladder in the **cupola**, with the Springfield in my arms.

(*DD* 70:L16, L20) Father ascended the ladder into the **cupola**, where I had been so recently. He there accomplished what Marco Maritimo later said should have been impossible for one man with such small and inappropriate tools. He cut away the base of the **cupola**, and he capsized it. It twisted free from its last few feeble moorings, and it went bounding down the slate roof, and it went crashing, weather vane and all, onto Chief Morissey's police car in the driveway below.

(*DD* 78:L2) They *(Gino and Marco Maritimo)* had received the obscene invitation *(to view Rudy in jail)*, offered as though nothing could be more civilized, soon after capping the hole in our roof where the **cupola** had been.
(*DD* 91:L24) His headlights picked out a strange broken form in the driveway. It hadn't been there on the previous morning. It was of course the wreckage of the **cupola** and the famous weather vane. It had been pulled off the top of the police chief's car and left there in the driveway.
(*DD* 153:L13) Guess what it was. It was the conical slate roof of my childhood home, only a few blocks away. The peak of the cone, where the **cupola** used to be, was capped with very light gray tar roofing, with bits of sand stuck to it. In the light of a full moon, it was glittering white-like snow. *Rudy tells of a Japanese person new to Midland City who asks him to come out from the pharmacy into the night air to see the image which reminds him of "Fujiyama. . . . the sacred volcano of Japan."*
(*DD* 215:L2) In this case, the government was about as careless as a half-wit boy up in a **cupola** with a loaded Springfield rifle—on Mother's Day. *Rudy compares his carelessness with the government's negligence in knowingly selling radioactive cement as war surplus. Exposure to the cement eventually kills his mother.*
(*HP* 27:L9) The 1 bell that was going to get to sing at once was installed in the **cupola** of the mansion, with its rope running all the way down to the first floor. It would call people to classes and, if need be, also serve as a fire alarm.
(*HP* 27:L14) The rest of the bells, it turned out, would slumber in the loft for 30 years, until 1899, when they were hanged as a family, the 1 from the **cupola** included, on axles in the belfry of the tower of a splendid library given to the school by the Moellenkamp family of Cleveland.

Cuthrell, William K. *The State Department representative who patronizingly responds to Professor Barnhouse's estimation of the potential peaceful uses for dynamopsychism. Cuthrell sides with General Barker's sense of realism and hopes Barnhouse will, too.* (*MH* 165:L10-16 *Report on the Barnhouse Effect*) "Unfortunately, the general is right in his own way," he said. "I wish to heaven the world were ready for ideals like yours, but it simply isn't. We aren't surrounded by brothers, but by enemies. It isn't a lack of food or resources that has us on the brink of war—it's a struggle for power. Who's going to be in charge of the world, our kind of people or theirs?"

Cuyahoga Bridge and Iron Company. *Founded by Daniel McCone, the company became the single largest employer in Cleveland by 1913. The neighborhood around the company, the shops and homes, all belonged to Cuyahoga Bridge. It became the sight of the Cuyahoga Massacre in 1894 after a long and bitter strike.* (*JB* 8:L4) **Cuyahoga Bridge and Iron**, incidentally, lost its identity, save in labor history, long ago. It was absorbed by Youngstown Steel shortly after the Second World War, and Youngstown Steel itself has now become a mere division of The RAMJAC Corporation.

Cuyahoga Massacre. (*JB* xxi:L19-20) There is mentioned in this book a violent confrontation between strikers and police and soldiers called the **Cuyahoga Massacre**. It is an invention, a mosaic composed of bits taken from tales of many such riots in not such olden times.

After a long dissertation about the political favors called in by Daniel McCone to put down the strikers and vivid descriptions of the unprofessional behavior by the National Guard, the impressions of the incident left on McCone's heir are simple and ominous. (*JB* xxxiv:L5-6) Years later Alexander McCone, when asked by Starbuck what he thought the principal cause of the **Cuyahoga Massacre** had been, would reply: "American am-am-am-amateurism in muh-muh-matters of luh-life and duh-duh-duh-death." (*JB* 7:L29-32, 8:L1-3) . . . the man who sent me to Harvard, Alexander Hamilton McCone, watched it *(the massacre)* from the factory clock tower in the company of his father and his older brother John. That was when he ceased to be a slight stammerer and became, when the least bit anxious about anything, a bubbling booby of totally blocked language instead.

cylinder, **cylindrical** (*PP* 60:L38) On the long grade past the golf course, the engine seemed to be hitting on no more than three **cylinders**, and a squad from the Reconstruction and Reclamation Corps, putting in a spruce windbreak to the north of the clubhouse, turned to watch the car's enervated struggle with gravity.
(*ST* 16:L31) The mower's swath skirted a dry fountain. The man who ran the mower had become creative at this point, had made the path fork. Constant could choose the side of the fountain on which he preferred to pass. Constant stopped at the fork, looked up. The fountain itself was marvelously creative. It was a cone described by many stone bowls of decreasing diameters. The bowls were collars on a **cylindrical** shaft forty feet high.
(*ST* 123:L27) He (*Unk—Malachi Constant*) found an aluminum **cylinder** with a screw cap. Inside the **cylinder** was a very long letter written in pencil. *The letter was written by Unk to himself after having had his memory wiped clean prior to the Martian invasion of Earth. His brainwashing was not totally successful, and he wrote this letter to himself in order to piece together the small bits of information he still had rattling around inside.*
(*CC* 177:L11-12) Around his (*Papa Monzano's*) neck hung a chain with a **cylinder** the size of a rifle cartridge for a pendant. I supposed that the **cylinder** contained some magic charm. I was mistaken. It contained a splinter of *ice-nine*.
(*CC* 192:L7, 9, 23-24) "He took it! Whatever was in that **cylinder**, "Papa" took—and now he's dead."

I remembered the **cylinder** "Papa" had hung around his neck, and I made an obvious guess as to its contents. "Cyanide?" . . .

That he had died of the contents of the **cylinder** around his neck was obvious. One hand held the **cylinder** and the **cylinder** was uncapped. And the thumb and index finger of the other hand, as though having just released a little pinch of something, were stuck between his teeth.

(*SL5* 64:L9, 21, 23) The formation flew backwards over a German city that was in flames. The bombers opened their bomb bay doors, exerted a miraculous magnetism which shrunk the fires, gathered them into **cylindrical** steel containers, and lifted the containers into the bellies of the planes. . . .

When the bombers got back to their base, the steel **cylinders** were taken from the racks and shipped back to the United States of America, where factories were operating night and day, dismantling the **cylinders**, separating the dangerous contents into minerals. Touchingly, it was mainly women who did this work. The minerals were then shipped to specialists in remote areas. It was their business to put them into the ground, to hide them cleverly, so they would never hurt anybody ever again.

(*SL5* 65:L24) The saucer was one hundred feet in diameter, with portholes around its rim. . . . It came down to hover over Billy, and to enclose him in a **cylinder** of pulsing purple light.

(*MH* 261:L8 *The Manned Missiles*) Stepan made pleasant jokes about his little house in the sky. He said it was a **cylinder** ten meters long and four meters in diameter. It could be very cozy.

(*BC* 150:L27, 29) There was a sexual revolution going on in the country, and women were demanding that men pay more attention to women's pleasure during sexual intercourse, and not just think of themselves. The key to their pleasure, they said, and scientists backed them up, was the clitoris, a tiny meat **cylinder** which was right above the hole in women where men were supposed to stick their much larger **cylinders**.

(*WFG* 176:L9 *Address to the National Institute of Arts and Letters, 1971*) I began with physical anthropology. I was taught how to measure the size of the brain of a human being who had been dead a long time, who was all dried out. I bored a hole in his skull, and I filled it with grains of polished rice. Then I emptied the rice into a graduated **cylinder**. I found this tedious.

(*WFG* 177:L4 *Address to the National Institute of Arts and Letters, 1971*) Dr. Redfield is dead now. Perhaps some physical anthropologist of the future will fill his skull with grains of polished rice, and empty it out again—into a graduated **cylinder**.

(*Slap* 107:L12-13) Be that as it may, our hands were busy—which is often the case with the hands of dying people. We had brought what we thought were the best of our writings with us. We rolled them into a **cylinder**, which we hid in an empty bronze funerary urn. *These were the treatises which would eventually lead to a disruption in the Earth's gravitational force.*

(*DD* 43:L14) The engine *(on the 1932 Keedsler touring car)* had sixteen **cylinders**, and the two spare tires were mounted in shallow wells in the front fenders.

D

"D.P." (1953). (see also **Karl Heinz**) *The short story about Karl Heinz, the product of a black American soldier and a German woman, according to Peter—an older orphan living in the same Karlswald orphanage. Karl lives in the hope that among the American military stationed nearby, someone will reunite him with his father.*

D'Arthanay, Barbara *Vonnegut's daughter-in-law by her marriage to his adopted son/nephew, James Adams.* (*PS* 244:L28 *Children*) He *(James Adams)* is married to a former New England schoolteacher who lived and worked with him for several years on his goat farm on a mountaintop in Jamaica. They are as uninterested in social rank and property as was Henry David Thoreau.

The Daffy-nition. *The privately published newspaper for those in the extended family of Daffodils.* (*Slap* 180:L22) There were editorials calling for family health insurance programs and sports teams and so on. There was one interesting essay, I remember, either in ***The Daffy-nition*** or *The Goober Gossip*, which said that families with high moral standards were the best maintainers of law and order, and that police departments could be expected to fade away.

dagonite. *Vonnegut—through Leon Trout—discusses the ancestry of this explosive as another means of discussing the interconnectedness of all activity.* (*Gal* 212:L15-27) The happy Colombianos were chewing and swallowing some of that poor cow's meat when they were blown to bits by the latest advance in the evolution of high explosives, which was called "**dagonite**." **Dagonite** was the son, so to speak, of a considerably weaker explosive made by the same company, and called "glacco." Glacco begat dagonite, so to speak, and both were descendants of Greek fire and gunpowder and dynamite and cordite and TNT.

So it might be said that the Colombianos had treated the cow abominably, but that retribution had been swift and terrible, thanks largely to the big-brained inventors of **dagonite**.

(*Gal* 214:L12) The detonation of **dagonite**, son of glacco, direct descendant of noble dynamite, caused a tidal wave in the estuary, which was six meters high when it swept the bus off the wharf at the Guayaquil waterfront and drowned Siegfried von Kleist, who wanted to die anyway.

The Daily Pancreas. *The newspaper of Sweetbread College in the play "The Chemistry Professor."*

"The Dancing Fool." *This Kilgore Trout short story was printed in a 1962 edition of* Black Garterbelt *magazine, a pornographic publication which used any text as filler between pictures of naked women. Trout found the magazine while browsing through an adult book store in Times Square. He was looking for materials he previously published to prepare himself for the Midland City Arts Festival. He was unaware this story was ever picked up for publication.*

(*BC* 58:L25-26) As for the story itself, it was entitled "The Dancing Fool." Like so many Trout stories, it was about a tragic failure to communicate.

Here was the plot: A flying saucer creature named Zog arrived on Earth to explain how wars could be prevented and how cancer could be cured. He brought the information from Margo, a planet where the natives conversed by means of farts and tap dancing.

Zog landed at night in Connecticut. He had no sooner touched down than he saw a house on fire. He rushed into the house, farting and tap dancing, warning the people about the terrible danger they were in. The head of the house brained Zog with a golfclub.

(*FWD* 209:L22) Because the most visible of the antiwar protestors, who included many returned Vietnam veterans, were so young, all they stood for could be dismissed by their enemies as symptoms of immaturity. They were attempting to save lives and resources, but their appearance and manners (and music, and excitement and confusion about sex) made them unfit, so went the argument, for such a serious role.

I memorialized this prejudice in a plot scheme for a short story (never written) to be called **"The Dancing Fool."** I included the plot in a novel.

Darlington, Edward Seward. *In* Sirens of Titan, *the half-wit stable boy at the Rumfoord Mansion during Winston's childhood. He was teamed with the Japanese gardener and his daughter against Winston, the butler, and Miss MacKenzie for games of German batball.*

Darwin, Alton. *Alton Darwin is the leader of the prison revolt in* Hocus Pocus. *Befriended by Eugene Debs Hartke, Darwin is a complex character* *who provokes Hartke's comparisons with both Jack Patton and himself. The following selected quotes help illustrate Darwin's enigmatic hold on Hartke. Darwin is killed by a sniper's bullet while ice skating at night on the frozen lake between the college and the prison.* (*HP* 71:L31-35, 72:L1-3) When I later went to work at the prison, I encountered a mass murderer named **Alton Darwin** who also could do arithmetic in his head. He was Black. Unlike Claudia Roosevelt, he was highly intelligent in the verbal area. The people he had murdered were rivals or deadbeats or police informers or cases of mistaken identity or innocent bystanders in the illegal drug industry. His manner of speaking was eloquent and thought-provoking.

(*HP* 75:L20-27) **Alton Darwin** was the first example I had ever seen of leadership in the raw. He was a man without any badges of rank, and with no previously existing organization or widely understood plan of action. He had been a modest, unremarkable man in prison. The moment he got out, though, sudden delusions of grandeur made him the only man who knew what to do next, which was to attack Scipio, where glory and riches awaited all who dared to follow him.

(*HP* 77:L35, 78:L1-2) **Alton Darwin** had the same untightened screw *(as Jack Patton)*. He was a convicted mass murderer, but never showed any remorse that I could see.

(*HP* 78:L8-11, 26-28) **Alton Darwin**, and this was true of Jack Patton, too, spoke of trivial and serious matters in the same tone of voice, with the same gestures and facial expressions. Nothing mattered more or less than anything else. . . .

So I was pondering the desertion problem when **Alton Darwin** said with exactly the same intensity, "I can skate on ice. Do you believe that?"

(*HP* 80:L1-10) SOMETIMES **Alton Darwin** would talk to me about the planet he was on before he was transported in a steel box to Athena. "Drugs were food," he said. "I was in the food business. Just because people on one planet eat a certain kind of food they're hungry for, that makes them feel better after they eat it, that doesn't mean people on other planets shouldn't eat something else. On some planets I'm sure there are people who eat stones, and then feel wonderful for a little while afterwards. Then it's time to eat stones again."

(*HP* 149:L16-22) I have long had a sort of ballpark figure in my head. I am quite sure that I killed more people than did my brother-in-law. I hadn't been working as a teacher at Athena very long before it occurred to me that I had almost certainly killed more people than had the mass murderer **Alton Darwin** or anybody else serving time in there. That didn't trouble me, and still doesn't. I just think it is interesting.

(*HP* 184:L16-18) The convicts didn't create a new flag. They flew the Stars and Stripes from the bell tower *(of Tarkington College)*. **Alton Darwin** said they weren't against America. He said, "We are America."

(*HP* 257:L1-7) "STAR Wars," said **Alton Darwin**.

He was alluding to Ronald Reagan's dream of having scientists build an invisible dome over this country, with electronics and lasers and so on, which no enemy plane or projectile could ever penetrate. Darwin believed that the social standing of his hostages was an invisible dome over Scipio.

Darwin, Charles (also **Darwinian** and **Darwinists**). *Vonnegut injects the father of evolution theory a number of times throughout his work, perhaps nowhere more continuously than in* Galápagos.

After Vonnegut recounts the deaths of Robert Kennedy, Martin Luther King, Jr., the government's body counts in Vietnam, and the natural death of his father, he continues with this passage. (*SL5* 182:L12-21) On Tralfamadore, says Billy Pilgrim, there isn't much interest in Jesus Christ. The Earthling figure who is most engaging to the Tralfamadorian mind, he says, is **Charles Darwin**—who taught that those who die are meant to die, that corpses are improvements. So it goes.

The same general idea appears in *The Big Board* by Kilgore Trout. The flying saucer creatures who capture Trout's hero ask him about **Darwin**. They also ask him about golf.

(*WFG* 205:L10-30, 206:L1-43 *In a Manner That Must Shame God Himself*) And looking at one day's news or a few days' news or a few years' news is a lot like staring at the radiator ornament of a Stutz Bearcat, it seems to me. Which is why so many of us would love to have a visitor from another planet, who might have a larger view of our day-to-day enterprises, who might be able to give us some clue as to what is really going on.

He would tell us, I think, that no real Winner fears God or believes in a punitive afterlife. He might say that Earthlings put such emphasis on truthfulness in order to be believed when they lie. President Nixon, for instance, was free to lie during his acceptance speech at the convention, if he wanted to, because of his famous love for the truth. And the name of the game was "Survival." Everything else was hokum.

He might congratulate us for learning so much about healing the planet, and warn us against wounding the planet so horribly during our real estate dealings, that it might never heal.

The visitor might say by way of farewell what **Charles Darwin** seemed to say to us, and we might write his words in stone, all in capital letters, like the words of the mayor of Birmingham: THE WINNERS / ARE AT WAR / WITH THE LOSERS, / AND THE FIX / IS ON. / THE PROSPECTS / FOR PEACE ARE / AWFUL.

Vonnegut muses that if he were a visitor from another planet, he would like to address earthlings based on his observations. (*WFG* 185:L8, 186:L4-23 *In a Manner That Must Shame God Himself*) I would say, "The two real political parties in America are the *Winners* and the *Losers*. The people do not acknowledge this. They claim membership in two imaginary parties, the *Republicans* and the *Democrats*, instead.

"Both imaginary parties are bossed by Winners. When Republicans battle Democrats, this much is certain: Winners will win.

"The Democrats have been the larger party in the past because their leaders have not been as openly contemptuous of Losers as the Republicans have been.

"Losers can join imaginary parties. Losers can vote.

"Losers have thousands of religions, often of the *bleeding heart* variety," I would go on. "The single religion of the Winners is a harsh interpretation of ***Darwinism***, which argues that it is the will of the universe that only the fittest should survive.

"The most pitiless **Darwinists** are attracted to the Republican party, which regularly purges itself of suspected bleeding hearts. It is in the process now of isolating and ejecting Representative Paul N. McCloskey, for instance, who has openly raged and even wept about the killing and maiming of Vietnamese."

(*WFG* 238:L1-13 *Playboy Interview*) PLAYBOY: What *is* in control?
VONNEGUT: Mankind's wish to improve itself.
PLAYBOY: In a **Darwinian** sense?
VONNEGUT: I'm not very grateful for **Darwin**, although I suspect he was right. His ideas make people crueler. **Darwinism** says to them that people who get sick deserve to be sick, that people who are in trouble most deserve to be in trouble. When anybody dies, cruel **Darwinists** imagine we're obviously improving ourselves in some way. And any man who's on top is there because he's a superior animal. That's the social **Darwinism** of the last century, and it continues to boom. But forget **Darwin**. . . .

(*Gal* 12:L17-32, 13:L1-14) **Darwin** Bay was named in honor of the great English scientist **Charles Darwin**, who had visited Genovesa and several of its neighbors for five weeks back in 1835—when he was a mere stripling of twenty-six, nine years younger than Wait. **Darwin** was then the unpaid naturalist aboard Her Majesty's Ship *Beagle*, on a mapping expedition that would take him completely around the world and would last five years.

In the cruise brochure, which was intended to delight nature-lovers rather the pleasure-seekers, **Darwin**'s own description of a typical Galápagos Island was reproduced, and was taken from his first book, *The Voyage of the Beagle:*

"Nothing could be less inviting than the first appearance. A broken field of black basaltic lava, thrown into the most rugged waves, and crossed by great fissures, is everywhere covered by stunted, sun-burnt brushwood, which shows little signs of life. The dry and parched surface, being heated by the noon-day sun, gave to the air a close and sultry feeling, like that from a stove: we fancied even that the bushes smelt unpleasantly."

Darwin continued: "The entire surface. . . seems to have been permeated, like a sieve, by the subterranean vapours: here and there the lava, whilst soft, had been blown into great bubbles; and in other parts, the tops of caverns similarly formed have fallen in, leaving circular parts with steep sides." He was vividly reminded, he wrote, ". . . of those parts of Staffordshire, where the great iron foundries are most numerous."

(*Gal* 16:L1-17) The Anglo-Saxon **Charles Darwin**, underspoken and gentlemanly, impersonal and asexual and blankly observant in his writings, was a hero in teeming, passionate, polyglot Guayaquil because he was the inspiration for a tourist boom. If it weren't for **Darwin**, there would not have been a Hotel El Dorado or a *Bahía de **Darwin*** to accommodate James Wait. There would have been no boutique to clothe him so comically.

If **Charles Darwin** had not declared the Galápagos Islands marvelously instructive, Guayaquil would have been just one more hot and filthy seaport, and the islands would have been worth no more to Ecuador than the slag heaps of Staffordshire.

Darwin did not change the islands, but only people's opinion of them. That was how important mere opinions used to be back in the era of great big brains.

(*FWD* 15:L10) Q: What is the trait you most deplore in others?

A: Social **Darwinism**.

(*FWD* 145:L2) "If you go to the Galápagos Islands, and see all the strange creatures, you are bound to think what **Charles Darwin** thought when he went there: How much time Nature has in which to accomplish simply anything. If we desolate this planet, Nature can get life going again. All it takes is a few million years or so, the wink of an eye to Nature."

(*FWD* 156:L19) Bishop Moore, as I've said, went to war a religious skeptic and came out of it a profoundly convinced Trinitarian. He told me he had a vision during the fighting on Guadalcanal. He went on from his vision (although he was born rich and had a rich Anglo-Saxon's education and tastes and friends) to minister to the poor in parishes where the prosperous had fled to the suburbs, to speak loathingly of social **Darwinists** (Neo-Cons, the FBI, the CIA, humorless, anal-retentive Republicans, and so on).

Das Reich der Zwei. *Translated to "***Nation of Two***," this is the play Howard Campbell thinks of writing about his relationship with Helga Noth.* (*MN* 27:L1-4) It was going to be about the love my wife and I had for each other. It was going to show how a pair of lovers in a world gone mad could survive by being loyal only to a nation composed of themselves—a **nation of two**. (*MN* 33:L20) *Das Reich der Zwei*, the **nation of two** my Helga and I had—its territory, the territory we defended so jealously, didn't go much beyond the bounds of our great double bed.

While contemplating the play, Campbell is approached by his soon to be Blue Fairy Godmother and asked to become an American agent. His double agent status eventually made Campbell a "stateless schizophrenic." (*MN* 34:L12-13) And when that nation ceased to be, I became what I am today and what I always will be, a stateless person.

This image of a "nation of two" is also used in Slapstick *when Wilbur and Eliza decide to bring true their mother's wish for any sign of intelligence among the twins. They paint a sign on a bedsheet telling their parents they can be as smart or dumb as the world wants them to be. This prompts the intelligence testing conducted by Dr. Cordelia Swain Cordiner and the twins' eventual separation.* (*Slap* 71:L2) THUS did Eliza and I destroy our Paradise—our **nation of two**.

Davis, Alvin. *The subject of Vonnegut's dedication to* God Bless You, Mr. Rosewater. *For Alvin Davis, / the telepath, / the hoodlums' friend.*

Davis, Benjamin. *Toward the close of* Breakfast of Champions, *Vonnegut admits to a lack of attention which prompts him to reveal that in an earlier version of the book Benjamin Davis took care of Kazak, the Doberman pinscher guarding the supply yard of the Maritimo Brothers Construction Company. In that previous version, Vonnegut explains that Benjamin Davis is the husband of Lottie Davis, Dwayne Hoover's maid. Aside from training Kazak to be mean and turning him loose at sundown, Davis is also first trumpet with the Midland City Symphony Orchestra—without pay. In the text as it finally appears, Benjamin Davis is outside the story except as Vonnegut chronicles this false allusion* (see *BC* 285-286).

Davis, Lottie. *Dwayne Hoover's black housekeeper, married to Benjamin Davis. Lottie is the only one to cry at the funeral service for Celia Hoover in* Deadeye Dick.

The Day the World Ended (see also ***Cat's Cradle***). The title of John/Jonah's opening chapter to his memoirs is revealed as the unlikely start of his journey toward enlightenment and the frozen apocalypse. (*CC* 13:L15, 14:L6) When I was a much younger man, I began to collect material for a book to be called ***The Day the World Ended***.

The book was to be factual.

The book was to be an account of what important Americans had done on the day when the first atomic bomb was dropped on Hiroshima, Japan.

It was to be a Christian book. I was a Christian then.

I am a Bokononist now.

I would have been a Bokononist then, if there had been anyone to teach me the bittersweet lies of Bokonon. But Bokononism was unknown beyond the gravel beaches and coral knives that ring this little island in the Caribbean Sea, the Republic of San Lorenzo.

We Bokononists believe that humanity is organized into teams, teams that do God's Will without ever discovering what they are doing. Such a team is called a *karass* by Bokonon, and the instrument, the *kan-kan*, that brought me into my own particular *karass* was the book I never finished, the book to be called ***The Day the World Ended***.

While in Ilium, researching the legacy of Dr. Felix Hoenikker, John/Jonah considered using a picture of the scientist's tombstone for a cover shot. The irony is that John/Jonah thought he was looking at the tomb of one of the principal participants in constructing the atom bomb, yet the moment foreshadowed the ice-nine destruction of the planet. (*CC* 57:L22-23) Sleet was still coming down, acid and gray. I thought the old man's tombstone in all that sleet might photograph pretty well, might even make a good picture for the jacket of ***The Day the World Ended***.

de la Madrid, Dr. Jose Sepulveda. *The president of Ecuador who had planned a state breakfast and parade in honor of the many luminaries expected to arrive for the "Nature Cruise of the Century." The event was called off when nearly all the expected adventurers failed to attend reservations for the cruise.*

de Medici, Innocenzo. *A member of the famed de Medici family, Innocenzo "the Invisible" was a banker and first owner of the palatial estate Marilee Kemp lived in when she became the Countess Portomaggiore. Designed by Leon Battista Alberti in the fifteenth century,* It was a cruciform structure whose four wings abutted on a domed rotunda twelve meters in diameter and in whose walls were half embedded eighteen Corinthian columns four and a half meters high. Above the capitals of the columns was a clerestory, a wall pierced with thirty-six windows. Above this was the dome—on whose underside was an epiphany, God Almighty and Jesus and the Virgin Mary and angels looking down through clouds, painted by Paolo Uccello. The terrazzo floor, its designer unknown, but almost surely a Venetian, was decorated with the backs of peasants planting and harvesting and cooking and baking and making wine and so on (*Blue* 213:L6-12, 214:L1-7).

De Mille, Hippolyte Paul. *The creole-speaking Haitian headwaiter at the Grand Hotel Oloffson in Port au Prince who becomes the employee of Rudy and Felix Waltz when they purchase the resort. De Mille claims to be eighty years old and counts fifty-nine descendants. More importantly, he practices voodoo, swearing he can make spirits rise and haunt their surroundings. De Mille accompanies Rudy and Felix on their trip back to the neutron-bombed Midland City. After visiting the graves of their parents and Celia Hildreth Hoover in Mount Calvary Cemetery, De Mille* argued that we owed it both to the past and to the future to raise some sort of representative ghost which would haunt the city, no matter who lived there, for generations to come. . . . So he raised the ghost of Will Fairchild. The old barnstormer was wearing goggles and a white silk scarf and a black leather helmet and all, but no parachute (*DD* 239:L13-16, 240:L21-23). *Rudy tells the reader the ghost of Will Fairchild will haunt Midland City looking for the parachute he failed to wear. In his amazement over the voodoo resurrection, Rudy comes to understand that differences in culture should not be so feared, that the amount we don't know about the capabilities of various cultures should cease to amaze us. In an apparent reference to the mysteries of his own culture, which he believes neutron-bombed his hometown as a test in the name of national security, Rudy leaves the text with the cryptic line,* You want to know something? We are still in the Dark Ages. The Dark Ages—they haven't ended yet (*DD* 240:L10-11).

de Stael-Holstein, Baronne. (*ST* 71:L4-5) The family *(Malachi Constant's)* could trace its line back through an illegitimacy to Benjamin Constant, who was a tribune under Napoleon from 1799 to 1801, and a lover of Anne Louise Germaine Necker, **Baronne de Stael-Holstein**, wife of the then Swedish ambassador to France.

de Sucre, Antonio Jose. (*Gal* 30:L20) A similar decay in imagined value was happening to the British pound and the French and Swiss francs and the West German mark. The Ecuadorian sucre, meanwhile, named in honor of **Antonio Jose de Sucre** (1795-1830), a national hero, had come to be worth less than a banana peel.
(*Gal* 114:L9) Without knowing anything about naval architecture, he had made a ship more attractive by persuading its owners not to call it, as they were about to do, the ***Antonio Jose de Sucre***, but the *Bahia de Darwin*. He had transformed what was to have been a routine, two-week trip out to the islands and back into the nature cruise of the century. How had he worked such a miracle? By never calling it anything but "the Nature Cruise of the Century."

de Wet, Mrs. Marthinus. *A 1924 graduate of Tarkington College who writes a letter taking exception to any retooling or tuning of the great Lutz Carillon bells. She married the owner of a gold mine in South Africa. For Eugene Debs Hartke, her overly romantic views about the project typified the objections forwarded by some alumni. Her concern for the school's loss of history, the bells were formed from discarded Civil War weapons, is put into ironic contrast by Hartke:* If my Socialist grandfather, nothing but a gardener at Butler University, could read the letter from **Mrs. de Wet** and note its South African return address, he would be grimly gratified. There was a clear-as-crystal demonstration of a woman living high on profits from the labor of black miners, overworked and underpaid (*HP* 67:L17-22).

Deadeye Dick. *The nickname Anthony Squires gave to Rudy Waltz after shooting to death Eloise Metzger. As long as Rudy was in Midland City someone somewhere would utter the nickname. He received nightly phone calls at Schramm's Pharmacy asking if he really was Deadeye Dick. While visiting New York for the production of "Katmandu," Rudy came to understand his fascination with John Fortune.* (*DD* 130:L25-30) I no longer cared about the play. It was **Deadeye Dick**, tormented by guilt in Midland City, who had found old John Fortune's quite pointless death in Katmandu, as far away from his hometown as possible, somehow magnificent. He himself yearned for distance and death.

Deadeye Dick (1982) (see also **Rudy Waltz**). *Institutionalized schizophrenia and a jerry-rigged world are central concerns in Deadeye Dick. The narrative* *revolves around a series of four murders. Two of the murders are accidental; the other two are not so accidental. As a group, they tend to point out the hypocrisy and schizophrenic tendencies of those in power to retain power. Rudy Waltz, the "neutered" pharmacist known as "Deadeye Dick" for his accidental murder of Mrs. Eloise Metzger and her unborn child, writes this memoir which includes: the accidental murder of August Gunther by Midland City Police Chief Morissey, the radiation death of Rudy's mother whose fireplace was constructed with contaminated cement from the Manhattan project and sold by the Nuclear Regulatory Commission, and the neutron-bombing of Midland City, Ohio.*

Chief Morissey blew off the head of August Gunther while on a hunting trip with Rudy's father, Morissey's son, and John Fortune. They were standing next to each other when Morissey's shotgun accidentally went off. None of his hunting buddies thought it would be fair to crucify him for an accident that could have happened to anybody, tragic though it was. Together they conspired to protect Morissey by letting Gunther's body drift down Sugar Creek.

Rudy's mother was the victim of a more calculating plot. Apparently, bureaucrats at the NRC believed selling off contaminated cement would make the Manhattan Project more cost effective than just the mere avoidance of invading the Japanese mainland. The only evidence linking Emma Waltz's brain tumors to the fireplace was the accidental exposure of a pack of film left in the house by Cliff McCarthy. Rudy and his brother Felix successfully sued the government, the Maritimo Brothers Construction Company, and the Ohio Valley Ornamental Concrete Company.

As for the neutron bombing of Midland City, there were two theories about how it occurred. The government said the bomb accidentally exploded when it fell off a truck transporting it out west. The farmers in surrounding communities hired a university professor to study the blast configuration using the pattern of livestock deaths to determine the outer perimeter of the bomb. He determined that the blast occurred sixty feet above the pavement. The farmers were convinced this was the purposeful act of unnamed forces which were forever in motion. Lawyer Bernard Ketchum asked the farmers who they thought it was that nuked the city. (*DD* 232:L28-34, 233:L1-12) This was the answer he got: "They don't want us to know their name, so they don't have a name. You can't fight back against something that don't have a name."

"The military-industrial complex?" said Ketchum archly. "The Rockefellers? The international conglomerates? The CIA? The Mafia?"

And the farmer said to him, "You like any of them names? Just help yourself. Maybe that's who it is, maybe it ain't. How's a farmer supposed to find out? It's whoever it was shot President Kennedy and his brother—and Martin Luther King."

So there we had it—the ever-growing ball of American paranoia, the ball of string a hundred miles in diameter, with the unsolved assassination of John F. Kennedy at its core.

"You mention the Rockefellers," said the farmer. "If you ask me, they don't know any more'n I do about who's really running things, what's really going on."

As for Rudy, My own guess is that the American Government had to find out for certain whether the neutron bomb was as harmless as it was supposed to be. So it set one off in a small city which nobody cared about, where people weren't doing all that much with their lives anyhow, where businesses were going under or moving away. The Government couldn't test a bomb on a foreign city, after all, without running the risk of starting World War Three.

There is even a chance that Fred T. Barry, with all his contacts high in the military, could have named Midland City as the ideal place to test a neutron bomb (*DD* 234:L25-34, 235:L1-2).

Rudy's own tale of murder takes place on Mother's Day 1944 (the same day Vonnegut's mother committed suicide). Though only twelve years old at the time, Rudy is given the key to the gun room and told to clean some of the weapons. Feeling at one with himself and the Springfield .30-06, Rudy loads the weapon while surveying Midland City from the attic gun room. Though knowing better, he fires off one round without any thought of aiming. Eight blocks away Mrs. Metzger goes down with a bullet between the eyes. Rudy recalls, So this was Mother's Day to most people, but to me it was the day during which, ready or not, I had been initiated into manhood (*DD* 61:L12-14). *Rudy believes the world is cruel and duplicitous.* (*DD* 112:L23-27) I wasn't to touch anything on this planet, man, woman, child, artifact, animal, vegetable, or mineral—since it was likely to be connected to a push-pull detonator and an explosive charge.

Despite ominous speculations about the neutron bombing and Rudy's incredulity about the possibilities for innocent personal activity, Vonnegut manages a denouement of a voodoo resurrection with hope as its message. Rudy's chef from his hotel in Haiti, Hippolyte Paul De Mille, is capable of resurrecting the dead. Together they stand in Midland City's Calvary Cemetery while Hippolyte raises the spirit of Will Fairchild. Fairchild was a stunt flyer who died in an air show, though he could have been saved had he been wearing his parachute. His spirit roams the empty city perhaps looking for his chute. In the midst of all he concocted, Vonnegut looks to undo irrational and fatal impulses in a search for survival.

Deal, Selena. *The young upstairs maid working for Amanda and Stewart Buntline. At the time we meet her in* God Bless You, Mr. Rosewater, *Selena had been working for only a month of her one-year commitment. She was raised by Wilfred Parrot in an orphanage founded by Castor Buntline, Stewart's great-grandfather, and bound by his oath mixing capitalism and predestination.* (*GBR* 154:L30-32, 155:L1-11) I do solemnly swear that I will respect the sacred private property of others, and that I will be content with whatever station in life God Almighty may assign me to. I will be grateful to those who employ me, and will never complain about wages and hours, but will ask myself instead, "What more can I do for my employer, my republic, and my God?" I understand that I have not been placed on Earth to he happy. I am here to be tested. If I am to pass the test, I must be always unselfish, always sober, always truthful, always chaste in mind, body, and deed, and always respectful to those to whom God has, in His Wisdom, placed above me. If I pass the test, I will go to joy everlasting in Heaven when I die. If I fail, I shall roast in hell while the Devil laughs and Jesus weeps. *Selena is far more knowledgeable about cultural matters than are her employers and is forever vexed by Amanda's corrections. In a letter to Mr. Parrot, Selena unleashes her frustrations and provides the basis for the novel's subtitle.* (*GBR* 158:L7-24) What gets me most about these people, Daddy, isn't how ignorant they are, or how much they drink. It's the way they have of thinking that everything nice in the world is a gift to the poor people from them or their ancestors. The first afternoon I was here, Mrs. Buntline made me come out on the back porch and look at the sunset. So I did, and I said I liked it very much, but she kept waiting for me to say something else. I couldn't think of what else I was supposed to say, so I said what seemed liked a dumb thing. "Thank you very much," I said. That was exactly what she was waiting for. "You're entirely welcome," she said. I have since thanked her for the ocean, the moon, the stars in the sky, and the United States Constitution.

Maybe I am just too wicked and dumb to realize how wonderful Pisquontuit really is. Maybe this is a case of pearls before swine, but I don't see how. I am homesick. Write soon. I love you.

Debs, Eugene V. *The labor leader from Terre Haute, Indiana, and for whom Vonnegut named two of his characters: Eugene Debs Hartke the narrator of* Hocus Pocus, *and Eugene Metzger—the son of Eloise and George Metzger in* Deadeye Dick.

Hocus Pocus *is dedicated to Debs with the inscription,* This work of pure fiction is dedicated to the memory of

EUGENE VICTOR DEBS

1855-1926

"While there is a lower class I am in it. While there is a criminal element I am of it. While there is a soul in prison I am not free." (*HP* 9:dedication) (*HP* 13:L6) **Debs** was a Socialist and a Pacifist and a Labor Organizer who ran several times for the Presidency of the United States of America, and got more votes than has any other candidate nominated by a third party in the history of this country.

"Deer in the Works" (1955). *The short story about the chaos caused by the unexpected entrance of a deer into the Ilium Works of the Federal Apparatus Corporation—very similar to the Ilium Works in* Player Piano. *On David Potter's first day as a public relations writer for the facility, he was assigned* *to cover the massive hunt by security personnel. When the photographer flashes a few pictures before Lou Flammer prepares to give the orders to shoot, the deer bolts toward Potter who opens the gate, letting the deer escape. His actions are taken as a sign of compassion and humanity in the midst of an overly technologized and desensitized society—most unappreciated by the stunned posse.*

Deer Park, Long Island. *In* Hocus Pocus, *the location of the New York state prison for Orientals.*

Deerfield Academy. *In* Hocus Pocus, *the Massachusetts prep school attended by Eugene Debs Hartke, Jr., contemptuously recalled by Vonnegut in nonfiction.* (*FWD* 98:L10-11) In Indianapolis back then, it was only the really dumb rich kids who got sent away to prep school. (I knew some of them, and after they graduated from Andover or Exeter or St. Paul's or wherever, they were *still* dumb and rich.) So I was astonished and annoyed, when I took up permanent residence in the East, to meet so many people who thought it only common sense that they be allowed to set the moral and intellectual tone for this country because they had been to prep school. (It was my personal misfortune that so many of them had become literary critics. I'm about to be judged by **Deerfield Academy**? **Deerfield** ***Academy***? Give me a break!)

Del Prado Hotel. *The Ilium hotel where the narrator of* Cat's Cradle *stays while researching for his book* The Day the World Ended.

Delbert. *The tourist outside the Rumfoord Mansion wearing a Robin Hood hat with Rumfoord's picture on it and embroidered with his own name on it. He's browsing at Sergeant Brackman's booth awaiting the materialization.*

Delgado, Private Geraldo. *The Ecuadorian soldier who kills Andrew MacIntosh and Zenji Hiroguchi. He broke into a souvenir shop looking for food amid the chaos that broke out all over South America. He was an eighteen-year-old paranoid schizophrenic who* thought his big problem was enemies with little radios (*Gal* 149:L12-13). *He killed the two men because Hiroguchi was playing with Mandarax, which Delgado mistook for a radio.*

Delgado's break-in established a pathway for the cruise passengers to make it to safety in the hotel. Leon Trout points out that if not for Delgado, the next million years of history would take place without any human beings.

Delta Upsilon. *Vonnegut's Cornell fraternity, which can also claim among its members Buck Young (the football player sought after by Cornell coach Doctor Roseberry in* Player Piano*), John/Jonah (the narrator of* Cat's Cradle*), Newt Hoenikker (though he got only so far as pledging before flunking out of Cornell), and bicycle manufacturer H. Lowe Crosby.*

Denny, Kyle. *Walter Starbuck's football-playing Harvard classmate from Philadelphia who* died in a fall in his bathtub on the day the Japanese bombed Pearl Harbor. He cracked his head open on a faucet (*JB* 99:L4-6). *He had also taken out Sarah Wyatt.*

Denton, Reverend Bobby. *The holy man conducting his Love Crusade in Wheeling, West Virginia, who sees the construction of the spacecraft* The Whale *and man's search of the heavens as analogous to the biblical Tower of Babel. The discovery of the chrono-synclastic infundibula halts that search as God had dispersed the nations of man for building the tower.* (*ST* 31:L26-32, 32:L1) "Are these not Bible times?" he said. "Have we not builded of steel and pride an abomination far taller than the Tower of Babel of old? And did we not mean, like those builders of old, to get right into Heaven with it? And haven't we heard it said many times that the language of scientists is international? They all use the same Latin and Greek words for things, and they all talk the language of numbers."

Derby, Edgar. *The forty-four-year-old Indianapolis high school teacher who is captured at the Battle of the Bulge and sent to a POW camp on the same train with Billy Pilgrim. Derby's character is drawn from Vonnegut's POW experience. While digging bodies out of the ashen rubble of Dresden, Derby is executed for looting. He had innocently picked up a Dresden china teapot. In the first chapter of* Slaughterhouse, *Vonnegut muses that Derby's death should be the fitting ironic conclusion.* (*SL5* 4:L19) "I think the climax of the book will be the execution of poor old **Edgar Derby**," I said. "The irony is *so* great. A whole city gets burned down, and thousands and thousands of people are killed. And then this one American foot soldier is arrested in the ruins for taking a teapot. And he's given a regular trial, and then he's shot by a firing squad."

Derby protected Billy Pilgrim, stood up to the bullying of Paul Lazzaro, and spoke out against the preachings of Howard Campbell while taking shelter in the slaughterhouse. Derby had a son in the Marines serving in the Pacific theater.

Derby, Howard. *The hospital mail clerk in the play "Fortitude," reprinted in* Wampeters, Foma & Granfalloons.

Destouches, Louis-Ferdinand (see **Céline**).

di Capistrano, Paulo. *When Wayne Hoobler is picked up for suspicious behavior outside the back gate of Barrytron, Ltd., the police find di Capistrano's Playboy membership card on him. He got it out of the garbage cans behind the Holiday Inn.*

di Sanza, Dr. Carlo. *The convicted felon serving his time at Finletter Air Force Base in* Jailbird, *holds a doctorate in law from the University of Naples.* (*JB* 50:L13-15) He was a naturalized American citizen and was serving his second term for using the mails to promote a Ponzi scheme. He was ferociously patriotic. *This reference to the nature of di Sanza's crimes allows Starbuck to explain what a Ponzi scheme is and create an analogy between this and the operation of government.* (*JB* 50:L27—52:L4) "In America I have been a millionaire two times," he said, "and I will be a millionaire again."

"I'm sure of it," I said, and I was. He would simply start up his third Ponzi scheme—consisting, as before, of offering fools enormous rates of interest for the use of their money. As before, he would use most of the money to buy himself mansions and Rolls-Royces and speedboats and so on, but returning part of it as the high interest he had promised. More and more people would come to him, having heard of him from gloatingly satisfied recipients of his interest checks, and he would use their money to write more interest checks—and on and on.

I am now convinced that **Dr. di Sanza**'s greatest strength was his utter stupidity. He was such a successful swindler because he himself could not, even after two convictions, understand what was inevitably catastrophic about a Ponzi scheme. . . .

I am now moved to suppose, with my primitive understanding of economics, that every successful government is of necessity a Ponzi scheme. It accepts enormous loans that can never be repaid. How else am I to explain to my polyglot grandchildren what the United States was like in the nineteen-thirties, when its owners and politicians could not find ways for so many of its people to earn even the most basic necessities, like food and clothes and fuel. It was pure hell to get shoes!

And then, suddenly, there were formerly poor people in officers' clubs, beautifully costumed and ordering filets mignon and champagne. There were formerly poor people in enlisted men's clubs, serviceably costumed and clad and ordering hamburgers and beer. A man who two years before had patched the holes in his shoes with cardboard suddenly had a Jeep or a truck or an airplane or a boat, and unlimited supplies of fuel and ammunition. He was given glasses and bridgework, if he needed them, and he was immunized against every imaginable disease. No matter where he was on the planet, a way was found to get hot turkey and cranberry sauce to him on Thanksgiving and Christmas.

What had happened?

What could have happened but a Ponzi scheme?

Dillon University. *Caroline Rosewater's alma mater in Dodge City, Kansas. She was a Phi Beta Kappa in philosophy.*

Dina and Donna. *Originally from Kokomo, Indiana, these identical twins were out joyriding when* Deadeye Dick*'s Felix Waltz drove into their car,* *sending Donna through the windshield. She was severely scarred. Donna and Felix were later married.*

Dobrowitz, Alvin. *Howard Campbell's Israeli lawyer who earnestly tries to defend him from the allegations of war crimes.* (*MN* 199:L4) Hope springs eternal, they say, in the human breast. It springs eternal, at any rate, in the breast of **Dobrowitz**, which is, I suppose why he costs so much.

Dodge, Dr. Ned. *The manager of Chicago's Proteus Park,* a postwar development of three thousand dream houses for three thousand families with presumably identical dreams (*PP* 138:L27-29). *He anxiously guides the Shah of Bratpuhr on a tour through the home of Edgar and Wanda Hagstrohm, which is filled with dozens of electrical appliances intended to instantaneously perform menial household chores.*

Dole, Dr. Helen. *The twenty-six-year-old, unmarried candidate to fill Hartke's physics position at Tarkington College.* (*HP* 265:L10-20) She was born in South Korea, and had grown up in what was then West Berlin. She held a Doctorate in Physics from the University of Berlin. Her father had been a Master Sergeant in the Quartermaster Corps of the Regular Army, serving in Korea and then in our Army of Occupation in Berlin. When her father retired after 30 years, to a nice enough little house in a nice enough little neighborhood in Cincinnati, and she saw the horrible squalor and hopelessness into which most black people were born there, she went back to what had become just plain Berlin and earned her Doctorate.

Tarkington's Board of Trustees asked Dr. Dole to promise never to discuss politics, history, economics, or sociology. She became infuriated and called them a bunch of European planters.

She asserted that Europeans like them were robbers with guns who went all over the world stealing other people's land, which they then called their plantations. And they made the people they robbed their slaves. She was taking a long view of history, of course. Tarkington's Trustees certainly hadn't roamed the world on ships, armed to the teeth and looking for lightly defended real estate. Her point was that they were heirs to the property of such robbers, and to their mode of thinking, even if they had been born poor and had only recently dismantled an essential industry, or cleaned out a savings bank, or earned big commissions by facilitating the sale of beloved American institutions or landmarks to foreigners. . . .

"Now," she said to them, "you are selling this plantation because the soil is exhausted, and the natives are getting sicker and hungrier every day, begging for food and medicine and shelter, all of which are very expensive. The water mains are breaking. The bridges are falling down. So you are taking all your money and getting out of here" (*HP* 264:L14-15, 18-30, 265:L21-26).

Hartke finds common ground with Dr. Dole. (*HP* 265:L33-36, 266:L1-3) So she and I, working independently, had noticed the same thing: That even our natives, if they had reached the top or been born at the top, regarded Americans as foreigners. That seems to have been true, too, of people at the top in what used to be the Soviet Union: to them their own ordinary people weren't the kinds of people they understood and liked very much.

Domesday Book. *Eliot Rosewater's ledger in which he kept coded information on all the Foundation's operations in Rosewater, Indiana. In the back of the* Domesday Book *was an unfinished novel Eliot started years before. The novel is about reincarnation.* (*GBR* 96:L22-31) Heaven is the bore of bores, *Eliot's novel went on*, so most wraiths queue up to be reborn—and they live and love and fail and die, and they queue up to be reborn again. They take pot luck, as the saying goes. They don't gibber and squeak to be one race or another, one sex or another, one nationality or another, one class or another. What they want and what they get are three dimensions—and comprehensible little packets of time—and enclosures making possible the crucial distinction between inside and outside.

Don. *The astronaut dreamed up by Kilgore Trout while he sat in a pornographic movie house. Don travels to a planet* where all the animal and plant life had been killed by pollution, except for humanoids. The humanoids ate food made from petroleum and coal (*BC* 59:L14-16). *His hosts manage to scrape together a feast in his honor, and their discussions turn to pornography and censorship on their respective planets. They take Don to a pornographic movie house where he views films of humanoids salivating and slobbering over a feast of food.*

(*BC* 61:L8-18) When **Don** and his friends left the theater, they were accosted by humanoid whores, who offered them eggs and oranges and milk and butter and peanuts and so on. The whores couldn't actually deliver these goodies, of course.

The humanoids told **Don** that if he went home with a whore, she would cook him a meal of petroleum and coal products at fancy prices.

And then, while he ate them, she would talk dirty about how fresh and full of natural juices the food was, even though the food was fake.

Donald. *The golden retriever roaming around Ilium and adopted by Roy and Mary Hepburn in* Galápagos. *Donald made Roy very happy as he lay dying from cancer.*

Donna. *A Manhattan slave of Vera Chipmunk-5 Zappa who brought Wilbur a fancy candlestick for his birthday, in* Slapstick.

Donner, John (also **Donner Party**). *The shop teacher who drives Eugene Debs Hartke from Scipio to the prison in Athena so both can apply for teaching* *jobs. Donner is proud of his appearance on the* Donahue *show concerning people who were raised in foster homes and were frequently beaten. Hartke doesn't believe this was a real "Donner," because he didn't know about* the infamous **Donner Party**, which got caught in a blizzard back in 1846 while trying to cross the Sierra Nevada Mountains in wagons to get to California. Their wagons were very likely made right here in Scipio. . . .

Those who survived the blizzard did so by becoming cannibals. The final tally, and several women and children were eaten, was 47 survivors out of 87 people who had begun the trip (*HP* 214:L19). *Hartke claims to have known several Donners including two unrelated Tarkington students as well as a sergeant in Vietnam. Hartke's experience indicated that all Donners knew the infamous legacy attached to the name.*

Donnini, Jim *In the caption accompanying a photograph in* Fates Worse Than Death (218-219), *Vonnegut reveals that Jim Donnini was one of the POWs with whom he was released at the end of World War II. Donnini is sitting on a bench playing a harmonica while Vonnegut rests with his head against the rear of a wagon.*

Until the recent publication of FWD, *however, Jim Donnini was better known as the Chicago youth being brought up by his uncle Bert Quinn in the short story "The Kid Nobody Could Handle." Though Quinn got the better of the real estate deal with band director George M. Helmholtz foreseeing the expansion that would occur and allow Quinn's restaurant to flourish, he didn't share Helmholtz's vision where it concerned young Jim. As Quinn describes him,* "His mother's dead. His old man married my sister, walked out on her, and stuck her with him. Then the court didn't like the way she was raising him, and put him in foster homes for a while. Then they decided to get him clear out of Chicago, so they stuck me with him." He shook his head. "Life's a funny thing, Helmholtz."

"Not very funny, sometimes," said Helmholtz. He pushed his eggs away.

"Like some whole new race of people coming up," said Quinn wonderingly. "Nothing like the kids we got around here. Those boots, the black jacket—and he won't talk. He won't run around with the other kids. Won't study. I don't think he can even read and write very good" (*MH* 246:L33-38, 247:L1-7).

Helmholtz reforms Jim Donnini by first shaming him (he took away his tough guy boots) and then offering him John Philip Sousa's trumpet. After a long silence, Helmholtz picked up the trumpet. He kissed the cold mouthpiece and pumped the valves in a dream of a brilliant cadenza. Over the bell of the instrument, Helmholtz saw **Jim Donnini**'s face, seemingly floating in space—all but deaf and blind. Now Helmholtz saw the futility of men and their treasures. He had thought that his greatest treasure, the trumpet, could buy a soul for **Jim**. The trumpet was worthless (*MH* 254:L35). *Helmholtz destroys the instrument thinking he had failed, that Jim was already beyond reach.*

However, at the close of the story, Jim sits in the band room with the repaired trumpet, waiting for practice to begin.

Donoso, Dr. Teodoro. *The one Ecuadorian official in the United States with whom Bobby King closely consulted about the Nature Cruise of the Century.* (*Gal* 118:L32) And the last call King made before leaving his office was to a man who had become a very close friend during the past ten months, who was **Dr. Teodoro Donoso**, a poet and physician from Quito, who was Ecuador's ambassador to the United Nations. He earned his medical degree at Harvard.

He recognizes the economic failure of the entire region is a foregone conclusion. He was preparing an elegy to "The Last Kanka-bono," unaware the Kanka-bonos would help restock humanity with the help of Mary Hepburn.

Donovan, General. *General Donovan was one of only three people who knew about the espionage work conducted by Howard Campbell. The other two were Harold J. Sparrow, Campbell's Blue Fairy Godmother, and Franklin Delano Roosevelt.*

Doris. *The daughter of the genetically mutated Akiko Hiroguchi, the first human to be born with a furry coat similar to a seal. Akiko had a number of children but it is not clear where in the birth order Doris falls. However, Leon Trout says* The father of Akiko's daughter was the oldest of the Captain's children, Kamikaze, only thirteen years old (*Gal* 64:L7-8). *Akiko names her daughter after Doris Wojciehowitz, whom she learned about from the real-life romance stories told by Mary Hepburn.*

Dornberger, General Walter. *It was at the general's birthday party that Howard Campbell met Werner von Braun in* Mother Night.

Dorset. *The small town ten miles from Ilium which is home to David Potter and his family in the short story "Deer In The Works." Potter owns the Dorset newspaper, which could be put out of business if one of the surrounding small town papers printed a one-page Dorset supplement.*

Dostoevski, Feodor (also **Fedor** and **Dostoyevsky**). *One of Vonnegut's favorite authors and one whom he frequently writes into his work. They share the same birthday, though 101 years apart.* (*SL5* 87:L28) Rosewater said an interesting thing to Billy one time about a book that wasn't science fiction. He said that everything there was to know about life was in *The Brothers Karamazov*, by **Feodor Dostoyevsky**. "But that isn't enough any more," said Rosewater.

Vonnegut finds kinship with Dostoyevsky in their shared sense of the interdependence of all activities. (*BC* 228:L32) The proper ending for any story about people it seems to me, since life is now a polymer in which the

Earth is wrapped so tightly, should be that same abbreviation, which I now write large because I feel like it, which is this one:

ETC.

"It's all like an ocean!" cried **Dostoevski**. I say it's all like cellophane.

(*WFG* 86:L22) "One sacred memory from childhood is perhaps the best education," said **Feodor Dostoevski**. I believe that, and hope that many Earthling children will respond to the first human footprint on the moon as a sacred thing. We need sacred things. The footprint could mean, if we let it, the Earthlings have done an unbelievable difficult and beautiful thing which the Creator, for Its own reasons, wanted Earthlings to do.

(*Slap* 90:L1-2) **FEDOR Mikhailovich Dostoevski**, the Russian novelist, said one time that, "One sacred memory from childhood is perhaps the best education." I *(Wilbur Swain)* can think of another quickie education for a child, which, in its way, is almost as salutary: Meeting a human being who is tremendously respected by the adult world, and realizing that that person is actually a malicious lunatic.

Dougie. *Mentioned as one of Corporal Fuller's long-lost friends serving with the Strategic Air Command in the short story "Miss Temptation."*

Drano. *Celia Hoover committed suicide by eating Drano and Vonnegut makes comparisons between her suicide and his mother's. Though Rudy Waltz suggests Celia's abuse of amphetamines caused her to eat Drano, Vonnegut suggests that it was simply the will of each woman to take their own lives.* (*BC* 65:L12) He *(Dwayne)* even forgot that his wife Celia had committed suicide, for instance, by eating **Drano**—a mixture of sodium hydroxide and aluminum flakes, which was meant to clear drains. Celia became a small volcano, since she was composed of the same sorts of substances which commonly clogged drains.

(*BC* 181:L11) Listen: Bunny's mother and my mother were different sorts of human beings, but they were both beautiful in exotic ways, and they both boiled over with chaotic talk about love and peace and wars and evil and desperation, of better days coming by and by, of worse days coming by and by. And both our mothers committed suicide. Bunny's mother ate **Drano**. My mother ate sleeping pills, which wasn't nearly as horrible.

(*BC* 259:L5) "All you robots want to know why my wife ate **Drano**?" Dwayne asked his thunderstruck audience. "I'll tell you why: She was that kind of machine!"

(*DD* 80:L17) Celia knew the arts center was going to open, and the newspaper and the radio station and the politicians and so on all said what a difference it was going to make in the quality of life in Midland City. But there was the can of **Drano**, with all its dire warnings, and she just couldn't wait around anymore.

(*DD* 190:L31) I would be glad to attempt a detailed analysis of Celia Hoover's character, if I thought her character had much of anything to do with her suicide by **Drano**. As a pharmacist, though, I see no reason not to give full credit to amphetamine.

The seeming inevitability of self-destruction is contemplated by Rudy while attending Celia's funeral. (*DD* 197:L25) The corpse was a mediocrity who had broken down after a while. The mourners were mediocrities who would break down after a while.

The city itself was breaking down. Its center was already dead. Everybody shopped at the outlying malls. Heavy industry had gone bust. People were moving away.

The planet itself was breaking down. It was going to blow itself up sooner or later anyway, if it didn't poison itself first. In a manner of speaking, it was already eating **Drano**.

In Palm Sunday *Vonnegut describes the desperation in the voice of a friend on the phone who, together with Vonnegut, was asked to write a blurb for the dust jacket of a book by one of their friends. After reading the book Vonnegut declined to write a blurb, but the other writer* called me up in the middle of the night, long distance and sounding as though he had just swallowed **Drano**. "My God," he said, "you just can't leave me on that book jacket all alone" (*PS* 309:L17).

Dresden. *Undoubtedly, the single most influential moment of Vonnegut's life occurred while a POW assigned to a work camp in Dresden. In one way or another, Dresden is brought up in* Mother Night, God Bless You, Mr. Rosewater, Slaughterhouse-Five, Wampeters, Foma & Granfalloons, Slapstick, Palm Sunday, *and* Bluebeard. *His most dispassionate account of the incident appears in the introduction to* Mother Night. (*MN* vi:L1-32, vii:L1-10) After a while the war came, and I was in it, and I was captured, so I got to see a little of Germany from the inside while the war was still going on. I was a private, a battalion scout, and, under the terms of the Geneva Convention, I had to work for my keep, which was good, not bad. I didn't have to stay in prison all the time, somewhere out in the countryside. I got to go to a city, which was **Dresden**, and to see the people and the things they did.

There were about a hundred of us in our particular work group, and we were put out as contract labor to a factory that was making a vitamin-enriched malt syrup for pregnant women. It tasted like thin honey laced with hickory smoke. It was good. I wish I had some right now. And the city was lovely, highly ornamented, like Paris, and untouched by war. It was supposedly an "open" city, not to be attacked since there were no troop concentrations or war industries there.

But high explosives were dropped on **Dresden** by American and British planes on the night of February 13, 1945, just about twenty-one years ago, as I now write. There were no particular targets for the bombs. The hope was that they would create a lot of kindling and drive firemen underground.

And then hundreds of thousands of tiny incendiaries were scattered over the kindling, like seeds on freshly turned loam. More bombs were dropped to keep firemen in their holes, and all the little fires grew, joined one another, became one apocalyptic flame. Hey presto: fire storm. It was the largest massacre in European history, by the way. And so what?

We didn't get to see the fire storm. We were in a cool meat-locker under a slaughterhouse with our six guards and ranks and ranks of dressed cadavers of cattle, pigs, horses, and sheep. We heard the bombs walking around up there. Now and then there would be a gentle shower of calcimine. If we had gone above to take a look, we would have been turned into artifacts characteristic of fire storms; seeming pieces of charred firewood two or three feet long—ridiculously small human beings, or jumbo fried grasshoppers, if you will.

The malt syrup factory was gone. Everything was gone but the cellars where 135,000 Hansels and Gretels had been baked like gingerbread men. So we were put to work as corpse miners, breaking into shelters, bringing bodies out. And I got to see many German types of all ages as death had found them, usually with valuables in their laps. Sometimes relatives would come to watch us dig. They were interesting, too.

(*FWD* 30:L4-5, 16, 19, 21, 26,35) "Elie Wiesel made his reputation with a book called *Night*, which is about the horrors of the holocaust as witnessed by the boy he used to be. I made my reputation with a book called *Slaughterhouse-Five*, which is about a British and American response to that Holocaust, which was the firebombing of **Dresden** as witnessed by the young American Infantry Private First Class I used to be. We both have German last names. . . .

"The Holocaust explains almost everything about why Elie Wiesel writes what he writes and is what he is. The firebombing of **Dresden** explains absolutely nothing about why I write what I write and am what I am. I am sure you are miles ahead of me in thinking of a thousand clinical reasons for this being true. I didn't give a damn about **Dresden**. I didn't know anybody there. I certainly hadn't had any good times there before they burned it down. I had seen some **Dresden** china back home in Indianapolis, but I thought then and still think now that it's mostly kitsch. . . .

"And **Dresden** china isn't made in **Dresden** anyway. It's made in Meissen. That's the town they should have burned dow. . . .

"Before I was a soldier I was a journalist, and that's what I was in **Dresden**—a voyeur of strangers' miseries. I was outside the event. Elie Wiesel, seeing what he saw and he was just a boy, and I was a young man was the event itself. The firebombing of **Dresden** was quick, was surgical, as the military scientists like to say, fitting the Aristotelian ideal for a tragedy, taking place in less than twenty-four hours. The Holocaust ground on and on and on."

(*FWD* 100:L17) "The firebombing of **Dresden** was an emotional event without a trace of military importance. The Germans purposely kept the city free of

major war industries and arsenals and troop concentrations so that it might be a safe haven for the wounded and refugees. There were no air-raid shelters to speak of and few antiaircraft guns. It was a famous world art treasure, like Paris or Vienna or Prague, and about as sinister as a wedding cake. I will say again what I have often said in print and in speeches, that not one Allied soldier was able to advance as much as an inch because of the firebombing of **Dresden**. Not one prisoner of the Nazis got out of prison a microsecond earlier. Only one person on earth clearly benefited, and I am that person. I got about five dollars for each corpse, counting my fee tonight."
(*FWD* 102:L26) "Among the unidentified, not-even-counted dead in the cellars of **Dresden** there were, without doubt, war criminals or loathsomely proud relatives of war criminals, SS and Gestapo, and so on. Whatever they got was too good for them. Maybe most of the Germans killed in **Dresden**, excepting the infants and children, of course, got what was coming to them. I asked another great German writer, Heinrich Böll, what he thought the dangerous flaw in the character of so many Germans was, and he said, 'Obedience.'"
(*FWD* 103:L5) "The firebombing of **Dresden**, which had no military significance, was a work of art. It was a tower of smoke and flame to commemorate the rage and heartbreak of so many who had had their lives warped or ruined by the indescribable greed and vanity and cruelty of Germany. The British and Americans who built the tower had been raised, like me, and in response to World War I, to be pacifists." *See also: FWD* 54:L8; 95:L34; 98:L16,35; 99:L4,24; 101:L16,23,34; 102:L8,13; 104:L18,34; 105:L2; 106:L18; 107:L31,34; 108:L2; 215:L20,24; 216:L5,8,19,28; 217:L7,15; 221:L6,10,18,27,29,31; 222:L6-7,9-11,20.

Dresden, History, Stage and Gallery (see **Mary Endell**).

Dresser, Paul. *According to Eugene Debs Hartke in* Hocus Pocus, *Henry Moellenkamp and Paul Dresser teamed up to write the ballad, "Mary, Mary, Where Have You Gone?" Henry brought the words to Dresser to be set to music, then Henry rewrote the lyrics into Tarkington's alma mater* (*HP* 30:L4-9). *Dresser wrote "On the Banks of the Wabash" (the state song of Indiana), "My Gal Sal," and was the brother of author Theodore Dreiser.*

drupelets. *Vonnegut describes the overpopulation problem which precipitated such measures as Ethical Suicide Parlors and ethical birth control pills at the beginning of "Welcome to the Monkey House."* (*MH* 27:L10-15 *Welcome to the Monkey House*) This was at a time when the population of Earth was 17 billion human beings. That was far too many mammals that big for a planet that small. The people were virtually packed together like **drupelets**.

Drupelets are the pulpy little knobs that compose the outside of a raspberry.

(*MH* 37:L20 *Welcome to the Monkey House*) There were 80 miles of sewers under Greater Hyannis, which had a population of 400,000 **drupelets**, 400,000 souls.

DSM (Dog Story of the Month). *One of the smaller book clubs established by the National Council of Arts and Letters authorized by the ruling technocracy in* Player Piano.

duffle (see also **Bokononism**). (*CC* 163:L3-7) "Do you know anybody who *might* want the job?" Frank was giving a classic illustration of what Bokonon calls ***duffle***. ***Duffle***, in the Bokononist sense, is the destiny of thousands upon thousands of persons when placed in the hands of a *stuppa*. A *stuppa* is a fogbound child.

Duke of Oklahoma. *In* Slapstick, *one of the military leaders at war with Stewart Oriole-2 Mott, the King of Michigan. The Duke had promulgated the "Urbana Massacre," in which the father of Melody Oriole-2 von Peterswald was killed.*

Dumas, Alexandre. *Alexandre Dumas (1802-1870), the French novelist and dramatist whose works include such historical romances and swashbucklers as* The Count of Monte Cristo, The Three Musketeers, *and* The Black Tulip. (*Gal* 61:L10) If you punched out on its back *1802*, for example, the year of Charles Darwin's birth, Mandarax would tell you that **Alexandre Dumas** and Victor Hugo were also born then, and that Beethoven completed his Second Symphony, and that France suppressed a Negro rebellion in Santo Domingo.

Dun Roamin. *Winston Niles Rumfoord's home on Titan which was a reproduction of India's Taj Mahal.* (*ST* 267:L7) It was Rumfoord's wry fancy to call his Titan home ***Dun Roamin***.

Dunkel, Stan. A grinning, bald, big-toothed man, wearing a badge that said, "Stan Dunkel, Sales," *tries to sell David Potter an X-ray Spectrogoniometer* (*MH* 212:L33 *Deer in the Works*). *Potter is the recently hired public relations man at the Ilium Works of the Federal Apparatus Corporation sent to cover the encroaching deer, and who releases the deer when given the chance.*

duprass. *In Bokononist terms, a* duprass *is a* karass *composed of only two people.* (*CC* 78:L10) "A true *duprass*," Bokonon tells us, "can't be invaded, not even by children born of such a union." *Members of a duprass always die within a week of each other.*

(*CC* 105:L6, 9) A ***duprass***, Bokonon tells us, is a valuable instrument for gaining and developing, in the privacy of an interminable love affair, insights that are queer but true. The Mintons' cunning exploration of indexes was surely a case in point. A *duprass*, Bokonon tells us, is also a sweetly conceited establishment. The Mintons' establishment was no exception.

Dürer, Albrecht. *Walter Starbuck claims to have been the first to ask for a sculpted rendition of Dürer's drawing of two hands held in prayer.* (*JB* 28:L6) My wedding gift to Ruth was a wood carving commissioned by me. It depicted hands of an old person pressed together in prayer. It was a three-dimensional rendering of a drawing by **Albrecht Dürer**, a sixteenth-century artist, whose house Ruth and I had visited many times in Nuremberg, during our courting days. That was my invention, so far as I know, having those famous hands on paper rendered in the round. Such hands have since been manufactured by the millions and are staples of dim-witted piety in gift shops everywhere. *Ruth loved the sculpture to the extent that it influenced their decision about which house to purchase when they moved to Chevy Chase, Maryland. She thought the mantlepiece was a "perfect resting place for her hands."*

As an aside to Circe Berman in Bluebeard, *Rabo Karabekian modestly speaks of his considerable drawing talent by saying that he* "wasn't an **Albrecht Dürer**" (*Blue* 264:L33, 265:L1).

The Dutch. *The Ithaca bar which serves as a gathering spot for Cornell fans in* Player Piano. *It is there that Dr. Roseberry, Cornell's football coach, and the State Department's Dr. Ewing J. Halyard meet prior to Halyard's attempted make-up for his lacking physical education course requirement.*

Duty-Dance, A Duty-Dance With Death. *The term denotes an obligatory commitment, and the title page of Vonnegut's masterpiece reads:*

Slaughterhouse-Five
or
THE CHILDREN'S
CRUSADE
A DUTY-DANCE WITH DEATH
BY
Kurt Vonnegut, Jr.
A FOURTH-GENERATION GERMAN-AMERICAN
NOW LIVING IN EASY CIRCUMSTANCES
ON CAPE COD
[AND SMOKING TOO MUCH],
WHO, AS AN AMERICAN INFANTRY SCOUT
HORS DE COMBAT,
WITNESSED THE FIRE-BOMBING OF DRESDEN, GERMANY,
"THE FLORENCE OF THE ELBE,"
A LONG TIME AGO,
AND SURVIVED TO TELL THE TALE.
THIS IS A NOVEL

SOMEWHAT IN THE TELEGRAPHIC SCHIZOPHRENIC
MANNER OF TALES
OF THE PLANET TRALFAMADORE,
WHERE THE FLYING SAUCERS
COME FROM.
PEACE.

The phrase is extracted from a book Vonnegut took with him on his return to Dresden in preparation for writing the text. (*SL5* 18:L22-33) My other book was Erika Ostrovsky's *Céline and His Vision.* Céline was a brave French soldier in the First World War—until his skull was cracked. After that he couldn't sleep, and there were noises in his head. He became a doctor, and he treated poor people in the daytime, and he wrote grotesque novels all night. No art is possible without a **dance with death**, he wrote.

The truth is death, he wrote. *I've fought nicely against it as long as I could. . . danced with it, festooned it, waltzed it around. . . decorated it with streamers, titillated it. . . .*

Time obsessed him.

Duveneck, Frank. *Duveneck taught at the Cincinnati School of Art and was part of the American expatriate group of artists touring Europe prior to World War I. Vonnegut notes in the preface to* Deadeye Dick, There really was a **Frank Duveneck**, and I in fact own a painting by him, "Head of a Young Boy." It is a treasure left to me by my father. I used to think it was a portrait of my brother Bernard, it looks so much like him (*DD* xii:L14).

Within the text Cliff McCarthy tells Rudy over the phone that Otto Waltz was mentioned in Duveneck's diary. According the McCarthy, "**Duveneck** heard about this wonderful studio a young painter was building in Midland City, and on March 16, 1915, he went and had a look at it" (*DD* 212:L15-18). *When Rudy presses McCarthy for Duveneck's opinion about his father, McCarthy relents and reads the entry.* (*DD* 212:L31-34) "'. . . . Otto Waltz should be shot. He should be shot for seeming to prove the last thing that needs to be proved in this part of the world: that an artist is a person of no consequence.'"

Dynamic Tension (*CC* 89:2, 22, 24) 47 **Dynamic Tension**

. . . Midgets are, after all, diversions for silly or quiet times, and I was serious and excited about Bokonon's theory of what he called "**Dynamic Tension**," his sense of a priceless equilibrium between good and evil.

When I first saw the term "**Dynamic Tension**" in Philip Castle's book, I laughed what I imagined to be a superior laugh. The term was a favorite of Bokonon's, according to young Castle's book, and I supposed that I knew something that Bokonon didn't know: that the term was one vulgarized by Charles Atlas, a mail-order muscle-builder. . . .

It was the belief of Charles Atlas that muscles could be built without bar bells or spring exercisers, could be built by simply pitting one set of muscles against another.

It was the belief of Bokonon that good societies could be built only by pitting good against evil, and by keeping the tension between the two high at all times.

And, in Castle's book, I read my first Bokononist poem, or "Calypso." It went like this: "Papa" Monzano, he's so very bad, / But without bad "Papa" I would be so sad; / Because without "Papa's" badness, / Tell me, if you would, / How could wicked old Bokonon / Ever, ever look good?

dynamopsychic, **dynamopsychism** (see also **Barnhouse**). (*MH* 157:L1-2 *Report on the Barnhouse Effect*) The name he *(Dr. Barnhouse)* chose for the phenomenon was "***dynamopsychism***," or *force of the mind.*
(*MH* 157:L38 *Report on the Barnhouse Effect*) Their total energy can be brought to bear on any single point the professor chooses, and that energy is undiminished by distance. As a weapon, then, **dynamopsychism** has an impressive advantage over bacteria and atomic bombs, beyond the single fact that it costs nothing to use: it enables the professor to single out critical individuals and objects instead of slaughtering whole poplulations in the process of maintaining international equilibrium.
(*MH* 158:L14, 30, 34 *Report on the Barnhouse Effect*) There is talk of screening the population for men potentially as powerful **dynamopsychically** as the professor. . . so another costly armaments race, with a new twist, has begun. . . .

Popularly, the "Age of Barnhouse" is said to have begun a year and a half ago, on the day of Operation Brainstorm. That was when **dynamopsychism** became significant politically. Actually, the phenomenon was discovered in May, 1942, shortly after the professor turned down a direct commission in the Army and enlisted as an artillery private. Like X-rays and vulcanized rubber, **dynamopsychism** was discovered by accident.
(*MH* 159:L37 *Report on the Barnhouse Effect*) In time, he came to recognize another startling feature of **dynamopsychism**: *its strength increased with use.*
(*MH* 162:L30 *Report on the Barnhouse Effect*) It was then that he told me of **dynamopsychism**. He knew only that there was such a force; he could not explain it. "It's me and me alone—and it's awful." *See also: MH—Report on the Barnhouse Effect* 157:L30; 158:L22; 159:L22; 160:L7; 164:L2; 168:L6.

Dyot. *In the San Lorenzan dialect this means God.*

dyslexia. *The disease suffered by Mohiga Valley Free Institute founder Aaron Tarkington. Though he overcame the resulting handicap and his own four children were unaffected by being carriers, the marriages of his descendants endangered a broad spectrum of the wealthy and powerful.* (*HP* 22:L1) All 3 of Aaron Tarkington's daughters married into prosperous and enterprising families in Cleveland, New York, Wilmington, Delaware—innocently making the threat of **dyslexia** pandemic in an emerging ruling class of bankers and industrialists, largely displaced in my time by Germans, Koreans, Italians, English, and, of course, Japanese. *Because a Mollenkamp married one of Aaron Tarkington's daughters, the families' common descendants suffered eleven times over from the disorder. All eleven* had all gone to college in Scipio, since no other institution of higher learning would take them in.

The first Moellenkamp to graduate from here was Henry, who enrolled in 1875, when he was 19, and when the school was only 6 years old. It was at that time that its name was changed to Tarkington College (*HP* 27:L20-26). *The narrator presumes the name change came about because Henry's grandfather was a trustee of The Mohiga Valley Free Institute, as were other men whose families married Tarkintgons and suffered from dyslexia, and that it* sounded too much like a poorhouse or a hospital. It is my guess that he would not have minded having the place sound like a catchment for the poor, if only he had not suffered the misfortune of having his own grandson go there (*HP* 27:L3-7). *Hartke goes on to muse that if not for the birth of Henry Mollenkamp, The Mohiga Valley Free Institute would have succumbed to the economic depression which eventually hit the rest of the region, that the 800,000-volume library would not have been built, the Lutz Carillon would never have been hung in the bell tower, that there would have been no one in Scipio for the 10,000 prisoners at Athena to terrorize after they broke out.*

E

Eagle-1 (see **Captain Bernard O'Hare**).

Eaker, Ira C., Lieutenant General, U.S.A.F. *Professor Rumfoord cites Eaker as one of his friends and a contributor to David Irving's* The Destruction of Dresden. *Vonnegut freely quotes some of Eaker's remarks as follows:* (*SL5* 161:L16-33) I find it difficult to understand Englishmen or Americans who weep about enemy civilians who were killed but who have not shed a tear for our gallant crews lost in combat with a cruel enemy. . . . I think it would have been well for Mr. Irving to have remembered, when he was drawing the frightful picture of the civilians killed at Dresden, that V-I's and V-2's were at that very time falling on England, killing civilian men, women, and children indiscriminately, as they were designed and launched to do. It might be well to remember Buchenwald and Coventry, too. . . .

I deeply regret that British and U.S. bombers killed 135,000 people in the attack on Dresden, but I remember who started the last war and I regret even more the loss of more than 5,000,000 Allied lives in the necessary effort to completely defeat and utterly destroy nazism.

Eastman, George. *The inventor of the Kodak camera and founder of the Rochester based Eastman Kodak company, who committed suicide in 1932. According to Eugene Debs Hartke in* Hocus Pocus, *Eastman's suicide note said nothing more than "My work is done." Hartke notes that his mentor, Sam Wakefield, retired Lieutenant General and President of Tarkington College, committed suicide in 1978 and left the same note. In* Fates Worse Than Death, *Vonnegut uses the phrase to mark the occasion of Voyager 2's leaving our Solar System.*

echolalia. *Also called "echophrasia," this is the involuntary repetition of words or phrases uttered by others. It is a symptom of both schizophrenia and* *autism, among other diseases. Professor Rumfoord believes Billy Pilgrim suffers it when they share a hospital room after Billy's plane crash.* (*SL5* 166:L8) **Echolalia** is a mental disease which makes people immediately repeat things that well people around them say. But Billy didn't really have it. Rumfoord simply insisted, for his own comfort, that Billy had it. Rumfoord was thinking in a military manner: that an inconvenient person, one whose death he wished for very much, for practical reasons, was suffering from a repulsive disease. *Despite Vonnegut's doubting words about Billy's possible affliction,* Slaughterhouse-Five *is "a novel somewhat in the telegraphic schizophrenic manner of tales of the planet Tralfamadore."*

In Breakfast of Champions, *Dwayne Hoover's echolalia precedes his violent outburst in Midland City.*

Edel, Israel and Norma. *In* Jailbird, *Israel Edel is the slovenly thirty year old night clerk at the Hotel Arapahoe when Walter Starbuck arrives in Manhattan after his first imprisonment at the Finletter Federal Prison facility in Georgia. Edel holds a Ph.D. in history from Long Island University, was graduated summa cum laude, and is a member of Phi Beta Kappa, but can't find an academic appointment. After making small talk with Starbuck, Edel is counted among those who showed him kindness and is rewarded for his deed by Mary Kathleen O'Looney, who makes him the vice president in charge of purchasing for Hospitality Associates, Ltd., a RAMJAC subsidiary. Despite Edel's Ph.D. in history, Starbuck is dismayed by Edel's lack of knowledge about Sacco and Vanzetti, confusing them with "thrill-killers" Leopold and Loeb.*

Norma is Israel's black wife who suffered the miscarriage of twins. She dislikes Starbuck, which he supposes is part of the hormonal legacy of her miscarriage. Once Israel becomes a RAMJAC executive, they buy and renovate a brownstone in Brooklyn Heights, an area ripe for yuppie gentrification.

Edison, Thomas. *Edison is a revered figure by Paul Proteus in* Player Piano *and maintains his memory by keeping intact Edison's elaborate laboratory. Proteus is so enamored by Edison's achievements that he refers to the whir of the lab's machinery as the* Building 58 Suite.

Edison is a central figure in Vonnegut's "Tom Edison's Shaggy Dog" *collected in* Welcome to the Monkey House. *Edison is seen in his Menlo Park, New Jersey, laboratory in the process of looking for a filament for his new invention, the electric light bulb. After a series of failures and an accidental meeting with his neighbor Harold K. Bullard and his faithful dog Sparky, Edison hooks up Sparky to another invention—the intelligence analyzer.* (*MH* 105:L16-19 *Tom Edison's Shaggy Dog*) "And the last words that Sparky ever spoke were to **Thomas Edison**. 'Try a piece of carbonized cotton thread,' he said. Later, he was torn to bits by a pack of dogs that had gathered outside the door, listening."

Vonnegut also makes mention of Edison in "The Mysterious Madame Blavatsky," *collected in* Wampeters, Foma & Granfalloons, *as a notable member of the Theosophical Society. In* Slapstick, Professor Swain died of his fatness in the mansion, at a dinner he gave in honor of Samuel Langhorne Clemens and **Thomas Alva Edison** (*Slap* 39:L7-9).

Edison Park. *A public park at the edge of Homestead in* Player Piano. *Both locations are on the opposite side of the river from the Ilium Works.*

Ehrens, Kurt and Heinrich. *The brothers whom Heinz Schildknecht's unnamed wife reveres as models of success and upward mobility, constantly berating Heinz for his comparatively low station in the new Nazi order. Heinz, of course, is the undercover Israeli agent prepared to testify against his best friend, Howard Campbell, Jr. Campbell sees Mrs. Schildknecht's appreciation of the Ehrens brothers as typically totalitarian and twisted.* (*MN* 87:L16-33) As for the kind of woman Heinz's wife had been: I knew her only slightly, though I saw her fairly often. She was a nonstop talker, which made her hard to know, and her theme was always the same: successful people, people who saw opportunities and grasped them firmly, people who, unlike her husband, were important and rich.

"Young **Kurt Ehrens**—" she would say, "only twenty-six, and a full colonel in the S.S.! And his brother **Heinrich**—he can't be more than thirty-four, but he has eighteen thousand foreign workers under him, all building tank traps. **Heinrich** knows more about tank traps than any man alive, they say, and I used to dance with him."

On and on she would talk this way, with poor Heinz in the background, smoking his brains out. And one thing she did to me was make me deaf to all success stories. The people she saw as succeeding in a brave new world were, after all, being rewarded as specialists in slavery, destruction, and death. I don't consider people who work in those fields successful.

Eichmann, Adolf. *The "bureaucratic Genghis Khan" of Nazi Germany, "the architect of Auschwitz, the introducer of conveyor belts into crematoria, the greatest customer in the world for the gas called Cyklon-B," who was kidnapped in South America by the Israeli secret service, convicted for war crimes and executed in 1961. He and Howard Campbell, Jr. briefly met once in Germany while having their official portraits photographed by Arndt Klopfer, and are later jailed together for a short period in Tel Aviv. Eichmann is serene about his incarceration, telling Campbell* Life is divided up into phases. . . . Each one is very different from the others, and you have to be able to recognize what is expected of you in each phase. That's the secret of successful living (*MN* 125:L14-17).

Eichmann is dumbfounded by Campbell's guess that he will plead innocent to his charges on the grounds he was simply following orders. (*MN* 125:L11-14) This man actually believed that he had invented his own trite defense, though a whole nation of ninety some-odd million had made the same defense before him. Such was his paltry understanding of the God-like human act of invention. *This prompts Campbell to compare the nature of Eichmann's crimes to his own and make the following judgment.* (*MN* 125:L15-31) The more I think about **Eichmann** and me, the more I think that he should be sent to the hospital, and that I am the sort of person for whom punishments by fair, just men were devised.

As a friend of the court that will try **Eichmann**, I offer my opinion that **Eichmann** cannot distinguish between right and wrong—that not only right and wrong, but truth and falsehood, hope and despair, beauty and ugliness, kindness and cruelty, comedy and tragedy, are all processed by **Eichmann**'s mind indiscriminately, like birdshot through a bugle.

My case is different. I always know when I tell a lie, am capable of imagining the cruel consequences of anybody's believing my lies, know cruelty is wrong. I could no more lie without noticing it than I could unknowingly pass a kidney stone.

If there is another life after this one, I would like very much, in the next one, to be the sort of person of whom it could truly be said, "Forgive him—he knows not what he does."

This cannot be said of me now.

As evidence of Eichmann's detachment, he later has a note smuggled to Campbell's Old Jerusalem cell asking if he thought it necessary to have a literary agent. Campbell replies it is if one plans to successfully cope with book clubs and movie rights.

Vonnegut's continuing interest in society's loss of historical perspective prompts him to wonder why, in his review of Webster's New International Dictionary, is the memory of John Dillinger perpetuated, while of **Adolf Eichmann** there is neither gibber nor squeak? (*MH* 110:L15)

Einstein, Albert. *Vonnegut uses the image of Einstein as an object of comparison for extremely intelligent people to express their disgust over being asked to do a menial mental chore (*Slapstick*'s Dr. Cordelia Swain Cordiner and Dr. Jekyll of "Jekyll and Hyde Revisited" exclaim "That's like asking Einstein to balance a checkbook"). The title hare in Kilgore Trout's* The Smart Bunny *is compared to Einstein and Shakespeare (*Breakfast of Champions*). Vonnegut admires both Einstein's intelligence and humanity as expressed by Walter Starbuck and as he steps into the narrative.* (*JB* 91:L3) I had been to the Arapahoe once before—in the autumn of Nineteen-hundred and Thirty-one. Fire had yet to be domesticated. **Albert Einstein** had predicted the invention of the wheel, but was unable to describe its probable shape and uses in the language of ordinary women and men. *A satirically oblique reference to nuclear fission.*
(*JB* 180:L11) During their deliberations, they received thousands of telegrams, some in favor of the executions, but most opposed. Among the telegraphers were Romain Rolland, George Bernard Shaw, **Albert Einstein**, John Galsworthy, Sinclair Lewis, and H. G. Wells. *This is in reference to those*

notables who telegraphed their opposition to the executions of Sacco and Vanzetti.

Einstein is the major character in Kilgore Trout's short story "Asleep at the Switch," whose premise is that before anyone is permitted past heaven's gates, God's auditors give them an IRS-type interrogation. (*JB* 185:L2, 11, 15, 18, 20, 28, 30) "Asleep at the Switch" was quite a sacrilegious story. The hero was the ghost of **Albert Einstein**. He himself was so little interested in wealth that he scarcely heard what his auditor had to say to him. It was some sort of balderdash about how he could have become a billionaire, if only he had gotten a second mortgage on his house in Bern, Switzerland, in Nineteen-hundred and Five, and invested the money in known uranium deposits before telling the world that $E=Mc^2$.

"But there you were—asleep at the switch again," said the auditor.

"Yes," said **Einstein** politely, "it does seem rather typical."

"So you see," said the auditor, "life really was quite fair. You did have a remarkable number of opportunities, whether you took them or not."

"Yes, I see that now," said **Einstein**.

"Would you mind saying that in so many words?" said the auditor.

"Saying what?" said **Einstein**.

"That life was fair."

"Life was fair," said **Einstein**.

"If you don't really mean it," said the auditor, "I have many more examples to show you. For instance, just forgetting atomic energy: If you had simply taken the money you put into a savings bank when you were at the Institute for Advanced Studies at Princeton, and you had put it, starting in Nineteen-hundred and Fifty, say, into IBM and Polaroid and Xerox—even though you had only five more years to live—" The auditor raised his eyes suggestively, inviting **Einstein** to show how smart he could be.

"I would have been rich?" said **Einstein**.

"'Comfortable,' shall we say?" said the auditor smugly. "But there you were again—" And again his eyebrows went up.

(*JB* 186:L29) All the auditing stories that **Einstein** heard were told by Americans. He had chosen to settle in the American part of heaven. Understandably, he had mixed feelings about Europeans, since he was a Jew. (*JB* 187:L5, 19, 21-23) It was in character for **Einstein** to be offended first by the mathematics of the system the auditors wanted everybody to be so grateful for. He calculated that if every person on Earth took full advantage of every opportunity, became a millionaire and then a billionaire and so on, the paper wealth on that one little planet would exceed the worth of all the minerals in the universe in a matter of three months or so. Also: There would be nobody left to do any useful work. . . .

The story ended abruptly. **Einstein** did not get to see God. But God sent out an archangel who was boiling mad. He told **Einstein** that if he continued to destroy ghosts' respect for the audits, he was going to take **Einstein**'s fiddle away from him for all eternity. So **Einstein** never discussed the audits with anybody ever again. His fiddle meant more to him than anything.

Einstein is also one of heaven's active shuffleboard afficionados in Happy Birthday, Wanda June. *See also: ST* 33:L15; *WJ* 135:L22; *BC* 233:L4; *Slap* 92:L28; *JB* 186:L1-3,5,7,12; *PS—Jekyll and Hyde Revisited* 269:L26.

El Greco. *In* God Bless You, Mr. Rosewater, *Eliot authorizes the family foundation to purchases an El Greco painting for Tampa, Florida. In* Breakfast of Champions, *Eliot loans his own El Greco painting of Saint Sebastian to the Midland City Arts Festival. Tarkington College benefactor Robert Moellenkamp loses all his possessions including an El Greco, when he is bankrupt by the failure of Microsecond Arbitrage, in* Hocus Pocus. (*BC* 217:L30) Mary Alice was smiling at a picture of Saint Sebastian, by the Spanish painter **El Greco**. It had been loaned to the Festival by Eliot Rosewater, the patron of Kilgore Trout. Saint Sebastian was a Roman soldier who had lived seventeen hundred years before me and Mary Alice Miller and Wayne and Dwayne and all the rest of us. He had secretly become a Christian when Christianity was against the law. *See also: GBR* 26:L21; *BC* 34:L2; *HP* 147:L4.

Empire State Building. *The landmark Manhattan skyscraper where* Mother Night*'s Howard Campbell was taken after being arrested in Dr. Jones' basement. Though he is quickly released, once in front of the building he has a quiet discussion with a policeman about the role chemicals have on human behavior.*

Eliot Rosewater moved the Rosewater Foundation into the building. (*GBR* 26:L10) He hired a suite of offices in the **Empire State Building**. He had them painted lime, burnt-orange and oyster white. He proclaimed them the headquarters for all the beautiful, compassionate and scientific things he hoped to do.

Wilbur Swain lives in the landmark building once it's abandoned after the Green Death, the Albanian Flu, and unstable gravity destroys present geopolitical structures. This is where Wilbur writes his memoirs and is joined by his granddaughter and her lover, Melody Oriole-2 von Peterswald and Isadore Raspberry-19 Cohen. It is there he dies in a funeral scene which includes a thousand candles lit along the great lobby of the building.

Endell, Mary. *The author of the 1908 book* Dresden, History, Stage and Gallery. *In the opening chapter of* Slaughterhouse-Five, *Vonnegut recounts that when he visited his old wartime buddy Bernard V. O'Hare and his wife Mary, she placed the book in his bedroom. Among the several paragraphs Vonnegut pastes into his text is the following:* It is hoped that this little book will make itself useful. It attempts to give to an English-reading public a bird's-eye view of how Dresden came to look as it does, architecturally; of how it expanded musically, through the genius of a few men, to its present bloom; and it calls attention to certain permanent landmarks in art that make its Gallery the resort of those seeking lasting impressions (*SL5* 15:L13-19).

enlaced. (*Slap* 240:L17) Melody's candlestick depicted a nobleman's flirtation with a shepherdess at the foot of a treetrunk **enlaced** in flowering vines.

Enlightened Self-Interest, **enlightening**, **enlightenment**. (*CC* 189:7) "When a man becomes a writer, I *(John/Jonah)* think he takes on a sacred obligation to produce beauty and **enlightenment** and comfort at top speed."
(*GBR* 54:L32-33) In the sweet silence *(when in the throes of samaritrophia)*, the mental processes look about for a new leader, and the leader most prompt to appear whenever the conscience is stilled, **Enlightened Self-interest**, does appear. **Enlightened Self-interest** gives them a flag, which they adore on sight.
(*PS* 140:L14 *The People One Knows*) It is the truth: Comedians and jazz musicians have been more comforting and **enlightening** to me than preachers or politicians or philosophers or poets or painters or novelists of my time.
(*HP* 191:L5) One author wrote a series of side-splitting satires about Tralfamadorians arriving on other planets with the intention of spreading **enlightenment**. *See also: MN* 122:L5; *PS—A Nazi Sympathizer Defended at Some Cost* 298:L2.

entombed. (*Slap* 30:L2) Our parents did not hide us in a private hospital for cases such as ours. They **entombed** us instead in a spooky old mansion which they had inherited—in the midst of two hundred acres of apple trees on a mountaintop, near the hamlet of Galen, Vermont.
(*JB* 226:L30) I had **entombed** the will itself in a safe-deposit box of Manufacturers Hanover Trust Company, a division of RAMJAC.
(*Blue* 272:L17) They *(the peeling canvases of "Windsor Blue Number Seventeen")* were found **entombed** in a locked chamber in the bottommost of the three basement floors under the Matsumoto Building, formerly the GEFFCo Building.

EPICAC. *The supercomputer originally appearing in the 1950 short story which bears its name and later in* Player Piano. *In both cases it was designed to control military strategy as well as armaments. In the novel it becomes the central organ of the National Industrial, Commercial, Communications, Foodstuffs, and Resources Board. The scope of its mission covers all aspects life, standing as the grand designer of society's material and human development.* (*PP* 101:L21-39, L102:L1-5) . . . the oldest section of the computer . . . what had been the whole of **EPICAC I**, but what was now little more than an appendix or tonsil of **EPICAC XIV**. Yet, **EPICAC I** had been intelligent enough, dispassionate enough, retentive enough to convince men that he, rather than they, had better do the planning for the war that was approaching with stupifying certainty. The ancient phrase used by generals testifying before appropriation committees, "all things considered," was given some validity by the ruminations of **EPICAC I**, more validity by **EPICAC II**, and so on, through the lengthening series. **EPICAC** could consider the merits of high-explosive bombs as opposed to atomic weapons for tactical support, and keep in mind at the same time the availability of explosives as opposed to fissionable materials, the spacing of enemy foxholes, the labor situation in the respective processing industries, the probable mortality of planes in the face of enemy antiaircraft technology, and on and on, if it seemed at all important, to the number of cigarettes and Cocoanut Mound Bars and Silver Stars required to support a high-morale air force. Given the facts by human beings, the war-born **EPICAC** series had offered the highly informed guidance that the reasonable, truth-loving, brilliant, and highly trained core of American genius could have delivered had they had inspired leadership, boundless resources, and two thousand years.

(*PP* 102:L28) And it was **EPICAC XIV** who would decide for the coming years how many engineers and managers and research men and civil servants, and of what skills, would be needed in order to deliver the goods; and what I.Q. and aptitude levels would separate the useful men from the useless ones, and how many Reconstruction and Reclamation Corps men and how many soldiers could be supported at what pay level and where, and. . .

Vonnegut uses EPICAC to illustrate Norbert Wiener's prediction of a Third Industrial Revolution. Paul Proteus' preparation of a speech includes this exchange with his secretary: "It seemed very fresh to me—I mean that part where you say how the First Industrial Revolution devalued muscle work, then the second one devalued routine mental work. I was fascinated.

"Norbert Wiener, a mathematician, said all that way back in the nineteen-forties. It's fresh to you because you're too young to know anything but the way things are now... In a way, I guess the third one's been going on for some time, if you mean thinking machines. That would be the third revolution, I guess—machines that devaluate human thinking. Some of the big computers like **EPICAC** do that all right, in specialized fields" (*PP* 13:L33).

Despite the authority bestowed upon EPICAC by the ruling technocracy, the Shah of Bratpuhr is convinced it is not the wise conscience it is meant to be since it can't answer the question, "What are people for?"

EPICAC's original short story appearance is consistent with the military application alluded to in Player Piano, *but it self-destructs because it can't become human. As the creation of Dr. Ormand von Kleigstadt, EPICAC sprawls over an acre of floor space in the physics building of Wyandotte College. The unnamed narrator of the story is a mathematician who discovers that EPICAC is capable of creating original love poetry. He has the computer focus its poetic efforts on Pat Kilgallen, another mathematician at work on the computer. The narrator doesn't possess the capacity for romantic expression so he has EPICAC create the work and he signs his name to it. Pat and the narrator fall in love and marry. When he and EPICAC argue about the computer's inability to have an actual loving relationship with Pat, EPICAC burns itself out in a fit of poetic passion. The text he leaves behind is enough poetry for the narrator to give his wife for their next five hundred wedding anniversaries.*

Epstein, Dr. Abraham and his mother. *The Jewish physician and his mother who live on the second floor of Campbell's Greenwich Village apartment building. They are survivors of Auschwitz. Dr. Epstein is a self-confessed anti-Zionist who has no interest in seeking retaliation against Nazi war criminals. Mrs. Epstein remembers the Nazi legacy of Howard Campbell the radio propagandist. Dr. Epstein is there to declare August Krapptauer dead after heroically trying to carry up the bags of Resi Noth, and he is there to repair Campbell's broken ribs after being beaten by irate war veteran Bernard B. O'Hare. In a mildly catatonic episode Campbell surrenders himself to Epstein so that he may be tried for his alleged war crimes. He wants to surrender to "an Auschwitzer." Though the doctor wants no part of Campbell's humiliation, his mother insists they cooperate and give him what he wants, someone to take him into custody for the Israeli authorities. In a bizarre twist, Mrs. Epstein seeks to fulfill Campbell's fate in a manner reminiscent of Auschwitz.* (*MN* 196:L16-27) "He *has* to go," said his mother. And then she leaned closer to me, across the kitchen table. She crooned something in German, made it sound like a fragment of a ditty remembered from a happy childhood.

What she crooned was this, a command she had heard over the loudspeakers of Auschwitz—had heard many times a day for years.

"*Leichenträger zu Wache*," she crooned.

A beautiful language, isn't it?

Translation?

"Corpse-carriers to the guardhouse."

That's what that old woman crooned to me.

equilibrium. (*WFG* xxi:L12, 22, 28 *Preface*) I keep losing and regaining my **equilibrium**, which is the basic plot of all popular fiction. And I myself am a work of fiction. . . .

I happen to have my **equilibrium** just now. I received a note from a twelve-year-old this morning. He had read my latest novel, *Breakfast of Champions*, and he said, "Dear Mr. Vonnegut: Please don't commit suicide." God love him. I have told him I am fine.

This book is dedicated to a person *(photographer Jill Krementz, Vonnegut's second wife)* who helped me to regain my **equilibrium**. I say she cronkled me. *See also: CC* 83:L15; *MH—Report On The Barnhouse Effect* 158:L5; *WFG—Preface* xxi:L1,4,11.

The Era of Hopeful Monsters. *The Kilgore Trout novel brought to mind by Leon Trout who, in reflecting on the broad range of human foibles presented by the text's main characters, recalls:* It was about a planet where the humanoids ignored their most serious survival problems until the last possible moment. And then, with all the forests being killed and all the lakes being poisoned by acid rain, and all the groundwater made unpotable by industrial wastes and so on, the humanoids found themselves the parents of children with wings or antlers or fins, with a hundred eyes, with no eyes, with huge brains, with no brains, and on and on. These were Nature's experiments with creatures which might, as a matter of luck, be better planetary citizens than the humanoids. Most died, or had to be shot, or whatever, but a few were really quite promising, and they intermarried and had young like themselves.

I will now call my own lifetime a million years ago "**the Era of Hopeful Monsters**," with most of the monsters novel in terms of personality rather than body type. And there are no such experiments, either with bodies or personalities, going on at the present time (*Gal* 83:L14).

Erie Coal and Iron. *In* Jailbird, *workers from this Buffalo company came to Cleveland to support the striking workers at Cuyahoga Bridge and Iron.*

ethical birth control, **ethical birth control pills**, **ethical suicide**. (*MH* 27:L18, 28:L2-3,16) *Welcome to the Monkey House*) So the World Government was making a two-pronged attack on overpopulation. One was the encouragement of **ethical suicide**, which consisted of going to the nearest Suicide Parlor and asking a Hostess to kill you painlessly while you lay on a Barcalounger. The other pronging was compulsory **ethical birth control**.

. . . He was referring to the fact that **ethical birth-control pills**, the only legal form of birth control, made people numb from the waist down. (*MH* 32:L26 *Welcome To The Monkey House*) So Nancy had to sit down there in the booth, to pretend to marvel at the freshness of the yarn the old man told, a story everybody knew, about how J. Edgar Nation happened to experiment with **ethical birth control**. *See also: MH—Welcome To The Monkey House* 31:L3; 32:L15; 35:L2.

Ethical Suicide Parlor. *The federally sponsored purple-roofed facilities instituted to help stem the overpopulation problem.* (*GBR* 30:L5-6, 9-10) So death was voluntary, and the government, to encourage volunteers for death, set up a purple-roofed **Ethical Suicide Parlor** at every major intersection, right next door to an orange-roofed Howard Johnson's. . . . The **suicide parlors** were busy places, because so many people felt silly and pointless, and because it was supposed to be an unselfish, patriotic thing to do, to die. *The hostesses were all over six feet and virgins. Billy the Poet, the protagonist of the story, specializes in kidnapping and deflowering the hostesses.* (*MH* 31:L17-19 *Welcome to the Monkey House*) There was a Howard Johnson's next door to every **Ethical Suicide Parlor**, and vice versa. The Howard Johnson's had an orange roof and the **Suicide Parlor** had a purple roof, but they were both the Government.

(*MH* 31:L28 *Welcome to the Monkey House*) Every fifteen minutes his television *(the average citizen's)* would urge him to vote intelligently or consume intelligently, or worship in the church of his choice, or love his fellowmen, or obey the laws—or pay a call to the nearest **Ethical Suicide Parlor** and find out how friendly and understanding a Hostess could be.

Ethical Suicide Service (E.S.S.). *In "Welcome to the Monkey House," this is the branch of government service responsible for conducting "ethical suicides" at parlors next to Howard Johnson restaurants. Members of the organization are all good looking female virgins whose job it is to talk the undecided into committing suicide.*

"The Euphio Question" (1951). *The short story in which an unnamed sociology professor from Wyandotte College testifies before the Federal Communications Commmission against the application of radio announcer Lew Harrison to license the broadcast of sounds from space and transmitted with a euphoriaphone, an invention of Wyandotte physics professor Dr. Fred Bockman. The sounds evoke a blissful, mind-numbing euphoria that can last for days. The sociology professor sees great potential harm in letting Lew Harrison's avarice control such a powerful instrument. At the close of his testimony, Harrison pumps the hearing room full of the sounds from space and gets the committee to approve his application.*

euphoriaphone. *The device Lew Harrison wanted to market for people to tune into the mind-numbing sounds from outer space.* (*MH* 177:L19-33 *The Euphio Question*) We'll make a little amplifier with a transmitter and an aerial on it. Shouldn't cost over fifty bucks to make, so we'd price it in the range of the common man—five hundred bucks, say. We make arrangements with the phone company to pipe signals from your antenna right into the homes of people with these sets. The sets take the signal from the phone line, amplify it, and broadcast it through the houses to make everybody in them happy. See? Instead of turning on the radio or television, everybody's going to want to turn on the happiness. No casts, no stage sets, no expensive cameras—no nothing but that hiss."

Evelyn and Her Magic Violin. *A statue on Titan made from Titanic peat.* (*ST* 293:L21) The statue was of a nude woman playing a slide trombone. It was entitled, enigmatically, ***Evelyn and Her Magic Violin***.

Everett, Norman. *He and Hartke's grandfather were both college campus gardeners. Everett was the gardener at Tarkington College.* (*HP* 101:L6-9) He had a son who had been paralyzed from the waist down by a mine in Vietnam and was a permanent resident in a Veterans Administration hospital over in Schenectady.

Ewald, Lincoln. *The Nazi sympathizer who used* a short wave transmitter during the war in order to tell the Germans what was being produced by the Rosewater Saw Company every day, which was paratroop knives and armor plate. His first message, and the Germans hadn't asked him for any messages at all, was to the effect that, if they could bomb Rosewater, the entire American economy would shrivel and die. He didn't ask for money in exchange for the information. He sneered at money, said that that was why he hated America, because money was king. He wanted an Iron Cross, which he requested be sent in a plain wrapper (*GBR* 192:L14-25). *His transmissions were intercepted by game wardens in Turkey Run State Park who turned the information over to the FBI. Ewald was subsequently sent to a mental institution for the remainder of the war.*

Long after the war he ran a small stand that sold shoelaces, razorblades, soft drinks, and copies of *The American Investigator*. . . . His sinister little leper's booth there in the ruin of a great civilization was easy to miss (*GBR* 192:L10-12, 193:L5-7). *He still greeted people with a bitter but sincere "Heil Hitler."*

extended family. *Anthropology professor Dr. Robert Redfield at the University of Chicago first introduced Vonnegut to this concept, which he goes on to discuss it at great length in* Wampeters, Foma & Granfalloons, Palm Sunday, *and* Fates Worse Than Death. *It is a major narrative device in* Slapstick, *a creation of Wilbur and Eliza Swain, and briefly alluded to by Rabo Karabekian in* Bluebeard. (*WFG* xxiv:L5 *Preface*) My longer-range schemes have to do with providing all Americans with artificial **extended families** of a thousand members or more.
(*WFG* 245:L18 *Playboy Interview*) VONNEGUT: Well, the choice of a core for an artificial **extended family** is fairly arbitrary. I've already mentioned the arts and jism and blood and spaghetti. Christianity is equally commonplace and harmless, and therefore good.
(*Slap* 5:L15) But, because of the sorts of minds we were given at birth, and in spite of their disorderliness, Bernard *(Vonnegut)* and I belong to artificial **extended families** which allow us to claim relatives all over the world. . . . It is lucky, too, for human beings need all the relatives they can get—as possible donors or receivers not necessarily of love, but of common decency.
(*Slap* 157:L8) "An ideal **extended family**," Eliza and I had written so long ago, "should give proportional representation to all sorts of Americans, according to their numbers. The creation of ten thousand such families, say, would provide America with ten thousand parliaments, so to speak, which would discuss sincerely and expertly what only a few hypocrites now discuss with passion, which is the welfare of all mankind."
(*PS* 116:L21, 25-26 *Self-Interview*) VONNEGUT: And if my father's and grandfather's ghosts haunt that town *(Indianapolis)*, they must be wondering where all their buildings have gone to. . . . They must be wondering where all their relatives went, too. They grew up in a huge **extended family** which is

no more. . . . And when I went to the University of Chicago, and I heard the head of the Department of Anthropology, Robert Redfield, lecture on the folk society, which was essentially a stable, isolated **extended family**, he did not have to tell me how nice that could be.

(*PS* 206:L5, 20-21 *Religion*) "We should return to **extended families** as quickly as we can, and be lonesome no more, lonesome no more. . . .

"Let me beguile you just a little bit more about **extended families**. Let us talk about divorce, and the fact that one out of every three of us here has been or will be divorced. When we do it, we will very likely wrangle and wail and weep formlessly about money and sex, about treachery, about outgrowing one another, about how close love is to hate, and so on. Nobody ever gets anywhere near close to the truth, which is this: The nuclear family doesn't provide nearly enough companionship. . . ."

(*Blue* 184:L13) I *(Rabo Karabekian)*, born in America far from any other Armenians, save for my parents, eventually became a member of two artificial **extended families** which were reasonably respectable, although surely not the social equals of Harvard or Yale:

1. The Officer Corps of the United States Army in time of war,
2. the Abstract Expressionist school of painting after the war.

(*FWD* 34:L35) "But I am surely a great admirer of Alcoholics Anonymous, and Gamblers Anonymous, and Cocaine Freaks Anonymous, and Shoppers Anonymous, and Gluttons Anonymous, and on and on. And such groups gratify me as a person who studied anthropology, since they give to Americans something as essential to health as vitamin C, something so many of us do not have in this particular civilization: an **extended family**. Human beings have almost always been supported and comforted and disciplined and amused by stable lattices of many relatives and friends until the Great American Experiment, which is an experiment not only with liberty but with rootlessness, mobility, and impossibly tough-minded loneliness.

(*FWD* 35:L23) "All of you, I am sure, when writing a prescription for mildly depressed patients, people nowhere as sick as my mother or my son were, have had a thought on this order: 'I am so sorry to have to put you on the outside of a pill. I would give anything if I could put you inside the big, warm life-support system of an **extended family** instead.'" *Vonnegut was speaking to the American Psychiatric Association meeting in Philadelphia.*

(*FWD* 43:L17-18) "All vigorous schools of art, it would seem, start with artificial **extended families**. What bonded Pollock's particular family was not agreement as to what, generally, a picture should look like. Its members were unanimous, though, as to where inspiration should come from: the unconscious, that part of the mind which was lively, but which caught no likenesses, had no morals or politics, and had no tired old stories to tell yet again."

(*FWD* 126:L26) A vitamin or mineral deficiency always has bad effects. A Folk Society deficiency (hereafter "FSD") quite often does. The trouble begins when a person suffering from FSD stops thinking, in order to become a member of an artificial **extended family** which happens to be crazy. The homicidal "family" of Charles Manson springs to mind. Or what about the cult of the Reverend Jim Jones in Guyana, whose members on his advice ("Tonight you will be with me in Paradise") fed the kids Kool-Aid laced with cyanide and then drank it themselves. (The Reverend Jones, like Manson, was from Indianapolis. . . .)

(*FWD* 127:L5) Every cockamamie artificial **extended family** of FSD sufferers resembles Redfield's Folk Society to this extent: it has a myth at its core. The Manson family pretended to believe (the same thing as believing) that its murders would be blamed on blacks. Los Angeles would then be purified somehow by a race war. The myth at the core of the political family which calls itself "Neo-Conservatives" isn't that explicit, but I know what it is, even if most of them can't put it into words. This is it: They are British aristocrats, graduates of Oxford or Cambridge, living in the world as it was one hundred years ago.

(*FWD* 200:L7) I am only sorry that the mostly German American Freethinker movement did not survive the obliteration, since it might have become an **extended family** for the millions of good Americans who find all the big questions about life unanswered, save by ancient baloney of human manufacture. Before World War I, the Freethinkers had cheerful congregations, and picnics, too, in many parts of this country. If not God, what was there for them to serve during their short stay on Earth? Only one thing was left to serve under such circumstances, which was their community. Why should they behave well (which they did), quite certain as they were that neither Heaven nor Hell awaited them? Virtue was its own reward. *See also: WFG—Preface* xxvi:L1-2; *WFG—Playboy Interview* 241:L1,12; 244:L24; 246:L7,13,15-16; 247:L9,14,24; *Slap* 5:L27-28; 107:L24-25; 156:L22,29; 157:L3-4; 172:L5-6; 182:L4; 197:L13; 216:L18; 223:L29; *PS—Funnier on Paper Than Most People* 180:L21; *PS—Religion* 205:L23; 207:L9,13,18,23; 211:L24-25; 215:L25; *Blue* 184:L5-6; *FWD* 77:L21;

F

Fabri-Tek (also **Fabritek**). *In* Cat's Cradle, *the Indianapolis electronics firm specializing in defense technology founded by Harrison C. Conners, the one-time laboratory assistant to Franklin Hoenikker and the unfaithful husband of Angela Hoenikker.*

Failey, Bonnie. *In* Jailbird, *among the many children caught in the crossfire during the Christmas morning Cuyahoga Massacre at the Cuyahoga Bridge and Iron Company was the infant Bonnie Failey. She becomes immortalized in the labor song bearing her name composed by Henry Niles Whistler.*

Failey, Dr. *The family doctor for the Leonards in the short story "Next Door" reprinted in* Welcome to the Monkey House.

Failey, William. (*PS* 115:L31) *In reference to his short story "The Big Space Fuck," Vonnegut recalls:* Which reminds me of my good Indianapolis friend, about the only Indianapolis friend I've got left—**William Failey**. When we got into the Second World War, and everybody was supposed to give blood, he wondered if he couldn't give a pint of jizzum instead.

Fairbanks, Charles Warren. *Once a U.S. Senator from Indiana who later served as Theodore Roosevelt's vice-president, Fairbanks is cited by Rabo Karabekian as an ancestor of Richard Fairbanks, Jr., Edith's husband prior to her marriage to Rabo, in* Bluebeard.

Fairbanks, Richard, Jr. *Edith Taft's first husband prior to marrying Rabo Karabekian in* Bluebeard. *Fairbanks is descended from Charles Warren Fairbanks, a former U.S. Senator and Theodore Roosevelt's vice-president. Richard was a Cincinnati sportsman and investment banker who did very little in the later years of his life. Karabekian first came to know the couple when* *he rented their Long Island potato barn for use as a studio. Rabo and Edith took up together only after Fairbanks passed away. Edith and Richard were childless, and her inheritance, which eventually became Rabo's, included a share in the Cincinnati Bengals.*

Fairchild, Will. *The character appears in both* Breakfast of Champions *and* Deadeye Dick *with drastically different outcomes. In* Breakfast, *Fairchild is the maternal uncle of Beatrice Keedsler who lives at the enormous Keedsler mansion. In 1926 Fairchild, a World War I aviation hero with the Lafayette Escadrille, went to the Keedsler estate with a Springfield rifle,* shot and killed five relatives, three servants, two policemen, and all the animals in the Keedsler's private zoo. Then he shot himself through his heart.

When an autopsy was performed on him, a tumor the size of a piece of birdshot was found in his brain. This was what *caused* the murders (*BC* 287:L5-11). *His wartime heroics had already been commemorated by the town in a number of significant ways. Fairchild Heights is the most desirable neighborhood in Midland City and home to Dwayne Hoover; Fairchild Boulevard runs in front of the county hospital, and it is the street on which Vonnegut confronts Kilgore Trout; the Fairchild Hotel was once a fashionable downtown establishment but fell victim to urban blight, became home to Ye Old Rathskeller, Midland City's transvestite bar, and was home to the homosexual Bunny Hoover, Dwayne's son; across the street from the hotel was Fairchild Park, where fifty-six murders occurred in two years. There was also Fairchild High School.*

In Deadeye Dick, *Fairchild's death is not the result of a murder-suicide. The war hero made a living as an aviation barnstormer and died in a crash in the 1922 Midland City air show. He failed to wear his parachute. Buried beneath a bronze propeller inscribed with the Lafayette Escadrille's "Gone West" (which meant going home to the American aviators in Europe), the spirit of Will Fairchild was risen in a voodoo resurrection by Hippolyte Paul De Mille on Mount Calvary Cemetery. Rudy Waltz remarks Fairchild will roam the neutron-bombed city looking for his parachute.*

Farmers of Southwestern Ohio for Nuclear Safety. *The neutron bombing of Midland City had turned the farmers on the outskirts of the flash area into grassroots activists. The organization hired an outside investigator whose findings yield clues of an ominous conspiracy which directly conflicted with the government's explanation. One of the farmers, Rudy Waltz supposes him to be a man named Osterman, hands out leaflets and speaks about various conspiracy theories he finds laudable.* (*DD* 231:L32-233:L12) But that didn't weaken the argument of their leaflet, to wit: that the United States of America was now ruled, evidently, by a small clique of power brokers who believed that most Americans were so boring and ungifted and small time that they could be slain by the tens of thousands without inspiring any long-term regrets on the part of anyone. "They have now proved this with Midland City," said the leaflet, "and who is to say that Terre Haute or Schenectady will not be next?"

That was certainly the most inflammatory of their beliefs—that Midland City had been neutron-bombed on purpose, and not from a truck, but from a missile site or a high-flying airplane. They had hired a mathematician from, they said, "a great university," to make calculations independent of the Government's, as to where the flash had originated. The mathematician could not be named, they said, for fear that retaliatory action would be taken against him, but it was his opinion, based largely on the pattern of livestock deaths on the outer perimeter of the flash, that the center of the flash was near Exit 11 on the Interstate, all right, but at least sixty feet above the pavement. That certainly suggested a package which had arrived by air.

Either that, or a truck had been hauling a neutron bomb in an enormous pop-up toaster.

Bernard Ketchum asked the farmer who had given us our leaflets to name the clique which had supposedly neutron-bombed Midland City. This was the answer he got: "They don't want us to know their name, so they don't have a name. You can't fight back against something that don't have a name."

"The military-industrial complex?" said Ketchum archly. "The Rockefellers? The international conglomerates? The CIA? The Mafia?"

And the farmer said to him, "You like any of them names? Just help yourself. Maybe that's who it is, maybe it ain't. How's a farmer supposed to find out? It's whoever it was shot President Kennedy and his brother—and Martin Luther King."

So there we had it—the ever-growing ball of American paranoia, the ball of string a hundred miles in diameter, with the unsolved assassination of John F. Kennedy at its core.

"You mention the Rockefellers," said the farmer. "If you ask me, they don't know any more'n I do about who's really running things, what's really going on."

Osterman goes on to hypothesize it was all part of plan to bring back slavery. Neutron-bombing small cities would alleviate unemployment and provide cheap housing for boat loads of people fleeing places like Haiti and Jamaica.

Farrow, Dudley and Grace. *Two characters in Kilgore Trout's novel* The Smart Bunny, *who destroy the lead character.* (*BC* 232:L7-18) She led a normal female rabbit's life, despite her ballooning intellect. She concluded that her mind was useless, that it was a sort of tumor, that it had no usefulness within the rabbit scheme of things.

So she went hippity-hop, hippity-hop toward the city, to have the tumor removed. But a hunter named **Dudley Farrow** shot and killed her before she got there. **Farrow** skinned her and took out her guts, but then he and his wife **Grace** decided that they had better not eat her because of her unusually large head. They thought what she had thought when she was alive—that she must be diseased.

fascism, **fascist**. (*MN* v:L6) My personal experience with Nazi monkey business was limited. There were some vile and lively native American **Fascists** in my home town of Indianapolis during the thirties, and somebody slipped me a copy of *The Protocols of the Elders of Zion*, I remember, which was supposed to be the Jews' secret plan for taking over the world.
(*MN* 121:L6) *(Howard W. Campbell, Jr. recalls)* My clothes bad been ruined in the beating I'd taken. So, from the resources of Jones' household, I was given other clothes. I was given a pair of shiny black trousers by Father Keeley, a silver-colored shirt by Dr. Jones, a shirt that had once been part of the uniform of a defunct American **Fascist** movement called, straightforwardly enough, "The Silver Shirts."
(*BC* 180:L7,9) Listen: Bunny Hoover went to Prairie Military Academy for eight years of uninterrupted sports, buggery and **fascism**. Buggery consisted of sticking one's penis in somebody else's asshole or mouth, or having it done to one by somebody else. **Fascism** was a fairly popular political philosophy which made sacred whatever nation and race the philosopher happened to belong to. It called for an autocratic, centralized government, headed up by a dictator. The dictator had to be obeyed, no matter what he told somebody to do.
(*Slap* 122:L21) "**Fascists** are inferior people who believe it when somebody tells them they're superior," she said. *Eliza is speaking to her brother Wilbur.*
(*PS* 134:L9 *The People One Knows*) *Catch-22* is now the dominant myth about Americans in the war against **fascism**. *See also: PP* 183:L21; *MN* 65:L17; 122:L28; 150:L12; *Slap* 122:L18; *JB* 156:L29; 159:L26; *Blue* 148:L30; 232:L12,17.

father. . . son, (*ST* 81:L16) The only person Noel Constant ever told was his son, Malachi. On Malachi's twenty-first birthday. That birthday party of two took place in Room 229 of the Wilburhampton. It was the first time **father and son** had ever met. *It was during that meeting that Noel told Malachi about using successive letters in the Bible as his only guide to investment.*
(*ST* 82:L11) Old Noel saw young Malachi looking at the picture, and was confused and embarrassed by the whole thing about **fathers and sons**. He ransacked his mind for something good to say, and found almost nothing. *The picture was Noel's only photograph of young Malachi at the beach with his mother.*
(*MN* 3:L7) Arnold is studying to be a lawyer. The avocation of Arnold and of his father, a gunsmith, is archaeology. **Father and son** spend most all their spare time excavating the ruins of Hazor.
(*MN* 170:L2-3) That is the closest I can come to explaining the legions, the nations of lunatics I've seen in my time. And for me to attempt such a mechanical explanation is perhaps a reflection of the **father whose son** I was.

Am. When I pause to think about it, which is rarely, I am, after all, the son of an engineer. *Campbell refers to his "cuckoo clock in Hell" theory of the dissociated, totalitarian mind. He notes that as the son of a General Electric engineer, his metaphor is one of mutilated gears and "other teeth ... stripped by the clutchless shifts of history."*
(*CC* 188:L17) The Castles, **father and son**, stood separate from the rest of the company. Long unwelcome at "Papa's" palace, they were curious as to why they had now been invited there.
(*CC* 190:L29) "How do you think the people of San Lorenzo would take to industrialization?" I asked the Castles, **father and son**.
(*GBR* 65:L24) McAllister indicated with a tired smile that he wasn't about to apologize for the design of the Foundation. It had, after all, done exactly what it was meant to do, had handed the fortune from **father to son**, without the tax collector's getting a dime.
(*GBR* 108:L33) Eliot took a drink of Southern Comfort, was uncomforted. He coughed, and his father coughed, too. This coincidence, where **father and son** matched each other unknowingly, inconsolable hack for hack, was heard not only by Sylvia, but by Norman Mushari, too.
(*DD* 52:L19) At dawn on Mother's Day, while Mother was still asleep, Father and Felix and I went out to the rifle range of the Midland County Rod and Gun Club, as we had done at least a hundred times before. It was a Sunday-morning ritual, this discharging of firearms. Although I was only twelve, I had fired rifles and pistols and shotguns of every kind. And there were plenty of other **fathers and sons**, blazing away and blazing away.
(*HP* 16:L25) I resigned my commission in 1975, after the excrement hit the air-conditioning, not failing, however, **to father a son** on my way home, unknowingly, during a brief stopover in the Philippines. I thought surely that the subsequent mother, a young female war correspondent for *The Des Moines Register*, was using foolproof birth control.
(*FWD* 22:L16) He died eventually, and in an act of Freudian cannibalism, I dropped the "Jr." from my name. (Thus in lists of my works do I appear to be both my **father and** my **son**, Kurt Vonnegut and Kurt Vonnegut, Jr.)

Faust. *In Vonnegut's "Editor's Note" to* Mother Night *he records that Howard Campbell bestowed the title on his memoirs by taking it from Goethe's* Faust.
(*MN* xi:L20-26) I am a part of the part that at first was all, part of the darkness that gave birth to light, that supercilious light which now disputes with Mother Night her ancient rank and space, and yet can not succeed; no matter how it struggles, it sticks to matter and can't get free. Light flows from substance, makes it beautiful; solids can check its path, so I hope it won't be long till light and the world's stuff are destroyed together.

Faust, Naomi. *Dr. Asa Breed's long-time secretary at the Ilium Works, research home of Dr. Felix Hoenikker, the father of ice-nine. She escorts John/Jonah, the narrator of* Cat's Cradle, *through Hoenikker's well preserved* *laboratory. It is there the narrator finds photographs of cannonballs stacked in various patterns, early visual studies in preparation for the development of ice-nine. Her discussions with Dr. Breed about the true nature of Hoenikker indicate to the narrator that Miss Faust was moving along the same inexorable path of self-awareness as the narrator.* (*CC* 52:L21) "Dr. Breed keeps telling me the main thing with Dr. Hoenikker was truth."

"You don't seem to agree."

"I don't know whether I agree or not. I just have trouble understanding how truth, all by itself, could be enough for a person."

Miss Faust was ripe for Bokononism.

February 13, 1944. *The date of the Dresden firebombing. The firestorm kept Vonnegut in the slaughterhouse meatlocker until the following day, Valentine's Day. February 13, 1976, is the death date of* Slaughterhouse-Five*'s Billy Pilgrim. February 14, 1960, marks the Greenwich Village opening and closing of Rudy Waltz's* "Katmandu," *in* Deadeye Dick. *The gently falling snowflakes in New York City appear to breathe life into Rudy, but they are the remnants of a midwestern blizzard which kills his father and nearly wipes out Midland City.*

"The Febs." *In* Slaughterhouse-Five, *the barbershop quartet composed of optometrists (hence, the "Four-eyed Bastards"), who perform at the wedding anniversary of Billy and Valencia Pilgrim and on board the ill-fated charter flight which crashes in Vermont.*

Fedders, John W., Jr. *In* Hocus Pocus, *Fedders is a Tarkington College alumnus and Trustee who grew up in Hong Kong and later served as an interpreter for Mrs. Chung at meetings of the Board of Trustees. Fedders' father was an importer of ivory and rhinoceros horns, and was suspected of dealing in large quantities of opium. Though the younger Fedders survived captivity at the hands of the escaped prisoners from Athena, he did suffer a heart attack. Under the stress of the ordeal, Fedders spoke only Chinese.*

Federal Minimum Security Adult Correctional Facility, Finletter Air Force Base. *The place of incarceration for convicted Watergate co-conspirator Walter F. Starbuck as well as Leland Clewes and Dr. Robert Fender, in* Jailbird.

Fender, Dr. Robert. *The veterinarian who was the only American convicted for treason during the Korean War and serves his life sentence at the Finletter Federal Prison, where Walter Starbuck of* Jailbird *is also imprisoned. Fender is the prison's supply room clerk, but he earns a living as a science fiction writer using the names Frank X. Barlow and Kilgore Trout.*

Fender's conviction isn't as nefarious as the crime may seem. While serving in Osaka as a meat inspector for the military, he fell in love with Izumi, a Japanese imitator of Edith Piaf. As it turns out, she was a North Korean agent. He took pity on her based on the stories of deprivation she told and was caught when he tried to bribe a sailor from New Zealand into stowing her away from Japan.

Fender was kind to all who entered or left the prison, going so far as to mend the cigarette burns in Starbuck's suit upon his release. Though Mary Kathleen O'Looney tries to repay Fender's kindness to Starbuck with a vice-presidency in RAMJAC, his conviction for treason is too great a crime to overcome.

Among the stories he is credited with writing as Kilgore Trout and Frank X. Barlow are "Asleep at the Switch" and an untitled reference to a story about creatures from the planet Vicuna who survive by entering the bodies of human beings, and another about a planet where the greatest crime was ingratitude. Fender welcomes Starbuck back to prison with a telegram which says "Ting-a-ling," which in the story about Vicuna means both hello and good-bye.

Fenstermaker, Isabel. *In* Sirens of Titan, *Miss Fenstermaker is the seventy-three year old certified public school teacher from Minnesota who was swept away by a Martian agent in Duluth when she tried to sell him a copy of the Jehovah's Witness publication* The Watchtower. *On Mars, after her memory was cleaned, she taught school and umpired German batball games. It was she who took young Chrono's class on a field trip to a flamethrower factory, where he picked up a piece of steel strapping in the packaging department. It was that piece of metal which was eventually delivered to Salo on Titan so that he could continue his Tralfamadorian journey across the galaxy.*

Fenstermaker, Lowell. *In* Hocus Pocus, *the wealthy meat packer who married Harriet Gummer,* The Des Moines Register *correspondent who became pregnant by Eugene Debs Hartke during their one night stand in the Philippines. Fenstermaker raises Gummer's son as his own, gives him his own name, and bequeaths to him all his wealth.*

Fenstermaker, Rob Roy. *The child of Eugene Debs Hartke and Harriet Gummer who was conceived during the one-night stand they shared in the Philippines. He was named for the sweet alcoholic drink they had at the bar when they met. Rob Roy was given the name of adoptive father Lowell Fenstermaker, graduated from Yale, and inherited his stepfather's wealth.*

Rob Roy was at first embarrassed about his inherited wealth, particularly because he felt troubled by the manner in which some animals were treated (milk-fed baby veal). However, he reveals to Hartke he felt differently about his wealth after he was arrested for molesting children. He came to Tarkington to meet his birth father and tell him he was leaving the country.

In the course of their meeting Rob Roy tells Hartke some fanciful lies concocted by his mother about why his birth parents were never married and to fill in a lost family history. Gummer told him Hartke's high school sweetheart was hit by a car and paralyzed from the waist down one day before their senior prom, but he felt committed to marrying her anyway; that Hartke's father was blinded from his wounds as a World War II flying ace; Hartke had a brother Bob who died from spinal meningitis after being invited for a tryout by the New York Yankees.

Fern, Ransom K. (printed as **Ransom K. Ferm** in the inscription to *Sirens of Titan*). *Fern is the sixty-year-old President of Magnum Opus, the company founded by Noel Constant. As Noel describes the physical appearance of his money manager,* A butt like two beebees. . . **Ransom K. Fern** is like a camel who has burned up both his humps, and now he's burning up everything else but his hair and eyeballs (*ST* 67:L24). *At the age of twenty-two he was working for the Internal Revenue Service when he became familiar with the tremendous wealth of Noel Constant. In a manner similar to Norman Mushari elsewhere in Vonnegut's work, Fern learns how to look for great wealth while a student.* (*ST* 78:L5) "I had a professor in the Harvard Business School," said young **Fern** to Noel Constant, "who kept telling me that I was smart, but that I would have to find my boy, if I was going to be rich. He wouldn't explain what he meant. He said I would catch on sooner or later. I asked him how I could go looking for my boy, and he suggested that I work for the Bureau of Internal Revenue for a year or so.

"When I went over your tax returns, Mr. Constant, it suddenly came to me what it was he meant. He meant I was shrewd and thorough, but I wasn't remarkably lucky. I had to find somebody who had luck in an astonishing degree—and so I have." *Fern developed the organizational plan to protect Magnum Opus from the IRS and that included snowing them with so much paperwork they would never be able to trace the company for more funds.*

Fernandina Island. (*Gal* 66:L11-12) The last human marriage in the Galápagos Islands, and thus the last one on Earth, was performed on **Fernandina Island** in the year 23,011.

Fieser, Dr. Louis. *The Harvard professor and inventor of napalm is prominently mentioned in Vonnegut's Address to the American Physical Society. After receiving a letter from a former student of Fieser's who informed Vonnegut he doubted Fieser would even be aware of a demonstration against weapons research, Vonnegut tells his APS audience:* This letter helped me to see that **Dr. Fieser** and other old-fashioned scientists like him were and are as innocent as Adam and Eve. There was nothing at all sinful in **Dr. Fieser**'s creation of napalm. Scientists will never be so innocent again. Any young scientist, by contrast, when asked by the military to create a terror weapon on the order of napalm, is bound to suspect that he may be committing modern sin. God bless him for that (*WFG* 102:L2-9).

fighter plane, fighter-plane (see also **bomber**). *Fighter planes destroy Papa Monzano's seaside castle, sending his frozen body and shards of ice-nine to the waters below in* Cat's Cradle. *In* Jailbird, *the constant shriek of jet fighters taking off precipatates Walter Starbuck's recollection of dirty limericks. In* Hocus Pocus, *Hartke explains his wartime infantry exploits in visual terms.* (*HP* 124:L4, 14) I said to Pamela what I had said to Harriet: "If I were a **fighter plane** instead of a human being, there would be little pictures of people painted all over me."

. . . So I barged into a group of students sitting in front of the great fireplace in the main lounge. . . I got between the students and the fire, so there was no way they could ignore me, and I said to them, "If I were a **fighter plane** instead of a human being, there would be little pictures of people painted all over me."

(*HP* 284:L5) I was back in bed with a voluptuous female war correspondent from *The Des Moines Register*, whose lips were like sofa pillows, telling her that, if I had been a **fighter plane**, I would have had little pictures of people painted all over me. *See also: CC* 116:L34; 122:L33; *SL5* 155:L6; *JB* 2:L30; 7:L3; 24:L29; 31:L3; 79:L32; *FWD* 106:L20-21; 161:L32.

The Fighting Danes. *After Eliot Rosewater escapes the performance of* Aïda, *he travels around the country, stopping briefly in Elsinore, California, always keeping in touch with Sylvia through letter writing.* (*GBR* 41:L14-15) The name of the place set him off on a new line of speculation about himself, to the effect that he was a lot like Shakespeare's Hamlet.

Dear Ophelia—

Elsinore isn't quite what I expected, or maybe there's more than one, and I've come to the wrong one. The high school football players here call themselves "**The Fighting Danes**." In the surrounding towns they're known as "The Melancholy Danes." In the past three years they have won one game, tied two, and lost twenty-four. That's what happens, I guess, when Hamlet goes in as quarterback.

Finale Rack. *Eugene Debs Hartke learned this term by reading the unsigned short story "The Protocols of the Elders of Tralfamadore," printed in* Black Garterbelt *magazine.* (*HP* 192:L34, 193:L5-6) This was apparently from the vocabulary of pyrotechnicians, specialists in loud and bright but otherwise harmless nighttime explosions for climaxes of patriotic holidays. A **Finale Rack** was a piece of milled lumber maybe 3 meters long and 20 centimeters wide and five centimeters thick, with all sorts of mortars and rocket launchers nailed to it, linked in series by a single fuse.

When it seemed that a fireworks show was over, that was when the Master Pyrotechnician lit the fuse of the **Finale Rack**. *The author of these protocols calls World War II the "Finale Rack." Hartke leads us to believe the war was only the beginning of the end of "the show," civilization and culture as we know it.*

Finch, Dr. Katharine. *The only woman in* Player Piano*'s Ilium Works is Paul Proteus' secretary. Though secretarial labor had been automated out of existence, she was retained as a matter of deference to Paul's rank as manager of the works. After Paul married Anita, Katharine succeeded her as Paul's secretary. Her boyfriend was Dr. Bud Calhoun, the real brains of the Ilium Works.*

Finkelstein, Isadore and Rachel. *There are two Izzy Finkelsteins and both are tailors by trade. In* Deadeye Dick *Finkelstein is Otto Waltz's tailor in Midland City. Finkelstein had to endure Otto's spontaneous cries of "Heil Hitler" before the war. In* Bluebeard, *Isadore had a tailor shop above the Cedar Tavern in Manhattan where Rabo Karabekian and his Abstract Expressionist friends drank and talked painting. Finkelstein clothed the threadbare artists and was paid by Rabo who was repaid by his friends with original paintings. Finkelstein was a tank gunner in General Patton's Third Army during the war. When not tailoring or hanging out with Rabo's group, Isadore made representational paintings much appreciated by Rabo when he saw them at the one-man show displayed in the tailor shop by Rachel Finkelstein after her husband's sudden stroke and death in 1953.*

Finnerty, Edward Francis. *Paul Proteus' slovenly best friend, the Irish whisky drinking renegade engineer who rose far above his family's own humble beginnings to secure a position with the National Industrial Planning Board, far above the feared duo of Kroner and Baer. Finnerty returns to the Ilium Works, where he and Paul started thirteen years earlier, to visit Proteus and tell him he was quitting his exalted position. When the two go drinking in Homestead, Finnerty decides to stay with Rev. Lasher, a member of the Ghost Shirt Society. Paul leaves Finnerty in the Homestead bar, where he is the only one to manually play the player piano, the central image of the text. Finnerty eventually joins the neo-Luddite revolutionary organization. Paul saw the stark differences between Finnerty and himself and often wondered about the comparative depth of his friend's innate intelligence.* (*PP* 31:L7-14) Paul envied **Finnerty**'s mind, for **Finnerty** could be anything he wanted to be, and be brilliant at it. Whatever the times might have called for, **Finnerty** would have been among the best. If this had been the age of music, **Finnerty** would have been, and in fact was, a top-flight pianist—or he might have been an architect or physician or writer. With inhuman intuition, **Finnerty** could sense the basic principles and motives of almost any human work, not just engineering. *It is Finnerty who balks at Kroner's laundry list of the technocrats' material accomplishments by reminding everyone that at the same time* dope addiction, alcoholism, and suicide went up proportionately. . . . And organized vice and divorce and juvenile delinquency, all parallel the growth of the use of vacuum tubes (*PP* 47:L7-8, 12-13).

Finnerty is responsible for the shame brought to Fred Berringer during Paul's championship match with Checker Charley. He noticed some of the robot's connections were loose but failed to reveal this to Berringer. This was his way of asserting the dominance of people over machines. Later, when Paul is a Ghost Shirt captive in the underground shelter, Finnerty tells him their sole purpose is to "get back to basic values, basic virtues! . . . Men doing men's work, women doing women's work. People doing people's thinking" (*PP* 259:L4-5). *These sentiments are far removed from the days when he, Paul, and Lawson Shepherd devised a machine to replicate the labor of lathe operator Rudy Hertz.*

Finnerty, Noyes. *In* God Bless You, Mr. Rosewater, *Noyes Finnerty swept floors in the Rosewater Volunteer Fire Department. Despite the glory brought by centering the 1933 and 1934 undefeated Noah Rosewater Memorial High School basketball teams, he was better known for strangling to death his unfaithful sixteen-year-old wife in 1934. Eliot Rosewater managed to arrange parole from his life sentence after reading about the case in back issues of* The Rosewater County Clarion Call. *Noyes never thanked Eliot. Drawing on his prison experience and his own criminal neuroses, Finnerty diagnoses Eliot's dissociative split to Charley Warmergram.* (*GBR* 188:L28) **Noyes Finnerty** spoke up. "All he hears is the big click." He came forward for a closer examination of Eliot. His approach was not sympathetic. It was clinical. Eliot's response was clinical, too, as though a nice doctor were shining a bright light in his eyes, looking for something. "He heard that *click*, man. Man, did he ever hear that *click*... It ain't a thing that happens just in prison. In prison, though, you get to listening for things more and more. You stay there long enough, you go blind, you're all ears. The click is one thing you listen for... You get to know a man, and down deep there's something bothering him bad, and maybe you never find out what it is, but it's what makes him do like he does, it's what makes him look like he's got secrets in his eyes. And you tell him, 'Calm down, calm down, take it easy now.' Or you ask him, 'How come you keep doing the same crazy things over and over again, when you know they're just going to get you in trouble again?' Only you know there's no sense arguing with him, on account of it's the thing inside that's making him go. It says, 'Jump,' he jumps. It says, 'Steal,' he steals. It says, 'Cry,' he cries. Unless he dies young, though, or unless he gets everything all his way and nothing big goes wrong, that thing inside of him is going to run down like a wind-up toy. You're working in the prison laundry next to this man. You've known him twenty years. You're working along, and all of a sudden you hear this *click* from him. You turn to look at him. He's stopped working. He's all calmed down. He looks real dumb. He looks real sweet. You look in his eyes, and the secrets are gone. He can't even tell you his own name right then. He goes back to work, but he'll never be the same. That thing that bothered him so will never click on again. It's dead, it's *dead*. And that part of that man's life where he had to be a certain crazy way, that's *done!*"

Firehouse Harris (see **Herbert Foster**).

The First District Court of Thankyou. *Eliot Rosewater was instrumental in securing the prison release of Noyes Finnerty, once the center on the championship Noah Rosewater Memorial High School basketball team. Finnerty was serving a life sentence for strangling his sixteen year old wife in 1934. Vonnegut points out that Finnerty's cynicism and lack of gratitude was a common experience.* (*GBR* 187:L8-9) He *(Eliot)* was used to ingratitude. One of his favorite Kilgore Trout books dealt with ingratitude and nothing else. It was called, ***The First District Court of Thankyou***, which was a court you could take people to, if you felt they hadn't been properly grateful for something you had done. If the defendant lost his case, the court gave him a choice between thanking the plaintiff in public, or going into solitary confinement on bread and water for a month. According to Trout, eighty per cent of those convicted chose the black hole.

Fishbein, Mrs. *Code-named X-229, Mrs Fishbein is the seamstress sewing together all the ghost shirts for the rebellious forces in* Player Piano. *In stark contrast to the mass production techniques in the rest of society, Mrs. Fishbein has already prepared 758 shirts before her developing cataracts put her six weeks behind in production.*

Fitzgerald, Bernard. *A distant relative of John F. Kennedy's (they had a common great-grandfather) Fitzgerald is the eighty-year-old Roman Catholic priest responsible for saving six young Kanka-bono girls, in* Galápagos. *They are eventually impregnated with the sperm of Captain von Kleist through the scientific know-how of Mary Hepburn.*

Flammer, Lou. *Flammer is the fat, thirtyish publicity director at the Ilium Works of the Federal Apparatus Corporation in the short story "Deer in the Works." He is an ideal company man, prepared at a moment's notice to lecture visiting Boy Scouts about the positive values scouting imparts to young men in preparation for becoming corporate managers (fifty-six percent of the managers were Eagle scouts). Earlier in his life, Flammer became disenchanted with the financial headaches of running his own weekly newspaper. He also grew disappointed trying to save parts of his community which seemed fated to destruction by the sprawling corporations. By selling out to a national chain, something his protege David Potter was contemplating, Flammer prospered and consistently hawked the positive company line. It is Flammer who assigns Potter the task of covering the deer in the Works.*

Flemming, Pearl. *One of the Rosewater County citizens who was physically afflicted (she needed crutches to get around), but was apparently cured by Eliot, in* God Bless You, Mr. Rosewater.

Flemming, Willard and Mary (see also **James Wait** and **Mary Hepburn**). *In* Galápagos, *James Wait traveled with the name Willard Flemming on his fake*

Canadian passport. As Flemming, he proposed to Mary Hepburn, who was posing as Mary Kaplan. Mary agreed to marry "Willard" when he was near death on the Bahía de Darwin. *Married by Captain Von Kleist, "Flemming" died only minutes after the wedding.*

"Flocka Butt" (see **Dr. Stewart Rawlings Mott**).

Florio, General Lucas. *In* Hocus Pocus, *the Schenectady, New York, commander of the Rainbow Division, the 42nd Division of the National Guard, who was ordered to quell the prison riot in Athena. His division was all white due to the resegregation of the military, though there were some Orientals classified as Honorary White People. Florio drafted Eugene Debs Hartke to act as the new warden when the riot was silenced. Florio later claimed Tarkington College for the government in order to use the college's and Scipio's state-of-the-art sanitary facilities. Despite Florio's respect for Hartke, political hacks looking for a scapegoat and an opportunity to turn the uprising to their political advantage forced him to arrest Hartke for insurrection.*

folk society (see also **extended family**). (*WFG* 177:L5 *Address to the National Institute of Arts and Letters, 1971*) Dr. Redfield is dead now. . . . While he lived, he had in his head a lovely dream which he called "The **Folk Society**." He published this dream in *The American Journal of Sociology*, Volume 52, 1947, pages 293 through 308. *Vonnegut goes on to paraphrase Redfield's idea by stating that folk societies* were so small that everybody knew everybody well, and associations lasted for life. The members communicated intimately with one another, and very little with anybody else.
(*WFG* 178:L13-14, 26, 28-29 *Address to the National Institute of Arts and Letters, 1971*) Moreover [Dr. Redfield goes on], in the **folk society** much besides human beings is treated personally. The pattern of behavior which is first suggested by the inner experience of the individual—his wishes, fears, sensitivities, and interests of all sorts—is projected into all objects with which he comes in contact. Thus nature, too, is treated personally; the elements, the features of the landscape, the animals, and especially anything in the environment which by its appearance or behavior suggests the attributes of mankind—to all these are attributed qualities of the human person. [I *(Vonnegut)* stop quoting now.]

And I say to you that we are full of chemicals which require us to belong to **folk societies**, or failing that, to feel lousy all the time. We are chemically engineered to live in **folk societies**, just as fish are chemically engineered to live in clean water—and there aren't any **folk societies** for us anymore.
(*PS* 211:L23, 28 *Religion*) "Channing grew up in what the late anthropologist Robert Redfield called a **folk society**, a relatively isolated community of like-thinking friends and relatives, a stable extended family of considerable size. Redfield said that we were all descended from persons who lived in such

societies, and that we were likely to hanker to live in one ourselves from time to time. A **folk society**, in his imagination and in our imaginations, too, is an ideal scheme within which people can take really good care of one another, can share fairly, and can distribute honors to one and all."

(*FWD* 122:L12, 13) When I studied anthropology long ago at the University of Chicago, my most famous professor was Dr. Robert Redfield. The idea that all societies evolved through similar, predictable stages on their way to higher (Victorian) civilization, from polytheism to monotheism, for instance, or from the tom-tom to the symphony orchestra, had by then been ridiculed into obscurity. It was generally agreed that there was no such ladder as cultural evolution. But Dr. Redfield said in effect, "Wait just a minute." He said that he could describe to every fair-minded person's satisfaction one (and only one) stage every society had passed through or would pass through. He called this inevitable stage and his essay on it "**The Folk Society**."

First of all, a **Folk Society** was isolated, and in an area it considered organically its own. It grew from that soil and no other. The break between the living and the dead was indistinct, and bonds of kinship crisscrossed every which way. There was such general agreement as to what life was all about and how people shouldbelieve in every conceivable situation that very little was debatable.

(*FWD* 126:L23-24) A **Folk Society** deficiency (hereafter "FSD") quite often does *(have a chemical imbalance)*. The trouble begins when a person suffering from FSD stops thinking, in order to become a member of an artificial extended family which happens to be crazy. The homicidal "family" of Charles Manson springs to mind. Or what about the cult of the Reverend Jim Jones in Guyana, whose members on his advice ("Tonight you will be with me in Paradise") fed the kids Kool-Aid laced with cyanide and then drank it themselves. *See also: WFG—Address to the National Institute of Arts and Letters, 1971* 177:L23,27; 178:L9; 179:L4,10,19-22,30-31; 180:L20; *PS—Self-Interview* 116:L24-25; *PS—Religion* 212:L3-4,10,12,21,28; *FWD* 123:L3,6,25; 124:L19,27,33-34; 126:L6,7; 127:L6; 156:L24.

foma (see also **Bokononism**). (*CC inscription page*) Nothing in this book is true.

"Live by the ***foma**** that make you brave and kind and healthy and happy."
The Books of Bokonon. I:5

**Harmless untruths*

(*CC* 156:L33-36, 157:L1-10) I learned some things, but they were scarcely helpful. I learned of the Bokononist cosmogony, for instance, wherein *Borasisi*, the sun, held *Pabu*, the moon, in his arms, and hoped that *Pabu* would bear him a fiery child.

But poor *Pabu* gave birth to children that were cold, that did not burn; and *Borasisi* threw them away in disgust. These were the planets, who circled their terrible father at a safe distance.

Then poor *Pabu* herself was cast away, and she went to live with her favorite child, which was Earth. Earth was *Pabu*'s favorite because it had people on it; and the people looked up at her and loved her and sympathized.

And what opinion did Bokonon hold of his own cosmogony? "***Foma!*** Lies!" he wrote. "A pack of ***foma!***"

(*CC* 214:L23-31) I turned to *The Books of Bokonon*, still sufficiently unfamiliar with them to believe that they contained spiritual comfort somewhere. I passed quickly over the warning on the title page of *The First Book:*

"Don't be a fool! Close this book at once! It is nothing but **foma**!"

Foma, of course, are lies.

(*WFG* xv:5 *Preface*) DEAR READER: The title of this book is composed of three words from my novel *Cat's Cradle*. A *wampeter* is an object around which the lives of many otherwise unrelated people may revolve. The Holy Grail would be a case in point. **Foma** are harmless untruths, intended to comfort simple souls. An example: "Prosperity is just around the corner." A *granfalloon* is a proud and meaningless association of human beings. Taken together, the words form as good an umbrella as any for this collection of some of the reviews and essays I have written, a few of the speeches I have made. Most of my speeches were never written down.

Ford, Henry. *In* Hocus Pocus, *Eugene Debs Hartke credits the famed industrialist with accepting the virulently anti-Semitic* Protocols of the Elders of Zion *to the extent that he provided financial support for its publication in the United States.*

Ford's involvement with publishing the forged tract is well delineated in Carol Gelderman's Henry Ford: The Wayward Capitalist *(The Dial Press, 1981). In 1919 Ford purchased the Dearborn* Independent, *a small rural weekly newspaper at the time. Ford appointed his friend and fellow anti-Semite Ernest Liebold general manager. The two men shared the belief that international Jewish bankers, particularly the Rothschilds and Warburgs, manipulated geopolitical relations for their own financial benefit. In 1920 the Dearborn* Independent *published a series entitled "The International Jew: The World's Problem." Soon after the series went into production, Liebold established a private detective agency dedicated to finding scandal in the private lives of Jews or suspected Jews and to the acquisition of anti-Semitic writings. The agency acquired* The Protocols of the Wise Men of Zion *in 1920, and had them translated for publication in the* Independent. *Despite the fact that international scholars had already established the text's false and fabricated background, excerpts were continually published through December 1921.*

Though the Independent *was a small rural weekly when Ford bought it, he convinced his automobile dealers to sell subscriptions to their customers. Ford's* Independent *quickly grew to three-quarters of a million subscribers while the anti-semitic articles were appearing in the paper.*

Ford, Rose Aldrich. (*Slap* 142:L13) Somewhere in there I *(Wilbur Swain)* married an equally wealthy woman, actually a third cousin of mine, whose maiden name was **Rose Aldrich Ford**. She was very unhappy, because I did not love her, and because I would never take her anywhere. I have never been good at loving. We had a child, Carter Paley Swain, whom I also failed to love.

Fort Belvoir. (*Blue* 206:L31) I *(Rabo Karabekian)* was a master sergeant at **Fort Belvoir** when I read of the deaths of Dan Gregory and Fred Jones in Egypt.

Fort Benjamin Harrison. *Located outside Indianapolis, it was there that Roland Barry in* God Bless You, Mr. Rosewater *suffers a nervous breakdown ten minutes after being sworn in when he is ordered to take a shower with 100 other men. It is also the location where Rabo Karabekian in* Bluebeard *has an operation repairing the orbital socket around the eye he lost when wounded. Rabo chose not to endure all the surgery required to make the socket hold a glass eye, so he is left wearing an eye patch.*

Fort Benning. (*WFG* 160:L12 *Address to Graduating Class at Bennington College, 1970*) I demand that the administration of Bennington College establish an R.O.T.C. unit here. It is imperative the we learn more about military men, since they have so much of our money and power now. It is a great mistake to drive military men from college campuses and into ghettos like **Fort Benning** and Fort Bragg. Make them do what they do so proudly in the midst of men and women who are educated.

In Deadeye Dick, *Felix Waltz went for his basic training at Fort Benning, Georgia, before Rudy killed Mrs. Metzger. While at Fort Benning, Felix never found out about the tragedy.*

In Bluebeard, *Rabo Karabekian is awarded the Soldier's Medal for saving the lives of two soldiers while an instructor at Fort Benning.* (*Blue* 223:L4) In 1941, I was giving a course in camouflage techniques to officer candidates at **Fort Benning**, Georgia. I saw a barracks on fire, and I gave the alarm, and then went in twice, without regard for my own safety, and carried out two unconscious enlisted men.

Fort Bragg. *The army base from which Private Francis J. Thompson was abducted only to become Sergeant Brackman after his memory was wiped clean by Rumfoord's Martian forces in* Sirens of Titan.

In "Long Walk To Forever," Newt (not Hoenikker) goes A.W.O.L. from Fort Bragg to be with his best friend Catharine. He came to realize he loved her and left Fort Bragg to propose marriage, only to find out she was engaged to someone else.

In Breakfast of Champions, *Francine Pefko, Dwayne Hoover's secretary, lived at Fort Bragg after her husband Robert was graduated from West Point and went to parachute school in South Carolina.*

In Hocus Pocus, *while Eugene Debs Hartke was in Vietnam, his family lived at Fort Bragg. Eventually his wife moved the family so they could live at her mother's house while she studied physical therapy at Johns Hopkins University.*

Fort Jesus. *The training camp for the soldiers of San Lorenzo in* Cat's Cradle.

"Fortitude" (1968). *The short play in which medical genius Dr. Norbert Frankenstein uses an advanced computer set-up to mechanically control the bio-chemical status of Sylvia Lovejoy, the one-hundred-year-old billionaire's widow. All that remains of Sylvia is her head, which sits atop miles of electrical cables and tubes. She longs to kill herself but her mechanical arms are built to guard against such an incident. Her hairdresser takes pity on her and smuggles a gun to her room, but because she can't kill herself she instead shoots Dr. Frankenstein. His wounds would be fatal if not for the quick-thinking medical team, which removes his head and attaches it to a device similar to Sylvia's. Such was his wish if his own death were imminent, along with the playing of the Jeanette MacDonald-Nelson Eddy recording of "Ah, Sweet Mystery of Life" upon waking next to Sylvia.*

Fortune, John. *In* Deadeye Dick, *John Fortune the dairy farmer was Otto Waltz's best friend when both men were in their twenties. Fortune served as Otto's best man at his wedding. While helping Otto do some household construction, John dropped an oak timber on Otto's foot and the resulting injury kept him from military service in World War I. John went to war and received numerous medals. Like Waltz, Fortune was also of German heritage and his name was an anglicized version of the German word for luck—*cluck.

In 1916 Fortune was among the group of hunters (including Otto Waltz, Police Chief Morissey, his son Bucky, and August Gunther) when Chief Morissey's shotgun accidentally fired and shot off the head of August Gunther. All conspired to keep the killing a secret. John Fortune deeply disagreed with Otto Waltz's affection for Adolf Hitler and this caused an irrevocable split in their friendship.

After Fortune's wife passed away, he cast about for something to keep himself going. He became deeply influenced by James Hilton's 1933 imaginary Shangri-La as described in Lost Horizon. *He went to Asia, searched for tranquility, and died in 1938. His last words to those he left behind in Midland City were recorded from his last postcard and printed in the* Bugle-Observer: "To all my friends and enemies in the buckeye state. Come on over. There's room for everybody in Shangri-La" (*DD* 120:L3-5). *The message didn't reach Midland City until 1944 when the adventurer Dr. Brokenshire got around to mailing the note along with a map of Fortune's burial place.*

Young Rudy Waltz, only six when Fortune died in Nepal, grew up thinking this was the most admirable person in Midland City and he wrote an essay to that effect for his teacher Mrs. Shoup. She was so impressed by it that Rudy forever thought of doing more with the story. Eventually he turned it into the play "Katmandu," and in 1959 won the Caldwell Foundation playwriting contest. The prize was a professional production of the play at the Theatre de Lys in Greenwich Village (the same theater which produced Vonnegut's "Wanda June").

"The Foster Portfolio" (1951) (also **Herebert and Alma Foster**—and **Firehouse Harris**). *Herbert is the secretly wealthy working man (two jobs almost all the time) who struggles with living dichotomously as the pious, reverent, and committed family man while sneaking away three nights a week to play piano jazz in a low-class local bar as did his unfaithful and deserting father. The family was supported by the grandfather after Herbert's father left. Grandfather Foster left Herbert an estate of stocks and bonds worth $850,000. However, Herbert kept their wealth a secret from his wife Alma for fear it would disrupt the honest, hardworking life they created, one which pleases them to earn all their smallest pleasures. For her part, Alma was dutiful and respectful of all the effort Herbert put into earning a living, playing piano for the church choir and volunteering in the fire department. She was totally unaware of Herbert's secret life.* (*MH* 57:L20 *The Foster Portfolio*) My client, **Herbert Foster**, hadn't had a new suit in three years; he had never owned more than one pair of shoes at a time. He worried about payments on his secondhand car, and ate tuna and cheese instead of meat, because meat was too expensive. His wife made her own clothes, and those of Herbert, Jr., and the curtains and slipcovers—all cut from the same bargain bolt. **The Fosters** were going through hell, trying to choose between new tires or retreads for the car; and television was something they had to go two doors down the street to watch. Determinedly, they kept within the small salary Herbert made as a bookkeeper for a wholesale grocery house.

(*MH* 65:L29-38, 66:L6-15, 29-36 *The Foster Portfolio*) And then **Herbert Foster**, looking drab and hunted, picked his way through the crowd. His expression was one of disapproval, of a holy man in Babylon. He was oddly stiff-necked and held his arms at his sides as he pointedly kept from brushing against anyone or from meeting any of the gazes that fell upon him. There was no question that being in the place was absolute, humiliating hell for him.

I called to him, but he paid no attention. There was no communicating with him. **Herbert** was in a near coma of see-no-evil, speak-no-evil, hear-no-evil. . . .

Herbert dusted off the piano bench with his handkerchief, and sat down gingerly. He took a cigarette from his breast pocket and lighted it. And then the cigarette started to droop slowly from his lips; and, as it drooped, **Herbert** hunched over the keyboard and his eyes narrowed as though he were focusing on something beautiful on a faraway horizon.

Startlingly, **Herbert Foster** disappeared. In his place sat an excited stranger, his hands poised like claws. Suddenly he struck, and a spasm of dirty, low-down, gorgeous jazz shook the air, a hot, clanging wraith of the twenties. . . . Nobody could do anything for **Herbert**. **Herbert** already had what he wanted. He had had it long before the inheritance or I intruded. He had the respectability his mother had hammered into him. But just as priceless as that was an income not quite big enough to go around. It left him no alternative but—in the holy names of wife, child, and home—to play piano in a dive, and breathe smoke, and drink gin, to be **Firehouse Harris**, his father's son, three nights out of seven.

Foust, Senator Warren. *When the power of dynamopsychism is revealed, Senator Foust seeks federal funds to screen the population for men who may possess the potential weapon, declaring:* He who rules the Barnhouse Effect rules the world! (*MH* 158:L16-17 *Report on the Barnhouse Effect*).

Francis X. Donovan Post of the American Legion in Brookline. *The fictitious name Campbell gives the American Legion Post to which Bernard B. O'Hare belongs and where Kraft/Potapov sends news of Campbell's whereabouts, in* Mother Night.

Frank, Anne. *The martyred author of* The Diary of Anne Frank. *Vonnegut uses a line from her diary as the opening inscription of* Galápagos*—a story about humanity's bizarre and cruel mishandling of technology, which brings an end to the human species as we know it.* In spite of everything, I still believe people are really good at heart. *—**Anne Frank*** (1929-1944)

Frankenstein, Dr. Norbert. *The sixty-five-year-old physician in the play "Fortitude" who has kept Sylvia alive for thirty-six years (and seventy-eight operations). The remarkable aspect is that only Sylvia's head survives, connected to all sorts of pumps, filters, and electronic gear. He is busy showing Dr. Elbert Little the marvels he has wrought through the unique combination of his medical and technological expertise. Frankenstein is determined to keep her alive for all eternity. He limited the range of motion on Sylvia's mechanical arm so she couldn't kill herself. When she is smuggled a gun just for that purpose and realizes she can't commit suicide, she shoots Frankenstein instead. He is saved by Dr. Little who connects Frankenstein's head to a second set of identical apparatus next to Sylvia's bed. For as long as technologically feasible, the two bodiless wonders will remain alive subject to the amphetamine- and barbiturate-induced states prescribed by the medical team.*

Franklin, Benjamin. *Vonnegut uses a quote attributed to Franklin as a counterpoint to traditional wisdom in showing how Captain von Kleist's bumbling actually saves mankind.* (*Gal* 143:L26-30, 144:L1-12) One emergency plan the Captain didn't consider there in the shower was that he himself take full charge of the ship, with only Mary Hepburn to help him—and that he run it aground on Santa Rosalia, which would become the cradle of all humankind.

Here is a quotation well known to Mandarax:

> *A little neglect may breed great mischief . . . for want of a nail the shoe was lost; for want of a shoe the horse was lost; for want of a horse the rider was lost.*
>
> **Benjamin Franklin** (1706-1790)

Yes, and a little neglect can breed good news just as easily. For want of Hernando Cruz aboard the *Bahía de Darwin*, humanity was saved. Cruz would never have run the ship aground on Santa Rosalia.

Frascati, Marion and Lou. *Marion and Lou were best friends with Edgar Rice Burroughs Hagstrohm and his wife Wanda in* Player Piano. *One month after Lou passed away Edgar and Marion began an affair. For Hagstrohm, the guilt of his secret life and the absolute dreariness of life on the assembly line pushed him over the edge. One night he cut up his Chicago home with a blowtorch and ran naked to Marion's house, imploring her to flee to the woods with him. She refused and he eluded police, escaping into the bird sanctuary bordering their housing development.*

Free American Corps. *The creation of Howard W. Campbell in* Mother Night, *the organization is also mentioned in* Slaughterhouse-Five *when Campbell makes a recruitment trip to Dresden, arriving in time to take cover with the American POWs in the meat-locker during the firebombing.* (*MN* 71:L20-29) The **Free American Corps** was a Nazi daydream—a daydream of a fighting unit composed mainly of American prisoners of war. It was to be a volunteer organization. It was to fight only on the Russian front. It was to be a high-morale fighting machine, motivated by a love of western civilization and a dread of the Mongol hordes.

When I call this unit a Nazi daydream, incidentally, I am suffering an attack of schizophrenia—because the idea of the **Free American Corps** began with me. I suggested its creation, designed its uniforms and insignia, wrote its creed.

free thinker, **freethinker**, **free-thinker** (see also **Clemens Vonnegut**). *Vonnegut's perspectives on religion are due in large measure to the German Freethinker legacy passed down from his great-grandfather Clemens Vonnegut. Among his fictional characters, Vonnegut calls Ed Finnerty a freethinker* (Player Piano)*, Hartke's grandfather Wills, and Hermann and Sophia Shultz* (Hocus Pocus). *Beatrice Rumfoord* (Sirens) *dreamed of a freethinking companion.* (*PS* 193:L1 *Religion*) And it is to suggest to her *(Jane Vonnegut)* and to some others why it was painful that I chose for this book's epigraph a

quotation from a thin book, *Instruction in Morals*, published in 1900 and written by my **Free Thinker** great-grandfather Clemens Vonnegut, then seventy-six years old: "Whoever entertains liberal views and chooses a consort that is captured by superstition risks his liberty and his happiness."
(PS 235:L4 *Children)* MY first wife and both my daughters are born-again Christians now—working white magic through rituals and prayers. That's all right. I would be a fool to say that the **free thinker** ideas of Clemens Vonnegut remain as enchanting and encouraging as ever—not after the mortal poisoning of the planet, not after two world wars, with more to come.
(*HP* 175:L17) I *(Eugene Debs Hartke)* have looked up who the **Freethinkers** were. They were members of a short-lived sect, mostly of German descent, who believed, as did my Grandfather Wills, that nothing but sleep awaited good and evil persons alike in the Afterlife, that science had proved all organized religions to be baloney, that God was unknowable, and that the greatest use a person could make of his or her lifetime was to improve the quality of life for all in his or her community.
(*FWD* 157:L16-17) "There was a newspaper humorist named Kin Hubbard in my hometown of Indianapolis, where my ancestors were **Freethinkers** and then Unitarians or not much of anything as far as religious labels go. Kin Hubbard attended a graduation ceremony out there in Indiana. He commented afterward on the graduation address to the departing seniors. He said it might be better to spread out the really important stuff over four years instead of saving it all up until the very end.
(*FWD* 238:L5) I am a fourth generation German American religious skeptic ("**Freethinker**"). Like my essentially puritanical forebears, I believe that God has so far been unknowable and hence unservable, hence the highest service one can perform is to his or her community, whose needs are quite evident. I believe that virtuous behavior is trivialized by carrot-and-stick schemes, such as promises of highly improbable rewards or punishments in an improbable afterlife. (The punishment for counterfeiting in Henry VIII's reign, incidentally, was being boiled alive in public.) The Bible is a useful starting point for discussions with crowds of American strangers, since so many of us know at least a little something about it. It has the added virtue of having for contributors at least two geniuses Moses and Christ. *See also: PP* 41:L35; *ST* 249:L11; *PS—Roots* 35:L26; *PS—Religion* 210:L18; *HP* 175:illustration; *FWD* 200:L6,10,18,24.

free will, free-willed. (see also ***Now It Can Be Told***) (*SL5* 74:L19-20, 24, 26-27) "You sound to me as though you don't believe in **free will**," said Billy Pilgrim.

"If I hadn't spent so much time studying Earthlings," said the Tralfamadorian, "I wouldn't have any idea what was meant by '**free will**.' I've visited thirty-one inhabited planets in the universe, and I have studied reports on one hundred more. Only on Earth is there any talk of **free will**."

(*BC* 15:L4, 13) Only Dwayne Hoover had **free will**. *This is the message Dwayne interpreted from Kilgore Trout's story* Now It Can Be Told.

Trout did not expect to be believed. He put the bad ideas into a science-fiction novel, and that was where Dwayne found them. The book wasn't addressed to Dwayne alone. Trout had never heard of Dwayne when he wrote it. It was addressed to anybody who happened to open it up. It said to simply anybody, in effect, "Hey guess what: You're the only creature with **free will**. How does that make you feel?" And so on. *See also: PP* 276:L18; *ST* 116:L20-21; 249:L18; *MN* 197:L1; *CC* 155:L34-35; *BC* 58:L3; 73:L25-26; 173:L26; 253:L19; 256:L30; 269:L32; *HP* 267:L13.

Freeman, Sally. *Felix Waltz's high school girlfriend in* Deadeye Dick *who dumped him just before the senior prom in favor of basketball captain Steve Adams. Instead, Felix asked the beautiful but socially outcast Celia Hildreth. What should have been a proud moment for Felix and Sally turned into one of the most shameful for Felix and Celia when they were forced to endure the shenanigans of Otto Waltz.*

French, Mary Alice. *After the judges at the Ohio State Science Fair discovered that Eugene Debs Hartke had next to nothing to do with his crystallography display, they awarded first place to Mary Alice French for her original crystallography display. Though the Mayor of Cincinnati declared a "Mary Alice French Day," she lost in the national competition held in Washington, D.C. Hartke's revaluation of his life causes him some pain when considering the impact he and his father may have had on Mary Alice's life.* (*HP* 47:L16) I have to wonder now, with so much time in which to think about people I've hurt, if Father and I didn't indirectly help set up **Mary Alice French** for her terrible disappointment in Washington. There is a good chance that the judges in Cleveland gave her First Prize because of the moral contrast between her exhibit and ours.

Friedmann, Tuvia. *Howard Campbell writes his* Mother Night *memoirs at the behest of Tuvia Friedmann, Director of the Haifa Institute for the Documentation of War Criminals. Friedmann promises Campbell all the help he needs while he sits in his Old Jerusalem jail cell. He even provides Campbell with a Third Reich era typewriter complete with the twin lightning bolts of the S.S., the Schutzstaffel.*

fubar. (*Blue* 20:L1) During that war we had a word for extreme man-made disorder which was ***fubar***, an acronym for "fucked up beyond all recognition." Well—the whole planet is now **fubar** with postwar miracles, but, back in the early 1960s, I *(Rabo Karabekian)* was one of the first persons to be totally wrecked by one—an acrylic wall-paint whose colors, according to advertisements of the day, would ". . . outlive the smile on the 'Mona Lisa.'"

Fuller, Norman. *In the short story "Miss Temptation," Corporal Norman Fuller has just returned from service in the Korean War and is bitter about almost everything in his life. When he sees Susanna, a breathtakingly beautiful actress visiting the rural community to perform in a summer stock theater group, Fuller loudly shames her as a temptress. In reality, Susanna is tempting no one; Fuller sees in her all his disappointing experiences with women. He fails to sense she is as full of feelings as he, and she prepares to leave town and not go on with the theater group. When he is sent to her apartment to deliver her newspaper, Susanna shames him by showing her how hurt she was by his outrageous conduct and by others like him who never seem to appreciate that beautiful people are frequently degraded by those who fail to approach and learn how normal they are. Fuller apologizes by escorting Susanna through downtown, a sign of public penance.*

funnel, **funnel-shaped** (see also **blue tunnel**). (*ST* 15:L15-16) *Infundibulum (infun-dib-u-lum) is what the ancient Romans like Julius Caesar and Nero called a* ***funnel****. If you don't know what a* ***funnel*** *is, get Mommy to show you one. (From Dr. Cyril Hall's* A Child's Cyclopedia of Wonders and Things to Do.*)*

(*Gal* 165:L30) He didn't tell Wait about it, but his big brain put on quite a movie for him while he was unconscious. It showed him one end of a writhing piece of blue tubing, about five meters in diameter, big enough to drive a truck through, and lit up inside like the **funnel** of a tornado. It did not roar like a tornado, however.

(*WJ* 145:L24) MILDRED I never saw a tornado when I was alive, and I grew up in Oklahoma. There's this big, black, **funnel-shaped** cloud. Sounds like a railroad train without the whistle. I had to come to Heaven to see a thing like that.

G

Gabriel (see **Archangel Gabriel**).

Galápagos (1985). *At the close of* Deadeye Dick, *the resurrected spirit of Will Fairchild is left to walk the plains of Midland City. Vonnegut seems to have so well liked the idea of a risen phantom in search of survival that this next novel is narrated by another phantom, the decapitated spirit of Vietnam veteran and deserter Leon Trout, son of science fiction writer Kilgore Trout. Leon writes his tale one million years in the future about the time back in 1986 when Homo sapiens were embarking on their next evolutionary epoch. Man's newest development returned him to the sea in a manner resembling sea lions and, just as importantly, man's capacity for reason declined and gave way to instinct. Though not explicitly stated, the narrative assumption is that man had managed to temporarily destroy the environment to the extent that it would no longer sustain humanity in its present form. Though offered the opportunity to step through the blue tunnel to the afterlife and reunite with his father, Leon decides to roam the earth to satisfy his curiosity about what life is all about.*

Not surprisingly, Vonnegut traces the root cause of humanity's ills to our large and well-developed brains. (*Gal* 66:L22-28) That cumbersome computer could hold so many contradictory opinions on so many different subjects all at once, and switch from one opinion or subject to another one so quickly, that a discussion between a husband and wife under stress could end up like a fight between blindfolded people wearing roller skates.

According to the ensuing scheme of existence, which Leon traces back to an aborted cruise bound for the Galápagos Islands, artificial constructs of wealth and twentieth-century man's belief in the perfectibility and preferability of machines in place of man yield to a more harmonious placement of the species within the great chain of being. (*Gal* 122:L31, 123:L1-3) People have no such illusions today. They learn very early what kind of a world this really is, and it is a rare adult indeed who hasn't seen a careless sibling or parent eaten alive by a killer whale or shark.

In refusing immediate admission to the afterlife, Leon seeks the vision afforded Tralfamadorians in Sirens *and* Slaughterhouse*:* (*Gal* 253:10-17) I had chosen to be a ghost because the job carried with it, as a fringe benefit, license to read minds, to learn the truth of people's pasts, to see through walls, to be many places all at once, to learn in depth how this or that situation had come to be structured as it was, and to have access to all human knowledge.

But he hadn't really learned more by sticking around for an extra million years. His own life experiences should have been enough to satisfy his curiosity (particularly as part of a My Lai-type war atrocity and his unwitting co-conspirator status with his father in driving his mother from their home). However, in the new scheme, man no longer suffers the pain of living with the mental associations of community. Less gray matter means less unhappiness. No pain—the comforting final realization of Alice Vonnegut as she waited for death to claim her (see *MH* xiv:L7).

Despite Vonnegut's insistence that humanity will eventually destroy itself, the evolutionary leap into the water (a move which saves the species from annihilation) is made possible by the product of man's destructive will. The sperm of the nearly sexless German-American Captain Adolf von Kleist is used to artificially inseminate Akiko Hiroguchi, the daughter of an Hiroshima bombing victim whose genes mutated due to radiation exposure. Vonnegut seems to be saying that within the seeds of our destruction lays the promise of our salvation.

Galápagos Islands. *In the novel named for the islands made famous by Charles Darwin, the Galápagos Islands become the center of man's next great evolutionary step as they evolve into small-brained sea lion type creatures. This is made possible by the artificial insemination of the genetically deformed daughter of an Hiroshima bombing victim with the sperm from a German-American sea captain.*

Galen, Vermont. *In* Slapstick, *the town closest to the mansion of Professor Elihu Swain, where Wilbur and Eliza were raised by local people and out of their parents' sight.*

gallows humor (see **humor**).

Garland, Dorothy Daffodil-7. *Of all the thousands in attendance when Wilbur Swain goes to Indianapolis for a Daffodil family reunion, this eleven-year-old black girl wins the drawing to chair the meeting.*

Garr, Vernon and Mary. *Vernon is a mechanic at the Sunoco station next to Dwayne Hoover's Pontiac dealership in* Breakfast of Champions. *Vernon's wife is schizophrenic and thought he was trying to turn her brains into* *plutonium. Vernon and Dwayne are on friendly terms and in an ironic twist, Garr takes solace discussing with Dwayne the problems of living with a schizophrenic; Dwayne is soon to experience his own schizophrenic breakdown.*

Garth, Dr. Fred (and his children **Brud**, **Alice**, and little **Ewing**). *Fred Garth is first introduced as Paul's competition for the Pittsburgh Works position. As competitors for the same position, they are distinctly different characters. While at the Meadows he shares a bunk with Paul and despondently speaks about the affect on him as a parent worrying about his children's performance on the General Classification Tests.* (*PP* 166:L2-8) "It's a trial, though, watching your kids grow up, wondering if they've got what it takes, seeing 'em just about killing themselves before the General Classification Tests, then waiting for the grades—" The sentence ended in a sigh. "I've just gone through that GCT business with my oldest, Brud, and I've got to live through the whole nightmare twice more still, with Alice and little Ewing."
(*PP* 112:L3-18) "**Garth**'s a fine man," said Paul. **Garth** was, too: four-square, desperate to please, and he seemed to have an anthropomorphic image of the corporate personality. **Garth** stood in relation to that image as a lover, and Paul wondered if this prevalent type of relationship had ever been given the consideration it deserved by sexologists. On second thought, he supposed that it had—the general phenomenon of a lover's devotion to the unseen—in studies of nuns' symbolic marriages to Christ. At any rate, Paul had seen **Garth** at various stages of his love affair, unable to eat for anxiety, on a manic crest, moved to maudlin near-crying at recollections of the affair's tender beginnings. In short, **Garth** suffered all the emotional hazards of a perennial game of she-loves-me, she-loves-me-not. To carry out directions from above—an irritating business for Paul—was, for **Garth**, a favor to please a lady.

Paul and Garth eventually share a basement cell in police headquarters along with "a small, elegant young Negro named Harold, who was in jail for petty sabotage." It is there that Paul has Garth confirm that it was he who torched the sacred oak tree at the Meadows. He did it because his son Brud had again done poorly on the GCTs and "cracked up." Garth felt betrayed by the system he had worshipped.

Garu, Krishna (also **Krishna Gatu**). *Among the many Earthlings conscripted for the Army of Mars in* Sirens of Titan, *this Indian typesetter was captured during the invasion of India only after his gun blew up. He later sells trinkets to pilgrims from The Church of God the Utterly Indifferent outside the Rumfoord mansion. He has outstanding warrants in Calcutta for bigamy, pandering, and nonsupport.*

Gatch. *The Gatch brothers (no first names are offered) once worked for the Maritimo Brothers Construction Company in* Deadeye Dick. *One of them had a shoplifting daughter (vaguely remembered by Rudy Waltz as either Mary, Martha, or Marie), who tried to make new friends by making presents of the stolen items. One of the Gatch brothers was working as a floor waxer at the Midland City airport when Celia Hoover collapsed on the runway in a drugged stupor. Gatch went out to get her and returned Celia to her home.*

GCT (General Classification Tests). *The aptitude tests given to young teenagers in* Player Piano. *The results of the tests determined the extent to which one would be allowed to pursue education or career goals. One's entire future was shaped by the test, and it was, therefore, dreaded by most.*

GEFFCo. *First mentioned in* Galápagos *as the primary industry in Ilium and employer of Roy Hepburn, and later in* Bluebeard *as the owner of Rabo Karabekian's ill-fated "Blue Windsor Number Seventeen." Roy's employment with GEFFCo came to an end when the Japanese Matsumoto company was called in to modernize the plant's facilities. Nearly the entire workforce below the management level was laid off. Matsumoto made it possible to run the facility with only twelve workers. With GEFFCo's employment opportunities so severely curtailed, Ilium lost nearly all its young families. The 1986 graduating class of Ilium High School would be its last.*

In Bluebeard, *Karabekian's eight-panel abstract painting was originally purchased by GEFFCo to hang in the lobby of their Park Avenue headquarters. By the time he was notified of the painting's deterioration in the third subbasement of the building, Matsumoto had purchased GEFFCo and renamed the building for themselves.*

Gelhorne, Dr. Francis Eldgrin (also **Gelhorne Enterprises**). *The recipient of numerous honorary doctorates but never one earned by his own academic efforts, Dr. Gelhorne succeeded George Proteus in becoming the second National Industrial, Commercial, Communications, Foodstuffs, and Resources Director. It is he who presents the ruling technocracy's scheme to have Paul Proteus infiltrate the fledgling Ghost Shirt Society. He coined the oft-repeated phrase "God smiles on the Meadows."* (*PP* 196:L7-14) His spherical bulk was enclosed in a double-breasted, dark-blue suit. His single concession to the Meadows' tradition of informality was an unbuttoned collar and the sliding of his necktie knot a fraction of an inch below where it should have been. Though he was seventy, his hair was as thick and black as a twenty-year-old Mexican's. His fatness was turned into something impressive rather than comical by his perpetual I-smell-excrement expression.

The head of the ruling technocracy is an anomaly in that he had none of the qualifications for employment and responsibility programmed into EPICAC's computerized specifications. (*PP* 197:L11-39, 198:L5-10) He had no college degree of any kind, other than bouquets of honorary doctorates that had come to him in his late fifties and sixties.

He'd had nothing to do with industry, in fact, until he was thirty. Before that, he'd pulled a mail-order taxidermy business out of bankruptcy, sold his interest in it, and bought a trailer truck. He'd built his fleet to five trucks when he received a hot market tip, sold his business, invested the proceeds, and tripled his wealth. With this bonanza, he'd bought the largest, yet failing, ice-cream plant in Indianapolis, and put the business in the black inside of a year by building ice-cream routes servicing Indianapolis manufacturing plants during the lunch hour. In another year, he had his trucks carrying sandwiches and coffee along with ice cream. In another year, he was running plant cafeterias all over town, and the ice-cream business had become a minor division of **Gelhorne Enterprises**.

He'd found that many of the manufacturing firms were owned by third- or fourth-generation heirs who, by some seeming law of decay, didn't have the nerve or interest the plants' founders had had. **Gelhorne**, half playfully at first, had offered these heirs advice, and found them amazingly eager to surrender responsibility. He'd bought in, watched and learned, and, discovering nerve was as valuable as special knowledge, he'd become manager and part owner of a dozen small plants.

There he'd come to the attention of Paul's father in Washington, and Paul's father had made **Gelhorne** his general executive manager when the whole economy had been made one flesh. When Paul's father died, **Gelhorne** had taken over.

It could never happen again. The machines would never stand for it.

General Forge and Foundry Company. *The major employer of Ilium in* Cat's Cradle *and* Slaughterhouse-Five. *According to Dr. Asa Breed, Vice-president in charge of the Research Laboratory at General Forge and Franklin Hoenikker's former supervisor, there are more than 30,000 workers on the day shift at the plant. The company was stingy when it came to compensating its scientists for their inventions. They paid a $45 bonus for every patent they produced. In* Slaughterhouse-Five *it is noted that because GF&F has 68,000 employees, Billy Pilgrim and the other optometrists made good money providing all the required safety glasses.*

generation gap. (*WFG* 110:L4 *Why They Read Hesse*) Students of the famous **Generation Gap** might ponder this: Two of the leading characters in *Steppenwolf* are Johann Wolfgang von Goethe (1749-1832) and Wolfgang Amadeus Mozart (1756-1791), who appear as ghosts in dreams.
(*WFG* 179:L20-21 *Address to the National Institute of Arts and Letters, 1971*) The **generation gap** is an argument between those who believe folk societies are still possible and those who know they aren't.

Genesis, **Genesis Gang**. (*ST* 72:L29, 73:L29-30) This comes very close to describing the **genesis** of Magnum Opus. The materials with which Noel Constant built his fortune were hardly more nourishing in themselves than calendar dates and bedsprings. . . .

He took the Gideon Bible that was in his room, and he started with the first sentence in **Genesis**.

The first sentence in **Genesis**, as some people may know, is: "In the beginning God created the heaven and the earth." *Noel Constant divided the sequence of letters as they appeared in the Bible as his investment guide, starting with Genesis.*

(*WFG* xxii:L27 *Preface*) One tip of the string is forever vanishing. Its neighboring loop is forever retreating from extinction. The other end is forever growing. Its neighboring loop is forever pursuing **Genesis**. *This is Vonnegut's sense of the universe, which he depicts* as straight as a string, except for a loop at either end.

(*WFG* 202:L22 *In a Manner That Must Shame God Himself*) And one thing that fascinated me about the Super Realtors' Worship Service on Sunday *(the 1972 Republican National Convention in Miami)* was that Colonel Frank Borman was on the bill. He looked as tired of space opera as Abbie Hoffman was of clowning. He did his bit, which was to read about the Creation from **Genesis**, and that was that.

(*PS* 200:L5 *Religion*) "The Book of **Genesis** is usually taken to be a story about what happened a long time ago. The beginning of it, at least, can also be read as a prophecy of what is going on right now. It may be that Eden is this planet. If that is so, then we are still in it. It may be that we, poisoned by all our knowledge, are still crawling toward the gate. . . ."

The "Genesis Gang" is the nickname given to Rabo Karabekian and all his Abstract Expressionist friends by Marilee Kemp, then the Countess Portomaggiore. (*Blue* 242:L4, 27) She said that we should call ourselves the "**Genesis Gang**," since we were going right back to the beginning, when subject matter had yet to be created. . . .

I have dug one of hers *(Marilee's letters)* from the archives here . . . says that we have failed to paint pictures of nothing after all, that she easily identifies chaos in every canvas. This is a pleasant joke, of course. "Tell that to the rest of the **Genesis Gang**," she says.

geodesic dome. *In the short story "Welcome to the Monkey House," Billy the Poet kidnaps Nancy the suicide parlor hostess and hides her beneath the geodesic dome sheltering the Kennedy Compound Museum in Hyannis Port.*

In Slaughterhouse-Five, *Billy Pilgrim and Montana Wildhack are housed in a geodesic dome on Tralfamadore, which protects them from the cyanide atmosphere of the planet. Billy is later murdered in a Chicago geodesic dome by fellow former POW Paul Lazzaro. At the time of Billy's death, the United States had been Balkanized into twenty small nations,*

Chicago had been hydrogen-bombed by the Chinese, and the geodesic dome provided an artificial atmosphere capable of sustaining life.

German batball. *The national sport of Mars as well as the chief sport of the Army of Mars, a game plyed with particluar excellence by the eight-year-old Chrono, son of Malachi Constant and Beatrice Rumfoord.* (*ST* 139:L13, 20, 28) The game of **German batball** is played with a flabby ball the size of a big honeydew melon. The ball is no more lively than a ten-gallon hat filled with rain water. The game is something like baseball, with a batter striking the ball into a field of opposing players and running around bases; and with the fielders attempting to catch the ball and frustrate the runner. There are, however, only three bases in **German batball**—first, second, and home. And the batter is not pitched to. He places the ball on one fist and strikes the ball with his other fist. And if a fielder succeeds in striking the runner with the ball when the runner is between bases, the runner is deemed *out*, and must leave the playing field at once.

The person responsible for the heavy emphasis on **German batball** on Mars was, of course, Winston Niles Rumfoord, who was responsible for everything on Mars.

(*ST* 140:L1, 7) Howard W. Sams proves in his *Winston Niles Rumfoord, Benjamin Franklin, and Leonardo da Vinci* that **German batball** was the only team sport with which Rumfoord was at all familiar as a child. Sams shows that Rumfoord was taught the game, when a child, by his governess, a Miss Joyce MacKenzie.

Back in Rumfoord's childhood in Newport, a team composed of Rumfoord, Miss MacKenzie, and Earl Moncrief the butler, used to play **German batball** regularly against a team composed of Watanabe Wataru the Japanese gardener, Beverly June Wataru the gardener's daughter, and Edward Seward Darlington the half-wit stable boy. Rumfoord's team invariably won.

Gettysburg Address. *Howard Campbell records in his* Mother Night *memoirs that he was preparing to write a pageant entitled "Last Full Measure," an homage to the German soldier, but the idea was shelved. He told Goebbels the title comes from Lincoln's famous address. When Hitler reads the text of the Gettysburg Address, he writes to Campbell,* Some parts of this . . . almost made me weep. All northern peoples are one in their deep feelings for soldiers. It is perhaps our greatest bond (*MN* 16:L3-5).

Gibney, Peter. *A musical composer and Harvard classmate of Walter Starbuck's who turned on him once Starbuck testified against Leland Clewes. As Starbuck recalls,* **Gibney** sent me a picture postcard, so that my wife and the postman could read the message, too.

"Dear shithead, it said, why don't you crawl back under a damp rock somewhere?" The picture was of the Mona Lisa, with that strange smile of hers (*JB* 122:L27).

"Gilgongo." *The name of the short story Kilgore Trout was imagining while hitchhiking to the Midland City Arts Festival in* Breakfast of Champions. *It was an anticonservation story about a planet where new species were constantly being created. Because the planet was becoming so crowded, the story opens with a party in honor of a man who wiped out a species of panda bears. "Gilgongo" meant extinct in the native language of the planet. The planet was finally overcome by a blanket of life one hundred feet thick.*

Gingiva-Tru and **Viverine**. *Together with Dr. Lomar Horthy, the Reverend Dr. Lionel J.D. Jones co-invented both the gum-simulating substance for false teeth and the embalming fluid. By the time Jones was paroled in 1950 from his conviction for sedition, both inventions dominated their respective markets and made Jones a wealthy man. He earned enough wealth to republish* The White Christian Minuteman *which led him to his fateful meeting with* Mother Night's *Howard Campbell.*

Ginsberg, Allen. *The prominent poet from the Beat Movement whose "bardic improvisations" are largely attributed to his experimentation with hallucinogenic drugs, the teachings of Zen Buddhism, and the influence of William Blake.* (*PS* 156:L29 *Playmates*) "**ALLEN Ginsberg** and I were inducted into the National Institute of Arts and Letters in the same year, 1973. Somebody from *Newsweek* called me up to ask what I had to say about two such antiestablishment writers being embraced by such a conservative organization.

I said this, and I meant it, and my comment was not printed: "My goodness, if Mr. Ginsberg and I aren't already members of the establishment, I don't know who is." *This anecdote is repeated from an earlier telling by Vonnegut in the* Playboy Interview *included in* Wampeters (280:L16).

Glampers, Diana Moon. *Originally appearing as the authoritarian Handicapper General of the United States in the short story "Harrison Bergeron," she is probably better remembered as the neurotic domestic servant employed by Senator Rosewater to maintain the family home in Rosewater, Indiana. In "Harrison Bergeron" she shoots to death both the title character and the ballerina who dared to remove her government-issued handicap bags full of lead balls.*

In God Bless You, Mr. Rosewater, *Diana Moon Glampers is quite a different character. She is an illiterate* sixty-eight-year-old virgin who, by almost anybody's standards, was too dumb to live. . . . No one had ever loved her. There was no reason why anyone should. She was ugly, stupid, and boring. On the rare occasions when she had to introduce herself, she always said her full name, and followed that with the mystifying equation that had thrust her into life so pointlessly:

"My Mother was a Moon. My father was a Glampers" (*GBR* 70:L12-20).

Deathly afraid of lightning, Diana Moon Glampers calls Eliot whenever it storms. During one storm she rattles off a number of "miracles" wrought by Eliot, the savior of Rosewater. (*GBR* 74:L5-10) "Dawn Leonard had boils for ten years, and you cured 'em. Ned Calvin had that twitch in his eye since he was a little boy, and you made it stop. Pearl Flemming came and saw you, and she threw her crutch away. And now my kiddleys have stopped hurting, just hearing your sweet voice."

"I'm glad."

"And the thunder and lightning's stopped."

It was true. There was only the hopelessly sentimental music of rainfall now.

Glinko-X-3. *The home planet of the chaplain in Kilgore Trout's* Pan-Galactic Three-Day Pass *and who has to break the news of the Milky Way's death to the earthling Sergeant Boyle. It was this story which sends Eliot Rosewater into a catatonic trance, imagining that he sees Indianapolis going up in a firestorm.*

Globular Cluster M13. (*ST* prefatory heading) "Every passing hour brings the Solar System forty-three thousand miles closer to **Globular Cluster M13** in Hercules—and still there are some misfits who insist that there is no such thing as progress."—RANSOM K. FERM

(*WFG* 79:L13 *Excelsior! We're Going to the Moon! Excelsior!*) We have spent something like $33 billion on space so far. We should have spent it on cleaning up our filthy colonies here on earth. There is no urgency whatsoever about getting somewhere in space, much as Arthur C. Clarke wants to discover the source of the terrific radio signals coming from Jupiter. It isn't as though we aren't already going somewhere in space. Every passing hour rings the whole solar system 43,000 miles closer to **Globular Cluster M13** in Hercules.

Gloria. *The beautiful beautician in the play "Fortitude" who befriends Sylvia, the one-hundred-year-old woman whose head alone remains of her body. Sylvia is connected to a roomful of machines and watched over by Dr. Frankenstein. Gloria takes pity on Sylvia and smuggles a handgun into her room so her friend could commit suicide. However, Sylvia's mechanical arms were positioned to prevent just such an occurrence. Instead, Sylvia shoots Dr. Frankenstein, who winds up connected to a roomful of machines as well.*

Gluck, Werner. *The sixteen-year-old German guard of Billy Pilgrim and Edgar Derby. Together they looked like three wartime fools:* And there in the doorway were **Gluck** and Derby and Pilgrim—the childish soldier and the poor old high school teacher and the clown in his toga and silver shoes (*SL5* 137:L1). *Pilgrim and Gluck never find out they are distant cousins. They both get their first glimpse of completely nude women when Werner mistakenly leads them to a shower where refugee girls from Breslau are cleaning themselves. Werner grew up in Dresden and presumably dies in the firestorm.*

"Go Back to Your Precious Wife and Son" (1962). The short story narrated by the unnamed New Hampshire vendor and installer of storm windows and bathtub enclosures. He relates the tale of movie star Gloria Hilton and her fifth husband, screenwriter George Murra who left his wife to be with Hilton. She loses patience with him because he has failed to produce a screenplay for her and because he deeply misses his son who needs close guidance. Gloria Hilton leaves Murra, he reclaims his relationship with his son and returns to his wife, and Murra is left with the custom shower door with Hilton's image etched in glass.

"The Goblet" (also **"The Snow Rose"** and **"Seventy Times Seven"**). *Howard Campbell's play, which is stolen by Soviet plagiarist Stepan Bodovskov only to become a favorite of Stalin's. Frank Wirtanen reminds Campbell of the plot when he breaks the news to him about George Kraft/Iona Potapov.* (*MN* 152:L28-32, 153:L1-21) "A blindingly pure young maiden . . . guards the Holy Grail. She will surrender it only to a knight who is as pure as herself. Such a knight comes along, and is pure enough to win the Grail.

"By winning it, he causes the girl to fall in love with him, and he falls in love with her. . . . "The knight and the girl—" said Wirtanen, continuing the tale, "they begin to have impure thoughts about each other, tending, involuntarily, to disqualify themselves from any association with the Grail. The heroine urges the hero to flee with the Grail, before he becomes unworthy of it. The hero vows to flee without the Grail, leaving the heroine worthy of continuing to guard it.

"The hero makes their decision for them . . . since they have both become impure in thought. The Holy Grail disappears. And, stunned by this unanswerable proof of their depravity, the two lovers confirm what they firmly believe to be their damnation with a tender night of love.

"The next morning, confident of hell-fire, they promise to give each other so much joy in life that hell-fire will be a very cheap price to pay. The Holy Grail thereupon appears to them, signifying that Heaven does not despise love like theirs. And then the Grail goes away again, forever, leaving the hero and the heroine to live happily ever after."

As a sign of Campbell's success, "The Goblet" was running in Dresden and Berlin simultaneously, and "The Snow Rose" was also playing in Berlin. Rather than resting with such good fortune, Campbell just finished "Seventy Times Seven." (*MN* 26:L10-11) All three plays were medieval romances, about as political as chocolate *éclairs*.

God Bless You, Mr. Rosewater (1965) (subtitled ***Pearls Before Swine***) (see also **Eliot Rosewater**, **Kilgore Trout**, **Samaritrophia**, **uncritical love**). *Eliot Rosewater seeks to reestablish communal ties in his ancestral home (Rosewater County) not by pitting people or ideologies in opposition to each other as in* Cat's Cradle, *but by providing for people's needs as they ask for assistance. Unlike* Player Piano*'s insistence that man continually step back from labor* *because of automation's economy and a desire to avoid the drudgery of repetitious and menial activities, Eliot sees the need for human participation in production if for no other reason than it keeps people invloved with living. Kilgore Trout comes to Eliot's aid and phrases Eliot's views in ways that even Senator Rosewater understands.* (*GBR* 210:L34, 211:L1-3) "Poverty is a relatively mild disease for even a very flimsy American soul, but uselessness will kill strong and weak souls alike, and kill every time.

"We must find a cure."

At the close of Cat's Cradle, *the history Bokonon advises John/Jonah to write is one which would deny the cosmic paternalism of religion and, by implication, any benevolent constructions designed by man. Considering Eliot by this measure, we are left with a series of magnanimous gestures, yet we have to doubt the efficacy of his paternalism. Without direction and foresight, the rich orphans of Rosewater County could be as dangerous as Felix Hoenikker or as degenerate as the idle rich in Pisquontuit. As a literary product of the mid-1960s,* Rosewater*'s backdrop appears to concern itself with an historical guilt among the "haves" in relation to the "have-nots." Bequeathing gobs of money to the poor doesn't settle the more pressing problem of uselessness (as evidenced by Vonnegut's satire of the wealthy on Cape Cod).*

Goebbels, Paul Joseph. *In* Mother Night, *Reichsleiter Dr. Paul Joseph Goebbels, Head of the German Ministry of Popular Enlightenment and Propaganda, is also Howard Campbell's boss. It was Goebbels' idea to have Campbell write "The Last Full Measure," a pageant in honor of the German soldiers who lost their lives in the Jewish uprising in the Warsaw Ghetto. The project was abandoned before Campbell completed it.*

Gokubi. *The first generation of simultaneous language translators invented by Zenji Hiroguchi, an employee of Matsumoto in* Galápagos. *Capable of translating ten languages, Gokubi was eventually succeeded by Mandarax.*

The Golden House of the Roman Emperor Nero. *The Tralfamadorians used their Universal Will to Become to send messages concerning the status of the replacement part for Salo's spaceship. The messages were conveyed in great architectural monuments on Earth that could be monitored by Salo.* (*ST* 271:L27) **The Golden House of the Roman Emperor Nero** meant: *"We are doing the best we can."*

Goldwater, Barry. *In "The Hyannis Port Story" reprinted in* Welcome to the Monkey House, *the Rumfoord estate has a garishly displayed portrait of Barry Goldwater facing the Kennedy family compound.* (*MH* 137:L24-25 *The Hyannis Port Story*) On a second-floor balcony was a huge portrait of **Barry Goldwater**. It had bicycle reflectors in the pupils of its eyes. Those eyes stared right through the Kennedy gate. There were floodlights all around it, so I could tell it was lit up at night. And the floodlights were rigged with blinkers.

Golgotha (see also **Calvary Cemetery**). (*SL5* 119:L21) Billy dozed, awakened in the prison hospital again. The sun was high. Outside were **Golgotha** sounds of strong men digging holes for upright timbers in hard, hard ground. Englishmen were building themselves a new latrine. They had abandoned their old latrine to the Americans—and their theater, the place where the feast had been held, too.
(*JB* 172:L1) As for the last days of Sacco and Vanzetti as a modern Passion: As on **Golgotha**, three lower-class men were executed at the same time by a state. This time, though, not just one of the three was innocent. This time two of the three were innocent.

Gömbös, Miklós (see **Boone**).

Gomburg, Crowther. *The author of* Primordial Scales, *a chronicle of Noel Constant's Magnum Opus, Inc., predicated on the notion that* Magnum Opus was a product of a complex of inabilities to love. Reading between the lines of **Gomburg**'s book, it is increasingly clear that **Gomburg** is himself unloved and unable to love (*ST* 81:L5-8).

The Goober Gossip. *The privately published newspaper for those in the extended family of Peanuts.* (*Slap* 180:L22) There were editorials calling for family health insurance programs and sports teams and so on. There was one interesting essay, I remember, either in *The Daffy-nition* or ***The Goober Gossip***, which said that families with high moral standards were the best maintainers of law and order, and that police departments could be expected to fade away.

goofballs (see **Combat Respiratory Rations**).

Gooz. *A central character in Kilgore Trout's* The Barring-gaffner of Bagnialto, *or* This Year's Masterpiece, *Gooz is a cobbler who paints a picture of his cat, offers it to the Barring-gaffner, and through the luck of the wheel the painting is valued at one billion dollars.* (*BC* 129:L12) The Barring-gaffner awarded **Gooz** a check for that amount, most of which was taken back at once by the tax collector. The picture was given a place of honor in the National Gallery, and people lined up for miles for a chance to see a painting worth a billion dollars.

Goring, Reichsmarschall Hermann. Jailbird*'s Walter Starbuck records that he and Ruth were married on October 15, 1946 (and he assumes that was the day they conceived their one child), the same day Reichsmarschall Hermann Goring committed suicide.*

Gorky, Arshile (1904-1948). (*Blue* 294:L5) "Yup," I said. "We were extricating ourselves from Happy Valley, and returning to real life. The melancholy roll-call of real-life suicides among the Abstract Expressionists again: *(Arshile)* **Gorky** by hanging in 1948, Pollock and then almost immediately Kitchen, by drunken driving and then pistol in 1956 and then Rothko with all possible messiness by knife in 1970."

The Gospel from Outer Space (also **Gospels**). *In* Slaughterhouse-Five, *when Billy Pilgrim was hospitalized after his charter plane crashed, he was placed in a room with Eliot Rosewater. Rosewater told Billy about this Kilgore Trout tale.* (*SL5* 94:L1-33, 95:L1-11) It was about a visitor from outer space, shaped very much like a Tralfamadorian, by the way. The visitor from outer space made a serious study of Christianity, to learn, if he could, why Christians found it so easy to be cruel. He concluded that at least part of the trouble was slipshod storytelling in the New Testament. He supposed that the intent of the **Gospels** was to teach people, among other things, to be merciful, even to the lowest of the low.

But the **Gospels** actually taught this:

Before you kill somebody, make absolutely sure he isn't well connected. So it goes.

The flaw in the Christ stories, said the visitor from outer space, was that Christ, who didn't look like much, was actually the Son of the Most Powerful Being in the Universe. Readers understood that, so, when they came to the crucifixion, they naturally thought, and Rosewater read out loud again:

Oh, boy—they sure picked the wrong guy to lynch that time!

And that thought had a brother: *"There are right people to lynch."* Who? People not well connected. So it goes.

The visitor from outer space made a gift to Earth of a new **Gospel**. In it, Jesus really was a nobody, and a pain in the neck to a lot of people with better connections than he had. He still got to say all the lovely and puzzling things he said in the other **Gospels**.

So the people amused themselves one day by nailing him to a cross and planting the cross in the ground. There couldn't possibly be any repercussions, the lynchers thought. The reader would have to think that, too, since the new **Gospel** hammered home again and again what a nobody Jesus was.

And then, just before the nobody died, the heavens opened up, and there was thunder and lightning. The voice of God came crashing down. He told the people that he was adopting the bum as his son, giving him the full powers and privileges of The Son of the Creator of the Universe throughout all eternity. God said this: *From this moment on, He will punish horribly anybody who torments a bum who has no connections!*

Gottlieb, Adolph. *Part of Karabekian's huge collection of Abstract Expressiont paintings includes Gottlieb's "Frozen Sounds Number Seven."* (*Blue* 193:L4) Slazinger was a lamb when they unswaddled him. "Just put me to bed," he said. He named the room he wanted to be put in, the one on the second floor with **Adolph Gottlieb's** "Frozen Sounds Number Seven" over the fireplace and a bay window looking across the dunes to the ocean.

Gottwald's estate. *Gottwald's estate in* Player Piano *promises a pastoral refuge from an overtechnologized society for Paul and Anita Proteus. The farm was completely without motorized farming implements or electricity. Gottwald had long since passed away. The farm was on the market for fourteen years by the time Proteus brings Anita to see where he plans to spend his years after quitting the Ilium Works. Gottwald originally bought the farm from old Mr. Haycox. Haycox's son was guaranteed the right to run the farm until he passed away. Along with help from the Reeks and Wrecks, the now aged younger Mr. Haycox is adamant about remaining caretaker of the estate.*

Grace Daffodil-13 (Cousin Grace). *At the Daffodil family meeting in Indianapolis, "Cousin Grace" was a mentally unbalanced woman whom Wilbur uses to prove the viability of his and Eliza's scheme for large, artificially extended families.* (*Slap* 217:L19-25) What was more: She was a menace only to herself, so nobody was particularly mad at her. Her children had wandered off to better-run houses almost as soon as they were able to walk, I was told. That was surely one of the most attractive features of Eliza's and my invention, I think: Children had so many homes and parents to choose from.

Graham, Jack (see also **Mary Kathleen O'Looney**). *In* Jailbird, *Graham was born a multimillionaire, became a mining engineer, and took control of The RAMJAC Corporation (then a small company), which became the nation's dominating economic entity. He met Mary Kathleen O'Looney in the streets of a Kentucky coal mining town when she fled her cabin in fear of the drunken union organizer Kenneth Whistler. Jack Graham became a recluse and died in 1952, survived only by his wife, Mary Kathleen.*

Graham, James and **John (Fifth Earl** and **First Marquis of Montrose)**. *Fred Rosewater learns about the establishment of the family name and the founder of his family by reading* A History of the Rosewaters of Rhode Island, *by Merrihue Rosewater.* (*GBR* 163:L5-24) The Old World home of the Rosewaters was and is in the Scilly Islands, off Cornwall. The founder of the family there, whose name was **John**, arrived on St. Mary Island in 1645, with the party accompanying the fifteen-year-old Prince Charles, later to become Charles the Second, who was fleeing the Puritan Revolution. The name Rosewater was then a pseudonym. Until **John** chose it for himself, there were no Rosewaters in England. His real name was **John Graham**. He was the youngest of the five sons of **James Graham, Fifth Earl and First Marquis of Montrose**. There was need for a pseudonym, for **James Graham** was a leader of the Royalist cause, and the Royalist cause was lost. **James**, among other romantic exploits, once disguised himself, went to the Scotch Highlands, organized a small, fierce army, and led it to six bloody victories over the far greater forces of the Lowland Presbyterian Army of Archibald Campbell, the Eighth Earl of Argyll. **James** was also a poet. So every Rosewater is in fact a **Graham**, and has the blood of Scotch nobility in him. **James** was hanged in 1650.

Grand Hotel Oloffson. (*DD* x:L9-10) There is a real hotel in this book, the **Grand Hotel Oloffson** in Port au Prince, Haiti. I love it, and so would almost anybody else. My dear wife Jill Krementz and I have stayed there in the so-called "James Jones Cottage," which was built as an operating room when the hotel was headquarters for a brigade of United States Marines, who occupied Haiti, in order to protect American financial interests there, from 1915 until 1934.

The exterior of that austere wooden box has subsequently been decorated with fanciful, jigsaw gingerbread, like the rest of the hotel. *Vonnegut has the Waltz brothers purchase the hotel with the settlement they receive for the wrongful death of their mother due to radiation exposure. They are at the hotel when Midland City is neutron bombed.*

granfalloon. *In Bokononist terms, a* granfalloon *is a false* karass. (*CC* 82:L3-4, 9) Hazel's *(Crosby)* obsession with Hoosiers around the world was a textbook example of a false *karass*, of a seeming team that was meaningless in terms of the ways God gets things done, a textbook example of what Bokonon calls a ***granfalloon***. Other examples of ***granfalloons*** are the Communist party, the Daughters of the American Revolution, the General Electric Company, the International Order of Odd Fellows—and any nation, anytime, anywhere.

As Bokonon invites us to sing along with him:

> If you wish to study a ***granfalloon***,
> Just remove the skin of a toy balloon.

(*WFG* xv:L7 *Preface*) DEAR READER: The title of this book is composed of three words from my novel *Cat's Cradle*. A *wampeter* is an object around which the lives of many otherwise unrelated people may revolve. The Holy Grail would be a case in point. *Foma* are harmless untruths, intended to comfort simple souls. An example: "Prosperity is just around the corner." A ***granfalloon*** is a proud and meaningless association of human beings. Taken together, the words form as good an umbrella as any for this collection of some of the reviews and essays I have written, a few of the speeches I have made. Most of my speeches were never written down.

Grant, Robert. *In* Jailbird, *Vonnegut cites the retired probate judge as one of three men assigned to review the convictions and death sentences for Sacco and Vanzetti. Along with Harvard President A. Lawrence Lowell and MIT President Samuel W. Stratton, the committee agreed with Judge Thayer's sentence.*

Grasso, Elmer Glenville. *The skeptical voter attending a political rally during Wilbur Swain's campaign for president. Wilbur explains to Grasso how a society would function with his proposed artificially extended families. Grasso is concerned about the possibility of being artificially connected to relatives he doesn't like, and this prompts Wilbur to lecture him about how that could be different than having unpleasant biological relatives.* (*Slap* 163:L9-20) "Mr. Grasso," I said, "I personally will be very disappointed, if you do not say to artificial relatives you hate, after I am elected, 'Brother or Sister or Cousin,' as the case may be, 'why don't you take a flying fuck at a rolling doughnut? Why don't you take a flying fuck at the mooooooooooooon?'

"You know what relatives you say that to are going to do, Mr. Grasso?" I went on. "They're going to go home and try to figure out how to be better relatives!"

great becoming. (*ST* 39:L12) "Things fly this way and that, my boy," he *(Rumfoord)* said, "with or without messages. It's chaos, and no mistake, for the Universe is just being born. It's the **great becoming** that makes the light and the heat and the motion, and bangs you from hither to yon."

The Great Wall of China. *The Tralfamadorians used their Universal Will to Become to send messages concerning the status of the replacement part for Salo's spaceship. The messages were conveyed in great architectural monuments on Earth that could be monitored by Salo.* (*ST* 271:L24) **The Great Wall of China** means in Tralfamadorian, when viewed from above: *"Be patient. We haven't forgotten about you."*

Greathouse, Virgil (also **Greathouse and Smiley**). *The former Secretary of Health, Education, and Welfare and one of the richest men in the country arrives to serve his Watergate sentence at the Finletter Minimum Security Adult Correctional Facility on the same day Walter Starbuck is being released. Greathouse was a Quaker, as was his boss Richard Nixon.* (*JB* 36:L14-17, 37:L14) I knew **Greathouse** mainly by sight—and of course by reputation. He was a famous tough guy, the founder and still majority stockholder in the public relations firm of **Greathouse and Smiley**, which specialized in putting the most favorable interpretations on the activities of Caribbean and Latin American dictatorships, of Bahamian gambling casinos, of Liberian and Panamanian tanker fleets, of several Central Intelligence Agency fronts around the world, of gangster-dominated unions such as the International Brotherhood of Abrasives and Adhesives Workers and the Amalgamated Fuel Handlers, of international conglomerates such as RAMJAC and Texas Fruit, and on and on.

He was bald. He was jowly. His forehead was wrinkled like a washboard. He had a cold pipe clamped in his teeth, even when he sat on a witness stand. I got close enough to him one time to discover that he made music on that pipe. It was like the twittering of birds. He entered Harvard six years after I graduated, so we never met there. We made eye-contact only once at the White House—at the meeting where I made a fool of myself by lighting so many cigarettes. I was just a little mouse from the White House pantry, as far as he was concerned. He spoke to me only once, and that was after we were both arrested. We came together accidentally in a courthouse corridor, where we were facing separate arraignments. He found out who I was and evidently thought I might have something on him, which I did not. So he put his face close to mine, his eyes twinkling, his pipe in his teeth, and he made me this unforgettable promise: "You say anything about me, Buster, and when you get out of jail you'll be lucky to get a job cleaning toilets in a whorehouse in Port Said."

It was after he said that, that I heard the birdcalls from his pipe.

Greathouse was a Quaker, by the way—and so was Richard M. Nixon, of course. This was surely a special bond between them, one of the things that made them best of friends for a while.

(*JB* 38:L1) Emil Larkin, the Presbyterian, and **Virgil Greathouse**, the Quaker, had been thick as thieves back in the good old days. They had not only dominated the burglaries and the illegal wiretaps and the harassment of enemies by the Internal Revenue Service and so on, but the prayer breakfasts, as well.

The Green Death. *While the rest of the country had to deal with the Albanian Flu, those on Manhattan Island were forced to contend with "The Green Death." The plague was so deadly that all crossing points to Manhattan were cut off.* (*Slap* 206:L2-6) They *(the Raspberry family)* discovered the antidote through dumb luck. They ate fish without cleaning them, and the antidote, probably pollution left over from olden times, was somewhere in the guts of the fish they ate.

(*Slap* 234:L29) **The Green Death**, on the other hand, was caused by microscopic Chinese, who were peace-loving and meant no one any harm. They were nonetheless invariably fatal to normal sized human beings when inhaled or ingested.

Wilbur was saved when he was kidnapped by the Raspberries and force-fed a small trapezoid of what seemed to be a tasteless sort of peanut-brittle. It was in fact boiled and dried fish guts, which contained the antidote to **The Green Death** (*Slap* 238:L20). *Wilbur was captured so he could care for the ill patriarch of the family, Hiroshi Raspberry-20 Yamashiro. Yamashiro survived his bout with pneumonia and from among the many gifts brought to Wilbur for curing him, he chose only a single brass candlestick. From then on he became known as the King of Candlesticks.*

Green Diamond Plow. *In* Deadeye Dick, *the tank-producing facility near Midland City which brought Eleanor Roosevelt to town for a morale boosting visit. While there she visited the famous studio of Otto Waltz and left only hours before Rudy accidentally killed the pregnant Eloise Metzger.*

Green River Cemetery. *The Long Island cemetery in* Bluebeard *where Edith Karabekian, Rabo's wife, is buried. He plans to be buried there next to her, not far from the graves of Jackson Pollock and Terry Kitchen.*

Green Team. *The team at the Meadows executive retreat and competition festival captained by Dr. Lawson Shepherd, Paul Proteus' college friend and long-time associate who served as his second in command at the Ilium Works.* (*PP* 120:L9-12) Well, if one cared about such things, **Green** was the lowest in the unofficial hierarchy of teams. It was one of those things that was understood without anyone's saying anything about it.

Greenfield Bank and Trust Company. *The two lieutenants of the National Guard unit sent to put down the strike at the Cuyahoga Bridge and Iron Company were twin sons of the president of the Greenfield Bank and Trust Company.* (*JB* xxvii:L24-31) The postmaster and the banker had both done local favors for the governor. The commissions were their rewards. And the officers, in turn, had rewarded those who had pleased them in some way by making them sergeants or corporals.

Gregory, Dan. *Born Daniel Gregorian in Moscow, he came to the United States in 1907 and became* an illustrator of magazine stories and advertisements, and of books for young people (*Blue* 50:L12-14). *He became one of the most well paid artists in American history and frequently abused his live-in girlfriend, Marilee Kemp. She was once sent by Gregory to have an abortion. Gregory unwillingly accepted Rabo Karabekian as an apprentice after the aspiring artist accepted Marilee's invitation to travel to New York. Gregory's own talents were developed while an apprentice for Beskudnikov, an engraver of plates of paper currency and bonds for the Czar. Beskudnikov and his wife cared for Gregory from the time he was five years old, but it wasn't until he began his art training that Gregory fell victim to Beskudnikov's tormenting. This same treatment was repeated by Gregory when Karabekian came to study with him.*

Rabo Karabekian makes the following assessment of his old mentor. (*Blue* 83:L25-33, 84:L1-19) But let's forget me for the moment, and focus on the works of **Gregory**. They were truthful about material things, but they lied about time. He celebrated moments, anything from a child's first meeting with a department store Santa Claus to the victory of a gladiator at the Circus Maximus, from the driving of the golden spike which completed the transcontinental railroad to a man's going on his knees to ask a woman to marry him. But he lacked the guts or the wisdom, or maybe just the talent, to indicate somehow that time was liquid, that one moment was no more important than any other, and that all moments quickly run away.

Let me put it another way: **Dan Gregory** was a taxidermist. He stuffed and mounted and varnished and mothproofed supposedly great moments, all of which turn out to be depressing dust-catchers, like a moosehead bought at a country auction or a sailfish on the wall of a dentist's waiting room.

Clear?

Let me put it yet another way: life, by definition, is never still. Where is it going? From birth to death, with no stops on the way. Even a picture of a bowl of pears on a checkered tablecloth is liquid, if laid on canvas by the brush of a master. Yes, and by some miracle I was surely never able to achieve as a painter, nor was **Dan Gregory**, but which was achieved by the best of the Abstract Expressionists, in the paintings which have greatness birth and death are always there.

Gregory's best friend was Fred Jones and both were great admirers of Benito Mussolini. He and Jones asked permission to accompany the Italian Army in uniform and both were killed around December seventh of 1940 at Sidi Barrani, Egypt. . . . (*Blue* 108:L6-7)

Gregory's photorealistic talents and sentiments made him rage at Abstract Expressionism. When he saw Marilee and Rabo exiting the Museum of Modern Art he became livid. (*Blue* 167:L6-11) "I don't give a *hoot* what pictures you look at," he said. "All I asked was that you not pay your respects to an institution which thinks that the smears and spatters and splotches and daubs and dribbles and vomit of lunatics and degenerates and charlatans are great treasures we should all admire."

The largest collection of Dan Gregory paintings and illustrations is in a private museum in Lubbock, Texas.

GRIOT™. *The Parker Brothers computer game, which projects the outcome of one's life based on a series of demographic and life experience questions. Eugene Debs Hartke frequently uses the device and, in so doing, realizes the game's programming is based on a series of stereotypes generally held to be true by major media. When Hartke tells GRIOT™ about his life experiences up to Vietnam,* It made me a burned-out case, on the basis of my length of service over there, I think. It had me becoming a wife-beater and an alcoholic, and winding up all alone on Skid Row (*HP* 103:L30-33).

Though the game's programmers supposedly updated the software every three months with the latest demographic trends for various ethnic groups, its synthesized futures usually reflected worst-case scenarios for minority groups and optimistic outcomes for whites. Hartke's skepticism about the efficacy of GRIOT™ is underscored by Parker Brothers' change in ownership. (*HP* 104:L24) There is some question now, I've heard, about whether **GRIOT™** is as deep and up-to-date as it used to be, since Parker Brothers, the company that makes it, has been taken over by Koreans. The new owners are moving the whole operation to Indonesia, where labor costs next to nothing. They say they will keep up with American news by satellite.

One wonders.

Guayaquil, Ecuador. *The city due east of the Galápagos Islands which was the congregating point for passengers planning to take "the Nature Cruise of the Century."*

Guggenheim. *Vonnegut traveled back to Dresden in 1967 with a Guggenheim Foundation grant to research* Slaughterhouse-Five. *In* Bluebeard, *Rabo Karabekian's "Hungarian Rhapsody Number Six" was bought by the Guggenheim Museum and, as happened with all his paintings made with Sateen Dura-Luxe, it was flaking apart.*

Guido. *At the Mafia-run crematoria behind the Meadowdale Cinema Complex in* Hocus Pocus, *Guido has the black market concession on gasoline in the post-prison riot period.*

Gumbo. *The Gumbo tribe saves Beatrice Rumfoord and her son Chrono after the failed Martian invasion of Earth.* (*ST* 233:L223-32, 234:L1-12) Bee's upper front teeth were gold, and her skin, like the skin of her son, was the color of golden oak.

Bee had lost her upper front teeth when the space ship in which she and Chrono had ridden from Mars crash-landed in the **Gumbo** region of the Amazon Rain Forest. She and Chrono had been the only survivors of the crash, and had wandered through the jungles for a year.

The color of Bee's and Chrono's skins was permanent, since it stemmed from a modification of their livers. Their livers had been modified by a three-month diet consisting of water and the roots of the salpa-salpa or Amazonian blue poplar. The diet had been a part of Bee's and Chrono's initiation into the **Gumbo** tribe.

During the initiation, mother and son had been staked at the ends of tethers in the middle of the village, with Chrono representing the Sun and Bee representing the Moon, as the Sun and the Moon were understood by the **Gumbo** people.

As a result of their experiences, Bee and Chrono were closer than most mothers and sons.

(*ST* 237:L23) The good-luck piece had probably saved Chrono's and Bee's lives in the jungle. The **Gumbo** tribesmen had recognized the piece of metal as an object of tremendous power. Their respect for it had led them to initiate rather than eat its owners.

Gummer, Harriet. The Des Moines Register *correspondent who has a child from her brief sexual encounter with Eugene Debs Hartke after he escaped from the American embassy in Saigon on the last day of the war. Hartke is unaware that their brief moment in Manila produced a son, Rob Roy. She later married Lowell Fenstermaker, the owner of a meat packing company, who adopts Rob Roy as his son.*

Gumps, Andy. *Vonnegut uses this term in reference to the appearance his brother Bernard and he must have struck as they sat on the plane back to Indianapolis for the funeral of their Uncle Alex.* (*Slap* 11:L14) We were both over six feet tall. We still had most of our hair, which was brown. We had identical mustaches—duplicates of our late father's mustache.

We were harmless looking. We were a couple of nice old **Andy Gumps**.

Gunther. *In the short story "Brief Encounters on the Inland Waterway," Gunther was the unhappy Swedish captain of the* Golden Hind VI, *an ocean liner among yachts.*

Gunther, August. *The best friend of Rudy's father, Otto Waltz, Gunther was decapitated by an accidental shotgun blast discharged by Francis X. Morissey, Midland City's Chief of Police. Rudy Waltz's grandmother* hired a rapscallion German cabinetmaker, who had studied art in Berlin in his youth, to give Father drawing and painting lessons on weekends and after school.

It was a sweet racket for both teacher and pupil. The teacher's name was **August Gunther**, and his peephole must have opened in Germany around 1850. Teaching paid as well as cabinetmaking, and, unlike cabinetmaking, allowed him to be as drunk as he pleased.

After Father's voice changed, moreover, **Gunther** could take him on overnight visits by rail to Indianapolis and Cincinnati and Louisville and Cleveland and so on, ostensibly to visit galleries and painters' studios. The two of them also managed to get drunk, and to become darlings of the fanciest whorehouses in the Middle West (*DD* 2:L20, 23). *Gunther was fired and blacklisted by Otto's parents and is later suspected of setting fire to their mansion.*

In 1916, Gunther, Otto Waltz, Francis Morissey, and John Fortune went geese hunting when Morissey's weapon accidentally discharged, decapitating his friend. They all agreed it was an honest accident that could only ruin more lives if the identity of the killer was revealed. They decided to send the decapitated body of August Gunther floating down Sugar Creek.

Gunther, Grace. *The only child of the soon-to-be decapitated August Gunther, in* Deadeye Dick.

Gutman, Andor. *In* Mother Night, *Howard Campbell's guard from noon to six p.m. each day in the basement confines of the Old Jerusalem prison. Gutman is an Estonian Jew who survived two years at Auschwitz. For reasons unknown to himself, he joined the* Sonderkommando, *corpse-carrying inmates, just as Himmler closed down the camp's ovens. The* Sonderkommando *responded to the frequent call over the loudspeakers,* "Leichenträger zu Wache," *meaning "Corpse-carriers to the guardhouse." This is the same phrase Auschwitz survivor Mrs. Epstein murmurs to the catatonic Campbell* *when he seeks to turn himself in to the Israelis. Gutman was ashamed for having volunteered for the detail, and he reveals to Campbell the tragic paradox he faced in the concentration camp.* (*MN* 6:L17-32, 7:L1-13) "There were loudspeakers all over the camp," he said, "and they were never silent for long. there was much music played through them. Those who were musical told me it was often good music—sometimes the best."

"That's interesting," I said.

"There was no music by Jews," he said. "That was forbidden."

"Naturally," I said.

"And the music was always stopping in the middle," he said, "and then there was an announcement. All day long, music and announcements."

"Very modern," I said.

He closed his eyes, remembered gropingly. "There was one announcement that was always crooned, like a nursery rhyme. Many times a day it came. It was the call for the Sonderkommando."

"Oh?" I said.

"*Leichenträger zu Wache*," he crooned, his eyes still closed.

Translation: "Corpse-carriers to the guardhouse." In an institution in which the purpose was to kill human beings by the millions, it was an understandably common cry.

"After two years of hearing that call over the loudspeakers, between the music," **Gutman** said to me, "the position of corpse-carrier suddenly sounded like a very good job."

"I can understand that," I said.

"You can?" he said. He shook his head. "I can't," he said. "I will always be ashamed. Volunteering for the Sonderkommando—it was a very shameful thing to do."

"I don't think so," I said.

"I do," he said. "Shameful," he said. "I never want to talk about it again."

H

Hacketts, Elmo C., Jr. *In* Player Piano, *Pfc. Elmo Hacketts is the unintended object of scrutiny by the Shah of Bratpuhr, who declares Hacketts to be a "Takaru"—a slave. His commanders insist citizens in America become soldiers out of a sense of duty and patriotism. However, the thoughts of this two-year veteran are to serve out the next twenty-three years and retire to Evanston, Illinois, so he could hang out with his friends and have no employment commitments. He knew his only two choices were between the Army and the Reconstruction and Reclamation Corps, and decidedly felt the Army was the preferable fate. He longed for overseas duty so he could get a real weapon with live ammunition and feel more like a soldier.*

Paul Proteus rides a train through upstate New York and overhears a conversation among Hacketts' old Army unit. Proteus knows well the limited options open to such people and when he hears Hacketts' request for overseas duty was granted, that he was on his way to Tamanrasset in the Sahara Desert, Vonnegut has this to say about Paul's silent conclusion: Paul sighed for **Hacketts**, born into a spiritual desert, now being shipped to where the earth was sterile, too (*PP* 222:L27-28).

Haggedorn, Elbert. *In the short story "Tomorrow and Tomorrow and Tomorrow," Haggedorn is the focus of a televised news story from Council Bluffs, Iowa. The content of the story is interrupted by squabbling in the Schwartz home, but we do learn Haggedorn is 183 years old and wedged into something requiring 200 workers to dig him out.*

Hagstrohm, Delores and Edgar, Jr. *The children of Edgar and Wanda Hagstrohm, all residents of Proteus Park in Chicago. While eating dinner with the Shah of Bratpuhr, Delores and Edgar, Jr. fall all over themselves with conflicting stories about their father's supposed bowling date with Joe Prince. Edgar was having an affair, and his son tries to protect his secret though he* *hates him for it.* (*PP* 145:L26-33) "I remember now he said he was going bowling with Pop. Sis got it all wrong, Mom." His hands were trembling, and, clumsily, he knocked over his milk glass. Both he and his father jumped to their feet to catch it before it toppled all the way. Young **Edgar** caught it, and when his eyes met old Edgar's they were full of hate. "Guess I'm too tired to go to the ball game after all," he said. "Guess I'll stay home and watch television with Mom."

Hagstrohm, Edgar Rice Burroughs (and his wife **Wanda**). *The Shah of Bratpuhr requested a visit at the home of a typical family, and the Hagstrohms were chosen by computer. The Shah arrives while Edgar is rereading a Tarzan story and just before he was going to tell his wife Wanda about the long and deeply felt affair he was having with Marion Frascatti, the widow of his best friend Lou.*

(*PP* 138:L10-23) **EDGAR R. B. HAGSTROHM**, thirty-seven, R&R-131313, Undercoater First Class, 22nd Surface Preserving Battalion, 58th Maintenance Regiment, 110th Building and Grounds Division, Reconstruction and Reclamation Corps, had been named after his father's favorite author, the creator of Tarzan—Tarzan, who, far away from the soot and biting winter of the **Hagstrohms**' home town, Chicago, made friends with lions and elephants and apes, and swung through trees on vines, and was built like a brick outhouse with square wheels and Venetian blinds, and took what he wanted of civilization's beautiful women in tree houses, and left the rest of civilization alone. **E.R.B. Hagstrohm** liked Tarzan as much as his father had, and hated being a little man and being in Chicago ten times as much.

(*PP* 139:L8) The personnel machines had considered the problem and ejected the card of **Edgar R. B. Hagstrohm**, who was statistically average in every respect save for the number of his initials: his age (36), his height (5' 7"), his weight (148 lbs.), his years of marriage (11), his I.Q. (83), the number of his children (2; 1 m., 9; 1 f. 6), the number of his bedrooms (2), his car (3 yr. old Chev. 2 dr. sed.), his education (h.s. grad, 117th in class of 233; maj. in business practice; 2nd string f'ball, b'k'tb'l; soc. comm., sen'r play; no coll.) his vocation (R&R), his avocations (spec'r sports, TV, softb'l, f'sh'g), and his war record (5 yrs., 3 ov'sea; T-4 radioman; 157th Inf. Div.; battle stars: Hjoring, Elbesan, Kabul, Kaifen, Ust Kyakhta; wounded 4 times; P'ple H't, 3 cl.; Silv. Star; Br'ze Star, 2 cl.; G'd Cond. Med.).

The stress of Hagstrohm's average existence proves too much for him to endure. He becomes an outlaw and seeks to escape into a world much like the fictional one created by his namesake. (*PP* 228:L4-6) The portrait emerged from a slit in the top of the machine bit by bit—first the hair, then the brows, on line with the word WANTED, and then, on line with the large, fey eyes, the name: **Edgar Rice Burroughs Hagstrohm**, R&R-131313. **Hagstrohm**'s sordid tale emerged along with his nose: "**Hagstrohm** cut up his M-17 home in Chicago with a blowtorch, went naked to the home of Mrs. Marion Frascati, the widow of an old friend, and demanded that she come to the woods with him. Mrs. Frascatti refused, and he disappeared into the bird sanctuary bordering the housing development. There he eluded police, and is believed to have made his escape dropping from a tree onto a passing freight—"

Haifa Institute for the Documentation of War Criminals. *Under the direction of Tuvia Friedmann, the institute is responsible for providing Howard Campbell with the means and research assistance to write his* Mother Night *memoirs. The institute made it a practice to collect statements from accused war criminals to fill out their own documentation of the Holocaust.*

Hall, Dr. Cyril (see also **chrono-synclastic infundibula**). *The author of the entry on the chrono-synclastic infundibula in* A Child's Cyclopedia of Wonders and Things to Do, *in* The Sirens of Titan.

Hall, Pamela Ford. *Tarkington College's visiting Artist in Residence, a sculptor who worked in polyurethane. She was a childless divorcee and alcoholic whose preference was for blackberry brandy. Hall and Eugene Debs Hartke have a brief physical affair. Their first night together he got drunk on brandy and they made love in her art studio. She got him to talk about his killing in Vietnam, and the brandy made him so maudlin he went to the student union and cried about it in front of the students.*

Pamela Ford Hall's one woman show of her polyurethane sculptures at the Hanson Centre for the Arts in Buffalo was also the museum's inaugural installation. Entitled "Bagladies," the figures were no bigger than a shoe box. When the founder of the museum made her late arrival and all the entryway doors were thrown open, the lightweight polyurethane figures blew off their pedestals and against the baseboard heating system. They melted and gave off a terrific stench.

Hall had deep feelings for Hartke though she knew about his womanizing. Once, while drunk and depressed, Pamela provided a magnificently complex insight to Hartke's emotional capabilities. (*HP* 178:L13-17) "You know what you ought to say to any woman dumb enough to fall in love with you?" she asked me. Her gaze was on Musket Mountain, not on me.

"No," I said.

And she said, "Welcome to Vietnam."

Halporn, Amy. *A friend of Anita Proteus.* (*PP* 15:L22) "**Amy Halporn** said this morning she'd heard something about you *(Paul)* and Pittsburgh. Her husband was with Kroner today, and Kroner had the impression that you didn't want to go to Pittsburgh."

Halyard, Dr. Ewing J. *In* Player Piano, *Halyard is the State Department's guide assigned to escort the Shah of Bratpuhr on his tour of the United States. He continually battles the Shah's labeling Americans as slaves. Halyard's* *exalted position within the government is jeopardized when an audit of academic credentials reveals Halyard neglected to complete a physical education requirement while an undergraduate at Cornell University. He is instructed to report to Doctor Roseberry, Cornell's athletic director and head football coach, to make up the deficiency. Unfortunately for Halyard, Roseberry possesses a damning letter written by Halyard to Cornell President Herpers about the bad behavior displayed by the coach and his team while in a public restaurant. Halyard fails his physical education make-up test, is stripped of his Ph.D., and faces unemployment just as he and the Shah are caught in the Ghost Shirt uprising in Ilium.*

Hamilton, Alexander. *The author of* The Federalist Papers *and first Secretary of the Treasury (1789-1795). An elitist, he lacked faith in the abilities of the common man, advocated a strong centralized government, and recommended the creation of a national bank. Hamilton was killed in a duel by political foe Aaron Burr.* (*GBR* 38:L26) "I ask him *(Eliot)* what he dreams about," the doctor continued, "and he tells me, 'Samuel Gompers, Mark Twain, and **Alexander Hamilton**.' I ask him if his father ever appears in his dreams, and he says, 'No, but Thorsten Veblen often does.'"

Hamlet. *While Eliot Rosewater aimlessly travels across America, he stops for a time in Elsinore, California, and the name of the location provides him an opportunity to examine himself and see parallels with the tragic character. Addressing the letter to his wife Sylvia as "Dear Ophelia," Eliot goes on to say:* The last thing you said to me before I got out of the taxicab was that maybe we should get a divorce. I did not realize that life had become that uncomfortable for you. I do realize that I am a very slow realizer. I still find it hard to realize that I am an alcoholic, though even strangers know this right away.

Maybe I flatter myself when I think that I have things in common with **Hamlet**, that I have an important mission, that I'm temporarily mixed up about how it should be done. **Hamlet** had one big edge on me. His father's ghost told him exactly what he had to do, while I am operating without instructions. But from somewhere something is trying to tell me where to go, what to do there, and why to do it. Don't worry, I don't hear voices. But there is this feeling that I have a destiny far away from the shallow and preposterous posing that is our life in New York. And I roam.

And I roam (*GBR* 42:L8, 10). *Eliot signs the letter in Hamlet's name. See also:* *FWD* 39:L11, 13.

Handy, Fred. *In* Hocus Pocus, *the college roommate of Eugene Debs Hartke's father who also trained as a chemical engineer. Handy left engineering and became a highly successful junk bond broker. After Hartke's father was let go by Barrytron, Handy invited him on a cruise down the Inland Waterway to his estate in Palm Beach. When Hartke saw all the plastic jugs and bottles floating along the route, all the while realizing how much he contributed to the* *development of those plastics which would survive a thousand years, he came to feel that he had indeed prostituted his intellect.*

Hanfstaengl, Putzi. *In an effort to properly express the extent to which he had disgraced Harvard by implicating Leland Clewes in the congressional hearings about communists in the government,* Jailbird*'s Walter Starbuck compares himself with Putzi Hanfstaengl, Hitler's favorite pianist.*

Hansels and Gretels. (*MN* vii:L5) Everything was gone but the cellars where 135,000 **Hansels and Gretels** had been baked like gingerbread men.

Hanson, Miss (also **Hanson Centre for the Arts**). *In* Hocus Pocus, *the aged Miss Hanson is a Rockefeller heir and resident of Buffalo, New York, who establishes the Hanson Centre for the Arts, a gift to the city. The inaugural art exhibit is a series of polyurethane sculptures entitled "Bagladies" by Tarkington College Artist in Residence Pamela Ford Hall. When three sets of entryway doors are simultaneously thrown open to allow the late-arriving Miss Hanson free access in her wheelchair, the Lake Erie winds sweep the lightweight sculptures off their pedestals and bring them to rest against the baseboard heating system where they melt down into a stinking mess.*

The Hapgoods, Three Earnest Brothers. *The 1977 book by Michael D. Maraccio referred to by Vonnegut in his prologue to* Jailbird. *Vonnegut uses the text to round out information about the Hapgoods, one of whom he met upon his return from military service.*

Happy Birthday, Wanda June (1970) (see also **Wanda June**). *Loosely based on Odysseus' return from the Trojan War in the last book of Homer's* Odyssey, *Vonnegut wrote the play in response to what he saw as Odysseus' "cruelly preposterous" actions when he finds his wife Penelope surrounded by suitors. Harold Ryan is Vonnegut's Odysseus and in whom he sought to portray all the worst characteristics of Ernest Hemingway. His wife Penelope is courted by the pacifist physician Dr. Norbert Woodly and vacuum salesman and weight lifter Herb Shuttle. The latter is more taken with wooing the wife of the famous warrior and hunter. Harold Ryan and his companion Colonel Looseleaf Harper return eight years after mysteriously disappearing on a hunting trip. Harper is credited with piloting the bomber which atom-bombed Nagasaki. Their return falls on Ryan's birthday, and without any warniing of his arrival they hastily purchase a birthday cake intended for Wanda June, who was killed when run over by an ice-cream truck.*

Ryan challenges Woodly for Penelope. Woodly fails and admits his cowardice, something which Penelope admires next to her husband's bullying bravura. However, Woodly retreats, having to rethink his life's meaning. Herb Shuttle was more easily dispatched by Ryan since he was really most interested in serving a legendary character—he lacked his own identity.

The ghosts of Wanda June and Nazi Major von Konigswald (himself killed by Ryan after a long career of brutality and atrocity) wear pink jackets emblazoned with the words "Harold Ryan Fan Club."

Harger, Lemuel K. and Rose. *In the short story "Next Door," while Rose is out of the apartment Lemuel uses it for a rendezvous with another woman. Paul Leonard, the young boy who lives next door, is horrified by all he hears through the paper-thin walls. He calls late night radio disc jockey "All-Night Sam" and dedicates a song from Lemuel to his wife Rose. Harger and his lover hear the radio dedication and break up in a rage. Rose returns and Lemuel couldn't feel any better.*

Hari, Mata. *Howard Campbell originally decided to dedicate* Mother Night *to the famous spy, surmising:* She whored in the interest of espionage, and so did I. *Upon reconsideration he decides to dedicate it to himself:* I would prefer to dedicate it to one familiar person, male or female, widely known to have done evil while saying to himself, "A very good me, the real me, a me made in heaven, is hidden deep inside" (*MN* xi:L31-32, xii:L3-5).

harmonium. *In* The Sirens of Titan, *The only indigenous life form on the planet Mercury, they live deep in its caves. They are fed by vibrations and Mercury's natural hum was their only nourishment until the arrival of Unk and Boaz. The thin, translucent, kite-shaped creatures allow the colors of the cave walls to shine through them. They have no circulatory system; their four suction-cup-type organs are used to attach themselves to sound-emitting sources and directly feed the entire creature. Each harmonium is capable of reproduction; their young look no more substantial than dandruff. Their communication is limited to two telepathic phrases, "Here I am, here I am, here I am," and "So glad you are, so glad you are, so glad you are"* (*ST* 186:L28-30).

The harmoniums are used by Winston Niles Rumfoord to spell out different messages to the stranded space travelers. Through them he provides an answer to the problem of how to extricate their spaceship from the cavern. By turning the ship upside down, they can fool the automatic navigation device, which can only determine how to go down. Despite their newfound realization, the harmoniums weren't communicating their messages to Unk and Boaz, the latter refuses to leave. He knows he can provide what the harmoniums need and they give him their attention.

Harper, Alice. *The former wife of Colonel Looseleaf Harper in* Happy Birthday, Wanda June, *Alice couldn't stand her husband's job as a test pilot. He eventually gave up flying for her and briefly sold insurance. Alice does not appear in the play, though she frequently comes to Colonel Harper's mind when he speaks of his many frustrations.*

Harper, Colonel Looseleaf. *Harold Ryan's war buddy and constant hunting companion in* Happy Birthday, Wanda June. *Retired from the Army Air Corps, Harper is cited as the pilot who dropped the atom bomb on Nagasaki which killed 74,000 people. After the war he and Ryan crash-landed in a light plane in the Amazon Rain Forest in quest of diamonds. Ryan recalls Harper lost his little toe to piranha fish while taking shelter in a treetop during a flash flood.*

In Breakfast of Champions, *Colonel Harper is the charter airplane pilot who delivers Eliot Rosewater to the Midland City Arts Festival.*

Harrell, Reverend Charles. *The minister who delivers the eulogy for Celia Hoover and who had played the role of John Fortune opposite Celia's role as his wife in Rudy Waltz's play "Katmandu." At Celia's funeral service he publicly forgave Rudy for shooting Eloise Metzger. To say the least, the minister did not inspire confidence about religious matters.* (*DD* 197:L11-12) I daydreamed at Celia's funeral. There was no reason to expect that anything truly exciting or consoling would be said. Not even the minister, the **Reverend Charles Harrell**, believed in heaven or hell. Not even the minister thought that every life had a meaning, and that every death could startle us into learning something important, and so on. The corpse was a mediocrity who had broken down after a while. The mourners were mediocrities who would break down after a while.

Harrison, Dr. Edmund L. (also **Edmond**). *The young engineer from the Ithaca Works befriended by Paul Proteus at the Meadows. They took a sincere liking of each other, and when Proteus is supposedly thrown out of the ruling technocracy in a move to infiltrate the Ghost Shirt Society, Kroner sends Harrison to meet Paul at the docks with a drink and words of encouragement. Proteus advises Harrison to make a clear decision about whether he wants to live within the technology-driven society or make a go of life through his own hard work. Later in the text, Harrison has an opportunity to express these same choices to Buck Young, the much-sought- after Cornell football recruit.*

Harrison, Lew. *In "The Euphio Question," Harrison is the radio announcer who first interviews Wyandotte College's Dr. Fred Bockman, who developed a receiver and amplifier to listen to the sounds of space. It was Harrison's idea to develop a marketing scheme for the euphoriaphone. So scheming and unethical was Harrison, that as the story unfolds as testimony before a congressional committee, the narrator finishes his testimony by stating:* In closing, I'd like to point out that **Lew Harrison**, the would be czar of euphio, is an unscrupulous person, unworthy of public trust. It wouldn't surprise me, for instance, if he had set the clockwork on this sample euphio set so that its radiations would addle your judgments when you are trying to make a decision. In fact, it seems to be whirring suspiciously at this very moment, and I'm so happy I could cry. I've got the swellest little kid and the swellest bunch of friends and the swellest old wife in the world. And good old **Lew Harrison**

is the salt of the earth, believe me. I sure wish him a lot of good luck with his new enterprise (*MH* 185:L36, 186:L6).

"Harrison Bergeron" (1961) (see **Bergeron**).

Hartke, Eugene Debs. *The narrator of* Hocus Pocus *who sits in the library of Tarkington Prison, formerly Tarkington College, writing his memoirs on irregularly sized slips of paper, which accounts for the solid black lines studded throughout the narrative. Hartke taught at Tarkington College for twenty-five years, starting just after the end of the Vietnam War. He claims to have been the last American to leave Saigon in the helicopter evacuation from the U.S. Embassy when the city fell to the North Vietnamese. Hartke was a Lieutenant Colonel and winner of the Silver Star at the time he resigned. He received the medal for killing with a hand grenade five Vietnamese hiding in enemy tunnels. Among them were a grandmother, mother, and baby.*

Hartke makes a point of avoiding all profanity in his memoirs, going so far as to substitute euphemisms for the language of others, as well. He always conducted himself this way because, as he told his troops in Vietnam, clear communication could mean the difference between life and death for all. For this he was forever known as "The Preacher." Despite this pastoral nicknaming, Hartke admits to a large number of sexual affairs as well as legitimate killings (during his Vietnam service). In the course of writing, Hartke realizes the astonishing coincidence that the number of his 100-percent-legal military kills and . . . adulteries *is exactly the same and is also the number he would like to have engraved on his tombstone* (*HP* 301:L10-11). *Rather than come out and tell the number, Hartke frequently alludes to it and makes a riddle for the reader to decipher. Here is how the riddle breaks down:*

		RUNNING TOTAL
Eugene Debs' death date	*1926*	*1926*
subtract title of Arthur C. Clarke's science fiction movie	*-2001*	*-75*
add year of Hitler's birth	*+1889*	*1814*
add gestation period of opossum	*+ 12*	*1826*
divide by square root of 4	*(divide by) 2*	*913*
subtract 100 x 9	*- 900*	*13*
add most children by one woman	*+ 69*	*82*
TOTAL		*82*

Hartke closes out the riddle and his memoir with a statement undercutting all the cunning and inventiveness which marked humanity's achievements and reflects the decline in human development signified by (among other things) the cruel application of technology in Vietnam, the Japanese colonization of America, and the prison break at Athena: Just because some of us can read and write and do a little math, that doesn't mean we deserve to conquer the Universe (*HP* 302:L21-24).

Hartke is the second of three Vonnegut characters named for Indiana labor leader Eugene Debs. The first is Eugene Debs Metzger, son of the ill-fated Eloise Metzger killed by Rudy Waltz in Deadeye Dick. *The third character so named is Hartke's son, Eugene Debs Hartke, Jr. Hartke married Margaret Patton, sister of his West Point classmate Jack Patton. Upon Hartke's return from Vietnam and rejection from M.I.T., he finds out from a Patton family acquaintance that Margaret's family has a strong strain of hereditary insanity whose onset begins in middle age. Shortly thereafter, his wife and mother-in-law fall to the disease and become his full-time responsibility while teaching at Tarkington.*

Hartke was recruited for West Point by then Lieutenant Colonel Sam Wakefield while in attendance at the Cleveland Science Fair. Hartke and his father were roundly criticized and all but disqualified by the judges for the crystal display which was clearly not Eugene's work. Hartke is later recruited by former Major General Sam Wakefield, now President of Tarkington College, to teach physics and play the Lutz Carillon at the school in the Finger Lakes region of New York. He is eventually fired from his teaching post for repeating anti-American and anti-Christian historical anecdotes first uttered by his good friend and fellow teacher Damon Stern. He takes employment with the prison in Athena, teaching basic literacy skills to the inmates. After the prison break, Hartke is falsely imprisoned on the allegation he helped plan the bloody escape.

Aside from the children he raised with Margaret (Eugene Debs, Jr. and Melanie), he had an illegitimate child with Des Moines Register *reporter Harriet Gummer, conceived in the Philippines on his way home from Vietnam. Harriet named their son after the mixed drink they had when they met, Rob Roy. His own children came to hate both their parents for having children despite the hereditary insanity. In Hartke's defense, he didn't know about the genetic disorder until after his return from war.*

Hartke, Melanie and Eugene, Jr. *The resentful children of Eugene and Margaret Hartke. When Margaret Patton's family secret of hereditary insanity came out, the children were furious with their parents for having had children who would be forced to wait for their biological time bombs to go off.* (*HP* 84:L3-35, 85:L1-15) **Melanie** was 21, and studying mathematics at Cambridge University in England. **Eugene Jr.** was completing his senior year at Deerfield Academy in Massachusetts, and was 18, and had his own rock-and-roll band, and had composed maybe 100 songs by then.

But **Melanie** would have spoiled our tableau on the beach. Like my mother until she went to Weight Watchers, she was very heavy. That must be hereditary. If she had kept her back to the convicts, she might at least have concealed the fact that she had a bulbous nose like the late, great, alcoholic comedian W. C. Fields. **Melanie**, thank goodness, was not also an alcoholic.

But her brother was.

And I could kill myself now for having boasted to him that on my side of the family the men had no fear of alcohol, since they knew how to drink in moderation. We were not weak and foolish where drugs were concerned.

At least **Eugene Jr.** was beautiful, having inherited the features of his mother. When he was growing up in this valley, people could not resist saying to me, with him right there to hear it, that he was the most beautiful child they'd ever seen.

I have no idea where he is now. He stopped communicating with me or anybody in this valley years ago.

He hates me.

So does **Melanie**, although she wrote to me as recently as 2 years ago. She was living in Paris with another woman. They were both teaching English and math in an American high school over there.

My kids will never forgive me for not putting my mother-in-law into a mental hospital instead of keeping her at home, where she was a great embarrassment to them. They couldn't bring friends home. If I had put Mildred into a nuthouse, though, I couldn't have afforded to send **Melanie** and **Eugene Jr.** to such expensive schools. I got a free house at Tarkington, but my salary was small.

Also, I didn't think Mildred's craziness was as unbearable as they did. In the Army I had grown used to people who talked nonsense all day long. Vietnam was 1 big hallucination. After adjusting to that, I could adjust to anything.

What my children most dislike me for, though, is my reproducing in conjunction with their mother. They live in constant dread of suddenly going as batty as Mildred and Margaret. Unfortunately, there is a good chance of that.

Hatfield, Byron. *In* Slapstick, *the frontiersman who killed the courier carrying a letter from Wilma von Peterswald, wife of the inventor of The Hooligan (a device for communicating with the dead), to Wilbur Swain. He mistook the man for Newton McCoy, a hereditary enemy of his family's.*

Hausmännin, Walpurga. *In Eliot Rosewater's unfinished novel about reincarnation which he wrote at the back of his* Domesday Book, *the ledger recording transactions of the Rosewater Foundation in Rosewater County, Walpurga Hausmännin was the most recent incarnation of the now bodiless spirit who recalls why she refuses to come back to life in another body. She speaks as a free spirit, literally, existing in a kind of bodiless purgatory without any rewards or punishments.* (*GBR* 97:L13) Uncomfortable as it is here, however, there are a few of us who do not care to be reborn. I am among that number. I have not been on Earth since 1587 A.D., when, riding around in the meat of one **Walpurga Hausmännin**, I was executed in the Austrian village of Dillingen. The alleged crime of my meat was witchcraft. When I heard the sentence, I certainly wanted out of that meat. I was about to leave it anyway, having worn it for more than eighty-five years. But I had to stay right with it when they tied it astride a sawhorse, put the sawhorse on a cart, took my poor old meat to the Town Hall. There they tore my right arm and left breast with red-hot pincers. Then we went to the lower gate, where they tore my right breast. Then they took me to the door of the hospital, where they tore my right arm. And then they took me to the village square. In view of the fact that I had been a licensed and pledged midwife for sixty-two years, and yet had acted so vilely, they cut off my right hand. And then they tied me to a stake, burned me alive, and dumped my ashes into the nearest stream.

As I say, I haven't been back since.

Haycox. *Old Mr. Haycox is a direct descendant of the original owners of the farm which came to be known as the Gottwald estate in* Player Piano. *According to the deed his father constructed prior to selling out, his son was to be caretaker of the land for as long as he lived or as long as he wished. After Paul Proteus is shown the property by the snobbish Dr. Pond (whose degree is in real estate), Haycox's contempt for a society which displaces people by creating Ph.D.s for every imaginable walk of life is clearly shown when he proclaims himself to be a* doctor of cowshit, pigshit, and chickenshit. . . . When you doctors figure out what you want, you'll find me out in the barn shoveling *my* thesis. (*PP* 133:L39, 134:L1-3). *After Proteus purchases the estate, Haycox refuses to carry out his orders to prepare the house for Anita's arrival. It isn't until Paul's wishes are expressed as favors that Haycox goes out of his way to make everything perfect for Anita's first appearance at the farm. Not surprisingly, Haycox later appears as a member of the Ghost Shirt Society when Proteus is held captive by the rebels in an abandoned bomb shelter.*

Hazor. *As the eighteen-year-old prison guard Arnold Marx explains to Howard Campbell in* Mother Night, *Hazor* was a Canaanite city in northern Palestine that existed at least nineteen hundred years before Christ. About fourteen hundred years before Christ, Arnold tells me, an Israelite army captured **Hazor**, killed all forty thousand inhabitants, and burned it down (*MN* 3:L15). *Arnold and his father were amateur archaeologists who spent their spare time as part of an excavation team at Hazor. Arnold's fascination with the city stems not from the Israeli victory, but from the succeeding Israeli settlement there which was destroyed by "The Assyrian" Tiglath-pileser the Third in 732 B.C.*

Heath, Durling. *The red-headed Cockney midget and shoe repairman in Cohoes, New York, with whom Kilgore Trout had enjoyed a friendly relationship in* Breakfast of Champions. *Heath grew weary of Trout's polite but meaningless conversation and finally screamed at the writer to leave him alone.*

Hederich, Oberdienstleiter Karl. *In* Mother Night, *the ping-pong playing doubles partner of Reichsleiter Goebbels, Howard Campbell's boss at the Ministry of Propaganda and Popular Enlightenment. Hederich and Goebbels were roundly defeated by Campbell and his best friend Heinz Schildknecht, then a member of the underground anti-Nazi movement and an Israeli agent after the war.*

Heinz, Karl (also known as **Joe Louis** and **Brown Bomber**). *In the short story "D.P." Karl Heinz is the six-year-old American-German who was fathered by a black American soldier in World War II. He lives in a Catholic orphanage run by nuns in the village of Karlswald in the American Zone of Occupation. It was with great affection that the village carpenter gives him the nickname "Joe Louis," the most highly regarded black man he knew about. Young Heinz eventually becomes aware of a black American sergeant serving nearby with the occupation forces and steals away one evening to seek him out. The military unit showers him with the traditional chocolates and the sergeant gives him his own watch, promising that in the future he will try to visit again. Karl tells one of the boys at the orphanage that the soldier promised to return and take him back to America.*

Heliogabalus. *When Kilgore Trout senses the public is closing in on him because of his invitation to the Midland City Arts Festival in* Breakfast of Champions, *he likens it to his theory that the atmosphere would eventually become unbreathable. He tells Bill, his parakeet, that they would all become Heliogabalus. The precise meaning is a bit vague, but Vonnegut informs the reader that Heliogabalus was the Roman emperor who would imprison an individual inside a sculpted bull and have a fire lit beneath it. The last sounds of the dying individual would be heard through the bull's mouth.*

helix. (*MN* 190:L8) The railing stopped O'Hare, and he gazed down the stairwell, down a beckoning **helix** to the patch of sure death below.
(*GBR* 201:L16) Eliot, rising from his seat in the bus, beheld the firestorm of Indianapolis. He was awed by the majesty of the column of fire, which was at least eight miles in diameter and fifty miles high. The boundaries of the column seemed absolutely sharp and unwavering, as though made of glass. Within the boundaries, **helixes** of dull red embers turned in stately harmony about an inner core of white. The white seemed holy.
(*Blue* 161:L25) He (*Fred Jones*) must have felt like (*Terry*) Kitchen again when he fired his machine guns up in the wild blue yonder, and saw a plane in front of him draw a **helix** of smoke and flame—ending in a sunburst far below.

Heller, Charlene. *A veteran of the Army of Mars who has a concession booth outside the Rumfoord estate, down the line from Bee's and Chrono's booth. Prior to her Martian Army days she had been an* assistant dietitian of the cafeteria of Stivers High School in Dayton, Ohio (*ST* 241:L28).

Helmholtz, George M. *Helmholtz has two incarnations in Vonnegut's very early work. In the 1955 short story "The Kid Nobody Could Handle," Helmholtz is the caring head of the music department at Lincoln High School, responsible for turning around the wayward Jim Donnini.*

In Sirens of Titan, *they are recruiting agents for Rumfoord's Army of Mars. Helmholtz poses as a former high school bandmaster teamed with Roberta Wiley, supposedly a former algebra teacher and an apparent male cross-dresser. Moments after Malachi Constant reads his father's letter in the Wilburhampton Hotel, Helmholtz and Wiley enter the room and offer him a way out of his earthly mess.* (*ST* 92:L26-32, 93:L1-5) Your situation on Earth is hopeless. Your wife is a beast. Moreover, our intelligence informs us that here on Earth you will not only be made penniless by civil suits, but that you will be imprisoned for criminal negligence as well.

In addition to a pay scale and privileges well above those accorded lieutenant-colonels in Earthling armies, we can offer you immunity from all Earthling legal harassment, and an opportunity to see a new and interesting planet, and an opportunity to think about your native planet from a fresh and beautifully detached viewpoint.

Hepburn, Mary and Roy. *The childless Hepburns were lifelong Iliumites in* Galápagos. *Roy was a millwright at GEFFCo, Ilium's largest employer. For twenty-five years Mary was a much- loved high school biology teacher. So well loved was she that for twelve consecutive years the students voted her the most popular teacher. Her nickname among the students was "Mother Nature Personified" and the high school's last graduating class dedicated their yearbook to her.*

After years of service to GEFFCo and then to its successor Matsumoto, Roy was summarily discharged along with hundreds of other workers. Matsumoto had so well computerized the manufacturing process that only twelve workers were needed to run the mill. On the day he was discharged, Roy signed them up for "the Nature Cruise of the Century." They were the very first people to sign on for the trip. Shortly thereafter, Roy's brain tumor was detected and he died August 3, 1986, at the age of fifty-nine. Mary, then fifty-one, kept her promise to him and traveled down to Ecuador for the cruise.

A distant relative of Daniel Boone, Mary became the midwife to the next evolutionary step for Homo sapiens. She secretively used the sperm from Captain Adolf von Kleist to inseminate the Kanka-bono girls. One of the sons from this union paired off with the furry Akiko, the product of genetic mutation due to radiation fallout at Hiroshima, and the human race was well on its way to returning to the sea as something closely resembling sea lions.

Though deeply devoted to her husband Roy, she had a brief affair with Robert Wojciehowitz, head of the English Department at Ilium High School. Later, while on board the Bahía de Darwin, *she took pity on the dying con man James Wait, posing as Willard Flemming, and married him just before he expired. She lived with Adolf von Kleist for ten years after they were stranded, breaking up only after he found out about her use of his sperm. She died at the age of eighty-one when she was eaten by a shark.*

Herald, Randy. *The showgirl whose picture is on the cover of* The Investigator *with the headline "I WANT A MAN WHO CAN GIVE ME A GENIUS BABY!"* (*GBR* 115:L1-12) *Insurance salesman Fred Rosewater uses the headline as an opportunity to launch into a life insurance pitch to the few customers in the coffee shop.*

Herpers, Dr. Albert. *In* Player Piano, *President of Cornell University and the recipient of a five- year-old letter from Doctor Ewing J. Halyard, highly critical of the school's football program. Doctor Herpers shared the letter with football coach Roseberry, who was able to exact revenge upon Halyard when a computer check found that Halyard was short a physical education class and would have to return to Cornell or lose his advanced degrees.*

Herrick, Cleota. *Despite being dubbed "the ugliest woman in Indiana," Noah Rosewater married her* because she had four hundred thousand dollars. With her money he expanded the factory and bought more farms, all in Rosewater County. He became the largest individual hog farmer in the North. And, in order not to be victimized by meat packers, he bought controlling interest in an Indianapolis slaughterhouse. In order not to be victimized by steel suppliers, he bought controlling interest in a steel company in Pittsburgh. In order not to be victimized by coal suppliers, he bought controlling interest in several mines. In order not to be victimized by money lenders, he founded a bank (*GBR* 20:L7-17). *Cleota was the great-grandmother of Eliot Rosewater. She gave birth to Samuel Rosewater, who became a Republican Party king-maker.*

Hertz, Rudy. *In* Player Piano, *the aging lathe operator at the Ilium Works whose work motion was immortalized on a computer tape by Paul Proteus, Ed Finnerty, and Lawson Shepherd. The tape was then used to develop computerized manufacturing machines which copied the operations of master workers. The three young engineers' experiments greatly contributed to automating blue-collar workers out of employment.*

Hildreth, Celia (see **Celia Hoover**).

Hildreth, Gerald. *The sixty-year-old owner of an immaculately kept taxicab on eastern Long Island whose local roots go back three hundred years.* Bluebeard*'s Rabo Karabekian points out that when Hildreth was with the Rescue Squad, he found Jackson Pollock's body sixty feet from the tree his car hit and only weeks later was picking up the pieces of Terry Kitchen's head.*

Hildreth, Shirley. *The sister of Celia Hildreth Hoover who left Midland City and was never heard from again. In* Deadeye Dick *she was rumored to have been seen as an extra in the remake of "King Kong."*

Hilton, Gloria. *The movie star wife of writer George Murra in the short story "Go Back to Your Precious Wife and Son." She had previously been married to a motorcycle policeman, a sugar millionaire, a Tarzan movie star, her agent, and then Murra. The couple moved from Los Angeles to New Hampshire so Murra could be closer to his son (from his first marriage), who was attending a private high school. The unnamed narrator of the story is a bathtub enclosure salesman and installer who witnesses the breakup of Hilton and Murra. She had grown weary of Murra, who failed to write a word since their move. The bathtub man was there to install a custom-made shower door with a glass etching of Gloria Hilton's head. At the height of the marital spat she tells Murra to go back to his wife and son.*

Hilyer, Tom. *The middle-class Whitehill School classmate of the wealthy Dr. Remenzel, both of whom are escorting their sons to the ritzy private school for their first day. Hilyer and his son were both scholarship students, meaning their parents didn't have the means to send them. They earned their way into Whitehill on academic merit, the primary criterion for admission. Remenzel's son Eli didn't tell his parents he failed to meet the strict academic requirements, and this is why the short story is called "The Lie."*

Hinkley, Bearse. *The seventy-two-year-old pharmacist in the short story "Miss Temptation" who kindly prepares Susanna's New York newspapers for her alluring and barefoot arrival each afternoon. When the recently returned Corporal Fuller demeans Susanna for her Bohemian presence, she decides to leave the summer stock theater troop. Hinkley convinces Fuller he must deliver Susanna's newspapers and apologize for his jealousy.*

Hiroguchi, Akiko. *The daughter of Zenji and Hisako Hiroguchi, Akiko's genetic code was altered by her mother's exposure to radiation during the atomic bombing of Hiroshima. She was born on the "northern-most extremity of the Galápagos Islands." The result is that Akiko and Kamikaze, Captain von Kleist's son by one of the Kanka-bono women made possible by Mary Hepburn's unauthorized use of von Kleist's sperm, give rise to an entirely new, furry version of humans. Thus, Hiroshima's atomic bombing and an unwitting German-American provide the basis for man's return to the sea—a salvation of sorts considering the fate of the Earth from Leon Trout's perspective across a millennium.* (*Gal* 59:L7, 12) When **Akiko** became an adult on Santa Rosalia, she would be very much like her mother on the inside, but in a different sort of skin . . . **Akiko** was protected from sunburn, and from the chilly water when she swam, and the abrasiveness of lava when she chose to sit or lie down—whereas her mother's bare skin was wholly defenseless against these ordinary hazards of island life.

Hiroguchi, Hisako. *The wife of Zenji Hiroguchi and the mother of Akiko, the furry progenitor of humanity as it moved back to the oceans. Hisako's mother survived the atom-bombing of Hiroshima, but her genetic code was altered so that when Hisako gave birth to Akiko, she was covered with a fine fur coat. Hisako taught ikebana, the Japanese art of flower arranging. She became infuriated with Zenji when she learned he had programmed Mandarax to teach ikebana in hundreds of languages. After Zenji was killed by looters, Hisako paired off with the blind Selena MacIntosh. Together they died in a suicide pact thirty-one years after being stranded on Galápagos. Hisako suffered deep depression for her last twenty years.*

Hiroguchi, Zenji. *The husband of Hisako and father of Akiko, this twenty-nine year old computer genius created Gokubi and then Mandarax. Though an acknowledged computer genius, he was a salary worker for Matsumoto, and this allowed Andrew MacIntosh to approach Hiroguchi about opening his own company. MacIntosh invited Zenji and Hisako to visit his Mexican villa and then join him for "the Nature Cruise of the Century" in the hope he could get Hiroguchi to leave Matsumoto. They traveled to Mexico under the name Kenzaburo, listing Zenji's occupation as a veterinarian. Hiroguchi and MacIntosh were shot in the backs of their heads by the paranoid schizophrenic deserter Private Geraldo Delgado, who had been looting a store down on the docks of Guayaquil.*

Hiscock, Ernest Hubble. (*HP* 62:L18-22) He was a Tarkington graduate who at the age of 21 was a nose-gunner on a Navy bomber whose pilot crashed his plane with a full load of bombs onto the flight deck of a Japanese aircraft carrier in the Battle of Midway during World War II. *His divorced parents took up a collection to repair and mechanize the Lutz Carillon. This had been a source of displeasure for some alumni, who felt modernization took away from the college's tradition. Without the need for students to swing on the bell ropes, the bells could be played by keyboard, which is exactly what gave Eugene Debs Hartke so much pleasure years later.*

Hitler, Adolf (also **Adolph**). *Vonnegut mentions Hitler in* Mother Night, Cat's Cradle, Slaughterhouse-Five, Wanda June, Jailbird, Deadeye Dick, Galápagos, Bluebeard, and Hocus Pocus.

Hitz, Benjamin D. (*JB* dedication) For **Benjamin D. Hitz**, / Close friend of my youth, / Best man at my wedding. / **Ben**, you used to tell me about / Wonderful books you had just read, / And then I would imagine that I / Had read them, too. / You read nothing but the best, **Ben**, / While I studied chemistry. / Long time no see.

Hitz is also mentioned in the dedication of Galápagos *as one of Vonnegut's companions on a trip out west with Hillis L. Howie.*

Hitz, Lowell W. *The twenty-five-millionth child to be born in the Chicago Lying-in Hospital according to a news report in the life-without-aging short story "Tomorrow and Tomorrow and Tomorrow."*

Hocus Pocus (1990) (see also **Eugene Debs Hartke**, **Tarkington College**, **Hiroshi Matsumoto**). *Vonnegut uses the magicians' famous phrase in reference to man's ability to rationalize new, often misleading explanations of history. Outside of the novel named for such a "big-brained" skill, its only other occurrence is early in* Breakfast of Champions. *In that novel's opening pages, when Vonnegut debunks the myths we are taught as youngsters in elementary school, he says,* It was as though the country were saying to its citizens, *"In nonsense is strength."*

A lot of the nonsense was the innocent result of playfulness on the part of the founding fathers of the nation of Dwayne Hoover and Kilgore Trout. The founders were aristocrats, and they wished to show off their useless education, which consisted of the study of **hocus-pocus** from ancient times (*BC* 10:L10).

Considering Vonnegut's usage for the term, it is surprising it doesn't reappear until the novel Hocus Pocus. *Eugene Debs Hartke uses it to describe the tirades he would employ to encourage his troops in Vietnam to be the best, most ruthless soldiers they could be.* (*HP* 148:L28-29) In Vietnam, though, I really was the mastermind. Yes, and that still bothers me. During my last year there, when my ammunition was language instead of bullets, I invented justifications for all the killing and dying we were doing which impressed even me! I was a genius of lethal **hocus pocus**!

. . . If my list of women isn't to include high school or prostitutes, then my list of those whose lives I took shouldn't include possibles and probables, or those killed by artillery or air strikes called in by me, and surely not all those, many of them Americans, who died as an indirect result of all my **hocus pocus**, all my blah blah blah.

When Hartke reflects on the murder mystery of Letitia Smiley, he understands the college's position in relation to the investigation based on his Vietnam experience. (*HP* 182:L34) I have to wonder, too, in light of my own experiences in public-relations **hocus pocus** and the recent history of my Government, if there weren't a lot of people back in 1922 *(the year of Vonnegut's birth)* who could put 2 and 2 together as easily as I have now. For the sake of the reputation of what had become Scipio's principal business, the college, there could have been a massive cover-up.

As much as anything else, Hocus Pocus *is about the loss of history and culture. These memoirs of Eugene Debs Hartke, written in the library of what was Tarkington College and now part of the New York State prison system, include considerations of parental fraud, the legacy of genetic disabilities, and the loss of a traditionally dynamic relationship and communal bond held by the wealthy in common with the working classes (this harkens back to themes in* God Bless You, Mr. Rosewater*). Captivated by the search for a worthy perpetual-motion machine and his concern for those with learning disabilities, Elias Tarkington established The Mohiga Valley Free Institute in 1869. In 1875 the school's name was changed but its mission remained. Over time it became a beacon for learning-disabled children of wealthy families from around the world. The list of college benefactors includes historical figures noted for their brutality (Pahlavi, the family of the former Shah of Iran; Samoza, the former Central American dictator) and fictitious characters such as Jason Wilder, a William F. Buckley type whose extreme conservatism is the driving force behind Hartke's 1991 dismissal for "teaching pessimism."*

Vonnegut uses the time frame of the novel, from the rise of The Mohiga Wagon Company to the takeover of Tarkington College, to show the roots of American wealth and cultural dominance as well as its demise. Scipio and Tarkington prospered as long as people maintained meaningful occupations. Once America achieved such a high standard of living and people didn't want to work as hard as they once did, industry closed its domestic plants and reopened abroad, resulting in a shift of wealth. America became a consumer rather than a producer, eventually losing its ability to handle such central functions as maintaining its prison systems. Any idea of an enduring American Dream is doomed from the hocus pocus it inflicts on its people as a way of maintining its culture.

Hoenikker, Angela. *The oldest of Felix Hoenikker's three children, Angela is the source for most of Little Newt's childhood memories of his father. When she was sixteen her mother died while giving birth to Newt, leaving Angela to care for her father and brothers. She and her brothers each had chips of ice-nine from their father's first experiment, the one that killed him and the family's dog. It was she who had found their father dead on Christmas Eve, and it was she who helped John/Jonah clean up the shards of ice-nine splintered from the frozen sinkful of water attached to the equally stone-frozen body of Dr. von Koenigswald. Newt provides an important historical footnote about Angela.* (*CC* 23:L33-35, 24:L5-9, 17-19) "**Angela** was one of the unsung heroines of the atom bomb, incidentally, and I don't think the story has ever been told. Maybe you can use it. After the turtle incident *(Dr. Hoenikker wondered whether their spines buckled or contracted)*, Father got so interested in turtles that he stopped working on the atom bomb. Some people from the Manhattan Project finally came out to the house to ask **Angela** what to do. She told them to take away Father's turtles. So one night they went into his laboratory and stole the turtles and the aquarium. Father never said a word about the disappearance of the turtles. He just came to work the next day and looked for things to play with and think about, and everything there was to play with and think about had something to do with the bomb. . . . Father was all she had.

She didn't have any boy friends. She didn't have any friends at all. She had only one hobby. She played the Clarinet."

John/Jonah is crude in his initial description of her. (*CC* 96:L19-20, 100:L23) **Angela** was the horse-faced platinum blonde I had noticed earlier.

. . . And then **Angela**, a woman to whom God had given virtually nothing with which to catch a man, showed me a picture of her husband *(Harrison C. Conners, one-time lab assistant to her father and now president of Fabri-Tek in Indianapolis). Angela's marriage is a complete failure according to Newt, who tells John/Jonah how cruel and unfaithful Conners is to his sister.*

While having drinks on San Lorenzo with Newt, Julian Castle, and John/Jonah, Angela gets sentimentally sloppy and resentful of how little monetary compensation her father received for his scientific achievements. Newt asks her to play her clarinet for them since that always calms and pleases him. Newt sees this as a way of settling down Angela more than anything else. The ensuing scene startlingly reveals the true depth and talent of this hideous giant for John/Jonah. (*CC* 148:L28-36, 149:L30-35, 150:L1-13) I did not know what was going to come from **Angela**'s clarinet. No one could have imagined what was going to come from there.

I expected something pathological, but I did not expect the depth, the violence, and the almost intolerable beauty of the disease.

Angela moistened and warmed the mouthpiece, but did not blow a single preliminary note. Her eyes glazed over, and her long, bony fingers twittered idly over the noiseless keys. . . .

Meade Lux Lewis played four bars alone—and then **Angela Hoenikker** joined in.

Her eyes were closed.

I was flabbergasted.

She was great.

She improvised around the music of the Pullman porter's son; went from liquid lyricism to rasping lechery to the shrill skittishness of a frightened child, to a heroin nightmare.

Her glissandi spoke of heaven and hell and all that lay between.

Such music from such a woman could only be a case of schizophrenia or demonic possession.

My hair stood on end, as though **Angela** were rolling on the floor, foaming at the mouth, and babbling fluent Babylonian.

When the music was done, I shrieked at Julian Castle, who was transfixed, too, "My God—life! Who can understand even one little minute of it?"

"Don't try," he said. "Just pretend you understand."

"That's—that's very good advice." I went limp.

Angela's death was an equally moving scene for John/Jonah. (*CC* 230:L2-6) And I saw magnificence in the way poor **Angela** had died, too. She had picked up a clarinet in the ruins of Bolivar and had begun to play it at once, without concerning herself as to whether the mouthpiece might be contaminated with ice-nine.

"Soft pipes, play on," I murmured huskily.

Hoenikker, Celia. *In* Cat's Cradle, *Dr. Felix Hoenikker's unseen sister who lives on Shelter Island, New York, raising giant schnauzers.*

Hoenikker, Dr. Felix. *The Nobel prize winner for physics and father of ice-nine in* Cat's Cradle. *He stole away the heart of Emily from his future boss Dr. Marvin Breed, when both were students at M.I.T. A short man, Hoenikker sired a giantess, Angela, and a midget, Newton (Little Newt). Franklin was the middle child. There were rumors that Dr. Breed actually fathered Emily's children.*

The narrator of the text goes to Ilium as part of his research for the book The Day the World Ended, *a chronicle of the activities conducted by the scientists responsible for the atom bomb on the day it was dropped on Hiroshima. He was looking for the ironic Sunday family barbecue on the day the bomb was dropped. The narrator later learns from Newton that on that fateful day, Dr. Hoenikker was in his pajamas and bathrobe, smoking a cigar, and playing "cat's cradle" with a piece of string. What he finds at the Research Laboratory of the General Forge and Foundry Company is Hoenikker's legacy of playful absentmindedness. Ice-nine became a reality after a Marine general complained about all the mud the Marines traditionally had to get through.*

Hoenikker died of an apparent heart attack at his Cape Cod home on Christmas Eve after telling his children about his invention. He was busy melting down the sliver of ice-nine when he took a break, sat in his wicker chair, and died. The children returned, cleaned up the puddles of water in the kitchen, and when the family dog licked the towel he froze into a furry stone. The children then split up the remaining ice-nine between them.

Vonnegut's inspiration for Dr. Hoenikker is recounted in the "Playboy" Interview, reprinted in Palm Sunday. *(PS* 102:L4 *Playboy Interview)*
VONNEGUT: **Dr. Felix Hoenikker**, the absent-minded scientist, was a caricature of Dr. Irving Langmuir, the star of the G.E. Research Laboratory. I knew him some. My brother worked with him. Langmuir was wonderfully absent-minded. He wondered out loud one time whether, when turtles pulled in their heads, their spines buckled or contracted. I put that in the book. One time he left a tip under his plate after his wife served him breakfast at home. I put that in. His most important contribution, though, was the idea for what I called "Ice-9," a form of frozen water that was stable at room temperature. He didn't tell it directly to me. It was a legend around the Laboratory about the time H. G. Wells came to Schenectady. That was long before my time. I was just a little boy when it happened—listening to the radio, building model airplanes.

Hoenikker, Emily. *The wife of Felix Hoenikker and mother to Franklin, Angela, and Newt. She died during the birth of Newt because of a previously crushed pelvis she suffered after driving Felix's Marmon. She was driving his car because Felix snapped one day and left his car in traffic.*

Before meeting Felix, Emily and Marvin Breed, the tombstone carver and salesman, were starting to become good friends while still in high school. They were co-chairmen of the Class Colors Committee. Breed gave up football to take violin lessons because Emily was such a well- accomplished musician on a number of instruments. When Asa Breed came home from M.I.T. with schoolmate Felix Hoenikker, Emily broke Marvin's heart.

Emily's unusual tombstone is described as an alabaster phallus twenty feet high and three feet thick (*CC* 57:L27-28).

Hoenikker, Franklin. *The middle child of Emily and Dr. Felix Hoenikker, Frank grows up a solemn and solitary child. On the day Hiroshima was bombed, he was busy putting red and black ants in a jar to see them fight. In high school he got a job at Jack's Hobby Shop, where he spent all his earnings on constructing a realistic small-scale depiction of an entire country. Unknown to Jack, Frank was also having a sexual affair with his wife. Because he spent all his afternoon and evening time in the hobby shop, he often fell asleep in school and was derisively called "Secret Agent X-9" by the other students, who looked at him as an oddball.*

Frank left Ilium during the graveside funeral service for his father and hitched his way down to Sarasota, Florida. There he went to work at a model shop, which turned out to be a front for running stolen cars to Cuba. Two years after the death of his father, the Treasury Department secured a warrant for his arrest, but he fled the country in a boat which just made it to San Lorenzo before sinking. Though at first placed under arrest by the authorities, when Papa Monzano found out he was the son of Felix Hoenikker, he released him from prison and made him a Major General and Minister of Science and Progress in the Republic of San Lorenzo. In exchange, Frank gave him his sliver of ice-nine which he had since his father died. Frank was twenty-six at the time.

Hoenikker, Newton. *The youngest child of Emily and Dr. Felix Hoenikker, Little Newt was the midget of the family. The narrator of* Cat's Cradle *contacted Newt once he found out he was pledging the Delta Upsilon fraternity. The narrator was a Cornell alumnus and a DU brother. (Vonnegut attended Cornell before the war and became a DU brother, as well.) Little Newt had planned to major in pre-med, but he flunked out and was forced to resign his DU pledge. Along with his brother and sister, Newt received one-third of the remaining ice-nine after his father died. After only a brief acquaintance, he married Zinka, a Ukrainian midget and dancer with the Borzoi Dance Company which performed in Indianapolis. Shortly after their honeymoon, Zinka stole* *his chip of ice-nine and returned to the Soviet Union. She claimed to be twenty-three, but Newt later found out she was forty-two.*

Little Newt's birth caused the death of his mother. She had previously had her pelvis crushed in a car accident. She was not used to driving her husband's Marmon, which she retrieved from downtown Ilium when he abandoned it in traffic one morning.

Hoenikker, Rudolph. *Dr. Felix Hoenikker's identical twin who lives in Zurich and manufactures music boxes. As with their sister Celia, Rudolph is mentioned but not seen in* Cat's Cradle.

Hoess, Rudolf Franz. *The Commandant of Auschwitz who was hanged in 1947 with the assistance of Bernard Mengel, one of Howard Campbell's Jerusalem prison guards in* Mother Night. *Campbell credits Hoess with organizing the Sonderkommando, the corpse-carrying volunteers from the Auschwitz inmates. Campbell further cites Hoess as one of the prime illustrations of the cuckoo-clock in hell—his description of the totalitarian mind.*

Hoffman, Abbie. (*FWD* 187:L24) "I was willing to believe back in the 1960s that deep meditation as practiced in India might be a way to achieve happiness and wisdom which had not been previously available to people of European and African stock. The Beatles also believed this for a while. I doubt that the late, great (I mean it) **Abbie Hoffman** ever believed it. He wasn't about to give up his frenzied sense of humor, the sanest thing in this country during the Vietnam War, in exchange for personal, inner peace."
(*FWD* 189:L5, 30) I mentioned **Abbie Hoffman** in that piece about books as mantras for meditation. I realize that most people nowadays don't know who he was or what he did. He was a clowning genius, having come into the world that way, like Lenny Bruce and Jack Benny and Ed Wynn and Stan Laurel and W. C. Fields and the Marx Brothers and Red Skelton and Fred Allen and Woody Allen and so on. He was a member of my children's generation. He is high on my list of saints, of exceptionally courageous, unarmed, unsponsored, unpaid souls who have tried to slow down even a little bit state crimes against those Jesus Christ said should inherit the Earth someday. . . .

I doubt that **Abbie Hoffman**'s clowning shortened the Vietnam War by as much as a microsecond; nor did protests by anyone but the enemy. At a meeting of writers (P.E.N.) in Stockholm, when that war still had about a year to go, I said that almost all American artists of every sort were opposed to the war, forming a sort of laser beam of moral outrage. The power of this beam, I reported, turned out to be equivalent to that of a banana cream pie three feet in diameter when dropped from a stepladder four feet high.
(*FWD* 209:L5, 32) Mark's only crime against his government, and the only crime committed by **Abbie Hoffman** and so many others of that generation

during the Vietnam War, was a sublimely Jeffersonian form of treason. It was disrespect. . . .

If **Abbie Hoffman** had been my son, I would have told him that he was doing the right thing while the Vietnam War was going on. I would have warned him, too, that he was putting his life on the line for his countrymen.

Holdermann, Bill. *The engineer and manager from the Indianapolis Works who wrote the morality play performed at the Meadows in* Player Piano.

Holderness, Marvin Sharpe. *While serving a prison sentence for murdering his brother, Holderness sent a manuscript of his novel* 2000 A.D. *to Dr. Felix Hoenikker, asking his advice about what type of explosive to write into his tale. The string used to hold together the manuscript is the same used by Hoenikker to play "cat's cradle" on the morning of the Hiroshima bombing. Hoenikker never read the manuscript. Little Newt did and he told John/Jonah the following:* The novel was about the end of the world in the year 2000, and the name of the book was *2000 A.D.* It told about how mad scientists made a terrific bomb that wiped out the whole world. There was a big sex orgy when everybody knew that the world was going to end, and then Jesus Christ Himself appeared ten seconds before the bomb went off (*CC* 19:L15-24).

Holiday Inn. *("The World's Innkeeper") The Holiday Inn of the mythical Midland City, Ohio, is the center of activity in* Breakfast of Champions, *serving as the forum for Dwayne Hoover's announcement that his wife Celia committed suicide as well as his violent rampage after reading Kilgore Trout's* Now It Can Be Told. *Wearing mirrored sunglasses purchased at the Holiday Inn outside Ashtabula, Ohio, Vonnegut walks into the bar of Midland City's franchise to become a part of the confrontation involving Kilgore Trout, Dwayne Hoover, and Rabo Karabekian. Midland City's Holiday Inn is also ground zero for the neutron bombing in* Deadeye Dick.
(*BC* 64:L15) He went past his principal place of business, which was *Dwayne Hoover's Exit Eleven Pontiac Village*, and he turned into the parking lot of the new **Holiday Inn** next door. Dwayne owned a third of the Inn partnership with Midland City's leading orthodontist, Dr. Alfred Maritimo, and Bill Miller, who was Chairman of the Parole Board at the Adult Correctional Institution at Shepherdstown, among other things. *Dwayne's homosexual son Bunny, né George, played piano in the hotel's bar.*

In Slaughterhouse-Five, *Billy Pilgrim owns one-fifth of a Holiday Inn in Ilium, New York. One of Billy's business partners is the physician who gives Valencia Pilgrim a hysterectomy. See also: BC* 192:L19; 234:L12; *WFG—Playboy Interview* 242:L18; *PS—Playmates* 154:L22.

Home Sweet Home Moving and Storage. *In* Bluebeard, *Rabo Karabekian uses the company to store his great collection of abstract expressionist* *paintings. He also employs them to retrieve his decaying mural "Windsor Blue Number Seventeen" from the basement of the GEFFCo building in Manhattan.*

Homestead. *The southern part of Ilium, New York, across the river from both the Ilium Works and the neighborhood lived in by the employed Ph.Ds, in* Player Piano. *It is where the unemployed and the Reeks and Wrecks live.*

Homo sapiens. (*GBR* 138:L11-12) "They *(the poor)* stand today as a monumental caricature of **Homo sapiens**, the harsh and horrible reality created by us out of our own misguided pity. They are also, if we continue our present course, the living prophecy of what a great percentage of the rest of us will become." *This is from "A Rift Between Friends in the War of Ideas," a pamphlet sent to Stewart Buntline from Reed McAllister, lawyer to both Buntline and the Rosewater estate, to help undo Stewart's socialist notions, which he had long ago abandoned, though unknown to McAllister.*

homosexual, homosexuality. *As contentious as this subject is for many, Vonnegut never deals contemptuously with homosexuals in his stories. The fawning, obsequious Bunny Weeks (owner of the dockside restaurant The Weir in* God Bless You, Mr. Rosewater*), is ill-mannered and rude to all but his wealthy patrons. His cutting remarks, however, are based on economic class distinctions and have nothing to do with his homosexuality. Dwayne Hoover's homosexual son Bunny (né George) is the kindly piano player in the Tally-ho Room of the Midland City Holiday Inn (*Breakfast of Champions *and* Deadeye Dick*). Milo Maritimo is the Holiday Inn's night desk clerk (*Breakfast of Champions*), grandson of Guillermo "Little Willie" Maritimo, one of Al Capone's bodyguards. James Wait is a misled and slightly twisted homosexual prostitute (*Galápagos*). Marilee Kemp marries Count Portomaggiore, Mussolini's Minister of Culture and head of British Intelligence in Italy during the war (*Bluebeard*). He took a wife to avoid any suspicion of espionage, but he was eventually executed for being a homosexual pedophile. Bruce Bergeron is the homosexual Ice Capades chorus boy—Tarkington class of 1985—befriended by Andrea Wakefield, the college president's wife who enjoys him as a skating partner. He is eventually killed by someone presumed to hate gays. Kilgore Trout's* Plague on Wheels (Breakfast of Champions), *has a spaceship from Lingo-three carrying Kago and a crew of Zeltoldimarians, all homosexual. Aside from these notable instances, Vonnegut makes a few references to homosexuality undercutting society's ambiguous appreciations of maleness and gayness.*

(*PP* 74:L17) He *(Ed Finnerty)* had a candor about his few emotional attachments that Paul found disquieting. He used words to describe his feelings that Paul could never bring himself to use when speaking of a friend: love, affection, and other words generally consigned to young and inexperienced lovers. It wasn't **homosexual**; it was an archaic expression of friendship by an undisciplined man in an age when most men seemed in mortal fear of being mistaken for pansies for even a split second.

(*CC* 105:L20) "You know why Castle will never marry the girl, even though he loves her, even though she loves him, even though they grew up together?" he whispered.

"No, sir, I don't."

"Because he's a **homosexual**," whispered Minton. "She can tell that from an index, too." *Ambassador Minton speaking to John/Jonah about Philip Castle and Mona Aamons Monzano. Mrs Minton used to index books and claimed all sorts of revelations could be gleaned from one's method on indexing.*

(*SL5* 99:L9-10) The Tralfamadorians tried to give Billy clues that would help him imagine sex in the invisible dimension. They told him that there could be no Earthling babies without male **homosexuals**. There could be babies without female **homosexuals**. There couldn't be babies without women over sixty-five years old. There could be babies without men over sixty-five. There couldn't be babies without other babies who had lived an hour or less after birth. And so on.

(*BC* 181:L32-33) The armed forces knew he *(Bunny Weeks)* was a **homosexual**, that he was certain to fall in love with other fighting men, and the armed forces didn't want to put up with such love affairs.

(*WFG* 174:L9 *Address to the National Institute of Arts and Letters, 1971*) I wish in particular to call your attention to the work of Dr. M. Sydney Margoles, a Los Angeles endocrinologist, who is able to distinguish between male **homosexuals** and heterosexuals by means of urinalysis. He doesn't ever have to meet them. What other sweet mysteries of life are chemicals? All of them, I believe. Biochemistry is everything. The speculations of artists about the human condition are trash.

(*DD* 99:L32) I think I am a **homosexual**, but I can't be sure. I have never made love to anyone. *The private musings of Rudy Waltz.*

(*FWD* 29:L34) "A rule we used to be able to extrapolate from cultural history, one which doesn't seem to work anymore, is that an American writer had to be an alcoholic in order to win a Nobel Prize Sinclair Lewis, Eugene O'Neill, John Steinbeck, the suicide Ernest Hemingway. That rule no longer works, in my opinion, because artistic sensibilities are no longer regarded in this country as being characteristic of females. I no longer have to arrive at this lectern drunk, having slugged somebody in a bar last night, in order to prove that I am not what was a loathsome creature not long ago, which is to say a **homosexual**." *See also: ST* 274:L2; *GBR* 34:L13; 125:L21; *BC* 27:L25; 65:L18; 143:L8; 176:L1; 229:L17; 257:L31; *WFG—There's a Maniac Loose Out There* 69:L8; *WFG—In a Manner That Must Shame God Himself* 199:L15; *JB* 114:L25; 154:L8,11; *DD* 133:L28; 172:L2; 186:L4; *Gal* 14:L24; 163:L20,29; 165:L19; *Blue* 162:L11; 226:L3; 230:L11,16; 154:L8; *HP* 141:L17,19; 163:L33; *FWD* 65:L10,21; 118:L20; 196:L1.

Hoobler. *The original family name of Dwayne Hoover's stepparents.* (*BC* 130:L1-12) Dwayne Hoover's stepparents had come from. . . West Virginia to Midland City during the First World War, to make big money at the Keedsler Automobile Company, which was manufacturing airplanes and trucks. When they got to Midland City, they had their name changed legally from ***Hoobler*** to *Hoover*, because there were so many black people in Midland City named **Hoobler**.

As Dwayne Hoover's stepfather explained to him one time, "It was embarrassing. Everybody up here naturally assumed **Hoobler** was a *Nigger* name."

Hoobler, Cynthia. *Briefly hired by Rudy Waltz to care for his parents while he went to New York for the production of "Katmandu," Cynthia is the daughter of Mary Hoobler.*

Hoobler, Dwayne, Grace, and Wanda June. *In the short story "The Big Space Fuck" reprinted in the section of* Palm Sunday *entitled "Obscenity," the Hooblers are being sued by their daughter Wanda June. She was the head of a shoplifting ring and* The only way she could avoid prison was to prove that everything she was and did was her parents' fault (*PS* 231:L30-32).

Dwayne and Grace live in Elk Harbor, Ohio, on the shore of what used to be Lake Erie. Lake Erie was almost solid sewage now. There were man-eating lampreys in there thirty-eight feet long. **Dwayne** was a guard in the Ohio Adult Correctional Institution, which was two miles away. His hobby was making birdhouses out of Clorox bottles. He went on making them and hanging them around his yard, even though there weren't any birds any more (*PS* 227:L15-22 *Obscenity*). *Dwayne had an IQ under 115 and was therefore disqualified from contributing sperm to be carried aboard the spaceship* Arthur C. Clarke *on its way to Andromeda.*

Wanda June's charges against her parents were based on normal parental discipline and/or slovenliness. (*PS* 231:L1-23 *Obscenity*) **Dwayne** was reading charges against himself, so he didn't ask **Grace** what awful thing she was supposed to have done when **Wanda June** was only four, but here it was: Poor little **Wanda June** drew pretty pictures with a crayon all over the new living-room wallpaper to make her mother happy. Her mother blew up and spanked her instead. Since that day, **Wanda June** claimed, she had not been able to look at any sort of art materials without trembling like a leaf and breaking out into cold sweats. "Thus was I deprived," Wanda June's lawyer had her say, "of a brilliant and lucrative career in the arts."

Dwayne meanwhile was learning that he had ruined his daughter's opportunities for what her lawyer called an "advantageous marriage and the comfort and love therefrom." **Dwayne** had done this, supposedly, by being half in the bag whenever a suitor came to call. Also, he was often stripped to the waist when he answered the door, but still had on his cartridge belt and his revolver. She was even able to name a lover her father had lost for her: John

L. Newcomb, who had finally married somebody else. He had a very good job now. He was in command of the security force at an arsenal out in South Dakota, where they stockpiled cholera and bubonic plague.

Hoobler, Josephus. *The former slave who went north to Midland City after his master's liberation and settled on a piece of land called Bluebird Farm. His descendants lost the farm in the Great Depression when the Midland County Merchants Bank foreclosed on the mortgage. Due to the many black families in the area bearing his name, Dwayne Hoover's stepfather changed his name from Hoobler when he arrived from West Virginia.*

In 1937, after Dwayne's stepfather took possession of Bluebird Farm in an insurance settlement, Dwayne discovered what was later called Sacred Miracle Cave.

Hoobler, Mary. *The cook for the Waltz family in* Deadeye Dick, *the source of Rudy Waltz's culinary textual interludes (including recipes for corn bread, barbecue sauce, and chitlins). She claimed that Eleanor Roosevelt's visit to the Waltz's was the highlight of her life. Rudy spent a great deal of time with Mary in the kitchen and learned how to cook and clean from her.*

Hoobler, Wayne. *A descendant of Josephus Hoobler, Wayne is paroled from The Adult Correctional Institution at Shepherdstown on the authority of Parole Board Chair Don Miller, father of Mary Alice Miller, the Queen of the Arts Festival. He goes straight to Dwayne Hoover's Exit Eleven Pontiac Village because he has a strong desire to work for Dwayne Hoover. Wayne was without any social awareness and actually longed for the safer confines of Shepherdstown.* (*BC* 189:L14-22) He missed the clash of steel doors. He missed the bread and the stew and the pitchers of milk and coffee. He missed fucking other men in the mouth and the asshole, and being fucked in the mouth and the asshole, and jerking off—and fucking cows in the prison dairy, all events in a normal sex life on the planet, as far as he knew. *Vonnegut suggest the appropriate epitaph for Wayne should read,* BLACK JAILBIRD—HE ADAPTED TO WHAT THERE WAS TO ADAPT TO (*BC* illustration).

"The Hooligan." *The invention of Dr. Felix Bauxite-13 von Peterswald, which allows one to speak with the dead in* Slapstick. *It wasn't invented for this purpose. Its remarkable ability was accidentally discovered by Francis Iron-7 Hooligan, a janitor in the doctor's laboratory. When von Peterswald listened to the sounds from the other side, he described it as sounding like a poor phone connection to a badly run turkey farm. Wilbur Swain uses the device to speak with his dead sister Eliza.*

Hooligan, Francis Iron-7. *In* Slapstick, *the janitor at work in Dr. von Peterswald's office who stored away the doctor's invention intended for use with a particle-accelerator which is shut down for lack of electricity. In the* *process of putting the pieces away atop a file cabinet, Hooligan discovered he was listening to voices of the dead. Wilbur Swain later uses the device to speak with his sister dead Eliza.*

Hooper, Charlton. *The son of Lyle Hooper, owner of the Black Cat Café, notary public, and Chief of the Scipio Volunteer Fire Department. Despite the fact his father's café was really a whorehouse, Lyle was so well liked and respected that it never stigmatized Charlton.* (*HP* 202:L30) This kindly conspiracy protected Lyle's son **Charlton**, as well. **Charlton** grew to be 2 meters tall, and was a New York State High School All-Star basketball center in his senior year at Scipio High School, and all he ever had to say about his father was that he ran a restaurant. *Charlton was such a good athlete that he was invited to try out for the New York Knicks. He turned down basketball, became a physicist at the Supercollider in Waxahachie, Texas, left when funds dried up and returned to Western New York to teach at Hobart College in Geneva. He returned to Scipio only to claim his father's body after the prison break.*

Hooper, Lyle. *Chief of the Volunteer Fire Department, notary public, father of all-star basketball center Charlton Hooper, and owner of the Black Cat Café in Scipio, Hooper was eventually shot in the back of the head during the prison break at Athena. The Black Cat Café was openly known as a whorehouse of sorts. The prostitutes did their business out back in parked vans. The townspeople loved Lyle Hooper and never called his bar a whorehouse, but the trustees of the college were adamant about its true nature.*

Hooper's wife left him when she discovered she was a lesbian. She ran off with the town's high school gym teacher to Bermuda and earned a living giving sailing lessons.

Lyle Hooper and Whitey VanArsdale ambushed and killed three escaped convicts after the prison break. The prisoners were trying to surrender at the time, flying white pillowcases from broomsticks. VanArsdale was killed immediately, but Hooper was taken prisoner. Hooper was held in the bell tower and was ceaselessly called "pimp." Before his execution he admitted his restaurant really was a whorehouse. This prompts Hartke to surmise a lesson about life in general. (*HP* 207:L1) **LYLE Hooper**'s last words, I think we can say with the benefit of hindsight in the year 2001, might serve as an apt epitaph for a plurality of working adults in industrialized nations during the 20th Century. How could they help themselves, when so many of the jobs they or their mates could get had to do with large-scale deceptions, legal thefts from public treasuries, or the wrecking of the food chain, the topsoil, the water, or the atmosphere?

Hoover, Bunny (né **George**). *In* Breakfast of Champions *Bunny Hoover is the son of Dwayne and Celia Hoover, though we are led to believe by a reference in* Galápagos *that he was fathered by James Wait during a one-time sexual* *liason with Celia. Like Vonnegut, Bunny is the son of a suicide. When he was ten years old, Bunny was sent to military school when he told his father* he wished he were a woman instead of a man, because what men did was so often cruel and ugly. **Bunny Hoover** went to Prairie Military Academy for eight years of uninterrupted sports, buggery and fascism. Buggery consisted of sticking one's penis in somebody else's asshole or mouth, or having it done to one by somebody else. Fascism was a fairly popular political philosophy which made sacred whatever nation and race the philosopher happened to belong to. It called for an autocratic, centralized government, headed up by a dictator. The dictator had to be obeyed, no matter what he told somebody to do (*BC* 180:L5).

After military school, Bunny became the piano player in the cocktail lounge of his father's Holiday Inn. He lived in the Fairchild Hotel in the most dangerous part of Midland City. Despite working for his father, they hadn't spoken to each other in years.

Hoover, Celia. *Born Celia Hildreth, she first appears in* Breakfast of Champions *as Dwayne Hoover's wife and later in* Deadeye Dick *where she is variously seen as Felix Waltz's prom date, the starring actress in Rudy's play "Katmandu," and as a drug addict partial to amphetamines prior to her suicide with Drano. She and Dwayne are the parents of George—better known as Bunny, the homosexual piano player in the Tally-Ho room of the Holiday Inn. However, in* Galápagos *we are told that George is the result of a one-time sexual encounter between Celia and James Wait.*

Vonnegut draws some parallels between Celia and his own mother. (*BC* 181:L1-23) **Celia Hoover** was crazy as a bedbug.

My mother was, too.

Listen: Bunny's mother and my mother were different sorts of human beings, but they were both beautiful in exotic ways, and they both boiled over with chaotic talk about love and peace and wars and evil and desperation, of better days coming by and by, of worse days coming by and by. And both our mothers committed suicide. Bunny's mother ate Drano. My mother ate sleeping pills, which wasn't nearly as horrible.

And Bunny's mother and my mother had one really bizarre symptom in common: neither one could stand to have her picture taken. They were usually fine in the daytime. They usually concealed their frenzies until late at night. But, if somebody aimed a camera at either one of them during the daytime, the mother who was aimed at would crash down on her knees and protect her head with her arms, as though somebody was about to club her to death. It was a scary and pitiful thing to see.

Celia's first mention in Deadeye Dick *fills in her family history. Felix Waltz was the high school class president and had just been dumped by his girlfriend who was going to the prom with the captain of the football team.* (*DD* 40:L14-26) Felix executed a sociological master stroke. He invited a girl who was at the bottom of the social order, whose parents were illiterate and unemployed, who had two brothers in prison, who got very poor grades and engaged in no extracurricular activities, but who, nonetheless, was one of the prettiest young women anybody had ever seen.

Her family was white, but they were so poor that they lived in the black part of town. Also: The few young men who had tried to trifle with her, despite her social class, had spread the word that, no matter what she looked like, she was as cold as ice.

This was **Celia Hildreth**.

After being scared from Felix's home by his father's outrageous greeting, we later see Celia with Dwayne Hoover, then a civilian inspector for the Army Air Corps, coming to view Rudy in jail after killing Eloise Metzger. After the blizzard that wipes out most of Midland City, Rudy again meets Celia, who is behind the counter in the hospital assisting people in locating their displaced relatives. She directs Rudy to the basement of the hospital where his mother is recovering.

Her death occurs in 1970, a few months before the opening of the Mildred Barry Memorial Arts Center. Vonnegut takes a shot at the medical community through the grief expressed by Dwayne after Celia's suicide. (*DD* 196:L1-10) The word was all over town of how in need of support he was, of how vocally ashamed he was to have been such a bad husband that his wife had committed suicide. He had been quoted to me as having made a public announcement in the Tally-ho Room of the new Holiday Inn, the day after **Celia** killed herself: "I take half the blame, but the other half goes to that son-of-bitching Doctor Jerry Mitchell. Watch out for the pills your doctor tells your wife to take. That's all I've got to say."

Hoover, Dwayne. *The Midland City entrepreneur who began life as an adopted orphan. He married Celia Hildreth who committed suicide in 1970 by swallowing Drano. Their one child is the homosexual piano player George, better known as Bunny, though in* Galápagos *we are given to believe George is the issue of a one-time sexual encounter between Celia and James Wait.* Breakfast of Champions *is primarily focused on the mental breakdown of Dwayne Hoover. What pushed Dwayne over the edge was Kilgore Trout's novel* Now It Can Be Told. **Dwayne**'s incipient insanity was mainly a matter of chemicals, of course. **Dwayne Hoover**'s body was manufacturing certain chemicals which unbalanced his mind. But **Dwayne**, like all novice lunatics, needed some bad ideas, too, so that his craziness could have shape and direction. . . .

The bad ideas were delivered to **Dwayne** by Kilgore Trout. . . . Here was the core of the bad ideas which Trout gave to **Dwayne**: Everybody on Earth was a robot, with one exception—**Dwayne Hoover**. . . .

Trout did not expect to be believed. He put the bad ideas into a science-fiction novel, and that was where **Dwayne** found them. The book wasn't addressed to **Dwayne** alone. Trout had never heard of **Dwayne** when he wrote it. It was addressed to anybody who happened to open it up. It said to simply anybody, in effect, "Hey guess what: You're the only creature with free will. How does that make you feel?" (*BC* 13:L33, 14:L1-5, 19-20, 27-29, 15:L8-14)

Dwayne had an ongoing affair with the secretary from his Exit Eleven Pontiac Village, Francine Pefko. Aside from his automobile dealership, Dwayne owned one-third of the Holiday Inn, three Burger Chefs, too, and five coin-operated car washes, and pieces of the Sugar Creek Drive-In Theatre, Radio Station WMCY, the Three Maples Par-Three Golf Course, and seventeen hundred shares of common stock in Barrytron, Limited, a local electronics firm. He owned dozens of vacant lots. He was on the Board of Directors of the Midland County National Bank (*BC* 65:L1-8).

In 1937 Dwayne discovered Sacred Miracle Cave and explored it with his stepfather. He gained one-third ownership of the cave when he and his stepbrothers inherited it from his step-father who had been awarded it as part of a legal judgment for a car accident. Dwayne is briefly seen in Deadeye Dick *when he is invited to view Rudy Waltz sitting in jail. Dwayne is accompanied by Celia Hildreth as they walk past the cage. Rudy recalls that Dwayne somehow avoided serving in the military during the war, serving instead as a civilian inspector of the Army Air Corps.*

Hoover, Lyle and Kyle. *Dwayne Hoover's younger twin stepbrothers who take care of their joint ownership of Sacred Miracle Cave in* Breakfast of Champions. *They live in identical yellow ranch homes on opposite sides of the cave. In 1954 Lyle had his nose broken in a fight over a woman at the Roller Derby. Since that time, Lyle did most of the speaking for the twins. Dwayne shows a true and deep affection for his brothers, who came to his car dealership to inform him about the chemical contamination threatening the Sacred Miracle Cave.*

Though Dwayne's parents adopted him after long years of trying to conceive their own children, Mrs. Hoover conceived the twins soon after he joined them.

Horthy, Dr. Lomar. *The chemist who teamed with the Rev. Dr. Lionel J.D. Jones in* Mother Night *to develop the highly successful embalming fluid Viverine as well as Gingiva-Tru, a gum-simulating substance for false teeth.*

Horton. *The Cincinnati resident and owner of Schramm's pharmacy in Midland City where Rudy Waltz works as a pharmacist in* Deadeye Dick.

Horvath, Dr. Nilsak. *A surface chemist at the Research Laboratory of the General Forge and Foundry Company in* Cat's Cradle. *Francine Pefko is his secretary.*

Hotel Arapahoe (see also **Algonquin Hotel**). *The Hotel Arapahoe is the scene for one of the more embarrassing moments of the youthful Walter Starbuck as* *well as his refuge when newly released from federal prison. It is there he finds a drawer full of stolen clarinet parts and is rearrested when he tries to sell them. The Arapahoe is owned by The RAMJAC Corporation. Starbuck's first appearance at the Arapahoe was in the company of Sarah Wyatt.* (*JB* 104:L24-25) I was flabbergasted. I might have been peering into the twinkling prisms of a time machine. On the other side of the French doors was the famous dining room of the **Hotel Arapahoe** in pristine condition, complete with a Gypsy fiddler—almost atom for atom as it must have been in the time of Diamond Jim Brady. A thousand candles in the chandeliers and on the tables became billions of tiny stars because of all the silver and crystal and china and mirrors in there.

Later in its life, the Arapahoe has a distinctly different appearance and clientele. (*JB* 112:L5-10) No one ever made a reservation at the **Arapahoe** anymore. The only way to arrive there was unexpectedly, in response to some misfortune. As Israel said to me only the other day, when we happened to meet in an elevator, "Making a reservation at the **Arapahoe** is like making a reservation in a burn ward."

Hotel El Dorado. *Wilhelm and Gottfried von Kleist, paternal uncles of Siegfried and Captain Adolf von Kleist, own this Ecuadorian hotel, the planned collection point for passengers of "The Nature Cruise of the Century,"* a brand-new, five-story tourist accommodation—built of unadorned cement block. It had the proportions and mood of a glass-front bookcase, high and wide and shallow. Each bedroom had a floor-to-ceiling wall of glass looking westward—toward the waterfront for deep-draft vessels dredged in the delta three kilometers away (*Gal* 10:L1). *See also: Gal* 16:L6.

House of Hope and Mercy in the Jungle (see **Dr. Julian Castle**).

Hovanessian, Kevork (also **Hovanissian**). Bluebeard*'s Rabo Karabekian proudly lists Hovanessian among the many Armenians to have done well after their families immigrated to the United States. According to Rabo, Hovanessian owns the former J. P. Morgan estate in Southampton, recently sold his ownership of Twentieth Century-Fox, and offered Karabekian $3 million for all the art treasures in his potato barn without seeing them. The offer came after Hovanessian read an article that stated Rabo was holding on to a large collection of Abstract Expressionist masterpieces in order to drive up their value.*

How You Doin'? *When Kilgore Trout hitches a ride in a Ford Galaxie driven by a traveling salesman, Vonnegut recalls this Trout novel.* (*BC* 169:L14-15) Trout wrote a novel one time which he called ***How You Doin'?*** and it was about national averages for this and that. An advertising agency on another planet had a successful campaign for the local equivalent of Earthling peanut butter. The eye-catching part of each ad was the statement of some sort of average—the average number of children, the average size of the male sex organ on that particular planet—which was two inches long, with an inside diameter of three inches and an outside diameter of four and a quarter inches-and so on. The ads invited the readers to discover whether they were superior or inferior to the majority, in this respect or that one—whatever the respect was for that particular ad.

The ad went on to say that superior and inferior people alike ate such and such brand of peanut butter. Except that it wasn't really peanut butter on that planet. It was *Shazzbutter*.

And so on.

Chapter 16

And the peanut butter-eaters on Earth were preparing to conquer the shazzbutter-eaters on the planet in the book by Kilgore Trout. By this time, the Earthlings hadn't just demolished West Virginia and Southeast Asia. They had demolished everything. So they were ready to go pioneering again.

They studied the shazzbutter-eaters by means of electronic snooping, and determined that they were too numerous and proud and resourceful ever to allow themselves to be pioneered.

So the Earthlings infiltrated the ad agency which had the shazzbutter account, and they buggered the statistics in the ads. They made the average for everything so high that everybody on the planet felt inferior to the majority in every respect.

And then the Earthling armored space ships came in and discovered the planet. Only token resistance was offered here and there, because the natives felt so below average. And then the pioneering began.

Vonnegut goes on at various points to describe people according to their dimensions in relationship to national averages.

Howard Johnson's. *The orange-roofed restaurant chain which is next door to every purple-roofed Ethical Suicide Parlor in the 1968 short story "Welcome to the Monkey House." It was previously mentioned in the exact same context in Kilgore Trout's* 2BR02B, *within* God Bless You, Mr. Rosewater. *Those who came in for ethical suicides were entitled to a free meal at the Howard Johnson's restaurant.*

Huie, William Bradford. *The author of* The Execution of Private Slovik *which is found beneath a seat cushion and read by Billy Pilgrim while in the waiting room of the Pine Knoll nursing home. He was waiting to see his mother.*

Humana, Dr. Vox. *"Papa" Monzano's Christian minister who seems more ready for mystical sacrifices than traditional Christian ministry. He waits outside "Papa's" bedroom prepared to deliver last rites complete with a brass dinner bell, a tranquilized chicken in a hatbox, a Bible, and a butcher knife. He explains to* Cat's Cradle*'s narrator that along with Bokononism,*

Christianity and Protestantism had been outlawed for years. He received his doctorate from the Western Hemisphere University of the Bible of Little Rock, Arkansas. Their motto was "Make Religion Live!" Since there was no way for him to understand traditional Christian practices, he left it to himself to make things up as needed. When "Papa" called for last rites, he threw out Humana and insisted on Bokononist last rites.

Dr. Humana was also a talented artist. He drew the target posters of all the Communist and Fascist leaders to be shot at during the great celebration.

He was named for the organ stop that struck his mother when the San Lorenzo Cathedral was dynamited in 1923.

humane. (*GBR* 32:L4) I tell you, boys, I used to belong to a volunteer fire department, and I'd belong to one now, if there were such a human thing, such a ***humane*** thing, in New York City.
(*BC* 5:L32) I have no culture, no **humane** harmony in my brains. I can't live without a culture anymore.
(*BC* 16:illustration) The American Academy of Arts and Sciences caused a monument to be erected over his ashes. Carved in its face was a quotation from his last novel, his two-hundred-and-ninth novel, which was unfinished when he died. *The monument read,*

Kilgore Trout
1907-1981
"WE ARE HEALTHY ONLY TO THE EXTENT THAT
OUR IDEAS ARE **HUMANE**."

(*WFG* 218:L17 *Address at Rededication of Wheaton College Library, 1973*) The best example I know of goodness from vileness is the body of **humane** writing produced by Louis-Ferdinand Céline, a French physician and novelist, who was a convicted war criminal after World War Two.
(*WFG—Playboy Interview* 267:L23) VONNEGUT: Several years ago, Norbert Wiener, the MIT mathematician, wrote in *Atlantic* that he wasn't going to give any more information to industry or the Government, because they weren't gentle people, because they don't have **humane** uses for things.
(*WFG* 229:L11 *Address to P.E.N. Conference in Stockholm, 1973*) We will become influential when those who have listened to our myths have become influential. Those who rule us now are living in accordance with myths created for them by writers when *they* were young. It is perfectly clear that our rulers do not question those myths for even a minute during busy day after busy day. Let us pray that those terribly influential writers who created those our leaders' were **humane**.
(*FWD* 62:L17) "Hemingway was unquestionably an artist of the first rank, with an admirable soul, the size of Kilimanjaro. His choice of subject matter, though, bullfighting and nearly forgotten wars and shooting big animals for

sport, often makes him a little hard to read nowadays. Conservation and **humane** treatment of animals and contempt for the so-called arts of war rank high on most of our agendas nowadays." *See also: GBR* 71:L23; *MH—Report on the Barnhouse Effect* 167:L32; *WFG—Hello, Star Vega* 23:L22; *WFG—Address to Graduating Class at Bennington College, 1970* 165:L30; *WFG—Playboy Interview* 267:L272:L21; *Slap* 29:L29; 176:L28-29; *JB* 155:L14; 174:L20; *PS—The First Amendment* 16:L11; *PS—Self-Interview* 91:L32; *PS—Religion* 206:L13; *PS—Children* 254:L23; *PS—Jekyll and Hyde Updated* 286:L5; *FWD* 59:L35; 80:L7; 97:L25; 103:L33; 190:L7.

humanism, humanist. (*WFG* 24:L1 *Hello, Star Vega*) "Thus," says Sagan the **humanist**, "the characteristic signs of life on Earth which may be detectable over interstellar distance include the baleful contents of many American television programs." It is a sobering thought that Gomer Pyle and the Beverly Hillbillies may be among our chief interstellar emissaries.

(*WFG* 92:L10, 13, 94:L15-16, 18 *Address to the American Physical Society*) There was a safety officer in the laboratory who called on him regularly, begging him to clean up the death traps all around the room. One day my brother said to him, "If you think this is a mess, you should see what it's like up here." And my brother pointed to his own head. I loved him for that. We love each other very much, even though I am a **humanist** and he is physicist.

I am charmed that you should call me in your program notes here a **humanist**. I have always thought of myself as a paranoid, as an overreactor, and a person who makes a questionable living with his mental diseases. Fiction writers are not customarily persons in the best of mental health. . . .

You have called me a **humanist**, and I have looked into **humanism** some, and I have found that a **humanist** is person who is tremendously interested in human beings. My dog is a **humanist**.

(*WFG* 95:L9 *Address to the American Physical Society*) One of the things that I tell beginning writers is this: "If you describe a landscape, or a cityscape, or a seascape, always be sure to put a human figure somewhere in the scene. Why? Because readers are human beings, mostly interested in human beings. People are **humanists**. *Most* of them are **humanists**, that is."

(*JB* 28:L22) Soon after our marriage I was transferred to Wiesbaden, Germany, outside of Frankfurt am Main, where I was placed in charge of a team of civilian engineers, which was winnowing mountains of captured German technical documents for inventions and manufacturing methods and trade secrets American industry might use. . . . There was nothing that a **humanist** could not supervise—or so it was widely believed at the time.

humanistic physicist (*WFG* 95:L18-19, 27-33 *Address to the American Physical Society*) I saw with interest the announcement of the talk entitled "The Virtuous Scientist," to be delivered by you and Eames and Drexler ... Unfortunately, I will not be present at the New York meeting this year. However, as a **humanistic physicist**, I would very much appreciate receiving a copy of the talk. *From a letter to Vonnegut from George F. Norwood, Jr., University of Miami, Coral Gables.*

If Professor Norwood really is a **humanistic physicist**, then he is exactly my idea of what a virtuous physicist should be. A virtuous physicist is a **humanistic physicist**. Being a **humanistic physicist**, incidentally, is a good way to get two Nobel Prizes instead of one. What does a **humanistic physicist** do? Why, he watches people, listens to them, thinks about them, wishes them and their planet well.

humanitarian, humanitarianism. (*CC* 193:L21) Dr. von Koenigswald, the **humanitarian** with the terrible deficit of Auschwitz in his kindliness account, was the second to die of *ice-nine*.

(*WFG* 189:L26, 32, 190:L2, 5 *In a Manner That Must Shame God Himself*) But there was a Pavlovian thing going on, and it has been going on for many years now: The wishes of the hostile crowds were invariably **humanitarian**, and the crowds weren't even hostile most of the time. But wherever they went, armies of policemen went to—to protect nice people from them. . . . *(The "hostile crowds" of humanitarians were the protestors attending the 1972 Republican National Convention in Miami.)*

So a Pavlovian connection has been made in the minds of people who are really awfully nice: When more than two people show up with a **humanitarian** idea, the police should be called.

If the police don't act immediately, and if the **humanitarians** behave in a manner that is dignified or beautiful or heartbreaking, there is still something nice people can do.

They can ignore the **humanitarians**.

(*Gal* 146:L1) This new explosive was regarded as a great boon to big-brained military scientists. As long as they killed people with conventional rather than nuclear weapons, they were praised as **humanitarian** statesmen. *See also: CC* 185:L36; *GBR* 34:L9-10; 119:L18; *JB* 76:L16.

humanity. (*PP* 51:L27) "It was practically his life—away from the laboratory," said Berringer. He was shocked and scared. "Years and years. Why did it have to happen?" It was one more hollow echo to the question **humanity** had been asking for millenniums, the question men were seemingly born to ask. *Berringer is speaking after the demise of the robot Checker Charlie.*

(*PP* 191:L19) Their eyes had met, and an inexpressibly sweet sense of eternal tragedy had passed between them, between their generations—a legacy of *Weltschmerz* as old as **humanity**. *Paul Proteus remembers back to the first time his father brought him to the Meadows and he saw the morality play intended to sanctify the role of engineers and the ruling technocracy.*

(*PP* 273:L4, 10) "The witness will please tell what he considers to be a lie," said the judge.

"Every new piece of scientific knowledge is a good thing for **humanity**," said Paul. . . .

"Now a truth," said the judge.

"The main business of **humanity** is to do a good job of being human beings," said Paul, "not to serve as appendages to machines, institutions, and systems."

(*ST* 242:L26-27) "I *(Winston Niles Rumfoord)* can think of no more stirring symbol of man's **humanity** to man than a fire engine."

(*MN* 23:L2) I committed high treason, crimes against **humanity**, and crimes against my own conscience, and I got away with them until now.

(*MN* 55:L19) Keeley was unfrocked, and Pope Pius sent a long letter to the American Hierarchy in which he said, among other things: "No true Catholic will take part in the persecution of his Jewish compatriots. A blow against the Jews is a blow against our common **humanity**."

(*CC* 14:L1) We Bokononists believe that **humanity** is organized into teams, teams that do God's Will without ever discovering what they are doing.

(*MH* 161:L32 *Report on the Barnhouse Effect*) As though the pointlessness of my work were not bad enough, the professor annoyed me further with irrelevant questions. His favorites were: "Think we should have dropped the atomic bomb on Hiroshima?" and "Think every new piece of scientific information is a good thing for **humanity**?"

(*BC* 18:L30) He *(Kilgore Trout)* told Bill that **humanity** deserved to die horribly, since it had behaved so cruelly and wastefully on a planet so sweet.

Vonnegut recalls a favorite quote of his from Guy Murchie's Music of the Spheres. (*WFG* 88:L22 *Excelsior! We're Going to the Moon! Excelsior!*) I sometimes wonder whether **humanity** has missed the real point in raising the issue of mortality and immortality—in other words, whether mortality itself may be a finite illusion, being actually immortality and, even though constructed of just a few "years," that those few years are all the time there really is, so that, in fact, they can never cease.

(*WFG* 163:L30 *Address to Graduating Class at Bennington College, 1970*) I beg you to believe in the most ridiculous superstition of all: that **humanity** is at the center of the universe, the fulfiller or the frustrator of the grandest dreams of God Almighty.

(*Gal* 125:L5) I *(Leon Trout)* did not know that **humanity** was about to be diminished to a tiny point, by luck, and then, again by luck, to be permitted to expand again. I believed that the chaos involving billions of big-brained people thrashing around every which way, and reproducing and reproducing, would go on and on. It did not seem likely that an individual could be significant in such an unplanned uproar.

(*Gal* 215:L6) And the *Bahia de Darwin* wasn't just any ship. As far as **humanity** was concerned, she was the new Noah's ark.

(*Gal* 254:L14) "Leon! Leon! Leon!" he implored. "The more you learn about people, the more disgusted you'll become. I would have thought that your being sent by the wisest men in your country, supposedly, to fight a nearly endless, thankless, horrifying, and, finally, pointless war *(in Vietnam)*, would have given you sufficient insight into the nature of **humanity** to last you

throughout all eternity!" *Kilgore Trout implores his son Leon to enter the blue tunnel into the Afterlife.*
(*HP* 194:L18) I did not realize at the time how much that story *("The Protocols of the Elders of Tralfamadore")* affected me. . . . But down deep the story was beginning to work like a buffered analgesic. What a relief it was, somehow, to have somebody else confirm what I had come to suspect toward the end of the Vietnam War, and particularly after I saw the head of a human being pillowed in the spilled guts of a water buffalo on the edge of a Cambodian village, that **Humanity** is going somewhere really nice was a myth for children under 6 years old, like the Tooth Fairy and the Easter Bunny and Santa Claus.
(*FWD* 116:L22) "If flying-saucer creatures or angels or whatever were to come here in a hundred years, say, and find us gone like the dinosaurs, what might be a good message for **humanity** to leave for them, maybe carved in great big letters on a Grand Canyon wall?

"Here is this old poop's suggestion:

WE PROBABLY COULD HAVE SAVED OURSELVES,
BUT WERE TOO DAMNED LAZY TO TRY VERY HARD.

"We might well add this:
AND TOO DAMN CHEAP."

(*FWD* 118:118) "My brother got his doctorate in 1938, I think. If he had gone to work in Germany after that, he would have been helping to make Hitler's dreams come true. If he had gone to work in Italy, he would have been helping to make Mussolini's dreams come true. If he had gone to work in Japan, he would have been helping to make Tojo's dreams come true. If he had gone to work in the Soviet Union, he would have been helping to make Stalin's dreams come true. He went to work for a bottle manufacturer in Butler, Pennsylvania, instead. It can make quite a difference not just to you but to **humanity**: the sort of boss you choose, whose dreams you help come true.
(*FWD* 119:23-24) "And to show you how fruity, how feminine I have become in late middle age: If I were the President of MIT, I would hang pictures of Boris Karloff as the Monster of Frankenstein all over the institution. Why? To remind students and faculty that **humanity** now cowers in muted dread, expecting to be killed sooner or later by Monsters of Frankenstein. Such killing goes on right now, by the way, in many other parts of the world, often with our sponsorship—hour after hour, day after day.
(*FWD* 185:L21) "My Lord, I think I even said in fact I know I said that **humanity** itself had become an unstoppable glacier made of hot meat, which ate up everything in sight and then made love, and then doubled in size again. I topped that off with a stage aside to the effect that the Pope in Rome was of no help when it came to slowing down the meat. *See also: PP* 87:L23; 273:L35; *ST* 261:L31; *MN* 31:L10; 192:L17; *SL5* 64:L32-33; *MH—Tom*

Edison's Shaggy Dog 102:L11; *MH—Report on the Barnhouse Effect* 157:L15; *MH—Unready To Wear* 239:L24; *WFG—Thinking Unthinkable, Speaking Unspeakable* 209:L18,20; *WFG—Playboy Interview* 272:L28; *Gal* 25:L14; 39:L4; 65:L4; 82:L6; 126:L26,28; 144:L11; 145:L4; 156:L17; 158:L29; 179:L1; 182:L1; 183:L8; 184:L21; 192:L21; 233:L19,23,27,31; *HP* 45:L16; 166:L18; *FWD* 44:L18; 101:L14; 136:L20; 148:L6,16.

humankind. *With rare exception, this is a term Vonnegut reserves for speaking about the continuation of the species in* Galápagos *or when speculating about the future after recalling his visit to the Galápagos Islands.*

(*Gal* 125:L2) So without any idea that he was going to be the sire of all **humankind**, I got into the head of Captain Adolf von Kleist as he rode in a taxicab from Guayaquil International Airport to the *Bahía de Darwin*.

(*Gal* 153:L7) They *(the Kanka-bono girls)* would grow to womanhood on Santa Rosalia, where, along with Hisako Hiroguchi, they would become the mothers of all modern **humankind**.

(*Gal* 185:L15) But I have yet to see an octopus, or any sort of animal, for that matter, which wasn't entirely content to pass its time on earth as a food gatherer, to shun the experiments with unlimited greed and ambition performed by **humankind**.

(*Blue* 288:L17) While there were notorious disputes in Europe as to which races and subraces were vermin, all Europeans could agree that the thieving, fortune-telling, child-stealing Gypsies were the enemies of all decent **humankind**. So they were hunted down everywhere.

(*HP* 143:L2-3) I argued that it was a teacher's duty to speak frankly to students of college age about all sorts of concerns of **humankind**, not just the subject of a course as stated in the catalogue. "That's how we gain their trust, and encourage them to speak up as well," I said, "and realize that all subjects do not reside in neat little compartments, but are continuous and inseparable from the one big subject we have been put on Earth to study, which is life itself."

(*FWD* 144:L7) "If you go to the Galápagos Islands, and see all the strange creatures, you are bound to think what Charles Darwin thought when he went there: How much time Nature has in which to accomplish simply anything. If we desolate this planet, Nature can get life going again. All it takes is a few million years or so, the wink of an eye to Nature.

"Only **humankind** is running out of time.

"My guess is that we will not disarm, even though we should, and that we really will blow up everything by and by. History shows that human beings are vicious enough to commit every imaginable atrocity, including the construction of factories whose only purpose is to kill people and burn them up.

"It may be that we were put here on Earth to blow the place to smithereens. We may be Nature's way of creating new galaxies. We may be programmed to improve and improve our weapons, and to believe that death is better than dishonor.

"And then, one day, as disarmament rallies are being held all over the planet, *ka-blooey!* A new Milky Way is born." *See also: Gal* 79:L11; 137:L22; 140:L4; 143:L30; 148:L13; 151:L7; 162:L20; 169:L25; 185:L2; 190:L7-8; 194:L4; 195:L17; 214:L20; 219:L4,6; 222:L15-16; 259:L25; *FWD* 120:13-14.

humanness. (*Slap* 69:L14) "I would give anything, Caleb, for the faintest sign of intelligence, the merest flicker of **humanness** in the eyes of either twin."

humanoid (see also **Don** and ***Era of Hopeful Monsters***). *All of Vonnegut's references to humanoids refer to science fiction stories writen by Kilgore Trout except for the one in* Hocus Pocus. *Though "The Protocols of the Elders of Trlafamadore" is not specifically attributed to Trout, it appears in* Black Garterbelt, *a porn magazine which frequently published Trout's stories as filler for the photographs.* (*Gal* 82:L31) I am reminded of one of my father's novels, *The Era of Hopeful Monsters*. It was about a planet where the **humanoids** ignored their most serious survival problems until the last possible moment.
(*HP* 190:L15) The Elders, incidentally, had given up on influencing the **humanoids** of Tralfamadore, who were right below where they were meeting. The Tralfamadorians had senses of humor and so knew themselves for the severely limited lunkers, not to say crazy lunkers, they really were. They were immune to the kilovolts of pride the Elders jazzed their brains with. *See also: BC* 59:L1521,27; 60:L7; 61:L9,13; *Gal* 83:L4,10.

humor, **humorist** (**American**, **barracks**, **black**, **college**, **gallows**, **Hoosier**, **Jewish**, **middle-European**, **white**). (*CC* 106:L4) By contrast *(with the natives of San Lorenzo)*, Johnson and McCabe had the glittering treasures of literacy, ambition, curiosity, gall, irreverence, health, **humor**, and considerable information about the outside world.
(*SL5* 111:L26) *(The following is read by a German major from one of Howard W. Campbell, Jr.'s monographs.) America is the wealthiest nation on Earth, but its people are mainly poor, and poor Americans are urged to hate themselves. To quote the* ***American humorist*** *Kin Hubbard, "It ain't no disgrace to be poor, but it might as well be." It is in fact a crime for an American to be poor, even though America is a nation of poor.*
(*WJ* 136:L15) VON KONIGSWALD It was almost worth the trip—to find out that Jesus Christ in Heaven was just another guy, playing shuffleboard. I like his sense of **humor**, though—you know? He's got a blue-and-gold warm-up jacket he wears. You know what it says on the back? "Pontius Pilate Athletic Club." Most people don't get it. Most people think there really is a Pontius Pilate Athletic Club.
(*WFG* 107:L16 *Why They Read Hesse*) Hesse is no **black humorist**. **Black humorists**' holy wanderers find nothing but junk and lies and idiocy wherever

they go. A chewing-gum wrapper or a used condom is often the best they can do for a Holy Grail. Not so with the wanderers of Hesse; they always find something satisfying—holiness, wisdom, hope.

(*WFG* 256:L7, 12, 257:L6, 7, 9, 13-14, 17, 19, 26 *Playboy Interview*) PLAYBOY: Another way of dealing with sadness, of coming to terms with problems you can't solve, is through **humor**. Is that your way?

VONNEGUT: Well, I try. But laughter is a response to frustration, just as tears are, and it solves nothing, just as tears solve nothing. Laughing or crying is what a human being does when there's nothing else he can do. Freud has written very soundly on **humor**—which is interesting, because he was essentially such a humorless man. The example he gives is of the dog who can't get through a gate to bite a person or fight another dog. He digs dirt. It doesn't solve anything, but he has to do *something*. Crying or laughing is what a human being does instead.

(*WFG* 257:L4-29 *Playboy Interview*) VONNEGUT: So the biggest laughs are based on the biggest disappointments and the biggest fears.

PLAYBOY: Is that what's called **black humor**? Or is all **humor black**?

VONNEGUT: In a sense, it probably is. Certainly, the people Bruce Jay Friedman named as **black humorists** weren't really very much like one another. I'm not a whole lot like J.P. Donleavy, say, but Friedman saw some similarity there and said we were both **black humorists**. So critics picked up the term because it was handy. All they had to do was say **black humorists** and they'd be naming twenty writers. It was a form of shorthand. But Freud had already written about **gallows humor**, which is **middle-European humor**. It's people laughing in the middle of political helplessness. **Gallows humor** had to do with people in the Austro-Hungarian Empire. There were Jews, Serbs, Croats—all these small groups jammed together into a very unlikely sort of empire. And dreadful things happened to them. They were powerless, helpless people, and so they made jokes. It was all they could do in the face of frustration. The **gallows humor** that Freud identifies is what we regard as **Jewish humor** here: It's **humor** about weak, intelligent people in hopeless situations. And I have customarily written about powerless people who felt there wasn't much they could do about their situations.

(*PS* 130:L4 *The People One Knows*) Mr. *(Joseph)* Heller is a first-rate **humorist** who cripples his own jokes intentionally—with the unhappiness of the characters who perceive them.

(*PS* 142:L28 *The People One Knows*) And while other comedians show us persons tormented by bad luck and enemies and so on, Bob and Ray's characters threaten to wreck themselves and their surroundings with their own stupidity. There is a refreshing and beautiful innocence in Bob's and Ray's **humor**.

(*PS* 174:L5, 8 *Funnier on Paper Than Most People*) "When I was a boy in Indianapolis, there was a **humorist** there named Kin Hubbard. He wrote a few lines for *The Indianapolis News* every day. Indianapolis needs all the **humorists** it can get. He was often as witty as Oscar Wilde. He said, for instance, that Prohibition was better than no liquor at all. He said that whoever named near-beer was a poor judge of distance. He said that it was no disgrace to be poor, but that it might as well be. He went to a graduation ceremony one time, and he said afterward that he thought it would be better if all the really important stuff was spread out over four years instead of being saved up for the very end."

(*FWD* 65:L30) "The last time I was in Boise, also as a lecturer, I met a nice woman with a wry sense of **humor** about men. Her husband was then out hunting with heavy-duty equipment and pals. She laughed about that. She said men had to get out of doors and drink and kill things before they could show how much they loved each other. She thought it was ridiculous that they had to go to so much trouble and expense before they could express something as simple and natural as love."

(*FWD* 113:L6) "In the children's fable *The White Deer*, by the late **American humorist** James Thurber, the Royal Astronomer in a medieval court reports that all the stars are going out. What has really happened is that the astronomer has grown old and is going blind. That was Thurber's condition, too, when he wrote his tale. He was making fun of a sort of old poop who imagined that life was ending not merely for himself but for the whole universe. Inspired by Thurber, then, I choose to call any old poop who writes a popular book saying that the world, or at least his own country, is done for, a 'Royal Astronomer' and his subject matter 'Royal Astronomy.'"

(*FWD* 183:L20, 25; 184:L3 "For whatever reason, **American humorists** or satirists or whatever you want to call them, those who choose to laugh rather than weep about demoralizing information, become intolerably unfunny pessimists if they live past a certain age. If Lloyd's of London offered policies promising to compensate comical writers for loss of sense of **humor**, its actuaries could count on such a loss occurring, on average, at age sixty three for men, and for women at twenty nine, say."

"My generalization is happily or unhappily confirmed in a book called *Punchlines* (Paragon House, 1990) by William Keough of the English Department of Fitchburg State College in Massachusetts. The subtitle is *The Violence of **American Humor***. Mr. Keough, by means of essays on Mark Twain, Ring Lardner, Ambrose Bierce, myself, comedians in the movies (both silents and talkies), and radio and TV and nightclub comics right up to the present, persuades me that the most memorable jokes by Americans are responses to the economic and physical violence of this society. 'How often does it seem that the American **humorist**, having set out daringly and lightly as an amused observer of the American spectacle of violence and corruption, ends up mouthing sardonic fables in a bed of gloom,' he writes.

"So guess what: My latest novel, *Hocus Pocus* . . . is a sardonic fable in a bed of gloom."

(*FWD* 186:L7, 11) "As a good friend pointed out to me one time, my ideas have everything but originality. That was my fate. So I came up with the wholly unoriginal idea of writing a *Don Quixote* set in modern times. There

might be a certain amount of freshness to my tale, I hoped, if I gave an affectionate razzing to what had long been my dream of an ideal citizen. Although Mr. Keough doesn't say so, I think all American **humorists**, when saying how flawed American citizens really are, would not be interested in doing that if they did not have clear images in their heads of what American citizens ought to be. Dreams of ideal citizens are as essential to our **humorists**, in my opinion, as they were to Karl Marx and Thomas Jefferson." (*FWD* 194:L6) ". . . suicidal persons can be divided into two sorts. Styron's sort blames the wiring and chemistry of his brain, which could easily fit into a salad bowl. My sort blames the Universe. (Why mess around?) I don't offer this insight as yet another joke ("Why is cream more expensive than milk?"). It is my serious belief that those of us who become **humorists** (suicidal or not) feel free (as most people do not) to speak of life itself as a dirty joke, even though life is all there is or ever can be.
(*FWD* 198:L1) Many people feel that **humor** (professorial drolleries excepted) is a scheme of self defense which only members of famously maligned and oppressed minorities should be allowed to use. (Mark Twain cast himself as poor white trash.) It must seem very wrong to them that I, an educated, middle class person of German descent, should joke all the time. As far as they are concerned, I might as well be singing "Ol' Man River" with tears in my eyes. (*FWD* 215:L15-16, 25) In some reviews Kurt has been characterized as a **black humorist**. Those reviewers wouldn't know **black humor** from Good Friday. They don't know that what they read is only his reaction to the sight of the world gone mad and rushing headlong toward Dresden to the hundredth power.

And they miss his message, in which he pleads that world governments found their rule on something more akin to the Sermon on the Mount than the preachings of those who lead the world to Armageddon.

There is certainly nothing wrong with a man like that. And if such thinking constitutes **black humor**, it's too bad there is not an epidemic of it. *This passage is from Bernard V. O'Hare's comments on his friendship with Vonnegut in honor of his sixtieth birthday. See also:* *PP* 256:L29; *MN* 14:L14; 74:L26; *CC* 82:L32; 157:L36; 158:L6; *GBR* 185:L20; *WFG—Teaching the Unteachable* 28:L3,8; *WFG—Biafra: A People Betrayed* 145:L25,27,29-30; *JB* 188:L19; *JB* 201:L3,5; *PS—Roots* 48:L3; *PS—Self-Interview* 99:L26; 108:L3; 114:L20; *PS—The People One Knows* 133:L25; *PS—Mark Twain* 166:L9; *PS—Religion* 195:L18; *PS—In the Capital of The World* 327:L24; *Gal* 44:L1; 193:L31; 202:L20; 262:L16; *Blue* 246:L4; *HP* 55:L35; 116:L7; 126:L32; 127:L12; 190:L17; *FWD* 68:L12; 82:L31; 157:L15; 184:L9; 187:L26.

Hundred Martyrs to Democracy. *Shortly after the official speech-making honoring the memory of San Lorenzo's lost soldiers, their inept air force misfires and hits the seaside castle of Papa Monzano, precipitating the frozen destruction of the Earth when Papa's ice-nine cadaver falls into the sea.*

Narrator John/Jonah recalls the American ambassador's words. (*CC* 121:L14-15) Minton now spoke of the so-called Hundred Martyrs to Democracy, and he told a whopping lie. "There is not an American schoolchild who does not know the story of San Lorenzo's noble sacrifice in World War Two. The hundred brave San Lorenzans, whose day tomorrow is, gave as much as freedom-loving men can. The President of the United States has asked me to be his personal representative at ceremonies tomorrow, to cast a wreath, the gift of the American people to the people of San Lorenzo, on the sea."

John/Jonah gets the real truth about the martyrs from his cab driver. (*CC* 125:L34, 36, 127:L10-11) I asked the driver who the **Hundred Martyrs to Democracy** had been. The boulevard we were going down, I saw, was called the Boulevard of the **Hundred Martyrs to Democracy**.

The driver told me that San Lorenzo had declared war on Germany and Japan an hour after Pearl Harbor was attacked.

San Lorenzo conscripted a hundred men to fight on the side of democracy. These hundred men were put on a ship bound for the United States, where they were to be armed and trained.

The ship was sunk by a German submarine right outside of Bolivar harbor.

"Dose, sore," he said, *"yeeeara lo hoon-yera mora-toorz tut zamoo-crtz-ya."*

"Those, sir," he'd said in dialect, "are the **Hundred Martyrs to Democracy**."

Hurty, Phoebe. *The advice-to-the-lovelorn columnist for the defunct* Indianapolis Times *and for whom Vonnegut dedicated* Breakfast of Champions. *She also wrote ads for the William H. Block Company department store and hired Vonnegut to write ads for teenage clothing. Her impact on him seems understandable from the preface.* (*BC* 2:L5-7, 10-33) She wrote this ad for an end-of-the-summer sale on straw hats: "For prices like this, you can run them through your horse and put them on your roses. . . ."

She would talk bawdily to me and her sons, and to our girlfriends when we brought them around. She was funny. She was liberating. She taught us to be impolite in conversation not only about sexual matters, but about American history and famous heroes, about the distribution of wealth, about school, about everything.

I now make my living by being impolite. I am clumsy at it. I keep trying to imitate the impoliteness which was so graceful in **Phoebe Hurty**. I think now that grace was easier for her than it is for me because of the mood of the Great Depression. She believed what so many Americans believed then: that the nation would be happy and just and rational when prosperity came.

I never hear that word anymore: Prosperity. It used to be a synonym for Paradise. And **Phoebe Hurty** was able to believe that the impoliteness she recommended would give shape to an American paradise.

Now her sort of impoliteness is fashionable. But nobody believes anymore in a new American paradise. I sure miss **Phoebe Hurty**.

"The Hyannis Port Story" (1963). *The Camelot-inspired short story about the amiable but deeply divisive confrontation between Commodore Rumfoord, a staunch and lifelong Republican, and President Kennedy. Rumfoord insists on keeping a billboard-sized poster of Barry Goldwater on his front lawn, complete with floodlights—all directly across the street from the Kennedy Compound. Secret Service Agent Raymond Boyle informs Rumfoord that his son Robert was caught on the Kennedy's yacht* Marlin *preparing for a love tryst with Sheila Kennedy, the president's fourth cousin visiting from Ireland. Robert and the beautiful, endearing Sheila dine with his parents and the Commodore softens to the extent he turns off the Goldwater floodlights. The president drives by and asks Rumfoord to turn on the lights so Khrushchev's son-in-law could see them—and so he can find his own way home.*

Hyatt, Malcolm. *The pharmacist who preceded Rudy Waltz at Schramm's in* Deadeye Dick. *Hyatt was a high school classmate of Otto Waltz's and was killed by a robber with a sawed-off shotgun.*

I

I. G. Farben. *The name of this German corporation first appears as the entity which purchases RAMJAC's Down Home Records Division in* Jailbird, *and later in* Hocus Pocus *purchases Du Pont (which had previously purchased Barrytron). Eugene Debs Hartke points out that Tarkington College trustee Sydney Stone brokered the deal which bought out Du Pont. Hartke also adds that I. G. Farben is* the same company that manufactured and packaged and labeled and addressed the cyanide gas used to kill civilians of all ages, including babes in arms, during the Holocaust (*HP* 37:L11-14).

ice-nine. *The final creation of* Cat's Cradle*'s Dr. Felix Hoenikker while working at the Research Laboratory of the General Forge and Foundry Company in Ilium. Having gathered together his children and Labrador Retriever, the Hoenikkers take a Christmas vacation to their Cape Cod Cottage. On Christmas Eve Dr. Hoenikker was playing with his small quantity of ice-nine, melting it down and refreezing more water, when he took a break and suddenly died in his wicker rocking chair. Angela, Franklin, and Newt discover their father's creation and split it up between them. Angela's sliver is eventually acquired by her husband's defense company; Little Newt's chunk is stolen by his Ukrainian wife Zinka who returns with it to the Soviet Union; and Franklin surrenders his to "Papa" Monzano and this leads to an icy destruction of the earth.*

Dr. Hoenikker began work on ice-nine after a Marine Corps general complained to him about all the mud his troops traditionally had to overcome. Ice-nine is a new crystal formation which turns moisture into an elongated chain of ice upon contact. It has a melting point of 114^0 Fahrenheit, so that when one small crystal of ice-nine comes into contact with another body of water or surface moisture, it immediately freezes.

Vonnegut's original idea for ice-nine is recorded in the "Playboy" interview, reprinted in Palm Sunday. *He notes that at the G.E. Research*

Laboratory where his brother worked as a physicist and Vonnegut was a publicity writer, there was a legendary story about Dr. Irving Langmuir, the star of the lab, and his meeting with the visiting celebrated science fiction writer H. G. Wells. (*PS* 102:L20-28 *Playboy Interview*) VONNEGUT: Anyway—Wells came to Schenectady, and Langmuir was told to be his host. Langmuir thought he might entertain Wells with an idea for a science-fiction story—about a form of ice that was stable at room temperature. Wells was uninterested, or at least never used the idea. And then Wells died, and then, finally, Langmuir died. I thought to myself: "Finders, keepers—the idea is mine."

Ilium. *This mythical central New York community is modeled after Schenectady, New York, where Vonnegut worked as a publicity writer for General Electric before devoting himself full time to writing. Ilium is prominently featured in* Player Piano, Cat's Cradle, Slaughterhouse-Five, Galápagos, *and the short story "The Deer in the Works."*

In Player Piano, *Ilium is home to the Ilium Works (managed by Dr. Paul Proteus), one of the first manufacturing centers absorbed by the National Manufacturing Council. Ilium becomes the home of the Ghost Shirt Society, the neo-Luddite revolutionary group. The National Manufacturing Council tore down the building housing the Ilium Historical Society and in its place built the Ilium Atomic Reactor. The Ilium Putsch was the Ghost Shirt Society's attempt to overtake all manufacturing and governmental facilities. From the earliest point in the text Vonnegut lays out the present state of Ilium's geographical and population divisions as well as its history, a history which is faithful to the actual development of central New York.* (*PP* 1:L1, 3:L6-20) **ILIUM**, NEW YORK, IS DIVIDED INTO THREE PARTS.

In the northwest are the managers and engineers and civil servants and a few professional people; in the northeast are the machines; and in the south, across the Iroquois River, is the area known locally as Homestead, where almost all of the people live. . . .

He *(Paul Proteus)* was showing the cat an old battlefield at peace. Here, in the basin of the river bend, the Mohawks had overpowered the Algonquins, the Dutch the Mohawks, the British the Dutch, the Americans the British. Now, over bones and rotten palings and cannon balls and arrowheads, there lay a triangle of steel and masonry buildings, a half-mile on each side—the **Ilium** Works. Where men had once howled and hacked at one another, and fought nip-and-tuck with nature as well, the machines hummed and whirred and clicked, and made parts for baby carriages and bottle caps, motorcycles and refrigerators, television sets and tricycles—the fruits of peace.

Paul raised his eyes above the rooftops of the great triangle to the glare of the sun on the Iroquois River, and beyond—to Homestead, where many of the pioneer names still lived: van Zandt, Cooper, Cortland, Stokes. . . .

The Ilium of Cat's Cradle *is home to the General Forge and Foundry Company and Dr. Felix Hoenikker. When Hoenikker was recruited to work on the Manhattan Project, the government agreed to his demands to do all his work in Ilium. It was at his research lab in Ilium that he made his final creation, ice-nine. Vonnegut supplies more historical background by recalling Ilium was an important hub for outfitting settlers heading out to the Western territories. The present site of the Research Laboratory of the General Forge and Foundry Company was where the old stockade was and where public hangings were held.*

Slaughterhouse-Five*'s Billy Pilgrim was born in Ilium in 1922. He attended Ilium High School and then the Ilium School of Optometry, which was owned by his future father-in-law. Though Kilgore Trout is seen elsewhere living in Cohoes, New York, as well as Manhattan, in* Slaughterhouse *he lives in Ilium. Billy leaves a tape recording chronicling his time trips to Tralfamadore and beyond death in a safe-deposit box at the Ilium Merchants National Bank and Trust.*

Mary and Roy Hepburn of Galápagos *are lifelong residents of Ilium. Mary worked for twenty-five years as an outstanding biology teacher at Ilium High School, and Roy worked for GEFFCo. The high school closed when the Matsumoto company of Japan purchased GEFFCo, then the largest employer in town, and computerized its manufacturing process so no more than twelve workers were needed.*

The Ilium Works of the Federal Apparatus Corporation in the 1955 short story "The Deer in the Works" is not the highly computerized operation of Player Piano, *but it is similarly intended to represent the dehumanization of society in an increasingly mechanized society. Primarily an armaments contractor, it is the second-largest industrial plant in America and is in the midst of a hiring blitz to keep up with demand.*

Ilium Gazette. *In* Slaughterhouse-Five *the sixty-two-year-old Kilgore Trout works* as a circulation man for the ***Ilium Gazette***, manages newspaper delivery boys, bullies and flatters and cheats little kids (*SL5* 142:L27). *Billy Pilgrim was a fan of Trout's books and when he realized Trout lived only two miles from him, Billy sought him out and struck up a slight friendship. Later, when Billy prepares to go on a New York radio talk show, he tells the host he worked for the* Ilium Gazette.

Ilium Historical Society. *The society's building was torn down and replaced by the Ilium Atomic Reactor in* Player Piano.

Ilium Merchants National Bank and Trust. (*SL5* 123:L3) As a time-traveler, he has seen his own death many times, has described it to a tape recorder. The tape is locked up with his will and some other valuables in his safe-deposit box at the **Ilium Merchants National Bank and Trust**, he says.

I, Billy Pilgrim, the tape begins, *will die, have died, and always will die on February thirteenth, 1976. (This is the 31st anniversary of the firebombing of Dresden.)*

Ilium News Leader. *Billy Pilgrim sends a letter to the editor of his hometown newspaper explaining time travel and his experiences on Tralfamadore, in* Slaughterhouse-Five.

Ilium School of Optometry. *Billy Pilgrim's alma mater owned and operated by his father-in-law Lionel Merble, in* Slaughterhouse-Five.

Ilium Works (see **Ilium**).

incantation. (*PP* 277:L5) "I'm going to bat for you," his immediate superior had written, but it was, Halyard knew, an archaic **incantation** in a wilderness of metal, glass, plastic, and inert gas.
(*BC* 260:L33) The person who answered this **incantation** *("Olly-olly-ox-in-freeeeeeeeeeeeeeeeeeeeeeeeeee" was shouted by Dwayne Hoover)* was a person who had never played hide-and-seek in his life. It was Wayne Hoobler who had never played hide-and-seek in his life.

Indianapolis. *Vonnegut's hometown figures prominently in a number of narratives. In* Player Piano, *the head of the National Manufacturing Council is Dr. Gelhorne, who early on increased his modest business success by purchasing the largest ice-cream plant in Indianapolis. He scheduled the ice-cream truck routes to service the heavy industry manufacturing plants. He expanded their services to include cafeteria items, eventually running most of the plants' in-house cafeterias. The ice-cream business was a minor division of Gelhorne Enterprises.*

In Sirens of Titan, *Malachi Constant asks Salo to return him to Earth to live out his years in Indianapolis. Though he had never been there before, Constant remembers reading that* **Indianapolis**, Indiana . . . is the first place in the United States of America where a white man was hanged for the murder of an Indian. The kind of people who'll hang a white man for murdering an Indian . . . that's the kind of people for me (*ST* 314:L32).

Virginia Crocker, the mother of Mother Night*'s Howard Campbell, is the daughter of an Indianapolis portrait photographer. The Soviet spy George Kraft/Iona Potapov lied to Campbell, saying he was a widower from Indianapolis and that his wife was buried there. When Kraft/Potapov circulated letters to a number of civic organizations and publications about the whereabouts of the infamous Howard Campbell, he sent a copy to* The Legion Magazine *in Indianapolis.*

Angela Hoenikker of Cat's Cradle *lives at 4918 North Meridian Street, Indianapolis, Indiana, with her husband Harrison C. Connors. Connors owned the Indianapolis-based defense contractor Fabri-Tek, and presumably stored*

Angela's sliver of ice-nine at his manufacturing plant. Her brother Newt fell in love with Zinka, a Ukrainian midget and dancer with the Borzoi Dance Company performing in Indianapolis. He later saw her perform at Cornell, as well. After Zinka swiped his shard of ice-nine and fled back to the Soviet Union, Newt took refuge in his sister's Indianapolis home.

Noah Rosewater, the scheming entrepreneur who conned his brother out of his birthright and bought his way out of military service during the Civil War, maximized the profitability of his military contracts by purchasing the largest Indianapolis slaughterhouse to avoid being victimized by meatpackers. Eliot's wife Sylvia was treated for samaritrophia at Dr. Ed Brown's private mental institution in Indianapolis. After reading Kilgore Trout's Pan-Galactic Three Day Pass *on a bus to Indianapolis, Eliot falls into a catatonic trance and looks up to see the city being consumed in a fire-storm.* (*GBR* 201:L12) Eliot, rising from his seat in the bus, beheld the fire-storm of **Indianapolis**. He was awed by the majesty of the column of fire, which was at least eight miles in diameter and fifty miles high. The boundaries of the column seemed absolutely sharp and unwavering, as though made of glass. Within the boundaries, helixes of dull red embers turned in stately harmony about an inner core of white. The white seemed holy. *The novel's dénouement takes place on a tennis court in Dr. Brown's Indianapolis asylum where Eliot was treated for a year after the bus episode.*

Slaughterhouse-Five*'s Edgar Derby, whose summary execution in the ashes of Dresden for picking up a piece of unbroken china—intended to be Vonnegut's ironic climax, was an Indianapolis high school teacher.*

Phoebe Hurty, the columnist and ad writer to whom Vonnegut dedicated Breakfast of Champions, *was a witty Indianapolis widow. Also within this text, Vonnegut explains that he first suspected humans were robots of one sort or another when, as a young boy, he frequently saw men in downtown Indianapolis suffering locomotor ataxia, a symptom of the final stages of syphilis.*

Vonnegut's prefatory note to Slapstick *reveals that while flying back to Indianapolis for a family funeral, he was forced to realize the void in his life left by his sister's early death, that she was the audience he tried to keep in mind while writing. Indianapolis is later noted as the Daffodil capitol of North America, the artificially extended family to which Wilbur Swain belonged. It was also the location of the Eli Lilly Company, producer of tri-benzo-Deportamil, the Tourette's syndrome medication that Wilbur relied upon for so long.*

Jailbird*'s union organizer Kenneth Whistler was inspired by Indianapolis' legendary Powers Hapgood.*

Vonnegut describes Deadeye Dick*'s neutron bombing of Midland City as* the disappearance of so many people I cared about in **Indianapolis** when I was starting out to be a writer. **Indianapolis** is there, but the people are gone (*DD* xii:L32-33).

Bluebeard*'s Rabo Karabekian has one eye removed at Fort Benjamin Harrison outside Indianapolis, after being wounded in the war.*

I *(Eugene Debs Hartke)* was named at the behest of my maternal grandfather, Benjamin Wills, who was a Socialist and an Atheist, and nothing but a groundskeeper at Butler University, in **Indianapolis**, Indiana, in honor of Eugene Debs of Terre Haute, Indiana. Debs was a Socialist and a Pacifist and a Labor Organizer who ran several times for the Presidency of the United States of America, and got more votes than has any other candidate nominated by a third party in the history of this country (*HP* 13:L5). *Hartke later learns that his wife's mother and grandmother were inpatients in the State Hospital for the Insane in Indianapolis. The old family friend who reveals this information runs an Indianapolis medical-waste company.*

For more complete information about Vonnegut's Indianapolis history, readers should consult the chapter entitled "Roots" in Palm Sunday *and the more recently published* Fates Worse Than Death.

Iron Guard of the White Sons of the American Constitution. *The neo-Nazi youth group in* Mother Night*, which is organized by August Krapptauer and meets in the basement of a building owned by Dr. Lionel J.D. Jones. Though there are fewer than a dozen boys participating, their parents drive great distances so their children can attend.*

Iron Maiden. (*PP* 218:L34) "Nope. Guess not," said Paul. He filed this remark away for his next meeting with Bud Calhoun. He could see the device now—sort of an **Iron Maiden**, without the spikes, of course, and electronic, of course, that would grasp a little girl firmly at St. Louis, and eject her into the arms of relatives at Poughkeepsie.

(*CC* 213:chapter title) The **Iron Maiden** and the Oubliette

(*CC* 214:L1) Then he *(in* The Books of Bokonon*)* speaks of the rack and the peddiwinkus and the **iron maiden** and the *veglia* and the oubliette.

(*SL5* 31:L7-8) Weary's father once gave Weary's mother a Spanish thumbscrew in working condition—for a kitchen paperweight. Another time he gave her a table lamp whose base was a model one foot high of the famous "**Iron Maiden** of Nuremburg." The real **Iron Maiden** was a medieval torture instrument, a sort of boiler which was shaped like a woman on the outside—and lined with spikes.

(*SL5* 31:L18, 27) Weary had told Billy Pilgrim about the **Iron Maiden**, about the drain in her bottom—and what that was for. . . .

Weary scornfully bet Billy one time that he didn't even know what a blood gutter was. Billy guessed that it was the drain in the bottom of the **Iron Maiden**, but that was wrong.

(*WFG* 167:L11 *Torture and Blubber*) But it is not easy in real life to make a healthy man blubber, no matter how wicked he may be. So good men have invented appliances which make unconstrained weeping easier—the rack, the boot, the **iron maiden**, the pediwinkis, the electric chair, the cross, the thumbscrew.

Irving, David. *The publication of Irving's* The Destruction of Dresden *revealed to Vonnegut that it was "the largest massacre in European history." Vonnegut quotes extensively from the text in* Slaughterhouse-Five *by having Professor Rumfoord refer to it while sharing a hospital room with Billy Pilgrim.*

"The Island of Death." *In* Slapstick, *because of Manhattan's outbreak of "The Green Death" plague, people across the river call it "The Island of Death."*

Ivankov, Aksinia. *The wife of cosmonaut Major Stepan Ivankov, Aksinia is a pediatrician.* (*MH* 257:L7, 9 *The Manned Missiles*) This is my letter, and I will get **Aksinia**, Stepan's widow, to read it to me to make sure Alexei has made it say exactly what I wish it to say. **Aksinia**, too, understands English very well. She is a physician for children. She is beautiful. She works very hard so she can forget sometimes her grief for Stepan.

Ivankov, Alexei. *The seventeen-year-old brother of Major Stepan Ivankov, the dead cosmonaut in "The Manned Missiles." Alexei speaks and writes English and German, so is chosen by his father to translate his thoughts in a letter to Charles Ashland, the father of the dead American astronaut Captain Bryant Ashland. Mikhail Ivankov illustrates the one-time differences between his sons' appreciation for the use of advanced technologies in space:* It was not for the Soviet Union but for the beauty and truth in space, Mr. Ashland, that Stepan worked and died. He did not like to speak of the warlike uses of space. It was **Alexei** who liked to speak of such things, of the glory of spying on earth from baby moons, of guiding missiles to their targets from baby moons, of mastering the earth with weapons fired from the moon itself. . . . **Alexei** has not spoken well of war since (*MH* 260:L13-20, 27).

Ivankov, Major Stepan. *In the short story "The Manned Missiles," Ivankov is the first Soviet cosmonaut in orbit who, together with Captain Bryant Ashland, is stranded in space for eternity. Ashland was sent to observe and photograph the cosmonaut but his ship collided with Ivankov's.*

Ivankov, Mikhail. *The Ukrainian stone mason and father of cosmonaut Major Stepan Ivankov in the short story "The Manned Missiles." He and Charles Ashland exchange letters of condolence tinged with hope for world peace after both their sons lose their lives in a confrontation while in orbit.*

Ivanoff, Prokhor. *Mikhail Ivankov, the grieving father of the dead cosmonaut Major Stepan Ivankov in the short story "The Manned Missiles," makes a black joke using Ivanoff to illustrate the dimensions of his loss.* (*MH* 257:L16 *The*

Manned Missiles) I will tell you a joke, Mr. Ashland. When the second baby moon of the U.S.S.R. went up with a dog in it, we whispered that it was not really a dog inside, but **Prokhor Ivanoff**, a dairy manager who had been arrested for theft two days before. It was only a joke, but it made me think what a terrible punishment it would be to send a human being up there. I could not stop thinking about that. I dreamed about it at night, and I dreamed that it was myself who was being punished.

Izumi. *The North Korean spy posing as a nightclub singer who is wooed by veterinarian and military meat inspector Dr. Bob Fender, in* Jailbird. *Fender's fellow officers and drinking buddies led her to believe he was so gloomy because he had the solemn duty of commanding an elite unit guarding atomic weapons. She convinces him to take her back to where he lives and works and is dismayed to find out Fender is a meat inspector. After spending a night of romance, they awaken to radio reports announcing the capture of a North Korean spy ring except for Izumi. Fender had already fallen in love with Izumi and so concealed her for eleven days. He then tried to convince a New Zealand sailor to take her on board his ship, but the sailor turned them both in.*

J

Jackie. *A waffle with strawberries and cream at the First Family Waffle Shop in the short story "The Hyannis Port Story."*

Jack's Hobby Shop. *The Ilium, New York, hobby shop in* Cat's Cradle *which served as Frank Hoenikker's teenage refuge. There he worked and spent most of his earnings on lifelike miniatures which he used to construct a realistic country setting on a rectangular piece of plywood in the basement. Though Jack never realized it, Frank had a long-standing sexual affair with Jack's wife.*

Jailbird (1979). Jailbird *is the autobiographical saga of Walter F. Starbuck (formerly Stankiewicz), the Harvard-educated son of immigrant domestics in the service of Alexander Hamilton McCone. The course of Starbuck's life was largely determined by deaths which occurred long before he was born. McCone was an heir to the Cuyahoga Bridge and Iron Company. In October 1894, McCone's father laid off large numbers of workers because they refused to take a pay cut. After a long and failing strike, the bankrupt families planned a peaceful protest on Christmas day, but old man McCone called in his political debts by assembling the Ohio National Guard to protect his factory. Since the nature of protesters is to stand firm and the nature of ill-prepared militiamen is to make fatal mistakes, or as Alexander would later recall that there were "certain instabilities inherent in the pageant," that day became known as the Cuyahoga Massacre. Alexander withdrew from the family enterprise. He endured a childless marriage by befriending the son of his cook and chauffeur and promising that in return for his companionship (largely as a chess partner) he would send Walter to Harvard. For his part, Walter "was willing to spend his childhood and youth so unnaturally for this reason" (JB* xxxviii:L14-15).

Alexander's refusal to enter the firm and instead become a famous Cleveland art patron, as well as the benefactor of an immigrant family, is his own way of making amends with his father's legacy. Walter does his part to follow the lead of his mentor, though his story reveals a mindless fealty to authority. He studies liberal arts at Harvard because McCone planned it that way. While an undergraduate, he embarrasses himself by taking Sally Wyatt to the Hotel Arapahoe for a dinner date meticulously planned by McCone, but falls victim to his own carelessness by tipping a strolling violinist with the bulk of his money.

During the McCarthy hearings in the 1950s, Walter errantly blurts out the name of an old and trusted friend, Leland Clewes, as having been a communist. While working in a subbasement office of the White House as President Nixon's special advisor on youth affairs, his own passivity coaxes the Watergate braintrust to stash the payoff money in his safe. Unable to identify those responsible for framing him, and unwilling to commit the same error which landed Leland Clewes in jail, Walter takes the rap and goes to federal prison at the Finletter Air Force Base in Georgia.

Regardless of the task at hand, Walter always acts in accordance with the expectations of the moment. He did little requiring forethought, and whatever intellectual insights he expressed were ideas developed by others. Walter appreciates the fiasco of his extravagant date at the Arapahoe with full candor, "I was a robot programmed to behave like a genuine aristocrat" (*JB* 103:L20-21). *He also understands that just as his future was in part determined by Alexander McCone's disgust with the type of ruthless capitalism which brought about the Cuyahoga Massacre, he was fortunate to have been born before the computerized present era, which would have allowed McCone to indulge himself in games without the need for human competition. This realization hits Walter toward the close of the novel when he is presented with a computerized chess board prior to returning to jail.* (JB 236:L29-31, 237:L1-7) He (the computer "Boris") can even joke about the moves I make. "Really?" he will say; or, "Have you played this game before?" or, "Is this a trap?" or, "Spot me a queen."

Those are the standard chess jokes. Alexander Hamilton and I exchanged those same tired jokes endlessly when, for the sake of a Harvard education in my future, I agreed to be his chess-playing machine. If Boris had existed in those days, I probably would have gone to Western Reserve, and then become a tax assessor or an office manager, or an insurance salesman, or some such thing.

In a manner quite uncharacteristic for Vonnegut, the women in Jailbird *play central roles in presenting depth and understanding; Walter adapts to their sensibilities.* (JB 105:L21-22). "How would I ever have got through life without women to act as my interpreters." *Sarah Wyatt fills in his French void while on their date, but more importantly, she is capable of pattering their string of one line jokes, enabling Walter to travel back to a time less complicated with knowledge of the world. Walter's wife was his translator in post war Germany, and it was her talent which made him succeed and be recognized by the Allied powers for his efforts at repatriating displaced individuals. And as for Mary Kathleen O'Looney, when Walter tried to be a spokesman for communism as a Harvard student, it was she who knew how to speak with members of the working class.*

Walter realizes the negligible contributions he made to his own development. While awaiting his release from prison for the Watergate conviction, he senses the moment as the demarcation from one life to another. Fearing his past complacency, Walter takes focused refuge in a bawdy song from his youth he thinks "may really have been a way of honoring the powers of women, of dealing with the fears they inspired."

> *Sally in the garden,*
> *Sifting cinders,*
> *Lifted up her leg*
> *And farted like a man.*
> *The bursting of her bloomers*
> *Broke sixteen winders.*
> *The cheeks of her ass went—*

> Here the singers, in order to complete the stanza, were required to clap three times (*JB* 10:L29-31, 11:L3-11).

For Walter, "Those three claps completed a rowdy song I had never liked, and which I had not thought about for thirty years or more. I was making my mind as blank as possible, you see, since the past was so embarrassing and the future so terrifying" (*JB* 8:L12-15). *And yet another Vonnegut character is described with the traits of a schizophrenic,* "So there I was all alone on a bench in the middle of nowhere again. I entered a period of catatonia again—staring straight ahead at nothing, and every so often clapping my old hands three times" (*JB* 8:L10-13).

Beyond the subbasement of the White House and the high jinks which led to his imprisonment is Walter's growing awareness of the historical and economic forces which have shaped his life. Cleveland Lawes, the RAMJAC chauffeur who kindly offers Walter a ride back from the prison, advises Walter that his son's toy steering wheel could point out a valuable lesson to the President. "He said that the President of the United States ought to be given a wheel like that at his inauguration, to remind him and everybody else that all he could do was pretend to steer" (*JB* 89:L15-18). *The mindless engine of capitalism chugs along in such a way* "that nobody who is doing well in this economy ever even wonders what is really going on. We are chimpanzees. We are orangutans" (*JB* 106:L25-27).

This is set in stark relief for Starbuck when he encounters Mary Kathleen O'Looney in midtown Manhattan. (JB p. 140:L12-26) Sociologically, of course, this melodrama was as gripping as *Uncle Tom's Cabin* before the Civil War. Mary Kathleen O'Looney wasn't the only shopping-bag lady in the United States of America. There were tens of thousands of them in major cities throughout the country. Ragged regiments of them had been produced accidently, and to no imaginable purpose, by the great engine of the economy. Another part of the machine was spitting out unrepentant murderers ten years old, and dope fiends and child batterers and many other bad things. People claimed to be investigating. Unspecified repairs were to be made at some future time.

Good-hearted people were meanwhile as sick about all these tragic by-products of the economy as they would have been about human slavery a little more than a hundred years before.

Mary Kathleen and Walter take temporary refuge in the uppermost offices of the Chrysler Building, home of the American Harp Company—a RAMJAC subsidiary. Just as Walter had been victimized by unknown Watergate criminals, he again falls victim to the deeds of the unknown. He asks American Harp sales manager Delmar Peale if he knew of any dealers who might be interested in the clarinet parts he found in his room at the Hotel Arapahoe. The keen octogenarian remembers a police bulletin about a stolen truck-load of such parts and he cooly keeps Walter waiting as he contacts the police. Only one day since his release for crimes committed in the subbasement of the White House, Walter finds himself imprisoned in the basement padded cell of the local police precinct. None other than Roy Cohn, Senator McCarthy's chief counsel during the communist witch hunts of the 1950s, is employed by RAMJAC to free him. Ah, fate.

After his release and his meeting with Arpad Leen, Mrs. Jack Graham's right hand man at RAMJAC (which owns nineteen percent of the United States), Walter realizes that Mary Kathleen O'Looney is Mrs. Jack Graham, the Chief Executive Officer of RAMJAC. He returns to Mary's haunts in the catacombs of Grand Central Station and finds her in a bathroom stall dying from injuries she received when hit by a taxi (owned by RAMJAC). She was mailing instructions to Arpad Leen commanding him to hire Walter and a host of those who had been kind to him. Before dying, Mary Kathleen absolves Walter for his historic lack of sincerity. (*JB* 220:L7-10). "You couldn't help it that you were born without a heart. At least you tried to believe what the people with hearts believed—so you were a good man just the same."

Walter did bargain in good faith with destiny, however crude the slapstick may have become. Yet, he always lamented his lack of conviction. (*JB* 171:L11-15) The most embarrassing thing to me about this autobiography, surely, is its unbroken chain of proofs that I was never a serious man. I have been in a lot of trouble over the years, but that was all accidental. Never have I risked my life, or even my comfort, in the service of mankind. Shame on me.

Walter realizes that pretension to goodness is merely shadow-boxing. Whether or not he tried to believe in things others felt were good didn't matter. After all, societal values of goodness are neither universal nor permanent. He offers a glimpse of the dimension of the problem at a going away dinner held in his honor prior to returning to jail for concealing Mary Kathleen's will. (*JB*

238:L26-31) You know what is finally going to kill this planet? . . . A total lack of seriousness. Nobody gives a damn anymore about what's really going on, what's going to happen next, or how we ever got into such a mess in the first place.

Walter decries having to operate with only a limited understanding of the forces at work on life; moreover, neglecting history makes the foundations of the future that much more frightening. Arnold Marx, the eighteen-year-old archaeology student/prison guard in the opening of Mother Night, *can recall the atrocities of Tiglath-pileser the Third but is ignorant of events in his own time. Vonnegut's compulsion to tell the truth of American atrocities in the early chapters of* Breakfast of Champions *is meant to mock the false history taught in the myth- making days of our earliest education/indoctrination.*

This loss of history is further punctuated by Vonnegut's reference to Sacco and Vanzetti. When Walter is most aware of his lack of seriousness, he recalls a conversation he had concerning them. (*JB* 171:L19-32, 172:L1-4) And it seems strange to me now that I have to explain who Sacco and Vanzetti were. I recently asked young Israel Edel at Ramjac, the former night clerk at the Arapahoe, what he knew about Sacco and Vanzetti, and he told me confidently that they were rich, brilliant thrill-killers from Chicago. He had them confused with Leopold and Loeb.

Why should I find this unsettling? When I was a young man, I expected the story of Sacco and Vanzetti to be retold as often and as movingly, to be as irresistable, as the story of Jesus Christ some day. Weren't modern people, if they were to marvel creatively at their own lifetimes, I thought, entitled to a Passion like Sacco and Vanzetti's, which ended in an electric chair?

As for the last days of Sacco and Vanzetti as a modern Passion: As on Golgotha, three lower-class men were executed at the same time by a state. This time, though, not just one of the three was innocent. This time two of the three were innocent.

Sacco and Vanzetti also bargained in good faith with destiny. The irony of these two anarchists being falsely convicted and executed along with the confessed murderer is not lost in Vanzetti's last words as he is strapped into the chair, "Never in our full life could we hope to do such work for tolerance, for justice, for man's understanding of man, as now we do by accident" (*JB* 179:L14-16). *Lost, too, in unstudied history are Judge Thayer's remarks, also offered in good faith with his sense of destiny,* "This man, although he may not have actually committed the crime attributed to him, is nevertheless morally culpable, because he is the enemy of our existing institutions" (*JB* 177:L11, 178:L1-2).

Our willful ignorance of historical truth (whatever that may be) consigns us to continued vicitimization. Ignoring objective truth in the name of institutional salvation opens the way for establishment schizophrenia. As a result, people live by the designs of conspirators (the Judge Thayers) and participate in the conspiracy of design (by clinging to and perpetuating the myths presented in youth). Vonnegut asserts that we have already reached this institutionalized schizophrenia. What we are missing is the common decency and respect of The Sermon on the Mount.

James, Jesse, *In* Breakfast of Champions, *Dwayne Hoover's stepfather bought a human skeleton from a doctor's estate, laid the rusted pieces of a .45 caliber revolver in its right hand, and placed the sham in Sacred Miracle Cave. They told the tourists the skeleton must have belonged to a railroad robber who took refuge in the cave and was trapped by a rockslide.*

Jarvis, Colin and Ma *In the prologue to* Jailbird, *Colin Jarvis is cited as the leader of the striking workers at the Cuyahoga Bridge and Iron Company,* an ordinary foundryman with a gift for oratory (*JB* xxii:L4). *The company resumed production with scabs and had Colin Jarvis arrested on trumped-up murder charges. His wife, Ma Jarvis, picked up the leadership banner while her husband was imprisoned. Her message to Daniel McCone was that the workers were prepared to return to work at whatever terms he dictated, but McCone was so incensed he refused to take them back.*

Jason, Ed. *In the short story "Deer in the Works," Jason is David Potter's assistant at the small newspaper in Dorset, New York. He recently graduated from college and his father wanted to purchase the paper for him. Potter was thinking of selling because he was looking into a public relations job at the Ilium Works of the Federal Apparatus Corporation.*

Jefferson, Arthur Stanley (see also **Laurel and Hardy**). (*Slap* dedication) Dedicated to the memory of **Arthur Stanley Jefferson** and Norvell Hardy, two angels of my time.

Jefferson Observatory, Lenin Observatory, Mare Imbrium. Sirens of Titan*'s Martian invasion of Earth began when the Martian Imperial Commandos attacked the Earthling moon on April 23 (the year is not mentioned) and took possession of America's Jefferson Observatory, the Soviet Union's Lenin Observatory, and Holland's Mare Imbrium.*

Jekyll, Dr. Henry and Hortense. *The absent-minded chemistry professor calls his wife "Mildred."* (*PS* 264:L12-13, 31-32) . . . the venerable head of the chemistry department . . . the only faculty member with a statewide reputation" and Elbert Whitefeet's closest friend.

Jekyll concocts a growth potion for chickens (which contains, among other hazardous compounds, LSD) to compete with the compound given him by Fred Leghorn, the wealthy chicken magnate. He drinks his own fowl growth potion and becomes "an enormous, homicidal chicken"; his dying words in "chicken" are for him to be roasted and given to an orphanage. However, all agree it would be unchristian and ill-advised for Sweetbread College to let out any publicity on the matter, so he is buried in an unmarked grave.

Jesus (see **Christ**).

Jewish humor (see **humor**).

Johannsen, Nils (also **Johannsen Grinder Company**). Jailbird*'s union organizer Kenneth Whistler leads a rally of striking workers against the company young Nils inherited. Johannsen's Scandinavian grandfather started the company, but Nils was running the business into the ground. Nils was asked to leave Harvard after hardly attending any classes during his two years there. When his Harvard classmates caught him shooting craps with loaded dice, they stuck his head in a toilet bowl at the Ritz. Whistler uses his knowledge of the affair to compare Johannsen's use of the police to protect his property rights against their human rights as playing with loaded dice.*

John/Jonah. Cat's Cradle*'s Bokononist narrator begins his tale by parodying Melville's* Moby Dick. (*CC* 13:L1-9) Call me **Jonah**. My parents did, or nearly did. They called me **John**.

Jonah—John—if I had been a Sam, I would have been a **Jonah** still—not because I have been unlucky for others, but because somebody or something has compelled me to be certain places at certain times, without fail. Conveyances and motives, both conventional and bizarre, have been provided. And, according to plan, at each appointed second, at each appointed place this **Jonah** was there.

John/Jonah started out by researching a book covering the activities of the inventors of the atomic bomb on the day it was dropped on Hiroshima. He planned to call it The Day the World Ended. *He was hoping to find the ironic backyard barbecue on the day Hiroshima was fried. What he found instead was an amoral priesthood of scientists which gave little thought to the real-world applications made of their newfound scientific truth. Above all he found the legacy of Dr. Felix Hoenikker, ice-nine, which would eventually lock up all the moisture on Earth. Its boiling point was 114^0 Celsius. His research took him to Ilium's Research Laboratory of the General Forge and Foundry Company, the fictional counterpart to General Electric's Schenectady research facility where Vonnegut was a publicity writer and where he first learned of the Irving Langmuir suggestion to H. G. Wells of a storyline suggesting an ice-nine type substance. From there he goes to the perfectly rectangular island of San Lorenzo (mimicking Franklin Hoenikker's hobby shop construction of a society in microcosm). There he learns of the artificial dynamic tensions juxtaposing the Bokononist faith and "Papa" Monzano's dictatorship; together they help keep the people economically underdeveloped but spiritually fulfilled.*

John/Jonah started writing the text before his trip to San Lorenzo and continued writing after ice-nine is released into the seas. He starts every chapter with the three dot mathematical symbol for "therefore," and this may indicate that the beginning of the text presupposes its end—a true Bokononist conundrum. Though some reprints of the text dropped the three dots (presumably to save one hundred twenty-seven lines of text, roughly three and a half pages), Vonnegut assured me in a letter that those three dots were his which he included in the first edition.

Johnson, Clarence Daffodil-11. *While thumbing through the Daffodil family directory in the Empire State Building, Wilbur Swain learns he is related to* **Clarence Daffodil-11 Johnson**, the Chief of Police of Batavia, New York (*Slap* 179:L21).

Johnson, Henry "Tex." *The last president of Tarkington College who assumed the post after Sam Wakefield's suicide. When the prisoners broke out of the prison across the lake and came to Tarkington, Tex went to the library bell tower with his high-powered rifle and started sniping the escaped convicts. They eventually shot him out of the bell tower and crucified his body in the loft of the college's stables.*

Johnson previously served as Provost of Rollins College in Winter Park, Florida. He held an undergraduate degree in Business Administration from Texas Tech University. Though he claimed to have descended from one of the ill-fated soldiers at the Alamo, he was actually the son of a Lithuanian second mate on a Russian freighter who jumped ship when it put in for emergency repairs at Corpus Christi. Zuzu told me that **Tex**'s father was not only an illegal immigrant but the nephew of the former Communist boss of Lithuania (*HP* 131:L8).

Shortly after Tex and his wife Zuzu moved to Tarkington, she and Eugene Debs Hartke started a sexual relationship which lasted until about a month before Hartke was forced to resign by the Board of Trustees. A private investigator's report of their affair was disclosed to Tex as well as the board. Hartke had a solid friendship with Tex and was never troubled by his duplicity. This prompts Hartke to recall that Tex was a cuckold in the present, and crucifixion awaited him in the future. I wonder if his father would have jumped ship in Corpus Christi if he had known what an unhappy end his only son would come to under American Free Enterprise (*HP* 134:L31-38).

Johnson, Zuzu. *The wife of Tarkington College President Howard "Tex" Johnson and the long time lover of Eugene Debs Hartke in* Hocus Pocus. *Whenever Tex was out of town, she and Hartke would get together. At the meeting of Tarkington's Board of Trustees convened to fire Hartke, a private investigator's report indicated that in one semester the lovers had no less than thirty trysts. Though Hartke was able to separate his emotions from his lust, Zuzu could not. She eventually complained that Hartke never would act on their small talk about leaving their spouses and taking off for Venice where she would tend a flower shop and he would teach English. This led to their final breakup.*

Zuzu was killed when the prisoners from across the lake broke out and made their way to the college's campus. She and her husband were buried at the foot of Musket Mountain.

Jolson, Al. *The star of the first movie with sound, the Jewish entertainer was once a close friend of Dan Gregory, in* Bluebeard. *When Jolson and other notable guests argued with Gregory about Mussolini at a dinner party, the guests broke their ties with Gregory from that time forward. Rabo Karabekian uses Jolson as another example of the loss of history among the young when he recalls that his cook's daughter and friends couldn't identify him.*

Jones, Fred. *The World War I flyer who lost an eye (as did Rabo Karabekian in World War II) and who serves Dan Gregory as a valet and constant male companion. They weren't homosexuals nor was Jones treated as a servant. They were simply inseparable friends. Jones and Gregory eventually died dressed in uniforms of Mussolini's troops at Sidi Barrani, Egypt, one year before Pearl Harbor was attacked. Karabekian understands Jones because he is able to see him in ways that others may not appreciate. In so doing, Rabo sheds light not only on Jones but also on some of his Abstract Expressionist painter buddies.* (*Blue* 161:L18-33, 162:L1-5) His life had been all downhill since World War One, when he had discovered a gift for flying rattletrap kites which were machine-gun platforms. The first time he got his hands on the joystick of an airplane, he must have felt what Terry Kitchen felt when he gripped a spray gun. He must have felt like Kitchen again when he fired his machine guns up in the wild blue yonder, and saw a plane in front of him draw a helix of smoke and flame—ending in a sunburst far below.

What beauty! So unexpected and pure! So easy to achieve!

Fred Jones told me one time that the smoke trails of falling airplanes and observation balloons were the most beautiful things he ever expected to see. And I now compare his elation over arcs and spirals and splotches in the atmosphere with what Jackson Pollock used to feel as he watched what dribbled paint chose to do when it struck a canvas on his studio floor.

Same sort of happiness!

Except that what Pollock did lacked that greatest of all crowd pleasers, which was human sacrifice.

Jones, Lionel J.D. (the Reverend Doctor Lionel J. D. Jones, D.D.S., D.D.). *The publisher of* The White Christian Minuteman, *Jones* was born in Haverhill, Massachusetts, in 1889, was raised as a Methodist (*MN* 48:L9-10). *Jones flunked out of the University of Pennsylvania Dental School in 1910. He failed his examinations not so much because of his lack of dental knowledge, but because* regardless of the subject, **Jones** managed to go from it to a theory that was all his own—that the teeth of Jews and Negroes proved beyond question that both groups were degenerate (*MN* 49:L7-10). *His parents disowned him when they became aware of his activities at school, and he found work as an* *apprentice embalmer with Scharff Brothers Funeral Home. At the age of twenty-four he married the fifty-eight-year-old widowed owner of the funeral home, Hattie Scharff. She died in 1928.*

During the marriage he teamed with chemist Dr. Lomar Horthy and invented Viverine, an embalming fluid, and Gingiva-Tru, a "gum-simulating substance for false teeth."

After his wife died he sold the funeral home and started The White Christian Minuteman. *After fourteen issues Jones was wiped out in the 1929 stock market crash.* (*MN* 50:L20) In the next-to-the-last issue, **Jones** billed himself on the masthead as, "**Dr. Lionel J.D. Jones, D.D.S.**" *In 1939 he applied for the presidency of The Little Rock School of Embalming, and after attaining the position he married the widowed owner of the school, Mary Alice Shoup—she was sixty-eight. Jones liquidated the funeral school* and had it rechartered as The Western Hemisphere University of the Bible. The university held no classes, taught nothing, did all its business by mail. Its business was the awarding of doctorates in the field of divinity, framed and under glass, for eighty dollars a throw (*MN* 50:L32-33, 51:L1-3).

Jones took one of his school's doctorates, expanded his title, and revived The White Christian Minuteman *when his second wife passed away. He published a book entitled* Christ Was Not a Jew, *the thesis of which is that by evaluating all the artistic renditions of Jesus Christ it can be determined he was not Jewish. His newspaper picked up sponsorship by the Nazis. In 1942 he was arrested, tried, and convicted for sedition and served eight years of a fourteen-year sentence. Upon his release from prison he came into great wealth from his patent on Gingiva-Tru, and in 1955 he reissued* The White Christian Minuteman.

In 1960 he received a letter from George Kraft/Iona Potapov about the whereabouts of Howard Campbell. Jones seeks him out with his strange entourage to lend whatever support he can.

In the cellar of Jones' home, August Krapptauer led the Iron Guard of the White Sons of the American Constitution. Jones' inner circle includes Krapptauer, Father Keeley, and The Black Fuehrer of Harlem.

Joseph of Arimathea. *The story of the Holy Grail is the impetus for Fred T. Barry to show off some of his command of obscure "facts." Here he tries to prove that Sir Galahad was Jewish.* (*DD* 154:L4-5, 35) According to Fred T. Barry, a Jew named **Joseph of Arimathea** took Christ's goblet when the Last Supper was over. He believed Christ to be divine... But then Sir Galahad presented himself at Camelot, and it was evident to everyone that his heart was perfectly pure. And he did find the Grail. He was not only spiritually entitled to it. He was legally entitled to it as well, since he was the last living descendant of that wandering Jew, **Joseph of Arimathea**.

journalism, New Journalism. (*WFG* xix:L12, 29, *Preface*) Everything else in here shows me trying to tell the truth nakedly, without the ornaments of fiction, about this or that. Which brings us to a discussion of the place of the "**New Journalism**," as opposed to fiction, in the literature of modern times.

. . . There's some **New Journalism** in here—about Biafra, about the Republican Convention of 1972. It's loose and personal.
(*WFG* xx:L2-4, 32 *Preface*) I have wavered some on this, but I am now persuaded again that acknowledged fiction is a much more truthful way of telling the truth than the **New Journalism** is. Or, to put it another way, the very finest **New Journalism** is fiction. . . .

And fiction is melody, and **journalism**, new or old, is noise.
(*WFG* 234:L5, 9 *A Political Disease*) Insults of that sort, isolated in a review, convey the idea of **journalism** at least as contemptible as the man attacked. But in the context of such a long and passionate book, such lapses seem almost beautiful. Curiously, they are frenzied, so grotesque, that they can do no harm to *(Senator)* Eagleton. I am extremely grateful for the **New Journalism**, many responsible people are not. And what I think about it now is that it is the literary equivalent of Cubism: All rules are broken; we are shown pictures such as no mature well-trained artist ever painted before, and in the crazy new pictures we somehow see luminous new aspects beloved old truths.
(*PS* xv:L9 *Introduction*) It is a marvelous new literary form. This book combines the tidal power of a major novel with the bone-rattling immediacy of front-line **journalism**—which is old stuff now, God knows, God knows.
(*HP* 50:L6) There were plenty of other exits, and I should have headed for 1 of those. At that moment, every other exit led to the University of Michigan and **journalism** and music-making, and a lifetime of saying and wearing what I goshdarned pleased. *See also: MH—Deer In The Works* 206:L2; *PS—Introduction* xxii:L7.

journalist, New Journalist. (*WFG* xix:L16, 29 *Preface*) Thucydides is the first **New Journalist** I know anything about. He was a celebrity who put himself at the center of the truths he was trying to tell, and he guessed when he had to, and he thought it worthwhile to be charming and entertaining. He was a good teacher. He did not wish to put his students to sleep with the truth, and he meant to put the truth into strikingly human terms, so his students would remember. . . .

Am I a **New Journalist**? I guess. There's some New Journalism in here—about Biafra, about the Republican Convention of 1972. It's loose and personal.
(*WFG* xx:L5 *Preface*) The **New Journalist** isn't free to tell nearly as much as a fiction writer, to show as much. There are many places he can't take his reader, whereas the fiction writer can take the reader anywhere, including the planet Jupiter, in case there's something worth seeing there.
(*WFG* 223:L1 *Address to P.E.N. Conference in Stockholm, 1973*) **Journalists** and teachers are often bullied or fired in my country—for saying this or that. But writers of novels and plays and short stories and poems have never been hurt or hampered much. They haven't even been noticed much by federal,

state, or local governments, no matter how insolent or blasphemous or treasonous those writers may be. This has been going on now for nearly two hundred years.
(*WFG* 231:L4 *A Political Disease*) I WORRY about the health of Dr. Hunter Thompson. I think I am supposed to do that. He is the most creatively crazy and vulnerable of the **New Journalists**, seemingly, and scattered throughout his dispatches are alarming reports on his health. Nor are his sicknesses imaginary. In this, his latest book, he gives the opinion of a physician: "He'd never seen anybody with as bad a case of anxiety as I had. He said I was right on the verge of a complete mental, physical, and emotional collapse."
(*WFG* 234:L19, 24 *A Political Disease*) I can put it more gruesomely—calling attention to the way people behave under torture sometimes, the way they are likely to thrash around and say things they might not say under other circumstances: The **New Journalists** are Populists screaming in pain.

They believe that it is easy and natural for Americans to be brotherly and just. That illusion, if it is an illusion, is the standard for well-being in the **New Journalists'** minds. Any deviation from that standard is perceived as a wound or a sickness.
(*HP* 33:L21) When Du Pont took over Barrytron, the double fence, the Dobermans, my father and all, I was a high school senior, all set to go to the University of Michigan to learn how to be a **journalist**, to serve John Q. Public's right to know. *See also: CC* 182:L12; *MH—Deer In The Works* 204:L9-10; *WFG—Playboy Interview* 269:L30; *JB* xvii:L18; *HP* 14:L27.

Joyce, Leroy. *The focus of a story told by Holiday Inn cocktail waitress Bonnie MacMahon in* Breakfast of Champions, *Joyce was a convicted rapist on death row at the Shepherdstown Adult Correctional Institution. Bonnie's husband Ralph was Leroy's guard at the time, and only hours before his scheduled execution Joyce cut off his penis and handed it to MacMahon in a coffee cup. Vonnegut interjects that though this is only a novel, he gave Bonnie the jist of a real story that occurred in Arkansas.*

Judgment Day. (*PP* 6:L21) Objectively, Paul tried to tell himself, things really were better than ever. For once, after the great bloodbath of the war, the world really was cleared of unnatural terrors—mass starvation, mass imprisonment, mass torture, mass murder. Objectively, know-how and world law were getting their long-awaited chance to turn earth into an altogether pleasant and convenient place in which to sweat out **Judgment Day**.
(*PP* 295:L15) Von Neumann considered Paul and then the broken glass. "This isn't the end, you know," he said. "Nothing ever is, nothing ever will be—not even **Judgment Day**."
(*SL5* 147:L28) "That's right. And I'm not the only one who's listening. God is listening, too. And on **Judgment Day** he's going to tell you all the things you said and did. If it turns out they're bad things instead of good things,

that's too bad for you, because you'll burn forever and ever. The burning never stops hurting." *Trout speaks with Maggie White.*

(*BC* 151:L23) "On **Judgment Day**," said Francine, "when they ask me what bad things I did down here, I'm going to have to tell them, 'Well—there was a promise I made to a man I loved, and I broke it all the time. I promised him never to say I loved him.'"

(*Slap* 36:L18) But there was one tremendous monument, with thick granite walls, a slate roof, and great doors, which would clearly last past **Judgment Day**. It was the mausoleum of the founder of the family's fortune and the builder of our mansion, Professor Elihu Roosevelt Swain.

(*JB* 1:L2-3) Life goes on, yes—and a fool and his self-respect are soon parted, perhaps never to be reunited even on **Judgment Day**.

(*JB* 38:L12) "Virgil Greathouse is no more and no less my brother than you or any other man," he said. "I will try to save him from hell, just as I am now trying to save you from hell." He then quoted the harrowing thing that Jesus, according to Saint Matthew, had promised to say in the Person of God to sinners on **Judgment Day**.

This is it: "Depart from me, you cursed, into the eternal fire prepared for the devil and his angels." *(Matthew 25:41)*

(*JB* 102:L2) I speak only of Ruth as "my wife." It would not surprise me, though, if on **Judgment Day** Sarah Wyatt and Mary Kathleen O'Looney were also certified as having been wives of mine.

(*PS* 168:L10, 22 *Mark Twain*) "I am moved on this occasion to put into a few words the ideal my parents and Twain and the rest held before me, and which I have now passed on. The ideal, achieved by few, is this: 'Live so that you can say to God on **Judgment Day**, "I was a very good person, even though I did not believe in you."'

". . . Religious skeptics often become very bitter toward the end, as did Mark Twain. I do not propose to guess now as to why he became so bitter. I know why I will become bitter. I will finally realize that I have had it right all along: that I will not see God, that there is no heaven or **Judgment Day**."

(*Blue* 30:L3) In the imaginary galleries in the distance are my own Abstract Expressionist paintings, miraculously resurrected by the Great Critic for **Judgment Day**, and then Pictures by Europeans, which I bought for a few dollars of chocolate bars or nylon stockings when a soldier, and then advertisements of the sort I had been laying out and illustrating before I joined the Army—at about the time news of my father's death in the Bijou Theater in San Ignacio came.

(*Blue* 207:L8) Gregory, I remember, was bid farewell in the papers as possibly the best-known American artist in history. Fred *(Jones)* was sent on to **Judgment Day** as a World War One ace, which he wasn't, and an aviation pioneer.

(*Blue* 243:L7) What will be found written after the name of Rabo Karabekian in the Big Book on **Judgment Day**?

"Soldier: Excellent.

"Husband and Father: Floparroo.

"Serious Artist: Floparroo." *Rabo's self-evaluation.*

(*HP* 23:L10) He *(Elias Tarkington)* had no fewer than 27 contraptions built, which he foolishly expected to go on running, after he had given them an initial spin or whack, until **Judgment Day**.

(*HP* 150:L2, 14) "To speed things up on **Judgment Day**," I said. . . .

I told him I wanted to be buried with my 2 lists, so that, if there really was going to be a **Judgment Day**, I could say to the Judge, "Judge, I have found a way to save you some precious time in Eternity. You don't have to look me up in the Book in Which All Things Are Recorded. Here's a list of my worst sins. Send me straight to Hell, and no argument." *This is Hartke's answer to his lawyer when asked why he was making up the two lists: all the women with whom he had meaningful sexual relationships and all the people he knows he has killed.*

(*HP* 168:L36) Clarke's *(Arthur C. Clarke's)* big arrival wasn't a half-bad dress rehearsal for **Judgment Day**.

(*HP* 295:L8) If there really is a big book somewhere, in which all things are written, and which is to be read line by line, omitting nothing, on **Judgment Day**, let it be recorded that I, when Warden of this place, moved the convicted felons out of the tents on the Quadrangle and into the surrounding buildings. They no longer had to excrete in buckets or, in the middle of the night, have their homes blown down. The buildings, except for this 1, were divided into cement-block cells intended for 2 men, but most holding 5.

June, Wanda (see also ***Happy Birthday, Wanda June***). *There are four incarnations of the character Wanda June. Her first appearance is in* The Sirens of Titan *as a six-year-old girl being dragged through the crowded concession stands outside the Rumfoord Estate. Winston Niles Rumfoord and Kazak were about to materialize and banish Malachi, Beatrice, and Chrono to Titan.*

The second Wanda June is the title character of the play. An error in the text indicates she was either eight or ten years old at the time of her death. She was killed by the drunken driver of an ice-cream truck. Wanda is happy in heaven. Her description of heaven makes it sound like a wonderful carnival. The title of the play comes from the birthday cake left at the bakery by her parents after her sudden death. Wanda's companions in heaven run the gamut from war criminals to innocents. Vonnegut sees this flaw in the play as an inherent characteristic of his literature. He recalls in its preface, Somewhere in there my father died, and one of the last things he said to me was that I had never written a story with a villain in it. That was surely one of the troubles with my play—and that remains a major trouble with it to this day. Even after we opened ***Happy Birthday, Wanda June***, we experimented shamelessly with endings. We had various people shoot Harold, including children. We had Harold shoot various people, including children. We had Harold do the world the favor of shooting himself (*WJ* ix:L15-26).

In the short story "The Big Space Fuck," reprinted in the "Obscenity" chapter of Palm Sunday, *Wanda June is the only daughter of the degenerate Dwayne and Grace Hoobler. Wanda June is suing her parents for ruining her childhood, resulting in diminished opportunities for her as an adult.*

In Hocus Pocus, *Wanda June is the wife of Tarkington College Professor Damon Stern. When the Athena prison break occurred, Stern sent Wanda June and the kids to her brother's house in Lackawanna, New York. The Sterns had saved Japanese yen in a Brussels Sprouts container in their freezer, and that was all she took away from Scipio. Damon Stern stayed behind to wake others in Scipio, and was eventually killed by the marauding convicts.*

Juno. *In Roman mythology, Juno is the goddess of the Pantheon and sister of Jupiter. In the short story "Welcome to the Monkey House," Billy the Poet derisively applies the term to Nancy McLuhan, the hostess from the Ethical Suicide Parlor whom he has kidnapped. He plans to let her ethical birth control pills wear off and have sex with her.*

K

Kago (see also ***Plague on Wheels***). *In* Breakfast of Champions, *Kago is the spokesperson for the band of Zeltoldimarian space travelers who promise to keep alive the story of the automobile civilization of Lingo-Three, in Kilgore Trout's* Plague on Wheels.

Kairys, Anna. *Walter Starbuck's mother.* (*JB* 5:L3) And what was I to Mr. McCone, that I should have been born into the unhappy stillness of his mansion? My mother, born **Anna Kairys** in Russian Lithuania, was his cook. My father, born Stanislaus Stankiewicz in Russian Poland, was his bodyguard and chauffeur. They genuinely loved him.

Kankabonos (also **Kanka-bonos**). *In* Galápagos, *the Ecuadorian tribe descended from native Indians and escaped African slaves. The six Kankabono girls cared for by Roman Catholic priest Father Bernard Fitzgerald eventually become the mothers of humanity as it evolves and returns to the sea. Through the ingenuity of Mary Hepburn, the Kankabonos are artificially inseminated with the sperm of Captain Adolf von Kleist. Their offspring mate with the genetically altered and furry children of Akiko Hiroguchi.*

The Kankabono girls were the last remaining members of their tribe when Father Fitzgerald hitched a ride for them to Guayaquil with bush pilot Eduardo Ximénez. The girls had been orphaned by the effects of pesticides dropped in their jungle home. Once in Guayaquil, Domingo Quezeda volunteered to care for them and serve as their interpreter, but he proved to be a lecherous old man who took advantage of their naivete.

kan-kan (see also **Bokononism**). (*CC* 14:L1-6) Bokononists believe that humanity is organized into teams, teams that do God's Will without ever discovering what they are doing. Such a team is called a *karass* by Bokonon, and the instrument, the ***kan-kan***, that brought me into my own particular *karass* was the book I never finished, the book to be called *The Day the World Ended*.

Karabekian, Dorothy. *Rabo's first wife, a registered nurse, who is now widowed by her second husband and lives in a beachfront condominium in Sarasota, Florida. After Rabo spent eight years in the military,* Poor **Dorothy** thought she was marrying a mature, fatherly retired military gentleman. What she got instead was an impossibly self-centered and undisciplined jerk of nineteen or so! (*Blue* 258:L4) *She became despondent over Rabo's involvement with the starving Abstract Expressionist artists who paid off their loans to Rabo with their paintings. When she gets angry with Rabo about the lack of talent among his group—agreeing with the published comments of an Italian sculptor—he draws two portraits of their children on the blank walls of their home. She doesn't understand why he doesn't use that talent to get commissioned work. He responds, "It's just too fucking easy." When they split up, Dorothy cut the two pieces of Sheetrock from the wall and took them with her.*

Karabekian, Rabo. *The one-eyed Armenian-American war veteran, Abstract Expressionist painter, and art collector who writes his autobiography,* Bluebeard, *at the request of Circe Berman. Rabo first appears as one of three distinguished guests at the Midland City Arts Festival in* Breakfast of Champions. *The first piece of artwork purchased for The Mildred Barry Memorial Center for the Arts is Karabekian's "The Temptation of Saint Anthony," a $50,000 acquisition. Introduced as a "minimal painter" as opposed to a "minimalist painter," Rabo's painting is nothing more than a single band of luminescent color on a white background. Within the text, Vonnegut frequently makes mention that he is in his own text to be reborn. He finds himself unexpectedly "renewed" by Rabo's interpretation of his painting.* (*BC* 221:L7-20) "I now give you my word of honor," he went on, "that the picture your city owns shows everything about life which truly matters, with nothing left out. It is a picture of the awareness of every animal. It is the immaterial core of every animal—the 'I am' to which all messages are sent. It is all that is alive in any of us—in a mouse, in a deer, in a cocktail waitress. It is unwavering and pure, no matter what preposterous adventure may befall us. A sacred picture of Saint Anthony alone is one vertical, unwavering band of light. If a cockroach were near him, or a cocktail waitress, the picture would show two such bands of light. Our awareness is all that is alive and maybe sacred in any of us. Everything else about us is dead machinery."

Though Rabo's painting is briefly alluded to in Deadeye Dick, *it isn't until the appearance of* Bluebeard *that Rabo becomes more than the wisecracking snob he is in* Breakfast of Champions. *He was born in 1916 in San Ignacio, California, to Armenian refugees. He was a largely self-taught artist, though when Rabo began a correspondence with Marilee Kemp (believing she was merely relaying information from the famed New York illustrator Dan Gregory), he was instructed to copy Gregory's illustrations as part of his training. Rabo briefly worked as an illustrator for a San Ignacio newspaper and left for New York to become Gregory's apprentice. He was unaware that Gregory only agreed to send for him because of Gregory's assault on Marilee Kemp. Gregory suffered Rabo's presence, training his protege in the same brutal manner as he was tutored by Beskudnikov. Rabo and Marilee became constant companions, and they eventually developed a brief physical relationship.*

During World War II, Rabo served in the Army Engineers, charged with using his artistry to camouflage military outposts. He lost his left eye during a shelling attack while serving in Europe. Upon his return to the United States, and after his surgery and recuperation at Fort Benjamin Harrison outside Indianapolis, Rabo returned to New York. He took up with a number of fledgling artists and became one of the founders of the Abstract Expressionist school of art. Rabo married a registered nurse, Dorothy, and sired two sons, Terry and Henri. Dorothy became disturbed with the amount of time Rabo spent with the other artists and his participation in an art form which, to her, revealed nothing and was commercially worthless. She became despondent with Rabo's friends constantly borrowing money from him and repaying him with their original artwork. Though she had no way to know at the time, those repayments formed the basis of Rabo's world-class collection of Abstract Expressionist paintings.

After Dorothy took the children and left their home in the village of Springs, Long Island, Rabo moved into the potato barn (six miles away on the waterfront of East Hampton), which he previously rented from Edith and Richard Fairbanks, Jr. to store his art collection. After Edith was widowed and his own divorce became final, Rabo and Edith began a relationship which led to a twenty-five-year marriage. Rabo later learned he lost Edith the same week Marilee Kemp passed away in Italy.

Rabo went on to live a quiet life on Long Island until he met Circe Berman, who moved into his life and caused him to reexamine his past by writing his memoirs. He titles those memoirs Bluebeard, and it is through Rabo's recall that we learn about his disastrous decision to use Sateen Dura-Luxe paint for his Abstract Expressionist creations. He learns of the paint's peculiar and tragic defect when he is told his sixty-four-foot tryptic "Blue Windsor Number Seventeen," has nearly completely peeled itself clean down to the underlying canvas. After retrieving its remains from the third subbasement of the Matsumoto Building in New York City, Rabo returns to the potato barn and paints "Now It's the Women's Turn." This new tryptic depicts the scene Rabo saw in the meadows of Europe after its liberation. Over five thousand figures, some no larger than a cigarette, are realistically rendered. It is similar to Vonnegut's description of the scenes he saw in Europe after being liberated from a POW camp, and this is confirmed in Fates Worse Than Death. *Perhaps as a reference to his own past "single band" paintings, Rabo paints himself into the tryptic. With his back to the viewer, his image is divided by the space between two canvasses. Rather than a single band of luminescent color representing one's essential awareness, Rabo's single band of emptiness (the space between the canvasses) takes the place of his spine.*

Rabo keeps this new masterpiece locked away in the potato barn until Circe Berman convinces him to reveal it. The barn and the painting become a tourist Mecca.

Karabekian, Terry and Henri. *The sons of Rabo and Dorothy Karabekian in* Bluebeard. *They are named after Rabo's best friend Terry Kitchen and his favorite artist, Henri Matisse. After Rabo and Dorothy break up, the boys are resentful of Rabo and have nothing to do with him. They eventually assume the name of their stepfather Roy Steel. Terry grows up to work as a publicity man for the Chicago Bears, and Henri works for the Pentagon as a civilian contract compliance officer. Rabo feels a great deal of guilt about his failure to properly father the boys, but he decides to leave his valuable collection of Abstract Expressionist paintings to them in his will, provided they change their names back to Karabekian. Rabo does this out of respect for his mother's wishes that the family name live on.*

karass (see also **Bokononism**). (*CC* 14:L1-6) Bokononists believe that humanity is organized into teams, teams that do God's Will without ever discovering what they are doing. Such a team is called a ***karass*** by Bokonon, and the instrument, the *kan-kan*, that brought me into my own particular ***karass*** was the book I never finished, the book to be called *The Day the World Ended*. (*CC* 50:L35-37, 51:L1-12) Which brings me to the Bokononist concept of a *wampeter*.

A *wampeter* is the pivot of a ***karass***. No ***karass*** is without a *wampeter*, Bokonon tells us, just as no wheel is without a hub.

Anything can be a *wampeter*: a tree, a rock, an animal, an idea, a book, a melody, the Holy Grail. Whatever it is, the members of its ***karass*** revolve about it in the majestic chaos of a spiral nebula. The orbits of the members of a ***karass*** about their common *wampeter* are spiritual orbits, naturally. It is souls and not bodies that revolve. As Bokonon invites us to sing:

> Around and around and around we spin,
> With feet of lead and wings of tin. . . .

And *wampeters* come and *wampeters* go, Bokonon tells us.

At any given time a ***karass*** actually has two *wampeters*—one waxing in importance, one waning.

Karlswald. *In the short story "D.P." the German village on the Rhine within the American Zone of Occupation where the American-German youngster Karl*

Heinz lives in an orphanage, hoping for the return of his American father. Karl is nicknamed Joe Louis.

Karpinski, Big John, Dorene, and Little John. *Rabo's neighbors to the north in East Hampton. Little John was a poor student, was arrested for selling dope, joined the Army during the Vietnam War—which brought great pride to Big John—and came back in a body bag. Big John and Dorene are preparing to sell the family farm, which was in the family for three generations, in six-acre lots for a housing development. Big John is a wounded Korean War veteran. The six-acre lot Rabo lives on was sold to his second wife Edith and her first husband by Big John's father. This final series of sales liquidating the Karpinski ancestral homeland is brought into sharp contrast for Karabekian.* (*Blue* 291:L14) **Big John and Dorene** will become cash millionaires in a condominium in Florida, where winter never comes. So they are losing their own sacred plot of earth at the foot of their own Mount Ararat, so to speak—without experiencing that ultimate disgrace: a massacre.

Kasabian, F. Donald. *Rabo Karabekian recalls the achievements of Armenian-Americans, among them F. Donald Kasabian.* (*Blue* 31:L26) Armenians have done brilliantly in this country during the short time they've been here. My neighbor to the west is **F. Donald Kasabian**, executive vice-president of Metropolitan Life—so that right here in exclusive East Hampton, and right on the beach, too, we have two Armenians side by side.

"**Katmandu**" (see also **John Fortune**). *Rudy Waltz's play about his childhood hero, dairy farmer John Fortune, which originally began as a high school essay. Rudy's teacher Naomi Shoup went to pieces after reading the essay and urged him to become a writer. For years Rudy continued to work on changing the essay into a play, and in 1959 he won a contest for new playwrights. His prize included an engagement at New York City's Theatre de Lys, the same theater where Vonnegut's "Wanda June" was produced. "Katmandu" was such a disaster it ran for just one night on February 14, 1960, fifteen years and a day after the firebombing of Dresden. The next morning Rudy and his brother Felix flew back to the snowed- in Midland City in search of their parents, only to find out their father had died.*

Rudy stayed with his brother and sister-in-law in New York while the play was in rehearsal, and for the first time in his life he could separate himself from the Deadeye Dick legacy. Able to stand outside himself, Rudy realized, I no longer cared about the play. It was Deadeye Dick, tormented by guilt in Midland City, who had found old John Fortune's quite pointless death in **Katmandu**, as far away from his hometown as possible, somehow magnificent. He himself yearned for distance and death.

So, there in Greenwich village, looking up at my name on the marquee, I was nobody. My braincase might as well have been filled with stale ginger ale (*DD* 130:L25-33). *The play had two more performances in 1963 at Midland City's Fairchild High School by the Midland City Mask and Wig Club.*

Kazak (also **Kazakh**). *There are three dogs named either Kazak or Kazakh in Vonnegut's work. The first Kazak is Winston Niles Rumfoord's "hound of space," a female mastiff traveling with her master along the same chrono-synclastic infundibulum in the novel* The Sirens of Titan. *At the end of the text an explosion on the Sun caused Kazak to be transported through time and space without her master. Rumfoord was left holding his dog's choke collar. In an earlier part of the text Rumfoord named one of the Martian months after Kazak. Later on Titan, he named* a cluster of ninety-three ponds and lakes, incipiently a fourth sea . . . the **Kazak Pools** (*ST* 265:L17).

In Breakfast of Champions, *Kazak is the Doberman pinscher patrolling the supply yard of the Maritimo Brothers Construction Company. Toward the end of the text, when Vonnegut again enters the narrative to confront Kilgore Trout, Kazak leaps toward the top of the fence to get Vonnegut, who is standing next to his rented car. Vonnegut leaps over the hood of the car in mortal fear, though Kazak was restrained by the height of the fence.*

In Galápagos, *Kazakh is the seeing-eye German shepherd belonging to Selena Macintosh. Kazakh has been fixed and well trained to ignore her normal canine instincts. After being stranded on Santa Rosalia, the six Kanka-bono girls stole Kazakh while Selena slept. They choked her to death and cooked her in the ship's oven before eating her.*

Keedsler, Beatrice. *The Midland City native and gothic novelist invited to return home as an honored guest to the Arts Festival. In the course of Dwayne Hoover's violent outrage, he broke Beatrice Keedsler's jaw. Aviator and World War I hero Will Fairchild was Beatrice's maternal uncle. In 1926 he shot and killed five of her relatives at the Keedsler mansion.*

While sharing drinks with Rabo Karabekian in the lounge of the Midland City Holiday Inn, Keedsler echoes Vonnegut's sense that former regional distinctions in American life have become homogenized. (*BC* 196:L20-29) **Beatrice Keedsler**, the Gothic novelist, had grown up in Midland City. "I was petrified about coming home after all these years," she said to Karabekian.

"Americans are always afraid of coming home," said Karabekian, "with good reason, may I say."

"They *used* to have good reason," said **Beatrice**, "but not anymore. The past has been rendered harmless. I would tell any wandering American now, 'Of course you can go home again, and as often as you please. It's just a motel.'"

Vonnegut's assessment of Keedsler's written works and of art in general as it has affected the masses is rather brutal. (*BC* 208:L5-6) I had no respect whatsoever for the creative works of either the painter or the novelist. I thought Karabekian with his meaningless pictures had entered into a conspiracy with millionaires to make poor people feel stupid. I thought **Beatrice Keedsler** had joined hands with other old-fashioned storytellers to make people believe that life had leading characters, minor characters, significant details, insignificant details, that it had lessons to be learned, tests to be passed, and a beginning, a middle, and an end.

As I approached my fiftieth birthday, I had become more and more enraged and mystified by the idiot decisions made by my countrymen. And then I had come suddenly to pity them, for I understood how innocent and natural it was for them to behave so abominably, and with such abominable results: They were doing their best to live like people invented in story books. This was the reason Americans shot each other so often: It was a convenient literary device for ending short stories and books.

Keeley, Father Patrick (also **Keely**). *The seventy-three-year-old defrocked Paulist priest reclaimed from skid row by the Rev. Dr. Lionel J.D. Jones in* Mother Night. *Prior to World War II, Father Keeley served as the chaplain for a Detroit gun club established by Nazi agents. One of the club's fondest hopes was to shoot Jews. Keeley's involvement came to the attention of Vatican officials when they read a newspaper's account of one of Keeley's virulently anti-Semitic benedictions. As a result, Pope Pius XI unfrocked him. Keeley resorted to alcohol and was found homeless and hopeless by Dr. Jones. Howard Campbell reveals that the prayer offered by Keeley to the gun club was a paraphrase of one of his own anti-Semitic diatribes delivered on shortwave radio. More recently, Father Keeley serves as Jones' secretary and chaplain for the Iron Guard of the White Sons of the American Constitution.*

Keene, Patty. *The seventeen-year-old blonde waitress at Dwayne Hoover's Burger Chef restaurant. She took the job to help pay off the hospital bills accumulated by her father's fatal bout with colon cancer. She became pregnant when raped by Don Breedlove outside the Bannister Memorial Fieldhouse after the Regional High School Basketball Playoffs. She decided not to report the crime because her father was dying at the time. Vonnegut uses Patty to comment on the manner in which some women have been trained to succeed in our society.* (*BC* 136:L19) **Patty Keene** was stupid on purpose, which was the case with most women in Midland City. The women all had big minds because they were big animals, but they did not use them much for this reason: unusual ideas could make enemies, and the women, if they were going to achieve any sort of comfort and safety, needed all the friends they could get.

So, in the interests of survival, they trained themselves to be agreeing machines instead of thinking machines. All their minds had to do was to discover what other people were thinking, and then they thought that, too.

Patty hoped she could entice Dwayne Hoover to take an interest in her since his wealth could solve so many of her problems. She sincerely pitied Dwayne for the suicide of his wife and his shame about having a homosexual son.

Kelly, Colonel Bryan. *In "All The King's Horses," reprinted in* Welcome to the Monkey House, *Colonel Kelly, his wife and twin sons, and a group of military technical specialists crash land in an unnamed Far East communist country while traveling to India to become a military attaché. Kelly is forced into playing a game of chess with his captor Pi Ying, and later Major Barzov, the Soviet attaché, for their freedom. The bizarre twist is that all the Americans are chess pieces who will be put to death if taken during the game. Kelly precipitates the assassination of Pi Ying when he realizes he would have to sacrifice his son during the game to achieve victory. Pi Ying's mistress kills him when she realizes what is about to happen. Barzov takes over for Pi Ying and goes on to lose to Kelly's strategy. Barzov spares the life of Kelly's son.*

Kelly, Margaret (and her twin sons **Jerry** and **Paul**) *The wife of Colonel Bryan Kelly and the mother of twin ten-year-old sons (Jerry and Paul) in the short story "All The King's Horses." In a game of chess with Pi Ying, the Kellys' captor, she is forced to play the queen, her sons are the knights, and her husband is the king and chess rival to their captor. Lost chess pieces result in the deaths of some of Colonel Kelly's soldiers.*

Kemp, Marilee. *The daughter of an illiterate West Virginia coal miner, former Ziegfeld Follies showgirl, mistress to Dan Gregory (who sent her away for an abortion while they lived in Europe), and the eventual Countess Portomaggiori, Marilee is fondly remembered by* Bluebeard*'s Rabo Karabekian for posing as Gregory's assistant and providing him material and spiritual support through the mail. She took it upon herself to correspond with Rabo when Gregory ignored his letters. Marilee went so far as to send Karabekian some of Gregory's expensive art supplies. When Gregory found out, he beat her and threw her down a flight of stairs in his brownstone, breaking both her legs and one arm. As a result, Marilee limped for the rest of her life. While Marilee was recuperating in the hospital, a temporarily remorseful Gregory promised he would bring Rabo to New York City. She and Rabo, only two years apart in age, struck up a close friendship and eventually enjoyed a brief physical relationship.*

Marilee revealed to Rabo that she had a series of abusive relationships with men: her father used to beat her, her junior high school football team raped her after the prom, the stage manager of the Ziegfeld Follies was sexually coercive, and Dan Gregory had thrown her down the stairs.

After Dan Gregory and Fred Jones were killed at Sidi Barrani, Marilee stayed on in Italy in the company of Bruno, Count Portomaggiore, Mussolini's Oxford-educated Minister of Culture. The Count was homosexual and not physically interested in Marilee. He occasionally engaged in pedophilia. Mussolini was being pressured to get rid of the Count because he was viewed as a security risk, so Mussolini ordered the Count to marry Marilee. She later learns that her husband was the head of British Intelligence in Italy. After the war, Marilee became the most-high-volume Sony distributor in Europe and a great collector of American postwar modern art. Marilee Kemp and Rabo's second wife, Edith, passed away in the same week.

Kennedy, Robert. *During Vonnegut's writing of* Slaughterhouse-Five, *Robert Kennedy was assassinated and Vonnegut includes this historical moment, as well as the assassination of Martin Luther King, Jr., to chronicle the cycle of deaths and new births which occurs each day. It prompts Vonnegut to see some virtue in the Tralfamadorian view of the life cycle.* (*SL5* 182:L1, 23-24, 183:L1-3) **Robert Kennedy**, whose summer home is eight miles from the home I live in all year round, was shot two nights ago. He died last night. So it goes. . . .

If what Billy Pilgrim learned from the Tralfamadorians is true, that we will all live forever, no matter how dead we may sometimes seem to be, I am not overjoyed. Still—if I am going to spend eternity visiting this moment and that, I'm grateful that so many of those moments are nice.

(*BC* 285:L5) Parking lots were vacant, except for night watchmen's cars which were here and there. There was no traffic on Fairchild Boulevard, which had once been the aorta of the town. The life had all been drained out of it by the Interstate and by the **Robert F. Kennedy** Inner Belt Expressway, which was built on the old right-of-way of the Monon Railroad. The Monon was defunct.

Kern, Shirley. *As* Hocus Pocus' *Eugene Debs Hartke begins to take account of all the women he's made love to, his first memory of a meaningful sexual encounter was with Shirley Kern when he was twenty.*

Kestenbaum, Stanley. *The accountant who marries Alice, the first wife of Colonel Looseleaf Harper, in* Happy Birthday, Wanda June.

Ketchum, Bernard. *In* Deadeye Dick, *Ketchum lost an eye as a child when a playmate shot him with a beebee gun. The Midland City lawyer represents Eugene Metzger, the widower of Jane killed by Rudy Waltz's errant shot from the attic gun room. He is later hired by Felix and Rudy Waltz to sue anyone connected with the sale of the radioactive Oak Ridge cement, which caused the massive brain tumors that killed their mother. He successfully sues the Nuclear Regulatory Commission, the Maritimo Brothers Construction Company, and the Ohio Valley Ornamental Concrete Company. The Waltz brothers then buy the Hotel Oloffson in Haiti. Ketchum is a Harvard Law School graduate. One of his sons flunked out of his alma mater and became a welder in Alaska; the other son "deserted to Sweden during the Vietnam War" and worked with alcoholics. Ketchum arranged for fake affidavits enabling Hippolyte Paul de Mille, the Waltz's Haitian chef, to accompany the group to Midland City, eventually conducting a voodoo resurrection at Calvary Cemetery.*

Key, Eddie. *The young black ambulance driver who helps remove the wounded from the streets of Midland City after Dwayne Hoover's violent outburst. He was a direct descendant of Francis Scott Key as well as a* *descendant of the family which originally owned Bluebird Farm, the site of Sacred Miracle Cave. He knew stories about more than six hundred ancestors including Africans, Indians, and whites. He enjoyed a heightened spiritual awareness because of his knowledge, and for this reason he is unique among Vonnegut's characters; Eddie Key lived more fully because of his appreciation of history.* (*BC* 270:L21, 271:L1-27) **Eddie Key** knew so much about his ancestry because the black part of his family had done what so many African families still do in Africa, which was to have one member of each generation whose duty it was to memorize the history of the family so far . . . looking out through the windshield, he had the feeling that he himself was a vehicle, and that his eyes were windshields through which his progenitors could look, if they wished to.

Francis Scott Key was only one of thousands back there. On the off-chance that **Key** might now be having a look at what had become of the United States of America so far, **Eddie** focussed his eyes on an American flag which was stuck to the windshield. He said this very quietly: "Still wavin', man."

Eddie Key's familiarity with a teeming past made life much more interesting to him than it was to Dwayne, for instance, or to me, or to Kilgore Trout, or to almost any white person in Midland City that day. We had no sense of anybody else using our eyes—or our hands. We didn't even know who our great-grandfathers and great-grandmothers were. **Eddie Key** was afloat in a river of people who were flowing from here to there in time. Dwayne and Trout and I were pebbles at rest.

And **Eddie Key**, because he knew so much by heart, was able to have deep, nourishing feelings about Dwayne Hoover, for instance, and about Dr. Cyprian Ukwende, too. Dwayne was a man whose family had taken over Bluebird Farm. Ukwende, an Indaro, was a man whose ancestors had kidnapped an ancestor of **Key**'s on the West Coast of Africa, a man named Ojumwa. The Indaros sold him for a musket to British slave traders, who took him on a sailing ship named the "Skylark" to Charleston, South Carolina, where he was auctioned off as a self-propelled, self-repairing farm machine.

"The Kid Nobody Could Handle" (1955) (see **Jim Donnini**).

Kilgallen, Pat. *The love interest of both the unnamed narrator and EPICAC in the 1950 short story of the same name. Kilgallen and the narrator are mathematicians at work on EPICAC housed at Wyandotte College. Kilgallen refuses the narrator's inept advances until he has EPICAC compose love poetry for her. They marry and in the wake of EPICAC's self-destruction through a poetic fury, the narrator is left with five hundred years worth of poetry for his wife.*

Kilyer, Tom. *Once a "scholarship boy" at the elite and expensive Whitehill school, Kilyer's son is also accepted on academic merit and given financial* *assistance in the short story "The Lie." Kilyer had written the school song, which was engraved on a school monument.*

Kimberly. *A student at Sweetbread College despondent over the institution's bankruptcy, in the play "The Chemistry Professor."*

King, Bobby. *The middle-aged Manhattan publicity man who organized "the Nature Cruise of the Century"* in Galápagos.

King of Candlesticks. *Though known as the "King of New York,"* Slapstick*'s Wilbur Swain is also called the "The King of Candlesticks" for his huge collection of candlesticks.*

Kirk, Mary Selwyn and **Oveta Cooper**. *The two practical nurses who kindly saw to the needs of Wilbur and Eliza Swain at their Vermont estate in* Slapstick.

Kisco, Buddy. *In the corrupt world of intercollegiate athletics illustrated by Cornell's inability to purchase quality football players in* Player Piano, *Buddy Kisco is emblematic of a system which exploits its athletes. In* Player Piano *college football was operated as a professional enterprise complete with long-term, lucrative contracts. Kisco died while playing for Rutgers, but the system left his widow nothing more than a government pension.*

Kissinger, Henry. *Richard Nixon's Secretary of State was present when* Jailbird*'s Walter Starbuck made a fool of himself with multiply lit cigarettes at a White House staff meeting concerning the National Guard shootings of students at Kent State University. Later, Vonnegut includes Kissinger among the preliminary passenger list for "the Nature Cruise of the Century" in* Galápagos. *In* Hocus Pocus, *Kissinger is one of the revelers in the caravan accompanying Arthur Clarke on his trip to Tarkington College. Although most of Clarke's companions joined him on a motorcycle ride to the college from Rochester, New York, Kissinger rode down in a limousine. Nonetheless,* Just like the people on the motorcycles . . . the people in the limousines wore gold crash helmets decorated with dollar signs (*HP* 168:L27-29).

Eugene Debs Hartke recalls: Although I had been an instrument of his geopolitics, I felt no connection between him and me. His face was certainly familiar. He might have been, like Gloria White, somebody who had been in a lot of movies I had seen.

I dreamed about him once here in prison, though. He was a woman. He was a Gypsy fortune-teller who looked into her crystal ball but wouldn't say anything (*HP* 209:L17-25). *See also: FWD* 103:L31, 105:L16.

Kitchen, Terry. *Rabo Karabekian's best friend and fellow Abstract Expressionist painter in* Bluebeard. *Together with Jackson Pollock, the three of them were known as "The Three Musketeers" for their endless hours of* *drinking in New York's Cedar Tavern. Rabo named his first son after Kitchen; his second son was named after Terry's and Rabo's favorite painter, Henri Matisse. Unlike the first-generation Armenian-American Rabo Karabekian, Terry Kitchen came from an old and wealthy family. He was a graduate of Yale Law School and worked as a clerk to Supreme Court Justice John Harlan. He was a silver star winner and member of the Eighty-second Airborne during World War II. Shortly after Jackson Pollock committed suicide, Rabo's wife and children left him. Three weeks later, Kitchen stuck a pistol in his mouth and blew his brains out. Karabekian speculates that among Kitchen's many problems, he never gained his balance after shooting his father in the shoulder during an argument. He was buried on Long Island's Green River Cemetery near Jackson Pollock and Rabo's second wife, Edith.*

Kitchen introduces Rabo to his concept of the "non-epiphany." After Rabo describes the blank contentedness he felt after three hours of lovemaking to Marilee Kemp, Terry explains that the non-epiphany is "A concept of my own invention. . . . The trouble with God isn't that He so seldom makes Himself known to us. . . . The trouble with God is exactly the opposite: He's holding you and me and everybody else by the scruff of the neck practically *constantly.*"

He said he had just come from an afternoon at the Metropolitan Museum of Art, where so many of the paintings were about God's giving instructions, to Adam and Eve and the Virgin Mary, and various saints in agony and so on. "These moments are very rare, if you can believe the painters—but who was ever nitwit enough to believe a painter?" he said, and he ordered another double Scotch, I'm sure, for which I would pay. "Such moments are often called 'epiphanies' and I'm here to tell you they are as common as houseflies," he said. . . .

"'Contentedly adrift in the cosmos,' were you?" **Kitchen** said to me. "That is a perfect description of a non-epiphany, that rarest of moments, when God Almighty lets go of the scruff of your neck and lets you be human for a little while. How long did the feeling last?"

"Oh—maybe half an hour," I said.

And he leaned back in his chair and he said with deep satisfaction: "And there you are" (*Blue* 173:L1-33, 174:L1-2).

Kitchen admitted to having his own non-epiphanies only after sex and the two times he took heroin. (*Blue* 180:L13) As **Terry Kitchen** once said of a postcoital experience of his own: "The epiphany came back, and everybody had to put on their clothes and run around again like chickens with their heads cut off."

After the war, Karabekian and Kitchen became roommates in a Union Square apartment. Kitchen attached himself to Karabekian and wherever Rabo took his family, Kitchen was sure to follow. When Terry helped Rabo move his art collection out to the Long Island potato barn, Kitchen had Rabo purchase a paint sprayer for him similar to the type Rabo used for camouflage during the war. He then used it to spray paint a discarded piece of beaverboard and suddenly found his artistic medium. Until that point, Kitchen's artwork suffered from his lack of basic artistic talent. Kitchen previously displayed enormous talents for all his endeavors, but making art was his Mount Everest, which had yet to be scaled at the time he made the characterization.

So close was Rabo to Kitchen that when he committed suicide, Rabo considered himself dead as well. The only other time Rabo experienced such a loss was after his wife Edith passed away.

Kittredge, Waltham. *Kittredge's* The American Philosopher Kings *is cited as the preeminent chronicle of America's ruling class.* (*ST* 27:L17-25) It was **Kittredge** who proved that the class was in fact a family, with its loose ends neatly turned back into a hard core of consanguinity through the agency of cousin marriages. Rumfoord and his wife, for instance, were third cousins, and detested each other.

And when Rumfoord's class was diagramed by Kittredge, it resembled nothing so much as the hard, ball-like knot known as a *monkey's fist*.

Kittredge coined the term "un-neurotic courage" to describe the pure courage displayed by such acts as Rumfoord's flight straight into the known chrono-synclastic infundibulum. It is a courage without the conscious pursuit of fame or money, and without any hint of mental defect.

Kleindienst, Edward Strawberry-4. *President Wilbur Swain's valet who dies of the Albanian Flu in* Slapstick.

Klopfer, Arndt. (*MN* 124:L13-25) *The New York Times* published a portrait of me *(Howard Campbell, Jr.)* as a much younger man, my official portrait as a Nazi and idol of the international airwaves. I can only guess at the year in which the picture was taken—1941, I think.

Arndt Klopfer, the photographer who took the picture of me, did his best to make me look like a Maxfield Parrish Jesus covered with cold cream. He even gave me a halo, a judiciously placed spot of nebulous light in the background. The halo was no special effect for me alone. Everybody who went to **Klopfer** got a halo, including Adolf Eichmann.

I can say that for certain about Eichmann, without asking for confirmation from the Haifa Institute, because Eichmann had his picture taken just ahead of me at **Klopfer**'s studio.

Knechtmann, Avchen, Heinz, and **baby Peter Karl; Karl and Helga**. *In the short story "Adam," Avchen and Heinz are German Jews who survived life in Nazi concentration camps. Heinz is the orphaned son of Karl and Helga Knechtmann. Helga had delivery trouble due to the malnutrition she suffered as a child.*

"Adam" is as much about the hope new parents hold for their children as it is about the legacy and self-imposed responsibility Holocaust survivors feel about continuing life and the culture which was the target of so many evils.

Though many critics wonder about Vonnegut's feelings toward victims of the Holocaust when he repeatedly recalls the events of Dresden and Hiroshima (notably columnist George Will), the 1954 short story "Adam" is early evidence of his concern for all people subject to genocidal policies and the inferno of international politics. (*MH* 276:L17-21, 277:L1-6, 17-28 *ADAM*) The man he left behind, all alone now, was **Heinz Knechtmann**, a presser in a dry-cleaning plant, a small man with thin wrists and a bad spine that kept him slightly hunched, as though forever weary. His face was long and big-nosed and thin-lipped, but was so overcast with good-humored humility as to be beautiful. His eyes were large and brown, and deep-set and long-lashed. He was only twenty-two, but seemed and felt much older. He had died a little as each member of his family had been led away and killed by the Nazis, until only in him, at the age of ten, had life and the name of **Knechtmann** shared a soul. He and his wife, **Avchen**, had grown up behind barbed wire. . . .

When the numbness of weary wishing lifted momentarily during this second vigil, **Heinz**'s mind was a medley of proud family names, gone, all gone, that could be brought to life again in this new being—if it lived. Peter Knechtmann, the surgeon; Kroll Knechtmann, the botanist; Friederich Knechtmann, the playwright. Dimly recalled uncles. Or if it was a girl, and if it lived, it would be **Helga Knechtmann, Heinz**'s mother, and she would learn to play the harp as **Heinz**'s mother had, and for all **Heinz**'s ugliness, she would be beautiful. The **Knechtmann** men were all ugly, the **Knechtmann** women were all lovely as angels though not all angels. It had always been so—for hundreds and hundreds of years.

(*MH* 279:L18-24 *Adam*) "Hello, hello, hello, little **Knechtmann**," said **Heinz** to the red prune on the other side of the glass. His voice echoed down the hard, bare corridor, and came back to him with embarrassing loudness. He blushed and lowered his voice. "Little Peter, little Kroll," he said softly, "little Friederich—and there's **Helga** in you, too. Little spark of **Knechtmann**, you little treasure house. Everything is saved in you."

(*MH* 283:L31-36 *Adam*) "They couldn't kill us, could they, **Heinz**?"

"No."

"And here we are, alive as we can be."

"Yes."

"The baby, **Heinz**—" She opened her dark eyes wide. "It's the most wonderful thing that ever happened, isn't it?"

"Yes," said **Heinz**.

The Knights of Kandahar. *A fraternal order which savagely beat the state police to wrest control of Griffin Boulevard during the Ghost Shirt rebellion in Ilium, in* Player Piano.

Knowles, Lyman Enders. *The enigmatic old elevator operator at the Research Laboratory of the General Forge and Foundry Company, where Felix*

Hoenikker worked, who grabs his behind and exclaims "Yes, yes!" whenever making a witty remark. "'This here's a re-search laboratory. *Re*-search means *look again*, don't it? Means they're looking for something they found once and it got away somehow, and now they got to *re*-search for it? How come they got to build a building like this, with mayonnaise elevators and all, and fill it with all these crazy people? What is it they're trying to find again? Who lost what?' Yes, yes!" (*CC* 56:L15-21) *Knowles characterized the Hoenikker children as "Babies full of rabies . . . Yes, yes!"*

Kolhouri. *The Shah of Bratpuhr is the spiritual leader of this sect of 6,000,0000 members in* Player Piano.

Konigswasser, Dr. Ellis. *The mathematician in the short story "Unready to Wear" who "did all his living with his mind" and who was so distressed with caring for his body that he accidentally discovered how to separate his spiritual essence from his body. Those who followed his teachings were called amphibians. Amphibians put on bodies they keep in storage centers for whenever they feel like doing work or dressing up. "Unready to Wear" is perhaps Vonnegut's earliest attempt to address demands made on humans simply because of their dependence on chemistry.* (*MH* 232:L32-38 *Unready to Wear*) "The mind's the only thing about human beings that's worth anything. Why does it have to be tied to a bag of skin, blood, hair, meat, bones, and tubes? No wonder people can't get anything done, stuck for life with a parasite that has to be stuffed with food and protected from weather and germs all the time. And the fool thing wears out anyway—no matter how much you stuff and protect it!"

(*MH* 234:L17 *Unready to Wear*) By following the instructions in **Konigswasser**'s book for about two years, almost anybody could get out of his body whenever he wanted to. The first step was to understand what a parasite and dictator the body was most of the time, then to separate what the body wanted or didn't want from what you yourself—your psyche-wanted or didn't want. Then, by concentrating on what you wanted, and ignoring as much as possible what the body wanted beyond plain maintenance, you made your psyche demand its rights and become self-sufficient.

(*MH* 236:L7-15 *Unready to Wear*) Nobody but a saint could be really sympathetic or intelligent for more than a few minutes at a time in a body—or happy, either, except in short spurts. I haven't met an amphibian yet who wasn't easy to get along with, and cheerful and interesting—as long as he was outside a body. And I haven't met one yet who didn't turn a little sour when he got into one.

The minute you get in, chemistry takes over—glands making you excitable or ready to fight or hungry or mad or affectionate, or—well, you never know what's going to happen next.

Koradubian, Martin. *In* Sirens of Titan*, this Boston solar watch repairman, liar, and erstwhile writer authored a magazine article for $3,000 about one of Winston Niles Rumfoord's materializations to which he claimed he was invited. The article was completely false.* (*ST* 50:L5-19) **Koradubian** claimed in his story that Rumfoord had told him about the year Ten Million A.D.

In the year Ten Million, according to **Koradubian**, there would be a tremendous house-cleaning. All records relating to the period between the death of Christ and the year One Million A.D. would be hauled to dumps and burned. This would be done, said **Koradubian**, because museums and archives would be crowding the living right off the earth.

The million-year period to which the burned junk related would be summed up in history books in one sentence, according to **Koradubian**: *Following the death of Jesus Christ, there was a period of readjustment that lasted for approximately one million years.*

Koshevoi, Mr. *In the short story "The Manned Missiles," Koshevoi is the Soviet Ambassador to the United Nations who publicly delivers the letter from the bereaved Mr. Ivankov to Mr. Ashland. The tale is told through an exchange of letters by the two men who lost their sons in space when Captain Bryant Ashland's capsule collided with Ivankov's. Ashland was sent to observe and photograph the Soviet ship. Koshevoi at first speaks harshly about the American astronaut, but later agrees with both nations' finding that the deaths of the two astronauts was accidental.*

Kouyoumdjian, Marktich (see **Marc Coulomb**).

Kovacs, Arpad. (*MN* 8:L1-3) The guard who relieves Andor Gutman at six each night is Arpad Kovacs. Arpad is a Roman candle of a man, loud and gay. *Kovacs, one of the four Jerusalem prison guards taking shifts watching Howard Campbell, is a Hungarian Jew who joined the Nazi S.S. in order to stay alive. He is upset with the widespread image of Jews who complacently, quietly went to their deaths in the gas chambers. He calls those Jews briquets. One could make the case that Kovacs understands Campbell's apparent collaboration since he recognizes the incongruity of himself being a Jew in the Hungarian S.S. and this* fact is the basis for his sympathy with me *(Campbell)*. "Tell them the things a man does to stay alive! What's so noble about being a briquet?" (*MN* 9:L6-8) *He is a harsh critic of Campbell's propaganda invectives, conjecturing that* "Goebbels should have fired you and hired me as the radio scourge of the Jews. I would have raised blisters around the world! . . . What an Aryan I made!" (*MN* 9:L26-28) *Despite all his bravado, he reveals that his true work for the S.S. allowed him to frame fourteen Nazis for execution as traitors. Eichmann had personally congratulated Kovacs for ferreting out the alleged spies, though Kovacs was unaware at the time just how important Eichmann was—or else he would have killed him.*

Kraft, George. *Though Iona Potapov's true identity wasn't known by the government of the United States until 1941, the Soviet spy operated in America since 1935 posing as aspiring artist George Kraft. By chance after the war, Howard Campbell settles into the same Greenwich Village apartment house as Kraft. The two strike up a friendship based upon their mutual loneliness and interest in chess. Campbell had purchased a war surplus whittling kit, the product of which was a complete chess set. He introduced himself to Kraft and the two became constant companions. In 1931, Kraft beat chess Grand Master Tartakover in Rotterdam.*

Kraft's paintings become the object of much praise after he begins his sentence at the Federal Penitentiary at Fort Leavenworth, bringing as much as $10,000 each.

Kraft was a member of Alcoholics Anonymous. Despite his duplicity, he was sincere in his appreciation of the organization, frequently echoing Vonnegut's own admiration for the group. Kraft also used the A.A. meetings to make his spy contacts, which Campbell reasons was typical of his schizophrenia as a spy that he would use an institution he so admired for purposes of espionage (*MN* 41:L21-22).

Once Kraft learned who Howard Campbell was, he put a number of plots in motion. He notified Moscow that Stepan Bodovskov was a plagiarist who had taken Campbell's manuscripts as war booty and published them under his own name. He also notified a number of American publications and patriotic organizations about Campbell's whereabouts. Resi Noth was brought out of a Russian prison and sent to America to pose as her sister Helga, Campbell's wife who was presumed dead. Exposing Campbell and reuniting him with Helga was meant to force him to flee America. Kraft had arranged for them all to fly to Mexico for refuge, only he planned for a quick transfer to a flight to Moscow where Campbell would face a war crimes trial. Campbell's Blue Fairy Godmother foiled Kraft's plans and arrested him for espionage.

Kraft submitted a deposition to the Israelis in preparation for Campbell's war crime trials in which he declares under oath that Russian intelligence was never able to turn up any proof that I *(Howard Campbell)* had been an American agent. He offers the opinion that I was an ardent Nazi, but that I shouldn't be held responsible for my acts, since I was a political idiot, an artist who could not distinguish between reality and dreams (*MN* 198:L18-23).

Kraft, Mary. *One of the two hostesses at the Ethical Suicide Parlor in the short story "Welcome to the Monkey House."* (*MH* 28:L32 *Welcome to the Monkey House*) Nancy *(McLuhan)* was a strawberry blonde. **Mary** was a glossy brunette. Their uniforms were white lipstick, heavy eye makeup, purple body stockings with nothing underneath, and black-leather boots. They ran a small operation—with only six suicide booths. In a really good week, say the one before Christmas, they might put sixty people to sleep. It was done with a hypodermic syringe.

Kramm, Doris. *Delmar Peale's eighty-seven-year-old secretary at The American Harp Company's headquarters atop the Chrysler Building.* (*JB* 150:L25, 151:L3) **Doris** wept because she had had two hard blows in rapid succession. She had been notified on the previous afternoon that she was going to have to retire immediately, now that RAMJAC had taken over. The retirement age for all RAMJAC employees everywhere, except for supervisory personnel, was sixty-five. And then that morning, while she was cleaning out her desk, she got a telegram saying that her great-grandniece had been killed in a head-on collision after a high-school senior prom in Sarasota, Florida. **Doris** had no descendents of her own, he explained, so her collateral relatives meant a lot to her. *Mary Kathleen O'Looney cancels the RAMJAC retirement order in order to save Doris' job.*

Krapptauer, August. *The founder and Vice-Bundesfuehrer of the Iron Guard of the White Sons of the American Constitution, Krapptauer was in ill health and passes away shortly after he appears. His immediate cause of death could be considered chivalry, since his heart gives out after climbing up and down the stairs of Campbell's brownstone carrying Resi/Helga's luggage.* (*MN* 54:L27-28, 55:L1) Jones' bodyguard was **August Krapptauer**, former Vice-Bundesfuehrer of the German-American Bund. **Krapptauer** was sixty-three, had done eleven years in Atlanta, was about to drop dead. But he still looked garishly boyish, as though he went to a mortuary cosmetologist regularly. The greatest achievement of his life was the arrangement of a joint meeting of the Bund and the Ku Klux Klan in New Jersey in 1940. At that meeting, **Krapptauer** declared that the Pope was a Jew and that the Jews held a fifteen-million-dollar mortgage on the Vatican. A change of Popes and eleven years in a prison laundry had not changed his mind. *As Campbell later reveals, he was responsible for broadcasting those lies which Krapptauer so readily accepted. Just after Campbell delivers Krapptauer's eulogy to the basement throng of the White Sons of the American Constitution, the Blue Fairy Godmother reappears to save Campbell from the kidnapping plot of Kraft/Potapov.*

Krebbs, Sherman. *The impoverished nihilistic poet, "a platinum blond Jesus with spaniel eyes," and self-professed National Chairman of Poets and Painters for Immediate Nuclear War who borrows John/Jonah's New York City apartment. Krebbs wrecked the apartment, killed John/Jonah's cat, ran up hundreds of dollars in long distance bills, set the couch on fire, and used excrement to write poetry on the floor. When John/Jonah discovered his murdered cat with a sign around its neck that said "Meow," he became convinced that Krebbs was a* wrang-wrang. (*CC* 71:L17-28) A *wrang-wrang*, according to Bokonon, is a person who steers people away from a line of speculation by reducing that line, with the example of the *wrang-wrang's* own life, to an absurdity.

I might have been vaguely inclined to dismiss the stone angel as meaningless, and to go from there to the meaninglessness of all. But after I saw what **Krebbs** had done, in particular what he had done to my sweet cat, nihilism was not for me.

Somebody or something did not wish me to be a nihilist. It was **Krebbs**'s mission, whether he knew it or not, to disenchant me with that philosophy. Well done, **Mr. Krebbs**, well done.

Krementz, Jill. *One of America's most noted female photographers and Vonnegut's second wife (they were married in 1979) for whom he dedicated* **Wampeters, Foma & Granfalloons** *with the words,* FOR / JILL / WHO CRONKLED ME (*WFG* dedication page). *He wrote a much simpler dedication to her in* Deadeye Dick, *and notes that they stayed in the "James Jones Cottage" of Haiti's Grand Hotel Oloffson, the same hotel owned by the Waltz brothers in the text—their brothers' refuge during the neutron-bombing of Midland City.*

Ms. Krementz was a war photographer in Vietnam (The Face of Vietnam *with CBS correspondent Dean Brelis*), *and more recently produced books focusing on children* (A Very Young Dancer; How It Feels When a Parent Dies; Sweet Pea: A Black Girl Growing Up in the Rural South). *Vonnegut has a great number of stories about their life together in* Fates Worse Than Death, *and it is there he reveals his nickname for her—Xanthippe. He also includes an homage written in honor of her 50th birthday.* (*FWD* 90:L32-33) The Festschrift ended with this clever sonnet, "To **Jill** Turning Fifty," by one of **Jill's** favorite photographic subjects, the man of letters John Updike:

The comely soul of self-effacement, you
can be admired as the twinkle in
a thousand authors' eyes where you, unseen,
perform behind the camera. How do
you soften up those hardened visages,
pickled in the brine of daily words?—
Eudora, Tennessee, Anaïs, Kurt,
Saul, Gore, Bill, Jim, Joan, Truman, Toni, Liz?

And children, too, grow docile in your lens,
and stare like lilies toward your clicking sun
while how it feels to be a very young
whatever is elicited. Now ends
your fifth decade. Live henceforth, Leica queen,
as Jill all candle lit, the seeress seen.

Kremlin. *The Tralfamadorians used their Universal Will to Become to send messages concerning the status of the replacement part for Salo's spaceship.*

The messages were conveyed in great architectural monuments on Earth that could be monitored by Salo. (*ST* 271:L29) The meaning of the Moscow **Kremlin** when it was first walled was: *"You will be on your way before you know it."*

Kroner, Anthony. *One half of the Kroner and Baer duo, Anthony Kroner is the spiritual supervisor of the ruling technocracy in* Player Piano. *Along with Drs. Baer and Gelhorne, he devises a plan to infiltrate the Ghost Shirt Society, a Luddite group devoted to overthrowing the technocracy which has displaced humanity as the center of societal concern in favor of machines. At the center of the conspiracy is Paul Proteus, whom Kroner hopes to win over as part of a loyalty test in his bid for manager of the Pittsburgh Works. Kroner was very close to Proteus' father, Doctor George Proteus—"the nation's first National Industrial, Commercial, Communications, Foodstuffs, and Resources Director, a position approached in importance only by the presidency of the United States." Accordingly,* "**Kroner** . . . took a breeder's interest in his engineers' bloodlines" (*PP* 30:L33). *Most typically, however, Kroner is thought of in relationship with his alter ego, Dr. Baer.* (*PP* 35:L21) "**Kroner**'s with Baer, Baer's with **Kroner**," said Finnerty. (*PP* 36:L31) One of the older men, **Kroner**, tall, heavy and slow, listened to the youngsters with ponderous affectionateness. The other, Baer, slight and nervous, noisily and unconvincingly extroverted, laughed, nudged, and clapped shoulders, and maintained a continuous commentary on whatever was being said: "Fine, fine, right, sure, sure, wonderful, yes, yes, exactly, fine, good."
(*PP* 37:L15-27) Baer waved and called to them in his high-pitched voice. **Kroner** nodded almost imperceptibly, and stood perfectly still, not looking directly at them, waiting for them to come up so that greetings could be exchanged quietly and with dignity.

Kroner's enormous, hairy hand closed about Paul's, and Paul, in spite of himself, felt docile, and loving, and childlike. It was as though Paul stood in the enervating, emasculating presence of his father again. **Kroner**, his father's closest friend, had always made him feel that way, and seemingly wanted to make him feel that way. Paul had sworn a thousand times to keep his wits about him the next time he met **Kroner**. But it was a matter beyond his control, and at each meeting, as now, the power and resolve were all in the big hands of the older man.
(*PP* 38:L10-29) Baer was a social cretin, apparently unaware that he was anything but suave and brilliant in company. Someone had once mentioned his running commentary on conversations to him, and he hadn't known what they were talking about. Technically, there wasn't a better engineer in the East, including Finnerty. There was little in the Division that hadn't been master-minded by Baer, who here seemed to **Kroner** what a fox terrier seems to a St. Bernard. Paul had thought often of the peculiar combination of **Kroner** and Baer, and wondered if, when they were gone, higher management could possibly duplicate it. Baer embodied the knowledge and technique of industry;

Kroner personified the faith, the near-holiness, the spirit of the complicated venture. **Kroner**, in fact, had a poor record as an engineer and had surprised Paul from time to time with his ignorance or misunderstanding of technical matters; but he had the priceless quality of believing in the system, and of making others believe in it, too, and do as they were told.

The two were inseparable, though their personalities met at almost no point. Together, they made an approximately whole man.

(*PP* 45:L26) He smiled beatifically. **Kroner** was the rock, the fountainhead of faith and pride for all in the Eastern Division.

Paul is set off in stark contrast from Kroner and others who firmly believe in the ruling technocracy: (*PP* 55:L3, 4, 10) **Kroner**, too, kept alive the notion that Paul could be expected to follow in his father's footsteps. This faith of **Kroner**'s had had a lot to do with Paul's getting to be manager of Ilium; and now that faith might get him the managership of Pittsburgh. When Paul thought about his effortless rise in the hierarchy, he sometimes, as now, felt sheepish, like a charlatan. He could handle his assignments all right, but he didn't have what his father had, what **Kroner** had, what Shepherd had, what so many had: the sense of spiritual importance in what they were doing; the ability to be moved emotionally, almost like a lover, by the great omnipresent and omniscient spook, the corporate personality. In short, Paul missed what made his father aggressive and great: the capacity to really give a damn.

Kroner is often seen as the great protector of the technocracy and emblematic of the engineering mind-set. (*PP* 63:L38-39, 64:L1-2) As **Kroner** often said, eternal vigilance was the price of efficiency. And the machines tirelessly riffled through their decks again and again and again in search of foot draggers, free riders, and misfits. (*PP* 71:L25-36) The civic managers were the career administrators who ran the city. They lived on the same side of the river as the managers and engineers of the Ilium Works, but the contact between the two groups was little more than perfunctory and, traditionally, suspicious. The schism, like so many things, dated back to the war, when the economy had, for efficiency's sake, become monolithic. The question had arisen: who was to run it, the bureaucrats, the heads of business and industry, or the military? Business and bureaucracy had stuck together long enough to overwhelm the military and had since then worked side by side, abusively and suspiciously, but, like **Kroner** and Baer, each unable to do a whole job without the other.

Kroner also presents a distinct contrast from his engineering siblings, possessing an appreciation for "old world" craftsmanship and lifestyle not unlike Paul's, though Kroner's is based on luxurious creature comforts while Paul's is rooted in old-fashioned human labor (seen most graphically when Paul tries to convince Anita to leave Homestead and retire with him to life on a working farm). (*PP* 107:L1-9, 17-22) THE **KRONER** HOME, just outside Albany, was a Victorian mansion, perfectly restored and maintained down to the filigree along the eaves, and the iron spikes along the roof peak. The archprophet of efficiency, **Kroner**, preferred it to the gracile, wipe-clean-with-a-damp-cloth steel and glass machines almost all of the engineers and managers lived in. Though **Kroner** had never accounted for his having bought the place—beyond saying that he liked lots of room—it was so in keeping with him that no one gave the anachronism more than passing thought. . . .

The mansion was one more affirmation of **Kroner**'s belief that nothing of value changed; that what was once true is always true; that truths were few and simple; and that a man needed no knowledge beyond these truths to deal wisely and justly with any problem whatsoever.

Kroner also relied on the images of power from the old era as props for his power. (*PP* 108:L28-39, 109:L1-4) The fact was, **Kroner** never fired his guns. His pleasure seemed to be in owning and handling them. He also used them for props, to give an air of informality to his man-to-man talks. He announced raises and promotions, demotions and firings, and praised or warned, always in seemingly casual asides made while swabbing a bore.

Paul followed him into the dark-paneled study, and waited for him to choose his weapon from the gunrack that filled one wall. **Kroner** ran his index finger along the collection, like a stick along a picket fence. It had been a matter of speculation among **Kroner**'s underlings as to whether there was any significance in the guns he chose for a particular discussion. For a while the rumor was current that shotguns were bad news, rifles were good news. But it hadn't withstood the test of time. **Kroner** finally chose a ten-gauge shotgun, broke open the breach, and squinted through the bore at a streetlight outside.

Though generally appreciated as the spiritual head of the engineers, Kroner is often awkward in his sentimental expression. (*PP* 172:L6-11, 17-26, 29-39, 173:L1-11) **Kroner** detached himself from the crowd and walked soberly to the thick tree trunk. He turned and looked down at his hands thoughtfully. His first words were so soft, so choked with emotion, that few heard them. He inhaled deeply, threw back his shoulders, raised his eyes, and gathered strength to say them again. . . .

"It is our custom," said **Kroner**; "it is the custom here at the Meadows—our custom, our Meadows—to meet here under our tree, our symbol of strong roots, trunk, and branches, our symbol of courage, integrity, perseverance, beauty. It is our custom to meet here to remember our departed friends and co-workers."

And now he forgot the crowd, and talked to the fat cumulus clouds scudding over the blue sky. "Since last we met, Doctor Ernest S. Bassett has left our world for his reward in a better one. Ernie, as you all know, was....

"Ernie was manager of the Philadelphia Works for five years, of the Pittsburgh Works for seven. He was my friend; he was our friend: a great American, a great engineer, a great manager, a great pioneer at the head of the procession of civilization, opening new, undreamed-of doors to better things, for better living, for more people, at less cost."

Now and then brokenly, **Kroner** told of Ernie Bassett as a young engineer, and he traced his career from works to works.

"He gave himself unstintingly engineeringwise, managershipwise, personalitywise, Americanwise, and—" **Kroner** paused to look impressively from face to face. Again he talked to the clouds—"heartwise."

A man stepped from the crowd to hand **Kroner** a long white box. **Kroner** opened it slowly and studied it thoughtfully before showing its contents to anyone else. At last he reached in and unfurled a blue and white pennant, the Armed Forces "E" that Bassett had won during the war as manager of the Philadelphia Works.

A muted bugle played taps.

Kroner knelt at the foot of the tree and placed Ernie Bassett's pennant there.

Kroner, Janice. *Mrs. Anthony Kroner who* was a fat repository of truisms, adages, and homilies, and was usually addressed by the young engineers and managers as "Mom" (*PP* 107:L32-35).

Kropotnik, Commissar. *The Soviet leader who fears the power of the Barnhouse Effect and begins a new arms race.*

L

Lady's Slipper. *In* Cat's Cradle, *there are two boats called the* Lady's Slipper. *Both boats were owned by Bokonon. The first took him from his home in Tobago to England, where he studied at the London School of Economics and Political Science. On his return to the island, he was picked up by the Nazi* submarine U-99, *which sunk his vessel. The British naval ship* Raven *captured the sub, freed Bokonon, and sank the* U-99. *Upon Bokonon's return to Tobago, he built the* Lady's Slipper II. *Eventually, he and Corporal Earl McCabe wreck the schooner on the rocks of San Lorenzo in the middle of a storm. The lifeboat from the boat becomes the bed of "Papa" Monzano. "Papa" swallows ice-nine while in the bed, and when the walls of the castle crumble into the sea, the boat and "Papa" go crashing into the sea, turning the world's water into ice-nine.*

Lafayette Escadrille. *One of Vonnegut's early literary editors was Kenneth Littauer, who had been a member of the Lafayette Escadrille. In* Deadeye Dick, *doomed stunt flyer Will Fairchild was also a member of the World War I outfit.*

Lake Maxincuckee (also **Lake Maxinkuckee**). *The Vonnegut family summer home was on this lake in northern Indiana and its significance is fully described in* Fates Worse Than Death. (*FWD* 49:L2-18, 50:L1-35, 51:L1-15, 29-34) "No matter where I am, and even if I have no clear idea where I am, and no matter how much trouble I may be in, I can achieve a blank and shining serenity if only I can reach the very edge of a natural body of water. The very edge of anything from a rivulet to an ocean says to me: 'Now you know where you are. Now you know which way to go. You will soon be home now.'

"That is because I made my first mental maps of the world, in the summertime when I was a little child, on the shores of **Lake Maxincuckee**, which is in northern Indiana, halfway between Chicago and Indianapolis, where we lived in the wintertime. **Maxincuckee** is three miles long and two and a half miles across at its widest. Its shores are a closed loop. No matter where I was on its circumference, all I had to do was keep walking in one direction to find my way home again. What a confident Marco Polo I could be when setting out for a day's adventure!

"Yes, and I ask the reader of this piece, my indispensable collaborator: Isn't your deepest understanding of time and space and, for that matter, destiny shaped like mine by your earliest experiences with geography, by the rules you learned about how to get home again? What is it that can make you feel, no matter how mistakenly, that you are on the right track, that you will soon be safe and sound at home again?

"The closed loop of the lakeshore was certain to bring me home not only to my own family's unheated frame cottage on a bluff overlooking the lake, but to four adjacent cottages teeming with close relatives. The heads of those neighboring households, moreover, my father's generation, had also spent their childhood summertimes at **Maxincuckee**, making them the almost immediate successors there to the Potawatomi Indians. They even had a tribal name for themselves, which sounded like 'Epta-mayan-hoys.' Sometimes my father, when a grown man, would call out to **Maxincuckee** in general, 'Epta-mayan-hoy?' And a first cousin fishing from a leaky rowboat or a sister reading in a hammock, or whatever, would give this reply: 'Ya! Epta-mayan-hoy!' What did it mean? It was pure nonsense from their childhoods. If was German, if not transliterated as I have done, meaning this: 'Do abbots mow hay? Yes! Abbots mow hay!'

"So what? So not very much, I guess, except that it allows me to say that after the Potawatomis came the Epta-mayan-hoys, who have vanished from **Lake Maxincuckee** without a trace. It is as though they had never been there.

"Am I sad? Not at all. Because everything about that lake was imprinted on my mind when it held so little and was so eager for information, it will be my lake as long as I live. I have no wish to visit it, for I have it all right here. I happened to see it last spring from about six miles up, on a flight from Louisville to Chicago. It was as emotionally uninvolving as a bit of dry dust viewed under a microscope. Again: That wasn't the real **Maxincuckee** down there. The real one is in my head.

"The one in my head is the one I swam across, all two and one-half miles of it, when I was eleven years old, with my sister, five years older than me, and my brother, nine years older than me, in a leaky rowboat near me, urging me on. My sister died thirty years ago. My brother, an atmospheric scientist, is still going strong, daydreaming about clouds and electricity. Times change, but my lake never will.

"If I were ever to write a novel or a play about **Maxincuckee**, it would be Chekhovian, since what I saw were the consequences of several siblings' inheriting and trying to share a single beloved property, and with their own children, once grown, moving to other parts of the world, never to return, and on and on. Our cottage, owned jointly and often acrimoniously by my father and his brother and his sister, was sold to a stranger at the end of World War II. The buyer put off taking possession for a week in order that I, just married after being discharged from the Army, might take my bride there for a honeymoon. . . .

"We went out in an old, leaky rowboat, which all my life I had called 'The Beralikur,' a mixture of my first name with those of my siblings, Bernard and Alice. But that name was not painted on the boat, which would have been redundant. Everybody who was anybody at **Maxincuckee** already knew that the name of that leaky boat was the Beralikur."

Vonnegut used the setting in Slapstick. *The King of Michigan took over what was once the Culver Military Academy and established it as his palace. It is there the powerless President Wilbur Swain meets with the King. Though Swain noticed a number of killed and wounded soldiers on his helicopter flight over the sight of the Battle of Lake Maxinkuckee, families were reuniting and being kind to each other rather than fighting. He is told that since there were no more nations, the various extended families found it easier to be merciful towards each other.*

lambos. *In Kilgore Trout's* The Barring-gaffner of Bagnialto, *winners of the yearly art lottery are paid in lambos.* (*BC* 129:L11) The painting by Gooz had an unprecedented gush of luck on the wheel. It became worth eighteen thousand ***lambos***, the equivalent of one billion dollars on Earth. The Barring-gaffner awarded Gooz a check for that amount, most of which was taken back at once by the tax collector.

lamprey. *An eel with a jawless sucking mouth. In the short story "The Big Space Fuck," some of them have grown as large as the space ship* Arthur C. Clarke, *and have slithered out of the noxious slime polluting the Great Lakes. One of them eats Dwayne and Grace Hoobler as well as the sheriff.*

Lancer. *As part of Vonnegut's musings about the natures of our lives and the reasons we live as we do, he describes the life of Lancer the Greyhound and compares him with the troubled ex-convict Wayne Hoobler. Lancer lived* in a one-room apartment fourteen feet wide and twenty-six feet long, and six flights of stairs above street level. His entire life was devoted to unloading his excrement at the proper time and place. There were two proper places to put it: in the gutter outside the door seventy-two steps below, with the traffic whizzing by, or in a roasting pan his mistress kept in front of the Westinghouse refrigerator.

Lancer had a very small brain, but he must have suspected from time to time, just as Wayne Hoobler did, that some kind of terrible mistake had been made (*BC* 197:L8-18).

Landry, Cynthia. *The former childhood sweetheart of John F. Kennedy becomes the bride of Lance Rumfoord. The newlyweds are seen honeymooning* *on the yacht* Scheherezade *by Billy and Valencia Pilgrim, in* Slaughterhouse-Five.

Lapp, Marlin T. *In* Sirens of Titan, *long after Winston Niles Rumfoord was caught in the chrono-synclastic infundibulum and Beatrice was taken to Mars, the mortgage holders of his Newport estate leased it to Marlin T. Lapp, a showman who sold tickets to Rumfoord's and Kazak's materializations.*

Larkin, Emil. *President Nixon's "most vindictive advisor and dreaded hatchet man" is convicted of obstruction of justice in the Watergate case and serves his sentence in the Adult Correctional Facility at the Finletter Air Force Base.* (*JB* 34:L10) This was a big man, goggle-eyed and liver-lipped, who had been a middle linebacker for Michigan State at one time. He was a disbarred lawyer now, and he prayed all day long to what he believed to be Jesus Christ. **Larkin** had not been sent out on a work detail or assigned any housekeeping task, incidentally, because of what all his praying on hard prison floors had done to him. He was crippled in both legs with housemaid's knee. *So complete and sincere was his born again status that when RAMJAC's Heartland House Publishing Company prints Larkin's autobiography* Brother, Won't You Pray with Me?, *he donated all his royalties to the Salvation Army.*

"Last Full Measure" (see **Howard W. Campbell**).

Laurel and Hardy. Slapstick *is dedicated to the comedy team whom Vonnegut calls* two angels of my time. *Vonnegut goes on to write,* I have called it "Slapstick" because it is grotesque, situational poetry—like the slapstick film comedies, especially those of **Laurel and Hardy**, of long ago.

It is about what life *feels* like to me.

There are all these tests of my limited agility and intelligence. They go on and on.

The fundamental joke with **Laurel and Hardy**, it seems to me, was that they did their best with every test.

They never failed to bargain in good faith with their destinies, and were screamingly adorable and funny on that account.

There was very little love in their films. There was often the situational poetry of marriage, which was something else again. It was yet another test—with comical possibilities, provided that everybody submitted to it in good faith.

Love was never at issue. And, perhaps because I was so perpetually intoxicated and instructed by **Laurel and Hardy** during my childhood in the Great Depression, I find it natural to discuss life without ever mentioning love.

It does not seem important to me.

What does seem important? Bargaining in good faith with destiny (*Slap* 1:L2-14, 2:L1-13).

Bluebeard's Rabo Karabekian includes Laurel and Hardy as Estonians in German uniforms in his masterpiece "Now It's the Women's Turn."

Eugene Debs Hartke imagines his appearance with his father at the Ohio Science Fair as something resembling the comic duo. (*HP* 42:L3) Even as Father and I were setting up our exhibit, we were spotted by other contestants as a couple of comedians, as **Laurel and Hardy**, maybe, with Father as the fat and officious one and me as the dumb and skinny one. The thing was, Father was doing all the setting up, and I was standing around looking bored. All I wanted to do was go outside and hide behind a tree or something and smoke a cigarette. We were violating the most basic rule of the Fair, which was that the young exhibitors were supposed to do all the work, from start to finish. Parents or teachers or whatever were forbidden in writing to help at all.

Lawes, Cleveland and Eucharist ("Ukey"). *Cleveland Lawes is the black chauffeur who escorts Virgil Greathouse to the federal prison at Finletter Air Force Base. Before returning to Atlanta, Lawes becomes interested in Walter Starbuck, who is passing time at a bus stop by going through his handclapping of the "Sally" rhyme. Lawes had little formal education but is self-educated, reading an average of five books a week in his limousine while waiting for his employers. Because of his initial kindness to Starbuck, Lawes later becomes personnel director of the Transico Division of The RAMJAC Corporation, a limousine, taxicab, rental car, parking lot, and garage business.*

As a private in the Korean War, Lawes had been taken prisoner and later befriended by the Chinese major in charge of his prison—a Harvard man. Because of the harsh treatment and cruelties Lawes experienced growing up in the American South, he accepted his captor's invitation to live in China after the war. He eventually wanted to return home because he missed the church music and food he grew up with. The Chinese bargained on his behalf for his return to America with only a minimal amount of punishment.

Eucharist Lawes is Cleveland's wife, more frequently called "Ukey," which means happy gratitude.

Lazarus. (*PS* 189:L4 *Embarrassment*) We woke up in ambulances headed for different hospitals, so to speak, and would never get together again. We were alive, yes, but the marriage was dead.

And it was no **Lazarus**.

(*PS* 326:L8, 328:L18-19, 24-25 *In the Capital of the World*) "'Six days before the Passover, Jesus came to Bethany, where **Lazarus** was, whom Jesus had raised from the dead. There they made him a supper; Martha served, but **Lazarus** was one of those at table with him. . . .

"His male companions for this supper are themselves a mockery. One is Judas, who will betray him. The other is **Lazarus**, who has recently been dead for four days. **Lazarus** was so dead that he stunk, the Bible says. **Lazarus** is surely dazed, and not much of a conversationalist—and not necessarily grateful, either, to be alive again. It is a very mixed blessing to be brought back from the dead.

"If I had read a little farther, we would have learned that there is a crowd outside, crazy to see **Lazarus**, not Jesus. **Lazarus** is the man of the hour as far as the crowd is concerned."

(*Blue* 19:L25) It was a postwar miracle that did me in. I had better explain to my young readers, if any, that the Second World War had many of the promised characteristics of Armageddon, a final war between good and evil, so that nothing would do but that it be followed by miracles. Instant coffee was one. DDT was another. It was going to kill all the bugs, and almost did. Nuclear energy was going to make electricity so cheap that it might not even be metered. It would also make another war unthinkable. Talk about loaves and fishes! Antibiotics would defeat all diseases. **Lazarus** would never die: How was that for a scheme to make the Son of God obsolete?

(*Blue* 128:L28) "I brought you back to life," she said. "You're my **Lazarus**. All Jesus did for **Lazarus** was bring him back to life. I not only brought you back to life—I got you writing your autobiography."

(*Blue* 300:L4) "Twice now I've been a **Lazarus**," I said. "I died with Terry Kitchen, and Edith brought me back to life again. I died with dear Edith, and Circe Berman brought me back to life again." *See also: PS—In the Capital of the World* 328:L29.

Lazzaro, Paul. *In* Slaughterhouse-Five, *the car thief from Cicero, Illinois, who promises to have Billy Pilgrim killed after the war for contributing to the frostbite death of Roland Weary. Lazzaro relishes talking about how easy it is for him to have someone killed. With equal relish he describes the time he poisoned a troublesome dog with a steak laced with the cut up springs from a clock. Lazzaro manages to steal jewelry from the dead when mining corpses in the burned out cellars of Dresden. He eventually kills Billy Pilgrim on the evening of February 13, 1976, thirty-one years to the day after the firebombing of Dresden.*

Le Fèvre, Andre. *The photo assistant to Louis J. M. Daguerre whom Vonnegut cites as selling one of the earliest pornographic photographs*—a woman attempting sexual intercourse with a Shetland Pony (*SL5* 35:L3-4). *Vonnegut notes that in 1841, Le Fèvre was sentenced to six months in prison for the sale and that he died in prison. In* God Bless You, Mr. Rosewater, *Lila Buntline sells copies of that image to friends in Newport, Rhode Island. In* Slaughterhouse-Five, *Roland Weary has a copy of the photograph in his coat when captured at the Battle of the Bulge.*

leaks. Kilgore Trout's term for mirrors. The term also provides an illustration of the respectability Trout received after his death. (*BC* 19:L16-32) It amused him to pretend that mirrors were holes between two universes.

If he saw a child near a mirror, he might wag his finger at a child warningly, and say with great solemnity, "Don't get too near that **leak**. You wouldn't want to wind up in the other universe, would you?"

Sometimes somebody would say in his presence, "Excuse me, I have to take a **leak**." This was a way of saying that the speaker intended to drain liquid wastes from his body through a valve in his lower abdomen.

And Trout would reply waggishly, "Where I come from, that means you're about to steal a mirror."

And so on.

By the time of Trout's death, of course, everybody called mirrors ***leaks***. That was how respectable even his jokes had become. *See also: BC* 90:L2,4-5; 193:L2,21; 194:L15; 202:L2; 229:L5-7; 236:L11.

Leech, Leonard. *Norman Mushari's old law professor who taught him how to focus on succeeding, advice which Mushari lived by.* (*GBR* 17:L18-31, 18:L1-7) He recalled what his favorite professor, **Leonard Leech**, once told him about getting ahead in law. **Leech** said that, just as a good airplane pilot should always be looking for places to land, so should a lawyer be looking for situations where large amounts of money were about to change hands.

"In every big transaction," said **Leech**, "there is a magic moment during which a man has surrendered a treasure, and during which the man who is due to receive it has not yet done so. An alert lawyer will make that moment his own, possessing the treasure for a magic microsecond, taking a little of it, passing it on. If the man who is to receive the treasure is unused to wealth, has an inferiority complex and shapeless feelings of guilt, as most people do, the lawyer can often take as much as half the bundle, and still receive the recipient's blubbering thanks."

Leen, Arpad. *Walter Starbuck recalls* the very public and communicative president and chairman of the board of directors of The RAMJAC Corporation. He would become my boss of bosses, and Cleveland Lawes's boss of bosses, too, when we both became corporate officers of RAMJAC. I say now that **Arpad Leen** is the most able and informed and brilliant and responsive executive under whom it has ever been my privilege to serve. He is a genius at acquiring companies and keeping them from dying afterward.

He used to say, "If you can't get along with me, you can't get along with anybody."

It was true, it was true. (*JB* 87:L20)

Leghorn, Fred ". . . shrewd hayseed king of the mechanized chicken industry" (*PS* 262:L25-26 *Jekyll and Hyde Revisited*). *Jerry Rivers' fifth stepfather (soon to be divorced from his mother), Leghorn asks Dr. Henry Jekyll to analyze a secret growth potion from one of his competitors. Jekyll concocts his own fowl growth potion, tests it on himself, turns into a human-sized homicidal chicken, and is shot to death by Leghorn.*

LeGrand, Pierre. *One of Eugene Debs Hartke's more emotionally troubled students, LeGrand used his wealth to purchase expensive gifts as a way of winning friends. Debs recalls that his Mercedes* was a gift from the mother of a student of mine named **Pierre LeGrand**. His maternal grandfather had been dictator of Haiti, and had taken the treasury of that country with him when he was overthrown. That was why **Pierre**'s mother was so rich. He was very unpopular. He tried to win friends by making expensive gifts to them, but that didn't work, so he tried to hang himself from a girder of the water tower on top of Musket Mountain. I happened to be up there, in the bushes with the wife of the coach of the Tennis Team.

So I cut him down with my Swiss Army knife. That was how I got the Mercedes.

Pierre would have better luck 2 years later, jumping off the Golden Gate Bridge, and a campus joke was that now I had to give the Mercedes back (*HP* 83:L11-25).

Leidveld and Moore. *In* Bluebeard, *the New York advertising agency hired by Marc Coulomb on behalf of Coulomb Frères et Cie of France, on the stipulation that they hire Rabo Karabekian.*

Lembrig, Dr. Thor. *Lembrig's one appearance indicates that, late in life, Kilgore Trout and his science fiction stories would achieve an impressive measure of exposure.* (*BC* 186:L4-5) As an old, old man, Trout would be asked by **Dr. Thor Lembrig**, the Secretary-General of the United Nations, if he feared the future. He would give this reply:

"Mr. Secretary-General, it is the *past* which scares the bejesus out of me."

Lenin Observatory (see **Jefferson Observatory**).

Leonard, Dawn. *According to Diana Moon Glampers—and not disputed by Eliot Rosewater—Dawn Leonard's ten-year-old case of boils was cured by Eliot; further proof that Eliot was the savior of Rosewater County.*

Leonard, Paul. *The eight-year-old boy in the short story "Next Door" who is frightened and appalled by the sounds heard through his apartment wall of Mr. Harger and his mistress carrying on while Mrs. Harger was away. Paul eventually calls "All-Night Sam," a radio disc jockey taking record dedications, and dedicates a song from Mr. Harger to his wife. When the lovers hear the dedication, they have a loud and final parting of the ways.*

LeSabre, Harry and Grace. *In* Breakfast of Champions, *Harry is the sales manager at Dwayne Hoover's Pontiac dealership. Harry's twenty-year experience with Dwayne allows him to see that Dwayne was starting to lose his mind.*

Harry is a heterosexual transvestite. He never told Dwayne this secret, and Dwayne would never have suspected it since Harry always wore business suits in black or gray with white shirts. However, when Dwayne warned Harry to dress in a festive mood for the upcoming Hawaiian Week promotion at the car dealership, Harry suspected Dwayne knew his secret. He spent an entire Veterans' Day weekend worrying he would be publicly exposed. Only Grace, Harry's cigar-smoking wife, knew his secret and supported him for sharing an active and mutually pleasing sex life.

Harry had invested in Xerox stock years earlier (at $8.00 per share), and Grace suggested that they cash in the stock and leave Midland City for Maui, Hawaii. She deeply felt the discomfort and pain brought to Harry by the declining Dwayne. The text suggests they went to Hawaii.

Letzinger, Coach. *In the unfinished novel at the back of Eliot Rosewater's* Domesday Book, *reincarnation is very much its thematic center. It is not clear if Eliot creates Coach Letzinger or he is chronicling the exploits of a local townsman.* (*GBR* 96:L5-17) Coeur de Lion has found himself once again taken captive during his travels, imprisoned this time in the flesh of **Coach Letzinger**, a pitiful exhibitionist and freelance garbage man in Rosewater, Indiana. **Coach**, with poor old King Richard inside, goes to Indianapolis on the Greyhound bus three or four times a year, dresses up for the trip in shoes, socks, garters, a raincoat, and a chromium-plated whistle hung around his neck. When he gets to Indianapolis, **Coach** goes to the silverware department of one of the big stores, where there are always a lot of brides-to-be picking out silver patterns. **Coach** blows his whistle, all the girls look, **Coach** throws open his raincoat, closes it again, and runs like hell to catch the bus back to Rosewater.

"The Lie" (1962) (see **Tom Hilyer** or **Dr. Remenzel**).

Lieber, Albert. *Edith Vonnegut's father, Kurt's maternal grandfather.* (*PS* 36:L7-13 *Roots*) WE have come now to a rascal, whose emotional faithlessness to his children, in my humble opinion, contributed substantially to my mother's eventual suicide. As I have said, he was the son of the limping Civil War Veteran. When his father retired to Dusseldorf, Albert remained in Indianapolis to run the brewery that his father had sold to a British syndicate. He was born in 1863.

Lieber, Andy. *Kilgore Trout hitched a ride toward the Midland City Arts Festival and was picked up by Andy Lieber in his Ford Galaxie. Lieber becomes a point of departure for Vonnegut to recount the plot of Trout's novel* How You Doin'? *which "was about national averages for this and that."* (*BC* 167:L33-169:L11) Kilgore Trout, hitchhiking westward, ever westward had meanwhile become a passenger in a Ford *Galaxie*. The man at the controls of the *Galaxie* was a traveling salesman for a device which engulfed the rear ends of trucks at loading docks. It was a telescoping tunnel of rubberized canvas.

. . . The idea of the gadget was to allow people in a building to load or unload trucks without losing cold air in the summertime or hot air in the wintertime to the out-of-doors. *(He also sold wire, cable, rope, and Excelsior fire extinguishers.)* . . . He was his own boss, in that he represented products whose manufacturers couldn't afford salesmen of their own.

"I make my own hours, and I pick the products I sell. The products don't sell me," he said. His name was **Andy Lieber**. He was thirty-two. He was white. He was a good deal overweight like so many people in the country. He was obviously a happy man. He drove like a maniac. The *Galaxie* was going ninety-two miles an hour now. "I'm one of the few remaining free men in America," he said.

He had a penis one inch in wide and seven and a half inches long. During the past year, he had averaged twenty-two orgasms per month. This was far above the national average. His income and the value of his life insurance policies at maturity were also far above average.

Lind, Jenny. *"The Swedish Nightingale" who sang at the Opera House in Midland City in 1881. She is immortalized by an historical marker in front of the building which was across from Fairchild Park, the seediest part of town in* Breakfast of Champions.

Lingamon, Cynthia Anne. *Cynthia Anne is murdered by her father Ned Lingamon because she wouldn't stop crying. She wasn't more than an infant. Her brief mention is made by Vonnegut as he extemporizes an incident on the phone in the lounge of the Midland City Holiday Inn. The passage parallels the concept of narrative control and interaction between the author and his fictional creations as seen in Kilgore Trout's novel* Now It Can Be Told. (*BC* 204:L3) He had now also committed the lowest crime which an American could commit, which was to kill his own child. Her name was **Cynthia Anne**, and she certainly didn't live very long before she was made dead again. She got killed for crying and crying. She wouldn't shut up.

First she drove her seventeen-year-old mother away with all her demands, and then her father killed her.

And so on.

Lingamon, Ned. *In* Breakfast of Champions, *Midland City's most decorated Vietnam veteran (he had won the Congressional Medal of Honor) calls Harold Newcomb Wilbur, the bartender at the Holiday Inn, from jail after being charged with killing his daughter, Cynthia Anne.*

Lingo-Three (see also ***Plague on Wheels***). (*BC* 26:L26) The words in the book, incidentally, were about life on a dying planet named **Lingo-Three**, whose inhabitants resembled American automobiles.

(*BC* 27:L1) **Lingo-Three** was visited by space travelers, who learned that the creatures were becoming extinct for this reason: they had destroyed their planet's resources, including its atmosphere.

Littauer, Kenneth. *Vonnegut dedicates* Cat's Cradle *to Littauer,* a man of gallantry and taste, *and whom he credits as his literary mentor in* Palm Sunday. *Vonnegut recalls that Littauer, when only twenty-three, was a colonel in the Lafayette Escadrille* and the first pilot to strafe a trench (*PS* 113:L25). *Littauer was a literary agent introduced to Vonnegut by Knox Burger.*

Little, Dr. Elbert. *In the play entitled "Fortitude," reprinted in* Wampeters, Foma & Granfalloons, *Dr. Little is a general practitioner from Vermont recently named Family Doctor of the Year by the* Ladies' Home Journal *who comes to visit Sylvia, Dr. Frankenstein's experiment in life-extension techniques. Sylvia's head is connected to a roomful of wires and computers. She had written to Dr. Little after reading the magazine article about him and asked him to visit and bring cyanide. He shows up without the cyanide and is initially repulsed by all he sees. When Sylvia shoots Dr. Frankenstein with her mechanical arm, Little becomes an important member of the transplant team which detaches Frankenstein's head and reattaches it to a companion set of machines so he and Sylvia can live in perpetuity side by side.*

Little, Sherman Wesley. *In* God Bless You, Mr. Rosewater, *Sherman Little appears as an entry in Eliot's* Domesday Book, *his ledger for recording the Indiana transactions of the Rosewater Foundation.* (*GBR* 93:L14) "**Sherman Wesley Little**," wrote Eliot. "*Indy, Su-TDM-LO-V2-W3K3-K2CP-RF $300.*" Decoded, this meant that Little was from Indianapolis, was a suicidal tool-and-die maker who had been laid off, a veteran of the Second World War with a wife and three children, the second child suffering from cerebral palsy. Eliot had awarded him a Rosewater Fellowship of $300.

Little Bighorn. *The site of the American Indian victory over General Custer. Reverend Lasher compares the limited and short-lived victory of the modern-day Ghost Shirt Society over the ruling technocracy to that one Indian triumph, however hollow it would inevitably prove to be.* (*PP* 291:L31) "This is like the Indians' massacre of Custer and his men," said Lasher reflectively. "The Little Bighorn. One isolated victory against an irresistible tide. More and more whites where Custer came from; more and more machines where these came from. But we may win yet."

In Hocus Pocus, *Eugene Debs Hartke compares the swift dispatch of his fraudulent crystal exhibition with Custer's defeat. He further compares it with other such swift and just rebukes.* (*HP* 44:L9) Other people made short work of Father's and my invincible contest entry in Cleveland 43 years ago.

Generals George Armstrong Custer at the **Little Bighorn**, and Robert E. Lee at Gettysburg, and William Westmoreland in Vietnam all come to mind.

Lonesome No More (see ***Slapstick*** and **Sargent Shriver**). *The phrase was Vonnegut's campaign slogan suggestion to Sargent Shriver during his 1972 vice-presidential campaign, and later became the subtitle of* Slapstick, *capturing the philosophy behind Wilbur Swain's plan for artificially extended families.*

"Long Walk to Forever" (1960) (see **Newt** and **Catharine**).

Love Crusade. *The Christian Fundamentalist revival tour headed by the Reverend Bobby Denton. His preachments center on the chrono-synclastic infundibula and the analogy that this was another manifestation of the Tower of Babel. Those who attended the Wheeling, West Virginia, meeting were known as Love Crusaders.*

Lovejoy, Sylvia. *The one-hundred-year-old bodiless patient of Dr. Norbert Frankenstein in the play "Fortitude." When Lovejoy was sixty-four and Frankenstein was twenty-nine, he performed his first life-saving surgery on her. Since then she endured seventy-eight operations, which left her with only her head. She is attached to a series of tubes and computers controlled by Frankenstein's around-the-clock medical team. She is naturally despondent with her life, but Frankenstein controls her moods through the application of drugs. At the end of the play, Gloria, Sylvia's compassionate hairdresser, brings her a pistol so she could kill herself with her mechanical arm. However, Frankenstein anticipated she may want to eventually commit suicide, so he designed the arm with a limited range of motion, which effectively prevents her from succeeding. Instead, she turns the gun on her doctor, and they are next seen in side-by-side hospital beds, two heads connected to a labyrinth of tubes and wires.*

Lowell, A. Lawrence. *In* Jailbird, *Walter Starbuck notes that this former President of Harvard University was the chairman of the three-member committee which reviewed the court's death sentences for Sacco and Vanzetti. Despite the telegrams of thousands who took issue with the sentence, the committee felt electrocuting the two would serve justice. The incident serves to further Starbuck's continued jabs at Harvard's image as the embodiment of enlightenment and a training ground for society's elite social architects.*

Lubbock, Luke. *In* Player Piano, *Luke epitomizes the power of sartorial symbolism. He is first seen leading a parade bearing an enormous elephant tusk before changing uniforms and leading the Royal Parmesans in the same parade. Because the bathrooms were filled with bar patrons, Luke was forced to change costumes in the booth where Ed Finnerty, Reverend Lasher, and Paul Proteus were drinking and discussing societal divisions and the likelihood of class confrontation. As Luke begins to change costume,* Paul relaxed his vigil for an instant to glance at **Luke**, and he was shocked at the transformation.

The man was in his underwear now, ragged and drab, and none-too-clean. And **Luke** had somehow shrunk and saddened and was knobbed and scarred and scrawny. He was subdued now, talking not at all, and meeting no one's eyes. Almost desperately, hungrily, he ripped open the brown parcel and took from it a pale-blue uniform, encrusted with gold embroidery and piped in scarlet. He pulled on the trousers and black boots, and the jacket with its ponderous epaulets. **Luke** was growing again, getting his color back, and as he strapped on his saber he was talkative again—important and strong. He bundled up his other costume in the brown paper, left the parcel with the bartender, and rushed into the street, waving naked steel.

A whistle blew, and the Parmesans fell in behind him, to be led to glorious exploits in a dreamworld those on the sidewalk could only speculate about (*PP* 82:L20-36).

At the Meadows executive retreat, Luke appears as a busboy and is later audibly heard as the lone, loudly sobbing individual during the eulogy for the manager of the Pittsburgh Works. Later, Luke appears in Ghost Shirt garb as one of Proteus' interrogators in the Ilium air-raid shelter, then as one of the strategic planners of the Ghost Shirt upheaval. Luke informs the conspirators that their plan to infiltrate the upper echelons in major social organizations across the country was about sixty percent successful.

Lucretia A. Mott. *In* Slaughterhouse-Five, *the freighter named for American suffragette Lucretia Mott transported Billy Pilgrim back home after his liberation from a German prison camp. Vonnegut appropriated the incident from his own experience.* (*FWD* 108:L8) When a Liberty Ship (the *Lucretia C. Mott*, named for a women's rights advocate) had wallowed us back to the United States through severe storms in the North Atlantic, and it was time for me and my buddy to say good-bye for a while (a condition now quite permanent), I said to him, "What did you learn?" The future DA O'Hare replied, "I will never again believe my Government." This had to do with our Government's tall tales of delicate surgery performed by bombers equipped with Sperry and Norden bombsights.

Luma County Clarion. *Rabo Karabekian's first paying job as an artist came when he drew a picture of Benito Mussolini for the editor of this San Ignacio, California, newspaper* (*Blue* 62:L32).

Luma County Savings and Loan Association. *The San Ignacio bank which was nicknamed "El Banco Busto" because it had failed.* (*Blue* 57:L5-13) El Banco Busto, moreover, had held the mortgage on the little building whose first floor was Father's shop and whose second story was our home. Father used to own the building, thanks to a loan from the bank. After the bank failed, though, its receivers liquidated all its assets, foreclosing all the mortgages which were in arrears, which was most of them. Guess why they were in arrears? Practically everybody had been dumb enough to entrust their savings to El Banco Busto.

Lutz, Andre. (*HP* 25:L7) The chief engineer at the *(Mohiga)* wagon company, for example, whose name was **Andre Lutz**, was a native of Liege, Belgium, and had served as an apprentice to a bell founder there. He would teach Chemistry. His French wife would teach French and Watercolor Painting.
(*HP* 26:L15-16, 28) One week before the first class was held, which was in Latin, taught by the Episcopalian priest Alan Clewes, **Andre Lutz** the Belgian arrived at the mansion with 3 wagons carrying a very heavy cargo, a carillon consisting of 32 bells. He had cast them on his own time and at his own expense in the wagon factory's foundry. They were made from mingled Union and Confederate rifle barrels and cannonballs and bayonets gathered up after the Battle of Gettysburg. They were the first bells and surely the last bells ever to be cast in Scipio. . . .

Andre Lutz gave the new college all those bells, even though there was no place to hang them. He said he did it because he was so sure that it would 1 day be a great university with a bell tower and everything. He was dying of emphysema as a result of the fumes from molten metals that he had been breathing since he was 10 years old. He had no time to wait for a place to hang the most wonderful consequence of his having been alive for a little while, which was all those bells, bells, bells.

Lutz Carillon. *The Lutz Carillon were the enormous bells forged by Andre Lutz and donated to the Mohiga Valley Free Institute, later becoming Tarkington College. Among other things, the bell tower is the sight of composition, self-reflection, and spiritual delight for Eugene Debs Hartke.*
(*HP* 18:L13, 26) The greatest stroke of luck for me *(Eugene Debs Hartke)*, the biggest chunk of manna from Heaven, was that Tarkington had need of somebody to play the **Lutz Carillon**, the great family of bells at the top of the tower of the college library, where I am writing now. . . .

The happiest moments in my life, without question, were when I played the **Lutz Carillon** at the start and end of every day.
(*HP* 31:L23) If Henry Moellenkamp hadn't come out of his mother's womb dyslexic, there would never have been a tower in which to hang the **Lutz Carillon**.
(*HP* 62:L17) Judging from letters to *The Musketeer*, I think the change that generated the most passionate resistance was the modernization of the **Lutz Carillon** soon after World War II, a memorial to Ernest Hubble Hiscock. He was a Tarkington graduate who at the age of 21 was a nose-gunner on a Navy bomber whose pilot crashed his plane with a full load of bombs onto the flight deck of a Japanese aircraft carrier in the Battle of Midway during World War II.
(*HP* 63:L19) In the old days 4 of the bells were famously off-key, but beloved, and were known as "Pickle" and "Lemon" and "Big Cracked John" and

"Beelzebub." The Hiscocks had them sent to Belgium, to the same bell foundry where Andre Lutz had been an apprentice so long ago. There they were machined and weighted to perfect pitch, their condition when I got to play them.

(*HP* 66:L19) Most of the letters to *The Musketeer* protesting the modernization of the **Lutz Carillon** are from people who had somehow hung on to the wealth and power they had been born to.

(*HP* 133:L13) In the folder was a report by a private detective hired by Wilder to investigate my sex life. . . . He didn't miss a thing Zuzu and I did during the second semester. . . . There was only 1 misunderstood incident: when I went up into the loft of the stable, where the **Lutz Carillon** had been stored before there was a tower and where Tex Johnson was crucified 2 years ago. I went up with the aunt of a student. She was an architect who wanted to see the pegged post-and-beam joinery up there. The operative assumed we made love up there. We hadn't.

Lynn, Jonathan (see **Alfred Planck**).

M

MacCleary, Lou. *The Executive Manager of National Industrial Security in* Player Piano. *His one scene is in the Council House at the Meadows during which he, Kroner, and Gelhorne reveal to Paul Proteus their plan to use him to infiltrate the Ghost Shirt Society.*

Machu Picchu. *In* Slapstick, *Vonnegut uses Machu Picchu as a nexus joining the rise and fall of an ancient and mysterious culture to the fall of all modern culture. After Eliza and Wilbur Swain experience an orgasm of creativity which yields their treatise about extended families as well as their theories about relative gravity, Eliza moves to a condominium in Machu Picchu. There she is approached by Fu Manchu, a miniaturized Chinese agent sent to the ancient site in search of lost Inca secrets. She agrees to permit him access to the twins' theories stored in the family mausoleum in Vermont, provided he gets her a trip to the Mars colony established by the Chinese. After Fu Manchu secures the Swain secrets, China's experiments destroy the planet's gravity. Wilbur recalls:* And somewhere in there a night of actual bad gravity crumbled the foundations of **Machu Picchu**. The condominiums and boutiques and banks and gold bricks and jewelry and pre-Columbian art collections and the Opera House and the churches, and *all* that, sloped down the Andes, wound up in the sea.

I cried (*Slap* 187:L7). *Wilbur's divorced wife and their son had moved to the same condominium as Eliza before the disaster.*

MacIntosh, Andrew. *This widower in* Galápagos, *whom Vonnegut describes as* an American financier of great inherited wealth (*Gal* 19:L19-20), *generally believed to be patterned after Malcolm Forbes*. (*Gal* 78:L8-21) ***Andrew MacIntosh** didn't even care if he himself lived or died—as evidenced by his enthusiasms for skydiving and the racing of high-performance motor vehicles and so on.

So I have to say that human brains back then had become such copious and irresponsible generators of suggestions as to what might be done with life, that they made acting for the benefit of future generations seem one of many arbitrary games which might be played by narrow enthusiasts—like poker or polo or the bond market, or the writing of science-fiction novels.

More and more people back then, and not just ***Andrew MacIntosh**, had found ensuring the survival of the human race a total bore.

(*Gal* 98:L19-23) ***Andrew MacIntosh** certainly enjoyed his exposure on talk shows. He was a welcome guest on them because he was so outrageous. He held forth about what fun life was if you had unlimited money to spend. He pitied and scorned people who weren't rich, and so on.

(*Gal* 102:L24) It is a joke to me that this man should have presented himself as an ardent conservationist, since so many of the companies he served as a director or in which he was a major stockholder were notorious damagers of the water or the soil or the atmosphere. But it wasn't a joke to ***MacIntosh**, who had come into this world incapable of caring much about anything. So, in order to hide this deficiency, he had become a great actor, pretending even to himself that he cared passionately about all sorts of things.

MacIntosh is the sponsor of a number of guests gathered for "the Nature Cruise of the Century" including Zenji Hiroguchi, creator of Gokubi and Mandarax. Hiroguchi and MacIntosh are shot dead by Delgado, an Ecuadorian soldier foraging for food among stores which had been separated from the general population by barbed wire. They surprise Delgado, who panics and shoots.

His association with Hiroguchi is used by Leon Trout, the narrator of Galápagos, *to write a metaphor applicable to humans in the 20th century as well as one million years later when humanity has returned to the sea.* (*Gal* 52:L10-22) What he *(MacIntosh)* meant to get from *Zenji, probably in Yucatan, or surely during "the Nature Cruise of the Century," was *Zenji's signature on an agreement to head a new corporation, whose stock *MacIntosh would merchandize.

Like James Wait, ***MacIntosh** was a fisherman of sorts. He hoped to catch investors, using for bait not a price tag on his shirt but a Japanese computer genius.

And now it appears to me that the tale I have to tell, spanning a million years, doesn't change all that much from beginning to end. In the beginning, as in the end, I find myself speaking of human beings, regardless of their brain size, as fisherfolk.

MacIntosh's constant and frantic telephoning, together with his graceless pursuit of Hiroguchi's partnership was terribly unsettling for the Japanese inventor. The Hiroguchis' discomfort took final form with Mandarax's diagnosis. (*Gal* 55:L17, 56:L4) The Hiroguchis could no longer conceive of any good news for themselves which could be delivered by ***Andrew MacIntosh**. They honestly believed him to be a madman, which misconception, ironically, had been impressed upon them by *Zenji's own creation, which was Mandarax. . . . Mandarax . . . could diagnose with respectable accuracy one thousand of the most common diseases which attacked *Homo Sapiens*, including twelve varieties of nervous breakdown. . . .

In Yucatán, the Hiroguchis had followed such a daisy chain of questions and answers, describing for Mandarax the behavior of ***Andrew MacIntosh**. Mandarax had at last displayed these words in Japanese on the screen, which was about the size of a playing card: *Pathological personality*.

Leon Trout builds on Mandarax's diagnosis of MacIntosh and offers yet another parallel between the present state of humanity and its landed ancestors. (*Gal* 129:L9) There is another human defect which the Law of Natural Selection has yet to remedy: When people of today have full bellies, they are exactly like their ancestors of a million years ago: very slow to acknowledge any awful troubles they may be in. Then is when they forget to keep a sharp lookout for sharks and whales.

This was a particularly tragic flaw a million years ago, since the people who were best informed about the state of the planet, like ***Andrew MacIntosh**, for example, and rich and powerful enough to slow down all the waste and destruction going on, were by definition well fed.

So everything was always just fine as far as they were concerned.

MacIntosh, Selena. *When we first see Selena in* Galápagos, *the eighteen-year-old congenitally blind daughter of Andrew MacIntosh is preparing to take "the Nature Cruise of the Century." Her mother died while giving birth to Selena. Accompanied by her dog Kazakh, Selena is marooned on Santa Rosalia with Captain Adolf von Kleist, Hisako Hiroguchi, Mary Hepburn, and the six Kankabono girls. Once marooned, Selena and Hisako pair off to raise the latter's furry daughter, Akiko, born on the island. Vonnegut states that Selena and Hisako die in a suicide pact, but the details of the event are not recorded.*

MacIntyre, Carlyle F. *The translator of the 1941 New Directions edition of Goethe's* Faust *cited by Vonnegut in the editor's note to the text* (*MN* xi:L17-19).

Mackay, Charles. *When Vonnegut visited his friend Bernard V. O'Hare to jog his own memory about the bombing of Dresden while writing* Slaughterhouse-Five, *Mary O'Hare was insistent that Vonnegut not glorify the soldiers' personalities since they really were just children. This led him to think of the Crusades in relation to his own war experience. Bernard O'Hare then pulled down a copy of Mackay's 1841 book* Extraordinary Popular Delusions and the Madness of Crowds. (*SL5* 14:L3) **Mackay** had a low opinion of *all* Crusades. The Children's Crusade struck him as only slightly more sordid than the ten Crusades for grown-ups. O'Hare read this handsome passage out loud:

> *History in her solemn page informs us that the crusaders were but ignorant and savage men, that their motives were those of bigotry unmitigated, and that their pathway was one of blood*

> *and tears. Romance, on the other hand, dilates upon their piety and heroism, and portrays, in her most glowing and impassioned hues, their virtue and magnanimity, the imperishable honor they acquired for themselves, and the great services they rendered to Christianity. . . .*
>
> *Now what was the grand result of all these struggles? Europe expended millions of her treasures, and the blood of two million of her people; and a handful of quarrelsome knights retained possession of Palestine for about one hundred years!*

MacKenzie, Joyce. *The governess who taught German batball to Winston Niles Rumfoord as a young child in* The Sirens of Titan. *She was regularly teamed with Rumfoord and Earl Moncrief (the butler), against Watanabe Wataru (the gardener), his daughter Beverly June, and Edward Seward Darlington (the stable boy).*

MacMahon, Bonnie and Ralph. *In* Breakfast of Champions, *Bonnie is the cocktail waitress in the bar of the Holiday Inn who serves Rabo Karabekian a martini with the greeting "Breakfast of Champions." She becomes incensed over Karabekian's flippant remarks about champion swimmer Mary Alice Miller, the Queen of the Arts Festival. Bonnie lashes out at Rabo's $50,000 painting until he explains its significance to her and the patrons at the bar. Rabo mockingly suggests Bonnie offer some story with local color to Beatrice Keedsler, another invited artist to the festival. Vonnegut has Bonnie tell Keedsler about Leroy Joyce, a convicted rapist who avoided electrocution by slicing off his penis while on death row at the Shepherdstown Adult Correctional Institution. Joyce put his penis in a cup and handed it to Ralph Hoover, Bonnie's husband and a guard in the Sexual Offenders' Wing of the institution. Vonnegut says this was a true story which originally happened in Arkansas. Bonnie and Ralph lost most of their assets in a failed car wash in Shepherdstown, and Bonnie was punched by Dwayne Hoover when he went on his violent rampage, though she succeeds in getting Dwayne from further beating his son Bunny.*

Madeiros, Celestino. *As chronicled in* Jailbird, *Madeiros was already in prison when he admitted to the killings for which Sacco and Vanzetti had been convicted. All three were executed on the same evening in Charlestown Prison. As one of Vonnegut's many references to the deaths of innocents, he draws this pointed inversion of the traditional image of Christ's execution.* (*JB* 171:L31, 172:L1-4) As for the last days of Sacco and Vanzetti as a modern Passion: As on Golgotha, three lower-class men were executed at the same time by a state. This time, though, not just one of the three was innocent. This time two of the three were innocent.

the twins' fiftieth birthday, Wilbur receives birthday greetings from his sister and a letter from Fu Manchu informing him of Eliza's death in a Martian avalanche. At that moment, the Chinese experiments with gravity based on the Swains' theories caused tremendous destruction because of the ensuing cataclysmic geological shifts. The consequent failure of stable natural forces eliminates geopolitical confrontations and limits political enmity to neighboring communities.

Mandarax. *The second generation of voice translators invented by twenty-nine-year-old Zenji Hiroguchi in* Galápagos. *The first generation was called Gokubi, which could translate ten languages. Mandarax could identify and translate more than one thousand languages, diagnose more than a thousand diseases and prescribe remedies, recall poetry from a database of classic works appropriate to any topic, recall historical events by date, and was programmable for any course of instruction from surgery to ikebana, the Japanese art of flower arranging.*

Hiroguchi planned to give a copy of Mandarax to Jackie Onassis during "the Nature Cruise of the Century," and in preparing this gift, he programmed it with his wife's lectures about ikebana. This enraged his wife, who lectured him in a manner reminiscent of other moments in Vonnegut's work which pit man's increasing technological abilities against human work. (*Gal* 70:L21) "You, *Doctor Hiroguchi," she went on, "think that everybody but yourself is just taking up space on this planet, and we make too much noise and waste valuable natural resources and have too many children and leave garbage around. So it would be a much nicer place if the few stupid services we are able to perform for the likes of you were taken over by machinery. That wonderful **Mandarax** you're scratching your ear with now: what is that but an excuse for a mean-spirited egomaniac never to pay or even thank any human being with a knowledge of languages or mathematics or history or medicine or literature or ikebana or anything?"

Contrary to Hisako Hiroguchi's tirade, Leon Trout (the text's narrator) describes the appearance of Mandarax in organic terms rather than differentiating between humans and machinery. (*Gal* 59:L7-22) When Akiko became an adult on Santa Rosalia, she would be very much like her mother on the inside, but in a different sort of skin. The evolutionary sequence from Gokubi to **Mandarax**, by contrast, was a radical improvement in the contents of a package, but with few perceptible changes in the wrapper. Akiko was protected from sunburn, and from the chilly water when she swam, and the abrasiveness of lava when she chose to sit or lie down—whereas her mother's bare skin was wholly defenseless against these ordinary hazards of island life. But Gokubi and **Mandarax**, as different as they were inside, inhabited nearly identical shells of high-impact black plastic, twelve centimeters high, eight wide, and two thick.

Any fool could tell Akiko from Hisako, but only an expert could tell Gokubi from **Mandarax**.

"The Manned Missiles" (1958) (see also **Ashland** and **Ivankov**). *This Cold War short story is told through an exchange of letters between the fathers of Major Stepan Ivankov and Captain Bryant Ashland. The American astronaut was sent into orbit to observe the Soviet cosmonaut's mission when he lost control of his capsule and crashed into the other. Both vehicles are disabled in space and neither can return home. The fathers' letters express the emotions of men without political considerations. They are loving fathers seeking to comfort the other for their common loss.*

Maori. *A member of the aboriginal people of New Zealand appears twice in Vonnegut's work. In* Slaughterhouse-Five, *a Maori soldier of unknown rank and captured at Tobruk worked side by side with Billy Pilgrim the morning after the firebombing of Dresden, digging bodies and valuables out of the rubble. After the bodies started to rot, the Maori succumbed to the stink that* "was like roses and mustard gas" (*SL5* 185:L26-27), *developing the dry heaves and eventually dying.*

In Bluebeard, *a Maori corporal from the New Zealand Field Artillery, also captured at Tobruk, is painted into Rabo Karabekian's sixty-four-foot tryptic "Now It's the Women's Turn." He is sitting on a German ammunition box with three bullets left inside, reading an anti-Semitic weekly from Latvia.* (*Blue* 296:L2) It is six months old, and offers tips on gardening and home canning. The **Maori** is studying it very earnestly, in the hopes of leaning what we would all like to know about ourselves: where he is, what is going on, and what is likely to happen next.

Mare Imbrium (see **Jefferson Observatory**).

Margo. *The home planet of Zog, the flying saucer traveler who lands in Connecticut and is beaten to death with a golf club when he tries to warn a family about a fire in their house. Tragically, Zog communicates by farting and tap dancing. All this takes place in Kilgore Trout's short story "A Dancing Fool," published in 1962 in* Black Garterbelt *magazine. Trout learns of its publication after buying a back issue of the porn magazine in* Breakfast of Champions.

Maritimo, Dr. Alan. (*DD* 227:L1-2) **Dr. Alan Maritimo**, the veterinarian, and his wife. **Alan** was a maverick in the Maritimo family, who had declined to go into the building business. His entire household was killed by the flash. *The flash, of course, refers to the neutron bombing of Midland City, Ohio.*

Maritimo, Dr. Alfred. (*BC* 64:L17-18) Dwayne owned a third of the inn *(Holiday Inn)* partnership with Midland City's leading orthodontist, **Dr. Alfred Maritimo**, and Bill Miller, who was Chairman of the Parole Board at the Adult Correctional Institution at Shepherdstown, among other things.

Maritimo, Carlo. *One of the many relatives who works for the Midland City-based Maritimo Brothers Construction Company. In* Breakfast of Champions, *Carlo listens to Rabo Karabekian's explanation of his painting while in the Tally-ho Room of the Holiday Inn.*

Maritimo, Gino and Marco. *The founders and operators of Maritimo Brothers Construction Company appearing in both* Breakfast of Champions *and* Deadeye Dick. *Though Marco isn't mentioned by name in* Breakfast of Champions, *Gino is noted as Midland City's premier dope dealer. It was the Maritimo brothers' guard dog, a Doberman named Kazak, who frightens Vonnegut near the end of that text when he prepares to meet an unsuspecting Kilgore Trout.*

The history of the Maritimo brothers in Midland City is recounted in Deadeye Dick. *When Gino was eighteen and Marco was twenty, they were working as stokers aboard an Italian freighter. While the ship was loading cargo in Newport News, Virginia, they fled to avoid conscription which awaited them upon their return to Italy and because they thought they could make a better life for themselves in the United States. Assisted by members of the Newport News Italian-American community, the two stole a ride on an empty railway boxcar. After being robbed at knifepoint by four hoboes, the two left the train when found out by railway detectives in Midland City. From a distance they saw the conical slate roof of Otto Waltz's home and decided to head there. They came upon Otto, dressed in one of his ornate costumes picked up on his European excursion, and offered to work for food. Otto spoke to them in Italian and offered them all the food they needed. Otto clothed them, provided shelter in the cupola gun room, and put them to work around the house. They were forever grateful to Otto and all his family.*

The Maritimos became the most successful building contractors in Midland City. The night before the fateful Mother's Day when Rudy killed Mrs. Metzger, Marco and his family dined with the Waltzes to commemorate the drafting of each family's oldest son. Marco's son Julio was eventually killed in Germany.

When the enormous snow storm hit Midland City and destroyed the Waltz family home, Gino and Marco frantically drove a company bulldozer to the hospital just in time to learn of Otto's death. It was later learned they did hundreds of thousands of dollars worth of property damage with the dozer.

Marco and Gino purchased John Fortune's dairy farm and created the Avondale development (the land was previously used as a testing ground for tanks during the war). After the Waltzes were financially ruined, Rudy and his mother moved into the show unit in Avondale. Unknown to the Maritimos was the fact that they had purchased cement from the Nuclear Regulatory Commission, which was used in the construction of the fireplace. Eventually, Mrs. Waltz died from exposure to radiation, and the Waltz brothers were forced to sue the Maritimo Brothers Construction Company, the Nuclear Regulatory Commission, and the Ohio Valley Ornamental Concrete Company. Though they apparently didn't know in advance about the radioactive cement, Gino and Marco were overcome with guilt, and without any urging sent workers into the home to rip out the fireplace, making it look as though a fireplace never existed.

The Maritimos constructed the famed Mildred Barry Memorial Center for the Arts. Marco died of natural causes a month before Celia Hoover's suicide, and Gino was electrocuted inspecting the arts center's drawbridge a few months later, just prior to the center's opening.

Maritimo, Guillermo. *A first cousin to Gino and Marco Maritimo and the grandfather of Milo Maritimo, the homosexual desk clerk at the Midland City Holiday Inn, in* Breakfast of Champions. *Guillermo "Little Willie" Maritimo was one of Al Capone's bodyguards in Chicago and is not seen in the text.*

Maritimo, Julio. *In* Deadeye Dick, *the eldest son of Marco Maritimo. He and Felix Waltz were drafted into military service at the same time. Julio was killed fighting in Germany.*

Maritimo, Milo. *The homosexual desk clerk at the Midland City Holiday Inn, grandson of Guillermo "Little Willie" Maritimo (one of Al Capone's bodyguards), and first cousin to Gino and Marco Maritimo, owners of Maritimo Brothers Construction Company. Milo is overjoyed to be the first in town to welcome Kilgore Trout's arrival for the Arts Festival. Maritimo had taken the trouble to write to Eliot Rosewater so he could read some of Trout's work before his arrival. Rosewater lent Milo his Trout collection of forty-one novels and sixty-three short stories and was reading his novel* The Smart Bunny *when he arrived. The desk clerk is overjoyed that Midland City will become known as the first community to acknowledge the greatness of Trout. Much to Trout's consternation, Milo's effusive welcome indicates his high expectations for Trout's arrival.* (*BC* 231:L11-12) "We are so ready for a Renaissance, Mr. Trout! You will be our Leonardo!"

In preparation for the Arts Festival banquet, Milo made the crown and scepter to be borne by Mary Alice Miller, Queen of the festival. See also: BC 233:L11; 234:L4.

Martha. *In* Breakfast of Champions, *Vonnegut speaks in his own voice and offers the information that his psychiatrist's name is Martha, no last name is provided.* (*BC* 268:L1-5) She gathers jumpy people together into little families which meet once a week. It's a lot of fun. She teaches us how to comfort one another intelligently. She is on vacation now. I like her a lot.

Marx, Arnold. *The eighteen-year-old red-headed Israeli-born amateur archaeologist and law student, one of Howard Campbell, Jr.'s four prison guards at the opening of* Mother Night. *Arnold and his father, a gunsmith by trade, excavate the ruins of Hazor under the direction of Yigael Yadin. He* *provides Campbell with an interesting object lesson concerning the interpretation of history and its all-too-frequent misapplications, foreshadowing Campbell's "cuckoo clock in hell" syndrome.* (*MN* 3:L12-18) Hazor, Arnold tells me, was a Canaanite city in northern Palestine that existed at least nineteen hundred years before Christ. About fourteen hundred years before Christ, Arnold tells me, an Israelite army captured Hazor, killed all forty thousand inhabitants, and burned it down.

"Solomon rebuilt the city," said Arnold, "but in 732 B.C. Tiglath-pileser the Third burned it down again." *Campbell receives this lesson as Arnold's way of informing him about what he perceives to be one of the most vicious criminals in history—Tiglath-pileser the Third—though he never considers those 40,000 people killed by the ancient Israelis. But when Campbell mentions his own boss, the Nazi war criminal Paul Joseph Goebbels, Arnold has no idea who that is. Campbell resigns himself to the sweep of history and the relative obscurity both he and his alleged crimes will eventually suffer.* (*MN* 4:L6-10) And I felt the dust of the Holy Land creeping in to bury me, sensed how thick a dust-and-rubble blanket I would one day wear. I felt thirty or forty feet of ruined cities above me; beneath me some primitive kitchen middens, a temple or two—and then—

Tiglath-pileser the Third.

Mary. *The forty-foot fishing boat belonging to Harry Pena and on which he made his living with sons Manny and Kenny.* (*GBR* 141:L32) She was a gray, lapstreak tub whose purpose was to wallow home in all weather with tons of fresh fish on board. There wasn't any shelter on her, except for a wooden box to keep the big new Chrysler dry. The wheel and the throttle and the clutch were mounted on the box. All the rest of the ***Mary*** was a bare-boned tub.

Mashtots, Mesrob. *Among the many notable Armenians proudly recorded by Rabo Karabekian is Mesrob Mashots,* the inventor of the Armenian alphabet, unlike any other, about four hundred years before the birth of Christ. . . . There are about six million of us now, including my two sons and three grandchildren, who know nothing and care nothing about **Mesrob Mashtots** (*Blue* 16:L21, 17:L2). *Rabo estimates the number of Armenians when he writes his memoirs, all stigmatized by the Turkish massacre of Armenians.*

Masters, Barbara. (*WFG* 103:L2 *Good Missiles, Good Manners, Good Night*) I WENT to high school in Indianapolis with a nice girl named **Barbara Masters**. Her father was an eye doctor in our town. She is now the wife of our Secretary of Defense *(Melvin Laird)*.

Matheson. *Ilium's pompous manager in charge of testing and placement for the General Classification Test, in* Player Piano.

Matsumoto, Hiroshi. *The lifelong employee of the Sony Corporation is also Warden of the New York State Maximum Security Adult Correctional Facility at Athena and serves as Vonnegut's voice on some matters economic and social. Previous to his appointment to Athena (New York State had contracted with Sony to run their correctional facilities), Matsumoto served Sony as the manager of a "for profit" hospital in Lexington, Kentucky, a position which deeply vexed him because he was forced to turn away indigent patients. When only eight years old, Matsumoto survived the atomic bombing of Hiroshima and this left some indelible memories upon him. He led a solitary existence with almost no hint of close friends. However, to some small extent he did befriend Eugene Debs Hartke after hiring him to teach at the prison. Matsumoto was chased away from the commotion at Athena during the prison break and wound up lost in the nearby forest. Two days later he emerged from the forest frozen and demoralized. His feet required amputation due to frostbite and gangrene. Matsumoto returned to Hiroshima where he eventually took his life by committing hara-kiri.*

Matsumoto's experience as an atomic bomb survivor and a lifelong employee of Sony gave him a unique perspective on the economic and social ties which bind Japan and the United States, and he conveyed these thoughts to Hartke, who heartily agreed with him. (*HP* 222:L29-36, 223:L1-26) He *(Matsumoto)* said, "I only wish our Chairman of the Board back in Tokyo could have spent just one hour with me in our emergency room, turning away dying people because they could not afford our services."

"You had a body count in Vietnam, I believe?" he said. It was true. We were ordered to count how many people we killed so that higher headquarters, all the way back to Washington, D.C., could estimate how much closer, even if it was only a teeny-weeny bit closer, all our efforts were bringing us to victory. There wasn't any other way to keep score.

"So now we count dollars the way you used to count bodies," he said. "What does that bring us closer to? What does it mean? We should do with those dollars what you did with the bodies. Bury and forget them! You were luckier with your bodies than we are with all our dollars."

"How so?" I said.

"All anybody can do with bodies is burn them or bury them," he said. "There isn't any nightmare afterwards, when you have to invest them and make them grow.

"What a clever trap your Ruling Class set for us," he went on. "First the atomic bomb. Now this."

"Trap?" I echoed wonderingly.

"They looted your public and corporate treasuries, and turned your industries over to nincompoops, he said. "Then they had your Government borrow so heavily from us that we had no choice but to send over an Army of Occupation in business suits. Never before has the Ruling Class of a country found a way to stick other countries with all the responsibilities their wealth might imply, and still remain rich beyond the dreams of avarice! No wonder they thought the comatose Ronald Reagan was a great President!"

Hartke uses Matsumoto's sentiments to explain the decayed social conditions resulting from economic hedonism and the general lack of faith in the economic traditions which built small communities through local investment. Such a system thrived on the interdependence of the upper and working classes in a community, the very model which originally built Scipio and Tarkington College. (*HP* 225:L28) What Warden Matsumoto had said about people like them *(the rich in general, though Hartke makes specific reference here to members of the Tarkington Board of Trustees)* was accurate. They had managed to convert their wealth, which had originally been in the form of factories or stores or other demanding enterprises, into a form so liquid and abstract, negotiable representations of money on paper, that there were few reminders coming from anywhere that they might be responsible for anyone outside their own circle of friends and relatives.

They *(the board members)* didn't rage against the convicts. They were mad at the Government for not making sure that escapes from prison were impossible. The more they ran on like that, the clearer it became that it was their Government, not mine or the convicts' or the Townies'. Its first duty, moreover, was to protect them from the lower classes, not only in this country but everywhere.

Were people on Easy Street ever any different?

Think again about the crucifixions of Jesus and the 2 thieves, and the 6,000 slaves who followed the gladiator Spartacus.

Matsumoto Corporation. *This corporation appears in both* Galápagos *and* Bluebeard. *In both instances, Vonnegut makes reference to Matsumoto's takeover of GEFFCo. In* Galápagos, *Matsumoto's modernization of GEFFCo's Ilium manufacturing plant results in the loss of hundreds of jobs, since they can run the plant with only twelve workers. Ilium is driven into bankruptcy due to the loss of its largest workforce. One of the laid off workers is Roy Hepburn. Matsumoto is also the employer of Zenji Hiroguchi, creator of Gokubi and Mandarax.*

In Bluebeard, *Matsumoto assumes ownership of GEFFCo's Manhattan office building as well as its art collection, which includes Rabo Karabekian's "Blue Windsor Number Seventeen." One of their security guards calls Karabekian about the demise of his painting and offers him the opportunity to retrieve its remains.*

mausoleum. *Wilbur and Eliza Swain used the mausoleum of Professor Elihu Roosevelt Swain, founder of the family fortune, as a childhood escape and as the repository for their treatises on gravity and artificially extended families. As children they took refuge there to read books and sing songs (especially "We're Off to See the Wizard" from* The Wizard of Oz*). Later, Wilbur retrieved the gravity treatise for the Chinese at the request of a message sent* *by his sister.* (*Slap* 38:L8) It was actually possible for Eliza and me, for example, to vanish into a huge grandfather clock in the ballroom at the top of the northernmost tower, and to emerge almost a kilometer away—through a trap door in the floor of the **mausoleum** of Professor Elihu Roosevelt Swain. (*Slap* 42:L4) There were thousands of books in the mansion. By the time we were ten, we had read them all by candlelight, at naptime or after bedtime—in secret passageways, or often in the **mausoleum** of Elihu Roosevelt Swain. (*Slap* 149:L1) The exterior doors to the **mausoleum** had been welded shut. So Fu Manchu and I had to enter the secret passageways, the alternative universe of my childhood, and come up through the **mausoleum's** floor. *See also:* *Slap* 36:L19; 58:L3; 106:L25; 146:L23; 148:L2; 149:L23; 150:L2; 156:L14; 202:L3.

McAllister, Reed. *This may be an internal inconsistency of Vonnegut's in* God Bless You, Mr. Rosewater. *Vonnegut refers to Reed McAllister as "Old McAllister" (GBR* 137:L3), *the attorney from McAllister, Robjent, Reed and McGee representing Stewart Buntline of Newport, Rhode Island. It seems unlike Vonnegut to have two closely associated characters sharing the same last name, a first name which is part of the law firm, and a reference to "Old McAllister" when he doesn't mean the senior partner, Thurmond McAllister. In any case, Reed McAllister is responsible for transforming Stewart Buntline from an idealistic youth possessed of great inheritance to a conservative middle-aged man of wealth. McAllister was forever forwarding Buntline capitalist tracts such as "A Rift Between Friends in the War of Ideas," long after Buntline became comfortable with his wealth.*

McAllister, Thurmond (also **McAllister, Robjent, Reed and McGee**). *The seventy-six-year-old senior partner in the Washington, D.C., law firm McAllister, Robjent, Reed and McGee, representing the Indiana Rosewaters and Stewart Buntline of Rhode Island, in* God Bless You, Mr. Rosewater. *It was the senior partner who first suggested establishing the Rosewater Foundation as a way of avoiding inheritance taxes. Norman Mushari is hired by the firm and put to work as an aide to the senior partner in the hope of toughening the softening old lawyer.*

McBundy, Hortense Muskellunge-13. *The private secretary of President Wilbur Swain died of the Albanian Flu in* Slapstick.

McCabe, Earl. *Corporal Earl McCabe is the "idealistic Marine deserter" stationed in Port-au-Prince, Haiti, who stole his outfit's recreation fund and gave five hundred dollars to new friend Lionel Boyd Johnson to purchase a schooner so the two could sail back to the United States. They were shipwrecked in a gale on the coastal rocks of San Lorenzo. In comparison to the diseased and impoverished natives,* Johnson and **McCabe** had the glittering treasures of literacy, ambition, curiosity, gall, irreverence, health, humor, and considerable information about the outside world (*CC* 106:L2-5). *They arrived in 1922, announced they were taking charge of the island, and Castle Sugar quickly withdrew.*

Johnson and McCabe tried to reform society. Johnson invented a new religion, Bokononism, and McCabe tried to reform the economy and legal system. McCabe tried socialism, but there wasn't any real wealth to redistribute. Johnson asked McCabe to outlaw Bokononism so there would be a new and vital dynamic tension created among the people. The two friends were trapped by their own creation. Bokonon needed to live as a saint, and McCabe had to repress all his natural goodness so he could carry out his side of the artificial struggle between the government and Bokononism. As Julian Castle recalls, "The drama was very tough on the souls of the two main actors, **McCabe** and Bokonon. As young men, they had been pretty much alike, had both been half-angel, half-pirate.

"But the drama demanded that the pirate half of Bokonon and the angel half of **McCabe** wither away. And **McCabe** and Bokonon paid a terrible price in agony for the happiness of the people—**McCabe** knowing the agony of the tyrant and Bokonon knowing the agony of the saint. They both became, for all practical purposes, insane" (*CC* 144:L32-35, 145:L1). *Castle is so convinced about the effects of this personality split that he believes it eventually caused McCabe's death.* (*CC* 153:L10-11) "Unrelieved villainy just wore him out, is my guess."

Johnson and McCabe renamed the capital of San Lorenzo to Bolivar, and the highest peak on the island was named Mount McCabe.

McCarthy, Cliff. *The Ohio University art professor who was originally seen by Vonnegut on a local PBS documentary series about Ohio artists. He and Vonnegut have enjoyed a long friendship and correspondence. McCarthy is introduced in the preface to* Deadeye Dick *and later becomes important as a teller of documented truth about Otto Waltz's status in the art community and the crimes of the military-industrial complex.* (*DD* xi:L32) **Cliff McCarthy** is about my age and from my part of America, more or less. When he went to art school, it was drummed into him that the worst sort of painter was eclectic; borrowing from here and there. But now he has had a show of thirty years of his work, at Ohio University, and he says, "I notice that I have been eclectic." It's strong and lovely stuff he does. My own favorite is "The Artist's Mother as a Bride in 1917." His mother is all dressed up, and it's a warm time of year, and somebody has persuaded her to pose in the bow of a rowboat. The rowboat is in a perfectly still, narrow patch of water, a little river, probably, with the opposite bank, all leafy, only fifty yards away. She is laughing. *McCarthy's painting is later used by Vonnegut as a photograph of Rudy's mother. While she lay dying, imagining herself on a spaceship to Mars, she recalls* "That picture," . . . and she would smile and give my hand a squeeze. I was supposed to know which of all the pictures in the world she meant. I thought for a while that it was Father's unfinished masterpiece from his misspent youth in Vienna. But in a moment of clarity, she made it clear that it was a scrapbook photograph of her in a rowboat on a small river somewhere, maybe in Europe. Then again, it could have been Sugar Creek. The boat is tied to shore. There aren't any oars in place. She isn't going anywhere. She wears a summer dress and a garden hat. Somebody has persuaded her to pose in the boat, with water around her and dappled with shade. She is laughing. She has just been married, or is about to be married.

She will never be happier. She will never be more beautiful (*DD* 221:L34, 222:L1-15).

(*DD* 211-212) We probably never would have found out that it was the mantelpiece that killed her, if it weren't for an art historian from Ohio University over at Athens. His name was **Cliff McCarthy**. He was a painter, too. And **Cliff McCarthy** never would have got involved in our lives, if it hadn't been for all the publicity Mother received for objecting to the kind of art Fred T. Barry was buying for the arts center. He read about her in *People* magazine. Then again, Mother almost certainly wouldn't have become so passionate about taking Fred T. Barry on in the first place, if it hadn't been for little tumors in her brain, which had been caused by the radioactive mantelpiece.

Wheels within wheels!

People magazine described Mother as the widow of an Ohio painter. **Cliff McCarthy** had been working for years, financed by a Cleveland philanthropist, on a book which was to include every serious Ohio painter, but he had never heard of Father. So he visited our little shitbox, and he photographed Father's unfinished painting over the fireplace. That was all there was to photograph, so he took several exposures of that with a big camera on a tripod. He was being polite, I guess.

But the camera used flat packs of four-by-five film, and he had exposed some of it elsewhere, so he got several packs out of his camera bag.

He accidentally left one behind—on the mantelpiece. One week later he swung off the Interstate, on his way to someplace else, and he picked up the pack.

Three days after that, he called me on the telephone to say that the film in the pack had all turned black, and that a friend of his who taught physics had offered the opinion that the film had been close to something which was highly radioactive.

He gave me another piece of news on the telephone, too. He had been looking at a diary kept by the great Ohio painter Frank Duveneck at the end of his life. He died in 1919, at the age of seventy-one. Duveneck spent his most productive years in Europe, but he returned to his native Cincinnati after his wife died in Florence, Italy.

"Your father is in the diary!" said **McCarthy**. "Duveneck heard about this wonderful studio a young painter was building in Midland City, and on March 16, 1915, he went and had a look at it."

"What did he say?" I asked.

"He said it was certainly a beautiful studio, such as any artist in the world would have given his eyeteeth to have."

"I mean, what did he say about Father?" I said. "He liked him, I think," said **McCarthy**.

"Look, I said,—I'm aware that my father was a fraud, and Father knew it, too. Duveneck was probably the only really important painter who ever saw Father's masquerade. No matter how cutting it is, please tell me what Duveneck said."

"Well—I'll read it to you," said **McCarthy**, and he did: "'Otto Waltz should be shot. He should be shot for seeming to prove the last thing that needs to be proved in this part of the world: that an artist is a person of no consequence.'"

McCarthy, Senator Joseph. *The infamous focal point in the search for communist sympathizers during the 1950s is frequently mentioned in Vonnegut's work. In* Cat's Cradle, *Ambassador Minton loses his post after his wife's letter to the* New York Times *attracts the attention of congressional powers. In* God Bless You, Mr. Rosewater, *a young Norman Mushari is pictured papering his room with photos of the senator and his assistant, Roy Cohn. In* Jailbird, *Ben Shapiro, Walter Starbuck's best man and the man who delivered the Starbucks' first child, loses his promotion to full colonel when McCarthy learns Shapiro was a communist before the war. Later in the same text, RAMJAC hires Roy Cohn, McCarthy's chief counsel of the Senate Permanent Investigating Committee, to defend Starbuck.*

McCarty, Eddie (see **Irving Buchanon**).

McClellan, Grace and George, and their neighbors **Anne** and her **husband** (unnamed). *In the short story "More Stately Mansions," Anne and her unnamed husband, the narrator of the story, are subjected to the interior decorating schemes of the desperate Grace McClellan. Grace's husband George had suffered one financial setback after another, and Grace's dreams of remodeling worked themselves out on her unsuspecting neighbors. Though Grace is obnoxiously aggressive in her criticism and advice about such matters, Anne and her husband come to realize the McClellans' sad plight and humor them. When Grace falls seriously ill, George comes into an inheritance from a distant relative and is assisted by Anne and her husband in directing a remodeling job of the McClellans' house before Grace returns from the hospital. The small inconsistencies in the execution of her design mildly disturb Grace, but they become a source of inspiration for her to continue her interest and dreams in large scale remodeling.*

McCone, Alexander Hamilton and Clara. *The younger son of Daniel McCone, Alexander graduated without distinction from Harvard in 1894 and is notable for befriending Walter F. Starbuck, the son of his cook and* *chauffeur. McCone was forty-one when Walter was born into his mansion on Euclid Ave. in Cleveland. At the time, Alexander was married to Alice Rockefeller and father to a daughter named Clara. His wife and child were embarrassed by his terrible stammering and spent most of their time in Europe. A. H. McCone promised Walter a Harvard education if he would be his companion, and so began Walter's lifelong affection for chess, the game he learned at the knee of McCone. Alexander felt morally committed to the family firm, the Cuyahoga Bridge and Iron Company,* "I then believed that a rich man should have some understanding of the place from which his riches came. That was very juvenile of me. Great wealth should be accepted unquestioningly, or not at all" (*JB* xxiii:L9-13).

Alexander was present at the Cuyahoga Massacre, an event he felt was the result of American am-am-am-amateurism in muh-muh-matters of luh-life and duh-duh-duh-death (*JB* xxxiv:L6-7). *He felt this way after witnessing the assassins hired by his father to help quell the union strikers.*

McCone, Daniel and John. *Daniel McCone was the founder and owner of the Cuyahoga Bridge and Iron Company, which became Cleveland's largest employer by the time Walter Starbuck was born.* (*JB* xxi:L31) **McCone** was a hard-bitten and brilliant little mechanical engineer, self-educated, born of working-class parents in Edinburgh, Scotland. *In October 1894, McCone demanded his workers take a ten percent pay cut. They refused, went on strike, and in December McCone and his two sons watched from the factory windows while the authorities first pushed compliance with the riot act and quickly followed with an armed charge on the strikers and their families.* (*JB* xxxvii:L11) Old **Daniel McCone** would say to his sons as he looked out over the battlefield, vacant now except for bodies, "Like it or not, boys, that's the sort of business you're in."

(*JB* 22:L20) **Daniel McCone** had two sons, Alexander Hamilton McCone, then twenty-two, and **John**, twenty-five. Alexander had graduated without distinction from Harvard in the previous May. He was soft, he was shy, he was a stammerer. **John**, the elder son and the company's heir apparent, had flunked out of the Massachusetts Institute of Technology in his freshman year, and had been his father's most trusted aide ever since.

Starbuck records that McCone held some severe theories about race. (*JB* 173:L25-31, 174:L1-2) My parents were recruited at once by an agent of the Cuyahoga Bridge and Iron Company in Cleveland. He was instructed to hire only blond Slavs, **Mr. McCone** once told me, on his father's theory that blonds would have the mechanical ingenuity and robustness of Germans, but tempered with the passivity of Slavs. The agent was to pick up factory workers, and a few presentable domestic servants for the various **McCone** households, as well. Thus did my parents enter the servant class.

McCoy, Newton. *In* Slapstick, *Byron Hatfield mistakenly shoots a Beryllium messenger sent by Wilma Pachysandra-17 von Peterswald to deliver a message* *to President Wilbur Swain. Hatfield thought he was shooting at his old nemesis, Newton McCoy.*

"The McGarvey Family." *In the short story "Tomorrow and Tomorrow and Tomorrow," "The McGarvey Family" is a television series in production for at least one hundred twelve consecutive years.*

McLuhan, Nancy. *In the short story "Welcome to the Monkey House," Nancy McLuhan is the virginal Ethical Suicide Parlor hostess kidnapped by Billy the Poet (originally disguised as the Foxy Grandpa). Taken to the Hyannis Port Kennedy Compound, now a national monument underneath a geodesic dome, Nancy is subdued with drugs administered by deflowered former hostesses. In a drugged haze Nancy admits to being sixty-three and virgin. She is kept on the drydocked Kennedy yacht* Marlin, *until her ethical birth control pills wear off.*

McSwann, Ross L. *The swaggering Mayor of Boca Raton, Florida, who mockingly pleads* "Send us more Martians" *after the failed Martian invasion* (*ST* 170:L23). *The townspeople hung twenty-three from lamp posts, shot dead another eleven, and took Sergeant Brackman prisoner. McSwann went on to become a United States Senator.*

Meadow Lark (see **Queen of the Meadows**).

Meadows. (*PP* 34:L17) The **Meadows** was a flat, grassy island in the St. Lawrence, in Chippewa Bay, where the most important men, and the most promising men ("Those whose development within the organization is not yet complete," said the Handbook) in the Eastern and Middle-Western Divisions spent a week each summer in an orgy of morale building—through team athletics, group sings, bonfires and skyrockets, bawdy entertainment, free whisky and cigars; and through plays, put on by professional actors, which pleasantly but unmistakably made clear the nature of good deportment within the system, and the shape of firm resolves for the challenging year ahead.

The Meadows is where the ruling technocracy hatch their plan to have Paul Proteus infiltrate the Ghost Shirt Society. Of course, by the time Paul arrived at the Meadows, he had planned on quitting.

A central feature of the Meadows' experience was the morality play repeated each year. (*PP* 190:L39) The play was virtually the same play that had begun every **Meadows** session, even before the war, when the island had belonged to a steel company. Twenty years ago, Paul's father had brought him up here, and the play's message had been the same: that the common man wasn't nearly as grateful as he should be for what the engineers and managers had given him, and that the radicals were the cause of the ingratitude.

Fred Garth, a competitor of Paul's for manager of the Pittsburgh Works, becomes disaffected with the stringent social design of the ruling technocracy when one of his children does poorly on the all-important General Classification Tests. He takes out his frustration by peeling the bark off the Great Oak of the Meadows and setting it on fire.

Complementing the Meadows is the Mainland, a camp for wives and children, and women employees whose development wasn't yet complete, across the water from the **Meadows**, the island where the men went (*PP* 121:L28).

Mellon, Hortense. *The graduating Tarkington student and harpist whose uncle, University of Chicago economist Dr. Martin Peale Blankenship, was invited to deliver the keynote speech in* Hocus Pocus. *Eugene Debs Hartke remembers Hortense for her false teeth, the result of a violent mugging she endured after leaving a party at the Waldorf-Astoria. Her parents were among the many Tarkington parents who lost fortunes in the stock-swindling Microsecond Arbitrage fiasco.*

Memoirs of a Monogamous Casanova. *Howard Campbell's homage to the love he shared with his wife Helga. It celebrated their passion and sexuality. Russian plagiarist Stepan Bodovskov had it printed anonymously and it became a runaway best-seller in the Eastern Bloc nations. Campbell doesn't understand how it could have been printed in those countries, but Frank Wirtanen explains the odd appeal it enjoyed.* (*MN* 154:L6, 15) "***Memoirs of a Monogamous Casanova*** is a curious little chapter in Russian history," said Wirtanen. "It could hardly be published with official approval in Russia—and yet, it was such an attractive, strangely moral piece of pornography, so ideal for a nation suffering from shortages of everything but men and women, that presses in Budapest were somehow encouraged to start printing it—and those presses have, somehow, never been ordered to stop." Wirtanen winked at me. "One of the few sly, playful, harmless crimes a Russian can commit at no risk to himself is smuggling home a copy of ***Memoirs of a Monogamous Casanova***. And for whom does he smuggle it? To whom is be going to show this hot stuff? To that salty old crony, his wife.

"For years," said Wirtanen, "there was only a Russian edition. But now, it is available in Hungarian, Rumanian, Latvian, Estonian, and, most marvelous of all, German again."

Howard Campbell recalls the text's epigraph is a poem by William Blake called "The Question Answered":

What is it men in women do require?
The lineaments of Gratified Desire.
What is it women do in men require?
The lineaments of Gratified Desire. (*MN* 97:L10-15)

Inspired to love again by Resi Noth impersonating Campbell's wife Helga, he adds a final chapter 643 and prints it directly in Mother Night (97-98).

Mencken, Barbira. *In* Bluebeard, *the former screen star and ex-wife of Paul Slazinger living in the Turtle Bay section of Manhattan, near Greta Garbo and Katharine Hepburn.* (*Blue* 110:L22) This woman came out of the brownstone with the duplex and triplex. She was old and trembly, but her posture was good, and it was easy to see that she had been very beautiful at one time. I locked my gaze to hers, and a flash of recognition went off in my skull. I knew *her* but she didn't know *me*. We had never met. I realized that I had seen her in motion pictures when she was much younger. A second later, I came up with her name. She was **Barbira Mencken**, the ex-wife of Paul Slazinger.

Mendoza, Jose. *In* Breakfast of Champions, *Mendoza is the Puerto Rican gang member who paints the insignia of the Pluto Gang on the backs of members' jackets. The Pluto Gang hoped to get the drug dealers out of their neighborhood so the government would be more inclined to provide social services.*

Mengel, Bernard. *One of four guards assigned to Howard Campbell in the Old Jerusalem basement jail cell. Mengel is a Polish Jew who* once saved his own life in the Second World War by playing so dead that a German soldier pulled out three of his teeth without suspecting that **Mengel** was not a corpse (*MN* 11:L5). *Mengel helped hang Auschwitz commandant Rudolf Franz Hoess by tying his legs together with a leather strap.* (*MN* 12:L18-22) "After we finished hanging Hoess . . . I packed up my clothes to go home. The catch on my suitcase was broken, so I buckled it shut with a big leather strap. Twice within an hour I did the very same job—once to Hoess and once to my suitcase. Both jobs felt about the same."

Mengel also tells Campbell that judging from the way he sleeps compared with the other Nazi prisoners, he must have a very guilty conscience about his war activities. The other prisoners sleep soundly, but Campbell is restless and constantly calls out in his sleep.

Merble, Lionel. *The owner of the Ilium School of Optometry and father-in-law to Billy Pilgrim in* Slaughterhouse-Five. *After his death in the charter flight which crashed in the Sugarbush Mountains, Billy became the school's proprietor.*

Merganthaler, Corporal. *The corporal is the central figure in a war story told by a sergeant about how he received the Silver Star. The story is overheard by Paul Proteus while riding on a train through upstate New York, and it highlights the importance of technology over individual acts of bravery. The sergeant's unit was about to have its perimeter overrun when he sent Merganthaler back for help.* So over they come, screamin' bloody murder, and us with nothing but our goddamn rifles and bayonets workin'. Looked like a tidal wave comin' over at us. . . . Just then, up comes **Merganthaler** with a truck and generator he's moonlight-requisitioned from the 57th. We hooked her into our lines, cranked her up, and my God, I wish you could of seen it. The poor bastards fryin' on the electric fence, the proximity mines poppin' under 'em, the microwave sentinels openin' up with the remote-control machine-gun nests, and the fire-control system swiveling the guns and flamethrowers around as long as anything was quiverin' within a mile of the place. And that's how I got the Silver Star" (*PP* 220:L26).

Merrihue, Faith. (*GBR* 120:L2) And blind George *(General George Rosewater)* was given a fourteen-year-old girl, an orphan named **Faith Merrihue**, who was to be his eyes and his messenger. When she was sixteen, George married her. *She later gave birth to Abraham Rosewater.*

Messiah. *Paul Proteus (the Ghost Shirt Society), Eliot Rosewater, and Kilgore Trout are all cast as messiahs, though none ever tried to pose as such. Proteus is the victim of of the scheming Ghost Shirt Society, which seeks to reclaim human dignity in a world full of technomania. Eliot Rosewater's benevolence is ignorantly though innocently inflated by Diana Moon Glampers and Mary Moody, while Norman Mushari is quick to exploit his kindness. Kilgore Trout is viewed by Billy Pilgrim as one of the many holy men he saw go to waste in Dresden.* (*PP* 83:L15, 19-20) "You figure to be the new **Messiah**?" said Finnerty. *Ed Finnerty is speaking with Reverend Lasher.*

"Sometimes I think I'd like to be—if only in self-defense. Also, it'd be a swell way to get rich. Trouble is, I can be sold or unsold on anything too easily. I enjoy being talked into something. Pretty shaky outlook for a **Messiah**. Besides, who ever heard of a short, fat, middle-aged **Messiah** with bad eyesight? And I haven't got that common touch. Frankly, the masses give me a pain in the tail, and I guess I show it." He made clucking sounds with his tongue. "I'm going to get myself a uniform, so I'll know what I think and stand for."

(*PP* 99:L23) If his attempt to become the new **Messiah** had been successful, if the inhabitants of the north and south banks had met in the middle of the bridge with Paul between them, he wouldn't have had the slightest idea of what to do next. He knew with all his heart that the human situation was a frightful botch, but it was such a logical, intelligently arrived-at botch that he couldn't see how history could possibly have led anywhere else.

(*PP* 250:L12) "And the Ghost Dance religion," said Lasher, "was that last, desperate defense of the old values. **Messiahs** appeared, the way they're always ready to appear, to preach magic that would restore the game, the old values, the old reasons for being. There were new rituals and new songs that were supposed to get rid of the white men by magic. And some of the more warlike tribes that still had a little physical fight left in them added a flourish of their own—the Ghost Shirt."

(*GBR* 109:L26) Mushari did not register disappointment. The baptism would hold up very well in court as evidence that Eliot thought of himself as a **Messiah**.
(*SL5* 143:L16) Trout's paranoid face was terribly familiar to Billy, who had seen it on the jackets of so many books. But, coming upon that face suddenly in a home-town alley, Billy could not guess why the face was familiar. Billy thought maybe he had known this cracked **messiah** in Dresden somewhere. Trout certainly looked like a prisoner of war.
(*PS* 202:L28 *Religion*) "It may be that moral simplicity is not possible in modern times. It may be that simplicity and clarity can come only from a new **messiah**, who may never come. We can talk about portents, if you like. I like a good portent as much as anyone. What might be the meaning of the comet Kahoutek [sic], which was to make us look upward, to impress us with the paltriness of our troubles, to cleanse our souls with cosmic awe? Kahoutek was a fizzle, and what might this fizzle mean?" *See also: PP* 80:L16,18; 83:L35; 91:L7; 252:L3,5-6; 284:L34.

Metzger, Eloise. *In* Deadeye Dick*, the ill-fated pregnant woman who was vacuuming her home when Rudy Waltz unthinkingly fired a shot from the upstairs gunroom of his home. She was the wife of George Metzger, city editor of the* Bugle-Observer*, and the mother of Eugene Debs Metzger and Jane Addams Metzger.*

Metzger, Eugene Debs and **Jane Addams**. *The children of George and Eloise Metzger.* (*DD* 99:L13-16) **Eugene** and **Jane** were named . . . for Eugene V. Debs, the labor hero from Terre Haute, Indiana, and Jane Addams, the Nobel prize-winning social reformer from Cedarville, Illinois.
(*DD* 104:L22-31) **Eugene Debs Metzger**, it turned out, lived in Athens, Greece, and owned several tankers, which flew the flag of Liberia.

His sister, **Jane Addams Metzger**, who found her mother dead and vacuum cleaner still running so long ago, a big, homely girl, as I recall, and big and homely still, according to Ketchum, was living with a refugee Czech playwright on Molokai, in the Hawaiian Islands, where she owned a ranch and was raising Arabian horses.

Metzger, George. *The widowed husband of Eloise Metzger and the editor of the* Midland City Bugle-Observer. (*DD* 82:L35, 83:L1-18) He was bald on top. He was skinny, and his posture was bad, and he was dressed like almost no other man in Midland City—in gray flannel trousers and a tweed sport coat, what I would recognize much later at Ohio State as the uniform of an English professor. All he did was write and edit at the *Bugle-Observer* all day long. . . . He was a newspaper gypsy. He had been hired away from the *Indianapolis Times*. It would come out at legal proceedings later on that he was born to poor parents in Kenosha, Wisconsin, and had put himself through Harvard, and that he had twice worked his way to Europe on cattle boats. The adverse information about him, which was brought out by our lawyer, was that he had once belonged to the Communist party, and had attempted to enlist in the Abraham Lincoln Brigade during the Spanish Civil War.

Metzger was sickened by the behavior of the police officers who brought him to the jail in the hope he would beat Rudy Waltz for killing his wife. However, he left the station and forgave Rudy in a Bugle-Observer *editorial.* (*DD* 87:L25-34) "My wife has been killed by a machine which should never have come into the hands of any human being. It is called a firearm. It makes the blackest of all human wishes come true at once, at a distance: that something die.

"There is evil for you.

"We cannot get rid of mankind's fleetingly wicked wishes. We can get rid of the machines that make them come true.

"I give you a holy word: DISARM."

Metzger hires Bernard Ketchum to sue Otto Waltz and succeeds in taking most of the family's assets. He left for Florida and bought a weekly newspaper in Cedar Key, investing the rest of the Waltz family wealth in "two thousand acres of open land near Orlando." He made a fortune when the land was purchased to construct Disney World.

Aside from the weekly Metzger purchased, he tried and failed to produce a newspaper expressing his exotic views on war and firearms and the brotherhood of man and so on (*DD* 103:L18-19).

Miasma, Khashdrahr. *The nephew and interpreter for the Shah of Bratpuhr in* Player Piano.

Microsecond Arbitrage, Inc. *The center of a major stock swindle which left a number of Tarkington benefactors, and Tarkington College itself, nearly penniless.* (*HP* 108:L7-19) That swindle claimed to be snapping up bargains in food and shelter and clothing and fuel and medicine and raw materials and machinery and so on before people who really needed them could learn of their existence. And then the company's computers, supposedly, would get the people who really needed whatever it was to bid against each other, running profits right through the roof. It was able to do this with its clients' money, supposedly, because its computers were linked by satellites to marketplaces in every corner of the world.

The computers, it would turn out, weren't connected to anything but each other and their credulous clients like Tarkington's Board Chairman.

Board Chairman Robert W. Moellenkamp was so excited about Microsecond Arbitrage that he authorized the sale of all the college's property in Scipio (including the old wagon factory, brewery, and land), to a Japanese company and invested the cash in the fraudulent firm.

middle-European humor (see **humor**).

Midland City. *The locus of activity in both* Breakfast of Champions *and* Deadeye Dick. *In* Breakfast of Champions, *Vonnegut uses it as the meeting ground for Kilgore Trout, Dwayne Hoover, and himself during the October 1972 Midland City Arts Festival commemorating the opening of the Mildred Barry Memorial Center for the Arts. Trout was invited to take part in a symposium entitled "The Future of the American Novel in the Age of McLuhan." In* Deadeye Dick, *Midland City is where Rudy Waltz fires the errant and fateful shot which kills the pregnant Eloise Metzger, the blizzard of February 14, 1960 devastates the town, it is later neutron-bombed, and Hippolyte Paul de Mille resurrects World War One ace Will Fairchild at Calvary Cemetery.*

Many view Midland City as Vonnegut's stand-in for his hometown of Indianapolis. He borrowed the name of the real Crispus Attucks High School of Indianapolis and placed it in Midland City, and the tragic death of Mrs. Metzger occurs on Mothers' Day 1944, the same day Vonnegut's mother committed suicide.

Midland City is also the hometown of Galápagos' *James Wait, the product of a dysfunctional family in that his father and sister had an incestuous relationship and left town to live together. James studied auto mechanics in high school before going to New York City to become a male prostitute.* Hocus Pocus' *Eugene Debs Hartke, Jr. moved there with his family when only two-years-old so his father could work for Robo-Magic Corporation.*

Vonnegut's description of the sensibilities of Midland City residents sounds remarkably similar to his description of the totalitarian mind as understood through his cuckoo clock in Hell analogy. (*BC* 142:7-8) It didn't matter much what most people in **Midland City** said out loud, except when they were talking about money or structures or travel or machinery—or other measurable things. Every person had a clearly defined part to play—as a black person, a female high school drop-out, a Pontiac dealer, a gynecologist, a gas-conversion burner installer. If a person stopped living up to expectations, because of bad chemicals or one thing or another, everybody went on imagining that the person was living up to expectations anyway.

That was the main reason the people in **Midland City** were so slow to detect insanity in their associates. Their imaginations insisted that nobody changed much from day to day. Their imaginations were flywheels on the ramshackle machinery of the awful truth.

Notable Midland City events and institutions in Breakfast of Champions:

Adult Correctional Institution at Shepherdstown (nearby)

Blizzard of 1960 (February 14, the night of Rudy's opening/closing of "Katmandu" in Greenwich Village)

Crispus Attucks High School (Innocent Bystander High)

Dwayne Hoover's Exit Eleven Pontiac Village

Fairchild Hotel

Fairchild Boulevard-main street of town

George Washington Carver High School

Holiday Inn (sight of the Trout-Hoover-Vonnegut confrontation)
John F. Kennedy High School
Keedsler Automobile Company
Maharishi Mahesh Yogi once visited
*Maritimo Brothers Construction (*BC *and* DD*)*
*Mildred Barry Memorial Center for the Arts (*BC *and* DD*)*
Midland City Arts Festival, October 1972
Midland City Association of Women's Clubs
Midland City Bugle-Observer
Midland City Chamber of Commerce
Midland County General Hospital
*Midland County National Bank (*BC *and* DD*)*
The Opera House, home of the Midland City Symphony Orchestra, eventually became a movie house called The Bannister, and later became home of the Empire Furniture Company
Prairie Mutual
Radio Station WMCY
*Robo-Magic Corporation of America, later became The Midland City Ordnance Company and then Barrytron, Limited. Eventually purchased by Du Pont (*HP*)*
Sacred Miracle Cave
Saint Christopher High School, later changed to Saint Athanasius
Sugar Creek
Tomb of George Hickman Bannister
The violent emotional breakdown of Dwayne Hoover, and in the same week a 14 year old boy shoots his parents because he didn't want to show them his bad report card.
Western Electric
Notable Midland City events and institutions in Deadeye Dick*:*
Avondale, a suburb of Midland City developed by the Maritimo Brothers Construction Co. and where Emma Waltz died of exposure to radioactivity from cement used during the Manhattan Project.
*Calvary Cemetery (*BC *and* DD*)*
Fairchild High School, where Celia Hildreth starred in the local production of Rudy Waltz's "Katmandu"
Fairchild Park
Farmers of Southwestern Ohio for Nuclear Sanity
Liederkranz cheese invented by a local dairy around 1865
Midland County Fair (1922) during which World War One ace Will Fairchild of the Lafayette Escadrille crashed during an exhibition. He wasn't wearing a parachute, and it was Fairchild whom Hippolyte Paul de Mille resurrected at Calvary cemetery at the close of Deadeye Dick.
Midland County Mask and Wig Club

Midland County Rod and Gun Club
Mothers' Day 1944, Rudy kills Eloise Metzger and her fetus
The Quality Motor Court
Rudy Waltz born in 1932
Schramm's Drugstore (where Rudy Waltz worked as the night-shift pharmacist)
Tally-ho Room
YMCA

The Midland City Ordnance Co. *The base of Dwayne Hoover's financial nest egg enabling him to purchase his car agency, Dwayne Hoover's Exit Eleven Pontiac Village.* (*BC* 42:L8-9) Here is where Dwayne got the money to buy the agency: He borrowed it from the *Midland County National Bank*. For collateral, he put up stock he owned in a company which was then called ***The Midland City Ordnance Company***. It later became *Barrytron, Limited*. When Dwayne first got the stock, in the depths of the Great Depression, the company was called *The RoboMagic Corporation of America*.

The name of the company kept changing through the years because the nature of its business changed so much. But its management hung on to the company's original motto—for old time's sake. The motto was this:

GOODBYE, BLUE MONDAY.

Midland County Mask and Wig Club. *The community theater which fulfills the wishes of Fred T. Barry to perform an all-Ohio revival of Rudy Waltz's "Katmandu."*

Midland County Merchants Bank. *The bank which foreclosed on ex-slave Josephus Hoobler's Bluebird Farm, in* Breakfast of Champions. *Dwayne Hoover's father was awarded the farm in an insurance settlement for a car accident. Bluebird Farm is the location of Sacred Miracle Cave.*

Midnight Pussycats. *The pornographic magazine which features on its cover a story about the fate of Montana Wildhack. The editors suspected she was at the bottom of San Pedro Bay, the victim of a gangland-style murder.* (*SL5* 176:6-177:2) Billy *(Pilgrim)* wanted to laugh. The magazine, which was published for lonesome men to jerk off to, ran the story so it could print pictures taken from blue movies which Montana had made as a teen-ager. Billy did not look closely at these. They were grainy things, soot and chalk. They could have been anybody.

Mildred Peasely Bangtree Memorial Theater. *In the play "Jekyll and Hyde Updated" reprinted in* Palm Sunday, *the Sweetbread College theater where a student production of "Dr. Jekyll and Mr. Hyde" is rehearsing to raise funds for the bankrupt institution. The college's real life Dr. Jekyll dies from gun shots on stage as the transformed human sized chicken.*

Miller, Bill (Don?). *Mary Alice Miller's father is inexplicably named both Bill and Don. Bill/Don was a one-third owner of Midland City's Holiday Inn and Chairman of the Parole Board at the Adult Correctional Institution at Shepherdstown.* (*BC* 64:L18) Dwayne owned a third of the inn partnership with Midland City's leading orthodontist, Dr. Alfred Maritimo, and **Bill Miller**, who was Chairman of the Parole Board at the Adult Correctional Institution at Shepherdstown, among other things.
(*BC* 255:L12) Mary Alice's father, **Don Miller**, was, among other things, Chairman of the Parole Board at Shepherdstown. It was he who had decided that Wayne Hoobler, lurking among Dwayne's used cars again, was fit to take his place in society.
(*BC* 260:L10) Mary Alice Miller's father, **Don Miller**, was in his car near Dwayne, waiting for Mary Alice to come back with her crown and scepter, but he never saw anything of the show Dwayne put on. . . . Don was lying on his back, with his head well below window level, resting, staring at the ceiling. He was trying to learn French by means of listening to lessons recorded on tape.

Miller, Lydia and Verne (also **Miller's Hardware Store**). *In the short story "Who Am I This Time?" Verne owns Miller's Hardware Store and employs Harry Nash, the introvert who miraculously changes into character when performing on stage with the North Crawford Mask and Wig Club. Lydia often plays in the community theater, and she tries to warn Helene Shaw, a newcomer to the troupe, not to be seduced in by Nash's on-stage persona.*

Miller, Mary Alice. *The fifteen-year-old Women's Two Hundred Meter Breast Stroke Champion of the World, Mary Alice was the cover girl on the program for the Midland City Arts Festival and also the Queen of the Festival.* (*BC* 217:L29) The cover of the program showed her in a white bathing suit, with her Olympic Gold Medal hanging around her neck. . . . **Mary Alice** was smiling at a picture of Saint Sebastian, by the Spanish painter El Greco. It had been loaned to the Festival by Eliot Rosewater, the patron of Kilgore Trout. . . .
(*BC* 218:L5, 19) The picture **Mary Alice** smiled at with such uncritical bliss showed a human being who was so full of arrows that he looked like a porcupine. . . . *(Her father)*, a member of the Parole Board out at Shepherdstown, had taught **Mary Alice** to swim when she was eight months old, and that he had made her swim at least four hours a day, every day, since she was three.

Mary Alice's legacy is defamed by Rabo Karabekian in the bar at the Holiday Inn. Milo Maritimo hopes Midland City's fortunes will rise through the Arts Festival along with Mary Alice's fame. (*BC* 230:L12) "No longer will Midland City be known merely as the home of **Mary Alice Miller**, the Women's Two Hundred Meter Breast Stroke Champion of the World. It will also be the city which first acknowledged the greatness of Kilgore Trout."

Ministry of Propaganda and Enightenment (see **Howard W. Campbell**).

"The Minorite Church of Vienna." *When Rudy Waltz's father was an aspiring art student in Europe, he befriended another failing artist, Adolf Hitler. Rudy's father bought Hitler's watercolor of "The Minorite Church of Vienna," which hung for years over his parents' bed. At the time, it was the only money Hitler had earned in quite a while. When Hitler became chancellor of Germany, Otto Waltz sent his congratulations and the painting back to his old art buddy. Hitler invited the Waltzes to be his guests for a visit. Only Rudy stayed behind.*

Minot, Dr. Frank. *The author of* Are Adults Harmoniums? *takes issue with the popularity of Sarah Horne Canby's* Unk and Boaz in the Caves of Mercury *because he believes she romanticizes their exploits.* (*ST* 197:L14-25) **Dr. Frank Minot** . . . sees something more sinister in the love children have for the book. "Dare we consider," he asks, "how close Unk and Boaz are to the everyday experience of children when Unk and Boaz deal solemnly and respectfully with creatures that are in fact obscenely unmotivated, insensitive, and dull?" **Minot**, in drawing a parallel between human parents and harmoniums, refers to the dealings of Unk and Boaz with harmoniums. The harmoniums spelled out for Unk and Boaz a new message of hope or veiled derision every fourteen Earthling days—for three years.

Minton, Horlick and Claire. *Horlick Minton is the new American Ambassador to San Lorenzo and travels to the island republic on the same plane as bicycle manufacturer H. Lowe Crosby and John/Jonah, the narrator of the text. He and his wife are described as a* "duprass"—*"a* karass *built for two." Claire had once been a professional book indexer. Horlick had once been fired by the State Department during the McCarthy era* "for pessimism. Communism had nothing to do with it," *as Crosby had intimated in his loud barroom baiting* (*CC* 86:L7-8). *Both Mintons acknowledged it was Claire's letter to* The New York Times *which previously cost Horlick his job.* (*CC* 86:L19-22, 86:L1-13) "'Americans,'" he said, quoting his wife's letter to the *Times*, "'are forever searching for love in forms it never takes, in places it can never be. It must have something to do with the vanished frontier. . . .'"

"What was so awful about the letter?" I *(John/Jonah)* asked.

"The highest possible form of treason," said **Minton**, "is to say that Americans aren't loved wherever they go, whatever they do. **Claire** tried to make the point that American foreign policy should recognize hate rather than imagine love."

"I guess Americans *are* hated a lot of places."

"*People* are hated a lot of places. **Claire** pointed out in her letter that Americans, in being hated, were simply paying the normal penalty for being people, and that they were foolish to think they should somehow be exempted from that penalty. But the loyalty board didn't pay any attention to that. All they knew was that **Claire** and I both felt that Americans were unloved."

The Mintons die together as the walls of the presidential palace crumble into the sea when the San Lorenzan Air Force misfires at the target ships during a national celebration.

Miss Canal Zone. *Malachi Constant's* most recent conquest. There was no question about it—the girl in the photograph was staggeringly beautiful. She was **Miss Canal Zone**, a runner-up in the Miss Universe Contest—and in fact far more beautiful than the winner of the contest. Her beauty had frightened the judges (*ST* 36:L25). *Constant uses her photograph to convince Rumfoord he has no reason to accept his fate as a space traveler. Rumfoord tried to entice him with tales of the beautiful women to be had on Titan, and when he returns Malachi's photograph he slips in another with the image of the three sirens of Titan.* (*ST* 37:L12-21) Within the margins lay shimmering depths. The effect was much like that of a rectangular glass window in the surface of a clear, shallow, coral bay. At the bottom of that seeming coral bay were three women—one white, one gold, one brown. They looked up at Constant, begging him to come to them, to make them whole with love.

Their beauty was to the beauty of **Miss Canal Zone** as the glory of the Sun was to the glory of a lightning bug.

"Miss Temptation" (1956) (see **Norman Fuller**).

Mitchell, Allison. *In the opening chapter of* Slaughterhouse-Five, *Vonnegut explains who went with him on his trip to see his old war buddy Bernard V. O'Hare.* (*SL5* 10:L23) I took two little girls with me, my daughter, Nanny, and her best friend, **Allison Mitchell**. They had never been off Cape Cod before. When we saw a river, we had to stop so they could stand by it and think about it for a while.

Mitchell, Dr. Jerome. (*DD* 165:L25) **Dr. Jerome Mitchell** was married to the former Barbara Squires, the younger sister of Anthony Squires. Anthony Squires was the policeman who had given me the nickname Deadeye Dick. *Dr. Mitchell was Felix Waltz's worst enemy in high school and was believed to sadistically torture dogs and cats all the while claiming to perform scientific experiments. He built his practice by prescribing pain killers for anyone who wanted them. He and his wife lived next door to Dwayne and Celia Hoover and encouraged his wife and Celia to take amphetamines. At Celia's funeral service, Dwayne Hoover loudly blamed Dr. Mitchell for his part in turning her into a suicide.*

Moakely, George Minor. *Dr. Breed informs* Cat's Cradle*'s narrator that on the site of the Ilium Research Laboratory there once stood the town stockade complete with gallows. In 1782 mass murderer George Minor Moakely was* *publicly hanged for killing twenty-six people. The narrator quietly appreciates the irony which escapes Dr. Breed, who finds it mind-boggling that Moakely went to his death unrepentently. Of course, the site of his execution is the same location where Dr. Hoenikker worked on the Manhattan Project and later developed ice-nine.*

Mobutu, President. *In* Hocus Pocus, *Zaire's President Mobutu purchases a San Diego ice cream company which then lays off Jerry Peck. He and wife Muriel return to the family's eastern roots in Scipio, New York.*

Moby Dick. *The great white whale is recalled three times in Vonnegut's novels. In* Breakfast of Champions *Moby Dick is a huge painted boulder in Sacred Miracle Cave. Dan Gregory illustrated an edition of Melville's book in* Bluebeard, *and in* Hocus Pocus *the library display of bell clappers from the Lutz Carillon takes on mythic proportions,* it became a college tradition for upperclasspersons to tell incoming freshmen that the clappers were the petrified penises of different mammals. The biggest clapper, which had once belonged to Beelzebub, the biggest bell, was said to be the penis of none other than **Moby Dick**, the Great White Whale (*HP* 66:L8).

Moellenkamp, Henry. *In* Hocus Pocus, *the nineteen-year-old dyslexic student graduated from Tarkington College in 1875, the school's sixth year of operation and the year its name was changed from The Mohiga Valley Free Institute. Henry's grandfather was a board member and son-in-law of the institution's founder, Aaron Tarkington. He sought the name change because he was afraid his grandson's alma mater would sound like a poorhouse or hospital.*

The Moellenkamp family became great benefactors of the college. They donated the library, which Eugene Debs Hartke points out became the second best small private school library in the country, and they constructed the bell tower which housed the school's Lutz Carillon, which later housed Hartke as he wrote his memoirs. Hartke believes that without Henry's attendance and his family's great generosity, the school would long ago have failed along with the rest of Scipio.

Henry Moellenkamp graduated with honors and went on to Oxford University. He eventually became a congressman and then a six-term United States senator from Ohio. At the turn of the century, Henry wrote the lyrics to "Mary, Mary, Where Have You Gone?" a ballad composed by his friend Paul Dresser, the brother of novelist Theodore Dreiser.

Moellenkamp, Robert W. *In* Hocus Pocus, *Robert W. Moellenkamp is the last Chairman of the Board of Trustees of Tarkington College. He is the descendant of Tarkington's founder, previous board members, and father of two Tarkingtonians. He presides over the board meeting which ousts Eugene Debs Hartke, though he was unaware that at that moment the Microsecond Arbitrage* *stock swindle was becoming public knowledge. He lost his family's ancient fortune and was responsible for the financial failure of the college. As were many other members of the Tarkington and Moellenkamp families, Robert was illiterate due to his extreme dyslexia. However, he was also gifted with Aaron Tarkington's superior ability to memorize after listening to material read out loud two or three times.*

Mohiga Ice Cream Emporium (see **Jerry and Muriel Peck**).

The Mohiga Valley Free Institute (see **Tarkington College**).

Mohiga Wagon Company. *Founded by illiterate dyslexic Aaron Tarkington in* Hocus Pocus, *the company prospered by building the "Conestoga" wagon, the name commonly used to describe the covered wagons used by settlers heading to the western frontier. Aaron's son Elias stipulated in his Last Will and Testament that The Mohiga Valley Free Institute should be established and financially endowed with his shares in the family-owned wagon company, carpet company, and brewery.*

Moncrief, Earl. *Winston Niles Rumfoord's butler in his Newport, Rhode Island, mansion, a trusted friend from the time they played German batball together in Winston's youth. Moncrief is an integral part of Rumfoord's scheme to recruit people for the Army of Mars and their eventual invasion of Earth. While Rumfoord was split in time and space,* The man who managed the Martian investments, headed the Martian Procurement Program and the Martian Secret Service on Earth, the man who took orders directly from Rumfoord, was **Earl Moncrief**, the ancient Rumfoord butler. **Moncrief**, given the opportunity at the very close of his servile life, became Rumfoord's ruthless, effective, and even brilliant Prime Minister of Earthling Affairs (*ST* 172:L13-20). *At the direction of Rumfoord,* **Earl Moncrief**, the butler, built his financial, procurement, and secret service organizations with the brute power of cash and a profound understanding of clever, malicious, discontented people who lived behind servile facades.

It was such people who took the Martian money and the Martian orders gladly. They asked no questions. They were grateful for the opportunity to work like termites on the sills of the established order (*ST* 173:L14). *It was Moncrief's responsibility to parcel out the schematics of Salo's spaceship to different manufacturers around the world and energize them with Universal Will to Become from Salo's ship.*

Monzano, Miguel "Papa." *The self-educated septuagenarian dictator of San Lorenzo in* Cat's Cradle, *the first human being to die of ice-nine poisoning. Years earlier he spared the life of Franklin Hoenikker, who had fled to the island to avoid prosecution in Florida for smuggling cars to Cuba. "Papa" was so enamored to know that Franklin was the son of Felix Hoenikker that he* *made him the Minister of Science and Progress. "Papa" was part of the charade established by Bokonon and McCabe to make Bokononism taboo while working toward civil development of the island. Despite publicly professing to be a Christian, "Papa" was a Bokononist to the very end, receiving the Bokononist Last Rites of boko-maru from Dr. Schlichter von Koenigswald. Monzano fell ill and was laid out in his bed, the converted dinghy from Bokonon's schooner the* Lady's Slipper *and which delivered Bokonon and Corporal Earl McCabe to San Lorenzo when the schooner sank. Now, the dinghy was plated with gold. It was there that "Papa" took the vial from around his neck and ingested the chip of ice-nine given to him by Franklin Hoenikker when he first arrived on the island. When the walls of the castle begin to crumble, the dinghy and the body slip into the water below, turning all the world's water into crystalline ice-nine.*

Monzano, Mona Aamons. *The xylophone-playing blonde negro beauty in* Cat's Cradle. *Mona is the daughter of Finnish architect Nestor Aamons and an unnamed San Lorenzan. Nestor died shortly after completing Julian Castle's House of Hope and Mercy in the Jungle, and Mona was adopted by "Papa" Monzano. Philip Castle named the island's one hotel "Casa Mona," in her honor. After "Papa" Monzano slips into the sea during the catastrophic commemoration of the Hundred Martyrs of Democracy, Mona and John/Jonah take refuge in an oubliette prepared for "Papa" in case of emergency. When they emerge three days later, they find hundreds of bodies in the frozen base of what was a waterfall. John/Jonah sees misery and deceit wrought by Bokonon's suicidal suggestions to the throngs, but Mona sees those suicides as a simple way to solve so much for so many. She then touches her finger to the ground and lifts the specks of ice-nine to her lips.*

Moody, Mary (also **Foxcroft and Melody**). *Mary Moody is descended from a long line of Rosewater County natives well know for arson and bearing twins. Mary was* a suspected arsonist, convicted shoplifter, and a five-dollar whore (*GBR* 172:L14-15). *In the course of the novel, Mary gives birth to twin daughters, Foxcroft and Melody. Long before Norman Mushari convinces Mary to file a false paternity suit against Eliot, she asked Eliot to baptize the twins. This, too, would be used by Mushari in legal action to wrest control of the Rosewater Foundation. In a phone conversation with Sylvia, Eliot says he reluctantly agreed to the ceremony despite having no clerical authority.* (*GBR* 109:L32-34, 110:L1-7) "What will you say? What will you do?"

"Oh—I don't know." Eliot's sorrow and exhaustion dropped away for a moment as he became enchanted by the problem. A birdy little smile played over his lips. "Go over to her shack, I guess. Sprinkle some water on the babies, say, 'Hello, babies. Welcome to Earth. It's hot in the summer and cold in the winter. It's round and wet and crowded. At the outside, babies, you've got about a hundred years here. There's only one rule that I know of, babies—:

"'God damn it, you've got to be kind.'"

Eliot sent each of the twins his usual present for children born in the county: a share of IBM stock.

Moon, Fletcher. *Noah Rosewater paid to have Fletcher Moon take his place in the company of Indiana riflemen raised by his brother George for service in the Civil War. Moon's short service to the cause prompts an exchange of letters between the brothers which reveals the dry wit, greed, and lack of sentimentality so characteristic of their descendant, Senator Lister Ames Rosewater.* (*GBR* 116:L25-34, 117:L1-16) **Moon** was blown to hamburger by Stonewall Jackson's artillery at Second Bull Run.

During the retreat through the mud toward Alexandria, Captain Rosewater took time out to write his brother Noah this note:

> **Fletcher Moon** kept up his end of the deal to the utmost of his ability. If you are put out about your considerable investment in him being used up so quickly, I suggest you write General Pope for a partial refund. Wish you were here.
>
> George

To which Noah replied:

> I am sorry about **Fletcher Moon**, but, as the *Bible* says, "A deal is a deal." Enclosed find some routine legal papers for you to sign. They empower me to run your half of the farm and the saw factory until your return, etc., etc. We are undergoing great privations here at home. Everything is going to the troops. A word of appreciation from the troops would be much appreciated.
>
> Noah.

MoonMist Tobacco, Ltd. *In* The Sirens of Titan, *Malachi Constant tries to avoid the future as outlined by Winston Niles Rumfoord by selling his shares in Galactic Spacecraft and putting all the proceeds into MoonMist Tobacco. The most memorable advertisement for the company* was the picture of the three sirens of Titan. There they were—the white girl, the golden girl, and the brown girl.

The fingers of the golden girl were fortuitously spread as they rested on her left breast, permitting an artist to paint in a **MoonMist** Cigarette between two of three. The smoke from her cigarette passed beneath the nostrils of the brown and white girls, and their space-annihilating concupiscence seemed centered on mentholated smoke alone (*ST* 56:L12-21).

As it turns out, MoonMist assisted the collapse of Constant's empire. The Journal of the American Medical Association *published an article indicating that MoonMist was the principal cause for sterility in both sexes. Ransom K. Fern, manager of Magnum Opus, conservatively approximated Constant's financial exposure to be around $5 billion.*

The image of the three sirens stays with Malachi though his memory was nearly wiped clean on Mars. Malachi eventually sees statues of the three Sirens in a pool on Titan, placed there by Salo.

moral, moralist, morality, moralize, morally. (*ST* 21:L24) Winston Niles Rumfoord was something else again—**morally**, spatially, socially, sexually, and electrically.
(*ST* 72:L9-10) One night in Los Angeles, at any rate, Noel Constant got it into his head to become a speculator. He was thirty-nine at the time, single, physically and **morally** unattractive, and a business failure.
(*ST* 251:L12) At the height of his good luck, Malachi Constant was worth more than the states of Utah and North Dakota combined. Yet, I daresay, his **moral** worth was not that of the most corrupt little fieldmouse in either state.
(*MN* v:L1-2, vii:L16, 18) This is the only story of mine whose **moral** I know. I don't think it's a marvelous **moral**; I simply happen to know what it is: We are what we pretend to be, so we must be careful about what we pretend to be.

. . . There's another clear **moral** to this tale, now that I think about it: When you're dead you're dead.

And yet another **moral** occurs to me now: Make love when you can. It's good for you.
(*MN* 107:L12) "That **Moral** Rearmament movement," he said, "believes in absolute honesty, absolute purity, absolute unselfishness, and absolute love." *A barfly has a conversation with Howard Campbell.*
(*MN* 141:L12, 17,20, 22-23) "I admire form," I said. "I admire things with a beginning, a middle, an end—and, whenever possible, a **moral**, too." *Howard Campbell speaks with Frank Wirtanen.*

"If I'd killed myself when you expected me to kill myself," I said, "maybe a **moral** would have occurred to you. . . ."

"I'm not used to things having form—or **morals**, either," he said. "If you'd died, I probably would have said something like, 'Goddamn, now what'll we do?' A **moral**? It's a big enough job just burying the dead, without trying to draw a **moral** from each death," he said. "Half the dead don't even have names. I might have said you were a good soldier."
(*MN* 154:L9) "*Memoirs of a Monogamous Casanova* is a curious little chapter in Russian history," said Wirtanen. "It could hardly be published with official approval in Russia—and yet, it was such an attractive, strangely **moral** piece of pornography, so ideal for a nation suffering from shortages of everything but men and women, that presses in Budapest were somehow encouraged to start printing it—and those presses have, somehow, never been ordered to stop." *The depth of its passion and sensuality was made moral by its subject matter—the relationship between a husband and wife.*
(*MH* xiv:L17 *Preface*) I used to be a public relations man for General Electric, and then I became a free-lance writer of so-called "slick fiction," a lot of it

science fiction. Whether I improved myself **morally** by making that change I am not prepared to say.

(*MH* 32:L29 *Welcome to the Monkey House*) "He didn't have the slightest idea his pills would be taken by human beings someday," said the Foxy Grandpa. "His dream was to introduce **morality** into the monkey house at the Grand Rapids Zoo. Did you realize that?" he inquired severely. *Foxy Grandpa is actually "Billy the Poet," the outlaw specializing in kidnapping and deflowering Ethical Suicide Parlor hostesses.*

(*SL5* 76:L20) "There are no telegrams on Tralfamadore. But you're right: each clump of symbols is a brief, urgent message—describing a situation, a scene. . . . There is no beginning, no middle, no end, no suspense, no **moral**, no causes, no effects. What we love in our books are the depths of many marvelous moments seen all at one time."

(*WFG* 97:L27, 29 *Address to the American Physical Society*) I have already called the fictitious inventor of the fictitious Ice-9 an old-fashioned sort of scientist. There used to be a lot of **morally** innocent scientists like him. No more. Younger scientists are extremely sensitive to the **moral** implications of all they do. My fictitious old-time scientist asked, among other things, this question: "What is sin?" He asked that question mockingly as though the concept of sin were as obsolete as plate armor. Young scientists, it seems to me, are fascinated by the idea of sin.

(*WFG* 99:L1-28 *Address to the American Physical Society*) I have never seen a more depressed audience leaving a theater. *The Diary of Anne Frank* was a lighthearted comedy when compared with Lilienthal's performance for that particular audience, on that particular night, in that particular city, where science was king. The young scientists and their young wives had learned something which most scientists now realize: that their bosses are not necessarily sensitive or **moral** or imaginative men. Ask Wernher Von Braun. His boss had him firing rockets at London.

The old-fashioned scientist I described in *Cat's Cradle* was the product of a great depression and of World War Two and some other things, of course. The mood of technical people in World War Two can be expressed in slogans such as "Can do!" and "The difficult we do right away; the impossible takes a little longer!"

The Second World War was a war against pure evil. I mean that seriously. There was never any need to **moralize**. Nothing was too horrible to do to any enemy that vile. This **moral** certainty and the heartlessness it encouraged did not necessarily subside when the war was won. Virtuous scientists, however, stopped saying "Can do!"

I don't find this particularly congenial, **moralizing** up here. **Moralizing** hasn't really been my style up to now. But people, university people in particular, seem to be demanding more and more that persons who lecture to them put **morals** at the end of their lectures.

(*WFG* 100:L3-4, 11 *Address to the American Physical Society*) I asked one of my hosts in what way I had offended the audience. He replied that they had hoped I would **moralize**. They had hired me as a **moralist**.

So now when I speak to students, I do **moralize**. I tell them not to take more than they need, not to be greedy. I tell them not to kill, even in self-defense. I tell them not to pollute water or the atmosphere. I tell them not to raid the public treasury. I tell them not to work for people who pollute water or the atmosphere, or who raid the public treasury. I tell them not to commit war crimes or to help others to commit war crimes. These **morals** go over very well. They are, of course, echoes of what the young say themselves.

(*WFG* 267:L18 *Playboy Interview*) VONNEGUT: But my brother has always tried to be alert to the violent uses of what he might turn up, and it saddened him to find out that silver iodide had been used in warfare. So scientists *have* become concerned about the **morality** of what they're doing. It's been happening for some time. Several years ago, Norbert Wiener, the MIT mathematician, wrote in *Atlantic* that he wasn't going to give any more information to industry or the Government, because they weren't gentle people, because they don't have humane uses for things.

(*JB* 178:L1) He told the jury, "This man, although he may not have actually committed the crime attributed to him, is nevertheless **morally** culpable, because he is the enemy of our existing institutions." *Vonnegut quotes Judge Webster Thayer's remarks at the murder trial of Sacco and Vanzetti. He cites the quote from* Labor's Untold Story, *written by Richard O. Boyer and Herbert M. Morais.*

(*PS* xix:inscription)

Whoever entertains liberal views
and chooses a consort that is captured
by superstition risks his liberty
and his happiness.
—CLEMENS VONNEGUT (1824-1906)
Instruction in Morals
(The Hollenbeck Press,
Indianapolis, 1900)

(*PS* 192:L11 *Religion*) Toward the end of our marriage, it was mainly religion in a broad sense that Jane and I fought about. She came to devote herself more and more to making alliances with the supernatural in her need to increase her strength and understanding—and happiness and health. This was painful to me. She could not understand and cannot understand why that should have been painful to me, or why it should be any of my business at all.

And it is to suggest to her and to some others why it was painful that I chose for this book's epigraph a quotation from a thin book, ***Instruction in Morals***, published in 1900 and written by my Free Thinker great-grandfather Clemens Vonnegut, then seventy-six years old:

"Whoever entertains liberal views and chooses a consort that is captured by superstition risks his liberty and his happiness."

(*PS* 201:L6-7 *Religion*) Socrates told us that the unexamined life wasn't worth living. The Louds demonstrated that the **morally** unstructured life is a clunker, too. *The Louds were the subject of a film documentary on average American family life.*

(*PS* 202:L13, 15, 24, 26 *Religion*) "If I have offended anyone here by talking of the need of a new religion, I apologize. I am willing to drop the word religion, and substitute for it these three words: *heartfelt* ***moral*** *code*. We sure need such a thing, and it should be simple enough and reasonable enough for anyone to understand. The trouble with so many of the **moral** codes we have inherited is that they are subject to so many interpretations. . . .

"If we were to try to grow recent strains of hypocrisy in the laboratory, what would we grow them in? I think they would grow like Jack's beanstalk in a mulch of ancient **moral** codes.

"It may be that **moral** simplicity is not possible in modern times. It may be that simplicity and clarity can come only from a new messiah, who may never come."

(*PS* 203:L15, 24 *Religion*) "As an ordinary person, appalled as I am by the speed with which we are wrecking our topsoil, our drinking water, and our atmosphere, I will suggest an idea about good and evil which might fit into a modern and simple **moral** code. Evil disgusts us. Good fills us with joy and brings a sparkle to our eyes. That much remains the same. . . .

"But the worst thing about my **moral** code is that it invites people to have the fun of being glamorously wicked at first, which many of us feel is sexy, and then becoming almost swooningly virtuous at the end. This comes close to being the biography of Saint Augustine, and of several other famous holy men."

(*PS* 204:L21 *Religion*) "At any rate, I don't think anybody ever dreaded hell as much as most of us dread the contempt of our fellowmen. Under our new and heartfelt **moral** code, we might be able to horrify would-be evildoers with just that: the contempt of their fellowmen. . . .

"For that contempt to be effective, though, we would need cohesive communities, which are about as common as bald eagles these days. And it is curious that such communities should be so rare, since human beings are genetically such gregarious creatures. They need plenty of like-minded friends and relatives almost as much as they need B-complex vitamins and a heartfelt **moral** code."

(*Blue* 141:L3) "Painters—and storytellers, including poets and playwrights and historians," he said. "They are the justices of the Supreme Court of Good and Evil, of which I am now a member, and to which you may belong someday!" *(Spoken by Dan Gregory.)*

How was *that* for delusions of **moral** grandeur!

See also: PP 23:L29; 63:L2; 245:L28; 247:L25; *ST* 12:L30; 261:L29; *MN* 107:L8; 135:L1; 141:L15; 144:L27; *CC* 204:L13; *GBR* 22:L32; 35:L30;

36:L34; 37:L1; 70:L2; 101:L11,14; *SL5* 98:L31; *MH—Welcome To The Monkey House* 28:L29; 35:L11; *MH—The Foster Portfolio* 65:L23; *MH—New Dictionary* 111:L8; *WFG—Address to the American Physical Society* 97:L21,27; 101:L7; *WFG—Address at Rededication of Wheaton college Library, 1973* 215:L4; *Slap* 180:L28; 209:L16; *JB* xvi:L7; 217:L8; *PS—Roots* 26:L13; 28:L8; 45:L2; *PS—The People One Knows* 135:L4; *PS—Religion* 208:L12; *PS—Children* 243:L28; *PS—Jekyll and Hyde Updated* 271:L27; 290:L13; *DD* 72:L23; 79:L11; *Gal* 15:L7; 61:L14; 177:L12; 184:L5; *HP* 47:L18; 145:L9; 155:L12.

morale, morale-builders. (*PP* 34:L22) The Meadows was a flat, grassy island in the St. Lawrence, in Chippewa Bay, where the most important men, and the most promising men ("Those whose development within the organization is not yet complete," said the Handbook) in the Eastern and Middle-Western Divisions spent a week each summer in an orgy of **morale** building—through team athletics, group sings, bonfires and skyrockets, bawdy entertainment, free whisky and cigars; and through plays, put on by professional actors, which pleasantly but unmistakably made clear the nature of good deportment within the system, and the shape of firm resolves for the challenging year ahead.
(*PP* 40:L24) Kroner and Baer seemed delighted. They were forever suggesting that teams be formed and games be played as a method for building **morale** in the Eastern Division's family.
(*PP* 54:L17) Finnerty was a magical name again; Paul's feelings about him had swung a full circle. **Morale** and *esprit de corps*, which Paul hadn't felt in any undertaking for years, had sprung up between them in the course of the exhilarating humiliation of Checker Charley.
(*ST* 136:L29) Boaz had arranged things so that he and Unk would be on board the company mother ship for the invasion. . . . It was meant to carry only two men, the rest of the space being taken up by candy, sporting goods, recorded music, canned hamburgers, board games, goofballs, soft drinks, Bibles, note paper, barber kits, ironing boards, and other **morale-builders**.
(*MN* 52:L1) He *(Dr. Jones)* wasn't arrested until July in 1942, when he was indicted with twenty-seven others for: Conspiring to destroy the **morale** and faith and confidence of the members of the military and naval forces of the United States and the people of the United States in their public officials and republican form of government. . . .
(*PS* 70:L16 *When I Lost My Innocence*) I, for one, now know what is really going on, so I can plan more shrewdly and be less open to surprise. But my **morale** has been lowered a good deal, so I am probably not any stronger than I used to be.
(*PS* 212:L32 *Religion*) "Sermons deeply rooted in local history and sociology and politics are by and large harmless, and perhaps even charming in a relatively closed and isolated community. Why shouldn't a preacher in such a society raise the **morale** of his parishioners by implying they are better

servants of God than strangers ar. ? That is a very old type of sermon—very old indeed. As old as the hills. Read the Old Testament."
(*DD* 55:L16) She was none other than Eleanor Roosevelt, the wife of the President of the United States. She was visiting war plants in the boondocks to raise **morale**.
(*DD* 63:L3) ELEANOR Roosevelt, with her dreams of a better world than this one, was well on her way to some other small city by then—to raise **morale**. So she never got to hear me shoot.
(*Gal* 121:L9) He guessed right, at any rate, as to what was going to happen to the **morale** of the people of Ecuador within the next hour or so, when he said to Bobby King on the telephone: "Everybody down there is just going to fall apart when they find out that Mrs. Onassis isn't coming after all."
(*Gal* 145:L17) One thing which made the Air Force such a high **morale** unit was that its equipment, bought on credit and delivered before the bankruptcy, was so up to date.

"More Stately Mansions" (1951) (see **Grace and George McClellan**).

Morgan, Eunice Eliot (see **Eunice Eliot Morgan Rosewater**).

Morissey, Bucky. *The son of Midland City Police Chief Francis X. Morissey. The father and son were part of the infamous 1916 hunting party during which August Gunther's head was accidentally blown off by a point-blank shotgun blast from Chief Morissey. Aside from the victim, their hunting companions included Otto Waltz and John Fortune.*

Bucky was often around loose gun play. He and Felix Waltz used to sneak weapons out of Otto's gun room and shoot crows perched on headstones in Calvary Cemetery, and had cut off telephone service to several farms by shooting insulators along the Shepherdstown Turnpike, and had blasted God-only-knows how many mailboxes all over the county, and had actually loosed a couple of rounds at a herd of sheep out near Sacred Miracle Cave (*DD* 60:L21-27). *Felix once saved themselves from a beating by a gang of boys by pulling a loaded Colt 45 from his jacket.*

Morissey, Francis X. *In* Deadeye Dick, *the Midland City Police Chief who accidentally blew off the head of hunting companion August Gunther in 1916. The other hunters, Otto Waltz, John Fortune, and Bucky Morissey (the chief's son), agreed it didn't pay to ruin Morissey's life because of the accident, so they let Gunther's body drift down Sugar Creek. Years later it was Chief Morissey who came to the Waltz home with news about the death of Eloise Metzger. Morissey knew who used the kind of ammunition which killed her, and he tried to give Otto an opportunity to excuse any knowledge about the incident, but Waltz loudly claimed the blame for Rudy's indiscretion. Much to Morissey's consternation, he couldn't protect his friend from the harsh treatment handed out by the other officers.*

Mother Night (1961) (see also **Howard Campbell**, **cuckoo-clock in hell**, and **Faust**). (*MN* v:L1-4, vii:L12-15) This is the only story of mine whose moral I know. I don't think it's a marvelous moral; I simply happen to know what it is: We are what we pretend to be, so we must be careful what we pretend to be. . . .

If I'd been born in Germany, I suppose I would have *been* a Nazi, bopping Jews and gypsies and Poles around, leaving boots sticking out of snowbanks, warming myself with my secretly virtuous insides. So it goes. *Vonnegut's introduction to* Mother Night *alludes to the timeless dynamic tension pitting appearance versus reality. Musing about life as a German born and bred parallel to his own time frame as a German-American forces the issue of identity into a single dimension. His fantasizing is in recognition of the fact that one's place and function within a given moment of existence is simultaneously defined by outsiders considering the facades we present and by ourselves contemplating the various mitigating factors which prompt our actions. An obvious dilemma arises when the spectators of our lives disagree with our own perceptions about the motives and actions which define us. As difficult as life may be with those critical of our actions, it is all the more contentious when we can't coalesce our own motives and deeds with our preconceived notions of identity. Vonnegut's real concern is with his hyphenated sense of self and, as a result,* Mother Night *is a study of the stateless schizophrenic Howard Campbell, trapped by the peculiarities of heredity and environment which mitigate any attempt to produce a satisfying self-image. Vonnegut's exploration of hyphenated lineage is more concerned with circumstances contributing to the establishment of identity than it is with coalescing one's multiplicity into a satisfying whole.*

Mothers' Auxiliary of the Paul Revere Association of Militant Gentiles. *This civic association gave the racist Rev. Dr. Lionel J.D. Jones a star-sapphire ring in 1940, in* Mother Night.

Mott, Dr. Stewart Rawlings (affectionately known as **"Flocka Butt"**). *The Texas physician who relocated to Vermont to care for Eliza and Wilbur Swain. The twins hold genuine affection for Mott to the extent that Wilbur is excited about the prospect of seeing him in the afterlife along with Eliza. Mott was summarily discharged by the twins' parents when Wilbur and Eliza revealed their true intelligence. Mott's last words to Wilbur were contained in a birthday greeting after he learned of his patients' advanced standing,* "'If you can do no good, at least do no harm.' Hippocrates" (*Slap* 141:L19-20).

Mott's grandson became the King of Michigan.

Mott, Stewart Oriole-2 . *The King of Michigan and arch enemy of the Duke of Oklahoma in* Deadeye Dick. *President Wilbur Swain signed away all the territory governed by the 1803 Louisiana Purchase and turned it over to Mott,* *but the largest part of the land transaction was already in the hands of the Duke of Oklahoma.*

The King of Michigan was also the grandson of Dr. Stewart Rawlings Mott, the physician who took care of the Swain twins at the Vermont estate until they revealed their true intelligence.

Mozart, Wolfgang Amadeus. *Mozart is mentioned in seven Vonnegut works:* Happy Birthday, Wanda June, Breakfast of Champions, Wampeters, Foma & Granfalloons, Slapstick, Palm Sunday, *and* Hocus Pocus. *Mozart is known to play shuffleboard in heaven along with Hitler and Einstein in* Wanda June. *In* Breakfast of Champions, *busts of Mozart and Shakespeare still reside in the high niches of The Bannister, at one time Midland City's leading movie house. Vonnegut quotes from Hesse's Steppenwolf in his essay "Why They Read Hesse," pointing out that the two leading characters in the text are Goethe and Mozart—both favorites of his father.*

Dr. Cordelia Swain Cordiner is the enraged psychometric expert in Slapstick *who compares her talents with Mozart and Einstein.* (*Slap* 92:L24-29) ". . . let me say that asking a person of my calibre to come all this distance into the wilderness to personally administer tests to only two children is like asking **Mozart** to tune a piano. It is like asking Albert Einstein to balance a checkbook. Am I getting through to you, 'Mistress Eliza and Master Wilbur,' as I believe you are called?"

Vonnegut heaps more praise on Mozart when Eugene Debs Hartke recounts the plot of The Protocols of the Elders of Tralfamadore. (*HP* 193:L11-16) If the author was right that the whole point of life on Earth was to make germs shape up so that they would be ready to ship out when the time came, then even the greatest human being in history, Shakespeare or **Mozart** or Lincoln or Voltaire or whoever, was nothing more than a Petri dish in the truly Grand Scheme of Things.

Müller, Gerhard. *The Dresden taxi driver who befriended Vonnegut and Bernard V. O'Hare on their postwar trip to East Germany and the slaughterhouse which saved their lives. Müller was a German POW held by the Americans. His mother was killed in the Dresden firebombing. He sent O'Hare a Christmas card with a sentiment that apparently made a deep impression on Vonnegut.* (*SL5* 2:L1-4) "I wish you and your family also as to your friend Merry Christmas and a happy New Year and I hope that we'll meet again in a world of peace and freedom in the taxi cab if the accident will."

I like that very much: "If the accident will."

Vonnegut dedicated Slaughterhouse-Five *to Mary O'Hare and Gerhard Müller. Mary was the one who reminded Vonnegut that he and his war buddies were mere children in the war: hence, the subtitle, "The Children's Crusade."*

Murra, George and John. *George Murra is the fifth husband of Gloria Hilton in the short story "Go Back to Your Precious Wife and Son." He left his wife and son John after meeting Hilton in preparation for writing a screenplay for* *her. After the couple moves to New Hampshire to be closer to his son's private high school, Hilton becomes disenchanted with Murra, who failed to write anything since their marriage. She leaves Murra and he befriends the bathtub enclosure man, the story's narrator. John is aloof and furious with his father. George is only able to win back John's respect when he follows the advice of his bathtub man and kicks the boy in the ass. They call Murra's first wife back in Los Angeles and plan to reunite.*

Musa Dagh. *In a fit of rage about succeeding generations' ignorance of history, Rabo Karabekian's father apostrophizes the cherished memory of Armenian sacrifice and suffering,* "***Musa Dagh***!" he might say. This was the name of a place in Turkey where a small band of Armenian civilians fought Turkish militiamen to a standstill for forty days and forty nights before being exterminated—about the time my parents, with me in my mother's belly, arrived safe and sound in San Ignacio (*Blue* 17:L3).

Mushari, Norman. *After graduating first in his class from Cornell Law School, this Lebanese-American, son of a Brooklyn rug merchant, is hired by McAllister, Robjent, Reed and McGee, the firm representing the Rosewater Foundation. He was hired with the express purpose of assisting the senior partner, Thurmond McAllister, regain his viciousness. Mushari is viewed as so conniving that other members in the firm whistle "Pop Goes the Weasel" whenever he passes by. Mushari's cutthroat demeanor goes back to the days when as a boy, he papered his bedroom walls with pictures of Senator Joe McCarthy and Roy Cohn. As an adult, he took to heart Professor Leonard Leech's words:* In every big transaction . . . there is a magic moment during which a man has surrendered a treasure, and during which the man who is due to receive it has not yet done so. An alert lawyer will make that moment his own, possessing the treasure for a magic microsecond, taking a little of it, passing it on. If the man who is to receive the treasure is unused to wealth, has an inferiority complex and shapeless feelings of guilt, as most people do, the lawyer can often take as much as half the bundle, and still receive the recipient's blubbering thanks (*GBR* 17:L29-31, 18:L1-7). *Mushari spends all his time trying to find out as much information as possible about Eliot Rosewater's oddities in order to establish legal grounds to shift control of the Rosewater Foundation to Fred Rosewater of Pisquontuit, Rhode Island.*

Mushari, Norman, Jr. *In* Slapstick, *once Wilbur and Eliza reveal their true intelligence to their parents and physician, the twins are separated because it is felt only Wilbur has an opportunity for education and an independent life. While Wilbur is sent to school in Europe, Eliza is institutionalized. Eventually, she is released and hires Norman Mushari, Jr. to represent her in a suit against her mother (her father had previously died in an automobile accident) to regain her inheritance and in another suit against the institution.*

Musket Mountain. *The high hill on the western edge of the campus of Tarkington College, at the foot of which is the local cemetery, in* Hocus Pocus.

The Musketeer. *The Tarkington College alumni magazine first appearing in 1910, and named for Musket Mountain at the edge of campus, in* Hocus Pocus.

Mussolini, Benito. (*PP* 251:L14) "Childish—like Hitler's Brown Shirts, like **Mussolini**'s Black Shirts. Childish like any uniform," said Lasher. "We *(the Ghost Shirt Society)* don't deny it's childish. At the same time, we admit that we've got to be a little childish, anyway, to get the big following we need."
(*CC* 76:L16) In his selfish days he *(Julian Castle)* had been as familiar to tabloid readers as Tommy Manville, Adolf Hitler, **Benito Mussolini**, and Barbara Hutton. His fame had rested on lechery, alcoholism, reckless driving, and draft evasion. He had had a dazzling talent for spending millions without increasing mankind's stores of anything but chagrin.

Mussolini is Dan Gregory's hero. Mussolini's minister of culture, Count Portomaggiore, is also head of the British spy apparatus in Italy all through the war and eventually marries Gregory's lover, Marilee Kemp. (*Blue* 63:L2, 8, 11) The editor *(of the* Luma County Clarion*)* asked me *(Rabo Karabekian)* if I could draw a picture of the Italian dictator **Benito Mussolini**, Dan Gregory's hero of heroes, incidentally, and I did so in two or three minutes maybe, without having to refer to a photograph.

Then he had me draw a beautiful female angel, and I did that.

Then he had me draw a picture of **Mussolini** pouring a quart of something into the mouth of the angel. He had me label the bottle CASTOR OIL and the angel WORLD PEACE. **Mussolini** liked to punish people by making them drink a quart of castor oil. That sounded like a comical way to teach somebody a lesson, but it wasn't. The victims often vomited and shit themselves to death. Those who survived were all torn up inside.
(*Blue* 72:L3-4) **Mussolini** had thanked him *(Dan Gregory)* for a portrait of himself which Gregory had painted as a gift. **Mussolini** was depicted as a general of Alpine troops on a mountaintop at sunrise, and you can bet that every bit of leather and piping and braid and brass and pleating, and all the decorations, were exactly as they should be. Nobody could paint uniforms like Dan Gregory.
(*Blue* 91:L13) Gregory was giving a dinner party in the dining room right below me for, among others, Al Jolson and the comedian W. C. Fields, and the author whose stories Gregory had illustrated countless times, Booth Tarkington. I would never meet any of them because they would never come back to the house again—after a bitter argument with Gregory about **Benito Mussolini**.
(*Blue* 107:L30, 33) Dan Gregory's mansion became three separate brownstones again soon after he and Marilee and Fred Jones left for Italy to take part in **Mussolini**'s great social experiment. Although he and Fred were well into their fifties by then, they would ask for and receive permission from

Mussolini himself to don Italian infantry officers' uniforms, but without any badges of rank or unit, and to make paintings of the Italian Army in action.

Karabekian is forced to listen to Dan Gregory's invectives against modern art, and Gregory goes on to extend his authority as though he and Mussolini were in close agreement on the subject. (*Blue* 139:L28-33, 139:L1-3) "You know the first two things Mussolini would do if he took over this country?

". . . He would burn down the Museum of Modern Art and outlaw the word *democracy*. After that he would make up a word for what we really are, make us face up to what we really are and always have been, and then strive for efficiency. Do your job right or drink castor oil!"

"My work is done" (see **George Eastman**).

myth, mythological, mythology. (*WFG* 22:L20 *Hello, Star Vega*) The saucer **myths** represent a neat compromise between the need to believe in a traditional paternal God and the contemporary pressures to accept the pronouncements of science. . . . *Vonnegut quotes Carl Sagan.*
(*WFG* 229:L1,3, 5-6, 8 *Address to P.E.N. Conference in Stockholm, 1973*) Our influence *(that of writers)* is slow and subtle, and is mainly felt by the young. They are hungry for **myths** which resonate with the mysteries of their own times.

We give them those **myths**.

We will become influential when those who have listened to our **myths** have become influential. Those who rule us now are living in accordance with **myths** created for them by writers when they were young. It is perfectly clear that our rulers do not question those **myths** for even a minute during busy day after busy day. Let us pray that those terribly influential writers who created those our leaders' were humane.
(*PS* 134:L6, 8, 10, 12, 18 *The People One Knows*) The uneasiness which many people will feel about liking *Something Happened* has roots which are deep. It is no casual thing to swallow a book by Joseph Heller, for he is, whether he intends to be or not, a maker of **myths**. (One way to do this, surely, is to be the final and most brilliant teller of an oft-told tale.) *Catch-22* is now the dominant **myth** about Americans in the war against fascism. *Something Happened*, if swallowed, could become the dominant **myth** about the middle-class veterans who came home from that war to become heads of nuclear families. The proposed **myth** has it that those families were pathetically vulnerable and suffocating. It says that the heads of them commonly took jobs which were vaguely dishonorable or at least stultifying, in order to make as much money as they could for their little families, and they used that money in futile attempts to buy safety and happiness. The proposed **myth** says that they lost their dignity and their will to live in the process.

It says they are hideously tired now.

(*PS* 134:L21, 26-27 *The People One Knows*) To accept a new **myth** about ourselves is to simplify our memories—and to place our stamp of approval on what might become an epitaph for our era in the shorthand of history. This, in my opinion, is why critics often condemn our most significant books and poems and plays when they first appear, while praising feebler creations. The birth of a new **myth** fills them with primitive dread, for **myths** are so effective.
(*PS* 172:L2, 5 *Mark Twain*) "This is a miracle. There is a name for such miracles, which is **myths**.

"Imagine, if you will, the opinion we would now hold of ourselves and the opinions others would hold of us, if it were not for the **myths** about us created by Mark Twain. You can then begin to calculate our debt to this one man."
(*PS* 315:L26, 28 *The Sexual Revolution*) But then I said to myself, Wait a minute—those steps at the beginning look like the creation **myth** of virtually every society on earth. And then I saw that the stroke of midnight looked exactly like the unique creation **myth** in the Old Testament. And then I saw that the rise to bliss at the end was identical with the expectation of redemption as expressed in primitive Christianity.

The tales were identical. *Vonnegut notes the structural parallels between* Cinderella *and* Genesis.
(*DD* 44:L21) My mind had been trained by heirloom books of fairy tales, and by the **myths** and legends which animated my father's conversation, to think that way. It was second nature for me, and for Felix, too, and for no other children in Midland City, I am sure, to see candle flames as fireflies—and to invent a King of the Early Evening.
(*HP* 194:L18) But down deep the story *("The Protocols of the Elders of Tralfamadore")* was beginning to work like a buffered analgesic. What a relief it was, somehow, to have somebody else confirm what I had come to suspect toward the end of the Vietnam War, and particularly after I saw the head of a human being pillowed in the spilled guts of a water buffalo on the edge of a Cambodian village, that Humanity is going somewhere really nice was a **myth** for children under 6 years old, like the Tooth Fairy and the Easter Bunny and Santa Claus.
(*FWD* 127:L6, 10) Every cockamamie artificial extended family of FSD sufferers resembles Redfield's Folk Society to this extent: it has a **myth** at its core. The Manson family pretended to believe (the same thing as believing) that its murders would be blamed on blacks. Los Angeles would then be purified somehow by a race war. The **myth** at the core of the political family which calls itself "Neo-Conservatives" isn't that explicit, but I know what it is, even if most of them can't put it into words. This is it: They are British aristocrats, graduates of Oxford or Cambridge, living in the world as it was one hundred years ago. *See also:* *PP* 54:L37-38; *SL5* 35:L22, 25-26; *WFG—Address at Rededication of Wheaton College Library, 1973* 215:L3; *Slap* 189:L23; *PS—The Sexual Revolution* 313:L29; 314:L1-2; *JB* 139:L16; *DD* 38:L28; 156:L32; *HP* 189:L14,18; *FWD* 168:L14.

N

Nash, Harry. *The bland, introverted clerk at Miller's Hardware Store who makes an amazing transformation into each character he plays for the North Crawford Mask and Wig Club in the short story "Who Am I This Time?" Harry was an orphan, left on the steps of the Unitarian Church when only a baby. Helene Shaw, his co-star in the club's production of* "A Streetcar Named Desire," *finally succeeds in developing a relationship with him by giving him new scripts to read with her. She accepts that the only passion she will get from him will be through his portrayal of literary characters.*

Nation, J. Edgar. *The Grand Rapids pharmacist who invented the ethical birth control pill (which completely numbs any sexual urges) in the short story "Welcome to the Monkey House." According to the annual Easter television play about him, he and his eleven children were visiting the zoo when he became disturbed about the "immoral" acts they witnessed in the monkey house.* "He didn't have the slightest idea his pills would be taken by human beings someday. . . . His dream was to introduce morality into the monkey house at the Grand Rapids Zoo" (*MH* 32:L27-30 *Welcome to the Monkey House*). *The story is recounted by the Foxy Grandpa to Nancy, one of the hostesses in the Ethical Suicide Parlor. He turns out to be Billy the Poet, the outlaw specializing in kidnapping suicide parlor hostesses, depriving them of ethical birth control pills, and having sex with them once their minds and bodies are no longer numbed by the pills.*

Nation of Two (see ***Das Reich der Zwei***).

National Council of Arts and Letters. *In the controlling technocracy of* Player Piano *even culture is controlled by computer algorithms. The National Council of Arts and Letters has theorized there are only twelve types of readers and as a matter of economics has established book clubs for each. Plots are* *also limited in number and books are solicited on very strictly contrived terms. The same is true for fine art, as well.* (*PP* 210:L21-27) "Well, a fully automatic setup like that makes culture very cheap. Book costs [sic] less than seven packs of chewing gum. And there are picture clubs, too—pictures for your walls at amazingly cheap prices. Matter of fact, culture's so cheap, a man figured he could insulate his house cheaper with books and prints than he could with rockwool. Don't think it's true, but it's a cute story with a good point."

"And painters are well supported under this club system?" asked Khashdrahr.

"Supported—I guess!" said Halyard. "It's the Golden Age of Art, with millions of dollars a year poured into reproductions of Rembrandts, Whistlers, Goyas, Renoirs, El Grecos, Dégas', da Vincis, Michelangelos. . . ."

"These club members, they get just any book, any picture?" asked Khashdrahr.

"I should say not! A lot of research goes into what's run off, believe me. Surveys of public reading tastes, readability and appeal tests on books being considered. Heavens, running off an unpopular book would put a club out of business like that!" He snapped his fingers ominously. "The way they keep culture so cheap is by knowing in advance what and how much of it people want. They get it right, right down to the color of the jacket. Gutenberg would be amazed."

National Union of Belgium Opticians. *Billy Pilgrim is busy reading an article in* The Review of Optometry *in which Jean Thiriart, Secretary of the* ***National Union of Belgium Opticians,*** *is pressing for formation of a "European Optometry Society." Billy fails to be moved by Thiriart's appeal, but the noon fire siren which sounds simultaneously to his reading causes him to travel back in time to the war.* (*SL5* 50:L9-12) Billy closed his eyes. When he opened them, he was back in World War Two again. His head was on the wounded rabbi's shoulder. A German was kicking his feet, telling him to wake up, that it was time to move on.

"Nature Cruise of the Century." *The brainstorm of New York businessman Bobby King, the cruise was intended to be a two week cruise to the Galápagos Islands aboard the Bahía de Darwin, leaving port from Ecuador on Friday, November 28, 1986. Instead, the ship becomes the link between humanity as it presently exists and the sea lion-like creatures of humanity's future state.*

Necker, Anne Louise Germaine. *According to Malachi Constant's family history,* The family could trace its line back through an illegitimacy to Benjamin Constant, who was a tribune under Napoleon from 1799 to 1801, and a lover of **Anne Louise Germaine Necker**, Baronne de Stael-Holstein, wife of the then Swedish ambassador to France (*ST* 72:L3).

Newcomb, John L. *In the short story "The Big Space Fuck," reprinted in the "Obscenity" chapter of* Palm Sunday, *Newcomb is Wanda June's evidence to her parents that they ruined her prospects in life by their degenerate and uncaring actions. Newcomb rose in life to command a South Dakota security force at a government arsenal stockpiling cholera and bubonic plague. Dwayne Hoobler, Wanda June's father, allegedly chased away the potential suitor by answering the door shirtless, drinking beer, and armed with a holstered pistol.*

neuter. *Aside from a single reference to the neutered Kazakh, Selena MacIntosh's dog, the term is exclusively used by Vonnegut to describe those who willfully live without sex and only minimally participate in life's events.*
(*DD* xiii:L2) The **neutered** pharmacist who tells the tale is my declining sexuality.
(*DD* 133:L29, 34) People talk a lot about all the homosexuals there are to see in Greenwich Village, but it was all the **neuters** that caught my eye that day. These were my people—as used as I was to wanting love from nowhere, as certain as I was that almost anything desirable was likely to be booby-trapped.

I had a fairly funny idea. Someday all we **neuters** would come out of our closets and form a parade. I even decided what banner our front rank should carry, as wide as Fifth Avenue. A single word would be printed on it in letters four feet high:

EGREGIOUS

(*DD* 144:L34, 145:L2) RUDY: It's okay. I don't have any more feelings than a rubber ball. You said how nobody sees me, how I never can get waited on . . . ?
GENEVIEVE: You heard that, too.
RUDY: That's because I'm a **neuter**. I'm no sex. I'm out of the sex game entirely. Nobody knows how many **neuters** there are, because they're invisible to most people. I'll tell you something, though: There are millions in this town. They should have a parade sometime, with big signs saying, TRIED SEX ONCE, THOUGHT IT WAS STUPID, NO SEX FOR TEN YEARS, FEEL WONDERFUL, FOR ONCE IN YOUR LIFE, THINK ABOUT SOMETHING BESIDES SEX.
(*DD* 146:L6, 11) RUDY: **Neuters** don't love anybody. They don't hate anybody either. . . . **Neuters** make very good servants. They're not your great seekers of respect, and they usually cook pretty well.
(*DD* 176:L26-27) To have been a perfectly uninvolved person, a perfect **neuter**, I *(Rudy Waltz)* should never have written a play.

To have been a perfect **neuter**, I shouldn't have bought a new Mercedes, either. That's correct: Ten years after Father died, I had saved so much money, working night after night, and living so modestly out in Avondale, that I bought a white, four-door Mercedes 280, and still had plenty of money left over. *See also: DD* 136:L7; 151:L9,23; 179:L217; *Gal* 243:L23.

"New Dictionary" (1967). *Vonnegut's short essay reprinted in* Welcome to the Monkey House *praising the new* Random House Dictionary.

New York State Maximum Security Adult Correctional Institution at Athena. *Sitting across the lake from Scipio, New York, the home of Tarkington College, this prison houses Eugene Debs Hartke while he writes his memoirs. Once a teacher at Tarkington and later at the prison, Hartke is imprisoned after a massive and bloody jail break, though he did not incite the insurrection.* (*HP* 28:L19-21) When I came to work at Tarkington, there were only 300 students, a number that hadn't changed for 50 years. But the rustic work-camp across the lake had become a brutal fortress of iron and masonry on a naked hilltop, the **New York State Maximum Security Adult Correctional Institution at Athena**, keeping 5,000 of the state's worst criminals under lock and key.

Newt and Catharine. *In the short story "Long Walk to Forever," Catharine is startled by the sudden appearance of Newt, a close but platonic friend since childhood. Newt went AWOL from Fort Bragg to confess his love for her before her planned marriage to Henry Stewart Chasens. Newt's mother told him about Catharine's approaching wedding. Newt and Catharine take a long walk and nap in the woods, and when it comes time for Newt to leave, Catharine's resolve to wed yields, consigning herself to the long suppressed love she held for him.*

"Next Door" (1955) (see **Paul Leonard** and **Lemuel K. Harger**).

Niagara Falls. *In* Hocus Pocus, *the location of the New York state prison for American Indians. Vonnegut notes the Indians called the falls "Thunder Beaver."*

Nicholson, Robert. *Vonnegut's short essay "Where I Live," in the beginning of the collection of stories entitled* Welcome to the Monkey House, *describes the people and culture of Barnstable, Massachusetts. Among the many characters is Episcopalian minister Robert Nicholson. By way of describing the insularity of his neighbors, Vonnegut relates that* At a village cocktail party one time—and the villagers do drink a lot—Father Nicholson was talking to a Roman Catholic and a Jew, trying to find a word to describe the underlying spiritual unity of Barnstable. He found one. "We're Druids," he said (*MH* 6:L15).

In Wampeters, Foma & Granfalloons, *Vonnegut uses Father Nicholson to describe the inability of clerics to create more comforting lies for people.* (*WFG* 239:L24 *Playboy Interview*) VONNEGUT: And we do have the freedom to make up comforting lies. But we don't do enough of it. One of my favorite ministers was a guy named **Bob Nicholson**. He looked like Joseph Cotten, and he was a bachelor Episcopalian priest up on Cape Cod. Every time

one of his parishioners died, he went all to pieces. He was outraged by death. So it was up to his congregation and the relatives of the deceased to patch him up, get him pumped up on Christianity sufficiently to get through the funeral service. I liked that very much: Nothing he was going to say in the standard Episcopalian funeral oration was going to satisfy *him*. He needed better lies.
PLAYBOY: Did you come up with any?
VONNEGUT: I tried. Everybody did. It was a very creative situation, with a minister of God falling apart like that.

Nightmare Ages. *The time frame for* The Sirens of Titan *is set by recalling:* The following is a true story from the **Nightmare Ages**, falling roughly, give or take a few years, between the Second World War and the Third Great Depression (*ST* 8:L12-13).

Nocturnal Goatsucker. *The name given to the whippoorwill by Eliza and Wilbur Swain in* Slapstick. *Later, in a frenzy of creativity, they write a manual on childrearing and call it* The Cry of the Nocturnal Goatsucker *and use the names "Betty and Bobby Brown."*

non-epiphany (see **Terry Kitchen**).

Norman Rockwell Hall. *In* Hocus Pocus, *the one building on the Tarkington College campus not named after a donor family, though it was the Moellenkamps who funded it. The building housed the sculpture studio of Artist in Residence Pamela Ford Hall. When Eugene Debs Hartke took temporary command of the prison encampment established at Tarkington, he installed machine-gun nests in its windows and doorways.*

North Crawford Mask and Wig Club. *The community theater group in the short story "Who Am I This Time?" which brings together the unlikely but highly talented couple Helene Shaw and Harry Nash.*

Noth, Eva. *Howard Campbell's mother-in-law. She witnessed him execute the family's dachshund.* (*MN* 79:L24) Like Resi's dog, **Eva Noth** had fattened dropsically on wartime food. The poor woman, made into sausage by unkind time, stood at attention, seemed to think that the execution of the dog was a ceremony of some nobility.

Noth, Helga. *In* Mother Night, *the German actress and wife of Howard Campbell, Jr., also the daughter of Berlin's Chief of Police and older sister to Resi. Campbell wrote some of his best plays as vehicles for Helga's talents. They were an apolitical couple as far as world events were concerned. Together they formed "Das Reich Der Zwei" (Nation of Two), as described by Campbell. Campbell wrote* Memoirs of a Monogamous Casanova *to honor the* *eroticism and passion they shared for each other. Campbell often remarked that Helga's great gift to him was her uncritical love, never questioning his very public deeds at the Ministry of Propaganda. Helga was lost in the Crimea when the Russians broke through the German lines. Unknown to Campbell until long after the war, he relayed the news of her loss to the Americans during one of his encrypted radio broadcasts.*

Noth, Resi. *The younger sister of Helga in* Mother Night. *During the war she is taken prisoner by advancing Soviet forces, and long after the war she is put to work as an agent assisting George Kraft (Soviet sleeper-spy Iona Potapov) maneuver Howard Campbell out of the country. In order to do so, she is sent to New York posing as her long lost sister. Resi convinces Howard she is Helga, and he begins to trust her. It is left to Campbell's Blue Fairy Godmother, Frank Wirtanen, to tell Howard the truth. When the FBI breaks into Dr. Jones' basement to arrest the plotters, Resi decides to take cyanide rather than face deportation.*

An interesting minor development in the story occurs when Campbell stops by the Noth household and is asked to kill Resi's dog before they evacuate. The date is February 12, 1945, a day before the Dresden firebombing. In Slaughterhouse-Five, *Campbell spends the night of the firebombing with Billy Pilgrim in the underground meatlocker.*

Noth, Werner. *The Chief of Police of Berlin and father-in-law of Howard Campbell. Noth hated Campbell for marrying Helga because he wanted a German soldier for a son-in-law. Despite his hatred for Campbell and his suspicion that he really was an American spy, Noth told Campbell why he no longer cared about what the truth might be, highlighting the eternal dilemma faced by Campbell.* (*MN* 75:L17-27) "And do you know why I don't care now if you were a spy or not?" he said. "You could tell me now that you were a spy, and we would go on talking calmly, just as we're talking now. I would let you wander off to wherever spies go when a war is over. You know why?" he said.

"No," I said.

"Because you could never have served the enemy as well as you served us," he said. "I realized that almost all the ideas that I hold now, that make me unashamed of anything I may have felt or done as a Nazi, came not from Hitler, not from Goebbels, not from Himmler—but from you." He took my hand. "You alone kept me from concluding that Germany had gone insane." *Noth was hung shortly after Campbell left their home.*

nothinghead (see also **somethinghead**). *In the short story "Welcome to the Monkey House," those renegades who refused to take ethical birth control pills were called "nothingheads." The most famous nothinghead is Billy the Poet, also known as Foxy Grandpa. He specializes in kidnapping virgin hostesses from the Ethical Suicide Parlors, starving them of their ethical birth control*

pills, deflowering them, and leaving them with normal birth control pills. (*MH* 27:L7 *Welcome to the Monkey House*) A **nothinghead** was a person who refused to take his ethical birth-control pills three times a day. The penalty for that was $10,000 and ten years in jail.
(*MH* 28:L13 *Welcome to the Monkey House*) "I don't need to remind you girls," the sheriff went on, "that a **nothinghead** is very sensitive from the waist down. If Billy the Poet somehow slips in here and starts making trouble, one good kick in the right place will do wonders."
(*MH* 30:L9 *Welcome to the Monkey House*) It wasn't just Billy the Poet who was attracted to Hostesses in Ethical Suicide Parlors. All **nothingheads** were. Bombed out of their skulls with the sex madness that came from taking nothing, they thought the white lips and big eyes and body stocking and boots of a Hostess spelled sex, sex, sex.
(*MH* 40:L19 *Welcome to the Monkey House*) But Nancy dreamed that millions of insects were swarming about her from the waist down. They didn't sting. They fanned her. Nancy was a **nothinghead**. *Nancy was one of the kidnapped hostesses deprived of her ethical birth control pills, now becoming aware of sexuality. See also: MH—Welcome To The Monkey House* 27:L5; 38:L37; 40:L29; 43:L14; 44:L2; 44:L13; 44:L18-19; 44:L23-24; 45:L31.

Now It Can Be Told. *Kilgore Trout's novel which reveals that all human activity up to that point in time was merely preparation for monitoring the reactions of the reader, that the only purpose in life was to respond to what the creator had set before you.* (*BC* 253:L17-217, 256:L7-16) "Dear Sir, poor sir, brave sir. . . . You are an experiment by the Creator of the Universe. You are the only creature in the entire universe who has free will. You are the only one who has to figure out what to do next—and *why*. Everybody else is a robot, a machine. . . .

"The Creator of the Universe had them invent hundreds of religions, so you would have plenty to choose among. He had them kill each other by the millions, for this purpose only: that you be amazed. They have committed every possible atrocity and every possible kindness unfeelingly, automatically, inevitably, to get a reaction from Y-O-U." *Dwayne Hoover takes this message to heart and goes on a violent rampage.*

Trout had previously purchased copies of Plague on Wheels *and* Now It Can Be Told *to take on his trip to Midland City. Both were the property of pornographic publishers who used the text as filler for their photographs.* (*BC* 56:L22, 24) The jackets of *Plague on Wheels* and ***Now It Can Be Told*** both promised plenty of wide-open beavers inside. The picture on the cover of ***Now It Can Be Told***, which was the book which would turn Dwayne Hoover into a homicidal maniac, showed a college professor being undressed by a group of naked sorority girls.
(*BC* 269:L28-29) The two physicians on the disaster vehicle named Martha were Cyprian Ukwende, of Nigeria, and Khashdrahr Miasma, from the infant nation of Bangladesh. Both were parts of the world which were famous from

time to time for having the food run out. Both places were specifically mentioned, in fact, in ***Now It Can Be Told***, by Kilgore Trout. Dwayne Hoover read in that book that robots all over the world were constantly running out of fuel and dropping dead, while waiting around to test the only free-willed creature in the Universe, on the off-chance that he should appear.

"Now It's the Women's Turn" (see **"Windsor Blue Number Seventeen"**).

O

Oger, Anna Maria. (*PS* 23:L7 *Roots*) They *(Vonnegut's great-grandparents)* were preceded only by four of his sixteen great-great-grandparents, who were Jacob Schramm and his wife, Julia Junghans; and Johann Blank and his wife, **Anna Maria Oger**.

Oglethorpe, James E. *According to Merrihue Rosewater's account of the family, in 1731 John Rosewater II was placed in debtor's prison but* was freed in 1732 by **James E. Oglethorpe**, who paid his debts on the condition that John accompany **Oglethorpe** on an expedition to Georgia. John was to serve as chief horticulturalist for the expedition, which planned to plant mulberry trees and raise silk. John Rosewater would also become the chief architect, laying out what was to become the city of Savannah (*GBR* 164:L34, 165:L1-6).

O'Hare, Bernard B. *Inexplicably, Vonnegut approximates the name of his much-respected and valued war buddy to name the lieutenant who captures the double-agent Howard W. Campbell, Jr. O'Hare and Campbell appear on the cover of* Life *magazine. That capture was the highlight of O'Hare's existence. When he returned from the war he got married and fathered a number of children, all the while moving from one failed business to another. When George Kraft/Iona Potapov informs O'Hare of Campbell's presence in New York, he travels to New York to destroy him. However, O'Hare first tells all the major newspapers and magazines that the escaped war criminal is still alive and in the United States.*

O'Hare arrives at Campbell's Greenwich Village apartment, gets drunk while waiting for his return, and his animosity for Campbell becomes a religious quest. (*MN* 185:L24) **O'Hare** had a far more exciting view of what we were to each other. When drunk, at any rate, he thought of himself as St. George and of me as the dragon.

This meeting produces one of the clearest sentiments in the text by either Campbell or Vonnegut. (*MN* 188:L29, 189:L1-2) "You're pure evil," he said. "You're absolutely pure evil. . . . For all the good there is in you, you might as well be the Devil." *Campbell breaks O'Hare's arm, throws him out of the apartment, and chastises him.* (*MN* 190:L9-21) "I'm not your destiny, or the Devil, either!" I said. "Look at you! Came to kill evil with your bare hands, and now away you go with no more glory than a man sideswiped by a Greyhound bus! And that's all the glory you deserve!" I said. "That's all that any man at war with pure evil deserves.

"There are plenty of good reasons for fighting," I said, "but no good reason ever to hate without reservation, to imagine that God Almighty Himself hates with you, too. Where's evil? It's that large part of every man that wants to hate without limit, that wants to hate with God on its side. It's that part of every man that finds all kinds of ugliness so attractive.

"It's that part of an imbecile," I said, "that punishes and vilifies and makes war gladly."

O'Hare, Bernard V. *Vonnegut's best friend from World War II, O'Hare was a fellow battalion scout with whom Vonnegut was captured and sent to the prison camp in Dresden. They experienced the bombing of Dresden together in the slaughterhouse meatlocker. In 1964 Vonnegut went to visit O'Hare in preparation for writing* Slaughterhouse-Five. *At the time, O'Hare was a district attorney in Pennsylvania. Vonnegut and O'Hare visited Dresden after the war while it was part of East Germany. Vonnegut recounts that when he asked his friend what the bombing of Dresden meant to him, he replied that he no longer believed what his Government said. O'Hare and his wife Mary appear in the first chapter of* Slaughterhouse-Five, *as Vonnegut chronicles his search for materials and meaning of the event.*

O'Hare, Captain Bernard. *In* Slapstick, *Captain O'Hare is the sixty-year-old helicopter pilot who remained stationed in the underground silo in Rock Creek Park with the presidential helicopter. He stayed there throughout the gravitational shake-up and the renaming of all American citizens. Capt. O'Hare flies President Wilbur Swain to Indianapolis for a reunion of Daffodils, then Urbana, Illinois, for an electronic reunion with the dead Eliza via the Hooligan, and lastly to the Swain's childhood home in Vermont. Swain renames O'Hare with the middle name Eagle-1 and later dubs him a Daffodil, making them cousins. Captain O'Hare eventually delivers Wilbur to the observation deck of the Empire State Building, where he lives out the remainder of his life.*

O'Hare, Mary. *Trained as a nurse, Mary is the wife of Bernard V. O'Hare, Vonnegut's war buddy and fellow witness to the Dresden firebombing. Vonnegut dedicates* Slaughterhouse-Five *to Mary O'Hare and Dresden cab driver Gerhard Müller. Vonnegut had gone to the O'Hare house to meet with*

Bernard and jog his memory about experiences of the war in preparation for writing the text. Mrs. O'Hare gave Vonnegut a chilly reception, thinking he was going to glorify their exploits. She breaks in on the men's reminiscence and proclaims, "You were just babies in the war—like the ones upstairs!"

I nodded that this was true. We *had* been foolish virgins in the war, right at the end of childhood.

"But you're not going to write it that way, are you." This wasn't a question. It was an accusation.

"I—I don't know," I said.

"Well, *I* know," she said. "You'll pretend you were men instead of babies, and you'll be played in the movies by Frank Sinatra and John Wayne or some of those other glamorous, war-loving, dirty old men. And war will look just wonderful, so we'll have a lot more of them. And they'll be fought by babies like the babies upstairs."

So then I understood. It was war that made her so angry. She didn't want her babies or anybody else's babies killed in wars. And she thought wars were partly encouraged by books and movies.

So I held up my right hand and I made her a promise: "**Mary**," I said, "I don't think this book of mine is ever going to be finished. I must have written five thousand pages by now, and thrown them all away. If I ever do finish it, though, I give you my word of honor: there won't be a part for Frank Sinatra or John Wayne.

"I tell you what," I said, "I'll call it 'The Children's Crusade.'"

She was my friend after that (*SL5* 13:L21).

O'Hare Paint and Varnish Company. *In* Breakfast of Champions, *the Hellertown, Pennsylvania, manufacturers of* Hawaiian Avocado, *the paint used by Rabo Karabekian for* "The Temptation of Saint Anthony," *the $50,000 painting purchased for the opening of the Mildred Barry Memorial Center for the Arts. Against the painted background, Karabekian placed a single vertical stripe of orange reflecting tape.*

Ohio Adult Correctional Institution. *Dwayne Hoobler was a guard at this institution in the short story "The Big Space Fuck," reprinted in* Palm Sunday *in the chapter entitled "Obscenity."*

Ohio Valley Ornamental Concrete Company. *In* Deadeye Dick, *the company purchased radioactive cement from the Nuclear Regulatory Commission and then resold it to the Maritimo Brothers Construction Company, which used it to construct, among other things, the fireplace in the Avondale home of Rudy Waltz and his mother. The Waltz brothers found it necessary to sue the Maritimos, the NRC, and the Ohio Valley Ornamental Concrete Company for the wrongful death of their mother.*

Ojumwa. *Indicative of Vonnegut's abiding interest in the beginnings of things and the otherwise ironic connections they precipitate, Vonnegut's inclusion of Ojumwa in* Breakfast of Champions *is one such instance. Ojumwa is the African ancestor of Eddie Key, the Midland City ambulance driver who helps remove the wounded from the streets of Midland City after Dwayne Hoover's violent outburst. Ojumwa was captured by the Indaro ancestors of Dr. Cyprian Ukwende, and sold to British slave traders for a musket. Ukwende is one of the Midland City physicians treating those wounded by Hoover.*

oligomenorrhea. *Paul Proteus sarcastically informs his wife Anita exactly what it was about her which drew him to marry her.* (*PP* 153:L8, 10) She *(Anita)* blew her nose. "I must have had something these people don't, or you wouldn't have married me."

"**Oligomenorrhea**," he said.

She blinked. "What's that?"

"**Oligomenorrhea**—that's what you had that these others don't. Means delayed menstrual period."

Olly-olly-ox-in-free. *The "all clear" signal called out at the end of hide-and-seek when it is safe for all players to show themselves. Howard Campbell longs to hear the words which will never be called for him, and Dwayne Hoover deceitfully uses them during his violent rampage to draw out Wayne Hoobler.* (*MN* 18:L1, 5) There was one pleasant thing about my ratty attic: the back window of it overlooked a little private park, a little Eden formed by joined back yards. That park, that Eden, was walled off from the streets by houses on all sides.

It was big enough for children to play hide-and-seek in.

I often heard a cry from that little Eden, a child's cry that never failed to make me stop and listen. It was the sweetly mournful cry that meant a game of hide-and-seek was over, that those still hiding were to come out of hiding, that it was time to go home.

The cry was this: "**Olly-olly-ox-in-free**."

And I, hiding from many people who might want to hurt or kill me, often longed for someone to give that cry for me, to end my endless game of hide-and-seek with a sweet and mournful—

"**Olly-olly-ox-in-free**."

(*MN* 34:L24) I can't say I wasn't warned. The man who recruited me that spring day in the Tiergarten so long ago now—that man told my fortune pretty well.

"To do your job right," my Blue Fairy Godmother told me, "you'll have to commit high treason, have to serve the enemy well. You won't ever be forgiven for that, because there isn't any legal device by which you can be forgiven."

"The most that will be done for you," he said, "is that your neck will be saved. But there will be no magic time when you will be cleared, when America will call you out of hiding with a cheerful: **Olly-olly-ox-in-free**."

(*MN* 185:L7) I looked out through the back windows by the stove, looked down into the foreshortened enchantment of the little private park below, the little Eden formed of joined back yards. No one was playing in it now.

There was no one in it to cry, as I should have liked someone to cry: ***"Olly-olly-ox-in-freeeeeee."***

There was a stir, a rustle in the shadows of my attic. I imagined it to be the rustle of a rat.

I was wrong.

It was the rustle of Bernard B. O'Hare, the man who had captured me so long ago. It was the stir of my own personal Fury, the man who perceived his noblest aspect in his loathing and hounding of me.

(*BC* 260:L32) Dwayne went on calling for Niggers to come talk to him. He smiled. He thought that the Creator of the Universe had programmed them all to hide, as a joke.

Dwayne glanced around craftily. Then he called out a signal he had used as a child to indicate that a game of hide-and-seek was over, that it was time for children in hiding to go home.

Here is what he called, and the sun was down when he called it: "**Olly-olly-ox-in-freeeeeeeeeeeeeeeeeeeeeeeeeeee**."

O'Looney, Francis X. *In* Jailbird, *the Morristown, New Jersey, deputy sheriff who, through a series of odd events, becomes the downfall of the RAMJAC empire. Two years after Walter Starbuck had Mary Kathleen O'Looney quietly buried in Morristown, the engraver of the crypt's doors was arrested for drunken driving and commented on Deputy O'Looney's unusual name, mentioning he had seen it only once before. O'Looney became intrigued about the identity of the woman in the grave and eventually uncovered the truth that she was Mrs. Jack Graham. This led to charges against Starbuck, who admitted to caring for her burial and keeping secret her Last Will and Testament.*

As it turned out, the deputy was not related to Mary Kathleen, and his obsession for the mystery lady drove him to lose all interest in his grandchild, his wife, and his job. He was dismissed from the sheriff's office, and his wife sought divorce from their thirty-two year marriage.

O'Looney, Mary Kathleen. *Mary Kathleen was the daughter of one of the victims of the Wyatt Clock Company fiasco. Workers there used to lick their brushes into a point before applying the radium paint to the clock faces. More importantly, she was one of the four women Walter Starbuck could honestly say he loved. Mary Kathleen volunteered as the circulation manager for the* Bay State Progressive *while Walter was a student at Harvard and co-chairman of the paper. While he learned all about socialism at school, Mary Kathleen read* *his textbooks on her own. She came to believe in the rising tide of unionism breaking upon the country. Walter says that though Mary Kathleen was the only one of his loves not to speak another language, it was she who became his interpreter with the American workers. Though Walter was seeing Sarah Wyatt at the same time, it was Alexander Hamilton McCone who essentially broke up his relationship with Mary Kathleen. When Walter graduated from Harvard, he declined to see her or answer her letters.*

Once Walter and Mary Kathleen stopped seeing each other, she left to join forces with Kenneth Whistler, a union organizer in Kentucky. One night Whistler came home drunk and abusive, so Mary Kathleen left and came upon the kindly Jack Graham who later married her. The young mining engineer founded The RAMJAC Corporation, became a recluse, and died in 1952.

Mary Kathleen increased the company's holdings and eventually sought the same kind of protective measures as Howard Hughes. However, she found security in posing as a bag lady on the streets of New York. She would phone her corporate directives to Arpad Leen and confirm those instructions with a fingerprinted letter sent through the mail. Mary Kathleen escaped the terror of New York's streets by discovering a deep, discarded tunnel beneath Grand Central Station once used to repair steam locomotives.

Mary Kathleen never abandoned her love for Walter Starbuck. In her tattered basketball shoes she kept his love letters and a picture of him alongside Kenneth Whistler. In those shoes was another picture of bales of money from Saudi Arabia earned through the McDonald's Hamburgers Division of RAMJAC. Her Last Will and Testament, also in those shoes, left all of RAMJAC's earnings and businesses to the guardianship of the United States to benefit the people of the United States. (This is vaguely reminiscent of Eliot Rosewater's determination to accept the ridiculous paternity suits as a way of redistributing wealth.) The document is discovered by Walter after Mary Kathleen was sideswiped by a taxi and died in a bathroom stall in her underground refuge. Walter comments on the miscalculations of Mary Kathleen, in part to justify his concealment of her will. (*JB* 231:L1) What, in my opinion, was wrong with **Mary Kathleen**'s scheme for a peaceful economic revolution? For one thing, the federal government was wholly unprepared to operate all the businesses of RAMJAC on behalf of the people. For another thing: Most of those businesses, rigged only to make profits, were as indifferent to the needs of the people as, say, thunderstorms. Mary Kathleen might as well have left one-fifth of the weather to the people. The businesses of RAMJAC, by their very nature, were as unaffected by the joys and tragedies of human beings as the rain that fell on the night that Madeiros and Sacco and Vanzetti died in an electric chair. It would have rained anyway.

The economy is a thoughtless weather system—and nothing more.

Some joke on the people, to give them such a thing.

Two years later, when the will is discovered and the government gains control of RAMJAC's assets, Walter comments further about the inability of a bureaucracy to care for such money-making enterprises. (*JB* 238:L16-17) And

I was suddenly offended and depressed by how silly we were. The news, after all, could hardly have been worse. Foreigners and criminals and other endlessly greedy conglomerates were gobbling up RAMJAC. **Mary Kathleen**'s legacy to the people was being converted to mountains of rapidly deteriorating currency, which were being squandered in turn on a huge new bureaucracy and on legal fees and consultants' fees, and on and on. What was left, it was said by the politicians, would help to pay the interest on the people's national debt, and would buy them more of the highways and public buildings and advanced weaponry they so richly deserved.

Onassis, Jacqueline Bouvier Kennedy (see also ***Jackie***). *In* Galápagos, *she is considered one of the most admired women on the planet. Originally scheduled to take "The Nature Cruise of the Century" aboard the* Bahía de Darwin, *she—along with all the other luminaries—fail to appear.*

Operation Brainstorm. *The military's plan to test the extent of Professor Barnhouse's dynamopsychic abilities. When Barnhouse realizes the government wants to use him as a weapon of destruction rather than as a threat to force worldwide disarmament, he destroys the armaments, preventing their launch, and escapes to a life on the run. This brings on what is known as "The Age of Barnhouse."* (*MH* 164:L12, 27 *The Barnhouse Effect*) The dismay occasioned by this flat announcement was offset somewhat by the exciting anticipation of **Operation Brainstorm**. The general was in a holiday mood. "The target ships are on their way to the Caroline Islands at this very moment," he declared ecstatically. "One hundred and twenty of them! At the same time, ten V-2s are being readied for firing in New Mexico, and fifty radio-controlled jet bombers are being equipped for a mock attack on the Aleutians. Just think of it!" Happily he reviewed his orders. "At exactly 1100 hours next Wednesday, I will give you the order to concentrate; and you, professor, will think as hard as you can about sinking the target ships, *destroying* the V-2s before they hit the ground, and knocking down the bombers before they reach the Aleutians! Think you can handle it?"

The professor turned gray and closed his eyes. "As I told you before, my friend, I don't know what I can do." He added bitterly,"As for this **Operation Brainstorm**, I was never consulted about it, and it strikes me as childish and insanely expensive."
(*MH* 167:L29-32 *The Barnhouse Effect*) *"Gentlemen,"* I read aloud, *"As the first superweapon with a conscience, I am removing myself from your national defense stockpile. Setting a new precedent in the behavior of ordnance, I have humane reasons for going off. A. Barnhouse."*

Ophelia (see also **Hamlet**). *Two women in Vonnegut's work are referred to as Ophelia. Eliot Rosewater addresses his wife "Dear Ophelia" in a letter sent from Elsinore, California. He does so because he sees himself possessing the* *indecision of Hamlet, and his stay in Elsinore provides an apt literary metaphor for his letter home.*

When Walter Starbuck in Jailbird *first sees the emaciated Ruth, he recalls,* She was uninterested in ever trusting anybody with her destiny anymore. Her plan was to roam alone and out-of-doors forever, from nowhere to nowhere in a demented sort of religious ecstasy. "No one ever touches me," she said, "and I never touch anyone. I am like a bird in flight. It is so beautiful. There is only God—and me."

I thought this of her: that she resembled gentle **Ophelia** in *Hamlet*, who became fey and lyrical when life was too cruel to bear. I have a copy of *Hamlet* at hand, and refresh my memory as to the nonsense **Ophelia** sang when she would no longer respond intelligently to those who asked how she was.

This was the song: *How should I your true love know / From another one? / By his cockle hat and staff / And his sandal shoon. / He is dead and gone, lady, / He is dead and gone; / At his head a grass-green turf / At his heels a stone—*

And on and on.

Ruth, one of millions of Europe's **Ophelias** after the Second World War, fainted in my motorcar (*JB* 21:L13-31, 22:L1-3).

Starbuck later makes a comparison between two of the most significant women in his life. (*JB* 155:L7) And contrast Mary Kathleen, if you will, with my wife Ruth, the **Ophelia** of the death camps, who believed that even the most intelligent human beings were so stupid that they could only make things worse by speaking their minds. It was thinkers, after all, who had set up the death camps. Setting up a death camp, with its railroad sidings and its around-the-clock crematoria, was not something a moron could do. Neither could a moron explain why a death camp was ultimately humane.

organism *Vonnegut often describes individual as well as collective activity in terms of his biochemical theories of life.* (*SL5* 61:L2) To the guards who walked up and down outside, each *(railway)* car became a single **organism** which ate and drank and excreted through its ventilators.

(*WFG* 228:L3, 20-26 *Address to P.E.N. Conference in Stockholm, 1973*) Most writers I know, all over the world, do the best they can. They must. They have no choice in the matter. All artists are specialized cells in a single, huge **organism**, mankind. Those cells have to behave as they do, just as the cells in our hearts or our fingertips have to behave as they do. . . .

Where do these external signals come from? I think they come from all the other specialized cells in the **organism**. Those other cells contribute to us energy and little bits of information, in order that we may increase the **organism**'s awareness of itself—and dream its dreams.

But if the entire **organism** thinks that what we do is important, why aren't we more influential than we are?

(*WFG* 237:L11-12 *Playboy Interview*) VONNEGUT: Writers are specialized cells in the social **organism**. They are evolutionary cells. Mankind is trying to become something else; it's experimenting with new ideas all the time. And writers are a means of introducing new ideas into the society, and also a means of responding symbolically to life. I don't think we're in control of what we do. *See also:* *WJ* 154:L20; *BC* 207:L25; *Slap* 206:L13; *Gal* 184:L28; *Blue* 154:L31; *FWD* 104:L1.

Ortiz, Jesús. *The bartender in the Hotel El Dorado,* a twenty-year-old descendent of proud Inca noblemen. . . . Nature's experiment with admiration for the rich (*Gal* 6:L25, 82:L18-19).

Orwell, George. (*WFG* 94:L8-9) . . . a man I admire almost more than any other man.
(*HP* 197:L28-29, 32) Do I *(Eugene Debs Hartke)* resent rich people? No. The best or worst I can do is notice them. I agree with the great Socialist writer **George Orwell**, who felt that rich people were poor people with money. I would discover this to be the majority opinion in the prison across the lake as well, although nobody over there had ever heard of **George Orwell**. Many of the inmates themselves had been poor people with money before they were caught, with the most costly cars and jewelry and watches and clothes. Many, as teenage drug dealers, had no doubt owned bicycles as desirable as the one I found in the weeds in the highlands of Scipio. *See also: WFG—Science Fiction* 4:L18; *WFG—A Political Disease* 234:L27.

Osterman (see also **Farmers of Southwestern Ohio for Nuclear Sanity**). *In* Deadeye Dick, *Osterman is the farmer who tells Rudy Waltz and Bernard Ketchum his conspiracy theory about who neutron-bombed Midland City. He was handing out leaflets for Farmers of Southwestern Ohio for Nuclear Sanity, asking citizens to write their congressmen.*

Ostrovsky, Erika (see **Céline**).

oubliette. *Usually considered a dungeon with a trapdoor in the ceiling, Vonnegut uses the device for the savlation of his characters. In* Cat's Cradle, *Papa Monzano's lavishly outfitted oubliette was designed as a sort of fallout shelter. When his frozen body falls into the sea, John/Jonah and Celia Aamons Monzano take shelter there until the storms subside. Prior to this incident, John/Jonah uses the image of an oubliette to characterize Franklin Hoenikker's escape from becoming President of San Lorenzo.* (*CC* 184:L3) And I realized that my agreeing to be boss had freed Frank to do what he wanted to do more than anything else, to do what his father had done: to receive honors and creature comforts while escaping human responsibilities. He was accomplishing this by going down a spiritual **oubliette**.
(*CC* 214:L1-8) Then he *(Bokonon)* speaks of the rack and the peddiwinkus and the iron maiden and the *veglia* and the **oubliette**.

In any case, there's bound to be much crying,
But the **oubliette** alone will let you think while dying.

And so it was in Mona's and my rock womb. At least we could think. And one thing I thought was that the creature comforts of the dungeon did nothing to mitigate the basic fact of **oubliation**.

(*CC* 216:L4) "Today I will be a Bulgarian Minister of Education," Bokonon tells us. "Tomorrow I will be Helen of Troy." His meaning is crystal clear: Each one of us has to be what he or she is. And, down in the **oubliette**, that was mainly what I thought—with the help of *The Books of Bokonon*.

Bokonon invited me to sing along with him:

We do, doodley do, doodley, do, doodley do,
What we must, muddily must, muddily must, muddily must;
Muddily do, muddily do, muddily do, muddily do,
Until we bust, bodily bust, bodily bust, bodily bust.

I made up a tune to go with that and I whistled it under my breath as I drove the bicycle that drove the fan that gave us air, good old air.

The remaining reference to an oubliette comes from Dr. Brown's description of the mental processes one goes through when suffering Samaritrophia, as did Sylvia Rosewater. (*GBR* 54:L28) They rebel at last. They pitch the tyrannous conscience down an **oubliette**, weld shut the manhole cover of that dark dungeon. They can hear the conscience no more. In the sweet silence, the mental processes look about for a new leader, and the leader most prompt to appear whenever the conscience is stilled, Enlightened Self-interest, does appear. Enlightened Self-interest gives them a flag, which they adore on sight. It is essentially the black and white Jolly Roger, with these words written beneath the skull and crossbones, "The hell with you, Jack, I've got mine!" *See also:* *CC* 175:L13; 179:L28; 182:L21; 213:L28; 219:L13; 222:L7; *GBR* 55:L11.

P

Pabu (see also **Bokononism**). (*CC* 156:L33-36, 157:L1-10) I learned some things, but they were scarcely helpful. I learned of the Bokononist cosmogony, for instance, wherein *Borasisi*, the sun, held ***Pabu***, the moon, in his arms, and hoped that ***Pabu*** would bear him a fiery child.

But poor ***Pabu*** gave birth to children that were cold, that did not burn; and *Borasisi* threw them away in disgust. These were the planets, who circled their terrible father at a safe distance.

Then poor ***Pabu*** herself was cast away, and she went to live with her favorite child, which was Earth. Earth was ***Pabu***'s favorite because it had people on it; and the people looked up at her and loved her and sympathized.

And what opinion did Bokonon hold of his own cosmogony? "*Foma!* Lies!" he wrote. "A pack of *foma!*"

Padwee, Dr. Howard. *The veterinarian who diagnoses the false pregnancy of Walter Starbuck's Lhasa apso. The dog was caring for a rubber ice-cream cone as though it were her puppy. Starbuck takes this opportunity to reach for some greater insight as he prepares to return to prison.* (*JB* 236:L14-23) I observe how profoundly serious Nature has made her about a rubber ice-cream cone—brown rubber cone, pink rubber ice cream. I have to wonder what equally ridiculous commitments to bits of trash I myself have made. Not that it matters at all. We are here for no purpose, unless we can invent one. Of that I am sure. The human condition in an exploding universe would not have been altered one iota if, rather than live as I have, I had done nothing but carry a rubber ice-cream cone from closet to closet for sixty years.

Pahlavi Pavilion. *The student recreation center at Tarkington College in* Hocus Pocus. *In order to construct the building in 1995, the graves of Hermann and Sophia Shultz were moved to Musket Mountain. Aside from displacing graves, the facility's bowling alley, pool hall, and ice-cream parlor* *forced local Scipio businesses to close. One night Pamela Ford Hall got Eugene Debs Hartke drunk on blackberry brandy and he went to the Pahlavi Pavilion, gathered an audience of students, and told them of the atrocities committed during the Vietnam War. He was tape recorded by Kimberley Wilder, whose father used the incident as part of the Board of Trustees' case to fire Hartke, partly due to his "teaching pessimism." After the prison break in Athena, Hartke served as temporary warden on the Tarkington campus and ordered machine gun placements in the windows and doorways of the recreation center.*

Palace of the League of Nations. *The Tralfamadorians used their Universal Will to Become to send messages concerning the status of the replacement part for Salo's spaceship. The messages were conveyed in great architectural monuments on Earth that could be monitored by Salo.* (*ST* 271:L32) The meaning of the **Palace of the League of Nations** in Geneva, Switzerland, is: *"Pack up your things and be ready to leave on short notice."*

Palm Sunday (1981). *The second of Vonnegut's collections of essays. It is also the title of a sermon he delivered at St. Clement's Episcopal Church in Manhattan, included in the chapter entitled "In the Capital of the World." It is mostly about The Sermon on the Mount, a text of great significance in* Jailbird.

"Pan Galactic Straw-boss." *In* Breakfast of Champions, *one of Kilgore Trout's short stories, which found its way into publication in a pornographic magazine. It's title was changed to "Mouth Crazy" and illustrated with pictures of naked women. No information is provided about the narrative.*

Pan-Galactic Humbug (subtitled ***Three Billion Dupes***). *Written by Winston Niles Rumfoord's chief detractor Dr. Maurice Rosenau, in* Sirens of Titan, *the text asserts that despite all of Rumfoord's shortcomings and braggadocio, he never intimated he was God or an agent of God.*

The Pan-Galactic Memory Bank. (*BC* 278:L26) I *(Vonnegut)* could go on and on with the intimate details about the various lives of people on the super-ambulance, but what good is more information?

I agree with Kilgore Trout about realistic novels and their accumulations of nit-picking details. In Trout's novel, ***The Pan-Galactic Memory Bank***, the hero is on a space ship two hundred miles long and sixty-two miles in diameter. He gets a realistic novel out of the branch library in his neighborhood. He reads about sixty pages of it, and then he takes it back.

The librarian asks him why he doesn't like it, and he says to her, "I already know about human beings."

And so on.

Pan-Galactic Space Service. *Army of Mars recruiters George Helmholtz and Roberta Wiley are members of the Pan-Galactic Space Service in* Sirens of Titan.

Pan-Galactic Three-Day Pass. *In* God Bless You, Mr. Rosewater, *Eliot purchases this Kilgore Trout novel to read on his bus trip to Indianapolis to meet his wife Sylvia. The story is about Sergeant Raymond Boyle, an English teacher attached to an intergalactic crew of explorers. Boyle receives an emergency three-day pass because the Milky Way died. Thrown into a catatonic trance, Eliot looks up and hallucinates a vision of Indianapolis consumed by firestorm. Eliot's only recollection is of the book held so secretly in his bedroom in Rosewater County,* The Bombing of Germany *by Hans Rumpf.* (*GBR* 201:L11-18) Eliot, rising from his seat in the bus, beheld the firestorm of Indianapolis. He was awed by the majesty of the column of fire, which was at least eight miles in diameter and fifty miles high. The boundaries of the column seemed absolutely sharp and unwavering, as though made of glass. Within the boundaries, helixes of dull red embers turned in stately harmony about an inner core of white. The white seemed holy.

At this point in the narrative there is a one-year gap during which time Eliot is cared for in Dr. Brown's Indianapolis sanitarium.

Parachute Ski Marines. *One of the military units on Mars preparing to invade Earth, in* The Sirens of Titan. *Winston Niles Rumfoord wore their uniform when materializing on Mars for strategy meetings.*

Parrot, Wilfred. *The manager of the Pawtucket, Rhode Island, orphanage founded by Castor Buntline in 1878, in* God Bless You, Mr. Rosewater. *The sixty-year-old Parrot fought in the Abraham Lincoln Brigade and wrote for the radio series "Beyond the Blue Horizon" in the mid 1930s. The Buntlines regularly take in one of the female orphans to train as domestic servants. Selena Deal is one such girl, and she confides in her weekly letters to "Daddy Parrot" that she doesn't understand the Buntlines.*

Patton, Jack. *The West Point classmate, close friend, and eventual brother-in-law of Eugene Debs Hartke in* Hocus Pocus. *Remembered for his often-repeated phrase, "I had to laugh like hell," Patton never took anything too seriously, and Hartke compares him to prison-break leader Alton Darwin. Patton introduced Hartke to his mother Mildred and his sister Margaret when they visited West Point for graduation. Jack was last in his class. He was killed by a fifteen-year-old sniper in Vietnam while serving as a Lieutenant Colonel in the Combat Engineers. While in high school, Patton built an electric chair for rats, but never used it.*

It was Patton who sent Hartke a copy of "Black Garterbelt" magazine, containing the short story "The Protocols of the Elders of Tralfamadore." Hartke doesn't read it until around the same time the prisoners at Athena were learning how to read using the anti-Semitic forgery, The Protocols of the Elders of Zion.

Patton, Margaret and Mildred. *The wife and mother-in-law of Eugene Debs Hartke in* Hocus Pocus. *Margaret is the sister of Jack Patton, Hartke's best friend at West Point. She and Hartke met at his West Point graduation. Both Margaret and Mildred suffered from hereditary insanity which didn't set in until middle age. This was unknown to Hartke when they married and had children, but their children hated them for bringing them into the world so genetically fated. Hartke found out about the family's medical history while standing at the urinal in a Boston Chinese restaurant and speaking with a man who was a hometown acquaintance of the Pattons back in Peru, Indiana. After Hartke was incarcerated, Margaret and Mildred were taken to the "Laughing Academy" in Batavia, New York, in the same steel boxes which brought convicts to the prison.* (*HP* 16:L34) The biggest booby trap Fate set for me, though, was a pretty and personable young woman named **Margaret Patton**, who allowed me to woo and marry her soon after my graduation from West Point, and then had 2 children by me without telling me that there was a powerful strain of insanity on her mother's side of the family.

Peach, Delbert. *The town drunk in Rosewater, Indiana, who fears Eliot will leave for Indianapolis and never return. As a going-away gift to Eliot, Peach tells him that only ten minutes ago he swore off liquor. Eliot tells him his fate is to remain in Rosewater, that even if he tried to leave, forces of biblical proportion would bring him back.* (*GBR* 171:L8-19) "Mr. Peach—" and Eliot rubbed his eyes, "if I were to somehow wind up in New York, and start living the highest of all possible lives again, you know what would happen to me? The minute I got near any navigable body of water, a bolt of lightning would knock me into the water, a whale would swallow me up, and the whale would swim down to the Gulf of Mexico and up the Mississippi, up the Ohio, up the Wabash, up the White, up Lost River, up Rosewater Creek. And that whale would jump from the creek into the Rosewater Inter-State Ship Canal, and it would swim down the canal to this city, and spit me out in the Parthenon. And there I'd be."

Peale, Delmar. *In* Jailbird, *the only salesman of the American Harp Company located on the top floor of the Chrysler Building. He and his secretary, eighty-seven-year old Doris Kramm, are featured in* People *magazine as the oldest boss and secretary team known to man. Peale has Walter Starbuck arrested when he appears in the showroom with stolen clarinet parts as listed on a police circular. When RAMJAC takes over American Harp and Starbuck becomes the CEO, Delmar Peale makes a present of the police circular to Walter.*

Pearls Before Swine. Vonnegut uses this biblical phrase as the subtitle for *God Bless You, Mr. Rosewater*. The text is from Matthew 7:6, which reads, "Give not that which is holy unto the dogs, neither cast ye your pearls before swine, lest they trample them under their feet, and turn again and rend you."

Peck, Jerry and Muriel. *The owners of the Mohiga Ice Cream Emporium in Scipio, New York, in* Hocus Pocus. *Though both had graduated with degrees in English literature from Swarthmore College, neither became teachers until Muriel filled the vacated position at Tarkington created by Eugene Debs Hartke's dismissal. Jerry was a direct descendant of John Peck, the first President of The Mohiga Valley Free Institute, but was raised in San Diego. When the couple first married, Jerry worked for an ice cream company in his hometown, but he lost his job when the company was purchased by Zaire's President Mobutu. They decided to return to the home of the family's eastern roots, Scipio. They purchased a store on Clinton Street and Jerry went to work stripping all the paint and renovating the building for their new enterprise, the Mohiga Ice Cream Emporium. He failed to read the cautionary warnings on the cans of paint stripper, and by the time they opened for business, Jerry was wheelchair-bound and breathing with the assistance of an oxygen tank. Jerry's disabilities from the renovation eventually killed him. Six months after the ice-cream parlor opened the designers of the new Pahlavi Pavilion recreation center took photographs of its interior and incorporated a similar facility into their building. This was yet another business destroyed by Pahlavi Pavilion. Muriel went to work as a bartender at the Black Cat Café. She and Hartke eventually became lovers. Muriel was killed in the prison uprising when the escapees came across the frozen lake. She was buried with the others in the shadow of Musket Mountain.*

Peck, John. *The twenty-six-year old school teacher from Athena, New York, brought to nearby Scipio to become the first President of The Mohiga Valley Free Institute, in* Hocus Pocus. *Though a cousin of the founding Tarkington family, his branch of the family did not suffer the dyslexia so common to the others. Elias Tarkington moved John Peck and his family into his own home, which also served as the school's first building, and moved his own collection of perpetual-motion machines to the attic, where they were found in 1978 by Eugene Debs Hartke.*

Pefko, Captain Julian. *The officer in charge of visitation to the neutron-bombed Midland City, in* Deadeye Dick. *Pefko agrees to let Hippolyte Paul de Mille and the Waltz brothers visit Calvary Cemetery where de Mille raises the spirit of aviator Will Fairchild.*

Pefko, Francine. *There are two appearances of Francine Pefko, though they bear little resemblance to each other. Her first appearance occurs during the Ilium Research Laboratory tour conducted by Dr. Breed for the visiting* *narrator of* Cat's Cradle. *Miss Pefko is the secretary of Dr. Nilsak Horvath, and she is invited by Dr. Breed to accompany them on their way to Dr. Hoenikker's laboratory.* (*CC* 36:L14) **Miss Pefko** was twenty, vacantly pretty, and healthy—a dull normal. *Despite working at the lab for nearly a year, Miss Pefko seemed terminally baffled by all she typed. She is embarrassed by her ignorance, but even more flustered with her superiors.* (*CC* 37:L12) "You scientists *think* too much," blurted Miss Pefko. She laughed idiotically. Dr. Breed's friendliness had blown every fuse in her nervous system. She was no longer responsible. "You *all* think too much."

The vacant Miss Pefko is reinvented for Breakfast of Champions, *becoming the managing secretary at Dwayne Hoover's Exit Eleven Pontiac Village as well as his mistress. She was widowed when her husband Robert Pefko was killed in Vietnam. He died shortly after Dwayne's wife killed herself by drinking Drano. By the time Dwayne started to develop a severe case of paranoia, he mistook Francine's suggestion of starting a new Kentucky Fried Chicken store as her way of looking for repayment for all the sex they had. In reality, she thought it would simply be a wise investment since the visitors at the Shepherdstown Correctional Facility needed some place to eat. Her thinking was innocently pure toward Dwayne and the product of racial stereotyping since she felt fried chicken would be the best product for all the black visitors going to the prison. Later, when Dwayne begins his violent rampage, Francine is one of his first targets. He dragged her from the Pontiac showroom so he could beat her in the parking lot for all to see.* (*BC* 272:L28-33, 273:L1-2) Dwayne had already broken her jaw and three ribs in the office. When he trundled her outside, there was a fair-size crowd which had drifted out of the cocktail lounge and the kitchen of the new Holiday Inn. "Best fucking machine in the State," he told the crowd. "Wind her up, and she'll fuck you and say she loves you, and she won't shut up till you give her a Colonel Sanders Kentucky Fried Chicken franchise." *She was saved by Kilgore Trout, who paid for his chivalry by having his ring finger bitten off by Dwayne.*

Pefko, Robert. *The husband of the Francine Pefko appearing in* Breakfast of Champions. *A West Point graduate and career military officer, he took a Master's Degree in Anthropology from the University of Pennsylvania and returned to West Point to teach Social Science. He was sent to Midland City to supervise the construction of military booby traps. From there, he was sent to Vietnam, where he died around the same time Celia Hoover committed suicide.*

Pena, Harry (also **Manny and Kenny**). *The Chief of the Pisquontuit Volunteer Fire Department, son of a trap fisherman, and former insurance salesman, Harry falls victim to chemical exposure (from a carpet cleaner), is forced to work outdoors, and so returns to the sea to make his living as his father did.* (*GBR* 126:L16) **Harry** was middle-aged and bandy-legged, but he had a head and shoulders Michelangelo might have given to Moses or God. *He* *and his sons Manny and Kenny do their fish trapping from their boat the* Mary, *in Pisquontuit Bay, within viewing distance of the patrons at* The Weir, *the restaurant belonging to Bunny Weeks. Bunny used the opportunity to inform various guests about the labors of the Penas, using them as part of the restaurant's ambience.* (*GBR* 143:L5) **Harry Pena** and his boys knew about the salad and the cocktail and the opera glasses, though they had never visited *The Weir*. Sometimes they would respond to their involuntary involvement with the restaurant by urinating off the boat. They called this ". . . *making cream of leek soup for Bunny Weeks.*"

Bunny Weeks is disgusted with the romanticism attached to the Penas by some of his patrons, particularly Caroline Rosewater. He uses information known to him as one of the local bank's directors to inform her that their romanticism is groundless. (*GBR* 151:L9-20) "Real people don't make their livings that way any more. Those three romantics out there make as much sense as Marie Antoinette and her milkmaids. When the bankruptcy proceedings begin—in a week, a month, a year—they'll find out that their only economic value was as animated wallpaper for my restaurant here." Bunny, to his credit, was not happy about this. "That's all over, men working with their hands and backs. They are not needed."

"Men like Harry will always win, won't they?" said Caroline.

"They're losing everywhere." Bunny let go of Amanita.

Penfield, Frederic Courtland. (*DD* xiii:L12-13) This is fiction, not history, so it should not be used as a reference book. I say, for example, that the United States Ambassador to Austria-Hungary at the outbreak of the First World War was Henry Clowes, of Ohio. The actual ambassador at that time was **Frederic Courtland Penfield** of Connecticut.

Pennwalt Biphetamine. *This is the narcotic of choice for Celia Hoover (née Hildreth) in* Deadeye Dick. *She comes into Rudy Waltz's pharmacy and he mentally constructs a playlet of her demanding the drug. When Rudy turns her down, she has a fit and wrecks the pharmacy's counter displays.*

perpetual-motion machine. (*JB* 180:L19) And I am now compelled to wonder if wisdom has ever existed or can ever exist. Might wisdom be as impossible in this particular universe as a **perpetual-motion machine**? *This is Vonnegut's thinking after noting the social luminaries who telegrammed their support for Sacco and Vanzetti. Judge Thayer did not believe in the evidentiary guilt of the charges for which he would sentence them to death—it was their politics he despised.*

Perpetual-motion machines are the intellectual curiosity riveting the attention of Elias Tarkington, founder of the college bearing his name. (HP 23:L7) He was not well educated, and was more a mechanic than a scientist, and so spent his last 3 years trying to invent what anyone familiar with Newton's Laws would have known was an impossibility, a **perpetual-motion**

machine. He had no fewer than 27 contraptions built, which he foolishly expected to go on running, after he had given them an initial spin or whack, until Judgment Day.
(HP 24:L23) Still another **perpetual-motion machine** envisioned by Elias Tarkington was what his Last Will and Testament called "The Mohiga Valley Free Institute." Upon his death, this new school would take possession of his 3,000-hectare estate above Scipio, plus half the shares in the wagon company, the carpet company, and the brewery. The other half was already owned by his sisters far away. On his deathbed he predicted that Scipio would 1 day be a great metropolis and that its wealth would transform his little college into a university to rival Harvard and Oxford and Heidelberg.

Once Tarkington passes away, the machines are moved to the attic to make room for classrooms and a library. There they remain until Eugene Debs Hartke finds them in 1978 when he searches for the entrance to the bell tower. (*HP* 24:L7-13) Yes, and we took the 10 machines we agreed were the most beguiling, and we put them on permanent exhibit in the foyer of this library underneath a sign whose words can surely be applied to this whole ruined planet nowadays:

THE COMPLICATED FUTILITY OF IGNORANCE

The display and the sign become evidence against Hartke when the Board of Trustees seek to fire him for, among other things, "teaching pessimism." See also: HP 26:L9-10; 66:L3-4; 126:L2.

Peterson, Mrs. Lyman R. *One of the many citizens who answer the call to arms provoked by the invasion from Mars.* (*ST* 170:L4) At the Battle of Boca Raton, in Florida, U.S.A., for instance, **Mrs. Lyman R. Peterson** shot four members of the Martian Assault Infantry with her son's .22 caliber rifle. She picked them off as they came out of their space ship, which had landed in her back yard.

She was awarded the Congressional Medal of Honor posthumously.

Phi Beta Kappa. *A large number of Vonnegut's characters earned membership in this national academic honor society including: the ugly wife of a handsome dullard, both members of Reverend Redwine's Church of God the Utterly Indifferent in Newport, Rhode Island, as well as Winston Niles Rumfoord (*Sirens*); Caroline Rosewater and Bunny Weeks (*Rosewater*); Wilbur Swain (*Slapstick*); Israel Edel (*Jailbird*); and Jason Wilder (*Hocus Pocus*). In* Jailbird, *Walter Starbuck mentions that many of his fellow inmates during the Watergate era were members.*

Phoebe. *In* The Sirens of Titan, *Phoebe is the only city established on Mars by Winston Niles Rumfoord and powered by Salo's UWTB (Universal Will to Become). At its height, Phoebe is home to eighty-seven thousand people who* *work mainly in munitions factories. It is also the location of the Schliemann Breathing School and Mars' only grade school. Phoebe is destroyed when thermonuclear bombs are launched at Mars as part of a counterstrike to the invasion fleet.*

Phoebe is also the name of a moon of Titan. When Chrono, the son of Malachi Constant and Beatrice Rumfoord, joins the Titanic Bluebirds, he is frequently heard crying out to Phoebe as it passes in the night sky.

Piatigorsky, Dr. Albert Aquamarine-1. *In* Slapstick, *President Wilbur Swain's science advisor who succumbs to the Albanian Flu, expiring in the arms of his president in the Oval Office.*

Piatigorsky, Gregor. *In* Deadeye Dick, *the renowned cellist is among the many illustrious people brought to perform at the Midland City YMCA and later tour Otto Waltz's in-home art studio.*

Pilgrim, Barbara and Robert. *The children of Billy and Valencia Pilgrim.*
(*SL5* 21:L21-26) In time, his daughter **Barbara** married another optometrist, and Billy set him up in business. Billy's son **Robert** had a lot of trouble in high school, but then he joined the famous Green Berets. He straightened out, became a fine young man, and he fought in Vietnam.
(*SL5* 22:L18-27) Some night owls in Ilium heard Billy on the radio, and one of them called Billy's daughter **Barbara**. **Barbara** was upset. She and her husband went down to New York and brought Billy home. Billy insisted mildly that everything he had said on the radio was true. He said he had been kidnapped by the Tralfamadorians on the night of his daughter's wedding. He hadn't been missed, he said, because the Tralfamadorians had taken him through a time warp, so that he could be on Tralfamadore for years, and still be away from Earth for only a microsecond.
(*SL5* 24:L29-33, 25:L1-10) The orchestration of the moment was this: **Barbara** was only twenty-one years old, but she thought her father was senile, even though he was only forty-six—senile because of damage to his brain in the airplane crash. She also thought that she was head of the family, since she had had to manage her mother's funeral, since she had to get a housekeeper for Billy, and all that. Also, **Barbara** and her husband were having to look after Billy's business interests, which were considerable, since Billy didn't seem to give a damn for business any more. All this responsibility at such an early age made her a bitchy flibbertigibbet. And Billy, meanwhile, was trying to hang onto his dignity, to persuade **Barbara** and everybody else that he was far from senile, that, on the contrary, he was devoting himself to a calling much higher than mere business.
(*SL5* 102:L11-18) Now *(while time tripping)* he was in bed with Valencia in a delightful studio apartment which was built on the end of a wharf on Cape Ann, Massachusetts. Across the water were the lights of Gloucester. Billy was on top of Valencia, making love to her. One result of this act would be the

birth of **Robert Pilgrim**, who would become a problem in high school, but who would then straighten out as a member of the famous Green Berets.
(*SL5* 163:L21-32, 164:L1-2) Billy Pilgrim opened his eyes in the hospital in Vermont *(after his plane crashed on the mountain)*, did not know where he was. Watching him was his son **Robert**. **Robert** was wearing the uniform of the famous Green Berets. **Robert's** hair was short, was wheat-colored bristles. **Robert** was clean and neat. He was decorated with a Purple Heart and a Silver Star and a Bronze Star with two clusters.

This was a boy who had flunked out of high school, who had been an alcoholic at sixteen, who had run with a rotten bunch of kids, who had been arrested for tipping over hundreds of tombstones in a Catholic cemetery one time. He was all straightened out now. His posture was wonderful and his shoes were shined and his trousers were pressed, and he was a leader of men.

Pilgrim, Billy (also **Joe Crone**). *Drawing on Vonnegut's own war-time experiences, Billy Pilgrim, the main character of* Slaughterhouse-Five, *is unstuck in time and space as he travels across the many significant moments of his life including those of the planet Tralfamadore and the bombing of Dresden. He first gains an awareness of his space travels fifteen years after his slaughterhouse reprieve from the Allied bombing. This occurs in the evening following his daughter's wedding. Billy is assassinated by Paul Lazzaro, who swore revenge for the death of Roland Weary. This occurs thirty-one years after the bombing of Dresden, February 13, 1976. Billy is aware of his death and continued experience of life through his unique understanding of the Tralfamadorians. Billy felt compelled to tell the world of Tralfamadore after surviving the Vermont plane crash which took the lives of all the other convention-bound optometrists on board. Billy had been trained as an optometrist by his father-in-law and inherited a school of optometry.*

Billy received an emergency furlough to return to Ilium after his father was accidentally shot dead while hunting with a friend. Upon his return to service, Billy was assigned as a chaplain's assistant and soon after was captured behind enemy lines at the Battle of the Bulge. His mother resides in an old people's home called Pine Knoll on the edge of Ilium. (*SL5* 28:L20) **Billy** was preposterous—six feet and three inches tall, with a chest and shoulders like a box of kitchen matches.
(*SL5* 75:L1, 8) **Billy Pilgrim** says that the Universe does not look like a lot of bright little dots to the creatures from Tralfamadore. The creatures can see where each star has been and where it is going, so that the heavens are filled with rarefied, luminous spaghetti. And Tralfamadorians don't see human beings as two-legged creatures, either. They see them as great millepedes—"with babies' legs at one end and old people's legs at the other," says **Billy Pilgrim**.
(*SL5* 124:L9) "It is time for you to go home to your wives and children, and it is time for me to be dead for a little while—and then live again." At that moment, Billy's high forehead is in the cross hairs of a high-powered laser

gun. It is aimed at him from the darkened press box. In the next moment, **Billy Pilgrim** is dead. So it goes.
(*SL5* 182:L12) On Tralfamadore, says **Billy Pilgrim**, there isn't much interest in Jesus Christ. The Earthling figure who is most engaging to the Tralfamadorian mind, he says, is Charles Darwin—who taught that those who die are meant to die, that corpses are improvements. So it goes. *Vonnegut writes these lines two nights after Robert Kennedy's assassination, only two months after the murder of Martin Luther King, Jr.*

In Fates Worse Than Death, *Vonnegut for the first time reveals his true life model Billy Pilgrim.* (*FWD* 106:L1-18, 107:L1-14) The fellow ex-Dresden PW at my National Air and Space Museum lecture was Tom Jones, who had paired off (as ordered) in his 106th Division platoon with **Joe Crone**, the model for **Billy Pilgrim**, the leading character in *Slaughterhouse-Five*. Jones said, in a letter I got only yesterday, "I remember **Crone** in Camp Atterbury. When we went on a forced march I had to walk behind him and pick up all the utensils falling out of his backpack. He could never do it right.

"I bunked with him when he died. One morning he woke up and his head was swollen like a watermelon and I talked him into going on sick call. By midday word came back that he had died. You remember we slept two in a bunk so I had to shake **Crone** several times a night and say, 'Let's turn over.' I recall how in the early morning hours the slop cans at the end of the barracks overflowed. Everyone had the shits, and it flowed down the barracks under everyone's bunk. The Germans never would give us more cans."

Joe Crone is buried somewhere in Dresden wearing a white paper suit. He let himself starve to death before the firestorm. In *Slaughterhouse-Five* I have him return home to become a fabulously well-to-do optometrist. (Jones and **Crone** were stockpiled college kids like O'Hare and me. We all read a lot at Camp Atterbury.)

Jones, there in Washington, D.C., turned out to have been quite a packrat when it came to wartime memorabilia. He had a copy of a letter given to us by the Germans which urged us to join their army (and get plenty to eat) and go fight for civilization on the Russian Front. (Rumor was that five Americans somewhere else had accepted the offer. If those five didn't exist we would still have had to invent them.) Tom Jones had photographs of several of us, including O'Hare (but not **Joe Crone**, not **Billy Pilgrim**), taken right after the war ended.

Pilgrim, Valencia Merble. *In* Slaughterhouse-Five, *the daughter of Lionel Merble, owner of the Ilium School of Optometry, and Billy Pilgrim's wife. Valencia's severe weight problems are due to her voracious appetite for candy bars. When Valencia visits Billy in the hospital after his first breakdown, Billy realized that his desire to marry one so undesirable was a symptom of his illness. However, with the exception of one sexual affair during a drunken episode at a holiday party, Billy treated her well and lovingly. For her part, Valencia is as devoted to Billy as she is to fattening foods, forever promising*

Billy she will lose weight. When Billy's charter flight crashes on Sugarbush Mountain, Valencia takes her Cadillac El Dorado Coupe de Ville and recklessly tries to make her way to Vermont to be with Billy. Though suffering an accident which detaches the exhaust system, Valencia continues to drive. She makes it to the emergency room of the hospital where she dies from carbon monoxide poisoning.

Contrasting Billy's most memorable trait, **Valencia** wasn't a time-traveler, but she did have a lively imagination. While Billy was making love to her, she imagined that she was a famous woman in history. She was being Queen Elizabeth the First of England, and Billy was supposedly Christopher Columbus (*SL5* 102:4).

Pine Knoll. *The Ilium nursing home where Billy Pilgrim is forced to put his mother in 1965, in* Slaughterhouse-Five. *He places her there because she isn't expected to recover from pneumonia, though she lingers for years after that.*

Pisquontuit (also **Chief Pisquontuit**; see also **Buntline**). *The Rhode Island hometown of Fred Rosewater who, at the urging of Norman Mushari, becomes locked in a legal struggle with Eliot Rosewater for control of the family foundation.* (*GBR* 113:L21-34, 114:L1-5) About **Pisquontuit**: It was pronounced "Pawn-it" by those who loved it, and "Piss-on-it" by those who didn't. There had once been an Indian chief named **Pisquontuit**.

Pisquontuit wore an apron, lived, as did his people, on clams, raspberries, and rose hips. Agriculture was news to **Chief Pisquontuit**. So, for that matter, were wampum, feather ornaments, and the bow and arrow.

Alcohol was the best news of all. **Pisquontuit** drank himself to death in 1638.

Four thousand moons later, the village that made his name immortal was populated by two hundred very wealthy families and by a thousand ordinary families whose breadwinners served, in one way and another, the rich.

The lives led there were nearly all paltry, lacking in subtlety, wisdom, wit or invention—were precisely as pointless and unhappy as lives led in Rosewater, Indiana. Inherited millions did not help. Nor did the arts and sciences.

Pisquontuit is paired with Rosewater County, Indiana, enabling Kilgore Trout to point out that man's ability to live a purposefully employed life is the greater determinant in assessing the social conditions of our communities than is one's financial standing. (*GBR* 210:L31) "Well—" and Trout rubbed his hands, watched the rubbing, "what you *(Eliot)* did in Rosewater County was far from insane. It was quite possibly the most important social experiment of our time, for it dealt on a very small scale with a problem whose queasy horrors will eventually be made world-wide by the sophistication of machines. The problem is this: How to love people who have no use?

"In time, almost all men and women will become worthless as producers of goods, food, services, and more machines, as sources of practical ideas in the areas of economics, engineering, and probably medicine, too. So—if we can't find reasons and methods for treasuring human beings because they are *human beings*, then we might as well, as has so often been suggested, rub them out."

"Americans have long been taught to hate all people who will not or cannot work, to hate even themselves for that. We can thank the vanished frontier for that piece of common-sense cruelty. The time is coming, if it isn't here now, when it will no longer be common sense. It will simply be cruel."

"A poor man with gumption can still elevate himself out of the mire," said the Senator, "and that will continue to be true a thousand years from now."

"Maybe, maybe," Trout answered gently. "He may even have so much gumption that his descendents will live in a Utopia like **Pisquontuit**, where, I'm sure, the soul-rot and silliness and torpor and insensitivity are exactly as horrible as anything epidemic in Rosewater County. Poverty is a relatively mild disease for even a very flimsy American soul, but uselessness will kill strong and weak souls alike, and kill every time.

"We must find a cure." *See also: GBR* 59:L26; 112:L17,34; 113:L1; 114:L11; 120:L15,19; 125:L16; 126:L5,31; 128:L16,20; 129:L13; 130:L21,24; 135:L2; 141:L18; 142:L20,23; 153:L2; 157:L15-16; 158:L22.

Plague on Wheels. *Kilgore Trout's most popular novel—originally published with pornographic pictures—which opens on the planet Lingo-Three*, and whose inhabitants resembled American automobiles. They had wheels. They were powered by internal combustion engines. They ate fossil fuels. They weren't manufactured, though. They reproduced. They laid eggs containing baby automobiles, and the babies matured in pools of oil drained from adult crankcases (*BC* 26:L25-32).

Homosexual space travelers from the planet Zeltoldimar, all one inch high and led by Kago, could not fulfill the wishes of the dying automobile civilization to take one of its 48 lb. eggs to another planet to continue their race because the Zeltoldimarian spacecraft was no bigger than a shoe box. Lingo-Three was running out of fossil fuels and very nearly depleted its oxygen supply by the time Kago arrived. He promised to tell others in the universe how wonderful the automobile creatures had been. . . . "You will be gone, but not forgotten" (*BC* 27:L16-18).

(*BC* 22:L7) At the time he met Dwayne Hoover, Trout's most widely-distributed book was ***Plague on Wheels***. The publisher didn't change the title, but he obliterated most of it and all of Trout's name with a lurid banner which made this promise: WIDE-OPEN BEAVERS INSIDE!

(*BC* 26:L18) There had been a time when a copy of Trout's most popular book to date, ***Plague on Wheels***, had brought as much as twelve dollars, because of the illustrations. It was now being offered for a dollar, and people who paid even that much did so not because of the pictures. They paid for the words.

(*BC* 29:L1-13) Within a century of little Kago's arrival on Earth, according to Trout's novel, every form of life on that one peaceful and moist and nourishing blue-green ball was dying or dead. Everywhere were the shells of the great beetles which men had made and worshipped. They were automobiles. They had killed everything."

Little Kago himself died long before the planet did. He was attempting to lecture on the evils of the automobile. But he was so tiny that nobody paid any attention to him. He lay down to rest for a moment, and a drunk automobile worker mistook him for a kitchen match. He killed Kago by trying to strike him repeatedly on the underside of the bar."

(*BC* 30:L8) The fan letter *(written by Eliot Rosewater)* reached him in his basement in Cohoes. It was hand-written, and Trout concluded that the writer might be fourteen years old or so. The letter said that ***Plague on Wheels*** was the greatest novel in the English language, and that Trout should be President of the United States.

(*BC* 56:L7-8, 22) Trout had come down from Cohoes late that afternoon. He had since visited many pornography shops and a shirt store. He had bought two of his own books, ***Plague on Wheels*** and *Now It Can Be Told*, a magazine containing a short story of his, and a tuxedo shirt. The name of the magazine was *Black Garterbelt*. . . .

The jackets of ***Plague on Wheels*** and *Now It Can Be Told* both promised plenty of wide-open beavers inside.

Planck, Alfred (also known as **President Jonathan Lynn**). *Alfred Planck, a high school drop out and one-time television personality, is President of the United States in* Player Piano. (*PP* 102:L39) The electric car pulled up to the platform, and **President Jonathan Lynn**, born **Alfred Planck**, stood and showed his white teeth and frank gray eyes, squared his broad shoulders, and ran his strong, tanned hands through his curly hair. The television cameras dollied and panned about him like curious, friendly dinosaurs, sniffing and peering. **Lynn** was boyish, tall, beautiful, and disarming, and, Halyard thought bitterly, he had gone directly from a three-hour television program to the White House.

"The Planet Gobblers." *Though this Kilgore Trout story appears nowhere in Vonnegut's fiction, it does appear in his nonfiction. As part of a longer illustration on his religious views, Vonnegut includes his address to the 1974 graduating classes of Hobart and William Smith Colleges.* (*PS* 209:L12 *Religion*) "Kilgore Trout wrote a science-fiction story called **'The Planet Gobblers'** one time. It was about us, and we were the terrors of the universe. We were sort of interplanetary termites. We would arrive on a planet, gobble it up, and die. But before we died, we always sent out spaceships to start tiny colonies elsewhere. We were a disease, since it was not necessary to inhabit planets with such horrifying destructiveness. It is easy to take good care of a planet.

"Our grandchildren will surely think of us as the Planet Gobblers. Poorer nations than America think of America as a Planet Gobbler right now. But that is going to change. There is welling up within us a willingness to say 'No, thank you' to our factories. We were once maniacs for possessions, imagining that they would somehow moderate or somehow compensate us for our loneliness.

"The experiment has been tried in this most affluent nation in all of human history. Possessions help a little, but not as much as advertisers said they were supposed to, and we are now aware of how permanently the manufacture of some of those products hurts the planet.

"So there is a willingness to do without them.

"There is a willingness to do whatever we need to do in order to have life on the planet go on for a long, long time. I didn't used to think that. And that willingness has to be a religious enthusiasm, since it celebrates life, since it calls for meaningful sacrifices.

"This is bad news for business, as we know it now. It should be thrilling news for persons who love to teach and lead. And thank God we have solid information in the place of superstition! Thank God we are beginning to dream of human communities which are designed to harmonize with what human beings really need and are.

"And now you have just heard an atheist thank God not once, but twice. And listen to this:

"God bless the class of 1974."

Player Piano (1952) (see also **Paul Proteus**, **Ghost Shirt Society**, **Norbert Wiener**). Player Piano *is Vonnegut's vision of how America will be restructured once the value of technocrats and the ramifications of the third industrial revolution take effect. This latter concept is extrapolated from Norbert Wiener's* The Human Use of Human Beings *(which Vonnegut read while witnessing the technological advances made by General Electric in Schnectady, and cited by Paul Proteus in discussion with Katharine Finch, his secretary). Wiener characterized the first industrial revolution as devaluing manual labor, and the second (describing the long-term effects of computers) as devaluing routine mental work. But the third industrial revolution, as envisioned by Vonnegut and illustrated by EPICAC, would devalue human thinking. Though Wiener feared massive unemployment in the semiskilled and skilled work sectors due to robotics, Vonnegut saw the advancement of unchecked technologies producing a society in which only some Ph.D.s would be employed at anything more than soldiers or road workers: the Reeks and Wrecks. The know-how and ability to produce would outrun our understanding of the purpose and effects of human labor. The ensuing plot, which Vonnegut admits was a rip-off of Eugene Zamiatin's* We, *and George Orwell's* 1984, *places Paul Proteus in the middle of two conspiracies. The ruling technocracy seeks to infiltrate the rebellious Ghost Shirt Society by making it seem as though Paul was thrown out of the hierarchy. At the same time, the Ghost*

Shirt Society kidnaps Paul and releases a declaration in his name for purposeful human labor (written by Professor Ludwig von Neumann).

Poe, Edgar Allan (1809-1849). *When Captain Adolf Von Kleist cries out "October!" Mandarax takes it as a command for citing a literary reference and complies with this from Poe.* (*Gal* 250:L4-7) The skies they were ashen and sober; / The leaves they were crisped and sere— / The leaves they were withering and sere; / It was night in the lonesome October / Of my most immemorial year.

Polk, Dalton. *The Scipio physician in* Hocus Pocus *who taught biology and Shakespeare at The Mohiga Valley Free Institute when it was first established.*

Pomerantz, Floyd. *One of Rabo Karabekian's East Hampton neighbors, in* Bluebeard. *Though only forty-three, he was given $11 million as severance pay to resign as the president of a television network. He asked Rabo if there was still enough time for him to become a painter.*

Pond, Dr. *The manager of the Ilium Real Estate Office in* Player Piano *who tries to talk Paul Proteus out of purchasing the Gottwald farm. He is very proud of his seven years in the Cornell Graduate School of Realty and his 896 page dissertation. Pond is keenly aware about the significance attached to one's real estate and the part it plays in the highly stratified social structure of the text.* (*PP* 130:L16-21) "For example, while the *Manual* doesn't tell me to do it, I make very sure that every man gets a house suited to his station on the ladder of life. The way a man lives can destroy or increase the stature of his job—can increase or decrease the stability and prestige of the entire system."

Pontius Pilate Athletic Club. *The ghost of Major Siegfried von Konigswald mentions that,* It was almost worth the trip *(to heaven)*—to find out that Jesus Christ in Heaven was just another guy, playing shuffleboard. I like his sense of humor, though—you know? He's got a blue-and-gold warm-up jacket he wears. You know what it says on the back? "**Pontius Pilate Athletic Club**." Most people don't get it. Most people think there really is a **Pontius Pilate Athletic Club** (*WJ* 136:L17, 19).

Ponzi scheme (see **di Sanza**)

pool-pah. (*CC* 198:L31, 33) "Sometimes the ***pool-pah***," Bokonon tells us, "exceeds the power of humans to comment." Bokonon translates ***pool-pah*** at one point in *The Books of Bokonon* as "shit storm" and at another point as "wrath of God."

Poo-tee-weet (also **Poo-tee-phweet**). *The dispassionate cry of birds flying above Vonnegut characters who either experience or imagine great atrocities.*

John/Jonah lived through the frozen death of the world due to ice-nine. (*CC* 211:L8-9) I dreamed for a moment of dropping to the platform, of springing up from it in a breath-taking swan dive, of folding my arms, of knifing downward into a blood-warm eternity with never a splash.

I was recalled from this dream by the cry of a darting bird above me. It seemed to be asking me what had happened. "**Poo-tee-phweet**?" it asked.

We all looked up at the bird, and then at one another.

Eliot Rosewater accidentally kills three volunteer firemen during the war in Germany, but when he reads Kilgore Trout's Pan-Galactic Three-Day Pass *(about the death of the Milky Way) he looks up from the book and imagines he sees Indianapolis consumed by firestorm. He falls into a catatonic trance and there is a one-year gap in the narrative while he is treated at Dr. Brown's Indianapolis sanitarium.* (GBR 203:L6-7, 204:L8) Everything went black for Eliot, as black as what lay beyond the ultimate rim of the universe. And then he awoke to find himself sitting on the flat rim of a dry fountain. He was dappled by sunlight filtering down through a sycamore tree. A bird was singing in the sycamore tree. ***"Poo-tee-weet?"*** it sang. ***"Poo-tee-weet. Weet, weet, weet."*** Eliot was within a high garden wall, and the garden was familiar. He had spoken to Sylvia many times in just this place. It was the garden of Dr. Brown's private mental hospital in Indianapolis, to which he had brought her so many years before. These words were cut into the fountain rim:

"Pretend to be good always, and even God will be fooled. . . ."

"Poo-tee-weet?"

Eliot looked up at the bird and all the green leaves, understood that this garden in downtown Indianapolis could not have survived the fire he saw. So there had been no fire. He accepted this peacefully.

(*GBR* 215:L24) ***"Poo-tee-weet?"***

Eliot looked up into the tree, and the memory of all that had happened in the blackness came crashing back—the fight with the bus driver, the straitjacket, the shock treatments, the suicide attempts, all the tennis, all the strategy meetings about the sanity hearing.

And with that mighty inward crash of memories came the idea he had had for settling everything instantly, beautifully, and fairly. *Eliot then decides to accept as valid the fifty-seven false paternity suits against him, settle with plaintiff and make a lump sum payment to his cousin Fred Rosewater. Fred was suing Eliot for control of the Rosewater Foundation—an action provoked by Norman Mushari's greed.*

Perhaps the most memorable use of the phrase comes in Slaughterhouse-Five. *Vonnegut explains his use of the term to his publisher Seymour Lawrence in this, his Dresden book.* (*SL5* 17:L10) It is so short and jumbled and jangled, Sam, because there is nothing intelligent to say about a massacre. Everybody is supposed to be dead, to never say anything or want anything ever again. Everything is supposed to be very quiet after a massacre, and it always is, except for the birds.

And what do the birds say? All there is to say about a massacre, things like ***"Poo-tee-weet?"***
(SL5 19:L33) I've finished my war book now. The next one I write is going to be fun.

This one is a failure, and had to be, since it was written by a pillar of salt. It begins like this:

Listen:

Billy Pilgrim has come unstuck in time.

It ends like this:

Poo-tee-weet?

(*SL5* 86:L16) Night came to the garden of the giraffes, and Billy Pilgrim slept without dreaming for a while, and then he traveled in time. He woke up with his head under a blanket in a ward for nonviolent mental patients in a veterans' hospital near Lake Placid, New York. It was springtime in 1948, three years after the end of the war.

Billy uncovered his head. The windows of the ward were open. Birds were twittering outside. "**Poo-tee-weet**?" one asked him. The sun was high. There were twenty-nine other patients assigned to the ward, but they were all outdoors now, enjoying the day. They were free to come and go as they pleased, to go home, even, if they liked—and so was Billy Pilgrim. They had come here voluntarily, alarmed by the outside world.
(*SL5* 186:L24) And somewhere in there was springtime. The corpse mines were closed down. The soldiers all left to fight the Russians. In the suburbs, the women and children dug rifle pits. Billy and the rest of his group were locked up in the stable in the suburbs. And then, one morning; they got up to discover that the door was unlocked. World War Two in Europe was over.

Billy and the rest wandered out onto the shady street. The trees were leafing out. There was nothing going on out there, no traffic of any kind. There was only one vehicle, an abandoned wagon drawn by two horses. The wagon was green and coffin-shaped.

Birds were talking

One bird said to Billy Pilgrim, ***"Poo-tee-weet?"*** *See also: GBR* 214:L5.

Pops. *In Vonnegut's updated musical version of "Dr. Jekyll and Mr. Hyde," Pops is "the doddering campus cop."* (*PS* 267:L14-17 *Jekyll and Hyde Revisited*) "I was on my way to being a star of stage, screen, and radio. But then my dog was run over, and I entered a period of deep depression from which I never recovered. Nobody starts out to be a campus cop."

Portomaggiore, Count Bruno. *In* Bluebeard, *Mussolini's Minister of Culture and head of British Intelligence in Italy during the war. The Oxford-educated Count Bruno is one of Italy's largest landowners and marries Marilee Kemp* *because Mussolini orders it (to suppress rumors of his homosexuality). He is eventually executed by firing squad by Italian authorities for being a pedophile.*

Potapov, Ilya. *A famous rocket scientist and eldest son of George Kraft/Iona Potapov in* Mother Night.

Potapov, Iona (see **George Kraft**).

Potapov, Tanya *In* Mother Night, *the wife of Soviet spy George Kraft/Iona Potapov dutifully waits for him in Borisoglebsk. Separated by occupation for more than twenty-five years, she raises their nine children and would never again see her husband due to his imprisonment.*

Potter, David. *In the short story "Deer in the Works," Potter is the new publicity man hired by the Ilium Works of the Federal Apparatus Corporation sent to cover the story of the deer which somehow entered the grounds of the plant. When unexpectedly close enough to the deer, Potter helps the deer escape through the fence, much to the chagrin of his superiors.*

Powers, Dr. *The obstetrician for both the Knechtmann and Sousa families in the short story "Adam." He breaks the unfortunate news to Mr. Knechtmann that his wife's malnutrition during the war makes it unlikely she will have any more children, though they are overjoyed about another generation since they both survived Nazi death camps.*

Prairie Military Academy (see also **Culver Military Academy**). *The military academy in* Cat's Cradle *where Bunny Hoover was sent when only ten years old. As a senior he was unanimously elected Cadet Colonel, the highest student rank. The circumstances leading to Bunny's removal there and Vonnegut's opinion of such institutions are included in the following description.* (*BC* 179:L31-33, 180:L1-14) Listen: Bunny was sent away to military school, an institution devoted to homicide and absolutely humorless obedience, when he was only ten years old. Here is why: He told Dwayne that he wished he were a woman instead of a man, because what men did was so often cruel and ugly.

Listen: Bunny Hoover went to **Prairie Military Academy** for eight years of uninterrupted sports, buggery and fascism. Buggery consisted of sticking one's penis in somebody else's asshole or mouth, or having it done to one by somebody else. Fascism was a fairly popular political philosophy which made sacred whatever nation and race the philosopher happened to belong to. It called for an autocratic, centralized government, headed up by a dictator. The dictator had to be obeyed, no matter what he told somebody to do.

prakhouls. (*PP* 207:L1) EN ROUTE BY air from Miami Beach to Ithaca, home of Cornell University, the Shah of Bratpuhr caught a nasty cold. When seven ***prakhouls*** (that quantity of fluid that can be contained in the skin of an adult male Bratpuhrian marmot) of *Sumklish* improved the Shah's spirits but did nothing for his respiratory system, it was decided that the plane should land in Harrisburg, Pennsylvania, in order that the Shah might rest and try the magic of American medicine.

Pratt, Mary. *Eugene Debs Hartke's high school English teacher who demanded the class learn Hamlet's "To be, or not to be" speech, in* Hocus Pocus. *He recalls her memory when resigning under the pressure of Tarkington's Board of Trustees, but before leaving he recites the speech. He felt it would provide a suitable shock to the Trustees, who feared the idea of another Vietnam veteran faculty member committing suicide at the school. The first to do so was the late President Sam Wakefield.*

Prince, Joe. *In* Player Piano, *Edgar Rice Burroughs Hagstrohm invokes the name of bowling buddy Joe Prince to avoid staying home with his wife so he could rendezvous with Marion Frascati. His children play along though they know what he is doing, and even Edgar's wife Wanda knows and approves of his relationship with Marion.*

Prince of Candlesticks. *The stillborn child of twelve-year-old Melody Oriole-2 von Peterswald (Wilbur Swain's daughter) who had been raped on her way to New York. Wilbur calls the unnamed child the "Prince of Candlesticks" because he was known as the "King of Candlesticks." Wilbur references the child to convey the significance he attaches to his memoirs.* (*Slap* 80:L16-24) Yes, and if archaeologists of the future find this book of mine, they will be spared the fruitless labor of digging through the pyramid in search of its meaning. There are no secret treasure rooms in there, no chambers of any kind.

Its meaning, which is minuscule in any event, lies beneath the manhole cover over which the pyramid is constructed. It is the body of a stillborn male.

Prince Richard of Croatia-Slavonia. *The owner of a Madison Avenue antique shop who hires homosexual prostitute James Wait to participate in a bit of sexual hijinks, in* Galápagos. *The Prince wanted to masturbate while Wait strangled him with a silken sash. Wait was supposed to count to twenty after the Prince ejaculated and lost consciousness, but Wait decides to count to three hundred and kills the shop owner.*

Princess Charlotte. *The daughter of a Staten Island roofer who married* "Prince Richard of Croatia-Slavonia, a direct descendant of James the First of England and Emperor Frederick the Third of Germany and Emperor Franz Joseph of Austria and King Louis the Fifteenth of France" (*Gal* 164:L24-28). *After his death, which was assisted by James Wait, she became the designer of neckties bearing his family's crest.*

Proteus, Anita. *Anita is the wife of Paul Proteus in* Player Piano. *If not for her ambition and cunning during an affair with Paul while employed as his secretary, they might never have married; she had a history of delayed menstruation.* (*PP* 2:L8-13) As for the Proteus genes' chances of being passed down to yet another generation, there were practically none. Paul's wife, **Anita**, his secretary during the war, was barren. Ironically as anyone would please, he had married her after she had declared that she was certainly pregnant, following an abandoned office celebration of victory. *Their marriage thrives but there is no lasting joy. As it turns out, Anita is barren and this causes a long-felt depression for her and Paul. Though fiercely loyal and protective of Paul, his lack of ambition always disappoints her. While married, they had fallen into clearly defined roles and their verbal patter became as predictably mechanical as the Ilium Works ("I love you, Paul." "And I love you, Anita.") Anita was also fiercely jealous of Dr. Katharine Finch, the woman who succeeded her as Paul's secretary.* (PP 16:L2-7) **Anita** had the mechanics of marriage down pat, even to the subtlest conventions. If her approach was disturbingly rational, systematic, she was thorough enough to turn out a creditable counterfeit of warmth. Paul could only suspect that her feelings were shallow—and perhaps that suspicion was part of what he was beginning to think of as his sickness.

(*PP* 28:L37-39, 29:L1-3) The expression "armed to the teeth" occurred to Paul as he looked at her over his glass. With an austere dark gown that left her tanned shoulders and throat bare, a single bit of jewelry on her finger, and very light make-up, **Anita** had successfully combined the weapons of sex, taste, and an aura of masculine competence.

(*PP*116:L33-35) **Anita** slept—utterly satisfied, not so much by Paul as by the social orgasm of, after years of the system's love play, being offered Pittsburgh. *Of course it is Paul who is offered the Pittsburgh position, though Anita's efforts to be the perfect corporate manager's wife are widely seen as significantly rounding out Paul's candidacy.*

(*PP* 117:L3-10) She made the carnage so vivid that he was obliged for a moment to abandon his own thoughts, to see if there was the slightest truth in what she was saying. He went over the scalps she was counting one by one—men who had competed with him for this job or that—and found that they all had done well for themselves and were quite unbroken either financially or in spirit. But to **Anita** they were dead men, shot squarely between the eyes, and good riddance of bad rubbish.

The competing conspiracies for Paul's allegiance by Kroner and Baer on one side and the Ghost Shirt Society on the other eventually force a break in their marriage. She takes up with Paul's nemesis, Dr. Lawson Shepherd. See also: *PP* 2:L29-36; 54:L29-38; 55:L1-2; 95:L18-25; 137:L14-23; 271:L22-35.

Proteus, Dr. Paul. *In* Player Piano, *the son of the late Dr. George Proteus (the first National Industrial, Commercial, Communications, Foodstuffs, and*

Resources Director), Paul is presented as the heir apparent to direct the overwhelming (and overbearing) industrial technocracy that spawned as a result of the engineering achievements during the war. Grooming Paul as his father's successor is an attempt to affirm the rightness of the system the engineers devised and EPICAC sustains. George (father of technocracy's first regime) and Paul (son of EPICAC's first guardian and himself the creator and overseer of lifeless machines which contain the working essence of once-productive human spirits) together with their inventions form the new trinity: the father, the son, and the ghost in the machine.

But Paul will not wind up as a messiah uniting all to an abiding faith in technocracy. For all Paul's intellectual achievements and rapid advancement in the ruling technocracy (nepotism notwithstanding), his conflict is due to his growing awareness that the system designed to relieve man from physical and mental labor also strips people of their dignity. Developing this awareness is as much the result of his own sheltered experiences becoming juxtaposed with the Homesteaders and the misgivings of Finnerty and Lasher, as it is the result of diabolical scheming on the part of Kroner and Gelhorne.

Paul stands at the center of the scheme developed by the technocrats, which demands he publicly resign so that he could infiltrate the upstart Ghost Shirt Society. At the same time, those in the Ghost Shirt movement seek to use Paul's name regardless of his true allegiance. Neither side is particularly interested in his true convictions.

Proteus' decision to claim leadership of the Ghost Shirt Society enables him to climb atop Vonnegut's soap box (more rightly, the witness stand in his treason trial). Citing the obvious polarities of life in the technocratic age, Paul reasons that not Every new piece of scientific knowledge is a good thing for humanity, *and that,* The main business of humanity is to do a good job of being human beings . . . not to serve as appendages to machines, institutions, and systems (*PP* 273:L3-4, 10-12).

Proteus, George. *The fabled father of Paul Proteus and the nation's first National Industrial, Commercial, Communications, Foodstuffs, and Resources Director. Though he was succeeded by Dr. Francis Gelhorne, it was believed Paul would eventually fill his father's post. For his part, however, Paul saw one significant difference between himself and his father.* (*PP* 55:L7-15) When Paul thought about his effortless rise in the hierarchy, he sometimes, as now, felt sheepish, like a charlatan. He could handle his assignments all right, but he didn't have what his father had, what Kroner had, what Shepherd had, what so many had: the sense of spiritual importance in what they were doing; the ability to be moved emotionally, almost like a lover, by the great omnipresent and omniscient spook, the corporate personality. In short, Paul missed what made his father aggressive and great: the capacity to really give a damn.

Proteus Park. *Managed by Dr. Ned Dodge, this Chicago development is* a postwar development of three thousand dream houses for three thousand families with presumably identical dreams (*PP* 138:L27-29). *It is there the Shah of Bratpuhr is given a guided tour of the home of Edgar and Wanda Hagstrohm. All these prefabricated homes are filled with dozens of electrical appliances intended to instantly perform menial household chores.*

"The Protocols of the Elders of Tralfamadore." *The unsigned science fiction short story appearing in the* Black Garterbelt *porn magazine given to Eugene Debs Hartke by his military buddy and brother-in-law, Jack Patton. It is similar to Vonnegut's* Sirens of Titan *and Kilgore Trout's* Now It Can Be Told *in that it displaces traditional Western and patriarchal monotheistic beliefs in a God which expects his creation to act in accordance with His given laws, and replaces them with a no-fault explanation of outside interference. By the time Hartke has an opportunity and the inclination to read the story, he welcomes the harmless untruths it has to offer.* (*HP* 194:L8-20) I did not realize at the time how much that story affected me. Reading it was simply a way of putting off for just a little while my looking for another job and another place to live at the age of 51, with 2 lunatics in tow. But down deep the story was beginning to work like a buffered analgesic. What a relief it was, somehow, to have somebody else confirm what I had come to suspect toward the end of the Vietnam War, and particularly after I saw the head of a human being pillowed in the spilled guts of a water buffalo on the edge of a Cambodian village, that Humanity is going somewhere really nice was a myth for children under 6 years old, like the Tooth Fairy and the Easter Bunny and Santa Claus.

The Elders of Tralfamadore were no more than germs which sought to spread themselves throughout the universe. Though their own physiology enabled them to easily attach themselves to other life forms, humans were particularly attractive because of their "extra-large brains." (*HP* 189:L1-5) So the Elders focused in on them, and wondered if people's brains might not invent survival tests for germs which were truly horrible.

They saw in us a potential for chemical evils on a cosmic scale. Nor did we disappoint them.

The short story points out that the critical difference between the humanoids on Tralfamadore, which the germs decided not to infect, and the humanoids on Earth was the inherent failing of Tralfamadorians to take anything seriously while Earthlings were deadly serious about any scheme which placed themselves at the center of attention. (*HP* 190:L14-23, 191:L1-18) The Elders, incidentally, had given up on influencing the humanoids of Tralfamadore, who were right below where they were meeting. The Tralfamadorians had senses of humor and so knew themselves for the severely limited lunkers, not to say crazy lunkers, they really were. They were immune to the kilovolts of pride the Elders jazzed their brains with. They laughed right away when the idea popped up in their heads that they were the glory of the Universe, and that they were supposed to colonize other planets with their incomparable magnificence. They knew exactly how clumsy and dumb they were, even though they could talk and some of them could read and write and do math. One author wrote a series of side-splitting satires about Tralfamadorians arriving on other planets with the intention of spreading enlightenment.

But the people here on Earth, being humorless, found the same idea quite acceptable.

It appeared to the Elders that the people here would believe anything about themselves, no matter how preposterous, as long as it was flattering. To make sure of this, they performed an experiment. They put the idea into Earthlings' heads that the whole Universe had been created by one big male animal who looked just like them. He sat on a throne with a lot of less fancy thrones all around him. When people died they got to sit on those other thrones forever because they were such close relatives of the Creator.

The people down here just ate that up!

The complete synopsis of "The Protocols of the Elders of Tralfamadore" appears on pages 188-194 of Hocus Pocus.

The Protocols of the Elders of Zion (see also **Henry Ford**). *In the introduction to* Mother Night, *Vonnegut recalls being handed a copy of the fraudulent anti-Semitic tract back in the 1930s.*

In Hocus Pocus, *the book was broadly distributed among the convicts in Athena by the Black Brothers of Islam, which had received copies from a publisher in Libya. It became the de facto textbook for Hartke's literacy campaign though he denounced the text's philosophy. Hartke notes the text's title was later appropriated for a science fiction story entitled "The Protocols of the Elders of Tralfamadore," which appeared in the issue of* Black Garterbelt *magazine bestowed upon him by his military buddy and brother-in-law, Jack Patton.* (*HP* 235:L19) *The Protocols of the Elders of Zion* was an anti-Semitic work first published in Russia about 100 years ago. It purported to be the minutes of a secret meeting of Jews from many countries who planned to cooperate internationally so as to cause wars and revolutions and financial busts and so on, which would leave them owning everything. Its title was parodied by the author of the story in *Black Garterbelt*, and its paranoia, too.

The great American inventor and industrialist Henry Ford thought it was a genuine document. He had it published in this country back when my father was a boy.

Pruitt, Major General Earl. *Pfc. Elmo Hacketts' division commander on hand to greet the visiting Shah of Bratpuhr in* Player Piano.

Pulsifer, Borders M., General of the Armies. (*ST* 117:L1) The nominal commander of the entire *(Martian)* Army, **General of the Armies Borders M. Pulsifer**, was in fact controlled at all times by his orderly, Corporal Bert Wright. Corporal Wright, the perfect orderly, carried aspirin for the General's almost chronic headaches . . . *due to the mind-riveting sounds run through the general's skull by Wright's electronic transmitter.*

punctual (experiencing time in a **punctual manner**). (*ST* 13:L10-14) Constant smiled at that—the warning to be **punctual**. To be **punctual** meant to exist as a point, meant that as well as to arrive somewhere on time. Constant existed as a point—could not imagine what it would be like to exist in any other way. That was one of the things he was going to find out—what it was like to exist in any other way. Mrs. Rumfoord's husband existed in another way.

When Malachi Constant asks Winston Niles Rumfoord if he can see into the future, Rumfoord responds, "In a **punctual** way of speaking—yes. . . . When I ran my space ship into the chrono-synclastic infundibulum, it came to me in a flash that everything that ever has been always will be, and everything that ever will be always has been" (*ST* 25:L30).

Rumfoord draws this comparison between his own chrono-synclastic infundibulated existence and those who experience time in a linear fashion. (*ST* 57:L23-31) "Look," said Rumfoord, "life for a **punctual** person is like a roller coaster." He turned to shiver his hands in her face. "All kinds of things are going to happen to you! Sure," he said, "I can see the whole roller coaster you're on. And sure—I could give you a piece of paper that would tell you about every dip and turn, warn you about every bogeyman that was going to pop out at you in the tunnels. But that wouldn't help you any."

Purdy and McCloud. *Two aging Cornell football linemen (thirty-seven and thirty-six years old, respectively) who worry that the economic realities of maintaining the Ivy League championship might cost them their jobs, in* Player Piano.

purity. (*WFG* xxiii:L24 *Preface*) Mr. Nixon himself is a minor character in this book. He is the first President to hate the American people and all they stand for. He believes so vibrantly in his own **purity**, although he has committed crimes which are hideous, that I am bound to conclude that someone told him when he was very young that all serious crime was sexual, that no one could be a criminal who did not commit adultery or masturbate.
(*WFG* 213:L15 *Address at Rededication of Wheaton College Library, 1973*) And one idea that was put into our heads *(as a result of the revealed atrocities committed by the Nazis)* was that our enemies were so awful, so evil, that we, by contrast, must be remarkably pure. That illusion of **purity**, to which we were entitled in a way, has become our curse today. *See also: ST* 216:L3-4; 261:L26; *MN* 107:L13; *WFG—The Mysterious Madame Blavatsky* 129:L7; 134:L31.

Q

Queen Margaret. *Queen Margaret of the planet Shaltoon is one of the main characters in Kilgore Trout's* Venus on the Half-shell, *in* God Bless You, Mr. Rosewater. *On the back flap of the novel she is characterized as the seductress of the story's hero, the Space Wanderer. There is no reason to believe this reference has any relation to Malachi Constant in* Sirens of Titan. *Fred Rosewater reads the back cover.* (*GBR* 133:L) Fred, thinking Lila wasn't paying any attention to him, now put down Better Homes and Gardens, picked up what looked like one hell of a sexy paperback novel, *Venus on the Half-shell*, by Kilgore Trout. On the back cover was an abridgment of a red-hot scene inside. It went like this:

> **Queen Margaret** of the planet Shaltoon let her gown fall to the floor. She was wearing nothing underneath. Her high, firm, uncowled bosom was proud and rosy. Her hips and thighs were like an inviting lyre of pure alabaster. They shone so whitely they might have had a light inside. 'Your travels are over, Space Wanderer,' she whispered, her voice husky with lust. 'Seek no more, for you have found. The answer is in my arms.'
>
> 'It's a glorious answer, **Queen Margaret**, God knows,' the Space Wanderer replied. His palms were perspiring profusely. 'I am going to accept it gratefully. But I have to tell you, if I'm going to be perfectly honest with you, that I will have to be on my way again tomorrow.'
>
> 'But you have found your answer, you have found your answer,' she cried, and she forced his head between her fragrant young breasts.
>
> He said something that she did not hear. She thrust him out at arm's length. 'What was that you said?'
>
> 'I said, **Queen Margaret**, that what you offer is an awfully good answer. It just doesn't happen to be the one I'm primarily looking for.'

Queen of the Meadows. *Symbolic of the strict hierarchy imposed by the ruling technocracy in* Player Piano, *the* Queen of the Meadows *is the ferry which takes the top one hundred men (by classification number) from the mainland to the island that is the Meadows for their annual retreat. Those with numbers from one hundred to two hundred fifty board the* Meadow Lark; *the remainder board the* Spirit of the Meadows.

Quezeda, Domingo. *The twisted old man who answered a call to serve as interpreter for the orphanage housing the Kanka-bono girls.* An old drunk and petty thief appeared, a purebred white man who, amazingly, was a grandfather of the lightest of the girls. When a youngster, he had gone prospecting for valuable minerals in the rain forest, and had lived with the Kanka-bonos for three years. . . . He was from excellent stock. His father had been head of the Philosophy Department of the Central University of Quito. If they were so inclined, then, people today might claim to be descended from a long line of aristocratic Spanish intellectuals (*Gal* 156:L26-31, 157:L3-8). *Quezeda taught the Kanka-bono girls to be thieves and introduced them to the world of prostitution.* He would do this in order to feed his big brain's thirst for self-esteem and alcohol. He was at last going to be a man of wealth and importance. . . . During their bad old days in Guayaquil, old **Quezeda** offered his stinking body for their experimentation as he taught them, as little as they were, the fundamental skills and attitudes of prostitutes (*Gal* 158:L11-14, 159:L17).

Quinn, Bert. *Quinn purchased a restaurant from George M. Helmholtz, the head of the music department at Lincoln High School, ten years before the opening of the short story "The Kid Nobody Could Handle." Quinn and Helmholtz have differing visions and values. The former looks only at monetary gain, the latter looks to music for self-fulfillment. Quinn gives up on his juvenile delinquent step-nephew Jim Donnini, while Helmholtz reforms the boy by enticing him with John Philip Sousa's trumpet.*

R

The RAMJAC Corporation. *In* Jailbird, *RAMJAC was once a small company but was transformed by multimillionaire mining engineer Jack Graham, who developed it into a multinational corporation. After Graham's death in 1952, his wife, Mary Kathleen O'Looney, took control. She hired Arpad Leen to serve as president and chairman of the board. His only orders were to acquire as many properties as possible, and at its height, RAMJAC controlled nineteen percent of everything in the country. Mary Kathleen's Last Will and Testament left RAMJAC to the American people, but government saw its liquidation as the answer to its short-term economic woes rather than managing the enterprise and realizing a steady income.*

The copyright for Deadeye Dick, *Vonnegut's succeeding novel, is held by The RAMJAC Corporation.*

Rauch, John G. *The husband of Gertrude Schull Rauch, a first cousin to Kurt Vonnegut, Sr., and the author of "An Account of the Ancestry of Kurt Vonnegut, Jr., by an Ancient Friend of His Family," reprinted in the "Roots" chapter of* Palm Sunday. *It is a most informative piece about the family's history and the influences at work on Vonnegut. Uncle John (1890-1976), as he was known to the family, gave the manuscript to Vonnegut as a gift.* (*PS* 19:L13-29) He was a Harvard graduate and a distinguished Indianapolis lawyer. Toward the end of his life, he made himself an historian, a *griot*, of his wife's family—in part my family, too, although he was not related to it by blood, but only by marriage.

It was painstakingly researched and better written, by Uncle John himself, than much of my own stuff, sad to say. That manuscript is the most extravagant gift I ever expect to receive—and it came from a man who had never spoken favorably of my work in my presence, other than to say that he was "surprised by my convincing tone of authority," and that he was sure I would make a great deal of money.

Raven. *The British destroyer which captured the Nazi submarine* U-99 *in* Cat's Cradle. *The sub had previously captured Bokonon and had sunk his schooner, the* Lady's Slipper.

reborn. (*MN* 50:L7, 8) When *(Rev. Lionel J.D.)* Jones' wife died, Jones felt the need to be **reborn**. He was **reborn** a thing he had been latently all along. Jones became the sort of racial agitator who is spoken of as having crawled out from under a rock. Jones crawled out from under his rock in 1928. He sold his funeral home for eighty-four thousand dollars, and he founded *The White Christian Minuteman*.
(*GBR* 96:L22, 23, 97:L11, 98:L13) Heaven is the bore of bores, Eliot's novel went on, so most wraiths queue up to be **reborn**—and they live and love and fail and die, and they queue up to be **reborn** again. They take pot luck. . . . They don't gibber and squeak to be one race or another, one sex or another, one nationality or another, one class or another. What they want and what they get are three dimensions—and comprehensible little packets of time—and enclosures making possible the crucial distinction between inside and outside.

. . . Uncomfortable as it is here, however, there are a few of us who do not care to be **reborn**. . . .

"Who are these people?" I ask myself. "What is this unimaginably horrible thing that has happened to them?" And I realize that, in order to get proper answers, I am going to have to cease to be dead. I am going to have to let myself be **reborn**." *These excerpts are from the novel Eliot Rosewater writes at the back of his* Domesday Book.
(*MH* 33:L5 *Welcome to the Monkey House*) "There is nothing like an Easter morning to make a man feel clean and **reborn** and at one with God's intentions."
(*WJ* 20:L12) WOODLY: Maybe God has let everybody who ever lived be **reborn**—so he or she can see how it ends. Even Pithecanthropus erectus and Australopithecus and Sinanthropus pekensis and the Neanderthalers are back on Earth—to see how it ends. They're all on Times Square—making change for peepshows. Or recruiting Marines.
(*BC* 218:L27) And my own pre-earthquake condition must be taken into consideration, too, since I was the one who was being **reborn**. Nobody else in the cocktail lounge was **reborn**, as far as I know. The rest got their minds changed, some of them, about the value of modern art. *This is at the point when Vonnegut enters the text and comments in his own voice.*
(*Slap* 50:L12) Thus did we *(Wilbur and Eliza Swain)* give birth to a single genius, which died as quickly as we were parted, which was **reborn** the moment we got together again.
(*Blue* 71:L20) Only after the war did Marilee, **reborn** as the Contessa Portomaggiore, tell me that I was the reason she had been pushed down the stairs back in 1932. *See also: PP* 74:L21; *CC* 94:L3; *WFG* 233:L7; *PS* 307:L3.

Reconstruction and Reclamation Corps (also known as the **Reeks and Wrecks**). *As explained by Dr. Ewing J. Halyard, the designated host for the visiting Shah of Bratpuhr,* "any man who cannot support himself by doing a job better than a machine is employed by the government, either in the Army or the Reconstruction and Reclamation Corps" (*PP* 18:L25-26). *More explicitly, the "Reeks and Wrecks" perform menial labor, mostly road repair.*

Redfield, Colonel George. *In* Jailbird, *the Sandusky lumber mill owner and son-in-law of the Ohio governor, commissioned to lead the National Guard troops during the strike at the Cuyahoga Bridge and Iron Company. Though lacking any military experience, he dressed as a cavalryman and stood with his troops when he ordered them to advance against the strikers. After the shooting broke out, Redfield was found crazed and naked in a side street.*

Redfield, Dr. Robert. *Vonnegut's faculty advisor in the Department of Anthropology at the University of Chicago. Vonnegut recalls that* While he lived, he had in his head a lovely dream which he called "The Folk Society." He published this dream in *The American Journal of Sociology*, Volume 52, 1947, pages 293 through 308. *He goes on to quote Redfield at great length to fully illustrate his sense of "folk society"* (*WFG* 177-178). *At another point, Vonnegut summarizes Redfield when commemorating the 200th anniversary of the birth of William Ellery Channing.* (*PS* 211:L22-23 *Religion*) "Channing grew up in what the late anthropologist **Robert Redfield** called a folk society, a relatively isolated community of like-thinking friends and relatives, a stable extended family of considerable size. Redfield said that we were all descended from persons who lived in such societies, and that we were likely to hanker to live in one ourselves from time to time. A folk society, in his imagination and in our imaginations, too, is an ideal scheme within which people can take really good care of one another, can share fairly, and can distribute honors to one and all."

(*FWD* 122:L2, 8) When I studied anthropology long ago at the University of Chicago, my most famous professor was **Dr. Robert Redfield**. The idea that all societies evolved through similar, predictable stages on their way to higher (Victorian) civilization, from polytheism to monotheism, for instance, or from the tom-tom to the symphony orchestra, had by then been ridiculed into obscurity. It was generally agreed that there was no such ladder as cultural evolution. But **Dr. Redfield** said in effect, "Wait just a minute." He said that he could describe to every fair-minded person's satisfaction one (and only one) stage every society had passed through or would pass through. He called this inevitable stage and his essay on it "The Folk Society."

(*FWD* 123:L3, 9) **Dr. Redfield** gave a public lecture on the Folk Society in the springtime each year. It was popular, I think, because so many of us took it as scientific advice about how to find deep and enduring contentment: join or create a Folk Society. (This was back in the 1940s, remember, long before the communes and flower children and shared music and ideals of my children's generation.) **Dr. Redfield** denounced sentimentality about life in Folk Societies, saying they were hell for anyone with a lively imagination or an insatiable curiosity or a need to experiment and invent—or with an irrepressible sense of the ridiculous. But I still find myself daydreaming of an isolated little gang of likeminded people in a temperate climate, in a clearing in a woodland near a lake. . . .

(*FWD* 125:L29, 33) If I am ever going to find a Folk Society for myself (and time is growing short), it will not be on Manhattan. The members of such a society, **Dr. Redfield** taught me, must feel that a particular piece of land gave birth to them, and has been and always will be theirs. As I say, nobody can really own anything in Skyscraper National Park.

I have said in speeches that **Dr. Redfield**, by describing a Folk Society, deserved to be honored alongside the identifiers of vitamins and minerals essential to our good health and cheerfulness.

(*FWD* 126:L15) I visited the Anthropology Department of the University of Chicago a few months ago. Dr. Sol Tax was the only faculty member from my time who was still teaching there. I asked him if he knew what had become of my own classmates (including Lisa Redfield, **Dr. Redfield**'s daughter). Many of them, Lisa, too, he said, were practicing what he called "urban anthropology," which sounded an awful lot like sociology to me. (We used to look down on the sociologists. I couldn't imagine why and can't imagine why.) If I had stayed with anthropology as a career, I would now be doing, probably, what I am doing, which is writing about the acculturated primitive people (like myself) in Skyscraper National Park.

Redwine, Reverend C. Horner. *The forty-nine-year-old minister of the Barnstable First Church of God the Utterly Indifferent, subtitled The Church of the Weary Space Wanderer, in* The Sirens of Titan. *He is the first to come upon the naked Malachi Constant (also known as The Space Wanderer) emerging from his spaceship.*

religion, religious. *Religion is a frequent concern for Vonnegut. He often mentions his family's legacy of German Freethinking, and his first marriage began to unravel when his wife became a born-again Christian. Religion is a major plot device in* Player Piano, The Sirens of Titan, *and* Cat's Cradle. (*PP* 104:L7) And Halyard suddenly realized that, just as **religion** and government had been split into disparate entities centuries before, now, thanks to the machines, politics and government lived side by side, but touched almost nowhere.

(*PP* 249:L17, 36-37, 250:L11) "Toward the end of the nineteenth century," said Lasher, "a new **religious** movement *(the Ghost Shirt Society)* swept the Indians in this country, Doctor. . . .

"With the game and land and ability to defend themselves gone," said Lasher, "the Indians found out that all the things they used to take pride in doing . . . were going or gone . . . Great **religious** leaders could no longer show that the old **religious** beliefs were the way to victory and plenty. . . .

"And the Ghost Dance **religion**," said Lasher, "was that last, desperate defense of the old values. . . ."

(*ST* 66:L9) The Magnum Opus Building was a slender, prismatic, twelve-sided shaft, faced on all twelve sides with blue-green glass that shaded to rose at the base. The twelve sides were said by the architect to represent the twelve great **religions** of the world. So far, no one had asked the architect to name them.

(*ST* 174:L18) As he says in his *Pocket History of Mars*: "Any man who would change the World in a significant way must have showmanship, a genial willingness to shed other people's blood, and a plausible new **religion** to introduce during the brief period of repentance and horror that usually follows bloodshed. . . ."

(*ST* 180:L3-28) "To that end, devoutly to be wished," said Rumfoord, "I bring you word of a new **religion** that can be received enthusiastically in every corner of every Earthling heart. . . .

"The name of the new **religion**," said Rumfoord, "is The Church of God the Utterly Indifferent. . . .

"The two chief teachings of this **religion** are these," said Rumfoord: "Puny man can do nothing at all to help or please God Almighty, and Luck is not the hand of God.

"Why should you believe in this **religion**, rather than any others" said Rumfoord. "You should believe in it because I, as head of this **religion**, can work miracles, and the head of no other **religion** can. What miracles can I work? I can work the miracle of predicting, with absolute accuracy, the things that the future will bring."

(*ST* 255:L3) "You have had the singular accident, Mr. Constant," he said sympathetically, "of becoming a central symbol of wrong-headedness for a perfectly enormous **religious** sect. . . ."

(*ST* 282:L25) "Didn't I give you half my UWTB?" said Salo. ". . . Didn't I spend day after day helping you to design the new **religion**?"

(*ST* 305:L20-21) He *(Malachi)* respected what his son *(Chrono)* was trying to do with **religion**.

(*CC* 16:L11) Anyone unable to understand how a useful **religion** can be founded on lies will not understand this book either.

(*CC* 142:L36-37) "When Bokonon and McCabe took over this miserable country years ago," said Julian Castle, "they threw out the priests. And then Bokonon, cynically and playfully, invented a new **religion**."

(*CC* 143:L4, 10, 18) "Well, when it became evident that no governmental or economic reform was going to make the people much less miserable, the **religion** became the one real instrument of hope. . . .

He asked McCabe to outlaw him and his **religion**, too, in order to give the religious life of the people more zest, more tang. . . .

Castle quoted this poem, which does not appear in The Books of Bokonon: So I said good-bye to government, / And I gave my reason: / That a really good **religion** / Is a form of treason.
(*CC* 173:L33) "I agree with one Bokononist idea. I agree that all **religions**, including Bokononism, are nothing but lies."
(*CC* 228:L34) "As far as I know, Bokononism is the only **religion** that has any commentary on midgets."
(*GBR* 109:L20, 29) Mushari was gratified to hear the anxiety in her voice *(Sylvia's)*. It meant to him that Eliot's lunacy was not stabilized, but was about to make the great leap forward into **religion**. . . .

"I told her," said Eliot, and Mushari's mind, which was equipped with ratchets, declined to accept this evidence, "that I wasn't a **religious** person by any stretch of the imagination. I told her nothing I did would count in Heaven, but she insisted just the same." *Eliot tells Sylvia that he reluctantly agreed to baptize Mary Moody's twins.*
(*SL5* 33:L19) His father *(Billy Pilgrim's)* had no **religion**. *However, Billy had a large crucifix on his bedroom wall and became a chaplain's assistant in the military.*
(*MH* 264:L35-36 *The Manned Missiles*) The more we think about it, the more we're sure it was meant to be. I never got it straight in my mind about **religion** in Russia. You don't mention it. Anyway, we are **religious**, and we think God singled out Bud and your boy, too, to die in a special way for a special reason.
(*WFG* 16:L7 *Brief Encounters on the Inland Waterway*) "Thinking the guy up ahead knows what he's doing is the most dangerous **religion** there is," he said.
(*WFG* 166:L27 *Address to Graduating Class at Bennington College, 1970*) A great swindle of our time is the assumption that science has made **religion** obsolete. All science has damaged is the story of Adam and Eve and the story of Jonah and the Whale. Everything else holds up pretty well, particularly the lessons about fairness and gentleness. People who find those lessons irrelevant in the twentieth century are simply using science as an excuse for greed and harshness.
(*WFG* 186:L13-14 *In a Manner That Must Shame God Himself*) "Losers have thousands of **religions**, often of the *bleeding heart* variety," I would go on. "The single **religion** of the Winners is a harsh interpretation of Darwinism, which argues that it is the will of the universe that only the fittest should survive."
(*WFG* 200:L13-14 *In a Manner That Must Shame God Himself*) One of the things the Indians had come to beg from President Nixon, who never begged anything from anybody, was that their **religions** be recognized as respectable **religions** under law.
(*WFG* 203:L12 *In a Manner That Must Shame God Himself*) It was perhaps unkind of me to associate Dr. Kissinger with evil. That is no casual thing to do in a country as deeply **religious** as ours is.
(*WFG* 216:L26-27 *Address at Rededication of Wheaton College Library, 1973*) Our minds aren't crippled anymore by good taste. And I can see now all the

other more sinister taboos which mingled with sexuality and excretion, such as **religious** hypocrisy and ill-gotten wealth. If we are to discuss truthfully what America is and what it can become, our discussion must be in absolutely rotten taste, or we won't be discussing it at all.

(*WFG* 240:L10,13-15, 20, 31 *Playboy Interview*) PLAYBOY: What's your **religious** background?

VONNEGUT: My ancestors, who came to the United State a little before the Civil War, were atheists. So I'm not rebelling against organized **religion**. I never had any. I learned my outrageous opinions about organized **religion** at my mother's knee. My family has always had those. They came here absolutely crazy about the United States Constitution and about the possibility of prosperity and the brotherhood of man here. They were willing to work very hard, and they were atheists.

PLAYBOY: Do you think organized **religion** can make anybody happier?

VONNEGUT: Oh, of course. Lots of comforting lies are told in church—not enough, but some. I wish preachers would lie more convincingly about how honest and brotherly we should be. I've never heard a sermon on the subject of gentleness or restraint; I've never heard a minister say it was wrong to kill. No preacher ever speaks out against cheating in business. There are fifty two Sundays in a year, and somehow none of the subjects comes up.

PLAYBOY: Is there any **religion** you consider superior to any other?

VONNEGUT: Alcoholics Anonymous. Alcoholics Anonymous gives you an extended family that's very close to a brotherhood, because everybody has endured the same catastrophe.

(*WFG* 255:L1-2 *Playboy Interview*) I'm grateful that I learned from them *(Vonnegut's parents)* that organized **religion** is anti-Christian and that racial prejudices are stupid and cruel. I'm grateful, too, that they were good at making jokes.

(*Slap* 13:L7) Since Alice had never received any **religious** instruction, and since she had led a blameless life, she never thought of her awful luck as being anything but accidents in a very busy place.

(*Slap* 19:L24) The old man *(Wilbur Swain)* is writing his autobiography. He begins it with words which my late Uncle Alex told me one time should be used by **religious** skeptics as a prelude to their nightly prayers.

These are the words: "To whom it may concern."

(*JB* 35:L17-18) I do not mean to sketch this blubbering leviathan *(Emil Larkin)* as a **religious** hypocrite, nor am I entitled to. He had so opened himself to the consolations of **religion** that he had become an imbecile.

(*PS* 15:L21 *The First Amendment*) What you may not know about our own culture is that writers . . . are routinely attacked by fellow citizens as being pornographers or corrupters of children and celebrators of violence and persons of no talent and so on. In my own case, such charges are brought against my works in court several times a year, usually by parents who, for **religious** or political reasons, do not want their children to read what I have to say.

(*PS* 69:L2, 4 *When I Lost My Innocence*) An enthusiasm for technological cures for almost all forms of human discontent was the only **religion** of my family during the Great Depression, when I first got to know that family well. It was **religion** enough for me, and one branch of the family owned the largest hardware store in Indianapolis, Indiana.

(*PS* 69:L12 *When I Lost My Innocence*) But I learned how vile that **religion** of mine could be when the atomic bomb was dropped on Hiroshima.

(*PS* 69:L29 *When I Lost My Innocence*) But the bombing of Hiroshima compelled me to see that a trust in technology, like all the other great **religions** of the world, had to do with the human soul.

(*PS* 101:L8, 13 *Self-Interview*) INTERVIEWER: Did the study of anthropology later color your writings?

VONNEGUT: It confirmed my atheism, which was the faith of my fathers anyway. **Religions** were exhibited and studied as the Rube Goldberg inventions I'd always thought they were. We weren't allowed to find one culture superior to any other. We caught hell if we mentioned races much. It was highly idealistic.

INTERVIEWER: Almost a **religion**?

VONNEGUT: Exactly. And the only one for me. So far.

(*PS* 106:L29 *Self-Interview*) VONNEGUT: It's my **religion** the censors hate. They find me disrespectful toward their idea of God Almighty. They think it's the proper business of government to protect the reputation of God.

(*PS* 168:L14, 18 *Mark Twain*) "We **religious** skeptics would like to swagger some in heaven, saying to others who spent a lot of time quaking in churches down here, 'I was never worried about pleasing or angering God—never took Him into my calculations at all.'

"**Religious** skeptics often become very bitter toward the end, as did Mark Twain. I do not propose to guess now as to why he became so bitter. I know why I will become bitter. I will finally realize that I have had it right all along: that I will not see God, that there is no heaven or Judgment Day."

(*PS* 194:L31 *Religion*) "We cannot believe that this Being formed a human being from clay and breathed into it an Immortal Soul, and then allowed this human being to procreate millions, and then delivered them all into unspeakable misery, wretchedness and pain for all eternity. Nor can we believe that the descendents of one or two human beings will inevitably become sinners; nor do we believe that through the criminal executions of an Innocent One may we be redeemed." *(From Clemens Vonnegut's funeral oration.)*

SUCH is my ancestral **religion**.

(*PS* 198:L6, 8-9 *Religion*) "Our politicians like to say that we have **religion** and the Communist countries don't. I think it is just the other way around. Those countries have a **religion** called Communism, and the Free World is where sustaining **religions** are in very short supply."

(*PS* 198:L32 199:L1, 4-5, 14-15 *Religion*) "I suggest that we need a new **religion**. If suggesting that we need a new **religion** is sacrilege, then the emperor Constantine was guilty of sacrilege, and the emperor Nero was an admirably pious man. And I want to point out that it is impossible to discard an old **religion** entirely. The **religion** of Nero survives today, determining as it does the dates and even moods of so many of our so-called Christian holidays...

"What makes me think we need a new **religion**? That's easy. An effective **religion** allows people to imagine from moment to moment what is going on and how they should behave. Christianity used to be like that. Our country is now jammed with human beings who say out loud that life is chaos to them, and that it doesn't seem to matter what anybody does next. This is worse than being seasick."

(*PS* 200:L3 *Religion*) "We know too much for old-time **religion**; and in a way, that knowledge is killing us."

(*PS* 202:L11-12 *Religion*) "If I have offended anyone here by talking of the need of a new **religion**, I apologize. I am willing to drop the word **religion**, and substitute for it these three words: heartfelt moral code."

(*PS* 210:L3 *Religion*) "There is a willingness to do whatever we need to do in order to have life on the planet go on for a long, long time. I didn't used to think that. And that willingness has to be a **religious** enthusiasm, since it celebrates life, since it calls for meaningful sacrifices."

(*PS* 215:L11-12, 27 *Religion*) "The faith of my ancestors, going back at least four generations, has been the most corrosive sort of agnosticism—or worse. When I was a child, all my relatives, male and female, agreed with H. L. Mencken when he said that he thought **religious** people were comical. Mencken said that he had been widely misunderstood as hating **religious** people. He did not hate them, he said. He merely found them comical. . . .

"Any time I see a person fleeing from reason and into **religion**, I think to myself, There goes a person who simply cannot stand being so goddamned lonely anymore."

(*PS* 216:L23 *Religion*) "I have spoken of the long tradition of **religious** skepticism in my family. One of my two daughters has recently turned her back on all that. Living alone and far from home, she has memorized an arbitrary Christian creed, Trinitarianism, by chance. She now has her human dignity regularly confirmed by the friendly nods of a congregation. I am glad that she is not so lonely anymore. This is more than all right with me."

(*Blue* 16:L26) Armenians, incidentally, were the first people to make Christianity their national **religion**.

(*HP* 97:L31-32) The origin of this most poisonous misunderstanding was in my account in Chapel of riding around with Grandfather *(Wills)* in his car one Sunday morning in Midland City, Ohio, when I was a little boy. He, not I, was mocking all organized **religions**.

When we passsed a Catholic church, I recalled, he said, "You think your dad's a good chemist? They're turning soda crackers into meat in there. Can your dad do that?"

(*FWD* 77:L7) So the Reverend was not a hypocrite. He was perfectly willing to say in so many words that there was nothing sacred about the First

Amendment, and that many images and ideas other than pornography should be taken out of circulation by the police, and that the official **religion** of the whole country should be his sort of Christianity. He was sincere in believing that my *Slaughterhouse-Five* might somehow cause a person to wind up in a furnace for all eternity (see the mass promulgated by Pope St. Pius V), which would be even worse (if you consider its duration) than being raped, murdered, and then mutilated by a man maddened by dirty pictures.

(*FWD* 156:L12-13, 34) My late war buddy O'Hare was born a Roman Catholic in Pennsylvania but came home from the war a **religious** skeptic. Bishop Moore, as I've said, went to war a religious skeptic and came out of it a profoundly convinced Trinitarian. He told me he had a vision during the fighting on Guadalcanal. He went on from his vision (although he was born rich and had a rich Anglo-Saxon's education and tastes and friends) to minister to the poor in parishes where the prosperous had fled to the suburbs, to speak loathingly of social Darwinists (Neo-Cons, the FBI, the CIA, humorless, anal-retentive Republicans, and so on). . . .

My second wife is another Episcopalian, and like my first one thinks that I have no **religion** and am a spiritual cripple on that account. When Jill's and my daughter Lily was baptized by the Bishop of New York in the biggest Gothic church in the world (in a neighborhood so poor that the Bishop couldn't get cable service for his TV), I did not attend.

(*FWD* 158:L9, 17-19) "I listen to the ethical pronouncements of the leaders of the so-called religious revival going on in this country, including those of our President, and am able to distill only two firm commandments from them. The first commandment is this: 'Stop thinking.' The second commandment is this: 'Obey.' Only a person who has given up on the power of reason to improve life here on Earth, or a soldier in Basic Training could accept either commandment gladly: 'Stop thinking' and 'Obey.'"

"I was an Infantry Private during World War II and fought against the Germans in Europe. My **religion** as well as my blood type was stamped into my dogtags. The Army decided my **religion** was P, for 'Protestant.' There is no room on dogtags for footnotes and a bibliography. In retrospect, I think they should have put S on my dogtags, for 'Saracen,' since we were fighting Christians who were on some sort of utterly insane Crusade. They had crosses on their flags and uniforms and all over their killing machines, just like the soldiers of the first Christian Emperor Constantine. And they lost, of course, which has to be acknowledged as quite a setback for Christianity.

(*FWD* 163:L29-31) "When I say that the Unitarian Universalists, the people who know pure baloney when they hear it, are something like the early Christians in the catacombs, am I suggesting that contempt for baloney will someday be as widespread as Christianity is today? Well the example of Christianity is not encouraging, actually, since it was nothing but a poor people's **religion**, a servant's **religion**, a slave's **religion**, a woman's **religion**, a child's **religion**, and would have remained such if it hadn't stopped taking the Sermon on the Mount seriously and joined forces with the vain and rich and

violent. I can't imagine that you would want to do that, to give up everything you believe in order to play a bigger part in world history.
(*FWD* 164:L31) "And stay clear of the Ten Commandments, as do the television evangelists. Those things are booby-trapped, because right in the middle of them is one commandment which would, if taken seriously, cripple modern **religion** as show business. It is this commandment: 'Thou shalt not kill.'"
(*HP* 176:L1) Freethinkers . . . believed . . . that science had proved all organized **religions** to be baloney, that God was unknowable, and that the greatest use a person could make of his or her lifetime was to improve the quality of life for all in his or her community.
(*FWD* 238:L11) I am a fourth generation German American **religious** skeptic ("Freethinker"). Like my essentially puritanical forebears, I believe that God has so far been unknowable and hence unservable, hence the highest service one can perform is to his or her community, whose needs are quite evident. I believe that virtuous behavior is trivialized by carrot-and-stick schemes, such as promises of highly improbable rewards or punishments in an improbable afterlife. (The punishment for counterfeiting in Henry VIII's reign, incidentally, was being boiled alive in public.) The Bible is a useful starting point for discussions with crowds of American strangers, since so many of us know at least a little something about it. It has the added virtue of having for contributors at least two geniuses Moses and Christ. *See also: PP*103:L32; 105:L9; *ST* 7:L8; 149.L22; 175:L1; 176:L25-26; 178.L18-19; 181:L3; 186:L19; 218:L3; 219:L21; 231:L28; 238:L4-5; 240:L9; 261:L2; *MN* 36:L32; *CC* 91:L8; 109:L1; 150:L31; 162:L14,15; 171:L14,22; 176:L18; 223:L21; *GBR* 90:L24,28; 128:L8; *SL5* 108:L17; 174:L22; *MH—Harrison Bergeron* 8:L31; *BC* 18:L29; 256:L11; *MH—Miss Temptation* 72:L13; *WFG—Yes, We Have No Nirvanas* 33:L8-9,13,17,21; 34:L12; 35:L21; 40:L20; *WFG—Why They Read Hesse* 114:L9; *WFG—The Mysterious Madame Blavatsky* 122:L32; 127:L8; 132:L26; *WFG—In a Manner That Must Shame God Himself* 198:L15,17; *WFG—Address at Rededication of Wheaton College Library, 1973* 214:L22; *Slap* 6:L5; 184:L16; *JB* 15:L24; 21:L16; 24:L29; 29:L23,27; 35:L27; 37:L20; 69:L1; 88:L5; 120:L8; 129:L15; 196:L31; 197:L3; *PS—The First Amendment* 3:L31; 9:L13; *PS—Roots* 24:L30; 31:L17,19; *PS—Self-Interview* 107:L3; *PS—Religion* 192:L1-2; 199:L21,24; 201:L2; 202:L1; 207:L32; 208:L5; 215:L15,18; 217:L10; *PS—Children* 250:L23; *DD* 59:L21; *Gal* 44:L27; 110:L21; 159:L8,14; *Blue* 24:L14; 31:L16; 40:L1 62:L14; *HP* 16:L15-16; 25:L1; 131:L26; 180:L16; *FWD* 43:L1; 73:L5; 77:L1; 79:L17; 143:L20; 152:L20; 153:L7; 159:L14; 164:L19; 164:L35; 165:L10,13; 167:L18; 222:L23.

Remenzel, Dr., Sylvia, and Eli. *In the short story "The Lie," Dr. Remenzel, wife Sylvia, and thirteen-year-old Eli travel to Whitehill School for Boys, a private preparatory school in North Marston, Massachusetts. The lie concerns Eli's deception about his failure to pass the entrance examinations for the elite* *boarding school. When the rejection letter arrived, he snatched it from the mail.*

Dr. Remenzel, a member of the class of 1939, is also a member of the school's Board of Overseers. Since the 18th century, generations of Remenzels attended Whitehill. While traveling in their chauffeured limousine to the campus, Dr. Remenzel reviews plans for the latest family donation, the Eli Remenzel Memorial Dormitory, named in honor of his great-great-grandfather. *Dr. Remenzel* was a massive, dignified man, a physician, a healer for healing's sake, since he had been born as rich as the Shah of Iran (*MH* 216:L13-15 *The Lie*). *Despite his dignity, when Dr. Remenzel learns of his son's deceit, he focuses on getting the other Board members to overrule the entrance exam requirements for his son. When young Eli learns of his father's demeaning act of asking for a special favor, he shames his father. Rather than being upset by his son's own lie, Dr. Remenzel leaves the campus in disgrace for his own behavior.*

Old Eli funded the school's Scholarship Fund in 1799 by donating forty acres in Boston. The Scholarship Fund enabled boys to attend who were academically gifted but from economically disadvantaged families. Among the many Remenzel gifts were the Sanford Remenzel Bird Sanctuary and the George MacLellan Remenzel Skating Rink.

"Report on the Barnhouse Effect" (1950) (see **Professor Arthur Barnhouse** and **dynamopsychism**).

Rettig, John (1860-1932). *The Cincinnati native was one of the expatriate artists working in Europe prior to World War I. In* Deadeye Dick, *Otto Waltz purchases Rettig's "Crucifixion in Rome," around 1913 while touring Volendam, Holland (though the painting is signed and dated 1888). The Waltz's are forced to sell it along with most of their other treasures when George Metzger sues them for his wife's wrongful death. Representatives from the Cincinnati Art Museum make their way to Midland City just to purchase the painting by their native son.* (*DD* 169:L16-35, 170:L1-2) "Crucifixion in Rome" is indeed set in Rome, which I have never seen. I know enough, though, to recognize that it is chock-a-block with architectural anachronisms. The Colosseum, for example, is in perfect repair, but there is also the spire of a Christian church, and some architectural details and monuments which appear to be more recent, even, than the Renaissance, maybe even nineteenth century. There are sixty-eight tiny but distinct human figures taking part in some sort of celebration amid all this architecture and sculpture. Felix and I counted them one time, when we were young. Hundreds more are implied by impressionistic smears and dots. Banners fly. Walls are festooned with ropes of leaves. What fun.

Only if you look closely at the painting will you realize that two of the sixty-eight figures are not having such a good time. They are in the lower left-hand corner, and are harmonious with the rest of the composition, but they have in fact just been hung from crosses.

The picture is a comment, I suppose, but certainly a bland one, on man's festive inhumanity to men—even into what to **John Rettig** were modern times.

Reyes, Colonel Guillermo. *The Peruvian pilot in* Galápagos *who fires the first shot in the war between Peru and Ecuador. He blew up the radar dish atop the control tower at Guayaquil International Airport.*

"**A Rift Between Friends in the War of Ideas**." *One of the many publications sent to Stewart Buntline by attorney Reed McAllister, who had forever feared his client might relapse into the socialist thinking he demonstrated when just a teenager. The pamphlet* was supposedly a letter from a conservative to close friends who were socialists without knowing it. Because he did not need to, Stewart had not read what the pamphlet had to say about the recipients of social security and other forms of welfare (*GBR* 137:L22-26).

Riley, James Whitcomb. *"The Hoosier Poet" is frequently mentioned as part of Vonnegut's litany of notable Indianans. Vonnegut mentions that his mother knew Riley (JB* x:L6-7), *and that his first mother-in-law, Riah Fagan Cox, his sister, and his parents are all buried in the same cemetery as Riley, the Crown Hill Cemetery in Indianapolis. When Vonnegut's family lost much of its wealth during the Great Depression, he was sent to Public School 43, "the James Whitcomb Riley school" (PS* 58:L19). *Hoosier Ambassador and Mrs. Minton in* Cat's Cradle, *are proud to claim Riley as well.*

Rivera, Jerry Cha-cha. *The first husband of Walter Starbuck, Jr.'s wife, herself a black nightclub singer. Together they had two children later adopted by Starbuck, who had since changed his name to Stankiewicz.* (*JB* 16:L1-2) The former nightclub comedian of Puerto Rican extraction named **Jerry Cha-cha Rivera** . . . was shot as an innocent bystander during the robbery of a RAMJAC carwash in Hollywood.

Rivera, Wanda Chipmunk-5 *The intoxicated slave who, at the close of* Slapstick, *kicks over the Dresden candlestick brought by Melody to her grandfather, Wilbur Swain. The event occurs on his final birthday.* (*Slap* 240:L15-17) Melody's candlestick depicted a nobleman's flirtation with a shepherdess at the foot of a treetrunk enlaced in flowering vines.

Rivers, Jerry. *The Mickey Rooney look-alike boyfriend of Sally Cathcart and student body president of Sweetbread College, in the play "The Chemistry Professor" reprinted in* Palm Sunday. *He suggests holding a Broadway musical to raise funds for the bankrupt college. He is the stepson of Fred Leghorn, though he is getting a divorce from Jerry's mother.*

Robbins, Eldon. *The ex-con who spent time at the Shepherdstown Adult Correctional Institution and is now a dishwasher at the Midland City Holiday Inn. He found Wayne Hoobler scavenging around the garbage cans and brought him into the kitchen for steak dinner. He was wearing a "Support the Arts" button and gave one to Wayne with the warning,* "Wear this at all times... and no harm can come to you" (*BC* 213:L24-26).

Robert, Henry Martyn (also ***Roberts Rules of Order***). *In* Slapstick, *when Wilbur Swain attends an extended family meeting, he applauds the efforts of Henry Martyn Robert (1837-1923), the West Point graduate and Civil War general who authored* Robert's Rules of Order *(1876). He also designed the defenses around Washington D.C. during the Civil War. Swain views* Robert's Rules *as one of the four great inventions by Americans, the other three being: The Bill of Rights, Alcoholics Anonymous, and the concept of artificially extended families he developed with his sister Eliza.*

The Robo-Magic Corporation. *In* Breakfast of Champions, *Fred T. Barry's company started advertising his new fully automatic washing machines in 1933, though he didn't begin production until 1934. His motto for the company "Goodbye Blue Monday," is also the subtitle of the novel. During World War II, the company stopped producing washing machines and became The Midland City Ordnance Company. The main mechanism of the washer became the central component in the "BLINC System" (Blast Interval Normalization Computer) a bomb release mechanism for heavy bombers. The company's emblem was a Greek goddess reclining on an ornate chaise lounge and holding a pennant with the company's motto.*

In Hocus Pocus, *Eugene Debs Hartke's father was sent to Robo-Magic by Du Pont to determine how to use plastics technology to lighten the military products. Mr. Hartke became the Vice-President in Charge of Research and Development for Barrytron, Ltd., the successor to Robo-Magic.*

The corporate genealogy of Fred T. Barry's is as follows: Robo-Magic Corporation of America later became The Midland City Ordnance Company and then Barrytron, Limited. In Hocus Pocus, *Barrytron, Limited is eventually purchased by E.I. Du Pont de Nemours & Company.*

Rockefeller, Alice (see **Alexander Hamilton McCone**).

Rockefeller, Geraldine Ames (see **Geraldine Ames Rockefeller Rosewater**).

Rockmell, Dr. Eli W. *The pseudonym used by Wilbur Swain to publish the childrearing manual he wrote with his sister Eliza. The pseudonym is "a garbling" of their two names: Wilbur Rockefeller Swain and Eliza Mellon Swain. They wrote the manuscript of* The Cry of the Nocturnal Goatsucker *by Betty and Bobby Brown, during one of their heads-together telepathic frenzies.*

When it was published under the Rockmell pseudonym, the publisher retitled it, So You Went and Had a Baby.

Roethke, Theodore. *When Vonnegut travels back to Dresden, he mentions taking along two books to read on the flight. One is Erika Ostrovsky's* Céline and His Vision, *and the other is Roethke's* Words for the Wind, *from which he quotes, "I wake to sleep, and take my waking slow. / I feel my fate in what I cannot fear. / I learn by going where I have to go"* (*SL5* 18:L19-21).

Roosevelt, Claudia. *In* Hocus Pocus, *the girlfriend of equestrian star Lowell Chung from whom he borrows a horse to teach Eugene Debs Hartke how to ride. Claudia is a mathematical whiz who lacks personality.*

Roosevelt, Eleanor. *In* Deadeye Dick, *Mrs. Roosevelt goes on a morale-boosting visit to the Green Diamond Plow facility, which was producing tanks during World War II. The first lady was given the usual tour and luncheon at Otto Waltz's home studio provided for all visiting dignitaries to Midland City. She arrived the morning Felix left for military service and left hours before Rudy's fateful shot killed the pregnant Eloise Metzger.*

Roseberry, Dr. Harold. *In* Player Piano, *the Cornell football coach who relishes the opportunity to ruin the life of Cornell alumnus Dr. Ewing J. Halyard. Halyard somehow graduated without completing the physical education requirement. Five years before the opening of the text, Halyard wrote a scathing letter to Cornell's president complaining about the behavior of the football team when on a road trip. Roseberry took the letter from his files in preparation for meeting Halyard.*

Rosenau, Dr. Maurice. *There are two Dr. Rosenaus in Vonnegut's early novels. In* Player Piano, *Dr. Rosenau is a lubrication engineer at the Ilium Works. In* Sirens of Titan, *Dr. Maurice Rosenau is one of Winston Niles Rumfoord's great detractors and has written* Pan-Galactic Humbug *(subtitled* Three Billion Dupes*) to forward his position.*

Rosenfeld, Franklin Delano. *This is how Howard Campbell would refer to President Roosevelt during his broadcasts in* Mother Night. *Roosevelt was one of the three individuals who knew Campbell's true mission as an American agent.*

Rosenquist, Per Olaf. *In* Galápagos, *the Swedish shipyard foreman who died of a defective heart, prompting Hjalmar Arvid Boström to recite a bit of black humor which would become Leon Trout's refrain when recording the deaths of various characters.* (*Gal* 244:L19-21) Oh, well—he wasn't going to write Beethoven's Ninth Symphony anyway.

Rosewater, Abraham. *The grandfather of Fred Rosewater, son of General George Rosewater and Faith Merrihue,* who became a Congregationalist minister. **Abraham** went as a missionary to the Congo, where he met and married Lavinia Waters, the daughter of another missionary, an Illinois Baptist.

In the jungle, **Abraham** begat Merrihue. Lavinia died at Merrihue's birth. Little Merrihue was nursed on the milk of a Bantu.

And **Abraham** and little Merrihue returned to Rhode Island. **Abraham** accepted the call to the Congregationalist pulpit in the little fishing village of Pisquontuit (*GBR* 103:L5-15).

Rosewater, Caroline. *The wife of Fred Rosewater and mother of Franklin, the Rhode Island cousins of Eliot Rosewater. Her best friend is Amanita Buntline who treats her like her own poorer relation. Her existence is one of bland futility.* (*GBR* 128:L26-30, 129:L1-23) She was a pretty, pinched, skinny, lost little woman, all dolled-up in well-made clothes cast off by her wealthy, Lesbian friend, Amanita Buntline. **Caroline Rosewater** clinked and flashed with accessories. Their purpose was to make the second-hand clothing distinctly her own. . . .

When she spoke to Fred, with Harry Pena watching, she behaved like a woman who was keeping her dignity while being frog-walked. With the avid help of Amanita, she pitied herself for being married to a man who was so poor and dull. That she was exactly as poor and dull as Fred was a possibility she was constitutionally unable to entertain. For one thing, she was a Phi Beta Kappa, having won her key as a philosophy major at Dillon University, in Dodge City, Kansas. That was where she and Fred had met, in Dodge City, in a U.S.O. Fred had been stationed at Fort Riley during the Korean War. She married Fred because she thought everybody who lived in Pisquontuit and had been to Princeton was rich.

She was humiliated to discover that it was not true. She honestly believed that she was an intellectual, but she knew almost nothing, and every problem she ever considered could be solved by just one thing: money, and lots of it. She was a frightful housekeeper. She cried when she did housework, because she was convinced that she was cut out for better things.

As for the Lesbian business, it wasn't particularly deep on **Caroline**'s part. She was simply a female chameleon trying to get ahead in the world.

Rosewater, Eliot. *The enigmatic alcoholic and obese title character who prods science fiction writers out of their disrepute by asking their continued efforts to consider the really great challenges in life, including economic challenges. While on a drunken binge in 1953, Eliot crashes a science fiction writers conference in Milford, Pennsylvania, and extemporaneously admonishes the crowd.* (*GBR* 27:L13-25, 31:L14-17) "I love you sons of bitches," **Eliot** said in Milford. "You're all I read any more. You're the only ones who'll talk about the *really* terrific changes going on, the only ones crazy enough to know that life is a space voyage, and not a short one, either, but one that'll last for billions of years. You're the only ones with guts enough to *really* care about the future, who *really* notice what machines do to us, what wars do to us, what cities do to us, what big, simple ideas do to us, what tremendous misunderstandings, mistakes, accidents and catastrophes do to us. You're the only ones zany enough to agonize over time and distances without limit, over mysteries that will never die. . . . I leave it to you, friends and neighbors, and especially to the immortal Kilgore Trout: think about the silly ways money gets passed around now, and then think up better ways."

Eliot becomes the target of Norman Mushari, the venal young lawyer who is already aware of the silly ways money gets passed around. Mushari seeks to have Eliot declared insane and have the courts declare Fred Rosewater president of the Rosewater Foundation. The legal fees for such a transaction drive Mushari's dreams.

As President of the Rosewater Foundation, Eliot spent $14 million from 1947 to 1953 on a series of public service projects and fine art donations, but he felt detached from the lives of ordinary people. This was due to a number of factors. His parents insulated themselves from the rest of society by traveling only in the rarefied circles of the wealthy and politically influential on the East Coast, despite the fact their ancestral hometown was the poverty-stricken area known as Rosewater County, Indiana. The family returned there each year to keep their legal residency, a political necessity for Senator Lister Ames Rosewater. On those brief visits, Eliot was made the mascot of the volunteer fire department, sparking a lifelong love for those who selflessly and without reward cared for their neighbors.

When only nineteen, Eliot unintentionally committed matricide. While sailing with his mother in Cotuit Harbor, he swung the boom around and knocked his mother overboard. As a captain in the U.S. Army a few years later, Eliot and his troops invaded a Bavarian clarinet factory supposedly infested with S.S. troops. Eliot tossed a grenade through a window, and led his men into the smoke-filled structure. (*GBR* 76:L33-34, 77:L1-22) He took a step forward, stumbled over one body, fell on another. They were Germans who had been killed by his grenade. He stood up, found himself face-to-face with a helmeted German in a gas mask.

Eliot, like the good soldier he was, jammed his knee into the man's groin, drove his bayonet into his throat, withdrew the bayonet, smashed the man's jaw with his rifle butt.

And then **Eliot** heard an American sergeant yelling somewhere off to his left. The visibility was apparently a lot better over there, for the sergeant was yelling, "Cease fire! Hold your fire, you guys. Jesus Christ—these aren't soldiers. They're firemen!"

It was true: **Eliot** had killed three unarmed firemen. They were ordinary villagers, engaged in the brave and uncontroversial business of trying to keep a building from combining with oxygen.

When the medics got the masks off the three **Eliot** had killed, they proved to be two old men and a boy. The boy was the one **Eliot** had bayoneted. He didn't look more than fourteen.

Eliot seemed reasonably well for about ten minutes after that. And then he calmly lay down in front of a moving truck.

The driver of the truck stopped in time, but Eliot suffered his first catatonic episode. Through innocent actions, Eliot had killed four people with whom he shared a deep spiritual bond.

His marriage to Sylvia suffered due to bouts with alcohol and his depression over not doing enough for the poor. She eventually broke down with Samaritrophia, an "hysterical indifference to the troubles of those less fortunate than oneself" (*GBR* 54:L7-8). *Eliot's final breakdown in New York came while attending a performance of* Aïda. *He stood up and yelled at the singers to stop singing because they would surely die sooner in the air-tight chamber.*

From the theater he went on an alcoholic cross-country trek, moving from one volunteer fire department to the next. Writing from the Elsinore, California, volunteer fire department, Eliot feels he found an apt literary analogy for himself—Hamlet. (*GBR* 42:L7-17) Maybe I flatter myself when I think that I have things in common with Hamlet, that I have an important mission, that I'm temporarily mixed up about how it should be done. Hamlet had one big edge on me. His father's ghost told him exactly what he had to do, while I am operating without instructions. But from somewhere something is trying to tell me where to go, what to do there, and why to do it. Don't worry, I don't hear voices. But there is this feeling that I have a destiny far away from the shallow and preposterous posing that is our life in New York. And I roam.

And I roam.

Eliot eventually finds himself in Rosewater, Indiana, where he sets up new Foundation offices above the volunteer fire department. There he dispenses money in accordance with the citizens needs, provided they ask, recording his transactions in his Domesday Book. *At the back of the ledger is his novel-in-progress about resurrection. Eliot becomes a spiritual solace to the community to the extent he is asked to perform a baptism for Mary Moody's twins.*

All the while, however, his guilt over driving Sylvia from his life and the legal pursuits of Norman Mushari keep closing upon him. Senator Rosewater's scheme to ward off Mushari includes Eliot traveling to Indianapolis for a reconciliation meeting with Sylvia. He reads Kilgore Trout's Pan-Galactic Three Day Pass *while on the bus, and as he reaches the outskirts of Indianapolis (Vonnegut's hometown) Eliot looks up and imagines the city consumed by firestorm.*

This episode is followed by a one-year gap in the narrative, during which time Mushari has pressed ahead with the court challenge. Eliot snaps out of his trance on the tennis courts of Dr. Brown's sanitarium, dressed in tennis whites, and surrounded by the doctor, his father and Kilgore Trout. It is left to Trout to explain the sanity of Eliot's life and times in Rosewater County. (*GBR* 213:L23-34, 214:L1-2) "It seems to me," said Trout, "that the main lesson Eliot learned is that people can use all the uncritical love they can get."

"This is *news*?" the Senator raucously inquired.

"It's news that a man was able to *give* that kind of love over a long period of time. If one man can do it, perhaps others can do it, too. It means that our hatred of useless human beings and the cruelties we inflict upon them for their own good need not be parts of human nature. Thanks to the example of **Eliot Rosewater**, millions upon millions of people may learn to love and help whomever they see."

Trout glanced from face to face before speaking his last word on the subject. The last word was: "Joy."

Eliot settles with Fred Rosewater for $100,000, cutting Mushari out of his contingency fee, and declares all fifty-seven participants in Mushari's false paternity suits to be his offspring. Though a lie, it eliminates Mushari from profit. Moreover, it is perhaps Eliot's single greatest experiment with redistributing wealth, the very subject he asked the science fiction writers to consider.

Eliot Rosewater also appears in Slaughterhouse-Five. *He shares a Lake Placid Veterans' Hospital room with Billy Pilgrim, who suffers a mental breakdown while attending the Ilium School of Optometry. Rosewater was there for alcoholism treatment. Eliot coaxes Billy back from his silence by talking about the science fiction stories of Kilgore Trout. Rosewater has a tremendous stack of Trout's books beneath his bed and lets Billy read all he wants. Billy eventually becomes an enormous fan of Trout's, as well.*

Rosewater, Eunice Eliot Morgan. *The wife of Senator Lister Ames Rosewater and mother of Eliot. The following information is from a letter Eliot wrote to be opened after his death.* (*GBR* 22:L19-27) As a curious footnote to history, **Eunice** became Woman's Chess Champion of the United States in 1927, and again in 1933.

Eunice also wrote an historical novel about a female gladiator, *Ramba of Macedon*, which was a best-seller in 1936. **Eunice** died in 1937, in a sailing accident in Cotuit, Massachusetts. She was a wise and amusing person, with very sincere anxieties about the condition of the poor. She was my mother . *A later description of Eunice's death concludes:* The statement that Eliot had killed his beloved mother was, in a crude way, true. When he was nineteen, he took his mother for a sail in Cotuit Harbor. He jibed. The slashing boom knocked his mother overboard. **Eunice Morgan Rosewater** sank like a stone (*GBR* 38:L19-23).

Rosewater, Franklin. *The young son of Fred and Caroline Rosewater in* God Bless You, Mr. Rosewater. *He purchases a pornographic photograph from*

Lila Buntline and prevents his father from committing suicide by calling down the basement stairs that Norman Mushari wanted to speak with him.

Rosewater, Fred. *The Rhode Island cousin of Eliot Rosewater manipulated by Norman Mushari in an attempt to transfer control of the Rosewater Foundation. Though Fred is a Princeton graduate, he makes a meager living selling insurance policies to the working class of Pisquontuit. Despondent over his poor lot in life, Fred frequently contemplates suicide. He comes within a moment of hanging himself in his basement when Norman Mushari comes knocking at his door. Fred started to read the history of his ancestors as chronicled by his father, Merrihue Rosewater. He became elated to find out about their illustrious beginnings in England but was crestfallen to find the rest of the history had been eaten by worms.*

Fred likes to think that his purpose in life as an insurance salesman is to make sure the survivors of the insured have secure financial futures. His customers understood the underlying irony of the situation. (*GBR* 114:L26-32) The workmen had an uneasy respect for **Fred**. They tried to be cynical about what he sold, but they knew in their hearts that he was offering the only get-rich-quick scheme that was open to them: to insure themselves and die soon. And it was **Fred**'s gloomy secret that without such people, tantalized by such a proposition, he would not have a dime. *He often thought about the value of his own death: $42,000. Both Fred and Eliot enjoy the moment when others turn to them and say, "God bless you, Mr. Rosewater." Fred hears it from the survivors who benefit from his policies, and Eliot hears it from the people in Rosewater County who enjoy his charity.*

Fred is the son of a suicide. His father shot himself in the head. His wife Caroline maintains an odd friendship with the lesbian Amanita Buntline, and though they don't have a sexual relationship, Caroline wears Amanita's second-hand clothes. Fred and Caroline met when he was stationed at Fort Riley during the Korean War and she was a student at Dillon University. She married him thinking people from Pisquontuit were all rich. Their son buys pornographic pictures from Lila Buntline.

In order for Eliot to prevent Norman Mushari from succeeding in his plans to transfer control of the foundation to Fred, he gives Fred a check for $1 million, thus preventing Mushari from profiting. Fred never was an active participant in the scheme to uproot the foundation.

Rosewater, George. *The younger brother of Noah, George had trustingly signed away his share of the family business while going off to serve the Union during the Civil War. He raised a company of riflemen from Rosewater County, joining forces with the Black Hat Brigade. He suffered a number of crippling wounds but in all respects was an exemplary and brave soldier.* (*GBR* 117:L19-29) By the time of Antietam, **George Rosewater** had become a Lieutenant Colonel, and had, curiously, lost the little fingers from both hands. At Antietam, he had his horse shot out from under him, advanced on foot, grabbed the regimental colors from a dying boy, found himself holding only a shattered staff when Confederate cannister carried the colors away. He pressed on, killed a man with the staff. At the moment he was doing the killing, one of his own men fired off a musket that still had its ramrod jammed down the bore. The explosion blinded **Colonel Rosewater** for life.

He returned home a blind brevet brigadier general without any rights in the family business. Noah was busy in Washington, but George refused to take any legal actions to reclaim his share of their enterprise. He chose instead to make formal calls on all the families who trusted their sons to his rifle company, and then he went to his brother's new mansion and One morning the workmen found the brigadier's uniform nailed to the front door as though it were an animal skin nailed to a barn door to dry (*GBR* 119:L1-3).

He traveled to Providence, Rhode Island, seeking work at the Buntline Broom factory, which had a reputation for employing disabled Civil War veterans. Castor Buntline hired General Rosewater and named the whiskbrooms after him. (*GBR* 119:L34) A "**General Rosewater**" was a *whiskbroom.*

Fourteen-year-old Faith Merrihue was assigned to the general as "his eyes and messenger." They later married and had Abraham, who eventually took a pulpit position in Pisquontuit, Rhode Island. General Rosewater is the great-grandfather of insurance salesman Fred Rosewater.

Rosewater, Geraldine Ames Rockefeller. *The wife of Samuel Rosewater and mother to Lister Ames Rosewater, in* God Bless You, Mr. Rosewater.

Rosewater, Merrihue. *Born in the Congo to missionaries Abraham Rosewater and Lavina Waters, he became a realtor in Pisquontuit, Rhode Island.* (*GBR* 120:L20-28) **Merrihue**, the Parson's son, became a realtor, divided his father's land into lots. He married Cynthia Niles Rumfoord, a minor heiress, invested much of her money in pavement and streetlights and sewers. He made a fortune, lost it, and his wife's fortune, too, in the crash of 1929.

He blew his brains out.

But, before he did that, he wrote a family history and he begat poor Fred, the insurance man. *The title of Merrihue's family chronicle is* A History of the Rosewaters of Rhode Island. *It was the discovery of the family history which convinced Fred not to commit suicide.*

Rosewater, Noah. *Together with his brother George, Noah inherited six hundred fertile acres of Indiana farmland and a saw factory. When the Civil War started, George raised a rifle company while Noah bought his way out by hiring Fletcher Moon to take his place. Noah convinced George to give him control of the company while he was off at the war. By marrying the notoriously ugly Cleota Herrick (she possessed $400,000)* he expanded the factory and bought more farms, all in Rosewater County. He became the largest individual hog farmer in the North. And, in order not to be victimized by meat packers, he bought controlling interest in an Indianapolis slaughterhouse. In order not to be victimized by steel suppliers, he bought controlling interest in a steel company in Pittsburgh. In order not to be victimized by coal suppliers, he bought controlling interest in several mines. In order not to be victimized by money lenders, he founded a bank (*GBR* 20:L8-17).

When his brother returned from the war, penniless and disabled by blindness, Noah's representatives explained to George he no longer had a share in the family enterprise. Noah was in Washington at the time, which became the center of the family business.

Noah's son Samuel became powerful in Republican Party politics, and his grandson is Senator Lister Ames Rosewater. Great-grandson Eliot is the undoing of the great family fortune.

Rosewater, Samuel. *The son of Noah Rosewater, husband of Geraldine Ames Rockefeller, and father of Lister Ames Rosewater. He advanced the family's standing in Republican Party politics and expanded the family's influence and wealth by purchasing newspapers.* (*GBR* 22:L4-14) And **Samuel** bought newspapers, and preachers, too. He gave them this simple lesson to teach, and they taught it well: *Anybody who thought that the United States of America was supposed to be a Utopia was a piggy, lazy, God-damned fool.* **Samuel** thundered that no American factory hand was worth more than eighty cents a day. And yet he could be thankful for the opportunity to pay a hundred thousand dollars or more for a painting by an Italian three centuries dead. And he capped this insult by giving paintings to museums for the spiritual elevation of the poor. The museums were closed on Sundays.

Samuel constructed the Samuel Rosewater Veterans' Memorial Park which honored the memory of local veterans.

Rosewater, Senator Lister Ames. *The father of Eliot, U.S. Senator Rosewater presided over the fourteenth largest family fortune in the United States and created The Rosewater Foundation* in order that tax-collectors and other predators not named Rosewater might be prevented from getting their hands on it (*GBR* 15:L13-15). *The Senator is distraught over his son's alcoholism, obesity, childless marriage, and return to Rosewater County. His attempts to reconcile Eliot's marriage to Sylvia go for naught. He is left to call in Kilgore Trout at Eliot's request prior to the sanity hearing which threatens to strip Eliot of the foundation presidency, allowing Norman Mushari to grab some of the fortune before Fred Rosewater's bogus claim could be achieved.*

Senator Rosewater's legislative masterpiece is called the Rosewater Law. (*GBR* 85:L15-24) It made the publication or possession of obscene materials a Federal offense, carrying penalties up to fifty thousand dollars and ten years in prison, without hope of parole. It was a masterpiece because it actually defined obscenity.

> Obscenity, *it said*, is any picture or phonograph record or any written matter calling attention to reproductive organs, bodily discharges, or bodily hair.

Eliot's ministrations to the poor prompt the Senator's fears that his son has become a communist. Except for a brief stay each election cycle, Senator Rosewater had long since divorced himself from the impoverished county which bears his name.

Rosewater, Sylvia. *Eliot Rosewater's faithful wife who is eventually diagnosed by Dr. Ed Brown as the first sufferer of "Samaritrophia,* which he said meant, *"hysterical indifference to the troubles of those less fortunate than oneself"* (*GBR* 54:L6-8).
(*GBR* 47:L11-20) This was a pale and delicate girl, cultivated, wispy. She played the harpsichord, spoke six languages enchantingly. As a child and young woman, she had met many of the greatest men of her time in her parents' home—Picasso, Schweitzer, Hemingway, Toscanini, Churchill, de Gaulle. She had never seen Rosewater County, had no idea what a night-crawler was, did not know that land anywhere could be so deathly flat, that people anywhere could be so deathly dull.

Dr. Brown's treatment made her an uncaring disconnected, almost disembodied individual. As Brown writes, I had blocked the underground rivers that connected her to the Atlantic, Pacific, and Indian Oceans, and made her content with being a splash pool three feet across, four inches deep, chlorinated, and painted blue (*GBR* 55:L15-18).

Sylvia resists Senator's Rosewater's attempts to have her reconcile with Eliot in the hopes of producing an heir to continue the family legacy. (*GBR* 66:L3) This was, of course, a medical decision, and a wise one, too. Her second breakdown and recovery had not turned her back into the old **Sylvia** of the early Rosewater County days. It had given her a distinctly new personality, the third since her marriage to Eliot. The core of this third personality was a feeling of worthlessness, of shame at being revolted by the poor and by Eliot's personal hygiene, and a suicidal wish to ignore her revulsions, to get back to Rosewater, to very soon die in a good cause.

So it was with self-conscious, medically-prescribed, superficial opposition to total sacrifice that she said again, "No."

The Rosewater County Clarion Call. *Eliot read back issues of this local newspaper and learned of the imprisoned Noyes Finnerty, star center on the 1933 undefeated basketball team from Noah Rosewater Memorial High School.* (*GBR* 187:L2) In 1934, Noyes strangled his sixteen-year-old wife for notorious infidelity, went to prison for life. Now he was paroled, thanks to Eliot. He was fifty-one. Eliot found out about his being in prison by accident, while leafing through old copies of ***The Rosewater County Clarion Call***, made it his business to get him paroled.

Rosewater Creek, Rosewater Inter-State Ship Canal. *Part of the circuitous route which Eliot Rosewater is convinced would form no more than a thoroughfare returning him to Rosewater County should he ever try to leave.* (*GBR* 171:L15-16) "if I were to somehow wind up in New York, and start living the highest of all possible lives again, you know what would happen to me? The minute I got near any navigable body of water, a bolt of lightning would knock me into the water, a whale would swallow me up, and the whale would swim down to the Gulf of Mexico and up the Mississippi, up the Ohio, up the Wabash, up the White, up Lost River, up **Rosewater Creek**. And that whale would jump from the creek into the **Rosewater Inter-State Ship Canal**, and it would swim down the canal to this city, and spit me out in the Parthenon. And there I'd be."

The Rosewater Foundation (also **The Rosewater Corporation**). *The first line of* God Bless You, Mr. Rosewater *defines the centrality of these two entities to the plot:* A sum of money is a leading character in this tale about people, just as a sum of honey might properly be a leading character in a tale about bees (*GBR* 15:L1-3). *The Rosewaters possessed "the fourteenth largest family fortune in America," so in 1947 Senator Lister Ames Rosewater had the family's law firm McAllister, Robjent, Reed and McGee create* a foundation in order that tax-collectors and other predators not named Rosewater might be prevented from getting their hands on it. And the baroque masterpiece of legal folderol that was the charter of the **Rosewater Foundation** declared, in effect, that the presidency of the **Foundation** was to be inherited in the same manner as the British Crown. It was to be handed down throughout all eternity to the closest and oldest 15 heirs of the **Foundation**'s creator, Senator Lister Ames Rosewater of Indiana.

Siblings of the President were to become officers of the **Foundation** upon reaching the age of twenty-one. All officers were officers for life, unless proved legally insane. They were free to compensate themselves for their services as lavishly as they pleased, but only from the **Foundation**'s income.

As required by law, the charter prohibited the Senator's heirs having anything to do with the management of the **Foundation**'s capital. Caring for the capital became the responsibility of a corporation that was born simultaneously with the **Foundation**. It was called, straightforwardly enough, **The Rosewater Corporation**. Like almost all corporations, it was dedicated to prudence and profit, to balance sheets. Its employees were very well paid. They were cunning and happy and energetic on that account. Their main enterprise was the churning of stocks and bonds of other corporations. A minor activity was the management of a saw factory, a bowling alley, a motel, a bank, a brewery, extensive farms in Rosewater County, Indiana, and some coal mines in northern Kentucky (*GBR* 15:L13-20, 16:L1-26).

The foundation's money became the focus of attention for Norman Mushari, a young attorney at McAllister, Robjent, Reed and McGee. In 1965 he focused on the insanity clause of the foundation's charter to wrest control away from Eliot for Fred Rosewater.

Eliot became the foundation's first president in 1947. Though there weren't any limitations on how the foundation's money could be used, he rented offices in the Empire State Building and proclaimed them the headquarters for all the beautiful, compassionate and scientific things he hoped to do (*GBR* 26:L12-13). *The Rosewater Foundation spent $14 million in its first six years by supporting a Detroit birth control clinic, supporting research in cancer, mental illness, race prejudice and police brutality, and purchasing acclaimed art works.*

After Eliot moves to the family's ancestral home in Rosewater, Indiana, he sets up a new foundation office in an attic atop both a luncheonette and a liquor store, across the street from the new volunteer firehouse built with foundation support. The foundation makes an anonymous gift to the fire department of the loudest alarm in the Western Hemisphere. It was driven by a seven-hundred-horsepower Messerschmitt engine that had a thirty-horsepower electric starter. It had been the main air-raid siren of Berlin during the Second World War. **The Rosewater Foundation** had bought it from the West German government and presented it to the town anonymously (*GBR* 92:L20-26).

Eliot kept a ledger he called his Domesday Book, *listing all the charitable deeds done on the foundation's behalf while in Rosewater County. All the entries were kept in code.*

Eliot's way of avoiding the upheaval wrought by Mushari's legal maneuvering is to offer Fred Rosewater an out-of-court settlement and accept responsibility for the fifty-seven paternity suits lodged against him by his neighbors, all of whom were duped by Mushari.

Rosewater Golden Lager Ambrosia Beer. (*GBR* 50:L7-8) A Utopian community in the southwest corner of the *(Rosewater)* county, New Ambrosia, invested everything it had in the *(Rosewater Inter-State Ship)* canal, and lost. They were Germans, communists and atheists who practiced group marriage, absolute truthfuless, absolute cleanliness, and absolute love. They were now scattered to the winds, like the worthless papers that represented their equity in the canal. No one was sorry to see them go. Their one contribution to the county that was still viable in Eliot's time was their brewery, which had become the home of **Rosewater Golden Lager Ambrosia Beer**. On the label of each can of beer was a picture of the heaven on earth the New Ambrosians had meant to build. The dream city had spires. The spires had lightning-rods. The sky was filled with cherubim. *Along with Southern Comfort, the alcoholic Eliot drank Rosewater Golden Lager (GBR* 60:L13).

Roswell Moose and **Elks**. *In* Player Piano, *these two civic organizations are teamed together to sabotage EPICAC during the Ghost Shirt rebellion. They failed, and the implication is that they blew themselves up when trying to pour nitro glycerin into Coke bottles which they intended to place in soda machines in Carlsbad Caverns, EPICAC's home.*

Rothko, Mark (1903-1970). *The Abstract Expressionist painter mentioned by Rabo Karabekian as a drinking buddy, but Rabo more frequently alludes to*

Rothko's horribly messy suicide. (*Blue* 151:L3) Yes, and **Mark Rothko**, with enough sleeping pills in his medicine cabinet to kill an elephant, slashed himself to death with a knife in 1970.

In Hocus Pocus, *one of Rothko's paintings is sold to the Getty Museum for $37,000,000. Perhaps this is another of the text's signs of America's pending economic collapse. This is in stark contrast with Karabekian's sale of a Rothko for $1,500,000 in* Bluebeard.

Rowley, Jonah K. *The alias used by Malachi Constant during his getaway from the Rumfoord mansion after attending the materialization of Winston Niles Rumfoord and Kazak, in* The Sirens of Titan.

Rowley, Mrs. Theodore. *In the Editor's Note to* Mother Night, *Vonnegut mentions that he hired Mrs. Theodore Rowley, of Cotuit, Massachusetts, a linguist and poetess, to restore three Howard Campbell poems offered in Chapter Twenty-two. Campbell's memoirs are nearly illegible due to his many revisions, so it was left to Mrs. Rowley to make them whole and poetic.*

Rumfoord, Beatrice. *The wife of Winston Niles Rumfoord, space mate of Malachi Constant (Unk), mother of Chrono, and an instructress at the Schliemann Breathing School on Mars. She was enraged that her husband, who had knowledge of the future, refused to help her fend off financial ruin or Malachi Constant. Bea was sexually assaulted by Malachi on their way to Mars, and the result was the birth of Chrono, the German batball star and deliverer of the spare part to Salo the Tralfamadorian voyager. When Beatrice Rumfoord is on Mars, the spelling of her name is "Bee." All other times she is either "Beatrice" or "Bea."* (*ST* 153:L4) **Bee** . . . had a strong face—high cheek-boned and haughty. She looked strikingly like an Indian brave. But whoever said so was under an obligation to add quickly that she was, all the same, quite beautiful.
(*ST* 156:L28, 30) **Bee** daydreamed. She daydreamed of a little girl in a starched white dress and white gloves and white shoes, and with a white pony all her own. **Bee** envied that little girl who had kept so clean. *Bee's daydream is actually a remembrance of the painting "**Beatrice Rumfoord** as a Young Girl" that hung in the Rumfoord mansion.*

When she and Chrono crash-landed in the Gumbo region of the Amazon Rain Forest, they were held captive and later initiated into the tribe. (*ST* 234:L8, 11) During the initiation, mother and son had been staked at the ends of tethers in the middle of the village, with Chrono representing the Sun and **Bee** representing the Moon, as the Sun and the Moon were understood by the Gumbo people.

As a result of their experiences, **Bee** and Chrono were closer than most mothers and sons.

Beatrice and Chrono sell Malachi dolls outside the Rumfoord estate after their capture in the Martian invasion of Earth. Before Malachi, Chrono, and Beatrice are exiled to Titan, Winston Niles Rumfoord explains to the crowd in Newport why she must be sent packing. Included in his diatribe against her is the veiled message that she had cuckolded Rumfoord while on her trip to Mars. (*ST* 261:L18, 22, 28, 262:L3) "The excesses of **Beatrice** were excesses of reluctance," said Rumfoord. "As a younger woman, she felt so exquisitely bred as to do nothing and to allow nothing to be done to her, for fear of contamination. Life, for **Beatrice** as a younger woman, was too full of germs and vulgarity to be anything but intolerable.

"We of the Church of God the Utterly Indifferent damn her as roundly for refusing to risk her imagined purity in living as we damn Malachi Constant for wallowing in filth.

"It was implicit in **Beatrice's** every attitude that she was intellectually, morally, and physically what God intended human beings to be when perfected, and that the rest of humanity needed another ten thousand years in which to catch up. Again we have a case of an ordinary and uncreative person's tickling God Almighty pink. The proposition that God Almighty admired **Beatrice** for her touch-me-not breeding is at least as questionable as the proposition that God Almighty wanted Malachi Constant to be rich. . . ."

In their old age on Titan, Malachi came to love Beatrice. And though age and circumstances weren't very kind, Bea's strength and bearing remained. She spent her time on Titan writing a refutation of Winston's Tralfamadorian grand scheme. (*ST* 307:L28-31, 308:L1-16) **Beatrice Rumfoord** was a springy, one-eyed, gold-toothed, brown old lady—as lean and tough as a chair slat. But the class of the damaged and roughly-used old lady showed through.

To anyone with a sense of poetry, mortality, and wonder, Malachi Constant's proud, high-cheekboned mate was as handsome as a human being could be.

She was probably a little crazy. On a moon with only two other people on it, she was writing a book called *The True Purpose of Life in the Solar System*. It was a refutation of Rumfoord's notion that the purpose of human life in the Solar System was to get a grounded messenger from Tralfamadore on his way again.

Beatrice began the book after her son left her to join the bluebirds. The manuscript so far, written in longhand, occupied thirty-eight cubic feet inside the Taj Mahal.

Every time Constant visited her, she read aloud her latest additions to the manuscript.

Rumfoord, Bertram Copeland. *The uncle of Lance Rumfoord of Newport, Rhode Island, Bertram is a seventy-year-old Harvard professor and the official Historian of the United States Air Force. Rumfoord broke his leg in a skiing accident and shares a hospital room with Billy Pilgrim in Vermont after his plane crash. Rumfoord's twenty-three-year-old wife, Lily, brings him research materials for his latest book, a one-volume history of the United States Army Air Corps in World War Two. Rumfoord comments on Billy and Vonnegut* *supplies a short description of the professor in the following passage.* (*SL5* 159:L11, 13) "He *(Billy)* bores the *hell* out of *me!*" **Rumfoord** replied boomingly. "All he does in his sleep is quit and surrender and apologize and ask to be left alone." **Rumfoord** was a retired brigadier general in the Air Force Reserve, the official Air Force Historian, a full professor, the author of twenty-six books, a multimillionaire since birth, and one of the great competitive sailors of all time. His most popular book was about sex and strenuous athletics for men over sixty-five. Now he quoted Theodore Roosevelt, whom he resembled a lot: "'I could carve a better man out of a banana.'"

Lily brings Rumfoord the book entitled The Destruction of Dresden, *because he needed to cover the event in his text.* (*SL5* 164:L34, 165:L14, 19) **Rumfoord** had a problem about Dresden. His one-volume history of the Army Air Force in World War Two was supposed to be a readable condensation of the twenty-seven-volume *Official History of the Army Air Force in World War Two*. The thing was, though, there was almost nothing in the twenty-seven volumes about the Dresden raid, even though it had been such a howling success. . . .

"Americans have finally heard about Dresden," said **Rumfoord**, twenty-three years after the raid. "A lot of them know now how much worse it was than Hiroshima. So I've got to put something about it in my book. From the official Air Force standpoint, it'll all be new."

"Why would they keep it a secret so long?" said Lily.

"For fear that a lot of bleeding hearts," said **Rumfoord**, "might not think it was such a wonderful thing to do."

Rumfoord and Billy eventually talk about Dresden and agree the destruction of Dresden had to be. Rumfoord looks at it from a military standpoint; Billy sees it in the Tralfamadorian perspective.

Rumfoord, Commodore William Howard Taft and Clarice. *The 1946 Commodore of the Hyannis Port Yacht Club and his wife meet the unnamed narrator and storm window salesman while attending a lecture given by their teenage son at the North Crawford (New Hampshire) Lions Club. After the Commodore gets into an argument with Hay Boyden, who had thrown some disrespectful remarks toward the youthful speaker, he engages the narrator in conversation because he and Boyden had also argued—about a bathtub enclosure, not politics. However, the Commodore thought the salesman was defending conservative causes against Boyden and orders windows for his entire Hyannis Port home.*

The Commodore hadn't been employed since 1946 and had made a full-time career of raging about whoever was President of the United States, including Eisenhower.

Especially Eisenhower (*MH* 136:L5-8 *The Hyannis Port Story*).

The Commodore's world is turned upside down when his son Robert becomes engaged to Sheila Kennedy, President Kennedy's fourth cousin visiting from Ireland. He is so shaken that he begins to believe he is nothing but an unproductive rich old man content to let his investments have a life of their own. That night he decides to let the Goldwater poster portrait go without the floodlights. President Kennedy asks that he turn the lights on so Khrushchev's visiting son-in-law could enjoy the view.

(*MH* 134:L18-28 *The Hyannis Port Story*) The **Commodore** was a short man with very shaggy eyebrows, and pale blue eyes. He looked like a gruff, friendly teddybear, and so did his son. I found out later, from a Secret Service man, that the Kennedys sometimes called the Rumfoords "*the Pooh people*," on account of they were so much like the bear in the children's book *Winnie the Pooh*.

The **Commodore's wife** wasn't a Pooh person, though. She was thin and quick, and maybe two inches taller than the **Commodore**. Bears have a way of looking as though they're pretty much satisfied with everything. The **Commodore's lady** didn't have that look. I could tell she was jumpy about a lot of things.

Rumfoord, Cynthia Niles. *The wife of realtor Merrihue Rosewater and mother of Fred, the insurance salesman.* (*GBR* 120:L22-25) He married **Cynthia Niles Rumfoord**, a minor heiress, invested much of her money in pavement and streetlights and sewers. He made a fortune, lost it, and his wife's fortune, too, in the crash of 1929.

Rumfoord, Lance. *In* God Bless You, Mr. Rosewater, *Lance is the six-foot, eight-inch Rumfoord heir who shabbily treats Norman Mushari on the one day out of the year the public is invited to tour the Rumfoord estate.* (*GBR* 159:L18) As Mushari was leaving the estate, **Lance Rumfoord** came loping after him. Predatorily genial, he towered over little Mushari, explained that his mother considered herself a great judge of character, and had made the guess that Mushari had once served in the United States Infantry.

"No."

"Really? She so seldom misses. She said specifically that you had been a sniper."

"No."

Lance shrugged. "If not in this life, in some other one, then." And he sneered and whinnied again.

In Slaughterhouse-Five, *Lance is momentarily seen with new bride Cynthia Landry honeymooning on the yacht* Scheherezade. *His uncle is Professor Bertram Copeland Rumfoord, the Air Force historian who is writing about Dresden and later shares a hospital room with Billy Pilgrim.*

Rumfoord, Lily. *The twenty-three-year-old fifth wife of Bertram Copeland Rumfoord, in* Slaughterhouse-Five. *She was a high school dropout and "go-go" dancer when they met. Lily dutifully brings Rumfoord's research materials* *to the hospital so he could continue writing his history of the United States Army Air Corps in World War II.*

Rumfoord, Remington, IV. *Though briefly mentioned, Remington Rumfoord, IV, enables Lyndon Boyd Johnson (later to become Bokonon) to travel the world and gain exposure to other cultures and insights.* (*CC* 93:L1) When the war ended, the young rakehell of the Rumfoord family, **Remington Rumfoord, IV**, proposed to sail his steam yacht, the *Scheherazade*, around the world, visiting Spain, France, Italy, Greece, Egypt, India, China, and Japan. He invited Johnson to accompany him as first mate, and Johnson agreed.

Johnson saw many wonders of the world on the voyage.

The *Scheherazade* was rammed in a fog in Bombay harbor, and only Johnson survived. He stayed in India for two years, becoming a follower of Mohandas K. Gandhi. He was arrested for leading groups that protested British rule by lying down on railroad tracks. When his jail term was over, he was shipped at Crown expense to his home in Tobago.

Rumfoord, Robert Taft. *The son of Clarice and Commodore William Howard Taft Rumfoord, an ardent Goldwater Republican and neighbor of the Kennedys in the short story "The Hyannis Port Story." He is the national president of a conservative student organization and is first encountered by the story's narrator when guest lecturing at the North Crawford Lions Club in New Hampshire. He becomes the fulcrum for his father's softening when the Secret Service unveils the relationship between young Robert and Sheila Kennedy, President Kennedy's fourth cousin visiting from Ireland.*

Rumfoord, Winston Niles. *The Newport millionaire in* The Sirens of Titan *whose style and gallantry make him a perfect tool for the Tralfamadorian scheme to get a spare part to their inter-galactic messenger, Salo.* (*ST* 28:L13-27) When **Rumfoord** became the first person to own a private space ship, paying fifty-eight million dollars out of his own pocket for it—that was style.

When the governments of the earth suspended all space exploration because of the chrono-synclastic infundibula, and **Rumfoord** announced that he was going to Mars—that was style.

When **Rumfoord** announced that he was taking a perfectly tremendous dog along, as though a space ship were nothing more than a sophisticated sports car, as though a trip to Mars were little more than a spin down the Connecticut Turnpike—that was style.

When it was unknown what would happen if a space ship went into a chrono-synclastic infundibulum, and **Rumfoord** steered a course straight for the middle of one—that was gallantry indeed.

Rumfoord and Kazak existed as wave phenomena—apparently pulsing in a distorted spiral with its origin in the Sun and its terminal in Betelgeuse (*ST* 13:L22-24). *Every fifty-nine days their spiral intersects with Earth. At the same time, they are permanently materialized on Titan. Rumfoord's materializations end the same as the Cheshire Cat's, with only his grin remaining.*

The Tralfamadorians use Rumfoord in an elaborate scheme taking hundreds of thousands of years to complete. Parts of the scheme include: telling his wife Beatrice and Malachi Constant a bit about their space traveling futures; using his tremendous wealth to finance the Pan-Galactic Space Service (the Army of Mars) in preparation for their foretold failure in the invasion of Earth; establishing the worldwide Church of God the Utterly Indifferent; excommunicating Beatrice, Malachi, and Chrono to Titan, an act which finally ends Salo's long wait for a spare part.

For all the knowledge Rumfoord possesses about the Tralfamadorian scheme, more than anything else he wishes to know what message Salo carries on his journey to the far side of the galaxy. Despite badgering Salo into opening the sealed wafer containing the message, Salo's acquiescence comes too late. (*ST* 295:L10-16) An explosion on the Sun had separated man and dog. A Universe schemed in mercy would have kept man and dog together.

The Universe inhabited by **Winston Niles Rumfoord** and his dog was not schemed in mercy. Kazak had been sent ahead of his master on the great mission to nowhere and nothing. *Shortly after, unaccompanied by his faithful companion, Winston Niles Rumfoord is spiralled straight out of the Solar System.*

Rumfoord mansion. (*ST* 18:L19-32) The **Rumfoord mansion** was marble, an extended reproduction of the banqueting hall of Whitehall Palace in London. The mansion, like most of the really grand ones in Newport, was a collateral relative of post offices and Federal court buildings throughout the land.

The **Rumfoord mansion** was an hilariously impressive expression of the concept: People of substance. It was surely one of the greatest essays on density since the Great Pyramid of Khufu. In a way it was a better essay on permanence than the Great Pyramid, since the Great Pyramid tapered to nothingness as it approached heaven. Nothing about the **Rumfoord mansion** diminished as it approached heaven. Turned upside down, it would have looked exactly the same.

The density and permanence of the mansion were, of course, at ironic variance with the fact that the quondam master of the house, except for one hour in every fifty-nine days, was no more substantial than a moonbeam.

Rumpf, Hans (see ***The Bombing of Germany***).

Ryan, Mildred. *The ghost of Harold Ryan's third wife. Mildred claims Harold drove her and his previous two wives to drink because of his habit of premature ejaculation. She exposes the truth behind Ryan's mystique.* (*WJ* 139:L1) **MILDRED** No grown woman is a fan of premature ejaculation. Harold would come home trumpeting and roaring. He would kick the furniture with his boots, spit into corners and the fireplace. He would make me presents of stuffed fish and helmets with holes in them. He would tell me that he had now earned the reward that only a woman could give him, and he'd tear off my clothes. He would carry me into the bedroom, telling me to scream and kick my feet. That was very important to him. I did it. I tried to be a good wife. He told me to imagine a herd of stampeding water buffalo. I couldn't do that, but I pretended I did. It was all over—ten seconds after he'd said the word "buffalo." Then he'd zip up his pants, and go outside, and tell true war stories to the little kids. Any little kids.

Ryan, Penelope, Harold and Paul. *In* Happy Birthday, Wanda June, *Penelope is the fourth wife of Harold Ryan. Penelope thought she lost her husband eight years earlier when he went on Safari and never returned. Since then, she had him declared legally dead and was being courted by effeminate physician Dr. Norbert Woodly and vacuum cleaner salesman Herb Shuttle. Penelope was a car-hop when she met Harold, but in his absence she attended college. By the time Harold returns, Penelope can no longer accept Harold's Hemingway lifestyle.*

Harold was a fearless soldier and voracious hunter. He and his sidekick, Colonel Looseleaf Harper, crashed their aircraft while on a hunting trip. The ghost of Mildred Ryan, Harold's third wife, exposes Harold's false macho facade.

Paul is the Ryans' twelve-year-old son. Though without his father since the age of four, Paul idolized him in his absence. Once Harold reappears, Paul rejects his coarse ways, as well.

S

Sacco and Vanzetti (also **Dante and Inez Sacco**) *Sacco and Vanzetti were falsely convicted of murder and later electrocuted in 1927 despite the confession of Celestino Madeiros. Much of the preface to* Jailbird *concerns their case. They are also alluded to in* Palm Sunday. *In both cases they are held up as symbols of America's inability to deal equitably with immigrants and those with radical social theories.*

The inscription to Jailbird, *appearing after Vonnegut's preface and before the actual novel, includes the following material from Sacco's last letter to his thirteen-year-old son, Dante.* (*JB* xxxix) Help the weak ones that cry for help, help the prosecuted and the victim, because they are your better friends; they are the comrades that fight and fall as your father and **Bartolo** fought and fell yesterday for the conquest of the joy of freedom for all the poor workers. In this struggle of life you will find more love and you will be loved. —**NICOLA SACCO** (1891-1927)

*"**Bartolo**" was **Bartolomeo Vanzetti** (1888-1927), who was executed after Sacco in the same electric chair. He was followed by history's forgotten man, Celestino Madeiros (1894-1927), who confessed to the crime of which **Sacco and Vanzetti** had been convicted, even while his own conviction for another murder was being appealed.*

(*JB* 171:L25, 29, 31) When I was a young man, I expected the story of **Sacco and Vanzetti** to be retold as often and as movingly, to be as irresistible, as the story of Jesus Christ some day. Weren't modern people, if they were to marvel creatively at their own lifetimes, I thought, entitled to a Passion like **Sacco and Vanzetti's**, which ended in an electric chair?

As for the last days of **Sacco and Vanzetti** as a modern Passion: As on Golgotha, three lower-class men were executed at the same time by a state. This time, though, not just one of the three was innocent. This time two of the three were innocent.

(*JB* 179:L13) "Never in our full life," said **Vanzetti**, "could we hope to do such work for tolerance, for justice, for man's understanding of man, as now we do by accident."
(*JB* 182:L1) **Sacco and Vanzetti** never lost their dignity—never cracked up. Walter F. Starbuck finally did.

Sacred Miracle Cave. *Located on the outskirts of Midland City and mentioned in* Breakfast of Champions *and* Deadeye Dick, *the cave was part of Bluebird Farm, originally owned by the former slave Josephus Hoobler. Dwayne's stepfather gained ownership of Bluebird Farm as part of a claims settlement for an auto accident. The owner of the land had bought the mortgage from Midland County Merchants Bank after Josephus Hoobler's descendants failed to meet the payments. The cave was discovered in 1937 by Dwayne Hoover after an earthquake. Dwayne and his stepfather opened up the small crack in the earth with crowbars and dynamite. Dwayne owned Sacred Miracle Cave in partnership with his younger stepbrothers Lyle and Kyle Hoover.*

The cave became polluted with plastic molecules flowing in Sugar Creek, which ran through Midland City and beneath the cave. The Maritimo Brothers Construction Company had been hired by Barrytron Ltd. to build a system which would get rid of the waste, but they built a simple pipeline emptying into Sugar Creek instead. Lyle and Kyle become concerned that the many natural and man-made attractions in the cave were threatened. Among the many sites in danger were the Cathedral of Whispers, Moby Dick, the Pipe Organ of the Gods, and the slaves.

St. Andres. (*PS* dedication page) *For my cousins the* ***de St. Andres*** *everywhere. Who has the castle now?*
(*PS* xvii:L29-30) I have dedicated this book to the **de St. Andres**. I am a **de St. Andre**, since that was the maiden name of a maternal great-grandmother of mine. My mother believed that this meant that she was descended from nobles of some kind.
(*PS* 23:L4 *Roots*) *From John Rauch's history of the Vonneguts in America:* "All of Kurt Vonnegut, Jr.'s eight great-grandparents were part of the vast migration of Germans to the Midwest in the half century from 1820 to 1870. They were: Clemens Vonnegut, Sr., and his wife, Katarina Blank; Henry Schnull and his wife, Matilde Schramm; Peter Lieber and his wife, Sophia **St. Andre**; Karl Barus and his wife, Alice Mollman." *See also: PS—Roots* 28:L31; 34:L6; *PS—Children* 238:L12; 247:L8.

St. Augustine. (*CC* 91:L14-15) Young Lionel Boyd Johnson was educated in Episcopal schools, did well as a student, and was more interested in ritual than most. As a youth, for all his interest in the outward trappings of organized religion, he seems to have been a carouser, for he invites us to sing along with him in his "Fourteenth Calypso": When I was young, / I was so gay and mean, / And I drank and chased the girls / Just like young **St.**

Augustine. / **Saint Augustine**, / He got to be a saint. / So, if I get to be one, also, / Please, Mama, don't you faint.

Saint Elmo's fire. *Both Winston Niles Rumfoord and his dog Kazak arrive and depart their chrono-synclastic infundibulated rounds in a shower of Saint Elmo's fire,* a luminous electrical discharge, and any creature afflicted by it is subject to discomfort no worse than the discomfort of being tickled by a feather. All the same, the creature appears to be on fire, and can be forgiven for being dismayed (*ST* 279:L10).

In Slaughterhouse-Five, Ever since Billy had been thrown into shrubbery for the sake of a picture, he had been seeing **Saint Elmo's fire**, a sort of electronic radiance around the heads of his companions and captors. It was in the treetops and on the rooftops of Luxembourg, too. It was beautiful (*SL5* 55:L7). *The photograph was staged by Billy Pilgrim's captors as part of their own propaganda effort, and, as was the case in* Sirens, *relates to time travel.* (*SL5* 50:L33-34, 51:L1-4). Billy's smile as he came out of the shrubbery was at least as peculiar as Mona Lisa's, for he was simultaneously on foot in Germany in 1944 and riding his Cadillac in 1967. Germany dropped away, and 1967 became bright and clear, free of interference from any other time. Billy was on his way to a Lions Club luncheon meeting.

Saint Elmo's fire presages the coming of "the blue tunnel into the Afterlife" for the spirit of Leon Trout in Galápagos. *He saw it on four distinct occasions. One incident occurred when Mary Hepburn was up in the crow's nest searching for land, but as Leon narrates,* I had seen it three times before: at the moment of my decapitation, and then at the cemetery in Malmö, when Swedish clay was thumping wetly on the lid of my coffin and Hjallar Arvid Boström, who certainly was never going to write Beethoven's Ninth Symphony, said of me, "Oh, well—he wasn't going to write Beethoven's Ninth Symphony anyway." Its third appearance was when I myself was up in the crow's nest—during a storm in the North Atlantic, in the sleet and spray, holding my severed head on high as though it were a basketball.

The question the blue tunnel implies by appearing is one only I can answer: Have I at last exhausted my curiosity as to what life is all about? If so, I need only step inside what I liken to a vacuum cleaner. If there is indeed suction within the blue tunnel, which is filled with a light much like that cast off by the electric stoves and ovens of the *Bahía de Darwin*, it does not seem to trouble my late father, the science fiction writer Kilgore Trout, who can stand right in the nozzle and chat with me (*Gal* 251:L19-31, 252:L1-8).

Saint Elmo's Remedy. *The foundation of the Waltz family wealth as described by Rudy.* (*DD* 2:L4) My father was Otto Waltz, whose peephole opened in 1892, and he was told, among other things, that he was the heir to a fortune earned principally by a quack medicine known as "**Saint Elmo's Remedy**." It was grain alcohol dyed purple, flavored with cloves and sarsaparilla root, and laced with opium and cocaine. As the joke goes: It was absolutely harmless unless discontinued.

St. Francis of Assisi. (*ST* 288:L15-16) Constant leaned against a statue of **St. Francis of Assisi**. **St. Francis** was trying to befriend two hostile and terrifyingly huge birds, apparently bald eagles. Constant was unable to identify the birds properly as Titanic bluebirds, since he hadn't seen a Titanic bluebird yet. He had arrived on Titan only an hour before.

St. George and the Dragon. *The literary metaphor Howard Campbell uses to describe the imaginary confrontation between pure good and pure evil supposed by former Lt. Bernard B. O'Hare in his quest to get Campbell in New York.* (*MN* 185:L25-26) He wasn't my nemesis. . . . To me, O'Hare was simply one more gatherer of wind-blown trash in the tracks of war.

O'Hare had a far more exciting view of what we were to each other. When drunk, at any rate, he thought of himself as **St. George and of me as the dragon**.

Vonnegut uses this hollow image in "The First Amendment" to describe those who ban books in public schools. (*PS* 7:L31-32, 8:L1-13) A school board has denounced some books again—out in Levittown this time. One of the books was mine. I hear about un-American nonsense like this twice a year or so. One time out in North Dakota, the books were actually burned in a furnace. I had a laugh. It was such an ignorant, dumb, superstitious thing to do.

It was so cowardly, to—to make a great show of attacking artifacts. It was like **St. George** attacking bedspreads and cuckoo clocks.

Yes, and **St. Georges** like that seem to get elected or appointed to school committees all the time. They are actually proud of their illiteracy. They imagine that they are somehow celebrating the bicentennial when they boast, as some did in Levittown, that they hadn't actually read the books they banned.

Such lunks are often the backbone of volunteer fire departments and the United States Infantry and cake sales and so on, and they have been thanked often enough for that. But they have no business supervising the educations of children in a free society. They are just too bloody stupid.

Salo. *The mechanical messenger from the planet Tralfamadore located in a universe known as the Small Magellanic Cloud. Salo is eleven million years old.* (*ST* 268:L17-24, 270:L15) In the Earthling year 483,441 B.C., he was chosen by popular telepathic enthusiasm as the most handsome, healthy, clean-minded specimen of his people. The occasion was the hundred-millionth anniversary of the government of his home planet in the Small Magellanic Cloud. The name of his home planet was Tralfamadore, which old Salo once translated for Rumfoord as meaning both *all of us* and the *number 541*. . . .

In the Earthling year 203,117 B.C., **Salo** was forced down in the Solar System by mechanical difficulties. He was forced down by a complete disintegration of a small part in his ship's power plant, a part about the size of an Earthling beer-can opener.

The disintegrated part was eventually duplicated through a series of lengthy Tralfamadorian schemes affecting all of Earth's history, resulting in the strip of chrome cherished by Chrono.

Salsedo, Andrea. (*JB* 176:L3, 7, 11) A printer named **Andrea Salsedo**, who was a friend of Vanzetti's, was also on the list *(a secret list compiled by the Department of Justice to monitor the political activities of foreigners)*. He was arrested in New York City by federal agents on unspecified charges, and held incommunicado for eight weeks. On May third of Nineteen-hundred and Twenty, **Salsedo** fell or jumped or was pushed out of the fourteenth-story window of an office maintained by the Department of Justice.

Sacco and Vanzetti organized a meeting that was to demand an investigation of the arrest and death of **Salsedo**. It was scheduled for May ninth in Brockton, Massachusetts, Mary Kathleen O'Looney's home town.

Sam *A student at Sweetbread College despondent over the institution's bankruptcy, in the play "The Chemistry Professor."*

Samaritrophia. *The term coined by Dr. Ed Brown, the Indianapolis psychiatrist who diagnoses Sylvia Rosewater's malady and which he describes as an* hysterical indifference to the troubles of those less fortunate than oneself.

. . . **Samaritrophia** . . . is the suppression of an overactive conscience by the rest of the mind. "You must all take instructions from me!" the conscience shrieks, in effect, to all the other mental processes. The other processes try it for a while, note that the conscience is unappeased, that it continues to shriek, and they note, too, that the outside world has not been even microscopically improved by the unselfish acts the conscience has demanded.

They rebel at last. They pitch the tyrannous conscience down an oubliette, weld shut the manhole cover of that dark dungeon. They can hear the conscience no more. In the sweet silence, the mental processes look about for a new leader, and the leader most prompt to appear whenever the conscience is stilled, Enlightened Self-interest, does appear. Enlightened Self-interest gives them a flag, which they adore on sight. It is essentially the black and white Jolly Roger, with these words written beneath the skull and crossbones, "The hell with you, Jack, I've got mine!" (*GBR* 54:L7-8, 18).

Samoza Hall. *The Tarkington College administration building which housed the meeting room of the Board of Trustees, in* Hocus Pocus. *It was in the Board Room that Eugene Debs Hartke lost his faculty position, and later, escaped prisoner Alton Darwin declared himself president of a new country. Lyle Hooper, owner of the Black Cat Café, was executed in front of the* *building. After Hartke assumed temporary position as warden in control of Tarkington, he used Samoza Hall as a makeshift prison wall, outfitting its doors and windows with machine-gunners guarding convicts housed in tents on the campus quad.*

Sams, Howard W. *In* The Sirens of Titan, *Sams is the author of* Winston Niles Rumfoord, Benjamin Franklin, and Leonardo da Vinci, *which documents that German batball was Rumfoord's only exposure to team sports as a child.*

San Lorenzo Cathedral. *After a British slave ship was overtaken by African slaves and they landed on San Lorenzo, formerly claimed by the Spanish, their new emperor Tum-Bumwa* "erected the **San Lorenzo Cathedral** and the fantastic fortifications on the north shore of the island, fortifications within which the private residence of the so-called President of the Republic now stands" (*CC* 108:L1-4). *It is from those fortifications that the Ambassador and Mrs. Minton plunge to their deaths and Papa Monzano's ice-nine-contaminated body also plunges into the sea. It also contains the oubliette in which John/Jonah and Mona Aamons take refuge from the storms which swirl as a result of the oceans icing over.*

Sandler, Bea (Bea Sandler's *The African Cookbook*). (*DD* x:L1) There are several recipes in this book, which are intended as musical interludes for the salivary glands. They have been inspired by *James Beard's American Cookery*, Marcella Hazan's *The Classic Italian Cook Book*, and **Bea Sandler's *The African Cookbook***. I have tinkered with the originals, however—so no one should use this novel for a cookbook.

Sandra. *In* Cat's Cradle, *the former high school classmate of Franklin Hoenikker, now working as a prostitute in the Cape Cod Room of the Del Prado Hotel in Ilium, New York. Sandra chaired the school's Class Colors Committee, and was in a position to know much about the student body. She and the text's narrator wind up spending the night together prior to his tour of the Ilium Research Laboratory. Before they leave the bar, however, Sandra tells him some little known facts and rumors: that Franklin was derisively called Secret Agent X-9 because he always seemed involved in some clandestine activity outside of school, and that it was generally assumed that Dr. Asa Breed enjoyed a long term affair with Emily Hoenikker and fathered her three children.*

Interestingly, Sandra's high school Colors Committee chose orange and black for their prom's colors, the same colors used to decorate the anniversary party on the lawn of Billy Pilgrim's home—the same colors which cause Billy to time travel back to the prisoner-of-war train he rode in World War II.

Sandy. *The sheep dog which Vonnegut adopted along with three children from his sister and brother-in-law after they passed away in 1958. Vonnegut became* *deeply enamored of Sandy and once recalled to a group of scientists,* You have called me a humanist, and I have looked into humanism some, and I have found that a humanist is person who is tremendously interested in human beings. My dog is a humanist. His name is **Sandy**. He is a sheep dog. I know that **Sandy** is a dud name for a sheep dog, but there it is (*WFG* 94:L18-19).

Santa Cruz. *The home of the Darwin Research Station from which guides, trained by resident scientists, were to conduct tours of the Galápagos Islands for "the Nature Cruise of the Century."*

sarooned (see also **Bokononism**). (*CC* 165:L9-15) All things conspired to form one cosmic *vin-dit*, one mighty shove into Bokononism, into the belief that God was running my life and that He had work for me to do.

And, inwardly, I ***sarooned***, which is to say that I acquiesced to the seeming demands of my *vin-dit*.

Inwardly, I agreed to become the next President of San Lorenzo.

Sateen Dura-Luxe. *The miracle paint advertised to "outlive the smile on the 'Mona Lisa'" and which Rabo Karabekian used in the early 1960s. Karabekian's* own most famous painting, which no longer exists, and which was sixty-four feet long and eight feet high, and used to grace the entrance lobby of the GEFFCo headquarters on Park Avenue, was called simply, "Windsor Blue Number Seventeen." Windsor Blue was a shade of **Sateen Dura-Luxe**, straight from the can (*Blue* 35:L20). *The great tragedy of any artist using the miracle paint was that after a period of time the paint would peel off the canvas in huge sheets. The canvas used for Karabekian's "Windsor Blue Number Seventeen" was wiped clean by the degrading paint and became the base for his eventual masterpiece, "Now It's the Women's Turn."*

Karabekian still had sixty-three gallons in his basement. Because it was found to degrade into a deadly poison, he would have had to ship the paints to a special repository near Pitchfork, Wyoming.

Karabekian makes a comparison between Sateen Dura-Luxe's ability to self-destruct and thereby eradicate cultural artifacts of a given epoch with Christian fundamentalism of another era. While visiting Marilee Kemp's home in Florence, Italy, Rabo notices that large rectangular white spaces at the base of the clerestory once held murals. (*Blue* 217:L12) The murals were destroyed by the insistence of the Dominican monk Girolamo Savonarola, who wished to dispel every trace of paganism, which he felt had poisoned the city during the reign of the Medicis.

The murals were the work of Giovanni Vitelli, about whom almost nothing else is known, except that he was said to have been born in Pisa. One may assume that he was the Rabo Karabekian of his time, and that Christian fundamentalism was his **Sateen Dura-Luxe**.

Savonarola, Girolamo. *Rabo Karabekian learned that the clerestory in the palazzo of Innocenzo "the Invisible" de Medici, later owned by the Countess Portomaggiore (the former Marilee Kemp), was scraped bare of frescos depicting lightly clad pagan gods and goddesses. The Medicis were exiled from Florence in 1494, and in their absence,* The murals were destroyed by the insistence of the Dominican monk **Girolamo Savonarola**, who wished to dispel every trace of paganism, which he felt had poisoned the city during the reign of the Medicis (*Blue* 217:L5). *Karabekian goes on to rejoice:* **Girolamo Savonarola**, incidentally, was hanged and burned in the piazza in front of what had been the Palazzo of Innocenzo "the Invisible" de Medici in 1494.

I sure love history. I don't know why Celeste and her friends aren't more interested (*Blue* 217:L19).

In 1981 Vonnegut used Savonarola to illustrate his frustration with would-be censors. (*PS* 9:L3 *The First Amendment*) Whenever ideas are squashed in this country, literate lovers of the American experiment write careful and intricate explanations of why all ideas must be allowed to live. It is time for them to realize that they are attempting to explain America at its bravest and most optimistic to orangutans.

From now on, I intend to limit my discourse with dim-witted **Savonarolas** to this advice: "Have somebody read the First Amendment to the United States Constitution out loud to you, you God damned fool!"

Saw City Kandy Kitchen. *The candy store which doubled as the Greyhound Bus depot,* in God Bless You, Mr. Rosewater.

Sawyer, Doris. *The theatrical director for the North Crawford Mask and Wig Club in the short story "Who Am I This Time?" She assists the narrator in casting their new production of "A Streetcar Named Desire," and plays a key role in bringing out the acting talents of Helene Shaw and Harry Nash.*

Scharff, Hattie. *In* Mother Night, *the widowed owner of Pittsburgh's Scharff Brothers Funeral Home who hired Lionel J.D. Jones as an apprentice embalmer. Three years later the twenty-four-year-old Jones, by that time the manager of the firm, married Mrs. Scharff, then fifty-eight. She passed away in 1928. Their marriage was good and satisfying enough for Jones to avoid any anti-Semitic activities. After his wife's death, Jones sold the funeral home for $84,000 and started publishing* The White Christian Minuteman.

Schildknecht, Heinz. *The best wartime friend of* Mother Night*'s Howard Campbell. As with almost every other significant character in the text, Heinz had two personas. While working for the German Ministry for Popular Enlightenment and Propaganda as an expert at propagandizing Australians and New Zealanders, he was simultaneously working as a Jewish member of the anti-Nazi underground. He remained an Israeli agent long after the war, posing as chief groundskeeper for Baron Ulrich Werther von Schwefelbad, a* *former Nazi residing in Ireland. The Haifa Institute for the Documentation of War Criminals informs Campbell that Heinz verified the death of Hitler after wandering into his bunker while his gasoline soaked body was still recognizable.*

Campbell and Schildknecht forged their friendship by becoming a championship doubles team in ping-pong at the Ministry. Heinz's wife was killed in an air raid, and the two friends became roommates and drinking buddies. Nevertheless, Heinz eagerly traveled to Jerusalem prepared to testify against Campbell at his war crimes trial.

schizophrenia (*MN* 41:L21, 23) It was typical of his **schizophrenia** as a spy that he would use an institution he so admired for purposes of espionage. *Campbell comments on George Kraft's use of Alcoholics Anonymous as part of his espionage cover.*

It was typical of his **schizophrenia** as a spy that he should also be a true friend of mine, and that he should eventually think of a way to use me cruelly in advancing the Russian cause.

(*MN* 71:L27) When I call this unit a Nazi daydream, incidentally, I am suffering an attack of **schizophrenia**—because the idea of the Free American Corps began with me. I suggested its creation, designed its uniforms and insignia, wrote its creed.

(*MN* 136:L25) I've always been able to live with what I did. How? Through that simple and widespread boon to modern mankind—**schizophrenia**.

(*MN* 172:L28) Kraft thought his situation over, and **schizophrenia** rescued him neatly. "None of this really concerns me," he said, and his urbanity returned.

(*CC* 150:L6) Such music from such a woman *(Angela Hoenikker)* could only be a case of **schizophrenia** or demonic possession.

(*GBR* 57:L1) She was not a **schizophrenic**, but, whenever her husband visited her, which he did three times a week, she manifested all of the sick cutenesses of paranoia.

(*GBR* 132:L25-26) Fred's gory shins were victims of his wife's interior decorating scheme, which called for an almost **schizo-phrenic** use of little tables, dozens of them all through the house. . . . And Caroline was forever rearranging the tables, as though for this kind of party one day and another the next. So poor Fred was forever barking his shins on the tables.

(*SL5* title page)

THIS IS A NOVEL
SOMEWHAT IN THE TELEGRAPHIC **SCHIZOPHRENIC**
MANNER OF TALES
OF THE PLANET TRALFAMADORE,
WHERE THE FLYING SAUCERS
COME FROM.
PEACE.

(*BC* 42:L30) As it happened, Vernon was having trouble at home. His wife, Mary, was a **schizophrenic**, so Vernon hadn't noticed whether Dwayne had changed or not. Vernon's wife believed that Vernon was trying to turn her brains into plutonium.

(*BC* 193:L30) There in the cocktail lounge, peering out through my leaks at a world of my own invention, I mouthed this word: ***schizophrenia***.

(*PS* 127:L22 *The People One Knows*) ARE many novelists **schizophrenic**—at least marginally so? . . . if writers themselves aren't lunatics, perhaps a lot of their ancestors were.

(*PS* 199:L32 *Religion*) "They are told to have faith. Faith in what? Faith in faith, as nearly as I can tell. That is as detailed as many contemporary preachers care to be, except when amazing audiences of cavemen. How can a preacher tell us about men and women who heard voices without raising questions about **schizophrenia**, a disease which we know is common in all places and all times."

(*PS* 241:L31 *Children*) "Mark has taught me never to romanticize mental illness, never to imagine a brilliant and beguiling **schizophrenic** who makes more sense about life than his or her doctor or even the president of Harvard University. . . ."

(*PS* 242:L1-2, 5, 11-12 *Children*) Mark says that **schizophrenia** is as ghastly and debilitating as smallpox or rabies or any other unspeakable disease you care to name. Society cannot be blamed, and neither, thank God, can the friends and relatives of the patient. **Schizophrenia** is an internal chemical catastrophe. It is a case of monstrously bad genetic luck, bad luck of a sort encountered in absolutely every sort of society—including the Australian aborigines and the middle class of Vienna, Austria, before the Second World War.

"Plenty of other writers at this very moment are writing a story about an admirable, perhaps even a divine **schizophrenic**. . . . Why? Because the story is wildly applauded every time it is told. It blames the culture and the economy and the society and everything but the disease itself for making the patient unwell. Mark says that is wrong."

(*DD* 191:L3) "The most severe manifestation of chronic intoxication is psychosis, often indistinguishable from **schizophrenia**."

(*Gal* 149:L4) He was only eighteen years old *(Private Geraldo Delgado)*, and was a paranoid **schizophrenic**. He should never have been issued live ammunition.

(*FWD* 32:L31-35, 32:L1-14) "He was diagnosed, when I took him to a private laughing academy in British Columbia, where he had founded a commune, as **schizophrenic**. He sure looked **schizophrenic** to me, too. I never saw depressed people act anything like that. We mope. We sleep. I have to say that anybody who did what Mark did shortly after he was admitted, which was to jump up and get the light bulb in the ceiling of his padded cell, was anything but depressed.

"Anyway Mark recovered sufficiently to write his book and graduate from Harvard Medical School. He is now a pediatrician in Boston, with a wife and two fine sons, and two fine automobiles. And then, not very long ago, most members of your profession decided that he and some others who had written books about recovering from **schizophrenia** had been misdiagnosed. No matter how jazzed up they appeared to be when sick, they were in fact depressives. Maybe so.

"Mark's first response to news of this rediagnosis was to say, 'What a wonderful diagnostic tool. We now know if a patient gets well, he or she definitely did not have **schizophrenia**.'"

Toward the close of Fates Worse Than Death, *Vonnegut includes a section entitled "What My Son Mark Wanted Me to Tell the Psychiatrists in Philadelphia, Which Was Also The Afterword to a New Edition of His Book* The Eden Express." (*FWD* 205:L12-23, 206:L5-16) The clinical definition of **schizophrenia** has been changed. Under the old definitions there was considerable ambiguity about what to call people like me. Under the new definitions I would be classified as manic depressive rather than **schizophrenic**. I wasn't sick for very long and I didn't follow a downhill course, so I did not fit what has now become a definition of someone who is **schizophrenic**. While it's tempting to dismiss this as an insignificant change in labels and be more than a little irritated that they went and changed the rules after I went and built a book around the old definitions, I have to admit that this too is probably a positive change. It should mean that fewer people with acute breakdowns will be written off as hopeless. . . .

There are probably a dozen or so separate diseases responsible for what we now call **schizophrenia** and manic depression. Until the definitive work is done, many things are plausible and almost anything is possible. This lack of certainty makes mental illness wonderful ground for intellectual speculation and absolute hell for patients and their families.

At the time I wrote my book I felt that the large doses of vitamins with which I was treated, along with more conventional therapies, had a great deal to do with my recovery. It was my hope that many people diagnosed as **schizophrenic** would get better if only their doctors would become more open minded and treat them with vitamins.

Schlesinger, Arthur Jr. (*MH* 137:L11-12 *The Hyannis Port Story*) The next thing I knew, I was in Hyannis, going past the Presidential Motor Inn, the First Family Waffle Shop. . . . It was late in the afternoon, and I'd missed lunch, so I decided to have a waffle. All the different kinds of waffles were named after Kennedys and their friends and relatives. A waffle with strawberries and cream was a *Jackie*. A waffle with a scoop of ice cream was a *Caroline*. They even had a waffle named ***Arthur Schlesinger, Jr.***
(*FWD* 193:L1) I said to the historian **Arthur Schlesinger, Jr.**, one time, "If you had to say that the world was divided into only two kinds of people, not counting the sexes, what would they be?" It took him maybe ten seconds before replying, "Roundheads and Cavaliers." (I thought that was a swell answer. I am a Roundhead. Xanthippe is a Cavalier.) I said to the graphic

artist Saul Steinberg one time, "There are some novelists I can hardly talk to. It is as though we were in two very unlike professions, like podiatry and deep sea diving, say. What do you think is going on?" He replied, "It is very simple. There are two types of artists, neither superior to the other. One responds to life itself. The other responds to the history of his or her art so far." (Jill and I are both artists of the first sort, which could be why we got married. We are both barbarians, too ignorant to respond to the histories of our arts so far.) *Xanthippe is Vonnegut's nickname for his wife Jill Krementz.*

Schliemann Breathing School for Recruits. *Beatrice Rumfoord is one of six instructors at the school located in Phoebe, Mars' only city.* (*ST* 148:L10) **Schliemann breathing**, of course, is a technique that enables human beings to survive in a vacuum or in an inhospitable atmosphere without the use of helmets or other cumbersome respiratory gear.

It consists, essentially, of taking a pill rich in oxygen. The bloodstream takes on this oxygen through the wall of the small intestine rather than through the lungs. On Mars, the pills were known officially as Combat Respiratory Rations, in popular parlance as goofballs.

Martian attempts to erase Beatrice's memories and sentimental inclinations failed and the result was a sonnet about Schliemann breathing, considered seditious by her superiors. For this, she was sent back to the hospital. (*ST* 152:L18-31) Break every link with air and mist, / Seal every open vent; / Make throat as tight as miser's fist, / Keep life within you pent. / Breathe out, breathe in, no more, no more, / For breathing's for the meek; / And when in deathly space we soar, / Be careful not to speak. / If you with grief or joy are rapt, / Just signal with a tear; / To soul and heart within you trapped / Add speech and atmosphere. / Every man's an island as in / lifeless space we roam. / Yes, every man's an island: / island fortress, island home.

Schneider, Kurt. *In* The Sirens of Titan, *the alcoholic manager of a failed travel agency in Bremen, Germany, who was recruited for the Army of Mars, captured during the invasion of Earth, and later sells trinkets outside the Rumfoord estate in Newport, Rhode Island. His booth is near that of Beatrice Rumfoord's.*

Schramm's Drugstore. *The Midland City establishment where Rudy Waltz worked as the all-night pharmacist six days a week. He got the job right out of pharmacy school after his predecessor, Malcolm Hyatt, was killed by a thief. Because so little business was transacted in the middle of the night, Rudy spent much of his time writing "Katmandu," his play about farmer John Fortune. Despite the solitude of the graveyard shift, it brought* one unsettling aspect of the all-night job at **Schramm's**, one I hadn't anticipated . . . the telephone there. Hardly a night passed that some young person, feeling wonderfully daring and witty, no doubt, would telephone to ask me if I was Deadeye Dick.

I always was. I always will be (*DD* 125:L16).

Though the store was once owned by the Schramm family in Midland City, they had long since sold the business and left the area. The pharmacy belonged to Mr. Horton of Cincinnati.

Schwartz, Harold D. (also known as **Gramps**). *The patriarch of the Schwartz family living in Alden Village in the short story "Tomorrow and Tomorrow and Tomorrow." He was seventy before the anti-aging compound "anti-gerasone" was invented. Consequently, he is wrinkled but a quite healthy 172 years old. Anti-gerasone has extended the span of life so greatly that it has precipitated a crushing housing shortage. The Schwartz's living conditions are so crowded that great-grandchildren old enough to give birth can't afford to because of the lack of space. Space allocation is accorded by age, so Gramps is free to impose himself in any room of the house.*

Gramps is well aware that members of the family want to dilute his anti-gerasone to kill him off and get him out of the apartment. One night he leaves a suicide note and disappears. In the note he leaves all his possessions to be divided equally among the entire family. Some assume age should continue to rule the division of space. Others disagree and a huge family brawl ensues. All the Schwartzes are hauled off to jail and face a year in jail. Jail seems nice because everyone has their own bed and sink. They want to stay.

Gramps sees the television coverage of the brawl while sitting in the Alden Village Green, a local bar. He sends away for a new anti-gerasone formula which promises to remove the wrinkles from those over 150, and returns to the apartment, its only inhabitant.

Schwartz, Louis J. and Emerald. *Two of the besieged family members forced to endure the cramped living conditions of their extended family due to the life-prolonging drug anti-gerasone, in the short story "Tomorrow and Tomorrow and Tomorrow." Louis is one hundred twelve and Emerald is ninety-three. Despite being disinherited by great-grandpa Harold D. Schwartz, Lou refills the patriarch's anti-gerasone prescription to full strength after witnessing Mortimer Schwartz dilute the solution. Louis feared the prospect of a chaotic family power struggle should the old man die.*

Schwartz, Mortimer. *The great-grandnephew of Harold D. Schwartz in the short story "Tomorrow and Tomorrow and Tomorrow." Mortimer and his new wife move into the extended family's cramped dwelling, and he dilutes Harold's anti-gerasone in the hope of eventually freeing up some living space. Louis Schwartz witnessed the event and, fearing a family power struggle, restores the drug to full strength.*

Schweitzer, Albert. *The spirit of the legendary medical missionary and theologian who founded a hospital in French Equitorial Africa in 1913, is invoked a number of times throughout Vonnegut's work.* Cat's Cradle*'s John/Jonah travels to San Lorenzo intending to write a magazine story about*

Julian Castle, the American sugar millionaire who apparently followed the Schweitzer's path by opening a free hospital in the island's jungle. Castle, however, sneeringly tells the narrator Schweitzer was not his hero. As a child Sylvia Rosewater (GBR) met Schweitzer along with Picasso, Hemingway, Toscanini, Churchill, and de Gaulle as a parade of the world's notable figures were frequent guests in her parents' home. When Dwayne Hoover goes into a violent rage, the advanced ambulance called to aid his victims was *the Martha Simmons Memorial Mobile Disaster Unit*, named in honor of the wife of Newbolt Simmons, a County Commissioner of Public Safety. She had died of rabies contracted from a sick bat she found clinging to her floor-to-ceiling livingroom draperies one morning. She had just been reading a biography of **Albert Schweitzer**, who believed that human beings should treat simpler animals lovingly (*BC* 265:L14-15). *Young Kimberly in "The Chemistry Professor" (reprinted in* Palm Sunday*'s "Jekyll and Hyde Revisited") declares she is a follower of Dr. Schweitzer.*

Vonnegut's most recent reference sarcastically ties in the humanitarian with our continued military insouciance. (*FWD* 103:L34) "**Albert Schweitzer**, a physician as well as a musician and a philosopher, hoped to teach us reverence for life. He felt that we should not kill even the tiniest, most contemptible organism if we could possibly avoid doing that. On the face of it, this ideal is preposterous, since so many diseases are caused by germs. **Dr. Schweitzer** himself must have killed germs by the billions. Either that, or most of his patients died.

"If I were to speak tonight of the agony experienced by individual germs in the bodies of patients dosed by **Dr. Schweitzer**, the men in white coats would be entitled to cart me off to St. Elizabeth's. And our frame of mind now, not just in this country but in many, many others, including, no doubt, Libya, is such that civilians attacked from the air are as unworthy of being discussed as individual germs."

science fiction, **science-fiction**. *Infamy and adulation—in not so equal measures—will forever be Vonnegut's dual legacy as a result of his forays into the genre.* (*WFG* 1:L8, 13 *Science Fiction*) Years ago I was working in Schenectady for General Electric, completely surrounded by machines and ideas for machines, so I wrote a novel about people and machines, and machines frequently got the best of it, as machines will. (It was called *Player Piano*, and it was brought out again in both hard cover and paperback.) And I learned from the reviewers that I was a **science-fiction** writer.

I supposed that I was writing a novel about life, about things I could not avoid seeing and hearing in Schenectady, a very real town, awkwardly set in the gruesome now. I have been a soreheaded occupant of a file drawer labeled "**science fiction**" ever since, and I would like out, particularly since so many serious critics regularly mistake the drawer for a urinal.

To be sure, one of Vonnegut's most famous creations is science fiction writer Kilgore Trout, who plays a significant role in God Bless You, Mr.

X

Rosewater, Slaughterhouse-Five, *and* Breakfast of Champions, *all novels from his perceived creative pinnacle. Moreover,* Galápagos *is told by the spirit of the decapitated Leon Trout—Kilgore's son;* Jailbird*'s Dr. Bob Fender uses Trout's name as one of his pen names; and* Hocus Pocus *has a wealth of references to science fiction author Arthur C. Clarke (highly esteemed by Vonnegut). There are a number of science fiction tropes throughout his short stories, and the topic is a main concern in his anthologized interviews.*

Vonnegut uses science fiction as an extension of his personal experience but always as a means for social commentary. (*WFG* 261:L26, 29 *Playboy Interview*) PLAYBOY: What attracted you to using the *(science fiction)* form yourself?
VONNEGUT: I was working for General Electric at the time, right after World War Two, and I saw a milling machine for cutting the rotors on jet engines, gas turbines. . . . This was in 1949 and the guys who were working on it were foreseeing all sorts of machines being run by little boxes and punched cards. *Player Piano* was my response to the implications of having everything run by little boxes. The idea of doing that, you know, made sense, perfect sense. To have a little clicking box make all the decisions wasn't a vicious thing to do. But it was too bad for the human beings who got their dignity from their jobs.
PLAYBOY: So **science fiction** seemed like the best way to write about your thoughts on the subject?
VONNEGUT: There was no avoiding it, since the General Electric Company was **science fiction**.

The short version of how Vonnegut invented ice-nine, arguably one of his most memorable creations: (*PS* 102:L22 *Self-Interview*) VONNEGUT: Anyway—*(H.G.)* Wells came to Schenectady, and Langmuir was told to be his host. Langmuir thought he might entertain Wells with an idea for a **science-fiction** story—about a form of ice that was stable at room temperature. Wells was uninterested, or at least never used the idea. And then Wells died, and then, finally, Langmuir died. I thought to myself: "Finders, keepers—the idea is mine."

Eliot Rosewater introduces readers (fictional and real) to Kilgore Trout in GBR, SL5, *and* BC. *In the first case, Eliot crashes a convention of science fiction writers and speaks warmly of the prolific Trout. He exhorts the crowd to use their talents to construct a book in which money is the key science fiction device—the very key to Vonnegut's novel.* (*GBR* 16:L30-31) And it occurred to him that a really good **science-fiction** book had never been written about money. "Just think of the wild ways money is passed around on Earth!" he said.

In SL5, *Rosewater shares a hospital room with Billy Pilgrim and introduces him to the scores of Trout books beneath his bed. In an interesting connection between Vonnegut's own creation and one of his all time favorite writers,* Rosewater said an interesting thing to Billy one time about a book that wasn't **science fiction**. He said that everything there was to know about life was in *The Brothers Karamazov*, by Feodor Dostoevsky. "But that isn't enough any more," said Rosewater (*SL5* 87:L26). *Rosewater is also responsible for bringing Trout to the Midland City Arts Festival in* Breakfast of Champions.

(*MH* xiv:L17, 27 *Preface*) I used to be a public relations man for General Electric, and then I became a free-lance writer of so-called "slick fiction," a lot of it **science fiction**. . . .

I asked him what the very lowest grade of fiction was, and he told me, "**science fiction.**" I asked where he was bound in such a rush, and learned that he had to catch a Fan-Jet. He was to speak at a meeting of the Modern Language Association in Honolulu the next morning. Honolulu was three thousand miles away. *Vonnegut alludes to an unnamed college professor identified by Jerome Klinkowitz as Robert Scholes of Brown University.*

(*WFG* 2:L10 *Science Fiction*) English majors are encouraged, I know, to hate chemistry and physics, and to be proud because they are not dull and creepy and humorless and war-oriented like the engineers across the quad. And our most impressive critics have commonly been such English majors. . . . So it is natural for them to despise **science fiction**.

(*WFG 85:L15, 19-20 Excelsior! We're Going to the Moon! Excelsior!*) Good **science-fiction** writers of the present are not necessarily as eager as Arthur C. Clarke to found kindergartens on Jupiter, to leave the poor Maine ape and his clam rake far behind. Isaac Asimov, who is a great man, perceives three stages so far in the development of American **science fiction**, says we are in stage three now:

1. Adventure dominant.
2. Technology dominant.
3. Sociology dominant.

(*WFG* 262:L3, 6, 12 *Playboy Interview*) PLAYBOY: *Slaughterhouse-Five* is mainly about the Dresden fire bombing, which you went through during World War Two. What made you decide to write it in a **science-fiction** mode?
VONNEGUT: These things are intuitive. There's never any strategy meeting about what you're going to do; you just come to work every day. And the **science-fiction** passages in *Slaughterhouse-Five* are just like the clowns in Shakespeare. When Shakespeare figured the audience had had enough of the heavy stuff, he'd let up a little, bring on a clown or a foolish innkeeper or something like that, before he'd become serious again. And trips to other planets, **science fiction** of an obviously kidding sort, is equivalent to bringing on the clowns every so often to lighten things up.

(*WFG* 273:L17 *Playboy Interview*) VONNEGUT: His opponent *(George McGovern's 1972 foe—President Richard Nixon)* had too powerful an issue: the terror and guilt and hatred white people feel for the descendants of victims of an unbelievable crime we committed not long ago—human slavery. How's that for **science fiction**? There was this modern country with a wonderful Constitution, and it kidnaped human beings and used them as machines. It stopped it after a while, but by then it had millions of descendants of those

kidnaped people all over the country. What if they turned out to be so human that they wanted revenge of some kind? McGovern's opinion was that they should be treated like anybody else. It was the opinion of the white electorate that this was a dangerous thing to do.
(*Gal* 78:L18) So I *(Leon Trout)* have to say that human brains back then had become such copious and irresponsible generators of suggestions as to what might be done with life, that they made acting for the benefit of future generations seem one of many arbitrary games which might be played by narrow enthusiasts—like poker or polo or the bond market, or the writing of **science-fiction** novels.
(*PS* 174:L24 *Funnier on Paper Than Most People*) "Perhaps you have read the novel *Childhood's End* by Arthur C. Clarke, one of the few masterpieces in the field of **science fiction**. All of the others were written by me. In Clarke's novel, mankind suddenly undergoes a spectacular evolutionary change. The children become very different from the parents, less physical, more spiritual—and one day they form up into a sort of column of light which spirals out into the universe, its mission unknown."
(*HP* 167:L9) I *(Eugene Debs Hartke)* read a lot of **science fiction** when I was in the Army, including Arthur C. Clarke's *Childhood's End*, which I thought was a masterpiece. He was best known for the movie *2001*, the very year in which I am writing and coughing now. *See also: GBR* 13:L3,30; 14:L18; *SL5* 87:L4,6,13,23; 93:L29; 100:L15; 142:L17; *BC* 7:L3; 15:L8,31-32; 106:L3; 123:L11; 231:L30; 238:L19; *MH—Tomorrow and Tomorrow and Tomorrow* 288:L11-12; *WFG—Preface* xix:L7; *WFG—Science Fiction* 1:essay title; 2:L12,18,27-29; 3:L2,11,28-29; 4:L16,19,26; 5:L7,14,21; *WFG—Address to the American Physical Society* 97:L4; *WFG—Thinking Unthinkable, Speaking Unspeakable* 209:L7; *WFG—Playboy Interview* 247:L17; 259:L24,26,29-30; 260:L1,8,13-14; 261:L4; 269:L8,13; *JB* 39:L12; 54:L24; 64:L9; 74:L11-12; 160:L12; 233:L14,26; *PS—Religion* 209:L11; *Gal* 70:L31-32; 183:L28; 219:L13; 234:L25; 252:L6; *HP* 135:L18; 166:L17; 251:L34; 301:L22.

Scilly Islands. *In Merrihue Rosewater's* A History of the Rosewaters of Rhode Island, *he writes:* The Old World home of the Rosewaters was and is in the **Scilly Islands**, off Cornwall. The founder of the family there, whose name was John, arrived on St. Mary Island in 1645, with the party accompanying the fifteen-year-old Prince Charles, later to become Charles the Second, who was fleeing the Puritan Revolution. . . . John Graham, rechristened John Rosewater in the **Scilly Islands**, apparently found the mild climate and the new name congenial, for he remained there for the rest of his life, fathering seven sons and six daughters (*GBR* 163:L6, 164:L7).

Scipio. *The fictional town in the Finger Lakes region of New York, ancestral home of the Tarkington family, founders of the Mohiga Wagon Company and The Mohiga Valley Free Institute, which later became Tarkington College, in* Hocus Pocus.

Seitz, Al and Sue. (*DD* x:L33) I found one such bill *(a faded and shrunken American dollar)* in my wallet when I got home from Haiti a couple of years ago, and I mailed it back to **Al** and **Sue Seitz**, the owners and host and hostess of the Oloffson, asking them to release it into its natural environment. It could never have survived a day in New York City. *Rudy Waltz and his brother eventually purchase the hotel from Al and Sue.*

Sermon on the Mount. *Among the many references Vonnegut makes to the Sermon on the Mount, perhaps the most insightful one for his readers, comes from Bernard V. O'Hare's letter commemorating his sixtieth birthday. O'Hare is, of course, Vonnegut's war buddy and fellow survivor of the Dresden firebombing. He and Vonnegut returned to Dresden during the writing of* Slaughterhouse-Five. (*FWD* 216:L22) In some reviews Kurt has been characterized as a black humorist. Those reviewers wouldn't know black humor from Good Friday. They don't know that what they read is only his reaction to the sight of the world gone mad and rushing headlong toward Dresden to the hundredth power.

And they miss his message, in which he pleads that world governments found their rule on something more akin to the **Sermon on the Mount** than the preachings of those who lead the world to Armageddon.

There is certainly nothing wrong with a man like that. And if such thinking constitutes black humor, it's too bad there is not an epidemic of it.

I am glad Kurt and I did not die.

And I would go back to Dresden with him again.

Happy Birthday, Kurt.

God Bless You, Mr. Rosewater *is Vonnegut's novel about money, the poor, and man's responsibility for both. This passage recalls a time twenty years earlier when Stewart Buntline's youth and compassion are hammered into a lifelong conservatism by his lawyer and financial advisor, Mr. McAllister.* (*GBR* 139:L29) "Every year at least one young man whose affairs we manage comes into our office, wants to give his money away. He has completed his first year at some great university. It has been an eventful year! He has learned of unbelievable suffering around the world. He has learned of the great crimes that are at the roots of so many family fortunes. He has had his Christian nose rubbed, often for the very first time, in the **Sermon on the Mount**.

"He is confused, tearful, angry! He demands to know, in hollow tones, how much money he is worth. We tell him. He goes haggard with shame, even if his fortune is based on something as honest and useful as Scotch Tape, aspirin, rugged pants for the working man, or, as in your case, brooms. You have, if I'm not mistaken, just completed one year at Harvard?"

"Yes."

"It's a great institution, but, when I see the effect it has on certain young people, I ask myself, 'How dare a university teach compassion without teaching history, too?' History tells us this, my dear young Mr. Buntline, if it tells us nothing else: Giving away a fortune is a futile and destructive thing. It makes whiners of the poor, without making them rich or even comfortable. And the donor and his descendents become undistinguished members of the whining poor."

Jailbird*'s Kenneth Whistler is based on the real union organizer Powers Hapgood (as drawn in the following passage), and the succeeding passage recalls Walter Starbuck's reply to Richard Nixon during hearings of the House Un-American Activities Committee.* (*JB* xix:L12, 17) Moon Claycomb's father, according to Powers Hapgood, asked him this final question just before lunch: "Mr. Hapgood," he said, "why would a man from such a distinguished family and with such a fine education choose to live as you do?"

"Why?" said Hapgood, according to Hapgood. "Because of the **Sermon on the Mount**, sir."

And Moon Claycomb's father said this: "Court is adjourned until two P.M."

What, exactly, was the **Sermon on the Mount**?

It was the prediction by Jesus Christ that the poor in spirit would receive the Kingdom of Heaven; that all who mourned would be comforted; that the meek would inherit the Earth; that those who hungered for righteousness would find it; that the merciful would be treated mercifully; that the pure in heart would see God; that the peacemakers would be called the sons of God; that those who were persecuted for righteousness' sake would also receive the Kingdom of Heaven; and on and on.

(*JB* 241:L2-3) Congressman Nixon had asked me why, as the son of immigrants who had been treated so well by Americans, as a man who had been treated like a son and been sent to Harvard by an American capitalist, I had been so ungrateful to the American economic system.

The answer I gave him was not original. Nothing about me has ever been original. I repeated what my one-time hero, Kenneth Whistler, had said in reply to the same general sort of question long, long ago. Whistler had been a witness at a trial of strikers accused of violence. The judge had become curious about him, had asked him why such a well-educated man from such a good family would so immerse himself in the working class.

My stolen answer to Nixon was this: "Why? **The Sermon on the Mount**, sir."

(*PS* 325:L3 *In the Capital of the World*) "I am enchanted by the **Sermon on the Mount**. Being merciful, it seems to me, is the only good idea we have received so far. Perhaps we will get another idea that good by and by—and then we will have two good ideas. What might that second good idea be? I don't know. How could I know? I will make a wild guess that it will come from music somehow. I have often wondered what music is and why we love it so. It may be that music is that second good idea's being born."

(*PS* 329:L28-29) "There are two sisters of Lazarus there—Martha and Mary. They, at least, are sympathetic and imaginatively helpful. Mary begins to massage and perfume the feet of Jesus Christ with an ointment made from the spikenard plant. Jesus has the bones of a man and is clothed in the flesh of a man—so it must feel awfully nice, what Mary is doing to his feet. Would it be heretical of us to suppose that Jesus closes his eyes?

"This is too much for that envious hypocrite Judas, who says, trying to be more Catholic than the Pope: 'Hey—this is very un-Christian. Instead of wasting that stuff on your feet, we should have sold it and given the money to the poor people.'

"To which Jesus replies in Aramaic: 'Judas, don't worry about it. There will still be plenty of poor people left long after I'm gone.'

"This is about what Mark Twain or Abraham Lincoln would have said under similar circumstances.

"If Jesus did in fact say that, it is a divine black joke, well suited to the occasion. It says everything about hypocrisy and nothing about the poor. It is a Christian joke, which allows Jesus to remain civil to Judas, but to chide him about his hypocrisy all the same.

"'Judas, don't worry about it. There will still be plenty of poor people left long after I'm gone.'

"Shall I regarble it for you? 'The poor you always have with you, but you do not always have me.'

"My own translation does no violence to the words in the Bible. I have changed their order some, not merely to make them into the joke the situation calls for, but to harmonize them, too, with the **Sermon on the Mount**. The **Sermon on the Mount** suggests a mercifulness that can never waver or fade.

Eugene Debs Hartke recalls how he was clandestinely taped by Kimberly Wilder to gather evidence for her father's denunciation of him at the meeting of Tarkington's Board of Trustees. (*HP* 97:L2-3) She asked me about my own lecture in Chapel only a month earlier. She hadn't attended and so hadn't taped it. She was seeking confirmation of things other people had said I said. My lecture had been humorous recollections of my maternal grandfather, Benjamin Wills, the old-time Socialist.

She accused me of saying that all rich people were drunks and lunatics. This was a garbling of Grandfather's saying that Capitalism was what the people with all our money, drunk or sober, sane or insane, decided to do today. So I straightened that out, and explained that the opinion was my grandfather's, not my own.

"I heard your speech was worse than Mr. Slazinger's," she said.

"I certainly hope not," I said. "I was trying to show how outdated my grandfather's opinions were. I wanted people to laugh. They did."

"I heard you said Jesus Christ was un-American," she said, her tape recorder running all the time.

So I unscrambled that one for her. The original had been another of Grandfather's sayings. He repeated Karl Marx's prescription for an ideal society, "From each according to his abilities, to each according to his needs." And then he asked me, meaning it to be a wry joke, "What could be more un-American, Gene, than sounding like the **Sermon on the Mount**?"

(*FWD* 78:L8-9) The Attorney General's Commission on Pornography, a traveling show about dirty books and pictures put on the road during the administration of Ronald Reagan, was something else again. At least a couple of the panel members would later be revealed as having been in the muck of financial or sexual atrocities. There was a clan feeling, to be sure, but the family property in this case was the White House, and an amiable, sleepy, absentminded old movie actor was its totem pole. And the crazy quilt of ideas all its members had to profess put the Council of Trent to shame for mean-spirited, objectively batty fantasias: that it was good that civilians could buy assault rifles; that the contras in Nicaragua were a lot like Thomas Jefferson and James Madison; that Palestinians were to be called "terrorists" at every opportunity; that the contents of wombs were Government property; that the American Civil Liberties Union was a subversive organization; that anything that sounded like the **Sermon on the Mount** was socialist or communist, and therefore anti-American; that people with AIDS, except for those who got it from mousetrapped blood transfusions, had asked for it; that a billion-dollar airplane was well worth the price; and on and on.
(*FWD* 132:L19) British imperialism was armed robbery. The British class system (which seems so right to the Neo-Cons) was and still is unarmed robbery. (Just because the Soviet Union, which used to brag about being such a friend of the common people, has collapsed, that doesn't mean the **Sermon on the Mount** must now be considered balderdash.)
(*FWD* 163:L32) "When I say that the Unitarian Universalists, the people who know pure baloney when they hear it, are something like the early Christians in the catacombs, am I suggesting that contempt for baloney will someday be as widespread as Christianity is today? Well the example of Christianity is not encouraging, actually, since it was nothing but a poor people's religion, a servant's religion, a slave's religion, a woman's religion, a child's religion, and would have remained such if it hadn't stopped taking the **Sermon on the Mount** seriously and joined forces with the vain and rich and violent. I can't imagine that you would want to do that, to give up everything you believe in order to play a bigger part in world history.

shaft. (*PP* 7:L4) The rafters still bore the marks of what Edison had done with the lonely brick barn: bolt holes showed where overhead **shafts** had once carried power to a forest of belts, and the wood-block floor was black with the oil and scarred by the feet of the crude machines the belts had spun.
(*PP* 10:L8) Now, by switching in lathes on a master panel and feeding them signals from the tape, Paul could make the essence of Rudy Hertz produce one, ten, a hundred, or a thousand of the **shafts**.
(*ST* 16:L31) The fountain itself was marvelously creative . . . a cone described by many stone bowls of decreasing diameters. The bowls were collars on a cylindrical **shaft** forty feet high. *This is the fountain outside the Rumfoord estate.*

(*ST* 66:L6) The Magnum Opus Building was a slender, prismatic, twelve-sided **shaft**, faced on all twelve sides with blue-green glass that shaded to rose at the base. The twelve sides were said by the architect to represent the twelve great religions of the world. So far, no one had asked the architect to name them.
(*ST* 269:L27) The wafer itself was contained in a gold mesh reticule which was hung on a stainless steel band clamped to the **shaft** that might be called Salo's neck. *The reticule around the Tralfamadorian messenger's neck held the one word message, "Greetings."*
(*CC* 62:L3) I asked Marvin Breed if he'd known Emily Hoenikker, the wife of Felix; the mother of Angela, Frank, and Newt; the woman under that monstrous **shaft**. *The shaft is an enormous obelisk.*
(*SL5* 22:L34, 23:L2) Their suction cups were on the ground, and their **shafts**, which were extremely flexible, usually pointed to the sky. At the top of each **shaft** was a little hand with a green eye in its palm. *Part of Billy's description of the Tralfamadorians.*
(*PS* 232:L29 *Obscenity*) Codpieces were very much in fashion, and many men were wearing codpieces in the shape of rocket ships, in honor of the Big Space Fuck. These customarily had the letters "U.S.A." embroidered on the **shaft**. Senator Snopes' **shaft**, however, bore the Stars and Bars of the Confederacy. *From Vonnegut's short story "The Big Space Fuck."*
(*DD* 25:L5) *Rudy describes his parents' weather vane:* Its arrow alone was twelve feet long, and one hollow copper horseman chased another one down that awesome **shaft**. The one in back was an Austrian with a lance. The one in front, fleeing for his life, was a Turk with a scimitar.
(*DD* 27:L30) And as soon as those relatives of mine got home, according to the paper, Father flew his favorite gift from Hitler from the horizontal **shaft** of the weather vane. It was a Nazi flag as big as a bedsheet. *See also: PP* 9:L4,7,11; 126:L26; *ST* 85:L25; 164:L11; 263:L11,23; *CC* 58:L1; 58:L30; 63:L19; 183:L33; 213:L2; *Slap* 79:L7; *JB* 88:L30; *HP* 65:L2.

Shah of Bratpuhr. *The spiritual leader of 6,000,000 members of the Kolhouri sect is the visiting head of state in* Player Piano. *He travels across the United States and is eventually trapped within his limousine during the Ghost Shirt uprising in Ilium. He sees EPICAC as a false god and the Reeks and Wrecks as slaves.*

He is mentioned again in Hocus Pocus. *Eugene Debs Hartke's long lost son, Rob Roy, is raised by Lowell Fenstermaker, the owner of a Dubuque meatpacking business. Fenstermaker was bought out by the Shah, and now Rob Roy Fenstermaker is "fabulously well-to-do."*

Shaltoon. *In* God Bless You, Mr. Rosewater, *the home planet of Queen Margaret in Kilgore Trout's sexy science fiction novel* Venus on the Half-shell—*not to be confused with the novel of the same name authored by real life science fiction author Philip Jose Farmer.*

Shapiro, Dr. Ben. *The Harvard classmate of Walter F. Starbuck who became a physician and a lieutenant colonel in the Army Medical Corps. He was the commander of the "twenty-bed hospital in the* Kaiserburg, *the imperial castle," when Starbuck brought the emaciated war refugee Ruth to him for care. Shapiro eventually serves as Walter's best man when he weds Ruth and later, as a full colonel, delivers their child by cesarean section in Wiesbaden. Unfortunately, Shapiro fell victim to McCarthyism.* (*JB* 28:L26-30) In a few years Senator Joseph R. McCarthy would find that promotion to have been sinister, since it was well known that **Shapiro** had been a communist before the war. "Who promoted **Shapiro** to Wiesbaden?" he would want to know.

Starbuck later finds out the unhappy though honored end to his friend's life. (*JB* 38:L31, 39:L1-3) He had gone to Israel long ago and gotten himself killed in the Six Day War. I had heard that there was a primary school named in his honor in Tel Aviv.

Shaw, Helene. *In the short story "Who Am I This Time?" Helene is the beautiful but uninspired newcomer to the North Crawford Mask and Wig Club teamed with the mercurial Harry Nash in a new production of* A Streetcar Named Desire. *Helene is transferred to North Crawford by the phone company so that she may train the local branch how to work the automatic billing machine. She decides to accept a friendly invitation to the club's tryouts as a way of meeting new people. Though her first reading is poor, once she reads opposite Harry, the two make the roles come alive. By the end of the story Helene realizes that the only way to maintain a relationship with Harry is to offer him various roles to rehearse. Together, they privately share a rich and romantic life moving from one play to the next, always fully becoming the characters they read.*

Shaw, Marilyn. *One of the many women fondly remembered by Eugene Debs Hartke. Both were veterans of Vietnam and recruited by Sam Wakefield to teach at Tarkington College. While serving as a nurse in the war, Marilyn's husband divorced her for another woman. After the war she gave up nursing and studied computer science at New York University, which is where Wakefield found her. She agreed to teach provided Scipio had a chapter of Alcoholics Anonymous. At Tarkington she became a tenured Full Professor and Chair of the Department of Life Sciences. When Wakefield committed suicide, she went on a week-long drinking binge at the Black Cat Café. Killed by a stray bullet when the escaped convicts took over Scipio, Marilyn was buried at the foot Musket Mountain. Eugene recalls,* I never considered making a pass at **Marilyn**, although she was reasonably attractive and unattached. I don't know why that is. There may have been some sort of incest taboo operating, as though we were brother and sister, since we had both been in Vietnam. . . .

Remembering her now, I wonder if I wasn't in love with her, even though we avoided talking to each other as much as possible.

Maybe I should put her on a very short list indeed: all the women I loved (*HP* 101:L14).

Shazzbutter (see ***How You Doin?***).

Shepherd, Lawson. *Second-in-command at the Ilium Works under the direction of Paul Proteus, Shepherd is in charge of buildings 53 through 71. Paul, Lawson, and Ed Finnerty graduated college together and joined in the project, which recorded the movements of lathe operator Rudy Hertz as part of the movement toward mechanizing repetitive manual labor. While Finnerty was elevated to the national board level and Proteus became the Ilium chief, Shepherd felt slighted in being passed by. Unlike his friends who cared little for the competitiveness of the system,* When **Shepherd** had first arrived in Ilium, he had announced to his fellow new arrivals, Paul and Finnerty, that he intended to compete with them. Baldly, ridiculously, he talked of competitiveness and rehashed with anyone who would listen various crises where there had been a showdown between his abilities and those of someone else, crises that the other participants had looked upon as being routine, unremarkable, and generally formless. But, to **Shepherd**, life seemed to be laid out like a golf course, with a series of beginnings, hazards, and ends, and with a definite summing up—for comparison with others' scores—after each hole. He was variously grim or elated over triumphs or failures no one else seemed to notice, but always stoical about the laws that governed the game. He asked no quarter, gave no quarter, and made very little difference to Paul, Finnerty, or any of his other associates. He was a fine engineer, dull company, and doggedly master of his fate and *not* his brother's keeper (*PP* 43:L13-29).

Shepherd achieves a measure of notice by being named captain of the Green Team at the Meadows. However, his team goes down to humiliating defeat because he tried to win all the events by himself.

When Paul's marriage to Anita breaks down (due to the ruling technocracy's plot to infiltrate the Ghost Shirt Society), Anita and Shepherd pair off. Though she previously found Shepherd contemptuous for his public and often hostile competitiveness, it was his desire for upward mobility that she found sorely lacking in Paul. Despite remaining in love with Paul, she plans to divorce him and marry Shepherd.

Shoup, Martin. *Rabo Karabekian recounts that after being rejected as an art student by Nelson Bauerbeck because his art had "no internal message," he sought expression through writing. However, Bauerbeck's perceptions about Rabo's painting were echoed by Shoup's critique of his writing.* (*Blue* 191:L11-23) So I signed up for a course in creative writing instead—taught three nights a week at City College by a fairly famous short-story writer named **Martin Shoup**. His stories were about black people, although he himself was white. Dan Gregory had illustrated at least a couple of them—with the customary delight and sympathy he felt for people he believed to be orangutans.

Shoup said about my writing that I wasn't going to get very far until I became more enthusiastic about describing the looks of things—and particularly people's faces. He knew I could draw, so he found it odd that I wouldn't want to go on and on about the looks of things.

Shoup, Mary Alice. *In* Mother Night, *the sixty-eight-year-old widowed owner of The Little Rock School of Embalming advertises for a new president and winds up hiring and marrying Lionel J.D. Jones.*

Shoup, Naomi. *The high school English teacher who encourages Rudy Waltz in his writing after reading his essay* on this assigned subject: "The Midland City Person I Most Admire." My hero was John Fortune, who died in Katmandu when I was only six years old. She turned my ears crimson by saying that it was the finest piece of writing by a student that she had seen in forty years of teaching. She began to weep (*DD* 109:L21-26). *Rudy hangs on to Miss Shoup's encouraging words, eventually producing the play "Katmandu" which sparks horrendous reviews. Rudy had drawn a brief sketch contrasting his play's critical reception with its initial encouraging influence by citing* How pathetic they would have found it, if only they had known, that I had been told that I should become a writer, that I had the divine spark, by a high school English teacher who had never been anywhere, either, who had never seen anything important, either, who had no sex life, either. And what a perfect name she had for a role like that: **Naomi Shoup** (*DD* 107:L7-14). *Rudy's father worried about the gifts Miss Shoup believed he possessed because he felt that once such a pronouncement is made the receiver has no choice but to follow that calling until it leads to ruin. Mr. Waltz decries that* "She is obviously a siren. . . . A siren is half woman, half bird . . . you know they lure sailors with their sweet songs to shipwrecks on rocks" (*DD* 111:L27-32).

Shriver, Sargent. *The 1972 vice-presidential candidate of the Democratic Party. In a passage indicating Vonnegut's emerging sense of extended families, which became a central concern for President Wilbur Swain in the 1976 novel* Slapstick, *he recalls an incident which gave early shape to this idea.* (*PS* 204:L31 *Religion*) "I know **Sargent Shriver** slightly. When he was campaigning for vice-president, he asked me if I had any ideas. You remember that there was plenty of money around, but as far as ideas went, both parties were in a state of destitution. So I told him, and I am afraid he didn't listen, that the number one American killer wasn't cardiovascular disease, but loneliness. I told him that he and McGovern could swamp the Republicans if they would promise to cure that disease. I even gave him a slogan to put on buttons and bumpers and flags and billboards: Lonesome No More!

"The rest is history." *Vonnegut also recounts this episode in the "*Playboy *Interview" reprinted in* Wampeters, Foma, & Granfalloons. *Also,*

"Lonesome No More!" became the battle cry of Swain's presidency and serves as Slapstick*'s subtitle.*

Shultz, Hermann and Sophia. *In* Hocus Pocus, *Elias Tarkington brought brewmaster Hermann Shultz and his wife from Leipzig, Germany, to Scipio to run his new brewery. Hermann became a teacher of botany, German, and the flute when Tarkington opened The Mohiga Valley Free Institute. The couple died during a diphtheria epidemic in 1893, and at their request were buried on campus. Their bodies were moved to the cemetery at the foot of Musket Mountain in 1987, to make way for the Pahlavi Pavilion recreation center. They shared a common gravestone with the single-word inscription, "FREETHINKERS."*

Shuttle, Herb. *The vacuum cleaner salesman and suitor of Penelope Ryan's in* Happy Birthday, Wanda June. *Though supremely confident in his own sales abilities, he fawns over the returning Harold Ryan. It would appear that Herb is more pleased with dating the wife of Harold Ryan than Penelope herself.*

Sidi Barrani. *The Egyptian site where the artist and Nazi sympathizer Dan Gregory meets his fate.* (*Blue* 108:L7) They *(Dan Gregory and Fred Jones)* would be killed almost exactly one year before the United States joined the war—against Italy, by the way, and against Germany and Japan and some others. They were killed around December seventh of 1940 at **Sidi Barrani**, Egypt, where only thirty thousand British overwhelmed eighty thousand Italians, I learn from the *Encyclopaedia Britannica*, capturing forty thousand Italians and four hundred guns.

Simmons, Newbolt and Martha. *Mrs. Simmons is remembered by having the Martha Simmons Memorial Mobile Disaster Unit named in her honor. The wife of Newbolt Simmons, a County Commissioner of Public Safety, Martha died of rabies contracted from a bat she found clinging to her drapes.* (*BC* 265:L14-15, 266:L1-4) She had just been reading a biography of Albert Schweitzer, who believed that human beings should treat simpler animals lovingly. The bat nipped her ever so slightly as she wrapped it in *Kleenex*, a face tissue. She carried it out onto her patio, where she laid it gently on a form of artificial grass known as *Astro-turf*.

The special ambulance is a converted transcontinental bus complete with an operating room and space for thirty-six patients. It is called into action when Dwayne Hoover goes on a violent rampage near the end of the text.

Simpkins, Darlene. *The International Committee for the Identification and Rehabilitation of Martians had difficulty determining Beatrice Rumfoord's true identity. They thought she was either Florence White or* **Darlene Simpkins**, a plain and friendless girl who had last been seen accepting a ride with a swarthy stranger in Brownsville, Texas (*ST* 241:L21).

sin-wat*. In* Cat's Cradle, *the Bokononist term for someone who wants all of somebody's love for themselves, unwilling to share that individual with others—a monogamist.*

sinookas*. In Bokononist terms, "the tendrils of one's life."* (*CC* 16:L19, 21)
Dr. Hoenikker himself was no doubt a member of my *karass*, though he was dead before my ***sinookas***, the tendrils of my life, began to tangle with those of his children.

The first of his heirs to be touched by my ***sinookas*** was Newton Hoenikker, the youngest of his three children, the younger of his two sons.

The Sirens of Titan (1959) (see also **Malachi Constant**, **Winston Niles Rumfoord**, **Tralfamadore**, **chrono-synclastic infundibulum**, **structured moment**, **Salo**, **Universal Will to Become**). *The premise of the novel is that all of human history has been one great Rube Goldberg invention designed by the Tralfamadorians for the singular purpose of getting a spare part to their stranded messenger, Salo. Any attempt to impose meaning on the apparent linearity of "history" is futile. The text comes to us long ago yet far beyond the "punctual" time of Rumfoord and Malachi Constant (because the universe is described by the chrono-synclastic infundibulum: all is-as-it-was-and-is-supposed-to-become).* Sirens *recounts man's plight before having learned the true state of cosmic affairs (Tralfamadorian intervention); the narration opens as a book of revelations promising to detail the shallow concerns which had riveted man's attention up to the close of* the Nightmare Ages, falling roughly, give or take a few years, between the Second World War and the Third Great Depression (*ST* 8:L12-15).

Perhaps the most distinguishing narrative feature of Sirens *is the chrono-synclastic infundibulum. "These places are where all different kinds of truths fit together as nicely as the parts in your daddy's solar watch"* (*ST* 14:L28-30) *It isn't that all truths are correct at the intersection of the chrono-synclastic infundibulum, but that all truths combine into the greater order of the universe as they always have and always will. The sum of these truths is not a greater all-encompassing, meaningful truth but rather a greater sense of the cosmic composition.*

Aside from absorbing the polarities of the various truths, the more prominent feature of the chrono-synclastic infundibulum is its explanation that time is a continuum, that those riding its electronic waves can see a full-formed future as well as past. Vonnegut's Ancient Mariner, Winston Niles Rumfoord, declares "it's a thankless job telling people it's a hard, hard Universe they're in. . . . When I ran my space ship into the chrono-synclastic infundibulum, it came to me in a flash that everything that ever has been always will be, and everything that ever will be always has been" (*ST* 25:L13-16,31-32, 26:L1-2). *Having been caught within the great whirlwind of World War II and the more particular flash point which was Dresden (while his genetic ancestors fought for their truths against the truths of his more recent homeland), Vonnegut's career long obligation has been to tell others how cruel our tensions sometimes appear. Fated to an eternity of conflict without any particular truth above the rest, the chrono-synclastic infundibulum describes a physical trap. Though man tends to believe he is on a linear track toward perfection, Vonnegut's wrinkle in time prompts the rhetorical question, "What makes you think you're going anywhere?"* (*ST* 31:L1-2).

The chrono-synclastic infundibulum denies man's inherent yearning to attach meaning to each succeeding moment in time. "Things fly this way and that, my boy," *Rumfoord tells Malachi,* "with or without messages" (*ST* 39:L9-11). *The eternal strife of dynamic tensions (in which man finds himself groping to understand the meaning of his particular moment) is merely a part of the redundant waves of history. Moving from one instance to the next, from the uncertain designs of others to our own self-interested prodding, man's focus is too narrowly obsessed with his finitude. Rumfoord (Vonnegut), our Ancient Mariner, is here to dispel such existential myopia,* "It's chaos, and no mistake, for the Universe is just being born. It's the great becoming that makes the light and the heat and the motion, and hangs you from hither to yon" (*ST* 39:L11-14).

The tale that follows is supposed to reveal how man came to understand the fifty-three portals to the soul. Instead, the main focus is "the great becoming" of man's understanding. Malachi's story reveals why such a Copernican shift in man's thinking became necessary—why even the Tralfamadorians weren't the center of the universe. Whether machines of flesh or steel, all were caught on the roller coaster known as the chrono-synclastic infundibulum.

Malachi's exit from the Rumfoord mansion, after witnessing Winston's materialization and hearing his explanation of the past which is Malachi's future, establishes the pre-Copernican state of thinking before Salo's eventual return of the aged Malachi: In crossing the bright zodiac on the foyer floor, he sensed that the spiral staircase now swept down rather than up. Constant became the bottommost point in a whirlpool of fate. As he walked out the door, he was delightfully aware of pulling the aplomb of the Rumfoord mansion right out with him (*ST* 42:L18-24).

As a metaphor for the narrative, the spiral staircase is the chrono-synclastic infundibulum, and Malachi imagines his centrality at either end. As he senses it, his destiny as the end point of some larger fate has already begun (or, in the chrono-synclastic infundibulated sense of things, already finished) in that he arrived at the mansion disguised as Jonah K. Rowley. This Jonah portends not the destruction of another Nineveh, but the destruction of man's inflated sense of self within all time. Insisting on the validity of man's contrived meanings for his existence is as false as personifying a physical structure, the mansion, with "aplomb."

The three Sirens of Titan were sculptures made by the Tralfamadorian messenger Salo and inspired by his observations of man's development on Earth. Of the millions of Titanic peat statues created by Salo, these alone were painted to look like real people. (*ST* 278:L35-38) It had been necessary to paint them in order to give them importance in the sumptuous, oriental scheme of things in Rumfoord's palace. *Rumfoord's palace was a re-creation of the Taj Mahal.*

In order to entice Malachi Constant with the idea of space travel, Rumfoord showed him a picture of the statues and passed them off for the way all women looked on Titan. Malachi stole the photograph and eventually used them for MoonMist Cigarette ads. (*ST* 56:L13) *Pleasure in Depth!* said the headline on the ad. The picture that went with it was the picture of the three **sirens of Titan**. There they were—the white girl, the golden girl, and the brown girl.

The fingers of the golden girl were fortuitously spread as they rested on her left breast, permitting an artist to paint in a MoonMist Cigarette between two of them. The smoke from her cigarette passed beneath the nostrils of the brown and white girls, and their space-annihilating concupiscence seemed centered on mentholated smoke alone.

On Titan, the three statues are in the middle of the rectangular pool at Rumfoord's Taj Mahal, which he called Dun Roamin. They were covered with bacterial growth ever since Malachi had taken over caring for the house and pool. (*ST* 309:L23) Constant knew of the significance of the three **sirens** in his life. He had read about it—both in the *Pocket History of Mars* and *The Winston Niles Rumfoord Authorized Revised Bible*. The three great beauties didn't mean so much to him now, really, except to remind him that sex had once bothered him.

Skag, Delmore. *The lead character in an unnamed Kilgore Trout novel. Skag was* a bachelor in a neighborhood where everybody else had enormous families. And **Skag** was a scientist, and he found a way to reproduce himself in chicken soup. He would shave living cells from the palm of his right hand, mix them with the soup, and expose the soup to cosmic rays. The cells turned into babies which looked exactly like **Delmore Skag**.

Pretty soon, **Delmore** was having several babies a day, and inviting his neighbors to share his pride and happiness. He had mass baptisms of as many as a hundred babies at a time. He became famous as a family man.

And so on.

Skag hoped to force his country into making laws against excessively large families, but the legislatures and the courts declined to meet the problem head-on. They passed stern laws instead against the possession by unmarried persons of chicken soup (*BC* 21:L15-33).

Skinner, Cornelia Otis. *Noted as a famous monologist and one of the many celebrities brought to the Midland City YMCA for a performance and given the routine tour of the Waltz home because of Otto's well-outfitted art studio, in* Deadeye Dick.

***Skylark**. The British ship which transported Ojumwa to Charleston, South Carolina, in* Breakfast of Champions. *Ojumwa is the ancestor of ambulance driver Eddie Key. He was captured and sold into slavery by Dr. Cyprian Ukwende's Indaro ancestors.*

Skyscraper National Park. *Wilbur Swain's nickname for Manhattan, in* Slapstick.

Slapstick (1976) (see also **Wilbur Swain** and **extended family**). *As is the case with* Slaughterhouse-Five, Slapstick *is also conceived while Vonnegut contemplated the dead. In this case, while flying to Indianapolis to bury their Uncle Alex, Vonnegut and his brother Bernard sit with an open seat between them. Uncle Alex was typical of the Vonneguts who had remained in Indianapolis in that he had more than a little trouble accepting Kurt's literature. The empty airline seat reminds Vonnegut of his sister, and in light of the rest of the family's displeasure with his lifestyle (getting divorced), Alice appears to have been Kurt's creative focal point.* (*Slap* 15:L19-26) For my own part, though: It would have been catastrophic if I had forgotten my sister at once. I had never told her so, but she was the person I had always written for. She was the secret of whatever artistic unity I had ever achieved. She was the secret of my technique. Any creation which has any wholeness and harmoniousness, I suspect, was made by an artist or inventor with an audience of one in mind. *More than simply writing with Alice in mind, Vonnegut employs her spirit to complement his own by creating the freakish fraternal twins Eliza and Wilbur Swain, whose intellectual synergism soars beyond the genius level when they literally place their heads together.*

Since so many of Vonnegut's novels concern schemes for restructuring communal relationships, it isn't surprising that Slapstick, *conceived in the midst of a lost familial spirituality, has as its centerpiece the creation of artificially extended families, a theory developed by the joint efforts of Eliza and Wilbur Swain. In actuality, Vonnegut witnessed a highly prized form of the extended family in January 1970, the final days of the Biafran independence campaign. Closer to home, he and Jane Cox Vonnegut adopted three of Alice's children after her death. Two days before Alice succumbed to cancer, her husband died in a commuter train accident.*

Despite the fact that the Chinese ruin the planet's stable gravity by experimenting with the Swains' scientific treatises, Wilbur is proud of what he and Eliza had done to restructure human relationships. As president, Wilbur successfully instituted their scheme for artificially extended families. In response to the "grotesque situational poetry," reminiscent of slapstick films, Wilbur Swain did his best with every test. Moreover, he reaffirms Vonnegut's denial of suicide as a logical extension of problem solving, as did the finale of Breakfast of Champions. *As autobiography, Vonnegut concludes for himself that "bargaining in good faith with destiny" is the supreme achievement one can strive for. It was Alice Vonnegut who labeled as "slapstick" the bizarre events which would orphan her children within a forty-eight hour period. The only thing to do was precisely what Kurt Vonnegut did: adapt as best he could.*

Slaughterhouse-Five (1969) (subtitled *THE CHILDREN'S CRUSADE—A DUTY-DANCE WITH DEATH*) (see also **Billy Pilgrim**, **Tralfamadore**, **structured moment**, **Dresden**, **Yon Yonson**). Slaughterhouse-Five *is born from death. In some sense, Vonnegut's life as a novelist was conceived in the death of Dresden. Just as the life of the biblical Adam is described in sensory terms, "And the Lord God formed man of the dust of the ground, and breathed into his nostrils the breath of life; and man became a living soul," Vonnegut, too, is infused through the olfactory senses.* (*SL5* 185:L24-27) There were hundreds of corpse mines operating by and by. They didn't smell bad at first, were wax museums. But then the bodies rotted and liquefied, and the stink was like roses and mustard gas. *To paraphrase the fictive Rudy Waltz, Vonnegut had caught life; he had come down with life. To "have come down with life," much as one would describe the onset of a disease, is precisely the effect the corpse mines had on Vonnegut.* (*SL5* 3:L33, 4:L1-6) I have this disease late at night sometimes, involving alcohol and the telephone. I get drunk, and I drive my wife away with a breath like mustard gas and roses. And then, speaking gravely and elegantly into the telephone, I ask the telephone operators to connect me with this friend or that one, from whom I have not heard in years.

Having risen from the meatlocker sepulchre inhaling the death stench of Dresden, Vonnegut continually struggles with the disease of life, not so much pondering the meaning of life as much as tracing the inertial forces which describe life. And so, breathing mustard gas and roses, attempting to look back with compassion and love for the innocents, Vonnegut calls war buddy Bernard O'Hare to aid his own failing memory.

At the time, Vonnegut is concerned with finding meaning in the moment that was Dresden, and he thinks the final illustration should concentrate on the ironic death of Edgar Derby. Though Derby's fate is considered by Vonnegut as a properly ironic closing for the novel, he is not the powerfully tragic figure to reinforce some grand statement about the meaninglessness of war. He is lost within the uncountable carnage reviewed by Vonnegut when considering the Crusades, World War II, (both military and civilian casualties), Dresden, Bobby Kennedy, Martin Luther King, Jr., and Vietnam.

As Billy Pilgrim comes to understand life according to the Tralfamadorian fourth-dimensional perspective, Vonnegut's narrative is a world defined by the recurrence of experience. The inevitable failure of the Ghost Shirt rebellion in Player Piano, *the predetermined history of humanity in* Sirens, *the netherworld existence of Howard Campbell, Eliot Rosewater's vision of Indianapolis in a firestorm (Vonnegut's hometown), and* Cat's Cradle*'s time-looped fatalism all have their roots in Billy Pilgrim's* Slaughterhouse *experience. Billy Pilgrim is caught within Vonnegut's* *structured moment which was Dresden, but Billy's predecessors have their roots in the defining moment of Pilgrim/Vonnegut.*

The title of the text is taken from Vonnegut's barracks' location while a POW in Dresden.

Slazinger, Paul. *Harvard-educated novelist Paul Slazinger appears in both* Bluebeard *and* Hocus Pocus *with greatly varying fortunes. He first appears as the ever-present sidekick of the one-eyed Rabo Karabekian. Though Slazinger officially resides in the house next to Karabekian's, he spends nearly all his waking hours at his friend's larger house. Paul is a novelist with eleven books to his credit, though he hadn't written anything in ages. According to Rabo, every three years or so Paul suffered a mental breakdown. On Okinawa in World War II, Slazinger won a Silver Star for throwing himself on a grenade to save his friends. The grenade failed to explode but he was badly injured. Rabo recalls he had a scar extending from his sternum to his crotch and had only one nipple. Paul's wit once prompted him to ask Rabo the riddle,* "What has three eyes, three nipples and two assholes?"

"I give up," I said.

And he said, "**Paul Slazinger** and Rabo Karabekian" (*Blue* 126:L10).

Slazinger the war hero is descended from a Hessian soldier serving as a mercenary under the leadership of British General John Burgoyne during the Revolutionary War. The mercenary was captured at the second Battle of Freeman's Farm by forces commanded by General Benedict Arnold.

Slazinger was briefly married to actress Barbira Mencken. Years later while living next door to Rabo, Paul went to Poland as part of a delegation from "PEN" to observe the plight of writers living under communist rule. On his return, he began suffering a slow mental decline. One evening the local volunteer fire department is called to his home because he was hysterical. He convinced them to take him to Karabekian's house. Later, Paul commits himself to the psychiatric ward at the Veterans Administration hospital in Riverhead, Long Island.

In Hocus Pocus, *Slazinger is an out-of-print novelist who takes a last-minute offer to become Tarkington College's 1990-1991 Writer in Residence. He spends some of his time playing pool with fellow Silver Star winner Eugene Debs Hartke. In December 1990, Paul received a Genius Grant from the MacArthur Foundation, $50,000 a year for 5 years. During a speech at the school's chapel just before Christmas break, Slazinger* predicted . . . that human slavery would come back, that it had in fact never gone away. He said that so many people wanted to come here because it was so easy to rob the poor people, who got absolutely no protection from the Government. He talked about bridges falling down and water mains breaking because of no maintenance. He talked about oil spills and radioactive waste and poisoned aquifers and looted banks and liquidated corporations. "And nobody ever gets punished for anything," he said. "Being an American means never having to say you're sorry" (*HP* 95:L26-35). *When these sentiments are later recalled* *by Hartke, Kimberley Wilder is nearby to tape-record his comments for future use during his dismissal hearing. After receiving notice about the Genius Grant, Slazinger left for the Florida Keys. There he was eventually joined by Tarkington's Artist in Residence, Pamela Ford Hall, with whom he enjoyed a secret affair while on campus. They planned to wed, but the relationship fell apart. Hartke assumes it was probably due to a combination of her alcoholism and his general attitude.*

Slezak, Premier. *The Soviet leader who called Professor Barnhouse's terrifying displays of power* a bourgeois plot to shackle the true democracies of the world (*MH* 159:L33-34 *Report on the Barnhouse Effect*).

Small Magellanic Cloud. *The galaxy containing the planet Tralfamadore, in* The Sirens of Titan.

The Smart Bunny. *Hotel clerk Milo Maritimo is reading this Kilgore Trout novel when the author checks in for the Midland City Arts Festival. There is a thematic connection between Trout's story and Karabekian's paintings of wavering bands of light representing one's essential core of awareness. The Farrows have no awareness of the bunny's consciousness and those in Midland City can't fathom the meaning of Karabekian's work. The bunny also suffers from the same mental isolation as Dwayne Hoover in that both suffer from an exaggerated sense of self brought on by bad chemicals.* The novel in question, incidentally, was ***The Smart Bunny***. The leading character was a rabbit who lived like all the other wild rabbits, but who was as intelligent as Albert Einstein or William Shakespeare. It was a female rabbit. She was the only female leading character in any novel or story by Kilgore Trout.

She led a normal female rabbit's life, despite her ballooning intellect. She concluded that her mind was useless, that it was a sort of tumor, that it had no usefulness within the rabbit scheme of things.

So she went hippity-hop, hippity-hop toward the city, to have the tumor removed. But a hunter named Dudley Farrow shot and killed her before she got there. Farrow skinned her and took out her guts, but then he and his wife Grace decided that they had better not eat her because of her unusually large head. They thought what she had thought when she was alive—that she must be diseased.

And so on (*BC* 232:L1-2).

Smiley (see **Greathouse and Smiley**).

Smiley, Letitia. *Named Tarkington College's 1922 Lilac Queen, Letitia disappeared the night after winning the Women's Barefoot Race from the bell tower to the President's House and back again, in* Hocus Pocus. *When the graves of Hermann and Sophia Shultz were moved to make room for the Pahlavi Pavilion, an unexpected skull was unearthed. Eugene Debs Hartke* *presumes it belongs to Letitia Smiley, and he conducts his own investigation, which leads him to presume her killer was Tarkington College Provost Kensington Barber. Hartke believes Barber made her pregnant.*

Snopes, Senator Flem. *The Mississippi senator and Chairman of the Senate Space Committee who managed* to locate the biggest jizzum-freezing plant in his "l'il ol' home town," which was Mayhew (*PS* 232:L6-8 *The Big Space Fuck*). *He wore a codpiece embroidered with the Confederate Stars and Bars. Snopes made a campaign pledge to change the national symbol from the eagle to the lamprey, since eagles were long since extinct and therefore symbolized degradation rather than survival, let alone supremacy.*

Solomon, Syd. *An artist acquaintance of Vonnegut's for whom he once wrote an essay for inclusion in an exhibition catalogue for a Solomon retrospective. Vonnegut asked him what he was trying to do with paint when working, and Solomon answered that he had no idea. This episode is recounted in the essay "Playmates," reprinted in* Palm Sunday.

Rabo Karabekian tries to answer Circe Berman's question about telling good pictures from bad by invoking Syd Solomon. (*Blue* 156:L17-23) "How can you tell a good painting from a bad one?" he said. This is the son of a Hungarian horse trainer. He has a magnificent handlebar mustache.

"All you have to do, my dear," he said, "is look at a million paintings, and then you can never be mistaken."

It's true! It's true!

Solzhenitsyn, Aleksandr. (*JB* 81:L9) Cleveland Lawes was reading *The Gulag Archipelago* now, an account of the prison system in the Soviet Union by another former prisoner, **Aleksandr Solzhenitsyn**.

somethinghead (see also **nothinghead**). *Those who continue to follow the government dictum and take their ethical birth control pills, effectively numbing all sexual urges and sensations below the waist.* (*MH* 34:L23 *Welcome to the Monkey House*) The sheaf proved to be photocopies of poems Billy had sent to Hostesses in other places. Nancy read the top one. It made much of a peculiar side effect of ethical birth-control pills: They not only made people numb—they also made people piss blue. The poem was called *What the* ***Somethinghead*** *Said to the Suicide Hostess*, and it went like this:

I did not sow, I did not spin,
And thanks to pills I did not sin.
I loved the crowds, the stink, the noise.
And when I peed, I peed turquoise.

I ate beneath a roof of orange;
Swung with progress like a door hinge.

'Neath purple roof I've come today
To piss my azure life away.

Virgin hostess, death's recruiter,
Life is cute, but you are cuter.
Mourn my pecker, purple daughter—
All it passed was sky-blue water.

Son of God (see **Christ**).

The Son of Jimmy Valentine. *At the suggestion of Darlene Trout, Kilgore's second wife, he* once wrote a short novel about the importance of the clitoris in love-making. . . . She told him that the hero should understand women so well that he could seduce anyone he wanted. So Trout wrote ***The Son of Jimmy Valentine***. . . .

Kilgore Trout invented a son for Jimmy Valentine, named Ralston Valentine. Ralston Valentine also sandpapered his fingertips. But he wasn't a safe-cracker. Ralston was so good at touching women the way they wanted to be touched, that tens of thousands of them became his willing slaves. They abandoned their husbands or lovers for him, in Trout's story, and Ralston Valentine became President of the United States, thanks to the votes of women (*BC* 151:L14-15).

Sonderkommando. *Former concentration camp inmate Andor Gutman explains to Howard Campbell the nature of the unique group he joined while held captive.* (*MN* 5:L11, 15) **Sonderkommando** means special detail. At Auschwitz it meant a very special detail indeed—one composed of prisoners whose duties were to shepherd condemned persons into gas chambers, and then to lug their bodies out. When the job was done, the members of the **Sonderkommando** were themselves killed. The first duty of their successors was to dispose of their remains.

Later, when Howard Campbell seeks out the Epstein family so that he may surrender to them, Mrs. Epstein understands his apparent catatonia. (*MN* 196:L9-13) What she crooned was this, a command she had heard over the loudspeakers of Auschwitz—had heard many times a day for years.

"*Leichentrager zu Wache*," she crooned.

A beautiful language, isn't it?

Translation?

"Corpse-carriers to the guardhouse."

That's what that old woman crooned to me.

Sony. *The Japanese electronics firm is mentioned twice in Vonnegut's work. In* Bluebeard, *Marilee Kemp, then the Countess Portomaggiori, became Europe's largest Sony distributor after World War II. In* Hocus Pocus, *Hiroshi Matsumoto, the Warden of the New York State Maximum Security Adult*

Correctional Facility at Athena, is a lifelong employee of Sony. The Japanese firm contracted with New York to manage its penal system. A previous reference in the text indicates Sony had purchased a Lexington, Kentucky, hospital and that Matsumoto managed that facility prior to moving to Athena.

The Soul Merchants. *Eugene Debs Hartke's high school rock band.* (*HP* 15:L18) What I would really like to have been, given a perfect world, is a jazz pianist. I mean jazz. I don't mean rock and roll. I mean the never-the-same-way-twice music the American black people gave the world. I played piano in my own all-white band in my all-white high school in Midland City, Ohio. We called ourselves **"The Soul Merchants."**

How good were we? We had to play white people's popular music, or nobody would have hired us. But every so often we would cut loose with jazz anyway. Nobody else seemed to notice the difference, but we sure did. We fell in love with ourselves. We were in ecstasy.

(*HP* 33:L22-23) When Du Pont took over Barrytron, the double fence, the Dobermans, my father and all, I was a high school senior, all set to go to the University of Michigan to learn how to be a journalist, to serve John Q. Public's right to know. Two members of my 6-piece band, **The Soul Merchants**, the clarinet and the string bass, were also going to Michigan.

We were going to stick together and go on making music at Ann Arbor. Who knows? We might have become so popular that we went on world tours and made great fortunes, and been superstars at peace rallies and love-ins when the Vietnam War came along.

(*HP* 36:L26) During my last 2 years in high school, I don't think my parents even suspected that I was half in the bag a lot of the time. All they ever complained about was the music, when I played the radio or the phonograph or when **The Soul Merchants** rehearsed in our basement, which Mom and Dad said was jungle music, and much too loud.

(*HP* 38:L3-4) "You let those 4 years slip by without doing anything but making jungle music," he said.

It occurs to me now, a mere 43 years later, that I might have said to him that at least I managed my sex life better than he had managed his. I was getting laid all the time, thanks to jungle music, and so were the other **Soul Merchants**. Certain sorts of not just girls but full-grown women, too, found us glamorous free spirits up on the bandstand, imitating black people and smoking marijuana, and loving ourselves when we made music, and laughing about God knows what just about anytime.

Sousa, Mr. *The father of seven girls in the short story "Adam." He envies waiting-room companion Mr. Knechtmann, whose wife gave birth to a boy, their first and probably only child. Mrs. Knechtmann's malnutrition during the war makes it unlikely she will be capable of bearing more children.*

space and time (see **time and space**).

Space Wanderer (see **Malachi Constant** and **Queen Margaret**).

Sparks, Jon. *In* Breakfast of Champions, *Vonnegut writes that he was wearing a commemorative bracelet inscribed with the name of Warrant Officer First Class Jon Sparks. He goes on to mention that he left the bracelet so Wayne Hoobler could find it. Hoobler believes it belongs to a woman romantically involved with someone named WO1 Jon Sparks, and he can't figure out how to pronounce "WO1."*

Sparky. *There are two dogs named Sparky in Vonnegut's work. The first is in the short story "Tom Edison's Shaggy Dog." Sparky yields the canine secret that dogs* can *talk when he solves Edison's search for a light bulb filament by suggesting a piece of carbonized thread. A pack of dogs later kills Sparky for divulging their secret.*

Sparky is also the name of Dwayne Hoover's Labrador retriever. Sparky lost his tail in a car accident, so he had no way of telling other dogs how friendly he was. He had to fight all the time. His ears were in tatters. He was lumpy with scars (*BC* 17:L8-11). *Vonnegut says Sparky is modeled after a dog once owned by his brother Bernard.*

Sparrow, Harold J. (see also **Frank Wirtanen**). *In the Editor's Note to* Mother Night, *Vonnegut discloses that he altered the names of various people including that of Howard Campbell's American sponsor. Previously known as the Blue Fairy Godmother and Colonel Frank Wirtanen, Harold J. Sparrow, serial number 0-61134, is the name used in the intelligence officer's letter to Israeli war crimes investigators. Sparrow is prepared to testify on Campbell's behalf about his espionage activities.*

Speer, Albert. *Hitler's grand architect for the Third Reich.* (*WFG* 170:L21 *Torture and Blubber*) Agony never made a society quit fighting, as far I know. A society has to be captured or killed—or offer things it values. While Germany was being tortured during the Second World War, with justice, may I add, industrial output and the determination of its people increased. Hitler, according to **Albert Speer**, couldn't even be bothered with marveling at the ruins or comforting the survivors.

spiral (also **spiral nebula**). (*ST* 13:L23, 25) Winston Niles Rumfoord had run his private space ship right into the heart of an uncharted chrono-synclastic infundibulum two days out of Mars. Only his dog had been along. Now Winston Niles Rumfoord and his dog Kazak existed as wave phenomena—apparently pulsing in a distorted **spiral** with its origin in the Sun and its terminal in Betelgeuse.

The earth was about to intercept that **spiral**.

(*ST* 24:L3, 21) With a limp right hand, he *(Winston Niles Rumfoord)* made the magical sign for **spiral** staircase. . . .

There was also the empty suit of armor of an armadillo, a stuffed dodo, and the long **spiral** tusk of a narwhal, playfully labeled by Skip, *Unicorn Horn*.
(*ST* 40:L7) She *(Beatrice Rumfoord)* wore a long white dressing gown whose soft folds formed a counter-clockwise **spiral** in harmony with the white staircase. The train of the gown cascaded down the top riser, making Beatrice continuous with the architecture of the mansion.
(*ST* 42:L3) It startled her *(Beatrice)* so much that she took a step back from the head of the staircase, separated herself from the rising **spiral**. The small step backward transformed her into what she was—a frightened, lonely woman in a tremendous house. *This action was a result of Malachi Constant's telling Beatrice that he had access to the world's biggest space ship,* The Whale.
(*ST* 42:L19) In crossing the bright zodiac on the foyer floor, he *(Malachi Constant)* sensed that the **spiral** staircase now swept down rather than up. Constant became the bottommost point in a whirlpool of fate. As he walked out the door, he was delightfully aware of pulling the aplomb of the Rumfoord mansion right out with him.
(*ST* 109:L1) He *(Unk/Malachi Constant)* could have stared happily at the immaculate **spiral** of the rifling for hours, dreaming of the happy land whose round gate he saw at the other end of the bore. The pink under his oily thumbnail at the far end of the barrel made that far end seem a rosy paradise indeed. Some day he was going to crawl down the barrel to that paradise.
(*ST* 143:L5) At the end of the tour, in the packaging department, the manager's ankle became snarled in a **spiral** of steel strapping, a type of strapping that was used for binding shut the packaged flamethrowers. *The school children of Mars were on a tour of the flamethrower factory. In anger, the manager stomps flat the spiral of steel strapping before it is quietly picked up by Chrono, the son of Malachi and Beatrice. This is the spare part for which Salo had been waiting.*
(*ST* 266:L20-29) Titan describes, as a consequence, a **spiral** around the Sun.

Winston Niles Rumfoord and his dog Kazak were wave phenomena—pulsing in distorted **spirals**, with their origins in the Sun and their terminals in Betelgeuse. Whenever a heavenly body intercepted their **spirals**, Rumfoord and his dog materialized on that body.

For reasons as yet mysterious, the **spirals** of Rumfoord, Kazak, and Titan coincided exactly.
(*CC* 51:L4) Whatever it is *(wampeter)*, the members of its *karass* revolve about it in the majestic chaos of a **spiral nebula**.
(*CC* 205:L1) So I once again mounted the **spiral** staircase in my tower; once again arrived at the uppermost battlement of my castle; and once more looked out at my guests, my servants, my cliff, and my lukewarm sea.
(*PS* 174:L28 *Funnier on Paper Than Most People*) "Perhaps you have read the novel *Childhood's End* by Arthur C. Clarke, one of the few masterpieces in the field of science fiction. All of the others were written by me. In Clark's [*sic*] novel, mankind suddenly undergoes a spectacular evolutionary change. The children become very different from the parents, less physical, more

spiritual—and one day they form up into a sort of column of light which **spirals** out into the universe, its mission unknown."
(*Blue* 160:L32) Fred Jones told me one time that the smoke trails of falling airplanes and observation balloons were the most beautiful things he ever expected to see. And I now compare his elation over arcs and **spirals** and splotches in the atmosphere with what Jackson Pollock used to feel as he watched what dribbled paint chose to do when it struck a canvas on his studio floor.
(*Blue* 171:L23) Marilee's and my canvas, so to speak, called for more and wetter kisses, and then a groping, goosey, swooning tango up the **spiral** staircase and through the grand dining room.
(*HP* 218:L30) Warden Hiroshi Matsumoto was a survivor of the atom-bombing of Hiroshima, when I was 5 and he was 8. . . . There was a flash and wind. When he straightened up, his city was gone. He was alone on a desert, with little **spirals** of dust dancing here and there. *See also: ST* 39:L32; 46:L29; 50:L3; 143:L8-14; 287:L4; 298:L1-6; *MN* 137:L7; *CC* 185:L10; 191:L34; *Blue* 86:L27; 88:L11,28; 92:L6; 141:L18.

spire. (*GBR* 50:L11) On the label of each can of beer *(Rosewater Golden Lager Ambrosia Beer)* was a picture of the heaven on earth the New Ambrosians had meant to build. The dream city had **spires**. The **spires** had lightning-rods. The sky was filled with cherubim.
(*MH* 222:L18 *The Lie*) The *(Holly House)* inn was on the edge of the Whitehill Sward, glimpsing the school's rooftops and **spires** over the innocent wilderness of the Sanford Remenzel Bird Sanctuary.
(*DD* 169:L20) "Crucifixion in Rome" is indeed set in Rome, which I have never seen. I know enough, though, to recognize that it is chock-a-block with architectural anachronisms. The Colosseum, for example, is in perfect repair, but there is also the **spire** of a Christian church, and some architectural details and monuments which appear to be more recent, even, than the Renaissance, maybe even nineteenth century.
(*Gal* 5:L5) But when this story begins, they were still ugly humps and domes and cones and **spires** of lava, brittle and abrasive, whose cracks and pits and bowls and valleys brimmed over not with rich topsoil or sweet water, but with the finest, driest volcanic ash.

Spirit of the Meadows (see ***Queen of the Meadows***).

Squires, Anthony. *Patrolman Anthony Squires is the one who gives Rudy Waltz the nickname "Deadeye Dick" while escorting him home after visiting with his father in the Midland City jail. Rudy's father was jailed because Rudy was too young to be charged with the accidental murder of Mrs. Eloise Metzger. Squires, who had two punctured ear drums as a result of being an abused child, is particularly mean spirited toward Rudy. He tells Rudy that if he were him, he would consider committing suicide since he would have to face* *years of anxiety about one of Metzger's relatives coming after him. Rudy completes his account of Squires with the following information:* Patrolman **Anthony Squires**, incidentally, would many years later become chief of detectives, and then suffer a nervous breakdown. He is dead now. He was working as a part-time bartender at the new Holiday Inn when he had his peephole closed by ye olde neutron bomb (*DD* 92:L1-6).

Squires, Barbara. *Married to Dr. Jerome Mitchell, she is the younger sister of policeman Anthony Squires, the man who gave Rudy Waltz the nickname "Deadeye Dick."*

SS Psychiatrist. (*FWD* 31:L35) "Like most writers, I have at home the beginnings of many books which would not allow themselves to be written. About twenty years ago, a doctor prescribed Ritalin for me, to see if that wouldn't help me get over such humps. I realized right away that Ritalin was dehydrated concentrate or pure paranoia, and threw it away. But the book I was trying to make work was to be called ***SS Psychiatrist***. This was about an MD who had been psychoanalyzed, and he was stationed at Auschwitz. His job was to treat the depression of those members of the staff who did not like what they were doing there. Talk therapy was all he or anybody had to offer back then. This was before the days of—Never mind.

"My point was, and maybe I can make it today without having to finish that book, that workers in the field of mental health at various times in different parts of the world must find themselves asked to make healthy people happier in cultures and societies which have gone insane.

"Let me hasten to say that the situation in our own country is nowhere near that dire. The goal here right now, it seems to me, is to train intelligent, well-educated people to speak stupidly so that they can be more popular.

"Look at Michael Dukakis.

"Look at George Bush."

Stacks, Dr. Herb. *Rudy Waltz's globe-trotting dentist who was vacationing with his family in Katmandu when Midland City was neutron-bombed, in* Deadeye Dick.

stairs, staircase, stairheads, stairway, stairwell (*ST* 24:L3) "This room," said Rumfoord. With a limp right hand, he made the magical sign for spiral **staircase**. "It was one of the few things in life I ever really wanted with all my heart when I was a boy—this little room." *Rumfoord's chimneylike room under the spiral staircase sported the sign "Skip's Museum."*

(*ST* 35:L2) "Well—" murmured Malachi Constant, there in the chimneylike room under the **staircase** in Newport, "it looks like the messenger is finally going to be used."

(*ST* 40:L7) She wore a long white dressing gown whose soft folds formed a counter-clockwise spiral in harmony with the white **staircase**. The train of the gown cascaded down the top riser, making Beatrice continuous with the architecture of the mansion.

(*ST* 42:L3) It startled her so much that she took a step back from the head of the **staircase**, separated herself from the rising spiral. The small step backward transformed her into what she was—a frightened, lonely woman in a tremendous house.

(*ST* 42:L19-20) In crossing the bright zodiac on the foyer floor, he sensed that the spiral **staircase** now swept down rather than up. Constant became the bottommost point in a whirlpool of fate. As he walked out the door, he was delightfully aware of pulling the aplomb of the Rumfoord mansion right out with him.

(*MN* 181:L3, 13-14, 182:L1, 3, 14) While the column of air enclosed by the **stairs** had carried in the past a melancholy freight of coal dust and cooking smells and the sweat of plumbing, that air was cold and sharp now. Every window in my attic had been broken. All warm gases had been whisked up the **stairwell** and out my windows, as though up a whistling flue. . . .

The feeling of a stale old building suddenly laid open, an infected atmosphere lanced, made clean, was familiar to me. I had felt it often enough in Berlin. Helga and I were bombed out twice. Both times there was a **staircase** left to climb.

One time we climbed the **stairs** to a roofless and windowless home, a home otherwise magically undisturbed. Another time, we climbed the **stairs** to cold thin air, two floors below where borne had been.

Both moments at those splintered **stairheads** under the open sky were exquisite. . . .

I remember one time, when Helga and I went from the head of a splintered **staircase** in the sky down into a shelter deep in the ground, and the big bombs walked all around above.

(*MN* 190:L7, 24) The railing stopped O'Hare, and he gazed down the **stairwell**, down a beckoning helix to the patch of sure death below.

. . . Whether it was my words or humiliation or booze or surgical shock that made O'Hare throw up, I do not know. Throw up he did. He flashed the hash down the **stairwell** from four stories up.

(*MN* 191:L6) I am in jail because I could not bring myself to walk through or leap over another man's vomit. I am referring to the vomit of Bernard B. O'Hare on the foyer floor at the foot of the **stairwell**.

(*CC* 136:L19) Stanley led me to my room; led me around the heart of the house, down a **staircase** of living stone, a **staircase** sheltered or exposed by steel-framed rectangles at random.

(*GBR* 167:L17, 24, 26) When Caroline had clumped back up the cellar **stairs**, tremulous with disgust, Fred calmly advised himself that the time had come to *really* die. . . .

He was putting the noose over his head, when little Franklin called down the **stairway** that a man wanted to see him. And the man, who was

Norman Mushari, came down the **stairs** uninvited, lugging a fat, cross-gartered, slack-jawed briefcase.
(*SL5* 141:L24) The Americans and their guards and Campbell took shelter in an echoing meat locker which was hollowed in living rock under the slaughterhouse. There was an iron **staircase** with iron doors at the top and bottom.
(*SL5* 153:L1) A guard would go to the head of the **stairs** every so often to see what it was like outside, then he would come down and whisper to the other guards. There was a fire-storm out there.
(*BC* 282:L3) And Trout found **stairs**, but they were the wrong **stairs**. They led him not to the lobby and the finance office and the gift shop and all that, but into a matrix of rooms where persons were recovering or failing to recover from injuries of all kinds.
(*MH* 20:L20 *Who Am I This Time?*) There was heavy clumping on the library **stairs**. It sounded like a deepsea diver coming upstairs in his lead shoes. It was Harry Nash, turning himself into Marlon Brando.
(*MH* 242:L19 *Unready to Wear*) I took a couple of steps, headed my spirit in another direction, and that beautiful field marshal, medals and all, went crashing down the **staircase** like a grandfather clock.
(*Slap* 38:L2) This was the secret: There was a mansion concealed within the mansion. It could be entered through trap doors and sliding panels. It consisted of secret **staircases** and listening posts with peepholes, and secret passageways. There were tunnels, too.
(*Slap* 40:L3-4;) Our servants would tell each other now and then that the mansion was haunted. They heard sneezing and cackling in the walls, and the creaking of **stairways** where there were no **stairways**, and the opening and shutting of doors where there were no doors.
(*JB* 34:L5) But then the person began to sing "Swing Low, Sweet Chariot" as he clumped up the **stairway**, and I knew he was Emil Larkin, once President Nixon's hatchet man.
(*JB* 145:L11) I had assumed that we were as deep in the station as anyone could go. How wrong I was! Mary Kathleen opened the iron door on an iron **staircase** going down, down, down. There was a secret world as vast as Carlsbad Caverns below.
(*JB* 146:L17) She led me through a tunnel under Lexington Avenue, and up a **staircase** into the lobby of the Chrysler Building.
(*JB* 236:L11) She carries it up and down the **stairs** of my duplex. She is even secreting milk for it. She is getting shots to make her stop doing that. *Starbuck's Lhasa apso is experiencing a false pregnancy and carries a toy rubber ice-cream cone around the house.*
(*PS* 313:L32, 314:L1 *The Sexual Revolution*) An American Indian creation myth, in which a god of some sort gives the people the sun and then the moon and then the bow and arrow and then the corn and so on, is essentially a **staircase**, a tale of accumulation. . . .

Almost all creation myths are **staircases** like. . . . Our own creation myth, taken from the Old Testament, is unique, so far as I could discover.
(*DD* 88:L7, 10) The police actually threw him down a flight of **stairs**. They didn't just pretend that was what had happened to him. There was a lot of confused racist talk, evidently. Father would later remember lying at the bottom of the **stairs**, with somebody standing over him and asking him, "Hey, Nazi—how does it feel to be a nigger now?"
(*DD* 209:L7-8) He was heroically honorable and truthful. He *(Otto Waltz)* was thrown down the **staircase**—like so much garbage.
(*Blue* 70:L21) He *(Dan Gregory)* had given her *(Marilee Kemp)* a shove in his studio which sent her backwards and down the **staircase**. She looked dead when she hit the bottom, and two servants happened to be standing there—at the bottom of the **stairs**.
(*Blue* 71:L22) Only after the war did Marilee, reborn as the Contessa Portomaggiore, tell me that I was the reason she had been pushed down the **stairs** back in 1932.
(*Blue* 97:L18) But think of this: there were fifty-two mirrors of every conceivable period and shape, many of them hung in unexpected places at crazy angles, to multiply even the bewildered observer to infinity. There at the top of the **stairs**, with Dan Gregory invisible to me, I myself was everywhere!
(*Blue* 172:L23) Marilee's and my canvas, so to speak, called for more and wetter kisses, and then a groping, goosey, swooning tango up the spiral **staircase** and through the grand dining room.
(*HP* 118:L19) White cotton strips spliced end to end crisscrossed every which way in the front hall and living room. The newel post of the **stairway** was connected to the inside doorknob of the front door, and the doorknob was connected to the living room chandelier, and so on ad infinitum. *See also: PP* 33:L27; 36:L2; 223:L26; *ST* 39:L2; 46:L30; 47:L2; 178:L30; 181:L12; 296:L13; *MN* 44:L14; 53 chapter title; 54:L14,17; 55:L32; 56:L17; 59:L10; 60:L1,5; 64:L2; 167:L27,30; 171:L2; 181:L2, 7; 191:L15; 195:L14; *CC* 171:L19; 185:L11; 191:L34; 205:L3; 212:L5,10; *GBR* 64:L15; 65:L1; 133:L4; 165:L25; 170:L3,12; *SL5* 53:L27; *BC* 197:L9; *MH—Who Am I This Time?* 19:L22; *MH—Miss Temptation* 68:L5; 74:L36; 76:L9; 79:L21; *MH—More Stately Mansions* 123:L29,34; *MH—Report on the Barnhouse Effect* 165:L22; *MH—Welcome to the Monkey House* 198:L1-2; 200:L13; *MH—Deer in the Works* 210:L31; *Slap* 99:L13; 184:L20; 191:L92; 236:L23; *JB* 35:L3,5,9; 144:L29; 213:L3; 217:L27; *PS—The People One Knows* 127:L9,12; *PS—Playmates* 145:L7; *PS—Obscenity* 222:L29; *DD* 82:L27; 83:L21; 84:L7; 85:L34; 86:L29; 105:L8,15; 160:L5; 208:L16; *Blue* 5:L11; 72:L28; 75:L3; 86:L27; 87:L33; 88:L11,28; 91:L2; 92:L7; 95:L22,25,28; 98:L26; 141:L18,28; 171:L13; 194:L19; 221:L24; *HP* 26:L12; 34:L15; *FWD* 89:L21; 149:L10.

Stankiewicz, Juan and Geraldo. *The estranged grandchildren of Walter Starbuck. Starbuck's son changed his name to the original European spelling* *to distance himself from his father, whom he believed behaved disgracefully during the McCarthy era. Starbuck recalls:* In accordance with my wife's will, incidentally, **Juan** and his brother, **Geraldo**, were receiving reparations from West Germany for the confiscation of my wife's father's bookstore in Vienna by the Nazis after the *Anschluss*, Germany's annexation of Austria in Nineteen-hundred and Thirty-eight. My wife's will was an old one, written when Walter was a little boy. The lawyer had advised her to leave the money to her grandchildren so as to avoid one generation of taxes. She was trying to be smart about money (*JB* 228:L22).

Stankiewicz, Stanislaus. *The Russian-Polish chauffeur and bodyguard to the McCone family, in* Jailbird. *He married Anna Kairys, the McCone's Russian-Lithuanian cook, and together they had Walter F. Stankiewicz, who later changed his name to Starbuck.*

Stankiewicz, Walter F. *Walter F. Starbuck, Jr. was so distraught and embarrassed by his father's behavior during the McCarthy era that when he turned twenty-one, he changed his name to its original European spelling. Once his mother passed away, he cut himself off from any further contact with his father. (Jailbird* 40:L12-17) Our son said this to me, before showing his back to me and the open pit and hastening to a waiting taxicab: "I pity you, but I can never love you. As far as I am concerned, you killed this poor woman. I can't think of you anymore as a father or as any sort of relative. I never want to see or hear of you again."

Stankiewicz earns his living as a book reviewer for The New York Times, *eventually a property The RAMJAC Corporation.*

Stankowitz. *In* Slapstick, *the original Polish name of Dr. Cordelia Swain Cordiner's grandfather. He changed his name to Swain when he came to America. Dr. Cordiner insists she is not related to Eliza and Wilbur Swain, in* Slapstick.

Stanley. *Franklin Hoenikker's valet on San Lorenzo, in* Cat's Cradle. *He grudgingly produces a copy of* The Books of Bokonon *for the narrator to read.*

Starbuck, Ruth. *The Jewish survivor of a concentration camp near Munich who later marries Walter Starbuck. Starbuck meets her as she helps American military police sort out displaced people after the war. Ruth is a master of languages because she made it a point of learning to speak with the fellow prisoners. Ruth's prewar* family owned a rare-book store there before the Nazis took it away from them. She was six years younger than I. Her father and mother and two siblings were killed in concentration camps. She herself was hidden by a Christian family, but was discovered and arrested, along with the head of that family, in Nineteen-hundred and Forty-two. So she herself was in a concentration camp near Munich, finally liberated by American troops, for the last two years of the war. She herself would die in her sleep in Nineteen-hundred and Seventy-Four—of congestive heart failure, two weeks before my own arrest. Whither I went, and no matter how clumsily, there did my **Ruth** go—long as she could. If I marveled at this out loud, she would say, "Where else could I be? What else could I do?" (*JB* 16:L7-21)

Aside from learning a multiplicity of languages, Ruth taught herself portraiture using lampblack while in Auschwitz. Before the war, when only sixteen, she photographed one hundred beggars in Vienna, all of whom were terribly wounded veterans of World War One (*JB* 17:L3-5). *She was also an accomplished pianist. She tried to draw on her artistic talents to make a living as a wedding photographer when Walter was down on his luck. However,* There was always an air of prewar doom about her photographs, which no retoucher could eradicate. It was as though the entire wedding party would wind up in the trenches or the gas chambers by and by (*JB* 17:L23-26). *She eventually developed a thriving business as an interior decorator.*

On October 15, 1946, Ruth and Walter were married. (*JB* 22:L26-29) On the day we were married, and probably conceived our only child as well, *Reichsmarschall* Hermann Göring cheated the hangman by swallowing cyanide. (*JB* 23:L24-31) She believed, and was entitled to believe, I must say, that all human beings were evil by nature, whether tormentors or victims, or idle standers-by. They could only create meaningless tragedies, she said, since they weren't nearly intelligent enough to accomplish all the good they meant to do. We were a disease, she said, which had evolved on one tiny cinder in the universe, but could spread and spread.
(*JB* 155:L6-14) . . . my wife **Ruth**, the Ophelia of the death camps . . . believed that even the most intelligent human beings were so stupid that they could only make things worse by speaking their minds. It was thinkers, after all, who had set up the death camps. Setting up a death camp, with its railroad sidings and its around-the-clock crematoria, was not something a moron could do. Neither could a moron explain why a death camp was ultimately humane.

Starbuck, Walter (né Stankiewicz). *The narrator and title character of* Jailbird. *The son of a chauffeur and cook, Walter is brought up in the home of Alexander Hamilton McCone, heir to the Cuyahoga Bridge and Iron Company. In exchange for becoming the chess partner and constant companion of the socially withdrawn McCone, Walter is promised a Harvard education. After Harvard he serves in the military as an officer in charge of resettling displaced persons in postwar Europe. This is how he meets Ruth, the multilingual Jewish concentration camp survivor who eventually becomes his wife.*

During the McCarthy communist witchhunts of the 1950s, Walter is called before a congressional investigative committee and asked by then Congressman Nixon if he knew anyone in government who had been a communist. Starbuck volunteers the name of Leland Clewes, thereby ruining his friend's career in government.

When Nixon becomes president, Starbuck is appointed the President's Special Advisor on Youth Affairs and given an office in the White House third subbasement. Nixon's Watergate cronies use the safe in Starbuck's office to hide illegal campaign contributions eventually used as hush money. This leads to Walter's imprisonment as a co-conspirator in the Watergate cover-up.

Upon release from prison, Walter takes a room in the once-fashionable Hotel Arapahoe in New York, where he finds stolen clarinet parts in a dresser. When he and Mary Kathleen O'Looney take refuge in The American Harp Company's Chrysler Building offices and he offers the clarinet pieces to Delmar Peale, he finds himself once again in jail (though is shortly released).

Starbuck is given control of O'Looney's RAMJAC Corporation upon her death. However, because Starbuck withheld her Last Will and Testament in order to fulfill his promise to her, he is forced to return to prison for another five years.

Walter continually notes there were only four women in his life whom he loved: his mother, Sarah Wyatt, Ruth, and Mary Kathleen O'Looney. (*JB* 9:L19-21) I will describe them all by and by. Let it be said now, though, that all four seemed more virtuous, braver about life, and closer to the secrets of the universe than I could ever be.

(*JB* 105:L18-26) Sarah had spent many summers in Europe. I had never been there. She was fluent in French, and she and the owner performed a madrigal in that most melodious of all languages. How would I ever have got through life without women to act as my interpreters? Of the four women I ever loved, only Mary Kathleen O'Looney spoke no language but English. But even Mary Kathleen was my interpreter when I was a Harvard communist, trying to communicate with members of the American working class.

Starr, Harrison. *In the opening pages of* Slaughterhouse-Five, *Vonnegut recounts how his Dresden experience was forever on his mind in an attempt to give it some literary structure. His exchange with movie producer Harrison Starr expresses his own futility about structuring another antiwar novel.* (*SL5* 3:L15) "You know what I say to people when I hear they're writing anti-war books?"

"No. What *do* you say, **Harrison Starr**?"

"I say, 'Why don't you write an anti-*glacier* book instead?'"

What he meant, of course, was that there would always be wars, that they were as easy to stop as glaciers. I believe that, too.

And, even if wars didn't keep coming like glaciers, there would still be plain old death.

Steel, Roy. *The second husband of Dorothy Karabekian in* Bluebeard. *Terry and Henri Karabekian, Rabo's and Dorothy's sons, took Steel's name as their own.*

Steel, Terrence W., Jr. *The private detective hired by Jason Wilder to document the activities of Eugene Debs Hartke in preparation for his dismissal, in* Hocus Pocus. *"Terry" posed as a gardener working at Tarkington College. In order to gain Hartke's confidence, Steel told him that his wife ran off their three children and her lesbian lover, a junior high school dietitian.*

Stern, Damon. *The head of Tarkington's history department and Eugene Debs Hartke's best and most entertaining friend. He* spoke as badly of his own country as Slazinger and I did, and right into the faces of students in the classroom day after day. I used to sit in on his course and laugh and clap. The truth can be very funny in an awful way, especially as it relates to greed and hypocrisy (*HP* 115:L10-15). *Damon Stern was the cause for Hartke's dismissal from Tarkington because Hartke frequently repeated some of the more shocking material Stern told his students. Stern told his students Hitler was a Roman Catholic and that it was no coincidence one of the Nazis' highest medals was the Iron Cross.* (*HP* 130:L32-33) **Damon Stern**, who was always turning up little-known facts of history, told me, incidentally, that the Battle of the Alamo was about slavery. The brave men who died there wanted to secede from Mexico because it was against the law to own slaves in Mexico. They were fighting for the right to own slaves.

Stern died during the Athena prison break. While his wife Wanda June left town with their children, he stayed behind to warn the people of Scipio. He was killed by an escaped prisoner who was "gut shooting" horses in the Tarkington Stable. Hartke is led to believe Stern asked the convict to spare the horses. Dammon Stern is buried in the shadow of Musket Mountain.

Stevenson, Adlai. *Losing Democratic Party candidate for president in 1952 and 1956.* (*MH* 136:L22 *The Hyannis Port Story*) I was feeling pretty sorry for myself, because I was just an ordinary citizen, and had to get stuck in lines like that. But then I recognized the man in the limousine up ahead of me. It was **Adlai Stevenson**. He wasn't moving any faster than I was, and his radiator was boiling, too.

Stevenson, Stony. *Though once a British military unit commander, Stony was recruited for a leadership position in the Army of Mars, in* The Sirens of Titan. *In order to conceal his rank, he and the other Martian leaders posed as privates. Stony was a large, gregarious man often amused by the more difficult or odd characters on Mars. Stony took an interest in Unk (Malachi Constant) because they had such difficulty erasing his mind. Stony became intrigued with Unk's strong desire to understand what was going on in his world despite Unk's numerous visits to the hospital to erase his memory and limit his cognitive abilities. Information about Stony is gleaned through Unk's letter to himself. Though Stony first thought he would be amused by Unk's ramblings, he quickly realized that his friend's bits of memory called into question all that he remembered as well as the information he was privy to as one of the Martian* *leaders. Stony and Unk shared all they knew in an effort to understand their predicament. It finally dawns on Stony that the invasion fleet would be doomed if it landed on Earth. It was Stony's suggestion that Unk write down everything he could remember. Together, Stony and Unk decided that Rumfoord and Kazak were the real commanders of the Martian Army. For their efforts, both had their minds wiped clean and Unk was radio-controlled into publicly strangling Stony.*

Boaz witnessed Stony's execution but never revealed this knowledge to Unk while they lived in the caves of Mercury. Whenever Unk upset Boaz with the truth about the harmoniums, Boaz would warn him, "Don't *truth* me, and I won't *truth* you" (*ST* 203:L28-29). *Though Boaz let Unk enjoy his own harmless untruths, Winston Niles Rumfoord was not so considerate. He reveals the truth about Stony's execution as part of the ceremony banishing the Space Wanderer to Titan.*

It is left to Salo to restore Malachi Constant's pleasant memories of Stony. In Malachi's final moments on the snowy outskirts of Indianapolis, he slips into Salo's posthypnotic suggestion reuniting the two comrades. (*ST* 319:L6-32) As the snow drifted over Constant, he imagined that the clouds opened up, letting through a sunbeam, a sunbeam all for him.

A golden space ship encrusted with diamonds came skimming down the sunbeam, landed in the untouched snow of the street.

Out stepped a stocky, red-headed man with a big cigar. He was young. He wore the uniform of the Martian Assault Infantry, Unk's old outfit.

"Hello, Unk," he said. "Get in."

"Get in?" said Constant. "Who are you?"

"**Stony Stevenson**, Unk. You don't recognize me?"

"**Stony**?" said Constant. "That's you, **Stony**?"

"Who else could stand the bloody pace?" said **Stony**. He laughed. "Get in," he said.

"And go where?" said Constant.

"Paradise," said **Stony**.

"What's Paradise like?" said Constant.

"Everybody's happy there forever," said **Stony**, "or as long as the bloody Universe holds together. Get in, Unk. Beatrice is already there, waiting for you."

"Beatrice?" said Unk, getting into the space ship.

Stony closed the airlocks, pressed the on button.

"We're—we're going to Paradise now?" said Constant. "I—I'm going to get into Paradise?"

"Don't ask me why, old sport," said **Stony**, "but somebody up there likes you."

Stockmayer, Walter H. *The Dartmouth chemistry professor in* Breakfast of Champions *who provides a drawing of the plastic molecule seeping into Sugar Creek running through Midland City. The endlessness of the molecular* *representation prompts Vonnegut to continue,* And when he sketched a plausible molecule, he indicated points where it would go on and on just as I have indicated them—with an abbreviation which means sameness without end.

The proper ending for any story about people it seems to me, since life is now a polymer in which the Earth is wrapped so tightly, should be that same abbreviation, which I now write large because I feel like it, which is this one: ETC.

And it is in order to acknowledge the continuity of this polymer that I begin so many sentences with "And" and "So," and end so many paragraphs with ". . . and so on."

And so on.

"It's all like an ocean! cried Dostoevski. I say it's all like cellophane (*BC* 228:L7-33).

Stone, Sydney and Fred. *Sydney is a member of Tarkington College's Board of Trustees, and Fred is his son and a student at the school, in* Hocus Pocus. *Eugene Debs Hartke witnessed Fred take a mug from the school bookstore in plain view of the cashier. After following Fred out to the quadrangle and confronting him with his deed, Hartke stood by in astonishment while Stone smashed the mug against the Vonnegut Memorial Fountain. Hartke wrote a letter to the Board of Trustees and became an eternal enemy of Sydney Stone's.*

Stone was worth more than a billion dollars earned in commissions for selling American properties to foreign interests, a main concern of the text's in general. He engineered the sale of Hartke's father's former employer, E.I. Du Pont de Nemours & Company, to I.G. Farben in Germany. Stone refuses to believe Hartke's accusations about Fred's theft.

Stonehenge. *The Tralfamadorians used their Universal Will To Become to send messages concerning the status of the replacement part for Salo's spaceship. The messages were conveyed in great architectural monuments on Earth that could be monitored by Salo.* (*ST* 271:L14-19) The reply was written on Earth in huge stones on a plain in what is now England. The ruins of the reply still stand, and are known as **Stonehenge**. The meaning of **Stonehenge** in Tralfamadorian, when viewed from above, is: *"Replacement part being rushed with all possible speed."*

Stratton, Samuel W. *In* Jailbird, *the physicist and President of the Massachusetts Institute of Technology who served on the three-member board which reviewed the death sentences of Sacco and Vanzetti.*

structured moment. *The Tralfamadorian concept which explains, in the fourth dimension, that all existence is-as-it-was-and-is-supposed-to-become, that all moments exist simultaneously.* (*SL5* 23:L13-24) "The most important thing I learned on Tralfamadore was that when a person dies he only *appears* to die. He is still very much alive in the past, so it is very silly for people to cry at his funeral. All moments, past, present, and future, always have existed, always will exist. The Tralfamadorians can look at all the different moments just the way we can look at a stretch of the Rocky Mountains, for instance. They can see how permanent all the moments are, and they can look at any moment that interests them. It is just an illusion we have here on Earth that one moment follows another one, like beads on a string, and that once a moment is gone it is gone forever.

stuppa (see **Bokononism**). (*CC* 163:L3-7) "Do you know anybody who *might* want the job?" Frank was giving a classic illustration of what Bokonon calls *duffle*. *Duffle*, in the Bokononist sense, is the destiny of thousands upon thousands of persons when placed in the hands of a ***stuppa***. A ***stuppa*** is a fogbound child.

subbasement (see also **basement**). (*JB* 12:L6, 10) I had an office, but no secretary, in the **subbasement** of the Executive Office Building, directly underneath, as it happened, the office where burglaries and other crimes on behalf of President Nixon were planned. I could hear people walking overhead and raising their voices sometimes. On my own level in the **subbasement** my only companions were heating and air-conditioning equipment and a Coca-Cola machine that only I knew about, I think.
(*JB* 15:L24) At the end of every futile day in the **subbasement** I would go home to the only wife I have ever had, who was Ruth—waiting for me in our little brick bungalow in Chevy Chase, Maryland.
(*JB* 52:L29-30) It became necessary to hide it when the contents of all White House safes were to be examined by the Federal Bureau of Investigation and men from the Office of the Special Prosecutor. My obscure office in the **subbasement** was selected as the most promising hiding place. I acquiesced. *An old steamer trunk was used to store illegal campaign contributions totalling $1 million in unmarked and circulated twenty-dollar bills—eventually used as Watergate payoff money.*

Sugar Creek. *Mentioned as a waste dumping ground in "Happy Birthday, Wanda June,"* Breakfast of Champions, *and* Deadeye Dick, *Sugar Creek is the waterway which runs through Midland City and beneath the Mildred Barry Memorial Center for the Arts.* (*BC* 94:L29-33, 95:L1-3) **Sugar Creek** flooded now and then. Dwayne remembered about that. In a land so flat, flooding was a queerly pretty thing for water to do. **Sugar Creek** brimmed over silently, formed a vast mirror in which children might safely play.

The mirror showed the citizens the shape of the valley they lived in, demonstrated that they were hill people who inhabited slopes rising one inch for every mile that separated them from **Sugar Creek**.

When Dwayne Hoover was younger and dumping the family's weekly trash in Sugar Creek, he and his father witnessed the brutal murder of a black man.

Sugar Creek is the threshold crossed by Kilgore Trout on the way to the arts festival. The creek was severely polluted with waste from the Barrytron manufacturing plant. When Trout emerged from the creek, his feet were coated at once with a clear plastic substance from the surface of the creek. When, in some surprise, Trout lifted one coated foot from the water, the plastic substance dried in air instantly, sheathed his foot in a thin, skin-tight bootie resembling mother-of-pearl. He repeated the process with his other foot (*BC* 224:L1-7). *The Maritimo Brothers Construction Company was hired by Barrytron to build a waste removal system, but instead the gangster-controlled company built a simple outlet into Sugar Creek. When Dwayne Hoover goes on a rampage, he bites off Trout's right ring finger and spits it into the creek.*

Dr. Cyprian Ukwende was used to seeing children come to the hospital with the mysterious plasticized sheet on their legs after having played in Sugar Creek. He used a pair of tinsnips to cut away the cast-like forms.

In Deadeye Dick, *Sugar Creek is also the threshold crossed by Gino and Marco Maritimo when they enter Midland City after being forced from the freight train they had been riding. It is also where the headless body of August Gunther is found after being accidentally killed by Police Chief Morissey. In an attempt to save Morissey from the criminal investigation which would have ruined him, Otto Waltz and the other hunting buddies tried to send Gunther's body down Sugar Creek which eventually flowed out to the Mississippi River and the Gulf of Mexico.*

Despite the history of open sewage flowing into the creek, the Waltz's cook, Mary Hoobler, often prepared catfish and crayfish for the family.

Sugar Creek High School. *The "elite white high school" in Midland City back when Dwayne Hoover went there. At the time* Breakfast of Champions *unfolds, it had become nearly all black. The only bit of learning Dwayne remembers is a poem he was forced to learn as a sophomore.* (*BC* 194:L26-29) The Moving Finger writes; and, having writ, / Moves on: nor all your Piety nor Wit / Shall lure it back to cancel half a Line / Nor all your Tears wash out a Word of it.

Sugarbush Mountain, Vermont. *Billy Pilgrim's charter flight from Ilium carrying optometrists on their way to an international convention in Montreal crashes on top of Sugarbush Mountain, in* Slaughterhouse-Five. *Except for Billy, everyone died.*

suicidal, suicide (see also **Ethical Suicide Parlor**). (*PP* 47:L7) "And dope addiction, alcoholism, and **suicide** went up proportionately," said Finnerty. *Finnerty alludes to societal ills which mushroomed while the promise of "peacetime uses of atomic energy" were receiving all the attention.*
(*ST* 129:L2) *The big attack on Earth would be* **suicide** *for sure.*
(*ST* 173:L12) Salo generously donated half of his supply of UWTB *(Universal Will to Become)* to the **suicide** of Mars.

(*ST* 174:L14) He *(Rumfoord)* wished to change the World for the better by means of the great and unforgettable **suicide** of Mars.
(*CC* 193:L34) "It's what Bokononists always say when they are about to commit **suicide**." *The phrase is "Now I will destroy the whole world."*
(*GBR* 93:L9, 16) The book *(Eliot's* Domesday Book*)* was nearly full. . . . What he wrote now was the name of the **suicidal** man who had called him, who had come to see him, who had just departed. . . .

"Sherman Wesley Little," wrote Eliot. "Indy, Su-TDM-LO-V2-3K3-RF $300." Decoded, this meant that Little was from Indianapolis, was a **suicidal** tool-and-die maker who had been laid off, a veteran of the Second World War with a wife and three children, the second child suffering from cerebral palsy.
(*GBR* 120:L32) Sons of **suicides** seldom do well.
(*GBR* 125:L29) Since he *(Fred Rosewater)* was the son of a **suicide**, it was hardly surprising that his secret hankerings were embarrassing and small.
(*GBR* 159:L33) Sons of **suicides** often think of killing themselves at the end of a day, when their blood sugar is low.
(*MH* xv:1, 4, 14 *Preface*) "I am committing **suicide** by cigarette," I replied.

My brand is Pall Mall. The authentic **suicides** ask for Pall Malls. The dilettantes ask for Pell Mells. . . .

The public health authorities never mention the main reason many Americans have for smoking heavily, which is that smoking is a fairly sure, fairly honorable form of **suicide**.
(*BC* 65:L11-12) He even forgot that his wife Celia had committed **suicide**, for instance, by eating Drano—a mixture of sodium hydroxide and aluminum flakes, which was meant to clear drains.
(*BC* 86:L6, 8) "In the long run, *he's* committing **suicide**," said the driver. "Seems like the only kind of job an American can get these days is committing **suicide** in some way."
(*BC* 181:L10) Listen: Bunny's mother and my mother were different sorts of human beings, but they were both beautiful in exotic ways, and they both boiled over with chaotic talk about love and peace and wars and evil and desperation, of better days coming by and by, of worse days coming by and by. And both our mothers committed **suicide**. Bunny's mother ate Drano. My mother ate sleeping pills, which wasn't nearly as horrible.
(*BC* 294:L14) His *(Trout's)* voice was my father's voice. I *heard* my father—and I *saw* my mother in the void. My mother stayed far, far away, because she had left me a legacy of **suicide**.
(*WFG* xxi:L25 *Preface*) I received a note from a twelve-year-old this morning. He had read my latest novel, *Breakfast of Champions*, and he said, "Dear Mr. Vonnegut: Please don't commit **suicide**." God love him. I have told him I am fine.
(*WFG* 105:L22 *Good Missiles, Good Manners, Good Night*) Word of honor—if I had been invited into the Laird home *(Melvin Laird, former Secretary of Defense)*, I would have smiled and smiled. I would have

understood that the defense establishment was only doing what it had to do, no matter how **suicidally**.

(*WFG* 175:L2 *Address to the National Institute of Arts and Letters, 1971*) That was a happy day. My father was the widower of a **suicide** when he told me about that happiest day. *The story is about Vonnegut's parents breaking into the Indianapolis 500-Mile Speedway and running their new Oldsmobile around the track—prior to the First World War.*

(*WFG* 281:L32-33 *Playboy Interview*) PLAYBOY: Most of the people in *Breakfast* seem jangled and desperate—in situations they can't get out of—and a number of them consider **suicide**.

VONNEGUT: Yes, **suicide** is at the heart of the book. It's also the punctuation mark at the end of many artistic careers.

(*WFG* 283:L9 *Playboy Interview*) I want to start believing in things that have shapeliness and harmony. *Breakfast of Champions* isn't a threat to commit **suicide**, incidentally. It's my promise that I'm beyond that now. Which is something for me. I used to think of it as a perfectly reasonable way to avoid delivering a lecture, to avoid a deadline, to not pay a bill, to not go to a cocktail party.

(*PS* 36:L9 *Roots*) WE have come now to a rascal, Albert Lieber, whose emotional faithlessness to his children, in my humble opinion, contributed substantially to my mother's eventual **suicide**.

(*PS* 71:L8-9 *When I Lost My Innocence*) "We Americans have guided our destinies so clumsily, with all the world watching, that we must now protect ourselves against our own government and our own industries.

"Not to do so would be **suicide**. We have discovered a brand-new method for committing **suicide**—family style, Reverend Jim Jones style, and by the millions. What is the method? To say nothing and do nothing about what some of our businessmen and military men are doing with the most unstable substances and the most persistent poisons to be found anywhere in the universe.

"The people who play with such chemicals are so *dumb!*"

(*PS* 75:L23 *Triage*) MY mother, who was also a **suicide** and who never saw even the first of her eleven grandchildren, is another one, I gather, who would not like to see her name anywhere. *Vonnegut groups his mother with his thesis advisor from the University of Chicago who had also committed suicide.*

(*PS* 196:L29 *Religion*) Some guesses are more **suicidal** than others. The belief that a true lover of God is immune to the bites of copperheads and rattlesnakes is a case in point.

(*PS* 304:L12 *The Sexual Revolution*) As for real death—it has always been a temptation to me, since my mother solved so many problems with it. The child of a **suicide** will naturally think of death, the big one, as a logical solution to any problem, even one in simple algebra.

(*DD* 80:L7) Celia would commit **suicide** by eating Drano, a drain-clearing compound of lye and zinc chips, in 1970, twelve years ago now. She killed

herself in the most horrible way I can think of—a few months before the dedication of the Mildred Barry Memorial Center for the Arts.
(*DD* 190:L3) I would be glad to attempt a detailed analysis of Celia Hoover's character, if I thought her character had much of anything to do with her **suicide** by Drano. As a pharmacist, though, I see no reason not to give full credit to amphetamine.
(*DD* 196:L4) The word was all over town of how in need of support he *(Dwayne Hoover)* was, of how vocally ashamed he was to have been such a bad husband that his wife had committed **suicide**. He had been quoted to me as having made a public announcement in the Tally-ho Room of the new Holiday Inn, the day after Celia killed herself: "I take half the blame, but the other half goes to that son-of-bitching Doctor Jerry Mitchell. Watch out for the pills your doctor tells your wife to take. That's all I've got to say."
(*DD* 208:L10) Some people, of course, find inhabiting an epilogue so uncongenial that they commit **suicide**. Ernest Hemingway comes to mind. Celia Hoover, née Hildreth, comes to mind.
(*Gal* 140:L16) The best-run nations commonly had such symbiotic pairings at the top. And when I think about the **suicidal** mistakes nations used to make in olden times, I see that those polities were trying to get along with just an Adolf von Kleist at the top, without an Hernando Cruz.
(*Blue* 49:L21) And if an artist wants to really jack up the prices of his creations, may I suggest this: **suicide**.
(*Blue* 66:L19) "If I had my way," he said, "American geography books would call those European countries by their right names: 'The Syphilis Empire,' 'The Republic of **Suicide**,' 'Dementia Praecox,' which of course borders on beautiful 'Paranoia.'"
(*Blue* 294:L4) The melancholy roll-call of real-life **suicides** among the Abstract Expressionists again: Gorky by hanging in 1948, Pollock and then almost immediately Kitchen, by drunken driving and then pistol in 1956—and then Rothko with all possible messiness by knife in 1970.
(*HP* 59:L22-23, 26, 29) Three years after that, Sam Wakefield would commit **suicide**. So there is another loser for you, even though he had been a Major General and then a College President. I think exhaustion got him. I say that not only because he seemed very tired all the time to me, but because his **suicide** note wasn't even original and didn't seem to have that much to do with him personally. It was word for word the same **suicide** note left way back in 1932, when I was a negative 8 years old, by another loser, George Eastman, inventor of the Kodak camera and founder of Eastman Kodak, now defunct, only 75 kilometers north of here.
(*HP* 102:L32) Afterward, he *(Sam Wakefield)* had hired both of us for Tarkington, and then committed **suicide** for reasons unclear even to himself, judging from the plagiarized note he left on his bedside table.
(*HP* 296:L10) Hiroshi Matsumoto's **suicide** has hit me so hard, I think, because he was innocent of even the littlest misdemeanors.

(*HP* 14:L34) During World War II, he *(Hartke's father)* was too valuable as a civilian deep-thinker about chemicals to be put in a soldier suit and turned into a **suicidal**, homicidal imbecile in 13 weeks.

(*FWD* 34:19) "We were able to keep her insanity a secret, since it became really elaborate only at home and between midnight and dawn. We were able to keep her **suicide** a secret thanks to a compassionate and possibly politically ambitious coroner." *Vonnegut refers to his mother's suicide.*

(*FWD* 61:L8) "We were born in the Middle West, we set out to be reporters, our fathers were gun nuts, we felt profoundly indebted to Mark Twain, and we were the children of **suicides**." *Vonnegut draws a parallel between Hemingway and himself.*

(*FWD* 67:L3, 7) "I am reminded of the **suicide** of another American genius, George Eastman, inventor of the Kodak camera and roll film, and founder of the Eastman Kodak Company. He shot himself in 1932. Eastman, who was not ill and was not suffering from grief, said in his **suicide** note what Ernest Hemingway must have felt when he was close to the end: 'My work is done.'"

(*FWD* 143:L10) And here is a fascinating statistic: They committed **suicide** less often than their masters did. *Vonnegut refers to the low incidence of suicide among American slaves as opposed to their owners.*

(*FWD* 162:L2) My own theory is that the little girl, by allowing herself to be adopted by a dark-skinned Muslim absolutely nobody watching American television could love, in effect committed **suicide**. *Vonnegut sarcastically remarks on America's shallow perceptions of the air-raid targeting Lybia's Qaddafi which failed to hit their target but succeeded in killing his adopted infant daughter.*

(*FWD* 182:L4, 17) The great fiction writer Ray Bradbury (who can't drive an automobile) made up a story called "The Kilimanjaro Device," which was about a person who could somehow undo ignominious **suicides** (or maybe ignominious anythings). . . .

It is possible in Ray Bradbury country that my own **suicide** was as successful as Hemingway's, that I am dead, that all I am seeing now is what might have been, if only I hadn't ended it all. This could be a lesson.

(*FWD* 193:L18, 194:L1, 7) Yes, and I, having just finished reading William Styron's short and elliptical account of his recent attack of melancholia, *Darkness Visible* (a **suicide** attempt may or may not have been involved), am now prepared to say that **suicidal** persons can be divided into two sorts. Styron's sort blames the wiring and chemistry of his brain, which could easily fit into a salad bowl. My sort blames the Universe. (Why mess around?) I don't offer this insight as yet another joke ("Why is cream more expensive than milk?"). It is my serious belief that those of us who become humorists (**suicidal** or not) feel free (as most people do not) to speak of life itself as a dirty joke, even though life is all there is or ever can be. *See also: PP* 54:L22-23; 72:L37; 204:L30; *ST* 172:L4; 172:L6,27; *MN* 39:L24; 141:L9,10; *CC* 193:L15; 210:L62; *GBR* 66:L8; 91:L23; 121:L21; 215:L28; *SL5* 77:L10; *MH—Unready to Wear* 233:L26; *WJ* 19:L21; 30:L15; 180:L17; *BC* 28:L13;

40:L17-18; 85:L28; 129:L20-21; *WFG—"There's a Maniac Loose Out There"* 75:L32; *WFG—Fortitude* 55:L15; *WFG—Why They Read Hesse* 114:L10; *WFG—Address to Graduating Class at Bennington College, 1970* 168:L18; *WFG—In a Manner That Must Shame God Himself* 186:L32; *Slap* 48:L5-6; 69:L6; 99:L22,24-25; 145:L25; *JB* 93:L14; 186:L14; 214:L1; *PS—Playmates* 158:L18; *PS—Jekyll and Hyde Updated* 266:L20; *PS—In the Capital of the World* 319:L11; *DD* 32:L1; 90:L19; 151:L12; 204:L31-32; 205:L3; *Gal* 25:L22; 27:L12; 81:L13; 139:L16; 213:L28-30; *Blue* 7:L17; 26:L5; 151:L10,16; 178:L14; *HP* 71:L16; 86:L10; 95:L11; 118:L8; 120:L12; 130:L29; 134:L28; 162:L17; 209:L7; 268:L25; 272:L3; 299:L18.

Suk, Dr. Kim Bum. *Rabo Karabekian learns the history of Marilee Kemp's Italian palazzo by reading Suk's* Private Art Treasures of Tuscany, *given to him by Circe Berman. The text started out as Dr. Suk's doctoral thesis at MIT. Suk explains the reason for the blank rectangular sections in the rotunda. Those spaces once held frescos of barely dressed pagan gods and goddesses. The Dominican monk Girolamo Savonarola had ordered the paintings sanded from the surface.*

Karabekian goes on to include that **Kim Bum Suk**, incidentally, was thrown out of his native South Korea for forming a union of university students which demanded improvements in the curricula (*Blue* 217:L15).

Sultan of Brunei. *In* Hocus Pocus, *the Sultan purchases Cincinnati's remaining newspaper and leading television station. He later purchases the Bank of Rochester, prompting Eugene Debs Hartke's mother-in-law to withdraw her life savings ($45,000) and bury it in their backyard in Scipio.*

Sumklish (see also ***prakhouls***). *The Bratpuhrian alcoholic drink of choice for the Shah of Bratpuhr. During the Shah's tour of the United States, which is woven throughout the plot of* Player Piano, *his aide Khashdrahr always has a flask at the ready for the seemingly alcoholic monarch.*

Surrasi. *An extinct infidel tribe in Bratpuhr which used to make mud and straw holy figures considered by some to be false gods. In* Player Piano, *the Shah of Bratpuhr compares Dr. Halyard's faith and wonder in EPICAC with that of the Surrasi.*

Susann, Jacqueline. *In* Slaughterhouse-Five, *the Tralfamadorians had one English-language book on the ship transporting Billy Pilgrim to their home planet. Billy read Jacqueline Susann's* Valley of the Dolls *while en route, and the Tralfamadorians planned on putting it in one of their museums.*

Susanna (see also **Norman Fuller**). *The title character of the short story "Miss Temptation."*

Sutton, Mrs. *Sarah Wyatt's grandmother in* Jailbird. *Though she was not from the side of the family which lost their wealth in the radium dial liability suit, she lost most of her wealth in the 1929 stock market crash. Her husband jumped out the window of his Wall Street office. Mrs. Sutton lives in a cramped two-bedroom apartment just large enough to house the few aged servants she insisted on maintaining despite her comparative poverty from former days. Two weeks after Tillie died, Mrs. Sutton's longest surviving servant, she also died.*

In her younger days, Mrs. Sutton showed horses in competition. When Walter admires the many ribbons she won, she wittily points out it was the horses who won the ribbons. By her own admission, she had no way to improve her standard of living since she was old and brought up to rely on the efforts of men.

Sarah was staying with her grandmother when Walter Starbuck came to pick her up for a date. Sarah and Walter deceived her into thinking his father was an art curator employed by Mr. McCone.

Swain, Caleb Mellon and Letitia Vanderbilt. *The parents of the dizygotic twins Wilbur and Eliza. Wilbur goes on to describe that,* Our parents were two silly and pretty and very young people named **Caleb Mellon Swain** and **Letitia Vanderbilt Swain**, née Rockefeller. They were fabulously well-to-do, and descended from Americans who had all but wrecked the planet with a form of Idiot's Delight—obsessively turning money into power, and then power back into money again, and then money back into power again (*Slap* 28:L22-23). *Because of the twins' deformities at birth, the Swains were advised to avoid raising the children themselves. They left the children with caretakers at their Vermont mansion, visiting infrequently at best.*

Swain, Carter Paley. *The son of Wilbur Swain and his third cousin Rose Aldrich Ford. In describing his son, Wilbur reveals more of himself than he does about his child.* (*Slap* 141:L15-25) I have never been good at loving. We had a child, **Carter Paley Swain**, whom I also failed to love. **Carter** was normal, and completely uninteresting to me. He was somehow like a summer squash on the vine—featureless and watery, and merely growing larger all the time.

After our divorce, he and his mother bought a condominium in the same building with Eliza, down in Machu Picchu, Peru. I never heard from them again even when I became President of the United States.

Swain, Elihu Roosevelt. *The founder of the Swain family fortune whose name at birth was Elihu Witherspoon Swain. Wilbur and Eliza believe he changed his middle name when he went to M.I.T. so that he would "seem more aristocratic when he enrolled." This is what gave the twins their idea for assigning new middle names to everyone in order to create artificially extended families.*

He graduated from M.I.T. at the age of eighteen and at twenty-two started the Department of Civil Engineering at Cornell University. He founded the Swain Bridge Company, which went on to construct "half the railroad bridges in the entire planet." He built the Swain family mansion on their ancestral land in Vermont and told no one about all the hidden passageways, though Wilbur and Eliza enjoy them immensely. (*Slap* 38:L8-9) This was the secret: There was a mansion concealed within the mansion. It could be entered through trap doors and sliding panels. It consisted of secret staircases and listening posts with peepholes, and secret passageways. There were tunnels, too.

It was actually possible for Eliza and me, for example, to vanish into a huge grandfather clock in the ballroom at the top of the northernmost tower, and to emerge almost a kilometer away—through a trap door in the floor of the mausoleum of **Professor Elihu Roosevelt Swain**.

In the midst of one of the twins' creative frenzies, they wrote theoretical papers about squaring circles, their utopian scheme for artificially extended families, a critique of Darwin's Theory of Evolution, and an essay on the nature of gravity (which they found to be unstable) and hid them in Professor Swain's empty funeral urn in his mausoleum. They often played in the mausoleum. The gravity paper becomes significant when one of Eliza's Chinese associates asks Wilbur to retrieve the paper. Their ensuing experiments confirm the twins' theories that gravity was indeed unstable. (*Slap* 39:L7) Yes, and **Professor Swain** died of his fatness in the mansion, at a dinner he gave in honor of Samuel Langhorne Clemens and Thomas Alva Edison.

Swain, Eliza Mellon (see **Wilbur Swain**).

Swain, Sophie Rothschild. *When Wilbur Swain was seventy years old and President of the United States, he married twenty-three-year-old Sophie Rothschild, a descendant of the famous international banking family, in* Slapstick. *Sophie becomes enraged when Wilbur's scheme for extended families places her in the Peanut clan. She divorces Wilbur and takes refuge in Machu Picchu, Peru, where many of her relatives had already moved.*

Swain, Wilbur Rockefeller and Eliza Mellon. *The intellectually brilliant, telepathically gifted, physically grotesque Swain twins. Wilbur and Eliza Swain* were christened in a hospital rather than in a church, and we were not surrounded by relatives and our parents' friends. The thing was: **Eliza** and I were so ugly that our parents were ashamed.

We were monsters, and we were not expected to live very long. We had six fingers on each little hand, and six toes on each little footsie. We had supernumerary nipples as well—two of them apiece.

We were not mongolian idiots, although we had the coarse black hair typical of mongoloids. We were something new. We were *neanderthaloids*.

We had the features of adult, fossil human beings even in infancy—massive brow-ridges, sloping foreheads, and steamshovel jaws (*Slap* 27:L11-14, 28:L1-10).

Because of their appearance, they were sent to the family's Vermont estate to be raised by servants. Their parents visited only on the twins' birthday. Wilbur and Eliza reasoned from an early age that since all the servants treated them so well but imagined them to be idiots, that it was a good thing to be an idiot. So they hid their intelligence, especially the potency of their intellect when they literally touched their heads together and communicated telepathically. Wilbur wrote about the depth of thought which went into their decision to hide their intelligence. (*Slap* 40:L8-24) Consider: We were at the center of the lives of those who cared for us. They could be heroically Christian in their own eyes only if **Eliza** and I remained helpless and vile. If we became openly wise and self-reliant, they would become our drab and inferior assistants. If we became capable of going out into the world, they might lose their apartments, their color televisions, their illusions of being sorts of doctors and nurses, and their high-paying jobs.

So, from the very first, and without quite knowing what they were doing, I am sure, they begged us a thousand times a day to go on being helpless and vile.

There was only one small advancement they wished us to make up the ladder of human achievements. They hoped with all their hearts that we would become toilet-trained.

Again: We were glad to comply.

The unique nature of their intelligence is also recorded by Wilbur. (*Slap* 50:L9-30, 51:L1-15) **Eliza** and I used bodily contact only in order to increase the intimacy of our brains.

Thus did we give birth to a single genius, which died as quickly as we were parted, which was reborn the moment we got together again.

We became almost cripplingly specialized as halves of that genius, which was the most important individual in our lives, but which we never named.

When we learned to read and write, for example, it was I who actually did the reading and writing. **Eliza** remained illiterate until the day she died.

But it was **Eliza** who did the great intuitive leaping for us both. It was **Eliza** who guessed that it would be in our best interests to remain speechless, but to become toilet-trained. It was **Eliza** who guessed what books were, and what the little marks on the pages might mean.

It was **Eliza** who sensed that there was something cockeyed about the dimensions of some of the mansion's rooms and corridors. And it was I who did the methodical work of taking actual measurements, and then probing the paneling and parquetry with screwdrivers and kitchen knives, seeking doors to an alternate universe, which we found.

Hi ho.

Yes, I did all the reading. And it seems to me now that there is not a single book published in an Indo-European language before the First World War that I have not read aloud.

But it was **Eliza** who did the memorizing, and who told me what we had to learn next. And it was **Eliza** who could put seemingly unrelated ideas together in order to get a new one. It was **Eliza** who *juxtaposed.*

When the twins are kept from exercising telepathy, they refer to themselves as the very average "Betty and Bobby Brown." Wilbur went on to Harvard Medical School and became a pediatrician. When coming together later in life they co-wrote a childrearing manual which they called The Cry of the Nocturnal Goatsucker, by Betty and Bobby Brown. *It eventually became an all-time best seller next to* The Bible *and* The Joy of Cooking. *He and Eliza also wrote papers criticizing Darwin's theory of evolution, the United States' Constitution, gravity (musing on the likelihood gravity could become as changeable as the weather), and extended families. They got the idea of dispensing new middle names from the example set by the founder of the family fortune, Professor Elihu Roosevelt Swain, whose baptismal certificate reads Elihu Witherspoon Swain.* (*Slap* 38:L15-17) He had given himself that middle name in order to seem more aristocratic when he enrolled as a student at M.I.T. (*Slap* 157:L8-15) "An ideal extended family," **Eliza** and I had written so long ago, "should give proportional representation to all sorts of Americans, according to their numbers. The creation of ten thousand such families, say, would provide America with ten thousand parliaments, so to speak, which would discuss sincerely and expertly what only a few hypocrites now discuss with passion, which is the welfare of all mankind." *Wilbur got a chance to put into effect their scheme for extended families when he became President of the United States. He lived to be just over one hundred years old and was the nation's last president.*

Wilbur's first wife was Rose Aldrich Ford, a third cousin. Together they had a son, Carter Paley Swain. He loved neither and after their divorce Rose and Carter went to live in Machu Picchu, Peru. His second marriage to Sophie Rothschild was childless.

Swift, Dr. Tom. *The number-one assistant to Dr. Norbert Frankenstein in the play "Fortitude." He has degrees in engineering and medicine, as does his mentor. When asked if he's tired after a full day managing the medical and psychological status of Sylvia Lovejoy, their bodiless patient, he replies,* It's a good kind of tiredness—as though I'd flown a big jet from New York to Honolulu, or something like that. *(Taking hold of a lever)* And now we'll bring Mrs. Lovejoy in for a happy landing. *(He pulls the lever gradually and the machinery slows down)* There (*WFG* 56:L5-9 *Fortitude*).

Szombathy, Lazlo and Miklos. *In* Mother Night, *Lazlo was a respected veterinarian in Hungary who became a Freedom Fighter and killed his brother Miklos, the Second Minister of Education in Hungary. Despite his successful* *veterinary practice in Hungary, he was not permitted to practice in America. He became a New York City garbage-man and hanged himself with the noose he found in the garbage outside Howard Campbell's apartment house. The noose was brought by an unnamed man for Campbell to hang himself once his whereabouts were publicized. Resi Noth threw the noose in the trash and Lazlo hanged himself the next day. His suicide note indicated his only lament was that he couldn't convince American physicians that he knew how to cure cancer.*

T

Taft, Edith. *Rabo Karabekian's second wife, formerly married to Cincinnati sportsman and investment banker Richard Fairbanks, Jr. Rabo and Edith were married for twenty years, living in the Long Island Victorian estate where she had lived with her first husband. They met after Rabo's first wife passed away and he convinced the Fairbankses to let him rent their potato barn as his apartment and art studio. Edith had no children by either of her husbands.*

Edith so well loved Rabo and desired to make him feel at home that she had the estate renovated and outfitted with track lighting to accommodate his large collection of Abstract Expressionist paintings. (*Blue* 116:L13-18) And then she said, "Call Home Sweet Home Moving and Storage," in whose warehouse I had stored my collection for years and years. "Let them tell your glorious paintings as they bring them out into the daylight, 'You are going *home*!'"

Edith loved uncritically, as Rabo fondly remembers. (*Blue* 6:L30) Dear **Edith**, like all great Earth Mothers, was a multitude. Even when there were only the two of us and the servants here, she filled this Victorian ark with love and merriment and hands-on domesticity. As privileged as she had been all her life, she cooked with the cook, gardened with the gardener, did all our food shopping, fed the pets and birds, and made personal friends of wild rabbits and squirrels and raccoons. (*Blue* 261:L14-22) She was a magical tamer of almost any sort of animal, an overwhelmingly loving and uncritical nurturer of anything and everything that looked half alive. That's what she would do to me when I was living as a hermit in the barn and she needed a new husband: she tamed me with nature poems and good things to eat which she left outside my sliding doors. I'm sure she tamed her first husband, too, and thought of him lovingly and patronizingly as some kind of dumb animal.

Rabo felt as though he died with the suicide of his friend Terry Kitchen, and that it was Edith who brought him back to life. Edith died the same week as another of Rabo's great loves, Marilee Kemp, the Contessa Portomaggiore.

Takaru. *In* Player Piano, *the Shah of Bratpuhr consistently calls Americans "Takaru," which means "slave" in his native language.*

Tamanrasset. *While Paul Proteus travels by train through upstate New York, he overhears soldiers (those who chose not to join the Reconstruction and Reclamation Corps) playing cards and bemoaning the fate of one of their buddies, Elmo C. Hacketts.* (*PP* 222:L22-23) "Where's Hacketts going? You know?"

". . . Yeah, Hacketts gets his overseas duty all right. Shipping out for **Tamanrasset** tomorrow morning."

"**Tamanrasset**?"

"The Sahara Desert, you dumb bastard. Don't you know any geography?" He grinned wolfishly. "How about a little blackjack for laughs?"

Paul sighed for Hacketts, born into a spiritual desert, now being shipped to where the earth was sterile, too.

Tappin, Al. *The regular staff photographer who misses the opportunity to photograph the deer in the Works.* (*MH* 210:L14 *Deer in the Works*) "Murder! The story will go all over the country, Potter. Talk about human interest. Front page! Of all the times for **Al Tappin** to be out at the Ashtabula Works, taking pictures of a new viscometer they cooked up out there!"

Tarkington, Aaron. (*HP* 20:L21-22) The founder of the Mohiga Wagon Company was **Aaron Tarkington**, a brilliant inventor and manufacturer who nevertheless could not read or write. He now would be identified as a blameless inheritor of the genetic defect known as dyslexia. He said of himself that he was like the Emperor Charlemagne, "too busy to learn to read and write." He was not too busy, however, to have his wife read to him for 2 hours every evening. He had an excellent memory, for he delivered weekly lectures to the workmen at the factory that were laced with lengthy quotations from Shakespeare and Homer and the Bible, and on and on.

The gene for dyslexia was inherited by all his children, and though his son Elias never married or fathered children, the marriage of his three daughters to prominent families in Cleveland, New York, and Wilmington, Delaware, made "the threat of dyslexia pandemic in an emerging ruling class of bankers and industrialists, largely displaced in time by Germans, Koreans, Italians, English, and, of course, Japanese" (*HP* 21:L36, 22:L1-3).

Tarkington, Elias. *Aaron Tarkington's only son and author of* "a technical account of the construction of the Onondaga Canal, which connected the northern end of Lake Mohiga to the Erie Canal just south of Rochester" (*HP* 21:L15-18). *Elias never married or sired any children.*

After inheriting his father's properties he added a brewery and a steam-driven carpet factory, and was shot at Gettysburg when mistaken for Abraham Lincoln. (*HP* 22:L11-18) **Elias Tarkington** never married. He was severely wounded at the age of 54 while a civilian observer at the Battle of Gettysburg, top hat and all. He was there to see the debuts of 2 of his inventions, a mobile field kitchen and a pneumatic recoil mechanism for heavy artillery. The field kitchen, incidentally, with slight modifications, would later be adopted by the Barnum & Bailey Circus, and then by the German Army during World War I.

He is better remembered as the Tarkington who tried to invent a perpetual-motion machine and who founded The Mohiga Valley Free Institute, the forerunner of Tarkington College. Eugene Debs Hartke records that Elias was poorly educated, "more a mechanic than a scientist, and so spent his last three years trying to invent what anyone familiar with Newton's Laws would have known was an impossibility, a perpetual-motion machine. He had no fewer than 27 contraptions built, which he foolishly expected to go on running, after he had given them an initial spin or whack, until Judgment Day.

"I found 19 of those stubborn, mocking machines in the attic of what used to be their inventor's mansion, which in my time was the home of the College President, about a year after I came to work at Tarkington. I brought them back downstairs and into the 20th Century. Some of my students and I cleaned them up and restored any parts that had deteriorated during the intervening 100 years. At the least they were exquisite jewelry, with garnets and amethysts for bearings, with arms and legs of exotic woods, with tumbling balls of ivory, with chutes and counterweights of silver. It was as though dying **Elias** hoped to overwhelm science with the magic of precious materials" (*HP* 23:L4-22).

(*HP* 24:L17) I have discovered from reading old newspapers and letters and diaries from back then that the men who built the machines for **Elias Tarkington** knew from the first that they would never work, whatever the reason. Yet what love they lavished on the materials that comprised them! How is this for a definition of high art: "Making the most of the raw materials of futility"?

(*HP* 24:L24) Still another perpetual-motion machine envisioned by **Elias Tarkington** was what his Last Will and Testament called "The Mohiga Valley Free Institute." Upon his death, this new school would take possession of his 3,000-hectare estate above Scipio, plus half the shares in the wagon company, the carpet company, and the brewery. The other half was already owned by his sisters far away. On his deathbed he predicted that Scipio would 1 day be a great metropolis and that its wealth would transform his little college into a university to rival Harvard and Oxford and Heidelberg.

Tarkington, Felicia. *The youngest daughter of Aaron Tarkington and author of* "a novel called *Carpathia*, about a headstrong, high-born young woman in the Mohiga Valley who fell in love with a half-Indian lock-tender on that same canal" *(Onondaga)* (*HP* 21:L19-21). *She was a carrier of the gene for dyslexia.*

Tarkington College. *Originally established in 1869 by Elias Tarkington's Last Will and Testament as The Mohiga Valley Free Institute, in 1875 the name was changed to Tarkington College to avoid sounding like a home for the impoverished, and in 1999 the name again changed to the Tarkington State Reformatory to reflect its new status as part of the New York State correctional system. Eugene Debs Hartke characterizes the genesis of Tarkington College as another "perpetual-motion machine" envisioned by Elias Tarkington.* (*HP* 24:L34, 25:L1-22) It was to offer a free college education to persons of either sex, and of any age or race or religion, living within 40 miles of Scipio. Those from farther away would pay a modest fee. In the beginning, it would have only 1 full-time employee, the President. The teachers would be recruited right here in Scipio. They would take a few hours off from work each week, to teach what they knew. The chief engineer at the wagon company, for example, whose name was Andre Lutz, was a native of Liege, Belgium, and had served as an apprentice to a bell founder there. He would teach Chemistry. His French wife would teach French and Watercolor Painting. The brewmaster at the brewery, Hermann Shultz, a native of Leipzig, would teach Botany and German and the flute. The Episcopalian priest, Dr. Alan Clewes, a graduate of Harvard, would teach Latin, Greek, Hebrew, and the Bible. The dying man's physician, Dalton Polk, would teach Biology and Shakespeare, and so on.

And it came to pass.

In 1869 the new college enrolled its first class, 9 students in all, and all from right here in Scipio. Four were of ordinary college age. One was a Union veteran who had lost his legs at Shiloh. One was a former black slave 40 years old. One was a spinster 82 years old.

The college becomes a haven for dyslexics and those with various learning disabilities which prevented their attendance at any other institution of higher education. Many of the students come from extremely wealthy families who show their gratitude by erecting new buildings and purchasing books for the library. Tarkington becomes so well endowed that among small private schools its only rival, in terms of library holdings, is Oberlin College.

Hartke's continuous comparisons between Tarkington College and the prison across the lake is highlighted by the fact that, Every year, 30 inmates at Athena died for every student who was awarded an Associate in the Arts and Sciences Degree by **Tarkington** (*HP* 86:L10-12).

Tartakover. *While doing research from his Jerusalem cell in* Mother Night, *Howard Campbell learns that his friend, chess partner, and Soviet spy, George Kraft/Iona Potapov, beat chess Grand Master Tartakover in Rotterdam in 1931.*

Tcherkassky, Maria Daffodil-11. *The Prima Ballerina of the Chicago Opera Ballet and a member of Wilbur Swain's artificially extended family, in* Slapstick.

Tennyson, Alfred. *Alfred, Lord Tennyson (1809-1892) was appointed England's poet laureate in 1850. In* God Bless You, Mr. Rosewater *Tennyson is the answer to a question of bathroom graffiti:* (*GBR* 95:L20) "Where can I get a good lay around here?" asks a bawdy soul, drawing this reply: "Try 'Lay of the Last Minstrel, by **Alfred, Lord Tennyson**."

Tennyson is also used as an example of Mandarax's ability to recall popular quotations from literature, if you punched out on its back the word *Sunset*, for example, these lofty sentiments would appear on its screen: *Sunset and evening star / And one clear call for me! / And may there be no moaning of the bar, / When I put out to sea.* **Alfred, Lord Tennyson** (*Gal* 61:L30)

Tharp, Naomi. *The woman who lived next door to Kilgore and Leon Trout and who tried to help raise Leon after Mrs. Trout abandoned the family. She appears at the mouth of the blue tunnel to the Afterlife trying to coax Leon to the other side.* (*Gal* 258:L4) "It's **Mrs. Tharp**," she called. "You remember me, don't you, Leon? You come in here just like you used to come in through my kitchen door. Be a good boy now. You don't want to be left out there for another million years."

Thayer, Webster. *The judge who tried Sacco and Vanzetti and recalled by Vonnegut for his anti-immigrant bigotry. Prior to the Sacco and Vanzetti murder trial, Thayer tried Vanzetti for robbery. Vonnegut writes:* Was Vanzetti guilty of this lesser crime? Possibly so, but it did not matter much. Who said it did not matter much? The judge who tried the case said it did not matter much. He was **Webster Thayer**, a graduate of Dartmouth College and a descendent of many fine New England families. He told the jury, "This man, although he may not have actually committed the crime attributed to him, is nevertheless morally culpable, because he is the enemy of our existing institutions" (*JB* 177:L9). *Because Sacco and Vanzetti were admitted anarchists, Thayer felt conviction on any grounds was justified. Vonnegut cites the source of his information as* Labor's Untold Story, *by Richard O. Boyer and Herbert M. Morais. Thayer's unremitting bigotry was publicized on a banner held by Kenneth Whistler outside the funeral parlor handling the executed pair.* (*JB* 181:L27) On the banner were painted the words that the man who had sentenced Sacco and Vanzetti to death, **Webster Thayer**, had spoken to a friend soon after he passed the sentence: DID YOU SEE WHAT I DID TO THOSE ANARCHIST BASTARDS THE OTHER DAY?

Theatre de Lys. *The Greenwich Village theater where* Happy Birthday, Wanda June *opened on October 7, 1970. Due to an off-Broadway actors' strike, the play was moved to the Edison Theatre, where it closed after 142 performances, on March 14, 1971.*

In Deadeye Dick, *Rudy Waltz's "Katmandu" played for one performance at the Theatre de Lys in 1960.*

Theodorides, Mildred Helium-20. *Wilbur Swain's vice-president who dies of the Albanian flu, in* Slapstick.

therefore (when represented by the mathematical symbol ∴). *This mathematical symbol precedes each chapter of* Cat's Cradle. *The effect, theoretically, creates a narrative-in-the-round, a plausible Bokononism. In a letter to the editor, Vonnegut confirms that the three-dot symbol was his contribution to the text. Some reprints were made without the symbol, probably because each appearance took its own line and a couple of pages were saved in the process. More recent reprints restore the symbol.*

Thiriart, Jean. *In* Slaughterhouse-Five, *the Secretary of the National Union of Belgium Opticians has an editorial in a 1968 issue of* The Review of Optometry *advocating the establishment of a "European Optometry Society." Thiriart believes the profession is at a crossroads and the professional status of optometrists is in danger of being reduced to "spectacle sellers." Billy Pilgrim reads the editorial between time travel episodes but can't muster any compassion for his colleagues across the sea.*

Thomas Jefferson High School. *When Kilgore Trout takes his fungi-ridden tuxedo from the steamer trunk in preparation for his trip to the Midland City Arts Festival, he recalls attending his senior prom at Dayton, Ohio's Thomas Jefferson High School, in 1924.* (*BC* 34:L24-26) His high school was named after a slave owner who was also one of the world's greatest theoreticians on the subject of human liberty.

thumbscrew. (*SL5* 31:L5) Weary's father once gave Weary's mother a Spanish **thumbscrew** in working condition—for a kitchen paperweight.
(*WFG* 169:L12-13 *Torture and Blubber*) But it is not easy in real life to make a healthy man blubber, no matter how wicked he may be. So good men have invented appliances which make unconstrained weeping easier—the rack, the boot, the iron maiden, the pediwinkis, the electric chair, the cross, the **thumbscrew**. And the **thumbscrew** is alluded to in the published parts of the secret Pentagon history of the Vietnam war.

Tiglath-pileser the Third. *In* Mother Night, *eighteen-year-old prison guard Arnold Marx tells Howard Campbell about Tiglath-pileser the Third, an Assyrian who in 732 B.C. captured and burned down Hazor. The Canaanite city was captured 700 years earlier by Solomon who killed its 40,000 inhabitants, burned it down, and rebuilt it for the Jews. Arnold Marx concentrates on the savagery of the Assyrians against the Jews and gives not a thought to Solomon's deeds. For all his knowledge of archaeology and history, young Arnold is unaware of people such as Paul Joseph Goebbels, Campbell's old boss in Nazi Germany. This prompts Campbell to look again at his life with a longer view of history.* (*MN* 4:L10) And I felt the dust of the

Holy Land creeping in to bury me, sensed how thick a dust-and-rubble blanket I would one day wear. I felt thirty or forty feet of ruined cities above me; beneath me some primitive kitchen middens, a temple or two—and then—

Tiglath-pileser the Third.

Tillie. *In* Jailbird*, Tillie is the long-devoted maid to Mrs. Sutton, Sarah Wyatt's grandmother. She is the last of the servants to pass away, and two weeks later Mrs. Sutton also passes away.*

time and space (also **space and time**). (*ST* 205:L10) The explanation of the bizarre emphasis on the music carried by the Martian mother ships is simple: Rumfoord was crazy about good music—a craze, incidentally, that struck him only after he had been spread through **time and space** by the chrono-synclastic infundibulum.
(*ST* 278:L14) Man and dog spent most of their time by the pool, monitoring signals from their other selves through **space and time**.
(*SL5* 65:L15-16) It was a flying saucer from Tralfamadore, navigating in both **space and time**, therefore seeming to Billy Pilgrim to have come from nowhere all at once. Somewhere a big dog barked.
(*PS* 163:L18 *Playmates*) "Even more magically, perhaps, we readers can communicate with each other across **space and time** so cheaply. Ink and paper are as cheap as sand or water, almost."
(*PS* 230:L14 *The Big Space Fuck*) There were at least eighty-seven chrono-synclastic infundibulae, time warps, between Earth and the Andromeda Galaxy. If the *Arthur C. Clarke* passed through any one of them, the ship and its load would be multiplied a trillion times, and would appear everywhere throughout **space and time**.
(*Blue* 96:L7) So I was unprepared for the vista on the top floor, which seemed to violate all laws of **time and space** by going on and on and on. *This is part of Rabo's first impression of Dan Gregory's triple-sized brownstone house in New York.*
(*FWD* 50:L1) "Yes, and I ask the reader of this piece, my indispensable collaborator: Isn't your deepest understanding of **time and space** and, for that matter, destiny shaped like mine by your earliest experiences with geography, by the rules you learned about how to get home again? What is it that can make you feel, no matter how mistakenly, that you are on the right track, that you will soon be safe and sound at home again?

ting-a-ling. Jailbird*'s Dr. Robert Fender (using the name Frank X. Barlow) publishes a story in* Playboy *about the disembodied beings from Vicuna who temporarily inhabit the bodies of earthlings. "Ting-a-ling" is the Vicunian way of saying "hello" and "goodbye."*

Titan. *The largest moon of Saturn serves for 200,000 earthling years as the home of Salo, the Tralfamadorian messenger whose space ship broke down on* *the way to another galaxy. It is also where the chrono-synclastic infundibulated Winston Niles Rumfoord and his dog Kazak are permanently materialized until a sunstorm interrupts their wavelike existence and sends them on separate journeys across time and space. It becomes home to Malachi Constant, Beatrice Rumfoord, and their son Chrono. Beatrice dies on Titan in her old age and Chrono joins a flock of Titanic bluebirds, but not before he unknowingly delivers the spare part for Salo's ship. Salo brings Malachi back to Earth, where he freezes to death waiting for a bus on the outskirts of Indianapolis.*

Vonnegut makes life on Titan sound idyllic. (*ST* 265:L5-10) The atmosphere of **Titan** is like the atmosphere outside the back door of an Earthling bakery on a spring morning.

Titan has a natural chemical furnace at its core that maintains a uniform air temperature of sixty-seven degrees Fahrenheit.

Titanic bluebird. Native inhabitants of Saturn's moon Titan, they are befriended by Chrono who does his best to live as they do. He wears a cloak made of their feathers, sits on their eggs, shares their food and speaks their language.

"Tom Edison's Shaggy Dog" (1953) (see **Harold K. Bullard**).

tomb. (*ST* 192:L3) They *(Unk and Boaz)* determined that their **tomb** was deep, tortuous, endless—airless, uninhabited by anything remotely human, and uninhabitable by anything remotely human.
(*MN* 71:L12) Werner Noth lived on the outskirts of Berlin, well outside the target area. He lived with his wife and daughter in a walled white house that had the monolithic, earthbound grandeur of a Roman nobleman's **tomb**.
(*CC* 51:17) There was one more thing I wanted to do in Ilium. I wanted to get a photograph of the old man's **tomb**. *John/Jonah refers to the tomb of Dr. Felix Hoenikker.*
(*BC* 109:L7, 9) A pyramid was a sort of huge stone **tomb** which Egyptians had built thousands and thousands of years before. The Egyptians didn't build them anymore. The **tombs**... tourists would come from far away to gaze at them. . . .
(*WFG* 68:L21 *"There's a Maniac Loose Out There"*) I myself have spoken to a few young people about the Provincetown drug scene, have put this question to them: "If the person who committed the Truro murders was high on something when he killed, what drug do you think he swallowed?" I remind them how crude the butcher was, how shallow the graves were, even though it would have been easy to dig deep **tombs** in the woodland floor which was sand.

The answer, invariably: "Speed."
(*WFG* 173:L24 *Address to the National Institute of Arts and Letters, 1971*) My own son asked me a month ago what the happiest day of my life had been so

far. He called down into my grave, so to speak. This speech is full of **tombs**. My son considered me practically dead, since I smoked so many Pall Malls every day. (He's right, too.)
(*WFG* 175:L19, 21 *Address to the National Institute of Arts and Letters, 1971*) My father and grandfather were good artists. I'm sorry they can't be here today. They deserved your warm company in this cool **tomb**.
(*Slap* 10:L6) He *(Kurt's Uncle Alex)* uncovered a scandal involving large expenditures for the maintenance of **Grant's Tomb**, which required very little maintenance indeed.
(*Slap* 81:L17) Since the infant was an heir of mine, the pyramid might be called this: "The **Tomb** of the Prince of Candlesticks."
(*Slap* 98:L27) "To the extent he can read and write," said Dr. Cordiner. "He isn't nearly as socially outgoing as his sister. When he is away from her, he becomes as silent as a **tomb**."
(*Gal* 95:L29) And there are no **tombs** in the Galápagos Islands. The ocean gets all the bodies to use as it will. But if there were a **tomb**stone for Mary Hepburn, no other inscription would do but this one: "Mother Nature Personified."
(*FWD* 223:L17) The trumpet's wondrous call sounding abroad / in **tombs** throughout the world / shall drive everybody toward the throne. *Vonnegut quotes a translation of the traditional Latin mass, then follows with his own mass:* Let no trumpet's wondrous call sounding abroad / in **tombs** throughout the world / drive ashes toward any Throne (*FWD* 227:L22).

"Tomorrow and Tomorrow and Tomorrow" (1953) (see also **Schwartz** and **anti-gerasone**). *The science fiction short story which envisions severe family strife and hellishly cramped living quarters due to anti-gerasone, a potion which can indefinitely extend life.*

top floor (also **the top of the northernmost tower**). (*CC* 47:L22) The room that had been the laboratory of Dr. Felix Hoenikker was on the sixth floor, the **top floor** of the building.
(*SL5* 172:L12) The room *(in the Royalton Hotel)* was small and simple, except that it was on the **top floor**, and had French doors which opened onto a terrace as large as the room.
(*Slap* 37:L6) It was actually possible for Eliza and me, for example, to vanish into a huge grandfather clock in the ballroom at the **top of the northernmost tower**, and to emerge almost a kilometer away—through a trap door in the floor of the mausoleum of Professor Elihu Roosevelt Swain.
(*JB* 119:L12) I *(Walter Starbuck)* sat down on the edge of my bed, wide awake at last, and drenched in sweat. I took an inventory of my condition. Yes, I had gotten out of prison only that morning. Yes, I had sat in the smoking section of the airplane, but had felt no wish to smoke. Yes, I was now on the **top floor** of the Hotel Arapahoe.

(*JB* 217:L25) And so it came to pass that she *(Mary Kathleen O'Looney)* was staying on the **top floor** of a RAMJAC hotel in Managua, Nicaragua.
(*PS* 96:L17 *Self-Interview*) VONNEGUT: And my father painted pictures in a studio he'd set up on the **top floor** of the house.
(*PS* 324:L5 *In the Capital of the World*) Jill *(Krementz)* runs her photographic business out of the bottom floor. I run my writing business out of the **top floor**. We share the two floors in between.
(*DD* 73:L11) But he was led off to cells in the basement of police headquarters, and I was taken to a much smaller cellblock on the **top floor**, the third floor, which was reserved for women and for children under the age of sixteen.
(*Gal* 77:L17) Turning to look at Ortiz, who had just come in with the filet mignons, *MacIntosh was rehearsing in his head the first thing he was going to say to Gottfried von Kleist in Spanish: "Before you tell me the rest of the good news, dear colleague, give me your word of honor that I am gazing at my own ship in the distance, from the **top floor** of my own hotel."
(*Blue* 96:L6-9) I had supposed that he owned only the townhouse with the oak door and the Gorgon knocker infected with verdigris. So I was unprepared for the vista on the **top floor**, which seemed to violate all laws of time and space by going on and on and on. Down on the lower floors, including the basement, he had joined up to three houses with doors and archways. On the **top floor**, though, he had ripped out the dividing walls entirely, from end to end and side to side, leaving only those six free-standing fireplaces.
(*Blue* 109:L27) I was mostly curious, though, about the **top floor**, which used to be the part of Gregory's studio with the big, leaky skylight.

topmost. (*PP* 12:L25) Paul glimpsed the only life visible through a narrow canyon between Buildings 57 and 59, a canyon that opened onto the river and revealed a bank of gray porches in Homestead. On the **topmost** porch an old man rocked in a patch of sunlight.
(*ST* 17:L5) Standing now in the **topmost**, in the smallest of the baroque fountain's bowls, standing with his feet in the ruins of birds' nests, Malachi Constant looked out over the estate, and over a large part of Newport and Narragansett Bay.
(*BC* 275:L5) Trout's right ring finger somehow slipped into Dwayne's mouth, and Dwayne bit off the **topmost** joint.
(*JB* 146:L22) . . . into the lobby of the Chrysler Building . . . we got into the elevator before he could stop us. The doors shut in his angry face as Mary Kathleen punched the button for the **topmost** floor.
(*DD* 61:L31) I slid forward the bolt, which caught the **topmost** cartridge and delivered it into the chamber.

tower, **Eiffel Tower**, **Leaning Tower of Pisa**, **Tower of Babel**, **Waldorf Towers** (see also **belfry**, or **cupola**). (*ST* 31:L11, 28, 32:L7, 15) Two hours after the firing of *The Whale* was called off indefinitely, the Reverend Bobby Denton shouted at his Love Crusade in Wheeling, West Virginia:

"'And the Lord came down to see the city and the **tower**, which the children of men builded. And the Lord said, "Behold, the people is one . . .'"

Bobby Denton spitted his audience on a bright and loving gaze, and proceeded to roast it whole over the coals of its own iniquity. "Are these not Bible times?" he said. "Have we not builded of steel and pride an abomination far taller than the **Tower of Babel** of old? . . .

"So why should we cry out in surprise and pain now when God says to us what He said to the people who builded the **Tower of Babel**: 'No! Get away from there! You aren't going to Heaven or anywhere else with that thing! Scatter, you hear? Quit talking the language of science to each other! Nothing will be restrained from you which you have imagined to do, if you all keep on talking the language of science to each other, and I don't want that! I, your Lord God on High *want* things restrained from you, so you will quit thinking about crazy **towers** and rockets to Heaven, and start thinking about how to be better neighbors and husbands and wives and daughters and sons! Don't look to rockets for salvation—look to your homes and churches!'"

(*CC* 209:L14, 16) And then there was the sound of a rockslide—and one great **tower** of "Papa's" castle, undermined, crashed down to the sea.

The people on the seaward parapet looked in astonishment at the empty socket where the **tower** had stood.

(*GBR* 50:L28, 31) To the west of the Parthenon was the old Rosewater Saw Company, red brick, too, green-roofed, too. The spine of its roof was broken, its windows unglazed. It was a New Ambrosia for barn swallows and bats. Its four **tower** clocks were handless. Its big brass whistle was choked with nests.

To the east of the Parthenon was the County Courthouse, red brick, too, green-roofed, too. Its **tower** was identical with that of the old saw company. Three of its four clocks still had their hands, but they did not run.

(*SL5* 6:L8) He had to show somebody what was in the bag, and he had decided he could trust me. He caught my eye, winked, opened the bag. There was a plaster model of the **Eiffel Tower** in there. It was painted gold. It had a clock in it.

(*SL5* 100:L24) "How the inhabitants of a whole planet can live in peace! As you know, I am from a planet that has been engaged in senseless slaughter since the beginning of time. I myself have seen the bodies of schoolgirls who were boiled alive in a water **tower** by my own countrymen, who were proud of fighting pure evil at the time." *Billy speaks in response to a Tralfamadorian's question about the most valuable thing he has so far learned on Tralfamadore.*

(*BC* 222:L4) Dwayne Hoover, incidentally, wasn't taking any of this in. He was still hypnotized, turned inward. He was thinking about moving fingers writing and moving on, and so forth. He had bats in his bell **tower**. He was off his rocker. He wasn't playing with a full deck of cards.

(*Slap* 38:L6) It was actually possible for Eliza and me, for example, to vanish into a huge grandfather clock in the ballroom at the top of the northernmost **tower**, and to emerge almost a kilometer away—through a trap door in the floor of the mausoleum of Professor Elihu Roosevelt Swain.

(*Slap* 239:L12) As a reward, the Raspberries brought their most precious possessions to Dr. Swain on the floor of the New York Stock Exchange. There was a clock-radio, an alto saxophone, a fully-fitted toiletries kit, a model of the **Eiffel Tower** with a thermometer in it—and on and on.

(*JB* xxv:L21) It was from the belfry of that **tower** that Alexander and his father and his brother would watch the Cuyahoga Massacre on Christmas morning. Each would have his own binoculars. Each would have his own little revolver, too.

(*JB* 218:L25) Mary Kathleen went to New York City soon after that. She began to watch shopping-bag ladies through field glasses from her suite in the **Waldorf Towers**. *She eventually assumes the persona of a bag lady because she fears for her safety.*

(*PS* 239:L13 *Children*) "When I thought I was going to talk about reference points, I had in mind the fixtures in a simpler and more stable civilization than what we have today. Examples: Shakespeare's *Hamlet*, Beethoven's Fifth Symphony, Leonardo's *Mona Lisa*, Lincoln's Gettysburg Address, Mark Twain's *Huckleberry Finn*—the Great Wall of China, the **Leaning Tower of Pisa**, the Sphinx. These few works of art used to be enormous monuments in the minds of public school graduates in every corner of this country. They have now been drowned in our minds, like Atlantis, if you will, by the latest sensations on television and radio, and in our motion picture palaces and *People* magazine."

(*Gal* 106:L30) What those birds did on camera, though, was supremely erotic all the same. Already breast to breast and toe to toe, they made their sinuous necks as erect as flagpoles. They tilted their heads back as far as they would go. They pressed their long throats and the undersides of their jaws together. They formed a **tower**, the two of them—a single structure, pointed on top and resting on four blue feet.

(*Gal* 187:L20) Colonel Reyes had already activated the brain of the tremendous self-propelled weapon slung underneath his airplane. That was its first taste of life, but already it was madly in love with the radar dish atop the control **tower** at Guayaquil International Airport, a legitimate military target, since Ecuador kept ten of its own warplanes there.

(*HP* 18:L14) The greatest stroke of luck for me, the biggest chunk of manna from Heaven, was that Tarkington had need of somebody to play the Lutz Carillon, the great family of bells at the top of the **tower** of the college library, where I am writing now.

(*HP* 31:L27) If Henry Moellenkamp hadn't come out of his mother's womb dyslexic, there would never have been a **tower** in which to hang the Lutz Carillon.

(*HP* 77:L16) Tex, meanwhile, was ascending the **tower** of the library here with a rifle and ammunition. He was going clear to the top, to turn the belfry itself into a sniper's nest.
(*HP* 83:L18) He *(Pierre LeGrand)* tried to win friends by making expensive gifts to them, but that didn't work, so he tried to hang himself from a girder of the water **tower** on top of Musket Mountain. I happened to be up there, in the bushes with the wife of the coach of the Tennis Team.
(*HP* 203:L27) At the very end of his life 2 years ago, though, when Lyle Hooper was a prisoner of the escaped convicts up in the bell **tower**, he was addressed by his captors as "Pimp."
(*HP* 250:L27) At dawn the valley was as quiet as ever, and the red light on top of the water **tower** on the summit of Musket Mountain, as though nothing remarkable had happened over there, winked off and on, off and on.
(*FWD* 103:L5-17) "The firebombing of Dresden, which had no military significance, was a work of art. It was a **tower** of smoke and flame to commemorate the rage and heartbreak of so many who had had their lives warped or ruined by the indescribable greed and vanity and cruelty of Germany. The British and Americans who built the **tower** had been raised, like me, and in response to World War I, to be pacifists.

"Two more such **towers** would be built by Americans alone in Japan. When they were built and then blew away, leaving nothing but ashes and cinders, I was on furlough in Indianapolis, my home. And even though I had seen on the ground the effects of a similar total conflagration, I myself regarded those twin **towers** as works of art. Beautiful! *See also: PP* 88:L31; 285:L2; *ST* 95:L23; *CC* 184:L18; 185:L11; 205:L1; *SL5* 15:L27; *MH—Long Walk To Forever* 46:L3; 51:L20; 52:L8; *MH—The Hyannis Port Story* 137:L22; *BC* 56:L27,29; 140:L18; 143:L11; *Slap* 93:L12; 94:L6; *JB* xxviii:L21; xxix:L31; xxxii:L6; xxxiii:L15; 7:L31; 78:L24; *PS—Children* 241:L17; *DD* 175:L10; *Blue* 293:L16; *HP* 26:L31; 27:L15; 67:L9; 70:L28; 95:L15; 99:L1; 133:L14; 152:L12; 180:L34; 184:L15; 185:L26,28; 204:L16,26; 205:L14; 206:L1; 220:L3; 239:L13; 241:L30; 246:L23; 117:L11; *FWD* 118:L28.

Tralfamadore (see also **"The Protocols of the Elders of Tralfamadore"**). *The planet in the Small Magellanic Cloud which is a central feature to both* The Sirens of Titan *and* Slaughterhouse-Five. *The nature of life on Tralfamadore, however, is not consistent across the texts. In* Sirens, *Tralfamadorians are a race of machines. Though they had living beings which originally created them, they had long since exterminated their creators and reproduced on their own.* (*ST* 274:L15, 275:L14) The legend was this:

*Once upon a time on **Tralfamadore** there were creatures who weren't anything like machines. They weren't dependable. They weren't efficient. They weren't predictable. They weren't durable. And these poor creatures were obsessed by the idea that everything that existed had to have a purpose, and that some purposes were higher than others.*

These creatures spent most of their time trying to find out what their purpose was. And every time they found out what seemed to be a purpose of themselves, the purpose seemed so low that the creatures were filled with disgust and shame.

And, rather than serve such a low purpose, the creatures would make a machine to serve it. This left the creatures free to serve higher purposes. But whenever they found a higher purpose, the purpose still wasn't high enough.

So machines were made to serve higher purposes, too.

And the machines did everything so expertly that they were finally given the job of finding out what the highest purpose of the creatures could be.

The machines reported in all honesty that the creatures couldn't really be said to have any purpose at all.

The creatures thereupon began slaying each other, because they hated purposeless things above all else.

*And they discovered that they weren't even very good at slaying. So they turned that job over to the machines, too. And the machines finished up the job in less time than it takes to say, "**Tralfamadore**."*

Their present form of government is "hypnotic anarchy," *which Salo declines to explain* (*ST* 268:L30-31). *According to Salo, the word Tralfamadore means* "both *all of us* and the *number 541*" (*ST* 268:L24). *They use the Universal Will to Become to power their vehicles and transmit messages to Salo. It enables them to influence the psychology and efforts of humans on Earth in order to have them unwittingly write messages to Salo. Among their many messages were Stonehenge, the Great Wall of China, the Palace of the League of Nations, and the Moscow Kremlin. When Winston Niles Rumfoord discovered that the meaning of life for human beings, and for himself in particular, was to get a spare part to Salo for his intergalactic journey, he dejectedly exclaims:* "**Tralfamadore** . . . reached into the Solar System, picked me up, and used me like a handy-dandy potato peeler!" (*ST* 285:L3) *Rumfoord never learned that the message Salo carried across the galaxies was the one word, "Greetings."*

Undercutting his own creation, Vonnegut has Eliot Rosewater address the science fiction writers' convention in Milford, Connecticut. (*GBR* 30:L33) And it occurred to him that a really good science fiction book had never been written about money. "Just think of the wild ways money is passed around on Earth!" he said. "You don't have to go to the **Planet Tralfamadore** in Anti-Matter Galaxy 508 G to find weird creatures with unbelievable powers. Look at the powers of an Earthling millionaire! Look at me! I was born naked, just like you, but my God, friends and neighbors, I have thousands of dollars a day to spend! . . . I leave it to you, friends and neighbors, and especially to the immortal Kilgore Trout: think about the silly ways money gets passed around now, and then think up better ways."

Billy Pilgrim explains the nature of time as understood by Tralfamadorians. (*SL5* 23:L13) "The most important thing I learned on **Tralfamadore** was that when a person dies he only *appears* to die. He is still very much alive in the past, so it is very silly for people to cry at his funeral. All moments, past, present, and future, always have existed, always will exist. The Tralfamadorians can look at all the different moments just the way we can look at a stretch of the Rocky Mountains, for instance. They can see how permanent all the moments are, and they can look at any moment that interests them. It is just an illusion we have here on Earth that one moment follows another one, like beads on a string, and that once a moment is gone it is gone forever.

"When a Tralfamadorian sees a corpse, all he thinks is that the dead person is in bad condition in that particular moment, but that the same person is just fine in plenty of other moments. Now, when I myself hear that somebody is dead, I simply shrug and say what the Tralfamadorians say about dead people, which is 'So it goes.'"

The unnamed Tralfamadorian who acts as Billy's host on board the flying saucer explains how they see time. (*SL5* 74:L13-18) I am a Tralfamadorian, seeing all time as you might see a stretch of the Rocky Mountains. All time is all time. It does not change. It does not lend itself to warnings or explanations. It simply is. Take it moment by moment, and you will find that we are all, as I've said before, bugs in amber. *Billy learns that reading a Tralfamadorian novel requires the same shift in perception.* (*SL5* 76:L12-22) . . . you're right: each clump of symbols is a brief, urgent message—describing a situation, a scene. We Tralfamadorians read them all at once, not one after the other. There isn't any particular relationship between all the messages, except that the author has chosen them carefully, so that, when seen all at once, they produce an image of life that is beautiful and surprising and deep. There is no beginning, no middle, no end, no suspense, no moral, no causes, no effects. What we love in our books are the depths of many marvelous moments seen all at one time.

This unique vision of time and space yields the Tralfamadorian secret about how the universe comes to an end. A Tralfamadorian pilot testing a new and faulty fuel explodes all existence. They are incapable of altering his actions because that is how the moment is structured.

Tralfamadorians in Slaughterhouse-Five *are sentient beings who communicate via telepathy. They use computers and speakers to converse with Billy Pilgrim and Montana Wildhack. In a letter to the* Ilium News Leader, *Billy describes their physiology.* (*SL5* 22:L32-34, 23:L1-8) The letter said that they were two feet high, and green, and shaped like plumber's friends. Their suction cups were on the ground, and their shafts, which were extremely flexible, usually pointed to the sky. At the top of each shaft was a little hand with a green eye in its palm. The creatures were friendly, and they could see in four dimensions. They pitied Earthlings for being able to see only three. They had many wonderful things to teach Earthlings, especially about time. *Billy sees his own role as a cosmic optometrist capable of enabling others to see time through his knowledge of Tralfamadorian philosophy.*

Tralfamadorians recognized five distinct sexes on their planet, all necessary for reproduction. Billy fails to understand this as well as their claim to have identified seven sexes among humans. Similar to Kilgore Trout's Now It Can Be Told *in* Breakfast of Champions, *Tralfamadorians see all creatures in the universe as being various sorts of machines. Billy continues:* On **Tralfamadore** . . . there isn't much interest in Jesus Christ. The Earthling figure who is most engaging to the Tralfamadorian mind, he says, is Charles Darwin—who taught that those who die are meant to die, that corpses are improvements (*SL5* 182:L12).

Vonnegut whimsically describes how his father preserved a letter informing him of his son's first commercial success as a writer. (*FWD* 25:L32) I am moved to add that Father tried to make good times revisitable (a trick which was easy as pie for the **Tralfamadorians** in my novel *Slaughterhouse-Five*) by gluing cheerful documents to sheets of masonite and protecting them with varnish.

tri-benzo-Deportamil. *Wilbur Swain endures a thirty-year addiction to the medication developed by the Eli Lilly Company for those who suffer "the socially unacceptable symptoms of Tourette's Disease."* (*Slap* 155:L7-9) The "Deport" part of the name had reference to good deportment, to socially acceptable behavior. *He started taking the medication after becoming disoriented due to the Chinese experiments which made gravity unstable. Wilbur gave his remaining small supply to David Daffodil-11 von Peterswald, a true sufferer of Tourette's and the son of Wilma Pachysandra-17, wife of the inventor of The Hooligan. Swain was out of his mind from the severe withdrawal symptoms and this necessitated tying him to a bed in the von Peterswald home for six days. During that time Wilbur got the widow pregnant and she eventually gave birth to the son who sired Melody Oriole-2 von Peterswald, the granddaughter who comforts him in his final days in the Empire State Building. It was also in that confused state that Wilma explains to Wilbur that* the Chinese . . . had become successful manipulators of the Universe by combining harmonious minds (*Slap* 237:L7-9). *They had succeeded in proving the Swain twins' theories which were taken from the mausoleum by the old Wilbur, the tri-benzo-Deportamil addict, and delivered to Fu Manchu.*

trinity. (*PP* 261:L36) "These are radical proposals *("that men and women be returned to work as controllers of machines, and that the control of people by machines be curtailed")*, extremely difficult to put into effect. But the need for their being put into effect is far greater than all of the difficulties, and infinitely greater than the need for our national holy **trinity**, Efficiency, Economy, and Quality."

(*BC* 212:L5) His biographer *(Saint Anthony's)* was another Egyptian, Saint Athanasius, whose theories on the **Trinity**, the Incarnation, and the divinity of

the Holy Spirit, set down three hundred years after the murder of Christ, were considered valid by Catholics even in Dwayne Hoover's time.
(*PS* 217:L1, 4 *Religion*) She *(Vonnegut's first wife)* believes that Jesus was the Son of God, or perhaps God Himself—or however that goes. I have had even more trouble with the **Trinity** than I had with college algebra. I refer those who are curious about it to what is known about the Council of Nicea, which took place in anno Domini 325. It was there that the **Trinity** was hammered into its present shape. Unfortunately, the minutes have been lost. It is known that the emperor Constantine was there, and probably spoke a good deal. He gave us the first Christian army. He may have given us the Holy Ghost as well.

Trippingham, Mona Lisa. *The security guard at the old GEFFCo Building, now the Matsumoto Building, who telephones Rabo Karabekian with the sad news that his "Blue Windsor Number Seventeen" has shredded and peeled itself from its canvas. She calls to ask if wants to come retrieve its remains. The irony of the situation lies in the fact that Rabo's choice of paint, Sateen Dura-Luxe, was advertised to* "outlive the smile on the 'Mona Lisa'" (*Blue* 20:L7). *Now, Mona Lisa was calling to tell Rabo to pick up his scraps.*

Trout, Darlene. *Kilgore's wife is mentioned only once.* (*BC* 151:L11) Kilgore Trout once wrote a short novel about the importance of the clitoris in love-making. This was in response to a suggestion by his second wife, **Darlene**, that he could make a fortune with a dirty book. She told him that the hero should understand women so well that he could seduce anyone he wanted. So Trout wrote *The Son of Jimmy Valentine*.

Trout, Kilgore. *The fabled science fiction writer first appearing in* God Bless You, Mr. Rosewater. *Trout is Eliot Rosewater's favorite author and is responsible for his nominal recovery at the end of the text. Vonnegut leaves it to Trout to express the meaning of Eliot's antics.* (*GBR* 213:L22, 214:L1) "It seems to me," said **Trout**, "that the main lesson Eliot learned is that people can use all the uncritical love they can get."

"This is *news*?" the Senator raucously inquired.

"It's news that a man was able to *give* that kind of love over a long period of time. If one man can do it, perhaps others can do it, too. It means that our hatred of useless human beings and the cruelties we inflict upon them for their own good need not be parts of human nature. Thanks to the example of Eliot Rosewater, millions upon millions of people may learn to love and help whomever they see."

Trout glanced from face to face before speaking his last word on the subject. The last word was: "Joy."

In Breakfast of Champions, *Kilgore Trout is asked to come to the Midland City Arts Festival as one of the honored guests. Eliot Rosewater bargained for Kilgore's invitation in exchange for the loan of an El Greco painting. Trout's novel* Now It Can Be Told *contributes to Dwayne Hoover's mental breakdown. Vonnegut records that Trout died in 1981 at the of seventy-four, and The American Academy of Arts and Sciences placed a monument over his grave with a quote from his unfinished 209th novel,* WE ARE HEALTHY ONLY TO THE EXTENT THAT OUR IDEAS ARE HUMANE (*BC* 16:illustration).

We learn a little about Trout's personal history in Breakfast of Champions. *He was born in Bermuda, the son of Leo Trout, a scientist working for the Royal Ornithological Society responsible for protecting the only remaining nesting grounds of the Bermuda Ern. We also learn that he had three failed marriages, though the only spouse mentioned by name is Darlene. He also had a son named Leo who ran away from home when only fourteen.*

In Galápagos, *Trout's son is named Leon, the narrator of the text. Kilgore comes back from beyond the grave at regular though distant intervals of time, asking his son to step through the blue tunnel into the afterlife. In* Jailbird, *imprisoned veterinarian and science fiction writer Dr. Bob Fender alternately publishes under the pseudonyms Frank X. Barlow and Kilgore Trout.*

The list below contains all the titled Trout works followed by tales without titles and one tale which probably belongs to Trout, though Vonnegut leaves its authorship unspecified. Not included are stories Trout makes up in his head but never puts on paper.

1. *2BR02B* (*GBR* 28:L23)
2. *Venus on the Half-shell* (*GBR* 133:L14)
3. *Oh Say Can You Smell?* (*GBR* 179:L4)
4. *The First District Court of Thankyou* (*GBR* 187:L8-9)
5. *Pan-Galactic Three Day Pass* (*GBR* 196:L28-29)
6. *Maniacs in the Fourth Dimension* (*SL5* 90:L3-4)
7. *The Gospel from Outer Space* (*SL5* 93:L33, 94:L1)
8. *The Gutless Wonder* (*SL5* 144:L7-8)
9. *The Big Board* (*SL5* 173:L32)
10. "Pan Galactic Straw-boss" became "Mouth Crazy" (*BC* 21:L10-11)
11. *Plague on Wheels* (*BC* 22:L7)
12. "The Dancing Fool" (*BC* 58:L25-26)
13. "This Means You" (*BC* 73:L1-2)
14. "Hail to the Chief" (*BC* 88:L6)
15. *The Barring-gaffner of Bagnialto*, or *This Year's Masterpiece* (*BC* 128:L24-25)
16. *The Son of Jimmy Valentine* (*BC* 151:L14-15)
17. *How You Doin'?* (*BC* 169:L14-15)
18. *The Smart Bunny* (*BC* 232:L1-2)
19. *Now It Can Be Told* (*BC* 253:L10)
20. *The Pan-Galactic Memory Bank* (*BC* 278:L26)

21. "Asleep at the Switch" (*JB* 184:L20) *(published by Dr. Robert Fender under Kilgore Trout's name)*

22. The Planet Gobblers (*PS* 209:L11-12 *Religion*)

— (*SL5* 174:L31) *A Trout novel about a man who builds a time machine and visits Jesus as a young boy learning carpentry from his father and grateful for the work order coming from Roman soldiers for a crucifixion stand.*

— (*BC* 184:L7) **Kilgore Trout** wrote a story one time about a town which decided to tell derelicts where they were and what was about to happen to them by putting up actual street signs . . . *which read* SKID ROW.

— (*WFG* 247:L15 *Playboy Interview*) *Vonnegut mentions that he is at work on a Kilgore Trout novel about "extended families," a central concept in* Slapstick *though not told as a Trout story.*

— (*JB* 54:L28) *Dr. Fender, who previously published under Trout's name, publishes a story in* Playboy *magazine about disembodied spirits from the planet Vicuna. Fender writes this story under the name Frank X. Barlow.*

— (*HP* 135:L18-19) *Though not specifically attributed to Kilgore Trout, "The Protocols of the Elders of Tralfamadore" appears in a magazine which published Trout's work in the past.*

Trout, Leo (see also **Leon Trout**). *There are citations for two Leo Trouts in* Breakfast of Champions. *The first is Kilgore's father, an American citizen working in Bermuda for the Royal Ornithological Society. He was protecting the remaining nesting ground for the endangered Bermuda Ern. Kilgore was born and brought up on Bermuda, assisting his father in monitoring the habitat.*

The second Leo is Kilgore's son, though in Galápagos, *Kilgore's son is named Leon. The history of the* Galápagos *Leo is significantly different from the one in* Breakfast of Champions. *In* Galápagos, *Leo did not join the Viet Cong, though he did desert.* (*BC* 111:L1-12) **Leo** left home forever at the age of fourteen. He lied about his age, and he joined the Marines. He sent a note to his father from boot camp. It said this: "I pity you. You've crawled up your own asshole and died."

That was the last Trout heard from **Leo**, directly or indirectly, until he was visited by two agents from the Federal Bureau of Investigation. **Leo** had deserted from his division in Viet Nam, they said. He had committed high treason. He had joined the Viet Cong.

Here was the F.B.I. evaluation of **Leo**'s situation on the planet at that time: "Your boy's in bad trouble," they said.

Trout, Leon. *The only child of Kilgore Trout and narrator of* Galápagos. *While a U.S. Marine serving in Vietnam, Leon recalls* how I felt after I shot a grandmother in Vietnam. She was as toothless and bent over as Mary Hepburn would be at the end of her life. I shot her because she had just killed my best friend and my worst enemy in my platoon with a single hand-grenade.

This episode made me sorry to be alive, made me envy stones (*Gal* 127:L11-17). *Leon was soon hospitalized for nervous exhaustion, and it was then he found out that his unit took revenge by killing all fifty-nine villagers. He was ordered to keep it a secret.*

While enjoying a pass from the hospital, Leon contracted syphilis from a prostitute in Saigon. He feared getting treatment from a military physician because his pay would be docked and the period of treatment would be added to his tour in Vietnam. Instead, he went to a Swedish physician working at a local medical school. It turned out that the doctor was a great fan of his father's books. Instantly, Leon felt a strong emotional attachment with the doctor, who then convinced Leon to desert to Sweden.

He went to work as a welder in the Malmö shipyard where the Bahía de Darwin *was being constructed.* (*Gal* 127:L18-21) I was painlessly decapitated one day by a falling sheet of steel while working inside the hull of the *Bahía de Darwin*, at which time I refused to set foot in the blue tunnel leading into the Afterlife. *He stayed behind because he was curious about how humanity would develop. He haunted the ship and observed humanity from the shores of the Galápagos Islands. It fell to Kilgore to convince Leon about the futility of his continued observations.* (*Gal* 254:L8) "**Leon**! **Leon**! **Leon**!" he implored. "The more you learn about people, the more disgusted you'll become. I would have thought that your being sent by the wisest men in your country, supposedly, to fight a nearly endless, thankless, horrifying, and, finally, pointless war, would have given you sufficient insight into the nature of humanity to last you throughout all eternity!

"Need I tell you that these same wonderful animals, of which you apparently still want to learn more and more, are at this very moment proud as Punch to have weapons in place, all set to go at a moment's notice, guaranteed to kill everything?

"Need I tell you that this once beautiful and nourishing planet when viewed from the air now resembles the diseased organs of poor Roy Hepburn when exposed at his autopsy, and that the apparent cancers, growing for the sake of growth alone, and consuming all and poisoning all, are the cities of your beloved human beings?

"Need I tell you that these animals have made such a botch of things that they can no longer imagine decent lives for their own grandchildren, even, and will consider it a miracle if there is anything left to eat or enjoy by the year two thousand, now only fourteen years away?

"Like the people on this accursed ship, my boy, they are led by captains who have no charts or compasses, and who deal from minute to minute with no problem more substantial than how to protect their self-esteem."

The True Purpose of Life in the Solar System. *Beatrice Rumfoord spent much of her time on Titan writing this text, which* was a refutation of Rumfoord's notion that the purpose of human life in the Solar System was to get a grounded messenger from Tralfamadore on his way again.

Beatrice began the book after her son left her to join the bluebirds. The manuscript so far, written in longhand, occupied thirty-eight cubic feet inside the Taj Mahal (*ST* 308:L7-14).

Tucci, Alfy. *Alfy Tucci is "the master of silent television," a title given him for his ability to watch musicians on television without sound and still discern the song being played, though he admits classical music is his weakest area. He is also one of the cooks at The Meadows retreat.* (*PP* 170:L32) As Paul's teammates carried him back to his seat, he realized fleetingly, as a fragment of a nightmare, that the cook had been **Alfy**, the master of silent television.

Tum-bumwa. *The enslaved African who took part in a 1786 insurrection aboard a British slave ship and set it ashore on San Lorenzo. He became the island's first emperor.* (*CC* 107:L23-24, 108:L1-4) "The emperor was **Tum-bumwa** the only person who ever regarded the island as being worth defending. A maniac, **Tum-bumwa** caused to be erected the San Lorenzo Cathedral and the fantastic fortifications on the north shore of the island, fortifications within which the private residence of the so-called President of the Republic now stands."

(*CC* 173:L36, 174:L1-11) Its parapets to the north were continuous with the scarp of a monstrous precipice that fell six hundred feet straight down to the lukewarm sea.

It posed the question posed by all such stone piles: how had puny men moved stones so big? And, like all such stone piles, it answered the question itself. Dumb terror had moved those stones so big.

The castle was built according to the wish of **Tum-bumwa**, Emperor of San Lorenzo, a demented man, an escaped slave. **Tum-bumwa** was said to have found its design in a child's picture book.

A gory book it must have been.

The fortification also held the oubliette in which John/Jonah and Mona Aamons Monzano took refuge when "Papa" Monzano slipped into the oceans, causing ice-nine to lock the world's surface moisture.

tunnel (see also **blue tunnel**). (*PP* 155:L9) He *(Paul)* led her *(Anita)* to the front door of the low little house through a dark, fragrant **tunnel** roofed and walled by lilacs.

(*ST* 236:L28) The effect of the closing inside the booths was to turn the line of concessions into a twilit **tunnel**.

(*ST* 236:L29-30) The isolation of the concessionaires in the **tunnel** had an extra dimension of spookiness, since the **tunnel** contained only survivors from Mars.

(*ST* 238:L1) It was the proud and impudent custom of all concessionaires to stay away from ceremonies—to stay in the twilit **tunnel** of their booths until Rumfoord and his dog had come and gone.

(*SL5* 80:L27) They *(the British POWs)* could **tunnel** all they pleased. They would inevitably surface within a rectangle of barbed wire, would find themselves greeted listlessly by dying Russians who spoke no English, who had no food or useful information or escape plans of their own.

(*BC* 83:L8) He *(Rabo Karabekian)* got a ride in a truck. . . . It picked him up at the mouth of the Lincoln **Tunnel**, which was named in honor of a man who had had the courage and imagination to make human slavery against the law in the United States of America.

(*BC* 168:L4) The man at the controls of the *Galaxie* was a traveling salesman for a device which engulfed the rear ends of trucks at loading docks. It was a telescoping **tunnel** of rubberized canvas.

(*WFG* 162:L15-16 *Address to Graduating Class at Bennington College, 1970)* I saved our marriage many times by exclaiming, "Wait! Wait! I see light at the end of the **tunnel** at last!" And I wish I could bring light to *your* **tunnels** today. My wife begged me to bring you light, but there is no light. Everything is going to become unimaginably worse, and never get better again.

(*Slap* 146:L1) It must have been a horrible sight—the **tunnel** with all the hair and bits of wax inside.

(*JB* 146:L17) She led me through a **tunnel** under Lexington Avenue, and up a staircase into the lobby of the Chrysler Building.

(*JB* 169:L1) He said he had been working as "a robber," taking out supporting pillars of coal from a **tunnel** where the seam had otherwise been exhausted. Something had fallen on him *(Kenneth Whistler)*.

(*Gal* 166:L6) This, of course, was the **tunnel** into the Afterlife.

(*Gal* 259:L13) The decision was made for me by Mary Hepburn, by "Mrs. Flemming," whose joy in the crow's nest held my attention so long that when I looked back at the **tunnel**, the **tunnel** was gone.

(*Blue* 67:L30) Yes, and when the Twentieth Century Limited from Chicago plunged into a **tunnel** under New York City, with its lining of pipes and wires, I was out of the womb and into the birth canal.

(*HP* 58:L4) I had won my Silver Star for finding and personally killing 5 enemy soldiers who were hiding in a **tunnel** underground.

(*HP* 220:L17) During our interview, he used all the antiwar rhetoric he had heard at Harvard in the '60s to denounce his own country's overseas disaster. We were a quagmire. There was no light at the end of the **tunnel** over here, and on and on. *Hartke notes the parallel drawn by Hiroshi Matsumoto between America's intervention in Vietnam with Japan's corporate occupation of America.*

(*HP* 236:L21) But as I've said, there were other veterans there who had heard of me and knew, among other things, that I had pitched a grenade into the mouth of a **tunnel** one time, and killed a woman, her mother, and her baby hiding from helicopter gunships which had strafed her village right before we got there.

The Turkey Farm. *Dr. von Peterswald coins this term after accidentally inventing The Hooligan, a device with which one can speak with the dead.* (*Slap* 231:L23) The talkers identified themselves as persons in the afterlife. They were backed by a demoralized chorus of persons who complained to each other of tedium and social slights and minor ailments, and so on.

As Dr. von Peterswald said in his secret diary: "It sounded like nothing so much as the other end of a telephone call on a rainy autumn day—to a badly run **turkey farm**."

Turner, Jeffrey. *The head of the Jamaican drug cartel whose televised trial lasted eighteen months. Though given twenty-five consecutive life sentences, he was serving time at Athena for only six months before his associates executed the enormously elaborate and high-powered jail break.* (*HP* 88:L14-30) Now a well-rehearsed force of his employees, variously estimated as being anything from a platoon to a company, had arrived outside the prison with explosives, a tank, and several halftracks taken from the National Guard Armory about 10 kilometers south of Rochester, across the highway from the Meadowdale Cinema Complex. One of their number, it has since come out, moved to Rochester and joined the National Guard, swearing to defend the Constitution and all that, with the sole purpose of stealing the keys to the Armory.

The Japanese guards were wholly unprepared and unmotivated to resist such a force, especially since the attackers were all dressed in American Army uniforms and waving American flags. So they hid or put their hands up or ran off into the virgin forest. This wasn't their country, and guarding prisoners wasn't a sacred mission or anything like that. It was just a business. *The half-hour precision attack on the prison left the facility's armory and gates wide open. This precipitated the escape of large numbers of prisoners and the subsequent takeover of nearby Scipio and Tarkington College.*

Turtle Bay. *Vonnegut has lived in this mid-Manhattan East Side neighborhood. Among his fictional characters, the parents of Wilbur and Eliza Swain preferred to live there than share their Vermont estate with their freakish offspring. At one point Eliza exclaims,* "**Turtle Bay, Turtle Bay**," she mused. "Did it ever occur to you, dear Brother, that dear Father was not our Father at all?"

"What do you mean?" I said.

"Perhaps Mother stole from the bed and out of the house on a moonlit night," she said, "and mated with a giant sea turtle in **Turtle Bay**."

Hi ho (*Slap* 18-25).

Dan Gregory's cook meets her fate in the same neighborhood. (*Blue* 144:L9) I don't know where this fits into my story, and probably it doesn't fit in at all. It is certainly the most trivial footnote imaginable in a history of Abstract Expressionism, but here it is:

The cook who had begrudgingly fed me my first supper in New York City, and who kept asking, "What next, what next?" died two weeks after I got there. That finally became what was going to happen next: she would drop dead in **Turtle Bay Chemists**, a drugstore two blocks away.

But here was the thing: the undertaker discovered that she wasn't just a woman, and she wasn't just a man, either. She was somewhat both. She was a hermaphrodite.

U

U-99. The Nazi submarine which intercepts Bokonon on his return voyage from England to Tobago. They take him prisoner and sink his schooner, the Lady's Slipper. *The sub is then captured and sunk by the British destroyer* Raven.

Ubriaco, Frank and Marilyn. *Frank is the fifty-three-year-old owner of the Coffee Shop in the Hotel Royalton, which in turn is owned by Hospitality Associates, Ltd., a RAMJAC subsidiary, in* Jailbird. *Frank is anxious to participate in every aspect of the restaurant's operation, from taking orders to cooking to working the cash register. Despite feeling ugly and dirty, Walter Starbuck is greeted warmly and treated well by Frank and his employees. For the humane way Walter is treated, Mary Kathleen O'Looney makes Ubriaco an executive vice-president of RAMJAC's McDonald's Hamburgers Division.*

Ubriaco is most notable for his misshapen hand. A year before Walter met him, Frank dropped his Accutron Bulova watch into the Fry-o-lator and mindlessly stuck his hand in to retrieve it.

Once living the high life as a RAMJAC executive, Frank meets the seventeen-year-old Marilyn at a discotheque and marries her. He plays on Marilyn's intrigue over the single white glove worn over his bad hand, by telling her he was burned by a Chinese communist flame thrower in the Korean War. He eventually tells the truth.

Frank's one great innovation for McDonald's is to replace the numbers on the cash registers with pictures of food items. This is necessary because of the increasing difficulty getting new employees smart enough to deal with basic restaurant arithmetic.

Ukwende, Dr. Cyprian. *From the Indaro tribe in Nigeria and equipped with a medical degree from Harvard, Ukwende is an intern at the Midland City County Hospital.* (*BC* 63:L20-21) He felt no kinship with . . . any American blacks. He felt kinship only with Indaros. *He is the presiding physician when*

108-year-old Mary Young dies, the black woman from Kentucky whose "parents had been slaves in Kentucky" (*BC* 63:L3-4).

Ukwende was staying at Dwayne Hoover's Holiday Inn until he could find a suitable apartment. He was one of the physicians on the ambulance which responded to the havoc wrought by Dwayne Hoover's violent outburst.

Ukwende's ancestors had kidnapped an ancestor of *(Eddie)* Key's on the West Coast of Africa, a man named Ojumwa. The Indaros sold him for a musket to British slave traders, who took him on a sailing ship named the "Skylark" to Charleston, South Carolina, where he was auctioned off as a self-propelled, self-repairing farm machine (*BC* 271:L22-27).

Ulm, Arthur Garvey. *One of the many examples of Eliot Rosewater's altruism gone awry.* (*GBR* 79:L19) "That poor **Arthur** told Eliot he wanted to be free to tell the truth, regardless of the economic consequences, and Eliot wrote him a tremendous check right then and there." *Eliot's belief in and hopes for an unfettered and truthful arts community come crashing down after giving Ulm the freedom to produce without the perpetual fear of poverty. Under the spell of Eliot's beneficence and cryptic quips, Ulm takes the money and is transformed into a novelist whose sense of truth and courage become manifested in an 800-page pornographic novel.* (*GBR* 82:L28,34 83:L1, 30) The name of the book was *Get With Child a Mandrake Root*, a line from a poem by John Donne. The dedication read, "For Eliot Rosewater, my compassionate turquoise." And under that was another quotation from Donne:

> A compassionate turquoise which doth tell
> By looking pale, the wearer is not well.

A covering letter from **Ulm** explained that the book was going to be published by Palindrome Press in time for Christmas, and was going to be a joint selection, along with *The Cradle of Erotica*, of a major book club.

> You have no doubt forgotten me, Compassionate Turquoise, *the letter said in part*. The **Arthur Garvey Ulm** you knew was a man well worth forgetting. What a coward he was, and what a fool he was to think he was a poet! And what a long, long time it took him to understand exactly how generous and kind your cruelty was! How much you managed to tell me about what was wrong with me, and what I should do about it, and how few words you used! Here then (fourteen years later) are eight hundred pages of prose by me. They could not have been created by me without you, and I do not mean your money. (Money is shit, which is one of the things I have tried to say in the book.) I mean your insistence that the truth be told about this sick, sick

> society of ours, and that the words for the telling could be found on the walls of restrooms*. . . .
>
> "Let them shoot me, let them hang me, but I have told the truth. The gnashing of the teeth of the Pharisees, Madison Avenue phonies and Philistines will be music to my ears. With your divine assistance, I have let the Djin of truth about them out of the bottle, and they will never, never, never ever get it back in!"

Eliot began to read avidly the truths **Ulm** expected to get killed for telling:

> "CHAPTER ONE"
>
> "I twisted her arm until she opened her legs, and she gave a little scream, half joy, half pain (how do you figure a woman?): as I rammed the old avenger home."

Ulm, Lowell. *The owner of a local car wash and the director of Midland County's civil defense response unit. Rudy Waltz asks Ulm to take radioactivity measurements with his government-issued Geiger counter inside the Waltz's Avondale home. Ulm contacts the federal government with news about the extremely hot mantelpiece.* (*DD* 218:L32, 219:L5) Mother and I had not yet begun to speculate seriously about what the radioactive mantelpiece might have done to our health, nor had we been encouraged to do so. Nor would we ever be encouraged to do so. **Ulm**, the director of civil defense and car-wash tycoon, had been getting advice on our case over the telephone from somebody at the Nuclear Regulatory Commission in Washington, D.C., to the effect that the most important thing was that nobody panic. In order to prevent panic, the workmen who had torn out our fireplace, wearing protective clothing provided by **Ulm**, had been sworn to secrecy—in the name of patriotism, of national security.

uncritical, uncritically (love, bliss, companionship, respect, nurturer). (*ST* 126:L22) Unk had no way of judging the quality of the information contained in the letter. He accepted it all hungrily, **uncritically**.
(*MN* 33:L12, 17-18) No matter what I was really, no matter what I really meant, **uncritical love** was what I needed—and my Helga was the angel who gave it to me.

No young person on earth is so excellent in all respects as to need no **uncritical love**. Good Lord—as youngsters play their parts in political tragedies with casts of billions, **uncritical love** is the only real treasure they can look for.

---

*The reference is to the couplet Eliot had earlier recalled as one of his more favorite and telling rhymes: "We don't piss in your ashtrays, / So please don't throw cigarettes in our urinals" (*GBR* 81:L23-24).

(*GBR* 70:L5) There was a tough element among the Rosewater County poor who, as a matter of pride, stayed away from Eliot and his **uncritical love**, who had the guts to get out of Rosewater County and look for work in Indianapolis or Chicago or Detroit.
(*GBR* 213:L24) "It seems to me," said Trout, "that the main lesson Eliot learned is that people can use all the **uncritical love** they can get."
(*BC* 218:L6) And somebody squealed on him. The Emperor Diocletian had him shot by archers. The picture Mary Alice smiled at with such **uncritical bliss** showed a human being who was so full of arrows that he looked like a porcupine. *The painting as described by Vonnegut is an El Greco depicting the death of Saint Sebastian.*
(*WFG* 111:L27 *Why They Read Hesse*) Again and again, his *(Hesse's)* holy wanderers love wine too much. They do something about it, too. They resolve to keep out of taverns, though they miss the **uncritical companionship** they've had there.
(*Slap* 2:L27-28) When a child, and not watching comedians on film or listening to comedians on the radio, I used to spend a lot of time rolling around on rugs with **uncritically** affectionate dogs we had.
(*PS* 213:L23 *Religion*) What is human dignity, then? It is the favorable opinion, respectful and **uncritical**, which we hold of those most familiar to us. It has been found that we can hold that same good opinion of strangers, if those who teach us and otherwise lead us tell us to.
(*PS* 214:L19 *Religion*) "There is this drawback, though: If you give to that sort of a stranger the **uncritical respect** that you give to friends and relatives, you will also want to understand and help him. There is no way to avoid this."
(*Blue* 74:L9) The other fillip was the undertaker's assumption that Father was a Mohammedan. This was exciting to him. It was his biggest adventure in being **uncritically pious** in a madly pluralistic democracy.
(*Blue* 260:L15) She *(Edith Taft Fairbanks, Rabo's second wife)* was a magical tamer of almost any sort of animal, an overwhelmingly loving and **uncritical nurturer** of anything and everything that looked half alive.
(*FWD* 28:L8) Our father when I, his youngest child, got to know him was, understandably, desperate for **uncritical friendship** from a member of the reputedly compassionate sex, since our mother (his wife) was going insane. Late at night, and always in the privacy of our home, and never with guests present, she expressed hatred for Father as corrosive as hydrofluoric acid. Hydrofluoric acid can eat its way out of a glass bottle, and then through a tabletop and then through the floor, and then straight to Hell.
(*FWD* 114:L14) "Back in the Great Depression, the Royal Astronomers used to say that a United States deprived of that wisdom was nothing but a United States of radio quiz shows and music straight out of the jungles of Darkest Africa. They say now that the same subtraction leaves us a United States of nothing but television quiz shows and rock and roll, which leads, they say, inexorably to dementia. But I find **uncritical respect** for most works by great thinkers of long ago unpleasant, because they almost all accepted as natural and

ordinary the belief that females and minority races and the poor were on earth to be uncomplaining, hardworking, respectful, and loyal servants of white males, who did the important thinking and exercised leadership.

underground. (*PP* 254:L36) There were circles under Katharine's gentle, wondering eyes, and she looked startled when Lasher called on her, as though Lasher, the meeting, the **underground** chamber, had suddenly risen about her in her clean, girlish world. "Oh," she said, and rattled the papers on the table before her.
(*MN* vi:L20) There were no particular targets for the bombs. The hope was that they would create a lot of kindling and drive firemen **underground**.
(*MN* 39:L21) He had a wife, all right, but not **underground** in Indianapolis. *George Kraft/Iona Potapov lied to Campbell about his marital status.*
(*MN* 193:L10) That was the undiluted evil in me, the evil that had had its effect on millions, the disgusting creature good people wanted dead and **underground**—
(*MN* 198:L4) Surprise: Heinz is a Jew, a member of the anti-Nazi **underground** during the war, an Israeli agent after the war and up to the present time.
(*CC* 208:L10) During our first day and night **underground**, tornadoes rattled our manhole cover many times an hour.
(*CC* 216:L9) The menage consisted of Frank, little Newt, and the Crosbys. They had survived in a dungeon in the palace, one far shallower and more unpleasant than the oubliette. They had moved out the moment the winds had abated, while Mona and I had stayed **underground** for another three days.
(*GBR* 39:L15) I had blocked the **underground** rivers that connected her to the Atlantic, Pacific, and Indian Oceans, and made her content with being a splash pool three feet across, four inches deep, chlorinated, and painted blue. *This is part of Dr. Brown's description of his treatment of Sylvia Rosewater.*
(*MH* 223:L22 *Unready to Wear*) "You're right about how fast things change," said Doctor Remenzel. "You're wrong about the colored people who've eaten here. This used to be a busy part of the **Underground** Railroad."
(*BC* 116:L10) The **underground** stream which passed through the bowels of Sacred Miracle Cave was polluted by some sort of industrial waste which formed bubbles as tough as ping-pong balls.
(*Slap* 198:L13) The truth was, though, that he was perfectly sane. He had been stationed for the past eleven years in the bottom of a secret, **underground** silo in Rock Creek Park. I had never heard of the silo before. *This is Wilbur Swain's recollection of his meeting with Captain Bernard O'Hare.*
(*PS* 90:L29 *Self-Interview*) VONNEGUT: The Germans got funeral pyres going, burning the bodies to keep them from stinking and from spreading disease. 130,000 corpses were hidden **underground**. It was a terribly elaborate Easter egg hunt.

(*Blue* 34:L3, 21, 25) "I wrote a book about it," she said. "Rather—I wrote about people like you: children of a parent who had survived some sort of mass killing. It's called ***The Underground***. . . ."

The formidable widow Berman told me the plot of ***The Underground***, which is this: Three girls, one black, one Jewish and one Japanese, feel drawn together and separate from the rest of their classmates for reasons they can't explain. They form a little club which they call, again for reasons they can't explain, "***The Underground***."

(*Blue* 272:L23) They *(the canvases of the tryptic* "Blue Windsor Number Seventeen"*)* were recognized for what they were, with shreds of Sateen Dura-Luxe clinging to them here and there, by an inspector from Matsumoto's insurance company, who was looking for fire hazards deep **underground**.

(*Blue* 285:L31) And I had made a schematic cut through the earth below them, so as to show their cellars, too, just as a museum display might give away the secrets of animals' burrows **underground**. *This is part of Karabekian's description of his* "Now It's the Women's Turn."

(*HP* 58:L4) I had won my Silver Star for finding and personally killing 5 enemy soldiers who were hiding in a tunnel **underground**.

(*FWD* 150:L6) What I should have said from the pulpit was that we weren't *going* to Hell. We were *in* Hell, thanks to technology which was telling us what to do, instead of the other way around. And it wasn't just TV. It was weapons which could actually kill everything half a world away. It was vehicles powered by glurp from **underground** which could make a fat old lady go a mile a minute while picking her nose and listening to the radio. And so on. (In what spiritual detail, I should have asked, did the glurp-powered automobile or Harley-Davidson differ from freebased cocaine? And was there anything we wouldn't do to ensure that the glurp kept on coming?) *See also: PP* 182:L24; *CC* 49:L15; 65:L4; *Blue* 34:L12; 35:L5.

The Underground. *The name of Circe Berman's book thematically centered around survivor's syndrome. Rabo recalls:* The formidable widow Berman told me the plot of ***The Underground***, which is this: Three girls, one black, one Jewish and one Japanese, feel drawn together and separate from the rest of their classmates for reasons they can't explain. They form a little club which they call, again for reasons they can't explain, "**The Underground**."

But then it turns out that all three have a parent or grandparent who has survived some man-made catastrophe, and who, without meaning to, passed on to them the idea that the wicked were the living and that the good were dead.

The black is descended from a survivor of the massacre of Ibos in Nigeria. The Japanese is a descendant of a survivor of the atom-bombing of Nagasaki. The Jew is a descendant of a survivor of the Nazi Holocaust (*Blue* 34:L21-35:L2).

Unification Church Korean Evangelical Association. *The church owns the Niagara Power and Light Company, which shuts off the electricity running to* *the prison and Tarkington College after the inmates break out* (*HP* 121:L13-14).

Unitarian, Unitarian Universalist. *Vonnegut often claims to be Unitarian, though how he distinguishes unitarianism from agnosticism is unclear—and maybe irrelevant. His parents were married in Indianapolis' First Unitarian Church. His son Mark was interested in becoming a Unitarian minster when an undergraduate at Swarthmore.*

Vonnegut's first expression of Unitarian uncertainty is meant as a partial explanation of the mercurial Harry Nash. (*MH* 16:L29 30 *Who Am I This Time*) Somebody said one time that Harry ought to go to a psychiatrist so he could be something important and colorful in real life, too—so he could get married anyway, and maybe get a better job than just clerking in Miller's Hardware Store for fifty dollars a week. But I don't know what a psychiatrist could have turned up about him that the town didn't already know. The trouble with Harry was he'd been left on the doorstep of the **Unitarian Church** when he was a baby, and he never did find out who his parents were.
(*WFG* 31:L1, 5 *Yes, We Have No Nirvanas*) A **UNITARIAN** minister heard that I had been to see Maharishi Mahesh Yogi, guru to The Beatles and Donovan and Mia Farrow, and he asked me, "Is he a fake?" His name is Charley. **Unitarians** don't believe in anything. I am a **Unitarian**.

Walter Starbuck's religious background is somewhat complex, though his son took a more determined position. (*JB* 37:L29) I myself was nothing. My father had been secretly baptized a Roman Catholic in Poland, a religion that was suppressed at the time. He grew up to be an agnostic. My mother was baptized a Greek Orthodox in Lithuania, but became a Roman Catholic in Cleveland. Father would never go to church with her. I myself was baptized a Roman Catholic, but aspired to my father's indifference, and quit going to church when I was twelve. When I applied for admission to Harvard, old Mr. McCone, a Baptist, told me to classify myself as a Congregationalist, which I did.

My son is an active **Unitarian**, I hear. His wife told me that she was a Methodist, but that she sang in an Episcopal Church every Sunday for pay. Why not?
(*PS* 204:L8 *Religion*) "I went to a **Unitarian** church for a while, and it might show. The minister said one Easter Sunday that, if we listened closely to the bell on his church, we would hear that it was singing, over and over again, 'No hell, no hell, no hell.' No matter what we did in life, he said, we wouldn't burn throughout eternity in hell. We wouldn't even fry for ten or fifteen minutes. He was just guessing, of course.
(*PS* 211:L14 *Religion*) "In this dream, if it is a dream, it is the two-hundredth anniversary of the birth of William Ellery Channing, a principal founder of **Unitarianism** in the United States. I wish that I had been born into a society like his—small and congenial and prosperous and self-sufficient. The people around here had ancestors in common then. They looked a lot like each other,

dressed a lot like each other, enjoyed the same amusements and food. They were generally agreed as to what was good and what was evil—what God was like, who Jesus was.
(*PS* 213:L6 *Religion*) "When Channing began preaching a new sort of sermon in this town, a sort of sermon we now perceive as **Unitarian**, he was urging his parishioners to credit with human dignity as great as their own persons not at all like their friends and relatives. The time to acknowledge the dignity of strangers, even black ones, had come.
(*FWD* 157:L9, 17) In order not to seem a spiritual quadriplegic to strangers trying to get a fix on me, I sometimes say I am a **Unitarian Universalist** (I breathe). So that denomination claims me as one of its own. It honored me by having me deliver a lecture at a gathering in Rochester, New York, in June 1986. I began (almost exactly as I would begin at the graduation ceremonies at the University of Rhode Island):

"There was a newspaper humorist named Kin Hubbard in my hometown of Indianapolis, where my ancestors were Freethinkers and then **Unitarians** or not much of anything as far as religious labels go. Kin Hubbard attended a graduation ceremony out there in Indiana. He commented afterward on the graduation address to the departing seniors. He said it might be better to spread out the really important stuff over four years instead of saving it all up until the very end."
(*FWD* 163:L24) "When I say that the **Unitarian Universalists**, the people who know pure baloney when they hear it, are something like the early Christians in the catacombs, am I suggesting that contempt for baloney will someday be as widespread as Christianity is today? Well the example of Christianity is not encouraging, actually, since it was nothing but a poor people's religion, a servant's religion, a slave's religion, a woman's religion, a child's religion, and would have remained such if it hadn't stopped taking the Sermon on the Mount seriously and joined forces with the vain and rich and violent. I can't imagine that you would want to do that, to give up everything you believe in order to play a bigger part in world history. *See also: ST* 216:L27; *MN* 49:L17; 168:L9; *PS—Roots* 31:L21; 51:L5-6; *PS—Playmates*164:L15; *PS—Religion* 210:L18-19; *FWD* 72:L22-23; 85:L5; 154:L28; 162:L9.

Universal Will to Become (UWTB). *The mystical Tralfamadorian source of energy and intergalactic communication.* (*ST* 138:L17) **UWTB** is what makes universes out of nothingness—that makes nothingness insist on becoming somethingness. *UWTB powers Salo's spaceship, and he uses half his supply for Winston Niles Rumfoord's Martian colonization and invasion force.*

As a communications medium, UWTB not only transmits messages but helps affect behavioral changes in other life forms. (*ST* 272:L14) It is grotesque for anyone as primitive as an Earthling to explain how these swift communications were effected. Suffice it to say, in such primitive company, that the Tralfamadorians were able to make certain impulses from the

Universal Will to Become echo through the vaulted architecture of the Universe with about three times the speed of light. And they were able to focus and modulate these impulses so as to influence creatures far, far away, and inspire them to serve Tralfamadorian ends.

It was a marvelous way to get things done in places far, far away from Tralfamadore. It was easily the fastest way. *In this manner, all sorts of famous architectural landmarks were used over centuries of Earthling time to transmit messages to Salo. This included The Great Wall of China, the Golden House of the Roman Emperor Nero, the Kremlin, and the Palace of the League of Nations.*

Unk (see **Malachi Constant**).

un-neurotic courage (see **Waltham Kittredge**).

"Unready to Wear" (1953) (see **Dr. Ellis Konigswasser**). *The science fiction short story about Dr. Ellis Konigswasser's discovery which helps people leave their bodies and be free of the illnesses associated with such an existence. Those who practice Kongiswasser's techniques are called amphibians. The government, however, viewed amphibians as traitors.* (*MH* 239:L20-24) The charge against us was a capital offense on the books of the enemy—*desertion*. As far as the enemy was concerned, the amphibians had all turned yellow and run out on their bodies, just when their bodies were needed to do brave and important things for humanity.

Updike, Norman. *The droll mortician in* Hocus Pocus *in charge of moving the graves of Hermann and Sophia Shultz from the nearby Tarkington stables to make room for the new Pahlavi Pavilion.* (*HP* 173:L23) The mortician, who is himself now in a covered trench by the stable, was **Norman Updike**, a descendant of the valley's early Dutch settlers. He went on to tell me with bow-wow cheerfulness back in 1987 that people were generally mistaken about how quickly things rot, turn into good old dirt or fertilizer or dust or whatever. He said scientists had discovered well-preserved meat and vegetables deep in city dumps, thrown away presumably years and years ago. Like Hermann and Sophia Shultz, these theoretically biodegradable works of Nature had failed to rot for want of moisture, which was life itself to worms and fungi and bacteria.

"Even without modern embalming techniques," he said, "ashes to ashes and dust takes much, much longer than most people realize."

Urbana Massacre. *Wilbur Swain's illegitimate son by Wilma Pachysandra-17 von Peterswald was one of the few survivors in this victory by the Duke of Oklahoma. He was forced to become a drummer boy in the Duke's army. At fourteen he paired off with a forty-year-old laundress and sired Melody Oriole-2 von Peterswald.*

Utopia. (*CC* 229:L21, 25) I directed our conversation into the area of **Utopias**, of what might have been, of what should have been, of what might yet be, if the world would thaw.

But Bokonon had been there, too, had written a whole book about **Utopias**, *The Seventh Book*, which he called "Bokonon's Republic." In that book are these ghastly aphorisms:

> The hand that stocks the drug stores rules the world.
>
> Let us start our Republic with a chain of drug stores, a chain of grocery stores, a chain of gas chambers, and a national game. After that, we can write our Constitution.

(*GBR* 20:L27, 21:L21) When the United States of America, which was meant to be a **Utopia** for all, was less than a century old, Noah Rosewater and a few men like him demonstrated the folly of the Founding Fathers in one respect: those sadly recent ancestors had not made it the law of the **Utopia** that the wealth of each citizen should be limited. This oversight was engendered by a weak-kneed sympathy for those who loved expensive things, and by the feeling that the continent was so vast and valuable, and the population so thin and enterprising, that no thief, no matter how fast he stole, could more than mildly inconvenience anyone.

Noah and a few like him perceived that the continent was in fact finite, and that venal office-holders, legislators in particular, could be persuaded to toss up great hunks of it for grabs, and to toss them in such a way as to have them land where Noah and his kind were standing.

Thus did a handful of rapacious citizens come to control all that was worth controlling in America. Thus was the savage and stupid and entirely inappropriate and unnecessary and humorless American class system created. Honest, industrious, peaceful citizens were classed as bloodsuckers, if they asked to be paid a living wage. And they saw that praise was reserved henceforth for those who devised means of getting paid enormously for committing crimes against which no laws had been passed. Thus the American dream turned belly up, turned green, bobbed to the scummy surface of cupidity unlimited, filled with gas, went bang in the noonday sun.

E pluribus unum is surely an ironic motto to inscribe on the currency of this **Utopia** gone bust, for every grotesquely rich American represents property, privileges, and pleasures that have been denied the many. An even more instructive motto, in the light of history made by the Noah Rosewaters, might be: *Grab much too much, or you'll get nothing at all.*

(*GBR* 23:L15) And Eliot became a drunkard, a **Utopian** dreamer, a tinhorn saint, an aimless fool.

Begat he not a soul.

(*GBR* 87:L30) "'Good,' he said again. 'The most exquisite pleasure in the practice of medicine comes from nudging a layman in the direction of terror, then bringing him back to safety again. Eliot certainly has his wires crossed, but the inappropriate thing to which the short circuit has caused him to bring his sexual energies isn't necessarily such a very bad thing.'

"'What is it?' I cried, thinking in spite of myself of Eliot stealing women's underwear, of Eliot snipping off locks of hair on subways, of Eliot as a Peeping Tom." The Senator from Indiana shuddered. "'Tell me, Doctor—tell me the worst. Eliot is bringing his sexual energies to what?'

"'To **Utopia**,' he said."

Frustration made Norman Mushari sneeze.

(*WFG* xxiv:L3 *Preface*) Mr. Nixon himself is a minor character in this book. He is the first President to hate the American people and all they stand for. He believes so vibrantly in his own purity, although he has committed crimes which are hideous, that I am bound to conclude that someone told him when he was very young that all serious crime was sexual, that no one could be a criminal who did not commit adultery or masturbate.

He is a useful man in that he has shown us that our Constitution is a defective document, which makes a childlike assumption that we would never elect a President who disliked us so. So we must amend the Constitution in order that we can more easily eject such a person from office and even put him in jail.

That is my chief **Utopian** scheme for the moment.

(*WFG* 243:L30 *Playboy Interview*) VONNEGUT: It's a sunny little dream I have of a happier mankind. I couldn't survive my own pessimism if I didn't have some kind of sunny little dream. That's mine, and don't tell me I'm wrong: Human beings will be happier—not when they cure cancer or get to Mars or eliminate racial prejudice or flush Lake Erie but when they find ways to inhabit primitive communities again. That's my **utopia**. That's what I want for me.

(*PS* 16:L20, 28 *The First Amendment*) And all that argle-barging that goes on between educated persons in the United States and the Soviet Union is so touching and comical, really, as long as it does not lead to war. It draws its energy, in my opinion, from a desperate wish on both sides that each other's **utopias** should work much better than they do. We want to tinker with theirs, to make it work much better than it does—so that people there, for example, can say whatever they please without fear of punishment. They want to tinker with ours, so that everybody here who wants a job can have one, and so that we don't have to tolerate the sales of fist-fucking films and snuff films and so on.

Neither **utopia** now works much better than the Page typesetting machine, in which Mark Twain invested and lost a fortune. That beautiful contraption actually set type just once, when only Twain and the inventor were watching. *See also: PP* 291:L11; *CC* 108:L34; *GBR* 22:L7; 49:L18; 135:L2; 141:L5 210:L21; *WFG—Address to Graduating Class at Bennington College, 1970* 168:L17; *Slap* 107:L24; 156:L21; *JB* xxvii:L5; *HP* 149:L30; 258:L5; 259:L1.

V

Valentine, Ralston (see *The Son of Jimmy Valentine*).

Valley of the Dolls (see **Jacqueline Susann**).

Van Arsdale, Herbert. (*HP* 183:L8) The President of Tarkington at that time, who was **Herbert Van Arsdale**, no relation to Whitey VanArsdale, the dishonest mechanic, ascribed the Provost's crackup *(Kensington Barber's)* to exhaustion brought on by his tireless efforts to solve the mystery of the disappearance of the golden-haired Lilac Queen.

van Curler, Dr. Ormand. *The manager of Ilium County's farming establishment. What was once a series of family farms throughout the Iroquois Valley was now a single farming entity managed with one hundred workers and machines. So vast was Dr. van Curler's responsibility that he declined to take over the mere two hundred acres of the Gottwald Estate.* (*PP* 132:L33-34) As though to point up the anachronism of Mr. Haycox and the Gottwald place for Paul, one of **Doctor Ormand van Curler**'s men, riding on a tractor, appeared on the other side of the windbreak, snappy in spotless white coveralls, a red baseball cap, cool sandals which almost never touched the ground, and white gloves which, like Paul's hands, rarely touched anything but steering wheels, levers, and switches.

VanArsdale, Whitey. *In* Hocus Pocus, *Whitey is the unscrupulous auto mechanic who tries to sell everyone a new transmission. During the prison break, he and Lyle Hooper ambush and kill three escaped convicts carrying a white flag on their way to negotiate with the legal authorities. Ten minutes later, Whitey was shot dead by another escapee and Hooper was taken prisoner.*

Vanzetti, Bartolomeo (see **Sacco and Vanzetti**).

Veblen, Thorstein. *Eliot Rosewater doesn't recall dreaming of his father, but he frequently dreams of Veblen. Vonnegut also recalls his first exposure to the famous economist.* (*PS* 59:L20-21 *Roots*) But Father's younger brother, Uncle Alex, a Harvard graduate and life insurance salesman, was responsive and amusing and generous with me, was my ideal grown-up friend.

He was also then a socialist, and among the books he gave me, when I was a high school sophomore, was **Thorstein Veblen**'s *Theory of the Leisure Class*. I understood it perfectly and loved it, since it made low comedy of the empty graces and aggressively useless possessions which my parents, and especially my mother, meant to regain someday.

Venus on the Half-shell (see also **Queen Margaret**). *A Kilgore Trout novel lightly skimmed by Fred Rosewater in* God Bless You, Mr. Rosewater. *On the back cover of the novel,* There was a photograph of Trout. He was an old man with a full black beard. He looked like a frightened, aging Jesus, whose sentence to crucifixion had been commuted to imprisonment for life (*GBR* 134:L8-11).

Science fiction writer Philip Jose Farmer appropriated both the name Kilgore Trout and the title Venus on the Half-shell *for his own book. Vonnegut wasn't happy about the event, but he declined to sue over the issue.*

Vicuna *A fictitious planet in a science fiction short story by Frank X. Barlow and published in* Playboy. *Walter Starbuck recalls:* they ran out of time on **Vicuna**, he says. The tragedy of the planet was that its scientists found ways to extract time from topsoil and the oceans and the atmosphere—to heat their homes and power their speedboats and fertilize their crops with it; to eat it; to make clothes out of it; and so on. They served time at every meal, fed it to household pets, just to demonstrate how rich and clever they were. They allowed great gobbets of it to putrefy to oblivion in their overflowing garbage cans.

"On **Vicuna**," says the judge, "we lived as though there were no tomorrow" (*JB* 56:L7, 16). *The Vicunians are forced to take their souls and leave their bodies behind as they search the galaxy for compatible bodies to inhabit. The judge's soul hovers over the Finletter Air Force Base and imagines the compound houses philosophers in a meditation center.* (*JB* 59:L1-10, 60:L1-4) The judge in Dr. Bob Fender's story tries to guess which of the philosophers in the meditation center is the wisest and most contented. He decides that it is a little old man sitting on a cot in a second-story dormitory.

Every so often that little old man is so delighted with his thoughts, evidently, that he claps three times.

So the judge flies into the ear of that little old man and immediately sticks to him forever, sticks to him, according to the story ". . . as tightly as Formica to an epoxy-coated countertop." And what does he hear in that little old man's head but this: *Sally in the garden, / Sitting cinders, / Lifted up her leg / And farted like a man. . . .*

That philosopher, of course, is Walter Starbuck.

Villavicencio, Carlos Daffodil-11. *The dishwasher embraced as a brother by Wilbur Swain because they shared the same extended family name designation. Carlos became a devoted "Sancho Panza" to Wilbur* (*Slap*: 192:L27-28). *Transported by helicopter pilot Captain Bernard O'Hare, Wilbur decides to leave Carlos in Indianapolis where he would be cared for in his later years by the large population of Daffodils living there who had already greeted their arrival with parades and feasts.*

vin-dit (see also **Bokononism**). (*CC* 64:L1-5) It was in the tombstone salesroom that I had my first ***vin-dit***, a Bokononist word meaning a sudden, very personal shove in the direction of Bokononism, in the direction of believing that God Almighty knew all about me, after all, that God Almighty had some pretty elaborate plans for me.
(*CC* 165:L9-15) All things conspired to form one cosmic ***vin-dit***, one mighty shove into Bokononism, into the belief that God was running my life and that He had work for me to do.

And, inwardly, I *sarooned*, which is to say that I acquiesced to the seeming demands of my ***vin-dit***.

Inwardly, I agreed to become the next President of San Lorenzo.

virtue. (*PP* 7:L17) On his office wall, Paul had a picture of the shop as it had been in the beginning. . . . In each face was a defiant promise of physical strength, and at the same time, there was the attitude of a secret order, above and apart from society by **virtue** of participating in important and moving rites the laity could only guess about—and guess wrong.
(*PP* 259:L3) "And then we get back to basic values, basic **virtues**!" said Finnerty. "Men doing men's work, women doing women's work. People doing people's thinking."
(*PP* 262:L4, 6, 8, 10) "That there must be **virtue** in imperfection, for Man is imperfect, and Man is a creation of God.

"That there must be **virtue** in frailty, for Man is frail, and Man is a creation of God.

"That there must be **virtue** in inefficiency, for Man is inefficient, and Man is a creation of God.

"That there must be **virtue** in brilliance followed by stupidity, for Man is alternately brilliant and stupid, and Man is a creation of God." *Excerpted from the Ghost Shirt Society declaration letter written by Professor Ludwig von Neumann and signed by Paul Proteus.*
(*ST* 22:L7) Constant found his memory stuffed with rumpled, overexposed snapshots of all the women he had had, with preposterous credentials testifying to his ownership of even more preposterous enterprises, with testimonials that

attributed to him **virtues** and strengths that only three billion dollars could have.
(*MN* 100:L23) "**Virtues** and vices, pleasures and pains cross boundaries at will." *Howard Campbell protests when, on their very first meeting, Colonel Frank Wirtanen asks/assumes he hates America.*
(*SL5* 14:L12) History in her solemn page informs us that the crusaders were but ignorant and savage men, that their motives were those of bigotry unmitigated, and that their pathway was one of blood and tears. Romance, on the other hand, dilates upon their piety and heroism, and portrays, in her most glowing and impassioned hues, their **virtue** and magnanimity, the imperishable honor they acquired for themselves, and the great services they rendered to Christianity. *Vonnegut quotes from Charles Mackay's* Extraordinary Popular Delusions and the Madness of Crowds, *read aloud by Bernard O'Hare while Vonnegut visits him to help refresh his memory in preparation for writing* Slaughterhouse-Five.
(*SL5* 44:L8) He *(Roland Weary)* dilated upon the piety and heroism of "The Three Musketeers," portrayed, in the most glowing and impassioned hues, their **virtue** and magnanimity, the imperishable honor they acquired for themselves, and the great services they rendered to Christianity. *The Three Musketeers in this case are Roland Weary and two unnamed battalion scouts.*
(*BC* 153:L18) A booby trap was an easily hidden explosive device, which blew up when it was accidentally twiddled in some way. One of the **virtues** of the new type of booby trap was that it could not be smelled by dogs.
(*WFG* 34:L15 *Yes, We Have No Nirvanas*) This new religion (which-is-not-a-religion-but-a-technique) *(transcendental meditation)* offers tremendous pleasure, opposes no existing institutions or attitudes, demands no sacrifices or outward demonstrations of **virtue**, and is risk free.
(*WFG* 207:L7 *Thinking Unthinkable, Speaking Unspeakable*) THE prohibition of the sale of alcoholic beverages in this country was called "The Noble Experiment," among other things. . . . The war in Vietnam might aptly be called "Noble Experiment II," since it is a similarly narrow-minded adventure in **virtue**.
(*JB* xxv:L30) The architect had also been matter-of-fact about the **virtues** of the factory as a fort. Any mob meaning to storm the front gate would first have to cross all that open ground.
(*PS* 64:L10 *When I Lost My Innocence*) "I pity you *Sun* people of today for not having truly great leaders to write about—Roosevelt and Churchill and Chiang Kai-shek and Stalin on the side of **virtue**, and Hitler and Mussolini and Emperor Hirohito on the side of sin. *On May 3, 1980, Vonnegut addressed the celebrants of the 100th anniversary of* The Cornell Daily Sun.
(*PS* 194:L12 *Religion*) "We also wish Knowledge, Goodness, Sympathy, Mercy, Wisdom, Justice, and Truthfulness. We also strive for and venerate all of those attributes from which the fantasy of man has created a God. We also strive for the **virtues** of Temperance, Industriousness, Friendship, and Peace.

We believe in pure ideas based on Truth and Justice." *From Clemens Vonnegut's self-eulogy.*

(*PS* 235:L9 *Children*) Can I say now, with all my heart, what he *(Clemens Vonnegut)* said in his little book in 1900: "We believe in **virtue**, in perfectibility, in progress, in stability of the laws of nature, in the necessity of improving the social conditions and relations, which should be in harmony with that benevolence which conditions the coherence of men"? *Vonnegut's answer—No.*

(*PS* 279:L31 *Jekyll and Hyde Updated*) *(The following is stage direction.) Dr. Jekyll played by JERRY comes out of his house, the image of civic decency, and is recognized and adored by all. . . . While biding his time, he performs acts of civic* ***virtue*** *which are noted and admired by one and all. He picks up a piece of trash dropped by somebody else, puts it in a waste barrel, gives money to a beggar, politely declines an invitation from SALLY the whore, giving her a gentle lecture, and so on.*

(*DD* 39:L19) On his deathbed at the County Hospital, when Father was listing all his **virtues** and vices, he said that at least he had been wonderful with children, that they had all found him a lot of fun. "I understand them," he said.

(*DD* 117:L17) I made no reply and he went on: "You and I and your mother and your brother are descended from solid, stolid, thick-skulled, unimaginative, unmusical, ungraceful German stock whose sole **virtue** is that it can never leave off working."

(*HP* 74:L32) And of course, this enriched their dreams of escaping, but what were those but what we could call in any other context the **virtue** hope?

(*HP* 143:L10) I said that the doubts I might have raised in the students' minds about the **virtues** of the Free Enterprise System, when telling them what my grandfather believed, could in the long run only strengthen their enthusiasm for that system. . . . "People are never stronger," I said, "than when they have thought up their own arguments for believing what they believe. They stand on their own 2 feet that way."

(*FWD* 15:L31) Q: What do you consider the most overrated **virtue**?
A: Teeth.

(*FWD* 39:19) "That confession will seem as damning and barbarous to humorless persons as my sister's fantasy of whizzing through the Louvre on roller skates. At least it has the **virtue** of truthfulness. *Vonnegut refers to the ultimately predictable—if not cliché—construction of most artistic creations. His confession is that he sees the end point of the work long before the machinery has worked itself out, and he longs for its completion.*

(*FWD* 115:L16) "So what is going on over there is really a touching thing for us to watch and hear about, an honest effort to give the common people of a powerful nation more liberty than they or their ancestors have ever known. If the experiment goes on for any length of time—and just a few people could shut it down instantly—we can expect to see it dawn on the citizens of the Soviets that liberty, like **virtue**, is its own reward, which can be a disappointment.

There as here and, in fact, almost everywhere on the planet, the great mass of human beings yearns for rewards that are more substantial.
(*FWD* 200:L17) Before World War I, the Freethinkers had cheerful congregations, and picnics, too, in many parts of this country. If not God, what was there for them to serve during their short stay on Earth? Only one thing was left to serve under such circumstances, which was their community. Why should they behave well (which they did), quite certain as they were that neither Heaven nor Hell awaited them? **Virtue** was its own reward.
(*FWD* 238:L15) The Bible is a useful starting point for discussions with crowds of American strangers, since so many of us know at least a little something about it. It has the added **virtue** of having for contributors at least two geniuses—Moses and Christ.

Vitelli, Giovanni. *The artist whose frescos of scantily dressed gods and goddesses once adorned the walls of the de Medici palazzo in Italy, later owned by Marilee Kemp. After Rabo reads about the Dominican monk Girolamo Savonarola and his successful efforts to scrape the paintings from the walls, he jibes:* One may assume that he was the Rabo Karabekian of his time, and that Christian fundamentalism was his Sateen Dura-Luxe (*Blue* 217:L10-12).

von Braun, Werner. *The German engineer who headed the Nazi rocket program against England. In* Mother Night, *he is an acquaintance of Howard W. Campbell's and danced with Helga at the birthday party of General Walter Dornberger. Campbell tells Kraft/Potapov he ran into von Braun while walking on 52nd street in Manhattan.*

von Furstenberg, Rudolf. *The Salzburg, Austria, friend of the Waltz family who was killed in World War I. Rudy Waltz is named for him. When Rudy's parents went to visit the remaining members of old Rudolf's family, they found only his mother and youngest brother. Impoverished by the war, they were selling their entire estate.* (*DD* 24:L7-14, 28-29) And Mother and Father bought a lot of the **von Furstenbergs**' furniture and linens and crystal, and some battle-axes and swords, chain maces, and helmets and shields.

My brother and I were both conceived in a **von Furstenberg** bed, with a coat of arms on the headboard, and with "The Minorite Church of Vienna," by Adolf Hitler, on the wall over that. . . .

Father and Mother also bought the enormous weather vane from the gatehouse of the **von Furstenberg** estate, and put it atop their cupola back home, making the studio taller than anything in the county, except for the dome of the county courthouse, a few silos, the Fortunes' dairy barn, and the Midland County National Bank.

That weather vane was instantly the most famous work of art in Midland City. Its only competition was a statue of a Union soldier on foot in Fairchild Park. Its arrow alone was twelve feet long, and one hollow copper horseman chased another one down that awesome shaft. The one in back was an Austrian with a lance. The one in front, fleeing for his life, was a Turk with a scimitar.

This engine, swinging now toward Detroit, now toward Louisville, and so on, commemorated the lifting of the Turkish siege of Vienna in 1683.

They also purchased a marble bust of Voltaire, which the Waltz's placed out in the yard where the family slaughtered chickens.

von Killinger, Baron Manfred Freihert. *In 1939 the Baron was German Consul General of San Francisco. He bestowed upon Dr. Lionel Jones the gift of* a diamond swastika on an onyx field (*MN* 56:L10-11).

von Kleigstadt, Dr. Ormand. *The Wyandotte College professor who creates EPICAC in the 1950 short story of the same name.*

von Kleist, Adolf. (*Gal* 49:L24) **Adolf von Kleist**, the Captain of the *Bahía de Darwin*, would in fact become the ancestor of every human being on the face of the earth today.
(*Gal* 119:L6) The Captain of the *Bahía de Darwin*, **Adolf von Kleist**, was a graduate of the United States Naval Academy at Annapolis.
(*Gal* 122:L20) **Adolf von Kleist** . . . was regularly bailed out by his parents from gambling debts and charges of drunken driving and assault and resisting arrest and vandalism and so on until he was twenty-six—when his father came down with Huntington's chorea and murdered his mother. Only then did he begin to assume responsibility for mistakes he made. *Deemed incompetent by* Galapagos' *narrator, Leon Trout, Adolf von Kleist unwittingly becomes the sire of the human race once Mary Hepburn is able to steal his sperm. He feared having children of his own because his father had Huntington's chorea, yet his offspring are free of the disease and begin man's return to the sea as something resembling sea lions.*

von Kleist, Gottfried and Wilhelm. *The uncles of Adolf and Siegfried von Kleist, in* Galápagos. *Gottfried is chairman of Ecuador's largest bank and co-owner with older brother Wilhelm of the* Bahía de Darwin *and the Hotel El Dorado.*

von Kleist, Sebastian. *The highly successful Ecuadorian sculptor, architect, and father of Adolf and Siegfried was also afflicted with Huntington's chorea.* (*Gal* 86:L15-23) It *(the disease)* usually lay in ambush, and undetectable by any known test, until the wretch who had inherited it was well into his or her adult years. The father of the brothers, for example, led an unclouded and productive life until he was fifty-four—at which time he began to dance involuntarily, and to see things which weren't there. And then he killed his wife, a fact which was hushed up. The murder was reported to the police, and so treated by them, as a household accident.

von Kleist, Siegfried. *The manager of the Hotel El Dorado and the younger brother of Captain Adolf von Kleist. Both he and his brother were fearful of carrying the gene for Huntington's chorea, so neither ever married or reproduced. Siegfried* was generally an idler, having inherited considerable money, but had been shamed by his uncles into, so to speak, "pulling his own weight" in this particular family enterprise (*Gal* 49:L1-4). *On the afternoon of November 27, 1986, the same day Peru declared war on Ecuador, Siegfried came down with the same frightful symptoms of the disease his father suffered. After watching Zenji Hiroguchi and Andrew MacIntosh get shot to death and listening to the beginning of the air attack, Siegfried bravely took a bus and gathered together the few travelers who booked passage on "the Nature Cruise of the Century" and made his way down to the docks. He and his drunken brother managed to get them on board the* Bahía de Darwin. *The prospects of the disease so horrified him that he planned on committing suicide by ramming the bus into a downtown building. However, a Peruvian pilot exploded a rocket in a nearby estuary, which caused a surging six-meter wave to wash the bus off the dock, simultaneously snapping the ship's mooring line. All in the same moment Siegfried was killed and his brother set free in the harbor to become the unwitting father of humanity's next step along the evolutionary chain.*

von Koenigswald, Dr. Schlichter. *The fourteen-year veteran of the Nazi S.S. and former Auschwitz camp physician who becomes "Papa" Monzano's personal physician as well as an attending physician at Julian Castle's House of Hope and Mercy in the Jungle. Jokingly considered penance, Castle says,* If he keeps going at his present rate, working night and day, the number of people he's saved will equal the number of people he let die—in the year 3010 (*CC* 153:L32-34). *When "Papa" lay dying in the castle, it was von Koenigswald who climbed in his bed (Bokonon's boat the* Lady's Slipper*) and delivered the Bokononist last rites. After "Papa" swallowed the bit of ice-nine hanging in the cylinder around his neck, von Koenigswald became the second person to die from Dr. Hoenikker's creation. He touched the dusty whiteness on Monzano's stone cold lips, went to the basin to wash it off and turned the water into a solid sphere of ice. Out of curiosity, he touched his tongue to the orb and solidified.*

von Konigswald, Major Siegfried. *The Nazi S.S. officer known as "The Beast of Yugoslavia," killed in hand-to-hand combat with Harold Ryan. Unabashedly, he recalls,* They used to call me "The Beast of Yugoslavia," on account of all the people I had tortured and shot—and hanged. We'd bop 'em on the head. We'd hook 'em up to the electricity. We'd stick 'em with hypodermic syringes full of all kinds of stuff. One time we killed a guy with orange juice. There was a train wreck, and two of the freight cars were loaded with oranges, so we had oceans of orange juice. It was a joke—how much orange juice we had. And we were interrogating a guy one day, and he wouldn't talk, and the next thing I know—somebody's filling up this big syringe with orange juice.

There was a guerrilla war going on. You couldn't tell who was a guerrilla and who wasn't. Even if you got one, it was still a civilian you got. Telling Americans what a guerrilla war is like—that's coals to Newcastle. How do you like that for idiomatic English? "Coals to Newcastle" . . . .

I'm up in Heaven now, like that little Wanda June kid. I wasn't hit by no ice-cream truck. Harold Ryan killed me with his bare hands. He was good. My eyes popped out. My tongue stuck out like a red banana. I shit in my pants. It was a mess (*WJ* 76-78).

von Neumann, Ludwig. *The former political science professor at Union College in Schenectady, New York, who becomes the chief public information officer in the Ghost Shirt Society's rebellion. The professor's academic life was displaced by the decision to tear down the university's Social Sciences Building and replace it with a Heat and Power Laboratory. Both he and Paul Proteus were members of the Ilium Historical Society before that was torn down for the Ilium Atomic Reactor.*

Professor von Neumann forges Paul's name on the Ghost Shirt press release outlining their philosophy and demands. The letter asserts that technology is, indeed, an overall benefit to mankind; however, when society abdicates self-governance in favor of designs determined by inanimate entities, the result goes against natural law. (*PP* 260-262) "Again, let me say we are all in this together, but the rest of us, for what we perceive as good, plain reasons, have changed our minds about the divine right of machines, efficiency, and organization, just as men of another age changed their minds about the divine right of kings, and about the divine rights of many other things.

"During the past three wars, the right of technology to increase in power and scope was unquestionably, in point of national survival, almost a divine right. Americans owe their lives to superior machines, techniques, organization, and managers and engineers. For these means of surviving the wars, the Ghost Shirt Society and I thank God. But we cannot win good lives for ourselves in peacetime by the same methods we used to win battles in wartime. The problems of peace are altogether more subtle.

"I deny that there is any natural or divine law requiring that machines, efficiency, and organization should forever increase in scope, power, and complexity, in peace as in war. I see the growth of these now, rather, as the result of a dangerous lack of law.

"The time has come to stop the lawlessness in that part of our culture which is your special responsibility. . . .

"I propose that men and women be returned to work as controllers of machines, and that the control of people by machines be curtailed. I propose, further, that the effects of changes in technology and organization on life patterns be taken into careful consideration, and that the changes be withheld or introduced on the basis of this consideration.

"These are radical proposals, extremely difficult to put into effect. But the need for their being put into effect is far greater than all of the difficulties, and infinitely greater than the need for our national holy trinity, Efficiency, Economy, and Quality.

"Men, by their nature, seemingly, cannot be happy unless engaged in enterprises that make them feel useful. They must, therefore, be returned to participation in such enterprises.

"I hold, and the members of the Ghost Shirt Society hold:

"That there must be virtue in imperfection, for Man is imperfect, and Man is a creation of God.

"That there must be virtue in frailty, for Man is frail, and Man is a creation of God.

"That there must be virtue in inefficiency, for Man is inefficient, and Man is a creation of God.

"That there must be virtue in brilliance followed by stupidity, for Man is alternately brilliant and stupid, and Man is a creation of God.

"You perhaps disagree with the antique and vain notion of Man's being a creation of God.

"But I find it a far more defensible belief than the one implicit in intemperate faith in lawless technological progress—namely, that man is on earth to create more durable and efficient images of himself, and, hence, to eliminate any justification at all for his own continued existence."

The professor and the other leaders of the rebellion are more understanding about the benign benefits of technology than is the great mass of rebels. He pays for this understanding by getting struck in the head by a rioter wielding the Sacred Mace of The Order of the Aurora Borealis while trying to prevent the destruction of a radio tower. Paul thinks of von Neumann as the consummate academician: He had been less interested in achieving a premeditated end than in seeing what would happen with given beginnings (*PP* 294:L38, 295:L1-2). *As the Ghost Shirt leadership looks out over the ruins of Ilium and prepares to surrender, von Neumann concludes,* "This isn't the end, you know. . . . Nothing ever is, nothing ever will be—not even Judgment Day" (*PP* 295:L14-15).

von Peterswald, David Daffodil-11. *The Tourette's stricken, fifteen year old son of Wilma Pachysandra-17 von Peterswald and the brother of Wilbur Swain—related through the government-sponsored extended family program.*

von Peterswald, Dr. Felix Bauxite-13. *The husband of Wilma von Peterswald, Felix invented "The Hooligan," which enabled people to talk with the dead (named after the janitor who first discovered the device's unique feature and whose lunch pail acted as the antennae). Wilbur uses the device to speak with his sister Eliza.* (*Slap* 193:L24-24) "It was the Chinese who told me about the astonishing discovery my husband, **Dr. Felix Bauxite-13 von Peterswald**, made just before he died. My son, who is incidentally a

Daffodil-11, like yourself, and I have kept this discovery a secret ever since, because the light it throws on the situation of human beings in the Universe is very demoralizing, to say the least. It has to do with the true nature of what awaits us all after death. What awaits us, Dr. Swain, is tedious in the extreme."

(*Slap* 230:L20) The talkers identified themselves as persons in the afterlife. They were backed by a demoralized chorus of persons who complained to each other of tedium and social slights and minor ailments, and so on.

As **Dr. von Peterswald** said in his secret diary: "It sounded like nothing so much as the other end of a telephone call on a rainy autumn day—to a badly run turkey farm."

von Peterswald, Melody Oriole-2. *The sixteen-year-old granddaughter of Wilbur Swain and Wilma Pachysandra-17 von Peterswald. Melody came to live with Wilbur when she was only twelve. She had already been impregnated by the King of Michigan who kept her in his harem. Shortly after she made her way to her grandfather, Melody gave birth to a stillborn son, which Wilbur cryptically cites as symbolic of his memoirs's meaning.* (*Slap* 80:L16-24, 81:L3-6) Yes, and if archaeologists of the future find this book of mine, they will be spared the fruitless labor of digging through the pyramid in search of its meaning. There are no secret treasure rooms in there, no chambers of any kind.

Its meaning, which is minuscule in any event, lies beneath the manhole cover over which the pyramid is constructed. It is the body of a stillborn male.

. . . The pyramid itself is entirely the idea of **Melody** and Isadore, who became her lover later on. It is a monument to a life that was never lived—to a person who was never named.

Melody was the daughter of Swain's illegitimate son by the widowed Mrs. von Peterswald. Her father survived the Urbana Massacre and became a drummer in the victorious army of the Duke of Oklahoma. At fourteen, the (unnamed) son and a forty-year-old laundress working for the army gave birth to Melody. Melody's middle name was given to guard against future confrontations with the King of Michigan, the Duke of Oklahoma's arch rival. Nevertheless, she was orphaned at age six after the Battle of Iowa City, and placed in the King of Michigan's harem composed of children with the same middle name as his. Melody stole a Dresden candlestick from the king and escaped one night to search for her grandfather, whom her father often told her was also a king.

As Wilbur begins to write his memoirs, Melody is pregnant again. The father is Isadore Raspberry-19 Cohen, and he also lives with Swain. Vonnegut's prologue to Slapstick, *in which he explains the special relationship he shared with his sister Alice, closes with his musings about the true identities of both Wilbur and Melody.* (*Slap* 19:L11-19) He *(Wilbur)* lives there *(Manhattan)* with his illiterate, rickety, pregnant little granddaughter, **Melody**. Who is he really? I guess he is myself—experimenting with being old.

Who is **Melody**? I thought for a while that she was all that remained of my memory of my sister. I now believe that she is what I feel to be, when I experiment with old age, all that is left of my optimistic imagination, of my creativeness.

von Peterswald, Wilma Pachysandra-17. *The Urbana, Illinois, wife of Dr. von Peterswald, inventor of "The Hooligan," a device which enables one to speak with the dead. After her husband died, she earned a living for herself and David, her Tourette's stricken son, by giving piano lessons. (Most members of the Pachysandra extended family were musical.) Mrs. von Peterswald writes to Wilbur Swain on behalf of his sister Eliza, asking him to visit and use "The Hooligan," to speak with her. After Wilbur donated part of his large supply of tri-benzo-Deportamil to help control David's affliction, Wilbur went into a six-day fit of withdrawal during which he had sex with Wilma. The result was a son who eventually sired Melody Oriole-2 von Peterswald.* (*Slap* 237:L6-9) Yes, and somewhere in there the widow passed on to him *(Wilbur)* what she had learned from the Chinese—that they had become successful manipulators of the Universe by combining harmonious minds.

von Schwefelbad, Baron Ulrich Werther. *While imprisoned in Jerusalem, Howard Campbell received news that his best friend in Germany, Heinz Schildknecht, was employed in Ireland by the former German aristocrat. In fact, Heinz was a double-agent during the war and never left the intelligence game.* (*MN* 88:L29-30) The Institute delights me with the news that Heinz is now in Ireland, is chief grounds-keeper for **Baron Ulrich Werther von Schwefelbad**. **Von Schwefelbad** bought a big estate in Ireland after the war.

von Strelitz, Arthur. *In* Jailbird*, the Harvard associate professor of anthropology who befriends Walter Starbuck and Mary Kathleen O'Looney, allowing them to use his house on Brattle Street to make love. His academic specialty was the headhunters of the Solomon Islands.*

Born into an aristocratic Prussian family, von Strelitz was lecturing at Harvard in 1933 when Hitler took power in Germany. He never returned home. His father died of pneumonia during the Siege of Leningrad while commanding a corps of S.S. troops. Arthur von Strelitz disappeared while an American spy on the Japanese occupied Solomon Islands.

Vonnegut, Alice. *Alice Vonnegut and her husband, James Carmalt Adams, died within forty-eight hours of each other. He died first in a commuter train accident and Alice saw the notice in the* New York Daily News. *Kurt Vonnegut adopted their three oldest children.* (*MH* xiv:L3-4) My only sister, five years older than I, died when she was forty. She was over six feet tall, too, by an angstrom unit or so. She was heavenly to look at, and graceful, both in and out of water. She was a sculptress. She was christened "**Alice**," but she used to deny that she was really an **Alice**. I agreed. Everybody agreed. Sometime in a dream maybe I will find out what her real name was.

Her dying words were, "No pain." Those are good dying words. It was cancer that killed her.

And I realize now that the two main themes of my novels were stated by my siblings: "Here I am cleaning shit off of practically everything" and "No pain." The contents of this book are samples of work I sold in order to finance the writing of the novels. Here one finds the fruits of Free Enterprise.

(*Slap* 11:L15-27) There was an empty seat between us, which was spooky poetry. It could have been a seat for our sister **Alice**, whose age was halfway between mine and Bernard's. She wasn't in that seat and on her way to her beloved Uncle Alex's funeral, for she had died among strangers in New Jersey, of cancer—at the age of forty-one.

"Soap opera!" she said to my brother and me one time, when discussing her own impending death. She would be leaving four young boys behind, without any mother.

"Slapstick," she said.

Hi ho.

(*Slap* 13:L7-11) Since **Alice** had never received any religious instruction, and since she had led a blameless life, she never thought of her awful luck as being anything but accidents in a very busy place.

Good for her.

(*FWD* 27:L8) In the household of my childhood and youth, my sister **Alice**, dead for many years now (and missed like heck by me), was the maiden and our father was the elusive and spookily enchanted unicorn. My only other sibling, my own big brother who went to MIT, Bernard, and I could never catch him. To him we weren't all that interesting. As far as the two of us are concerned, this is not a remotely tragic tale. We were tough. We could take it. We had other fans.

(*FWD* 37:L11, 13, 22, 25) But to get back to the thing between my father and my sister, the unicorn and the maiden: Father, no more a Freudian than Lewis Carroll, made **Alice** his principal source of encouragement and sympathy. He made the most of an enthusiasm they had in common, which was for the visual arts. **Alice** was just a girl, remember, and aside from the embarrassment of having a unicorn lay its head in her lap, so to speak, she was traumatized mainly by having every piece of sculpture or picture she made celebrated by Father as though it were Michelangelo's Pieta or the ceiling of the Sistine Chapel. In later life (which was going to last only until she was forty-one) this made her a lazy artist. (I have often quoted her elsewhere as saying, "Just because people have talent, that doesn't mean they have to do something with it.")

"My only sister, **Alice**," I wrote, again in *Architectural Digest*, "possessed considerable gifts as a painter and sculptor, with which she did next to nothing. **Alice**, who was six feet tall and a platinum blonde, asserted one time that she could roller-skate through a great museum like the Louvre, which

she had never seen and which she wasn't all that eager to see, and which she in fact would never see, and fully appreciate every painting she passed. She said that she would be hearing these words in her head above the whir and clack of her wheels on the terrazzo: 'Got it, got it, got it.'"
(*FWD* 51:L30) "We went out in an old, leaky rowboat, which all my life I had called 'The Beralikur,' a mixture of my first name with those of my siblings, Bernard and **Alice**. But that name was not painted on the boat, which would have been redundant. Everybody who was anybody at Maxincuckee already knew that the name of that leaky boat was the Beralikur.
(*FWD* 73:L13) (Speaking of composers: My sister **Alice** asked our father when she was about ten years old if he and Mother used to dance to Beethoven.)
(*FWD* 96:L16) One nice thing: Camp Atterbury was so close to Indianapolis that I was able to sleep in my own bedroom and use the family car on weekends. But Mother died on one of those. My sister **Alice** gave birth to Mother's first grandchild (whom I would adopt along with his two brothers when he was fourteen) maybe six weekends after that, about the time of the D-Day landings in France.
(*FWD* 187:L6-7) Not only would I have written that if I hadn't died, but I would have rejoiced in the birth of three more grandchildren. I already had three. My mother never saw any of her one dozen grandchildren, although my sister **Alice** was pregnant with her first one, Jim, when **Alice** and I found Mother dead. (No prospect of good news, obviously, could rescue Mother. She felt as awful as anybody does nowadays in Mozambique, where there is no end to murdering but almost no suicide.)

Vonnegut, Bernard. *There are two Bernard Vonneguts, Kurt's paternal grandfather as well as his older brother. His grandfather was artistic from an early age, and when he grew older he didn't want to work in the family hardware business. He eventually became an architect in New York City and returned to Indianapolis at the insistence of his parents. He married Nannette Schnull, a sociable woman uninterested in the arts. Their three children were Kurt, Irma, and Alex.*

Bernard Vonnegut's son Kurt sired Bernard (named for the grandfather), Alice, and Kurt Jr. This younger Bernard was a chemistry professor at the State University of New York at Albany. He helped invent the method for seeding rain clouds. He received his undergraduate and doctoral degrees from the Massachusetts Institute of Technology. (*WFG* 91:L3-11) He was notorious in Schenectady for having a horrendously messy laboratory. There was a safety officer in the laboratory who called on him regularly, begging him to clean up the death traps all around the room. One day my brother said to him, "If you think this is a mess, you should see what it's like up here." And my brother pointed to his own head. I loved him for that. We love each other very much, even though I am a humanist and he is physicist.

Vonnegut, Carl Hiroaki and Emiko Alice. *Vonnegut's grand-nephew and grand-niece, the children of Peter Vonnegut and Mishi Minatoya.* (*PS* 238:L10-12) ". . . my brother's only grandchildren. They, too, are, among other things, de St. Andrés. Strange and nice."

Vonnegut, Clemens. *Vonnegut's great-grandfather who wrote an* Instruction in Morals, *from which Vonnegut took the following quotation for his inscription to* Palm Sunday, "Whoever entertains liberal views and chooses a consort that is captured by superstition risks his liberty and his happiness."

Born in Munster in Westphalia in 1824, Clemens Vonnegut came to the United States in 1848, settling in Indianapolis in 1850. His father had been a tax collector for the Duke of Westphalia. In Indianapolis he met another German immigrant named Vollmer who had been settled here a few years and was already established in business for himself in a small way as a retail merchant in hardware and sundry merchandise. The two became friends, and Vollmer invited **Vonnegut** to join him in this enterprise. The firm then became known as Vollmer & **Vonnegut**. After a short association Vollmer decided to make a journey out West to explore the new country and visit the gold fields recently discovered in California. He was never heard from again, and presumably lost his life in the 'Wild West' (*PS* 25:L7-16 *Roots*). *Vollmer & Vonnegut became the Vonnegut Hardware Company, a family business which thrived into the 20th century. In 1852 he married Katarina Blank.*
(*PS* 27:L1-15) "Many tales were told of **Clemens Vonnegut**. When he was elected to the Board of School Commissioners, he found that the local banks did not pay interest on the somewhat large deposits which the Board carried to finance its operations. He demanded that the banks pay interest on the Board's deposits. This was then considered to be an offensive innovation in the customary and comfortable practice which until then had prevailed. The banker John P. Frenzel then called upon **Clemens** at his office and loudly upbraided him. **Clemens** pretended to be hard of hearing, and capped his ears. Frenzel shouted louder. Still **Clemens** pretended not to hear. Frenzel raised his voice and interjected profanity, but to no avail. **Clemens** would not 'hear' him. Finally Frenzel stormed out—still not heard. But thenceforth the banks paid interest and have continued to do so to this day."

Clemens Vonnegut is a significant character because he was a self-professed Free Thinker, though he was raised Roman Catholic. Vonnegut says Clemens was what he only aspires to be, "a cultivated eccentric." He also calls him "a skeptic, one who rejects faith in the unknowable," something Vonnegut wishes to ascribe to himself, as well.

More significantly, Vonnegut and his great-grandfather seemingly share more than a similarity of views upon such weighty matters as religion; they share a manner of expression which is wholly original for each. In 1874 Clemens planned his own funeral, including his eulogy. In 1981, while Vonnegut was preparing Palm Sunday, *his brother Bernard sent him a copy of Clemens'* Instruction on Morals *as well as some of his "comments on life and death." The similarity of expression is so close, some scholars thought Kurt Vonnegut wrote it.* (*PS* 193:L18-31, 194:L1-32) "Friends or Opponents: To all of you who stand here to deliver my body to the earth:

"To you, my next of kin:

"Do not mourn! I have now arrived at the end of the course of life, as you will eventually arrive at yours. I am at rest and nothing will ever disturb my deep slumber.

"I am disturbed by no worries, no grief, no fears, no wishes, no passions, no pains, no reproaches from others. All is infinitely well with me.

"I departed from life with loving, affectionate feelings for all mankind, and I admonish you: Be aware of this truth that the people on this earth could be joyous, if only they would live rationally and if they would contribute mutually to each others' welfare.

"This world is not a vale of sorrows if you will recognize discriminatingly what is truly excellent in it; and if you will avail yourself of it for mutual happiness and well-being. Therefore, let us explain as often as possible, and particularly at the departure from life, that we base our faith on firm foundations, on Truth for putting into action our ideas which do not depend on fables and ideas which Science has long ago proven to be false.

"We also wish Knowledge, Goodness, Sympathy, Mercy, Wisdom, Justice, and Truthfulness. We also strive for and venerate all of those attributes from which the fantasy of man has created a God. We also strive for the virtues of Temperance, Industriousness, Friendship, and Peace. We believe in pure ideas based on Truth and Justice.

"Therefore, however, we do not believe, cannot believe, that a Thinking Being existed for millions and millions of years, and eventually and finally out of nothing—through a Word—created this world, or rather this earth with its Firmament, its Sun and Moon and the Stars.

"We cannot believe that this Being formed a human being from clay and breathed into it an Immortal Soul, and then allowed this human being to procreate millions, and then delivered them all into unspeakable misery, wretchedness and pain for all eternity. Nor can we believe that the descendents of one or two human beings will inevitably become sinners; nor do we believe that through the criminal executions of an Innocent One may we be redeemed." (*PS* 236:L11 *Children*) "Truth," he *(Clemens Vonnegut)* says, "must always be recognized as the paramount requisite of human society." As I myself said in another place, I began to have my doubts about truth after it was dropped on Hiroshima.

CLEMENS Vonnegut wrote of powerful and rich families founded by criminals. He despised them. He himself founded a dynasty based on hard work, prudence, and honest dealing.

Vonnegut, Dr. Mark. *The oldest of Vonnegut's natural children. After graduating from Swarthmore and experimenting with nontraditional lifestyles, Mark Vonnegut suffered a schizophrenic breakdown. He recovered and wrote* *about his experiences in the critically acclaimed* The Eden Express. *He went on to graduate from Harvard Medical School.*

Interestingly, Kurt Vonnegut was writing about schizophrenia long before his son's illness. He has since referred to his son's affliction, recovery, and writing on numerous occasions in his speeches. Toward the close of Fates Worse Than Death, *Vonnegut includes the full text of his afterword to a new edition of his son's book. He chiefly speaks about the medical community's struggle with treating mental disorders and Vietnam, both symptoms of man's inability to communicate. Vonnegut illustrates his point by summarizing Kilgore Trout's short story "The Dancing Fool."* (*PS* 241:L19-32, 242:L1-20 *Children*) "But I am a storyteller, not a cultural anthropologist, no matter what the diploma says. And I am not even the best storyteller in my own family when it comes to the relationship of culture to mental health. My son **Mark** is the best storyteller in that area. He wrote an excellent book about going crazy and recovering. It is called *The Eden Express*. **Mark** remembers everything. His wish is to tell people who are going insane something about the shape of the roller coaster they are on. It helps sometimes to know the shape of a roller coaster. How many of you here have taken Thorazine?

"**Mark** has taught me never to romanticize mental illness, never to imagine a brilliant and beguiling schizophrenic who makes more sense about life than his or her doctor or even the president of Harvard University. **Mark** says that schizophrenia is as ghastly and debilitating as smallpox or rabies or any other unspeakable disease you care to name. Society cannot be blamed, and neither, thank God, can the friends and relatives of the patient. Schizophrenia is an internal chemical catastrophe. It is a case of monstrously bad genetic luck, bad luck of a sort encountered in absolutely every sort of society—including the Australian aborigines and the middle class of Vienna, Austria, before the Second World War.

"Plenty of other writers at this very moment are writing a story about an admirable, perhaps even a divine schizophrenic. Why? Because the story is wildly applauded every time it is told. It blames the culture and the economy and the society and everything but the disease itself for making the patient unwell. **Mark** says that is wrong.

"As his father, though, I am still free to say this, I think: I believe that a culture, a combination of ideas and artifacts, can sometimes make a healthy person behave against his or her best interests, and against the best interests of the society and the planet, too.

In his inscription to Bluebeard, *Vonnegut quotes his son,* "We are here to help each other get through this thing, whatever it is."

—**Dr. Mark Vonnegut, M.D.** *(Letter to Author, 1985)*

Vonnegut, Edith. *The name of both Vonnegut's mother and one of his daughters. His mother's maiden name was Lieber. She committed suicide in the early morning hours of Mother's Day, 1944. This is the same date Vonnegut gives to the death of the pregnant Eloise Metzger when Rudy Waltz* *fires an errant shot from the upstairs gun room of their Midland City home in* Deadeye Dick. *In Vonnegut's public lectures he has stated Rudy did no more than he had done as a young boy in Indianapolis.*

Vonnegut, Jane Cox. *Vonnegut's childhood sweetheart and first wife to whom he was married for twenty-five years until they separated and divorced in 1970. He dedicates* Player Piano *to her with a quote from the* Bible,

> *For Jane—God Bless Her*
>
> CONSIDER THE LILIES OF THE FIELD, HOW THEY GROW:
> THEY TOIL NOT, NEITHER DO THEY SPIN;
> AND YET I SAY UNTO YOU,
> THAT EVEN SOLOMON IN ALL HIS GLORY
> WAS NOT ARRAYED LIKE ONE OF THESE . . .
> MATTHEW 6:28.

About their breakup Vonnegut writes: We are still good friends, as they say. Like so many couples who are no longer couples these days, we have been through some terrible, unavoidable accident that we are ill-equipped to understand. Like our six children, we only just arrived on this planet and we were doing the best we could. We never saw what hit us. It wasn't another woman, it wasn't another man.

We woke up in ambulances headed for different hospitals, so to speak, and would never get together again. We were alive, yes, but the marriage was dead.

And it was no Lazarus.

It was a good marriage for a long time—and then it wasn't. The shock of having our children no longer need us happened somewhere in there. We were both going to have to find other sorts of seemingly important work to do and other compelling reasons for working and worrying so. But I am beginning to explain, which is a violation of a rule I lay down whenever I teach a class in writing: "All you can do is tell what happened. You will get thrown out of this course if you are arrogant enough to imagine that you can tell me why it happened. You do not know. You cannot know."

SO I am embarrassed about the failure of my first marriage (*PS* 188:L26-32, 189:L1-15 *Embarrassment*).

(*PS* 192:L2 *Religion*) TOWARD the end of our marriage, it was mainly religion in a broad sense that **Jane** and I fought about. She came to devote herself more and more to making alliances with the supernatural in her need to increase her strength and understanding—and happiness and health. This was painful to me. She could not understand and cannot understand why that should have been painful to me, or why it should be any of my business at all.

And it is to suggest to her and to some others why it was painful that I chose for this book's epigraph a quotation from a thin book, *Instruction in*

Morals, published in 1900 and written by my Free Thinker great-grandfather Clemens Vonnegut, then seventy-six years old:

"Whoever entertains liberal views and chooses a consort that is captured by superstition risks his liberty and his happiness."

Vonnegut, Kurt, Sr. *Kurt Vonnegut's father worked as an architect in Indianapolis, as did his father. In the "Roots" chapter of* Palm Sunday, *there is a fairly lengthy treatment of the family. That particular section of the chapter is excerpted from John Rauch's "An Account of the Ancestry of Kurt Vonnegut, Jr., by an Ancient Friend of His Family." In the preface to* Wanda June, *Vonnegut recalls,* Somewhere in there my father died, and one of the last things he said to me was that I had never written a story with a villain in it (*WJ* ix:L15-17).

Vonnegut, Uncle Alex. (*ST* dedication) FOR **ALEX VONNEGUT**, SPECIAL AGENT, WITH LOVE

(*WFG* 181:L1, 4 *Reflections on My Own Death*) My **Uncle Alex** has just calculated in a letter to me that he is a thousand months old, and he told me another time that dying is like a candle's going out. Combustion stops. **Uncle Alex** is right.

(*Slap* 8:L2-3) We went back *(to Indianapolis)* last July for the funeral of our **Uncle Alex Vonnegut**, the younger brother of our late father—almost the last of our old-style relatives, of the native American patriots who did not fear God, and who had souls that were European.

(*Slap* 9:L6, 10) At any rate, if **Uncle Alex**, the atheist, found himself standing before Saint Peter and the Pearly Gates after he died, I am certain he introduced himself as follows:

"My name is **Alex Vonnegut**. I'm an alcoholic."

Good for him.

(*Slap* 11:L19) There was an empty seat between us, which was spooky poetry. It could have been a seat for our sister Alice, whose age was halfway between mine and Bernard's. She wasn't in that seat and on her way to her beloved **Uncle Alex**'s funeral, for she had died among strangers in New Jersey, of cancer—at the age of forty-one.

(*Slap* 12:L12-13) She *(Kurt's sister Alice)* died at about the same time of day that **Uncle Alex** died—an hour or two after the sun went down.

(*Slap* 16:L3) Be that as it may, she *(Alice)* had vanished entirely as my audience by the time **Uncle Alex** died.

(*Slap* 17:L16) "People from our great-grandfathers' generation would mingle with our own, when we were young—" I said, "and all the generations in between. Arrivals and departures would be announced. **Uncle Alex** would leave for his job as a spy in Baltimore. You would come home from your freshman year at M.I.T."

(*Slap* 19:L23) The old man is writing his autobiography. He begins it with words which my late **Uncle Alex** told me one time should be used by religious skeptics as a prelude to their nightly prayers.

These are the words: "To whom it may concern." *Vonnegut sets up the opening of* Slapstick, *which is the autobiography of Wilbur Swain, the "old man" referred to here.*

(*JB* xi:L1, 19, 27) I had lunch with him *(Powers Hapgood)* and Father and my **Uncle Alex**, my father's younger brother, in Stegemeier's Restaurant in downtown Indianapolis after I came home from the European part of World War Two. That was in July of 1945. The first atomic bomb had not yet been dropped on Japan. That would happen in about a month. Imagine that.

Powers Hapgood is fictionalized as Kenneth Whistler in Jailbird.

It was **Uncle Alex** who had arranged the lunch. He and Powers Hapgood had been at Harvard together. . . .

Uncle Alex was so conservative politically that I do not think he would have eaten lunch with Hapgood gladly if Hapgood had not been a fellow Harvard man. Hapgood was then a labor union officer, a vice-president of the local CIO. His wife Mary had been the Socialist Party's candidate for vice-president of the United States again and again.

(*JB* xii:L11, 15, 22) The meeting with Hapgood came about because I had told **Uncle Alex** that I might try to get a job with a labor union after the Army let me go. . . .

Uncle Alex must have thought something like this: "God help us. Against stupidity even the gods contend in vain. Well—at least there is a Harvard man with whom he can discuss this ridiculous dream.". . .

So **Uncle Alex** and I sat down at a front table in Stegemeier's and ordered beers and waited for Father and Hapgood to arrive.

(*JB* xiii:L9) **Uncle Alex**, by the way, could do nothing with his hands. Neither could my mother. She could not even cook a breakfast or sew on a button.

(*JB* xvi:L13) So we ordered more beers. **Uncle Alex** would later become a cofounder of the Indianapolis chapter of Alcoholics Anonymous, although his wife would say often and pointedly that he himself had never been an alcoholic. He began to talk now about The Columbia Conserve Company, a cannery that Powers Hapgood's father, William, also a Harvard man, had founded in Indianapolis in 1903. It was a famous experiment in industrial democracy, but I had never heard of it before. There was a lot that I had never heard of before.

(*JB* xvii:L8, 31) "It went bust," said **Uncle Alex**, with a certain grim, Darwinian satisfaction. . . .

It did not go completely bust for a while. In fact it still existed when **Uncle Alex** and Father and Powers Hapgood and I had lunch.

(*JB* xviii:L8, 16) Now Powers Hapgood came into the restaurant, an ordinary-looking Middle Western Anglo-Saxon in a cheap business suit. He wore a union badge in his lapel. He was cheerful. He knew my father slightly. He knew **Uncle Alex** quite well. . . .

He was a talker, with far more wonderful stories than Father or **Uncle Alex** had ever told. He was thrown into a lunatic asylum after he led the pickets at the execution of Sacco and Vanzetti.

(*PS* 59:L16 *Roots*) But Father's younger brother, **Uncle Alex**, a Harvard graduate and life insurance salesman, was responsive and amusing and generous with me, was my ideal grown—up friend.

(*PS* 185:L12 *Embarrassment*) I would describe the hum that is with me all the time as *embarrassment*. I have somehow disgraced myself.

My Indianapolis relatives may actually feel that I have done so. They are not enthusiastic about my work. I have already described my Uncle John's distaste for it. As for my **Uncle Alex**: I dedicated *The Sirens of Titan* to him, and he said he could not read it. He supposed that beatniks would think it was wonderful.

(*PS* 187:L18-19 *Embarrassment*) In Indianapolis his aunts, cousins and old friends call him Kay, and their memories of him are fond and lively. His Aunt, Irma Vonnegut Lindener, says warmly, "He's a dear, awfully nice," and her eyes light up with affection as she recounts thoughtful things he has done for the family over the years. He shared an enviable rapport with his uncle, **Alex Vonnegut** . . . though they were worlds apart in their convictions. *This is an excerpt about Vonnegut in the October 1976 issue of* Indianapolis Magazine.

(*FWD* 22:L5) It was a tradition in the Indianapolis branch of our once large and cohesive family that we should go east to college but then come back to Indianapolis. My **Uncle Alex** went to Harvard, and his first assignment was to write an essay about why he had chosen to study there. His opening sentence, he told me, was, "I came to Harvard because my big brother is at MIT."

(*FWD* 34:L24,26) "Dr. Bruetsch couldn't have helped my mother, and he was the greatest expert on insanity in the whole State of Indiana. Maybe he knew she was crazy. Maybe he didn't. If he did know she was crazy after midnight, and he was very fond of her, he must have felt as helpless as my father. There was not then an Indianapolis chapter of Alcoholics Anonymous, which might have helped. One would be founded by my father's only brother, **Alex**, who was an alcoholic, in 1955 or so.

"There—I've told you another family secret, haven't I? About **Uncle Alex**?

(*FWD* 37:L4-21) "And I think yet again about my father, who struggled to become a painter after he was forced into early and unwelcome retirement by the Great Depression. . . . I remember a portrait he did of his only brother, **Alex**, who was an insurance salesman, which he called Special Agent. When he roughed it in, his hand and eye conspired with a few bold strokes to capture several important truths about **Alex**, including a hint of disappointment. **Uncle Alex** was a proud graduate of Harvard, who would rather have been a scholar of literature than an insurance man.

"When Father finished the portrait, made sure of every square inch of masonite had its share of paint, **Uncle Alex** had disappeared entirely. We had a drunk and lustful Queen Victoria instead." *See also: FWD* 35:L9; 61:L1.

Vonnegut Memorial Fountain. *In* Hocus Pocus, *the fountain is outside the Tarkington College campus book store. When Eugene Debs Hartke confronts Fred Stone about stealing a mug from the store, Stone smashes it on the rim of the fountain.*

W

Wainwright, Right Reverend William Uranium-8. *In* Slapstick, *the evangelistic Founder of the Church of Jesus Christ the Kidnapped, located at 3972 Ellis Avenue, Chicago, Illinois.*

Wainwright, Tawny. *When Eliot Rosewater goes to the Saw City Kandy Kitchen to catch the Greyhound bus for a planned reunion with Sylvia, he startles the teenager inside.* (*GBR* 196:L4) The customer was a fourteen-year-old nymphet, pregnant by her stepfather, which stepfather was in prison now. The *(Rosewater)* Foundation was paying for her medical care. It had also reported the stepfather's crime to the police, had subsequently hired for him the best Indiana lawyer that money could buy.

The girl's name was **Tawny Wainwright**. When she brought her troubles to Eliot, he asked her how her spirits were. "Well," she said, "I guess I don't feel too bad. I guess this is as good a way as any to start out being a movie star."

Wait, James (also known as Willard Flemming). "Nature's experiment with purposeless greed" (*Gal* 82:L24-25), *Wait has one of the most checkered histories of all Vonnegut's characters. The incestuous issue of a father and daughter in Midland City, Ohio, he was placed in a foster home shortly after birth when his parents fled town. He grew up in five different foster homes, often enduring the cruelty of his foster parents. In Midland City he studied auto mechanics at a vocational high school. While still in high school, Wait fathered Celia Hoover's only child, George. Wait was mowing the lawn at the home of Dwayne and Celia when she invited James in for iced tea. Dwayne was in Cincinnati on business at the time. Though this scenario is not mentioned in* Breakfast of Champions, *it does not conflict with previous character histories.*

James Wait ran away to New York City after completing only two years of high school. A pimp taught him to become a homosexual prostitute. He also worked as a ballroom dancing instructor, a talent he apparently inherited from his parents. He eventually made his living, however, as a bigamist using various identities. By the time he is introduced to Mary Hepburn, he is already a millionaire, having swindled seventeen brides and stashing their assets in various accounts across the country. He travels down to Guayaquil to escape his most recent wife, a seventy-year-old widow in Skokie, Illinois, right outside Chicago. Guayaquil sounded to him like the last place she would ever think of looking for him.

This woman was so ugly and stupid, she probably never should have been born. And yet **Wait** was the second person to have married her (*Gal* 11:L17).

Wait decides to make a play for Mary Hepburn after learning she may be a wealthy widow. He introduces himself as Willard Flemming, an engineer from Moose Jaw, Saskatchewan. Mary becomes convinced of his goodness when she sees him feeding the Kanka-bono girls at the bar in the Hotel El Dorado. He and Mary later throw their bodies over the girls when the glass on their bus shatters during the air raid. The excitement of the moment taxes his congenitally weak heart, and he dies the next day due to a heart attack. (Both his parents died of heart attacks in their forties.) Before dying, however, Captain Adolf von Kleist married Mary Hepburn to "Willard Flemming."

Earlier in the text, while Wait was working as a homosexual prostitute in Manhattan, he killed Prince Richard of Croatia-Slavonia. The Prince hired Wait to strangle him with a silken sash while masturbating. Wait was supposed to count to twenty after the Prince ejaculated and lost consciousness, but he decided to count to three hundred.

Wakeby, Stella. *A poor though proud old woman in Rosewater County who fought calling Eliot for any help from the Foundation. One rainy evening, Stella comes to her wits end and asks a neighbor to drive her to a pay phone. Her pride and independence are characterized by her admission,* "Oh, Mr. Rosewater—if you only knew—" And she burst into violent tears. "We always said we were *Senator* Rosewater people and not *Eliot* Rosewater people!" (*GBR* 98:L5-7) *Though she doesn't explain the exact nature of her problem, just hearing Eliot's voice soothes her. He easily gets Stella to relax and agree to visit him in person the next day to help solve her problem.*

Wakefield, Andrea. *The wife of General Sam Wakefield, the man who recruited Hartke for both West Point and Tarkington College, she becomes close friends with Hartke.* (*HP* 162:L15-20) He *(Sam Wakefield)* had a very rich wife, **Andrea**, who would become Tarkington's Dean of Women after he committed suicide. **Andrea** died 2 years before the prison break, and so is not buried with so many others next to the stable, in the shadow of Musket Mountain when the Sun goes down.

Andrea Wakefield is a graduate of the Sorbonne in France. (*HP* 163:L9-20) In addition to her duties as Dean, dealing with unwanted pregnancies and drug addiction and the like, she also taught French and Italian and oil painting. She was from a genuinely distinguished old Philadelphia family, which had given civilization a remarkable number of educators and lawyers and physicians and artists. She actually may have been what Jason Wilder and several of Tarkington's Trustees believed themselves to be, obviously the most highly evolved creatures on the planet.

She was a lot smarter than her husband.

I always meant to ask her how a Quaker came to marry a professional soldier, but I never did.

(*HP* 163:L24-25) Even at her age then, which was about 60, 10 years older than me, **Andrea** was the best figure skater on the faculty. I think figure skating, if **Andrea Wakefield** could find the right partner, was eroticism enough for her. General Wakefield couldn't skate for sour apples. The best partner she had on ice at Tarkington, probably, was Bruce Bergeron....

(*HP* 163:L34) **Andrea** and I had never been lovers. She was too contented and old for me.

(*HP* 164:L1) "I want you to know I think you're a Saint," said **Andrea**. *Andrea says so because she admires Hartke's commitment to caring for his wife and mother-in-law.*

Wakefield, Sam. *The man who recruited Eugene Debs Hartke for West Point and later hired him to teach physics at Tarkington College. In both instances Wakefield showed up when Hartke reached new lows in his life. In the first instance Wakefield was at the Cleveland Science Fair when Hartke and his father were shamed by the judges who quickly saw the crystal display was fraudulently submitted as student work. He stopped Eugene with the innocent introduction, "What's the hurry, son?" Wakefield arranged Eugene's appointment to West Point through his father. In the second instance, Wakefield was on the street outside the Boston Chinese restaurant when Hartke exploded at another customer who harassed him about his military uniform. This was right after Hartke's visit to the bathroom where, through casual conversation with a family friend of his wife's, he found out about the hereditary insanity which would soon strike his wife. Wakefield was there to calm down Eugene and offer him a teaching post at Tarkington.* (*HP* 156:L29) I ran outside. Everybody and everything was my enemy. I was back in Vietnam!

But a Christ-like figure loomed before me. He was wearing a suit and tie, but he had a long beard, and his eyes were full of love and pity. He seemed to know all about me, and he really did. He was **Sam Wakefield**, who had resigned his commission as a General, and gone over to the Peace Movement, and become President of Tarkington College.

He said to me what he had said to me so long ago in Cleveland, at the Science Fair: "What's the hurry, Son?"

Wakefield was a veteran of World War II, Korea, and Vietnam. Wakefield became a Major General in Vietnam and awarded Hartke a Silver Star for his heroism in enemy tunnels. A year before the war ended, Wakefield resigned his commission to join the peace movement. He became President of Tarkington and committed suicide three years later by shooting himself in the head. Hartke doesn't believe Wakefield was depressed as much as he was exhausted. He believes this because Wakefield "plagiarized" his suicide note. (*HP* 59:L24-33) I think exhaustion got him. I say that not only because he seemed very tired all the time to me, but because his suicide note wasn't even original and didn't seem to have that much to do with him personally. It was word for word the same suicide note left way back in 1932, when I was a negative 8 years old, by another loser, George Eastman, inventor of the Kodak camera and founder of Eastman Kodak, now defunct, only 75 kilometers north of here.

Both notes said this and nothing more: "My work is done."

Walker, Shelton. *Walker served as Assistant Secretary of the Army in President Eisenhower's administration.* (*JB* 71:L17-21) He had been in the war and had risen to the rank of major in the Field Artillery and had made the landings in North Africa and then, on D-Day, in France. But he was essentially an Oklahoma businessman. Someone would tell me *(Walter Starbuck)* later that he owned the largest tire distributorship in the state. *Two years after Starbuck testified before Congress and implicated Leland Clewes in the McCarthy witch-hunt against communists in the government, it falls to Walker to gently fire Starbuck.* (*JB* 72:L3-8) I am unable to say even now whether he was being unkind or not when he said to me, rising and extending his hand, "You can now sell your considerable skills, Mr. Starbuck, for their true value in the open marketplace of the Free Enterprise System. Happy hunting! Good luck!"

Waltz, Barbara. (*DD* 103:L25-34) Felix's *(Waltz)* fifth wife, Barbara, and the first loving wife he had ever had, in my opinion, found the solitude of old George Metzger in Cedar Key intolerable. She was a native of Midland City like the rest of us, and a product of its public schools. She was an X-ray technician. That was how Felix had met her. She had X-rayed his shoulder. She was only twenty-three. She was pregnant by Felix now, and so happy to be pregnant. She was such a true believer in how life could be enriched by children.

Waltz, Charlotte. *The socialite wife of Felix Waltz who, in his opinion, was more interested in being married to the president of the National Broadcasting Company. At the peak of her hurt and fury over their divorce, Charlotte cut all the buttons off Felix's clothes and tossed the buttons down the incinerator.*

Waltz, Donna. *Felix Waltz's first wife and twin sister of Dina (no last name given). She and her sister were joyriding in a car when Felix crashed into them. Donna suffered disfiguring scars and later married Felix.*

Waltz, Emma Wetzel. *The mother of Rudy Waltz. She was born in 1901 and died in 1978 due to cancer brought about by radiation exposure. She died before the famous neutron bombing of Midland City. Her exposure was due to the radioactive cement used to build the fireplace in her Avondale home. The cement was sold by the Nuclear Regulatory Commission—against its own rules—as surplus from the government's work on the Manhattan Project.*

Though Emma was nine years younger than Otto Waltz, their two families lived side-by-side in their respective mansions in Midland City. She died penniless save for the money brought in by Rudy. They lost their wealth in the wrongful-death lawsuit brought by George Metzger after his wife's death.

Waltz, Felix. *Rudy Waltz's older brother, Felix frequently fell victim to his father's eccentricities. In 1934, when the Waltzes were invited to Germany by Otto's old friend Adolf Hitler, Otto dressed Felix in a Hitler Youth brown shirt uniform (though only twelve years old), and the family photo depicting the scene was eventually published in* The Midland City Bugle-Observer. *Later, Otto so scared Felix's prom date, Celia Hildreth, that she ran from the Waltz house across town to her own home.*

Felix was drafted in 1944 while a student at Ohio State University. Scheduled to leave the afternoon of Mothers' Day, 1944, Felix's family obligations fell to Rudy. Among the many responsibilities was caring for the small arsenal in the upstairs gun room. Felix handed the key to Rudy, caught the bus for boot camp, and that evening Rudy shot Eloise Metzger from the cupola. Years later Felix explains to Rudy why their father so readily surrendered: "You know why the old man confessed? . . . It was the first truly consequential adventure life had ever offered him. He was going to make the most of it. At last something was happening to him! He would keep it going as long as he could!" (*DD* 69:L20-26)

Felix returned from the war and became general manager of radio station WOR in New York, and later President of NBC. Along the way he collected five wives. He met Donna in a car accident and married her out of sympathy for the horrible facial scars she suffered. Genevieve was the second or third wife (there is an inconsistency in the text); she worked at WOR, and Felix called her "Anyface." She had almost no eyebrows, and very thin lips, so that, if she wanted anything memorable in the way of features, she had to paint them on (*DD* 127:L19-22). *Charlotte, wife number three or four, got so enraged with him that she cut the buttons off all his clothes. She was upset about his being released from NBC. Depressed and disheveled, he returned to Midland City (in time for Celia Hildreth Hoover's funeral) addicted to prescription drugs. Felix truly loved Barbara, wife number five. She was a*

Midland City X-ray technician and was carrying Felix's first child at the close of the text.

Though Rudy took personal care of their parents, Felix regularly contributed large sums of money to support them. After Mrs. Waltz died from radiation exposure, he and Rudy sued the Nuclear Regulatory Commission, the Maritimo Brothers Construction Co., and the Ohio Valley Ornamental Concrete Co. With the proceeds they bought the Grand Hotel Oloffson in Port au Prince, Haiti, which is where they were when Midland City was neutron bombed. While visiting Calvary Cemetery after the bombing, Felix declined an offer from the chef and voodoo priest Hippolyte Paul De Mille to raise the spirit of Celia Hoover.

Waltz, Genevieve. *Either the second or third wife of Felix Waltz, depending on which reference is cited from the text* (*DD* 106:L14-15, 135:L15). *Rudy stays with them in their Greenwich Village apartment when he comes to New York for the theater production of "Katmandu." During his stay, Rudy witnesses his brother's marriage dissolve, and in his mind he writes a comic play about it called "Duplex." Long after the marriage is over, Felix started calling her* "Anyface." She had almost no eyebrows, and very thin lips, so that, if she wanted anything memorable in the way of features, she had to paint them on (*DD* 127:L19-22). *She worked for WOR radio in New York when Felix was its general manager.*

Waltz, Otto (1892-1960). *The eccentric father of Rudy and Felix Waltz, his family indulged his slight art talent, but he never learned to apply himself.* (*DD* 2:L2-8) . . . he was told, among other things, that he was the heir to a fortune earned principally by a quack medicine known as "Saint Elmo's Remedy." It was grain alcohol dyed purple, flavored with cloves and sarsaparilla root, and laced with opium and cocaine. As the joke goes: It was absolutely harmless unless discontinued. *Otto was placed under the tutelage of August Gunther. Gunther did little to advance the knowledge or skill of the aspiring artist, but he did take him on trips around the Midwest under the guise of visiting art museums. Instead, the two were visiting whorehouses. Otto was sent to Vienna for treatment of gonorrhea, contracted on his trips with Gunther, and to enroll in the Academy of Fine Arts. After being turned down by the art school, he met up with another rejected and despondent artist, Adolf Hitler. Otto purchased Hitler's painting, "The Minorite Church of Vienna," eventually hanging it in his Midland City bedroom. At the time, however, Otto and Adolf paired off on their daily excursions with Otto paying their way. It was a friendship which lasted until Hitler declared war on Europe. It also prompts Rudy to surmise:* Think of that: My father could have strangled the worst monster of the century, or simply let him starve or freeze to death. But he became his bosom buddy instead.

That is my principal objection to life, I think: It is too easy, when alive, to make perfectly horrible mistakes (*DD* 6:L10-15).

Otto left Vienna at the start of World War I after foolishly seeking a commission in the Hungarian Life Guard. He liked their panther-skin uniforms. Henry Clowes, the American ambassador to the Austro-Hungarian Empire, chased Otto home, threatening to tell his parents how he had really been spending his days while they thought he was studying art.

Back in Midland City, Otto renewed his friendship with August Gunther. While on a hunting trip with Police Chief Morissey, his son Bucky Morissey, John Fortune, and August Gunther, it was Otto's idea to conceal the truth about Gunther's death: his head was blown off by an accidental shotgun blast from Chief Morissey. Otto took charge and instructed the others to help send Gunther's headless body down Sugar Creek. Later, when Chief Morissey came to the Waltz home knowing the bullet which killed Eloise Metzger had to have come from Otto's gun collection, Otto refused Morissey's entreaties to feign knowledge about the incident. Waltz loudly took the blame for Mrs. Metzger's death.

For all of Otto's eccentricities, including chasing away Celia Hildreth on the night of her prom date with Felix, he became a god to the Maritimo brothers. Otto sheltered and fed the illegal aliens, earning their lifelong respect and loyalty.

Otto died from the effects of the February 1960 snow storm which buried Midland City. It was only days after the February 14th performance of Rudy's "Katmandu" at New York City's Theatre de Lys.

Waltz, Rudy. *The lead character in* Deadeye Dick, *received his nickname for killing the pregnant Eloise Metzger with an errant shot fired from his home's cupola on the evening of Mother's Day, 1944. (That is the same date Edith Vonnegut committed suicide. Moreover, in a speaking engagement in Iowa, in April 1989, Vonnegut admitted to firing off a shot from his family's home in the same manner.) Rudy was twelve years old at the time. Otto Waltz claimed responsibility for his son's action.*

Despite the handicap of his legacy, Rudy grew up to become a pharmacist. He is a self-described "neuter," living without any female companionship. His teachers encouraged his small writing talent exhibited in a short sketch about his boyhood hero, John Fortune. Years later, while working the graveyard shift at Midland City's Schramm's Pharmacy (after receiving his pharmacy degree from Ohio State University), he turned the essay into the play "Katmandu." He entered and won a new playwrite's contest. His prize was a professional production in New York City. "Katmandu" played for one night in Greenwich Village's Theatre de Lys (the same theater which staged Vonnegut's "Wanda June"). The occasion meant that Rudy was in New York when Midland City was hit with a record-breaking blizzard. Rudy's father Otto died from the pneumonia he contracted in the storm.

Rudy and his mother moved into Avondale, a real estate development of the Maritimo Brothers Construction Company. Unknown to the builders, the mantlepiece was built with contaminated concrete left over from the Manhattan

Project. Rudy's mother died from her exposure, but whenever Rudy wasn't working, he was in the kitchen and avoided a fatal dose.

Rudy and his brother Felix sued the Nuclear Regulatory Commission, the Maritimo Brothers Construction Company, and the Ohio Valley Ornamental Concrete Company for the wrongful death of their mother. They retired to Port au Prince, Haiti, where they purchased the Grand Hotel Oloffson. Their new wealth meant the brothers were out of Midland City for a second disaster, the neutron bombing.

wampeter (see also **Bokononism**); ***Wampeters, Foma & Granfalloons*** (1965 – *Vonnegut's first collection of essays*). (*CC* 50:L35-37, 51:L1-12) Which brings me to the Bokononist concept of a ***wampeter***.

A ***wampeter*** is the pivot of a *karass*. No *karass* is without a ***wampeter***, Bokonon tells us, just as no wheel is without a hub.

Anything can be a ***wampeter***: a tree, a rock, an animal, an idea, a book, a melody, the Holy Grail. Whatever it is, the members of its *karass* revolve about it in the majestic chaos of a spiral nebula. The orbits of the members of a *karass* about their common ***wampeter*** are spiritual orbits, naturally. It is souls and not bodies that revolve. As Bokonon invites us to sing: Around and around and around we spin, / With feet of lead and wings of tin. . . .

And *wampeters* come**Warmergram, Charley** (also **Warmergran**) and ***wampeters*** go, Bokonon tells us.

At any given time a *karass* actually has two ***wampeters***—one waxing in importance, one waning.

(*CC* 158:L32) The contents of those jugs, of course, were parts of the legacies from Dr. Felix Hoenikker, were parts of the ***wampeter*** of my *karass*, were chips of *ice-nine*.

(*WFG* xv:L3 *preface*) DEAR READER: The title of this book is composed of three words from my novel *Cat's Cradle*. A ***wampeter*** is an object around which the lives of many otherwise unrelated people may revolve. The Holy Grail would be a case in point. *Foma* are harmless untruths, intended to comfort simple souls. An example: "Prosperity is just around the corner." A *granfalloon* is a proud and meaningless association of human beings. Taken together, the words form as good an umbrella as any for this collection of some of the reviews and essays I have written, a few of the speeches I have made. Most of my speeches were never written down.

Warmergram, Charley (also **Warmergran**). *Aside from being an insurance salesman in Rosewater, Indiana,* "He was one of about seven in the county who had actually done quite well under real free enterprise. Bella of Bella's Beauty Nook was another. Both of them had started with nothing, both were children of brakemen on the Nickel Plate. **Charley** was ten years younger than Eliot. He was six-feet-four, had broad shoulders, no hips, no belly. In addition to being Fire Chief, he was Federal Marshal and Inspector of Weights and

Measures. He also owned, jointly with Bella, La Boutique de Paris, which was a nice little haberdashery and notions store in the new shopping center for the well-to-do people in New Ambrosia. Like all real heroes, **Charley** had a fatal flaw. He refused to believe that he had gonorrhea, whereas the truth was that he did" (*GBR* 186:L6-22).

Charley was a good friend of Eliot's and drove Sylvia Rosewater to the private mental hospital in Indianapolis when she broke down with Samaritrophia. He was also the butt of a local Rosewater joke concerning the air-raid siren Eliot brought to town and discharged every day at noon. (*GBR* 175:L25-29) And wits throughout the county poised themselves to tell a tired and untruthful joke about Fire Chief **Charley Warmergran**, who had an insurance office next to the firehouse: "Must have scared **Charley Warmergram** half out of his secretary."

He had won the 1962 Young Hoosier Horatio Alger Award from the Indiana Federation of Conservative Young Republican Businessmen's Clubs. Eliot got him to return the award when he learned that thirteen of the sixteen previous recipients were either in jail, under indictment, had falsified military records, or had been executed. Charley was genuinely fond of Eliot and enchanted by the memories he had of their battling fires together.

Warren, Dr. Donald. *The elderly headmaster of Whitehill School in the short story "The Lie." The story centers on the fact that Eli Remenzel, the thirteen year old son of Sylvia and Dr. Remenzel, tore up Dr. Warren's letter informing the family Eli wasn't up to the academic demands necessary for admission to Whitehill. The family rides in their limousine to the school only to find out the truth from an embarrassed Dr. Warren.*

Washington, Elgin. *After Kilgore Trout is treated at the hospital for the thumb he lost to Dwayne Hoover's bite, he meets Midland City's well-to-do black pimp who recently had his leg amputated. Washington is snorting cocaine after being visited by his ladies. He is yet another Vonnegut character living life compulsively as a dedicated machine, as do Trout's characters in* Now It Can Be Told, *the story which sent Dwayne Hoover over the edge to insanity.* (*BC* 282:L27, 283:L7-8) And, in the midst of the uproar, **Elgin Washington** said something wheedlingly to Trout. "Hey man, hey man, hey man," he wheedled. He had his foot amputated earlier in the day by Khashdrahr Miasma, but he had forgotten that. "Hey man, hey man," he coaxed. He wanted nothing particular from Trout. Some part of his mind was idly exercising his skill at making strangers come to him. He was a fisherman for men's souls. "Hey man—" he said. He showed a gold tooth. He winked an eye.

Trout came to the foot of the black man's bed. This wasn't compassion on his part. He was being machinery again. Trout was, like so many Earthlings, a fully automatic boob when a pathological personality like **Elgin Washington** told him what to want, what to do.

Wataru, Watanabe and Beverly June. *The Rumfoord family gardener and his daughter against whom young Winston played German batball. Rounding out the opposition was* Edward Seward Darlington, the half-wit stable boy (*ST* 140:L10-11).

Waterman, Earl. *The Congressman for the Ashland family of Titusville, Florida, in the short story "The Manned Missiles." He apparently found out the truth about the death of their astronaut son but was unable to disclose the information.* (*MH* 266:L4 *The Manned Missiles*) **Mr. Waterman** came and talked to us personally, and he looked like he had seen God. He said he couldn't tell us what Bud had done, but it was one of the most heroic things in United States history.

Waters, Lavinia. *In* God Bless You, Mr. Rosewater, *the daughter of an Illinois Baptist missionary, Lavinia marries Abraham Rosewater, travels with him on his mission to the Congo, and dies while giving birth to their son Merrihue (the maiden name of Rosewater's mother, Faith Merrihue). In* Sirens of Titan, *Lavina is the author of* Too Wild a Dream, *which details the strange history of Noel Constant and Florence Whitehill.*

Watson, Myron S. *In* The Sirens of Titan, *the alcoholic Watson mysteriously disappeared from his job as a bathroom attendant at Newark Airport. He is next seen selling trinkets outside the Rumfoord mansion in advance of the materializations. Apparently, he was recruited for the Army of Mars and survived their invasion of Earth.*

Watson Brothers. *In Midland City,* ***Watson Brothers*** was the name of the funeral parlor for white people who were at least moderately well-to-do (*BC* 46:L15). *Dwayne Hoover suggests to Harry LeSabre that if he fails to wear colorful attire for the Hawaiian Week sale at the Pontiac dealership, he should wear his usual funeral director's suit and take a job at Watson Brothers, or perhaps get embalmed.*

Weary, Roland. *The eighteen-year-old antitank gunner from Pittsburgh, Pennsylvania, captured with Billy Pilgrim behind German lines at the Battle of the Bulge. Weary's tank crew fired one shot and missed before a Sherman tank fired and killed the rest of his crew.*

Back home, Weary had been unpopular because he was stupid and fat and mean, and smelled like bacon no matter how much he washed. He was always being ditched in Pittsburgh by people who did not want him with them (*SL5* 30:L19-23). *He became violent with the few friends he did have. He shared his father's great interest in weaponry, and he openly brandished a triple-edged dagger to Billy Pilgrim when the two were captured. Upon capture, Weary's new combat boots were taken and exchanged for the wooden clogs of his captor. His feet became infected and he eventually died on the train to the prison camp. However, before dying, he blamed Billy for his death, thinking that it was his timidity in the snow which caused their capture in the first place. It also didn't help that Billy frequently, though accidentally, stepped on Weary's bloody feet. Paul Lazzaro, another captured American prisoner on the train, vowed to avenge Weary's death, and he did.*

One of Roland Weary's prize possessions was a photo of the daguerreotype depicting a woman having intercourse with a pony. A copy of that photo is sold by Lila Buntline to Fred Rosewater, Jr., in God Bless You, Mr. Rosewater.

Weeks, Bunny. *The flamingly gay owner of The Weir restaurant who fawningly waits on the wealthy Amanita Buntline while suffering her companion, Caroline Rosewater. He is the great-grandson of Captain Hannibal Weeks of New Bedford, the man who killed Moby Dick.*

Weeks, Captain Hannibal. *The great-grandfather of Bunny Weeks, owner of The Weir restaurant in Pisquontuit, Rhode Island. Captain Weeks was from New Bedford and killed the famed Moby Dick. Out at Bunny's restaurant,* No less than seven of the irons resting on the rafters overhead were said to have come from the hide of the Great White Whale (*GBR* 127:L25-27).

The Weir. *In* God Bless You, Mr. Rosewater, *The Weir is Bunny Week's restaurant on the outskirts of Pisquontuit, overlooking the favorite fishing bed of Harry Pena and his sons. It contained the world's largest private collection of harpoons and was decorated with the bones of Moby Dick, captured by his great-grandfather Captain Hannibal Weeks. Bunny placed opera glasses on the tables so customers could watch the Pena men haul in their catch. Amanda Buntline and Caroline Rosewater were frequent guests at The Weir.*

Welcome to the Monkey House (1968) (see also **Billy the Poet**, **ethical birth control** and **ethical suicide**). *Named for one of his short stories, this is Vonnegut's only collection of short stories.*

Weltschmerz. *The first time Vonnegut uses this term is in* Player Piano. *Paul is reminded of the first time he saw the allegory on stage at the Meadows. He was with his father.* (*PP* 191:L19) The play was virtually the same play that had begun every Meadows session, even before the war, when the island had belonged to a steel company. Twenty years ago, Paul's father had brought him up here, and the play's message had been the same: that the common man wasn't nearly as grateful as he should be for what the engineers and managers had given him, and that the radicals were the cause of the ingratitude.

When Paul had first seen the allegory, as a teenager, he'd been moved deeply. He had been struck full force by its sublime clarity and simplicity. It was a story in a nutshell, and the heroic struggle against ingratitude was made so vivid for his young mind that he'd worshipped his father for a little while as a fighter, a latter-day Richard the Lionhearted.

"Well," his father had said after that first play, years ago, "what are you thinking, Paul?"

"I had no idea—no idea that's what was going on."

"That's the story," his father had said sadly. "The whole story. That's the way it is."

"Yessir." Their eyes had met, and an inexpressibly sweet sense of eternal tragedy had passed between them, between their generations—a legacy of ***Weltschmerz*** as old as humanity.

The next citation of the term occurs in John Rauch's biography of the Vonneguts, reprinted in Palm Sunday. (*PS* 56:L19 *Roots*) "AFTER Edith's death Kurt lived almost as a recluse, for some ten years. But his sister, Irma Vonnegut Lindener, who was then a resident of Hamburg, Germany, paid him protracted visits—sometimes for months at a time. They were very congenial and deeply attached to each other. She understood his vagaries, respected his privacy and fierce independence, and gave him the only sort of companionship which he would tolerate. They resembled each other in many ways and were deeply empathetic. They were both blond and blue-eyed. They both spoke German fluently and shared their attachment to their German traditions of music and literature. Kurt acquired a sort of skeptical and fatalistic contempt for life—what the Germans call ***Weltschmerz***."

The final citation is from Vonnegut's essay on the religious traditions of his family. After quoting Freethinker Clemens Vonnegut's "comments on life and death," Vonnegut continues, SUCH is my ancestral religion. How it was passed on to me is a mystery. By the time I got to know them, my parents were both so woozy with **Weltschmerz** that they weren't passing anything on—not the German language, not their love for German music, not the family history, nothing. Everything was all over with. They were *kaput* (*PS* 195:L1 *Religion*).

The Western Hemisphere University (also **Western Hemisphere University of the Bible**). *There are two references to this mail-order diploma mill. The first appears in* Mother Night, *the creation of Lionel J.D. Jones. The second occurs in* Cat's Cradle *by way of the enigmatic Dr. Vox Humana.* (*MN* 50:L33) The school he headed was named, straightforwardly enough, The Little Rock School of Embalming. It was losing eight thousand dollars a year. Jones took it out of the high-overhead field of embalming education, sold its real estate, and had it rechartered as **The Western Hemisphere University of the Bible**. The university held no classes, taught nothing, did all its business by mail. Its business was the awarding of doctorates in the field of divinity, framed and under glass, for eighty dollars a throw.

And Jones helped himself to a W.H.U.B. degree, out of open stock, so to speak. When his second wife died, when he brought out *The White Christian Minuteman* again, he appeared on the masthead as, "The Reverend Doctor Lionel J.D. Jones, D.D.S., D.D."

(*CC* 176:L10-11) He turned out to be an intelligent man. His doctorate, which he invited me to examine, was awarded by the **Western Hemisphere University of the Bible** of Little Rock, Arkansas. He made contact with the University through a classified ad in *Popular Mechanics*, he told me. He said that the motto of the University had become his own, and that it explained the chicken and the butcher knife. The motto of the University was this:

MAKE RELIGION LIVE!

Westlake, Ian. *The Englishman liberated from a German P.O.W. camp by advancing Soviet forces and who later witnessed the hanging of Werner Noth. He took photographs and wrote a skillful account of the incident, only to be published in the pages of a lurid girly magazine (a manner reminiscent of Kilgore Trout's publishing history). In the late 1950s, while Howard Campbell waited his turn in a Greenwich Village barber shop, his eye caught the provocative title "Hangwomen for the Hangman of Berlin." Ironically, Westlake's article informed Campbell more about his father-in-law's activities than he ever knew.* (*MN* 82:L31, 83:L4) "Terror and torture were the provinces of other branches of the German police," said **Westlake**. "Werner Noth's own province was what is regarded in every big city as ordinary law and order. The force he directed was the sworn enemy of drunks, thieves, murderers, rapists, looters, confidence men, prostitutes, and other disturbers of the peace, and it did its best to keep the city traffic moving.

"Noth's principal offense," said **Westlake**, "was that he introduced persons suspected of misdemeanors and crimes into a system of courts and penal institutions that was insane. Noth did his best to distinguish between the guilty and the innocent, using the most modern police methods; but those to whom he handed over his prisoners found the distinction of no importance. Merely to be in custody, with or without trial, was a crime. Prisoners of every sort were all to be humiliated, exhausted and killed."

Campbell also learned that it took nine attempts to hang Werner Noth.

Wetzel, Richard. *In* Deadeye Dick, the founder and principal stockholder of the Midland County National Bank and father of one child, Emma. Emma Wetzel married Otto Waltz in her parents' mansion, next door to the Waltz family home. Both families were agnostics, so a local judge performed the ceremony.

The Whale. *In* The Sirens of Titan, *the three-hundred-foot-high spacecraft with living quarters for five, built by Malachi Constant's Galactic Spacecraft Corporation. It's launch was suspended when scientists made the discovery of the chrono-synclastic infundibulum. After Winston Niles Rumfoord told Constant and his wife about their futures together on Titan, Malachi tried to divest his holdings in Galactic Spacecraft. At the same time, Beatrice used her wealth to buy into Galactic in order to prevent its launch. Nevertheless, the*

President declared a New Age of Space, rechristened The Whale *as* The Rumfoord*, and Malachi and Beatrice were on a collision course to a future on Titan.*

Wheeler, Elm. *Professional barber Homer Bigley delivers a monologue to Dr. Ewing J. Halyard about the virtues of military service over civilian life and holds up the life and death of Sergeant Elm Wheeler as proof there was more opportunity for heroism and greatness in the military than anywhere else. In recalling the war Bigley tells Halyard,* "But you know, terrible as that mess was—not just **Wheeler**, but the whole war—it brought out the greatness in the American people. There's something about war that brings out greatness. I hate to say that, but it's true. Of course, maybe that's because you can get great so quick in a war. Just one damn fool thing for a couple of seconds, and you're great. I could be the greatest barber in the world, and maybe I am, but I'd have to prove it with a lifetime of great haircutting, and then nobody'd notice. That's just the way peacetime things are, you know?

"But **Elm Wheeler**, you couldn't help but notice him when he went hog-wild after he got a letter from his wife saying she'd had a baby, and he hadn't seen her for two years. Why, he read that and ran up to a machine-gun nest and shot and hand-grenaded everybody in it something awful, then he ran up to another one and mashed up all the people there with his rifle butt, and then, after he'd busted that, he started after a mortar emplacement with a rock in each hand, and they got him with a shell fragment. You could of paid a surgeon a thousand dollars, and he couldn't of done a nicer job. Well, **Elm Wheeler** got the Congressional Medal for that, and they laid it in his coffin with him. Just laid it there. Couldn't hang it around his neck, and if they'd put it on his chest, I expect they'd of had to use solder, he was so full of lead and scrap iron.

"But *he* was great, and nobody'd argue about that, but do you think he could of been great today, in this modern day and age? **Wheeler**? **Elm Wheeler**? You know what he would be today? A Reek and Wreck, that's all. The war made him, and this life would of killed him" (*PP* 177:L33-39, 178:L1-22).

Wheelock, Harley, II and III. *Lieutenant Colonel Harley Wheelock III, is the West Point graduate in charge of the 62nd Airborne Division which vanquished the marauding prisoners from Athena who overran Scipio. He was preparing for leave from his post in the South Bronx when the prison break occurred. Wheelock knew Eugene Debs Hartke by his nickname, "The Preacher." He put Hartke in charge of the troops he left behind, securing for him a commission to become a Brigadier General in the National Guard.*

The two military men became quick comrades. Harley II was three years ahead of Hartke at the academy. Harley III shared with Hartke information about his father's death. (*HP* 272:L1-7) He told me his father drowned while trying to rescue a Swedish woman who committed suicide by opening the windows of her Volvo and driving it off a dock and into the Ruhr River at Essen, home, as it happens, of that premier manufacturer of crematoria, A.J. Topf und Sohn.

Small World.

Harley III and his wife were infertile, so they adopted twin orphaned girls from Peru, South America.

"Where I Live" (1964). *The opening essay in* Welcome to the Monkey House *describing Vonnegut's life and cultural underpinnings while living in West Barnstable, Cape Cod.*

Whistler, Henry Niles. *In* Jailbird, *the Harvard graduate and poet who comes to Cleveland to lend his support to the striking workers at the Cuyahoga Bridge and Iron Company. He writes the letter sent by the workers to Daniel McCone.* (*JB* xxx:L7-12) "We wish only . . . to take one last look at the factory to which we gave the best years of our lives, and to show our faces to all who may care to look upon them, to show them to God Almighty alone, if only He will look, and to ask, as we stand mute and motionless, 'Does any American deserve misery and heartbreak such as we now know?'" *McCone's response was to have the Riot Act read to the strikers just before the ensuing massacre. When it was learned an infant was shot dead in the fracas, Whistler wrote the song "Bonnie Failey," which includes the couplet, "Damn you, damn you, Dan McCone, / With a soul of pig iron and a heart of stone. . . ."* (*JB* xxxii:L1-2)

Whistler, Kenneth. *The spellbinding Harvard-educated labor organizer in* Jailbird, *patterned after real-life organizer Powers Hapgood. Whistler repeats Hapgood's unionization efforts in Kentucky's coalfields and his leadership in protest of the executions of Sacco and Vanzetti. Walter Starbuck and Mary Kathleen O'Looney first hear Whistler speak at a labor rally in Boston for the International Brotherhood of Abrasives and Adhesives Workers. Mary Kathleen became so infatuated with Whistler that after Walter graduated from Harvard and no longer communicated with her, she took off to Kentucky in search of Whistler. Mary moved into his life and had a brief relationship. However, Whistler drank heavily and physically abused Mary. One night he came home drunk and dangerous, so Mary fled into the street, where she literally ran into Jack Graham, the young mining engineer and owner of the fledgling RAMJAC Corporation—soon to become her husband. Whistler died in a 1941 mining disaster. Mary's infatuation for Whistler-the-socialist sustains her long after the death of her husband. As she roams the streets of New York City disguised as a bag lady, she keeps a picture of Whistler and Starbuck in her raggedy sneakers.*

Starbuck was also influenced by Whistler. At his farewell dinner before returning to prison, his RAMJAC colleagues play a recording of his testimony before a 1949 session of the House Un-American Activities Committee: Congressman Nixon had asked me why, as the son of immigrants who had been treated so well by Americans, as a man who had been treated like a son and been sent to Harvard by an American capitalist, I had been so ungrateful to the American economic system (*JB* 240:L20-24). *Starbuck confides that his answer was the same one he heard his "one-time hero" confess in response to a similar question by a judge presiding over a case of alleged violence by strikers,* My stolen answer to Nixon was this: "Why? The Sermon on the Mount, sir" (*JB* 241:L1-2).

White, Allison. *The mother of Celeste and the cook and housekeeper for Rabo Karabekian. Though she didn't care for Karabekian's collection of Abstract Expressionist paintings, she was extremely curious about what kind of painting was locked inside the potato barn. She did, however, express great admiration for a Dan Gregory painting of black and white boys squaring off in an alley.*

White, Celeste. *The fifteen-year-old daughter of Allison, Rabo Karabekian's live-in cook in* Bluebeard. *She is a devoted fan of the Polly Madison novels, having read the entire collection. Celeste spends her time lounging with her friends around Karabekian's home. She takes birth control pills, much to Rabo's consternation, and constantly disappoints him with her inability to identify historical figures whom he considers to be the principal figures of a basic education.*

White, Gloria. *The traveling companion of billionaire hot-air balloonist and motorcyclist Arthur K. Clarke.* (*HP* 166:L7) He himself was on a motorcycle, and on the saddle behind him, holding on for dear life, her skirt hiked up to her crotch, was **Gloria White**, the 60-year-old lifelong movie star! They wore gold helmets festooned with dollar signs as they motored into Scipio.

White, Maggie. *The beautiful former dental assistant who became a homemaker when she married an Ilium optometrist.* (*SL5* 147:L10-13) She was a dull person, but a sensational invitation to make babies. Men looked at her and wanted to fill her up with babies right away. *At Billy and Valencia Pilgrim's eighteenth wedding anniversary, the vacuous and gullible Maggie has a terrifying conversation with Kilgore Trout, a specially invited guest. Trout first makes up a story about the funeral of a great French chef over whose body the mourners sprinkled parsley and paprika before closing the casket. Maggie believes Trout when he swears it is no fiction. She fears Trout when he says that everything he experiences is later used in his stories. Then he tells her that God is listening as well,* "And on Judgment Day he's going to tell you all the things you said and did. If it turns out they're bad things instead of good things, that's too bad for you, because you'll burn forever and ever. The burning never stops hurting."

Poor **Maggie** turned gray. She believed that, too, and was petrified.

Kilgore Trout laughed uproariously. A salmon egg flew out of his mouth and landed in **Maggie**'s cleavage (*SL5* 148:L1-4).

The White Christian Minuteman. ". . . a scabrous, illiterate, anti-Semitic, anti-Negro, anti-Catholic hate sheet published by the Reverend Doctor Lionel J.D. Jones, D.D.S. (*MN* 45:L17-18) *Jones founded the paper in 1928 after his wife died. His latent racism was expressed in the paper he began after selling his funeral home for $84,000. He suspended publication in 1929 after the stock market crash, though he had managed to send free copies of all fourteen issues to everyone in* Who's Who. *He originally used the paper to publish his theories about racial superiority which had long ago gotten him thrown out of dental school.*

When his second wife died, Mary Alice Shoup—the sixty-eight-year-old owner of the Little Rock Embalming School, Jones again brought out the paper. However, the paper increased in size and style because "Jones had been recruited and financed as a propaganda agent for Hitler's then-rising Third German Reich. Jones' news, photographs, cartoons and editorials were coming straight from the Nazi propaganda mills in Erfurt, Germany" (*MN* 51:L22-26).

In 1955, after serving fourteen years in prison for a federal conviction of conspiracy to commit seditious acts, Jones again brought out the paper. George Kraft/Iona Potapov sent a notice to the newspaper, among many others, chronicling the postwar existence of Howard Campbell.

Whitefeet, Elbert. *The president of the bankrupt Sweetbread College in the play "Jekyll and Hyde Revisited." He had withdrawn the college's funds from IBM, Xerox, and Polaroid and reinvested them in cocoa futures. This sets in motion the students' musical production of "Dr. Jekyll and Mr. Hyde," to raise funds for the college. It also spurs the college's Dr. Jekyll to search for a new discovery to raise funds.*

Whitehall, Major General Daniel. *The highly suggestible commander of the Corps of Engineers combat troops who asked that Private Rabo Karabekian be permitted to paint his portrait prior to his retirement (he was being retired because of failing kidneys). Whitehall wanted Karabekian for the task because he* believed that somebody with a foreign-sounding name could do the best job (*Blue* 204:L16-18). *The general left the service before America's involvement in World War II, having joined the military shortly after World War I.* (*Blue* 204:L27-31) If I had realized that at the time *(that this painting "might actually outlive the 'Mona Lisa'")* I might have given him a puzzling half-smile, whose meaning only I knew for certain: he had become a general, but had missed the two big wars of his lifetime.

Rabo took the opportunity presented by long hours alone with the general to make small talk about the strategic impact brought about by aerial photography, suggesting it should be the Corps of Engineers, Whitehall's command, which should lead the way in camouflage techniques to counteract aerial surveillance. (*Blue* L17-24, 206:L2-6) In what must surely have been the manner of powerless Armenian advisors in Turkish courts, I congratulated him on having ideas he might never have had before. An example: "You must be thinking very hard how important aerial photography is going to be, if war should come." War, of course, had come to practically everybody but the United States by then.

"Yes," he said. . . . And then I added almost absentmindedly as I laid the paint on: "Every branch of the service is claiming camouflage from the air as their specialty, even though it's obviously the business of the Engineers."

At the general's retirement party and portrait unveiling, He lectured on aerial photography, and the clear mission of the Engineers to teach the other branches of the service about camouflage. He said that among the last orders he would ever give was one which called for all enlisted men with what he called "artistic experiences" to be assigned to a new camouflage unit under the command of, now get this: "Master Sergeant Rabo Karabekian. I hope I pronounced his name right" (*Blue* 206:L21-28).

Whitehall Palace (see **Rumfoord mansion**).

Whitehill, Florence. *The chambermaid at the Wilburhampton Hotel who becomes Noel Constant's only visitor during his first two years there. She* spent one night out of ten with him for a small, flat fee (*ST* 75:L19-20).

An account of the affair between Noel Constant and Florence Whitehill is included in Lavina Waters' Too Wild a Dream? (*ST* 80:L22-31) Miss Waters' volume, while fuddled as to business details, contains the better account of the chambermaid **Florence Whitehill**'s discovery that she was pregnant by Noel Constant, and her discovery that Noel Constant was a multi-multi-millionaire.

Noel Constant married the chambermaid, gave her a mansion and a checking account with a million dollars in it. He told her to name the child Malachi if it was a boy, and Prudence if it was a girl. He asked her to please keep coming to see him once every ten days in Room 223 of the Wilburhampton Hotel, but not to bring the baby.

white humor (see **humor**)

"Who Am I This Time" (1961). *The short story about the North Crawford Mask and Wig Club, particularly the mercurial Harry Nash. The otherwise silent and rather vapid hardware clerk assumes the persona of his stage roles. In order to maintain any sort of relationship with him, his new co-star Helene Shaw keeps bringing him scripts to rehearse. Under such circumstances, they share a rich and passionate life.*

Wiener, Norbert. *The MIT mathematician whose essays gave Vonnegut a central image and thematic focus for* Player Piano, *Vonnegut's vision of how American society will become restructured once the value of technocrats and the third industrial revolution take effect. This latter concept is extrapolated* *from Wiener's* The Human Use of Human Beings: Cybernetics and Society *(1950). Wiener characterized the first industrial revolution as devaluing muscle work, and the second (describing the long-term effects of computerization) as devaluing routine mental work. But the third industrial revolution, as envisioned by Vonnegut and illustrated by EPICAC, would devalue human thinking. Though Wiener feared massive unemployment in the semiskilled and skilled work sectors due to robotics, Vonnegut saw the advancement of unchecked technologies producing a society in which only some Ph.D.s would be employed at anything more than soldiers or road workers: the Reeks and Wrecks. The know-how and ability to produce would outrun our understanding of the purpose and effects of production. Paul Proteus outlines these ideas and credits Wiener for his industrial revolution model in a conversation with Katharine Finch, his secretary* (*PP* 13:L3).

The entire dilemma of technological "know-how" and the engineers' role in shaping society, as well as the source of Vonnegut's tile, are bound within a few sentences from Wiener's seminal text: Our papers have been making a great deal of American *know-how* ever since we had the misfortune to discover the atomic bomb. There is one quality more important than *know-how* and we cannot accuse the United States of any undue amount of it. This is *know-what* by which we determine not only how to accomplish our purposes, but what our purposes are to be. I can distinguish between the two by an example. Some years ago, a prominent American engineer bought an expensive player-piano. It became clear after a week or two that this purchase did not correspond to any particular interest in the piano mechanism. For this gentleman, the player-piano was not a means of producing music, but a means of giving some inventor the chance of showing how skillful he was at overcoming certain difficulties in the production of music. This is an estimable attitude in a second-year high school student. How estimable is it in one of those on whom the whole cultural future of the country depends *(Wiener, 1950)*.

Vonnegut praises Wiener because he wrote in *Atlantic* that he wasn't going to give any more information to industry or the Government, because they weren't gentle people, because they don't have humane uses for things (*WFG* 267:L20-24 *Playboy Interview*).

Wilbur, Harold Newcomb. *The second-most-decorated veteran in Midland City, next to child-killer Ned Lingamon. Wilbur fought in the Pacific Theater of World War II and earned the Silver Star, the Bronze Star, the Soldier's Medal, the Good Conduct Medal, and a Purple Heart with two Oak-Leaf Clusters. Lingamon had all those and a Congressional Medal of Honor, as well. Wilbur is the bartender in Dwayne Hoover's Holiday Inn. Through Wilbur, Vonnegut illustrates the relationship he has with his literary creations, highlighting one of the text's central conflicts—freewill.* (*BC* 202:L1-26) The bartender took several anxious looks in my direction. All he could see were the *leaks* over my eyes. I did not worry about his asking me to leave the establishment. I had created him, after all. . . .

And he went on staring at me, even though I wanted to stop him now. Here was the thing about my control over the characters I created: I could only guide their movements approximately, since they were such big animals. There was inertia to overcome. It wasn't as though I was connected to them by steel wires. It was more as though I was connected to them by stale rubberbands.

So I made the green telephone in back of the bar ring. **Harold Newcomb Wilbur** answered it, but he kept his eyes on me. I had to think fast about who was on the other end of the telephone.

Wild Bob. *In* Slaughterhouse-Five, *the commanding officer and sole survivor of the 451st Infantry Regiment who wants to be known as "Wild Bob." He tells everyone "If you're ever in Cody, Wyoming, just ask for Wild Bob!" Wild Bob dies in a boxcar on the same train transporting Billy Pilgrim and others to a POW camp. His invitation to Cody, Wyoming, becomes a refrain repeated by Billy Pilgrim and Kurt Vonnegut. When in the Vermont hospital after the airplane crash, Billy hears his roommate Bertram Copeland Rumfoord recite the carnage of Dresden and Hiroshima and drones out the colonel's* "If you're ever in Cody, Wyoming, just ask for Wild Bob!" (*SL5* 162:L23-23) *Billy nervously repeats the invitation to himself while being introduced by a radio talk show host. Vonnegut says it later in the text when, after recalling how many people were killed in Dresden, he and Bernard V. O'Hare had survived and prospered* (*SL5* 183:L24-25).

Wilder, Jason. *A Rhodes Scholar and graduate of either Yale or Princeton (there is an inconsistency in the text) and member of the Tarkington Board of Trustees, it was Wilder who led the investigation which culminated in the firing of Eugene Debs Hartke. Aside from hiring a private detective to take surveillance photos, he enlisted his learning-disabled daughter Kimberley to tape Hartke's lectures and informal conversations. Wilder was a very high profile individual, an esteemed conservative newspaper columnist, lecturer, and television talk-show host. Hartke reflects on his firing that,* He saved my life by doing that. If it weren't for him, I would have been on the Scipio side of the lake instead of the Athena side during the prison break (*HP* 90:L22-23, 91:L1-2). *He threatened the other Board members that if they wouldn't fire Hartke, then he would publicly denounce the college through his various media outlets.*

Wilder, Kimberley. *The learning-disabled daughter of Jason Wilder, enlisted by her father to surreptitiously tape the lectures and informal conversations of Eugene Debs Hartke for evidence at his dismissal hearing. For the most part, what she actually taped was Hartke repeating stories and lectures he heard from other Tarkington faculty, particularly Damon Stern and Paul Slazinger.* (*HP* 99:7-20) She was pitiful because she was a dimwit from a brilliant family and believed that she at last had done something brilliant, too, in getting the goods on a person whose ideas were criminal. I didn't know yet that her

Rhodes Scholar father, a Phi Beta Kappa from Princeton, had put her up to this. I thought she had noted her father's conviction, often expressed in his columns and on his TV show, and no doubt at home, that a few teachers who secretly hated their country were making young people lose faith in its future and leadership.

I thought that, just on her own, she had resolved to find such a villain and get him fired, proving that she wasn't so dumb, after all, and that she was really Daddy's little girl.

Wrong.

Wildhack, Montana. *The twenty-year-old porn queen abducted from a Palm Springs poolside and transported to a dome in a Tralfamadorian zoo to be the mate of Billy Pilgrim. She wore a locket around her neck* containing a photograph of her alcoholic mother—a grainy thing, soot and chalk. It could have been anybody. Engraved on the outside of the locket were these words: God grant me the serenity / to accept the things I / cannot change, courage / to change the things / I can, and the wisdom / always to tell the / difference (*SL5* 180:L3-5, 181 illustration).

Billy loved Montana, adored her. (*SL5* 115:L28) Billy switched on a floor lamp. The light from the single source threw the baroque detailing of **Montana**'s body into sharp relief. Billy was reminded of fantastic architecture in Dresden, before it was bombed. *Eventually, she learned to love Billy, and only then did she invite him into her bed. Together they had a baby. Billy often told her about the firebombing of Dresden, and she never tired of listening.*

Wiley, Roberta (see also **George Helmholtz**). *The former algebra teacher teamed with former high school bandmaster George Helmholtz to work as recruiting agents for the Pan-Galactic Space Service, Rumfoord's Army of Mars. Roberta is actually a man dressed up as a woman to avoid suspicion about the couple's activities. Wiley's true name is not revealed. They successfully recruit over 14,000 people.* (*ST* 89:L9) Their usual technique was to dress like civil engineers and offer not-quite-bright men and women nine dollars an hour, tax free, plus food and shelter and transportation, to work on a secret Government project in a remote part of the world for three years. It was a joke between Helmholtz and **Miss Wiley** that they had never specified what government was organizing the project, and that no recruit had ever thought to ask. *They were among the few in the Pan-Galactic Space Service who did not have their minds wiped clean.*

Rumfoord tells Helmholtz and Wiley the precise moment to enter Malachi Constant's Wilburhampton Hotel room to offer him a commission in the service. It is just after he reads his father's letter asking what life is all about. A short while later, Helmholtz and Wiley pose as estate appraisers and kidnap Beatrice Rumfoord.

Wills, Ben. (*HP* 227:L1) Unlike my *(Eugene Debs Hartke's)* Socialist grandfather **Ben Wills**, who was a nobody, I have no reforms to propose. I think any form of government, not just Capitalism, is whatever the people who have all our money, drunk or sober, sane or insane, decide to do today.

Wilson, Robert Sterling. *The self-styled "Black Fuehrer of Harlem," imprisoned in 1942 for spying for Japan, Wilson is the seventy-three-year-old chauffeur and butler for Rev. Dr. Lionel J.D. Jones. Wilson gave Dr. Jones a ring to wear among all his other baubles,* an American eagle carved in jade and mounted in silver, a piece of Japanese craftsmanship (*MN* 56:L13-14). *Howard Campbell sees Wilson's joining forces with Jones and August Krapptauer as symptomatic of the "cuckoo-clock in hell," the totalitarian mind. As further evidence of the inexplicable associations made by the totalitarian mind, Campbell offers this bit of conversation with Wilson.* (*MN* 68:L3-18) "I tell this Reverend gentleman here the same thing every morning, the same thing I tell you now. I give him his hot cereal for breakfast, and then I tell him: 'The colored people are gonna rise up in righteous wrath, and they're gonna take over the world. White folks gonna finally lose!'"

"All right, **Robert**," said Jones patiently.

"The colored people gonna have hydrogen bombs all their own, he said. "They working on it right now. Pretty soon gonna be Japan's turn to drop one. The rest of the colored folks gonna give them the honor of dropping the first one."

"Where they going to drop it?" I said.

"China, most likely," he said.

"On other colored people?" I said.

He looked at me pityingly. "Who ever told you a Chinaman was a colored man?" he said.

"Windsor Blue Number Seventeen" *Blue Windsor was a shade of the ill-fated Sateen Dura-Luxe paint used by Rabo Karabekian in his Abstract Expressionist days. This particular painting was an eight-panel, sixty-four-foot painting purchased by GEFFCo and hung in their Park Avenue headquarters as proof it was a company in tune with the latest developments in business and culture. Years later Karabekian was contacted and asked to retrieve his canvas from GEFFCo's subbasement storage facility where the painting had been shedding its defective paint.* (*Blue* 275:L29) I had the eight panels purged of every trace of faithless Sateen Dura-Luxes, and restretched and reprimed. I had them set up in the barn, dazzling white in their restored virginity, just as they had been before I transmuted them into "**Windsor Blue Number Seventeen**."

I explained to my wife that this eccentric project was an exorcism of an unhappy past, a symbolic repairing of all the damage I had done to myself and others during my brief career as a painter. That was yet another instance, though, of putting into words what could not be put into words: why and how a painting had come to be. *Karabekian used the freshened canvasses to create his masterpiece "Now It's the Women's Turn" (shortened from his first impulse, "I Tried and Failed and Cleaned Up Afterwards, so It's* Your *Turn Now"). It is the scene Karabekian (Vonnegut) saw when he was released from his prison camp at the end of the war. Karabekian painted in realistic detail over five thousand individuals he saw in the countryside.*

Winkler, Kermit. *In* Jailbird, *Winkler was two years behind Walter Starbuck at Harvard and Secretary of the Treasury when Starbuck was released from prison for his Watergate conviction.*

Winslow, Bernard K. *One of the Martian veterans who survived the invasion and now sells "twittering mechanical birds" outside the Rumfoord mansion nearby Beatrice Rumfoord's stall.* (*ST* 241:L6-7) The International Committee for the Identification and Rehabilitation of Martians had, with the help of fingerprints, identified the bird man as **Bernard K. Winslow**, an itinerant chicken sexer, who had disappeared from the alcoholic ward of a London hospital. . . . "Thanks very much for the information. . . . Now I don't have that lost feeling any more."

Wirtanen, Carly. *The first mate and son of Frank Wirtanen, skipper of the Kennedy yacht* Marlin. *Carly is not seen, but a statue of him and his father are on display at the Kennedy Museum, in the short story "Welcome to the Monkey House."*

Wirtanen, Major Frank. *Called by Howard Campbell his "Blue Fairy Godmother" and later revealed to be Colonel Harold J. Sparrow, Wirtanen is responsible for recruiting Campbell to serve as a spy before the United States entered World War II, in* Mother Night. *Wirtanen releases Campbell from custody after the war and sets him up with money and a new life. He later bails Campbell out of trouble when the FBI plans its raid on Dr. Jones' meeting of the Iron Guard of the White Sons of the American Constitution, but not before Wirtanen discloses the fate of Campbell's manuscripts in the hands of Stepan Bodovskov and the secret transmission of Helga Noth's death. At the close of the text, Wirtanen sends Campbell a letter in his Jerusalem jail cell offering to appear at his trial in Israel and testify that Campbell's wartime activities were on behalf of the United States government. It is then he reveals his true name.*

In the short story "Brief Encounters on the Inland Waterway," reprinted in Wampeters, Foma & Granfalloons, *Wirtanen is a native of West Barnstable, Cape Cod, skipper of the yacht* Marlin, *for the Kennedy family.*

Witherspoon, Withers. *A staff member at the Swain mansion in Galen, Vermont, serving variously as guard, chauffeur and handyman. He was the only one of the Witherspoons to travel outside Vermont, and that was only because he served in the military. In keeping with the theme of extended* *families, Wilbur notes that Witherspoon was* of course distantly related to Eliza and me, too, since our Vermont ancestors had once been content to dogpaddle endlessly, so to speak, in the same tiny genetic pool.

But, in the American scheme of things at that time, they were related to our family as carp were related to eagles, say—for our family had evolved into world-travelers and multimillionaires (*Slap* 31:L13-20).

Wojciehowitz, Doris, Robert and Joseph. *Akiko Hiroguchi enjoyed hearing the true life love stories told by Mary Hepburn and one of them involved her own affair with Robert Wojciehowitz. He chaired the English Department at Ilium High School before it closed. While Doris lay dying, she decided to buy her loving husband a Jaguar automobile as a sign of her love. Their son Joseph got drunk and wrecked the car.*

After Doris died, Robert proposed to Mary Hepburn. Her rejection so embarrassed Robert he climbed a tree for an hour. Mary coaxed him down and he threw up all over himself. Doris is so revered by Akiko that she names her daughter after her.

womb, womblike. (*PP* 53:L12) Paul had the comforter pulled up over his face and was trying to get to sleep tightly curled in the dark, muffled **womb** he made of his bed each night.
(*PP* 243:L4) "Do?" said Harrison. "Do? That's just it, my boy. All of the doors have been closed. There's nothing to do but to find a **womb** suitable for an adult, and crawl into it. One without machines would suit me particularly."
(*CC* 214:L6) And so it was in Mona's and my rock **womb**. At least we could think. And one thing I thought was that the creature comforts of the dungeon did nothing to mitigate the basic fact of oubliation.
(*GBR* 112:L8) A child in her **womb** *(Sylvia Rosewater's)* would have an unbreakable claim to control of the Foundation, whether Eliot was crazy or not.
(*Gal* 63:L17) And when Mandarax was asked to come up with quotations from world literature which could be used in a celebration of some event on the slag heap of Santa Rosalia, the instrument almost always came up with clunkers. Here were its thoughts when Akiko gave birth. . . . *In the dark **womb** where I began / My mother's life made me a man. / Through all the months of human birth / Her beauty fed my common earth. / I cannot see, nor breathe, nor stir / But through the death of some of her.*

John Masefield (1878-1967)*

(*Gal* 225:L15) He *(James Wait)* wasn't having any visions of the future or the past. He was little more than a fibrillating heart, just as Hisako Hiroguchi, wedged between the vibrating toilet and washbasin below, was little more than a fetus and a **womb**.

---

*Masefield's poem is one of three poems and one biblical inscription Mandarax provides for the occasion.

(*Blue* 67:L27, 32) Yes, and my mind really was as blank as an embryo's as I crossed this great continent on **womblike** Pullman cars. It was as though there had never been a San Ignacio. Yes, and when the Twentieth Century Limited from Chicago plunged into a tunnel under New York City, with its lining of pipes and wires, I was out of the **womb** and into the birth canal.
(*Blue* 71:L3) Circe Berman has just suggested that I was a replacement for the Armenian baby which had been taken from her **womb** in Switzerland.
(*Blue* 112:L4, 6) What a satisfactory form of transportation that proved to be! That Cadillac was better than **womblike**. The Twentieth Century Limited, as I have said, really was **womblike**, in constant motion, with all sorts of unexplained thumps and bangs outside. But the Cadillac was *coffin*like. Pomerantz and I got to be *dead* in there. The hell with this baby stuff. It was so cozy, two of us in a single, roomy, gangster-style casket. Everybody should be buried with somebody else, just about anybody else, whenever feasible.
(*HP* 30:L23, 34) If Henry Moellenkamp had not come out of his mother's **womb** dyslexic, Tarkington College wouldn't even have been called Tarkington College. . . .

If Henry Moellenkamp hadn't come out of his mother's **womb** dyslexic, and if that mother hadn't been a Tarkington and so known about the little college on Lake Mohiga, this library would never have been built and filled with 800,000 bound volumes.
(*HP* 31:L22, 29) If Henry Moellenkamp hadn't come out of his mother's **womb** dyslexic, there would never have been a tower in which to hang the Lutz Carillon. . . .

If Henry Moellenkamp had not come out of his mother's **womb** dyslexic, these heights above Scipio might have been all darkness on the cold winter night 2 years ago, with Lake Mohiga frozen hard as a parking lot, when 10,000 prisoners at Athena were suddenly set free.
(*HP* 32:L2) REGARDLESS of whether Henry Moellenkamp came out of his mother's **womb** dyslexic or not, I was born in Wilmington, Delaware, 18 months before this country joined the fighting in World War II.
(*HP* 289:L18) His stepfather had been very good to him. Rob Roy said that the only thing he didn't like about him *(his stepfather)* was the way he raised calves for veal. The baby animals, scarcely out of the **womb**, were put in cages so cramped that they could hardly move, to make their muscles nice and tender.
(*HP* 302:L5) Add the greatest number of children known to have come from the **womb** of just 1 woman, and there you are, by gosh. *This is one of the steps in Hartke's riddle about how many people he killed in war—equivalent to the number of women he made love to throughout his life.*
(*FWD* 78:L6) The Attorney General's Commission on Pornography, a traveling show about dirty books and pictures put on the road during the administration of Ronald Reagan, was something else again. At least a couple of the panel members would later be revealed as having been in the muck of financial or sexual atrocities. There was a clan feeling, to be sure, but the

family property in this case was the White House, and an amiable, sleepy, absentminded old movie actor was its totem pole. And the crazy quilt of ideas all its members had to profess put the Council of Trent to shame for mean-spirited, objectively batty fantasias: that it was good that civilians could buy assault rifles; that the contras in Nicaragua were a lot like Thomas Jefferson and James Madison; that Palestinians were to be called "terrorists" at every opportunity; that the contents of **wombs** were Government property; that the American Civil Liberties Union was a subversive organization; that anything that sounded like the Sermon on the Mount was socialist or communist, and therefore anti-American; that people with AIDS, except for those who got it from mousetrapped blood transfusions, had asked for it; that a billion-dollar airplane was well worth the price; and on and on.

Woodcock, Sheldon. *In* Deadeye Dick*, Woodcock is chosen to play the part of John Fortune in the New York production of Rudy Waltz's "Katmandu." Woodcock is frustrated because Rudy can't explain Fortune's inarticulate behavior. The actor points out that Fortune says something about Shangri-La thirty-four times, seventeen times proclaiming that no one dies there. And yet, the climax of the play shows John Fortune dying in Shangri-La.*

Woodly, Dr. Norbert. *The effeminate physician dating Penelope Ryan, in "Happy Birthday, Wanda June." Woodly is such a pacifist, that despite Penelope's disgust with her husband's Hemingway lifestyle, she comes to view Woodly as too wimpish for her tastes.*

The Woodpile. *The title of the family newspaper for those whose government-issued middle name is "Chipmunk."* (*Slap* 181:L1) . . . the motto of *The Woodpile* used to be this: "A Good Citizen is a Good Family Woman or a Good Family Man."

Woollcott, Alexander Humphreys. *Alexander Humphreys Woollcott (1887-1943) was born into the North American Phalanx commune in Red Bank, New Jersey, and became the* New York Times *drama critic (1914-1922), moving to the* New York World *from 1925 to 1928. He hosted "The Town Crier" radio show from 1929 to 1942 while writing for* The New Yorker. *He was a member of the Algonquin Round Table and through the 1930s was known as an arbiter of popular literary tastes. (Benet's Reader's Encyclopedia, Third Edition)*
(*DD* 55:L24) Whenever a famous visitor came to Midland City, he or she was usually brought to Father's studio at one point or another, since there was so little else to see. . . . That was how I got to meet Nicholas Murray Butler, the president of Columbia University, when I was a boy—and **Alexander Woollcott**, the wit and writer and broadcaster, and Cornelia Otis Skinner, the monologist, and Gregor Piatigorsky, the cellist, and on and on.

(*DD* 78:L6) I have mentioned **Alexander Woollcott**, the writer and wit and broadcaster and so on, who was a guest at our house one time. He coined that wonderful epithet for writers, "ink-stained wretches."

wrang-wrang. *John/Jonah reflects on the purpose served by the destructive nihilistic poet Sherman Krebbs in association with himself.* (*CC* 71:L15-20) I have not seen Krebbs since. Nonetheless, I sense that he was my *karass*. If he was, he served it as a ***wrang-wrang***. A ***wrang-wrang***, according to Bokonon, is a person who steers people away from a line of speculation by reducing that line, with the example of the ***wrang-wrang***'s own life, to an absurdity.

Wright, Bert. (*ST* 117:L2-3) The nominal commander of the entire Army, General of the Armies Borders M. Pulsifer, was in fact controlled at all times by his orderly, **Corporal Bert Wright**. **Corporal Wright**, the perfect orderly, carried aspirin for the General's almost chronic headaches.

Wu, Sam. *In* Bluebeard, *Wu was once the cook for Dan Gregory before World War II. He also sat for Gregory when he needed to illustrate Fu Manchu. Later, Wu opened a Chinese laundry in New York City. Wu heard about how lonesome it was for soldiers stationed overseas, so he asked Rabo for his address before the young apprentice went abroad. While stationed in France, Rabo came across a number of valuable paintings that he sent to Wu for safekeeping. After the war, Wu had everything ready for Rabo's arrival.*

Wyandotte College. *The institution which employed the dynamopsychic Professor Barnhouse in* "Report on the Barnhouse Effect," *and the first known home of the computer EPICAC, designed by Dr. Ormand von Kleigstadt of Wyandotte's physics department in the 1950 short story "EPICAC." Both stories are reprinted in* Welcome to the Monkey House.

Wyatt, Radford Alden. *Walter Starbuck's roommate at Harvard and twin brother of Sarah Wyatt. Though an heir to the fortunes of the Wyatt Clock Company, the terrible losses it suffered because of the radium dial disaster caused him to drop out of Harvard. He went to work in a tuberculosis sanitarium and, as a consequence, contracted the disease which kept him out of the armed forces during World War II. He then went to work as a welder in a Boston shipyard, and* died of a heart attack in Nineteen-hundred and Sixty-five—in a cluttered little welding shop he ran singlehanded in the village of Sandwich, on Cape Cod (*JB* 107:L12-14).

Wyatt, Sarah. *One of the four great loves of Walter Starbuck's life, the twin sister of Radford Alden (Starbuck's Harvard roommate), and wife of Leland Clewes. Her early relationship with Starbuck was marred by her innocence and naivete.* (*JB* 98:L17-29) This would continue to be the case for the next seven years. **Sarah Wyatt** believed that sex was a sort of pratfall that was easily avoided. To avoid it, she had only to remind a would-be lover of the ridiculousness of what he proposed to do to her. The first time I kissed her, which was in Wellesley the week before, I suddenly found myself being played like a tuba, so to speak. **Sarah** was convulsed by laughter, with her lips still pressed to mine. She tickled me. She pulled out my shirttails, leaving me in humiliating disarray. It was terrible. Nor was her laughter about sexuality girlish and nervous, something a man might be expected to modulate with tenderness and anatomical skill. It was the unbridled hee-hawing of somebody at a Marx Brothers film. *She and Starbuck paired off into a great friendship which grew out of their disastrous date at the Hotel Arapahoe.* (*JB* 111:L11-20) I told her brokenly in the taxicab that nothing about the evening had been my own idea, that I was a robot invented and controlled by Alexander Hamilton McCone. I confessed to being half-Polish and half-Lithuanian and nothing but a chauffeur's son who had been ordered to put on the clothing and airs of a gentleman. I said I wasn't going back to Harvard, and that I wasn't even sure I wanted to live anymore.

I was so pitiful, and **Sarah** was so contrite and interested, that we became the closest of friends, as I say, off and on for seven years.

Wyatt Clock Company. *The seemingly ancient Brockton, Massachusetts, firm partly owned by the parents of Sarah and Radford Wyatt. The company, the workers, and the Wyatt family were all victimized by the terrible error in management instruction given by the foreman.* (*JB* 101:L1-17) It went like this: In the nineteen twenties the United States Navy awarded Wyatt Clock a contract to produce several thousand standardized ships' clocks that could be easily read in the dark. The dials were to be black. The hands and the numerals were to be hand-painted with white paint containing the radioactive element radium. About half a hundred Brockton women, most of them relatives of regular **Wyatt Clock Company** employees, were hired to paint the hands and numerals. It was a way to make pin money. Several of the women who had young children to look after were allowed to do the work at home.

Now all those women had died or were about to die most horribly with their bones crumbling, with their heads rotting off. The cause was radium poisoning. Every one of them had been told by a foreman, it had since come out in court, that she should keep as fine point on her brush by moistening it and shaping it with her lips from time to time. *Among the victims was Mary Kathleen O'Looney's mother. Sarah Wyatt's father was an inactive partner in the company but still shouldered financial liability for the radium-poisoning. He had been the largest yacht broker in Massachusetts, but by 1931 the effects of the depression and the radium case had left them penniless.*

Wysocki, Mary Ann. *One of the unfortunate victims of mass murderer Anthony Costa, included in Vonnegut's essay "There's a Maniac Loose Out There."* (*WFG* 76:L14-16 *There's a Maniac Loose Out There*) Young women in America will continue to look for love and excitement in places that are as dangerous as hell. Salute them for their optimism and their nerve. *Vonnegut is unnerved about the innocence of Costa's victims, recalling that his daughter Edith also spent a summer in Provincetown, and had been involved with a man who often said he wanted to kill her. He goes on to say,* When Tony was arrested, I called her up in Iowa City, and I said, "Edith—that guy who kept saying he was going to kill you: was his name Tony Costa?"

"No, no," she said. "Tony wouldn't say anything like that. Tony wasn't the one."

Then I told her about Tony Costa's arrest (*WFG* 76:L24-29).

X

X, Muhammad Daffodil-11. *While reading through the Daffodil Directory, Wilbur learns he is artificially related to the former Light-Heavyweight Boxing Champion of the World, in* Slapstick.

Ximénez, Eduardo. *The Ecuadorian bush pilot who saw the SOS tramped in the riverbank of the Tiputini River, landed his amphibious plane, and met Father Bernard Fitzgerald, the Roman Catholic priest living with the Kanka-bonos for the past fifty years. Fitzgerald convinces Ximénez to take the last remaining six Kanka-bonos (all young girls) to Guayaquil. They eventually wind up on the Galápagos Islands with Mary Hepburn and Captain von Kleist and unwittingly participate in Hepburn's procreation schemes which also involve Akiko Hiroguchi. Leon Trout sees a parallel between the efforts of Ximénez and bomber pilot Paul W. Tibbets, the man who dropped the atomic bomb on Hiroshima.* (*Gal* 156:L16-23) So **Ximénez** was one aviator who had quite a lot to do with the future of humanity. And another one was an American named Paul W. Tibbets. It was Tibbets who had dropped an atomic bomb on Hisako Hiroguchi's mother during World War Two. People would probably be as furry as they are today, even if Tibbets hadn't dropped the bomb. But they certainly got furrier faster because of him.

Y

Yadin, Yigael. *Arnold Marx and his father are amateur archaeologists working on the ruins of Hazor.* (*MN* 3:L9) They do so under the direction of **Yigael Yadin**, who was Chief of Staff of the Israeli Army during the war with the Arab States *(in 1948 when Israel was granted independence by the United Nations)*.

Yamashiro, Hiroshi Raspberry-20. *In* Slapstick, *the patriarch of the Manhattan Roseberry clan who is near death when Wilbur Swain arrives in the city. Swain is abducted by the Raspberries not because he's president but because he's a physician. Wilbur's abductors give him the antidote to The Green Death, the plague of the city, and bring him to the Financial District where he is expected to treat Hiroshi Yamashiro. After curing his patient, the Raspberries bring Wilbur all sorts of prized possessions. Rather than taking all their valuables, Wilbur selects a single brass candlestick. His legend grew, and he became known as the King of Candlesticks.*

Ying, Pi (see also **Colonel Bryan Kelly** and **Major Barzov**). *The sadistic military commander of a brigade in an unnamed Far East communist country in the short story "All the King's Horses," reprinted in* Welcome to the Monkey House. *He challenges Colonel Bryan to a game of chess using Kelly's wife, children, and soldiers as various chess pieces to be killed if captured during the game. Ying's mistress kills him when she realizes he is preparing to kill Kelly's son.*

Yonson, Yon. *In the opening chapter of* Slaughterhouse-Five, *Vonnegut writes about the frequency with which he has returned to Dresden as literary subject. In some ways he feels spent by the recurring desire to write about the firebombing, and at the same time the desire to write about it defines him. These feelings are expressed in both the limerick and poem he recites.* (*SL5*

2:L31, 3:L3) There was a young man from Stamboul, / Who soliloquized thus to his tool: / "You took all my wealth / And you ruined my health, / And now you won't *pee*, you old fool."

and,

"My name is **Yon Yonson**, / I work in Wisconsin, / I work in a lumbermill there. / The people I meet when I walk down the street, / They say, "What's your named?" / And I say, / "My name is **Yon Yonson**, / I work in Wisconsin. . . . "

Young, Buck. *In* Player Piano, *Buck Young is the "young buck" Cornell football coach Doctor Roseberry is trying to lure into playing for the university rather than his Delta Upsilon fraternity. Buck is determined to become an engineer, insisting he plays football for fun. As a commentary on the often-perceived sham of intercollegiate athletics, Vonnegut characterizes college football in the days of the ruling technocracy as a business without pretense of student-athletes. Doctor Roseberry is prepared to sell linemen to Harvard to offer Buck Young a $35,000 contract. Similarly, the linemen see no reason why a well trained college athlete couldn't play into their forties.*

Buck Young decides to play ball when Doctor Edmond L. Harrison of the Ithaca Works appears in The Dutch bar while Roseberry is proposing to the football star. Harrison is drunk and depressed about the apparent fall from grace of Paul Proteus while at the Meadows. Buck Young had been brought up to believe that people do lousy work when compared to machines and can't understand Harrison's disenchantment. Harrison tells him that machines are slaves and "Anybody that competes with slaves becomes a slave" (*PP* 243:L13). *Buck Young will apparently sign with Coach Roseberry.*

Young, Ida. *The Vonnegut family cook when Kurt was a young child. He writes lovingly about her, acknowledging a debt accrued during long hours in a warm kitchen.* (*WFG* xxiv:L27, xxv:L19 *Preface*) One of the lost pieces of mine which I hope Professors Klinkowitz and Somer will never find has to do with my debt to a black cook my family had when I was a child. Her name was **Ida Young**, and I probably spent more time with her than I spent with anybody—until I got married, of course. She knew the *Bible* by heart, and she found plenty of comfort and wisdom in there. She knew a lot of American history, too—things she and other black people had seen and marveled at, and remembered and still talked about, in Indiana and Illinois and Ohio—and Kentucky and Tennessee. She would read to me, too, from an anthology of sentimental poetry about love which would not die, about faithful dogs and humble cottages where happiness was, about people growing old, about visits to cemeteries, about babies who died. I remember the name of the book, and wish I had a copy, since it has so much to do with what I am.

The name of the book was *More Heart Throbs*; and it was an easy jump from that to *The Spoon River Anthology*, by Edgar Lee Masters, to *Main Street*, by Sinclair Lewis, to *U.S.A.*, by John Dos Passos, to my thinking now. There is an almost intolerable sentimentality beneath everything I write. British critics complain about it. And Robert Scholes, the American critic, once said I put bitter coatings on sugar pills.

It's too late to change now. At least I am aware of my origins—in a big, brick dreamhouse designed by my architect father, where nobody was home for long periods of time, except for me and **Ida Young**.

Young, Mary. *Loosely modeled after Ida Young, the Vonnegut family cook when Kurt was a small boy, Mary Young is 108 years old when she dies of pneumonia at the Midland County Hospital. She was Midland's oldest citizen. Her parents were slaves in Kentucky. Mary worked as a laundress for Dwayne Hoover's family when he was quite young.* (*BC* 63:L8-11, 33) She told Bible stories and stories about slavery to little Dwayne. She told him about a public hanging of a white man she had seen in Cincinnati, when she was a little girl.

. . . Here is all she had to say about death: "Oh my, oh my."

Like all Earthlings at the point of death, **Mary Young** sent faint reminders of herself to those who had known her. She released a small cloud of telepathic butterflies, and one of these brushed the cheek of Dwayne Hoover, nine miles away.

Dwayne heard a tired voice from somewhere behind his head, even though no one was back there. It said this to Dwayne: "Oh my, oh my."

Z

zah-mah-ki-bo. *In Bokononist thinking,* "Fate—inevitabe destiny" (*CC* 152:L1).
(*CC* 155:L33) Frank's servants brought us gasoline lanterns; told us that power failures were common in San Lorenzo, that there was no cause for alarm. I found that disquiet was hard for me to set aside, however, since Frank had spoken of my ***zah-mah-ki-bo***.

He had made me feel as though my own free will were as irrelevant as the free will of a piggy-wig arriving at the Chicago stockyards.

Zamiatin, Eugene. *Russian author Yevgeny Zamyatin's 1920 novel* We *is credited by Vonnegut as the source for novels about regimented totalitarian societies including his own* Player Piano. (*WFG* 261:L31 *Playboy Interview*)
VONNEGUT: This was in 1949 and the guys working on it *(a computer-operated milling machine at General Electric)* were foreseeing all sorts of machines being run by little boxes and punched cards. *Player Piano* was my response to the implications of having everything run by little boxes. . . .
PLAYBOY: So science fiction seemed like the best way to write about your thoughts on the subject?
VONNEGUT: There was no avoiding it, since the General Electric Company *was* science fiction. I cheerfully ripped off the plot of *Brave New World*, whose plot had been cheerfully ripped off from **Eugene Zamiatin**'s *We*.

Zappa, Lee Razorclam-13. *The husband of Vera Chipmunk-5 Zappa. Together they served as cooks in the King of Michigan's field kitchens during the battle of Lake Maxinkuckee in* Slapstick.

Zappa, Vera Chipmunk-5 (also cited as **Vera Chipmunk-17 Zappa**). *After the world is in a shambles and Wilbur Swain is living on the first floor of the Empire State Building, his* nearest neighbor is **Vera Chipmunk-5 Zappa**, a woman who loves life and is better at it than anyone I ever knew. She is a strong and warm-hearted and hard-working farmer in her early sixties. She is built like a fireplug. She has slaves whom she treats very well. And she and the slaves raise cattle and pigs and chickens and goats and corn and wheat and vegetables and fruits and grapes along the shores of the East River (*Slap* 22:L20).

It is she who supplied the thousand candles eventually used in the closing death scene of Wilbur.

Zeltoldimar (see also ***Plague on Wheels***). *The home planet of Kago and his band of space travelers who make stops at Lingo-Three and Earth, in* Breakfast of Champions.

Zinka. *In* Cat's Cradle, *the Ukrainian midget working as a dancer with the Borzoi Dance Company. Newt Hoenikker saw her perform in Indianapolis and again while attending Cornell. His infatuation with her led to a whirlwind romance, a quickie marriage, and a honeymoon at the Hoenikker Cape Cod cottage, all with the United States granting political asylum. Just as quickly, Zinka returned to the Soviet Union claiming disgust over American materialism. An American correspondent in Moscow discovered that Zinka was not twenty-three, but forty-two years old. When she left Newt, she took his chip of ice-nine with her and gave it to her government.*

Zircon-212 (see also ***The Big Board***). *Billy Pilgrim read Eliot Rosewater's copy of Kilgore Trout's* The Big Board *when in the Veterans' Hospital in Ilium. The story takes place on the planet Zircon-212, and partially parallels Billy's Tralfamadorian experience.* (*SL5* 173:L5) It was about an Earthling man and woman who were kidnapped by extra-terrestrials. They were put on display in a zoo on a planet called **Zircon-212**. *Billy read the story again in a Times Square bookstore while time-tripping.*

Zog (see also **"The Dancing Fool"**). *In Kilgore Trout's "The Dancing Fool," Zog is the diminutive creature from the planet Margo who comes in friendship to Earth, prepared to offer cures for cancer and world peace. He is killed by a golf-club-wielding homeowner who is startled by Zog and his crude speech, a series of farts and tap dancing. Zog was trying to tell the man his house was on fire.*

Index

Aamons, Celia, **1**, 445
Aamons, Nestor, **1**, 102, 131, 415
A-bomb, American bomb, atomic bomb, atom-bombed, atom-bombing, atombombed, atomic weapons, hydrogen bomb, the bomb (when clearly meaning a nuclear device), neutron bomb, **1-3**, 26, 50, 68, 72, 128, 133, 139, 196, 199-200, 216, 225, 233-234, 261, 281, 283, 292, 294, 313, 299, 329, 336, 363, 394, 407, 445, 451, 481, 544-545, 596, 621, 642, 645, 653
aboriginal, 125, 145, 390, 515, 618
Academy of Fine Arts, 629
"Adam," **3**, 357-358, 465, 541
Adams, James Carmalt (also James Carmalt Adams, Jr.), **3**, 190, 613
Adams, Steve, **3-4**, 253
Adams, Tiger, **4**
Adult Correctional Institution at Shepherdstown, **4**, 87, 96, 111, 115, 299, 303, 341, 386, 390, 407, 410, 422, 452, 487
afterlife (*see also* blue tunnel), **4-5**, 40, 60, 138, 193, 252, 256, 423, 484, 589, 612
Agnes and Agnes (Barbara and Martha), **5**
Agnew, Spiro, **5**
agnosticism, 30, 482, 597, 636
Aïda, **5**
AIDS, 7, 20, 526, 649
Aiken, Conrad, **5-6**
Ainus, **6**, 12
air-raid, air raid, air-raid shelter, air-raid siren (also raid and raids as they refer to Dresden or to wartime bombing), **5-7**, 36, 114, 212, 380, 498, 514, 560, 625, 632
A.J. Topf und Sohn, **7**, 20, 638
Ajax, **8**
Akbahr, Abdullah, **8**, 57, 117
Al, **8**
Alamo, 337, 552
Albanian Flu, **8**, 223, 271, 357, 396, 455, 572
Alberti, Leon Battista, **8**, 164, 183, 197
Alburger, J.T., 151
Algonquin Hotel, **8**, 137
Algonquins, **8-9**, 323
Algren, Nelson, **9**, 141
Alice in Wonderland, **9**
"All the King's Horses," **9**, 36, 69, 352, 654
All-Night Sam, **9-10**, 110, 123, 282, 375
Allen, Lester, **10**
Amazon Rain Forest, 145, 274, 283, 499
Amphibious Pioneers Society (also

Amphibians), **10**, 387
Anderson Trailer, **10**
Annapolis (United States Naval Academy), 12, 185, 608
Anschluss, **10**, 549
anthropoids, **10**
anthropological, anthropologist, anthropology, **10-11**, 52, 59, 77, 108, 111, 128-129, 150, 152, 189, 229-230, 244-245, 452, 476-477, 481, 613, 618
anthropomorphic, **12**, 133, 257
anti-gerasone, **12**, 518, 575
anti-Semitism, 57, 112, 139, 246, 351, 390, 450, 470, 513, 640
apocalyptic, **12**, 33, 67, 78, 109, 211
Arapahos, **12**
Archangel Gabriel (also Gabriel horn), **13**
Archimedes screw, **13**
Aristotle, **14**
Arnold, General Benedict, **14**, 357
Arthur, Chester Alan, **15**
Ashland, Captain Bryant, **15**, 328
Ashland, Charlene, **15**
Ashland, Charles, **15**, 328-329
Asimov, Isaac, **15-16**, 521
"Asleep at the Switch" (*see also* Albert Einstein, Dr. Robert Fender, and Kilgore Trout), 16, 222, 238, 585
Astor, Madelaine, **16**, 165
atheism, 4, 11, 16, 43, 108, 165, 327, 461, 480-481, 498, 620
Atlas, Charles, **16**, 43, 65, 106, 215-216
Augustus, Caesar, **16-17**
Aurelius, Marcus, 14, **17-18**
Auschwitz, 7, **18-21**, 128, 185, 220, 226, 275, 298, 312, 403, 540, 545, 550, 609
Auschwitzer, 19, **21**, 226
Auschwitzian, **21**
Averageman, John, **21**
Avondale, **22**, 184, 391, 408, 431, 439, 593, 628, 630

B-1, **23**
B-17, **23**, 73-74
B-36, **23**
B-52, **23-24**, 70
Babel (also Tower of Babel), **24**, 203, 379, 576, 577
Babylon, Babylonian, **25**, 182, 249, 295
Bach, Johann Sebastian, **25-26**
bacteria, bacterium, **26**, 53, 216, 599
Baer (*see also* Kroner), **26-27**, 104, 241, 364-365, 421, 467
"Bagladies" (*see also* Pamela Ford Hall), 27, 279, 281
Bagnialto (*see also* Barring-gaffner of Bagnialto), **27-28**, 33, 266, 370, 584
Bahía de Darwin, 5, 7, **28**, 60, 61, 176, 184, 195, 198, 244, 251, 289, 313, 315, 430, 443, 508, 586, 608-609
Baku, **28**
Baltra, **28**, 73
The Bannister, **28**, 408, 424
Bannister, George Hickman (also Bannister Memorial Fieldhouse), **28-29**, 84, 96, 351
Bannister, Lucy, **29**
baptism, baptismal, Baptist, baptized, baptizing, **29-31**, 97, 405, 415, 479, 483, 489, 491, 534, 565, 597, 633,
Barber, Kensington, **31**, 539, 602
Barca-Lounger, Barcalounger, **31**, 56, 227
Barker, General Honus, **31-32**, 187
Barkley, Ben, **32**
Barlow, Frank X., **32**, 167, 237-238, 573, 584-585, 603
Barnhouse, Professor Arthur (*see also* dynamopsychism), 3, 31-32, 72, 92, 99-100, 115, 132, 187, 216, 313, 443, 538, 650
Barnstable, Barnstable First Church of God the Utterly Indifferent, West Barnstable, West Barnstable Volunteer Fire Department, 12, **33**, 122, **147-148**, 172, 257, 454, 477-478, 500, 504, 638, 646
barracks humor (*see also* humor)
The Barring-gaffner of Bagnialto, or

This Year's Masterpiece, 27-28, **33-34**, 266, 370, 584
Barry, Fred T., 4, 22, 31, **34**, 35, 42, 200, 339, 398, 409, 487
Barry, Mildred (also The Mildred Barry Memorial Center for the Arts), **34**, 306, 346, 392, 407-408, 439, 555, 559
Barry, Roland, **34-35**, 247
Barrytron, 34, **35**, 203, 280, 307, 322, 341, 408-409, 487, 507, 541, 556
Barus, Karl, **35-36**, 41, 507
Barzov, Major, 9, **36**, 352, 654
basement (*see also* air-raid shelter, cellar and subbasement), 7, 18, **36-38**, 89, 109, 116-117, 155, 156, 159, 223-224, 257, 275, 300, 306, 327, 330, 333, 362, 403, 434, 460, 512, 541, 555, 576
Bassett, Earnest S., **38**, 366-367
Batavia, 31, **38**, 337, 450
Batten, Barton, Durstine & Osborn, **38**
Battle of Boca Raton, **39**, 62, 78, 401; Mrs. Lyman R. Peterson, 454
Battle of Iowa City, 612
Battle of the Bulge, **39**, 203, 373, 456, 633
Bauerbeck, Nelson, **39**, 529
Bavaria, **39**, 490
Bay State Progressive, **39**, 441
Beagle, Her Majesty's Ship (also *The Voyage of the Beagle*), **39**, 194
Beame, Timothy, **39-40**
Bearse, Alfy, **40**
Beelzebub, **40**, 382, 413
Beethoven (also Beethoven's Ninth Symphony), **40**, 77, 213, 488, 508, 578, 615
begat, beget, begetting, 25, 30, 35, **40-41**, 190, 494, 600
beginning, middle... and end, **41-42**, 169, 351, 417-418, 581
Begum, Arjumand Banu, **42**
belfry (*see also* cupola and tower), **42**, 186-187, 576, 578-579
belief, 16, **43-44**, 65-66, 106, 130, 171, 216, 234, 246, 255, 320, 366, 469, 478, 512, 558, 560, 592, 595, 604, 611
Bella (also Bella's Beauty Nook), 37, **44**, 631-632
Beralikur, 370, 615
Bergeron, Bruce, **44-45**, 300, 626
Bergeron, Ed, **44-45**
Bergeron, George and Hazel, **45**
Bergeron, Harrison, **45-46**
Berman, Abe, **46**
Berman, Circe, 26, **46**, 61, 70, 75, 118, 136, 173, 177, 181, 214, 346, 347-348, 373, 387, 539, 561, 596, 648
Berringer, Fred and Dave, **46-47**, 75, 123, 170, 241-242, 312
Bert (*see also* Quinn; Wright), **47**, 122
Beryllium, **47**, 400
Beskudnikov, **47-48**, 272, 347
Betelgeuse (also Betelguese), B48, 503, 542, 543
Bethlehem (also Star of Bethlehem), **48**
Bethune, **48**, 168
BIBEC, **49**
Bierce, Ambrose, **49**, 166, 319
The Big Board, **49**, 193, 584, 658
big eye, **49-50**
"The Big Space Fuck," **50**, 54-55, 116, 147, 153-154, 232, 302, 344, 370, 431, 439, 527, 539, 573
Bigley, Homer and Clara, **50**, 637
Bijou Theater, **50**, 342
Bikini Atoll, **50**
Bill, **51**, 288, 313
Billy the Poet, **51**, 227, 260, 344, 401, 418, 429, 434-435, 634
biochemical-anthropological, anthropology and biology, biochemistry, 10-11, 48, **52-53**, 77, 79, 108, 111, 130, 150, 152, 189, 229-230, 245, 289, 301, 324, 444, 452, 462, 476-477, 481, 570, 613
biodegradable, 26, **52-53**, 599

Birch (John Birch Society), **53**
bird, birdhouses, birdlike (*see also* Titanic Bluebird), 51, **53-55**, 98, 158, 167, 178, 251, 270, 279, 302, 444, 462-464, 485, 509, 530, 544, 567, 576, 578, 646
Birkenau, 21, 128
birth (*see also* ethical birth control), 3, 40-41, **55-57**, 58, 66, 76-77, 113, 120, 173, 208, 213, 217, 227, 229, 238, 245, 273, 284, 290, 292-294, 297-298, 301, 385, 393, 404, 415, 428, 447, 456, 475-477, 489, 499, 501, 518, 541, 562, 564, 582, 588, 597, 612, 615, 624, 633, 647-648
Black Brothers of Islam, 8, **57**, 470
Black Cat Café, **57-58**, 154-155, 304, 451, 510, 528
Black Garterbelt (*see also Plague on Wheels*), **58**, 191, 240, 316, 390, 449, 460, 469, 470
black humor (*see also* humor), 58, **316-320**, 320, 488, 523
Blackbeard, **58**, 64
Blake, William, **58-59**, 262, 402
Blank, Katarina, 41, **59**, 507, 616
Blankenship, Dr. Martin Peale, **59**, 402
BLINC System, **59**, 70, 72, 487
blivit, **60**
Blue Fairy Godmother (*see also* Frank Wirtanen), 37, **60**, 97, 119, 149, 158, 195, 208, 361-362, 434, 440, 542, 646
blue tubing, blue tunnel (also tunnel and tube when used to mean the blue tunnel of the Afterlife; *see also* Afterlife and funnel), 4-5, 56, **60-61**, 254-255, 314, 508, 571, 584, 586
Bluebeard (*see also* Rabo Karabekian for), 37, 46, 50, **61-62**, 93, 111, 149, 173, 210, 214, 229, 232, 241, 258, 272, 274, 290, 292, 299, 327, 338, 346-348, 352, 355, 387, 390, 395, 403, 413, 462, 499, 537, 540, 551, 618, 639, 650
Bluebird, 61
Bluebird Farm, **62**, 303, 354, 409, 507
Boaz, 19, 39, 54, **62**, 92, 98, 110, 131, 172, 282, 411, 421, 553, 574
Bob (*see also* Wild Bob)
Bob & Ray, **62-63**
Bockman, Dr. Fred and Marion, **63**, 228, 283
Bodovskov, Stepan, **63**, 264, 361, 402, 646
Bohn, Arthur, **63-64**
Boko-maru, boko-maruing, **64**, 66, 102, 415
Bokonon, 16, 43, 58, **64-67**, 76, 101-103, 106-107, 139, 196, 213-216, 245-246, 265, 269, 327, 345, 348, 362, 368, 397, 415, 445-447, 462, 475, 478-479, 503, 549, 555, 591, 600, 609, 631, 650
Bokononism, Bokononist, 43, 64, **65-67**, 76, 83-84, 102, 105, 107, 139, 171, 196, 213, 216, 237, 245, 269, 309-310, 313, 336, 345, 348, 397, 415, 447, 479, 512, 532, 555, 557, 604, 609, 631, 657
Bolivar, **67**, 101, 112, 295, 321, 397
bomb, bomb proof, bomb shelter, bombed, bombed-out, bombing, bombproof, bombshells, timebomb (These bomb references are for non-nuclear devices only. *See also* A-bomb for all other references to nuclear bombs.), 30, 35, 50, 59, **67-70**, 71-72, 94, 148, 189, 203, 229, 287, 435, 487, 546
bombardier, 23, 59, 69, **70**, 72, 74, 122, 133
bombardment, **70-71**
bombenfest, **71**
bomber, fighter bomber, fighter-bomber (*see also* fighter plane), 2, 20, 23, 28, 59, 68-70, **71-74**, 133, 145, 189, 218, 281, 288,

292, 380-381, 443, 487, 653
The Bombing of Germany, **74**, 78, 162, 449, 504
bomb-release, 23, 73, **74**
bombsight, 69-70, **74**, 133, 380
Bonesana, Cesare, Marchese di Beccaria, **74**
booby trap, booby-trap, boobytrapped, **74-75**, 188, 431, 450, 452, 484, 605
book-banning, **76**
Boone, Michael, **76**, 266, 289
Borasisi, 66, **76**, 245, 447
Borders, Lance and Leora, **76**
Boris, **76-77**, 101, 156, 314, 331
Borisoglebsk, **77**, 465
Borman, Frank, 260
Bormann, Martin, **77**
born again, born-again, **77**, 81, 120, 140, 252, 371, 477
Borzoi Dance Company, **77**, 297, 326, 658
Boström, Hjalmar Arvid, 40, **77**, 488, 508
Boyden, Hay, **77-78**, 501
Boyer, Richard O., **78**, 419, 571
Boyle, Raymond, **78**, 263, 322, 449
Brackman, Sergeant Henry, 39, **78**, 174, 202, 247, 401
Braxton, Carter, **78**
Breakfast of Champions, 4, 28-29, 34-35, 37, 40, 56, 58, 62, **78-84**, 87-88, 96, 111, 119, 129, 149, 162, 196, 219, 221, 223, 226, 233, 247, 256, 262, 283, 287-288, 293, 299-300, 304-307, 321, 326, 334-335, 341, 345-346, 350, 375, 377, 386, 390-392, 403, 407, 409, 413, 424, 439-440, 448, 452, 487, 507, 520-521, 535, 542, 553, 555-558, 582-585, 624, 658
Breed, Dr. Asa, **82-83**, 84, 236, 259, 297, 511
Breed, Marvin and Avram, **84**, 296-297, 299, 527
Breedlove, Don, **84-85**, 87, 319, 351
Breslaw, **85**
Breslau, 263
Brewer, Ansel (also Irving Buchanon and Eddie McCarty), **85**
briquet, **85**, 360
Brokenshire, Dr. David, **85-86**, 248
Bromley, Milford S., **86**
Brown, Betty and Bobby, **86**, 184, 433, 487, 565
Brown, Dr. Ed, **86**, 326, 496, 510
Brown, Payton, **87**
Brown Bomber (*see also* Karl Heinz), **288**
Browning, Gloria, 85, **87**
Buchanon, Irving (*see also* Ansel Brewer), **85**
Buchenwald, 19, **87**, 218
Buffalo Works, **87**
bugger, buggered, buggery, **87-88**, 235, 305, 309, 465
Bugle-Observer (the *Midland City Bugle-Observer*), 85, **88**, 248, 405-406, 408, 628
Building 58 Suite, **88-89**, 219
Bullard, Dr. Brainard Keyes, **89**
Bullard, Harold K., **89**, 219, 574
Bunker, Archie, **89-90**, 514
Buntline, Amanita, **90**, 91-92, 453, 489, 493, 634
Buntline, Castor, **90-91**, 200, 426-427, 449, 494
Buntline, Elihu, 90, **91**
Buntline, Lila, 90, **91**, 373, 472, 493, 634
Buntline, Stewart, 90, **91**, 139, 200, 300, 396, 486, 523
Bunty, **92**
Burch, Captain Arnold, **92**
Burger, Knox, **92-93**, 161, 378
Burgoyne, General John, 14, **93**, 537
Bush, George, 54
Butler, Nicholas Murray, **93**, 649
Butler, Pennsylvania, 314
Butler University, 198, 327

calcimine, 68, **94**, 211
Caldwell Foundation, **94**, 249
Calhoun, Doctor Bud, 75, **94-95**, 241, 327
Calvary Cemetery (*see also* Golgotha), 28, **95-96**, 197, 200,

233, 266, 353, 407-408, 422, 451, 629
Calvin, Ned, **96**, 263
Calypso, 64, 66, **96**, 216, 507
Camelot, 144-145, 322, 339
Campbell, Archibald, **96**, 269
Campbell, Howard W. Jr., 6-7, 14, 18, 21, 29, 37, 42, 48, 56, 58, 60, 63, 85, **96-97**, 105, 114, 119, 121, 123, 138, 158, 168, 178-179, 195, 203, 205, 208, 220, 223, 226, 235-236, 251, 253, 261-262, 264-265, 275, 279, 282, 287-288, 298, 316, 325, 339, 351, 357, 360-361, 371, 392, 402-403, 411, 417, 423, 433-434, 437, 440, 488, 499, 509, 513, 536, 540, 542, 566, 570, 572, 605, 607, 613, 636, 640, 645, 646
canary, canary-in-the-coal-mine, canary-bird-in-the-coal-mine, 51, 53, **98**
Canby, Sarah Horne, **98**, 411
capitalism, 200, 246, 331-332, 396, 524-525, 639, 645; *The Wayward Capitalist*, 246
Capone, Al, **98**, 300, 392
Carlsbad Caverns, **99-100**, 498, 547
The Carlyle Hotel, **100**
Caroline, **100**, 132, 516
Caroline Islands, **100**, 443
Carpathia, **100**, 569
Carroll, Madeleine, **100**
Carson, Johnny, **100**
Carter, Clyde and Claudia, **100-101**
Carter, Jimmy, 101
Carver, George Washington—George Washington Carver High School, **101**, 127, 407
Casa Mona, **101**, 103, 415
Casey, Dwight, **102**, 175
Castle, Dr. Julian, 1, 19, 64, **102**, 103, 295, 397, 415, 426, 478, 519, 609
Castle, Dr. Morris N., **102-103**
Castle, Philip, 58, 101-102, **103**, 215, 301, 415
Castle Sugar, Incorporated, 64, **103**, 397
catacombs, 67, **103-104**, 183, 333, 483, 526, 598
Cathcart, Sally, **104**, 486
Cathedral of Whispers (*see also* Sacred Miracle Cave), 111, 507
Cat's Cradle, 1-2, 10, 16, 19, 37, 77, 82, 84, 87, 96, **104-109**, 110, 112, 168, 175, 179, 196, 202, 232, 236, 240, 246, 248, 259, 264-265, 269, 292, 296-299, 307, 309, 322-325, 330, 336, 368, 378, 399, 412, 414-415, 418, 445, 452, 465, 475, 477, 486, 511, 518, 532, 536, 549, 572, 631, 635, 658
cave, cave dweller, **109-112**, 131, 172, 282, 307, 335, 507
Carlsbad Caverns (also cavern), **99-100**, 194, 282, 498, 547
Caz-ma-cas-ma, 67, **112**
Cedar Key, 406, 627
Cedar Tavern, **112**, 241, 356
Céline, Louis-Ferdinand, **112-114**, 310
cell, cellblock (*see also* jail and organism), 7, 37, 56, **114-118**, 221, 253, 257, 333, 403, 515, 570, 576, 646
cellar, cellars, 36, 44, **118-119**, 211-212, 281, 339, 373, 546, 596,
chaos, chaotic, 65, 77, **119-121**, 143, 151, 201-202, 209, 260, 270, 305, 313, 348, 482, 518, 533, 543, 557, 631
Chaplin, Charlie, 70, **121-122**, 165
chaplinesque, 121
Charity Anne Browning, 47, **122**
Charlestown Prison, **122**, 386
Charley, **122-123**, 597
Charlotte, **123**
Chasens, Henry Stewart, **123**, 432
Checker Charley, 46-47, 75, **123**, 170, 241, 312, 421
chemical, chemically, 12, 52, **123-127**, 152, 160, 223, 244-245, 280, 301, 306-307, 407, 452, 469, 515, 538, 558, 560, 574, 618

chemist, 21, 59, 101, **127-128**, 129, 307, 339, 482, 590
chemistry, 52, 104, 123, 125-128, **129-130**, 175, 191, 292, 320, 335, 359, 381, 486, 510, 519, 521, 553, 560, 570, 615
"The Chemistry Professor," 104, **130**, 191, 355, 486, 510
Chessman, Caryl, **131**
Chetniks, 1, **131**
Chevy Chase, Md., **131**, 214, 555
chimney, chimneylike, 69, 74, **131-133**
Christ, Jesus Christ, Christ's (*see also* The Church of Jesus Christ the Kidnapped), 2, 12, 29, 30, 59, 91, 95, **133-138**, 139-141, 143, 145, 148, 161, 164, 176, 178-183, 193, 197, 201, 248, 252, 257, 267, 287, 298-299, 316, 334, 336, 339, 342, 357, 360, 362, 371-373, 386, 393, 395, 457, 462, 484, 490, 506, 524-525, 540, 582-583, 585, 598, 603, 607, 624
christen, **138-139**, 563, 613
Christian (also Young Men's Christian Association, Christian Scientists; *see also* The White Christian Minuteman), 48, 77, 90, 104, 129-130, 136-137, **139-142**, 144, 180, 183, 196, 223, 252, 267, 309-310, 379, 415, 477, 482-483, 485, 512, 523, 525-526, 544, 549, 564, 583, 598, 607
Christianity, 104, 120, 137, 139, 141, **142-145**, 150, 223, 229, 267, 310, 386, 428, 433, 482-483, 526, 598, 605
Chrono, 29, 33, 54, 78, **145-146**, 147, 171-172, 178, 238, 261, 274, 288, 343, 455, 478, 499, 504, 510, 543, 574
chrono-synclastic infundibula, 24, 48, 82, 98, 104, **146-147**, 148, 154, 158, 172, 203, 254, 279, 350, 357, 371, 379, 471, 503, 508, 532-533, 542, 573-574, 636
Chrysler Building, **147**, 333, 362, 450, 547, 551, 576, 588
Chung, Lowell, **147**, 488
Chung, Mrs., **147**, 237
Church of God the Utterly Indifferent, 12-13, 33, **147-148**, 172, 257, 454, 477-478, 500, 504
Church of Jesus Christ the Kidnapped, **148**, 624
Churchill, Winston, **148-149**, 496, 519, 605
Cincinnati Bengals, **149**, 233
Cinderella, 60, **149-150**, 428
civic, civic managers, civics, junior civics, 27, 91, 121, **150-151**, 325, 365, 423, 498, 606
Claessen, **151**
Claggett, Noble, **151**
clan, 47, 125, **152**, 526, 563, 648, 654
Clarke, Arthur C., 15, 50, 55, 147, **152-154**, 163, 263, 284, 302, 343, 370, 520-522, 543, 573
Clarke, Arthur K., **154-155**, 639
Claycomb, Judge and Moon, **155**, 524
Cleveland Science Fair, 111, **155**, 181, 285, 626
Clewes, Dr. Alan, **155**, 381, 570
Clewes, Leland and Sarah (*see also* Sarah Wyatt), 37, 76, 101, **155-156**, 237, 261, 281, 331, 550, 627, 650
Clinton Street, **157**, 451
Clough and Higgins, **157**
Clowes, Henry, **157**, 453, 630
Club Cybernetics, **157**, 642
Coates, Arnold, **157-158**
cocoon, **158**
Coggin's Pond, **158**
Cohen, Abe, **158-159**
Cohen, Isadore Raspberry-19, **159**, 223, 612
Cohen, Israel (also Cohen Rink), **159**
Cohn, Roy, **159**, 333, 399, 425
Cohoes, 37, 134, **159-160**, 287, 324, 460
coil, **160**

college humor (*see also* humor)
Collier's, **92**, 132, 161
Colson, Charles W., **161**
The Columbia Conserve Company, **161**, 621
column, 16, **161-165**, 175, 183-184, 197, 288, 326, 449, 522, 544, 546, 644
Combat Respiratory Rations (also called CRR's or goofballs), **165**, 214, 218, 266, 421, 449, 466, 517, 609, 633, 640
comedians, 62-63, 121, **165-166**, 224, 285, 317, 319, 372, 426, 486
common decency, **166**, 229, 335
communism, 1, 21, 36, 128, 131, 156, 168, 176, 269, 281, 310, 331-333, 337, 352, 399, 406, 411, 481, 496, 498, 526, 528, 537, 550-551, 591, 627, 649, 654
cone, cone-shaped, conical, **166-168**, 187-188, 391, 447, 526, 544, 547
Conestoga, **168**, 414
    stogies, 168
Conners, Harrison C., **168**, 232, 295
conspiracy, 42, 119, **168-169**, 233, 304, 334, 350, 364, 445, 461, 467, 640
conspiratorial, **170**
conspirators, **170**, 334, 380
conspire, 66, **170-171**, 199, 248, 421, 512, 604, 622
Constant, Benjamin, **171**, 198, 430
Constant, Malachi, 7, 10, 24, 29, 33, 54, 62, 78, 92, 104-105, 109, 131, 145, 161, 170, **171-172**, 173, 178, 184, 188, 198, 235, 239, 261, 289, 325, 343, 387, 412, 416, 417, 430, 455, 471-472, 477-478, 499, 500, 504, 509, 532-534, 542-543, 545-546, 552-553, 574, 576, 599, 604, 636-637, 641, 644
Constant, Noel, 10, 13, 157, 171, **172-173**, 235, 239, 260, 266, 387, 417, 641
Constant, Sylvanus, **173**
Cooley, Franklin, **173**
Cooper, Oveta and Mary Selwyn Kirk, **173**, **355**
Copernican (*also* pre-Copernican), 533
Corbett, General William K., **173**
Cordiner, Dr. Cordelia Swain, **173-174**, 196, 221, 224, 549, 575
cork, corkscrew-shaped, corkscrews, 155, **174-175**
Cormody, **175**
Cornell University, 59, 85, 102, 127-129, 157, **175**, 179, 202, 214, 280, 283, 290, 297, 326, 355, 425, 462, 465, 471, 488, 563, 605, 655, 658; *Cornell Daily Sun*, **175**, 605
Corpus Christi, **175-176**, 337
Cortes, Hernando, **176**
Cortez, Major Ricardo, **176**
Corwin, Lance, 135, **176**
Costa, Antone C., 10, 33, 160, **176**, 651-652
Cotuit Harbor, **177**, 490, 492
Coulomb, Marc, **177**, 360, 375
Count Dracula, **177**
counter-clockwise, counterclockwise, **177-178**, 543, 545
Cowper, William, **178**
The Cradle of Erotica, 592
Crimea, 97, **178**, 434
Crispus Attucks High School, **178**, 407
Crocker, Harry, **178**
Crocker, Pete, **179**
Crocker, Virginia, **179**, 325
Crone, Joe, **179**, 456-457
Crosby, H. Lowe and Hazel, 101, 175, **179**, 202, 269, 411, 595
Crown Hill Cemetery, **179**, 486
crucifix, **179-183**, 479
    crucifixion, 25, 95, 133-134, 137, 180-184, 267, 337, 395, 485, 544, 585, 603; "Crucifixion in Rome," 180-181, 485, 544
    crucify, 25, 42, 104, 180-183, 199, 337, 382; crurifragium, 180, 182

cruciform, 164, 183, 197
Cruz, Hernando, **184**, 451, 512, 559
The Cry of the Nocturnal Goatsucker, 86, **184**, 433, 487, 565
cuckold, cuckolding, 182, **184**, 337, 500
cuckoo clock in Hell, 18, **184-185**, 236, 298, 393, 407, 423, 509, 645
Culver Military Academy, **185**, 370, 465
cupola (*see also* belfry and tower), 42, 56, 88, 167, **186-187**, 391, 576, 607, 628, 630
Cuthrell, William K., **187**
Cuyahoga Bridge and Iron Company, 42, **187**, 227, 232, 272, 330, 335, 400, 476, 550, 638
Cuyahoga Massacre, 25, 42, 155, 187, **188**, 232, 330, 331, 400, 578
cylinder, cylindrical, 68, 71, 166, **188-189**, 526, 609

"D.P." **190**, 288, 348
D'Arthanay, Barbara, **190**
The Daffy-nition, **190**, 266
dagonite, 28, 41, **190-191**
The Daily Pancreas, **191**
"The Dancing Fool," **191**, 390, 584, 618, 658
Darlington, Edward Seward, **191**, 261, 386, 633
Darwin, Alton, 159, **191-193**, 449, 510
Darwin, Charles, 39, **193-195**, 213, 256, 315, 457, 582; Darwinian, 98, 193-194, 621; Darwinism, 194-195, 479; Darwinists, 193-195, 483
Das Reich der Zwei, **195-196**, 429, 433
"Nation of Two," 97, 195-196, 429, 433
Davis, Alvin, **196**
Davis, Benjamin, **196**
Davis, Lottie, **196**
The Day the World Ended, 65, 82, 105, **196-197**, 202, 296, 336, 346, 348
de la Madrid, Dr. Jose Sepulveda, **197**
de Medici, Innocenzo, 8, 164, 183, **197**, 513, 607
De Mille, Hippolyte Paul, 29, 95, 111, **197-198**, 200, 233, 353, 407-408, 451, 629
de Stael-Holstein, Baronne, 171, **198**, 430
de Sucre, Antonio Jose, **198**
de Wet, Mrs. Marthinus, **198**
Deadeye Dick, 37, **198**, 199, 349, 412, 517, 544-545
Deadeye Dick, 2, 4, 22, 28-29, 34-35, 37-38, 56 **198-200**, 201, 204, 215, 233, 237, 241, 247-248, 253, 255, 258, 271, 275, 285, 291-292, 299-300, 303, 305, 307, 322, 326, 346, 353, 363, 368, 391-392, 397, 405, 407-408, 422-423, 439, 445, 451, 453, 455, 474, 485, 488, 507, 534, 545, 555, 556, 571, 619, 630, 636, 649
Deal, Selena, **200-201**, 449
Debs, Eugene V., **201**, 285, 327, 405
"Deer in the Works," 127, 175, **201-202**, 208, 213, 243, 323-324, 335, 340-341, 465, 548, 568
Deer Park, Long Island, **202**
Deerfield Academy, **202**, 285
Del Prado Hotel, **202**, 511
Delbert, **202**
Delgado, Private Geraldo, **202**, 292, 384, 515
Delta Upsilon, 175, **202**, 297, 655
Denny, Kyle, **203**
Denton, Reverend Bobby, 24, **203**, 379, 577
Derby, Edgar, 60, 103, 149, **203**, 263, 326, 536
Derby, Howard, **203**
Destouches, Louis-Ferdinand (*see also* Céline)
di Capistrano, Paulo, **203**
di Sanza, Dr. Carlo, **204**
Dillon University, **204**, 489, 493
Dina and Donna, **204-205**

Dobrowitz, Alvin, **205**
Dodge, Dr. Ned, **205**, 468
Dole, Dr. Helen, **205-206**
Domesday Book, **206**, 286, 376, 378, 475, 491, 498, 557
Don, **206**
Donald, **206**
Donna, **206**
Donner, John, 6, **206-207**
    Donner Party, 206-207
Donnini, Jim, **207-208**, 289, 354, 473
Donoso, Dr. Teodoro, 73, **208**

Donovan, 597
Donovan, General, **208**
Doris, **208**, 362, 450, 513, 647
Dornberger, General Walter, **208**, 607
Dorset, New York, **208**, 335
Dostoevski, Feodor (also Fedor and Dostoyevsky), 174, **208-209**, 521, 554
Dougie, **209**
Drano, 79, 117, 120, **209-210**, 305-306, 452, 557-559
Dresden, 2, 6-7, 30, 36-37, 39, 67-69, 70-72, 74, 80, 106, 112, 118, 203, **210-212**, 214-215, 218, 223, 237, 251, 263-264, 274, 320, 325-326, 328, 349, 358, 373, 385, 390, 404-405, 424, 434, 438, 456-457, 463, 486, 488, 501-502, 521, 523, 532, 536-537, 551, 579, 612, 643-644, 654
Dresden, History, Stage and Gallery, 71, 223
    Mary Endell, 71, **223**
Dresser, Paul, 172, **212**, 413, 551
drupelets, **212-213**
DSM (Dog Story of the Month), **213**
duffle, 66, **213**, 555
Dukakis, Michael, 545
Duke of Oklahoma, **213**, 423-424, 599, 612
Dumas, Alexandre, **213**
Dun Roamin, **213**, 534
Dunkel, Stan, **213**
duprass, **213-214**, 411
Dürer, Albrecht, **214**
The Dutch, **214**, 265
Duty-Dance (A Duty-Dance With Death), **214-215**, 536
Duveneck, Frank, **215**, 398-399
Dynamic Tension, 16, 65-66, 106, **215-216**, 336, 397, 423, 533
dynamopsychic, dynamopsychism, 26, 31-32, 100, 132, 187, **216**, 250, 443, 485, 650
Dyot, **216**
dyslexia, 168, **216-217**, 381, 413-414, 451, 568-570, 578, 648

Eagle-1 (*see also* Captain Bernard O'Hare), 438
Eaker, Ira C., Lieutenant General, U.S.A.F., **218**
Eastman, George, **218**, 427, 559-560, 627
echolalia, **218-219**
    echophrasia, 218
Edel, Israel and Norma, 167, **219**, 334, 454
The Eden Express, 52, 118, 260, 440-441, 516, 618
Edison, Thomas, **219-220**, 526, 563
    Edison Theatre, 571
Edison Park, **220**
Ehrens, Kurt and Heinrich, **220**
Eichmann, Adolf, 114, **220-221**, 357, 360
Einstein, Albert, 127, **221-223**, 424, 538
El Greco, **223**, 410, 430, 583, 594
Empire State Building, 148, 159, **223**, 337, 438, 498, 582, 657
Endell, Mary, 71, **223-224**
enlaced, **224**, 486
Enlightened Self-Interest, enlightening, enlightenment, 62, 81, 97, 165, 196, **224**, 265, 288, 379, 446, 470, 510, 513
entombed, **224**
EPICAC, 1, 28, 87, 99, 160, **224-226**, 258, 354, 461, 468, 498, 527, 561, 608, 642, 650
Epstein, Dr. Abraham and his

mother, 18-19, 21, **226**, 275, 540
equilibrium, 26, 215-216, **226**
The Era of Hopeful Monsters, **226-227**, 316
Erie Coal and Iron, **227**
ethical birth control, ethical birth control pill, ethical suicide, 51, 55-56, 212, **227**, 344, 401, 429, 434-435, 539, 634
Ethical Suicide Parlor, 31, 51, 55-56, 212, 227-228, 260, 309, 344, 361, 401, 418, 429, 434-435, 447, 451, 483, 539, 556, 571, 633-634
Ethical Suicide Service (E.S.S.), **228**
"The Euphio Question," 63, 87, **228**, 283
euphoriaphone, 63, **228**, 283
Evelyn and Her Magic Violin, **228**
Everett, Norman, **228**
Ewald, Lincoln, **229**
extended family, 11, 124, 135, 143, 163, 190, **229-231**, 244-245, 266, 268, 270, 326, 370, 379, 383, 388, 395, 428, 476, 480, 487, 518, 530, 535, 562-563, 565, 570, 585, 604, 611, 613, 646

Fabri-Tek (also Fabritek), 168, **232**, 295, 325
Failey, Bonnie, **232**, 638
Failey, Dr., **232**
Failey, William, **232**
Fairbanks, Charles Warren, **232**,
Fairbanks, Richard Jr., **232-233**, 347, 567
Fairchild, Will, 29, 95, 197, 200, **233**, 255, 350, 368, 407-408, 451; Fairchild Boulevard, 233, 353, 407; Fairchild Heights, 233; Fairchild High School, 233, 305, 408; Fairchild Hotel, 233, 350, 407; Fairchild Park, 233, 377, 408, 607; Will Fairchild Memorial Airport, 4
Farmers of Southwestern Ohio for Nuclear Safety, **233-234**, 408, 445
Farrow, Dudley and Grace, **234-235**, 538, 597
fascism, fascist, 88, 114, **235**, 306, 310, 427, 465
father. . . son, fathers. . . sons, 173, 185, 199, **235-236**, 422, 468, 493, 505
Faust, 56, **236**, 385
Faust, Naomi, **236-237**
February 13, 1944, 67, 210, **237**, 373, 456
"The Febs," **237**
Fedders, John W. Jr., 147, **237**
Federal Minimum Security Adult, Correctional Facility, Finletter Air Force Base, 156, **237**
Fender, Dr. Robert, 16, 32, 167, **237-238**, 329, 520, 573, 584-585, 603
Fenstermaker, Isabel, 171, **238**
Fenstermaker, Lowell, **238**, 274, 527
Fenstermaker, Rob Roy, **238-239**, 274, 527, 648
Fern, Ransom K., 14, **239**, 387, 416
  Ferm, Ransom K., 239, 263
Fernandina Island, **239**
Fieser, Dr. Louis, **239**
fighter plane, fighter-plane (*see also* bomber), 71, 145, **240**
The Fighting Danes, **240**
  The Melancholy Danes, 240
Finale Rack, 20, **240**
Finch, Dr. Katharine, 94, **241**, 461, 467, 642
Finkelstein, Isadore and Rachel, **241**
Finnerty, Edward Francis, 5, 9, 27, 47, 89, 114, 123, 170, **241-242**, 251, 290, 300, 364, 379, 404, 421, 468, 529, 556, 604
Finnerty, Noyes, **242**, 243, 496
Firehouse Harris (*see also* Herbert Foster), 242, 249, 250
The First District Court of Thankyou, **423**, 584
Fishbein, Mrs., **243**
Fitzgerald, Bernard, **243**, 345, 653
Flammer, Lou, 202, **243**
Flemming, Pearl, **243**, 263
Flemming, Willard and Mary (*see*

also Mary Hepburn and James Wait), **243-244**, 289, 624-625
"Flocka Butt" (*see also* Dr. Stewart Rawlings Mott)
Florio, General Lucas, **244**
folk society (*see also* extended family), 11, 124-125, 230, **244-245**, 259, 476
"The Folk Society," 11, 230-231, 244-245, 428, 476-477
foma (*see also* Bokononism), 65-66, **245-246**, 269, 447
Ford, Henry, **246**, 470
Ford, Rose Aldrich, **247**, 562, 565
Fort Belvoir, **247**
Fort Benjamin Harrison, **247**, 327, 347
Fort Benning, **247**
Fort Bragg, **247-248**, 432
Fort Jesus, 178, **248**
"Fortitude," 122, 203, **248**, 250, 263, 378-379, 565
Fortune, 154
Fortune, John, 22, 85-86, 186, 198-199, **248-249**, 275, 283, 349, 391, 422, 517, 530, 607, 630, 649
"The Foster Portfolio," 25, 38, **249-250**, 421
Alma and Herbert Foster, 249
Firehouse Harris, 249-250
Foust, Senator Warren, **250**
Francis X. Donovan Post of the American Legion in Brookline, **250**
Frank, Anne, 114, **250**, 418
Frankenstein, Dr. Norbert, 88, 122-123, 248, **250**, 263, 314, 378-379, 565
Franklin, Benjamin, **250-251**, 261, 511
Frascati, Marion and Lou, 54, **251**, 278, 466
Free American Corps, 97, 121, 176, **251**, 337, 514
free thinker, freethinker, free-thinker, 4, 11, 41, 43, 138, 140, 231, **251-252**, 419, 477, 484, 531, 598, 607, 616, 620, 635
free will, free-willed, 81, 114, 135, **252-253**, 307, 435-436, 657
Freeman, Sally, 4, **253**
French, Mary Alice, 111, **243**, 253
Freud, 19, 236, 317, 614
Friedman, Bruce Jay, 317
Friedmann, Tuvia, **253**, 279
fubar, **253**
Fuller, Norman, **254**
funnel, funnel-shaped (*see also* blue tunnel), 60, 147, **254**

Gabriel (*see also* Archangel Gabriel)
Galápagos, 2, 4-5, 28, 40, 50, 55, 60, 76-77, 100. 107, 147, 157, 159, 175-176, 193, 206, 243, 250, **255-256**, 258, 265, 289, 293, 300, 304-306, 315, 323-324, 345, 350, 355, 383-385, 389, 395, 407, 433, 466, 486, 488, 508, 520, 584-585, 608
Galápagos Islands, 28, 39, 45, 168, 184, 195, 239, 255-256, 274, 291-292, 315, 430, 512, 575, 586, 653
Galen, Vermont, 224, **256**, 646
gallows humor, 316-317
Garland, Dorothy Daffodil-7, **256**
Garr, Vernon and Mary, **256-257**, 515
Garth, Dr. Fred (and his children Brud, Alice, and little Ewing), 12, 87, 114, 133, **257**, 401
Garu, Krishna (also Krishna Gatu), **257**
Gatch, **248**
GCT (General Classification Tests), **257**, 258, 393, 402
GEFFCo, 37, 224, **258**, 289, 300, 324, 395, 512, 583, 645
Gelderman, Carol (*The Wayward Capitalist*), 246
Gelhorne, Dr. Francis Eldgrin (also Gelhorne Enterprises), **258-259**, 325, 364, 383, 468
General Forge and Foundry Company, 82-83, **259**, 296, 307, 322, 324, 336, 358
generation gap, **259**

Genesis, Genesis Gang, 173, **260**, 260, 428
Genius Grant (MacArthur Foundation), 537-538
geodesic dome, **260-261**, 401
German batball, 145, 191, 238, **261**, 386, 414, 499, 511, 633
Gettysburg Address, **261**, 578
  Gettysburg, 378, 381, 568-569
Gibney, Peter, **261**
"Gilgongo," **262**
Gingiva-Tru and Viverine, 127, **262**, 307, 339
Ginsberg, Allen, 10, **262**
Glampers, Diana Moon, 46, 96, **262-263**, 375, 404
Glinko-X-3, 78, **263**
Globular Cluster Ml3, 153, **263**
Gloria, 88, **263**, 379
Gluck, Werner, **263**
"Go Back to Your Precious Wife and Son," 179, **264**, 291, 424
The Goblet (also *The Snow Rose* **264** and *Seventy Times Seven* **264**), 63, **264**
God Bless You, Mr. Rosewater, 22, 37, 39-40, 74, 78, 91-92, 177, 196, 210, 223, 242-243, 247, 262, **264-265**, 294, 300, 309, 373, 378, 396, 399, 449, 451, 472, 492-494, 497, 502, 513, 523, 527, 571, 583, 603, 625, 633-634
Goebbels, Paul Joseph, 261, **265**, 288, 360, 393, 434, 572
Gokubi, 41, 117, **265**, 292, 384, 389, 395
Goldberg, Rube (inventions), 11, 95, 108, 481, 532
The Golden House of the Roman Emperor Nero, **265**, 599
Goldwater, Barry, **265-266**, 322
  Goldwater Republican, 78, 502-503
Golgotha (*see also* Calvary Cemetery), 95, **266**, 334, 386, 506
Gömbös, Miklós (*see also* Michael Boone), **76**
Gomburg, Crowther, **266**, 387
Gompers, Samuel, 280
The Goober Gossip, 190, **266**
goofballs (*see also* Combat Respiratory Rations)
Gooz, 33, **266**, 370
Goring, Reichsmarschall Hermann, **266**
Gorky, Arshile, **267**, 559
The Gospel from Outer Space, 134, 139, 142, **267**, 584
Gottlieb, Adolph ("Frozen Sounds Number Seven"), **267-268**
Gottwald's estate, **268**, 287, 462, 602
Grace Daffodil-13 (Cousin Grace), **268**
Graham, Jack, **268**, 333, 441-442, 474, 638
Graham, James and John (Fifth Earl and First Marquis of Montrose), 96, **268-269**, 522
Grand Hotel Oloffson, 197, **269**, 353, 363, 523, 629, 631
granfalloon, 179, **269**
Grant, Robert, **269**
Grasso, Elmer Glenville, **270**
great becoming, 119, **270**, 533
The Great Wall of China, **270**, 578, 580, 599
Greathouse, Virgil (also Greathouse and Smiley), **270-271**, 342, 372
The Green Death, 8, 223, **271**, 328, 654
Green Diamond Plow, **271**, 488
Green River Cemetery, **272**, 356
Green Team, **272**, 529
Greenfield Bank and Trust Company, **272**
Gregory, Dan, 37, 47, 56-57, 132, 151, 177, 184, 247, **272-273**, 338, 347, 352, 413, 420, 426-427, 529, 531, 548, 573, 589, 639, 650
GRIOT™, **273**, 474
Guayaquil, Ecuador, 28, 73, 117, 184, 191, 195, **274**, 292, 315, 345, 473, 486, 578, 625, 653
Guber, Lee, 130
Guggenheim, **274**

Guido, **274**
Gumbo, 145, **274**, 499
Gummer, Harriet, 238-239, **274**, 285
Gumps, Andy, **275**
Gunther, **275**
Gunther, August, 199, 248, **275**, 422, 556, 629-630
Gunther, Grace, **275**
Gutman, Andor, 18, 85, **275-276**, 360, 540

Hacketts, Elmo C., Jr., **277**, 470, 568
Haggedorn, Elbert, **277**
Hagstrohm, Delores and Edgar, Jr., **277**
Hagstrohm, Edgar Rice Burroughs (and his wife Wanda), 205, **278-279**, 466, 469
Haifa Institute for the Documentation of War Criminals, 253, **279**, 357, 514
Hall, Dr. Cyril, 254, **279**
Hall, Pamela Ford, 27, **279**, 281, 433, 448, 538
Halporn, Amy, **279**
Halyard, Dr. Ewing J., 50, 99, 199, 157, 175, 214, **279-280**, 290, 325, 430, 460, 476-477, 488, 561, 637
Hamilton, Alexander, **280**, 331, 399
Hamlet, 240, **280**, 443-444, 466, 491, 578
Handy, Fred, **280-281**
Hanfstaengl, Putzi, **281**
Hansels and Gretels, 118, 211, **281**
Hanson, Miss (also Hanson Centre for the Arts), 279, **281**
The Hapgoods, Three Earnest Brothers, **281**
Happy Birthday, Wanda June, 2, 94, 146, 223, **281-282**, 283, 343, 353, 424, 505, 531, 555, 571, 649
Harger, Lemuel K. and Rose, 9-10, 110, 123, 174, **282**, 375, 432
Hari, Mata, **282**
harmonium, 62, 110, 114, **282**, 411, 553
Harper, Alice, **282**
Harper, Colonel Looseleaf, 2, 281-282, **283**, 353, 505
Harrell, Reverend Charles, 117, **283**
Harrison, Dr. Edmund L. (also Edmond), **283**, 655
Harrison, Lew, 63, **283-284**
"Harrison Bergeron," (*see also* Bergeron) 45, **46**, 148, 262, 484
Hartke, Eugene Debs, 4, 7-8, 14, 16, 19, 23, 25, 31, 35, 38, 44, 57-58, 68, 74-75, 102, 111, 125, 129, 137, 147-148, 155, 160, 168, 191, 198, 201-202, 206, 212, 218, 238, 240, 244, 246, 248, 252-253, 273-274, 279-280, **284-285**, 292-293, 322, 327, 337, 353, 355, 372, 375, 378, 381, 394, 402, 407, 413, 424, 432-433, 445, 448-451, 454, 466, 469, 487-488, 510, 522, 525, 527, 528, 537-538, 541, 552, 554, 561, 569-570, 623, 626, 637, 643, 645
Hartke, Melanie and Eugene Jr., **285-286**
The Harvard Lampoon, 116
Hatfield, Byron, 47, **286**, 400-401
Hausmännin, Walpurga, **286-287**
Haycox, 268, **287**, 602
Hazor, 235, **287**, 392-393, 572, 654
Heath, Durling, **287**
Hederich, Oberdienstleiter Karl, **288**
Heinz, Karl, 190, **288**, 348, 357
Heliogabalus, **288**
helix, 162, **288**, 326, 338, 449, 546
Heller, Charlene, **288**
Helmholtz, George M., 207, **289**, 449, 473, 644
Hepburn, Mary and Roy, 50, 76, 117, 151, 206, 208, 243-244, 251, 258, **289-290**, 291, 324, 345, 385, 395, 403, 508, 575, 585-586, 588, 608, 625, 647, 653
Herald, Randy, **290**
Herpers, Dr. Albert, 157, 175, 280, **290**
Herrick, Cleota, **290**, 494

Hertz, Rudy, 242, **290**, 526, 529
Hildreth, Celia (*see also* Celia Hoover), 4, 149, 197, 253, 290-291, 305-307, 408, 453, 559, 628, 630
Hildreth, Gerald, **290**
Hildreth, Shirley, **291**
Hilton, Gloria, 179, 264, **291**, 424
Hilyer, Tom, **291**
Hinkley, Bearse, 40, **291**
Hiroguchi, Akiko, 41, 60, 208, 256, 289, **291-292**, 345, 385, 389, 647, 653
Hiroguchi, Hisako, 2, 292, **292**, 315, 385, 389, 647, 653
Hiroguchi, Zenji, 41, 202, 265, 291, **292**, 384, 389, 395, 609
Hiscock, Ernest Hubble, 73, **292**, 381
Hitler, Adolf (also Adolph), 21, 77, 102, 128, 140, 171, 181, 229, 241, 248, 261, 281, 284, 292, 314, 411, 424, 426, 434, 514, 527, 542, 552, 605, 607, 613, 628-629, 640
Hitz, Benjamin D., **292-293**
Hitz, Lowell W., **293**
Hocus Pocus, 2, 4, 35, 38, 42, 57-59, 155, 157, 168, 175, 191, 201-202, 212, 218, 223, 237-238, 240, 244, 246, 248, 251, 274, 280-281, 284, 292, **293-294**, 316, 319, 322, 337, 344, 353, 355, 378, 402, 407, 413-414, 424, 426, 432-433, 447, 449-451, 454, 462, 466, 470, 487-488, 499, 510, 520, 522, 527, 531, 537-538, 540, 552, 554, 561, 599, 602, 623
Hoenikker, Angela, 25, 168, 232, **294-296**, 297, 322, 325-326, 514, 527
Hoenikker, Celia, **296**
Hoenikker, Dr. Felix, 82, 84, 108-109, 133, 168, 196, 236-237, 265, 294, **296**, 297-299, 322, 324, 336, 413, 452, 532, 574-575, 609, 631
Hoenikker, Emily, 84, 296, **297**, 511, 527
Hoenikker, Franklin, 37, 40, 110, 232, 259, 296, **297**, 322, 336, 414-415, 445, 489, 511, 546, 549
Secret Agent X-9, 110, 297, 511
Hoenikker, Newton, 67, 77, 106, 109, 175, 179, 202, 294-296, **297-298**, 299, 322, 326, 527, 532, 595, 658
Hoenikker, Rudolph, **298**
Hoess, Rudolf Franz, 18, 185, **298**, 403
Hoffman, Abbie, 137, 260, **298-299**
Holdermann, Bill, **299**
Holderness, Marvin Sharpe, **299**
Holiday Inn, 40, 42, 80, 85, 203, **299**, 300, 305-307, 341, 350, 377, 386, 390-392, 408, 410, 452, 487, 545, 559, 592, 642
Home Sweet Home Moving and Storage, **299-300**, 567
Homestead, 5, 220, 241, **300**, 323, 365, 468, 576
Homo sapiens, 255, 289, **300**, 385
homosexual, homosexuality, 16, 21, 44, 52, 75, 98, 128, 233, 299, **300-301**, 305-306, 338, 351, 392, 431, 459, 465-466, 625
Hoobler, **302**
Hoobler, Cynthia, **302**
Hoobler, Dwayne, Grace and Wanda June, 50, 54, 115-116, **302-303**, 344, 370, 410, 431, 439, 507
Hoobler, Josephus, **303**, 409, 507
Hoobler, Mary, 302, **303**, 556
Hoobler, Wayne, 4, 87, 115, 203, **303**, 325, 370, 410, 440, 487, 502
"The Hooligan," 4, 47, 286, **303**, 438, 582, 589, 611, 613
Hooligan, Francis Iron-7, **303-304**
Hooper, Charlton, **304**
Hooper, Lyle, 8, 57, 169, **304**, 510, 579, 602
Hoover, Bunny (née George), 88, 120, 209, 233, 235, 299-301, **304-305**, 306, 386, 465, 557
Hoover, Celia, 196-197, 209-210,

258, 283, 290-291, 304, **305-306**, 392, 412, 452-453, 559, 624, 628-629
Hoover, Dwayne, 4, 35, 56, 79-81, 85, 87-99, 101, 111, 117, 124, 149, 178, 196, 219, 233, 247, 253, 256, 293, 299-300, 302-305, **306-307**, 325, 335, 350-351, 353-354, 375, 407-409, 412, 435-436, 440, 452, 459, 465, 507, 519, 531, 538, 542, 555-556, 559, 577, 583-584, 592, 624, 632-633, 642, 656
Hoover, Lyle and Kyle, 62, 111, 304, **307**, 507
Horthy, Dr. Lomar, 127, 262, **307**, 339
Horton, **307**
Schramm's Pharmacy, 198, 307, 322, 409, 437, 507, 517-518, 630
Horvath, Dr. Nilsak, 127, **307**, 452
Hotel Arapahoe, 219, **307-308**, 331, 333, 551, 575, 651
Hotel El Dorado, 195, **308**, 445, 608-609, 625
House of Hope and Mercy in the Jungle (*see also* Dr. Julian Castle), 1, 19, 64, 102-103, 178, 415, 609
Hovanessian, Kevork (also Hovanissian), **308**
How You Doin'? **308-309**, 376, 529, 584
Howard Johnson's, 31, 175, 182, 227, **309**
Huie, William Bradford, **309**
Humana, Dr. Vox, **309-310**, 635
humane, 32, 112, 141, **310-311**, 419, 427, 443-444, 550, 584, 591, 642
humanism, humanist, 8, **311**, 512, 615
humanistic physicist, **311-312**
humanitarian, humanitarianism, 16, 19, 54, 90, **312**, 519
humanity, 2, 12-13, 15, 20, 40, 65, 97, 120, 154, 171, 184, 196, 202, 208, 221, 250-251, 255-256, 284, 292, **312-315**, 345, 348, 364, 384-385, 428, 430, 468-469, 500, 536, 586, 599, 609, 635, 653
humankind, 184, 251, **315-316**
humanness, **316**
humanoid, 206, 227, **316**, 469
humor, humorist (American, barracks, black, college, gallows, Jewish, Hoosier, middle-European, white), 15, 44, 63, 130, 135, 165-166, 175, 202, 298, **316-319**, 320, 396, 399, 462, 469, 488, 523, 560, 598
Hundred Martyrs to Democracy, 101, **319-320**, 415
Hurty, Phoebe, 162, **320-321**, 326
"The Hyannis Port Story," 77-78, 100, 122, 132, 213, 265, **321**, 330
Hyatt, Malcolm, **321**, 517

I. G. Farben, **322**, 554
ice-nine, 7, 19, 53, 77, 83, 105-108, 110, 133, 179, 188, 197, 236-237, 240, 294, 296-298, 312, 320, **322-323**, 324-326, 336, 368, 413-415, 418, 451, 463, 511, 520, 587, 609, 631, 658
Ilium (*see also* GEFFCo, General Forge and Foundry, and Pine Knoll), 8, 47, 82, 84, 157, 179, 196, 206, 208, 258-259, 280, 296, 298-300, 322, **323-324**, 330, 336, 358, 365, 395, 574, 602; Ilium air-raid shelter, 36, 114, 380; Ilium Atomic Reactor, 323, 610; Ilium High School, 258, 647; Ilium Police Headquarters, 37; Ilium Real Estate Office, 462; Veteran's Hospital, 658
Ilium Gazette, 324
Ilium Historical Society, 323, **324**, 610
Ilium Merchants Bank, **324-325**
Ilium News Leader, **325**, 581
Ilium School of Optometry, **325**, 403, 457

Ilium Works, 8, 27, 46, 88, 94, 150, 201, 220, 236, 241, 268, 272, 290, 300, 323, 365, 465, 467, 488, 527, 529

incantation, **325**

Indianapolis, 35-36, 41, 52, 59-60, 63-64, 78, 86, 99, 119, 155, 168, 172, 178-179, 202-203, 211, 229, 231-232, 235, 247, 259, 275, 297, 317, **325-327**, 368, 376, 378, 393, 407, 419, 438, 449-450, 463, 474, 481, 491, 535, 557-558, 579, 594-595, 604, 615-616, 619-622, 632, 658; Ahtenaeum, 64; Alcoholics Anonymous, 621-622; Borzoi Dance Company, 297, 658; brewer, 41, 376; Butler University, 198, 327; Camp Atterbury, 615; Chamber of Commerce, 64; Clemens Vonnegut, 41, 59, 252, 419, 481, 616, 620; Columbia Conserve Company, 161, 621; Crispus Attucks High School, 178, 407; Crown Hill Cemetery, 179, 486; Das Deutsche Haus, 35; Daffodil family reunion, 256, 268, 604; Dr. Brown's Indianapolis sanitarium, 86, 449, 463, 510, 632; Edgar Derby, 203; Fabri-Tek, 168, 232, 295; firestorm, 74, 78, 162, 263, 288, 449, 463, 536; First Unitarian Church, 597; Fletcher Trust Building, 64; Fort Benjamin Harrison, 247, 347; *Indianapolis Magazine*, 622; *Indianapolis News*, 317; *Indianapolis Times*, 163, 321, 405; Indianapolis Works, 299; John G. Rauch, 474; John Herron Art Museum, 64; Kin Hubbard, 252, 317, 598; L.S. Ayres store, 64; Midland City, 407; Nazi, 235; outskirts, 170, 172, 491, 553, 574; Powers Hapgood, 155, 621; Public School 43, 150; "Roots," 620; Shortridge High School, 52; slaughterhouse, 290, 495; State Hospital for the Insane, 327; Stegemeier's Restaurant, 621; Virginia Crocker, 179; William Failey, 232

Iowa Writer's Workshop (*also* University of Iowa), 9, 113

Iron Guard of the White Sons of the American Constitution, 119, **327**, 339, 351, 362, 646

Iron Maiden, **327-328**, 445, 572

Irving, David, 2, 218, **328**

"The Island of Death" (Manhattan), **328**

Ivankov, Aksinia, **328**

Ivankov, Alexei, **328**

Ivankov, Major Stepan, 15, **328**, 390

Ivankov, Mikhail, 15, **328**

Ivanoff, Prokhor, **328-329**

Izumi, 237, **329**

Jackie, **330**, 516

Jack's Hobby Shop, 37, 297, **330**

Jailbird, 32, 37, 42, 49, 55, 76-78, 99-100, 122, 147, 155, 161, 204, 219, 227, 232, 237, 240, 266, 268-269, 281, 292, 303, 322, 326, 329, **330-335**, 336, 355, 379, 386, 399, 441, 444, 448, 450, 454, 474, 476, 506, 520, 524, 549-550, 554, 562, 573, 584, 591, 613, 621, 638, 646

James, Jesse, **335**

Jarvis, Colin and Ma, **335**

Jason, Ed, **335**

Jefferson, Arthur Stanley (*see also* Laurel and Hardy), **335**

Jefferson Observatory, Lenin Observatory, Mare Imbrium, **335**, 375, 390

Jekyll, Dr. Henry and Hortense, **335**, 374

Jesus (*see also* Christ)

Jewish humor (*see also* humor)

Johannsen, Nils (also Johannsen Grinder Company), **336**

John/Jonah, 2, 7, 19, 25, 53, 67, 82-84, 101-102, 104-105, 109-110, 175, 179, 196, 202, 224, 236,

265, 294-295, 299, 301, 321, **336-337**, 362, 411, 415, 445, 463, 511, 518, 574, 587, 650
Johnson, Clarence Daffodil-11
Johnson, Henry "Tex," 25, 42, 154, 175, 181-182, 184, **337**, 382,
Johnson, Zuzu, 176, 181, **337-338**, 382
Jolson, Al, **338**, 426
Jones, Fred, 247, 273, 288, **338**, 342, 352, 426, 531, 544
Jones, Lionel J. D. (the Reverend Doctor Lionel J. D. Jones, D.D.S., D.D.), 125, 139, 231, 245, 262, 307, **338-339**, 351, 423, 475, 558, 635, 640, 645
Joseph of Arimathea, **339**
journalism, New Journalism, **339-340**
journalist, New Journalist, 107, 211, **340-341**, 541
Joyce, Leroy, **341**, 386
Judgment Day, 154, **341-343**, 454, 481, 569, 611, 639
June, Wanda (also *Happy Birthday, Wanda June*), 2, 9, 50, 94, 135, 146, 223, 249, 281-283, 292, 302, **343-344**, 349, 353, 424, 431, 505, 531, 552, 555, 571, 610, 620, 630, 649
Jungian, 19
Juno, **344**

Kago (*see also Plague on Wheels*), 300, **345**, 459, 460, 658
Kairys, Anna, **345**, 549
Kankabonos (also Kanka-bonos), 208, 243, 289, 291, 315, **345**, 350, 385, 473
kan-kan, 65, 196, **345-346**
Karabekian, Dorothy, 256, **346**, 347-348, 551
Karabekian, Rabo, 7-8, 37, 39, 46, 48, 50, 56-57, 61-62, 70, 75, 77, 81, 100, 111-112, 115, 118, 120, 122, 132, 147, 149, 151, 157, 164, 173, 175, 177, 214, 229-230, 232, 241, 247, 253, 258, 260, 272, 274, 290, 299, 308, 327, 338, 342, **346-348**, 349-350, 352, 355-356, 372, 375, 380, 386-387, 390-391, 393, 395, 410, 425-426, 439, 462, 498, 512-513, 529, 537, 539, 551, 561, 567, 583, 588, 607, 639-641, 645
Karabekian, Terry and Henri, 347, **348**, 551
karass, 65, 106, 120, 196, 213, 269, 345-346, 348, 411, 532, 543, 631, 650
Karloff, Boris (*also* Monsters of Frankenstein), 314
Karlswald, 190, 288, **348-349**
Karpinski, Big John, Dorene and Little John, **349**
Kasabian, F. Donald, **349**
"Katmandu," 86, 94, 198, 237, 249, 283, 302, 305, **349-350**, 407-409, 517, 530, 545, 571, 629-630, 649
Kazak (also Kazakh), 48, 146-147, 196, 343, **350**, 371, 385, 391, 431, 499, 503-504, 508, 542-543, 553, 574
Keedsler, Beatrice, 42, 120, 169, 233, **350-351**, 386
Keeley, Father Patrick (also Keely), 185, 235, 313, 339, **351**
Keene, Patty, 84, 115, 149, **351**
Kelly, Colonel Bryan, 9, 36, **352**, 654
Kelly, Margaret (and her twin sons Jerry and Paul), **352**
Kemp, Marilee, 100, 121, 151, 157, 164, 175, 184, 197, 260, 272-273, 300, 346-347, **352-353**, 356, 387, 426, 464, 475, 512-513, 540, 544, 548, 561, 567, 607
Kennedy, Robert, 193, **353**, 457
Kennedy, Sheila, 78, 322, 501
Kenzaburo (*see also* Zenji Hiroguchi), 292
Keough, William (*also Punchlines*), 165-166, 319-320
Kern, Shirley, **353**
Kestenbaum, Stanley, **353**
Ketchum, Bernard, 199, 234, **353**,

405-406, 445
Key, Eddie, 62, **353-354**, 440, 535, 592
"The Kid Nobody Could Handle," 55, 130, 207, 289, 473
Kilgallen, Pat, 255, **354**
"The Kilimanjaro Device," 560
Kilyer, Tom, **354-355**
Kimberly, **355**, 519
King, Bobby, 147, 208, **355**, 422, 430, 536
King of Candlesticks, 271, **355**, 466, 612, 654
Kirk, Mary Selwyn, 173, **355**
Kisco, Buddy, **355**
Kissinger, Henry, **355**, 479
Kitchen, Terry, 6, 9, 46, 70, 112, 122, 272, 288, 290, 338, 348, **355-357**, 373, 567
non-epiphany, 356
Kittredge, Waltham, **357**, 599
un-neurotic courage, 357
Kleindienst, Edward Strawberry-4, **357**
Klopfer, Arndt, 220, **357**
Knechtmann, Avchen, Heinz and baby Peter Karl; Karl and Helga, 3, **357-358**
The Knights of Kandahar, **358**
Knowles, Lyman Enders, 10, **358-359**
Kolhouri, **359**, 527
Konigswasser, Dr. Ellis, 10, **359**, 387, 599
Koradubian, Martin, 133, **360**
Koshevoi, Mr., **360**
Kouyoumdjian, Marktich (*see also* Marc Coulomb), 177
Kovacs, Arpad, 105, **360**
Kraft, George, 14, 63, 77, 97, 119, 121, 168, 250, 264, 325, 339, **361**, 362, 434, 437, 465, 514, 570, 595, 607, 640
Kraft, Mary, 339, **361**, 362, 640
Kramm, Doris, **362**, 450
Krapptauer, August, 119, 226, 327, 339, **362**, 645
Krebbs, Sherman, **362-363**, 650
Krementz, Jill, **363**
Kremlin, **363-364**, 580, 599
Kroner, Anthony, 26-27, 38, 47, 89, 104, 170, 241, 279, 283, **364-367**, 383, 421, 467-468
Kroner, Janice, **367**
Kropotnik, Commissar, **367**

Lady's Slipper, 34, **368**, 415, 475, 591, 609
Lafayette Escadrille, 233, **368**, 378, 408
Laird, Melvin, 393, 537
Lake Maxinkuckee (also Lake Maxincuckee), 185, **368-370**, 615, 657
lambos, 33, **370**
lamprey, 50, 154, 302, **370**, 539
Lancer, **370**
Landry, Cynthia, **370-371**, 502
Lapp, Marlin T., **371**
Lardner, Ring, 166, 319
Larkin, Emil, 140, 163, 271, **371**, 480, 547
"Last Full Measure," 251, 261, 265
Laurel and Hardy, 70, 121-122, 137, 165, 298, 335, **371-372**
Lawes, Cleveland and Eucharist ("Ukey"), 332, **372**, 374, 539
Lazarus, 46, 136, **372-373**, 524, 619
Lazzaro, Paul, 60, 118, 149, 203, 260, **373**, 456, 634
Le Fèvre, Andre, **373**
leaks, 79, **373-374**, 515, 642
Leech, Leonard, **374**, 425
Leen, Arpad, 49, 333, **374**, 442, 474
Leghorn, Fred, 130, 335, **374**, 486
LeGrand, Pierre, **375**, 579
Leidveld and Moore, 177, **375**
Lembrig, Dr. Thor, **375**
Lenin Observatory (*see also* Jefferson Observatory)
Leonard, Dawn, 263, **375**
LeSabre, Harry and Grace, 4, **375-376**, 633
Levittown, 509
Letzinger, Coach, **376**
"The Lie," 32, 54-55, 121, 291, 355, **376**, 484-485, 544, 622
Lieber, Albert, 41, **376**, 558

Lieber, Andy, **376-377**
Lind, Jenny, **377**
Lingamon, Cynthia Anne, **377**
Lingamon, Ned, **377**, 642
Lingo-Three (*see also Plague on Wheels*), 300, 345, **377-378**, 459, 658
Littauer, Kenneth, 92, 161, 368, **378**
Little, Dr. Elbert, 250, **378**
Little, Sherman Wesley, **378**, 557, 650
Little Bighorn, **378**
"Long Walk to Forever," 123, 247, **379**, 432, 579
Love Crusade, 24, 203, **379**, 577
Lovejoy, Sylvia, 248, **379**, 565
Lowell, A. Lawrence, 269, **379**
Lubbock, Luke, **379-380**
Lucretia A. Mott, 133, **380**
Luma County Clarion, **380**, 426
Luma County Savings and Loan, Association, **380-381**
Lutz, Andre, 155, **381**, 382, 570
Lutz Carillon, 34, 40, 155, 181, 198, 217, 285, 292, **381-382**, 413, 578, 648
Lynn, Jonathan (*see also* Alfred Planck), 99, 119, **382**, 460

MacCleary, Lou, **483**
Machu Picchu, **382**, 562-563, 565
MacIntosh, Andrew, 202, 292, **383-385**, 609
MacIntosh, Selena, 292, 350, **385**, 431
MacIntyre, Carlyle F., 56, **385**
Mackay, Charles, 142, **385-386**, 605
MacKenzie, Joyce, 191, 261, **386**
MacMahon, Bonnie and Ralph, 140, 341, **386**
Madeiros, Celestino, **386**, 442, 506
Madge, **387**
Madison, Polly, 46, **387**, 639
Magnum Opus, Incorporated, 13, 157, 171-172, 239, 260, 266, **387**, 416, 478, 527
Mainland (*see also* Meadows), 402
Mamigonian, Leo, **387**
Mamigonian, Vartan, **388**
Manchu, Fu, **388-389**, 396, 582, 650
Mandarax, 41, 49, 74, 117, 151, 202, 213, 251, 265, 292, 384-385, **389**, 395, 462, 571, 647
"The Manned Missiles," 15, 69, 139, 189, 328-329, 360, 479, 633
Maori, **390**
Mare Imbrium (*see also* Jefferson Observatory)
Margo, 191, **390**, 658
Maritimo, Dr. Alan, **390**
Maritimo, Dr. Alfred, 299, **390**, 410
Maritimo, Carlo, **391**
Maritimo, Gino and Marco, 22, 187, **391-392**, 556
The Maritimos, 391-392, 439
Maritimo, Guillermo ("Little Willie"), 73, 98, 300, **392**
Maritimo, Julio, 391, **392**
Maritimo, Milo, 80-81, 98, 300, **392**, 410, 538
Martha, **392**
Marx, Arnold, 287, 334, **392-393**, 572, 654
Mary, **393**
Mashtots, Mesrob, **393**
Masters, Barbara, **393**
Matheson, **393**
Matsumoto, Hiroshi, 2, 6-7, 53, 68, 293, **394-395**, 540, 544. 559, 588
Matsumoto Corporation, 324, **395**
mausoleum, 7, 342, 383, 388, **395-396**, 563, 575, 578, 582
McAllister, Reed, **396**
McAllister, Thurmond (also McAllister, Robjent, Reed and McGee), 86, 91, 139, 236, 300, **396**, 425, 486, 497, 523
McBundy, Hortense Muskellunge-13, **396**
McCabe, Earl, 16, 64-65, 67, 102-103, 106, 316, 368, **396-397**, 415, 478
McCarthy, Cliff, 110, 199, 215, **397-399**
McCarthy, Senator Joseph, 37, 156, 159, 331, 333, **399**, 411, 425, 528, 549-550, 627

McCarty, Eddie (*see also* Irving Buchanon)
McClellan, Grace and George, and their neighbors Anne and her husband (unnamed), **399**
McCone, Alexander Hamilton and Clara, 39, 42, 76, 188, 330-331, **399-400**, 442, 550, 651
McCone, Daniel and John, 42, 76, 187-188, 335, 399, **400**, 638
McCoy, Newton, 47, 286, **400-401**
The McGarvey Family, **401**
McLuhan, Nancy, 344, 361, **401**
McSwann, Ross L., **401**
Meadow Lark (*see also* Queen of the Meadows), 473
Meadows, 21, 38, 166, 257-258, 272, 283, 299, 312, 347, 366, 380, 383, 387, **401-402**, 421, 473, 529, 544, 587, 634, 655
Mellon, Hortense, 59, **402**
Memoirs of a Monogamous Casanova, 58, 63, **402**, 417, 433
Mencken, Barbira, **403**, 537
Mendoza, Jose, **403**
Mengel, Bernard, 18, 298, **403**
Merble, Lionel, 325, **403**, 457
Merble, Valencia (*see also* Valencia Merble Pilgrim)
Merganthaler, Corporal, **403-404**
Merrihue, Faith, **404**, 489, 494, 633
messiah, 13, 30, **404-405**, 420, 468
Metzger, Eloise, 7, 37, 56, 88, 95, 117, 198-199, 201, 271, 283, 285, 306, **405**, 407, 409, 422, 488, 544, 618, 628, 630
Metzger, Eugene Debs and Jane Addams, 301, 285, 353, **405**
Metzger, George, 37, 88, 201, **405-406**, 485, 627-628
Miasma, Khashdrahr, 99, **406**, 435, 561, 632
Microsecond Arbitrage, Inc., 223, 402, **406**, 413
middle-European humor (*see also* humor), 316-317
Midland City, 2, 4, 7, 22-23, 28-29, 34-35, 37, 40, 42, 51, 56, 58, 73-75, 77, 79-81, 85, 88, 93, 95-96, 101, 111, 120, 159, 167, 178, 187, 191, 196-200, 209, 215, 219, 223, 233-234, 237, 241, 248, 255, 258, 262, 269, 271, 275, 283, 288, 291, 299-300, 302-303, 305-307, 326, 346, 349-351, 353-354, 363, 376-377, 390-392, 398, 405, **407-409**, 410, 422, 424, 428, 435, 440, 445, 451-452, 455, 482, 485, 487-488, 507, 517-518, 521, 530, 534, 538, 541, 544-545, 553, 555-556, 572, 583, 607, 619, 624, 627-633, 642, 649
The Midland City Ordnance Co., 35, 408, **409**, 487
Midland County Mask and Wig Club, 350, 408, **409**,
Midland County Merchants Bank, 303, 409, 507
Midnight Pussycats, **409**
Mildred Peasely Bangtree Memorial Theater, **409**
Miller, Bill (Don?), 299, 390, **410**
Miller, Lydia and Verne (also Miller's Hardware Store), **410**, 429, 597
Miller, Mary Alice, 159, 223, 303, 386, 392, **410**
Ministry of Propaganda and Enlightenment, 97, 265, 288, 513
"The Minorite Church of Vienna," 411, **607**, 629
Minot, Dr. Frank, *Are Adults Harmoniums?*, **411**
Minton, Horlick and Claire, 213-214, 301, 321, 399, **411-412**, 486, 511
Miss Canal Zone, **412**
"Miss Temptation," 72, 142, 209, 254, 291, 412, 484, 548, 561
Mitchell, Allison, **412**
Mitchell, Dr. Jerome, **412**, 545
Moakely, George Minor, **412-413**
Mobutu, President, **413**, 451
Moby Dick, 111, 336, **413**, 507, 634
Moellenkamp, Henry, 212, 381, **413**, 578, 648

Moellenkamp, Robert W., 223, 406, **413-414**
Mohiga Ice Cream Emporium (*see also* Jerry and Muriel Peck), 451
The Mohiga Valley Free Institute (*see also* Tarkington College), 155, 216-217, 294, 381, 413-414, 451, 454, 462, 522, 531, 569-570
Mohiga Wagon Company, 168, 294, 381, **414**, 454, 522, 568-570
Moncrief, Earl, 261, 386, **414**
Monzano, Miguel ("Papa"), 7, 66, 188, 216, 240, 297, 309, 320, 322, 336, 368, **414-415**, 445, 511, 587, 609
Monzano, Mona Aamons, 1, 67, 101, 103, 131, 253, 261, 301, **415**, 446, 508, 511-512, 578, 583, 587, 595, 640, 647
Moody, Mary (also Foxcroft and Melody), 30, 404, **415-416**, 479, 491
Moon, Fletcher, 64, **416**, 494
MoonMist Tobacco, Ltd., **416**, 534
moral, moralist, morality, moralize, morally, 16-17, 20-21, 42, 104, 108, 190, 202, 230, 252-253, 266, 298-299, 312, 334, 400-402, 405, **417-421**, 423, 429, 482, 500, 571, 581, 616, 620
morale, morale-builders, 73, 171, 271, 401, **421-422**, 488
"More Stately Mansions," 38, 142, 399, **422**, 548
Morgan, Eunice Eliot (*see also* Eunice Eliot Morgan Rosewater), 41, 177, 492
Morissey, Bucky, 95, 111, 248, **422**, 630
Morissey, Francis X., 186, 199, 248, 275, **422**, 556, 630
Mother Night, 37, 48, 56, 63, 67, 77, 85, 96, 105, 119, 158, 178, 208, 210, 223, 236, 250-251, 253, 261-262, 265, 275, 279, 282, 287-288, 292, 298, 307, 325, 327, 334, 351, 392, 402, **423**, 433-434, 465, 470, 488, 499, 513, 530, 542, 565, 570, 572, 607, 635, 646
Mothers' Auxiliary of the Paul Revere Association of Militant Gentiles, **423**
Mott, Dr. Stewart Rawlings, **423**, 424
Mott, Stewart Oriole-2, 185, 213, **423-424**
Mozart, Wolfgang Amadeus, 259, **424**
Müller, Gerhard, **424**, 438
Murra, George and John, 264, 291, **424-425**
Musa Dagh, **425**
Mushari, Norman, 5, 29-30, 159, 175, 236, 239, 374, 396, 399, 404-405, 415, 425, 458, 463, 479, 490-493, 495, 497-498, 502, 547, 601
Mushari, Norman Jr., **425**
Musket Mountain, 181, 279, 338, 375, **426**, 447, 451, 528, 531, 552, 579, 625
The Musketeer, 381-382, **426**
Mussolini, Benito, 108, 273, 300, 314, 338, 352, 380, **426-427**, 464-465, 605
"My work is done." (*see also* George Eastman), 54, 218, 516, 560, 627
myth, mythological, mythology, 57, 82, 162, 169, 293, 310, 334, 413, **427-428**, 528
myth-making, 334
mythic, mythical, 82, 299, 323, 413
mythologizing, 105

Nash, Harry, 410, **429**, 433, 513, 528, 547, 597, 641
Nation, J. Edgar, 55, 227, **429**
Nation of Two (*see also Das Reich der Zwei*), 97, 195-196, 429, 433
National Council of Arts and Letters, 213, **429-430**
National Manufacturing Council, 323, 325
National Union of Belgium Opticians, **430**, 472
Nature Cruise of the Century, 28,

147, 197-198, 208, 274, 289, 292, 308, 355, 384-385, 389, **430**, 443, 512, 609
Necker, Anne Louise Germaine, 171, 198, **430**
Newcomb, John L., 302-303, **431**
neuter, 34, 75, 199, **431**, 630
"New Dictionary," 69, 221, 421, **432**
New York State Maximum Security Adult Correctional Institution at Athena, 6, 8, 20, 57, 117, 192, 206, 217, 237, 244, 284-285, 304, 344, 394, **432**, 448-449, 470, 541, 552, 570, 589, 637, 643, 648
Newt and Catharine, **432**
"Next Door," 9, 110, 123, 174, 232, 282, 375
Niagara Falls, 99, **432**
Nicholson, Robert, 142, **432-433**
Nightmare Ages, **433**, 532
Nixon, Richard, 89, 156, 163, 193, 270-271, 331, 355, 371, 471, 479, 521, 524, 547, 550-551, 555, 601, 638-639
Nocturnal Goatsucker (*see also The Cry of the Nocturnal Goatsucker*), **433**
non-epiphany, 356
Norman Rockwell Hall, **433**
North Crawford Mask and Wig Club, 410, 429, **433**, 513, 528, 641
Noth, Eva, **433**
Noth, Helga, 18, 63, 97, 121, 178, 195, 361-362, 402, **433-434**, 546, 593, 607, 646
Noth, Resi, 18, 85, 97, 119, 121, 138, 178, 226, 361-362, 402, 433, **434**, 566
Noth, Werner, 17, 97, **434**, 574, 636
nothinghead, 51, 179, **434-435**, 539
Now It Can Be Told, 76, 80, 115, 252-253, 299, 306, 377, 435-436, 460, 469, 582, 584, 592, 632
"Now It's the Women's Turn" (*see also* "Windsor Blue Nuber Seventeen"), 7, 38, 62, 70, 118, 122, 173, 177, 347, 372, 390, 436, 512, 596, 646

Oger, Anna Maria, **437**
Oglethorpe, James E., **437**
O'Hare, Bernard B., 97, 226, 250, **437-438**, 441, 509, 546
O'Hare, Bernard V., 39, 62, 69, 74, 132-133, 223, 320, 380, 385, 412, 424, **438**, 457, 483, 523, 536, 605, 643
O'Hare, Captain Bernard, 218, 288, **438**, 595, 604
O'Hare, Mary, 385, 424, **438-439**
O'Hare Paint and Varnish Company, **439**
Ohio Adult Correctional Institution, 302, **439**
Ohio Valley Ornamental Concrete Company, 199, 353, 391, **439**, 629, 631
Ojukwu, General, 71
Ojumwa, 354, **440**, 535, 592
oligomenorrhea, **440**
Olly-olly-ox-in-free, 325, **440-441**
O'Looney, Francis X., **441**
O'Looney, Mary Kathleen, 7, 11, 37, 39, 90, 99, 101, 103, 132, 156, 163, 219, 238, 268, 332-333, 342, 362, **441-443**, 444, 474, 510, 547, 551, 576, 578, 591, 613, 638, 651
Onassis, Jacqueline Bouvier Kennedy (*see also Jackie*), 73, 90, 389, 422, **443**
Operation Brainstorm, 31, 100, 216, 430, **443**
Ophelia, 54, 240, 280, **443-440**, 550
The Order of the Aurora Borealis, 611
organism, 114-116, **444-445**, 519
Ortiz, Jesús, **445**, 576
Orwell, George, **445**, 461
Osterman, 233-234, **445**
Ostrovsky, Erika (*see also* Céline), 112, 215, 445, 488
oubliette, 7, 53, 86, 179, 327, 415, **445-446**, 510-511, 587, 595
oubliation, 446, 647

Pabu, 66, 76, 245-246, **447**
Padwee, Dr. Howard, 167, **447**
Pahlavi Pavilion, 294, **447-448**, 451, 531, 538, 599
Shah of Iran, 294
Palace of the League of Nations, **448**, 580, 599
Palm Sunday, 2-3, 35, 50, 54, 60, 62, 107, 114, 126, 130, 136, 147, 149, 150, 167, 175, 210, 229, 296, 302, 322, 327, 344, 378, 409, 424, 431, 439, **448**, 474, 486, 506, 519, 539, 616, 620, 635
"Pan Galactic Straw-boss," **448**, 584
"Mouth Crazy," 584
Pan-Galactic Humbug, **448**
The Pan-Galactic Memory Bank, **448**, 584
Pan-Galactic Space Service, **449**, 504, 644
Pan-Galactic Three-Day Pass, 78, 263, **449**, 463
Parachute Ski Marines, 71, **449**
Parrot, Wilfred, 200-201, **449**
Patton, Jack, 58, 75, 192, 285, **449-450**, 469-470
Patton, Margaret and Mildred, 75, 285, **450**
Peach, Delbert, **450**
Peale, Delmar, 330, 362, **450**, 551
Pearls Before Swine, 201, 264, **451**
Peck, Jerry and Muriel, 102, 155, 413-414, **451**
Peck, John, **451**
Pefko, Captain Julian, 95, **451**
Pefko, Francine, 75, 87, 247, 307, 342, **451-452**
Pefko, Robert, 10, **452**
Pena, Harry (also Manny and Kenny), 393, **452-453**, 489, 634
Penfield, Frederic Courtland, 157, **453**
Pennwalt Biphetamine, **453**
perpetual-motion machine, 294, 451, **453-454**, 569-570
Peterson, Mrs. Lyman R., **454**
Phi Beta Kappa, 204, 219, **454**, 489, 644
Phoebe, 162, 321-322, 326, **454-455**, 517
Piatigorsky, Dr. Albert Aquamarine-1, **455**
Piatigorsky, Gregor, 649
Pilgrim, Barbara and Robert, **455-456**
Pilgrim, Billy (*see also* Joe Crone), 6-7, 25, 31, 37, 39, 49, 53, 60, 68, 71, 80, 99, 106, 115, 119, 132, 134-135, 149, 171, 176, 179, 186, 193, 203, 219, 237, 252, 259-260, 263, 267, 299, 309, 324-325, 327-328, 353, 371, 373, 380, 390, 403-404, 409, 430, 434, 455, **456-457** , 458, 464, 479, 492, 500, 502, 508, 511, 520, 536, 556, 561, 572-573, 580-581, 633, 639, 643-644, 658
Pilgrim, Valencia Merble, 72, 237, 299, 371, 455, **457-458**, 639
Pine Knoll, 309, 456, 458
Pisquontuit (also Chief Pisquontuit; *see also* Buntline), 91, 119, 201, 265, 425, 452-453, **458-459**, 489, 493-494, 634
Plague on Wheels, 58, 300, 345, 377, 435, **459-460**, 584, 658
Planck, Alfred (also known as President Jonathan Lynn), **460**
"The Planet Gobblers," **460-461**, 585
Player Piano, 1, 6, 21, 28, 31, 36, 43, 50, 54, 85-87, 99, 104, 157, 175, 201-202, 213-214, 219-220, 224-225, 241, 243, 251, 257-258, 264, 268, 277, 279, 287, 290, 299, 300, 323-325, 355, 358-359, 364, 379, 383, 393, 406, 429, 460. **461-462**, 466-467, 470-471, 473, 477, 488, 498, 519-520, 527, 536, 561, 568, 619, 634, 641, 655, 657; player-piano, 642
Poe, Edgar Allan, **462**
Polk, Dalton, **462**, 570
Pomerantz, Floyd, 177, **462**, 648
Pond, Dr., 158, 175, 287, **462**
Pontius Pilate Athletic Club, 135,

316, **462**
Ponzi scheme (*see also* di Sanza), 204
pool-pah, **462**
Poo-tee-weet (also Poo-tee-phweet), 53, **462-464**
Pops, **464**
Portomaggiore, Count Bruno (*see also* Marilee Kemp), 300, 352, 426, **464-465**
Potapov, Ilya, **465**
Potapov, Iona (*see also* George Kraft), 63, 77, 97, 119, 121, 168, 250, 264, 325, 339, 361-362, 434, 437, **465**, 570, 595, 607, 640
Potapov, Tanya, 77, **465**
Potter, David, 201-202, 208, 213, 243, 335, **465**, 568
Powers, Dr., **465**
Prairie Military Academy (*see also* Culver Military Academy), 88, 235, 305, **465**
prakhouls, **465-466**, 561
Pratt, Mary, **466**
Prince, Joe, 277, **466**
Prince of Candlesticks, **466**, 575
Prince Richard of Croatia-Slavonia, **466**, 625
Princess Charlotte, **466**
Proteus, Anita, 42, 89, 170, 241, 268, 279, 287, 365, 440, **467**, 529, 587
Proteus, Dr. Paul, 6-8, 27, 36, 43, 46, 75, 88, 94, 104, 114, 123, 170, 219, 225, 241, 258, 268, 272, 277, 283, 287, 290, 312, 323, 364, 379, 383, 401, 403-404, 440, 461-462, **467-468**, 529, 568, 604, 610, 642, 655
Proteus, George, 88, 258, 312, 364, 404, 461, **467**, 468
Proteus Park, 205, 277, **468-469**
"The Protocols of the Elders of Tralfamadore," 58, 182, 240, 314, 424, 428, 449, **469-470**, 579, 585
The Protocols of the Elders of Zion (*see also* Henry Ford), 8, 57, 235, 246, 450, **470**
Pruitt, Major General Earl, **470**
Pulsifer, Borders M., General of the Armies, **470**, 650
punctual (experiencing time in a punctual manner), 8, 57, 235, 246, 450, **471**
Purdy and McCloud, **471**
purity, 417, **471**, 500, 601

Queen Margaret, **472**, 527, 542, 603
Queen of the Meadows, 401, **473**, 544
Quezeda, Domingo, 345, **473**
Quinn, Bert, 47, 207, **473**

Rankian, 19
Ramba of Macedon, 492
The RAMJAC Corporation, 49, 76, 90, 100-101, 103, 147, 156, 159, 187, 219, 224, 238, 268, 270, 308, 322, 332-334, 362, 371-372, 374, 399, 441-443, 450, **474**, 486, 549, 551, 576, 591, 638
Rauch, John G., 35, 38, 152, 175, **474**, 507, 620, 635
Raven, 368, **475**, 591
Reagan, Ronald and Nancy, 6, 152, 192, 395, 526, 648
reborn (*see also* born again), 206, 286, 346, **475**, 548, 564
Reconstruction and Reclamation Corps (also known as the Reeks and Wrecks), 95, 188, 225, 268, 277-278, 300, 461, **476**, 527, 568, 642
Redfield, Colonel George, **476**
Redfield, Dr. Robert (*see also* folk society), 11, 189, 229, 244-245, **476-477**
Redwine, Reverend C. Horner, 33, 454, **477**
Barnstable First Church of God the Utterly Indifferent, 12-13, 33, 147-148, 172, 257, 454, 477-478, 500, 504
religion, religious, 2, 4, 11, 14, 29-30, 33, 43-44, 49, 51, 53, 57,

64-65, 67-68, 75, 102, 104, 106-108, 120, 138, 140-145, 148, 152, 172, 179-180, 194-195, 230-231, 244-245, 251-252, 260, 265, 283, 310-311, 320, 342, 387, 397, 404-405, 419-421, 435, 437, 444, 460-461, 476, **477-484**, 507, 515, 522, 526-527, 530, 558, 570, 583, 585, 594, 597-598, 605, 614, 616, 621, 635-636
Remenzel, Dr., Sylvia and Eli, 32, 54, 291, 376, **484-485**, 544, 595, 632
"Report on the Barnhouse Effect" (*see also* dynamospsychism and Professor Arthur Barnhouse), 3, 26, 32, 72, 92, 99-100, 115, 132, 161, 187, 216, 226, 250, 311, 313, 315, 485, 538, 548, 650
Republican National Convention (1972), 43, 260, 312
Rettig, John, 180-181, **485-486**
Reyes, Colonel Guillermo, 73, **486**, 578
Rhodes Scholar, 39, 59, 643-644
"A Rift Between Friends in the War of Ideas" (*see also* Stewart Buntline), 300, 396, **486**
Riley, James Whitcomb, 99, 179, **486**
Rivera, Jerry Cha-cha, **486**
Rivera, Wanda Chipmunk-5, **486**
Rivers, Jerry, 34, 48, 86, 104, 374, **486**, 496, 595
Robbins, Eldon, **487**
Robert, Henry Martyn (also *Roberts Rules of Order*), **487**
The Robo-Magic Corporation, 23, 34-35, 59, 73, -74, 407-409, **487**
Rockefeller, Alice (*see also* Alexander Hamilton McCone),
Rockefeller, Geraldine Ames (*see also* Geraldine Ames Rockefeller Rosewater)
Rockmell, Dr. Eli W., 86, 184, **487-488**
Roethke, Theodore, **488**
Roosevelt, Claudia, 192, **488**
Roosevelt, Eleanor, 61, 271, 303, 422, **488**
Roseberry, Dr. Harold, 85, 157, 175, 202, 214, 280, 290, **488**, 654-655
Rosenau, Dr. Maurice, 448, **488**
Rosenfeld, Franklin Delano, **488**
Rosenquist, Per Olaf, 40, **488**
Rosewater, Abraham, 404, **489**, 494, 633
Rosewater, Caroline, 40, 90, 204, 453-454, **489**, 492, 634
Rosewater, Eliot, 5-6, 13, 29-30, 34, 39, 41, 58, 74, 78, 80, 86, 91, 121, 177, 206, 223, 240, 242-243, 263-265, 267, 280, 283, 286, 290, 375-376, 378, 392, 404, 410, 422, 425, 442-443, 449-450, 458, 460, 463, 475, **489-492**, 493, 495-498, 520, 536, 580, 583, 592, 603, 624-625, 632, 658
Rosewater, Eunice Eliot Morgan, 41, 177, 422, **492**
Rosewater, Franklin, 489, **492**
Rosewater, Fred, 37, 119, 268, 290, 425, 458, 463, 472, 489, 490, 492, **493**, 494-495, 498, 502, 557, 603, 634
Rosewater, George, 90, 404, 489, **493-494**
Rosewater, Geraldine Ames Rockefeller, **494**, 495
Rosewater, Merrihue, 37, 41, 96, 119, 268, 404, 437, 489, 493, **494**, 502, 522, 633
Rosewater, Noah, 242-243, 290, 326, 416, 493, **494-495**, 496, 600
Rosewater, Samuel, 41, 290, 494, **495**
Rosewater, Senator Lister Ames, 13, 16, 29, 41, 86, 91, 262, 265, 416, 490-492, **495-496**, 497, 625
Rosewater, Sylvia, 5, 30, 446, **496**, 510, 519, 595, 632, 647
The Rosewater County Clarion Call, 242, 426, **496**

Rosewater Creek, Rosewater Inter-State Ship Canal, 450, **497**, 498
Rosewater Foundation (also Rosewater Corporation), 22, 29, 206, 223, 286, 378, 396, 415, 425, 458, 463, 490-491, 493, 495, **497-498**, 624
Rosewater Golden Lager Beer, **498**, 544
Roswell Moose and Elks, **498**
Rothko, Mark, 9, 267, **498-499**, 559
Rowley, Jonah K., **499**, 533
Rowley, Mrs. Theodore, **499**
Rumfoord, Beatrice, 131, 145, 165, 172, 251, 261, 274, 455, **499-500**, 517, 531, 543, 574, 586, 637, 644, 646
Rumfoord, Bertram Copeland, **500-501**, 502, 643
Rumfoord, Commodore William Howard Taft and Clarice, 78, 322, **501-502**, 503
Rumfoord, Cynthia Niles, 494, **502**
Rumfoord, Lance, 370, 500, **502**
Rumfoord, Lily, 500-501, **502-503**
Rumfoord, Remington, IV, **503**
Rumfoord, Robert Taft, 77-78, 322, **503**
Rumfoord, Winston Niles, 13, 33, 48, 104, 110, 131, 147, 172, 184, 191, 213, 261, 282, 313, 343, 350, 360, 371, 386, 414, 416-417, 448-449, 454, 471, 488, 499-500, **503-504**, 508, 511, 532-534, 542-543, 553, 574, 580, 598, 636
Rumfoord mansion, 40, 191, 202, 257, 414, 499, 504, 533, 543, 546, 633, 641, 646
Rumpf, Hans (*see also The Bombing of Germany*), 74, 78, 162, 449
Rutgers, 102, 355
Ryan, Mildred, **504-505**
Ryan, Penelope, Harold and Paul, 281-283, 504, **505**, 531, 609-610, 649

Sacco and Vanzetti (also Dante and Inez Sacco), 78, 98, 122, 135-136, 219, 222, 266, 269, 334, 379, 386, 419, 442, 453, **506-507**, 510, 554, 571, 603, 622, 638
Sacred Miracle Cave, 62, 96, 104, 111, 303, 307, 335, 354, 408-409, 413, 422, **507**, 595
St. Andres, **507**
St. Augustine, 14, 64, **507-508**
Saint Elmo's fire, 171, **508**
Saint Elmo's Remedy, **508-509**, 629
St. Francis of Assisi, **509**
St. George and the Dragon, 437, **509**
Salo, 50, 110, 145, 158, 170, 172, 238, 265, 270, 325, 363-364, 414, 417, 448, 454, 478, 499, 503-504, **509-510**, 527, 532, 533, 543, 553-554, 556, 573-574, 580, 598-599
Salsedo, Andrea, **510**
Sam, **510**
Samaritrophia, 86, 224, 264, 326, 446, 491, **510**, 632
Samoza Hall, **510-511**
Samoza, 294
Sams, Howard W., 261, **511**
San Lorenzo Cathedral, 310, **511**, 587
San Lorenzo, 1, 7, 16, 19, 37, 58, 64-67, 101-103, 105, 106, 109-110, 112, 176, 178-179, 196, 236, 248, 295, 297, 310, 316, 320-321, 336, 368, 396-397, 411, 414-415, 445, 511-512, 518, 549, 587, 604, 657
Sandler, Bea (Bea Sandler's *The African Cookbook*), **511**
Sandra, 82, **511**
Sandy, **511-512**
Santa Cruz, **512**
Saracen, 141, 144, 483
sarooned, 66, **512**, 604
Sateen Dura-Luxe, 7, 37, 274, 347, **512**, 583, 596, 607, 645
Savonarola, Girolamo, 76, 512, **513**, 561, 607
Saw City Kandy Kitchen, 121, **513**, 624

Sawyer, Doris, **513**
Scharff, Hattie, 339, **513**; Scharff Brothers Funeral Home, 339, 513
Scheherazade (*also Scheherezade*), 371, 502-503
Schildknecht, Heinz, 220, 288, **513-514**, 613
schizophrenia, schizophrenic, 18, 79, 105-106, 125, 195, 198-199, 202, 215, 218-219, 251, 256-257, 292, 295, 332, 334-335, 361, 423, **514-516**, 617-618
Schlesinger, Arthur Jr., **516-517**
Schliemann Breathing School for Recruits, 165, 455, 499, **517**
Schneider, Kurt, **517**
Schramm, Jacob, and Julia Junghans, 437
Schramm's Drugstore, 198, 307, 322, 409, **517-518**, 630
Schwartz, Harold D. (also known as Gramps), **518**
Schwartz, Louis J. and Emerald, **518**
Schwartz, Mortimer, **518**
Schweitzer, Albert, 102, 496, **518-519**
science fiction, science-fiction, 5, 15, 32, 37, 50, 55, 58, 61, 79, 107, 109, 129-130, 152-154, 163, 208, 237, 253, 255, 284, 306, 316, 323, 375, 384, 418, 445, 460, 469, 470, 489, 492, 508, **519-522**, 527, 543, 575, 580, 583-584, 599, 603, 657
Scilly Islands, 96, 268, **522**
Scipio, 7, 20, 31, 42, 45, 48, 157, 159, 168-169, 192-193, 206-207, 217, 244, 293-294, 304, 344, 381, 395, 406, 413, 432, 445, 448, 451, 454, 462, **522**, 528, 531, 552, 561, 569, 570, 589, 637, 639, 643, 648
Seitz, Al and Sue, **523**
Sermon on the Mount, 104, 137, 139, 155, 320, 335, 448, 483, **523-526**, 598, 639, 649
shaft, 166, 188, 387, 478, **526-527**, 581, 607
Shah of Bratpuhr, 28, 50, 86, 99, 173, 205, 225, 277-279, 359, 406, 465, 469-470, 476, **527**, 561, 568
Shah of Iran (*see also* Pahlavi Pavilion), 294, 485
Shaltoon, 472, **527**
Shapiro, Dr. Ben, 399, **528**
Shaw, Helene, 410, 429, 433, 513, **528**, 641
Shaw, Marilyn, **528-529**
Shazzbutter (*see also How You Doin?*), 88, 309
Shepherd, Lawson, 242, 272, 290, 467, **529**
Shoup, Martin, **529-530**
Shoup, Mary Alice, 339, **530**, 640
Shoup, Naomi, 249, **530**
Shriver, Sargent, 90, 379, **530-531**
Shultz, Hermann and Sophia, 26, 52, 251, 447, 431, **538**, 570, 599
Shuttle, Herb, 281, 505, **531**
Sidi Barrani, 273, 338, 352, **531**
Simmons, Newbolt and Martha, 519, **531**
Simpkins, Darlene, **531**
sin-wat, **532**
sinookas, **532**
The Sirens of Titan, 9, 33, 39, 44, 62, 78, 82, 104, 109, 111, 131, 146, 157, 191, 238-239, 247, 251, 256-257, 279, 282, 289, 325, 335, 343, 350, 360, 371, 386, 412, 416-417, 443, 448-449, 454, 469, 472, 477, 488, 499, 503, 508, 511, 517, **532-534**, 536, 538, 552, 579, 622, 633, 636
sirens (as sculptures), 533-534
Skag, Delmore, 30, 115, **534**
Skinner, Cornelia Otis, **534**, 649
Skylark, 354, **535**, 592
Skyscraper National Park, 477, **535**; Chrysler Building, 101, 103, 147, 333, 362, 393, 450, 547, 551, 576, 588; Empire State Building, 148, 159, 223, 337, 438, 498, 582, 657
Slapstick, 3-4, 8, 38, 89, 94, 173, 175, 184, 195, 206, 210, 213,

220-221, 229, 256, 286, 303, 326, 328, 333, 355, 357, 370-371, 379, 383, 388, 396, 400, 424-425, 433, 438, 454-455, 486-487, 530-531, **535-536**, 549, 563, 570, 572, 585, 612, 614, 621, 624, 653-654, 657
Slaughterhouse-Five, 2, 6, 25, 31, 37, 39, 53, 60, 79, 87, 96-97, 99, 112-113, 141, 144, 179, 203, 210, 211, 214, 219, 223, 237, 251, 256, 259-260, 267, 274, 292, 299, 323-326, 328, 353, 371, 373, 380, 385, 390, 403, 412, 424, 434, 438, 456-458, 463, 483, 492, 502, 508, 520-521, 523, 535, **536-537**, 551, 556, 561, 572, 579, 581-582, 605, 643, 654
Slazinger, Paul, 14, 93, 403, **537-538**, 643
Slezak, Premier, **538**
Small Magellanic Cloud, 509, **538**, 579
The Smart Bunny, 221, 234, 392, **538**, 584
Smiley (*see also* Greathouse and Smiley) 270
Smiley, Letitia, 31, 293, **538-539**
Snopes, Senator Flem, 527, **539**
socialism, 137, 198, 201, 300, 327, 397, 441, 445, 486, 525-526, 603, 621, 645, 649
Solomon, Syd, **539**
Solzhenitsyn, Aleksandr, **539**
somethinghead, 434, **539-540**, 598
Son of God (*see also* Christ), 140, 176, 373, 492, 583
The Son of Jimmy Valentine, **540**, 583-584, 602
Sonderkommando, 18, 275, 298, **540**
Sony, 352, 394, **540-541**
The Soul Merchants, 465, **541**
Sousa, John Philip, 207, 473
Sousa, Mr., **541**
space and time (*see also* time and space)
Space Wanderer (*see also* Malachi Constant and Queen Margaret), 13, 33, 161, 172, 472, 477, 553
Sparks, Jon, **542**
Sparky, 89, 219, **542**
Sparrow, Harold J. (*see also* Frank Wirtanen), 60, 97, 158, 208, **542**, 646
Speer, Albert, **542**
spiral, 13, 48, 131, 153, 158, 164, 177, 338, 503-504, 522, 533, **542-544**, 545-546, 548; spiral nebula, 65, 120, 348, 542-543, 631
spire, 168, 485, 498, **544**
Spirit of the Meadows (*see also* Queen of the Meadows), 473
Squires, Anthony, 37, 198, 412, **544-545**
Squires, Barbara, 412, **545**
SS Psychiatrist, 20, **545**
Stacks, Dr. Herb, **545**
stairs, staircase, stairheads, stairwell, 58-59, 100, 131-132, 162, 177, 288, 352, 362, 370, 475, 493, 533, 542-544, **545-548**, 563, 588
Stankiewicz, Juan and Geraldo, **548-549**
Stankiewicz, Stanislaus, 345, **549**
Stankiewicz, Walter F., 163, 330, **549**
Stankowitz, **549**
Stanley, 546, **549**
Starbuck, Ruth, 10, 53, 266, **549-550**
Starbuck, Walter, 7, 10, 25, 32, 37, 39, 53, 76, 99-100, 103, 116, 131, 155, 159, 161, 163, 203, 214, 219, 221, 237, 240, 261, 266, 270, 281, 307, 345, 355, 372, 374, 379, 399-400, 441-442, 444, 447, 450, 454, 486, 507, 524, 528, 548-549, **550-551**, 562, 575, 591, 597, 603-604, 613, 627, 638, 646, 650
Starr, Harrison, **551**
Steel, Roy, 438, **551**
Steel, Terrence W., Jr., **552**
Stern, Damon, 20, 285, 344, **552**, 643
Stevenson, Adlai, **552**
Stevenson, Stony, 105, **552-553**

Stockmayer, Walter H., 127, **553-554**
Stone, Sydney and Fred, 322, **554**, 623
Stonehenge, **554**, 580
Stratton, Samuel W., 269, **554**
structured moment, 79, 106, 532, 536-537, **554-555**, 581
stuppa, 66, 213, **555**
subbasement (*see also* basement), 7, 36-37, 99, 109, 258, 331-333, 347, 551, **555**, 645
Sugar Creek, 34-35, 199, 275, 307, 398, 408, 422, 507, 553, **555-556**, 630
Sugar Creek High School, **556**
Sugarbush Mountain, Vermont, 403, 458, **556**
suicidal, suicidally, suicide (*see also* Ethical Suicide Parlor), 5, 34, 37, 43-44, 46, 67, 79, 97, 105, 119-120, 124-125, 130, 142, 166, 200, 209-210, 218, 226-227, 241, 250, 260, 263, 266-267, 292, 299, 301, 305-306, 320, 337, 351, 356-357, 376, 378-379, 385, 392, 407, 412, 415, 452, 463, 466, 493-494, 496, 499, 518, 528, 535, 544, **556-561**, 566-567, 609, 615, 618, 625, 627, 630, 634, 637; Mona Aamons, 415; Conrad Aiken, 5; American slave masters more often than their slaves, 560; Barring-gaffner, 34; Circe Berman (her father), 46; Ray Bradbury ("The Kilimanjaro Device"), 560; Howard Campbell, 97; George Eastman, 218, 559-560, 627; Hermann Goring, 266; Arshile Gorky, 267, 559; Ernest Hemingway, 301, 559-560; Hisako Hiroguchi, 292, 385; Celia Hoover, 79, 120, 209-210, 299, 305-306, 351, 392, 407, 452, 557, 559; Rev. Jim Jones, 125; Terry Kitchen, 267, 357, 559, 567; Selena MacIntosh, 292, 385; Mars, 557; Hiroshi Matsumoto, 559; "Papa" Monzano, 67; Resi Noth, 119; Jackson Pollock, 267, 356, 559; Fred Rosewater (his father), 493; Merrihue Rosewater, 119; Mark Rothko, 267, 499, 559; Harold D. ("Gramps") Schwartz, (fakes suicide) 518; William Styron (*Darkness Visible*), 560; Lazlo Szombathy, 566; Edith Vonnegut, 79, 119-120, 125, 200, 209, 305, 376, 407, 557-558, 560, 618, 630; Sam Wakefield, 218, 337, 466, 528, 559, 625, 627; Harvey Wheelock, II (died in suicide rescue attempt), 637
Suk, Dr. Kim Bum, **561**
Sultan of Brunei, **561**
Sumklish, 99, 466, **561**
Super Realtors' Worship Service (1972 Republican National Convention), 260
Surrasi, 28, **561**
Susann, Jacqueline, **561**
Susanna (*see also* Norman Fuller), 254, 291, **561**
Sutton, Mrs., **562**, 573
Swain, Caleb Mellon and Letitia Vanderbilt, **562**
Swain, Carter Paley, 247, **562**, 565
Swain, Elihu Roosevelt, 175, 256, 342, 395-396, **562-563**, 565, 575, 578
Swain, Eliza Mellon (*see also* Wilbur Swain), 4, 47, 86, 111, 139, 173-174, 177, 184, 195-196, 229, 235, 256, 268, 303-304, 355, 383, 388-389, 395-396, 423-425, 433, 438, 475, 487, 535, 549, 562-565, 575, 578, 589, 611, 613, 647
Swain, Sophie Rothschild, **563**
Swain, Wilbur Rockefeller, 4, 7, 15, 38, 47, 86, 135, 139, 148, 159, 173, 184-185, 209, 223, 229, 247, 256, 270, 286, 303-304, 326, 337, 355, 357, 370, 379, 383, 388, 395-396, 401, 423, 433, 438, 454-455, 466, 475, 480, 486-487, 530, 535, 549,

562, **563-565**, 570, 572, 582, 589, 595, 599, 604, 611-613, 621, 654, 657
Swift, Dr. Tom, **565**
Szombathy, Lazlo and Miklos, **565-566**

Taft, Edith, 232, **567**, 594
Takaru, 86, 99, 377, **568**
Tamanrasset, 277, **568**
Tappin, Al, **568**
Tarkington, Aaron, 100, 168, 216-217, 280, 413-414, **568**, 569
Tarkington, Elias, 294, 343, 414, 451, 453-454, 531, **568-569**, 570
Tarkington, Felicia, 100, **569**
Tarkington College, 16, 23, 31, 40, 42, 44, 48, 57, 59, 102, 147, 155, 160, 175, 181, 192, 198, 205, 217-218, 223, 228, 237, 244, 279, 281, 284-285, 293-294, 322, 337, 344, 355, 381, 395, 406, 413-414, 426, 432-433, 447, 453, 466, 510, 522, 525, 528, 537-539, 552, 554, 569, **570**, 589, 596, 623, 625-626, 643, 648
Tartakover, 361, **570**
Tcherkassky, Maria Daffodil-11, **570**
Tennyson, Alfred (Alfred, Lord Tennyson), **571**
Tharp, Naomi, **571**
Thayer, Webster, 78, 269, 334, 419, 453, **571**
Theatre de Lys, 94, 249, 349, **571**, 630
Theodorides, Mildred Helium-20, **572**
therefore (∴), 105, 336, **572**
Thiriart, Jean, 430, **572**
Thomas Jefferson High School, **572**
Thucydides, 340
thumbscrew, 327-328, **572**
Thurber, James, 319
Tibbets, Paul W., 653
Tiglath-pileser the Third, 287, 334, 393, **572-573**
Tillie, 562, **573**
time and space, space and time, 104, 147, 154, 350, 369, 414, 456, **573**, 574, 576, 581
Titan, 33, 54, 146, 172, 213, 228, 238, 343, 350, 412, 455, 500, 503-504, 509, 534, 543, 553, **573-574**, 586, 636-637
Titanic bluebird, 53-54, 146, 455, 509, **574**
"Tom Edison's Shaggy Dog," (*see also* Harold K. Bullard), 89, 219, 315, 542
tomb, 196, 408, **574-575**
"Tomorrow and Tomorrow and Tomorrow," 12, 89, 115, 277, 293, 401, 446, 518, 522, **575**
Too Wild a Dream (*see also* Lavina Waters), 387, 641
top floor (also the top of the northernmost tower), 6, 56, 117, 147, 396, 450, 563, 573, **575-576**, 578
topmost, **576**
tower, 21, 24, 29, 70, 122, 128, 181, 187-188, 192, 212, 304, 337, 375, 381-382, 396, 413, 454, 486, 538, 543, 563, 575, **576-579**, 611, 648; belfry, 24, 42, 187; cupola, 186; Eiffel Tower, 578; Leaning Tower of Pisa, 578; Tower of Babel, 203, 379; Waldorf Towers, 578
Tralfamadore, Tralfamadorian (*see also* "The Protocols of the Elders of Tralfamadore"), 25-26, 31, 42, 58, 68, 78, 104, 110, 135, 139, 142, 145, 148, 158, 172, 182, 193, 215, 219, 224, 238, 240, 252, 256, 260, 265, 267, 270, 301, 314, 316, 324-325, 353, 363, 418, 424, 428, 448-449, 455-457, 469-470, 499-501, 503-504, 509-510, 514, 527, 532-533, 536, 538, 554-555, 561, 573, 577, **579-582**, 585, 587, 598-599, 644, 658
tri-benzo-Deportamil, 326, **582**, 613
trinity, 140, 468, **582-583**, 611
Trippingham, Mona Lisa, **583**
Trout, Darlene, 540, **583**, 584

Trout, Kilgore, 5, 8, 16, 27-28, 30-35, 37, 40, 48-49, 51, 58, 61, 74, 78-82, 86, 88, 101, 134-135, 139, 142, 176, 178, 191, 193, 206, 221-223, 226, 233-234, 237-238, 243, 253, 255, 262-267, 287-288, 293, 299-300, 306, 308-310, 313-314, 316, 324, 326, 345, 350, 354, 370, 373, 375-377, 390-392, 404, 407, 410, 435-436, 448-449, 452, 458-460, 463, 469, 472, 490-492, 495, 508, 519-520, 527, 534, 538, 540, 556, 571-572, 580, 582, **583-585**, 603, 618, 632, 636, 639, 658; Trout's bibliography, 584-585
Trout, Leo, 28, 584, **585**
Trout, Leon, 5, 7, 8, 40, 55, 60, 77-78, 120, , 159, 184, 190, 202, 208, 226, 255, 291, 313-314, 384-385, 389, 488, 508, 520, 522, 571, 584, **585-586**, 608, 653
The True Purpose of Life in the Solar System, 500, **586-587**
Tucci, Alfy, 40, **587**
Tum-bumwa, 511, **587**
tunnel (*see also* blue tunnel), 4-5, 7, 40, 56, 60-61, 254-255, 284, 314, 377, 442, 471, 508, 547, 563, 571, 584, 586, 587-589, 596, 627, 648
The Turkey Farm, 4, 303, **589**, 612
Turner, Jeffrey, **589**
Turtle Bay, 128, 403, **589-590**

U-99, 368, 475, **591**
Ubriaco, Frank and Marilyn, **591**
Uccello, Paolo, 164, 197
Ukwende, Dr. Cyprian, 354, 435, 440, 535, 56, **591-592**
Ulm, Arthur Garvey, **592-593**
Ulm, Lowell, **593**
uncritical, uncritically (love, bliss, companionship, respect, nurturer), 264, 410, 434, 492, 567, 583, **593-595**,
underground, 6-7, 36, 63, 67, 86, 109, 111, 118, 210, 242, 288, 434, 438, 442, 496, 513, 588, **595-596**
The Underground, **596**
Unification Church Korean Evangelical Association, **596-597**
Niagara Power and Light Company, 596
Unitarian, Unitarian Universalist, 12, 33, 104, 152, 252, 429, 483, 526, **597-598**
Universal Will to Become (UWTB), 148, 265, 270, 363, 414, 448, 454, 478, 532, 554, 556, 580, **598-599**
Unk (*see also* Malachi Constant), 29, 33, 39, 54, 62, 78, 92, 98, 109-110, 131-132, 172, 188, 282, 411, 421, 499, 543, 552-553, 574, 593
un-neurotic courage (*see also* Waltham Kittredge), 357
"Unready to Wear," 7, 10, 127, 130, 315, 359, 387, 547, 560, 595, 599
Updike, Norman, 26, **599**
Urbana Massacre, 213, **599**, 612
Utopia, 41, 91, 459, 495, 498, 563, **600-601**

Valentine, Ralston (*see also The Son of Jimmy Valentine*), 540, **602**
Valley of the Dolls (*see also* Jacqueline Susann), 561
Van Arsdale, Herbert, **602**
van Curler, Dr. Ormand, **602**
VanArsdale, Whitey, 8, 304, **602**
Vanzetti, Bartolomeo (*see also* Sacco and Vanzetti)
Veblen, Thorstein, 280, **603**
Venus on the Half-shell (*see also* Queen Margaret), 472, 527, 584, 589, **603**
Vicuna, 167, 238, 573, 585, **603-604**
Villavicencio, Carlos Daffodil-11, **604-605**
vin-dit, 66, 84, 171, 512, **604**
virtue, 4, 75, 138, 142, 151, 231, 242, 252, 311-312, 353, 386,

418, 420, 423, 484, 551, **604-607**, 611, 617, 637
Vitelli, Giovanni, 512, **607**
von Braun, Werner, 208, 418, **607**
von Furstenberg, Rudolf, 186, **607-608**
von Killinger, Baron Manfred Freihert, **608**
von Kleigstadt, Dr. Ormand, 87, 225, **608**, 650
von Kleist, Adolf, 12, 28, 184, 256, 289, 308, 315, 345, 385, 462, 559, **608**, 609, 625
von Kleist, Gottfried and Wilhelm, 308, 576, **608**
von Kleist, Sebastian, **608**
von Kleist, Siegfried, 175, 191, 308, 608, **609**
von Koenigswaid, Dr. Schlichter, 19, 415, **609**
von Konigswald, Major Siegfried, 282, 462, **609-610**
von Neumann, Ludwig, 341, 462, 604, **610-611**
von Peterswald, David Daffodil-11, 88, 582, **611**
von Peterswald, Dr. Felix Bauxite-13, 303, **611-612**
von Peterswald, Melody Oriole-2, 159, 213, 223, 466, 582, 599, **612-613**
von Peterswald, Wilma Pachysandra-17, 47, 286, 400, 582, 599, 611-612, **613**
von Schwefelbad, Baron Ulrich Werther, 513, **613**
von Strelitz, Arthur, 10, 77, **613**
Vonnegut, Alice, 3, 139, 179, 256, 535, **613-615**
Vonnegut, Bernard, 41, 59, 151, 166, 215, 229, 275, 370, 535, 542, 614, **615**, 616, 620
Vonnegut, Carl Hiroaki and Emiko Alice, 427, **616-617**
Vonnegut, Clemens, 41, 59, 140, 251-252, 419, 481, 507, 606, **616-617**, 620, 635
Vonnegut, Dr. Mark, 3, 52, 92, 117, 125, 218, 516, 558, 560, 597, **617-618**
Vonnegut, Edith, 3, 149, 152, 176, 353, 376, **618-619**, 630, 635, 652
Vonnegut, Jane Cox, 3, 251, 535, **619-620**
Vonnegut, Kurt, Sr., 152, 474, **620**
Vonnegut, Uncle Alex, 155, 535, 615, **620-623**
Vonnegut Memorial Fountain, 554, **623**
Voyager 2, 54, 218

Wainwright, Right Reverend William Uranium-8, 148, **624**
Wainwright, Tawny, **624**
Wait, James, 195, 243, 289, 300, 304-306, 384, 407, 466, **624-625**, 647
Wakeby, Stella, **625**
Wakefield, Andrea, 300, **625-626**
Wakefield, Sam, 155, 181, 218, 285, 337, 466, 528, 559, 625, **625-627**
Walker, Shelton, **627**
Waltz, Barbara, **627**
Waltz, Charlotte, **627**
Waltz, Donna, **628**
Waltz, Emma Wetzel, 199, 408, **628**, 636
Waltz, Felix, 4, 38, 95, 111, 149, 197, 204, 247, 253, 305, 353, 392, 412, 422, 627, **628-629**
Waltz, Genevieve, 431, 628, **629**
Waltz, Otto, 22, 149, 157, 215, 241, 248, 253, 271, 275, 322, 391, 397, 399, 406, 411, 422, 455, 485, 488, 508, 534, 548, 556, 628, **629-630**, 636
Waltz, Rudy (*see also* Deadeye Dick), 7, 22, 28-29, 31, 37, 56, 74, 86, 93-94, 111, 117, 164, 197-199, 209, 215, 233, 237, 247-248, 258, 271, 275, 283, 285, 301-303, 305, 307, 322, 349, 353, 405-409, 411, 422, 431, 439, 445, 453, 508, 517, 523, 530, 536, 544-545, 571, 593, 607, 618, 628-629, **630-**

631, 649
wampeter, 33, 148, 65, 119-120, 246, 262, 269, 348, 543, **631**
Wampeters, Foma & Granfalloons, 10, 33, 60, 107, 122, 203, 210, 219, 229, 363, 378, 424, 432, 530, **631**, 646
Warmergram, Charley (also Warmergran), 86, 242, **631-632**
Warren, Dr. Donald, **632**
Washington, Elgin, **632**
Wataru, Watanabe and Beverly June, 261, 386, **633**
Waterman, Earl, **633**
Waters, Lavinia (also Lavina), 30, 387, 489, 494, **633**, 641
Watson, Myron S., **633**
Watson Brothers, **633**
The Wayward Capitalist, 246
Weary, Roland, 142, 373, 456, 605, **633-634**
Weeks, Bunny, 300-301, 453-454, **634**
Weeks, Captain Hannibal, **634**
The Weir, 300, 453, **634**
Welcome to the Monkey House, 3, 9, 31-33, 36, 46, 51, 54-57, 63, 69, 87, 123, 127, 142, 162, 179, 212-213, 219, 227-228, 232, 260, 265, 309, 344, 352, 361, 401, 418, 421, 429, 432, 434-435, 475, 539, 548, **634**, 638, 646, 650, 654
Weltschmerz, 312, **634-635**
The Western Hemisphere University (also Western Hemisphere University of the Bible), 310, 339, **635-636**
Westlake, Ian, 17, **636**
Wetzel, Richard, **636**
The Whale, 24, 203, 543, **636-637**
Wheeler, Elm, **637**
Wheelock, Harley, II and III, **637-638**
"Where I Live," 55, 151, 167, 174, 432, 638
Whistler, Henry Niles, 232, **638**
Whistler, Kenneth, 132, 268, 326, 442, 524, 571, 588, 621, **638-639**
White, Allison, **639**
White, Celeste, **639**
White, Gloria, 154, 355, **639**
White, Maggie, 342, **639**
The White Christian Minuteman, 85, 139, 168, 262, 338-339, 475, 513, 635, **640**
Whitefeet, Elbert, 335, **640**
Whitehall, Major General Daniel, **640-641**
Whitehall Palace, 504
Whitehill, Florence, 171, 173, **641**
white humor (*see also* humor)
"Who Am I This Time," 70, 410, 429, 433, 513, 528, 547-548, 597, **641**
Wiener, Norbert, 225, 310, 419, 461, **641-642**
Wilbur, Harold Newcomb, 377, **642-643**
Wild Bob, 62, **643**
Wilder, Jason, 16, 45, 59, 164-165, 294, 454, 552, 626, **643**
Wilder, Kimberley, 16, 448, 525, 538, **643**
Wildhack, Montana, 119, 260, 409, 581, **645**
Wiley, Roberta (*see also* George Helmholtz), 289, 449, **644**
Wills, Ben, **645**
Wilson, Robert Sterling (the "Black Fuehrer of Harlem"), **645**
"Windsor Blue Number Seventeen," 7, 37, 173, 177, 224, 258, 300, 347, 395, 436, 512, 583, 596, **645-646**
Winkler, Kermit, **646**
Winslow, Bernard K., **646**
Wirtanen, Carly, **646**
Wirtanen, Major Frank, 33, 37, 60, 97, 122, 158, 264, 402, 417, 434, 542, 605, **646**
Witherspoon, Withers, **646-647**
Wojciehowitz, Doris, Robert and Joseph, 208, 289, **647**
womb, 56, 177, 381, 446, 526, 578, 588, **647-649**
Woodcock, Sheldon, **649**

Woodly, Dr. Norbert, 281, 505, **649**
The Woodpile, **649**
Woollcott, Alexander Humphreys, **649-650**
wrang-wrang, 362, **650**
Wright, Bert, 47, 470, **650**
Wu, Sam, **650**
Wyandotte College, 63, 89, 99, 225, 228, 283, 354, 608, **650**
Wyatt, Radford Alden, **650**, 651
Wyatt, Sarah, 155-156, 203, 308, 331, 342, 442, 551, 562, 573, **650-651**
Wyatt Clock Company, 441, 650, **651**
Wysocki, Mary Ann, 160, **651-652**

X, Muhammad Daffodil-11, **653**
Xanthippe, 363, 516-517
Ximénez, Eduardo, 345, **653**

Yadin, Yigael, 392, **654**
Yamashiro, Hiroshi Raspberry-20, 271, **654**
Ying, Pi, 9, 36, 352, **654**
Yonson, Yon, 536, **654-655**
Young, Buck, 202, 283, **655**
Young, Ida, **655-656**
Young, Mary, 158, 592, **656**

zah-mah-ki-bo, **657**
Zamiatin, Eugene (*also* Yevgeny Zamyatin), 461, **657**
Zappa, Lee Razorclam-13, **657**
Zappa, Vera Chipmunk-5 (also cited as Vera Chipmunk-17 Zappa), 206, **657-658**
Zeltoldimar (*see also Plague on Wheels*), 300, 345, 459, **658**
Zinka, 77, 297, 322, 326, **658**
Zircon-212 (*see also The Big Board*), 49, **658**
Zog (*see also* "The Dancing Fool"), 191, 390, **658**

About the Author

MARC LEEDS, a graduate of the University of Buffalo, New York University, and Brooklyn College, directed computer-based writing programs at East Tennessee State University and later at Shawnee State University in Ohio, commuting across five states to do so. Leeds recently resigned from teaching to become a free-lance writer in Boca Raton, Florida, where he also concentrates on developing hypermedia databases and teaching others to incorporate high technology in the classroom.